# THE

# CAMBRIDGE

# MODERN  HISTORY

London: C. J. CLAY AND SONS,
CAMBRIDGE UNIVERSITY PRESS WAREHOUSE,
AVE MARIA LANE.
Glasgow: 50, WELLINGTON STREET.

Leipzig: F. A. BROCKHAUS.
Bombay and Calcutta: MACMILLAN AND CO., Ltd.

# THE
# CAMBRIDGE
# MODERN HISTORY

PLANNED BY

THE LATE LORD ACTON LL.D.

REGIUS PROFESSOR OF MODERN HISTORY


EDITED BY

A. W. WARD Litt.D.

G. W. PROTHERO Litt.D.

STANLEY LEATHES M.A.


## VOLUME I

## THE RENAISSANCE

CAMBRIDGE

AT THE UNIVERSITY PRESS

1902

**Cambridge:**

PRINTED BY J. AND C. F. CLAY,
AT THE UNIVERSITY PRESS.

# PREFACE.

The plan of this History, as is indicated on the title-page, was conceived and mapped out by the late Lord Acton. To him is due, in its main features, the division of the work into the volumes and chapters of which it consists; and it was at his request that most of the contributors agreed to take a specified part in the execution of his scheme. In the brief statement which follows, intended to set forth the principles on which that scheme is based, we have adhered scrupulously to the spirit of his design, and in more than one passage we have made use of his own words. We had hoped during the progress of this work to be encouraged by his approval, and perhaps to be occasionally aided by his counsel; but this hope has been taken away by an event, sudden at the last, which is deeply mourned by his University and by all students of history.

The aim of this work is to record, in the way most useful to the greatest number of readers, the fulness of knowledge in the field of modern history which the nineteenth century has bequeathed to its successor. The idea of a universal Modern History is not in itself new; it has already been successfully carried into execution both in France and Germany. But we believe that the present work may, without presumption, aim higher than its predecessors, and may seek to be something more than a useful compilation or than a standard work of reference.

By a universal Modern History we mean something distinct from the combined History of all countries—in other words, we mean a narrative which is not a mere string of episodes, but displays a continuous development. It moves in a succession to which the nations are subsidiary. Their stories will accordingly be told here, not for their own sakes, but in reference and subordination to a higher process, and according to the time and the degree in which they influence the common fortunes of mankind.

A mere reproduction of accepted facts, even when selected in accordance with this principle, would not attain the end which we have in view. In some instances, where there is nothing new to tell, the contributors to this History must console themselves with the words of Thiers, "On est déjà bien assez nouveau par cela seul qu'on est vrai"; but it is not often that their labours will be found to have been confined to a recasting of existing material. Great additions have of late been made to our knowledge of the past; the long conspiracy against the revelation of truth has gradually given way; and competing historians all over the civilised world have been zealous to take advantage of the change. The printing of archives has kept pace with the admission of enquirers; and the total mass of new matter, which the last half-century has accumulated, amounts to many thousands of volumes. In view of changes and of gains such as these, it has become impossible for the historical writer of the present age to trust without reserve even to the most respected secondary authorities. The honest student finds himself continually deserted, retarded, misled by the classics of historical literature, and has to hew his own way through multitudinous transactions, periodicals and official publications, in order to reach the truth.

Ultimate history cannot be obtained in this generation; but, so far as documentary evidence is at command, conventional history can be discarded, and the point can be shown that has been reached on the road from the one to the other. To discharge this task satisfactorily, however, requires a judicious division of labour. The abundance of origina. records, of monographs and works of detail, that have been published within the last fifty years, surpasses by far the grasp of a single mind. To work up their results into a uniform whole demands the application of the cooperative principle—a principle to which we already owe such notable achievements of historical research as the *Monumenta Germaniae Historica,* our own *Rolls Series,* and the *Dictionary of National Biography.* Without such organised collaboration, an adequate and comprehensive history of modern times has become impossible. Hence the plan of the present work, the execution of which is divided among a large and varied body of scholars.

The general history of Europe and of her colonies since the fifteenth century, which it is proposed to narrate in accordance with the principles stated above, is to be treated in twelve volumes. For each of these some historical fact of signal importance has been chosen as the central idea round which individual developments are grouped, not accidentally, but of reasoned purpose. The Renaissance, the Reformation, the United States of America, the French Revolution, Napoleon, are examples of such ideas, achievements or figures which give to each of these volumes in succession a unity not of name alone. The use of such characteristic designations frees us, to some extent, from the necessity of adhering rigorously to the precise limits of chronology or geography.

Thus the subject of the present volume—the Renaissance—possesses a unity of subject matter rather than of time. Neither the anterior nor the posterior limits of the movement are precisely marked. Again, the history of the United States of America, although intimately connected with that of Europe, and with that of Great Britain in particular, has an inner coherence of its own, which is best preserved by a distinct and continuous treatment. In another part of this work, dealing with the same events from a British or French point of view, the American War of Liberation will again find its place, in so far as it affected the national progress or interests of either country. What in one volume or in one chapter constitutes the main subject, in another may form a digression or furnish an illustration. But, throughout the varied treatments of successive periods, each in its turn dominated by historic ideas or movements of prominent significance, we shall consistently adhere to the conception of modern history, and of the history of modern Europe in particular, as a single entity. This conception has regulated the choice and the distribution of matter and the assignment of space to each division.

Certain nations or countries may at times require relatively full treatment. Italy, for instance, fills an exceptionally large space in the present volume. And the reason is obvious. From Italy proceeded the movement which aroused the mind of Europe to fresh activity; in Italy this movement bore its earliest and, in some branches, its finest fruit. Moreover, in the general play of forces before the Reformation, it was on Italian soil that nearly all the chief powers of Europe met for battle and intrigue. If to these considerations are added the importance of Rome as the capital of the Catholic world and that of Venice as the capital of commercial Europe, it will be seen that there is nothing disproportionate in the share allotted to Italy and Italian affairs in this volume. Other countries within the geographical limits of the European continent had little influence during the period of the Renaissance, and are therefore comparatively neglected. The Scandinavian nations were still in the main confined to their own immediate sphere of action; and it needed the Reformation to bring them into the circle of general European politics. Russia remained, as yet, inert, while the other Eastern races of Europe played but a minor part either in its material or in its intellectual development.

Our first volume is not merely intended to describe and discuss the Renaissance as a movement of European history. It is also designed as an introductory volume whose business it is, as it were, to bring upon the stage the nations, forces, and interests which will bear the chief parts in the action. Each chapter of this volume includes so much of antecedent, especially of institutional history, as seemed necessary for the clear understanding of the conditions with which it is concerned. Such an introduction was not thought requisite, in the case of Great Britain, in a book written for English readers.

That no place has been found in this volume for a separate account of the development of the pictorial, plastic, and decorative art of the Renaissance, may appear to some a serious omission. But to have attempted a review of this subject in the period dealt with in our first volume, would have inevitably entailed a history of artistic progress during later periods—an extension of the scope of this work which considerations of space have compelled us to renounce. Politics, economics, and social life must remain the chief concern of this History; art and literature, except in their direct bearing on these subjects, are best treated in separate and special works; nor indeed is this direct influence so great as is frequently supposed.

A full index to the whole work will be published when the series of volumes has been completed. A carefully constructed table of contents and a brief index of names accompany each volume. Footnotes are deliberately excluded, and quotations, even from contemporary authorities, are sparingly introduced. On the other hand, each chapter is supplemented by a full working bibliography of the subject. These bibliographies are not intended to be exhaustive. Obsolete works are intentionally excluded, and a careful selection has been made with the view of supplying historical students with a compendious survey of trustworthy and accessible literature.

Some of the points of view, to which this preface has referred, have been urged again in the introductory note from the pen of the late Bishop of London which is prefixed to the present volume. We have printed it with a few changes of a kind which we had Dr Creighton's express authority to make, and we are glad to think that it shows both the cordial interest taken by him in the scheme designed by Lord Acton, and the agreement as to its main principles between the late Regius Professor and the eminent historian who like him formerly filled a chair in this University.

On behalf of the Syndics of the Press, and on our own behalf, we desire to express our thanks, in which we feel assured that Lord Acton would have cordially joined, for valuable assistance given in regard to the present volume by the Rev. J. N. Figgis, of St Catharine's College, and Mr W. A. J. Archbold, of Peterhouse. Mr Archbold was also of much service in advancing the general distribution of chapters and other editorial arrangements. The advice of Professor F. W. Maitland has been invaluable to all concerned, and will, we trust, continue to be given. The ready and courteous cooperation of the Secretary to the Syndics, Mr R. T. Wright, of Christ's College, has from the first been of the greatest advantage to the Editors. They confidently hope for a continuation of the aid which they have received and are receiving from historical scholars in this University and elsewhere. While all readers of this work will regret the loss of the guidance to which the undertaking had been originally entrusted, it is most keenly felt by those who are endeavouring to carry out the late Lord Acton's conception.

A. W. W.
G. W. P.
S. L.

CAMBRIDGE,
*August* 1902.

# TABLE OF CONTENTS.

## INTRODUCTORY NOTE.

By the late Right Rev. Mandell Creighton, D.D.,
Bishop of London.

## CHAPTER I.

### THE AGE OF DISCOVERY.

By E. J. Payne, M.A., Fellow of University College, Oxford.

## CHAPTER II.

### THE NEW WORLD.

By E. J. Payne, M.A., Fellow of University College, Oxford.

## CHAPTER III.

### THE OTTOMAN CONQUEST.

By J. B. BURY, Litt.D., LL.D., Fellow and Regius Professor of
Greek in Trinity College, Dublin.

## CHAPTER IV.

### ITALY AND HER INVADERS.

### By Stanley Leathes, M.A., Fellow and Lecturer of Trinity College.

# CHAPTER V.

## FLORENCE (I): SAVONAROLA.

### By E. Armstrong, M.A., Fellow and Tutor of Queen's College, Oxford.

# CHAPTER VI.

## FLORENCE (II): MACHIAVELLI.

### By L. ARTHUR BURD, M.A.

## CHAPTER VII.

### ROME AND THE TEMPORAL POWER.

### By Richard Garnett, C.B., LL.D.

# CHAPTER VIII.

## VENICE.

### By Horatio Brown, LL.D.

# CHAPTER IX.

## GERMANY AND THE EMPIRE.

By T. F. Tout, M.A., Professor of History in the Owens College,
Victoria University, Manchester.

## CHAPTER X.

### HUNGARY AND THE SLAVONIC KINGDOMS.

#### By Emil Reich, Dr. Jur.

## CHAPTER XI.

### THE CATHOLIC KINGS.

#### By H. Butler Clarke, M.A.

## CHAPTER XII.

### FRANCE.

By STANLEY LEATHES, M.A., Fellow and Lecturer of
Trinity College.

## CHAPTER XIII.

### THE NETHERLANDS.

### By A. W. Ward, Litt.D., LL.D., Master of Peterhouse.

# CHAPTER XIV.

## THE EARLY TUDORS.

### By James Gairdner, C.B., LL.D.

# CHAPTER XV.

## ECONOMIC CHANGE.

### By the Rev. WILLIAM CUNNINGHAM, D.D., Fellow of Trinity College.

## CHAPTER XVI.

### THE CLASSICAL RENAISSANCE.

### By Sir RICHARD C. JEBB, M.P., Regius Professor of Greek.

# CHAPTER XVII.

## THE CHRISTIAN RENAISSANCE.

### By M. R. James, Litt.D., Fellow of King's College.

## CHAPTER XVIII.

### CATHOLIC EUROPE.

### By the Rev. WILLIAM BARRY, D.D.

## CHAPTER XIX.

### THE EVE OF THE REFORMATION.

#### By Henry Charles Lea.

# BIBLIOGRAPHIES.

# ERRATUM.

p. 336, l. 19 from top.  *For* 1592 *read* 1492.

# INTRODUCTORY NOTE.

ANY division of history is doubtless arbitrary. But it is impossible for history to discharge all the obligations which, from a strictly scientific point of view, are incumbent upon it. If we accept the position that history is concerned with tracing the evolution of human affairs, we are continually being driven further back for our starting-point. The word "affairs" is generally supposed to indicate some definite movement; and the forces which rendered a movement possible must be supposed to have depended upon institutions which produced organised action. These institutions arose from attempts to grapple with circumstances by the application of ideas. We are thus carried back to an enquiry into the influence of physical environment and into the origin of ideas relating to society. We pass insensibly from the region of recorded facts into a region of hypothesis, where the qualities requisite for an historian have to be supplemented by those of the anthropologist and the metaphysician. A pause must be made somewhere. Humanity must be seized at some period of its development, if a beginning is to be made at all. The selection of that point must be determined by some recognisable motive of convenience.

The limitation implied by the term modern history depends on such a motive, and is to be defended on that ground only. Modern history professes to deal with mankind in a period when they had reached the stage of civilisation which is in its broad outlines familiar to us, during the period in which the problems that still occupy us came into conscious recognition, and were dealt with in ways intelligible to us as resembling our own. It is this sense of familiarity which leads us to draw a line and mark out the beginnings of modern history. On the hither side of this line men speak a language which we can readily understand; they are animated by ideas and aspirations which resemble those animating ourselves; the forms in which they express their thoughts and the records of their activity are the same as those still prevailing among us. Any one who works through the records of the fifteenth and the sixteenth century becomes conscious of an extraordinary change of mental attitude, showing itself on all sides in unexpected ways. He finds at the same time that all attempts to analyse and account for this change are to a great extent unsatisfactory. After marshalling all the forces and ideas which were at work to produce it, he still feels that there was behind all these an animating spirit which he cannot but most imperfectly catch, whose power blended all else together and gave a sudden cohesion to the whole. This modern spirit formed itself with surprising rapidity, and we cannot fully explain the process. Modern history accepts it as already in existence, and herein has a great advantage. It does not ask the reader to leave the sphere of ideas which he knows. It makes but slight claims on his power of imagination, or on his sympathy with alien modes of thought. He moves at his ease in a world which is already related at every point with the world in which he lives. Things are written clearly for his understanding.

It is of course possible to investigate the causes of this change, and to lay bare the broad lines of difference between the medieval and the modern world. In outward matters, the great distinction is the frank recognition in the latter of nationality, and all that it involves. The remoteness of the Middle Ages is partly due to the technicalities which arose from the persistent attempt to regard international relationships as merely forming part of a universal system of customary law. Motives which we regard as primary had to find expression in complicated methods, and in order to become operative had to wait for a convenient season. A definite conception had been promulgated of a European commonwealth, regulated by rigid principles; and this conception was cherished as an ideal, however much it might be disregarded in actual · practice. Practical issues had always to justify themselves by reference to this ideal system, so that it is hard to disentangle them accurately in terms of modern science. This system wore away gradually, and was replaced by the plain issue of a competition between nations, which is the starting point of modern history. This division of history is mainly concerned with the rise and fall of nations, and with an estimate of the contributions made by each to the stock of ideas or experiments which influenced the welfare of mankind.

The growth of national feeling, and its recognition as the dominant force in human affairs, went side by side with a fuller recognition of the individual. The strength of national life depended upon the force of the individuals of whom the nation was composed. International competition implied a development of national sentiment, which needed the aid of each and all. As the individual citizen became conscious of increased importance, he was inclined to turn to criticism of the institutions by which he had previously been kept in a state of tutelage. The Church was the first to suffer from the results of this criticism, and modern history begins with a struggle for liberty on the ground which was the largest, the right of free self-realisation as towards God. The conflict which ensued was long and bitter. The issue could not be restricted solely to the domain of religion, but rapidly invaded civil relations. The demands of the individual constantly increased, and every country had to readjust in some form or another its old institutions to meet the ever growing pressure.

Hence, the two main features of modern history are the development of nationalities and the growth of individual freedom. The interest which above all others is its own lies in tracing these processes, intimately connected as they are with one another. We delight to see how peoples, in proportion to their power of finding expression for their capabilities, became more able to enrich human life at large not only by adapting in each case means to ends, but also by pursuing a common progressive purpose.

Side by side with this increase of energy went an extension of the sphere with which European history was concerned. The discovery of the New World is a great event which stands on the threshold of modern history, and which has mightily influenced its course. New spheres of enterprise were opened for adventurous nations, and colonisation led to an endless series of new discoveries. The growth of sea power altered the conditions on which national greatness depended. Intercourse with unknown peoples raised unexpected problems. Trade was gradually revolutionised, and economic questions of the utmost complexity were raised.

These are obvious facts, but their bearing upon the sphere and scope of historical writing is frequently overlooked. It is no longer possible for the historian of modern times to content himself with a picturesque presentation of outward events. In fact, however much he may try to limit the ground which he intends to occupy, he finds himself drawn insensibly into a larger sphere. His subject reveals unsuspected relations with problems which afterwards became important. He perceives tendencies to have been at work which helped to produce definite results under the unforeseen conditions of a later age. He discovers illustrations, all the more valuable because they represent an unconscious process, of forces destined to become powerful. His work expands indefinitely in spite of his efforts to curtail it; and he may sigh to find that the main outline before him insensibly loses itself in a multitude of necessary details. If he is to tell the truth, he cannot isolate one set of principles or tendencies; for he knows that many of equal importance were at work at the same time. He is bound to take them all into consideration, and to show their mutual action. What wonder that his book grows in spite of all his efforts to restrain it within definite limits?

Indeed history, unlike other branches of knowledge, cannot prescribe limitations for itself. It is not only that men need the experience of the past to help them in practical endeavours, to enable them to understand the position of actual questions with which they and their age are engaged. For this purpose accurate facts are needed,—not opinions, however plausible, which are unsustained by facts. At the same time, the variety of the matters with which history is bound to concern itself steadily increases. As more interest is taken in questions relating to social organisation, researches are conducted in fields which before were neglected. It is useless for the science of history to plead established precedent for its methods, or to refuse to lend itself willingly to the demands made upon its resources. The writer of history has to struggle as he best may with multifarious requirements, which threaten to turn him from a man of letters into the compiler of an encyclopædia.

This continual increase of curiosity, this widening of interest introduces a succession of new subjects for historical research. Documents once disregarded as unimportant are found to yield information as to the silent growth of tendencies which gradually became influential. The mass of letters and papers, increasing at a rate that seems to be accelerated from year to year, offers a continual series of new suggestions. They not only supplement what was known before, but frequently require so much readjustment of previous judgments, that a new presentation of the whole subject becomes necessary. This process goes on without a break, and it is hard in any branch of history to keep pace with the stock of monographs, or illustrations of particular points, which research and industry are constantly producing. However much a writer may strive to know all that can be known, new knowledge is always flowing in. Modern history in this resembles the chief branches of Natural Science; before the results of the last experiments can be tabulated and arranged in their relation to the whole knowledge of the subject, new experiments have been commenced which promise to carry the process still further.

In sciences, however, which deal with nature, the object of research is fixed and stable: it is only man's power of observation that increases. But history deals with a subject which is constantly varying in itself and which is regarded by each succeeding generation from a different point of view. We search the records of the past of mankind, in order that we may learn wisdom for the present, and hope for the future. We wish to discover tendencies which are permanent, ideas which promise to be fruitful, conceptions by which we may judge the course most likely to secure abiding results. We are bound to assume, as the scientific hypothesis on which history is to be written, a progress in human affairs. This progress must inevitably be towards some end; and we find it difficult to escape the temptation, while we keep that end in view, of treating certain events as great landmarks on the road. A mode of historical presentation thus comes into fashion based upon an inspiring assumption. But the present is always criticising the past, and events which occur pass judgment on events which have occurred.

Time is always revealing the weaknesses of past achievements, and suggesting doubts as to the methods by which they were won. Each generation, as it looks back, sees a change in the perspective, and cannot look with the same eyes as its predecessor.

There are other reasons of a like kind which might further explain the exceeding difficulty of writing a history of modern times on any consecutive plan. The possibility of effective and adequate condensation is almost abandoned, except for rudimentary purposes. The point of view of any individual writer influences not only his judgment of what he presents, but his principle of selection; and such is the wealth of matter with which the writer of modern history has to deal, that selection is imperative. In the vast and diversified area of modern history, the point of view determines the whole nature of the record, or else the whole work sinks to the level of a mass of details uninformed by any luminous idea. The writer who strives to avoid any tendency becomes dull, and the cult of impartiality paralyses the judgment.

The present work is an attempt to avoid this result on an intelligible system. Every period and every subject has features of its own which strike the mind of the student who has made that period or subject the field of his investigations. His impressions are not derived from previous conceptions of necessary relations between what he has studied and what went before or after; they are formed directly from the results of his own labours. Round some definite nucleus, carefully selected, these impressions can be gathered together; and the age can be presented as speaking for itself. No guide is so sure for an historian as an overmastering sense of the importance of events as they appeared to those who took part in them. There can be no other basis on which to found any truly sympathetic treatment.

From this point of view a series of monographs, conceived on a connected system, instead of presenting a collection of fragments, possesses a definite unity of its own. The selection and arrangement of the subjects to be treated provides a general scheme of connexion which readily explains itself. Each separate writer treats of a subject with which he is familiar, and is freed from any other responsibility than that of setting forth clearly the salient features of the period or subject entrusted to him. The reader has before him a series of presentations of the most important events and ideas. He may follow any line of investigation of his own, and may supply links of connexion at his will. He may receive suggestions from different minds, and may pursue them. He is free from the domination of one intelligence—a domination which has its dangers however great that intelligence may be—striving to express the multifarious experience of mankind in categories of its own creation. He is free at the same time from the aridity of a chronological table,—a record of events strung round so slight a thread that no real connexion is apparent. Each subject or period has a natural coherence of its own.

If this be grasped, its relations to other divisions of the work will be readily apparent and may be followed without difficulty.

This is the main idea on which the method pursued in these volumes is founded. The mode of treatment adopted is not arbitrary, or dictated by considerations of convenience. It springs from the nature of the subject and its difficulties. Specialisation is absolutely necessary for the study of history, and it is impossible for any one master mind to co-ordinate in one product the results of all the special work that is being accomplished around it. Elements of interest and suggestiveness, which are of vital importance to the specialist, disappear before the abstract system which the compiler must, whatever may be the scale of his under-taking, frame for his own guidance. The task is too large, its relations are too numerous and too indefinite, for any one mind, however well stored, to appreciate them all. It is better to allow the subject-matter to supply its own unifying principle than to create one which is inadequate or of mere temporary value. At all events, this work has been undertaken with a desire to solve a very difficult problem, and to supply a very real need, so far as was possible under the conditions of its publication.

# CHAPTER I.

## THE AGE OF DISCOVERY.

AMONG the landmarks which divide the Middle Ages from modern times the most conspicuous is the discovery of America by the Genoese captain Cristoforo Colombo in 1492. We shall discuss in the next chapter the nature and consequences of this discovery; the present deals briefly with the series of facts and events which led up to and prepared for it, and with the circumstances in which it was made. For Colombo's voyage, the most daring and brilliant feat of seamanship on record, though inferior to some others in the labour and difficulty involved in it, was but a link in a long chain of maritime enterprise stretching backward from our own times, through thirty centuries, to the infancy of Mediterranean civilisation. During this period the progress of discovery was far from uniform. Its principal achievements belong to its earliest stage, having been made by the Phoenicians, Greeks and Carthaginians before the Mediterranean peoples fell under the dominion of Rome. By that time, the coasts of Southern Europe and Asia, and of Northern Africa, together with one at least—perhaps more—among the neighbouring island groups in the Atlantic, were known in their general configuration, and some progress had been made in the task of fixing their places on the sphere, though their geographical outlines had not been accurately ascertained, and the longitude of the united *terra firma* of Europe and Asia was greatly over-estimated. In consequence of this excessive estimate Greek geographers speculated on the possibility of more easily reaching the Far East by a western voyage from the Pillars of Hercules; and this suggestion was occasionally revived in the earlier days of the Roman Empire. Yet from the foundation of that Empire down to the thirteenth century of our era, such a voyage was never seriously contemplated; nor was anything substantial added to the maritime knowledge inherited by the Middle Ages from antiquity. About the beginning of the twelfth century maritime activity recommenced, and by the end of the fifteenth a degree of progress had been reached which forced the idea of a westward voyage to the Far East into prominence, and ultimately brought it to the test of experience.

These four centuries, the twelfth, thirteenth, fourteenth, and fifteenth, constitute what is called the Age of Discovery. The fifteenth century marks its greatest development; and in the last decade of that century it enters on its final stage, consequent on the discovery of America.

This period was an Age of Discovery in a wider sense than the word denotes when associated with maritime enterprise only. It beheld signal discoveries in the arts and sciences—the result of a renewed intellectual activity contrasting vividly with the stagnation or retrogression of the ten centuries preceding. It witnessed the rise and development of Gothic architecture, in connexion with the foundation or rebuilding of cathedrals and monasteries; the beginnings of modern painting, sculpture, and music; the institution of universities; the revival of Greek philosophy and Roman law; and some premature strivings after freedom of thought in religion, sternly repressed at the time, but destined finally to triumph in the Reformation. All these movements were in fact signs of increased vitality and influence on the part of Roman Christianity; and this cause stimulated geographical discovery in more than one way. Various religious and military Orders now assumed, and vigorously exercised, the function of spreading Christianity beyond the limits of the Roman Empire. By the end of the tenth century, the Danes, Norwegians, Swedes, Poles, and Hungarians had already been partly converted. During the twelfth century, the borders of the Roman faith were greatly enlarged. Missionary enterprise was extended to the Pomeranians and other Slavonic peoples, the Finns, Lieflanders, and Esthonians. The Russians had already been christianised by preachers of the Greek Church; Nestorians had penetrated Central Asia, and converted a powerful Khan who himself became a priest, and whose fame rapidly overspread Christendom under the name of Presbyter or "Prester" John. Prester John was succeeded by a son, or brother, who bore the name of David; but Genghis Khan attacked him, and towards the end of the twelfth century put an end to the Christian Khanate. In the thirteenth century, Roman missionaries sought to recover the ground thus lost, and Roman envoys made their way through Central Asia, though the Catholic faith never obtained in these Eastern parts more than an imperfect reception and a precarious footing. Traders and other travellers brought the Far East into communication with Europe in other ways; and Marco Polo, a Venetian adventurer who had found employment at the Great Khan's court, even compiled a handbook to the East for the use of European visitors.

While inland discovery and the spread of Christianity were thus proceeding concurrently in the North of Europe and Central Asia, a process somewhat similar in principle, but different in its aspect, was going on in the South, where the Mediterranean Sea divided the Christian world from the powerful "Saracens," or Mohammadans of

Northern Africa.  The conquests of this people, of mixed race, but united in their fanatical propagation of the neo-Arab religion, had been made when Southern Europe, weak and divided, still bore the marks of the ruin which had befallen the Western Empire.  The greater part of Spain had fallen into their hands, and they had invaded, though fruitlessly, France itself.  Charles the Great had begun the process of restoring the Christian West to stability and influence, and under his successors Western Christendom recovered its balance.  Yet the Saracen peoples still preponderated in maritime power.  They long held in check the rising maritime power of Venice and Genoa; they overran Corsica, Sardinia, and the Balearic Islands.  Nor was the domination of these vigorous peoples confined to the Mediterranean.  In the Red Sea and on the East coast of Africa, frequented by them as far south as Madagascar, they had no rivals.  Eastward from the Red Sea they traded to, and in many places settled on, the coasts of India, and the continental shores and islands of the Far East.  That branch which held Barbary and Spain was not likely to leave unexplored the Western coast of Africa and the Canary Islands.  It was on this coast that the principal work achieved in the Age of Discovery had its beginnings; and although maritime enterprise flourished at Constantinople and Venice, there can be little doubt that these beginnings are due to the Saracens.  The Moors, or Saracens of North-west Africa, must have made great progress in ship-building and navigation to have been able to hold the Mediterranean against their Christian rivals.  Masters of North Africa, they carried on a large caravan trade across the Sahara with the negro tribes of the Soudan.  It is certain that at the beginning of the Age of Discovery they were well acquainted with the dreary and barren Atlantic coast of the Sahara, and knew it to be terminated by the fertile and populous tract watered by the Senegal river; for this tract, marked "Bilad Ghana" or "Land of Wealth," appears on a map constructed by the Arab geographer Edrisi for Roger II, the Norman King of Sicily, about the year 1150.  That they habitually or indeed ever visited it by sea, is improbable, since it was more easily and safely accessible to them by land; and the blank sea-board of the Sahara offered nothing worthy of attention.  The Italians and Portuguese, on the contrary, excluded from the African trade by land, saw in Bilad Ghana a country which it was their interest to reach, and which they could only reach by sea.  Hence, the important events of the Age of Discovery begin with the coasting of the Atlantic margin of the Sahara—first by the Genoese, in the thirteenth and fourteenth centuries, then by the Portuguese, in the first half of the fifteenth—and with the slave-raiding expeditions of the latter people on the voyage to and in Bilad Ghana itself.  The name Ghana became known to the Genoese and Portuguese as "Guinea," and the negroes who inhabited it—a pure black race, easily distinguishable from the hybrid wanderers, half Berber and half black, of the

Western Sahara—were called "Guineos." Hitherto the Portuguese and Spaniards had purchased blacks from the Moors; by navigating the African coast they hoped to procure them at first hand, and largely by the direct process of kidnapping.

While we know nothing of any voyages made by the Moors to Bilad Ghana, and very little of the expeditions of the Genoese explorers who followed them, we possess tolerably full accounts of the Portuguese voyages from their beginning; and these accounts leave us in no doubt that the nature and object of the earliest series of expeditions were those above indicated. The slave-traders of Barbary, until the capture of Ceuta by the Portuguese in 1415, may have occasionally supplemented their supply of slaves obtained through inland traffic, by voyages to the Canary Islands, made for the purpose of carrying off the Guanche natives. Probably they also frequented the ports and roadsteads on the Barbary coast outside the Straits. But the possession of Ceuta enabled the Portuguese to gain a command of the Atlantic which the Moors were not in a position to contest. Dom Henrique, Iffante of Portugal, and third surviving son of King João I, by Philippa of Lancaster, sister of Henry IV, King of England, became Governor of Ceuta, in the capture of which he had taken part, and conceived the plan of forming a "Greater Portugal" by colonising the Azores and the islands of the Madeira group, all recently discovered, or rediscovered, by the Genoese, and conquering the "wealthy land" which lay beyond the dreary shore of the Sahara. The latter part of this project, commenced by the Iffante about 1426, involved an outlay which required to be compensated by making some pecuniary profit; and with a view to this Dom Henrique subsequently resolved to embark in the slave-trade, the principal commerce carried on by the Moors, over inland routes, with the Soudan and Bilad Ghana. Having given his slave-hunters a preliminary training, by employing them in capturing Guanches in the Canary Islands, he commissioned them in 1434 to pass Cape Bojador and make similar raids on the sea-board of the Sahara. The hardy hybrid wanderers of the desert proved more difficult game than the Guanches. For the purpose of running them down, horses were shipped with the slave-hunters, but the emissaries of the Iffante still failed to secure the intended victims. Vainly, says the chronicler, did they explore the inlet of the Rio do Ouro, and the remoter one of Angra de Cintra "to see if they could make capture of any man, or hunt down any woman or boy, whereby the desire of their lord might be satisfied." In default of slaves, they loaded their vessels with the skins and oil of seals. This poor traffic was scarcely worth pursuing, and for several years (1434–41) the project of conquering Bilad Ghana and annexing it to the Portuguese Crown remained in abeyance.

Yet Dom Henrique was not a mere slave-trader. The capture of slaves was destined to subserve a greater purpose—the conversion of

Bilad Ghana into a Christian dependency of Portugal, to be administered by the military Order of Jesus Christ. In Portugal this Order had succeeded to the property and functions of the dissolved Order of the Temple, and Dom Henrique was its Governor. His project was in substance similar to that carried out by the Teutonic Order in conquering and christianising the heathen Prussians; and the Order of Christ corresponded in its function to the Orders of Santiago and Alcantara, which were actively engaged in ridding Spain of the Moors. Dom Henrique's scheme represents the final effort of the crusading spirit; and the naval campaigns against the Muslim in the Indian seas, in which it culminated, forty years after Dom Henrique's death, may be described as the Last Crusade. We shall see that Albuquerque, the great leader of this Crusade, who established the Portuguese dominion in the East on a secure footing, included in his plan the recovery of the holy places of Jerusalem. The same object was avowed by Colombo, who thought he had brought its attainment within measurable distance by the successful voyage in which he had sought to reach the Far East by way of the West.

A curious geographical illusion served as a background and supplement to the scheme. The Senegal river, which fertilises Bilad Ghana, and is the first considerable stream to the southward of the Pillars of Hercules, was believed by Arab geographers to flow from a lake near those in which the Nile originated, and was itself described as the "Western Nile." The eastern branch of the true Nile flowed through the Christian kingdom of Abyssinia; and if the "Western Nile" could also be christianised from its mouth to its supposed source—no insuperable task, for Bilad Ghana had not fallen under the sway of Islam— Christian Europe would join hands with Christian East Africa, the flank of the Mohammadan power would be turned, and European adventure would have unmolested access to the Red Sea and the ports of Arabia, India, and China. How far in this direction the Iffante's imagination habitually travelled, is uncertain. His immediate object was to subjugate and convert the not yet Islamised heathen in the North-west of Africa, beginning with the Senegal river, and to create here a great Portuguese dependency, the spiritualities of which were, with the consent of the Holy See, to be vested in the Order of Jesus Christ, and were destined to furnish a fund for the aggrandisement of the Order, and the furtherance of its objects.

In recent times Dom Henrique has been named Prince Henry the Navigator,—a title founded on the supposition that his expeditions mainly aimed at the extension of nautical enterprise for its own sake, or had for their conscious though remote object the discovery of the sea-route to India and the westward exploration of the Atlantic Ocean. It has even been stated that the town founded by him on the southernmost point of the Sacred Promontory, the westernmost angle of which bears the name of Cape St Vincent—a town now represented by the little village of Sagres—was the seat of a school of scientific seamanship, and that his aim was to train up for the national service a continuous supply of intrepid and accomplished sailors, destined in the third and fourth generation to perform the memorable feats associated with the names of Da Gama and Magalhāes. All this must be dismissed as illusory, and the picturesque title "the Navigator" is calculated to mislead. There is nothing to show, or even to suggest, that Dom Henrique was ever further away from Portugal than Ceuta and its immediate neighbourhood, or that he had formed any plans for the extension of ocean navigation beyond a point long previously reached by the Genoese, or ever thought of the route round the southernmost point of Africa as a practical route to India. A more truthful clue to the aims of his life occurs near the beginning of his last will, wherein, after invoking "my Lord God" and "my Lady Saint Mary for that she is the Mother of Mercy," he beseeches "my Lord Saint Louis, to whom I have been dedicated from my birth, that he and all Saints and Angels will pray God to grant me salvation." The model of conduct and policy affected by Dom Henrique was the heroic and sainted French King who had flourished two centuries before. Louis, after ascertaining by disastrous experience the impracticability of driving the Saracens from the Holy Land and Egypt, had sought to convert the Sultanate of Tunis into a dependency of France as the first step in recovering northern Africa for Christendom. In some respects the plan of Dom Henrique was easier of achievement than that of Louis. Islam having not yet overspread Bilad Ghana, it would be far less difficult to conquer and convert its undisciplined savages to the Gospel, than to drive a wedge into the heart of Mohammadan North Africa by the conquest of Tunis. Both schemes were late offshoots of the crusading spirit; Dom Henrique's plan was among its last manifestations. As in the case of the later Crusades, this plan was largely inspired by political objects. The Villa do Iffante on the Sacred Promontory was destined to be the maritime centre of the united empire of Peninsular Portugal and Greater Portugal—the latter comprising the Madeira group and the Azores, together with Bilad Ghana, and whatever else the Iffante might annex to the ancient dominion of Portugal and Algarve. It was a sacred spot; for hither the Christians of Valencia had fled, seven centuries before, from the terrible Abd-ur'rahman Adahil, carrying with them the body of St Vincent, from whose last burial-place the westernmost promontory of Europe thenceforth took its name.

In 1441, twenty-six years after the capture of Ceuta, and the year after Terceira, the first among the Azores to be discovered, had been reached, a sudden impetus was given to the Iffante's project. Antam Gonçalvez had sailed to the Rio do Ouro for sealskins and oil. Having secured his cargo, he landed with nine armed men on the shore of the inlet, and after a desperate struggle with a solitary naked African succeeded in wounding and capturing him.  To this feat he added that of cutting off a female slave from her party, and securing her also. Shortly afterwards Nuño Tristam, a knight highly esteemed by Dom Henrique, arrived at the Rio do Ouro with a caravel, intending to explore the coast beyond Angra de Cintra in search of captives.  Fired by the exploit of Gonçalvez, Tristam landed, marked down a party of natives, and after killing several captured ten men, women, and children, including a personage who ranked as a chief.  After exploring the coast, with no further success, as far as Cape Branco, Tristam followed Gonçalvez to Portugal, where they joyfully presented to the Iffante the long-desired first-fruit of his projects.  Chroniclers dwell complacently on the joy experienced by the Iffante, commensurate not to the value of the slaves actually taken but to the hope of future captures, and on his pious rapture at the prospect of saving the souls of so many African heathen.  Dom Henrique now sought and obtained from the Pope a special indulgence for all who should fight under the banner of the Order of Christ for the destruction and confusion of the Moors and other enemies of Christ, and for the exaltation of the Catholic faith. He further procured from his brother Dom Pedro, regent of the kingdom, an exclusive right of navigation on the West African coast, and a surrender of the whole of the royalties due to the Crown on the profits of these voyages.  A new stimulus was given to the enterprise by the discovery that captives of rank could be held to ransom, and exchanged for several slaves.  In the following year (1442) Gonçalvez obtained ten slaves in exchange for two captured chiefs, and brought back a little gold dust and some ostrich eggs.  In the next year Tristam passed in his caravel beyond Cape Branco, and reached the island of Arguin. Fortune favoured him in an unusual degree, for he returned with his caravel laden with captives to its full capacity.  The success of the enterprise was now assured, and in the next year it was prosecuted on a more extensive scale.  The people of Lagos, the port where the captured slaves were landed, roused by the prospect of still greater gains, made preparations for seeking them, by way of joint-stock enterprise, on a larger scale than heretofore.  The Iffante licensed an expedition consisting of six caravels, the command being given to Lanzarote, receiver of the royal customs at Lagos, and presented each with a banner emblazoned with the cross of the Order of Christ, to be hoisted as its flag.  Lanzarote and his companions raided the coast as far as Cape Branco, shouting " Santiago! San Jorge! Portugal!" as their war-cry, and ruthlessly slaying all who resisted, whether men, women, or children.  They brought back to Lagos no less than 235 captives ; the receiver of customs was raised by the Iffante to the rank of knight, and the wretched captives were sold and dispersed throughout the kingdom. Large tracts, both of Portugal and Spain, remained waste or half culti-vated as a result of the Moorish wars : and the grantees of these lands eagerly purchased the human chattels now imported in increasing numbers.

The project of Dom Henrique had now made an important advance. Its ultimate success appeared certain; and the Iffante resolved that a direct effort should be made to reach Bilad Ghana itself, through which the "Western Nile" rolled its waters from the highlands of Abyssinia and the Christian realm of "Prester John." A certain equerry was commanded to go with a caravel straight for Guinea, and to reach it without fail. He passed Cape Branco, but was unable to resist the temptation of a profitable capture on his route. Landing on one of the islands near the Bank of Arguin, he and his men were surprised by a large party of natives, who put off from the mainland in canoes, and killed most of the raiders, including their commander. Five only returned to Portugal. Diniz Diaz, an adventurer of Lisbon, claimed about the same time to have passed the Senegal river, to have sailed along the thirty-four leagues of coast which separate it from Cape Verde, and on the strength of having on his way picked up a few natives in canoes, to have been the first to bring back real "Guinea negroes" for the Portuguese slave-market. How far his claim to this distinction is sustainable, is left an open question by the authorities. The wave of African enterprise was now steadily gaining strength. The Iffante readily licensed all intending adventurers, and the coast, long unfrequented by the European sailor, swarmed with caravels. In 1445 twenty-six vessels, fourteen of which belonged to Lagos, left that port under the command of the experienced Lanzarote, specially commissioned to avenge the Iffante's unfortunate equerry who had fallen as a protomartyr on the African shore, carrying the Cross-emblazoned banner of the Order of Christ. Six of these fulfilled the Iffante's direction to push on to the "River of Nile," and land in Bilad Ghana. The palm-trees and other rich vegetation, the beautiful tropical birds which flitted round their caravels, the strange kinds of fish observed in the waters, gave promise of the approaching goal; and at length the voyagers beheld the sea discoloured by the muddy waters of the Senegal to a distance of two leagues from land. Scooping these up in their hands, and finding them fresh, they knew that their object was attained, sought the river's mouth, anchored outside the bar, launched their boats, captured a few hapless negroes, and returned to Dom Henrique, picking up more captives on the way, with the welcome intelligence that his desires were at length accomplished, that the "River of Nile" had been reached, and the way opened to the kingdom of Prester John.

In the nineteenth year of his efforts to reach Bilad Ghana the Iffante thus saw them at length crowned with success; and his licensees pursued the trade thus opened up so vigorously that in 1448, seven years after the capture of the first natives, and three years after the Senegal had been reached, not less than 927 African slaves had been brought to the Portuguese markets, the greater part of whom, it is unctuously observed by Zurara, were converted to the true way of salvation. The rich field of commerce thus entered upon was rapidly developed by the continued exploration of the coast. We have seen that even before the Iffante's emissaries anchored at the mouth of the Senegal a navigator standing further out to sea claimed to have passed it, and reached Cape Verde. The year in which the Senegal river was actually reached (1445) was marked by another important advance. The Venetian captain Ca da Mosto and the Genoese Antonio de Nola, both in the Iffante's employ, passed beyond Cape Verde, and reached the Gambia river; the Iffante began also in this year the colonisation of San Miguel, which had been reached in the previous year, and was the second among the Azores Islands in order of discovery. In 1446 Ca da Mosto and Antonio de Nola not only discovered the four Cape Verde Islands, Boavista, Santiago, San Filippe, and San Cristovão, but passed Capo Roxo, far beyond the Gambia River, and coasted the shore to an equal distance beyond Capo Roxo, discovering the rivers Sant' Anna, San Domingos, and Rio Grande. From the coast south of Cape Verde new wonders were brought back to Portugal. The Iffante's eyes were gladdened by beholding tusks of the African elephant, and a living African lion.

How far southward along the coast the Iffante's licensees had actually sailed at the time of his death (1460), is uncertain. Could the distances reported by them as expressed in nautical leagues be accepted as trustworthy evidence, they must have passed the Bissagos and De Los Islands, and here reached the latitude of Sierra Leone, only eight degrees north of the equator. But the estimates given in the chronicle, founded only on dead reckoning, are in excess of actual geographical distances. We doubt whether before Dom Henrique's death Portuguese seamen had passed the tenth parallel of north latitude; and it is known that in his last years the complete discovery and colonisation of the Azores group chiefly occupied his attention. Dom Henrique's will, which specifies churches founded by him in each of the Azores, in Madeira, Porto Santo, and Deserta, as well as in various towns of Portugal and on the opposite coast of Morocco, speaks of the great dependency of Guinea, which he had secured for the Portuguese Crown, in general terms only. He looked on it as a certain source, in the future, of large ecclesiastical revenues. These, following a common practice of the age, were settled by him, with the Pope's assent, on the military and religious Order of which he was governor. Guinea was to be parcelled into parishes, each having a stipendiary vicar or chaplain, charged for ever with the duty of saying "one weekly mass of St Mary" for the Iffante's soul. We find nothing about the circumnavigation of Africa, or the extension of the enterprise to the Indian Ocean. Down to his death he probably expected that a junction with the

Christians of Abyssinia and the East would be ultimately effected by ascending the Western Nile or Senegal River to its sources, which were universally supposed to be near those of the Egyptian Nile. This expectation, however, he associated with the remote future; his present policy was to secure Guinea as a dependency for Portugal and a rich appanage for the Order of Christ, by the construction of forts, the establishment of parochial settlements, and the foundation of churches.

The economic character of the Iffante's enterprise was felt, even in his lifetime, to be so little in accordance with the character which history demands for its heroes, that a contemporary chronicle of the Guinea expeditions, compiled by one Cerveira, is known to have been suppressed, and replaced by the garbled work of Zurara, whose object it was to write the Iffante's panegyric as a great soldier and eminent Christian, and as the patriotic founder of the Greater Portugal which posterity would never cease to associate with his name. As the enterprise assumed larger proportions, the pretence that the negro was captured and shipped to Portugal for the salvation of his soul was abandoned. Even more valuable, for commercial purposes, than negro slaves, were the gold and ivory in which the tribes south of the Gambia River abounded. The Portuguese, who were now expert slave-raiders, found that the reward of their enterprise was best secured by disposing of their prey to the chiefs of other tribes, who were ready to give gold and ivory in exchange. The Guinea trade, which assumed this character almost exclusively soon after Dom Henrique's death, was now farmed out to the highest bidders. Affonso V in 1469 granted it to one Fernam Gomes for five years, at an annual rent of 500 crusados, on condition that the grantee should in each year discover a hundred leagues of coast, or five hundred leagues altogether during the term. Pursuant to these conditions Gomes pushed the task of exploration vigorously forward. His sailors rounded Cape Palmas, the south-western extremity of North Africa, whence the coast trends to the north-east, passed the "Ivory Coast," and reached what has ever since been known as "the Gold Coast" in a special sense—the land of the Fantee, having as a background the mountains of Ashantee; and here, a few years later, João II founded the fort of San Jorge da Mina, the first great permanent fortress of the Portuguese on the Guinea coast. Before the death of Affonso V (1481), his subjects had coasted along the kingdoms of Dahomey and Benin, passed the delta of the Niger, crossed the bight of Biafra, where the coast at length bends to southward, discovered the island of Fernam do Po, followed the southwards-trending coast-line past Cape Lopez, and reached Cape St Catherine, two degrees south of the equator. These explorations proved that the general outline of Southern Africa had been correctly traced on Italian charts dating from the preceding century; and the last steps in the process of exploration, which finally verified this outline, were taken with extraordinary rapidity. In 1484 Diego Cam reached the mouth of the Congo, sailed a short way up the river, and brought back with him four natives, who quickly acquired enough Portuguese to communicate important information regarding their own country and the coast beyond it. Returning with them in 1485, he proceeded some distance to the southward, but made no extensive discoveries; nor was it until the following year that Bartolomeo Diaz, charged by João II with the task of following the continent to its southern extremity, passed from the mouth of the Congo two degrees beyond the southern tropic, and reached the Sierra Parda, near Angra Pequeña. From this point he resolved to stand out to sea, instead of following the shore. Strong westerly gales drove him back towards it; and he at length reached Mossel Bay, named by him Bahia dos Vaqueiros, from the herdsmen who pastured their flocks on its shore. He was now on the southern coast of Africa, having circumnavigated the Cape of Good Hope unawares. From this point Diaz followed the coast past Algoa Bay as far as the Great Fish River. Its trend being now unmistakably to the north-east, he knew that he had accomplished his task. Returning towards the Cape, to which he gave the name Cabo Tormentoso, or Cape Tempestuous, he rounded it in the reverse direction to that which he had at first intended, and returned to Portugal.

As the Portuguese exploration of the African coast proceeded during sixty years, the objects with which it was pursued were almost completely transformed; and it illustrates perhaps more aptly than any other episode in European history the transition from the ideas of the crusading age to those of the age of dominant commerce and colonisation. Dom Henrique's conception of a "Greater Portugal" including the island groups of the Atlantic and Bilad Ghana on the Senegal River certainly recalls, and was probably founded on, the Mohammadan dominion which included Southern Spain, the Balearic Islands, and Northern Africa, and which St Louis proposed to replace by a Christian dominion equally comprehensive. To this strictly medieval conception the Iffante added some dim idea of a junction with the Christian sovereign of Abyssinia, to be effected by ascending the Western Nile. Beyond this point we have no reason to conclude that his imagination ever wandered. The transformation began after his death. The new dominion called "Guinea" was ascertained by a rapidly extending process of exploration to be of enormous size; this modest province, as it had seemed in prospect, assumed the proportions and character of a vast and hitherto unknown continent. Twenty-six years of discovery, after the Iffante's death, revealed three times the length of coast which had been made known in the course of a considerably longer period during his lifetime; and the Portuguese sailors had now been brought within measurable distance of the Red Sea and Persian Gulf— of India, China, and the Spice Islands. Europe's commerce with the

East—an object far exceeding in importance the conquest of Guinea—
was evidently within the grasp of Portugal. Ten years elapsed, and
a transcendent effort of seamanship had to be made, before actual
possession was taken of the prize. Meanwhile, the geographical knowledge attained during these twenty-six years wrought like a ferment in
the minds of European observers. It was felt that the little kingdom
of Portugal had effected something like a revolution in the intellectual
world: and the ideas inspired by this change, while the existence of
the New World, called afterwards America, was as yet unsuspected, are
admirably expressed in an epistle addressed to João II by Angiolo
Poliziano, professor of Greek and Latin literature at Florence. The
foremost scholar of the Renaissance tenders to the Portuguese King the
thanks of cultivated Europe. Not only have the Pillars of Hercules
been left behind, and a raging ocean subdued, but the interrupted continuity of the habitable world has been restored, and a continent long
abandoned to savagery, representing one-third of the habitable world,
has been recovered for Christianity and civilisation. What new commodities and economic advantages, what accessions to knowledge, what
confirmations of ancient history, heretofore rejected as incredible, may
now be expected! New lands, new seas, new worlds (*alii mundi*), even
new constellations, have been dragged from secular darkness into the
light of day. Portugal stands forth the trustee, the guardian, of a
second world (*mundus alter*), holding in the hollow of her hand a vast
series of lands, ports, seas, and islands, revealed by the industry of her
sons and the enterprise of her Kings. The purpose of Politian's epistle
is to suggest that the story of this momentous acquisition should be
adequately written while the memorials of it are yet fresh and complete, and to this end he offers his own services. Its significance for
ourselves lies in the fact that his admiration is couched in terms which
would apply with equal or greater propriety to the impending discovery
of the western continent. The existence of America was as yet unsuspected: and the mental fermentation produced in Europe by the
Portuguese voyages quickly led to its discovery. To cosmographers
this fermentation irresistibly suggested the revival of an idea evolved
eighteen hundred years previously by Greek geographers from the consideration of the recently ascertained sphericity of the earth and the
approximate dimensions of its known continental areas. A few days'
sail, with a fair wind, it had been long ago contended, would suffice
to carry a ship from the shores of Spain, by a westward course, to the
eastern shores of Asia. The argument had never been wholly lost
sight of; and the revival of science in the thirteenth century had once
more brought it into prominence. Roger Bacon had given it a conspicuous place in his speculations as to the distribution of land and
ocean over the globe. One is even tempted to think that those adventurous Genoese who in 1281 passed the Straits of Gibraltar with two

vessels, intending to make their way to the Indies, and were never again heard of, prematurely sought to bring it to the test of experience; but the better opinion is that they merely proposed to circumnavigate South Africa. As the African coast was progressively explored by the Portuguese and laid down on the chart, the realisation of the idea of reaching the East by way of the West became a practical matter. While Gomes was pushing forward the exploration of Southern Guinea, a canon of Lisbon, on a visit to Florence, consulted Toscanelli, the most celebrated of Italian physicists, on the feasibility of such a voyage, and brought back to Affonso V a verbal opinion favourable to it; and this opinion was shortly confirmed by a letter and a chart on which the proposed westward course was laid down. Twelve years were yet to pass before Diaz reached the Cape of Good Hope; the time for testing the scheme had not fully come. But as the Portuguese ships drew nearer to their goal, the western voyage more and more attracted attention; and the idea gained countenance through the extension of maritime enterprise further and further into the unknown westward expanses of the Atlantic Ocean, pursuant to the development of a Greater Portugal according to Dom Henrique's design.

Before his death the Iffante had provided for colonisation and church-building in each island of the Azores group. Beyond the Azores, medieval imaginative cartographers dotted the unknown Atlantic with numerous islands, some of which were distinguished by positive names. Scholars pondered over Pliny's account, based on a legend stated at length in Plato's *Timaeus*, of the great island Atlantis, believed to have formerly existed far to the westward of Mount Atlas, from which both island and ocean derived their familiar name. Later legends described various existing islands as having been actually reached in historical times. Arab sailors had discovered the "Isle of Sheep"; Welsh emigrants had peopled a distant land in the west; seven bishops, fleeing before the Mohammadan invaders, had sailed westward from the Spanish peninsula and founded Christian communities on an island which thenceforward bore the name of the Isle of the Seven Cities. Saint Brandan, an Irish missionary, had reached another rich and fertile island, traditionally named from its discoverer; another island, believed to lie not far to westward of the Irish coast, bore the name "Brasil." Far to the north-west, a perfectly truthful historical tradition embodied in the Sagas of Iceland, and repeated by geographers, placed the "New Land" or "New Isle" discovered in the tenth century by Northmen from Iceland, and by them named "Vineland," from the small indigenous American grape. All the Azores Islands had been colonised in the Iffante's lifetime. As after his death the Guinea coast was revealed in ever-lengthening extent, other adventurers dared to sail further and further westward into the unknown expanses of the Atlantic. The name commonly given among the Portuguese seamen to the object of such voyages was "Antilha,"—a word by some antiquaries derived from the Arabic, though more probably a compound Portuguese word meaning "opposite island," or "island in the distance," and denoting any land expected to be descried on the horizon. Year by year vessels from Lisbon scoured the sea beyond the Azores in search of " Antilha" or " Antilhas." In 1486, the year in which Diaz reached the Cape of Good Hope, Fernam Dolmos, lord of Terceira, procured from João II a grant of Antilha to his own use, conditionally upon its discovery by him within two years. The terms in which it was on this occasion described clearly illustrate the contemporary idea concerning it—"a great isle, or isles, or continental coast." The possibility of reaching Eastern Asia, with its continental coast and numerous islands, by a western passage was no doubt present to the minds of those who framed this grant. But Antilha was by no means conceived of as part of the Asiatic coast, or as one of the adjacent islands. It was believed to lie nearly midway between Europe and Asia, and would form the voyager's half-way station on his passage to and fro; hence its discovery was looked forward to as the first step in the achievement of the westward passage. The description of it as "a great isle, or isles, or continental coast" perhaps connects it with the " New Land" or " Vineland" of the North-men, which was represented as a continental shore bordering the northern expanses of the Atlantic, with islands of its own adjacent to it. Some such conception of the half-way land was probably present to the mind of John Cabot, who reached Labrador and Newfoundland by taking a northward route, passing by or near to Iceland, the maritime base of the Northmen's discovery of " Vineland."

The more usual conception of Antilha was that of a large solitary island in the midst of the Atlantic in more southern latitudes: and it had been so indicated on the chart sent by Toscanelli for the guidance of Portuguese explorers in 1474. Similar notions were entertained as to the islands of St Brandan, and Brasil, by the seamen of Bristol, who during these years were scouring the Atlantic further to the northward, with not less eagerness than those of Lisbon. The general object of all these voyages was the same. It was to find some convenient halfway island as an outpost of further exploration in the direction of the Far East, and a station in the new commercial route about to be established. Year by year sailors from Bristol sailed from Dingle Bay, on the south-west coast of Ireland, in search of "Brasil Island," pursuing the same plan as that of the Portuguese who sailed from Lisbon in quest of the " Antilha," or " Antilhas." No record exists of the course taken in these voyages: but we can have little doubt that after sailing for some distance due west the course was changed, and a zigzag mode of exploration was adopted, which could lead to nothing but failure. The explorer, ever haunted by the suspicion that he had left Antilha behind him, would at length change his course, and look out in the reverse direction. It is easy to see that the first condition of a westward voyage which was to produce a positive discovery was definitively to abandon this fruitless method, and to sail due west from the Old World; Colombo was the first to reach America because he was the first to take this view of the conditions of his task. His plan, early determined on and tenaciously adhered to, was to abandon Antilha and Brasil, and to assume that between the Azores and the Eastern shores and islands of Asia there were no lands to be discovered, and that there was accordingly nothing to be done but to cross the trackless Atlantic by as direct a course as possible. This perfectly accurate forecast, and the firmness with which he adhered to the plan founded upon it, rank among the most conspicuous indications of Colombo's greatness.

The execution of such a plan involved great preparations. Three ships, provisioned for twelve months, represented Colombo's estimate of what was necessary; and whatever power should accept his offer to sail with such an equipment for the Eastern shores and islands of Asia, was destined to acquire the substantial sovereignty of that New Continent whose existence remained as yet unsuspected. Both Cristoforo and Bartolomeo Colombo had been from their youth in the maritime service of Portugal, and Cristoforo had married a Portuguese wife. In early life he had found constant employment in the Guinea voyages; having also sailed to Bristol, and from Bristol far beyond Iceland, he knew the entire field of Atlantic navigation from the Arctic circle to the equator. It was natural that his first proposal for making a westward passage to the East should be made to the King of Portugal. It was equally natural that the proposal should be rejected. The circumnavigation of Africa was nearly accomplished; of this route to the wealthy East the Portuguese would enjoy a practical monopoly, and it could be effectively defended. Contemporary explorations in the Western Atlantic left doubtful the question whether any land, island or continent, existed in this direction within practical sailing distance. Even if the westward passage were successfully accomplished, it was manifest that Portugal would be unable to monopolise it, and that the discovery must ultimately enure for the benefit of the stronger maritime nations of Western Europe. Considerations of this kind sufficed to ensure the rejection of Colombo's proposals by the prudent counsellors of Affonso V; but the projector always remembered his repulse with bitter resentment, and mockingly remarked, in after years, that the Almighty had rendered Affonso "blind and deaf to the miracle about to be wrought by Him through the agency of the King and Queen of Castile." Having failed in the land of his adoption, Colombo carried his project to the republic of which he was born a citizen, where it met with no better reception. The interest of Genoa was to keep the Oriental trade in its existing overland channels; and the same consideration prevailed with the rival city of Venice, to whose Signoria the projector made his next application.

It was now clear that the project would only be taken up by some power which had no vested interest in maintaining the existing state of commercial intercourse—some power on the western sea-board of Europe, for which the establishment of the proposed route would open up a new field of enterprise. Such powers were Spain, England, and France; and Colombo astutely bethought himself of applying simultaneously to the two former, and playing them off against each other until one of them definitely accepted his proposals. He carried his plan in person to Spain, and commissioned his brother Bartolomeo to lay it before Henry VII of England (1485). Accidents, delays, and circumstances of various kinds put off for four years longer the momentous issue which of these two powers would accept the plan and obtain the inheritance of the unknown New World. Fortune inclined the balance in favour of Spain. When a message at length arrived summoning Colombo to a conference with the King of England, he had already come to a substantial agreement, though he had not yet concluded all the terms of his bargain, with Ferdinand and Isabella. Bartolomeo Diaz, at this juncture, had just returned from his cruise on the southernmost shore of Africa. On April 17, 1492, the contract was signed which secured to Colombo, not merely the usual rewards of maritime enterprise accorded to adventurers in Portuguese practice, but some additional advantages of a personal nature, including the dignity of Admiral and Viceroy in the islands and continental provinces to be acquired by him for the Castilian Crown. On August 3 he sailed from Palos; on September 6 he quitted the roadstead of Gomera; and three days later the breeze sprang up which carried his three caravels successfully across the Atlantic.

At this point it will be convenient to glance for a moment at the existing state of geographical knowledge, which had become considerably augmented during the fifteenth century. With one vast deduction—namely, the northern and north-eastern coasts of Europe and Asia from the North Cape of Norway eastward as far as Northern China, including Northern Russia and Siberia—the Old World had now been completely revealed. To Europeans, indeed, the contour of South-eastern Africa remained unascertained. Its true shape, nevertheless, must have been known to the Arab seamen who navigated the Indian ocean: many of these were also well acquainted with the Eastern Archipelago, known to Europeans only as passengers or overland travellers, as far as a point near the western end of New Guinea. Greenland was known, and in Northern and Western Europe the discovery of "Vineland" by Norse adventurers five hundred years previously was still a familiar tradition. From the point of view of scientific geography all this amounted to little. Not more than one-fourth of the earth's surface had been laid down on the map. Colombo's first expedition did no more than determine the breadth of the Atlantic in the latitude of the northern tropic, and prove that a numerous group of islands, from which the proximity of a continental shore or Terra Firma might fairly be inferred, existed on the other side. His subsequent voyages changed this inference into certainty: but the fact that the Terra Firma here encountered was a continent hitherto unknown, though its northern parts had been reached by the Northmen five centuries before, was never ascertained by him, and to the day of his death, fourteen years later, he believed himself to have merely reached the eastern parts of Asia. In fact, he was nearly at the opposite meridian, and a hemisphere raised its immense dome between. Colombo's five weeks' voyage, nevertheless, proved the great turning-point in man's slowly-progressing knowledge of the globe. Eighteen years after his death the general figure of the New World had been ascertained, its southernmost point rounded, the Pacific crossed, and the first furrow ploughed by a ship's keel around the sphere. Small as was his own actual contribution to geographical knowledge, it was his energy and enterprise, and his alone, which rapidly forced on a conception of geography sufficiently accurate to last with little improvement to the time of Cook, nearly three centuries later.

The consequences of this voyage must ever render all its details and circumstances matters of exceptional interest; but it is impossible here to enter into them. On October 12, 1492, Colombo landed on one of the Bahama Islands from his ship's boat, wearing the costume of Admiral of Castile, and holding aloft the Castilian banner; and in the course of a three months' cruise he visited Cuba and Hayti, and gained a general notion of the West Indian archipelago. The tidings of his voyage were joyfully received both in Spain and at Rome; and a petition was preferred to Pope Alexander VI for a confirmation to the Spanish Crown of the district comprising the newly-found islands, subject only to the rights of any Christian communities which might happen to be included in it. In answer to this two separate bulls were issued. One simply contained the confirmation desired; the other was framed in similar terms, but limited the area of Spanish enterprise to a meridian line to be drawn one hundred leagues west of the Azores and the Cape Verde Islands. The last, often singled out as a prominent illustration of Romish arrogance, was in fact only a suggestion intended to prevent disputes, probably due to some official of the papal chancery. It was never acted on by the parties, and was withdrawn in the same year by the Pope himself. For by a third bull, dated September 25, 1493, and superseding previous ones, the entire field of oceanic enterprise was expressly declared to be open to both nations, on the understanding that Spain should approach it by the westward passage only, and not infringe Portugal's monopoly of the African coast. The parties, thus remitted to their original rights, fixed as the boundary of their areas of enterprise a meridian of their own selection, 370 leagues west of the Cape Verde Islands, and intended to mark a midway line between the Azores, the westernmost of Portugal's possessions, and the new islands in the West Indies, supposed to be the easternmost parts of the Spanish acquisitions. The action of the Holy See in assuming to partition the globe between the sovereigns of Spain and Portugal has often been ridiculed. Such ridicule, it will be seen, is misplaced; and the papal claim to universal dominion, in its practical bearings, represented nothing more than a simple counterclaim against the more ancient and equally extravagant pretensions of the successors of Mohammad.

A second voyage made by Colombo in 1493, a third in 1498, and a fourth in 1502, added something, but not much, to the sum of his discoveries; and his administration as governor of the new Spanish acquisitions was only remarkable for demonstrating his utter incapacity for the post. Naturally enough, his conception of his duties and of the purpose which the new possessions of Spain were destined to serve, was based on the policy of the Portuguese on the coast of Guinea. Gold, and slaves as a means to gold, and as the only product immediately procurable and readily exchangeable for gold, were the only commodities worth carrying to Europe; and the scantier the supply of the former, the greater was the necessity for pushing the quest of the latter. The true riches of the Indies, Colombo wrote, are the Indians. The wretched natives, unable to procure the small quantity of gold demanded of them as a poll-tax, were provoked to resistance, and then captured and shipped by him in great numbers to Europe to be sold in the market of Seville. But the feeble and intractable Indians proved of little value as labourers; and it was at length ordered that this revolting traffic must cease. The Spanish adventurers who accompanied him frustrated his plans and procured his recall; and at his death in 1506, fourteen years after his unique nautical achievement, the first seaman in Europe, who might in half that time have revealed the whole American coast, had only added to the map the West Indian archipelago and the coasts of Honduras, Nicaragua, Costa Rica, Darien, and Paria in Venezuela. In a few years his name was almost forgotten; and, by a strange freak of fortune, one Americo Vespucci, a man of mercantile pursuits who happened more than once to visit the New World and wrote accounts of his adventures, was credited by an ignorant public with Colombo's discovery, and from him the new continent received its name.

Meanwhile, the success of Colombo's first and second voyages urged on the Portuguese the necessity of prosecuting to its conclusion their own national enterprise. Dom Manoel the Fortunate now succeeded to the throne (1495); and Vasco da Gama, a young seaman who had been selected by João II, after the return of Diaz, to command the expedition which was to complete the work of sixty years by carrying the Portuguese flag round the newly-discovered southern cape to the shores of India, was commissioned to undertake the task. A voyage from Lisbon to India was by far the greatest feat of seamanship ever attempted; even its first portion, the voyage to the Cape of Good Hope, which it was proposed to make as directly as possible from the Cape Verde Islands across the open ocean, avoiding the circuitous route by the Guinea coast and the mouth of the Congo, was a far greater undertaking than the voyage of Colombo. The discoverer of America had but to sail 36 days, with a fair wind, to traverse the 2,600 miles between Gomera and the Bahamas. The distance from the Cape Verde Islands to the Cape was 3,770 miles. It was impossible to make the voyage by great-circle sailing. Contrary winds and currents made it necessary to shape a course curving to the extent of almost half a circle, the direct line forming the chord of the arc; and 93 days elapsed after Da Gama had left the Cape Verde Islands before he reached the coast of South Africa. Leaving Lisbon on July 8, 1497, and the Island of Santiago, the southernmost of the Cape Verde group, on August 3, he first sighted land on November 4, and on the 8th anchored in the bay of St Helena, in the land of the Hottentots, where he remained eight days, careening his ships and taking in wood. Quitting his anchorage on the 16th, he doubled the Cape on the 22nd, and three days later reached Mossel Bay, where he remained thirteen days. Resuming his course on December 8, he eight days afterwards passed the mouth of the Great Fish river, the last point reached by Diaz, and was now in waters never before traversed by European vessels. Struggling against the Agulhas current, which had baffled his predecessor, he on Christmas Day reached the roadstead which from that circumstance obtained the name of Port Natal. After making halts in the bay of Lourenço Marques, and at the mouth of the Kiliman river, Da Gama once more stood out to sea, and on March 2, 1498, anchored in the roadstead of Mozambique. He had now effected the desired junction of the West with the East; for the Mohammadan population here spoke the Arabic language, and through his own interpreters he could freely communicate with them.

From this point Da Gama's task was easy. He had entered a field of navigation known in all its parts from remote times, and familiar ground to resident Mohammadan seamen and traders, who received him amicably and furnished him with pilots. From Mozambique he proceeded to Mombasa, where he fell in with non-Mohammadan residents, supposed by him to be Christians, but in reality Banyans of India. A still larger "Christian" population of the same nation was found in the port of Malindi. Here the adventurers were furnished with a "Christian" pilot, who conducted them safely across the Indian Ocean to Calicut, off which place Da Gama anchored on May 20, ten months and twelve days after leaving Lisbon. Calicut was the great emporium of Arab trade. It was the chief among the many ports of the Malabar coast, whence Europe drew its supplies of pepper and ginger. Here Mohammadan merchants purchased cinnamon brought from Ceylon and spices from the Molucca Islands, which they carried to the port of Jiddah in Arabia, and then to the port of Tor in the Sinaitic peninsula, whence they were carried overland to Cairo. Here they were shipped down the Nile to Rosetta, and the last stage of transport was performed on camels to Alexandria, where they were purchased by European merchants. At all these places duties had to be paid, in consequence of which the cost of the merchandise was quadrupled; and large profits could be reaped by merchants who carried them directly from the East to Western Europe. There was another trade route to Europe by way of the Persian Gulf, and so through Syria to Aleppo and Beyrut. Although frequent wars were waged between the native princes of the Malabar coast, they all maintained a good understanding with the Muslim sailors and traders, and many of the latter permanently resided on the Malabar coast and in the Far East. The arrival of the Portuguese was not altogether unexpected. Their intention of penetrating the Indian Ocean was well known; and on his arrival Da Gama pretended to be in search of some missing vessels of his squadron. Having landed to enquire concerning them, he asked permission to trade, which was granted. Meanwhile the Muslim residents intrigued with the native prince, entitled the "Samori," or "Zamorin," hoping to deal the Portuguese a crushing blow on the very threshold of their undertaking. Representing the new-comers as mere marauders, they so far succeeded as to induce the Zamorin to detain Da Gama and some of his companions as prisoners. He barely himself escaped assassination; but a good understanding was at length restored, and the Portuguese commander, after taking in a valuable cargo of pepper, ginger, cinnamon, cloves, and nutmegs, besides rubies and other precious stones, sailed on his return voyage on August 29, 1498, and in September 1499 at length made his triumphal entry into Lisbon. Besides the merchandise which he secured, he brought back precise information concerning the coasts of India as far as Bengal, Ceylon, Malacca, Pegu, and Sumatra.

Thus was the way opened for Europe's maritime invasion of the East; a process in modern history perhaps of even greater importance than the European occupation of the New World. Ever since Da Gama's great voyage Southern and Eastern Asia, comprising then as now the most populous nations on the globe, have been gradually falling under the sway of the European powers, who have first appropriated their foreign trade, making permanent settlements on their coasts in order to secure it, thence advanced to controlling their administration and usurping their government, and in some varying degree have succeeded in the more difficult task of gradually changing their habits of life and thought. In all this Europeans have been following in the footsteps of the Mohammadans of Western Asia and Northern Africa; and these had inherited their commercial sphere from remote antiquity. Greek tradition even ascribed the invention of ocean navigation to the aboriginal Erythraeans, who had ploughed the Red Sea long before Phoenicians and Greeks ventured to cross the Mediterranean ; and ancient ethnology distinguished these from the Semitic adventurers who in historical times had colonised the islands on the southern coast of Arabia, and not only traded by sea along this coast in its entire length, but frequented the adjacent shores of Africa, and regularly crossed the mouth of the Persian Gulf with the monsoon in search of the commodities of Western India.

The establishment of Islam gave a new and powerful stimulus to all Arabian enterprise. By the end of the fifteenth century there existed from the Red Sea to Japan a valuable and well-organised commerce, mainly in the hands of Arabian or other Muslim seamen and merchants. For the effect of the propagation of Islam had been to bring to the field of Asiatic trade a crowd of adventurers of many nations, many of whom were Turks of Anatolia or Europe. Others were Greeks, Albanians, Circassians, and other Levantines of European descent who had abandoned the Christian faith for gain, and had brought to the Muslim sailors and merchants of the Eastern ocean the knowledge and experience of the Mediterranean peoples. These were generally known in India and the Far East as " Rumes " (Arab. *Rumi*, a Greek) ; and Muslim opponents found in the East by the Portuguese thus included not only true Arabs, whether of Arabia, Africa, or India, generally known as " Moors," but large numbers of Turks and " Rumes," whose European experience and connexion greatly aided the Moors in their resistance to the European maritime invasion.

The course of trade in these seas was not exclusively from west to east and back again. From very early times a maritime commerce had been carried on in the reverse direction ; and the meeting-place of the two trades was the port of Calicut. Hither came, once a year—for only during the summer were the Chinese seas navigable for Chinese vessels— a large trading fleet from the ports of China. The huge Chinese junks, with their fixed sails of matted reeds, never lowered, even in harbour, and mainly propelled by oars of immense length, and having on board gardens of growing vegetables, and large chambers for the ships' officers and their families, so that each was as it were a floating town, were objects of curious interest to the Arabian sailors. The largest were reputed to carry a thousand persons, and each was attended by three smaller craft for the purpose of loading and unloading. It was natural for the Arabs, who had already secured a part of the Indian coasting trade, to push their way towards the Far East, and to claim a share in the trade of China and the Spice Islands. They found a convenient station in the port of Malacca, which in their hands quickly became the second great emporium of the Eastern trade. Nor did they rest here. Making their way to the ports of China itself, they were amicably received, and allowed to form settlements of their own. Many such settlements, each having its resident magistrate and Sheikh ul Islam, existed hard by the chief Chinese ports, and others were scattered through the Eastern Archipelago. Malacca became the western outpost of the Far-Eastern trade thus developed. Hither were brought the cloves of the Moluccas, the mace and nutmeg of Banda, the sandal wood of Timor, the camphire of Borneo, and many other spices, drugs, dyes, and perfumes from Java, Siam, China, and the Philippine Islands, all of which could be purchased here more cheaply of the resident Arab merchants than of those of Calicut, who obtained them in the ancient course of trade from the Chinese fleet. Hence the sailors of Africa and Arabia, at the arrival of the Portuguese, already resorted directly to Malacca for the produce of the Far East, and Calicut became chiefly a market for the cinnamon of Ceylon, and the ginger, pepper, and miscellaneous commodities of Malabar itself.

The ports of Arabia, and the Arab settlements in Eastern Africa, were the inlets through which the produce of India and the Far East were finally dispersed; and large quantities found their way through Suez, Jiddah, Mascat, and Hormuz, to the markets of Europe. It thus appears that the area of the Eastern trade naturally fell into two divisions, the mouth of the Persian Gulf marking the partition. Eastward of this lay the area of export, westward the area of import. Hence the fact that the Portuguese, having rounded Southern Africa, made straight for Calicut, the outpost of the exporting area. The ideas and expectations with which they approached this immense and unique field of enterprise were tinged with the arrogance of prolonged success. It was necessary, as a means to making themselves masters of the Eastern trade, before all else, not only to prove themselves masters of the Asiatic seas, but to be able to defy resistance on land, and to hold by military force whatever positions it might be desirable to occupy. For these purposes such demonstrations of force as had availed them on the African coast were insufficient. Society in the East rested everywhere on a military basis. The native Asiatic princes universally possessed numerous and not ill-equipped armies, though ill-supplied, or not at all, with firearms. By sea the Arabs and Rumes were more formidable. Wherever maritime trade exists it must defend itself against pirates; and piracy was rife on all the Indian and Chinese shores. Hence the larger vessels, both on the Malabar coast and on that of China, were usually manned with fighting men, and those of the Arabs and Rumes occasionally carried large guns. The Oriental fleets, if assembled in one place, would have immensely outnumbered the ships capable of being sent against them by Portugal. But in regard to construction, equipment, and the art of navigation the Portuguese had greatly the advantage. Even the Arabs knew nothing of the art of using a vessel mainly as a military machine, much less of manœuvring and combined action for attack, defence, pursuit, and co-operation with troops on land.  Eastern vessels, indeed, were scarcely capable of being so employed.  The hard woods used in constructing them forbade the use of iron nails, and their heavy planks were rudely made fast with cocoa-nut cordage and wooden pins.  Steering gear and ground-tackle were of a rudimentary sort : even a moderate gale rendered the ship scarcely manageable, and the guns were useless except at close quarters.  The Portuguese, who inherited the naval experience of two thousand years, had become through their African voyages the best seamen in Europe, possessed ships of the newest type, and attacked the Arabian vessels with the confidence begotten of their maritime successes against the Barbary Moors.

The treachery experienced by Da Gama from the Zamorin of Calicut made it still more necessary for the Portuguese to be strong enough to punish, as well as to invade, the enemy ; and when Pedro Alvarez Cabral sailed in 1500 in command of the second expedition to India his vessels were formidably armed with artillery.  By way of demonstrating his strength Cabral shortly after his arrival captured a large Moorish vessel as it passed the roadstead and presented her to the Zamorin.  Suspecting the Moors of obstructing him in procuring lading for his fleet, he attacked and captured a Moorish vessel in the roadstead itself.  In reprisal the Moors on shore destroyed the Portuguese factory and massacred its inhabitants.  Cabral seized and destroyed ten large Moorish ships, and bombarded the town.  He then sailed for Cochin, burning two more ships of Calicut on the way.  Cochin, the seat of a Rajah hostile to the Zamorin, was also a port frequented by the Moors, and a few of them resided there permanently.  Cabral was amicably received, completed his lading, and promised the Rajah to add Calicut to his dominions, his design in this being to gain the Rajah's assistance in conquering Calicut for the Portuguese.  Being now ready to return, Cabral declined invitations from the Rajahs of Cananor and Quilon, and sailed for Europe.  Having encountered a storm, he put into Cananor, where the Rajah promised free trade to the Portuguese, and sent on board an envoy with presents for the Portuguese king.  Before his return João de Nueva had sailed from Lisbon for India, with four ships and four hundred men.  In view of the hostile attitude of the Zamorin, De Nueva made for Cananor, where he learned that the Indian King was ready to attack him with forty ships.  Leaving his factors at Cananor, De Nueva sailed at once to attack the enemy in their own waters, and inflicted on them a signal defeat.  Successful though the Portuguese had been, the tidings of this continued hostility on the part of the Rajah who dominated the principal emporium of India gave rise at home to grave misgivings.  Some counselled the abandonment of an enterprise to which the strength of a small European power seemed unequal.  Even if the resistance of Calicut were broken, what would be the situation when Turkey and Egypt should combine with the Arabs to drive Portugal from the precarious lodgment she had acquired ? And if the mere threshold of the East had proved so hard to win, how much harder would it be to strike into the heart of the field, and attack the Muslim in the strong positions of the Far East, with the countless millions of China at their back ?

Against such arguments the honour of a Christian nation, the lust of territorial aggrandisement, and above all the greed of gold, prevailed in the end. Twenty ships were despatched, in three squadrons, under the general command of the first adventurer, Vasco da Gama, and other commanders followed in rapid succession. The original plan of campaign was still adhered to. Whatever the cost, the Moors must be dislodged from Calicut, the resistance of the native king broken, and the control of the trade transferred to the Portuguese, whose king the Zamorin must acknowledge as his sovereign. Beaten at every point in fair fight, the Zamorin maintained his ground by fraud and treachery. The stream of wealth still poured into Portugal through Cochin and Cananor, immensely augmented by the spoils of captured Moorish vessels, but the Zamorin still held his ground. In an interval during which the Portuguese forces were weakened by the withdrawal of returning ships, he attacked and destroyed Cochin. The Portuguese having retaken it, restored its prince, and built a strong fort for themselves, the infuriated Rajah, having roused such of his neighbours as were amenable to his appeal, seized a similar opportunity and assailed Cochin with fifty thousand men. In a campaign of five months he was defeated and slain by the Portuguese under Duarte Pacheco, who earned the title of the Portuguese Achilles; but his successor maintained the same attitude, and despatched an embassy to the Sultan of Egypt, asking for aid in resisting the invaders. The Sultan sent word to the Pope threatening to destroy the holy places at Jerusalem if the Portuguese persisted in their invasion of India. The only effect of this empty menace was to stimulate the Portuguese King to renewed efforts on a larger scale. The crisis of the struggle was approaching; and in view of this a more comprehensive scheme was adopted. Abandoning the attempt to reduce the obstinate resistance of a single prince, it was determined to attack the Muslim maritime system in all its parts, and to establish a new emporium on the Malabar coast as the commercial and naval centre of the new Portuguese eastern empire. Already the Moorish traders in search of the produce of the Far East had begun to avoid the Malabar coast, and to make their way from the Arabian and African ports by a new route to Malacca. It was resolved to seize this key of the Far East without delay, and to gain possession of the Moorish settlements on the African coast, and the Arabian ports of Hormuz and Aden. By exacting heavy duties at these places the whole trade would gradually be diverted, and the Portuguese would ultimately control the Red Sea itself.

The chief African settlements were seized with little difficulty by
Francisco de Almeida; and the rest of the programme was successfully
carried out by Affonso de Albuquerque (1509–15). The excellent
natural harbour of Goa had already been chosen as the new seat of the
Portuguese dominions. The town, built by the Muslim fifty years
previously, had lately fallen, together with the adjacent country, under
the sway of the powerful Adil Khan; and it was well known that here
the Muslim enemy intended to concentrate their forces with the view of
driving the Portuguese from the Indian seas. A Muslim pirate who
foresaw the issue of the contest allied himself with the Portuguese, on
the terms that he should be appointed *guazil* or port-admiral of Goa,
and farmer of the large demesne lands which the conquest would annex
to the Portuguese Crown; and on March 4, 1510, Albuquerque entered
Goa and received the keys of the fortress. The dispossessed Hindoo
inhabitants welcomed the Portuguese as deliverers; and although Adil
Khan forced his way again into the town, compelling the Portuguese to
evacuate, it was recaptured by Albuquerque (November 25), and strongly
fortified. Many Portuguese received grants of land, and married native
women; the confiscated estates of the Moorish mosques and Hindoo
temples were annexed to the great church of S. Catherina: a mint was
set up, the new coinage having on one side the cross of the Order of
Christ, on the other Manoel's device of a sphere, lately adopted by him
to signalise the vast accession which his dominions had now received.
Hindoos and Moors returned to the settlement, acknowledging the
Portuguese supremacy; and Goa thus became the most thriving port
of the Malabar coast.

Albuquerque followed up this success by sailing in person for Malacca,
where he arrived in June, 1511. A few Portuguese had already been
allowed to settle there for the purpose of trade. They had been treacherously attacked by the Moors, and their property confiscated; and
although a few effected their escape, several were still held prisoners.
Mohammad, the Sultan of Malacca, having refused Albuquerque's demand
for their liberation and the restitution of their property, Albuquerque
assaulted and sacked the town, capturing hundreds of guns, erected a
fortress, set up a mint, and built a church dedicated to the Virgin. The
native princes of the adjoining mainland and islands hastened to offer
their friendship and urge the Portuguese commander to make his
footing secure. In this he completely succeeded, for although repeated
attempts were made to dislodge the Portuguese, the settlement was
successfully defended, and became, as was foreseen, a base from which all
the Muslim settlements in the Far East were gradually reduced to
subjection.

The news of the capture of Malacca was in due time communicated
to the Court of Rome. A public thanksgiving was appointed, marked
by processions in which the Pope figured in person. Later came an

embassy from Portugal, headed by Tristão da Cunha, under whom Albuquerque had seen his first service in the East. The presents of gold, jewels, and oriental embroidery, an earnest of the future wealth to be drawn by the Holy See from the East, were borne in triumphal procession. They were followed by richly caparisoned Persian horses, leopards, a panther, and a gigantic elephant, which knelt thrice before the Holy Father; and in reply to an address Leo X delivered a Latin oration, in which he praised the maintenance of peace by the Christian powers, and spoke hopefully of the union of their forces against the Muslim. Meanwhile Albuquerque, having almost swept the Turkish and Arab ships from the Indian sea, was preparing to carry the war into their own waters. Early in 1513 he sailed from Goa with twenty vessels, and after an unsuccessful attack on Aden entered the Red Sea. His successes had filled his mind with the wildest expectations. By an alliance with the Christian sovereign of Abyssinia he dreamed of establishing himself on the Upper Nile, cutting a canal through the mountains separating it from the Red Sea, diverting the river, and thus turning into a desert the most flourishing of the Muslim countries. Another project was to land a force in the harbour of Yembo, plunder the temple of Medina, and carry away Mohammad's coffin, to be held until the holy places of Jerusalem should be surrendered in exchange for it. A fiery cross, seen over the African coast as he waited for a wind, was hailed as an omen of success; but prudence and the affairs of Goa suggested his return, and after a very limited reconnaissance of the Red Sea coasts he returned to India. The voyage confirmed his belief in the capture and fortification of Aden as the necessary means of effecting a junction with Abyssinia at the port of Massowah. This once accomplished, Suez, Jiddah, and Mecca itself would be practically at the invader's mercy.

At another important point Albuquerque strengthened the Portuguese position. Before succeeding to the chief command he had set up a small Portuguese factory at the ancient port of Hormuz, near the entrance of the Persian Gulf. From this the Portuguese had advanced to obtaining control of the customs payable on Persian exports to India. Albuquerque now obtained the surrender of the fort of Hormuz, with the command of the entire import trade from India to Persia, as well as through Mesopotamia to Aleppo, and Beyrut on the Mediterranean. At the time of his death he was preparing an expedition for the conquest of Aden, the only thing which seemed still undone in order to give Portugal complete control of the eastern seas, being, in his own words, " the closing of the gates of the Straits." He died at Goa, habited as a commendador of the Order of Santiago. By his will he desired that his bones should be carried to Portugal. This was strenuously opposed by the settlers of Goa, who believed their city to be only safe so long as the bones of the great commander remained among them; nor was it until fifty years later, when the Portuguese dominion seemed absolutely safe from attack, that they were at length removed to Lisbon. During these fifty years the main features of his scheme had been carried out. Unmolested access to all the trading stations in the Far East was obtained, and of many the Portuguese were in uncontrolled possession. In other places they shared the trade with those whom they had hoped to expel. Albuquerque's scheme for seizing and holding the Red Sea was abandoned: and the culmination of the Portuguese successes in the East was followed by the rapid decline of their power. We must now recur to the situation of other European powers at the time of Dom Manoel's succession to the throne in 1495.

Not merely were the Spaniards by this time actively preparing for the exploration and effective occupation of their newly acquired transatlantic islands; but Englishmen, who had so long been prosecuting westward discovery, and whose king, Henry VII, had barely missed the prize which had fallen to the lot of Spain, now bestirred themselves once more. Bristol was at this time one of the most considerable ports in Europe; its merchants and seamen vied with those of Genoa and Venice, and skilled navigators from those great ports here found ready employment. Doubtless in 1495, or earlier, the news of Colombo's success in a quest which Bristol men had long made an interest of their own roused its merchants to activity; and John Cabot, a citizen of Venice, though of Genoese extraction, became the chosen instrument of their designs. Cabot's three sons, Lewis, Sebastian, and Sanctus, had apparently all been educated to his own calling; and on March 5, 1496, Henry VII granted a petition preferred by the father and sons, praying the sanction of the Crown to a voyage contemplated by them in search of unknown countries, understood or believed to exist beyond the ocean in northern latitudes. Having regard to the large commerce carried on between Bristol and Iceland, and to the continuity of Icelandic tradition, embodied in the Sagas, we entertain no doubt that the intention was to seek the "New Land," "New Isle," or "Vineland" of the Northmen; and this conclusion is borne out by the course actually taken when the voyage was begun. Pursuant to this petition, still preserved in the Public Record Office, the Privy Seal was on the same day affixed to the first charter authorising its holders to hoist the English flag on shores hitherto unknown to Christian people, and to acquire the sovereignty of them for the English Crown. This charter, and the voyage made pursuant to it, were put forward in a later generation, and are still sometimes regarded, as the root of England's title to her American possessions; and the date of the letters patent (March 5, 1496) has not ineptly been styled the birthday of the British Empire. It is stipulated that the grantees, who are authorised to enter the Northern, Western, and Eastern seas, but not the Southern, shall after each voyage return to the port of Bristol; that they shall then and there pay to the Crown, in money or merchandise, one-fifth of their net profits: that they shall be allowed to import their goods free of customs: and that no English subject shall frequent the continents, islands, villages, towns, castles, and places generally frequented by them without their licence. While the Cabot grant disregards the Pope's supposed partition of the globe between Portugal and Spain, it forbids, by implication, any intrusion into those southern seas in which each of these powers had already acquired territory by actual occupation. Colombo's discoveries were as yet limited to the chain of islands separating the Caribbean Sea from the Atlantic; the Portuguese had not as yet set foot on American soil. The voyage of Cabot, which had no practical results, and was soon well-nigh forgotten, will be briefly noticed in our next chapter. Englishmen, eminently practical, saw in the intelligence brought back by him no promise of a profitable commerce, or indeed of commerce at all; nor did English colonial ideas take a definite shape until nearly a century later.

Meanwhile the Spanish monarchs, anxious to ascertain the extent of their trans-oceanic possessions and to secure them from intrusion, licensed Vicente Yañez Pinzon, who had commanded a vessel under Colombo in his first voyage, to prosecute the discovery of the supposed coast of Eastern Asia. Pinzon was directed to avoid interference with the private rights acquired by Colombo, and to visit only the coast to southward of the Orinoco, the limit of Colombo's explorations. Starting from the Cape Verde Islands on November 14, 1499, and having on board Americo Vespucci, through whose narrative the voyage became well known, though the name of the captain who conducted it was suppressed, Pinzon stood to the south-west and struck the coast of Brazil near Cape St Augustin in the State of Pernambuco. Sailing northwards along the coast, he rounded Cape San Roque, the north-western promontory of South America, coasted along the north-eastern shore of Brazil and the coasts of Guiana and Venezuela, passing the mouth of the Amazon river, the rivers of Guiana, and the Orinoco, and reached the Gulf of Paria, whence he made his way back to Europe, bringing with him thirty Indian captives and a quantity of strange vegetable products, including various dye-woods, whence the coast ultimately obtained its permanent name of "Brazil." When these new discoveries were laid down on the chart, it became manifest that a considerable part of them were to the east of the 370 leagues' line, agreed on in 1494 as the boundary between the Spanish and Portuguese areas of enterprise; and by a singular accident these very coasts were reached in the last year of the fifteenth century by Pedro Alvarez Cabral, the commander of the second Portuguese expedition to India and the Far East. Like Da Gama himself, Cabral proposed to cross from the Cape Verde Islands to the Cape of Good Hope athwart the open sea, making, for the reason already given in our description of Da Gama's voyage, an immense

circuit to the westward. In so doing he lost sight as might be anticipated, of one of his ships; while seeking her he lost his course, and
unexpectedly descried land. It was the Brazilian coast, the mountain
range called Pascoal, in the State of Bahia, to the south of the spot
where Pinzon had landed three months previously. Having discovered
a safe harbour, named by him Porto Seguro, Cabral proceeded on his
voyage to the Cape and India. Thus was America discovered for the
second time, and independently of the enterprise of Colombo. The
discovery was rapidly followed up. In May, 1501, Manoel despatched
three vessels commissioned to explore from Porto Seguro southwards,
as far as the coast within the Portuguese line might extend. They
returned in September, 1502, having discovered it as far south as 32
degrees of south latitude. Adding this coast to what had already
been discovered by Colombo and others in the Caribbean Sea, it will
be seen that at the time of Colombo's death in 1506, and in the
course of fourteen years from his first voyage, about seven thousand
miles of the Atlantic coast of America had been revealed. As a mere
matter of measurement, this fell short of the length of coast-line which
Portuguese enterprise had added to, or rather, had accurately traced
on, the map of Africa since the year 1426. But its geographical
importance and general significance were far greater, for it became
more and more doubtful whether this immense coast could possibly be
the eastern shore of Asia. Colombo himself, in writing of the lands
reached by him, occasionally referred to them as constituting "Another
world (*orbis*)" or "A new world." The former expression had been
commonly employed in late Roman times to denote regions separated,
or apparently separated, by the ocean from the continent of Europe,
such as the British Islands were, and the Scandinavian peninsula was
supposed to be. The latter expression came into general use. It was
employed by Vespucci in the narrative of his voyages, which he circulated
in manuscript with a view to his own promotion in the maritime
profession; a narrative which fell into the hands of an obscure printer,
one Walzmüller of St Dié in Lorraine, and was embodied in a brief
outline of geography compiled by him and printed in 1507. Half
in jest, half seriously, Walzmüller proposed to denominate the New
World from the seaman whom he supposed to be its discoverer, and gave
it the name AMERICA.

By similar steps proceeded the final stage of the great discovery, in
which the New World was revealed in something nearly approximating
to its real extent, and its discontinuity with Asia proved everywhere
except in the northernmost parts of the Pacific. From the Caribbean
Sea Spanish explorers advanced northwards to the Gulf of Mexico,
circumnavigated Cuba, reached the peninsula of Florida and the mouth
of the Mississippi, proved the continuity of these northern shores
with the "America" of the South, and showed them to be probably

continuous with the "New Land" of the Northmen which had been revisited by Cabot, and subsequently by the Portuguese navigator Cortereal. This probability was strengthened by the voyage of the Florentine seaman Giovanni da Verrazzano, commissioned for the purpose by Francis I of France, in 1524, in circumstances to be mentioned presently. Before this, not only had the Pacific been reached by crossing the continent in more than one place, but Magalhaẽs had discovered and passed the strait which bears his name. Juan Diaz de Solis in 1515 reached the Plate River, where he and several companions were killed in a kidnapping raid on the natives. Probably he supposed himself to have reached the southern extremity of the continent. Shortly afterwards the estuary was examined by a more famous captain, who ascertained its real geographical character. Fernão de Magalhaẽs, a skilful Portuguese seaman who had long been employed in the Portuguese trade to the Far East, having been refused an increase of pay to which he considered himself fairly entitled, quitted the service of Manoel, and sought to revenge himself by persuading Charles V that the Spice Islands were within the hemisphere assigned to Spain by the treaty of 1494. He undertook to demonstrate this, and to conduct Spanish vessels thither by a route round the southern cape of America; and on September 20, 1519, he sailed from San Lucar for this purpose. The enormous estuary of the Plate River had to be completely explored, in order to ascertain that it was not in fact the passage of which he was in search; and more than a year elapsed before this intrepid navigator found himself past the 50th parallel of latitude, painfully coasting the barren and apparently interminable coast of Patagonia. Nearly two months elapsed before he reached the Strait which bears his name. On November 27, 1520, having occupied twenty days in threading the Strait, he reached the Pacific; and fourteen months afterwards he was slowly nearing the Ladrones, after accomplishing the greatest feat of continuous seamanship the world has ever known. Magalhaẽs was fated not to complete his task. He fell by the spear of a native at Zebu, one of the Philippine Islands, on April 27, 1521; and his vessel, the "Victoria," was brought home on September 8, 1522, after making the first circumnavigation of the globe in a voyage which occupied three years less fourteen days. The feat which Colombo proposed to accomplish—a voyage to the Far East by a westward passage across the Atlantic—was at length achieved, thirty years after its projector made the first attempt to perform it, and twenty-four after he stumbled unexpectedly on the vast continent which barred the way.

# CHAPTER II.

## THE NEW WORLD.

THE story of the Age of Discovery naturally merges in that of the New World, the principal fruit of the strenuous labours to which that Age owes its name. The history, in the wider sense, of the New World begins in the remotest ages; for the habits of life and thought displayed among its aborigines at the time of the Discovery, and its indigenous languages, which stand nearer to the origin of speech than any group of languages in the Old World, carry the ethnologist back to a stage far more archaic than is indicated in any other quarter of the globe. Its history, in so far as history is a mere record of specific facts and events known to have taken place in particular districts, in a definite succession, and admitting of being distinctly connected with particular peoples and personages, is extremely limited. Its modern historical period, in fact, coincides very nearly with that of the Old World's "modern" history,— a circumstance partly due to the fact that its advanced peoples, though by no means devoid of the historical instinct, possessed but limited means of keeping historical records; and partly to the circumstance that their history, such as it was, consisted in changes of ascendancy happening in comparatively quick succession, in the course of which the memory of events connected with past dominations soon lapsed into oblivion, or dwelt but faintly and briefly in the remembrance of those peoples who happened to be dominant at the Spanish Conquest. Although the general series of American migrations, beginning with the entry of man into the New World from the Old in the remote age when Asia and America, afterwards parted by the shallow Strait of Behring, were continuous, has passed out of knowledge, it may be assumed to have proceeded on the principle of the stronger tribe expelling the weaker from districts yielding the more ample supplies of food. There is good reason to conclude that the peoples and tribes of low stature who still occur sporadically in various parts of America, represent the earliest immigrants. At the Discovery tribes and nations of tall stature, great physical strength and endurance, and a certain degree of advancement in the arts of life, were dominant in all the districts most favourable for human habitation; and it is possible in some measure to trace the movements by which their migrations had proceeded, and the steps by which they acquired dominion over lower or less powerful peoples in whose midst they settled. Foremost among these dominant peoples stand the Nahuatlacâ or Mexicans, who had their chief seat at Mexico on the plateau of Anahuac, and the Aymara-Quichua, or Peruvians, whose centre of dominion was at Cuzco in the Andes. On the subjugation of these two peoples the Spanish-American Empire was founded. Next in importance, but of lower grade, come the Caribs of Venezuela and the West Indian archipelago, the first ethnological group encountered by Colombo, and the only one known to him; the Tupi-Guarani of Brazil, who had conquered and occupied most of the shore which fell to the lot of Portugal; the Iroquois, who held the district colonised by France; and the Algonquins, who occupied with less power of resistance to invasion that colonised by England. It is remarkable that all these nations appear once to have been maritime and fishing peoples, to have multiplied and developed their advancement in the immediate neighbourhood of the sea, and thence to have penetrated and settled various tracts of the interior. We trace them to three maritime districts, all extremely favourable to practice in fishing, navigation, and exploration: (1) the Nahuatlacâ, Iroquois, and Algonquins, to British Columbia; (2) the Aymara-Quichua and the Tupi-Guarani to the ancient "Argentine sea"—a vast body of salt water which at no very remote period filled the great plain of Argentina—and to the chain of great lakes which once existed to the north of it; (3) the Caribs to the Orinoco, whence they spread by a natural advance to the West Indian archipelago, and probably to the valley of the Mississippi, where one branch of them, at no very remote period before the Discovery, perhaps founded large agricultural pueblos, still traceable in the earthworks which in many places line the banks of that great river and its tributaries, and threw up the "Animal Mounds" which are among the most curious monuments of ancient America.

The Nahuatlacâ or "Civilised People" (*nahua* = rule of life; *tlacatl*, pl. *tlacâ* = man) appear to have originally dwelt at no great distance from the Iroquois and Algonquins, on the North American coast opposite Vancouver Island, where their peculiar advancement had its first development. With them the history, in the ordinary sense, of aboriginal America begins. The Nahuatlacâ alone among American peoples possessed a true though inaccurate chronology, and kept painted records of contemporary and past events. Pinturas preserved at Tezcuco variously assigned the years 387 and 439 of the Christian era as the date of the earliest migration to the south from maritime lands far to the north of California. A more probable date—about A.D. 780—was furnished to the earliest Spanish enquirers as the time when the first swarm of the Aculhuaquê, or "Strong Men," arrived in Anahuac from Aculhuacan, their previous seat northward of Xalisco, founded the pueblos of Tollan and Tollantzinco, and entered the Mexican Valley, where they settled at Culhuacan and Cohuatlichan and built on an island in the Lake a few huts, which later grew into the pueblo of Mexico. By a long subsequent immigration were founded the Tecpanec pueblos in the South-Western corner of the Lake, to which Mexico was once tributary, and on whose subjugation by Mexico the dominion found by the Conquistadores was established about a century before the Conquest. The Tecpanec pueblos, five in number, the principal one being Azcapozalco, subjugated a rival confederacy, on the opposite shore, headed by Tezcuco, about 1406. In this conquest they were materially assisted by the people of two villages (Tenochtitlan and Tlatelolco), founded on the island of Mexico nearly a century before by a wandering tribe of non-Nahuatlacan origin, to whom the Tecpanecs had given the name of Aztecá, or "Crane-people." Over these lake villages, after the Tezcucans had been subdued by their aid, the Tecpanecs maintained a relentless tyranny, which at length produced a revolt, in the course of which the Mexican villagers obtained a complete victory. The Tezcucans, who rose against their Tecpanec conquerors shortly afterwards (1431), regained their liberty; and the two Mexican pueblos entered into an alliance with Tezcuco, in which Tlacopan, a Tecpanec pueblo which had remained neutral during the struggle, was also included. This confederacy conquered and considerably enlarged the dominion acquired by the Tecpanec confederacy, and held in subjection a large and populous tract extending from the Atlantic to the Pacific, and containing all the best parts of the southern extremity of North America, where it narrows towards the Isthmus of Tehuantepec. One important district only was excluded from it. This was a highland tract held by Tlaxcallan, Huexotzinco, and Cholollan,—pueblos of the Nahuatlacá, founded in early times, and never subjugated either by the Tecpanecs, or by the confederated pueblos who succeeded to their dominion. At the Spanish Conquest Cholollan, the largest and most prosperous of the three, was in alliance with the Lake pueblos; and there is little doubt that Tlaxcallan and Huexotzinco would have been admitted to the same status but for the Mexican Rule of Life, which demanded war every twenty days, ostensibly as a means of procuring sacrifices for the sun and other gods, but really to provide the material for the cannibal feasts by which each sacrifice was terminated. Had peace been made between the pueblos of the Lake and those of the highlands, both groups must have had recourse to distant frontiers for the means of fulfilling what was universally regarded by the Nahuatlacá as an imperative obligation. Human sacrifice, indeed, was understood to be necessary to the cosmic order, for without it the sun, who was conceived as a god of animal nature, subsisting by food and drink, would not merely cease to yield his warmth, but would perish out of the heavens.

The importance of the New World to Europe, in the first century after the Discovery, chiefly rested on the fact that it was found to be a huge storehouse of gold and silver. To a large extent its resources in this respect had already been worked by the aborigines. Gold is the only metal which occurs in its native or unmixed state, and is largely found in the débris of those rocks which are most exposed to atmospheric action. It therefore early attracts the attention of savages, who easily apply it to purposes both of use and ornament; and more elaborate working in gold is one of the first arts of advanced life. Silver attracts attention and acquires value from its similarity, in most qualities, to gold; in Mexico both metals were regarded as of directly divine origin. The Toltecs, or people of Tollan, were reputed the earliest workers in gold and silver; and as this pueblo was understood to have been founded by a Nahuatlacan tribe at least as early as A.D. 780, these metals had been sought and wrought in the Mexican district for at least 700 years. There is no reason for concluding that after being manufactured they were largely, or indeed at all, exported; hence the immense accumulations of metallic wealth which were found in the Mexican district—accumulations greedily seized by the Conquistadores, and poured through Spanish channels into the mints of Europe, where the stock of gold had probably not been substantially increased since the fall of the Roman Empire. Still larger accessions to the mineral wealth of Europe followed the discovery and conquest of Peru—especially after the Spaniards became masters of the mines of Potosi—and of New Granada, where an almost savage people had laid up great quantities of the precious metals in the form of utensils and rude works of art: and from the discovery and conquest of these richly endowed countries, and the plunder of their stored-up wealth, date the serious efforts of European nations other than Spain and Portugal to acquire territory in the New World.

Twenty-five years passed between Colombo's discovery and the first intelligence of Mexico. During this period Spanish America was limited to the four greater Antilles—Española, Cuba, Puerto Rico, and Jamaica. On the northern shore of the South American continent, in what is now Venezuela, attempts had been made to effect a lodgment, but in vain; this district, and indeed the continent generally, was long regarded as a mere field for slave-raiding, the captives being sold in Española and Cuba. The smaller islands, and the other adjacent continental coasts, remained unconquered and uncolonised; much as on the opposite side of the Atlantic the Canaries and the Madeira group were parcelled into feudal estates and parishes, while the neighbouring shore of Africa remained unattempted. The Spaniards, wholly new to their task, had to gain experience as colonists in a savage land. Often their settlements were founded on ill-chosen sites. When Isabella, Colombo's first colony in Española, had to be abandoned, San Domingo was founded on the opposite side of the island (1494); the site of this, again, was changed by Ovando, the successor of Colombo after his removal from the administration (1502); and the same thing happened at Santiago de los Caballeros. Of the eighteen towns founded in the early years of colonisation a century later only ten survived. A few towns were founded in Puerto Rico by Ovando; Cuba was colonised by Diego Velasquez, and Jamaica by Juan de Esquivel. But the settlements in both were few and unprosperous, Santiago de Cuba having in the course of a few years become almost deserted. Sugar was the only crop yielding profits; gold was procured in the smallest quantities; the best investment was to take over horned cattle, turn them loose to breed, and hunt the savage herd for its hides and tallow, which were shipped for sale to Europe.

By such means, and by mercilessly tasking the Indians as labourers in field and mine, many emigrants in time became rich men, and looked eagerly round for new and wider fields of adventure. Slave-raiding on the continental coasts was a favourite employment, and a certain quantity of gold was readily bartered for trifles by the natives, wherever the Spaniards landed; and by these pursuits the Cuban colonists at length reached the coast pueblos of Yucatan, which were comparatively recent outposts of Nahuatlacan advancement. Velasquez, the governor of Cuba, in 1518 sent a squadron of vessels to reconnoitre this coast more fully; Grijalva, who commanded, traced the shore-line as far as the *tierra caliente* of Mexico, and reached Vera Cruz, then as now the port of Mexico. Here Carib seamen shipped the surplus tributes and manufactured products of the Lake pueblos for barter in the southern parts of their extensive field of navigation. From Vera Cruz Grijalva coasted northwards as far as the Panuco river. Many large pueblos were descried in the distance; the names of Mexico and of Motecuhzoma, its Tlatohuani ("Speaker," in the sense of "Commander" or Supreme Chief), first fell on Spanish ears; and the description of the great Lake pueblo was listened to with more interest, because in these parts the exploring party obtained by barter an immense quantity of gold. Here, at length, signs of civilised life were found; large hopes of wealth, whether by commerce or plunder, were excited; and on the return of the expedition Velasquez ordered a new one to proceed thither without delay. His design was simply to prosecute the remunerative trade which Grijalva had begun. Others formed bolder schemes; and his secretary and treasurer, probably in collusion with the schemers, persuaded him to entrust the command to Hernan Cortes, who had conceived the plan of employing the whole military force of Santiago de Cuba at his disposal in invading Mexico and subjugating it at one blow. This Cortes accomplished only by fortune's favour; for he knew nothing of the imminent peril he was rashly encountering, and his force barely escaped annihilation.

The landing of Cortes, and his safe progress through a difficult country to the frontier of Tlaxcallan, were facilitated by the circumstance that the people of the country, who had groaned for the greater part of a century under the cruel tyranny of Mexico, welcomed him everywhere as a deliverer. The coast tribes mistook him for the ancient Toltec god Quetzalcohuatl. The Tlaxcaltecs, who had never beheld a friendly force on their borders, at first mistook him for an ally of the Mexicans; but on learning the true aspect of affairs they joined him as allies. Thus Cortes, from the territory of Tlaxcallan as his base, conducted his campaign against the Lake pueblos with the help of auxiliaries who possessed a complete knowledge of the country, and a military experience gained by a century's constant fighting. At first he posed as a friendly emissary of the great European monarch his master. Having on these terms obtained admittance to Mexico for himself and his armed force, he seized the Tlatohuani's person, put him in chains, and assumed the government. These proceedings naturally led to a rising on the part of the Mexican warriors, who attacked the Spaniards and drove them from the pueblo with great loss, taking many prisoners and sacrificing them to the Nahuatlacan gods. Driven ignominiously from Mexico, and chased by an infuriated enemy through and out of the Valley, Cortes retired by a circuitous route to Tlaxcallan, and laid his plans anew. Having refreshed his troops and renewed his supplies, he built two brigantines for action on the Lake; launched them from Tezcuco, which he occupied with little difficulty; assaulted Mexico by water; gained possession of its streets and buildings by slow degrees; and at length broke the resolute resistance of its warriors, and rased its clay-built edifices to the ground. He had won for the Castilian Crown the dominion of the confederated Lake pueblos—a tract of country extending from the Pacific to the Mexican gulf, 800 miles in length on the Pacific shore, and somewhat less on the other, comprising many large towns and above five hundred agricultural villages, and the seat of the most advanced communities of the New World.

This conquest was no barren victory over mere barbarians. Though no ethnologist would concede to the Nahuatlacan polity the title of a civilisation, it possessed the foundations on which all civilisation is built —a numerous and docile peasantry, an organised system of labour, and physical elements adequate to wealth-production. In these circumstances an unique social state had been evolved, to which the nearest analogue in the Old World is the gross barbarism of Ashanti or Dahomey. It was lower than these in that, except man himself, there were no animals kept for labour, nor were any kept for food except man and the dog. In other respects the arts of life were better developed: and to the superficial observation of the Conquistadores the large territory dominated by the Lake pueblos had an aspect sufficiently civilised to justify them in giving it the name of "New Spain." What was of most importance in the eye of the European invaders, it possessed stores of the precious metals, which had been accumulating in

the hands of dominant tribes for seven centuries.    Immense quantities of
treasure steadily poured henceforth into Spain; and America assumed an
entirely new aspect for the nations of Western Europe.    Almost from
the first Spain perceived that other European powers would dispute
with her, and perhaps one day wrest from her, the possession of the
rich New World which accident had given to her.    The conquest of
Mexico nearly corresponded with the opening of a period of hostility
between Spain and France, which lasted, though with considerable
intermissions, from 1521 to 1556.    Cortes, who entered Mexico in the
former year, despatched at the end of 1522 two vessels to Spain laden
with Mexican treasure; Giovanni da Verrazzano, a Florentine in the
French service, captured these near the Azores, and about the same time
took a large vessel homeward bound from Española, laden with treasure,
pearls, sugar, and hides.    Enriched by these prizes, he gave large compli-
mentary presents to the French King and High Admiral; and general
amazement was felt at the wealth which was pouring into Spain from
its transatlantic possessions.    "The Emperor," Francis exclaimed, "can
carry on the war against me by means of the riches he draws from the
West Indies alone!"    Of the immense inheritance obtained by Spain
in America the only parts actually reduced to possession by the
Spanish monarch were the four great Antilles, and those portions of the
continent which had been settled by the Nahuatlacâ.    Southward, the
shores from Yucatan as far as the Plate River had been explored by
Spain and Portugal; and all that seemed to remain to the future
adventurer was the North American shore from the Mexican Gulf to
Newfoundland.    Jocosely refusing to acknowledge the claim of the
peninsular powers to make a bipartite division of the sphere between
them until they should "produce the will of Adam, constituting them
his universal heirs," Francis commissioned the successful Florentine
captain to reconnoitre the whole shore from Florida to Newfoundland.
This being done, he intimated to Europe that he claimed it, by right
of discovery, as the share of France in the great American heritage.
He called it New France,—a term familiar in French ears since the
beginning of the thirteenth century as the title of the Latin Empire
of Constantinople, and now less inappropriately applied by transfer to
the New World.

The commission thus entrusted to and accomplished by Verrazzano
was masked under the pretence of seeking a North-west passage to the
Far East.    But its real object was to lay a foundation for the claim of
France to the whole of America north of Mexico, put forward in the
belief, which ultimately proved well warranted, that this tract would,
like Mexico, prove rich in the precious metals.    Having completed the
voyage by which his name is chiefly remembered, Verrazzano resumed the
profitable practice of plundering the Spanish homeward-bound ships,
and took some prizes between Spain and the Canaries.    On his return he

fell in with a squadron of Spanish war vessels, surrendered to them after
a severe engagement, and in 1527 was hanged as a pirate at Colmenar
de Arenas. France strenuously maintained, and sought by repeated
efforts to substantiate, the right to North America which Verrazzano's
coasting-voyage was supposed to have acquired. In periods of war no
attempts at possession were made; but in the intervals of peace expeditions were undertaken to the Gulf of St Lawrence, with the view of
exploring the passage to the Far East of which it was imagined to be
the beginning. Cartier made two voyages for this purpose in 1534 and
1535; and in 1540 he sailed up the great river of Canada, and selected
a site for the colony which in 1542 Roberval attempted to establish.
Cartier brought to France news of the two principal native nations
of North America—nations on which later French settlers bestowed the
names "Iroquois" and "Algonquin," each being a purely French word
embodying a peculiarity in the sound of their respective languages.
The Algonquins, who were the earlier immigrants, were partially cultivators of the soil, but chiefly relied for subsistence on hunting and
fishing. The more advanced Iroquois, who appear to have driven the
Algonquins from the choicest parts of their territory, had nearly reached
the stage in which agriculture is the main source of subsistence, though
they were accomplished hunters and formidable warriors : and their
compact territory was parcelled out among five tribes, who formed the
confederation so well known in later history as the "Five Nations."
Though Roberval's attempt failed, the example thus set was followed in
a later generation in other latitudes, and other nations were encouraged
to imitate it. Meanwhile the aspect of American enterprise was greatly
modified, and the effect produced by the discovery of the treasures of
Mexico greatly enhanced, by the discovery and conquest of Peru, the
richest district of the New World hitherto revealed.

Here, again, we are struck by the comparatively modern date of the
aboriginal dominion which the Spanish adventurers found established
along the coast and in the valleys of the Andes. This dominion, of
which the centre was at Cuzco, was very much more extensive than that
of the federated Mexican pueblos. Unlike the Nahuatlacâ, the Peruvian
people had no reckoning of years; nor can the date of any fact in
Peruvian history anterior to the conquest be accurately ascertained. All
that we know is that the settlement of the nation or people who then
dominated the sierra and the coast from Cuzco, where the traditions
of their arrival were still fresh, was of comparatively modern date.
They called themselves *Inca*, or "people of the sun" (*Inti*). They
were probably an offshoot from a large group of warlike tribes, in
which the Tupi-Guarani were included, long settled on the margins
of the vanished Argentine sea and of a chain of great lakes to the
north of it, where they subsisted by fishing and hunting. From this
district they ascended to the sierra, where the huanaco and vicuña,

two small cognate species of the camel genus, furnished abundant food and material for clothing.  These they domesticated as the *llama* and *paco*, both being Quichua words implying subjugation; they propagated by art the pulse and food-roots of the Cordillera, and established many permanent pueblos in and near the great lake basin of Titicaca, the earliest seat of Peruvian advancement.  From this district they advanced northwards, and occupied a canton almost impregnably situated in the midst of immense mountains and deep gorges, known to geographers as the "Cuzco district."  In historical times they had separated into two branches, speaking two languages, evidently divergent forms of a single original, called by Spanish grammarians *Aymara* and *Quichua*; names which it has been found convenient to use as ethnical terms for the peoples who spoke them.  Tradition carried back the history of the Aymara-Quichua in Cuzco and its neighbourhood about three hundred years, during which eleven Apu-Capac-Incas, or "head-chiefs of the Inca (people)" were enumerated; but it was generally considered, and is almost conclusively shown by balancing evidence, that not much more than a century had elapsed since they made their first conquests beyond the limited "Cuzco district," and that only the last five of the Apu-Capac-Incas—Huiracocha-Inca, Pachacutic-Inca, Tupac-Inca-Yupanqui, Huaina-Capac-Inca, and Tupac-atau-huallpa—all forming a chain of succession from father to son, had ruled over an extensive territory. The great expansion took place in the time of Pachacutic-Inca, and is traceable to an invasion by an alliance of tribes from the north, who had long dominated Middle Peru, and now sought to conquer the Cuzco district and the valley of Lake Titicaca.  Under Pachacutic this invasion was repelled; the allies were defeated at Yahuarpampa, and the war was carried into the enemy's country: the dominion of the invading tribes now fell almost at one blow into the hands of the chiefs of Cuzco.  These victories were rapidly followed by the conquest of the northern or Quito district, now forming the republic of Ecuador, and of the coast-valleys, where a remarkable and superior advancement, founded on fishing and agriculture, had existed probably from an earlier date than that of the stronger tribes of the sierra.

The Spaniards, who obtained information of the Inca people and their dominion soon after crossing the isthmus of Panama, reconnoitred the Peruvian coast in 1525, during the head-chieftaincy of Huaina-Capac.  But this chief had died, and a civil war, in which the succession was contested between his two sons Tupac-cusi-huallpa ("the sun makes joy"), commonly known by the epithet Huascar ("the chosen one"), and Tupac-atau-huallpa ("the sun makes good fortune"), had been terminated in favour of the latter, when Pizarro invaded the country in 1532 with a party of 183 soldiers.  Everywhere large accumulations of treasure were found; for gold and silver had been mined both in the coast-pueblos and in the sierra from remote times, and the whole of the produce still remained, largely accumulated in the numerous burial-places of a people who preserved with almost Egyptian care the corpses of the dead, depositing with them the gold and silver which had belonged to them when alive. The facilities for marching, which a century of well-organised aboriginal rule had established from one end of the dominion to the other, and in several places between the coast and the mountains, made Pizarro's progress easy. So soon as the supreme chief had been seized and imprisoned or put to death, the submission of his followers, and the subjugation of his territory, quickly followed. But it was an easier task for the vile and sordid adventurers who invaded Peru to destroy the tyranny of its aboriginal conquerors and sack its pueblos, than for the Spanish government to assert the authority of the Crown, and provide the Inca dominion with a suitably organised administration. After much bloodshed, extending over many years, this was at length accomplished; the lands which had belonged to the Inca, the sun, or the native chiefs, and the peasantry, were, with their peasant inhabitants, chiefly serfs attached to the soil, granted by the Crown to gentlemen immigrants, and held on similar terms to those annexed to the "commends" of the military Orders—the name "commend," indeed, becoming the technical term for estates so held. Here, as in Mexico, churches were built and endowed, diocesan organisations were established, and the difficult work of converting the Indians was begun and earnestly carried on by a devoted clergy; superior courts of justice were constituted, and law was administered in the village by alcaldes; the aboriginal population, freed from the grinding tyranny of their old masters, increased and throve; new mines, especially of silver, were discovered and wrought. Both Peru and Mexico gradually assumed the resemblance of civilised life; and their prosperity testified to the benefits conferred on them by conquests which, however unjustifiable on abstract grounds, in both cases redeemed the populations affected by them from cruel and oppressive governments, and bloody and senseless religions.

After the conquest of Peru the treasure sent by America to Spain was trebled; the silver mines of Europe were practically abandoned, and before long Europe's entire gold-supply was obtained from the New World. In these circumstances the naval enterprise not only of the enemies, but of the political rivals of Spain was stimulated to assume the form of piracy; and in this connexion a peculiar cause came into operation about this time, which had a strongly modifying effect on the destinies of the New World. Both Charles V and his son and successor in Spain, Philip II, had constituted themselves the champions of the Catholic Church; and they freely employed the gold of America in the pursuit of intrigues favourable to their policy in every European country. Hence, to cut off the supply at its source became the universal policy of Protestantism, now struggling for life throughout Western Europe. The persecution of the Huguenots drove large numbers of

French Protestants to join the roving captains who harassed Spanish commerce; and their efforts, begun in time of war, were continued in time of peace. Thus did the French wars with Spain develope into a general war on the part of the Protestants of Western Europe against Spain as the champion of the Papacy and the author of the Inquisition. In the New World this movement resulted in the plundering of Spanish vessels, attacks on the Spanish ports with the object of holding them to ransom, and finally attempts, unsuccessful at first, but effectual when experience in colonisation had once been gained, to found new European communities, in the teeth of all opposition, on the soil of a continent which the Spaniards regarded as most justly their own, and as before all things entrusted to them for the diffusion, and the ultimate extension over the whole globe, of the Catholic faith.

Here, at length, we reach a point of view from which the general bearing of the New World on the parallel growth of European economics and politics on the one hand, and of religious theory, philosophical thought, and scientific advancement on the other, might be brought under observation. Our remarks must be confined to the latter group of topics. For during the period covered by this chapter the political system of Europe was not sensibly disturbed, while the economic changes produced by the discovery and conquest of the New World were as yet imperfectly developed. But the sudden shattering of the old geography produced by the Discovery reacted at once in a marked way on European habits of thought. Religion is man's earliest philosophy; and what affects his habits of thought and alters his intellectual points of view cannot but modify his religious conceptions. The discovery of the New World, and its prospective employment as a place for the planting of new communities of European origin, greatly contributed to substitute for the medieval law of religious intolerance the modern principle of toleration. In the Old World the former theory had hitherto enjoyed general acceptance, and it rested on a logical basis. There was Scriptural warranty for the doctrine that the Supreme Being was a jealous God, visiting the sins of men not only upon their descendants to the third and fourth generation, but also upon the nation to which such men belonged; and it followed that to believe or conceive of Him, or to worship Him, otherwise than in accordance with the revelation graciously made by Him for the guidance of man, was something more than an offence against Himself. It was an intolerable wrong to society, for it exposed the pious many to the penalty incurred by an impious minority. Plague and pestilence, famine and destruction in war, were brought on a nation by religious apostasy; and it was therefore not merely lawful, but a national duty, to stamp out apostasy in its beginnings. The history of Christendom down to the Discovery of America is in the main one long series of more or less successful applications of this perfectly intelligible principle to the general conduct of human affairs. Had it not been for the New World, the Old World might perhaps to this day have been governed in accordance with it.

But the New World was virgin soil. All Christendom, with the approbation even of Jew and Islamite, would readily have united in the opinion that its gross aboriginal idolatries should be extinguished, and the worship of the One God introduced into it, in whatever form. And in the plantation or creation of new Christian communities in America the reason for intolerance as a necessary social principle no longer existed. Each colony—and colonies in this practically vacant continent could be planted at considerable distances from each other—could now settle its religious principles for itself, for it did so at its own risk. In this way the Old World found the solution of what in France and elsewhere had, by the middle of the sixteenth century, become a serious social and political difficulty. In France, in Germany, in England, the nation was coming to be divided into two hostile camps, Catholic and Protestant. Was the one half in each case to be extinguished by the other, in an internecine war? The banishment of the weaker party by migration—and already expatriation was substituted for the death penalty in the case of greater moral crimes than heresy—was a wise and merciful alternative. The French Protestants, who felt that the course of God's dealings with man must on the whole be in their favour, were the first to think of a new career, in a new world perhaps revealed for the purpose, as the beginning of a better order of things, if not as the fulfilment of the destiny of the Reformed faith; and, as the triumph of the Catholic party in France became more and more probable, Protestant leaders cast anxious eyes towards the American shore, as a possible place of refuge for their people, should they be worsted in the struggle. An attempt of this nature was made, with the sanction and help of Coligny, the head of the Protestant party, by Nicolas Durand, better known by his assumed name of Villegagnon, a Knight of the Maltese Order who had served in the expedition of Charles V against Algiers, and who also distinguished himself as an author and an amateur theologian. Durand had resided at Nantes, where the propriety of providing a transatlantic refuge for Protestants, and the capabilities of the Brazilian coast, now frequently visited for commercial purposes by French seamen, were matters of common discussion. He resolved to be the first to carry such a scheme into effect; and he found ample support among the partisans of the Reformed religion, including Coligny, through whose influence he obtained a large pecuniary grant from the French King. In May 1555 he sailed with two ships for the coast of South Brazil, where he settled on an island, still known as Ilha de Villagalhão, near the mouth of the bay of Rio de Janeiro, two miles from the mainland. Durand named the country he proposed to occupy "Antarctic France." The voyage was understood to mark, and did in fact mark, a new era in history. It was the actual beginning of the movement which brought to the New World, as a place where they might worship God in their own way, the Puritans of New England, the Quakers of Pennsylvania and the Catholics of Maryland. Scholars called it the Expedition of the Indonauts; and a French pedant, after the fashion of the time, celebrated its departure in an indifferent Greek epigram. God looked down, he said, from heaven, and saw that the corrupt Christians of Europe had utterly forgotten both Himself and His Son. He therefore resolved to transfer the Christian Mysteries to a New World, and to destroy the sinful Old World to which they had been entrusted in vain.

Preoccupied with the task of establishing themselves in India and the Far East, the Portuguese had for thirty years after the discovery of Brazil done almost nothing by way of reducing this district into possession. A few ships frequented the coast for the purpose of trading with the natives, and setting ashore criminals to take their chance of being adopted or eaten by them. The success of Madeira as a sugar-growing island suggested the extension of this form of enterprise in Brazil, to which attention had been drawn by a recent discovery of gold; and the soil, as in Madeira, was granted out in hereditary captaincies, each grantee receiving exclusive rights over 50 leagues of sea-board. Martim Affonso de Sousa, afterwards viceroy in India, obtained the first of the fiefs, and took possession in 1531. Eleven others followed, and in 1549 the direction of the whole colony was vested in a Governor-general, whose seat was fixed at Bahia. The Portuguese settlements were in North and Middle Brazil, and by choosing an insular site far to the south Durand expected to escape disturbance. His first care was to build a fort and mount his guns. He announced his arrival to the Church of Geneva, by whom two pastors were duly ordained and sent out with the next batch of emigrants. Durand began by sharing with these ministers the conduct of divine worship; and specimens of his extemporaneous prayers, in the course of which he gave thanks to God for mercifully visiting the mainland with a depopulating pestilence, whereby the enemies of the elect were destroyed, and the Lord's path made straight, have come down to us. He devoted to theological studies the abundant leisure left him by his administration. Convinced by the arguments of Cyprian and Clement, he ordered that water should be mingled with the sacramental wine, directed salt and oil to be poured into the baptismal font, and forbade the second marriage of a pastor, fortifying himself in the position he thus assumed by argu-mentative appeals to Holy Scripture. When he at last publicly announced his adherence to the doctrine of transubstantiation, a breach between him and his Calvinist flock was inevitable. Only one among them, a voluble doctor of the Sorbonne whom he associated with himself in the office of the pulpit, supported his pretensions. When the scandalised colonists absented themselves from public worship, he proceeded to severe disciplinary measures; and in the end they quitted the island, threw themselves on the kindness of the savages of the mainland, and made their way to trading vessels in which they sailed for Europe. Thus the Indonaut colony, the first Protestant community in the New World, ended in a ludicrous failure.

As the struggle between the Catholics and Protestants of France became more and more desperate, the idea of founding a Protestant colony in America was revived: and it was now resolved to use for this purpose the immense tract which Verrazzano's voyage was understood to have acquired for the French Crown. Coligny, with the assent of Charles IX, equipped two vessels which he despatched on February 18, 1562, under the command of Jean Ribault, to found the first colony attempted in North America since the return of Roberval in 1540. After exploring the coast, Ribault chose Port Royal Sound in the present State of South Carolina, as the most promising site for a colony; began the construction of a fort, to which he gave the name of Charles-fort, for the protection of those whom he intended to leave behind; and returned to Europe. Their supplies being exhausted, the colonising party fell into dissensions, mutinied against the rigorous discipline enforced by their captain, and assassinated him. No reinforcements arriving from Europe, they built a pinnace, intending to return, put to sea, suffered indescribable hardships, and put back again, more dead than alive, towards the American shore. They were picked up by a homeward-bound English barque, one of whose crew had been with Ribault on the outward voyage. Some were landed in France; while those who were not too exhausted to continue the voyage were taken on to England, where the liveliest interest was by this time felt in the question of North American colonisation. How this revived interest arose, may now be briefly explained.

The history of English enterprise in connexion with the New World goes back in substance to the period of the Discovery itself. Even before this, Bristol seamen had sought for the mythical St Brandan's in the expanses of the Atlantic; possibly the ancient connexion of that port with Iceland had brought the Norse sagas to their ears, and the quest pursued by them was in substance the search for "Vineland" or New England. John Cabot, having obtained on March 5, 1496, the patent referred to on an earlier page, evidently sailed in quest of the "New Land" or "New Island" of the Northmen, and between that date and August, 1497, when he returned to Bristol, reached and investigated the shores of Labrador and Newfoundland which represent the coast called by the Northmen "Hellu-Land" (stony land). A voyage was attempted by him to the New Land in 1498, but not accomplished, and thenceforward English interest in the continent of America relaxed, although the Newfoundland waters were increasingly frequented by fishermen of other nations; so that the voyage of 1496–7 was practically forgotten, when, nearly sixty years afterwards, English-men began once more to turn their attention to America. From the untroubled early years of Henry VIII, when America, as yet wholly savage, and its discovery received conspicuous notice in a serious philo-sophical drama, to the marriage of Philip and Mary, when it stood forth in the eyes of Europe as the source of more wealth than the world had ever seen, the New World is scarcely mentioned in English literature, though the continental press teemed with accounts of it and allusions to it. But an old dramatist's picture of the new continent, as it presented itself to English eyes about 1515, becomes all the more striking through its isolation. The play, or "interlude," is entitled *The Four Elements*; the leading personage, named *Experience*, discourses at some length on the "Great Ocean"—"so great that never man could tell it, since the world began, till now these twenty year"—and the new continent lately found beyond it; a continent "so large of room" as to be "much longer than all Christendom," for its coast has been traced above 5000 miles. The inhabitants, from the south, where they "go naked alway," to the north, where they are clad in the skins of beasts, are everywhere savages, living in woods and caves, and knowing nothing of God and the devil, of heaven and hell, but worshipping the sun for his great light. The fisheries, the timber, and the copper of America are named as its chief sources of wealth; and the speaker laments, in stanzas perfectly rhyth-mical, though the accent is somewhat forced, that England should have missed the opportunity of discovering and colonising this vast country :

> O what a [great] thing had been then,
> If that they that be Englishmen
>     Might have been the first of all
> That there should have taken possession,
> And made first building and habitation,
>     A memory perpetual !
>
> And also what an honourable thing,
> Both to the realm, and to the king,
> To have had his dominion extending
>     There into so far a ground,
> Which the noble king of late memory,
> The most wise prince the seventh Harry,
>     [Had] caused first for to be found !

Nor is this all that England has lost. Hers would have been the privilege of introducing civilisation and preaching the Gospel in this dark continent—of leading its brute-like tribes "to know of men the manner, and also to know God their Maker." This task, it is evidently felt, would more fittingly have fallen to the lot of England than of Castile and Portugal.

The American coast was doubtless occasionally sighted from English vessels. But it was only gazed on as a curious spectacle. The Northern shore, the only part accessible to English adventurers without encroachment on the transatlantic possessions of a friendly power, yielded little or nothing to commerce which could not be obtained with less trouble in Europe itself. During these sixty years, which saw no break in the friendly relations between England and Spain, many English merchants resided in the latter country, who must have heard with astonishment, and probably a certain envy, of the rich treasure-districts which exploration revealed in quick succession, and occasionally visited them, or some of them, in person. Not until the marriage of the English Queen with the Spanish heir-apparent was it ever suggested that England should aspire to share in the wealth which the fortune of events had poured into the lap of Spain. About this time Mexico and Potosi shone forth with tempting lustre in the eyes of Europe. These districts were mere patches on the map of a continent which probably contained gold and silver in all its parts, and which had been designed by nature to be the treasure-house of the world. Nine-tenths of it remained unexplored. The events of the Franco-Spanish wars had proved the Spaniards incapable of excluding from it other nations whose seamen were better than their own; and English seamen, then as now, acknowledged no superiors. Other Mexicos and Potosis doubtless awaited the first adventurer bold enough to strike the blow that should secure them. Why should England again neglect her opportunity?

It was not, however, exactly in this aspect that the suggestion of "America for the English" was first put forward. The writer who earned the credit of it—one Richard Eden, Hakluyt's precursor, who to book-learning added a keen personal interest in sailors and sailors' tales—was a clerk in Philip's "English Treasury." Possibly he owed this post to a volume published by him in the year preceding that of Philip's marriage, containing a translation of a somewhat meagre account of the New World compiled by a German geographer. The object of this volume, in his own words, was to persuade Englishmen to "make attempts in the New World to the glory of God and the commodity of our country," and the sole inducement held out was America's wealth in the precious metals. Only a few years had elapsed since the produce of the mines of Potosi was first registered in the books of the Spanish King. Had Englishmen, writes Eden, been awake to their interests, "that Rich Treasury called PERULARIA (the bullion-warehouse of Seville) might long since have been in the Tower of London!" At this date Edward VI, a Protestant, with whom Spain's papal title to the New World was not likely to find recognition, was on the throne. His future marriage remained undecided; but it was anticipated that he would intermarry with a French princess, and that England and France, henceforth in strict alliance, would continue the process of despoiling Spain, which France alone had so successfully begun. By the death of Edward and the succession of Mary the political outlook was changed. On July 19,

1554, Philip of Spain arrived in England, and in the next week was married to Mary at Winchester. He brought with him immense quantities of gold and silver borne on the backs of a hundred horses. Eden's regretful comment was now misplaced, for the contents of "that Rich Treasury called Perularia" were actually on their way to the Tower of London! On October 2 there arrived at the Tower £50,000 in silver, destined to form the nucleus of Philip's "English Treasury," in which Eden had obtained a clerkship. He watched the entry of the newly-married sovereigns into the metropolis; and his former vision, in a modified shape, now floated before him as a consequence of the match. An ancient commercial alliance was now fortified by a dynastic one; Spain and England must surely henceforth deal with the New World as partners. Eden now resolved to translate the first portion of the "Decades" of Peter Martyr, which contained a lively and popular account, in a series of Latin letters, written in the fashion of the day, of American history from the Discovery to the Conquest of Mexico. Other matter of a similar description filled up his volume; and in the preface he eloquently urges English sailors and merchants to quit the well-worn tracks of traditional commerce, and adventure boldly to the coasts of Florida and Newfoundland.

Although such ideas were doubtless widely entertained, the short reign of Mary afforded no scope for realising them; and the new Anglo-Spanish connexion left in the New World but a single and fleeting trace. A South-American official, when planning a town in a remote valley of the Argentine Andes, named it Londres, or London, in honour of the union of Philip and Mary. This was the first place in America named after an English city. Its existence was of short duration; the Indians expelled the colonists, who were fain to choose another site. The only noteworthy fact during this reign bearing upon the present subject was, that a remarkable maritime project was disastrously proved to be impracticable. Its aim was the discovery of a North-eastern passage to the Far East, answering to the South-eastern passage that was now commonly made by the Portuguese round the Cape of Good Hope. Shortly before Edward's death Sir Hugh Willoughby sailed for this purpose with three vessels. Winter came suddenly on; Willoughby laid up his ships in a harbour of Russian Lapland, where he and the crews of two of his vessels were frozen to death; while Chancellor, the captain of the third, with difficulty reached the White Sea, landed at Archangel, and returned by Moscow. This disaster stopped further search for the passage; seamen and traders henceforth turned in the opposite direction, and speculated on the discovery of a North-west passage. Elizabeth had been on the throne eighteen years, when Frobisher, a Yorkshireman who had constituted himself the pioneer of this project, obtained the means of bringing it to the test, and commenced a fruitless search, which lasted two centuries and a half, for a passage first proved in our own generation to have a geo-graphical existence, but to be nautically impossible. Frobisher's voyages did little towards effecting their ostensible purpose. Led astray by the quest of the precious metals, he loaded his ships with immense quantities of a deceptive pyrites, which contained a small proportion of gold, but far less than enough to pay the cost of extracting it; and the scheme, which had degenerated into a mere mining adventure, was quietly abandoned.

Meanwhile the attention of Western Europe was still concentrated on "Florida,"—a term denoting all the North American continent as far northward as the Newfoundland fishery, and bestowed on it by its dis-coverer Ponce de Leon, who reached it on Easter Day (*Pascua Florida*), 1513. Eden's preface conveys the impression that the Spaniards had neglected this vast tract of the continent; nothing however could be less true. The most strenuous efforts had been made to penetrate it, in the confident expectation that it would prove as rich in treasure as Mexico itself; and Pamphilo de Narvaez, chiefly known to fame by his futile mission to arrest the campaign of Cortes, had landed here in 1528 with the object of emulating that supremely fortunate adventurer's exploits. Repulsed and forced back to the coast, he took refuge in his ships and perished in a storm. Five only of his three hundred men regained Mexico, where they published the exciting news that Florida was simply the richest country in the world. This statement was probably made in irony rather than in seriousness; yet it was not without foundation in fact, for the Appalachian mountains contain mines of gold and silver which are profitably worked to this day. By the conquest of Peru adventure to Florida received for the second time a powerful stimulus. Hernan de Soto, a lieutenant of Pizarro, who had been appointed Governor of Cuba, undertook to annex it to the Spanish dominions (1538). His ill-fated expedition, commenced in the next year, forms a well-known episode in American history. During four years De Soto persevered in a series of zigzag marches through a sparsely peopled country, containing no pueblos larger than the average village of hunting tribes, and showing no trace whatever of either gold or silver. In descending the Mississippi he sickened and died; the miserable remnant of his troops sailed from its mouth to the Panuco river in Mexico, bringing back tidings of a failure more disheartening, because the result of a more protracted effort, than that of Narvaez. In 1549 some friars of the Dominican order, elsewhere so successful in dealing with the American aborigines, landed in Florida, only to be at once set upon and massacred. By this time the Indians knew the general character and aims of the new-comers who styled themselves "Christians," and dealt with them accordingly. Outside Spain it was generally thought that Providence had prescribed limits to Spanish conquest, and reserved the Northern continent for some other European people—obviously either the French or the English.

Hence, when in 1558 a Protestant princess succeeded to the English throne, she found the policy which she was expected to pursue in this direction defined for her in public opinion. Here was Florida, the "richest country in the world," still without any owner, or even any pretender to its ownership, though sixty years had passed since Colombo discovered the continent of which it formed a large and prominent part. A whole generation had passed away since the heroic period of Spanish-American history—the conquest of Mexico and Peru; and that period had evidently closed. Clearly Providence forbade Spain to cherish the hope of succeeding in any further attempt to subjugate Florida. France, though ambitious as ever, was hopelessly entangled in civil broils. Everyone expected Elizabeth, who was in truth no bigot, to found colonies in this vast and fertile tract, so near to England and so easily reached from it; where, perhaps, her Catholic and her Protestant subjects might settle in peace, each group respectively occupying some large and well-defined district of its own. The name itself, bandied about for half a century, had by this time become a household word which was not without humorous suggestions. Satirists travestied it as "Stolida," or land of simpletons, and "Sordida," or land of muckworms; pirates, arrested on suspicion and examined, mockingly avowed themselves bound for Florida. In France experiences of a certain kind—unedifying transactions of gallantry in the base sense of the word—were called "adventures of Florida." The world was eagerly expecting the impending revelation, which should disclose the future fate of the temperate regions of North America. To the pretensions of France the fortune of events soon gave a negative answer. Nothing daunted by the failure of Ribault's party, Coligny in 1565 despatched René Laudonnière, a captain who had served under Ribault, to make a second effort. Laudonnière chose as the site of his settlement the mouth of the river called by Ribault the River of May (St John's River), from its discovery by him on the first day of that month in 1562; and here he arrived in the midsummer of 1564, with a strong and well-armed party, built a fort, and began exploring the country. Most of the intending settlers had been pirates, whom, in the close proximity of St Domingo and Jamaica, it was impossible to keep from resuming their old trade; others joined an Indian chief, and followed him to war with a neighbouring tribe in hope of plunder. The stores of Fort Caroline were soon exhausted; and, but for the timely relief obtained from John Hawkins, who passed the Florida coast on his homeward way, the emigrants must have starved, or have returned to Europe, or have been dispersed among the wild aborigines. In the next year (1565) the Spaniards destroyed what was in effect a mere den of pirates, and built the fort of St Augustine to protect their own settlements and commerce, as well as the still unspoiled treasures of Appalachia, and to prevent the heretics of France from gaining a footing on American soil; and in a few years (1572) the massacre of St Bartholomew put an end to the Huguenot designs on Florida.

At this point, where France retires for a time from the stage, leaving England to enter upon it and open the drama of Anglo-American history, we drop the thread of events to resume our survey of the effect produced by the discovery and unveiling of the New World on European ideas and intellectual habits. The complete revolution in geography, which now suddenly revealed to man his gross ignorance in the most elementary field of knowledge—the earth beneath his feet—had a wider effect. It shook the existing system of the sciences, though it had not as yet the effect of shattering it, much less of replacing it by something more nearly in accordance with the truth of things. It produced in many—over and above the suspicion already long harboured in logical minds, that neither the accepted doctrine and practice of the Catholic Church nor any modification of it likely to meet with acceptance in its place, could possibly represent the true construction of God's will revealed in Scripture—that sense of general intellectual insecurity which is best named "scepticism." Charron's future motto, "Que sais-je?," became the leading motive in intellectual conduct. It is impossible to attempt here to trace this movement in its entirety; we can but select three writers, belonging to three successive generations, and all prominent among their contemporaries as pioneers of new paths of thought, and all of whom avowedly derived much of their inspiration from the events briefly noticed above. All three were laymen; a fact not in itself devoid of significance. The writings of ecclesiastics during this period, even in the case of distinguished humanists such as Bembo or Erasmus, show scarcely a trace of the same influence. The control of thought was passing away from the Church. All three, too, were lawyers, and two of them were Lord Chancellors of England. Sir Thomas More, born ten years before the voyage of Colombo, wrote and published his *Utopia* in 1516, soon after the Pacific had been first descried from a mountain in Darien, and while the Spaniards in the Antilles were gathering the information which led to the conquest of Mexico and Peru, both as yet unknown. This admirable classic of the Renaissance, too keen in its satire and too refined in its feeling to have any practical effect commensurate with the acceptance which it instantly won among cultivated and thoughtful contemporaries, was avowedly suggested by the discovery and settlement of the new Western World. What possibilities of discovery, not merely in the realm of geography, but in that of social organisation, morals, and politics, were laid open by this amazing revelation of a strange world of oceans, islands and continents, covering one-third of the sphere! The extent of America to the westward, with all that lay beyond, was as yet unknown; and More was not exceeding the limits of those possibilities when he described a traveller, who had accompanied Vespucci in his last voyage, as remaining in South America with a few companions and making their way westwards home by shore and sea, thus anticipating the circumnavigation of the globe which a few more years were to see achieved. The traveller's name is Hythlodaeus, or Expert in Nonsense; and none among the countries visited by him so strongly arrests his attention as the island of Utopia, or Nowhere, where the traditional absurdities dominant in the Old World are unknown, and society is constituted on a humane and reasonable basis. Utopia is an aristocratic republic, in which the officers of government, elected annually, are presided over by a chief magistrate elected for life. Everyone is engaged in agriculture, and drones are banished from the hive; it is an accepted principle that every man has a natural right to so much of the earth as is necessary for his subsistence, and may lawfully dispossess of his land any possessor who leaves it untilled. Even the generous imagination of More did not rise to the conception of a state of society in which slavery was unknown: and the labouring population of Utopia are still slaves. Not that they are held as private property, for private property is unknown. Whatever is valuable is held as it were on lease from the community, on condition of making such use of it as shall enure for the public benefit. The family is patriarchally governed; there is no coinage; gold and silver are not used as ornaments, but are only applied to the basest purposes, and precious stones serve only to adorn children. The energies of the Utopians, released from the empty employments of Old World life, are concentrated on the development of learning and science. Many of them worship the heavenly bodies and the distinguished dead, but the majority are theists. Their priests are chosen by popular election: they have few and excellent laws, but no professional lawyers; they detest war, but are well armed, and fight intrepidly when necessary, though by preference they employ a neighbouring nation of herdsmen as mercenaries. The temples of the Utopians are private buildings, and there is no worship of images. No living thing is offered in sacrifice, though incense is burned, and wax candles are lighted during the service of God, and vocal and instrumental music is practised in connexion with it. But in all religious matters there is absolute toleration. There is indeed a limited exception in favour of the immortality of the soul, and a future state of rewards and punishments, belief in both of which is thought to be essential to good citizenship. Yet even those who reject these doctrines are tolerated, on the principle that a man cannot make himself believe that which he might desire to believe, but which his reason compels him to reject: these, however, are regarded as base and sordid natures, and excluded from public offices and honours. The attitude of the Utopians towards Christianity, of which they hear for the first time from Hythlodaeus, is described as favourable: what chiefly disposes them to receive it is its original doctrine of community of goods. Before the strangers quit Utopia, many of the inhabitants have embraced Christianity and received baptism. The question of the Christian priesthood presents a difficulty. All the European travellers are laymen; how then can the Utopian Christians obtain the services of duly qualified pastors? They settle this question for themselves. Applying the established principle of popular election, they hold that one so chosen could effectually do all things pertaining to the priestly office, notwithstanding the lack of authority derived through the successors of St Peter. Although Christianity is thus permitted and even encouraged, its professors are forbidden to be unduly zealous for its propagation; a Christian convert who condemns other religions as profane, and declares their adherents doomed to everlasting punishment, is found guilty of sedition and banished. The *Utopia*, it will be seen, is no mere academic imitation of Plato's *Republic*. Specifically, the New World has little to do with its details. It was the mere possibilities suggested by the New World which occasioned this remarkable picture of a state of society diametrically opposed to the aspect of contemporary Europe. More's romance lost its hold on public attention, as soon as headstrong enthusiasts on the Continent endeavoured to realise some of its fundamental principles; but at a later date, through the founders of New Jersey and Pennsylvania, it had some ultimate effect on, as it took its motive from, the New World which was beginning to stir European minds to their depths at the time when it was written.

From More we turn to a writer of a later generation, remarkable for the freedom and independence of his mental attitude towards contemporary ideas and institutions, and who avows in more than one place that the New World profoundly modified his habits of thought. No close reader of Montaigne will dispute that the contemplation of the New World, in connexion with the events which happened after its discovery, greatly contributed to give him that large grasp of things, that mental habit of charity and comprehensiveness, something of which passed from him to Bacon and to Shakspere, both diligent students of his writings. Michel de Montaigne, a French advocate and country gentleman, who may be called the Plato of modern philosophical literature, was born in 1533, when Pizarro was overrunning Peru. During his life the New World was growing ever larger in the eyes of mankind; and as it drew him to itself, by a species of intellectual gravitation, it detached him from the standing-ground of his time, and raised him in a corresponding degree far above it. The facts of aboriginal American history and ethnology, narrated by the Conquistadores and by other travellers, sank deeply into his mind; and his knowledge of the New World was not mere book-learning. As a counsellor of Bordeaux, he often came in contact with merchants and seamen who were familiar with America; but his chief source of information was a man in his own service, who

had lived ten or twelve years in Brazil, whom he describes as a plain
ignorant fellow, but from whom he seems never to have been weary of
learning at first hand.  Before Colombo's voyage the savage or "brute
man" had been as little known in Europe, and was in fact as much of
a myth, as the unicorn or griffin.  When Montaigne wrote, he had
become as well known as the Moor, the Berber, or the Guinea negro,
and the spectacle of a new transatlantic continent, scarcely less extensive
than the aggregate of those Old World countries of which Europe
possessed any definite knowledge, and peopled by men scarcely above the
state of nature, seized the French philosopher with a strange fascination.
By its contrast with European life it suggested some startling reflections.
What if civilisation, after all, were a morbid and unnatural growth?
What if the condition of man in America were that for which the
Creator designed him?  What if those omnipotent powers, law and
custom, as at present constituted, were impudent usurpers, destined one
day to decline under the influence of right reason, and to give place, if
not to the original rule of beneficent Nature, at least to something
essentially very different from the systems which now passed under their
names?  Montaigne puts these questions very pointedly.  In the Tupi-
Guarani of Brazil, as described by one who had known them long and
intimately, he recognised nothing of the character associated with the
words "barbarous" and "savage."  They were rather a people permanently enjoying the fabled Golden Age of ancient poetry; strangers to
the toils, diseases, social inequalities, vices, and trickeries which chiefly
made up civilised life; dwelling together in vast common houses, though
the institutions of the family were strictly preserved, and enjoying with
little or no labour, and no fears for the future, all the reasonable commodities and advantages of human life, while knowing nothing of its
superfluities; refined in their taste for poetry, specimens of which were
recited to him by his domestic informant, and which appeared to him
Anacreontic in their grace and beauty: and employed chiefly in the
chase, the universal pleasure of the human race, even in the highest
state of refinement.  This they carried, perhaps, a stage too far.  They
hunted their neighbouring tribesman for his flesh, and, like others
among the more advanced American peoples, were cannibals—a name
which Montaigne used as the title of the laudatory tractate here
quoted.  What of that?  Civilised man, says the philosopher, who
practically enforces servitude on nine-tenths of the human race, consumes
the flesh and blood of his fellow-man alive.  Is it not worse to eat one's
fellow-man alive, than to eat him dead?  These Americans torture their
prisoners, it is true; worse tortures are inflicted in civilized Europe, in
the sacred names of justice and religion.  We Europeans regard these
our fellow-men with contempt and aversion.  Are we, in the sight of
God, much better than they?  Have we done, are we doing, by our fellow-
man at home, according to the light which is, or should be, within us?

Montaigne was perhaps only half serious. Yet such views commended themselves more or less to perfectly serious thinkers in other European countries; and they accorded with a feeling, which had long been gaining ground, of revolt against the hollow pageantry, the rigid social and political forms, the grasping at an empty show of power and dignity, which marked medieval life, and of expectation advancing towards more of simplicity, sincerity, and accordance with truth and nature. These views affected men's religious conceptions, and had something to do with the Protestant and Puritan views of religious duty and theory. They were more amply represented in the Quakerism of a later age; and while they originated in the Old World, they had their freest and fullest development, as will appear later on in this History, in the New. Held in check in Europe, where power tenaciously clung to the machinery of feudalism, they fermented in, and began to permeate, social strata on which that machinery rested with crushing weight, and produced those revolutionary and socialistic doctrines which have so largely affected modern European society, but have found less favour in America. The emigrant in the New World was conscious of breathing different air. In this spacious continent much seemed trifling, and even ridiculous, which had commanded his respect, and even devotion, at home. Much of the burden of the Past seemed to fall from his shoulders. Industry ensured subsistence, even to the poorest: security of subsistence led by an easy transition to competence, and often to affluence. In all these stages a general sense of independence was fostered, felt in different degrees in different parts, but common, to some extent, to the Spanish landowner among his Indian serfs, the sugar-planter among his slaves, the missionary among the converts he was reclaiming from savagery, and the peasant wrestling with the forest and turning it into an expanse of fertile fields. The political tie which bound the emigrant to the European power commanding his allegiance was scarcely felt. The merchant made large profits: capital earned high interest. There was everywhere a large measure of freedom in local government. Even in Spanish America the European distinction between the noble and the plebeian was never introduced, nor could the Courts of justice exercise jurisdiction of *hidalguia*. Such a condition of things necessarily had its reaction on the mother countries: and Europe almost from the first felt that reaction, in however slight a degree.

In one respect the medieval constitution of Europe received from the New World, in the period immediately subsequent to the Discovery, a decided accession of strength. The conquest and settlement of Spanish and Portuguese America opened an immense field of operations to the Catholic Church; and this field was forthwith entered upon with extraordinary vigour and success. During the sixteenth century Rome was gaining in the New World more than she was losing in the Old. In Mexico, in Peru, and in New Granada foundations already existed from which the missionary had but to sweep away an effete super-structure to erect a loftier and more durable one. The aborigines were deeply imbued with religious ideas, and trained from childhood to regular habits of worship and ritual; the houses of the gods, numerous and often magnificent, were held in deep veneration, and endowed with extensive estates; the superiority of the great "Dios" of the Spaniards—a title understood by the Indians to be the proper name of a deity to whose worship the people of Europe were especially devoted—had been abundantly manifested in the military successes of his votaries; con-version was insisted on by the conquerors; and as the images of the old deities were destroyed, their shrines defaced, and their rites forbidden, compliance was dictated by the very spirit of aboriginal paganism. In Mexico, where the ancient rites demanded human sacrifices in vast numbers, and in a cruel and repulsive form, their abolition was effected with comparative ease. In Peru, where human sacrifice was chiefly limited to infant victims, who were simply strangled and buried, the Indians were more firmly attached to their old religion; and a serious obstacle to its abandonment lay in their devotion to the practice of ancestor-worship. Long after the mass of them had accepted the doctrine and practice of Christianity, they secretly offered sacrifice to the desiccated bodies of the dead; and a rigorous and prolonged inquisition had to be organised and carried into effect before the idolatry of Peru was extirpated. Meanwhile the settlement of the Church proceeded on the general lines recognised in Europe; but in America, as in the Spanish districts conquered from the Moors, the Holy See forbore some of its prescriptive rights in favour of the Crown. Notwithstanding the ordinances of the Lateran Council, Alexander VI in 1501 granted to the Crown all tithes and firstfruits in the Indies. The consideration for this "temporalisation" of property which of right belonged to the Church was the conquest of territory from infidels, and their conversion to Christianity. The right of patronage in all sees and benefices was also vested by the Pope in the Spanish sovereigns, as fully as had already been done in the case of the Kingdom of Granada, subject only to the condition that it should remain in the Crown inalienably. The Crown was further appointed the Pope's legate in America. The limits of dioceses were at first laid down by the Popes; but even this right, together with the power of dividing and consolidating them, was granted to the Crown, and no American Bishop could return to Europe without the Viceroy's licence. The Church in America held its own Councils, under the direction of the metropolitans of Mexico and Lima; and no appeal in ecclesiastical matters was carried to Rome. The Crown obtained the income of vacant sees, a part of which was assigned to the defence of the coasts against heretic pirates. These concessions were amply justified by the immense revenue which poured into Rome from Spanish America in the form of donations, of proceeds of bulls for the Holy Crusade, and of the sale of indulgences and dispensations. What the Holy See bestowed with one hand it received back, in larger measure, with the other.

Outside the limits of settled life the work of evangelisation was vigorously pursued by Franciscan, Dominican, and Augustinian friars, who from the first flocked to the New World in all its parts; but the chief share in this labour was borne by the newly-founded Company of Jesus. Among the exigencies which led to its establishment may certainly be reckoned the need of adequately grappling with the task of preaching Christianity in America, as well as in India and the Far East; and the numerous " Reductions " in the savage districts of North and South America abundantly testify to the devotion and energy of the Jesuit Fathers. At first the regular clergy greatly outnumbered the secular. In many cases they received, by dispensation, valuable benefices; and being in all respects better educated and trained than the secular clergy, they more easily acquired the American languages. The surplus incomes of these regularised benefices were remitted to the superiors of their incumbents in Europe, and were ultimately applied to the foundation of houses of the several Orders in the New World. The Franciscan, Augustinian and Jesuit colleges in Peru were in effect the chief centres of European civilisation; and the Jesuits have left a durable monument of their zeal in the Republic of Paraguay. To those members of these Orders who engaged in missionary work the ethnologist and historian are greatly indebted. But for their labours the deeply interesting history and folk-lore of Mexico and Peru would have been inadequately preserved, and the languages of many tribes outside the pale of settled life must have perished. Together with the fine churches attached to the mission settlements, the cathedral and parish churches of Spanish America, often built on the sites of ancient temples, form an unique series of historical monuments. Entirely built by native labour, and largely by voluntary contributions from native sources, they were to a great extent served by pastors of Indian or partly Indian descent—a class whom it was the policy of Spain to foster, and through which her control of her vast American dominions was in some measure maintained.

What was the effect of the New World in the realm of learning and science? Here, on the whole, the New World, at least in the first eighty years of its history, figures rather as a consequence than a cause. At Montaigne's death Francis Bacon, designing to reconstruct the system of the sciences, was meditating and elaborating the great series of books and tractates in which his views were given to the world; and in many of his writings it is clear that America with its physical features, its plants and animals, and its aboriginal race, was largely the subject of his meditation, and that the vast array of facts associated with it enlarged and modified his opinions and forecasts. To some extent Bacon was the scholar of Montaigne, whose conception of America as the middle one of three island-continents which once lay westward of the Old World—the vanished Atlantis which gave its name to the Atlantic, the new-found America beyond it, and a third, still undiscovered, but probably soon to be revealed in the unknown expanses of the Pacific, and called by Bacon "New Atlantis," as bearing the same geographical relation to the New World which the earlier Atlantis had borne to the Old—underlies his noble philosophical romance bearing that name as its title.  Bacon's habit of thought and study had induced in him a broader and profounder conception of the New World than that presented in the pages of his French predecessor.  The phenomena of society, which chiefly attracted Montaigne, had for him only a secondary interest.  Thirsting to know the Causes of Things, he aspired to comprehend nature in her entirety, to penetrate her secret, and to interpret her message: and the New World lent him opportune and unexpected help.  The configuration of sea and land surfaces, the mountains, the tides and winds, the animals and plants of the New World, opened for the first time an enormous field of physical enquiry.  The New World, for example, threw new light on the distribution of terrestrial and maritime areas.  Like the continents of the Old World (Europe and Asia for the purpose of this comparison counting as one) both North and South America broadened out towards the north and tapered towards the south, the alternative principle of termination by variously shaped peninsulas being found here also to recur.  What, Bacon asked, was the shape of that supposed continent lying south of the Strait of Magalhães, and commonly called Terra Australis?  The conflicting or according phenomena of the tides in different places; the water-spouts; the refrigeration of the air by icebergs on the Canadian coast; the balmy breezes blowing to seaward from Florida; the trade-winds, which had lent Europe wings to carry her across the Atlantic: the constant westerly or anti-trade winds blowing towards the Portuguese shore, from which, it was sometimes said, Colombo had inferred the existence of a western continent generating them; the comparatively cold climate of North America, the frozen expanse of Labrador being in the latitude of Britain, and the contradictory phenomena of the Peruvian coast, which lay almost under the Equator, while its ocean breezes, blowing hardest at the full moons, were said to produce a climate like that of Southern Europe; the strange inequalities of temperature experienced in different parts of the Peruvian Cordilleras; the alleged phenomenon that the peaks of the Andes remain destitute of snow, while it thickly covers their lower elevations, with the effects produced on man by their attenuated air, not so much cold as keen, piercing the eyes and purging the stomach;—such enquiries as these, never previously formulated, make Bacon the founder of modern physical geography.  American man, in his physical and ethnological aspect, strongly attracted Bacon's attention.

Was the extraordinary longevity of the Brazilian and Virginian tribes, who retained manly vigour at the age of 120 years, connected with their practice of painting the skin? What was the cause of a similar phenomenon in Peru? Was it true, as some alleged, that the fearful "morbus gallicus," then for the first time raging in Europe, and supposed, though erroneously, to have been imported from America, had its origin in the loathsome practice of cannibalism? What was the effect on American man of maize, as his staple diet? In America, where flint was scarce, fire was universally kindled by the wooden drill. The American Prometheus, then, in Bacon's words, "had no intelligence with the European," and the arts of life must have originated independently in the New World;—an inference somewhat boldly made from a single pair of facts, but which accorded, though Bacon knew it not, with the traditions of Mexico and Peru, and is amply confirmed, in our own well-informed age, by everything known as to the general progress of the American aborigines. By an effort of judgment for which the materials scarcely existed, and which had certainly never been made before his time, Bacon mentally arrayed against each other the polished nations of Europe and the barbarous or savage ones of America, and asked himself the reason of the contrast. Was it to be sought in the soil, in the sky, in the physical constitution of man? These suggestions he answered negatively; the difference, he concluded, lay solely in the fact that the American peoples, for some as yet unknown reason, had made less progress in the arts of life. We know the reason to be Nature's parsimony in furnishing the western continent with animals capable of labour and amenable to domestication.

Here another question presented itself to this prince among thinkers. Was the project of planting the civilisation of Europe among the American savages—a project widely entertained in Western Europe— a feasible one? Bacon answered this also in the negative. Nor is it doubtful that, having regard to the contemporary idea of "planting," Bacon was right. The idea of teaching the Indians "to live virtuously, and know of men the manner, and also to know God their Maker," was not yet obsolete; and the Spaniards, according to their lights, were vigorously prosecuting the task in Mexico and elsewhere. It has been reserved for a later age, in most respects more advanced, to acquiesce in a system of colonisation which dispossesses the aboriginal owners of the soil, and deals with them as with vermin to be hunted down, or stamped out, or deported to holes and corners of the land, to dwindle and die out under the effect of poverty, chagrin, and vices introduced by their civilised conquerors. From the Discovery to the time when European nations adopted a commercial policy and a commercial morality—from Colombo to Penn—those of the natives who submitted to European rule were regarded as men to be civilised and christianised, and ultimately to be blended in one race with their

European brethren. Bacon discountenanced this view so far as concerned the savages of "Florida" or North Eastern America, and the foundation of English colonies there on a corresponding footing. He bade Englishmen throw aside ideas which to his thinking savoured less of reality than of antiquated romances like *Amadis de Gaul*, and take up Caesar's *Commentaries*. If Englishmen must perforce colonise, he pointed out to them as the proper field of colonial enterprise, the adjacent island of Ireland, whose aboriginal people were sunk in a barbarism more shameful than American savagery, because of their immediate proximity to, and close relations with, one of the most civilised nations on the globe.

These instances by no means represent the full influence exercised by the New World on the most powerful mind of modern times, and through him on ages which have realised his ideas without adding anything to their transcendent scope and penetration. There can be little doubt that Bacon's whole scheme for the reconstitution of knowledge on a broader basis and firmer foundation, in accordance with the truth of things and without regard to the routine of scholastic tradition, and with such fulness that, in his own words, the "crystalline globe" of the understanding should faithfully reflect all that the "material globe," or external world, offers to his apprehension, was suggested to him by the facts briefly sketched in the foregoing pages. Truth, he wrote, was not the daughter of Authority, but of Time. America was certainly "the greatest birth of time"; Bacon applied these words to the philosophic system of which he was the founder. The discovery of America gave the human intellect what is known to mechanics as a "dead lift." It dispelled a secular illusion; it destroyed the old blind reverence for antiquity, which Spenser might well have depicted as a sightless monster, stifling mankind in its serpentine embraces. Truth, to borrow from Milton an allegory worthy of Bacon, had been hewn, like the body of Osiris, into a thousand pieces. Philosophy, like Isis, the disconsolate spouse, wandered over the earth in quest of them: and the time would come when they should be "gathered limb to limb, and moulded into an immortal feature of loveliness and perfection." What "grounds of hope," to use Bacon's phrase, for that glorious reunion—or rather, what certain auguries of its ultimate attainment—he gathered from the New Cosmography, his writings abundantly testify. His own vast survey of knowledge, attained or that ought to be attained, he modestly described as a coasting voyage or periegesis of the "New Intellectual World." He loved to compare his own conjectures and anticipations of the boundless results which he knew his method destined to achieve in the hands of posterity with the faint indications which had inspired Colombo to attempt that "mirabilis navigatio," that daring six weeks' voyage westward across the Atlantic. Feebly, indeed, and through the darkness of night, he says, blew the breeze of hope from the shores of the New Continent of knowledge and power towards him, as from his lonely elevation he eagerly watched for those cheering signals which he knew would sooner or later greet the patient eye of expectant philosophy, though he himself might not be destined to behold them. Those signals, he wrote, must one day come, unless his own faith in the future should prove vain, and men were content to remain intellectual abjects. Humanity had waited long ages for the accomplishment of Seneca's prophecy—a prophecy which was in every mouth at the Discovery, and of which Bacon, like all his contemporaries, hailed the Discovery as the destined fulfilment ;

> Venient annis saecula seris
> Quibus Oceanus vincula rerum
> Laxet, et ingens pateat tellus,
> Tiphysque novos detegat orbes,
> Nec sit terris ultima Thule.

Possibly he had pondered over a less-known passage in the prose writings of the same author, who predicts that the time shall come when knowledge shall be vastly increased, and men shall look back with amazement at the ignorance of the Greeks and Romans. There was confirmation for such hopes in Holy Scripture. The anticipation of the Chaldean seer that in the latest times "many should run to and fro, and knowledge be increased" he interpreted as foreshadowing the opening of five-sixths of the globe, hitherto closed, to man's travel, study, and reinvigorated powers of reasoning. Into the future of history in the narrow sense of the word, Bacon ventured only by one memorable forecast, since abundantly verified, and more abundantly by momentous events of quite recent occurrence. He prophesied that the great inheritances of the East and the West, both at the time ready to slip from the feeble grasp of Spain, must alike fall to those who commanded the ocean—to that Anglo-Saxon race of which he will remain to all time one of the most illustrious representatives.

# CHAPTER III.

## THE OTTOMAN CONQUEST.

In the middle of the fourteenth century two powers which had recently sprung into unexpected prominence were closing in upon Constantinople from the west and from the east. But in the race for the stronghold on the Bosphorus the competitor which might have seemed to have the best chances of winning, suddenly fell out. With the death of Stephen Dušan (1356) the ill-consolidated empire of Servia collapsed: his successors were ciphers; whereas Orchan, the Sultan of the Ottomans, handed down a well-disciplined State, built on strong foundations, to a line of eminent princes. Under him the Ottoman Turks won (1358) their first foothold on European soil by the occupation of the fortress of Gallipoli,—somewhat less than a century before Mohammad II captured Constantinople. It was not long before Orchan's son Murad I had crept round and conquered the eastern half of the Balkan peninsula, cutting off Constantinople from Christian Europe. For the first time, since the days of Darius and Xerxes, Thrace passed under the sway of an Asiatic power,—often as the hosts of Sassanid kings and Saracen caliphs had lined the shores of the dividing straits. If the conquest had resembled in character the old Persian conquest, if the inhabitants had been required only to pay tribute to a distant ruler and receive his garrisons in their cities, the lot of these lands would have been light. But they were taken into full possession by their new lords; and oriental nomads of an alien and intolerant religion were planted as the dominant race amid the Christian population. The circumstance that the Ottomans were nomads (they were a clan of the Turkish tribe of Oghuz) gives their empire its significance in the history of mankind. In the perpetual struggle between the herdsmen and the tillers of the soil which has been waged from remote ages on the continents of Europe and Asia, the advance of the Ottomans was a decisive victory for the children of the steppes. This feature of their conquest is of no less fundamental importance than its aspect as a victory for Islam.

How the Ottomans were caught in the tide of the Mongol invasion and their power almost ruined; how they recovered under the prudent guidance of Mohammad I ; how the wave of conquest once more rolled on under Murad II, until a seal was set upon their European empire by the capture of Constantinople,—all this has been told by Gibbon.   The story is here taken up in 1453.

For a moment it was not clear whether the new lord of Constantinople would be content with a suzerainty over the neighbouring lands which had once been provinces of the Roman empire, or would reduce them to the condition of provinces of the Ottoman realm.   The princes of the Peloponnese, the despot of Servia, the lords of some of the island States of the Aegean, forthwith offered their submission.   Mohammad soon showed that he would not acquiesce in a system of vassal states paying him tribute as overlord, but aimed at compassing the complete and immediate subjection of the Balkan peninsula.   A typical oriental conqueror, he was driven on by the true instinct that it would be fatal to stand still or abandon aggression; he believed that it was the destiny of his people to spread the religion of the Prophet over the whole earth, and the task of his life was to further the accomplishment of this end. His next successors worked with varying vigour in the same direction, and the Ottomans throve so long as they conquered.   But it was constant success in war that quickened and strengthened the frame of their State ; and the hour in which limits were set to territorial advance marks the beginning of a rapid decline.   The nature of their institutions, as we shall see, demanded war.

Mohammad first turned his arms against Servia.   This step was determined by Servia's geographical position, lying on the road to Hungary.   For Mohammad saw that Hungary was the only country, John Hunyady the only leader, that he had seriously to fear.   The two western powers which had the greatest interests at stake in the east and were most gravely affected by the change of masters at Constantinople, were Venice and Genoa.   The Genoese were accustomed to dealings with the Ottomans; they were the first Christian power west of the Adriatic that had made a treaty with them, and they had not scrupled to use the alliance of the infidels against their fellow-Christians.   The Genoese colony of Galata sent the keys of their walled town to Mohammad on the fall of the City, and the Sultan though he slighted their walls granted them a favourable capitulation securing their liberties and commercial rights.   But Genoa was feeble and indifferent; and, feeling herself unequal to new efforts, she transferred, before the fatal year was over, her Pontic settlements to the Genoese Bank of St George, into whose hands the administration of Corsica passed about the same time.   But the financial resources of the Bank did not suffice for the task of supporting these colonies, and Genoese trade declined.   Venice, on the other hand, was not indifferent; and her first thought was, not to recover the bulwark of Christendom from the hands of the Muslim, but to preserve her own commercial privileges under the rule of the infidel sovereign.   She sent an envoy to Mohammad; and a treaty, which formed the basis of all subsequent negociations, was presently concluded. By it she secured freedom of trade for her merchants and the privilege of protecting Venetian settlers on Turkish soil by means of her own officers.

Hungary, then, was the only power that Mohammad, secure on the side of Venice, had immediately to fear. In the first month of 1454 the young and worthless King Ladislaus had assembled a diet at Buda and carried extraordinary measures for organising an army against the Turks. John Hunyady, appointed commander-in-chief, had a host ready to take the field in spring, when George Branković, the despot of Servia, arrived, suppliant for help, with the news that the Turk was advancing against his kingdom. Hunyady crossed the Danube and raided Turkish territory, while Mohammad beleaguered the Servian fortresses of Ostroviza and Semendra (Smederevo). He took Ostroviza, but Semendra—a stronghold of capital strategic importance for operations against Servia, Hungary, and Wallachia—was saved by the arrival of the Magyar general, and Mohammad retreated. A large detachment of the retreating army encountered Hunyady near Krusovać. No regular battle was fought; a panic seized the Turks and they were routed with slaughter. Hunyady completed his campaign by descending the Danube and reducing the Ottoman fortress of Widdin to ashes.

In the following year (1455) Mohammad—who claimed Servia through his step-mother, a Servian Princess—won a foothold in the south of the country by the capture of Novoberdo, with its important gold and silver mines; and he spent the next winter in making large and elaborate preparations for besieging Belgrade by land and water. The siege lasted three weeks in July, 1456, and hardly has a more brilliant feat been achieved in the course of the struggles between Europe and the Ottoman Turks than the relief of Belgrade by John Hunyady and his Magyar army. It was the second time that he saved this bulwark at the gates of Hungary. Pope Calixtus III had sent an able legate, Juan de Carvajal, to rally the people round the general in the holy cause; but it is a Minorite brother, John of Capistrano, who shares with Hunyady the glory of the triumph. The eloquence of this preacher, inspired with zeal against the misbeliever, could still move men's hearts to some faint semblance of that crusading fervour which had once strung Europe to madness. The greater part of the host which was collected was a tattered undisciplined rabble; but infinite patience and energy overcame all difficulties. With a few vessels Hunyady broke through the chain of barques by which Mohammad had barred the Save, and entered the besieged city. Though the defenders were far inferior in number and equipment, yet by valour and cunning they defeated all the efforts of the enemy and at last forced the whole army to retreat in confusion, and with tremendous losses, amounting to more than 50,000 killed and wounded, 300 guns, and 27 war-boats. In the first hour of delight the

victors overrated the importance of their achievement; they fancied
that the Turk was almost crushed and that but little was wanting
to drive him from Europe.  It could be done, wrote Hunyady in a letter
to the Pope, "if Christendom were to rise up against him."  But there
was no chance of such a rising, and in a few days Christendom lost her
ablest champion, Hunyady himself (August, 1456).  Hungary, crippled
by domestic feuds, without a leader in whom men trusted, receiving no
support from Germany in consequence of the hatred between King
Ladislaus and the Emperor, could not follow up her victory.  Presently
Ladislaus died and Hunyady's son, Matthias Corvinus, a lad of sixteen
years, came to the throne (January, 1458).

Meanwhile Mohammad was taking measures for the subjection of
Servia.  He was helped by its domestic circumstances.  After a struggle
for the succession to the crown, the government devolved upon a woman,
Helena, the widow of the despot George's youngest son ; and she took
the strange impolitic step of placing the country under the protection and
overlordship of Pope Calixtus, who had vowed his energies to the abolition
of the Turk.  But this act alienated the boyars, who liked the interference
of the Catholic no better, or even less, than the rule of the infidel.  In 1457
Mahmud Pasha (Beglerbeg, or Governor, of Rumelia) had overcome all
Servia; in 1458 Mohammad came himself, captured Semendra by treachery,
and received the voluntary submission of many of the boyars.  It is said
that 200,000 inhabitants were carried from the land, whether to be
trained for military service, or to be settled in other parts of the empire.

On the death of Hunyady only a single great warrior was left to fight
for the cause of Christendom—"standing almost alone, like a strong wall,"
said Pope Calixtus;—but it was as much as his strength could compass to
defend his own land.  This was George Castriotes, the Albanian, whom
we are accustomed to designate as Scanderbeg,—a name which always
reminds us that he had been brought up in the faith of Islam and held
high office under Murad II, before he returned to his own religion and
his own people.  Beneath the supremacy of his masterful and daring
spirit, the Albanian folk, which in the regions of northern Epirus preserved
the old Illyrian language, was raised into transient greatness.  For a brief
space, an united Albanian nation lifted up its voice amid the roar of the
world's tide, and admiring Europe applauded.  In the warfare on the
Illyrian hillsides, Scanderbeg was almost invariably successful ; and a
defeat which he suffered at the Albanese fortress of Belgrade, through an
indiscreet concession (1456), was avenged in the following year by a great
victory over Mohammad's able general Hamsa, who was himself taken
prisoner.  Mohammad was glad to make a truce for a year, and
Scanderbeg was persuaded to cross over, a second "Alexander" of
Epirus, to Apulia, to help the Spaniard Ferdinand of Naples to drive
out the French (1461).  On the Albanian chief's return, new discom-
fitures forced Mohammad, intent on more pressing enterprises, to seek a

permanent peace; and the Sultan acknowledged Scanderbeg as the absolute sovereign of Albania (April, 1463).

But the peace was broken before the year was out. It was the Albanian who violated the contract, under the importunate pressure of the Pope and the Venetian Republic. He reopened hostilities by a raid into Macedonia; and in 1464 he won a crushing victory over a Turkish army under Balaban (an Albanian renegade). His successes decided Mohammad to take the field himself at the head of a mighty host and lay siege to Kroja, the Albanian capital (1465). The last exploit of the hero was to render this expedition fruitless. Failing to storm the place, Mohammad retreated, leaving Balaban to starve it out; but before he left the country he massacred some thousands of Albanian families, whom he discovered in their refuge in the valley of Chidna. Having no forces sufficient to relieve Kroja, Scanderbeg visited Rome, hoping to obtain effectual help from Pope Paul II. He obtained a little money and much good will. On his return to Albania he found that some Venetian troops had come to his aid, and he was now able to act. But fortune relieved Kroja. A chance blow wounded Balaban mortally, and the blockading army immediately retreated, leaving Albania in a state of terrible devastation. The "athlete of Christendom," as Scanderbeg was called, died a year later at Alessio, recommending his son and his country to the protection of Venice (January, 1467). For Venice his death was a serious event, as he was the "buffer" between the Ottoman power and her possessions on the lower Adriatic, such as Scodra and Durazzo. Henceforward she would have to do her own work here.

Bosnia, which had borne its part in the fatal battle of Kosovo field (1389), was inevitably drawn into the vortex. The catastrophe of this land received a peculiar character from its religious condition. The mass of the people, high and low, was firmly devoted to the Patarine or Bogomilian tenets, which Catholics and Greeks branded as Manichaeanism. It is one of that series of religions which range from Armenia to Aquitaine, including Albigensians at one extremity and Paulicians at the other, all apparently descended from the ancient "heresies" of Adoptianism. But the Catholics were eager to crush the heresy; Franciscan missionaries worked with all their might in the land; and some of the kings embraced Catholicism. In 1412 the Bogomils threatened to Turcise, and in 1415 they executed the threat, fighting at Usora against Hungary. When King Stephen Thomas embraced Catholicism (1446), the Pope and the King of Hungary hoped that the false doctrines would be extirpated. In the south of the Bosnian kingdom was the large vassal state, practically independent, which had grown up out of the lordship of Chlum. The voivod of this country was Stephen Vukčić, and in 1448 he received from the Emperor the title of "Duke *(Herzog)* of St Sabas"; whence the complex of his lands derived the name of *Herzegovina*, the Duchy. His daughter married Stephen the King; but Stephen the Duke remained true to the national faith. He seems to have entered into a sort of vassal relation to Mohammad; for, when he makes peace with his neighbour Ragusa in 1454, we find him undertaking not to attack it, save at the command of the "Great ruler the Sultan of Turkey." On the fall of Constantinople the Bosnian King offered tribute; but Hunyady's feat at Belgrade, and the success of Scanderbeg in the south, raised up King Stephen's drooping hopes and heartened him to refuse the payment (1456). Before, however, any results ensued from his change of attitude, he made peace again (1458); his object was to have his hands free for laying hold of Servia. In the diet of Szegedin the Hungarian King agreed that the despot's son, Stephen Tomasević, should become despot of Servia and actual ruler of the little northern strip of Servia that was not in Turkish power. The position here depended entirely on holding the key-fortress of Semendra. But the inhabitants of this place were reluctant to submit to the Bosnian prince imposed upon them; and when in the next year Mohammad appeared with an army, they opened their gates to him. A cry of mortification at the fall of this bulwark arose in Hungary and Italy, and the disaster was attributed to the corruption and cowardice of Stephen Tomasević. The Hungarian king Matthias Corvinus never forgave him; but the evidence seems to show that the surrender was the act of the inhabitants of the town, done in his despite.

Two years later King Stephen Thomas died, hampered in his struggle with the Turk by his feuds with his vassal and father-in-law, the ruler of Herzegovina, and with the Ban of Croatia, and above all by the estrangement in religion between himself and his folk. The storm broke upon his son Stephen, who, having apparently convinced Pope Pius II of his innocence in the loss of Semendra, was crowned by the Pope's Legate, and reconciled with the Hungarian monarch. Meanwhile the anti-national policy of the kings was producing its effect. The oppressive measures adopted by them, at the instigation of the Pope and Hungary, towards the Patarenes, alienated many of that sect, who fled into Turkey or remaining in the country acted as spies for the Sultan, while some actually embraced Islam. Mohammad resolved to reduce Bosnia to complete subjection. When he sent an embassy to demand tribute, King Stephen, taking the envoy into a treasure-chamber, said, "Here is the tribute; but I have no mind to send it to the Sultan." "It is a fine treasure to keep," replied the envoy, "but I know not whether it will bring you luck; I fear, the reverse." When however Stephen failed to gain any aid from Venice or from Ragusa (itself trembling at the danger of a Turkish attack), and heard of the equipment of a great Turkish army, he repented his boldness, and sent to Mohammad to offer the tribute and ask for a truce for fifteen years. His ambassadors found the Sultan at Hadrianople. The historian of the Bosnian war, Michael Konstantinović, who was in the service of the Turks, was there at the time; and, hidden behind a chest, he overheard the conversation of two pashas who were in the confidence of Mohammad. They arranged that the demands of the Bosnian King should be granted, and the envoys dismissed on the Saturday; but on the following Wednesday the army was to start and overwhelm Bosnia, before any aid from Hungary or elsewhere could reach it. So it came to pass; and though Michael privately informed the Bosnian ambassadors of the perfidious intentions of the Sultan, they would not believe him. Having occupied the district of Podrinje, Mohammad attacked the royal residence, the mighty fortress of Bobovac; and here again the special condition of Bosnia affected the course of events. The defender, Prince Radak, was secretly a Patarine, though he had feigned to accept Catholicism; and he betrayed the town to the Turk. The Turk rewarded him by decapitation;—a strange policy on the part of a conqueror whose interest it was to encourage such treacheries. Jajce in the west of the land capitulated, and the King, who had fled to Kliuć, surrendered to Mahmud Pasha, receiving from him a written guarantee for his life and freedom. The lands directly under the Bosnian Crown were soon subdued, Stephen commanding the captains of his castles to yield; and Mohammad marched southward to subdue the Duchy and Ragusa. But in this difficult country he made little way; and, on failing to take the capital, Blagaj, he abandoned the enterprise. It was the Sultan's policy to put to death all rulers whom he dethroned; and, in order to release him from the obligation of keeping a promise which he had not authorised, a learned Persian *mufti* with his own hand beheaded the Bosnian King. It is said that Mohammad carried off 30,000 boys to be made into Janissaries, besides 100,000 other captives. The Catholics who were left fled from the country; and to prevent its utter dispeoplement, Mohammad gave the Franciscans a safeguard, allowing the Christians free exercise of their religion. Henceforward the Franciscan influence was predominant.

King Matthias Corvinus made a vigorous attempt to rescue Bosnia; and in the year 1463 he drove many of the Ottoman garrisons out. But he had not made timely preparations for encountering the return of Mohammad, who in the next spring (1464) came to recover Jajce, the most important stronghold of all. The hard-pressed place was relieved by a Hungarian force; but at the end of the year Matthias, who was besieging another fort, was constrained by Mahmud Pasha to retreat. Nothing more was done for Bosnia. A strip in the north, with a few fortresses including Jajce, remained in the power of Hungary, and gave the title of "King of Bosnia" to the voivod of Transylvania; but the land as a whole had passed under Muslim rule. Herzegovina was made fully subject nearly twenty years later (1483). All the Slavonic powers of the Balkan peninsula were thus gathered into the Asiatic empire, except the tributary republic of Ragusa and a part of the principality of Montenegro, whose recesses afforded a refuge to many of those who saved themselves from the wreckage of the neighbouring countries. Stephen Crnoiević, the maker of Montenegro, had spent his life in defending his country against Mohammad's father, Murad, and had fought hand in hand with Scanderbeg. He died in 1466. His son Ivan the Black continued the struggle with indomitable spirit, though the waves seemed to be closing over his head, when to south of him Albania was thrown open to the Turk by the death of Castriotes and Bosnia was conquered in the north. When the Venetians abandoned Scodra to Mohammad (1479), the very key of Montenegro seemed to have been surrendered; and so desperate appeared the outlook that Ivan burned Žabljak, the city which his father had founded, near the upper end of the lake of Scodra, and went up to lofty Cetinje, which has ever since remained the capital of the only Slavonic princes of the peninsula who never bowed the knee to Asiatic lords. Ivan the Black was more than a heroic patriot. To him belongs the distinction of having established (at Obod) the first Slavonic printing press, from which the earliest books in Cyrillic character were issued (1493).

Meanwhile Greece had been conquered, except a few forts which still remained to Venice. The Duchy of Athens, which had passed in the previous century to the Florentine merchant family of the Acciajoli, was won; the last Duke, Franco, surrendered the Acropolis to Omar son of Turakhan in 1456. When Mohammad visited the city, two years later, he was amazed at the beauty of its buildings and the handsome quays of the Piraeus, and cried: "Islam owes a debt to the son of Turakhan." Subsequently Franco was privately strangled, on account of a plot of some Athenians to restore him. But, on the whole, Athens had reason to be pleased with the change from the rule of Catholic princes to that of the unbelievers. The administration of justice and the collection of the tribute were assigned to local officers, and the only new burden was the tribute of children.

The Peloponnesus was misgoverned by the two brothers of the last Roman Emperor, Thomas and Demetrius, worthless and greedy despots, whose rule was worse than the worst Turkish tyranny. Thomas, notorious for his cruelty, resided at Patras, and oppressed the western part of the peninsula; Demetrius, distinguished by his luxury, ruled over the east, and his seat was in the rocky fortress of Mistra, at the foot of Mount Taygetus, three miles west of Sparta. The court officials, who were the ministers of their oppression, were detested throughout the land, which was further distracted by the hatred between the Greek inhabitants and the Albanian shepherds, who had come down and settled here in the previous century after the fall of the Servian empire. The invasion of the Turks in 1452 had desolated the land and given the Albanian herds a wider range; the Greek peasants overcrowded the towns, and the most thriving traders began to emigrate. The Albanians deemed that the right moment had come for making the Morea an

Albanian state; perhaps they were encouraged by the fame and success of Scanderbeg. But there was no Scanderbeg among them to unite and keep them together; they could not agree upon a leader of their own race; and they selected Manuel Cantacuzenus (a noble, of the family which had given an emperor to the East-Roman throne) who was now ruling informally over the hillsmen of Maina in Taygetus. He adopted the Albanian name of Ghin, and placed himself at the head of the insurgents. By themselves the despots would have been unable to hold out in their strong places; but they appealed to Mohammad, to whom after the fall of Constantinople they had become tributary; and, when the governor of Thessaly marched into the peninsula, the rebels sued for peace (1454). The Albanians received favourable terms; for it was Ottoman policy to preserve them as a make-weight to the Greeks. But the Morea was far from being tranquillised. Four years later Mohammad in person led an army thither to restore order, and captured and garrisoned the Acro-Corinth. The enmity of the two brothers Palaeologus led to new miseries. They took up arms against one another, Thomas posing as the champion of Christendom against the Turks; and Mohammad decided that an end must be made of Greek rule in the Peloponnese. In 1460 he descended for the second time, and he did not hold his hand when policy urged cruelty. Thus when the indwellers of Leondari (a place on the northern extremity of Taygetus, overlooking Megalopolis) abandoned their town and took refuge in the hills in the citadel of Gardiki—an ill-omened place where thirty-seven years before Turakhan had built pyramids of Albanian heads (1423)—Mohammad followed the luckless people to this sequestered fort, and on their surrender they were all gathered together and slain, six thousand of them. At Calavryta a renegade Albanian chief who had been in Turkish service was sawn in two. Here and elsewhere thousands were reduced to slavery. Demetrius had submitted without a blow at Mistra; Thomas fled to Corfu and ended his life at Rome as a pensioner of the Pope. It was thus that the Morea became perhaps the most miserable province in the Turkish realm; nor can there be any doubt but that Mohammad deliberately intended this to be its fate. He unpeopled and desolated it, so that it might present no allurements to a foreign invader and have no spirit to be restless. Six maritime places still belonged to Venice:—Argos, Nauplia and Thermisi in the east, and Coron, Modon and Navarino in the west, to which we must add Aegina. The little town of Monemvasia, which Frankish speech corrupted to Malvoisy, on the rocky east coast of Laconia, held out for four years, in the name of Thomas Palaeologus, and then placed itself under the protection of Venice (1464).

The withdrawal of Genoa from the field, and the conquest of the Morea and Bosnia, followed by the death of Scanderbeg, devolved the whole defence of the coasts of the Illyrian peninsula and the Aegean

upon the republic of St Mark. New Phocaea and the northern islands
(Lemnos, Imbros, Samothrace, Thasos) had been successively conquered
(1456–7); and in 1462 Lesbos, which had become a very nest of pirates
from Spain and Sicily, was annexed to the Turkish dominion. Its last
Genoese Lord, Nicolò Gattilusio, was strangled; one-third of the inhabitants were enslaved, one-third deported to augment the population
of Constantinople, and the rest, the poorest and the worst, were left to
till the land and gather in the vintage. As bases for maritime war in
the Aegean, Venice still possessed Negroponte, Candia, together with
Nauplia ("Romanian Naples"), and had command of the islands composing the Duchy of Naxos.

The inevitable War broke out in 1463, and its first scene was the
Morea. Singlehanded, Venice was scarcely equal to the work, and the
delay of ten years made the task more arduous.

Never was there a moment at which a common effort of the Christian
powers of Europe was more imperatively needed; never a moment at
which such an effort was less feasible. The monarchs were not blind
to the menace of the new and deadly ecumenical force which was hurled
within range of their kingdoms; they discerned and owned the peril;
but internal policy and the consolidation of their power at home so
wholly absorbed their interest, that nothing less than a Turkish advance
to the Upper Danube or the Rhine would have availed to stir them
into action. The Emperor Frederick III had not remained unmoved
by the fall of Constantinople, but his strained relations with Hungary
as well as the affairs of the Empire hindered him from stretching a hand
to save Servia. Yet at his side was a man who fully realised the
jeopardy and conceived the project, to which he devoted himself heart
and soul, of stirring up the princes of Europe to wage a holy war against
the infidel. This was Aeneas Sylvius, bishop of Siena. He utters his
idea immediately after the fall of the City in a letter to Pope Nicholas V:
"Mohammad is among us; the sabre of the Turks waves over our head;
the Black Sea is shut to our ships; the foe possess Wallachia, whence
they will pass into Hungary—and Germany. And we meanwhile live
in strife and enmity among ourselves. The Kings of France and
England are at war; the princes of Germany have leapt to arms against
one another; Spain is seldom at peace, Italy never wins repose from
conflicts for alien lordship. How much better to turn our arms against
the enemies of our faith! It devolves upon you, Holy Father, to unite
the kings and princes, and urge them to gather together to take counsel
for the safety of the Christian world."

A vain idea, inappropriate to the conditions of the age, but which was
to hover in the air for many years to come and inspire abundance of
useless talk and empty negotiations! The urgent words of Aeneas and a
letter of the Emperor roused the Pope to an action which neither of
them had contemplated; he issued a bull imposing a tithe for a war

against the infidel,—thus, as Aeneas himself owned, seeking to cure one evil by another.

The chief interest perhaps of the efforts made by Nicholas and his successors to bring about an European peace, for the sake of driving back the Turk and recovering Constantinople, lies in the measure which they suggest of the distance which the world had travelled since the age of the Crusades. In the eleventh and in the twelfth, even in the thirteenth century, a religious sentiment could stir the princes and the peoples of Europe to go forth, not to avert a danger, but to rescue a holy place of pilgrimage. But in the fifteenth, though the unbeliever had won his way into Europe, had reached the Danube and threatened the Adriatic, the imminent danger to Christendom left Christendom lukewarm. Except religious zeal, there was no force which could compel an European effort. With the growth of "humanism" the old kind of religious enthusiasm had passed away. Pope Nicholas himself illustrated the change of things since the days of Urban II, when, at the very time of his proclaiming a Crusade, he privately sent agents to the East, to rescue from the deluge all Greek manuscripts they could lay hands on.

There were however special reasons, besides the general lukewarmness, that accounted for the failure of the first papal efforts. Nothing could be effectually done without the co-operation of Venice ; and Venice, as we saw, made on her own account an advantageous treaty with Mohammad. The Emperor, who professed to support the idea of a Crusade, was hindered from energetic action by his ill relations with Hungary. The demand for money, which might have enabled the Pope to organise an armament, was highly unpopular. And not the least serious impediment was the intolerance which divided the Catholics from the Greek Church, and prevented them from feeling any true pity for the forlorn prospects of their fellow-Christians in Greece and Servia, or any sincere desire to save them. It was futile for Aeneas Sylvius to say that the Greeks were not heretics, but only schismatics ; they were generally regarded as worse than infidels. The only prince who might have been ready to make sacrifices, if any common action had been organised, was Duke Philip of Burgundy. In the spring of 1454 a diet was held at Ratisbon, but the essential business was deferred to a second diet at Frankfort in the autumn ; and it came to a third at Wienerisch-Neustadt (February, 1455). Aeneas Sylvius was persuasive and eloquent ; but the meetings had no result. At the two later diets the appeals of John of Capistrano produced a sensation from which much was hoped. Like Peter the Hermit, he possessed the faculty of stirring the common folk in open-air assemblies. On the death of Pope Nicholas, the papal chair was filled by a Spaniard, Calixtus III (March, 1455), who seemed to have no less burning zeal for the holy war than John of Capistrano and Aeneas himself. He made a solemn vow to dedicate all his strength to the recovery of Constantinople and to the extermination of the "devilish sect" of Mohammad. For three and a half years he wrought and hoped, but with all his efforts could do no more than send a few ducats to Scanderbeg, or float a few galleys to harass the shores of the eastern Aegean. He was succeeded by Aeneas Sylvius, under the name of Pius II (August, 1458). While the West had been talking, Mohammad had been advancing; and in a great Council, assembled with much trouble at Mantua (1459), Pius said: "Each of his victories is the path to a new victory; he will conquer the kings of the West, abolish the Gospel, and ultimately impose the law of Mohammad on all peoples." The insincere attitude of the Venetians frustrated any results that might have been brought about by the assembly at Mantua. These fruitless diets and councils are a dull and dead page in history; but they represent the efforts of the European states to discuss the same Eastern Question which we have seen them deal with in our own day at the Congress of Berlin.

One of the most obvious policies for the western enemies of Mohammad was to enter into communication with his enemies in the orient and attempt to concert some common action. Such negotiations had been set on foot by Popes Nicholas and Calixtus. The last two sovereigns of the dynasty of the Grand Comneni of Trebizond, who were now the representatives of the Roman Empire, John IV and David, had endeavoured to organise an alliance of the principalities of Asia Minor and Armenia, and to gain the support of Persia. It was upon Uzun Hasan, prince of the Turcomans of the White Sheep, that they above all relied. In 1459 David wrote to the Duke of Burgundy announcing the conclusion of such a league, and expressing the conviction that, if east and west were to strike together now, the Ottoman could be abolished from the earth. But the league availed not David, when two years later Mohammad came to destroy the empire of Trebizond (1461), and Uzun Hasan left him in the lurch. He surrendered on the offer of favourable treatment; but he was not more fortunate than the King of Bosnia; he and his family were afterwards put to death. At the same time Mohammad seized Genoese Amastris, and likewise Sinope, an independent Seljuk state; and thus he became master of the whole southern board of the Pontic sea.

It was about this time (1460) that Pope Pius indited a most curious letter to Mohammad, proposing that the Sultan should embrace Christianity, and become, under the patronage of the Roman see, "Emperor of the Greeks and the East." A little thing, he wrote, only a drop of water, will make you the greatest of mortals; be baptised, and without money, arms, or fleet, you will win the greatest lordship in Christendom. Had this chimerical proposal been seriously meant, it would argue in Aeneas an almost incredibly fanciful and unpractical mind; but, when we find that he himself composed Mohammad's answer, we may infer that the letter was written as a rhetorical exercise, and never intended to be sent.

The prospect looked brighter in 1463, when the breach at length came between Venice and the Sultan. An offensive and defensive alliance was concluded between the Pope, Venice, and the King of Hungary; the Duke of Burgundy joined it. The co-operation of Venice seemed a security that business was meant at last. The Pope, though he was advanced in years, resolved to lead the Crusade himself; Ancona was appointed as the mustering-place; and thither streamed from all countries bands of poor and ill-furnished people, drawn by the hope of booty (1464). But neither the Venetian vessels which were to transport them to Greece, nor the princes who were to lead them, appeared; and Ancona and the whole country round about groaned under their excesses. When Pius arrived in June, he found but the remnant of a disbanded rabble; and, overcome with disappointment, this victim of an idea out of season fell ill and died.

Venice, unlike the Pope, was in contact with realities. The war had broken out in Greece by the Turkish capture of Argos, which a Greek priest betrayed. The Venetians laid siege to Corinth, and built a wall— the old "Six-mile" wall—across the Isthmus; and had they been directed by a brave and competent commander, they would have captured the key of the Morea. But, disheartened by defeat in some small engagements with Omar Pasha who had marched up from the south of the peninsula to raise the siege, they abandoned the defence of the Isthmus, before Mahmud Pasha, the grand vezir, arrived with an army from the north (1463). Their failure at this favourable tide put a term to their chances of recovering ground in the Peloponnesus. An ineffectual maritime war was prosecuted for the next six years (1464–9); and then the great blow to Venetian power was struck. At the beginning of June 1470 a fleet of 108 large galleys and nearly 200 small sail, commanded by Mahmud, set sail for the Euripus, and by land Mohammad himself led an army probably numbering about 80,000. The usual size of his armies seems to have been from 80,000 to 100,000, though they are generally set at far larger figures by the vanity of his defeated foes. The Sultan had resolved to rob Venice of her most valuable station, the strong fort of Chalcis or Egripos (which the Latins further corrupted to Negroponte, with an allusion to the bridge which connected it with the mainland). Against this great double armament Venice had nothing ready to oppose but the strength of the well-provisioned city's walls, the resolution of the inhabitants, and thirty-five galleys which were in the Aegean under Nicolò da Canale. This captain could not venture to guard the Straits against the far superior squadron; but, had he remained hard by, he might, it was thought, have effectually impeded Mohammad's construction of a bridge of boats from the mainland to the shore of the island. But he sailed away to beat up reinforcements in Crete. The siege operations lasted for four weeks. In a final storm Mohammad, apparently aided by treachery, took the city in the teeth of a desperate defence (July 12). All the Italians who survived the conflict were executed; the Greeks were enslaved. At this crisis Canale covered himself with shame. He had returned to the Euripus; his small squadron was within sight of the city; the garrison was signalling to him; and he made no effort to save the place. If he had broken the boat-bridge, as Hunyady had done at Belgrade, he would probably have rescued Negroponte; it was his plainest duty to try, and Venice punished him for his *fainéance*. After the fall of its bulwark, the whole island passed into Turkish hands.

The event created in the West little less consternation than the fall of Constantinople itself. Pope Paul II and old Cardinal Bessarion were fluttered; and Sixtus IV (who succeeded in 1471), in conjunction with Ferdinand of Naples, accomplished something more considerable than the western powers had yet done. They sent a number of galleys to join Pietro Mocenigo, an able seaman whom Venice had chosen captain of her fleet. At Samos in 1472 Mocenigo commanded 85 vessels, of which 48 were furnished by Venice and her dependencies, 18 by the Pope, 17 by Ferdinand, and 2 by Rhodes: an armament notable as the greatest that the combination of Christian powers at this time achieved. The Venetian admiral who had taken on board a number of Albanian *stradioti* conducted a war of raids with skill, swooping down and plundering Passagio, a trading-town over against Chios; burning Smyrna; pillaging the quays of Satalia, then a mart of the oriental spice-trade; helping the royal house of Cyprus. One brilliant feat was wrought by a Sicilian, who venturing into the Dardanelles with six companions fired the Turkish arsenal of Gallipoli, and expiated his daring by a cruel death. Such warfare was highly agreeable to the mercenaries who were paid on the system of receiving a part of the booty; but it was hopelessly ineffectual, and Venice recognised that war must be waged by land. The scene was shifted to Albania, where Scanderbeg's legacy had fallen to Venice. Here all turned on the possession of Scodra (Scutari), the key of Albania, which had the same kind of strategic significance as Negroponte or Acrocorinth. The Sultan was determined to secure it, and Sulayman, governor of Rumelia, laid siege to it in 1474. He was repelled by its brave defender Antonio Loredano ; and the stress of need which the inhabitants endured was shown, the moment the siege was raised, by their general rush for the gates to quench their thirst in the waters of the Bojana. In 1477 the Turks renewed their designs in this quarter by besieging Kroja, and at the same time their light cavalry (*akindje*) harassed Venice in the north by overrunning Friuli. The garrison of Kroja, reduced to eating their dogs and receiving no aid from Venice, submitted in the ensuing year, and Mohammad advanced to the second siege of Scodra. The Venetian republic was hard pressed. In these days its yearly revenue did not touch 100,000 ducats; nor could the Venetians at this moment expect aid from other powers; Ferdinand of Naples was actually intriguing with the Turk, and Friuli was exposed to the inroads of the infidels from Bosnia; the plague was raging in the lagoons. Unable to relieve Scodra, Venice resolved to make peace and consented to hard conditions,

But the Wallachian overreached them, and impaled them all; then crossing the Danube, he laid waste the Turkish territory. In 1462 Mohammad arrived at the head of an army, bringing with him Radu, Vlad's brother, to take the place of the latter. Like Darius, he sent a fleet of transports to the Danube to carry the army across. Vlad withdrew his forces into the deep oak-forests, which formed a natural fortification. One night he penetrated in disguise into the Turkish camp, hoping to slay Mohammad; but he mistook the tent of a general for that of the Sultan. By his address and boldness he seems to have inflicted a serious repulse on the invaders; but he was presently attacked on the other side by Stephen, the prince of Moldavia. After his divided army had sustained a double defeat, he fled to Hungary, and his brother Radu was enthroned by the Turks.

The stress of the struggle now devolved upon the northern principality of Moldavia, and there too a strong man had arisen. In 1456 Peter Aron gave tribute to the Turk, but this prince was overthrown in the following year by Stephen the Great. At first Stephen did not rise to his rôle of a champion against the unbelievers. He set his desire on securing the fortress of Kilia (near the mouth of the Danube) which belonged to Hungary and Wallachia in common, and he actually urged Mohammad's invasion. But he failed to win Kilia at this moment, and his capture of it three years later, when Wallachia belonged to the Turk, was an act of hostility to Mohammad. Five years later he invaded Wallachia, dethroned Radu, and set up in his stead Laïot, a member of the Bassarab family which has given its name to Bessarabia. At this time Mohammad was occupied with other things, but the conflict would come sooner or later, and Stephen stirred himself to knit alliances and form combinations to east and to west. He was in communication with Venice, with the Pope, with Uzun Hasan. The victory of Terdshan left Mohammad free to throw an army into Moldavia under the command of Sulayman Pasha. Stephen, reinforced by contingents sent by the Kings of Poland and Hungary, gained at Racova (on the Birlad stream) a great victory—the glory of his reign—which entitles him to a place near Hunyady and Scanderbeg (1475). But a new element was brought into the situation in the same year by the simultaneous expedition which was sent against the Genoese settlements of the Crimea. Caffa capitulated—40,000 inhabitants were sent to Constantinople; and its fall was followed by the surrender of Tana (Azov) and the other stations. Mohammad could now launch the Tartars of this region against Moldavia on the flank; and next year (1476) this befell. Unassisted by Poland or Hungary, who were each suspicious of his relations with the other; attacked by the Wallachian prince whom he had himself enthroned; assailed on the other side by the Tartars,—Stephen was worsted with great loss by a Turkish army led by the Sultan, who had come to avenge the shame of Racova, in a forest glade which is called the Place of Battles (Rasboieni). But he rallied, and Mohammad retired without subduing the country. Eight years after this the Turks seized the two fortress-keys of Moldavia—Kilia and Tschetatea Alba (1484). Before his death, Stephen made a vain attempt to form an East-European league against the infidel—embracing Moscow and Lithuania, Poland and Hungary. But his experience convinced him that the struggle was hopeless, and on his death-bed (1504) the advice which he gave to his son Bogdan was to submit to the Turkish power. On the accession of the Sultan Selim (1512) Moldavia submitted, paying a yearly sum to the Porte, but keeping the right of freely electing her own princes.

The war with Venice and the struggle with Uzun Hasan had hindered Mohammad from concentrating his forces upon the subjugation of Rhodes, where the Knights of St John maintained an outpost of Christendom. On the conclusion of the Venetian peace he began preparations for a serious attack on Rhodes, and in 1480 Masih Pasha sailed with a considerable fleet and laid siege to the town. The whole of Europe had been aware that the blow was coming, and much had been done to meet it. The defence devolved upon the Grand-Master of the Order, Peter d'Aubusson, a man "endued with a martial soul," who had learned "the mappes, the mathematicks," as well as the art of war, "but history was his principal study." The Turks were aided by the local knowledge of a German renegade, and their guns, of immense size for that age, created a sensation. They had sixteen bombards, 64 inches long, throwing stone shot 9 and 11 inches in diameter. But the siege lasted two months, before they forced an entry into the outer parts of the city. In the terrible mellay which ensued the valour of the knights pressed the Turks backward, and at this moment, when the chance of success depended on heartening the troops to recover their lost ground, Masih Pasha, in foolish confidence that the day was won, issued an order that no soldier should touch the booty, since the treasures belonged to the Sultan. Thus deprived of a motive for fighting, the Turks fled to their camp, and their general raised the leaguer. But, after this shame dealt to his arms, Mohammad could not let the island continue to defy him. He equipped another armament and resolved to lead it in person. But even as he started he fell sick and death overtook him (May 3, 1481): an event which, as it proved, meant a respite of forty years to the Latin lords of Rhodes. The deeds of Mohammad show best what manner of man he was: a conqueror who saw in conquest the highest statesmanship, but who also knew how to consolidate and organise, and how to adapt the principles of Islam to political dealings with Christian States. We have portraits of him painted both by pen and brush. Contrary to the precepts of his religion, he had his picture painted by Gentile Bellini, and is the first great Mohammadan sovereign of whose outward appearance we have such evidence. The pale, bearded face, set on a short, thick neck, was marked by a broad forehead, raised eyebrows, and an eagle nose.

The situation and prospects of the Ottoman empire seemed changed on the death of the conqueror. The prosperity and growth of that empire depended wholly on the personality of the autocrat who ruled it; and the two sons whom Mohammad left behind were made in a different mould from their vigorous father. Bayazid the elder, who was governor of the province of Amasia, was a man of mild nature who cared for the arts of peace, and would have been well contented to rest upon the conquests which had been already achieved, and to enjoy the fruits of the labours of his fathers. Jem, governor of Caramania, was a bright, clever youth, endowed with a distinguished poetical talent; he might easily have been lured into a career of military ambition, but perhaps he hardly possessed the strength and steadfastness necessary for success. When Bayazid reached Constantinople, on the news of his father's death, he found that the Janissaries had begun a reign of terror in the city. They had slain the Grand Vezir, who, being disposed to espouse the cause of Jem, had, according to a common practice in such cases, concealed the Sultan's death; and they had plundered the habitations of the Jews and Christians. They favoured the claims of Bayazid, and were tranquillised when they had exacted from him a pardon for their outbreak and an increase of their pay. Meanwhile Jem—who claimed the throne on the ground that, though the younger, he was born in the purple—had advanced to Brusa, and was there proclaimed Sultan. But he was willing to compromise. Through his great-aunt he made a proposal to Bayazid that they should divide the empire—Bayazid to rule in Europe, and he in Asia. The question at stake was not merely a personal one, the extent of Bayazid's sovereignty, but the integrity and power of the Ottoman empire. Moreover, it involved a direct violation of one of the fundamental canons of Islam: that there shall be only one supreme Imam. Bayazid's decision accordingly influenced the history of the world. He refused to accept Jem's offer; "the empire," he said, "is the bride of one lord." The rival claims were settled by the award of battle in the plains of Yenishehr, where the treachery of some of Jem's troops gave the victory to Bayazid. The defeated brother fled to Cairo, and his attempt in the following year to seize Caramania in conjunction with an exiled prince of that country was repelled. Then he sought refuge at Rhodes; his chances of success lay in the help of the Christian powers of Europe.

Jem arrived at Rhodes under a safe-conduct from the Grand-Master and the Council of the Knights, permitting him and his suite to remain in the island and leave it at their will. But it was soon felt that it was not safe to keep the precious person of the prince at Rhodes, so near the realm of Bayazid, who was ready to resort to any foul means of seizing or destroying him; and Jem and the Grand-Master agreed that France would be the best retreat, pending the efforts which they hoped would be made to restore him. To France, accordingly, Jem sailed (September, 1482). After his departure, the Knights concluded first a treaty of peace with Bayazid for the Sultan's lifetime, and secondly a contract by which he agreed to pay them 45,000 ducats a year, in return for which the Grand-Master undertook to maintain and guard Jem in such a way as to cause no inconvenience to the Sultan. In an age when the violation of engagements was regarded as justifiable, and was even in certain cases recommended by the heads of the Church, there is no more shameless instance of perfidy than this. D'Aubusson had guaranteed Jem his freedom, and undertaken to espouse his cause; he now took Bayazid's money to be Jem's jailor. His conduct could not even be defended on the plea of the interests of religion, which in those days were often furthered by dishonesty and bad faith; on the contrary, it was a treachery to the cause of Christendom, to which Jem's ambitions —according to the letters which D'Aubusson himself wrote to the western powers—furnished so unique an opportunity against its foe. For six years Jem was kept a prisoner in France, being constantly removed from one castle to another by his Rhodian guards, and making repeated attempts to escape which were always frustrated; while the Pope, the King of Naples, and the King of Hungary were each seeking to induce D'Aubusson to deliver the prince into his hands. At length Innocent VIII came to an arrangement. The concession of various privileges, and a cardinal's hat for D'Aubusson, persuaded the Knights, who were already anxious to rid themselves of a charge which involved them in troublesome relations with both Bayazid and the Sultan of Egypt. Another series of negotiations was required to obtain from Charles VIII permission for Jem to leave France; and not till March 1489 did the Turkish prince arrive at Rome. Pope Alexander VI, who succeeded Innocent in 1492, and who was threatened by the invasion of Charles VIII, affected the most friendly relations with Bayazid and had recourse to him for money and other support. In 1494 the document containing this Pope's instructions to his envoy, together with letters from Bayazid, was intercepted at Sinigaglia, in the possession of Turkish envoys who had landed at Ancona and were on their way to Rome. The compromising papers were taken to Charles VIII at Florence, and the Pope's treachery to Christendom was exposed. One of the Sultan's communications to the Pope is significant. Considering—wrote Bayazid in Latin, a language with which he was well acquainted—that sooner or later Jem must die, it would be well, for the tranquillity of his Holinesss and the satisfaction of the Sultan, to hasten a death which for him would be life; and therefore he implored the Pope to remove Jem from the vexations of this life and send him to a better world. For the dead body of the prince he promised 300,000 ducats, with which the Pope might buy estates for his sons. Charles VIII advanced to Rome, and the terms which he made with Alexander VI comprised the transference of Jem into his own power. Jem accompanied the King southward, but he was in ailing health, and at Capua became so ill that he could go no further. He was taken in a litter to Naples, and died there in high fever (February, 1495). The Venetians, who were the first to inform the Sultan of his brother's end, wrote in a pointed way that he had died a natural death; but, as it was their policy at this moment to keep on good terms with the Pope, this testimony does not weigh much in deciding the question whether, as was certainly believed at the time, Jem's health was undermined by a deliberate system of intoxication. The insufficiency of our material compels us to leave the question open; but the circumstances are at least suspicious, and in any case the French were innocent.

Thus for thirteen years the western powers held Jem as a menace over the head of the Turkish Sultan; but this singular episode did not affect the course of Turkish history. A second ruler like Bayazid, Machiavelli thought, would have rendered the Ottoman power innocuous to Europe. The temper of the man was displayed at once not only by the abandonment of the Rhodian expedition, but by a reduction of tribute granted to Ragusa, and by a modification in Venice's favour of the treaty which had recently been concluded with that republic (1482). His reign was marked indeed by raids on Croatia and the Dalmatian coast, by intermittent hostilities with Hungary, by incursions into Moldavia and even into Poland; but the only serious war was with Venice, which broke out in 1499 after twenty years of peace. In that interval the republic had acquired the island of Cyprus (1489) and extended her influence in the Aegean, and the Sultan at last deemed it time to check her course. Active naval preparations in the Turkish arsenals stirred the alarm of Venice; but the Porte lulled her suspicions by furnishing her envoy, Andrea Zancani, with a document which renewed and confirmed the peace. An experienced Venetian resident at Constantinople, Andrea Gritti by name, well acquainted with Turkish methods, pointed out to Zancani that the document was drawn up in Latin, not in Turkish, and was therefore not considered binding by the Porte; but Zancani, unable to induce the Porte to give him a new deed in Turkish, omitted to explain the matter to the authorities at home. Gritti's surmises were true. Suddenly the Sultan threw him and all the other Venetians at Constantinople into prison, and presently sent forth a fleet of 270 sail. Its destination was Lepanto. It was intercepted by a Venetian squadron of about half that strength, hastily got together, off the coast of Messenia; but the brave seaman Antonio Loredano failed in his attack and perished himself. Besieged by land and sea, Lepanto fell; and, after its fall, the Turks made a terrible incursion, through Carniola and Friuli, into the Venetian territory, advancing as far as Vicenza. The next object of Bayazid was to drive Venice out of the Morea; and when she sued for peace he demanded the cession of Modon, Coron, and Nauplia. To this she would not consent; but in the following year Modon was besieged by Bayazid himself, and the garrison, seeing that they could not hold out, set the place on fire and perished in the flames. Hereupon Coron, Navarino, and Aegina capitulated, and nothing was left to the republic but Nauplia, which boldly and successfully defied the foe. But the Venetian fleet suddenly bestirred itself, recaptured Aegina, and, reinforced by a Spanish armament under the greatest captain of the day, Gonzalo of Cordova, conquered Cephalonia. These successes were followed up by neither side in 1501; and when Venice conquered Santa Maura in 1502, a peace ensued. Santa Maura was given back; Cephalonia remained to Venice; Lepanto and the places captured in the Morea were kept by Turkey. In the same year in which this peace was concluded (1503) a treaty for seven years was made between the Porte and Hungary; this was intended to include all the powers of Europe—France and England, Spain, Portugal, and Naples, the Pope and the various States of Italy, Rhodes and Chios, Poland, and Moldavia.

From this moment for the next seventeen years Europe had some respite from the Eastern Question. There was incessant fear of what the Turk might do next, incessant talk of resisting him, incessant negotiations against him; but there was no actual war; almost no Christian territory was won for Islam, and no Christian territory won back for Europe. The attention of the Sultan was drawn eastward; where he had to reckon with a new power; for the lordship of Persia had once more changed hands. The decline of the Turcomans of the White Sheep was clearly shown in the circumstance that on the death of Uzun Hasan nine dynasts (not to speak of rival claimants) succeeded in twenty-four years. Murad, the last of these, succumbed to the power of Ismail, a sheikh of Ardabil, who traced his descent to the Prophet. The decisive battle was fought at Shurur in 1502; and, from his new-won capital at Tavriz, Ismail advanced to the conquest of Persia and Khorasan. The history of modern Persia begins with Ismail, the first Shah—the first of the Safavid dynasty which endured till the middle of the eighteenth century (1736). He called himself a Safavi, from Safi, an ancestor illustrious for piety; and hence to contemporary Europe he was known as the Sofi.

A collision between the new Persian power and the Turks was rendered inevitable by religious fanaticism. To orthodox Sunnites like the Ottomans, the heresy of the Shiites is more obnoxious than the infidelity of the Giaours, who are altogether outside the pale; and, when Bayazid discovered that the Shiite doctrines were being propagated and taking root in certain parts of his Asiatic dominion, he took steps to check the evil by transporting suspected persons to Greece. The Shah Ismail then came forward as the protector of the Shiites, and called upon the Turkish Sultan to allow adherents of that belief to leave his realm. But, though the Shah is said to have insulted the Sultan by giving the name of *Bayazid* to a fattened swine, war did not break out in Bayazid's days. The Persian monarch showed his anticipation of trouble by entering into negotiations with the western powers, as Uzun Hasan had done before; and a Persian embassy was welcomed at Venice though the Signory openly declared that there was no intention of breaking the peace: two years before they had given up Alessio in Albania, in order to avoid a breach.

On the side of the south too, Bayazid's dominions had been threatened. The Mamluk Sultan of Egypt, Sayf ad-Din (1468–95), had espoused the cause of Jem, to whose mother he had given an asylum; had interfered in the affairs of Sulkadr, a small Turcoman lordship in Cappadocia; and had asserted authority in the regions of Lesser Armenia,—even as in ancient days the Ptolemies had thrown out an arm to grasp Cilicia. Tarsus, Adana, and other places passed under Egyptian rule, and in 1485 war openly broke out between the Mamluk and the Ottoman Sultans. An important victory was won by the Egyptian in 1488; but a peace was patched up in 1491, and lasted during the rest of Bayazid's reign.

The tremendous earthquake which sent a thrill through the world in 1509 laid Constantinople in ruins; the Sultan himself fled to Hadrianople. But an oriental autocrat in those days could rebuild quickly; and with a host of workmen, worthy of a Pharaoh or a Babylonian King, Bayazid restored the city in a few months. The last days of the old Sultan were embittered by the rebellion and rivalry of his sons, Ahmad, Corcud, and Selim. He destined Ahmad as his successor, and thought of abdicating the throne in his favour; but Selim, a man of action and resolution, was determined that this should not be. From the province of Trebizond of which he was the governor, he marched to Europe at the head of an army, and appearing at the gates of Hadrianople, demanded to be assigned an European province. He wished to be near the scene of action when the moment came. He demanded too that his father should not abdicate in favour of Ahmad. Both demands were agreed to. But at this juncture news arrived that Corcud had revolted; and thereupon Selim seized Hadrianople. This was too much. His sire took the field and defeated him in a battle; and he fled for refuge to the Crimea. But the cause of Ahmad was not won. The Janissaries, whose hearts had been captivated by the bold stroke of Selim, broke out in mutiny and riot when Ahmad drew nigh to take possession of the throne, and were pacified only by a pledge from Bayazid that this design should not be carried out. Ahmad thereupon sought to get Asia Minor into his power; Corcud intrigued at the same time for his own hand; and finally, in the spring of 1512, Selim advanced from the Crimea to the Danube, and, supported by the Janissaries who would brook no opposition, forced Bayazid to abdicate (April 25). A month later the old Sultan died, poisoned, it can hardly be questioned, by order of his son. It was not to be expected that Ahmad would submit; he seized Brusa; but Selim crossed over to Asia, drove him eastward, and deprived him of the governorship of Amasia. Next year Ahmad made another attempt, but was defeated in battle at Yenishehr and executed. Corcud had not dared to take the field; but in consequence of his intrigues he was likewise put to death. The next victims were the Sultan's nephews, children of other brothers who had died in the lifetime of their father. Thus Selim put into practice a ruthless law which had been enacted by the policy of Mohammad II, that it was lawful for a Sultan, in the interests of the unity of the realm, which was the first condition of its prosperity, to do his brothers and their children to death.

The spirit of Selim I was very different from that of his father. He was resolved to resume the old paths of forward policy from which the studious temper of Bayazid had digressed, and to follow in the way of Mohammad the Conqueror. Yet he was also unlike his grandfather. He revelled in war and death; all his deeds seem prompted rather by instinct than by policy. Mohammad seems almost genial beside this gloomy and restless soul. Selim the Grim delighted in cruelty, but he was extremely moderate in pleasure; like his father and uncle he was highly cultivated. He raised the pay of the Janissaries,—this was the meed of their support; but he soon showed that he was resolved to be their master. The truth is that the Janissaries were an institution ill compatible with a peace policy; amenable to the discipline of war, they were a perpetual danger for a pacific ruler.

The collisions with Persia and Egypt, which menaced the reign of Bayazid, actually came to pass after the accession of Selim. The Shah, Ismail, had given an asylum to the sons of Ahmad, and had made an incursion into the eastern districts of the Ottoman Empire (1513). But the fundamental cause of the Persian war was religious antagonism; it was a struggle between the great Sunnite and the great Shiite power. It was stamped with this character by a sweeping act of persecution on the part of Selim, who, seizing 40,000 Shiites, killed some and imprisoned others; and the mutual attitude of the rival superstitions was shown in a high-flown letter which Selim, when he took the field (1514), indited to his enemy. He marched into the dominions of Ismail, and the decisive battle was fought in the plain of Chaldiran, lying further east than the field which had seen the struggle of Mohammad with Uzun Hasan. The Ottomans were again successful; on this occasion too their superiority in artillery told; and Tavriz fell into the hands of Selim. In the following year Sulkadr was annexed; and in 1516 Northern

Mesopotamia (including among other cities Amida, Nisibis, Dara, and Edessa) was conquered and became a province of the Ottoman Empire.

This conquest led to designs on Syria and Egypt, a sufficient pretext being found in the alliance between the old Mamluk Sultan Kansuh Ghuri and the Shah Ismail. The Mamluk army awaited the invader at Aleppo; and Selim, here again conspicuously superior in artillery, won a victory which decided the fate of Syria (1516). The old Sultan's successor Tumanbeg was defeated in an equally disastrous battle at Reydaniya near Cairo (January, 1517). Thus Syria and Egypt were brought once more under the authority of the lords of Constantinople, to remain so actually or formally till the present day. The conquest of Egypt was followed by the submission of Arabia to the Sultan's sway.

The same year which saw the conquest of the Nile country witnessed an important exaltation of the dignity of the Ottoman ruler. The Ottoman princes had been originally Emirs under the Seljuks, and, even after they had become the strongest power of the Mohammadan world, though they might demean themselves as Caliphs, they had no legal claim to be considered its heads. It is one of the fundamental principles of Islam that all Muslims shall be governed by a single Imam, and that Imam must be a member of the Koreish, the tribe of the Prophet. At this time the Imamship was in the hands of a shadow, Mohammad Abu Jafar of the race of Hashim, who kept up the semblance of a court at Cairo. The last of the Caliphs of the Abbasid line, he resigned the caliphate to the Sultan Selim. This formal transference is the basis of the claims of the Sultans of Turkey to be the Imams or supreme rulers of Islam, though they have not a drop of Koreish blood in their veins. The translation of the Caliphate was confirmed by the recognition which Selim received at the same time from the Sherif of Mecca, who sent him the keys of the Kaaba, thus designating him as the protector of the Holy Places.

The Imam, according to the Ottoman code of Mohammadan law, has authority to watch over the maintenance of the laws and the execution of punishments; to defend the frontier and repress rebels; to raise armies and levy tribute; to celebrate public prayer on Fridays and in Bairam; to judge the people; to marry minors of both sexes who have no natural guardians; and to divide the spoils of war. He is thus supreme legislator and judge, the religious head of the State, the commander-in-chief, and he possesses absolute control of the finances. His ecumenical authority rests on a verse of the Koran: whoever dies without acknowledging the authority of the Imam of his day is dead in ignorance. The Imam must be visible to men; he cannot lurk in a cave like the Mahdi, for whose coming the heretical Shiites look. It is discreetly provided that the Imam need not be just or virtuous, or the most eminent man of his time; it is requisite only that he should be able to enforce the law, defend the frontiers, and sustain the oppressed.

Moreover the wickedness and tyranny of an Imam would not necessitate or justify his deposition.

The brilliant conquests of Selim in the East alarmed the powers of the West; "returning powerful and proud," such a monarch as he was a terrible menace to Europe. Leo X had thrown himself with zeal into the project of a Crusade; for the experience of sixty years of futilities had not killed that idea. In 1517 he issued a bull imposing a truce of five years on Christendom, in order that the princes of Europe might march against the Infidels. His hopes rested chiefly on the young French King, Francis I, who, after the victory of Marignano, had met him at Bologna and discussed with him the Eastern Question. A letter of Francis, written soon after that interview, breathes the spirit of a knight-errant dedicating his youth and strength to a holy war. But though Francis was in earnest, religious enthusiasm was not his moving inspiration or his guiding idea. His project was that the three great powers of Europe—the Empire, France, and Spain—should conquer the Turkish realm and divide it amongst them in three equal parts. Thus the Eastern Question began to enter upon its modern phase—assuming a political rather than a religious aspect; and the significance of the oriental policy of Francis I was that he definitely formulated the doctrine, now a commonplace of politics, that Turkey is a spoil to be parted among the great powers of Europe. The new conception of the French King was indeed more likely to lead to practical results than had been the arguments of Aeneas Sylvius and his successors; and the Emperor Maximilian composed a memoir of suggestions on the conduct of the proposed war. But his death in 1519 changed the situation, disconcerting the plan of the European powers; and the favourable hour for a common enterprise against the Turk had passed. Men were indeed still painfully afraid of the designs of the formidable Sultan. The logic of geography determined that after the acquisition of Egypt the next enterprise of Selim should be the conquest of Rhodes, which lay right in the track of communication between Egypt and Constantinople. He made preparations accordingly for the destruction of the "dogs" of Rhodes. But when his fleet and army were ready, he was smitten down by the plague (September 21, 1520), having in his short reign done as much as any of the Sultans for the extension and prestige of the Ottoman empire.

On his death Europe, full of apprehensions for the fate of Rhodes, breathed securely; but the feeling of relief was premature. The rumour had spread that his son and successor was, in complete contrast to his father, of a quiet unaggressive nature, and might prove another Bayazid. But these auguries were ill-based; for the youth who mounted the throne was Solyman (Sulayman) the Lawgiver—known to the west as Solyman the Magnificent, in whose reign Turkey climbed to the summit of its power and glory. He was as strong as his father, a soldier as well as a statesman; but his mind was well balanced; he felt none of Selim's grim delight in war and butchery. Perhaps no contemporary sovereign in Christendom was so unfeignedly desirous or so sincerely resolute to administer evenhanded justice as Solyman. His reign began without bloodshed; he was lucky enough to have no brother or nephew to remove; the only trouble was a rebellion in Syria, which was promptly crushed.

The wave which had flowed eastward under Selim turns westward again under Solyman. He had been viceroy in Europe during his father's absence in the orient, and he had occasion to observe the intolerable situation on the north-western frontier, where there was continuous friction with the Hungarian kingdom. On this side he could not feel safe, so long as the key-fortresses of Belgrade and Szabács were in the hands of the Hungarians; these places must be captured whether as a base for further advance or as the bulwarks of a permanent frontier. Envoys were sent to King Louis demanding tribute; he replied by murdering the envoys. When this news arrived, the Sultan's thought was to march straight on Buda; but his military advisers pointed out that he could not leave Szabács in his rear. The operations on the Save were protracted during the whole summer (1521). Szabács was taken under the eye of the Sultan himself, and a few days later Semlin was captured by his generals. But Solyman was compelled to recognise that Belgrade must also be secured, and after a difficult siege it was taken, through treachery. Solyman kept a diary of the campaign so that we can read his doings day by day. Other fortresses, such as Slankamen and Mitrović, fell into his hands; and thus the gates of Hungary were fully unlocked, whenever he chose to pass in. As yet he did not press on to Buda. A more urgent task lay before him in another quarter,—the conquest of Rhodes.

Where Mohammad had failed, his great-grandson was to succeed. Belgrade had fallen, Rhodes was now to fall. The pirate-ships of the Rhodian Knights were a pest to the eastern waters of the archipelago and the Asiatic coasts; and not only was it imperative for the Sultan that his line of communication with Egypt should be cleared of the corsair nest, but it was in the interest of public order that the island should be annexed to the Turkish realm. The lords of Rhodes had to depend entirely on themselves, without aid from the west. The first principle of Venetian policy at this time was to keep on good terms with the Turk. The Signory had congratulated Selim on his conquests, and had transferred to him the tribute for Cyprus previously paid by them to the Sultan of Egypt. They had congratulated Solyman on his accession, and of all foreigners they had the most advantageous commercial position in the Ottoman realm. They were therefore careful to lend no countenance to Rhodes. In summer 1522 the main army of the Turks under Solyman himself marched across Asia Minor to the Carian coast, and a fleet of about 300 ships carried select troops. In all, the Turkish army was about 200,000 strong, including 60,000 miners from Wallachia and Bosnia. The Grand-Master, L'Isle Adam, had made all possible preparations. An iron chain locked the harbour; and outside it a boom of timber floated from the windmill tower at the north-east point of the harbour to Fort St Nicholas, which stood at the end of a mole on the north-west side. The houses beyond the walls were demolished, to deprive the foe of shelter and supply stones for new defences. The precaution was taken of removing the slaves from the powdermills; freemen were set to work there day and night. The first great assault (in September) was repelled with such enormous loss, that Solyman resigned himself to the tactics of wearying the garrison out. In December, as the ammunition of the besieged was failing, the Grand-Master agreed to surrender. Free departure within ten days was conceded to all the Latin Knights; any who chose to remain in the island were to be free from taxes for five years, were not to be subject to the child-tribute, and were to enjoy free exercise of their religion. Hostages were exchanged, and Solyman withdrew his army some miles from the walls to allow the garrison to depart in peace. But it was hard to keep the Turkish troops under control, and on Christmas-day a body of soldiers burst in and sacked the city. The majority of the Knights sought refuge in Crete, to find eight years later an abiding home in Malta.

By the capture of the two bulwarks of Christendom which had defied the conqueror of Constantinople, the young Sultan established his fame. Belgrade and Rhodes fallen, as Pope Adrian wrote, "the passages to Hungary, Sicily, and Italy lie open to him." There was as much cause for alarm in the west as there had been on the captures of Negroponte and Scodra. But the conqueror could not immediately follow up his victories. Now, as often, events in the eastern dominions of the Sultan procured a respite for his western neighbours. A revolt in Egypt and disquiet in Asia Minor claimed Solyman's attention, and not till the fourth year after the fall of Rhodes could he march on Buda, "to pluck up" in the words of a Turkish historian "the strong-rooted tree of evil unbelief from its place beside the rose-bed of Islam." Sooner or later, this expedition was inevitable; but it may have been hastened by a year or two through the action of one of the Christian powers.

After the sudden disaster of Pavia (February, 1525) Francis I, a captive in his enemy's hands, looked abroad for succour, and the only European power he could discern strong enough to bear effectual help was the Turk, to whose extirpation he had devoted himself some years before. No scruple was felt in appealing to the common foe. The French King's mother dispatched an ambassador to Solyman with rich presents; but in passing through Bosnia he and his companions were slain and robbed by the *sanjak-beg*. A second envoy, with a letter written by the King himself in his captivity at Madrid, suggesting that the Sultan should attack the King of Hungary, arrived safely at Constantinople. Without committing himself Solyman returned a gracious answer in this style:

"I who am the Sultan of Sultans, the Sovereign of Sovereigns, the distributor of crowns to the monarchs of the surface of the globe, the shadow of God on the earth, the Sultan and Padishah of the White Sea, the Black Sea, Rumelia, Anatolia, Caramania, Rum, Sulkadr, Diarbekr, Kurdistan, Azerbijan, Persia, Damascus, Aleppo, Cairo, Mecca, Medina, Jerusalem, all Arabia, Yemen, and other countries which my noble ancestors (may God brighten their tombs) conquered and which my august majesty has likewise conquered with my flaming sword, Sultan Sulayman Khan, son of Sultan Selim, son of Sultan Bayazid; you who are Francis, King of France, you have sent a letter to my Porte the refuge of sovereigns"; then he heartens the captive, and observes, "night and day our horse is saddled, and our sword girt on."

This was the first embassy of a French King to the Porte, the beginning of France's oriental politics. It was naturally the interest of the Sultan to cultivate friendly relations with the western neighbours of Germany and the Empire. But Francis hardly looked beyond the immediate emergency; and at the beginning of 1526, when he won his freedom by the treaty of Madrid, he undertook to help the Emperor in an expedition against the Turks. The efforts of the Popes meanwhile to organise a Crusade had failed, as before. Adrian had proclaimed a holy truce for three years; the Minorites had dreamed of an army of crusaders furnished by all the monasteries of Europe "for the confusion and destruction of the Turks." The Reformation reacted on the Eastern Question. The mere fact that the Roman See continuously and consistently exhorted to a Crusade was to the adherents of the new religious movement an argument against a Turkish war. Luther himself announced the principle, that to resist the Turks was to resist God, who had sent them as a visitation. At a safe distance, this was a comfortable doctrine. But some years later, when the visitation drew nigh to the heart of Germany itself, the Reformer was somewhat embarrassed to explain away his earlier utterances.

The diffusion of the doctrine of the Reformers seems to have been one of the causes which slackened and weakened the resistance of Hungary to the Ottoman invasion. But the main cause was that King Louis was not competent as ruler or as leader; he had not the trust of his kingdom, and he was unable to cope with the opposition and dilatoriness of the Diet. The transactions of the Diet during the crisis are a melancholy comedy: the King and the councillors severally disclaiming any responsibility for consequences of the coming invasion and the safety of the realm. Help from his neighbours Louis could not expect. Venice had congratulated Solyman on the capture of Rhodes, and was still on most friendly terms with him; Poland had just concluded a peace with him. The distant kingdoms of England and

Portugal promised subsidies, but it was on his brother-in-law Charles V that Louis depended.  Charles sent reinforcements, but they came too late, two days after the decision of the campaign.  The most competent general the Hungarians could have chosen would have been John Zapolya, the voivod of Transylvania, but he was not trusted.  The command devolved upon Louis himself in default of a better man ; and at the start want of money rendered it difficult to mobilise.  It was decided to defend the line of the Save, but when it came to the point the lukewarmness of the magnates caused this plan to be abandoned.  The only really energetic man in the land was Archbishop Tomory, who did what he could to make defensible Peterwardein, the chief fortress of the Danube between the mouths of the Drave and the Save.

The Sultan set out towards the end of April with an army of 100,000 and 300 cannons; and his diary chronicles the heavy rainfalls which made his advance painful and slow, so that he did not reach Belgrade till July 9, when he was joined by his infantry (the Janissaries) which had been transported up the Danube by a flotilla.  Ibrahim, the Grand Vezir, had been sent forward to take Peterwardein, and it was in Turkish hands before the end of July.  After the fall of this bulwark, a bloody sword was carried, according to custom, throughout the Hungarian land, summoning men to help their country in the hour of her utmost jeopardy.  Zapolya was waiting uncertain what to do.  Receiving a command from the King to join the army he obeyed slowly, but only reached Szegedin on the Theiss where he remained.  There is not the least proof that he was acting in collusion with the Turk; the most that can be said is that he was secretly pleased at the embarrassing situation of King Louis.  The Hungarian army advanced to Tolna, and all told they were perhaps fewer than 30,000.  It was now a question whether the line of the Drave should be held ; but while the Hungarians were deliberating, the Turks had crossed that river at Essek (August 20–21).  The Chancellor Broderith gave the counsel to fall back to Buda, but messages from Tomory (at Neusatz) urged the King to give battle in the plain of Mohács (south of Tolna) where he had taken up a position.  On August 29 the Turks were known to be not far off, and the Hungarians spread out their two lines—a long thin line of foot in front, flanked by cavalry, and a rear line mainly of cavalry.  The plan was that the foot should open the attack all along the line, and when their attack began to tell the horse should charge.  In the afternoon the Rumelians who formed the vaward of the Turks became visible; they had no intention of fighting that day, and were about to camp.  The Hungarian centre and left attacked and dispersed them; the cavalry then struck in, and rode forward stimulated by the first easy success.  But nothing save a freak of chance could have averted the discomfiture of the Christian army; for the battle was controlled by no commander, and the divisions acted independently.  The cavalry were beaten back by the

steady fire of the enemy; and the Hungarian right wing, when the
Turks spread out leftwards and rounded on its flank, retired towards the
Danube. Twenty thousand of the Hungarian army were killed. The
King escaped from the field, but in crossing a brook his horse slipped on
the bank and he was drowned. The Sultan advanced and took possession
of Buda, but he did not leave a garrison; he was not yet prepared to
annex Hungary. His army was somewhat demoralised, and grave news
came of troubles in Asia Minor.

John Zapolya was crowned King, November 10, supported by a large
party; and his rivalry with Ferdinand, the late King's brother-in-law,
who claimed the throne, determined the course of the following events.
At first things looked ill for Zapolya. Ferdinand drove him out of
Buda back to Transylvania, and was himself crowned at Stuhlweissenburg
(November, 1527). Then Zapolya turned for help to the Sultan; who
after protracted parleys concluded a treaty of alliance with him
(February, 1528). Ferdinand also sent ambassadors; but they pleaded
in vain, and were even detained under arrest at the suggestion of some
Venetian envoys. On the other hand Francis I concluded a treaty with
Zapolya, who promised that if he died without male heir the crown of
Hungary should descend to the French King's son, the Duke of
Orleans. No French prince was destined ever to sit on the Hungarian
throne; but before half a century had passed a grandson of Francis was
to wear the crown of Poland, and the political idea was the same.

One of the results of the victory of Mohács was the consolidation
of Ottoman rule in the north-western countries, Bosnia and Croatia.
Jajce, which had so long defied the Sultans, was at last taken (1528), and
many other fortresses of less note. Early in 1529 it was known that
Solyman was preparing for a grand expedition northwards in that year.
Germany was alive to the danger. Luther changed his attitude and
acknowledged the necessity of war against the Turks, while he insisted
that all the disasters which had befallen Christendom from Varna to
Mohács had been due to the interference of Popes and bishops—
language which the deeds of Archbishop Paul Tomory of Kalocsa, the
defender of southern Hungary, might have been held to belie.

Solyman marched northwards—we can again follow his movements in
his own diary—at the head of an immense army, set at 250,000 men, an
exaggerated figure. King John met him on the field of Mohács, and the
crown of St Stephen on this occasion passed for safe keeping into the
possession of Solyman, who never gave it back. Buda was easily taken,
and the host advanced up the Danube, avoiding Pressburg, against
Vienna. The garrison numbered 22,000; the walls were not strong;
and Charles V, who ought to have hastened to the defence of the
eastern mark, was in Italy. Ferdinand waited in terrible anxiety at
Linz. He believed that it was the purpose of Solyman to winter in
Vienna and spend three years in the subjugation of Germany. The

garrison of Vienna in the meanwhile made suitable arrangements for encountering the storm. The houses outside the walls were levelled, the streets within torn up, buildings unroofed. The city was surrounded on September 26 and the operations began with mining. But the difficulty of procuring provisions and the approach of winter rendered the army impatient; and, when successive attempts at storming had been repelled with grave loss (October 9–12), it was decided to retreat after one more effort—especially as help was approaching, about 60,000 men from Bohemia, Moravia, and Germany. A half-hearted attack closed the episode of the first siege of Vienna, and at midnight the signal was given for a retreat which was marked by every horror. On December 16 Solyman records, he returned "fortunately" to Stambul. He had failed in Austria, but Hungary lay at his feet, and John Zapolya, though not a tributary, was absolutely dependent on his support.

The Ottoman State is marked off from the rest of Europe by a legal and political system which is based entirely on religious foundations. In Christian countries religion has frequently modified the principles of secular law; but in Turkey the problem of legislators has been to relax or adjust the interpretation of the canons of Islam, so as to permit it to take its place among European States, and to establish a *modus vivendi* with neighbouring unbelievers. Under Mohammad II a general code of law called "the Pearl" was drawn up by the Molla Khusrev in 1470; but this was superseded by Ibrahim Haleby of Aleppo, who in the reign of Solyman compiled a code which he named "the Confluence of the Seas" (*Multeka-ul-ubhar*). The sources from which these codes were compiled are four: the *Koran*; the *Sunnas* (the sayings of the Prophet which depend on early tradition, and inferences from his actions and his silences); the "apostolic laws" (explanations and decisions given by the Prophet's apostles and chief disciples in theological and moral matters); and the *Kiyas* (canonical decisions of "the four great Imams," who lived in the eighth and ninth centuries).

One of the universal duties of Islam on which the code of Ibrahim does not fail to insist was the conquest of the unbelievers; they must be converted to Islam, subjected to tribute, or destroyed by the sword. The fulfilment of this religious duty was the end and purpose of the Ottoman power, to which its institutions were designed and excellently adapted. Under the autocratic will of one man, possessing religious as well as secular supremacy, and holding a sovereignty which the Sacred Book forbade to be divided, the whole forces of the State could be directed to the execution of his policy. And these forces were organised in such a way that they could move swiftly and promptly at his command. The two features of this organisation were a feudal system of a peculiar kind, and the slave tribute.

The main part of the Turkish army was the feudal levy of cavalry (the *sipahis*). When a new country was conquered, it was parcelled out into a number of larger fiefs called *ziamets* and smaller called *timars*, which were assigned to Ottoman horse-soldiers in reward for military service in the past and with the obligation of military service in the future. The holder of each fief was bound to supply one or more mounted soldiers, according to the amount of its value. In the time of Solyman the total number of the levy of the *sipahis* is said to have amounted to 130,000. A number of districts or "sabres" was constituted as a *sanjak* or "standard," under the authority of a *sanjakbeg* ("sanjak lord"); and *sanjaks* were combined into larger districts (*eyalayets*) under *beglerbegs* ("lords of lords"). All these governors were subject to the two great *beglerbegs* of Europe and Asia (Rumelia and Anatolia), military and administrative powers being combined. When the word of the Sultan flew forth to summon the army to war, there was no delay; the horse of the *sipahi* was always ready at a moment's notice; all the sabres rallied round the *sanjak*; the *sanjaks* gathered to the mustering place appointed by the *beglerbeg*, and there awaited further orders. The feudal system of the Turks, founded by Othman, remodelled by Murad I (1375), differed from the feudal systems of the West in this one important respect, that the fief of the father did not necessarily descend to the son; each man had to win a right to a fief by his own valour. But on the other hand, only the son of a feudal tenant could become a feudal tenant. This provision was a safeguard of the military effectiveness of the system; and it must also be remembered that the Ottoman tenants were still nomads in spirit, and had not developed the instincts of a settled agricultural population.

Such a levy was almost equivalent to a standing army; but there was also a standing army in a precise sense,—an establishment of paid troops, recruited from captive children who were robbed from hostile or subject Christian countries and educated in Islam. A strict, but not cruel, discipline trained some of them to be foot-soldiers; while others, under an equally severe *régime*, served in the seraglio; thence rising gradually to offices of state, or being drafted into the brilliant corps of the paid mounted soldiery who were the bodyguard of the Sultan. The Turks had one enlightened principle of education: they observed carefully the particular qualifications of the individual youth, and adapted his work to his powers. Those of the Christian children—taken every five years or oftener as a tribute from the subject population—who had not the finer qualities which marked them out for service in the palace, were set to all kinds of hard work; but their stern discipline seems to have been compatible with acts of petulance and outrage in the city. In this preliminary stage they were called *ajami oghlanlars*. At the age of about twenty-five they were enrolled among the *yani chari* (new soldiery), whose name we have corrupted into Janissaries. The Janissaries, organised by the great Sultan Orchan, constituted the infantry of the Ottoman army, and at the beginning of Solyman's reign they numbered only about 12,000; yet this small body often decided battles; they had won Kosovo and Varna, and had never been known to flee. All except men of Christian birth, thus trained from childhood, were jealously excluded from the corps, which was under the command of the Aga of the Janissaries, one of the highest officers of the realm. The fundamental laws which regulated their discipline were absolute obedience to the commanders, abstinence from luxury, modest attire, fulfilment of the duties of Islam. They were unable to marry or exercise any trade, or leave their camp. It is clear that the existence of such a body of warriors was in itself a constant incentive or even compulsion to warlike enterprises; and peacefully inclined sultans like Bayazid II were unpopular with the Janissaries who were more fanatical in fighting for Islam even than men of Muslim race. Without any bonds of family or country, they were the creatures of the Sultan, in turn imposing their yoke on him. Scanderbeg's tenacious devotion to the memory of his father and the Albanian mountains was an isolated exception.

Against an army thus disciplined and organised, propelled by the single will of an able ruler, Europe without unity could do nothing. The *sipahis* were still the restless herdsmen of the waste, impatient of tillage, eager to go forth where there was fighting and plunder; only standing forces of mercenary troops could have availed against them, and such forces would have cost enormous sums of money which were not to be raised. The fanaticism of the Mohammadan faith, though not so tempestuous as in the first century of the Hijra, could still kindle and incite; and it was habitual; the Turks needed no John of Capistrano for the preaching of a holy war. The insidious doctrine of fatalism, which holds the minds of oriental nations, fosters some of the qualities which make a soldier a useful instrument; but it is worthy of notice that though *kismet* pervades the Turkish spirit it is not an article of Mohammadan belief. The doctrine of predestination applies only to the spiritual state and the future life,—a point at which Islam and Calvinism meet; but it does not apply to secular and political matters, in which freewill has full play. But notwithstanding the true doctrine, the Turkish nation believes in *kismet*, and regards murmurs of discontent against existing circumstances as irreligious; and this attitude of mind, which sustains the soldier in the hour of jeopardy, has helped to keep the Ottomans far behind in the march of civilisation—hindering them, for instance, from taking the ordinary precautions against plague or fire.

But an organisation admirably designed for its purpose was useless without brains to wield it. Everything depended on the strength and capacity of the Sultan; and, if there had been any means of securing a series of successors equal in ability to the Murads and Mohammads, to Selim I and Solyman the lawgiver, the Ottoman State need not have declined. The succession of exceptionally great rulers lasted in the Ottoman line longer than such successions usually last; but after Solyman their character changed; and even in his reign the first symptoms of decline appeared, and those inherent vices in the organisation which demanded constant precautions began to emerge. The discipline of the Janissaries was undermined, when the law which forbade their marrying was relaxed; and the feudal system was corrupted by the assignation of fiefs to others than the sons of feudal tenants, who had served in war. But this decline lies outside our present range.

In the theoretical morality of Islam nothing is of higher importance than justice and the protection of the oppressed; and it is probable that under the early Ottoman rulers the administration of justice was better in Turkey than in any European land; the Mohammadan subjects of the Sultans were more orderly than most Christian communities and crimes were rarer. Under Mohammad II there were two supreme *cadiaskers*, or military judges, one for Europe and one for Asia (the conquests of Selim added a third for Syria and Egypt); all the *cadis* (judges) of the empire were subordinate to them. From the sentences of the judges men could always appeal to the *mufti* or *sheikh-ul-Islam*, who was the religious oracle and interpreter of the law; holding the position of head of the *Ulema* (that is, all the litterati). But he was not a religious authority independent of the caliph; the caliph could depose him. He had no executive power; he could not enforce his pronouncements (*fetvas*); but their authority was recognised as morally binding, and the *mufti* took care not to endanger his position by issuing sentences which would run counter to the Sultan's known will.

It was Mohammad II who defined the position of the Grand Vezir as the Sultan's representative and regent. The Grand Vezir received the right of using the Sultan's seal and of holding a divan or State council in his own palace, which was called the High Porte. It was a position of which the political importance necessarily varied according to the character of the ruler. But it is not till the reign of Solyman that the Grand Vezir attains the plenitude of his power. In 1523 Solyman raised to the Grand Vezirate his friend Ibrahim, a Greek who had been captured by corsairs, and in the following year married him to his own sister. Ibrahim associated with his master more as a friend and equal than any Vezir with any Sultan; they were bound together by youthful friendship and common tastes. Ibrahim, says a contemporary Venetian report, is "the heart and breath" of the Padishah, who does nothing without consulting him; he is learned, fond of reading, and knows his law well. In 1529, before setting out for Hungary, Solyman increased his salary to 60,000 ducats and made him commander-in-chief (*serasker*) of the army: "all that he says is to be regarded as proceeding from my own pearl-raining mouth." This delegation of supreme military command is an innovation not in the spirit of Orchan or

Mohammad, and is a premonition of the new paths along which the empire is about to travel. It is a significant fact, that no sooner has the Vezirate reached a high elevation, than the influence of the harem begins to make itself felt for the first time in Ottoman history,—and as an influence hostile to the Vezir.

The income of the Ottoman State at the beginning of the sixteenth century was probably about four million ducats; and it went on increasing with new conquests till, towards the middle of the century, it seems to have approached ten millions. The head of the financial administration was the *Defterdar* of Rumelia, to whom those of Anatolia and, afterwards, of Aleppo, were subordinate. About three-fifths of the revenue were produced by the *kharaj* or capitation tax, levied on all unbelieving subjects with the exception of priests, old men, and children under ten. It does not seem to have been oppressive, it was generally paid with docility; and the duties on exports and imports were so reasonable that commerce, which was mainly in the hands of Christians, was in a flourishing condition. The worst feature in the fiscal system of the Turks was the stupid method employed in levying the land-tax (incident on all landowners without distinction of creed), which might amount to much more than a tithe of the produce. The farmer was not allowed to begin the harvest, until the tax-gatherer was on the spot to watch over the interests of the treasury, and he was forbidden to collect the produce until the fiscal portion was set aside. Apart from the incidental waste of time and injury to the crops, the inevitable consequence of this system has been that agriculture has never improved; certain primitive methods of work are prescribed by the law, and these and no others must be followed under the tax-officer's eye. Another weak point in the financial system has been the depreciation of the coinage, a process which had set in at least as early as the beginning of the sixteenth century.

Until the empire began to decline and the system became established of leaving the provinces to be exploited by officials who had paid heavy sums for their posts, the condition of the subject Christian population as a whole was perhaps more prosperous under Turkish rule than it had been before. The great oppression was the tribute of children, but even this was thought to have some compensations. Greeks, Albanians, and Servians rose to the highest positions in the State. Christians and Jews were, as a matter of policy, suffered to exercise their religions freely—a toleration which might indeed at any moment be withdrawn. In nothing had Mohammad shown astuter statesmanship than in his dealings with the Greek Church. He knew the "Romaic" language well, and had sounded the nature of the Greeks of that age; he was well aware how they were absorbed in narrow theological interests, utterly divorced from the principles of honour and rectitude, which they were always willing to sacrifice in order to gain a victory for their own religious party. He saw that the Greek Church under a Patriarch appointed by the Sultan would be a valuable engine of government, placing in the Sultan's hands a considerable indirect influence over the laity. It was, further, his policy to favour the Greek Church, in view of the crusading plans of the Latin powers; for, though the Roman pontiffs of this period showed themselves able to rise to the higher conception of the unity of Christendom, the bigoted hatred existing between the Latin and Greek Churches went far towards paralysing the sympathies of the Catholic countries. Mohammad aimed at fostering this ill-feeling, and he was thoroughly successful; the supremacy of the infidel Sultan seemed more tolerable than the supremacy of the heretical Pope. Naturally Mohammad chose for the Patriarchate one of those who were opposed to the union of the Greek and Latin Churches: George Scholarios, a man of learning and bigotry, who had thrown whatsoever obstacles he could in the way of the Emperor Constantine's forlorn defence of Constantinople. On his election George took the name of Gennadios. A church in the city was assigned to him, and the Sultan guaranteed that he and his bishops should be exempt from tribute and enjoy their former revenues. But the internal dissensions and intrigues of the Greek clergy and laity rendered the position of the Patriarch so difficult, that in a few years Gennadios resigned. His successors were equally helpless; and after the fall of Trebizond (1461) the struggle between the Trapezuntine and the Constantinopolitan Greeks, each anxious to secure the Patriarchate for a man of their own, made matters worse. A wealthy Trapezuntine, named Simeon, compassed his own election by paying a thousand ducats to the Sultan; and this was the beginning of a system of unveiled simony which has lasted in the Greek Church to our own times. This payment was increased at subsequent elections; afterwards a yearly contribution to the treasury was promised; but it is important to observe that these tributes were not originally imposed by the Sultans, but were voluntarily offered by the intriguing Greeks. The policy of Mohammad, who was solicitous to repeople Constantinople, had the effect of gathering thither a multitude of Greek families of the better class, who might otherwise have sought refuge in foreign lands. Settled in the quarter of the Phanar, in the north of the city, they were known as Phanariots, and came to be reputed a class of clever, unprincipled intriguers.

We have followed the expansion of Turkey up to the eve of its greatest splendour and widest extent. Subsequent pages will tell how the Ottomans advanced westwards by sea, and how the Austro-Spanish monarchy set limits to their expansion both in the north and in the south.

# CHAPTER IV.

## ITALY AND HER INVADERS.

In the latter half of the fifteenth century Italy presented the appearance of comparative calm. Frederick III, in spite of the motto attributed to him, "Alles Erdreich ist Oesterreich untertan," took no step to assert imperial claims in Italy. Conciliar storms had blown over. The *condottieri* had been tamed; secure for the most part in their little tyrannies they drew the pay of some neighbouring State, and spent it on luxury, literature, and art. If war was on foot, its bitterness was mitigated, at any rate to the soldier, by every courteous device. The clash of party strife was seldom heard, for most cities had bought internal peace at the price of liberty.

Italy possessed her own State system, her own great powers, intent on preserving a balance of forces, her own alliances, triple or dual. At first the north Italian powers had their own league; later the alliance of Milan, Florence, and Naples, promoted and sustained by Lorenzo de' Medici, kept in check the vigilant ambition of Venice, still almost at the height of her power and pride. The smaller powers, Mantua, Ferrara, and the tyrants of the Papal States, in constant dread of their covetous neighbours, leant for support on one or other of the great powers, and did what in them lay to preserve the balance. After the brilliant raid of John, the Angevin duke of Calabria, Ferrante, the bastard of Aragon, ruled Naples in comparative peace. The revolt of his barons was stamped out, without regard for faith or mercy, as befitted a man of that age. The seizure of Otranto by the Turks in 1480 was a warning of external danger that may have assisted to preserve the peace, although all projects of united and offensive resistance to the advancing Mohammadans came to nothing. The equilibrium was unstable, but on the whole it was preserved.

The death of Lorenzo de' Medici in 1492, soon followed by that of Innocent VIII, marks a turning-point in the history of Italy. It is easy to attach too much importance to such casual incidents, but they may at least delay or hasten the inevitable course of events. And in Lorenzo was removed the conscious guardian of the peace of Italy, while the successor of Innocent, Rodrigo Borgia, was neither fitted nor inclined to play a pacific part. This then is the moment to survey the scene of our drama, to name our chief *dramatis personae*, and to unfold our plot.

Three of our protagonists, Venice, Florence, the Holy See, have their own place for separate treatment in this volume. Nor is this the occasion to dwell on the petty politics of the many tyrants of the Romagna and central Italy. Naples, however, and Milan require some introduction.

The kingdom of Naples, though still styling itself kingdom of Sicily, had been separated from its island namesake since the Sicilian Vespers, when the Angevin successors of the Suabian kings were driven from the Trinacrian island. In 1435 this Angevin dynasty died out, and its inheritance fell to Alfonso of Aragon, the King of insular Sicily. On his death in 1458 the island kingdom had remained attached to Aragon, while Naples had been devised to his bastard Ferdinand or Ferrante. The political characteristics of the Neapolitan kingdom mark it off sharply from the rest of Italy. Here had survived, though in a debased form, the feudal economy which had long since disappeared further north. Here no elusive ideal of municipal liberty mocked, amid the realities of party strife, the citizens of independent cities. Great feudatories ground down their vassals with all the ingenuity that a new commercial and industrial wisdom inspired. The King, himself a feudatory and tributary of the Holy See, was master of Naples and its castles, and of certain royal dues and domains, but for the rest hung on the goodwill of a score of almost independent princes. Ferrante, greedy, capable, and ruthless, had done much to change all that. He had devised a system of commercial monopolies exercised for the royal benefit, which had considerably increased his revenues. The barons' war had restored to him by confiscation a part of the toll that his commercial partners had levied on his profits, and had crushed the greatest family of the kingdom, the princely house of San Severino. His relations to the papacy had been unfriendly, even warlike, but on the whole he had succeeded in withholding his tribute without losing his fief. But dangers now threatened him at home and abroad. At home, though feared, he was hated. His son Alfonso, the partner of his many cruel and treacherous acts, was equally detested. Zealous enemies were working against him, especially at the Court of France. The *de facto* ruler of Milan had wronged him in the person of his grand-daughter. The illegitimate son of an usurper, he held his crown by no hereditary right, and rumours came from beyond the Alps that a stronger claimant was astir.

The State of Milan, created by the vigour of the house of Visconti, and recognised as a duchy in 1395 by the Emperor Wenceslas, had fallen in 1450 to the house of Sforza, whose founder, the great *condottiere*, had risen from the plough. Francesco, the first Sforza duke, was succeeded in 1466 by his son Galeazzo Maria, who was assassinated in the Church of San Stefano in 1476, leaving a young son, Gian Galeazzo, then about eight years old. The government was carried on by his mother, Bona of Savoy, in the name of the infant and in her own. But dissensions soon arose between the regent and her brothers-in-law. In the first encounter Bona and her chief counsellor, Cicco Simonetta, were victorious, and the brothers of Galeazzo Maria were obliged to leave the city. But before long Ludovico, the ablest of the sons of Francesco Sforza, took advantage of the rivalry between Tassino, the favourite of the duchess, and Simonetta, to procure his own readmission. The fall and execution of Simonetta followed, and from 1479 the real government of Milan lay in the hands of Ludovico, whose power was further secured in 1480, when he seized the person of the young duke and the duchess was obliged to leave Milan. Henceforward the rule of Ludovico was not seriously challenged. The young duke was a prisoner, and Ludovico managed everything in his name. Nor was the condition of the unfortunate young man improved even after his marriage to Isabella, the grand-daughter of the King of Naples.

Thus at the time when our story begins, the whole force and policy of Milan was moved at the will of one man. Ludovico, called the Duke of Bari from the Neapolitan fief he owned, and known from his complexion as the Moor, made a great impression on the men of his time. He was a master of every political art as then understood by Italian statesmen. By his wisdom he had risen, and by it he aspired to dominate Italy. Mistakes he made, no doubt, as for instance in marrying his nephew to the Neapolitan princess. But his versatile and unscrupulous intelligence, well served by his agents with information from every Court, was never at a loss for an expedient to meet a difficulty. His weakness was partly the weakness of his school of statesmanship, in which good faith and consistency were not valued as political qualities. A more serious defect was the lack of courage and nerve which he showed under the stress of danger. His munificence towards artists and men of letters, his luxurious and noble ostentation, while they tended no doubt to diminish his unpopularity, proved a heavy burden on his finances, and increased the weight of his exactions.

The State over which he ruled was one of the richest of Italy. His annual revenue was estimated at 700,000 ducats, about the same sum as Ferrante raised from Naples. The Dukes of Milan, though frequently embarrassed, again and again surprise us by the enormous sums of which they disposed. Thus Ludovico was able to give to Maximilian with his niece, Bianca Maria, no less a sum as dowry than 400,000 ducats. Only Venice had more ample resources; and the fixed charges on the Venetian treasury were heavier than Milan had to bear. The Duke of Milan controlled Genoa and her navy, which, although no longer a match for that of Venice, could be employed with great effect on the western seaboard of Italy. Through the Genoese his influence extended over the chief part of Corsica, whence on occasion good foot-soldiers could be drawn. But the military strength of Milan, like that of the other Italian States, left much to be desired. While good infantry was scarce, the inferior infantry was very bad; and the brilliant troops of mercenary horse, on which principal reliance was put, were untrustworthy and unused to serious war. Moreover the old party animosities still survived in Milan; and, if policy prompted, Guelf could still be roused against Ghibelline. Again, the Sforza rule had not yet received imperial confirmation, and the claims of the Duke of Orleans were a permanent and a serious menace.

With full consciousness of their own weakness, and sincere mutual distrust, the Italian powers had watched the growth of France. French intervention in Italy was no new thing. While her strength was yet immature, France had given one race of kings to Naples, and had endeavoured to give another. Charles VII had driven the English from France, and before his death Genoa had asked and received French protection and a French governor. Louis XI found that Genoa had revolted, but was too wise to waste his resources on distant enterprises, and gave no material aid to the ill-fated quest of John of Calabria as a pretender to the kingdom of Naples. Louis devoted his whole energy to the union of France under his absolute rule; but he never lost sight of the affairs of Italy. The powers of Italy abased themselves before him in rivalry to win his favour. He answered them impartially with good words and maintained them in slavish expectation of good services. Thus the French King came to be more and more regarded as the arbiter of Italian fortunes. The presents made to his ambassadors and courtiers and their reception when they visited Italy assisted to foster the belief that Italy was rich, disunited, and helpless, an easy prey to a militant monarchy. There was no reason to believe that the successor of Louis would be hampered by his difficulties or inclined to his reserve.

The leagues formed among themselves by the Italian States served to prevent the undue aggrandisement of any one State at the expense of the others. But no such partial alliance could stand up against the French King, in view of the suspicion,—almost the certainty,—that the other powers would join the invaders, and that the members of the alliance itself could not be trusted. The union of Italy against a foreign foe was almost unthinkable. Charles VIII had hardly come to the throne when the Signoria of Venice approached his government with the proposal that the conquest of Milan and of Naples should be at once undertaken. This treacherous act, if treachery can be imputed where there is no mutual assurance of good faith, is explained by the position of Venice, then engaged in a single-handed struggle with almost the whole of Italy. But it proved, if proof was needed, that a French invasion, whatever its pretext, would find allies in the peninsula.

Ludovico deserves the doubtful credit of having been the first to bring his goods to market. French ambition had two excuses for intervention in Italy. The first was the claim of Orleans to Milan, resting on the marriage of Valentina Visconti to the first Duke of Orleans, and on the marriage contract of Valentina, confirmed by Clement VII, in which her right to succeed to her father in default of male heirs was recognised. There seems also to have been a will of Gian Galeazzo Visconti, securing the succession to her male issue in default of the direct male line; but Ludovico alone knew of this and caused all known copies to be destroyed. Legal objections might be urged against all these grounds of claim, but they were good enough to support a dynastic war. Louis of Orleans had in 1491 recovered his favour at Court, and it was not impossible that Milan would be made the object of the French attack. Milan lay dangerously near to France, and strategically was much less difficult of access than Naples. On the other hand Charles might well be unwilling to aggrandise one of the most powerful of his nobles, a possible heir to the throne, who, though reconciled, had not long ago been in arms against his King. It was Ludovico's natural policy to endeavour to divert this danger from himself.

The second French pretext was the claim to Naples, resting on similar grounds, and similarly open to cavil. Joanna I, Queen of Naples of the first Angevin line, had no heirs of her body. The lawful heir was Charles of Durazzo, descended from the younger son of Charles II of Naples. Being at enmity with Charles of Durazzo, Joanna adopted her remote cousin Louis, Duke of Anjou by the second creation. Charles and his descendants had successfully defended their rights against Louis and his heirs, until their line also died out in Joanna II. The latter, in order to defend herself against the attacks of Louis III of Anjou, adopted Alfonso of Aragon as her heir. When later Alfonso wished to make himself master of Naples without waiting for Joanna's death, Joanna revoked this act of adoption, adopted Louis III, and on her death (1435) made his brother René her heir. Thus Alfonso, who seized the kingdom, was legally only a successful usurper; and all the claims which Louis I derived from the adoption of Joanna I, together with the claims of the house of Durazzo, were united in the person of René, who more than once tried to recover his heritage. The rights of René passed in 1481, through his nephew the Count of Maine, by will and also, though not so certainly, by succession, to Louis XI, and after him to Charles VIII. Sixtus IV, although he refused to consider the application of Charles du Maine for the investiture of Naples, in 1482, moved by different thoughts, urged Louis to undertake the conquest of the kingdom, "which belongs to him." At the beginning of the reign of Charles VIII there was some talk of putting forward René of Lorraine, a descendant through the female line of the house of Anjou, as claimant to the kingdom, but these proposals seem never

to have been serious, and cannot be said to impair the rights of
Charles VIII.

Thus there were two paths open to the ambition of the French king,
when freed from the prudent tutelage of his sister Anne. The head of
the young monarch was filled with chimerical dreams. His domestic
troubles had been satisfactorily composed. His standing force of
cavalry, fitted alike for the shock of battle, for scouting and skirmishing,
and for missile tactics, was full of military enthusiasm and wanted work.
His artillery was far ahead of any other in Europe. His infantry was
less satisfactory, but could be strengthened from abroad. He had
himself but lately come to man's estate and was eager to prove himself
a man and a king. At his Court were the Neapolitan exiles, especially
the San Severino princes, eager to press on him a definite plan of conquest.
He was estranged from the wise counsellors who had kept him so long in
leading-strings. Supple courtiers and men of business, Étienne de Vesc,
and Guillaume Briçonnet, were at his side, ready to find means for the
execution of any scheme that pleased their royal master, and promised to
them incidental profits. The crown of Sicily carried with it the crown
of Jerusalem, thus suggesting at once and facilitating an ulterior project
of crusade ; and Europe needed a crusade.

The Moor was probably the first among the Italian princes to see
that French intervention in Italy, so often talked of, had at length
become a real danger. He approached the King of France in 1491, and
received from him in the name of his nephew the investiture of Genoa,
which had been similarly granted to Francesco, his father, by Louis XI.
In 1492 he obtained the renewal of the alliance formerly enjoyed
by his father, thus recovering the position of favour which his elder
brother had lost through his indiscreet leanings towards Charles the
Bold.

The Milanese embassy of unusual magnificence that soon afterwards
visited France had no compromising instructions. Its object was to win
the French courtiers by presents, to make all vague assurances of general
devotion, and to secure if possible the protection of the King for the
Duke of Bari himself. In all this it succeeded. Whatever may have
been spoken of in private—and Commines suggests that the most
important topics were discussed—it is probable that no promises were
made which Ludovico could not afterwards disavow. Yet it is clear
that he desired to secure a safeguard for himself, not only against
France, but also against Naples. For his relations with that country
were less than cordial. The King of Naples could hardly acquiesce
permanently in the humiliation of his grand-daughter, which Isabella
herself deeply resented. Hitherto he had been hampered by war with
the Pope, but peace was concluded at the end of 1491. Ludovico
looked to France to protect him against Naples; he hoped to achieve
this end without armed French intervention; but in any case, if invasion

occurred, he was determined that Naples and not Milan or the Duke of Bari should be the victim.

The events of the next two years illustrate the unstable nature of Italian policy and Italian alliances. Lorenzo de' Medici died in April, 1492, while the Milanese embassy was at Paris. The choice before his son Piero was a difficult one. It was the traditional policy of Florence to keep up intimate, almost subservient, relations with France, where the commercial and financial interests of the Medici Bank were important, but on the other hand to prevent, if possible, active foreign interference in Italy. These two aims were probably now no longer to be reconciled ; and Piero sacrificed the first without attaining the second. Following, as it seems, the counsels of Virginio Orsini, his wife's cousin, he drew closer to Naples, thus alarming and alienating Ludovico, who soon afterwards concluded an alliance with Venice and Rome. Piero rejected all overtures from France ; and the opening campaign was preceded by the expulsion of the Medici agents from French territory.

The accession of Alexander VI in August, 1492, seemed at first a great good fortune for Ludovico ; for his brother, the Cardinal Ascanio Sforza, was reputed to have supreme influence with the new pontiff. A little matter, the sale by Franceschetto Cibò, son of the late Pope, of two places in the Patrimonio, Anguillara and Cervetri, to Virginio Orsini, the friend of Piero and captain general of Naples, assisted the secret endeavours of Ascanio to animate the Pope against Naples and Florence. The league of the Pope with Milan and Venice, and an indirect encouragement of France in her plans against Naples, were results of this ill-feeling. But the dread of a General Council, of which Charles had rashly spoken, may have inclined Alexander to entertain the pressing solicitations of Ferrante, supported by the offer of an advantageous marriage for one of Alexander's sons to a Neapolitan princess. The Pope allowed his anger to be appeased, and in August, 1493, returned an evasive answer to the confident request of Perron de Baschi, the French envoy, for the investiture of Naples, with a free passage and the supply of provisions for French troops. After the death of Ferrante in January, 1494, Alexander confirmed the investiture to his son Alfonso, and in February he solemnly warned the French King against disturbing the peace of Christian Italy.

Leagued with Savelli, Colonna, and Orsini, the fiery Cardinal Giuliano della Rovere, afterwards Pope Julius II, was consistent only in his opposition to Alexander. So long as the Pope was hostile to Naples, Giuliano supported Ferrante, and, retiring from Rome, he occupied his strongly fortified castle at Ostia, a standing menace to the city. When Naples was reconciled, he returned sulkily to Rome. But when the certainty of the invasion was established, he saw his opportunity for striking a blow, left Rome in April, 1494, and joined the King of France at Lyons, to urge upon him the necessity of a Council, with a view to the deposition of Alexander.

Before the French King took the final step, it had been necessary for him to surmount serious difficulties. The marriage of Charles with Anne of Britanny had involved France in hostilities with a league of powers. On the north, Henry VII descended and laid siege to Boulogne. England was bought off, by the treaty of Etaples (November, 1492), with an exorbitant money ransom, which caused Henry VII to forget that he had ever felt himself threatened by the presence of the French in Britanny. On the south France was menaced by the recently consolidated and extended kingdoms of Aragon and Castile. Their neutrality was purchased (January, 1493) by the retrocession without indemnity of the counties of Roussillon and Cerdagne, on the northward slope of the Eastern Pyrenees, pledged in 1462 to Louis XI by John of Aragon for 300,000 crowns. Maximilian, King of the Romans, had not only been robbed of his Breton marriage, but had also a claim under the treaty of Arras to the restitution of Franche Comté and Artois, with some minor places, part of the heritage of Charles the Bold. Under that treaty these provinces had been given to France as the dowry of Maximilian's daughter, whom Charles had now repudiated. In the war which followed this double wrong Maximilian had achieved partial, though for him unusual, success. His honour was satisfied, moreover he was now deserted by his allies. He could the more willingly accept the terms of the treaty of Senlis (May, 1493), which gave him in effect almost all there was left to give. The opportunity offered by this reconciliation Ludovico was not slow to seize. With the consent of France he gave to Maximilian the hand of his niece, Bianca Maria, with her more than princely dowry. In the following year Maximilian, who had in the interval succeeded to the empire, redeemed his obligation by bestowing on Ludovico the investiture of Milan, a little before the opportune death of Gian Galeazzo.

The heavy price that Charles was paying for a free hand in Italy must have shown Ludovico that the expedition was probable, and by the end of the year he knew for certain that it was imminent. He could no longer hope to withdraw from the alliance he had sought. On the other hand his own position was extremely dangerous. By the end of 1493 it was clear that Florence, Rome, and Naples were against him. Venice maintained a watchful neutrality. A rapid advance on Milan or Genoa, or both, might have overthrown his precarious rule. It was his task to amuse his enemies with fair words, delusive proposals, and treacherous promises until the time for action was past. Meanwhile the French King delayed. Warlike preparations had been in progress since 1492. In 1493 Charles assumed the title of King of Sicily and of Jerusalem. Additional taxes and forced loans were exacted to raise the necessary funds, royal domains were sold, and the revenues pledged in advance. At the beginning of 1494 the Neapolitan ambassadors were dismissed. On the 6th of March Charles entered Lyons to press on the mobilisation in person. In the same month the composition of the proposed force was fixed. 1,900 French lances, six men to a lance, were to be supplemented by 1,500 Italian lances, four men to a lance, making with 1,200 mounted arblasters a total force of 18,600 horsemen, though a proportion of these were grooms and servants. The *bailli* of Dijon, Antoine de Bessey, was sent to raise 6,000 Swiss. French infantry, Picards, Gascons, Dauphinois, and infantry to be raised in Italy, with a few German *Landsknechte*, were to make up a total of 22,000 foot. Of this force, about one-fourth was to be transported by sea from Genoa, and orders were sent to prepare and collect a sufficient naval armament. It is probable that ultimately the above estimate was nearly realised. But everything, especially the preparation of the fleet, was retarded for lack of money. In vain Ludovico, who had now thrown aside all hesitation, urged through his agents the need of haste. Inexperience, incompetence, lack of goodwill in the royal surrounding, especially it would seem in Briçonnet, everything tended to delay. Toward the end of May a small instalment of troops crossed the Alps. The Duke of Orleans, appointed to the command of the fleet, was still detained at Asti, when a Neapolitan squadron appeared at Genoa, with native exiles on board, in hope of exciting a rising. The stroke failed, but the danger had been real, and was not past. However, by the end of July a sufficient fleet had been collected; Alfonso's chance was gone. On the 19th of August, Louis of Orleans took up his command at Genoa, and on the 8th of September the first collision occurred. The Neapolitan fleet had occupied Rapallo, and landed 4,000 men. On the advance of the French fleet the enemy, stronger in numbers, though weaker in artillery, sailed off. Their post on shore was attacked by land and cannonaded from the sea. The victory rested with the French and Genoese, and Italy was startled at a battle in which the shedding of blood had not been spared. The Swiss in particular had shown themselves ruthless and bloodthirsty.

Meanwhile the King had actually crossed the Alps by the Mont Genèvre, his heavy artillery being sent by sea to Genoa. In Savoy, subject to French influence since Louis XI, no courtesy or facility was denied him. The Marquis of Montferrat put himself and his lands at the King's service. At Asti, which belonged to Orleans, the Dukes of Bari and Ferrara greeted the King; and the news of the victory of Rapallo was brought. Here a mild attack of small-pox delayed the King for a short time, and the general disorganisation was increased by an access of fever which prostrated the Duke of Orleans. The King having recovered, it was determined that Louis should stay behind at Asti. In absolute lack of money the King had to raise a loan by the help of the credit of Ludovico, from whom much more liberal assistance had been expected.

The King of Naples had caused his army, strengthened by a papal contingent, to advance into the Romagna, where he could rely on Urbino and Cesena. The attitude of Bentivoglio at Bologna, and of Caterina

Sforza at Imola and Forlì was doubtful. These troops were opposed by Milanese under the Count of Caiazzo, and French under Aubigny; but, when Charles had decided to advance through Tuscany, the operations in Romagna lost their meaning and the allies withdrew. Charles passed through Pavia, where he visited Gian Galeazzo. At Piacenza he heard of the young duke's death. As far as Pontremoli he marched over Milanese soil. Thence, descending the Apennines, he advanced into Florentine territory and attacked Sarzana. Had Sarzana and Pietra Santa been strongly defended, the country at this point presented serious difficulties to an advancing army. The land on either side of the road was marshy, and the fortresses were well capable of defence. But Piero, unsupported and unprepared, had at length determined to give in. He knew that there were many in Florence who were favourable to France, and hostile to himself. Acting on his own responsibility, while Sarzana still held out, he came to the French camp at San Stefano and surrendered everything,—Sarzana, Pietra Santa, Pisa, and Livorno,—and promised the King a considerable loan. But his submission came too late. When he returned to Florence, he found the palace of the Signoria closed to him; the city rose against him, and he was obliged to fly with his brother, the young Cardinal Giovanni.

Nothing now remained to delay Charles' advance to Florence. Into Lucca the King made a triumphant entry. At Pisa he was received with acclamations, and in a hasty speech was understood to have restored its liberty to the city, where he left a small garrison. Finally, on the 17th of November, the King entered Florence with 8,000 horse and 4,000 infantry, in a martial array such as never had been seen before. The whole city received him with eager hopes and fervent affection. Before he had left, however, some change of feeling had set in. The behaviour of the French soldiers was not all that could be desired. Wages were in arrear, and they could not, if they wished, pay for all they needed. But to women it is admitted that they did no wrong; and, indeed, the conduct of the French towards non-combatants throughout these wars compares favourably with that of Italians, Spaniards, Germans, or Swiss. But there were other grievances. Charles had put off all negotiations until after his entry. The deliberations that followed were not always peaceful. The King was suspected, and not wholly without cause, of wishing to restore Piero. His financial demands were considered excessive, and even after abatement still remained large. He insisted on retaining Pisa and Livorno, Sarzana and Pietra Santa, till the end of the campaign. But the freedom of Pisa was not among the stipulations. A French envoy was to be present at all deliberations of the Signoria. In the discussions which ensued bold words were used. The Florentine Capponi threatened to call the citizens to arms. But the King was the stronger, and finally his principal demands were accepted.

The whole French army was now moving on Rome. Aubigny brought his men across the Apennines into Tuscany. Montpensier had gone on with the troops from Genoa. The heavy artillery had been disembarked at Spezia, and was following the King. A small force with Giuliano della Rovere joined the Colonna who were holding Ostia. The position of the Pope was critical. Rumour ran that he had not hesitated to call in the Turk in defence of Rome and Naples. It was certain that he was the pensioner of Bayazid, and the gaoler of his brother, Jem. The simony by which he had gained the triple crown and the scandals of his private life were well known, and even exaggerated by report. His bitterest enemies were with the French. Could he resist, should he fly, should he await the King, and come to terms? For a time he meditated resistance. The Duke of Calabria, Ferrantino, afterwards king, led his army into Rome. Alexander arrested the cardinals Ascanio and Colonna. Then wiser counsels prevailed. The city was not defensible. Ferrantino was dismissed, the cardinals released, and on the last day of the old year Charles VIII entered Rome with the consent of the Pope. Even in the strong places of the Orsini, who served the King of Naples, he had found no resistance.

Reluctantly, sullenly, Alexander came to terms. The King was to have the custody of Jem, who might be used in the proposed crusade to stir up rebellion against Bayazid. The Cardinal of Valencia, Cesare Borgia, was to accompany Charles, nominally as legate, really as a hostage. The Pope promised no investiture; indeed, he had every reason to be satisfied with the moderation, perhaps with the simplicity, of his visitor. The hostile cardinals were bitterly disappointed.

On the 28th of January, 1495, the King left Rome. Meanwhile his lieutenants, advancing in the Abruzzi, had occupied Aquila. The Neapolitans, retreating, had laid waste the country before him. But Alfonso, conscious of his own unpopularity, and tortured, it is said, by remorse, had lost all courage. On the 21st of January he resigned in favour of his son Ferrantino, an amiable youth, free from all complicity in the crimes of his father and grandfather. At Velletri the King of France received his first warning. Envoys from Spain reproached him with the injuries done to the Holy Father, whereby they declared the treaty of Barcelona had been violated; and summoned him to desist from his enterprise, and to accept the mediation of the Catholic King. The same day the Cardinal of Valencia escaped from the French camp. The best answer to such indications of ill-feeling was success. Ferdinand lay at San Germano defending the line of the Liris. At Monte San Giovanni the strong fortress ventured to defy the French. In a few hours the place was taken by assault and sacked. The advanced guard of the French crossing the Liris then threatened the enemy's flank and rear. Ferrantino retreated to Capua. Gaeta surrendered; and, during the absence of the King at Naples, Gian Giacomo Trivulzio made overtures to give up Capua, which were accepted. At Nola, the Orsini captains, Pitigliano and Virginio Orsini, were captured. At Aversa and Poggio Reale embassies from Naples saluted Charles, offering submission. On the 22nd of February Charles entered Naples. Ferrantino, who had destroyed the chief part of his fleet, still held the detached Castel dell' Uovo with five ships, and retired on the following day to Ischia, leaving garrisons in the fortresses. The last of these surrendered under the French fire on the 22nd of March.

Charles was thus master of the capital, and the more distant provinces showed willingness to accept his rule. He showed a praiseworthy desire to win the goodwill of his new subjects, remitting taxes, as he says, to the amount of more than 200,000 ducats. A general amnesty to those who had served the Aragon kings, restoration of property to the Angevin exiles, even the recognition of slavery as then existing, proved his desire to respect all rights. But impatient of business, given up to pleasure, indolently desirous to satisfy all petitioners, he not only squandered the royal domain, but created almost as many grievances as he bestowed favours. No serious attempt was made to settle the government on a firm basis.

The project of a crusade had received a grave blow in the death of Jem, which took place at Naples. The Archbishop of Durazzo undertook to organise a rising in Albania, but the project was frustrated by his accidental arrest at Venice. Charles' own position was too doubtful to allow any more determined effort. Since his refusal to confer Sarzana and Pietra Santa upon Ludovico, the latter had been intriguing against his ally. Ferdinand of Aragon had sent to Sicily the great captain Gonzalo de Cordova with a fleet, ostensibly for defensive purposes. Venice was arming, as she said, against the Turk. Maximilian was afraid that the successes of Charles in Italy might lead him to claim the Imperial Crown. Negotiations took place at Venice resulting in a league between the Pope, the Roman King, Ferdinand and Isabella, Venice and Milan, for the protection of the confederates against the aggression of other powers then possessing states in Italy. The league purported to be defensive, but was in reality offensive. Florence alone, still friendly to France and relying on her good offices to recover Pisa, was not a party to it. The transaction was communicated to Commines, French ambassador to Venice, on the 1st of April. Charles was soon informed of the danger rising in his rear, but did not leave Naples till the 21st of May.

Fortunately for the invader, Louis of Orleans was still at Asti with a handful of troops. In a few days he had collected 2,000 men. The Duke of Bourbon, the wise vicegerent of the King in France, was pressed to send aid, for the troops of Milan threatened an attack, if the place was not surrendered. But Ludovico, timid as usual, allowed the moment to pass. Reinforcements soon put Asti in a position for defence, and secured for the King his line of retreat. Meanwhile Ludovico was celebrating the investiture of Milan, which he had at length permission to proclaim. In June Louis was in a position to occupy the city of

Novara by the invitation of the citizens; shortly after, the citadel surrendered. Ludovico was paralysed; it is thought that if the Duke of Orleans had marched on Milan he would have met no serious resistance.

Meanwhile the King had left Naples with some 1,200 French lances, 4,000 Swiss, and 2,000 Gascon arblasters. The other half of his army, partly Italians, was left with Montpensier, the viceroy, to deal with Ferrantino, who had recently landed in Calabria with Spanish aid. On reaching Rome, the King found the Pope had fled to Orvieto. Florence Charles avoided, since the Florentines claimed, and he was determined to refuse, the surrender of the fortresses, especially of Pisa. At Pisa he found himself equally unable to satisfy the Pisans. At Spezia, against all sound advice, he detached 500 horse and 2,000 foot to operate against Genoa with the aid of the fleet and the Genoese exiles. But he had the forethought to send on a force to occupy Pontremoli, which capitulated. The Swiss, violating the terms of the surrender, sacked and burned the place, destroying valuable stores.

The possession of Pontremoli gave the French access to the pass. Beyond the summit lay the army of the League. The chief part of the army, about 40,000 strong, was in Venetian pay, and commanded by the Marquis of Mantua. Beside men at arms there were some thousands of *Stradioti*, the ferocious light cavalry of Albania. The chief part of the forces of Milan was engaged in the siege of Novara, but a Milanese contingent was present. Over the steep pass the Swiss, in sign of penitence for their late excesses, dragged by hand the heavy cannon, each ordinarily drawn by thirty-five horses; and French nobles, notably la Trémouille, did not disdain to work beside them. At Fornovo the French vanguard came into touch with the Stradiot advanced posts, and halted. The rest of the army, coming up, encamped for the night in great lack of provisions. Negotiations were opened for a free passage, but came to nothing. The next day the French advanced.

At Fornovo the valley of the Taro is of moderate width. On the right bank were posted the allies and there was their fortified camp. The French resolved to cross the river, and to force their way along the left bank. The river had been much swollen by a thunderstorm during the night and rain was still falling. Thus the French army, having once successfully effected its crossing, which it did undisturbed, was partly protected. The vanguard was expected to bear the main weight of the attack, and included the bulk of the artillery, with 3,000 Swiss, and a strong body of men-at-arms. This body, moving on too fast, became separated from the rest of the army, and had only to sustain a trifling charge of the Milanese horse under the Count of Caiazzo. Little use was made on either side of the artillery. The main attack was made by the Marquis of Mantua. Though it was originally directed on the centre, the necessity to deviate for a ford made it really an attack on the rear under Louis de la Trémouille. The King's main battle then wheeled round and took up a position to the left of the rear guard, facing to the rear. Fortunately, the baggage, which was moving along the hills and away from the river, attracted the Stradiots, and diverted them from serious work. The Italian horse, who charged the King's rear and centre, were outflanked and soon put to flight, and were pursued to the ford from which they came. More than half the army of the allies never came into action, but the whole of it was thrown into confusion and many fled. The rout was partly stopped by the King's prisoners Pitigliano and Virginio Orsini, who escaped during the battle. But another attack was out of the question, and the French even thought of assuming the offensive. Perhaps a well-timed charge by the Marshal de Gié with the vanguard might have turned the defeat into a rout, but the French had every reason to be satisfied. They were able after a rest to march off during the night, and reached Asti on the 15th of July practically unmolested. The Venetians claimed the victory, but the fruits of victory were with the French.

At Asti the King found things in forlorn case. The expedition against Genoa had failed. The French fleet was captured in Rapallo by a superior Genoese force and all the plunder of Naples was lost. The Duke of Orleans was besieged at Novara, and his garrison were at the last pinch. Bessey was sent in haste to raise a fresh force of Swiss, but by the time they arrived, 20,000 strong, Novara had capitulated on easy terms, and Ludovico showed himself inclined for peace. Louis of Orleans was anxious to use the Swiss against Milan, but Charles, perhaps disgusted with the shifting fortune of war, concluded at Vercelli a separate peace with Ludovico, and on the 15th of October he crossed the Alps.

Milan was left *in statu quo*, except that the Castelletto of Genoa was left for two years as a pledge of good faith to France in the hands of the Duke of Ferrara. Venice had profited by the trouble of Naples to acquire four ports, Monopoli, Trani, Brindisi, and Otranto, on the easterly coast of Apulia. Florence was by agreement to receive back her towns, but the corrupt disobedience of French lieutenants gave Pisa to the Pisans, Sarzana to the Genoese, and Pietra Santa to Lucca. In Naples the first descent of Gonzalo had not been fortunate. His army was defeated at Seminara by a band of Swiss. But Ferrantino, nothing daunted, presented himself at Naples with his fleet. Repulsed at first, a chance gave him the advantage, and his supporters gained the town. Montpensier, Yves d'Allègre, and Etienne de Vesc were shut up in the Castel Nuovo. The Provinces, North and South, rose against the French. The Colonna left them. Aubigny with difficulty held out against Gonzalo in Calabria. Montpensier in despair concluded a conditional capitulation, and, when Précy failed to relieve him, abandoned the city of Naples. In February, 1496, all the castles of Naples were in the hands of the Aragonese. The French still held Ariano, Gaeta, and a few other posts. In July Précy and Montpensier surrendered to

Gonzalo and Ferrantino at Atella. The chief part of the French prisoners, including Montpensier, succumbed to the climate and to disease. Aubigny gave up the struggle in Calabria. On the death of Ferrantino, October 6, 1496, Federigo, his uncle, succeeded. Soon after (November 19) Gaeta, the last important stronghold of the French, surrendered. The king of France still meditated another expedition, and concluded, towards the end of 1497, an alliance with Aragon for a joint conquest. Five months later an accident cut short his life. The only son of his marriage with Anne of Britanny had died in infancy. His successor, Louis of Orleans, inherited his plans of conquest, but with a difference.

The fear of a new French invasion, increased by the league concluded with France in 1496 by the majority of the Swiss Cantons, worked upon Italian nerves. The restless Ludovico first took the alarm, and approached the Venetian Signoria. It was agreed to call in the King of the Romans, who responded to the call. Maximilian agreed, like a mere *condottiere*, to take the pay of the league, which was composed as in 1495, with the addition of Henry VII of England. In July, 1496, a conference was held at Mals in the Tyrol near the frontier. The members of the league gave diplomatic support, but none were ready to give material help, except Milan and Venice; and even these doled out their pittance with a chary hand. Maximilian had a name to sell, but few men and less money to back it. The imperial Estates and the much discussed imperial subsidy afforded no help. However some Swiss were enrolled, and Maximilian raised a few horsemen from his own subjects and personal adherents. By the end of September a small army had collected around the Roman King at Vigevano in the Milanese.

The league, such as it was, still lacked a plan. The Duke of Milan was anxious to secure the north-western frontier. Gian Giacomo Trivulzio was at Asti with 700 French lances threatening Milan. Savoy under its new duke, Philippe de Bresse, was intimately linked with France. Montferrat was governed in the same interest. The Marquis of Saluzzo was a French vassal. To conquer Asti, to coerce the other north-western powers, great and small, and so to secure the Alpine passes, was an intelligible plan, though it carried risks and difficulties. But Venice, by this time reassured against the fear of an immediate invasion, was unwilling so far to strengthen her neighbour and ally. Her real wish was that Maximilian should retire. Failing that, there was one enterprise that Venice could, tolerantly though not cordially, support. Florence alone of the Italian powers was still friendly to France. Florence was at war with Pisa, where Venice had troops, and on which she had designs. Against Florence the blow must be directed, aided by Venetian galleys and Genoese ships. Maximilian readily fell into this plan, which he further enriched with fantastic additions, scheming to capture the vessels returning from Naples with the French prisoners, to invade Provence, and join hands with a Spanish force from Roussillon, and with Germans from the Rhine. Meanwhile a part of Maximilian's army and a Venetian contingent were needed to protect the north-west.

Delays were many, but at length the allied force moved from Genoa, partly by land, partly by sea. It was now October, and the autumnal gales imperilled and impeded the naval force. The land forces suffered equally from heavy rains. At length Maximilian reached Pisa. The united army reached the total of about 2,500 horse and 4,000 foot. With this inadequate power, ill-provided with heavy artillery, Maximilian, himself literally penniless, determined to undertake the siege of Livorno, the last outlet of Florence to the sea. The Venetian and Genoese fleet moved up and occupied the harbour, while Maximilian directed the land attack. The town was in evil case, supplies short, the garrison weak and demoralised. But aid was promptly sent from Florence, and on the 29th of October a French squadron sailed in, favoured by a stormy wind which prevented the allied fleet from offering opposition. A fortnight later, while the Genoese were disputing the orders of the King, the Frenchmen sailed out again, leaving 500 soldiers and abundant stores. The weather, rainy and cold, discouraged and incapacitated the besiegers. Discipline was bad, and money scarce. Maximilian therefore determined to raise the siege and discussed the chances of a direct attack on Florence. Soon that was also given up, and he left hurriedly for Lombardy, perhaps disturbed by rumours of an attack upon his line of retreat. By the beginning of December he was at Pavia. Here he heard that Ferdinand of Aragon had concluded a truce with France. Alarmed perhaps for his own hereditary dominions and for the empire, certainly disgusted with all he had seen and suffered in Italy, Maximilian hurried across the Alps, there to expend his desultory vigour in other plans, fruitless indeed and unpractical, but none more fantastic and fruitless than the enterprise of Pisa.

If Louis of Orleans had had his own way, the expedition of 1494 would have been directed against Milan. A year later he would have seized the welcome opportunity to punish Ludovico for his treachery. What the jealousy of Charles had perhaps prevented, Louis XII found himself in a position to carry out. On his accession he took the title of Duke of Milan in addition to that of King of Sicily; and a full year was spent in diplomatic and military preparations. The treaty with England was renewed. A treaty was concluded with the Catholic Kings of Aragon and Castile (July, 1498), in which no mention was made of the King of Naples. Though Louis could not secure the neutrality of Maximilian, he was able to win his son Philip, ruler of the Low Countries, by some concessions in Artois. With the Swiss the French King contracted a league (March, 1499), by which the cantons stipulated to supply the King with men at a fixed rate of pay, and received in return an annual pension of 20,000 florins, and a promise of pecuniary or other assistance in their own wars. The powers of Italy, except Milan and Naples, were individually approached, and Venice, already on bad terms with Milan over the question of Pisa, after long deliberations accepted in February, 1499, an agreement for the partition of Milan. Venice was to receive Cremona and the territories east of the Adda as her share, and promised a contribution of 100,000 ducats to the French expenses in the joint war. The Pope was seeking a rich marriage for his son Cesare, who had decided to lay down his dignity of Cardinal. Repulsed in Naples, he turned the more willingly to France. Louis purchased his divorce from Jeanne of France, and papal support in his war, by the gift to Cesare of the hand of Charlotte d'Albret, and of the duchy of the Valentinois. The marriage was celebrated in May, 1499, at Blois. Florence, aggrieved though she was by the Venetian support of Pisa, dared not promise aid to Milan, and secretly professed her friendship for France. The powers of the north-western frontier of Italy were all won for the invaders.

Meanwhile Ludovico had not been idle. At every court his envoys met the ambassadors of France, and fought an unequal diplomatic fight. Maximilian was friendly, but he was engaged during the crisis in unsuccessful warfare with the Swiss. He took Ludovico's money, but gave him no material aid. Naples, reduced to famine by the ravages of war, was benevolent but helpless. The smaller powers, Mantua, Ferrara, Bologna, jealous as they were of Venice, were yet more afraid. They gave willingly good words, but took no compromising step. The Marquis of Mantua indeed, after much haggling, accepted a *condotta* from Ludovico, but was careful not to carry out its obligations. One ally Ludovico had, or at least professed to have,—the enemy of Christendom, the Turk, who did much harm to Venice during and after the war of Milan, and even raided Friuli, and the march of Treviso. But Ludovico was not to gain by this.

Thrown thus upon his own resources, he was in fact beaten before the war began. His frontier was long, and not naturally defensible. He had to fear attacks from every side. The spring and summer of 1499 were spent in feverish attempts to organise defence. A large number of infantry was raised in the Milanese, and distributed in the strong towns and on the frontiers. A few Swiss and Germans were hired. Efforts were made to collect mercenary horse, with moderate success; but the most important contingent, that promised from Naples under Prospero Colonna, was detained at home. Much labour was spent on the frontier fortresses. Alessandria in particular was thought to have been made very strong. The brothers San Severino, in whom the Duke had complete confidence, were put in the chief commands, and returned favourable reports to their master. The Duke flattered himself that his State could hold out for a time even against the overwhelming odds. If time were allowed, the powers of Germany might be set in motion.

Far more methodical and effective were the measures taken beyond the Alps. Louis had improved the administration of the finances, and there was money to spare. The companies of regular cavalry (*ordonn-ances*) were recruited, and in great part remodelled. Not less than 1,500 lances were at the King's disposal for the invasion, besides the forces employed in watching Burgundy and the other frontiers. Some 6,000 Swiss foot were enrolled. The total infantry reached the sum of 17,000. The artillery was finer, more numerous, and better equipped than that of Charles VIII. At length about the 10th of August this army was concentrated at Asti. The chief command was given to Gian Giacomo Trivulzio, a Milanese exile, who had left the service of the King of Naples for that of France. The Venetians were at the same time in readiness to advance on the eastern frontier.

The French, after capturing the strong place of Annone, where they massacred the garrison, occupied Valenza, Tortona, and some places of less importance, and then (August 25) closed in upon Alessandria, which was held in strength by Galeazzo San Severino. Galeazzo could not rely on his troops, inferior as they were, and ill-paid. His communications were threatened. Faithful himself, he could not trust his own brothers. On the fourth day after the invading army had encamped before the town, Galeazzo and his principal officers took to flight, and the city at once fell to the French. This was practically the end of the war. On the 30th of August there were some signs of disquiet in Milan. The Duke's treasurer Landriano was killed in the street. On the 2nd of September Ludovico quitted Milan with his treasure, still considerable, and made his way by Como and the Valtellina into Tyrol. The castle of Milan, entrusted by the Duke to his most trusted friend, Bernardino da Corte, was sold by him to the French for the equivalent of some 150,000 ducats. No further opposition was made. The duchy was occupied by the French on the west of the Adda, by Venice to the east. Beyond the Po, Parma and Piacenza, with their dependent territory, submitted without resistance to the French.

Louis now resolved to cross the Alps to take possession of his new acquisition. On the 6th of October he made his solemn entry into Milan, accompanied by a brilliant following of cardinals, princes, and ambassadors. After spending about a month in regulating the affairs of his duchy, he returned to France, leaving Trivulzio in supreme command. With him was associated a Senate consisting of the Chancellor and seventeen councillors, partly French, and partly Italian. Its functions were both administrative and judicial. The task of Trivulzio was difficult. He was himself the head of the Guelf party, and secure of Guelf support, but he had to keep on good terms with the Ghibellines, many of whom had deserted the cause of Ludovico, and accepted the new *régime*. The inhabitants of the duchy, impoverished by the exactions of Ludovico made for the war, hoped for some remission of taxation. But the expenses of the army of occupation were heavy, trade and industry were interrupted, and it was found impossible materially to reduce the imposts. The French soldiers were quartered on the inhabitants, discipline was seriously relaxed, and there were many grave causes of complaint. The arrogance of Trivulzio gave general offence; his administrative incapacity was conspicuous; his personal greed was notorious. Supported by the knowledge that Ludovico was approaching, the nobles and people of Milan armed, and before the end of January, 1500, Trivulzio's position was clearly untenable. On the 3rd of February he retired with the French army from a city barricaded and in open revolt, leaving a sufficient garrison in the castle under Saint-Quentin.

Meanwhile Ludovico in the Tyrol had succeeded in procuring a truce between Maximilian and the Swiss (September 22). With the aid of Maximilian, more valuable in the Tyrol than elsewhere, and by the expenditure of a part of his hoard, he gradually collected a force. 1,500 men at arms reached him from Burgundy; the mercenary Swiss accepted his pay; finally he beat up a motley army of some 20,000 men. While Ludovico advanced from Bormio, Galeazzo came by Aosta through Savoy with a considerable body of Swiss. Ligny attempted to resist at Como, but his strength was insufficient. Trivulzio ordered him to retreat on Milan. Thence the French retired to Novara, and Mortara, where they were joined (February 13) by Yves d'Allègre with the lances and infantry that Louis had lent to Cesare for the conquest of Imola and Forlì. Other scattered forces having come in, the French could now hold their own until the arrival of reinforcements.

On the 5th of February Ludovico re-entered Milan, greeted by enthusiastic shouts of "Moro, Moro." His partisans showed some zeal in subscribing to replenish his partly exhausted treasury; but the most extreme measures were needed to supply the necessary funds. Even the treasures of the churches were not spared. Such resources could suffice for a time, but before the end of March they showed signs of failure. While vain efforts were made to reduce the Castle of Milan, Ludovico advanced with his army by Pavia to Vigevano, which he captured with its castle, and thence after some desultory warfare he moved against Novara (March 5), where was Yves d'Allègre with a sufficient garrison, still further strengthened a day or two later. But the inhabitants were hostile, and provisions scarce, so that the French were obliged to accept a favourable capitulation (March 21).

Here ended Ludovico's successes. On the 23rd of March la Trémouille reached Mortara with 500 men-at-arms and good artillery. Trivulzio was by this time not only hated but distrusted by his companions, and a new and trusted leader was worth as much as the new troops. On the 3rd of April a large body of Swiss joined the French under Antoine de Bessey. The French army was now, though perhaps not equal in numbers, superior in quality to that of Ludovico. In his army discontent caused by want of pay was general, and desertions were frequent.

There were Swiss in both armies, and it was likely that they would refuse to fight against their countrymen. The French levy had official authority; the French chests were full. Thus when the French army moved forward against the Milanese at Novara, almost the whole ducal army abandoned him. Further resistance was impossible. Ludovico attempted to escape in disguise among the Swiss, but was detected and became a prisoner (April 10). His captivity was only terminated by his death. His brother Ascanio was captured by the Venetians and handed over later to the French. The sons of Ludovico were safe in Germany. The little son of Gian Galeazzo fell into the hands of France.

For the reorganisation of the duchy the King sent his own right hand, the Cardinal of Rouen, Georges d'Amboise. Trivulzio was superseded in the civil government by Charles d'Amboise, Seigneur de Chaumont, the Cardinal's nephew, and in the military command by Aubigny.

With the completed conquest of Milan French predominance in the peninsula was established. Venice was content to accept the situation for the present, and to make use of her powerful friend, who sent ships to cooperate in her war with the Turks during the years 1499–1501. The Pope was fain to lean on France. French troops assisted Cesare in the conquest of Imola and Forlì and afterwards served him against Rimini, Pesaro and Faenza. His further conquests were limited by French sufferance. When he threatened Bologna or Florence, he was warned off by their august protector. In the enterprise of Naples, Cesare followed the French banner as a willing ally, almost as a subject. During the time of Ludovico's success several of the Italian States had given him help, or shown him goodwill. After his fall, the Duke of Ferrara, the Marquis of Mantua, Bentivoglio of Bologna, and others, were forced to pay compensation to France for their incautious actions. Florence reaped the reward of her more correct behaviour, when the King sent Beaumont with French troops to assist the Florentines against Pisa. The failure of the expedition brought Florence into temporary disgrace, but later she was allowed to buy her pardon. Thus in Lombardy, in Tuscany, in the Papal States, there was no power that did not accept as a fact the predominance of France.

It may be doubted whether Louis aimed at converting predominance into sovereignty. But he was determined to conquer Naples, and he hoped that an occasion would offer to establish the Cardinal of Rouen as pope. These ends achieved, he might be content with the substance, while the Emperor still enjoyed the shadow. Meanwhile no great effort would be required to keep Maximilian in check. But with regard to Naples Louis had in Aragon a more dangerous rival. Naples had been a part of the kingdom of Sicily, and Sicily was owned by Aragon. Moreover Alfonso of Aragon had been *de facto* King of Naples, and had established there the ruling race of kings. These claims were not convincing, but neither were Louis' claims beyond possibility of question.

Nor could the King of Sicily remain a tranquil spectator, while his neighbour and relative was displaced by a new and aggressive power. Louis determined to compromise, and (November, 1500) concluded at Granada a secret treaty with Aragon for a joint conquest of Naples, conceding to Ferdinand a fair half of the kingdom, and, provisionally, the provinces of Apulia and Calabria.

Strengthened by this compact, Louis was free to move. In May, 1501, his army was ready in Lombardy. With the certainty of Spanish aid, 1,000 lances, 4,000 Swiss, and 6,000 French infantry were held sufficient. The command was divided between Aubigny, the Count of Caiazzo (Francesco di San Severino), and the Duke of Valentinois. A fleet under Ravenstein was operating on the coast from the convenient base of Genoa. Federigo relied on help from Sicily, where was the great Gonzalo, who had recently returned from a successful expedition against the Turks, and who, acting under orders, was careful not to undeceive him. The first news of the coalition came to Naples from Rome, where in June Alexander issued a bull depriving Federigo of his throne and confirming the partition already arranged between the Kings of France and Aragon. In July the French army reached Capua, which was held by Fabrizio Colonna with a sufficient force. But the French artillery soon made a practicable breach, and, while terms of surrender were being discussed, the French were admitted into the town, which they sacked with every circumstance of cruelty and outrage. There was no further resistance. On August 2 Federigo retired to Ischia, and after a time decided to accept the asylum offered to him by Louis, who provided him with a rich endowment and an honourable position in France. On August 4 French garrisons occupied the castles of Naples, and la Palice was sent to hold the Abruzzi. Louis d'Armagnac, duke of Nemours, was appointed viceroy of the newly acquired kingdom.

Meanwhile Gonzalo without difficulty occupied his master's share of the kingdom of Naples, and was joined by Prospero and Fabrizio Colonna, whose family was about this time expelled from their possessions in papal territory, while Cesare, their bitterest enemy, was leagued with the French. Only at Taranto was there considerable resistance. Here lay Federigo's son, Ferrante. The town was strong, but a siege by sea and land compelled it after a stout resistance to come to terms (March, 1502). Gonzalo promised his liberty to Ferrante, but the Spanish King disregarded the promise, and caused the young prince to be sent in custody to Spain.

The treaty of Granada had not been so carefully drawn as to exclude all possibility of doubt. France was to have the Abruzzi, the Terra di Lavoro, Naples, and Gaeta, while Spain received Apulia and Calabria. But nothing was said about the province of the Capitanata, lying between Apulia and the Abruzzi, about the Basilicata, lying between Calabria and Apulia, or about the two Principati, lying between the Basilicata and the Terra di Lavoro.   Yet the clause stipulating that the incomes of the two shares should be approximately equal might, with a little goodwill, have pointed the way to an equitable settlement.   The main difficulty turned on the question of the Capitanata.   The inhabitants of the barren Abruzzi depended on the corn-lands of the Capitanata for their food-supplies.   The flocks that wintered in the plains were driven in summer to the mountain pastures, from Apulia proper into the Southern Apennines, and from the Capitanata into the Abruzzi, toll (*dogana*) being taken from them on the way for the King of Sicily.   The treaty settled that " the *dogana* of Apulia " should be collected by the commissaries of Spain and equally divided between the kings.   The French, supported by recent administrative usage, denied that the Capitanata was part of Apulia, and claimed it as a necessary complement of their own share.

No satisfactory agreement was reached on these dangerous points, although the question was referred to the kings for decision.   At Troia in the Capitanata, at Tripalda in the Principato *ultra*, collisions took place.   Finally, in July open war broke out.   Louis about the same time visited the Milanese, and apparently purchased the neutrality or support of Cesare by giving him a free hand in the Romagna, and even against Bologna.   Reinforcements were sent to the French, and the Spaniards were driven from Cerignola, and then from Canosa (August, 1502). Gonzalo was obliged to concentrate at Barletta on the northerly coast of Apulia, holding also Taranto.   The indecision of the French leaders saved the great captain.   While they were occupying unimportant places in Apulia and Calabria, and watching Gonzalo at Barletta, the time for a crushing blow went by.   The Venetians sent provisions if not money to Barletta.   Reinforcements were sent into Calabria from Sicily.   In March, 1503, a fresh army reached Reggio from Spain.   In April 3000 *Landsknechte* were sent by Maximilian from Trieste to Barletta. Gonzalo had already shown that he was to be feared, when he fell upon la Palice at Ruvo, defeated, and captured him.   On hearing that Aubigny had been routed at Seminara in Calabria, he was able to take a vigorous offensive.   He left Barletta with the chief part of his troops and seized Cerignola.   The French generals decided to strike a despairing blow. They attacked Gonzalo's army in a fortified position at Cerignola, and were completely defeated, Nemours being killed.   The news determined Allègre to evacuate Naples except the castles, and to retire to Gaeta. On the 16th of May Gonzalo entered the capital.   Prospero Colonna was sent to subdue the Abruzzi, while the great engineer, Pedro Navarra, employed the newest resources of military art against the castles of Naples.   In a short time they were made untenable.   At Gaeta however the French, strengthened by reinforcements from Genoa, repulsed the conquerors; while Louis d'Ars still held Venosa with a remnant of the army defeated at Cerignola.

At the very crisis of the war Louis had been entangled in a futile negotiation. Since the end of 1500 Philip, Archduke of Austria, had been busying himself with the double object of securing his dominions in the Netherlands against France, and of obtaining for his infant son, the Duke of Luxemburg, afterwards Charles V, additions by marriage to those vast possessions to which he was already heir presumptive. The outcome of these efforts was a contract of betrothal at Lyons (August, 1501) between Charles and Claude, the daughter of Louis XII: a provisional treaty at Trent between Maximilian and Louis (October, 1501) agreeing to this marriage, and stipulating the investiture of Milan for Louis: an interpretation of the same arranged between Philip and Louis in December of the same year at Blois, but never accepted by Maximilian: and finally a treaty concluded by Philip with Louis at Lyons (April 5, 1503), in the name of Ferdinand and Isabella, by which the whole of the kingdom of Naples was to be given to the infant pair. This last treaty was never ratified by Ferdinand and Isabella, who asserted that Philip had exceeded his powers, and Gonzalo paid no heed to it. But Louis showed less prudence. Relying on the treaty, he deferred, in the critical month of April, the despatch of a body of troops which he had ready in Genoa. It is true that the threatening movements of the Swiss, to whom Louis was obliged at this moment to cede Bellinzona, gave an additional reason for delaying what had been already too long delayed.

The disasters and humiliation of the year called for a great effort. The French raised three armies, one of which was directed on the Spanish frontier of Navarre and another against Roussillon, while the third was intended for the recovery of Naples. The Italian expedition was entrusted to la Trémouille. The northern powers of Italy remained to all appearance faithful. Ferrara, Mantua, Bologna, Florence furnished contingents. In August the French were beginning to move. The Pope and Cesare vacillated long between the parties, but at the crisis they were both stricken down by illness, and on the 18th of August the Pope expired. The ambassadors and the cardinals succeeded in freeing the town from the armed men of rival factions, Orsini, Colonna, Cesare; but Gonzalo was at Castiglione, and the French advanced guard at Nepi, so that the election took place as it were under the shadow of war. It wisely ended by giving the prize to neither of the foreign nations. The new Pope, Pius III (Francesco Piccolomini), treated Cesare with indulgence and left him in a position to bargain with both Spain and France. However, his final adhesion to the latter power proved to be of little value, while both Orsini and Colonna were thereby driven into the arms of Spain.

The French advance was delayed by the illness of la Trémouille, whose place was ultimately taken by the Marquis of Mantua. Finally they moved forward by the Latin Way, which was blocked by Gonzalo, holding San Germano, Aquino and Roccasecca. Joined by Allègre, from Gaeta, they attacked Roccasecca, but were beaten off and obliged to retire to Ceprano (October, 1503). They then determined to move southwards, along the right bank of the Garigliano, hoping to be able to advance by the Appian Way. On the Garigliano the two armies confronted each other for weeks. The French, vexed in the marshy land by rainy, wintry weather, deprived of supplies and of pay by the dishonesty of commissariat officers, were in bad case, but hardly in worse than their opponents. Having bridged but failed to cross the river, the French drew back a little, scattering themselves over a somewhat wide area for better provisioning. Discipline was bad, and the Marquis of Mantua, insulted by his troops, withdrew from the command. At length in the last days of December, the vigilance of the enemy being relaxed, Gonzalo crossed the Garigliano higher up, and fell upon the French, disunited and unprepared. A complete rout followed. The artillery was hurriedly embarked on boats and sent round by sea. The men fled in disorder for Gaeta, pursued to the gates of the town by the victorious Spaniards and Italians. During several days afterwards parties of fugitives were straggling into Rome, half naked and half starved. Some of the boats were swamped, and in one of them perished Piero de' Medici. The French captains in Gaeta soon surrendered; nor could Louis d'Ars in Apulia keep up the hopeless struggle. Such was the end of French lordship in Naples; where Gonzalo now held unquestioned sway, dispensing the royal bounty as if it was his own, and encouraging his soldiers to live at the expense of the inhabitants.

The fortune of war had decided against Louis. He was fain to heal his wounded pride by new treaties of marriage which recognised his rights and promised to enrich his offspring at the expense of France. By the treaty of Blois with Maximilian (September, 1504), Claude, already heiress of Britanny, was to receive Milan with Genoa and Asti, the duchy of Burgundy with Macon and Auxerre, and the county of Blois, as a dowry on her marriage with Charles. In return the King of the Romans conferred upon Louis the investiture of Milan for a cash consideration. A separate and secret treaty stipulated a joint attack on Venice. An arrangement made at Hagenau (April, 1505), between the same and Archduke Philip, contemplated the addition of Naples to this ample endowment. But in October of this year, at Blois, Louis preferred to give the kingdom of Naples as a dowry to his relative, Germaine of Foix, on her marriage with Ferdinand of Aragon; and Ferdinand so far recognised the rights of Louis that he promised a compensation of 1,000,000 ducats, and, in default of heirs of the marriage, the reversion of the kingdom to the Most Christian King. It was settled that an amnesty should be granted to the barons who had supported the Angevin cause, and that restitution of property should be made as far as possible. As a sign of restored amity, an interview took place at Savona, under circumstances of unusual trustfulness, between the sovereigns (June, 1507).

Gonzalo, who on this occasion received extraordinary marks of confidence and admiration from both the Kings, enjoyed his last and most memorable moments of good fortune. His master, who suspected his ambition, and disapproved of his methods of administration, enticed him by the promise of still higher honours to return with him to Spain. There he found himself deluded and disappointed. The wealth which he had accumulated in his master's service he was allowed to enjoy, but his days of public activity were over.

The arrangements mentioned above did not affect the actual position of Italian affairs. Indeed, all dispositions depending on the marriage of Claude and Charles were rendered void by the decision of Louis in 1506 to bestow his daughter's hand on the heir presumptive of France, Francis of Angoulême. The years following the disastrous wars of Naples were years of uneasy watchfulness, of bewildering arrangements and re-arrangements of unstable leagues and combinations, of mendacious protestations of friendship, and treacherous provocations addressed to jealousy and greed. The inheritance of the Duke of Valentinois was gathered in by his enemies, Orsini, Colonna, Venice, and Giuliano della Rovere, who as Julius II succeeded the short-lived Piccolomini. Cesare himself, a prisoner in Spain, added another to the list of those whose trust in Ferdinand proved their ruin. The war of Florence with Pisa continued, but barely interested any one besides the belligerents. Gradually, from an old man's passion, as from live fire hidden under blackened embers, infectious energy spread through Italy and through Europe. Cesare Borgia's conquests and fall had brought almost all of the Romagna and the March of Ancona under the direct control of the Holy See. The ambition of Julius would be satisfied with nothing less than the whole of what had ever been claimed by the successors of Peter. Venice first earned his hatred by refusing to give up Faenza and Rimini, which she had occupied after the death of Alexander. The secret treaty of Blois gave Julius hopes of a speedy revenge. But that treaty remained without effect, and Julius had to wait, exercising a violent self-restraint, and evincing qualities, not natural in him, of patience, reticence, and duplicity. Practising simony and extortion on the grand scale, he slowly replenished the papal treasury, which had been plundered by Cesare Borgia on Alexander's death. Then (1506), reckoning that swift and sudden action might reach its effect before either Venice or France decided to offer opposition, he struck a rapid blow at two usurpers of St Peter's rights. At Perugia Giampaolo Baglione made complete submission. Against Bologna the French themselves sent troops to aid the Pope, unwilling, when they saw he was in earnest, to risk the loss of his friendship. Giovanni Bentivoglio and his sons, hopeless of successful resistance, took to flight. The Pope set up his own government in the town.

While still at Bologna, Julius heard unwelcome news. In Genoa French rule had not led to peace. Genoa had always been noted for the violence of its civic feuds, which had largely contributed to its defeat in the commercial race with Venice. These disputes had in the past centred about the two great plebeian families of Adorno and Campo-Fregoso. The quarrel, which now arose, was a quarrel of class against class. The nobles had been perhaps unduly encouraged by their aristocratic French rulers. At any rate it seems clear that they were guilty, on more than one occasion, of arrogant and injurious conduct towards the common people, many of whom were in their own esteem, as in their wealth, equal to the nobles. In June and July, 1506, matters came to a head. An attack was made on the nobles, especially on the powerful family of Fiesco. Neither Ravenstein the governor, nor his deputy Rocquebertin, showed much zeal or capacity in dealing with the trouble. Matters were allowed to go from bad to worse. At first the common people were content with the concession of two-thirds of the public offices, instead of the half share hitherto allowed to them. Then the artisans, as opposed to the rich plebeian merchants and bankers, more and more got the upper hand. Tribunes of the people were appointed, and finally an artisan, a dyer, Paolo da Novi, was elected to be Doge. Meanwhile the cities on the sea-coast were taken by force from their noble governors, and in November siege was laid to Monaco, which was held by the noble Grimaldi. Five months the siege lasted, while in Genoa the French garrison was obliged first to vacate the Palace and retire to the Castle, and finally carried on an active war of bombardment against the town. Monaco held out with conspicuous bravery against great odds, until relieved in March by Yves d'Allègre.

Julius was disturbed in the enjoyment of his victorious sojourn at Bologna by the news that the French King was coming in person with a large army to punish his rebellious city. Himself a native of Savona and a favourer of the popular party in Genoa, the Pope, while opposed to the coercion of Genoa, feared also ulterior designs of the French King. The ambition of the Cardinal of Rouen was well known, and it could only be satisfied at the expense of the existing pontiff. In alarm Julius withdrew to Rome, where he followed events in the north with anxiety. The King, with nearly 10,000 Swiss, and an army apparently disproportionate to his task, was at Asti on April 16, 1507. His troops at once moved on Genoa, by Buzalla. The command of the army was in the hands of Charles d'Amboise. On the 25th of April he began the attack, ordering the capture of a bastion planted on the highest point of the hills surrounding Genoa, and commanding the whole position. The access was very difficult, and the Swiss disliked the task. However, they were shamed into doing their duty by a troop of dismounted men-at-arms who advanced to the assault. When the place at length was reached the Genoese took to flight without further resistance, but many of the assailants were wounded on the way. After some scattered fighting, that night the army held the heights overlooking Genoa. The next day envoys were sent to treat, but while terms were being discussed warlike views prevailed within the town, and the whole force of Genoa came out to fight. They were enticed to attack the well-ordered mass of the French infantry, and driven back in panic to their walls. The next day the citizens accepted the King's terms of unconditional surrender. On the 28th he rode into the town with drawn sword, cancelled the city's privileges, imposed on them a fine of 300,000 ducats, ordered a new castle to be built, and pay for a garrison of 2,000 foot to be henceforth provided. While imposing on Genoa his will he was careful to preserve it from plunder or outrage. Paolo da Novi fled, but was shortly afterwards captured and put to death.

The fears that had disturbed Julius when he heard of the powerful expedition against Genoa proved vain. Nothing was attempted, if anything had been imagined, against the Holy Father. But the interview at Savona (June, 1507), which followed shortly, was calculated to cause him not less serious alarm. Ferdinand had sought, but had not received, the investiture of Naples, and had shown his resentment by avoiding an interview at Ostia, which the Pope had wished. We do not know what the Kings may have discussed at Savona; the secrecy observed at the time still baffles the curiosity of investigators. There was grave matter for deliberation. Maximilian, the inveterate enemy of Louis, and the rival of Ferdinand for the regency of Castile, was making serious preparations for a descent into Italy, with the ostensible purpose of obtaining the imperial crown, and the probable intention of driving the French from Milan. Common measures may have been considered against this common foe; joint action against Julius may also have been proposed. But the document from Simancas published by Maulde seems to prove that the Kings finally decided to attempt a league in which Julius and Maximilian should be included as friends. The careful exclusion of all other powers from the projected league seems to indicate an intended victim, to whose sacrificial feast all four could be invited, with the prospect, if not the certainty, of a favourable reply. The oath of Louis at Savona foreshadows the League of Cambray. Venice is not mentioned, but no other solution satisfies the conditions of the enigma.

Venice had indeed run up a long account with the powers of Italy and Europe. Since 1495 she had held Brindisi, Otranto, and other ports of Apulia, and thus mutilated Ferdinand's new acquisition. By treaty with France and by older conquest she held the eastern portion of the duchy of Milan. Against Julius she held Rimini and Faenza, as well as her earlier possession, Ravenna. There had also been acrimonious discussion about the right of collation to Venetian prelacies, such as Vicenza and Cremona. Maximilian's imperial rights were ignored in Padua and Verona, his hereditary rights in Friuli. She had recently refused to Maximilian free passage with his army through her territory for his coronation at Rome. She had declined to renew her league with France, declaring the old league sufficient. The day of reckoning was at hand.

If such a league as that of Cambray was projected at Savona, Maximilian's unconcerted action assisted the plan. Enraged at the repeated refusals of Venice to grant him a free passage, he attacked the republic in February, 1508. The fortunes of war were against him. The French stood by their ally. Pitigliano held his own in the Veronese, while Alviano in the east took Görz and Trieste in the hereditary lands of the enemy and threatened a further advance. The "elected Roman Emperor," as he now called himself, was fain in June to conclude for three years a humiliating truce, by which Venice retained her conquests. In this truce the King of France was himself included, and he wished the Duke of Gelders, his own ally, and Maximilian's obdurate enemy, to be also comprised; but Venice, with unusual imprudence, allowed the wishes of her reputed friend to remain unsatisfied.

This inconsiderate conduct was an excuse, if not the reason, for the decided adhesion of France to the enemies of the Republic. We catch glimpses, during the eighteen months that followed the meeting of Savona, of the negotiations which led Maximilian to forget all the painful associations of slight or wrong connected with Milan, Burgundy, Gelders, and Britanny. His new rancour against Venice, the unsuccessful progress of the war in Gelders, the influence of his daughter Margaret, anxious to protect her nephew's dominions in the Netherlands, which were now entrusted to her charge, the secret and cautious instigations of the Pope,—all urged him towards the league at length concluded at Cambray in December, 1508, by Margaret and the Cardinal of Rouen. After a temporary settlement of the affairs of Gelders, a league was there secretly compacted, purporting to include not only France and the Empire, but also the Pope and Aragon. The Cardinal undertook to answer for the Pope; no one spoke for the King of Aragon, but it is probable that a secret understanding already existed. Each power was, by the united action of the league, to recover the places held against it by Venice. Thus Spain would recover Monopoli, Trani, Brindisi, Otranto; the Pope, Ravenna, Rimini, Faenza, and smaller places in the neighbourhood, a list which might be afterwards extended; Maximilian, Verona, Padua, Vicenza, Treviso, Friuli, and generally all places held or usurped by Venice from Austria or the Empire; while France was to receive Brescia, Bergamo, Crema, besides Cremona and the Ghiara d' Adda, ceded to Venice as her share of the spoils of Ludovico il Moro. The Italian powers were to open the war by the 1st of April, 1509, and Maximilian promised to join them within the space of forty days. The investiture of Milan was to be renewed to Louis for the sum of a hundred thousand crowns, still due under the earlier bargain. England and Hungary were to be invited to join the unwieldy coalition, and each contracting power was given four months for naming its allies.

Venice had long been aware that such a conspiracy would correspond to the Pope's inmost and deepest wishes, and that similar plans had frequently been discussed between France and Maximilian. She may, notwithstanding, have relied on the jealousies and hatreds of the powers for keeping them apart. Something of the truth, however, reached her soon after the meeting of Cambray. Early news of a more precise order came to her from the great Gonzalo, who offered his services to the Signoria. The results would have been interesting had this remarkable offer been accepted. While negotiations were carried on in the vain hope of detaching the Pope from the alliance, all preparations were hurried forward for resistance. France declared war on the 7th of April; on the 27th the Pope proclaimed his ban. The Venetians had more than 30,000 men on foot, Italian men-at-arms, picked infantry from Apulia and Romagna, with the excellent levies from the Val di Lamone under Dionigi di Naldi, Stradiots from Illyria and the Morea, Sagdars from Crete, and a considerable force of native militia. Of the allies, the French were first in the field, opposed on the Adda by the Venetians under Pitigliano and Alviano. The impetuous character of the latter was ill-yoked with the Fabian strategy of his colleague, and the policy of the Signoria was a compromise between the two. Alviano proposed to cross the Adda and take the offensive. This plan having been set aside, Pitigliano determined to recover Treviglio, which had given itself to the French. The place was captured and burned, but, owing to the delay thus caused, the Venetians were not ready to prevent the French from crossing the Adda at Cassano. The Venetian orders were to run no unnecessary risk. Thus the French were allowed to capture Rivolta undisturbed. But when (May 14) Louis began to move southwards towards Pandino, and threatened to cut off Venetian communications with Crema and Cremona, the Venetians hurried to anticipate him. The light horse were sent on to occupy Pandino and Palazzo, and the main force followed along the higher ground, while the French moved by the lower road parallel to the Adda. Between Agnadello and Pandino the French found an opportunity to attack the Venetian columns on the march. By this time the Venetian army was spread over some four miles of ground, the artillery was not at hand, and Alviano, who was not present when the fight began, was only able to bring into action a small portion of the heavy-armed horse and a part of the infantry. It is not certain whether he could have refused battle, it is certain that he did not expect it. Nor is it clear whether the French movement on Pandino was a feint, or whether their attack was an afterthought, when the movement on Pandino had failed. It is certain that the French were able to throw the whole weight of their force on a part of the Venetian army. Aided however by the higher

ground and the vineyards which clothed the slope, the Venetians held
their own for awhile, and even gained some advantage. But when the
main battle of the French came up, while Alviano received no further
support, the day was lost. The losses fell chiefly on the levies raised
by conscription from the Venetian peasantry, who did well. Alviano's
own band of infantry from Brisighella was almost annihilated. He
was himself captured, fighting desperately. Pitigliano, with the main
body of men-at-arms, was able to retreat in good order. But a great
part of the army was broken and fled. Thirty-six pieces of ordnance
were left behind and fell into the hands of the enemy. Pitigliano
at Brescia endeavoured to collect and reorganise the remnant of his
army. But the demoralisation was great, and the troops refused to
remain with the colours, deserting in numbers as soon as they received
their pay.

The first impulse of the proud Republic was to bow before the
storm. France was allowed to occupy Bergamo and Brescia, Crema
and Cremona, almost unopposed. The *visdomino*, whom the Signoria
had some years before set up at Ferrara as a mark of suzerainty,
was driven out. The restitution of the towns of Romagna and other
concessions were offered to the Pope, and shortly afterwards the Romagna
was actually evacuated. Verona, Vicenza, and Padua were allowed to
give themselves up to emissaries, real or pretended, of the Emperor.
Treviso was still held, but the recent conquests to the east of Venice
were given up. The towns in Apulia were abandoned. Meanwhile every effort was made to strengthen the narrower line of defence.
Fresh troops were raised, and money and stores collected ; while on the
other hand attempts were made to open negotiations with the allies
severally, and especially with the Pope.

Maximilian had appeared at Trent in June; but as his forces were slow
in collecting, the Venetians felt strong enough in July to re-establish
themselves in Padua, which was made as strong as possible. Thus, when
at length in August he was ready to move, the first thing necessary
was the recapture of this fortress-city. Supported by 500 French
lances under la Palice, and an army that seemed to contemporaries
nothing less than prodigious, he sat down to besiege the town in the
middle of August. The hostility of the peasantry, whose hearty loyalty
furnishes the best testimonial to Venetian good government, caused him
much difficulty, and his heavy guns were not in position till the middle
of September. Dissensions arose among the allies. La Palice was on
the worst of terms with Maximilian's chief military adviser, Constantin
Areniti. A famous legend represents Bayard himself and the French
men-at-arms as unwilling to go to the assault on foot unless accompanied
by the German nobles and gentlemen, who declined to derogate so
far. Finally the siege was given up on October 2. Soon afterwards the
Emperor took his departure to the Tyrol ; the French retired into the

Milanese, and the Pope withdrew his men.   Vicenza speedily returned to
Venetian rule, and Verona alone of the more important places remained
in imperial hands.

In February, 1510, the Venetians at length came to terms with the
Pope.   His conditions were hard, but they were accepted.   Venice
recognised in full the immunities of the clergy and the papal right
to provide to all Venetian benefices, renounced all unauthorised treaties
concluded with towns in the Papal States, abandoned all intention of
appealing to a council against the papal bans, and conceded free navigation of the Adriatic to all papal subjects, among whom Ferrara was
expressly included.   In return, the Pope admitted the humble request
of the Republic for pardon, and promised his good offices in future.
The Venetians were allowed to recruit in the Papal States, where they
engaged several famous *condottieri*, among others Giampaolo Baglione,
and Renzo da Ceri.   Thus the first aim of Julius was secured.   He
had humiliated the Queen of the Adriatic, and recovered all rights
usurped by Venice from the Holy See.   He was now at liberty to turn
his attention to his second object, the expulsion from Italy of the
"Barbarians"—in the first place of the French.   For this purpose he
hoped to win the aid of the Emperor and of Henry VIII.   But
abundant patience was needed before this could be brought about.
The first effect of the Pope's change of policy was rather to increase
the bitterness of Maximilian against the Venetians, so that he tried to
induce the Turk to attack them.   With the King of Aragon Julius
was not at first much more successful.   Ferdinand accepted the investiture of Naples, but showed no inclination to an open breach with the
league.   There remained the Swiss.

The Swiss were poor and ignorant, their general Diet ill-instructed
and impotent, their leading men needy and venal, their common men
ready to follow any liberal recruiting officer, and even the cantonal
governments lacked coercive force.   Thus the fine military qualities so
often displayed by them in these wars had hitherto served only to win
the mercenary's pittance.   French victories would have been impossible
without Swiss aid; French disasters had fallen mainly on the Swiss.
But latterly they had risen to a higher sense of their own value;
their arrogant behaviour and exorbitant demands had begun to fatigue
the French paymaster.   Relations, which had never been easy, had now
become decidedly unfriendly; for the French King had refused the
Swiss terms, and discharged his unruly levies, intending in future to
draw his infantry from Germany, the Grisons, and the Valais.   Moreover the ten years' treaty of 1499 had run to a close, and Louis showed
no great eagerness for its renewal.

Already in 1506–7 the Emperor had tried to shake the Franco-
Swiss alliance, and lavish expenditure had been needed to neutralise
his influence.   For the expedition against Imperial Genoa it had been

necessary first to hoodwink, afterwards to ignore, the Swiss authorities. The Swiss who fought at Agnadello were illicit volunteers. It was the task of Julius to turn Swiss dissatisfaction to his own ends, and for this purpose he had an admirable instrument in Matthäus Schinner, Bishop of Sion. A man of energy and ambition, plausible and energetic, the enemy of France, Schinner was early in 1510 set to win the Cantons and the Diet for the Pope, and a defensive alliance was concluded. In July the Diet was asked to give effect to this agreement by assisting the Pope in the invasion of Ferrara, which persisted in hostility against Venice. To comply was an act of open hostility to France, the ally of Ferrara; moreover, Ferrara could only be reached through Milanese territory. However, the influence of Schinner prevailed, and 10,000 men set out. The Diet still hesitated; French gold was at work; Chaumont d'Amboise was prepared to resist any attack on the Milanese; the Swiss, without artillery and scant of victual, did not venture to advance beyond the land which lies between Como and the Lago Maggiore. In all their movements they were closely followed by the French, and finally they were forced to retire without having effected anything (September). During the winter negotiations proceeded between the Pope and the Swiss, the latter pressing in vain for the pay of the troops supplied. Meanwhile the offers of the King of France were met by the determined opposition of the Forest Cantons, whose antagonism to the French was growing, increased by measures directed against their trade with Milan. Maximilian, on the other hand, succeeded in concluding (February, 1511) a defensive treaty with a majority of the Cantons in favour of his duchy of Austria and his county of Burgundy. Thus the greatest powers of Europe were treating as equals with the league of peasants and burghers.

Meanwhile in the war France had held her own. An attack by sea and land on Genoa failed ignominiously. The efforts directed by Julius against Ferrara led only to the capture of Modena. Nor did Louis despise ecclesiastical weapons. A synod of French clergy at Tours (September, 1510) declared the King justified in making war on the Pope in defence of his States and his allies, and called for the summons of a General Council. Embarking on this plan with the support of the Emperor, the King was able to attract five cardinals to his side, who not long after issued an invitation to a General Council to be held at Pisa in September, 1511. Pressing on at the same time in arms, Chaumont d'Amboise threatened Bologna, where the Pope lay ill. The danger was extreme; but the unconquerable vigour of the Pope and opportune assistance from Venice averted the worst. Having repulsed the French, the Pope urged forward his schemes against Ferrara; taking the field himself in the snows of winter, he occupied Concordia, and besieged and took Mirandola (January, 1511). There his successes stopped. Trivulzio, who assumed the command after the death of Chaumont (February, 1511), recovered Concordia and Mirandola, and in May Bologna was abandoned to him. The Pope retired to Ravenna. Misfortune brought with it dissension. The Pope's nephew and commander-in-chief, the Duke of Urbino, charged by the Pope's favourite, Cardinal Alidosi, legate of Bologna, with the blame for the loss of that city, and unable to get support from his uncle, fell upon his accuser and slew him. The Pope's fortunes were at their lowest ebb, but his will was unshaken. Returning to Rome, he met the hostile summons to a General Council by summoning a Council of his own to meet at the Lateran in April, 1512. For material help he turned to Spain; but in the crisis of discussion fell sick almost to death. Baffling his enemies by a complete recovery, he fortified himself against them by concluding with Venice and Spain in October, 1511, the Holy League for the recovery of all papal territory. It was soon afterwards joined by Henry VIII.

The Swiss also aided the papal plans, while making war for the first time on their own behalf. The failure of 1510 still rankled, and the commercial hostility of the Forest Cantons together with the hope of Milanese booty predisposed not only the soldiers of fortune, but also the governments, to warlike action. A grievance of Schwyz having been lightly treated by Louis, the Schwyzers took up arms (November, 1511) and summoned their allies. The call was obeyed, and towards the end of the month troops were collecting on the old marshalling ground between the lakes. Venetian aid was solicited and promised. Gaston de Foix, now Governor of Milan, was menaced at the same time on the side of Parma and Bologna. With the scanty forces at his disposal he could only impede, not prevent, the advance of the enemy towards Milan. But there the Swiss successes ended. They were unable to undertake the siege of Milan. No help came from Venice or the Pope; and the invaders were obliged to retreat, which they did in great disorder.

In spite of this second rebuff, the opening months of 1512 saw once more the King of France and the other Powers competing for the favour of the Swiss. The King of France was unable to satisfy their inordinate demands. Yet his need of an ally was extreme. The English and the Spaniards were threatening an invasion of France. Brescia and Bergamo had been recovered by Venice (January, 1512). The forces of the Holy League were menacing Ferrara and Bologna. Maximilian was vacillating, and in April concluded a truce with the Pope and Venice. Momentary relief was brought by the brilliant and brief career of Gaston de Foix, duke of Nemours. Early in the year 1512, the young general repulsed a dangerous attack of the allied forces directed against Bologna, and, on hearing of the fall of Brescia, he at once withdrew from Bologna all the forces that could be spared, crossed the Mantuan lands without leave, met and defeated Giampaolo at Isola della Scala, and in nine days presented himself before Brescia, assaulted, captured, and sacked the city. But in view of Maximilian's change of front it was urgent to achieve some still more notable success, before the Germans serving in the French army might be withdrawn. Having in vain endeavoured to induce the Spanish viceroy, Ramon de Cardona, to give battle in the Romagna, Gaston marched against Ravenna, and assaulted the town. To save this important place the forces of the league approached, and entrenched themselves to the south of the Ronco. During the night of the 10th of April Gaston threw a bridge over the river, and on the following morning, Easter-day, he led his troops across and attacked the position of his enemies. They were strongly fortified. On the left they were protected by the river, while their front was covered by a line of armed waggons guarded by the infantry of Pedro Navarra. The engagement opened with an artillery duel, which lasted some time without conspicuous result, until Alfonso d'Este, seeing an opportunity, led round his excellent and mobile artillery and directed it against the enemy's flank. The fire proved so galling that the Italian men-at-arms left their breastworks to attack the French. After the hand-to-hand engagement had begun between the cavalry on both sides, the Germans attacked the Spanish infantry behind their waggon wall, and a desperate battle resulted in a French victory. The Italian men-at-arms were defeated and broken, and Fabrizio Colonna was captured; but the Spanish infantry withdrew in good order. The French commander, rashly charging with a few horsemen on a body of Spanish foot who were retreating along a causeway, was unhorsed and killed. Yves d'Allègre also perished in the encounter. Navarra was a prisoner. Ramon de Cardona escaped by flight.

The complete victory, and the capture of Ravenna on the following day, were dearly bought by the loss of so vigorous a leader as Gaston de Foix. La Palice, who found himself by seniority in the chief command, was not qualified to make the most of a great victory, or to impose his authority on his motley army. The Pope amused the King with insincere negotiations, while pressing on the work of military reconstruction, and encouraging with Venetian help a fresh invasion of the Swiss. Unable to induce Venice to buy peace from the Emperor by the cession of Verona and Vicenza, Julius yet succeeded in procuring for her a truce. The Swiss, who began to move in May, were allowed free passage through Tyrol towards Verona. In May the adhesion of Maximilian to the League was proclaimed, though prematurely, by Julius, and in June the German infantry was ordered to leave the French army. The Council of Pisa had been a complete failure, and when removed to Milan fared no better. The Lateran Council, which met in May, 1512, though at first attended mainly by Italians, had far more of the appearance, and of the inner conviction, of authority. The pressure, which after Ravenna had appeared so urgent that there had been talk of bringing Gonzalo into the field as chief commander of the Holy League, was relaxing. The French were without a consistent policy. La Palice was first recalled to Milan, and then ordered into the Romagna to strike, if possible, a decisive blow. Part of his troops had been disbanded for financial reasons; others had been sent home. His enterprise in the Romagna could hardly have succeeded; but while yet on the way he was recalled for the defence of Milan.

The Swiss Diet had in April determined to act in concert with the League. The effort which followed was national and imposing. The Swiss army, not less than 20,000 strong, was mustered at Chur, and thence made its way by different paths to Trent, where Venetian emissaries welcomed them. The Spanish and papal army was advancing to occupy Rimini, Cesena, Ravenna, and threatening Bologna. The Venetian forces joined the Swiss at Villafranca in the Veronese, after Schinner had with difficulty dispelled the suspicions and satisfied the demands of these dangerous allies. La Palice had garrisoned the most important places, and lay in the neighbourhood ready to repeat the defensive strategy which had proved so useful in 1510 and 1511. But his forces were insufficient, and, on his retiring to Cremona, they were still further diminished by the loss of 4000 *Landsknechte*, withdrawn by the Emperor's command. Thence la Palice fell back to Pizzighetone, and again to Pavia, whence, a few days after the arrival of the enemy on the 14th of June, he again retreated, not without difficulty. Hereupon the French, abandoning all further resistance, made for the Alps. Meanwhile Trivulzio had evacuated Milan. Only the castles of Milan, Cremona, and Brescia, and the Lanterna of Genoa were still in French hands.

It remained to dispose of the conquered territory. Julius recovered without difficulty Ravenna, Bologna, and the rest of the Romagna. His commander, the Duke of Urbino, easily occupied Reggio and Modena, though Alfonso d'Este refused any settlement that would deprive him of Ferrara. The congress of allies which met at Mantua in August made over to the Pope Parma and Piacenza, to which he had at best a shadowy claim. The Emperor and Ferdinand would have been glad to give Milan to their grandson, Charles; but the Swiss were in possession and, supported by the Pope, made their will good. The duchy was given to Massimiliano Sforza, son of Ludovico, who in return ceded Locarno, Lugano, and Domo d' Ossola to his Swiss protectors. The Venetian claims were left unsettled. Brescia still held out. The Swiss claimed Cremona and the Ghiara d' Adda for the duchy. The Emperor demanded Vicenza and Verona. Florence, who in 1509 had ended her long war by the recovery of Pisa, was punished for her support of France by the restoration of the Medici, effected by the arms of Ramon de Cardona, and with the consent of the Pope. Julius' policy had reached a point of triumph. Much had been done for Rome, and something for Italy; but much yet remained to do, before the barbarians could be expelled.

The complicated problems had not been solved, and, before Julius' death in February, 1513, new difficulties had arisen. In order to secure the recognition of his Lateran Council by Maximilian, Julius had to make at least a show of sacrificing Venice, who obstinately refused to give up Vicenza and Verona. The new league of Pope and Emperor, compacted in November, 1512, was bound to suggest the reconciliation of Venice and France, and before the year was out overtures were made, which in March, 1513, led to a renewal of the Franco-Venetian league. On the other hand, the question of Ferrara was not decided, and imperial rights conflicted with papal pretensions in Parma and Piacenza, Modena and Reggio. The advance of the Spanish army into Lombardy, and its occupation of Brescia, threatened Italian freedom in every direction. The Swiss had been called into Milan as deliverers; they remained as masters. These problems were bequeathed by Julius to his successor, Giovanni de' Medici (Leo X).

During the period of the Swiss conquest of Milan Louis had been in great straits. The English had landed at Guipuscoa to join with the Spaniards in invading France, and although the only result was the conquest of Navarre, the danger had been serious. The retirement of the English, and a truce with Ferdinand on the Pyrenean frontier relieved the French King, and the Venetian alliance gave him strength. With the Swiss it was impossible to come to terms. But the dissatisfaction of the Milanese with the costly, oppressive, and disorderly rule of the Swiss, complicated as it was by the collateral authority of the Emperor's commissioners and of the Spanish viceroy, made the King hopeful of support in the duchy. In April the army of France, strengthened by a powerful force of *Landsknechte*, recruited in the Emperor's despite, was ready to cross the Alps, under Louis de la Trémouille and Trivulzio. The Guelf party rose to receive them. In May the Venetian army under Alviano, now at length released, began to advance and occupied the country to Cremona. The French party was set up in Genoa by the aid of a French fleet. Cardona remained inactive at Piacenza. At the end of the month only Novara and Como remained faithful to Sforza. On the third of June the French army lay before Novara, which was held by the Swiss. After a fruitless attack on the town, the French withdrew to Trecate, a place in the neighbourhood. Meanwhile Swiss reinforcements had reached Novara, and on the 6th of June the whole force swarmed out to attack the French. Advancing under cover of a wood they surprised the French outposts. When serious business began, the Swiss foot, unsupported by horse and artillery, carried the day by sheer force and fury. It is said that 8,000 fell on the side of the French, although the pursuit was ineffective for lack of horse. All the artillery and stores fell into the hands of the Swiss. Thus Milan was once more lost and won. The French retreated hastily by Vercelli, Susa, and the Mont Cenis. The power of Massimiliano, or rather of the Swiss, was easily restored throughout the duchy. The Venetians fell back, and their recent conquests were re-occupied by Cardona, and the imperial troops, who inflicted on them a serious defeat. But no combination of disasters could bend the Signoria to accept the Emperor's terms.

French prestige was low in 1513. Henry VIII routed the famous French cavalry at Guinegaste and captured Térouanne. The Swiss invaded Burgundy with imperial aid, and la Trémouille was forced to ransom the province and its capital, by the promise to surrender Milan and pay 400,000 crowns. The refusal of Louis to ratify this bargain hardly improved the situation. But towards the end of the year he recovered the papal friendship by recognising the Lateran Council, and abandoning the schismatic cardinals. The remainder of his reign, until his death in January, 1515, was spent in preparations, military and diplomatic, for the recovery of his lost position in Europe. Various marriage arrangements were mooted, of which only one came into effect, the third marriage of Louis, with Mary the sister of Henry VIII. The alliance with Venice was maintained; with the rest of the European powers a relation ensued of precarious hostility, tempered by more or less insincere offers of friendship.

Thus the accession of Francis of Angoulême found France prepared for war, and secured at least on the side of England. The gallant young King was eager for the paths of glory. His enemies made ready to receive him,—Ferdinand, the Swiss, and Maximilian with unequivocal hostility, the Pope prepared to accept a profitable compromise. But Francis could not pay Leo's price, which was nothing less than Naples for Giuliano de' Medici. Thus of the Italian powers Venice alone stood on his side.

The lack of Swiss foot-soldiers was supplied partly by German levies, partly by recruits raised by Pedro Navarra, who had entered French service, on the frontiers of France and Spain. The *ordonnances* were raised to 4,000 lances. Genoa was ready to join the French, and the Swiss, alarmed by rumours, sent a considerable reinforcement into Milan, which was employed to occupy Susa and the Alpine passes. In June and July a further and larger contingent entered the Milanese. Lack of pay and provision soon made itself felt, to the damage of discipline and goodwill. However the promise of papal and Florentine help eased the situation.

At length in August the French army, more powerful than any that had been hitherto raised in these wars, was ready to move. To avoid the passes held by the Swiss, Trivulzio led the bulk of the army by an unknown road over the Col d'Argentière, while another force advanced by the Maritime Alps towards Genoa. The French vanguard surprised by their unexpected arrival a body of Italian horse under Prospero Colonna, whom they defeated and captured at Villafranca near Saluzzo. The Swiss, surprised and disconcerted, short of pay and provisions, mistrustful of their allies, determined to retreat by Ivrea to Vercelli and wait for reinforcements.

Here disunion and divergent counsels led to further undecided and unconcerted movements and left the way open to the French, who only at Novara met some slight resistance. But reinforcements came across the Alps; and at the beginning of September considerable bodies of Swiss lay at Domo d' Ossola, Varese, and Monza, unable to agree on any plan for joint action or even for concentration. Meanwhile negotiations were in progress at Gallerate, the French showing themselves ready to make considerable money grants, and offering Sforza compensation in France. On the 9th of September an agreement was actually sealed. Foremost among the peace party were the towns of Bern, Freiburg, and Solothurn. But the army, now at length partly concentrated at Monza, was ill-satisfied with the terms, and especially the men of Uri, Schwyz, and Glarus. These determined to reject the treaty and move on Milan, where the party favourable to France had recently been overthrown.

At this moment the distribution of the various forces was as follows. The French lay at Binasco, the Swiss at Monza; Alviano near Cremona; Cardona with the Spanish, and Lorenzo de' Medici with the papal army, near Piacenza. Cardona and Lorenzo with good reason mistrusted each other, and were mistrusted by the Swiss. But the latter were at length determined by the influence of Schinner to reject all overtures for peace, and advance against the enemy. On the 10th of September the Swiss army was in Milan. Meanwhile the French army had moved to a position S.S.E. of Milan near Marignano, in order to be in easier touch with Alviano, who had occupied Lodi.

The Swiss were still undecided and discordant. Schinner and the enemies of peace built their hopes on the effects of a casual encounter, which actually took place on September 13 and precipitated a general engagement. The Forest Cantons led the way to the attack, the others followed, not altogether willing. The French lay encamped along the road from Milan to Marignano. The front lay near San Donato, the rear-guard between San Giuliano and Marignano. The camp was strongly fortified, and the land on each side of the road made difficult by irrigation canals. The attack began late in the day. The French vanguard, in spite of the damage caused by their artillery, was thrown into some confusion, and the *Landsknechte* were broken. Then the centre received the assault, but withstood it. Night fell upon the combatants, and the struggle was renewed with earliest dawn. Order had been in some measure restored. It was indeed a battle of the giants. The Swiss held their own before the repeated charges of the heavy-armed French horse, and had developed a formidable flank attack on the French rear-guard. Secure of victory they had sent a detachment to break down a bridge in the enemy's rear, when Alviano came up with a part of the Venetian horse, and, as much by the moral as by the material effect of his arrival, restored the tottering fortunes of the French. Towards mid-day the defeated army withdrew in good order with its wounded towards Milan. The pursuit was not vigorous, for the victors were exhausted, and their losses, if not so heavy as those of the Swiss, were serious. Two days after the fight the Swiss started for home, since no money was forthcoming for their needs. They made their retreat by Como, harassed by Venetian Stradiots.

The success of Francis was complete. Cardona withdrew to Naples. The Pope began to treat. The Swiss, though the Forest Cantons were opposed to peace, were sick of a league which had left all the hard work to them and did not even supply the sinews of war. Sforza surrendered the castles of Milan and Cremona and became a pensioner of France. In December the Pope and King met in Bologna, and conditions were arranged which restored peace between the Holy See and the Most Christian King. But the claims of Venice still presented difficulties, and Maximilian could not acquiesce in the occupation of Milan. The Swiss League was seriously divided. Eight cantons were ready for a peace, even for a league with France, but five were eager to renew the struggle. With the aid of these latter Maximilian invaded Milan in March, 1516; but the Swiss were unwilling to fight against their countrymen in French service, and finally the imperial host broke up. In November the whole Swiss League concluded an everlasting peace with Francis. Early in the same year Ferdinand had died, and his successor, Charles, was not for the present ready to take up his heritage of hostility to France. So at Noyon it was arranged between Charles and Francis to dispose of Naples by way of marriage (August, 1516); and at length, in December, the Emperor made terms at Brussels, which closed the war of Cambray by a precarious truce. Soon after Verona was restored to Venice, who had in the interval conquered Brescia.

Here we may halt, while war is hushed awhile, to glance at the results of all these years of strife. France is established temporarily in Milan, Spain more lastingly in Naples. The extent of the papal possessions has been increased, and the papal rule therein has been made firmer and more direct. A close alliance between the Papacy and the interests of the Medici family has been established. Venice has recovered all her territory, though the sacrifices of the war and the shifting of trade-routes will prevent her from ever rising again to her former pride of place. The short-lived appearance of the Swiss among the great and independent powers of Europe is at an end. The international forces of the West have assumed the forms and the proportions that they are to retain for many years to come.

Little has been accomplished to compensate for all this outpouring of blood and treasure. The political union of the Italian nation is as far removed as ever. Misfortune has proved no cure for moral degeneration. Little patriotism worthy of the name has been called out by these cruel trials; the obstinate resistance of Pisa, the steadfastness and endurance of Venice, show local patriotism at its best, but Italian patriotism is far to seek.

Though almost every province of Italy has been devastated in its turn, though many flourishing cities have been sacked, and the wealth of all has been drained by hostile or protecting armies, literature, learning, and art do not appear at first to feel the blight. The age of the war of Cambray is also the age of Bramante, Michel Angelo, and Raffaelle. Julius II is not only the scourge of Italy, but the patron of art. The greatest or at least the most magnificent age of Venetian art is the age of her political and commercial declension. The vigorous vitality that had been fostered in half a century of comparative peace served to sustain the Renaissance movement through many years of war and waste. Peace multiplies wealth, and art is the fosterchild of wealth; but wealth is not its true parent. No statistician's curve can render visible the many causes of the rise and fall of art. The definite decline, which is perceptible after the sack of Rome, may be due in part to economic changes, and those to the influence of war, but its fundamental causes are spiritual and moral, and elude all material estimation.

As a chapter in military history the period is full of interest. The individual heroism of panoplied knights still plays its part amid the shock of disciplined armies at Novara or at Marignano. Yet in all the battles and campaigns we see the tactics and strategy of infantry working towards a higher evolution, in which Swiss and German and Spaniard each bears his part. Hand fire-arms, though constantly employed, seldom appear to influence results. On the other hand at Ravenna the skilful use of artillery determined for the first time the issue of an important battle. And the art of military engineers, especially that of mining, shows considerable advance.

War plays its part in promoting the intercourse of nations and in spreading the arts of peace. Captive Italy made her domination felt, not only in France, but also in Germany and Spain. But apart from this meagre and indirect result we look in vain for any of the higher motives or tendencies that sometimes direct the course of armies and the movement of nations. Greed, ambition, the lust of battle, the interests of dynasties, such are the forces that seem to rule the fate of Italy and Europe. Yet amidst this chaos of blind and soulless strife the scheme and equilibrium of the western world is gradually taking shape.

# CHAPTER V.

## FLORENCE (I): SAVONAROLA.

HAD Girolamo Savonarola died before the French invasion of 1494 he would scarcely have been distinguished above other missionary friars, who throughout the fifteenth century strove faithfully to revive the flagging religion of Italy. The French King and the Italian Dominican were poles asunder in character and aims, yet their fortunes were curiously linked. On Charles VIII's first success Savonarola became a personage in history, and his own fate was sealed by the Frenchman's death. The Friar's public career was very short, less than four years in all, but, apostle of peace as he was, it was a truceless war. Nor did the grave bring peace. Savonarola's ashes were cast into the running Arno, yet they seem to be burning still. Twenty years after his death the old passions which his life had fired blazed up in Florence yet more fiercely; his followers held the town against Pope and Emperor without, against Medicean and aristocrat within. Until this very day Catholics and Protestants, Dominicans and Jesuits, men of spiritual and men of secular temperament, fight over Savonarola's memory with all the old zest of the last decade of the fifteenth century.

San Bernardino and Savonarola were both missionary friars; not half a century divided them; they made their homes in neighbour towns; their objects were similar or the same; neither could claim from the other the palm of personal holiness or unselfish sacrifice. Yet how very different were their ends, how different their fate in after history! The impersonal symbol of the one, the IHS, is set in its blue and primrose disc as in a summer sundown; the stern figure of the other, grasping the crucifix, stands out in its medal against a lowering sky rent by the sword of an avenging God. Why is the preacher of madcap Siena an admitted Saint, and why does the merest hint of the canonisation of the evangelist of sober Florence convert men of peace into fiery controversialists throughout Western Europe?

Savonarola's early life was as uneventful as that of most preaching friars. His grandfather, a Paduan, was a physician of repute at the court of Ferrara; his father a nonentity even for the hagiologist; his stronger characteristics have been attributed, as is usual, to his Mantuan mother. He thus had no inheritance in the keen, rarefied air from the Tuscan mountains, which is believed to brace the intellect and add intensity to the imagination of the dwellers in the Arno valley; he was a child of the north-eastern waterlands, more sluggish in intellectual movement but swept from time to time by storms of passion. Girolamo refused to enter his grandfather's profession for which he was brought up; he secretly left home to enter the Order of St Dominic at Bologna. He preached later at Ferrara, but was no prophet in his own country, and was thence ordered to Florence to join the convent of Lombard Dominican Observantists who had been established by Cosimo de' Medici in San Marco. Successful in teaching novices, he failed as a preacher until he found his natural gift of utterance among a more simple, less critical congregation at San Gimignano. His reputation was made at Brescia, and it is noticeable that in both these cases the fire of eloquence was kindled by a spirit of prophecy; the people were spell-bound by the denunciation of wrath to come. When he returned to Florence he stood on a different plane; the Florentines always gave a warm welcome to a reputation. In the following year (1491) he was elected Prior of San Marco. As this convent was under the peculiar patronage of the ruling house of Medici, Savonarola was in a position to become a leader of Florentine opinion.

The character of the new Prior had hitherto offered more features of interest than his career. He had been an unattractive, unchildlike child, shunning his playmates, poring over books often far beyond his years. He had no love for pleasure, for which Ferrara and its rulers lived; there is a tale that he was once taken to the palace and would never again cross its threshold. His peculiar characteristic was an overpowering sense of sin, a conviction of the wickedness of the world and more especially of the Church. He must have seen the festivities which greeted Pius II on his way to open the Congress of Mantua; it may have struck the serious child that they ill accorded with the sacred object of the Congress, the Crusade against the infidel. But after all, the court of Pius II was relatively decent. At all events in the most youthful of Savonarola's writings is expressed a loathing for the Court of Rome, a belief that throughout all Italy, and above all at Rome, virtue was spent and vice triumphant. The tribute which solitude exacts from those who court her is an abnormal consciousness of self. In Girolamo's letter to his father, excusing his flight from home, he urges that he at least must save himself. In his boyish poetical tirade against the Papacy, it is he who must break the wings of the foul bird; in praying for a new passage across the Red Sea, his own soul must traverse the waves which flow between the Egypt of Sin and the Promised Land of Righteousness.

In the conventual life of the fifteenth century absolute segregation was fortunately impossible. Savonarola's latent sympathies were awakened by contact with his fellows. He had the gift of teaching younger men; he was a good master. Occasionally in his later sermons he would inveigh against the futility of human knowledge; he would cry that a little old woman who held the faith knew more than did Aristotle and Plato. Nevertheless he was convinced of the merits of education, of the power of human reasoning. Reason justified his flying from his home; reason supported his attack upon astrology; his own prophecies found their proof in reason. His farewell letter to his father had concluded with the plea that his little brother might be taught, in order not to waste his time. Hereafter he was to urge the Florentines to have their children taught the art of grammar, and that by good masters. The old-fashioned Scholastic dialectics in which the Dominicans were trained were to Savonarola a real vehicle of thought; to the last he was always thinking, putting everything to the test of his own judgment; page upon page of his sermons form one long argument. Savonarola was in fact eminently argumentative. If the coarse and tightly compressed lips betokened obstinacy and self-assertion, sympathy shone in the expressive eyes. Savonarola held his audience with his eyes as well as with his voice. The small plain-featured Lombard with the awkward gestures and the ill-trained voice was early loved in Florence by those who knew him. Impatient of indifference or opposition, his sympathy readily went out to those who welcomed him, expanding into a yearning love for Florence, his adopted city, and her people. Sympathy and self-assertion are perhaps the two keys to his character and his career.

Until Savonarola steps into the full light of history the tales told by his early biographers must be received with caution. The temptation to exaggerate and ante-date is with hagiologists and martyrologists of all ages irresistible. The atmosphere of asceticism favours imagination, and the houses of the great Religious Orders were natural forcing-beds for legends relating to their members. Such legends, serving to edification, will be welcome to all but dry historians who are more perplexed by the unconscious exaggerations of devotees than by the deliberate falsehoods of opponents. Savonarola's party in 1497 destroyed the heads of the Medicean group; after the Medicean restoration of 1512 his name was indelibly stamped on the popular cause which had been overthrown; above all, his name became a watchword during the passionate struggle of the Second Republic. What then was more natural than to represent him as, from the moment of his settlement in Florence, promoting opposition to the Medici? The stories of his attitude of independence or incivility towards Lorenzo may or may not be true. The sermon which he preached before the *Signoria* on April 6, 1491, has been regarded as an attack upon the Medici. It is rather an academic lecture upon civic justice, which might have been appropriately preached before any European magistracy. Had the Friar been the recognised opponent of the ruling house, he would not have been invited to address the

*Signoria*, the creatures of the Medici. Lorenzo, at the request, as it is said, of Pico della Mirandola, had summoned him back to Florence; without Lorenzo's favour he would scarcely have been elected Prior. Lorenzo was all-powerful both at Rome and Milan; a word from him would have relegated the preacher against tyranny to a distant Lombard convent.

For Savonarola's independence at this period there are two scraps of personal evidence. On March 10, 1491, he wrote to his friend Frà Domenico that magnates of the city threatened him with the fate of San Bernardino of Feltre, who had been expelled. He added, however, that Pico della Mirandola was a constant attendant at his sermons and had subsidised the convent; now Pico was one of Lorenzo's most intimate friends. In his last sermon on March 18, 1498, Savonarola stated that Lorenzo sent five leading citizens to dissuade him, as of their own accord, from his prophetic utterances; he replied that he knew from whom they came: let them warn Lorenzo to repent of his sins, for God would punish him and his: he, the alien Friar, would stay, while Lorenzo, the citizen and first of citizens, would have to go. For this tale there are several good authorities, though the sermon may be their common source: Guicciardini, the best of them, omits the Friar's reply. It is certain that Lorenzo took no further measures; the chronicler Cerretani expressly affirms that, while Lorenzo lived, Savonarola was entirely quiet.

It is well known that Lorenzo summoned the Dominican to his death-bed at Careggi. This has been represented by modern writers as though it had been a strange and sudden thought, the result of an agony of repentance. But no act could have been more natural. Savonarola was now without question the greatest preacher in the city; he was Prior of Lorenzo's own convent, in the garden of which he often walked; the rival divine Frà Mariano da Genazzano was not in Florence. Lorenzo with all his faults was no lost soul; he had a singularly sympathetic nature; he was keenly alive to religious as to all other influences. Whom should he better call from Florence to Careggi than the Friar whom he had brought back from Lombardy? The details of the death-bed scene as related by the Dominican biographers are difficult to accept; they rest on third-hand authority, contain inherent improbabilities, and are contradicted by contemporary evidence both direct and indirect. Neither in Savonarola's writings, nor in the letters of Lorenzo, Politian, or Ficino, nor in the despatches of ambassadors, is there any statement as to the Dominican's alleged hostility to the powers that be. Among his devotees were numbered Lorenzo's two chief confidants, Pico and Pandolfini, his friend and teacher, Marsilio Ficino, the favourite painter Botticelli, and the youthful Michel Angelo, who had lived in the Medici palace almost as a son. Giovanni da Prato Vecchio, the financial adviser who did much to make the Medicean administration unpopular with the masses, was Savonarola's personal friend.

Later writers, living under the terrorism of a restoration, neglected distinctions between the stages of Medicean rule; but contemporaries drew a strong line between the veiled and amiable despotism of Lorenzo and the overt tyranny of his son. The young Piero, they said, was no Medici, no Florentine. Born as he was of an Orsini mother, and wedded to an Orsini wife, his manners were Orsini manners, his bearing was that of an insolent Campagna lordling. With some of the purely intellectual gifts of his father's house, he inherited none of its capacity for rule, none of the sympathy which attracted the men of culture and the men of toil, none of the political courage which could avert or brave a crisis. Savonarola's future foe was a brutal athlete who had angered his father by his youthful brawls,—who, in Guicciardini's phrase, had found himself at the death of a man or two by night. He and his disreputable train would all day long play ball in the streets of Florence, neglecting the business of the State, disturbing the business of the city. The weakness of the Medicean system stood confessed. An accepted monarchy may survive a weak and wicked ruler, but the Medici had no constitutional position, and were unprovided with props to a tottering throne, or with barriers to keep the crowd away. Their power rested only upon personal influence, upon the interests of a syndicate of families, on the material welfare of the middle classes, and the amusement of the lower. Even without the catastrophe of the French invasion Piero's government must have come crashing down.

From the outset of Medicean rule there had been a seesaw between monarchy and oligarchy. The ring of governmental families had admitted, not without some rubs, the superiority of Lorenzo; they showered upon Piero his father's honours, but were not prepared to concede his power. The ruling party began to split; the bureaucratic section, the secretaries, the financial officials, necessarily stood by the ostensible government, and, owing to the traditional maladministration of police and finance, determined popular feeling in its disfavour. The leading Medicean families, the younger branch of the House, and the Rucellai and Soderini connected with it by marriage, began to shadow forth an opposition.

It might seem as if Savonarola must now have chosen his side, but of this there is little sign. Cerretani relates that the heads of the opposition, fully conscious of his power over the people, tried to win him but completely failed. Savonarola himself has absolutely stated that he took no part in politics until after Piero's fall. In his sermons there is a passage against princes, but it was a cap that would fit royal heads of all shapes and sizes, and was intended, if for any in particular, for those of the rulers of Naples and Milan.

In 1492 and 1493 Savonarola was much away in Lombardy. It has been assumed that he was removed from Florence by Piero's influence but of this there is no evidence. Savonarola's journeys were in full accordance with the usual practice of his Order. On his return Piero energetically aided his endeavour to separate the Tuscan Dominican convent of stricter observance from the Lombard Congregation to which they had previously been united. The effect of this separation would be to confine Savonarola's activity to Tuscany, and thus to give him permanent influence at Florence. Savonarola's chief, if not his only desire, was to restore the convents, over which he already exercised a personal influence, to the poorer and simpler life of the Order as founded by St Dominic; it is a libel to suggest that he had ulterior political motives. The separation of San Marco, which had been definitely refounded within the century as a member of the Lombard Congregation, was a strong measure which cast reflection on the discipline of the parent body. The governments of Milan and Venice resisted the separation, which Piero warmly advocated. Savonarola became for the moment a figure of diplomatic importance. Alexander VI declared himself against the separation; but the story goes that when the Consistory had separated, the Cardinal of Naples playfully drew the signet ring from the Pope's finger and sealed the brief which he held in readiness. Piero's action makes it impossible to believe that Savonarola had assumed the *rôle* of a leader of political opposition. The only existing letter from the Friar to Piero expresses warm gratitude for his aid. Nevertheless the perpetual prophecies of impending trouble did undoubtedly contribute to political unrest, and Nerli ascribes Piero's fall in some measure to his placing no check upon the Friar's extravagant utterances.

At the moment of the French invasion (September, 1494) Savonarola was no politician, but a hard-working Provincial, throwing his heart into the reform of his new Congregation. This was no easy task, for he was thwarted by the particularist traditions of the larger Tuscan towns, where the Dominican convents resented subordination to that of the hated rival or mistress, Florence; they would more willingly have obeyed a distant Lombard Provincial. At Siena, Savonarola's failure was complete; the Convent of St Catharine's at Pisa was only united after the expulsion of the majority of the Friars. The new Congregation contained only some 250 members, whereas at the recent chapter at San Miniato more than a thousand Franciscans had been gathered.

Meanwhile all Florence was entranced by the eloquence of the Ferrarese Friar. What was the secret of his fascination? It consisted partly in the contagious force of terror. Italy had long been conscious of her military weakness, of her want of national unity. For fifty years her statesmen had nervously played with or warded off invasion; but, as the century closed, her generals were provoking the catastrophe. Disaster was in the air, and this atmospheric condition at once created the peculiar quality of Savonarola's eloquence, and the susceptibility of his audience. His confident forebodings gave definite expression to the terror which was in every heart, terror of storm and sack, of fierce foreign troopers who knew not the make-believe campaigns of Italy,

of antiquated fortresses crumbling before the modern French artillery.
The audacious attack upon the ecclesiastical hierarchy also fell upon
willing ears. Abuse of the clergy has always been popular, even when
ill-deserved; but with much reason Italy was ashamed of her priesthood
and her Pope. The moral standard of the clergy was absolutely, and
not relatively, lower than that of the laity. In every town, therefore,
Savonarola's invectives might find a hearing; but at Florence the seed
fell upon ground peculiarly well-prepared. Florentine wickedness has
often been painted in sombre colours to render her prophet's portrait
more effective. Nothing can be more unjust, more contradictory of
Savonarola's own utterances. His permanent success was due to the
moral superiority of Florence over other Italian capitals. For him,
she was the navel and the watch-tower of Italy, the sun from which
reform should radiate, the chosen city, the new Jerusalem. Florence
was a sober God-fearing State after a somewhat comfortable, material
fashion. There was much simplicity of life, a simplicity observed by
travellers down to the eighteenth century. Private letters and diaries,
which frankly relate such scandals as occur, testify to this. Her art and
literature at this period compare not unfavourably with those of modern
days. Accusations, when pressed home, usually reduce themselves to the
lewd carnival songs; but the *fêtes* of the city were altogether exceptional as a gross survival of medieval or pagan license. Florentines,
who were neither prudes nor prigs, looked with horror on the corruption
of the papal Court. Lorenzo de' Medici could warn his young Cardinal
son against this sink of iniquity. The youthful Guicciardini spoke
of the simony at Rome with all the disgust of a later Lutheran,
and incidentally mentions the character of Cardinal Soderini as being
"respectable for a priest." His father would not stain his conscience
by making any one of his five sons a priest, notwithstanding the rich
benefices which awaited them. The Florentines had recently been
shocked at their Milanese visitors, who ate meat in Lent. The rulers
of Florence had been religious men. San Marco had long set the
standard of religion, and the Medici were deeply interested in its
future. Both Cosimo and Piero were men of piety, notwithstanding
political *finesse*, and occasional moral lapses. Lorenzo's mother was
noted for her piety; her spiritual songs are among the city's heir-
looms. Lorenzo, whatever his backslidings, had the potentiality of a
religious nature. Paganism unabashed found scant favour at Florence.
Platonism became a serious religion, shaking off the slough of mate-
rialism, and searching for union with Christianity. The whole city
had worshipped Sant' Antonino; all upper-class Florence had lately
been moved by the eloquence of Frà Mariano da Genazzano, an
eloquence, indeed, of the polished, artificial type, enhanced by cadence
and gesture, garnished with classical allusion and quotation. Yet this
was the fashion of the day, and in matters intellectual Florence was

at fashion's height. The vices of Florence were those of a rich, commercial city, extravagance in clothes and furniture, in funerals and weddings. Young *bourgeois* might think the brothel and the tavern the ante-chambers of gentility. Men of all classes gambled and swore. Dowries were high, and it was becoming difficult to marry. Yet in Florentine society there was a healthy consciousness that all this was wrong, and a predisposition in favour of any preacher who would say so.

Savonarola's sympathetic nature, when once he had learned his method and his manner, touched this chord. The very novelty of his style was a merit with the Athens of the fifteenth century. The Florentines had forgotten the careful simplicity of San Bernardino of Siena, his fund of anecdote and his playful humour. Preaching was either too classical or too grotesque. Frà Mariano represented the former school, and there are hints that Savonarola's other rival, Frà Domenico da Ponzo, the Franciscan, was an exponent of the latter. The new preacher struck a middle note, captivating Florence by his directness, his naturalness, his fire. He abandoned the artificial division of the sermon into parts, a survival of the Roman art of rhetoric; his sermons are, indeed, lacking in composition; mystical flights often soar far beyond the subject of discussion. There are contradictions in his method, which receive curious illustration from two facts of his early life. Letters exist from the learned Garzoni of Bologna, which rally the youth on his revolt from the rules of Priscian, while his first teacher at Florence lectured him on his excessive subtlety in argument, and forced him to the simplicity which at the outset he exaggerated to a childlike "yea" and "nay." Such contradictions are explained by the preacher's impressionable nature; and this, combined with his power of expression, produced a contagious effect upon his audience. A thorough Dominican in his intellectual dialectic training and in the exposition of definite doctrine in his tracts, his sermons have much of the Franciscan style. The spirit of prophecy linked him closely to the Fraticelli of Monte Amiata, the believers in Abbot Joachim, and through them to the half-religious, half-political extravagances of Rienzi in the second stage of his development. As we look forwards, it seems rather the apocalyptic preachers of early Anabaptism that have a right to claim him as a precursor, than the Lutheran divines. His enemies actually accused him of holding the Fraticelli doctrine of Spiritual Poverty. This he directly denied, but he approached perilously near Wyclif's theory of the Dominion of Grace, which was in popular estimation nearly akin to it. So again, though a trained Aristotelian and Thomist, he was in feeling a Platonist; he employed his Aristotelian method in the exposition of the relation between the upper and the lower worlds. This mystical quality won him the early favour of the Neo-Platonists, Pico, Marsilio Ficino, and others of Lorenzo's circle. On the other hand he could employ the devices by which popular preachers fixed the attention of their congregation.   His flights of eloquence were varied by homely dialogues with God or angels, with imaginary enemies or timid friends.   Above all he knew his Bible by heart, and next only to this Aquinas.   From the Bible he always took his start, and to it he ever led his hearers back.   This it is which gives the peculiar tone to the religion of the *Piagnoni*, which carries the reader from the benches of San Marco to the Galloway hillside.

The residuum of old-fashioned simplicity in Florence favoured his desire to simplify not only private, but religious life.   The fifteenth century was everywhere marked by magnificence in ecclesiastical externals, in vestments and jewels, in banner, pyx and crucifix, in chapels built or restored by private families, with portraits frescoed and arms embossed upon their walls.   Church music had been elaborated; the organist had become a personage, and might aspire to be a knight; weary men repaired to the Cathedral, not to worship, but to be soothed by the music of Orcagna, the greatest executant of his day.   Against these jewels and broad phylacteries, against the monuments of family pride, against the substitution of sound for praise, Savonarola repeatedly inveighed.   One of his few humorous passages describes the solo-singer with a voice like a calf, while the choir howled round him like little dogs, none understanding what they meant.   His readers can still picture the abuses of society at church, the rows of gallants lining the nave, the ladies in their lowest and longest gowns filing between them, lending ear to unseemly jests and doubtful compliments.   Savonarola would have none of this; in church or in street processions he kept the sexes separate.

After Lorenzo's death Savonarola's sermons became more outspoken.   They were not as yet political, but two constant features might easily assume a political complexion—the one the invectives against the Church, the other the prophecy of immediate doom.   The two were in close connexion.   Not only the Neapolitan exiles but Alexander VI's enemy, the Cardinal della Rovere, had taken refuge in France; the French invasion therefore was aimed not only at the King of Naples, but also at the Pope, whose simoniacal election and scandalous life added fuel to the fire of Savonarola's diatribe.   For Charles VIII Naples should be the stepping-stone to the recovery of Jerusalem.   So too Savonarola had fondly dreamed that the reform of the Tuscan Congregation should be the pathway to the possession of the Holy Sepulchre.   The objects of the French invader and the Dominican reformer seemed identical, their enemies the same.

Within Florence, too, the threatened invasion might well give a political bearing to Savonarola's utterances.   Piero, deserting the traditions of his house, had abandoned the Milanese alliance, the keystone of its policy; he had flouted the friendship of France, the Guelfic ally of centuries; under Orsini influence he had flung himself into the arms of the King of Naples.   The great Medicean families resented this light-of-love diplomacy, and clung to the Milanese alliance.   The populace hated the Neapolitan dynasty, after having endured its cruelty as an enemy, and its insolence as a friend.   The whole town disliked and feared the armed opposition to the formidable hosts of France.   What then was more natural than that Florence should turn to Savonarola for his guidance ? Here was the very terror from the north which he had predicted; the sword that should strike the earth, and that quickly; the chastisement that should purge Italy of sin and then renew the world !   Who could so well conjure the phantom as he by whom it had been raised ?

The French had now crossed the Apennines and were besieging the strong Florentine fortress of Sarzana.   Before Piero set out on his fateful journey to the French King, discontent found expression in the very Seventy, the stronghold of Medicean power.   Diplomacy had been the palladium of the Medici.   Lorenzo knew this, when he made his perilous voyage to cajole the King of Naples.   Piero knew it when, in conscious imitation, he slipped away to meet the King of France before Sarzana.   He wrote himself, that he was being dragged to sacrifice. Lorenzo's success had saved the dynasty, and Piero's failure lost it.   A crushing defeat could have sacrificed no more.   With the fortresses of Sarzana, Pietra Santa, Pisa and Leghorn in French hands, Florence herself lay at the mercy of Charles.   High and low scorned this base surrender by one who had no commission from the State.   Piero's cowardice gave courage to his opponents.   Hitherto they had stammered and stuttered in criticising his proposals.   Now, in his absence, they sent envoys to the French camp.   On the morning after his return the very magistrates, picked from the adherents of the house, shut the wicket of the *Palazzo Pubblico* in his face.   As he rode sullenly homewards, the crowd shook their caps at him; the boys pelted the uncrowned King with stones and insulted him with cat-calls.   His adherents of the lower class soon melted from his side.   From the Palace windows issued cries of 'People and Liberty'; from the *piazza* were brandished nondescript weapons, long hung up to rust.   Paolo Orsini, Piero's cousin, was at the gates with 500 horse, but he perceived that the game was up, and Piero fled; the dynasty of four generations had fallen without stroke of sword. Piero's young brother, the Cardinal Giovanni, alone showed courage. He rode towards the Palace, but the crowd pushed him back.   Landucci saw him at his window on his knees, with his hands clasped in prayer. " I was much moved and judged that he was a good young man and of good understanding."   A little later, and the future Leo X likewise fled, disguised as a Franciscan friar.   Florence had let slip the really dangerous member of his house, for whom aristocrats and rabble, saints and sinners, *Piagnoni* and *Arrabbiati*, were to prove no match.

Piero had in the first instance been resisted not by the democracy but by the aristocracy, by malcontent members of the Medicean ring.   Young

Jacopo Nerli had closed the Palace door in Piero's face; yet Jacopo's brothers had dedicated the *editio princeps* of Homer, printed at their expense, to Piero as a boy. A few of the loyal Mediceans fled; the others, with the veteran statesman Bernardo del Nero, bowed to the storm. To the conquerors the spoils! The aristocrats intended to replace the rule of a single house by an oligarchy of a group of houses. But the people were excited; they sacked the Medici palace, ably assisted by French officers already in the town, on the improbable pretext that the Medici bank owed them money. The mob then burnt and plundered the houses of Piero's financial agents, but were drawn away to the *piazza*, where all ranks were shouting People and Liberty. Lungs pay no bills, and thus coinage and taxation are apt to be the first victims of revolution. The aristocrats felt obliged to make popular concessions. Francesco Gualterotti, an ardent Savonarolist to the end, sprang on the *ringhiera*, the platform projecting from the Palace, and on the *Signoria's* authority declared the white farthings withdrawn from circulation. These white farthings, the Wood's halfpence of the Medicean dynasty, had been issued to replace a medley of base and foreign coins of varying value. But the State made its profit, for all duties had to be paid in the new coinage, which stood to the black farthings in the relation of 5 to 4. Nevertheless the mob was still idle and therefore dangerous; shops and factories were closed; the artisans restlessly roamed the streets; the French officers were chalking the doors for quarters; unmarried girls were being hurried off to distant convents or country cousins. Prophecy seemed nearing its fulfilment. Why should men work, when either the Millennium or the Cataclysm was upon them!

Savonarola was not in Florence when Piero was expelled. He was chosen on November 5 as one of the envoys who were sent to the French King at Pisa. This was his entrance into history. It may seem surprising that he should have been elected. Yet a better choice could scarcely have been made. Piero Capponi, one of the leading aristocrats, had proposed him because the people loved him, and would have confidence in his embassy. No envoy could be more acceptable to Charles VIII, whose easy victories he had foretold, whom he had set on high as the chosen instrument of God. Errands of peace had long been among the express functions of the Friars. For two centuries past they had reconciled house and house and town and town during the cruel conflicts by which Italy had been rent. It seemed natural enough that the Dominican should accompany the heads of the aristocracy in their mission for persuading Charles to respect the liberties of Florence, and to abandon his intention of restoring Piero. Savonarola now or later won the respect of the French King, but his eloquence could not shake the resolution to make no terms except in the great city.

Before Charles VIII moved up the Arno, two great events had befallen Florence. The Medici had been expelled, and Pisa was in full revolt. The lives of the Florentine envoys and officials were in no small danger. When Charles VIII at length entered Florence, Savonarola seems to have taken no part in the negotiations; the hero of the week was not the Friar, but the merchant, statesman and soldier, Piero Capponi, who tore the draft of the shameful treaty in two before the French King's face, crying, "Blow your trumpets and we will clang our bells." Yet the ultimate conditions were sufficiently humiliating, for all the Florentine coast fortresses were left in French hands, and the city was pledged to a huge subsidy. She had, however, at least escaped the restoration of the Medici, although she was forced to withdraw the price upon their heads. The main desire was to rid Florence of her dangerous guests. The treaty was signed on November 28; but on the 29th Charles showed no signs of stirring. Then it was that Savonarola went to warn him that it was God's will that he should leave. More efficacious, perhaps, were the arguments of the Scotch general Stuart d'Aubigni, who had led a French corps from the Romagna into the Arno valley. He very bluntly told the King that he was wasting time, and that he must push on to Naples. Thus on November 30 the French marched out, to their hosts' infinite relief.

The next task was the reform of the constitution. The Palace bell summoned a *Parlamento,* a mass meeting of the people, to the great *piazza,* and the *Signoria* from its platform proposed a *Balìa,* or provisional government. The Medicean institutions, the Councils of the Hundred and of the Seventy, and the *Otto di Pratica,* a standing Committee for State affairs, which had already been suspended, were now abolished, while the members of the *Otto di Balìa,* the Ministry of Justice, were deposed. A board of Twenty was nominated to select the *Signoria* for one whole year; under the title of the Ten of War a commission was to be appointed for the subjection of Pisa. Within the year a register was to be drawn up of all citizens qualified for office, and at its expiration the popular traditional practice of appointing to all magistracies by lot should be resumed. This provisional government was virtually the substitution of oligarchy for monarchy; a group of aristocrats now held the power which Lorenzo de' Medici had striven to secure. Nevertheless the proposal was passed by acclamation in the *Parlamento,* and confirmed by the two older Councils of the People and the Commune.

It was impossible that such a piece of patchwork should stand the wear and tear of a restless people. The Councils of the Hundred, and of the Seventy, and the *Otto di Pratica* had been successively introduced, not merely for family or party purposes, but to strengthen administrative efficiency. The old municipal constitution was unequal to the needs of an expanding territory and of complicated international relations. This had been the justification for the rule of a family, or of groups of families who had no official place in the Constitution, of the Parte Guelfa, the Albizzi, the Medici. All the really operative elements in the State, whether official or non-official, were now removed; the normal constitution would be worked by twenty individuals with no coherence, and not much experience, divided by family and personal rivalries. Oligarchies, wrote Aristotle, fall from internal divisions, and almost invariably one section will appeal to the people for support against its fellows. It was certain from the first that this would happen at Florence, where in spite of monarchy or oligarchy there was a democratic atmosphere, and where, in the absence of soldiers or efficient police, public opinion could at any crisis find expression. Even before Piero's fall some of the aristocracy had paid their addresses to the people. And now the populace was in a dangerous state; unsatisfied with fire and plunder, it pleaded for blood; none had been let in Florence since the short fever of the Pazzi plot. The oligarchs sacrificed one of the Medicean government officials, Antonio di Bernardo, who was hanged from a window above the great *piazza*. His hands were clean, but his origin low, his manners rough, and his office—that of the public debt—the most unpopular in Florence. Others were condemned to imprisonment for life. To flatter the ingrained love of equality, the Twenty nominated insignificant persons to the chief magistracy, the Gonfalonierate of Justice. So again, men of no repute were sent on important embassies; Ludovico il Moro gibed at the diplomatic methods of the new republic. But all this was not enough; the oligarchs must satisfy not only the populace but each other, which was indeed impossible. One of the cleverest, the most experienced, the most ambitious aristocrats, Paol' Antonio Soderini, had been excluded from the Twenty, probably by the influence of his rival Piero Capponi. On the death of Lorenzo de' Medici he had tentatively resisted the advance of the monarchy, but when young Piero showed his teeth he shrank from the encounter. He now intrigued for the fall of the Twenty; and it was no difficult task to make the provisional government impossible. Soderini had just returned from an embassy to Venice; it was natural that he should sing the praises of her constitution. The cry caught up in the street was echoed from the pulpit. Soderini, it is said, first persuaded Savonarola to advocate a popular government on the Venetian model. It need not be assumed that Soderini was a hypocrite. He was virtuous and serious; but virtue and sobriety cast fantastic shadows which assume the forms of ambition and intrigue.

During and after the French occupation Savonarola had been untiring in preaching for the poor, especially for those who were ashamed to confess their poverty. He implored the idling artisans to return to work. Unity, peace, and mercy were his perpetual theme. The people, however, threatened to extend their vengeance from the financial officials to all adherents of the Medici. The more moderate aristocrats became alarmed; already exiles were returning, the victims of themselves or of their fathers; and titles to property confiscated in the past were endangered. The exiles might well bid for popular support. It was felt that the new oligarchy, the Whites, must stand by the Greys (*Bigi*), the families who still had Medicean proclivities. But these oligarchs could not stay the flood of popular hatred; if they stemmed it, they would be swept away in their turn. Their leader, Piero Capponi, turned for aid to Savonarola, and the Friar succeeded where others must have failed. Of all his claims to the gratitude of his adopted city this is the strongest.

Savonarola now fairly entered into politics. He had striven as a Ferrarese, he declared, to have nothing to do with the Florentine State; but God had warned him that he must not shrink, for his mission was the creation of the spiritual life, and this must have a solid material edifice wherein to dwell. To his political sermons he summoned the magistrates, admitting none but men. He sketched not only the form of the new constitution but the main lines of legislation, ethical and economic. Monarchy, he admitted, might be the ideal government, but it was unsuited for people of temperate climates, who had at once too much blood and too much cleverness to bear a king,—unsuited above all to high-spirited and subtle Florentines, for whom the Venetian popular government was the natural type. He suggested that the citizens should gather under their sixteen companies (*gonfaloni*), that each company should draft a scheme, that of these the sixteen gonfaloniers should select four, and from them the *Signoria* should choose the best: this, he assured his congregation, would be after the Venetian model.

In official circles there was resistance, but popular opinion was overwhelming. The aristocrats had overthrown the Medici, but the people claimed the spoils. After long debate the several magistracies, the Sixteen gonfaloniers, the Twelve *buonuomini*, the Twenty, the Eight, and the Ten of War each presented constitutions, and of these that of the Ten, to which Soderini belonged, was chosen. The old Councils of People and Commune were replaced by a Grand Council, which became the sovereign authority of the State. Membership was confined to those who had at any time been drawn for the three chief offices, the *Signoria*, the Twelve, and the Sixteen, or whose ancestors within three generations had been so drawn: the age limit was twenty-nine, and no one could be a councillor who had not paid his taxes. A small number of citizens, otherwise qualified, above the age of twenty-four was admitted, and in each year twenty-eight additional members, unqualified by office, might be elected; few of these, however, obtained the requisite majority of two-thirds of the votes. The chief function of the Council was electoral. Electors drawn by lot nominated candidates for the more important offices, and of those who secured an absolute majority of votes he who polled the highest number was elected. For the minor offices members of the Council were drawn by lot. The Council chose a Senate of eighty members, who sat for six months but were re-eligible; their duty was to

advise the *Signoria* and to appoint ambassadors and commissioners with
the army. The executive remained unchanged; at the head was the
*Signoria*, the Gonfalonier of Justice and the eight Priors, holding office
for two months. Its consultations were aided by the College, the Twelve
and the Sixteen; the Ten of War and the Eight of *Balìa* continued to
exist. Every legislative proposal, every money-bill, every question of
peace and war, was initiated in the *Signoria*, passed through the College
to the Senate and received completion in the Council. This was expected
to number about 3000 members, and, until a large hall in the Palace
could be built, it was divided into three sections which sat in turn.

This was a bold constitutional experiment, the boldest that had yet
been tried at Florence. It was not exactly the transplantation of an
exotic constitution which had matured under different conditions of soil
and climate, but rather an attempt to hybridise the Florentine executive
with the Venetian elective system. To all Italian statesmen it seemed
clear that Venice possessed the ideal constitution, but the essence of this
perfection was not so obvious. The academic explanation was that it
was mixed, combining the merits of monarchy, aristocracy and democracy.
Consequently Venice could serve as a model to artists of very different
schools. Lorenzo de' Medici, convinced of the weakness of the Florentine
system for diplomacy and war, had, in creating the Seventy and the
Committee of Eight, looked to the Senate and the Ten, which were
essentially the motive powers of the Venetian constitution. His last
political act, the creation of a *balìa* of Seventeen, was probably another
adaptation of the Venetian Ten, applied to the purposes most essential
to Medicean power, elections and finance; it is at least a curious coinci-
dence that the so-called Ten consisted really of seventeen members. His
intention is believed to have been that he should be elected life-Gonfalonier, or Doge; this would have legalised his irregular position, and
given him permanent influence in every department. Lorenzo, however,
while making a selection from both the aristocratic and monarchical
elements of his model, left out of sight its broad popular basis. At
Venice, the Grand Council was eminently the elective body, and the
electors could tolerate the supremacy of their representatives. Lorenzo
had entrusted elective functions above all to oligarchical councils and
committees.

The cry of the Florentines now was, People and Liberty. Overlooking therefore the administrative excellence of Venice, they gave
exclusive attention to the Grand Council, which had been, indeed, rather
the declining partner in the Venetian Constitution. They believed, not
unnaturally, that by directly interesting a large number of citizens in the
constitution they would shake off once for all the extra-legal influences,
which had for so long dominated the elections and through them the
administration; thus would cease the curious dualism between the real
and the apparent government, the cause of some oppression and much

heart-burning. There was, however, this great difference, that at Florence every legislative question and every important question of policy ultimately came before the Council, whereas at Venice almost all received their decision in the Senate. Thus while at Venice, if the Ten be momentarily set aside, the Senate was the determining body, at Florence it exercised little weight in the fortunes of the coming years, and was, indeed, overshadowed by the influence of the *Pratica*, an excrescence on the constitution, of which more anon. It is clear from this alone that in diplomacy and war, when speed, secrecy, and trained experience were required, Florence would be at a disadvantage. At Venice, again, the executive was more highly developed, there was greater differentiation. Each, for instance, of the *Savi da terra firma* had his own department, while the functions of the board differed from those of the *Savi da mar*. At Florence the *Signoria* with its consultative associates, the Twelve and the Sixteen, had undergone no process of evolution. Even between the *Signoria* and the two chief executive committees, the Ten and the Eight, there was no clear demarcation; conflicts of authority might and did arise. Moreover, Florence had no trained pilot; very ordinary seamen took their place on the bridge almost in turn. The Venetian Doge is traditionally called a figure-head, but this metaphor gives a false impression of his relation to the ship of State. He was, it is true, hemmed in by every precaution against absolutism, but he was usually elected as a citizen of high position and long experience. Chosen for life, he sat among officials most of whom were elected for short terms; he was in the closest touch with every branch of the administration; nor did his fortunes depend on the popularity of his opinions. His influence might not be obvious but it was all-pervading; every great movement in Venetian policy will be found to associate itself with the personality of a Doge. How different was the position of a Florentine Gonfalonier of Justice elected for two months, and welcomed by the citizens in proportion to his insignificance! Finally, at Florence there was no attempt as yet to emulate the Venetian judicial system with its three courts of forty citizens, and its admirable supervision of local justice by itinerary commissions from the capital. It was this organisation, partly representative and popular, partly expert, which made Venetian justice acceptable to the mainland cities and respected at home. Florence was left with her old faulty system, at once weak, cruel and partial, inspiring neither affection nor respect. The controlling dynastic power was now withdrawn which had at least striven to give some efficiency and regularity to justice. This was certain to become the sport of the political passions of the moment.

In spite of these defects the new constitution was popular, for it gave a constant interest in government to a larger number than had previously been the case. In this sense it may be termed democratic; it is frequently called the Florentine democracy even by those who stigmatise its Venetian model as a narrow oligarchy. This is so far correct, that the more democratic features of the model had been adopted, while the Florentine executive retained the democratic principle of rapid rotation, of ruling and being ruled in turn. The term nobility as applied to the ruling class at Venice created some little difficulty; it was explained that this was a misnomer,—that it implied only an official distinction, involving no personal rights over other men. Soderini indeed declared that as many possessed citizenship at Venice as were fit to enjoy it at Florence. The origin of the two systems was more alike than the Florentines probably knew. At the date of the "Closing of the Grand Council" at Venice (1296) a reform of the constitution had become imperative; and then, as at Florence in 1494, the alternative lay between an oligarchy and a more popular form, between a group of families and a considerable section of the citizens. In both cases it was decided in favour of the latter; in both, the new citizenship had an official basis, for at Venice membership of the old Council during several generations corresponded to the Florentine qualification of past office in the three greater magistracies. In both, all classes which had not previously enjoyed power were, subject to insignificant exceptions, permanently excluded. There was however this important difference, that in Florence the noble houses had, since the Ordinances of Justice, been disfranchised. The Medici had done much to break down this antiquated distinction, but many families still remained almost outside the State, some of them enjoying great social, and indirectly no little political influence. Hitherto there had been possibilities of recovering qualification through membership of the Arts; this avenue was now closed. Hitherto they could at all events belong to the Council of the Commune: this Council was now abolished. Thus, a wealthy and influential class was placed in inevitable opposition towards the new government.

If the highest class lost by the constitutional change, the lower classes did not gain. There was no extension of the franchise in the modern sense; no new class obtained a share in government. Citizenship still depended on membership of the *Arti* (the Greater or the Less); in each magistracy the former were represented in the proportion of three to one. Even in the Council, a little consideration will show that the same proportion must have been approximately maintained, unless it be urged that three generations of a poorer class will produce more children than three of a richer. Government was left, as before, in the hands of the upper middle classes, with a preponderance in favour of the uppermost.

The name of Savonarola has been indissolubly connected with this constitution. He did not probably first propose it, nor had he, as far as is known, any share in drafting its actual provisions. But unquestionably he created an overpowering public feeling in its favour. Henceforth he regarded the Grand Council as his offspring, whose life it was his most solemn duty to safeguard. His influence too induced the Twenty to resign before their term of office had expired, and from June 10, 1495, the Council assumed full sovereign authority. Even before this date his sermons had directly affected legislation. The first Act carried by the Council was an amnesty for the past; this was followed by a measure granting an appeal to the Council to any citizen qualified for office, who, for a political offence, had been sentenced by a vote of two-thirds of the *Signoria* or the Eight. This question of "appeal from the Six Beans" was the first which seriously agitated the new republic, and ultimately gravely affected Savonarola and his party. The *Signoria* and the Eight possessed by law an unlimited power of punishment. This they were usually too timid to exercise on their own responsibility, but they might easily be made the tools of a dominant faction for party purposes. Political opponents might be proscribed under legal forms without the chances afforded by delay or by an appeal to popular feeling. Hence this appeal to the Council was proposed and was warmly debated in that peculiar Florentine institution termed a *Pratica*.

The *Pratica* was no formal element in the constitution new or old, and yet so strong were its traditions that, when in later years the Gonfalonier Piero Soderini preferred to consult the regular magistracies, the innovation was almost regarded as unconstitutional. The upper magistracies and committees sometimes composed the *Pratica*, but on important occasions the executive added a considerable number of leading citizens and legal luminaries. The timid executive thus widened the area of responsibility, and obtained a preliminary test of the drift of public opinion. A *Pratica* was the only assembly in which questions were freely debated; hence it somewhat threw into the shade not only the Eighty, but the Council itself. In Savonarola's career, on the three most critical occasions, the interest centres in the debates of the *Pratica*.

The final vote in favour of appeal was large both in the Eighty and the Council, but during the discussion the result had seemed very doubtful. The aristocrats, who had hitherto manipulated the *Signoria*, could show that such a measure would still further weaken the already feeble executive. A section of them had, however, become aware that henceforth the executive would be wielded by the people, and that, after the Medicean leaders, the prominent oligarchs might be the victims of a sudden sentence: delay would be in favour of men of position, who in the Council would not be without adherents. On the other hand those who were irreconcilable with the Medici urged that the executive was the sword of the people, and that to blunt its edge was to weaken the people's power. Savonarola had previously proposed an appeal, not to the Council, but to a smaller body. He seems however to have attributed no importance to the distinction, and preached earnestly in favour of the government proposal. Against the Dominican his opponents set up the eloquent Franciscan Frà Domenico da Ponzo, and the populace flocked from San Marco to Santa Croce and back again, to be taught its politics from the pulpit. The triumph of the government was complete, and the law was carried; time only could show whether, amid party passions, it would be observed. Savonarola's share in this law has recently been denied; but contemporary friends and enemies ascribed to him its initiation and success. His panegyrists have no need to be ashamed of a measure which rightly gave the power of pardon to the sovereign authority. In a democracy, wrote Aristotle, the people should have the power of pardoning, but not of condemning. Savonarola's reputation was afterwards injured, not by the law of appeal, but by the failure of his party to observe it.

In a kindred proposal to pare the claws of the executive, Savonarola had a yet more direct share. From the pulpit of San Marco was uttered the death-warrant of the primeval Florentine assembly, the *Parlamento.* This was a curious survival of the old municipal life of a comparatively small city, in which the people at large was the ultimate resort on any change of government. Under altered conditions it was doubtless an abuse. Each dominant party could induce the *Signoria*, which was its nominee, to summon a Parliament, and there propose measures of greater or less importance, with the purpose of prolonging or enhancing its own authority. By this simple expedient the constitution was more than once suspended. Savonarola saw that a single *Signoria* with an aristocratic or Medicean majority might, through such a *plébiscite*, overthrow in an hour the fabric of the new republic. On no political subject was his language more intemperate. There was now, he cried, no need of Parliaments: the sovereignty of the people was vested in the Council, which could make every law that the people could desire: Parliament was the robbery of the people's power. He warned his congregation, if ever the bell of the *Palazzo* rang for Parliament, to hack to pieces every Prior that stepped upon the platform: the Gonfaloniers of the companies must swear that on the first stroke of the bell, they would sack the Priors' houses, and of each house sacked, the Gonfalonier and his company should divide the spoils. Within sixteen days of Savonarola's sermon this ferocious proposal, though modified in its penal details, became law. Thus the middle classes deprived the lower of even the semblance of a share in government. The Parliament which abolished the Medici *régime* had shouted away its own existence. Hitherto every insignificant *balìa* had required the assent of this popular assembly; but the sweeping change which established the new republic had never received its sanction. The time might come when even this faint echo of the people's voice might be regretted.

In these two deliberate attempts to weaken the executive, Savonarola was probably less influenced by theoretic democratic considerations, than by feverish anxiety to fend off the immediate danger, a recrudescence of

party strife and proscription executed under legal forms. But his dislike
of the rabble as a political power was genuine. He had all an Italian's
respect for family; he dwelt with complacency on the fact that many of
his novices were scions of the best Florentine houses. He knew, or soon
learned to know, the defects of a weak executive. During his trial
he confessed his wish to imitate yet further the Venetian constitution,
by the appointment of a Doge, a Gonfalonier for life. After his death,
this very method was adopted from sheer despair at the incompetence of
the republican administration. So again he opposed the most durable
democratic principle which flattered Florentine love of equality, election
by lot. When a combination of aristocrats, who wished to discredit the
Council, and of extreme men, who would carry democratic principles
to their logical conclusions, strove to eliminate nomination, and to
substitute a bare for an absolute majority, Savonarola preached against
this enfeeblement of administrative efficiency.

Savonarola taught his congregation that every vote entailed a solemn
responsibility; he amplified San Bernardino's warning that a single bean
wrongly given might prove the ruin of the State. The elector, he
preached, must have in view the glory of God, the welfare of the
community, the honour of the State: he ought not to nominate a candidate from private motives nor reject one who may have wronged him:
a candidate should be both good and wise, but if the choice lie between
a wise man and one who is good but foolish, the interest of the State
required the former: no man should be elected to an office by way of
charity, his poverty must not be relieved to the detriment of the public
service: the elector should not from temper or persuasion vote against a
candidate or throw his nomination paper on the ground, nor yet support
any who had canvassed him, nor ever give a party vote: in cases of reasonable doubt let the elector pray, and then without looking give the black
bean or the white, for God would guide his hand. This last characteristic reference to divine guidance was followed by a remarkable
instance of reliance upon miracle. There were rumours that the new
great hall of Council was unsafe, and nervous electors feared to take
their seats. Let them not fear, exclaimed the preacher, for if the
building were not sound, God would hold it up!

On the expulsion of the Medici, their financial system as well as
their constitution was cast into the melting-pot. The progressive tax
on all forms of income, which had been their favourite expedient, shared
in their unpopularity. Savonarola was prepared not only with a constitution but a budget. He preached that direct taxation should be
limited to a tenth on immovables, and that this should be levied once
only in the year. It was argued that such a tax was not liable to the
arbitrary assessment, which had been the curse of Florentine finance;
a tax on land was easy to collect and had solid security behind it;
it entailed no inquisitorial prying into credit, it suffered merchant and

artisan to ply unhindered those occupations which made the wealth of Florence; for she was poor in land but rich in commerce. The proposal became law, and a committee of sixteen was elected to assess all landed property in Florence and its territory. Apart from its being limited to immovables, the new tax differed from its predecessors in being regarded technically as a gift, and not as a loan. Extraordinary taxes had previously been credited to the tax-payer in the State-debt and nominally bore interest; the new tax was subject to no repayment.

For this suggestion Savonarola has won the fame of a great financier, and it is true that the tenth had a long life, when once its delicate youth was past, for it formed the basis of taxation under the Medici Grand-dukes. Yet the proposal was neither wise nor novel. Taxes had long been levied on revenue from land, and the limitation was but a return to earlier practice. The wealth of Florence, the source of luxurious expenditure, was commerce; the landed classes might live in easy circumstances, but not in state; yet commerce was now exempt. The arbitrary taxation of individuals was remedied by shifting it to the shoulders of a class. The new tax fell hardly on the nobles who were unrepresented in the State; it was therefore popular with the ruling middle-classes, who were jealous of their social influence. The French were still in Italy, while Pisa was in full revolt, and Florentine territory exposed to depredation. Yet the source of income taxed was that which was least protected; the lower classes would necessarily feel the pinch, for the impost would inevitably, in spite of State regulation, raise the price of grain and oil and wine.

Savonarola's financial scheme was predoomed to failure, for it was totally inadequate to its purpose. Even the assessment was not completed until the year of his death, and then only for the inhabitants of Florence. The republic from the first resorted to the old tainted sources of supply—forced loans from richer or less popular citizens; it still, as was said of Cosimo de' Medici, used the taxes instead of the dagger. The *arbitrio*, an impost on the profits of trades and professions, reappeared; and the duties on articles of consumption rose and rose again. Even before Savonarola's death it was proposed to restore the progressive tax, which could be levied several times within the year. The white farthings, the withdrawal of which had been the first concession to the populace, were reissued. The finances were incompetently and extravagantly administered; there was no permanent control, no subordination of private to public interests. Under the Medici a limited number had benefited from corruption; under the Republic each fresh group which came into momentary power, felt bound to gratify its adherents by the superfluous creation of commissaries and envoys. It became difficult to pass money-bills through the Council, and the consequent delay came to cost the State a hundred times the sum originally needed. So entire was the decay of the Florentine marine, that towards the close of the Pisan War, Florence was reduced to hiring a Genoese pirate with a brigantine or two to blockade the outlets of the Arno.

The defects of Florentine justice did not escape Savonarola's ken. His recommendation that the chief commercial court, the *Mercatanzia*, should be reformed by means of a representative committee, was carried out as far as statute went. Politicians however continued to manipulate the court through the agency of its permanent secretary, and this afterwards brought about a split in the liberal party, even as it was alleged to have caused the original breach between Medici and Albizzi. The Friar also proposed a new criminal court, which he called *Ruota*, composed of citizens sufficiently wealthy and well-paid to stand above fear or favour. A *Ruota* was after his death established, but bore no resemblance except in name to his proposal, which was undoubtedly borrowed from the admirable Venetian courts named *Quarantie*. When, still later, a *Quarantia* was introduced at Florence, it was a mere temporary criminal commission to ensure the condemnation of the over-mighty subject.

Savonarola's political programme might now seem complete, but he well knew that the constitution was not perfect. He stated plainly that time would show the defects and make them good; the essential was to establish the local popular base at once. Even this he came to see might need amendment; in a remarkable sermon preached in 1497, he hinted that the Grand Council itself might need a purge. He had to learn that there was no panacea for the inherited hysteria of a State. Not entirely without reason the hostile chronicler Vaglienti wrote that little reliance could be placed in what the Commune of Florence did, since what was done to-day was undone to-morrow; that truly Dante had said

> Quante volte nel tempo che rimembre
> Legge, moneta ed ufficio e costume
> Hai tu mutato, e rinnovato membre.

Notwithstanding Savonarola's political activity, politics were for him solely subordinate to ethics. The form of government was not an end in itself, but the means to moral purification; tyrants must be expelled, not because they were oppressive, but because they were morally perverting. He preached against Cosimo de' Medici's maxim that a State could not be governed by paternosters: the more spiritual a polity, the stronger it was: where there was grace, there were unity, obedience, sobriety, and therefore strength: riches followed grace and enabled the citizens to help each other and the Commune in times of need: in a State that kept its word, the soldiers were braver and more regularly paid: enemies feared the city that was at unity with itself, and friends more readily sought its alliance. For Savonarola the State was coextensive with the citizens' moral and religious welfare. His aim may almost be termed a system of State socialism applied to ethics rather than to economics. His programme was set out in four clauses—the fear of

God—the common weal—universal peace—political reform. He confessed that Florence had begun at the end, but hoped that she would
work backwards. Politics and ethics were so closely dovetailed, that
he regarded opposition to his political views as involving sin; and herein
lies his justification for his unmeasured denunciation of his opponents.

The Friar's influence upon the new government is proved by its
first legislative acts, especially by the terrible penalties attached to
unnatural vice. The deadly canker of Florentine life he, like other friars
before him, believed to be gambling. To eradicate this, he was prepared
to violate the privacy of family life, destroy individual liberty, and make
the servant an informer against his master. Gambling he would punish
with torture, blasphemy with piercing of the tongue. The dress and
the hair of women and children were made the subject of legislation.
The establishment of *monti di pietà*, State pawnbroking offices, would
nowadays be regarded as an economic measure; in Savonarola's eyes it
was mainly ethical, a form of State charity and a protest against usury;
indeed, he at first proposed that the State should lend free of interest. His
success in this measure proved his strength; for again and again Franciscans had advocated this check upon usurious Jews, who in bad seasons
gained a hold upon the poor. Invariably they had been shown the city-
gate by the upper citizens, themselves, as was believed, not averse to
usurious interest. Quite of late Piero de' Medici had favoured a *monte
di pietà*, but had found the opposition insuperable. Savonarola was no
professed Anti-Semite; he expressed in print his sympathy for the
Jews and his desire for their conversion; but for all that he virtually
rid Florence of them.

His enemies accused Savonarola of leading the poor to idle. The
general sense of excitement and unrest was no doubt intensified by
prophecy. Nevertheless he consistently preached the gospel of labour
for rich and poor. He had made every member of his own convent toil
for its support; from the pulpit he implored artisans to return to work,
and the employers to find them labour; to give work, he repeated, was
the best form of charity; no one need fear starvation who lived a godly
and industrious life. The rich, he preached, should labour even as the
poor; he denounced the princes who lived on their subjects without
protecting them, the wealthy who cornered grain, who scraped away the
wages of the poor, who would give their worn-out shoes in lieu of money.
But in the financial crisis through which Florence was passing an
exhortation to work was not enough; crowds of peasants were driven into
the towns by war and famine; wages must be supplemented by public
and private charity. Collections were raised in the churches, in the
processions, at the street corners, by house to house visitation; the
government was urged to buy up grain from abroad, to open a relief
office, to write off old arrears of taxes.

The reform of the public holidays was a natural consequence of the political and moral revolution, for the Medici had closely associated themselves with these, and their return was to be marked by a revival of the old magnificence.  Savonarola knew, as all earnest reformers know, that such holidays not only contain possibilities of irreparable evil in themselves, but taint the preceding and succeeding months, and permanently lower the standard of national purity and sobriety.  He insisted on the suppression by the State of the horse-races, the bonfires and allegorical processions, the gross carnival songs, which would have been tolerated at no other season; in the country-towns the *podestà* was to forbid the public dances.  His enemies accused him of imposing total abstinence on Florence; a Sienese satirist has jeered at Florentine teetotalism.  But this was an exaggeration, based apparently on recommendations for a short fast in time of national humiliation.  Savonarola was aware that men and children cannot live without amusement, and hence the processions, the religious dances, the burning of the vanities, which have become so celebrated.  Bands of urchins had been wont to stretch poles across the streets and levy black-mail upon the passers-by.  The proceeds were expended on a supper, while faggots and brooms were piled around the pole, and the stack converted into a bonfire, after which the rival bands would stone each other throughout the night, leaving some dead upon the square.  Savonarola stopped this disgraceful custom; the children used their poles with offertory-bags suspended to collect alms; and marched through the streets in thousands bearing crosses or olive-branches.  These bands of hope were organised into a moral police.  Gamblers fled at their approach; they freely tore veils, which they thought immodest, from girls' heads; no lady dared flaunt her finery in the street.  They visited houses to collect materials for the great public bonfires, known as the Burning of the Vanities.  This latter was no new custom; it had been a common practice with mission friars; so lately as 1493 Frà Bernardino of Feltre had made a bonfire of false hair and books against the faith.  Savonarola's bonfires have become more celebrated, because they replaced the great public feasts, and the process of collection was more elaborate and inquisitorial.  All the implements of gambling, false hair, indecent books and pictures, masks and amulets, scents and looking-glasses were cast into the flames.  It is impossible to decide whether objects of permanent value were destroyed.  Savonarola had some love for poetry and much for art; his denunciations against the realism of contemporary art referred usually to the introduction of portraiture or of nudities into sacred subjects, representations of which should be the picture-books by which to teach the young; among his devotees were several of the leading artists.  On the other hand, there is a passage which urges the destruction of objects representing the pagan deities.  Drawing from the life had lately been the chief novelty in the development of Florentine art; precisians could scarcely as yet accept this as a matter of course; it would not be surprising if among the indecencies were included scientific studies from the nude; two of Savonarola's artistic followers, Bartolommeo della Porta and Lorenzo di Credi, had, as is known, devoted themselves to the new study, and yet the examples that survive are extremely rare. In literature Burlamacchi, the Friar's biographer, speaks with delight of the destruction of Pulci and Boccaccio; and this sacrifice Savonarola's own sermons might lead us to think possible. The idea of the dances was perhaps derived from the well-known pictures of the Dominican artist, Frà Angelico. Three rings of dancers, novices with boys, young friars with young laymen, priests with aged citizens, tripped it round the square with garlands on their heads. Folly, Savonarola preached, had its proper seasons; had not David danced before the ark? There was in this some fantastic exaggeration which did the cause of righteousness no good; all Italy laughed, and this was a pity, for the Florentines were of all Italians the most sensitive; they were too clever to bear ridicule.

No one has questioned the moral transformation wrought by Savonarola. For many, no doubt, it was the beginning of a new life; many resisted the disillusion caused by the tragic circumstances of his end. Nevertheless in a city, where individual liberty was highly prized, the methods of transformation were not always welcome. Street urchins are no trained judges as to what luxuries are meet food for flames; it is not surprising that young bloods jostled the boys in their processions, and threw their crosses into the river. The savage penalties proposed for gambling affected a large proportion of the citizens; the very suggestion that slaves, who turned informers, should be liberated by the State, disturbed the peace of many a fairly decent household. All satirists and reformers believe that their own is an age of decadence, that luxury and vice are the mushroom growth of their own short day. Had Savonarola read his Dante, he would have found his own invectives applied to the golden age of Florence. The effective scene-painting of sin had been the task of generations of mission-friars. But in Savonarola's character there had been from childhood an element that was at once morbid and quixotic. His early isolation from his fellows, his vivid imagination, his premature and phenomenal horror of sin, his knowledge of the world through the confessional, all caused him to exaggerate the wickedness of his time. There was, moreover, in the religious exaltation of Florence an element of hysteria. The oft-repeated statement, that Savonarola broke up families by encouraging married women to enter nunneries, rests upon a single passage in a Mantuan ambassador's report, which has been strangely misunderstood. But it would seem true that women would rush at night to the Cathedral to struggle with the Friar's opponents, and that they saw in him the true light that was to come into the world. At the convent of Santa Lucia there was an epidemic of religious mania among nuns of good family; even Savonarola on his trial laughed at the memory of one who snatched away his crucifix and so belaboured him that he could scarce escape her clutches. At San Marco there was a case of hysteric epilepsy, while there can be small question that the fantastic visions of the somnambulist Frà Silvestro obscured, as time went on, the sounder sense of Savonarola himself.

A not unnatural reaction against the new puritanism showed itself, whenever Savonarola temporarily withdrew or lost his influence. Then the gambling-hells, the taverns, the brothels drove a roaring trade; and Savonarola's death was followed by scenes of profanity such as Florence had never before witnessed. It was a necessary result of the fusion of ethics and politics that the reformer regarded opposition to his political views as involving sin. Thus the dividing line in politics produced cleavage in morals and religion, and *vice versa*. Serious political opponents became confused with men of pleasure, and, indeed, scents and silks and sin were too apt to be the outward signs of the party loyalty of the *Arrabbiati*. Florence on a small scale prefigured our own Commonwealth and its results.

Although Savonarola seemed for a time all-powerful, yet from the first there were elements of opposition. Florence had been saved from bloodshed but not from discord; as the chemist Landucci put it, "some would have it roast and others liked it boiled"; there were those who muttered, "this dirty friar is bringing us to grief." Parties began to shape themselves. It was scarcely a conflict of class against class, though as yet Savonarola could usually rely upon the middle, and, perhaps, upon the lower classes. Most of the aristocrats who had been instrumental in Piero's expulsion were opposed to the Friar who had robbed them of their reward. Less moderate than their leader Piero Capponi were the Nerli, the Pazzi, the younger line of Medici, and the clever lawyer Vespucci, the more pronounced of whom were nicknamed *Arrabbiati*. But Francesco Valori, a leading member of the Twenty, after some hesitation became the recognised head of the Savonarolists, who were christened *Piagnoni* (snivellers) or *Colletorti* (wry-necks). They could boast of other members of good family, who before or afterwards played leading parts. Such were Paol' Antonio Soderini, Giovanni Battista Ridolfi, Luca Albizzi, Alamanno and Jacopo Salviati, and Piero Guicciardini, the historian's father. The remnants of the Medicean party lay low, thankful to have escaped with a sound skin, or attached themselves to the other groups. The Savonarolist party, writes Parenti, included many Mediceans who had owed their lives to him; and it was a common accusation against the Friar that he was a secret adherent of the Medici.

Family solidarity was the most permanent feature of Florentine life, yet so intense was the excitement that families were riven asunder, father standing against son and brother against brother; the Ridolfi, the Salviati, the Soderini were divided. It was said, indeed, that Paol' Antonio Soderini made the family fortunes safe by inducing his son to join the *Compagnacci*, a dining club of young bloods and swashbucklers irreconcilable to reform.  The line of demarcation was as much ethical as political.  Guicciardini has admirably analysed the parties: behind Capponi were ranged aristocrats who hated popular government, sceptics who disbelieved in prophecy, libertines who feared molestation in their pleasures, devotees of the Franciscans and other Orders.  Against these Valori led an equally heterogeneous force; serious men who believed in Savonarola's prophecies or welcomed his good works, hypocrites who drew a mantle of sanctity round secret sin, worldlings whose avenue to popularity and office lay through the stronger party.  The outward test was foreign policy.  Here the line was hard and fast.  The *Piagnoni* steadfastly looked to France for terrestrial salvation.  The *Arrabbiati*, in the phrase of the Spanish Pope and the Austrian Maximilian, would be "good Italians"; they would join the Italian League and close the Peninsula to the foreigner; they courted the Pope and the Duke of Milan, whose ambassador Somenzi became the receptacle or the source of all the scandal and intrigue against the Friar.  It was certain that sooner or later foreign politics would help to decide the issue.  All depended on the realisation of prophecies as to the recovery of Pisa. Florence could not permanently remain in isolation.  Prophecy, un- fortified by French aid, would prove a stimulant with inevitable reaction.

If Savonarola, in Machiavelli's words, was an unarmed prophet, the chosen city was a weak military State.  The rebellion of Pisa tasked her whole strength for many years to come.  When Charles VIII retired from Naples, Savonarola met him on the Florentine frontier at Poggibonsi (June, 1495),—and this on no public mission, but as one directly inspired by God.  The King was threatened with the condign punishment of heaven if he did not behave honestly towards Florence.  The prophecy seemed to receive fulfilment in the death of the King's children, but this was slight consolation to the injured town.  Charles, indeed, avoided Florence, but he demanded the third instalment of his subsidy, and dismissed the prophet with vague promises.  Indignation was already expressed against the folly of clinging to France at the instigation of a "foreign Friar."  "Believe now in your Friar," men cried, "who declared that he held Pisa in his fist!"  No sooner had Charles left Italy, than the French commandants, corrupt and insubordinate, sold the fortress of Pisa to its inhabitants, and Lorenzo de' Medici's conquests, Sarzana and Pietra Santa, to the Genoese and Lucchese respectively.  Beaumont, governor of Leghorn, alone restored his charge.  Thus Florence had lost her seaboard from the mouth of the Magra to the Pisan marshes, while the natural road northwards was blocked by unfriendly States.  Nor was this all ; in the far south Montepulciano revolted to Siena, whilst beyond the Apennines the protectorate of Faenza was abandoned and control lost of the well-worn route to the Adriatic by the Val di Lamone.  On the tableland of the Mugello, in the mountain basin of the Casentino, in the subject city of Arezzo and all down the Chiana valley, Florence had to fear a revival of local autonomy or lingering attachment to the Medici. From furthest North to extremest South, from the Pisan littoral to the backbone of the Apennines, the State was threatened with disintegration. The League, which in March, 1495, had been formed against the French, took Pisa under its protectorate ; Ludovico il Moro, indeed, soon withdrew his troops; he had no wish to exasperate the Florentines. His aim was the erection of an oligarchy which would re-connect the chain of Florentine-Milanese alliance, snapped by Piero. But Venice had come to stay. By her settlements in Romagna and Apulia she was making the Adriatic a *mare clausum*; Pisa should be a stepping-stone to the monopoly of the Tuscan Gulf.

The Pisan volunteers were now stiffened by the seasoned mercenaries of Venice, whose trained engineers strengthened the defences which her artillery could arm. Her incomparable Stradiot light-horse, swimming rivers and treating mountain watercourses as highroads, pushed far into Florentine territory, raided down the line of the modern railway towards Volterra, wasted the rich corn-lands of the Elsa, threaded the intricate hill country towards the Nievole, endangering Florentine communications with Pistoia. In 1509 their ubiquity was to be the bugbear of the finest French and Imperial troops; it is small wonder that they caused embarrassment to the inexperienced Florentines. Pisa controlled a large territory; she was protected to west and south by stagnant side-channels of the Arno and miasmatic marshes; to east and north-east lay a mass of tumbling hills. The Pisan peasantry fought desperately, and every hill-village became a fortress. Pisa could not be starved, for the sea was open to Genoese and Corsican cornfactors; Lucca afforded a ready market for the sale of Pisan property; through Lucchese and Pisan hills wound convoys, whose local knowledge enabled them to baffle the vigilance, or utilise the somnolence, of the Florentine *condottieri*.

Savonarola staked the truth of his inspiration on the recovery of Pisa; all that Florence had lost should be restored, and much that she had never possessed should be her prize. The prophet's reputation would necessarily rise or fall with every turn in the Pisan war. Amid all the new-born enthusiasm for liberty at Florence there was no sympathy for the Pisans, who so bravely asserted theirs. Sympathetic as Savonarola was by nature, while he had not been born to a share in the old Florentine hatreds, not a word escaped his lips on behalf of the revolted town. Towards the close of the war Florentines of the upper classes felt for the ruined peasantry and the women and children a pity which they scarcely dared express; but, when at this earlier stage a solitary canon of the Cathedral asserted that Pisa had a right to liberty, he was severely punished by the *Piagnone* government. The idea of liberty stretched but a yard beyond the four quarters of Florence, and even there its currency was conditional on its being stamped with the hallmark of her guilds; in the new constitution no reforms bettered the condition of her extensive territory.

Charles VIII had left Italy never to return, but the autumn of 1496 witnessed another flying royal visit. The King of the Romans had been induced by Milan and Venice to enter Italy in favour of the League. He came, however, as little more than Ludovico Moro's *condottiere*; he had few troops and less money; "he had sailed," as the saying went, "with a short supply of biscuit in his galley." His wider schemes shrank to the relief of Pisa. In welcoming a King of the Romans the Pisans felt a glow of their old Ghibelline enthusiasm. They had thrown the Florentine lion from their bridge into the Arno, and a statue of Charles VIII was reigning in its place; they now served the French king as they had served the lion. From Pisa Maximilian sailed to take Leghorn; its capture must have sealed the fate of Florence, for it was her last port, the last gate open to her French allies. But Leghorn was stoutly held. From the village of Impruneta was brought to Florence the sacred figure of the Madonna, and, as it reached the Ponte Vecchio, a horseman brought the news that a storm had scattered Maximilian's ships, and that a French squadron with supplies had broken the blockade. To Florentine imagination, kept at fever-heat by prophecy, this seemed a miracle wrought by Savonarola's intercession; and the belief became a certainty, when it transpired that the French had left Marseilles on the very day on which the Florentines had sent to Impruneta. The French alliance recovered its popularity; Maximilian hurried back to Tyrol, leaving Italy to wonder or to laugh.

Savonarola's fame was doubled by the salvation of Leghorn, and the close of the year 1496 was perhaps its zenith. In the previous spring a group of aristocrats of secondary importance had formed an electoral ring to reject all opposition candidates. This in Florence was a criminal offence; they were condemned by the Eight, and appealed to the Council without success, while their leaders were sentenced to life imprisonment. Then died Piero Capponi, shot before a paltry fortress in the Pisan hills. So fierce was faction that the people rejoiced at Capponi's death. Yet he was the hero of 1494, a passionate champion against French and Medici, the most, perhaps the only, capable soldier and statesman in the city. Nor was he an uncompromising opponent; he had cooperated with Savonarola in saving the Mediceans, and his attitude towards the Friar had not been consistently unfriendly. But marked character and high ambitions the Florentine love of equality could not brook; the ideal was a citizen who did everything that he was asked to do, and nothing very ill or very well.

Capponi's death disorganised his party, and the year closed with triumph for the *Piagnoni*, for Francesco Valori was elected Gonfalonier for January, 1497. In the long run Valori's leadership was no blessing to his party, but as yet he was the people's darling. One of the few citizens above suspicion of corruption, he was devoted heart and soul to the service of the State. He had no children; his leadership could not found a dynasty. It mattered little to humbler citizens that he was violent and eccentric, that his tongue was biting and abusive, and his temper impatient of contradiction; inasmuch as the victims of these qualities were their opponents. Valori used his two months of office without stint or scruple in the *Piagnone* cause. None but Valori's partisans were elected to salaried offices, or allowed to address the Council; every measure prepared by the Valori group must pass, however unpalatable to the public. The malcontents who had not paid their taxes were excluded from the Council; the age-limit was lowered to twenty-four in the hope that younger men, who had not tasted the loaves and fishes of the Medici, would favour the righteous cause. Many of the Franciscans who had preached against Savonarola were summarily expelled. Severe penalties were imposed upon priests and gentry who should hold intercourse with the Cardinal de' Medici at Rome.

Valori overshot his mark. Under the existing system of election the composition of the *Signoria* would immediately reflect the current of opinion in the Council, and from the close of Valori's term of office there were unmistakable signs of reaction. His successor was Bernardo del Nero, who had succeeded Capponi in the leadership of the aristocrats. This had a peculiar significance, for Bernardo was a veteran Medicean, opposed indeed to Piero's methods, but devoted to the house. The leaders of the *Bigi* had been regarded with as much hostility by the *Arrabbiati* as by the populace; but on Capponi's death the former, having no chief equal in talent to Valori, had turned to Bernardo. The union was still very far from complete, but it was a symptom that the oligarchy might be driven back to the monarchy for shelter against the people. Valori's character and conduct, which even alienated other Savonarolist leaders, had not, perhaps, been the only cause of the reaction. Pisa seemed as far as ever from recapture; the last French troops were leaving Italy; pitiless rain had fallen for eleven months, and the harvest of 1496 had been a total failure. In the early months of 1497 people dropped dead of famine in the very streets. The government did its best to supply grain to the poor; but once and again women were crushed to death in the throng that besieged the relief-office. Plague trod on the heels of famine. Savonarola's sanguine prophecies seemed a mockery to the poor. The rest of Italy, he repeated, would be scourged, but Florence, the elected city, would be saved. Now that the barbarian had retired, Italy had resumed her normal aspect; the Pope and the tyrants were enjoying their escape; only Florence had suffered from the flood, only Florence was shorn and starving.

The ruling classes, whether *Arrabbiati* or *Piagnoni*, were so occupied by faction that they forgot the possibility of a Medicean revival. There was no Medicean party, no appreciable number who would actively move in Piero's favour; but while the upper classes resented Valori's drastic methods, the poor were saying that under the Medici they had been better off. The hospitable house of the genial Cardinal was open to all Florentines who visited Rome on business or for pleasure; Valori had failed to check this practice, which slowly but surely sapped the republicanism of the aristocracy. A handful of citizens believed that they could work upon the general discontent, and invited Frà Mariano, the Augustinian, to Florence to preach against Savonarola and to act as intermediary between Piero and his friends. The conspirators relied upon the support of the League. Ludovico il Moro indeed drew back, feeling that there could be no sure friendship between himself and Piero. Venice however gave support, in the hope of procuring the cession of Pisa. Piero, sanguine as all exiles are, believed that indefinite discontent with the republic implied definite loyalty towards himself, and with some 1300 troops, led by the Orsini captain Alviano, moved from Siena upon Florence; but for heavy rain he might have surprised the Porta Romana at early dawn (April 29, 1497). Bernardo's term of office was just closing, and the new *Signoria* was hurriedly elected as being more trustworthy. The reported Medicean partisans were secured in the *Palazzo Pubblico*, the gates were guarded, the *condottieri* set in motion. Piero, hearing no rumours of a rising, retired upon Siena. No favour had been shown to the Medici, but few obeyed the order to join their companies; only the personal enemies of Piero took up arms, and that when he was already retreating. The citizens at large were too indifferent to risk their interests, when either aristocrats or Medici might prove victorious.

The *Signoria* for May and June, 1497, contained a majority of *Arrabbiati*; and Savonarola's position became critical. Under pretext of the plague, it forbade preaching in the Cathedral after Ascension day. The *Compagnacci* were gaining courage; they openly wagered that Savonarola should not preach the Ascension sermon. In the night they befouled the cathedral pulpit. Savonarola, undeterred, began to preach, when one of his enemies dashed a heavy alms-box to the ground. Amid cries of "Jesu, Jesu!" the terrified congregation rushed to the doors, while the *Compagnacci* shouted and hammered on the desks. The brawlers, including two members of the Eight, the very Ministry of Justice, made for the preacher, but were beaten off. At length the *Piagnoni*, returning with arms, escorted Savonarola to San Marco; but the convent was now from time to time surrounded by a howling mob. The *Piagnoni* and *Arrabbiati* boys stoned each other in the streets, and even an ex-Gonfalonier forgot his dignity, and became again a boy and stone-thrower. The Gonfalonier took advantage of the scandal to propose the Friar's dismissal as the only means of healing these passionate dissensions. The proposal was lost by a single vote; for five of the *Signoria* were for, and four against, and a majority of two-thirds was requisite. The government had a heavy responsibility to face; there was no police force which could control the *Compagnacci*; unless Savonarola could be silenced, civil war seemed certain.

Silence was soon imposed, not, indeed, from Florence but from Rome. In June arrived the brief of excommunication, which Savonarola at first obeyed. Other circumstances contributed to lull the popular excitement. The plague was raging; all who had the means left the city, and the younger Dominicans were sent to the hill convents. Either the violence of the *Compagnacci* or resentment at papal interference turned the tide of feeling. The *Signorie* until the close of 1497 were favourable to Savonarola, while public attention was diverted to an incident in which he had no direct part. Piero's attempt on Florence had been a farce, but its sequel was a tragedy. In August a disappointed Medicean agent, Lamberto della Antella, disclosed the details of the plot. Several leading citizens were arrested and others fled. It was proved that Bernardo del Nero, though Gonfalonier, was privy to the plot, together with at least two members of his *Signoria*, one of whom, Battista Serristori, was, curiously enough, a pronounced Savonarolist. The issue finally narrowed itself to the fate of five citizens, whose position well illustrates the composition of the *Bigi*. Bernardo had not, perhaps, favoured the conspiracy; he would have preferred an oligarchy with the younger line of Medici at its head; but he had information of the plot and would not betray his close associates. The soul of the attempt was Lorenzo Tornabuoni, a young man of thirty-two, the darling of Florentine society. Closely related to the Medici, he was well-nigh ruined by the revolution, but above all feared the apparently inevitable oligarchy; for he had been chief among the dandies who had been the personal rivals of Piero de' Medici's cousins. Of the others Niccolò Ridolfi was father-in-law to Piero's sister, and hoped for high position under a Restoration: Giannozzo Pucci belonged to the *parvenu* family in which the Medici had long found their cleverest and least scrupulous supporters: Giovanni Cambi was ruined by the Pisan war, for he had speculated in the Medicean syndicate for the development of land near Pisa. Money had been supplied by Lucrezia Salviati, Piero's sister, who frankly confessed that she wished her brother back.

The executive in Florence was notoriously timid in punishing criminals of high family; the term of office was so short that vengeance might speedily overtake the judge. Both *Signoria* and Eight hesitated to sentence the conspirators, and threw the responsibility on a large *Pratica*. Here opinion was almost unanimous in favour of death, and sentence was duly passed; whereon the friends of the accused demanded the right of appeal to the Council. The *Signoria* was divided, and once more referred the question to a *Pratica*. This meeting, with less unanimity than before, reported that delay was dangerous and that the safety of the State demanded a refusal of the appeal. Five of the Priors refused to break the law, but were threatened with personal violence by members of the *Pratica*. Valori, thumping the ballot box on the table, swore that either he or the prisoners should die, while Carlo Strozzi took Piero Guicciardini round the waist and tried to throw him from the window. Two of the five Priors were intimidated, and thus the appeal was rejected by six beans, Guicciardini and two colleagues courageously protesting to the end. On the same evening the sentenced men were executed.

The appeal would certainly have failed; it was merely a forlorn expedient to catch at the chances which time might offer. Yet when popular passion had cooled, men reflected that a fundamental law of the new constitution had on the supreme question of life or death been broken, and this threw discredit upon those concerned. It had hardly been a party issue. Valori and his Savonarolist followers shared the attack with aristocrats who had reason to fear Piero's restoration. For the defence Vespucci and the Nerli were most active because they regarded Bernardo as their party leader. Others were moved by friendship or relationship or the fear of giving the people a taste for blood. Piero Guicciardini, who throughout was opposed to extreme measures, was a moderate Savonarolist, and both the Priors for the Lesser Arts originally supported him. Two Savonarolist diarists, Landucci and Cambi, regard the sentence as cruel, and the historian Guicciardini condemns the refusal of appeal. Of Savonarola's attitude nothing certain is known; he was under excommunication, and not at this time preaching. After Piero's fall his entreaties had saved these very citizens; the law of appeal was universally regarded as his peculiar work. In the course of his own trial he confessed that he should have preferred Bernardo's exile; that he had recommended Lorenzo Tornabuoni to Valori, but in cold terms such as he was not wont to use when he wished his requests fulfilled.

A revulsion in public sympathy was only natural. Ordinary citizens had from the first resented the application of torture to the best blood of Florence. The well-known figure of the bright young Tornabuoni was soon missed; men remembered the brilliant marriage-feast, when he had led home the pride of Florence, the beautiful Giovanna d' Albizzi. The loss of territory and trade, the famine, the faction, the ferocity of the new republic were contrasted with what men began to call the joyous times before 1494. The responsibility for the judicial crime was fixed upon Valori; he desired, it was said, to lord it over the Council, and he struck down Bernardo del Nero because he alone was sufficiently able to withstand him. He would, indeed, gladly have saved Tornabuoni; but then his own rival would have escaped. The practice of old Roman proscription had prevailed—friends must be sacrificed that enemies might die. Meanwhile Valori alone profited; until the close of 1497 his will was law. Lorenzo de' Medici had been called a tyrant because, after his brother's murder, the State had voted him an escort of outriders. The dominant republican party now established a standing guard in the *Piazza* to protect itself, and there it stayed until Savonarola's death.

Henceforth the interest of Savonarola's career is rather ecclesiastical than political; the attack upon him is directed not from Florence but from Rome. Nevertheless the scourge which was manufactured in the Vatican was composed of several strands,—strands social and constitutional, moral and religious, personal and political,—all twisting in and out in the rope-walk of Italian diplomacy. Alexander VI has rightly left so terrible a repute that every act of his is exposed to a sinister interpretation. He had, perhaps, no positive virtues, but he was not entirely a conglomerate of vices. Abstemious in meat and drink, he had an equable temper; a healthy animal, he was not irritated by personalities; scandal has few terrors for those who habitually live in sin. Alexander was not cruel, if his immediate gratification were not concerned; in his official duties he had been regular and hardworking; he possessed a perfect knowledge of the etiquette and business of the Vatican, nor were the ecclesiastical interests of the Christian world neglected. It would be rash to assume that Alexander VI was actuated by personal hostility to Savonarola, although such hostility would have been only human. Under the zealous Popes of the Catholic Revival Savonarola would have met with less consideration, had their ideas and his been found in conflict.

Alexander VI was fully conscious that he would not a second time escape so lightly from the consequences of a French invasion. His personal enemy, Cardinal della Rovere, was influential at the French Court and, together with Cardinal Brissonet, would gladly make the Pope's simoniacal election a pretext for his deposition. He was thus the natural ally of Ludovico il Moro, who had everything to fear from French vengeance; the Duke's brother, Cardinal Ascanio Sforza, was still the leading figure at the Vatican. The refusal of Florence to abandon the French alliance and join the Italian League kept the peninsula in a condition of nervous agitation; it was known that Savonarola's party looked forward to a new invasion; it was guessed that he was himself corresponding with the French Court. Thus the Medici plots were hatched at Rome, but the Pope had no special interest in the Medici. Ludovico, as has been seen, was definitely opposed to a Medicean restoration. Alexander VI, on the other hand, would use the Medici, as he would use any other instrument, to embarrass a government which was a standing danger to himself, although it might be impolitic needlessly to exasperate the Republic, for this might only hasten an invasion.

Savonarola's relations to the Pope have hitherto been left unnoticed, because until the summer of 1497 they had little effect upon his action. They had opened with the brief of July 21, 1495, which summoned the Friar to Rome, and they reached a climax in the brief of excommunication.

The points of attack were the alleged gift of prophecy, the public invectives against Rome which brought the Papacy into contempt, and the artifices by which the separation of the Tuscan Congregation had been obtained. Savonarola defended himself point by point with great ability. He excused himself from visiting Rome on the plea of weak health, which was forcing him to abandon the pulpit, and of the danger from Milanese assassins on the road. He submitted his doctrines to the judgment of the Church, referring the Pope to his *Compendium Revelationum* for his defence of prophecy; his Holiness, he constantly repeated, had been deceived by the slanders of his enemies. Alexander vacillated; he was pressed on the one side by Ludovico il Moro and the Friar's Florentine enemies, on the other by the government and by the several Florentine envoys, all personally devoted to Savonarola. He was perhaps genuinely unwilling to take a decisive step against one whose holiness he respected; for sinners are not unable to value saints. In September, 1495, he adopted an obvious method of removing the Dominican from Florence by re-uniting the Tuscan to the Lombard Congregation. In answer to Savonarola's remonstrances he abandoned this intention, but in November, 1496, he ordered the union of all the Tuscan Dominican convents under a new Tusco-Roman Congregation. Even this brief contained no patent evidence of hostility. The papal consent to the independence of the Tuscan Congregation had been won almost by a trick; the Congregation had not proved an entire success, owing to the resistance of the larger Tuscan towns; even the union of the convent at Prato had only just been effected, and not without difficulty. The smallness of the Congregation virtually confined Savonarola's ministrations to Florence, which was most unusual. No previous hostility existed between the Roman and Tuscan Dominicans, like that which animated the latter against their Brethren of Lombardy; the new Vicar-General, the General, and the Protector of the Order were all of them Savonarola's friends. The Roman authorities might reasonably have doubted whether his temporary withdrawal from the city would prove an unmixed evil, either for Florence or for himself.

To this brief Savonarola's reply from the pulpit was almost a declaration of war. For he hinted not obscurely, that there were limits to obedience; that if a brief of excommunication were brought into the city on a spear-head he should know how to reply; and that his answer would make many a face turn pale. His Apology of the Brethren of San Marco was a formal appeal from the Pope to the public. Yet of Savonarola's resistance Alexander took little notice, until he felt assured that there were signs of a reaction within Florence. Then, he launched his brief of excommunication, which was solemnly read between lighted torches in the Florentine churches on the evening of June 18, 1497. To the clauses of the brief which condemned Savonarola for disobedience in not visiting Rome and for doctrinal heterodoxy, he could readily reply

that his excuses had been accepted, and that his doctrines had been submitted to the judgment of the Church; in further proof of his orthodoxy he now composed his most elaborate work, the *Triumphus Crucis,*
a noble tract on which his reputation as a theological writer mainly
rests.  The gist, however, of the brief was the Friar's resistance to the
Tusco-Roman Congregation, to which charge a reply was not so easy.  If
the Pope possessed the power to separate the Tuscan from the Lombard
Congregation, in spite of the protests of the latter, he could clearly unite
the Tuscan to the Roman.  But Savonarola was not daunted; in letters
addressed to the public he opposed a *non volumus* in the form of a *non
possumus,* protesting that it was not in his power to compel his Brethren,
and that they were fully justified in their resistance.  His answer implied
that the Pope had no powers in such a matter of discipline, if his command
were contrary to the wish of those affected; he forgot that in 1493 the
union of St Catherine's at Pisa with his own Congregation had been
effected against the declared wish of the great majority of the Brethren.

The brief after all seemed likely to fall harmless.  It was doubtful
how far the Pope was yet in earnest; more than a month had elapsed
between the dating and the publication of the sentence.  On June 14
occurred the mysterious murder of the Duke of Gandia.  Alexander,
in his passionate grief and remorse, initiated a project of reform such as
Savonarola would have welcomed.  It was a moment of strange concessions.  The excommunicated man wrote a letter of condolence on the
death of the Pope's bastard, tenderly urging him to lead a new life,
while Alexander assured the Florentine ambassador that the publication
of the brief had never been intended; the belief was current that he
would willingly withdraw it, if only the Friar would come to Rome.
From July, 1497, onwards until the spring the Florentine government
and its envoys pleaded ceaselessly for pardon.  Testimonials of the
Prior's orthodoxy were forwarded by the Brethren of San Marco and by
five hundred leading citizens; Savonarola himself in October addressed
a humble letter to the Pope praying for reconciliation.  For six months
he never preached; the excitement both at Rome and Florence had
subsided.

On Christmas day Savonarola committed his first act of open
disobedience.  He celebrated mass at San Marco, and then led a solemn
procession round the square.  This act scandalised many zealous supporters; but from Rome it provoked no violent protest.  The Pope's
interest was political; he would withdraw his brief for an equivalent—
the adhesion of Florence to the League.  On February 11, 1498, Savonarola
broke silence.  He preached in San Marco on the invalidity of the
excommunication, declaring that whosoever believed in its validity was
a heretic: that the righteous prince or good priest was merely an
instrument of God for the people's government, but that, when grace
was withdrawn, he was no instrument but broken iron: that if any Pope

12—2

had spoken against charity he too was broken iron. "If, O Lord," he cried, "I should seek to be absolved from this excommunication, let me be sent to hell; I should shrink from seeking absolution as from mortal sin." This sermon contains a summary of his correspondence with the Pope; Alexander, he concludes, resembled a *podestà* of Brescia who always agreed with the last speaker; he was like the king at chess, who moved backwards and forwards from square to square whenever check was called.

These utterances, followed by others fully as audacious, forced Alexander to a resolution. He demanded, under pain of interdict, that either the government must place Savonarola in his custody, subject to a promise that he should not be hurt, or at least confine him to his convent and prevent his preaching. The envoys assured the *Signoria* that the Pope was now in earnest, and after much debate Savonarola was ordered not to preach. On receiving this decision, the Friar preached his farewell sermon; he was willing to obey the State, for he could not force virtue upon the city against its will. This sermon contained his fiercest diatribe against the Roman Court; none could misunderstand the allusions to Alexander's concubines and children. It was time now, cried the preacher, to appeal from the Pope to Christ; the Power ecclesiastic was ruining the Church, it was therefore no longer Power ecclesiastic, but Power infernal, Power of Satan. Henceforth, if Savonarola was silent, he was not idle. In his seclusion he prepared an appeal to a General Council, and drafted letters calling upon the European princes to depose the Pope, who was no Pope, for his election was simoniacal, he was a heretic and unbeliever, since he disbelieved in the existence of God— the deepest depth of unbelief. Had his cause been as strong in Florence as of yore, had succeeding *Signorie* been as bold as that of January, 1498, a formal schism must have followed; and who can say that the revolt would have been limited to Florence, or that it would not have overstepped the frontier of discipline and doctrine? But the issue was to be decided by internal rather than by external politics, and the final conflict was provoked by circumstances almost accidental.

Savonarola's brethren were still preaching, and perhaps exaggerating, the apocalyptic features of his doctrine. From prophecy to miracle was but a step; an appeal to supernatural agency became almost a form of speech; it was boldly asserted that miracle, if necessary, would support prophecy. At length, on March 25, 1498, a Franciscan in Santa Croce threw down the challenge; he would pass through fire if Savonarola would do likewise: he knew that he should himself be burnt, but the Dominican would also perish, and the people would be freed from its delusion. Savonarola was averse to forcing a miracle from God; the Court of Rome expressed its abhorrence at this tempting of the Divine Power. The government, however, yielded to popular clamour; it was willing to clutch at any remedy for the civil conflict, which was wasting

the life of Florence.   Above all the *Piagnoni* were eager for the ordeal;
the more zealous offered to enter the fire in full reliance on a miracle,
while those who wavered thought that the prophet's success would render
his cause triumphant or his failure justify secession.

Neither Savonarola nor the Franciscan challenger, Francesco da
Puglia, were the champions of their Orders.   Domenico da Pescia,
Savonarola's right hand, represented the Dominicans, and Frà Ron-
dinelli the Franciscans.   The painful tale of the ordeal is too well
known to bear retelling in detail.   The Franciscans were gathered
in the *Loggia*, and the huge pile was laid in the great *Piazza*, when
the Dominicans entered in procession, two by two, amid lines of torch-
bearers, followed by Frà Domenico bearing the Host, and his Prior
bearing the Crucifix.   Their chant "Let God arise and let his enemies be
scattered" was caught up by the faithful on every side.   The square
was free but for the armed bands of the government, and the groups of
the leading supporters of each party; but every window and every roof
was dark with eager onlookers, hungering for miracles or horrors.
Then followed the unseemly wrangles between the Orders, Franciscans
insisting that Frà Domenico must be stripped of his robes for fear they
should be enchanted, Dominicans refusing to send their champion to the
flames without the Host.   Then came the drenching thunderstorm, and
their wrangles again till eventide, when the *Signoria* dismissed the
Friars to their convents.   The Dominican procession reached San Marco
amid the yells and threats of a disappointed mob.

The populace, long wavering, had made up its mind.   Some were
angry at their own credulity, others at the proposal to endanger the
Holy Sacrament.   Many were disgusted at losing a spectacle for which
they had waited wet and weary; others had hoped that the Dominican's death by fire would purify the State from faction.   Savonarola
preached to his disciples that he had won the victory; but in their
hearts they doubted it, for they gathered to defend the convent in
expectation of an onslaught.   This was not slow in coming.   On the
following day, Palm Sunday, the *Compagnacci* shouted down a Dominican preacher in the Cathedral, and amid cries of "To San Marco"
led the mob against the convent.   Valori escaped to rally adherents round
his palace and to attack the enemy from without.   But the assailants
were too quick; Valori reached his house with difficulty and hid himself;
his wife, looking from an upper window, was killed by a cross-bow.
Then came officials of the *Signoria* and took him from his hiding-place
towards the *Palazzo*.   The weak escort was overpowered; a Ridolfi and
a Tornabuoni hacked the *Piagnone* leader down, in vengeance for their
relation's death, and so the greatest citizen in Florence died unshriven in
the street.   Meanwhile San Marco was gallantly defended.   The bell
was tolling to rally the *Piagnoni*, who, however, were isolated in the
churches or in their houses in blank dismay.   Women were gathered in

the nave in prayer, while Savonarola stood before the altar, Sacrament in hand, with his novices around him, expecting martyrdom, for the convent doors were burnt and the enemies crowding in. It was high time that the *Signoria* should interfere in the cause of order. All lay citizens were commanded on their allegiance to leave the convent within an hour. Further resistance was hopeless. Savonarola and Frà Domenico surrendered under promise of safe conduct. For the last time the Prior gathered the Brethren in the library, and besought them to abide in faith, in prayer, in patience. The officers led their prisoners out into the street, and thence to the Palace, through the surging, howling mob, spitting, kicking and striking at its victims. On the following day Frà Silvestro left his hiding-place and was given up.

From the moment of Savonarola's arrest, his execution became a necessity of State; nothing else would satisfy the people, who would otherwise have clamoured for a proscription of his party; nothing else would have healed the divisions among the governing class. The religious strife had not only cleft the city in twain; it was making her alliance worthless to any foreign power. The news of Charles VIII's death had arrived, it seemed certain that Pisa could only be recovered through the League, and this would give no aid while Savonarola thundered from the pulpit against the Pope. Exile was an alternative to death, but exile would have removed the danger to a foreign and almost necessarily hostile State; the *Piagnoni* would never rest, while there was a possibility of their leader's return. The Pope at once urged the transference of the prisoner to Rome; the government, as a reward for silencing the prophet, pressed for a tithe upon the clergy for the Pisan war. Florentine independence declined to play the sheriff's officer for Rome, and Savonarola's extradition was refused; as a compromise the Pope sent commissioners to aid in his examination.

The trial of the three Friars lasted from April 9 until May 22. Their depositions and those of other citizens are not necessarily worthless, because they were extracted under torture. Torture was invariably applied, and such a view would invalidate, for instance, the whole of the evidence on which the Medicean conspirators were condemned. Savonarola was, however, a bad subject. His nervous, highly-strung constitution, weakened by asceticism and anxiety, shrank from physical pain. Though never abandoning his duty, he had always been haunted by the fear of personal violence; he frequently referred to his providential escapes from the poison or the dagger of Ludovico il Moro, although successive governments devoted to the Friar never contrived to arrest one of these Milanese agents, with whom he believed Florence to be teeming. The prosecution admitted that Savonarola retracted the confessions made under torture, and these retractations are set down in black and white. Not all of the Florentine Commission were pronounced enemies; and of the two Papal Commissioners, the General of the

Dominicans, Turriani, had, until Savonarola's final act of disobedience, been his consistent friend. More difficult is the question of the additions, alterations, and omissions attributed to the notary Ser Ceccone, a renegade; although, had this "editing" been absolutely unscrupulous, the confessions of the accused would have been more compromising. The depositions of Frà Domenico, whether in their original form or in the official copy, bear out the general authenticity of the evidence, as do even those of the hysterical somnambulist Frà Silvestro, who was believed by many to be more knave than fool, and with whom, it was suspected, the less scrupulous leaders of the *Piagnoni* conducted their political correspondence.

The Florentine commissioners directed the examination mainly to the gift of prophecy and political relations. It was essential to extort from Savonarola a denial of his prophecies; for nothing would so effectually alienate the large numbers who still silently clung to him. At first he stoutly asserted the divine origin of his gift, but under the strain of torture he broke down, and henceforth his answers were contradictory or confused. He was perhaps at war within himself on this mysterious subject, on which even his pulpit utterances are not consistent; in his agony of mind he now cried out that the spirit of prophecy had departed from him. The prosecution represented him as admitting that his alleged gift was an imposture, the result of ambition, of the desire to be thought wise and holy. He strenuously denied that his prophecies were founded on confessions made to Frà Silvestro or himself. With regard to his interference in party politics the depositions of the three Friars were very colourless. It was the wish of the government to narrow the issue to San Marco, and not to mark leading citizens out for popular vengeance. Even those who were arrested and tortured were soon released. Not Savonarola's old aristocratic enemies, but the people were the most vindictive. Parenti, whose own opinions are typical of the changes in public feeling, affirms that, to satisfy the people and to save the heads of the Savonarola party, the government replaced four of the Friar's judges, who might possibly be too favourable to his cause. The aristocracy could escape a revolution only by his condemnation. Valori and his associates, it was confessed, frequently visited the convent, as did other believers high and low; the Friars had heard their visitors speak of the prospects of the coming elections; their prayers had been sometimes asked in the cause of righteousness, but there had been nothing in the nature of an electoral organisation. Savonarola clearly avowed that he had supported the popular government, but had not meddled with its workings. Both he and Frà Domenico mentioned their design for a life-Gonfalonier or Doge. Their thoughts had naturally turned to Valori, but his violent and eccentric character made them hesitate; the excellent Giovanni Battista Ridolfi had been mentioned, but his large family connexion might lead to the predominance of a single house; Savonarola had protested against the tendency to form an oligarchical ring within his party. In all this there was no implication of any political association, nothing to compel the *Signoria* to extend enquiry further.

On the arrival of the papal commissioners the examination turned on Savonarola's appeal to a General Council; it was conducted chiefly by the Spanish lawyer Romolino, Bishop of Ilerda. Savonarola confessed that, having no friend in Italy, he had turned to foreign princes, and especially to those of France and Spain: he hoped for the aid of Cardinals Brissonet and della Rovere, both enemies of the Borgia; Matthæus Lang, Maximilian's confidential adviser (afterwards Bishop of Gurk and Cardinal), had spoken ill of Alexander in the Friar's presence, while the scandals of the Curia were odious to the Spanish sovereigns who could influence the Cardinal of Lisbon. In vain the commissary pressed for evidence to implicate the Cardinal of Naples; for confessions extracted by torture were afterwards withdrawn. The victim declared that he had no wish to be Pope or Cardinal; his reward would be enough, if by his agency so glorious a work as the reform of the Church could be effected.

Extorted and garbled as they were, these depositions showed no proof, in Guicciardini's words, of any fault except ambition. And who can say that in his last agony Savonarola himself may not have been conscious of past ambition, of the parasite which clings most closely to monastic walls? Pride was the fault which from the first Alexander VI had fixed on his future enemy.

The result of the trial was less the condemnation of Savonarola than that of the popular government on which he had pinned his faith. It would be vain to seek under Medici or Albizzi so violent a strain on the constitution, so shameless a disregard for individual rights. It was pitiful that the free constitution, the panacea against tyranny, should have been guilty of the worst crime with which Florence can be charged. Of physical or political courage there was none, save in the small band which in the heat of fight had held the convent. Only a short time before, the Milanese ambassador had assured his master that Savonarola controlled the great majority of the town; yet now no *Piagnone* dared mention his prophet in the streets. The Eight and the Ten were known to have Savonarolist sympathies; in defiance of the most fundamental constitutional traditions, without even the pretence of a *balìa*, they were dismissed before their office had expired. There was no protest from these lawfully elected bodies, and none from the Council which had given them their commission. When the new *Signoria* was elected, the well-known *Piagnoni* were forcibly excluded; the qualification for office became cowardice or party hate. The Council itself suffered the garbled depositions to be read, and did not insist on the appearance of the accused, because a *Signoria*, notoriously hostile, stated that he was voluntarily absent from fear of stoning. In the Council and in the magistracies, Savonarola, as was afterwards proved, must have numbered hundreds of secret adherents. Yet one citizen only, Agnolo Niccolini, dared to suggest that death should be commuted for perpetual imprisonment, so that posterity might not lose the fruits of the invaluable works which Savonarola might write in prison. The Florentine constitution was still a sham; there was still no correspondence between real and nominal power; the mandatories of the people were swayed by a ferocious faction, as they had been swayed by a cool-headed dynasty. It is small wonder that the hybrid constitution withered in the first fierce heat; that when a few thousand famished Spaniards rushed the walls of Prato, two audacious youths dragged the chief magistrate of the Florentine Republic from the *Palazzo Pubblico*, and condescendingly gave him their escort to his home.

In the sentence pronounced on May 22, 1498, Church and State concurred. Savonarola and his companions were declared heretics and schismatics, because they had denied that Alexander was true Pope and had compassed his deposition; because they had distorted Scripture and had revealed the secrets of the confessional under the pretext that they were vouchsafed by visions. Against the State they had sinned in causing the useless expenditure of countless treasure and the death of many innocent citizens, and in keeping the city divided against herself. Unity between the city and the Pope was now complete; Florence obtained the grant of three-tenths of Church revenues; the price, observed the *Piagnoni*, of them that sold innocent blood was three times ten. Even to the three Friars Alexander sent his absolution. On the morrow came the end. Unfrocked and degraded by the Archbishops Suffragan, condemned as heretics and schismatics by the Papal Commissaries, Savonarola and his Brethren were handed over to the secular arm, the Eight, who passed the formal sentence. Led from the *ringhiera* along a raised platform to the scaffold, they were hanged from the gibbet, and when life was extinct the pile was lit. The boys of Florence stoned the bodies as they hung. Four years ago they had stoned Piero de' Medici; then, in an access of righteousness, they had stoned notorious sinners. Now they stoned their prophet, and lastly they were to stone to death his executioner. The bodies were cut down into the flames, the ashes carefully collected and thrown into the Arno. The *Piazza* had been thronged with onlookers, for whom barrels were broached and food provided at government expense. For the crowd it was a vast municipal picnic; the burning of the Friars replaced the burning of the Vanities, even as this had superseded the fireworks and pageants of the Medici.

The horror of the tragedy lies not only in the character of the victims, but in its contrast to the high civilisation of the city which destroyed them. From the rising and suppression of the *Ciompi* until the fall of Piero, that is, in more than a century, no notable act of violence had been witnessed, save when the *Signoria* hanged from the palace windows, red-handed, the Pazzi conspirators who had murdered Giuliano de' Medici in the Cathedral and attempted to storm the palace. The next four years saw first the arson and bloodshed which followed Piero's fall, then the irregular condemnation of five chief citizens; then, the storming of San Marco and the murder of Valori and his wife; and now the fever of political passion reached its climax in Savonarola's death. The republican experiment cost Florence very dear, alike in territory, blood and treasure.

The tragedy had become inevitable. It is never easy to screw up the moral standard of a people. Yet in Florence there was such a genuine and permanent element of what may almost be called puritanism that, had she stood by herself and enjoyed a period of profound peace Savonarola's system might have been partially successful. It would have needed, perhaps, no very professional knowledge to administer the State; the good man might have been not only the good citizen but the good ruler. The experiment was, however, tried at a crisis of peculiar complexity, when the elements of violence abroad and at home were unusually strong—when ethics and politics had least chance of fusion. For such a task a novice in the art of government must needs prove unequal; he must consciously or unconsciously hand the reins to those who had the experience which he lacked.

The Pope and the Duke of Milan doubtless hastened the catastrophe, and Savonarola was in a measure the victim of his party's foreign policy. Causes, however, should not be multiplied without reason, and within Florence there was cause sufficient for the tragedy. If she were a good subject for ethical reform, it was otherwise with politics. It is easier to change the constitution than the character of a people. The Florentines, said Guicciardini, possessed two characteristics in apparent contradiction, the love of equality and the desire of each family to lead. If the new constitution could satisfy the former, it could not assuage the latter. The influence of family rivalry was the vital distinction in the working of the Venetian and Florentine republics. At Venice family jealousies rarely influenced the State; at Florence they overmastered and corrupted public life. In vain Savonarola, like San Bernardino before him, inveighed against the party nicknames which would surely bring back the horrors of the strife of Guelf and Ghibelline. He became himself the very subject of these factions; he could not shake himself free from a Valori or a Soderini; his opponents regarded him as the dangerous tool of the most ambitious of their rivals. To gain admirable ends he was forced to work through agents who were compromised. Disavowing democratic principles, it was only a question of time to which branch of the aristocracy he would attach himself; his religious achievements might have been greater under the unquestioned rule of the Medici. This impossibility of detachment from family strife is the tragedy of Savonarola; he fell because he was believed to be Valori's tool. The Florentines perhaps exaggerated the closeness of his intimacy with the party chiefs. In his sermons on Amos and on Ruth he implored his congregation to leave himself and his friars alone, and not to pester them with legislative proposals, with this or that man's candidature,—questions for magistrates and citizens, and not for friars. He repeated that he was no politician, that he had no finger in their government, nor in their foreign relations. Yet in these very sermons he stated that he was accused of constant interference; and the visits of the party leaders to San Marco seemed to support the accusation. His enemies not unnaturally thought that the midnight meetings of Medicean days on the eve of elections had been but transferred from the palace in the Via Larga to the parlour of San Marco. Parenti describes in detail the passage of Valori's measures from their initiation in San Marco to their consummation in the Council. The biographer Burlamacchi incidentally gives some slight colour to the charge of close intercourse with Valori, writing that Savonarola would not be interrupted in his prayers even when Valori called. The Friar himself protested to the Pope in 1495 that he could not obey the call to Rome because the new government needed his daily care. The pulpit was performing the functions of the modern press; its importance was heightened by the absence of debate in the assembly. If one party used this medium, the other was sure to follow. The pulpit of San Marco became the organ of the *Piagnoni*, that of Santa Croce the organ of the grandees.

It is not easy to time precisely the flow and ebb of public opinion towards and away from Savonarola. So early as June, 1497, a private letter written to Venice describes the populace as Medicean, the citizens as inclined towards Milan. From the early spring of 1498 the feeling against him had been strong. His preaching while under excommunication had scandalised earnest disciples; the threats of interdict were doubtless a terror to many more. Florence was not prepared for a breach with the visible head of her Church even at the bidding of her prophet. When the end came, the number of avowed supporters was not large; the pronounced *Piagnoni* whom the government excluded from the Council numbered sixty at the most. The lower classes had long been turning; with them Savonarola's constitution had found no place; they had lost the amusement and sense of importance which an occasional *Parlamento* provided. The puritanism which replaced the extravagant splendour of Florentine festivities entailed a diminution both of work and pleasure. Many of the poor were of course dependent on the great houses, most of which were opposed to Savonarola. The East end of Florence, the poorest quarter, had long been a Medicean stronghold; sooner or later it must feel the loss of Medicean charities. The great square of Santa Croce, the playground of the poor, missed the *fêtes* which had drawn thither the beauty and fashion of Florentine society. Life had now left it for the religious centres of the Cathedral and San Marco. *Monti di pietà* and burnings of the Vanities were poor substitutes for *panis et Circenses.* From the great Franciscan church the friars perpetually thundered against the rival Dominican; the Franciscans were after all the peculiar Order of the poor, and they gradually regained the influence which the eloquence of Savonarola had temporarily filched away from them.

The ordeal had decided all but zealous adherents, and the faith of these was widely, if only temporarily, shaken by the alleged confessions. This is clear from the piteous expressions of Landucci, who describes his grief and stupefaction at the fall of the glorious edifice built on the sorry foundation of lying prophecy, at the vanishing of the New Jerusalem which Florence had expected, and from which were to issue a code and an example of holy living, the renovation of the Church, and the conversion of the infidels. The disillusion was completed by Savonarola's silence at the stake and by the Divine refusal of a miracle to save him. Among thinking men it is unlikely that Marsilio Ficino, the Platonist, and Verino, the Humanist, should have been alone in deserting him, although they were no doubt the most distinguished of their class. It is needless to brand them as hypocrites and turncoats. Marsilio at least had led a blameless life; his devotion to Savonarola was of long standing; they had much in common in their speculative mysticism, in their groping after the unseen world. Marsilio was no politician; he could gain or lose nothing by the change of front, which he himself ascribed to the fierce family divisions produced by Savonarola's influence. The desertion of the Prior by the Brethren of San Marco must not be judged too harshly. Something was doubtless due to cowardice, the result of the fierce fight round the convent. But monastic life is subject to contagious waves of feeling; the belief might well run through the convent that its inmates had been befooled and duped by the saintly exterior and passionate eloquence of their Prior. The reaction from the spiritual excitement raised by prophecy brings with it the abandonment of the very foundations of belief. To Savonarola's modern biographers no language has seemed too hard for Frà Malatesta who headed the apostasy, and who had witnessed Savonarola's signature of the depositions. But he too had borne a spotless character; he was a man of high birth, a Canon of the Cathedral, who from genuine devotion had joined San Marco, abandoning a fine income and the certainty of advancement. Men of this type may in a moment of physical and spiritual disturbance be weak, but they seldom then begin to be deliberately wicked. Even Frà Benedetto, who spent the rest of his life in restoring his master's memory, for the moment fell away.

The passionate hatred which Savonarola had excited may seem hard to explain. It was otherwise with Sant' Antonino, who had laboured not less earnestly in the field of morality and religion, or with San Bernardino, who had found favour both with Guelf and Ghibelline. Saints are not necessarily unpopular. The cause may, perhaps, be sought in Savonarola's self-assertion, in his perpetual use of the first person, in the reiteration of all that he had done for Florence, of all the prophecies that had been fulfilled or were to be fulfilled, at the expense of those who would not listen. Whoever will force himself to read one of his more emphatic sermons from an opponent's point of view may find the key to the final verdict of the city. The child had grown into the man. Savonarola had striven to break the wings of the foul bird, and the bird had struck him with its talons; he had lifted his rod to part the waters, and the Red Sea had overwhelmed him.

The fascination which Savonarola exercised is almost as living to-day as it was when his congregation sat spell-bound round him. The object of these pages has been to discuss his influence upon political and constitutional history; but this is only one aspect of his career and to himself the least important. He was, perhaps, no skilled statesman, no wise political leader; but, as a spiritual force whose influence long survived him, he has had few equals. Those who would study this side of his character must leave the chroniclers, the despatches of ambassadors, and the biographies, and turn to his letters, his sermons, and his tracts. His zeal for righteousness, his horror of sin, his sympathy for the poor, his love of children appeal to the earnest and loving of all ages. There is little question that for most foreigners, certainly for those of the English-speaking race, the very thought of Florence centres in Dante, the exile of Ravenna, and in Savonarola, the alien of Ferrara.

# CHAPTER VI.

## FLORENCE (II): MACHIAVELLI.

By the year 1512 the downfall of the Florentine Republic was complete. Her failure was due to a variety of causes. A form of government which had worked satisfactorily while remaining outside the general stream of European politics, proved incapable of readjustment to novel conditions, and became an anachronism, more and more discredited as time went on. The character of the Florentine constitution rendered almost impossible any continuity of aim or persistence in policy. The *Signoria* changed every two months: the *Dieci della guerra*, who had *de facto* the largest control over foreign politics, changed every six months. No State could repose confidence in a government, in which political secrets could not be kept and where it appeared impossible to fix responsibility on anyone. From time to time efforts were made at Florence to remove this source of weakness, and the appointment in 1502 of a *Gonfaloniere* holding office for life seemed to many men, including Machiavelli, to have at last furnished some real guarantee for a stable policy. Not only, however, was the notion of a permanent official at variance with the theories of political liberty accepted at Florence, but the new *Gonfaloniere*, Piero Soderini, was in reality unequal to his position, and maintained his authority only at the cost of much unnecessary friction. He was firm only in his allegiance to France. Louis XII on his part was indifferent to the real interests of the city, though ready to make what use he could of Florentine assistance in his Italian expeditions. When the French were ultimately forced to withdraw from Italy, Florence was left isolated and impotent.

It was not merely the inherent defects of her constitution that weakened Florence; in the city itself there was never during these years any real union. The death of Savonarola neither removed the causes of internal discontent, nor mitigated the animosity of faction. The quarrels of individuals and of parties rendered it difficult to maintain order in the city or to conduct the daily business of government. The adherents of the Medici family were numerous, rich, and unscrupulous, and in the end proved successful. They were ready at any moment to cooperate with any foreigner or Italian, who might be an enemy of the Republic. The result was to create general distrust, and to render impossible any combined effort on a large scale.

A city so situated could only maintain its independence, if its military strength supplied more than a counterpoise to its constitutional weakness. An adequate army and trustworthy commanders were indispensable, and Florence possessed neither. The practice of hiring professional soldiers was general in Italy, and was adopted at Florence. It became the cause of incalculable evil. Not only was the city liable to be deserted or betrayed, even during a battle, by her mercenary troops, but the system necessarily involved a vast outlay of public money and a heavy taxation. By 1503 the financial crisis had in consequence become so acute that it was necessary to levy a tithe upon all real property. The evil was mitigated, but not removed, by the military reforms of 1506. Machiavelli, who carried into effect the new system, though the idea did not originate with him, was able, by means of his indomitable diligence and enthusiasm, to muster a force of about 5000 citizen soldiers; but in the end they proved to be of little service.

Florence was, moreover, set in the midst of many and great enemies. In the North, Ludovico il Moro at Milan, whether as open enemy or insidious friend, did what he could to damage the State, until he was taken prisoner by the French in 1500 and finally disappeared from Italian history. Venice had long ago abandoned her traditional policy and been seeking to acquire an inland empire, and, until the battle of Agnadello in 1509 crushed her power, harassed and impeded the Florentines at every turn. At Rome both Alexander VI and Julius II were indifferent or hostile to Florentine interests, and Cesare Borgia was believed, probably with reason, to include among his designs the incorporation of Tuscany with his other conquests. And besides the opposition of the larger Italian States, Florence had during this period to struggle against the hostility of nearly all the smaller towns in her neighbourhood. Pisa in particular was a source of endless trouble. From 1494, when Pisa, thanks to Charles VIII, threw off the Florentine dominion and became a free State, until 1509, Florence was at war with her; and any other Power, whose object was to damage Florence, was sure to intervene from time to time in the struggle.

To meet the dangers which threatened them from outside and the embarrassments and perplexities within the city, the Florentines possessed no statesmen of commanding ability or acknowledged pre-eminence, and no generals with real military genius. There were skilful diplomatists and mediocre captains in abundance, and even men who, like Antonio Giacomini and Niccolo Capponi, might under more favourable conditions have proved efficient commanders; but, speaking broadly, at Florence, as in most cities of Central Italy, intellect had outrun character, and the sterner virtues were almost unknown. The "corruption" of which Machiavelli complained so often and so bitterly, was to be found everywhere; and, though its effects were naturally most obvious in the military class, it was equally a source of weakness in the political world. The defensive attitude which was forced upon the city by the movements of the larger European Powers, and the constant vigilance and diplomatic manœuvring necessary to combat the shifting designs of Italian neighbours, prevented any elevation of view, and rendered inevitable the employment of all the familiar resources of small and weak States *in extremis.*

In the great events of the years 1499–1512 Florence played but a subordinate part. When Louis XII was preparing his expedition against Milan, Florence held aloof, awaiting the result of the struggle. While Louis XII was at Milan, ambassadors arrived from Florence. The hesitation of the city to declare her intentions before the event had aroused some distrust in the French; but it would have been obviously undesirable, in view of the proposed expedition against Naples, to alienate the Florentines, and hence an arrangement was without difficulty concluded, by which Florence was to receive aid from Louis for the war against Pisa, and in return to supply him with troops and money (October 12, 1499). Thenceforward the fortunes of Florence were intimately linked with the fortunes of France.

In the campaign of Cesare Borgia against Imola and Forlì there was nothing which directly menaced Florence; and when the Pope secretly endeavoured to influence Louis XII against the city, he was unsuccessful, and Louis gave definite instructions that Cesare was to do nothing detrimental to Florence. But it was becoming clear that the Borgian policy, in so far as it tended to consolidation, was a menace to the Republic: for even if Tuscany were not directly to suffer, one strong neighbour would take the place of many feeble ones.

While these events were in progress, the Florentines had devoted their best energies to the war against Pisa; but they were unable to make any real progress towards the capture of the town. In the summer of 1498 they had hired Paolo Vitelli as their general, and in 1499 it seemed as though Pisa would be forced to capitulate. But Vitelli failed at the last moment, and paid for his blunder with his life. Things became still worse when, in accordance with the agreement concluded at Milan, October 12, some Swiss and Gascons were sent by Louis XII to the assistance of the Florentines. The Gascons soon deserted, while the Swiss mutinied; and Louis XII blamed the Florentines for the fiasco. It was in connexion with these events that Machiavelli was sent to France. He was unable to obtain any satisfaction, and it was not until three years later (1504), when the French had been defeated at Naples and the danger threatened by Cesare Borgia had passed away, that Florence was able to resume operations with any vigour.

After the settlement of the Milanese question, Louis XII was occupied with the preliminaries of his expedition against Naples. The treaty by which he and Ferdinand of Aragon agreed to conquer the Neapolitan territory and to divide it between them, was concluded on November 11, 1500, and ratified by the Pope on June 25 of the following year. It affected Florence in so far as it implied an assurance that Cesare Borgia would not be molested by France in prosecuting his designs. But Louis XII hardly yet perceived the scope of Borgian ambition, and there was for the moment at least no certainty that a collision with Florence was impending. At the end of September Cesare started for the Romagna, and, after a series of successes which placed him in possession of Pesaro, Rimini, and Faenza, sent to Florence to demand provisions and a free pass through Florentine territory. Without, however, awaiting a reply, he advanced to Barberino and there renewed his demands, at the same time requiring the Florentines to alter the government of their State. His object was to secure Piero de' Medici more closely to his interests. This demand was not, however, insisted upon, as the restoration of the Medici was hardly practicable at this juncture, and, even if practicable, appeared likely to throw more power than was compatible with Cesare's interests into the hands of Vitellozzo Vitelli and the Orsini. But he pressed his demand for a *condotta* from Florence, and this was conceded, the Florentines also undertaking not to hinder his enterprise against Piombino. Such was the position of affairs when he started for Rome in June, in order to join the French army now advancing towards Naples. His work was successfully continued by his captains, and he returned early in the next year (1502) to take formal possession of Piombino.

The next six months witnessed a further development of the Borgian policy, and the Florentines began at length to realise in what peril they stood. It is not possible to determine with precision how far Cesare Borgia's movements during the year were definitely premeditated; considering the complexity of the conditions under which he was working, his actions could not be settled long beforehand, but were necessarily adjusted day by day in the face of momentary opportunities or emergencies. From Piombino he returned to Rome, leaving military operations in the hands of Vitellozzo Vitelli. Acting in conjunction with Piero de' Medici, Vitellozzo was able to effect the revolt of Arezzo, and rapidly made himself master of nearly all the places of any importance northwards as far as Forlì and southwards as far as the shores of Lake Trasimeno. At Florence the news of the revolt was received with consternation, and the alarm became general. It was clear that the city itself was being gradually and systematically shut in. Cesare's idea was to bring under his control all the country which lay, roughly speaking, between four points—Piombino, Perugia, Forlì, Pisa: the lines of country and towns which connected these four points were now practically secured to him. For on the south, the district between Piombino and Perugia was already won, and Pandolfo Petrucci, Lord of Siena, who, situated about midway between the two points and a little to the north, might have hampered his designs, had been brought over to his interests in 1501. The country along the eastern line from Perugia to Forlì was won by the rebellion of Arezzo and the Valdichiana. On the north, from Forlì to Pisa, his hold was not quite so secure, but Pistoia, ever rent by faction, could offer no effective resistance, Lucca was avowedly Medicean, and the Pisans definitely offered their city to Cesare Borgia before December 1502. About the coast-line from Piombino to the mouth of the Arno, there was no need to trouble. It seemed, therefore, as though everything were ready for an immediate and crushing attack upon Tuscany.

The situation of Florence was not, however, so desperate as it appeared to be. There were still a few places of importance lying outside the eastern line from Forlì to Perugia, which might at any moment prove troublesome to Cesare. Of these the most notable were Urbino, Camerino, and Perugia. The latter he could afford to disregard for the moment, as the *Signore*, Giovan Paolo Baglioni, was serving in his army and at the time seemed trustworthy. But Urbino, which blocked his way to the eastern coast and might cut off communication with Rimini and Pesaro which he had held since 1500, had to be subdued. The same could also be said of Camerino, as the point of junction between Perugia and Fermo. Cesare was, moreover, already aware that he could not trust to the loyalty of his mercenary captains. Seeing how town after town fell before him, it was inevitable that they should reflect how their own turn might come next. They distrusted their employer, and he distrusted them. Conspiracy and treachery were bound to ensue; the notions of right and authority had ceased to be regarded on either side, and the vital question was, who would have the dexterity and cunning to overreach his antagonist? Lastly, Louis XII was still the most important factor in the impending struggle. There had recently been some grounds of dispute between the Florentines and France, Louis complaining that he had not received proper assistance from the city during his Neapolitan campaign. But the misunderstanding had been removed by a new agreement (April 12, 1502); and the King had undertaken to supply troops for the defence of Florence whenever necessary. The French had no intention of allowing the Borgia to become masters of Florence; in that event, the road to Naples would have been blocked by a new Power commanding Central Italy from sea to sea. The capture of Urbino by Cesare Borgia at the end of June was an unmistakable revelation of his designs. It was at this juncture that France intervened, and obliged him to suspend operations. It became necessary to temporise, and he entered into negotiations with Florence. Arezzo and the other places which he had conquered in Tuscany were reluctantly restored to the Republic. But at the end of July he went in person to Milan to have an interview with Louis XII and succeeded in effecting a complete reconciliation with him. Florence was, however, relieved from immediate apprehension.

It was at this critical moment that the threatened conspiracy of Cesare Borgia's captains broke out. The exasperation which the Borgian projects had aroused at Florence led the conspirators to hope that the Republic would espouse their cause; and, after making themselves masters of the Duchy of Urbino, they appealed to Florence for assistance. But as soon as the existence of the conspiracy had become known, both the Pope and his son had in their turn applied to the Florentines and asked that ambassadors might be sent to confer with them. Machiavelli was deputed to visit Cesare Borgia, and remained with him till the end of the following January (1503). The arrival of French troops, for which Cesare Borgia applied to Louis XII and which were readily furnished, forced the recalcitrant captains to come to terms, and they were allowed to take service with him as before. But the hollow reconciliation deceived no one, and Machiavelli in particular had opportunities day by day to trace the stages by which Cesare Borgia, who never trusted twice to men who betrayed him once, lulled his opponents into a false sense of security, and finally took them prisoners at Sinigaglia (December 31). The ringleaders, including Vitellozzo Vitelli, were put to death by his orders. Thence he withdrew to Rome, where he arrived early in the following year (1503).

The year's work had not been, on the whole, unfavourable to the Borgias. Florence on the other hand had suffered seriously, and the incompetence of the government was generally obvious. The reform of 1502, which, carried as a compromise and supported by academic reasoning, provided for the election of a *Gonfaloniere* to hold office for life, did something to revive the spirits of the inhabitants, and met the wishes of Louis XII; but it added nothing to the real strength of the Republic. In the Neapolitan territory disputes had arisen between the French and the Spaniards, and all Northern Italy watched with anxiety the progress of the war. The defeat of the French at the battle of Cerignola (April 28, 1503) had a marked effect upon the policy of the Pope, who began in consequence to incline towards Spain; but on August 18 all the Borgian designs were cut short by the sudden and unexpected death of Alexander VI. His son was ill at the same time, and unable to do anything. The politics of the Italian States were thus completely disorganised, and Florence in common with the others looked anxiously for the election of the new Pope. Pius III's short reign of less than a month was without real influence upon the position of affairs. On November 1 he was succeeded by Julius II, whose election Cesare Borgia had not been able to prevent. With Julius II a new period begins not only in the history of Italy but of Europe.

Florence had now nothing to fear from Cesare Borgia. On the death of his father, he lost all his possessions except the Romagna, which remained faithful to him for about a month. He had governed the district with justice and integrity, and won the affections of the inhabitants. But his inopportune illness was fatal to his prospects. The Venetians, always on the watch for opportunities to enlarge their inland empire, obtained possession of Faenza and Rimini; Pesaro returned under the rule of its former Lord; Imola and Forlì surrendered themselves to the Pope. By the end of January, 1504, Cesare Borgia was forced to sign an agreement by which he abandoned to Julius II all his claims to the Romagna, in return for permission to withdraw wherever he might wish. In the spring he arrived at Naples and, taken prisoner by Gonzalo, was conveyed to Spain. He was killed in battle in Navarre (1507).

But whatever advantages the Florentines might have derived from the disappearance of Cesare Borgia, they were more than counterbalanced by several other events. The final defeat of the French at the battle of the Garigliano (December 28, 1503) placed the whole of southern Italy in the power of Spain; and the movements of Gonzalo, who was known to be willing to help Pisa, were a source of constant anxiety to the Republic. The presence of the Venetians in the Romagna, the ignorance which yet prevailed as to the intentions of the Pope, and the want of troops and of money, combined to produce a situation of extreme gravity at Florence. Within the city itself there was much discontent with the government of Soderini. He was, it is true, acceptable to the masses, having been able by rigid economy to lighten somewhat the burden of taxation; but the leading families in the State were irritated by neglect and by the filling up of the *Signoria* and Colleges with persons who were either nominees of the *Gonfaloniere*, or too insignificant to offer an effective opposition to his designs. His chief supporters were to be found among the younger men recently embarked upon political life and beginning to win a reputation for themselves. Among these Machiavelli in many unpretentious ways was of immense service to Soderini and, though sometimes disagreeing with him, proved ready to subordinate personal opinions to what seemed the general interest of the State. This was clearly seen early in 1504, when an attempt was made to reduce Pisa to extremities by diverting the course of the Arno. The plan had been strongly urged by Soderini and was supported by Machiavelli in his official capacity, though he had little hope that it could prove successful. Ultimately it had, of course, to be abandoned.

The French defeat at Naples naturally aroused hopes that they might be driven from Milan also. The Cardinal Ascanio Sforza, brother of Ludovico il Moro, was now at Rome and bestirring himself vigorously to win assistance in recovering the duchy. The project could not succeed if Florence blocked the way, and Soderini was too devoted to France ever to entertain the idea. Ascanio therefore turned for help to Gonzalo, and an arrangement was made by which Bartolommeo d' Alviano, one of Gonzalo's *condottieri*, was to invade Tuscany and to restore Giovanni and Giuliano de' Medici to Florence; when this was accomplished, the Medici were to help to reinstate Sforza at Milan. This intrigue had hardly been matured, when Ascanio Sforza died. Bartolommeo d' Alviano, however, continued to advance, but was defeated by the Florentines in the summer of 1505, the Republic thus escaping from a very serious danger. So elated were the Florentines by their victory, that they followed it up by an attempt to storm Pisa; but Gonzalo sent a force of Spanish infantry to defend the town and the attack had to be abandoned.

The regular failure of so many repeated attempts to overpower Pisa disheartened the Florentines, but their hatred was insatiable. Everything tended to confirm the opinion, to which many men had been long inclining, that success could only be achieved by a thorough reform of the military system. The year 1506 witnessed the actual carrying out of a scheme which was to supersede the employment of mercenary troops. Machiavelli was the leading spirit in the whole movement; he was supported both by Soderini and by Antonio Giacomini. A national militia was instituted and a body of troops enrolled from the *Contado*; they numbered about 5000, and were mustered before the close of the year. A new magistracy with the title *I Nove della milizia* was formed to manage all affairs connected with the militia in time of peace, while the authority in time of war would as usual rest with the *Dieci della guerra*. Machiavelli was in January, 1507, appointed chancellor of the *Nove della milizia*, and the main bulk of the work connected with the levy and organisation of the new troops fell to him.

During the following years Florence enjoyed a period of comparative repose, while Julius II was occupied with designs which did not directly concern Florence. The subjection of Perugia and Bologna, the War of Genoa, and the early operations of the War against Venice, left Florence to pursue her own designs, unattacked and unimpeded. But when in 1510 Julius decided to make peace with Venice, the consequence was a collision with France, and it was also clear that the Florentines would become involved in the struggle. To this they might, however, look forward with some measure of hopefulness; for they had at last (1509) reduced Pisa to submission, and one long-standing cause of weakness and waste was thus removed.

The year 1510 witnessed the first stages of the conflict between the Pope and France. At Florence it was common knowledge that Julius II was hostile both to Soderini and to the Republican government, and that he already entertained the idea of a Medicean restoration. The difficulties of the situation were not lightened by Louis XII's demand that the city should definitely declare her intentions. The danger from the papal troops was at the moment more directly pressing than any other: to declare for France would not only have exposed the Florentine territory to an immediate attack, but would have also alienated the sympathies of all those citizens who dreaded a conflict with the head of the Church, and wished also to stand well with the Medici. The city was full of antagonistic parties and irreconcilable interests, and an abortive conspiracy was formed to murder the *Gonfaloniere*. In order to gain time Machiavelli was sent upon a mission to France. On his arrival at Blois in July, 1510, he found Louis XII eager for war and inclined towards the idea of a General Council, which should secure the deposition of the Pope. This Council actually met in the following year (September), and although consisting of only a handful of members, held three sessions at Pisa, the Florentines allowing the use of the town for that purpose. It was powerless to harm Julius II, who replied by giving notice of a Council to be held at the Lateran, and thus *ipso facto* disqualified the Council of Pisa. It served, however, to embitter the Pope against Florence; and both Florence and Pisa were placed under an interdict.

During the winter of 1510–11 Julius II successfully continued his military operations, until his progress was checked by the appointment of Gaston de Foix to the command of the French forces, in conjunction with Gian Giacomo Trivulzio. Throughout the spring reverse followed reverse, and by June the Pope was back in Rome; indeed, if Louis XII had permitted it, Trivulzio might have followed him unhindered to Rome itself. Had he done so, France would have commanded the whole of Northern and Central Italy, and once more cleared the road to Naples. Knowing this, Ferdinand of Aragon had, so early as June, 1511, made proposals to Julius for the formation of a league to check the progress of the French. The idea, momentarily delayed by the illness of the Pope in August, was realised in October; and on the fifth of that month the Holy League was published at Rome. The contracting parties were Julius, Ferdinand and the Venetians: the ostensible object was the defence of Church interests and the recovery of Church property. The command of the allied forces was entrusted to the Viceroy of Naples, Ramon de Cardona.

Whichever side proved victorious in the inevitable struggle, the result would be equally disastrous to the Florentine Republic. Soderini still represented what might be considered the official policy of the State —friendship with France: but his authority was growing steadily weaker, and the collision of parties made any combined action impossible. It was the battle of Ravenna (April 11, 1512) that finally cleared the situation. Though the French were victorious, the death of Gaston de Foix deprived them of their most efficient general, and they were henceforward helpless. By the end of June they were driven from Lombardy and ceased for the time to exist at all as factors in the politics of Italy. Florence was at the mercy of the confederates. The supreme moment had come.

By the expulsion of the French the object for which the Holy League had been really formed was accomplished, and it was necessary for the allied Powers to readjust their policy and to determine their future movements. For this purpose they held a congress at Mantua in August, at which among other subjects the reconstitution of the Italian States was discussed. It was decided to restore the Medici at Florence. This had been the Pope's avowed object since 1510, and he was not likely at this stage to see that it was, from his point of view, an impolitic blunder. The work was entrusted to Ramon de Cardona, who joined his army at Bologna and began to march southwards. He arrived without resistance at Barberino, about fifteen miles north of Florence. From there he sent to the city to demand the deposition of Soderini and the return of the Medici as private citizens. The Florentines refused to depose Soderini, though willing to receive the Medici on those terms. At the same time they sent a force of troops to garrison Prato. Ramon de Cardona therefore continued his advance; Prato was captured on August 30, and its inhabitants were with ruthless barbarity tortured, debauched and butchered. Further resistance was impossible. On September 1 Soderini was deposed, and on the same evening Giuliano de' Medici entered Florence, to be followed on the 14th by Giovanni and other members of the family. Nothing remained but to fix the form of the new government. The *Consiglio Grande* and the *Dieci di balìa* were abolished, as well as the *Nove della milizia* and the national militia; *Accoppiatori* were appointed to select the *Signoria* and Colleges *a mano*, and it was resolved that the *Gonfaloniere* should henceforth hold office for two months only. During the close of the year Florence settled down quietly under Medicean rule. The revolution was accomplished with more moderation than might have been expected; and even those who, like Machiavelli, had been zealous servants of Soderini, suffered as a rule no more than loss of official employment or temporary banishment.

These years, in which the fate of Florence was decided, while the Republic was dragged helpless in the chain of events, helpless to determine her own fortunes, were the period in which Machiavelli's term of political activity was comprised.

Niccolò Machiavelli was born at Florence in 1469, and died, comparatively young, in 1527. For about fourteen years he was employed by the Florentine government in a subordinate official capacity, and even his intimate friends hardly recognised that he was a really great man. Although his position as Secretary to the *Dieci* kept him constantly in touch with political movements in Central Italy, and although he was employed almost without intermission from 1499 till 1512 upon diplomatic missions, he exerted hardly any influence upon the course of events; if he were known only by his official letters and despatches, there would be little in his career to arrest attention. It is only as an author that Machiavelli has any abiding place in the world's history. He has a claim upon the attention of the modern world because, living at a time when the old political order in Europe was collapsing and new problems both in State and in society were arising with dazzling rapidity, he endeavoured to interpret the logical meaning of events, to forecast the inevitable issues, and to elicit and formulate the rules which, destined henceforth to dominate political action, were then taking shape among the fresh-forming conditions of national life.

His natural gifts marked him out as peculiarly fitted to be an intellectual pioneer. He has more in common with the political thinkers of later generations than with the bulk of his contemporaries, on whom still pressed the dead hand of medievalism. It is true, of course, that he did not stand alone; both in Italy and in France there were a few men who worked along the same lines and were approaching the same goal. Commines had nothing to learn from Machiavelli; and Guicciardini, his equal in ability and his superior in moral detachment, was harder and colder, and more logical. And there were men of lesser note, Vettori and Buonaccorsi and the long line of eminent historians from Nardi to Ammirato, who helped, each in one way or another, to break the fetters of tradition and to usher in the modern world. But there is no one among them all, except Machiavelli, who has won ecumenical renown. And the ultimate reason is that, although the area which he was able to observe was small, the horizon which he guessed was vast; he was able to overstep the narrow limits of Central Italy and Lombardy, to think upon a large scale, and to reach some real elevation of view. He made, it is true, many mistakes, and there is much in his writings that is indefensible; but, on the whole, later history has done much to justify him, and the view which is most essentially Machiavellian, that the art of government, like the art of navigation, is out of relation to morals, has hardly ever lacked authoritative support.

It was in 1513 that Machiavelli, then living in retirement near San Casciano, began the composition of those works which were to make his name famous. They are not intelligible except when considered in relation to the historical background of his life, and to the circumstances in which they were written. But for many generations the ideas which they contained were censured or defended by men who were at least partially ignorant of the epoch and of the country in which they arose, and were often mere controversialists or the accredited champions of some branch of the Church. As the doctrines of which Machiavelli was the earliest conscious exponent were so important and so comprehensive, it was inevitable that attempts should be made to appraise their absolute value; they appeared to involve not only an unfamiliar, if not wholly novel, conception of the State, but to imply also the substitution of some new standards of judgment and principles of action which, while overriding the traditional rules and the accepted authorities in the political order, might be understood to apply also to the conduct of society and to the ordinary affairs of men. The consideration of these ideas and the attempt to gauge their effects upon religion or morals or politics, and to elicit the conclusions to which they appeared to lead, engrossed attention so largely, that their historical origin was forgotten, their classical antecedents were ignored, and step by step, for more than a century, criticism drifted away from Machiavelli and concerned itself with an ill-defined and amorphous body of doctrine known loosely under the name of Machiavellism. No fair judgment of Machiavelli's works is possible, unless they are separated from the literature and the controversies which have grown up around them. It is true that the accretions of later thinkers have an importance of their own, but they are of hardly any value in Machiavellian exegesis. All the necessary materials for judgment are to be found in the writings of Machiavelli and of his contemporaries.

The doctrines of Machiavelli are not systematically expounded or adequately justified in any one of his books. It is only by piecing together the scattered notices in different writings and by comparing the forms in which similar ideas are presented at different periods, that there emerges slowly a general conception of the character of the whole. Some of these ideas were not original, but as old as the beginnings of recorded thought. In certain cases they were part of the intellectual heritage transmitted by Greece and Rome, adapted to a new setting and transfused with a new potency and meaning. Sometimes they were common to other contemporary publicists. Often they were provisional solutions of primitive problems, claiming no universal or permanent validity. Often, again, they were the expression of beliefs which among any people and at any period would be regarded as innocuous and inoffensive and perhaps even as obvious. Efforts have often been made to summarise them all in a single phrase, or to compress them within one wide generalisation. Such attempts have been always unsatisfactory, because much that is essential cannot be included. Machiavelli himself is not rightly viewed as, in the strict sense, a *doctrinaire;* he had no systematic theories to press. There was at no time anything rigid or harshly exclusive in his views: they were formed after slow deliberation, as experience and study widened his range or quickened his insight. They embrace elements which come from many sources, and, though they are on the whole fairly consistent, his writings contain many indications of the diffident and tentative steps by which the conclusions were reached.

Portions of Machiavelli's works were intended to form a contribution to general questions of politics and ethics: there are other portions which were more directly determined by the pressure of an unusual problem and of ephemeral conditions. In nearly all his writings the dispassionate, scientific temper of the historian or thinker who records and explains is combined with the earnestness and the eagerness of the advocate who is pleading a cause. Aspiration and emotion were not foreign to the genius of Machiavelli, and at appropriate moments found impassioned utterance. Discussions of general principles of history and of the art of government are everywhere applied and enforced by examples of contemporary failures or successes, and the reasoning is thus brought home "to men's business and bosoms." In the *Discourses on Livy* the doctrinal and scientific interest predominated: in *The Prince*, which became the most influential of all his books, the local and temporary problems lay at the root of the whole discussion. It is therefore necessary to separate, within the limits of a legitimate analysis, the two elements found combined in his writings; and though no firm line can or ought to be drawn between the two parts, which at nearly every point touch and supplement each other, a divided discussion will best conduce to the clearness from which truth most quickly emerges.

The writings of nearly all the Florentine historians and publicists of the sixteenth century involve certain fundamental beliefs or hypotheses, upon which the whole structure of their reasoning rests; these are rarely stated *totidem verbis* in any passage, although implied in nearly all. The general body of their work forms a perpetual commentary upon a text, which is only incidentally enunciated; the method employed is expository only in appearance, but in reality genetic; the ultimate principles of the argument are the final result at which the reader arrives, and not a guide which he has with him from the beginning. Even with an author like Machiavelli, who was not averse to repeating himself, and less reticent than many others, it is not always easy to be certain that the latent hypotheses and scattered hints have been correctly elicited and grouped. Still, it is in any case clear that what controlled his views of the movement of events, whether in his own day or in earlier times, and of the lessons which they convey, was, in the last analysis, a specific notion of man's nature as a permanent force realising itself and imposing itself upon external things, shaping and subjecting them. The conception of human nature to which he adhered was used as the foundation for a definite theory of history as a whole. Then the process of reasoning was reversed, and from the collective activity of national life a return was made to the isolated unit or individual, and an ethical supplement added, thus completing a general conspectus of man both in the State and in society. For though Machiavelli inferred that ethics and politics are distinct, and that the art of government is out of relation to morals, he founded both upon the same assumptions. The ethical portion of his work is, of course, of little importance in comparison with the political, and is usually wholly ignored.

The conception which had the widest influence upon Machiavelli's teaching is that of the essential depravity of human nature. Men are born bad, and no one does good, unless obliged. This he regarded as a necessary axiom of political science. It was contested by a few of his contemporaries, but on the whole the political speculation of the Renaissance and the theological teaching of the Reformation issued, in this respect, in the assertion of the same truth. The result at which theologians arrived in their efforts to settle the controversies connected with original or "birth" sin, was reached by Machiavelli through the study of the past, and with the object of obtaining a fixed basis for discussion. For the most part he limited himself to an emphatic iteration of his belief, without attempting analysis or defence beyond a general appeal to the common experience of mankind. It is not certain through what channels the view was conveyed to him; he shared the belief with Thucydides. "Men never behave well," he wrote, "unless they are obliged; wherever a choice is open to them and they are free to do as they like, everything is immediately filled with confusion and disorder.—Men are more prone to evil than to good.—As is shown by all who discuss civil government, and by the abundance of examples in every history, whoever organises a State, or lays down laws in it, must necessarily assume that all men are bad, and that they will follow the wickedness of their own hearts, whenever they have free opportunity to do so; and, supposing any wickedness to be temporarily hidden, it is due to a secret cause of which, having seen no experience to the contrary, men are ignorant; but time, which they say is the father of all truth, reveals it at last." This view involved the corollary, that human nature could not be depended upon to reform itself; it is only through repression that evil can be kept below the suicidal point.

Combined with this conviction was another, resting also upon an assumption and likewise applied as a general principle to explain history. The maxim "Imitation is natural to man" would express it in its crudest and most vague form. "Men almost always walk in the paths which others have trodden and in their actions proceed by imitation, and yet cannot keep entirely to other men's paths, nor attain to the excellence which they imitate." The idea is often enforced directly by Machiavelli, sometimes expanded or spoken of in a figure. His meaning was that all men, at any given period, must necessarily be in the debt of the dead; the masses cannot help following the beaten paths; the tendency of history is not to initiate, but to reproduce in a debased form. Men, being lazy, are more willing to conform than to pioneer; it is less inconvenient to tolerate than to persecute. Of course such repetition as history appeared to reveal would still be, in the main, not the result of conscious imitation, but the inevitable product of the permanent passions in man, which he believed to have a larger power in determining events than the rational and progressive elements. "The wise are wont to say, and not at random or without foundation, that he who desires to foresee what is going to take place, should consider what has taken place; because all the things in the world, at all periods, have an essential correspondence with past times. This arises because, as they are the work of men who have and always have had the same passions, they must of necessity produce the same effects.—In all cities and among all peoples there exist the same appetites and the same dispositions that have always existed."

The uniformity of the forces at work in history might be expected to produce a monotonous movement in events, a mere recurring series in the life of nations. This is not the case, because whatever, whether in the intellectual or material order, is the outcome of man's activity is subjected to a law similar to that which controls the progress and decay of the individual life; everything contains within itself the seeds of its own dissolution; "in all things there is latent some peculiar evil which gives rise to fresh vicissitudes." No struggle against the tendency to corruption and extinction can be permanently successful, just as no man can prolong his existence beyond a certain point. But while decadence is in progress in one part of the world, the corresponding principle of growth may predominate elsewhere. In every case, when the highest point has been reached, the descent begins. Machiavelli did not flinch from the consequences of this reasoning, when translated into the moral order: evil is the cause of good, and good is the cause of evil. "It has been, is, and always will be true that evil succeeds good, and good evil, and the one is always the cause of the other." On this assumption, the variety of history became no more than the displacement or dislocation of permanent elements: "I am convinced that the world has always existed after the same manner, and the quantity of good and evil in it has been constant: but this good and this evil keep shifting from country to country, as is seen in the records of those ancient Empires which, as their manners changed, passed from the one to the other, but the world itself remained the same: there was this difference only, that whereas Assyria was at first the seat of the world's virtue [*virtù*], this was afterwards placed in Media, then in Persia, until at last it came to Italy and Rome: and though since the Roman Empire no other Empire has followed which has proved lasting, nor in which the world has concentrated its virtue, nevertheless it is seen to have been diffused throughout many nations, in which men lived virtuously [*virtuosamente*]." And what is true of institutions and civilisation in general, is a valid law also in the political world, where forms of government recur in a series which can be calculated upon. Monarchy passes into tyranny, aristocracy into oligarchy, democracy into anarchy: "so, if the founder of a State establishes in a city any one of these three governments, he establishes it for a short time only; for no remedy can be applied to prevent it sliding off into its opposite, owing to the resemblance which exists, in this case, between the virtue and the vice.—This is the circle within which all States have been and are governed." Many revolutions of this nature would exhaust the vitality of a State, and render it the prey of a stronger neighbour; but if any people could possess adequate recuperative power, the circular movement might continue for ever: "a State would be able to revolve for an indefinite period from government to government." Considering the inherent defects of each of these constitutional forms, Machiavelli accorded unreservedly a theoretical preference to a "mixed" government, while rejecting it as practically unsuited to the condition of Italy in his own day.

The next step was to consider, how this tendency to become corrupt and, ultimately, extinct, made itself manifest in a State; what were the symptoms of decay and what the more immediate causes which determined it; and, lastly, what were the methods by which the process of national dissolution might be, at least temporarily, arrested. Machiavelli furnished an answer by a reference to a primitive bias of human nature, a congenital failing in all men. Power breeds appetite; no rulers are ever satisfied; no one has ever reached a position from which he has no desire to advance further. "Ambition is so powerful in the hearts of men that, to whatever height they rise, it never leaves them. The reason is, that nature has created men so that they can desire everything, but they cannot get everything; thus, as the desire is always in excess of the power of gratifying it, the result is that they are discontented and dissatisfied with what they possess. Hence arise the vicissitudes of their fortunes; for as some desire to have more, and some fear to lose what they have already, enmities and wars ensue, which lead to the ruin of one country and the rise of another.—That which more than anything else throws down an empire from its loftiest summit is this: the powerful are never satisfied with their power. Hence it happens that those who have lost are ill-contented and a disposition is aroused to overthrow those who come off victors. Thus it happens that one rises and another dies; and he who has raised himself is for ever pining with new ambition or with fear. This appetite destroys States; and it is the more extraordinary that, while everyone recognises this fault, no one avoids it." The primary impulse towards evil thus comes from within the ruler: the direction in which political changes tend is not determined by the progress of general enlightenment among the citizens, by the growth of new ideas, or by the development of new needs in a country. Machiavelli deemed the individual supreme: a "new prince," like the Greek νομοθέτης, brought into existence an artificial structure, formed on arbitrary lines, and called a State: under this his subjects had to live. He also by his personal and individual failings led the way to ruin. On the other hand, having regard rather to the general body of citizens than to their rulers, Machiavelli believed, like Bacon, that wars were necessary as a national tonic; peace is disruptive and enervating; "war and fear" produce unity. So long as a community continued young, all would be well; but "virtue produces peace, peace idleness, idleness disorder, disorder ruin.—Virtue makes places tranquil; then, from tranquillity results idleness; and idleness wastes country and town. Then, when a district has been involved in disorder for a time, virtue returns to dwell there once again."

The periods within which these inevitable revolutions are accomplished, might, with certain limitations, be regulated by human effort. Man, inasmuch as he is by nature a disorderly being, needed, whatever the form of the government, to be held under control by some despotic power; hence the necessity of law. The rights, the duties, and even the virtues of individuals are the creatures of law. The duration of any constitutional form and the life of any State is in large measure determined by the excellence of its laws. "It is true that a Power generally endures for a larger or a shorter time, according as its laws and institutions are more or less good.—Let Princes know that they begin to lose their State at that hour in which they begin to violate the laws, and those customs and usages which are ancient and under which men have lived for a long time." If the laws are inadequate or unsound, or if they can be ignored with impunity, the obligations hitherto resting upon the citizens are simultaneously removed. Machiavelli, however, believed that there can be extremely few cases in which a man is entitled to judge for himself of the working of law. "Men ought to give honour to the past, and obedience to the present; they ought to wish for good princes, but to put up with them, whatever their character." Innovation is hazardous both for the subject and for the ruler. True political wisdom will be revealed in the organisation of government on a basis so firm that innovation becomes unnecessary. "The safety of a republic or a kingdom consists, not in having a ruler who governs wisely while he lives, but in being subject to one who so organises it that, when he dies, it may continue to maintain itself." Some element of permanence in the source of authority is the more indispensable, because there is a point in the career of every society at which laws would otherwise be too feeble to cope with the general corruption: "there are no laws and no institutions which have power to curb a universal corruption.—Laws, if they are to be observed, presuppose good customs."

Machiavelli by no means overestimated the power of laws; alone, they could never be an adequate instrument of empire. Their severity required to be mitigated, and their restraining force to be supplemented, by some influence potent to control not men's acts only but their minds. There was a sense, therefore, in which the State could not with advantage be separated from the Church; both were to cooperate to create national customs and habits of thought, not less than to enforce order and maintain the stability of society. Without confounding the domains of politics and theology, Machiavelli urged the familiar view that any community, which has lost or misdirected the religious sentiment, has greatly weakened itself and imperilled its own existence. "The observance of the ordinances of religion is the cause of the greatness of commonwealths; so also is their neglect the cause of ruin. For where the fear of God is wanting, a kingdom must either go to ruin, or be supported by the fear of a Prince as compensating for the lost influences of religion.—Rulers of a commonwealth or kingdom ought to preserve the existing foundations of religion; if they do this, it will be easy for them to keep their State religious, and consequently virtuous and united." A politician is not called upon to examine the truth or the absolute value of religion; in some cases it may even be incumbent upon a prince to protect a form of religion which he believes to be false; and thus religious toleration would rest, in the first instance, upon a secular sanction. The ruler must be careful to preserve his intellectual balance, and to allow neither religion nor sentiment to intrude inappropriately. Politics and paternosters are distinct. If the auspices are unfavourable, they must be set aside. On the other hand no ceremonies and no creed can of themselves secure success. "The belief that if you remain idle on your knees, God will fight for you in your own despite, has ruined many kingdoms and many States. Prayers are, indeed, necessary; and he is downright mad who forbids the people their ceremonies and devotions. For from them it seems that men reap union and good order, and upon these depend prosperity and happiness. Yet let no man be so silly as to believe that, if his house falls about his head, God will save it without any other prop; for he will die beneath the ruins." When the supports of law and of religion collapse, a State is approaching its dissolution. It is possible, indeed, that a reformer may be equal to the work of regeneration; but on the other hand it is "very easy for a reformer never to arise." Under such conditions abnormal methods find their justification; recourse must be had to "extraordinary remedies" and "strong medicines"; the diseased members must be cut away, to prolong, though but for a season, the life of a State.

Such, in broad outline, were the chief views of Machiavelli concerning the nature of man and the general movement of history, separated from the limitations of any particular time and place. At first sight they might perhaps appear visionary, remote, unreal; vitiated in some degree by ambiguities in the meaning of the terms employed and by hasty generalisation; academic in character, and out of relation to the storm and stress of a reawakening world. This impression would be only partially true. Machiavelli, living at a period of transition, endeavoured, in the presence of an unusual problem, to push beyond its barriers, and to fix the relations of what was local and temporal to the larger and more universal laws of political societies in general. It was only by enlarging the area of analysis, and embracing the wider questions of history and ethics, that it was possible to frame a scientific basis on which to erect the structure of practical politics. The theoretical foundation was essential. Interest was naturally most largely centred in that portion of his works which was the most unusual; but in reality it is hardly intelligible by itself. Ideas, long familiar in classical literature, may seem in their new context to bear little relation to what has come to be regarded as Machiavelli's main object; in reality they are not extraneous nor incidental, but the logical *prius* of the whole construction. Whoever began without securing his foundations, was obliged to secure them afterwards, though, as Machiavelli reflected, with discomfort to the architect and danger to the building. It was his conception of human nature and of history that logically entitled him to use the experience of the past as a guide for the future; to justify his rejection of constitutional reform where the material to be worked upon was thoroughly corrupt, and virtue imputed for a capital crime; to create new standards, to which appeal might be made in judging practical questions; to throw aside the fetters of medievalism and to treat politics inductively. It was thus that he was led to look to the past, and especially to ancient Rome, for examples and models. Often he repeated with enthusiastic emphasis his abiding conviction, that in his own day the teaching of the Romans might still be applied, their actions imitated, their principles adopted. He was criticised on this ground by Guicciardini and others, who, as they admitted only partially the postulates involved in Machiavelli's conception of history, rejected the appeal to ancient Rome as logically invalid.

This specifically historical theory required an ethical complement. Machiavelli had formed definite opinions upon some of the fundamental questions of moral science. He has recorded his views upon what is now called the origin of morality, and also attempted to determine the real nature of good and evil. Believing men naturally bad, and holding therefore that morality is non-natural, in the sense that it is distasteful to the untrained impulses in men and not to be arrived at by evolving anything of which perhaps they are, in some unexplained way, capable, the question confronted him, How is right action to be enforced? Where does the obligation reside? Only one answer could be consistent, In the laws. To explain this a reference was made to the origins of society. "In the beginning of the world, as the inhabitants were few, they lived for a time dispersed after the manner of wild beasts; afterwards, when they increased and multiplied, they united together, and in order the better to defend themselves, they began to look to that man among them who was the strongest and bravest, and made him their head and obeyed him. From this arose the knowledge of things honourable and good, as opposed to things pernicious and evil; because, seeing that, if a man injured his benefactor, hatred and pity were aroused among men, and that the ungrateful were blamed and the grateful honoured,— reflecting, moreover, that the same injury might be done to themselves,— they resorted to making laws and fixing punishments for whoever violated them: hence came the knowledge of justice. Consequently, when they had afterwards to elect a ruler, they did not seek out the strongest, but the most wise and the most just.—There is a saying that hunger and poverty make men industrious, and the laws make them good."

Thus moral action in a civil society meant for Machiavelli chiefly conformity to a code; the moral sense is the product of law or, in the last analysis, of fear. The sanction of conduct was derived from positive institutions; where no law existed, no action could be unjust. This admitted, the next stage was to interpret the notion of right, and to ask specifically, What *is* right? Machiavelli replied in words that furnished at once a moral criterion and a positive conception of right: "I believe good to be that which conduces to the interests of the majority, and with which the majority are contented." The scope and consequences of such a statement were not perhaps fully realised by him; yet the conception exercised some measure of control, possibly almost unconscious, upon his other views, and might be considered to furnish a sanction for much that is eccentric or immoral; even as an isolated and incidental utterance, it remains a curious forerunner of more modern theories. It is further possible to construct from Machiavelli's *data* a list of the particular virtues which, though not free from the vice of cross-division, nor to be regarded as exhaustive or scientific, helps to widen and complete the conception of his teaching. The virtues, the possession of which would in his judgment be most praiseworthy, are these: liberality, mercy, truthfulness, courage, affability, purity, guilelessness, good-nature, earnestness, devoutness. The last was indeed of supreme importance to all members of society, and so essential to a ruler that whosoever was not reputed religious had no chance of success, and was therefore forced to preserve, as the absolutely indispensable minimum, the appearances at least of a religious believer. For the masses do not discriminate between religion and morality; it is from religion that moral truths are believed by the uneducated conscience of mankind to derive their *ne varietur* character. Speaking more specifically of Christianity, Machiavelli was aware that it had effected a very fundamental change in ethical conceptions. "Our religion has glorified men of humble and contemplative life, rather than men of action. Moreover, it has placed the *summum bonum* in humility, in lowliness, and in the contempt of earthly things; paganism placed it in highmindedness, in bodily strength, and in all the other things which make men strongest. And if our religion requires us to have any strength in us, it calls upon us to be strong to suffer rather than to do." Christianity, as understood by medieval society, appeared to add to the difficulties of combining the characters of the good man and the good citizen. Machiavelli looked for power: "whereas this mode of living seems to have rendered the world weak, and given it over as a prey to wicked men, who can with impunity deal with it as they please; seeing that the mass of mankind, in order to go to Paradise, think more how to endure wrongs than how to avenge them." Such opinions provoked criticism, and were attacked at an early period; afterwards they were, without offence, excused, defended, or outbidden.

When the original obligation of morality and the standard of action had been fixed, it remained to enquire whether men were able to do what was right, *i.e.* whether they were free agents. The constant recurrence of the question in Machiavelli's writings is the measure of the importance it possessed for him. He gave much consideration to this primitive problem, which he called *il sopraccapo della filosofia*; he perceived that it was at least necessary to devise some intellectual compromise which, while in no way claiming to offer a logical solution, should be clear and manageable enough for practical life. His examination was neither thorough nor profound; he did not distinguish the senses which the word *freedom* may, in this context, assume; and his reasoning was complicated by the intrusion of ideas originating in a mythological and figurative conception of Fortune, and in some measure by the lingering influences of astrology. Through all his writings runs the idea of a personified Fortune,—a capricious deity, who is not merely the expression in a figure of the incalculable element in life, but a being with human passions and attributes. Here the suggestions and examples of classical authors, and especially of Polybius, were decisive for Machiavelli, in whom after the manner of his age ancient and modern modes of thought were fancifully blended. "I am not unaware," he wrote, "that many have held and still hold the opinion that human affairs are so ordered by Fortune and by God, that men cannot by their prudence modify them; rather, they have no remedy at all in the matter; and hence they may come to think they need not trouble much about things, but allow themselves to be governed by chance. This opinion has gained more acceptance in our own times, owing to the great changes which have been seen and are seen every day, beyond all human conjecture. I have sometimes thought about this, and have partly inclined to their opinion. Yet, in order that free-will may not be entirely destroyed, I believe the truth may be this: Fortune is the mistress of half our actions, but entrusts the management of the other half, or a little less, to us." This is the solution which, running all through Machiavelli's works, gave a special propriety to the repeated antithesis of *fortuna* and *virtù*. The same meaning would be expressed in modern phraseology by the statement that men determine their own lives, but only under conditions which they neither themselves create nor are able largely to control; or, that the will makes the act, but out of a material not made by it.

Upon the basis of these *data* Machiavelli attempted to fix some general rule of conduct for the guidance of the individual, applicable amid all the diversified conditions under which action can take place. Considering the relation in which the agent stands to the forces among which he has to assert himself, an ideal of conduct was needed which should enable a man, who could have but a limited power of control over the conditions of his life, to succeed. Failure was the seal of Divine disapproval, and to Machiavelli, as to all Italian politicians at his time, the one unpardonable sin. The essential requisite for success was, in his judgment, a constant adaptation between the individual and the surroundings of his life. Sufficient versatility of character, thus understood, would imply a perpetual adjustment of means to the needs of the moment, the ability to reverse a policy or a principle at the call of expediency, and a readiness to compromise or renounce the ideal. The world is rich in failures, because character is too rigid. The truism "Circumstances alter cases," was interpreted by Machiavelli to mean that the pressure of external forces is usually stronger than the resistance of individual principle. This formed the rational basis of his complaints that no one who attempted to govern in Italy would alter the courses to which his genius inclined him, when facts had altered; yet any one who was sufficiently versatile would always have good fortune, and the wise man would at last command the stars and fate. In political life such reasoning led to the rejection of morality, as the plain man understands it. A ruler was to remember that he lived in a world which he had not made, and for which he could not be held responsible; he was not obliged to act on any one principle; he was not to flinch if cruelty, dishonesty, irreligion were necessary; he was exempt from the common law; right and wrong had really nothing to do with the art of government. In furnishing what appeared a reasoned justification for such tenets, Machiavelli interpreted to itself the world of contemporary statecraft, and fixed upon politics the stamp of irremediable immorality—a result to which the rejection of medieval ideas need not necessarily have led.

Such are the general principles which lie at the root of all Machiavelli's teaching, and which serve to universalise all the particular rules and maxims with which his books are crowded. They have, with hardly an exception, their roots in the ancient world, and in nearly every case it can be shown how they were transmitted to him, and how by him the old material was forged and moulded into new shapes. It remains to enquire how they were applied to the necessities of his own age and country. In 1513, Machiavelli was ruined and discredited, ready to despair of Fortune's favour, and willing to accept even the humblest position which would enable him to be of use to himself and his city. Employment was slow in coming, and during enforced leisure he devoted himself to literature. *The Prince* and *The Discourses* were begun in 1513; *The Art of War* was published in 1521, and the eight books of *The Florentine Histories* were ready by 1525. All these works are closely related; in all the same principles are implied; no one of them is any more or less immoral than any of its fellows; they supplement each other, and by precept and example enforce the same conclusions. There is reason to believe that Machiavelli himself considered *The Art of War* the most

14—2

important of his books, but his fame in later generations has rested almost wholly upon *The Prince*.

The contents of *The Prince* were little, if at all, affected by Machiavelli's altered fortunes, though he hoped that if the book was read by the Medici, they might employ him in some official position, for which his past life qualified him. This did not prevent him from developing, without any reserve, the conclusions which his studies and experience had enabled him to mature. He was primarily concerned neither with his own interests nor with the Medici family, but with the problems presented by the condition of Italy in 1513. Ten years previously he had written the words: "Go forth from Tuscany, and consider all Italy." His early writings, and in particular his diplomatic letters, are crowded with suggestions of the form which the conclusions would ultimately take. Slowly, through at least fourteen years, his mind had moved in one direction, and new ideas of a wide compass and a lofty range had taken shape and asserted their claims to recognition. He had been a Florentine of the Florentines, hating Pisa and exulting over Venice. By 1513 he was almost persuaded to become an Italian, to merge the local in the national. Yet, although enthusiastic and at times even visionary, he was under no permanent delusion; the hope of an ultimate unity for Italy could not under the circumstances assume for him any precise form; only as a far-distant aspiration, a pervasive thought, it formed the large background of his speculation. He knew that union was not possible then; but he held, in opposition to Guicciardini, that it was only through union that national prosperity becomes possible; "truly no country was ever united or prosperous, unless the whole of it passes beneath the sway of one commonwealth or one prince, as has happened in the cases of France and Spain." When, however, the possibility of such a thing in his own day was suggested to him, he was, he said, ready to laugh; no progress could be made in the presence of a disruptive Papacy, worthless soldiers, and divided interests. But if autonomy and independence of foreign control could be secured the question would at once enter upon a new stage. Machiavelli did not mistake the problem; but he could not forecast the issues of the nineteenth century.

*The Prince*, though not a complete novelty, became for many reasons a work of primary importance. Machiavelli was the earliest writer who consistently applied the inductive or experimental method to political science. What was new in method produced much that was new in results. The earlier manuals of statecraft rested upon assumptions transmitted through the medieval Church. In Dante's time and long afterwards no man dared to discard the presuppositions of Christianity. Private judgment in politics, scarcely less than in theology, was disqualified, not because it might be incompetent, but as always *e hypothesi* wrong, wherever authority is recognised. Abstract principle of justice, duty, morality, formed the foundation upon which the political theories of the Middle Ages had been constructed. The reasoning from final causes was almost universal. So long as these primary postulates wcre not revised, speculation trod and re-trod the same confined area. What Machiavelli did, was to shift the basis of political science and, consequently, to emancipate the State from ecclesiastical thraldom. Henceforward, the fictions of the Realists, which had controlled the forms of medieval thought in nearly all departments, were set aside; the standard was to be no philosophic *summum bonum*, nor was the *sic volo* of authority to silence enquiry or override argument. An appeal was to be made to history and reason; the publicist was to investigate, not to invent,—to record, not to anticipate,—the laws which appear to govern men's actions. Machiavelli's method of reasoning was a challenge to existing authority, and was believed to entail the disqualification, at least in politics, of the old revealed law of God, in favour either of a restored and revised form of natural law, or at any rate of some new law which man might elicit, independently of God, from the accumulated records of human activity. *The Prince* was the first great work in which the two authorities, the Divine and the human, were clearly seen in collision, and in which the venerable axioms of earlier generations were rejected as practically misleading, and theoretically unsound. The simplicity and directness of its trenchant appeal to common experience and to the average intelligence won for the book a recognition never accorded to Machiavelli's other works.

In *The Prince* the discussion of the methods, by which a "new prince" might consolidate his power, developed into a contribution towards a new conception of the State. The book not only furnished a summary of the means by which, in the circumstances then existing, the redemption of Italy might be accomplished; but, inasmuch as the conditions of life repeat themselves and the recurrence of similar crises in the future was always possible, recommendations, primarily directed to the solution of an immediately pressing difficulty, were enlarged in scope, and came to have the intention of supplying in some measure and with perhaps some minor reservations a law of political action in all times. Beneath the special rules and maxims new principles were latent, and, though obscured occasionally by the form in which they are expressed, they can be disengaged without serious difficulty.

Machiavelli, though his sympathies were republican, knew that the times required the intervention of a despot. He had no hesitation in deciding the relative merits, in the abstract, of the democratic and the monarchical forms of government: "the rule of a people is better than that of a prince." When the problem was, not how to establish a new government in the face of apparently overwhelming obstacles, but only how to carry on what was already well instituted, a republic would be found far more serviceable than a monarchy; "while a prince is superior to a people in instituting laws, in shaping civil society, in framing new statutes and ordinances, a people has the same superiority in preserving what is established." It is doubtful whether Machiavelli ever contemplated the creation of an enduring monarchy in Italy; the continuance of an absolute power would, he believed, corrupt the State. He was on the whole sanguine as to the possibilities of popular rule; he thought it reasonable to compare the voice of the people to the voice of God, and held with Cicero that the masses, though ignorant, may come to understand the truth. But the drastic reform contemplated by him could not be achieved under republican institutions, which could only work satisfactorily among a people whose character was sound. Corruption had gone too far in Italy; "it is corrupt above all other countries." Moreover "a people, into whom corruption has thoroughly entered, cannot live in freedom, I do not say for a short time, but for any time at all." By "corruption" Machiavelli understood primarily the decay of private and civic morality, the growth of impiety and violence, of idleness and ignorance; the prevalence of spite, license, and ambition; the loss of peace and justice; the general contempt of religion. He meant also dishonesty, weakness, disunion. These things, he knew well, are the really decisive factors in national life. For the restoration of old ideals and the inauguration of a new golden age, he *ex hypothesi* looked to the State. And the State is plastic; it is as wax in the hands of the legislator; he can "stamp upon it any new form."

The drift of such arguments is obvious. "It may be taken for a general rule that a republic or kingdom is never, or very rarely, well organised at its beginning, or fundamentally renovated by a reform of its old institutions, unless it is organised by one man....Wherefore the wise founder of a commonwealth, who aims, not at personal profit but at the general good, and desires to benefit not his own descendants but the common motherland, ought to use every effort to obtain the authority for himself alone; and no wise intellect will ever find fault with any extraordinary action employed by him for founding an empire or establishing a republic. For though the act accuses him, the result excuses him." There were, besides, other reasons which led Machiavelli to believe that in 1513 the undivided force of a despot was needed. In every decaying State a class of men is to be found who, whether the degenerate survivors of the old feudal nobility or upstart *signori* with no authoritative title at all, are the enemies of all reform, and who cannot otherwise be suppressed. These *gentiluomini* "live in idleness and plenty on the revenues of their estates, without having any concern with their cultivation or undergoing any labour to obtain a livelihood. They are mischievous in every republic and in every country; yet more mischievous still are those who, besides being so situated, command fortified places and have subjects who obey them. The kingdom of Naples, the territory of

Rome, the Romagna, and Lombardy are filled with these two classes of men. For this reason there has never been in those provinces any republic or free State; for such kinds of person are absolutely antagonistic to all civil government. The attempt to introduce a republic into countries so circumstanced would not be possible. In order to reorganise them—supposing any one had authority to do it—there would be no other way than to establish a monarchy; the reason being this: where the body of the people is so corrupt that the laws are unable to curb it, it is necessary to establish together with the laws a superior force, that is to say, the arm of a King (*mano regia*), which with absolute and overwhelming power may curb the overwhelming ambition and corruption of the nobles." A republic, therefore, cannot initiate a fundamental reform; it is, moreover, too divided in counsel and too dilatory in action; "supposing a republic had the same views and the same wishes as a prince, it will by reason of the slowness of its movements take longer to come to a decision than he." Hence the remedies which republics apply are doubly hazardous, when they have to deal with a crisis which cannot wait.

On these grounds Machiavelli, in pleading for the liberation of Italy from her "barbarian" invaders, addressed a prince; the work of regeneration could logically be entrusted only to an armed despot. It remained to investigate the methods to be employed, and to consider what manner of man the reformer should be. The general principle enforced was that all reform must be retrograde, in the sense that it must bring back the State to its original condition, restoring the old $\eta\theta\sigma\varsigma$ and looking for the ideal in the past. "It is a certain truth that all things in the world have a limit to their existence; but those run the full course that Heaven has in a general way assigned them, which do not disorder their constitution, but maintain it so ordered that it either does not alter, or, if it alters, the change is for its advantage, not to its detriment....Those alterations are salutary, which bring States back towards their first beginnings. Those States, consequently, are best-ordered and longest-lived, which by means of their institutions can be often renewed, or else, apart from their institutions, may be renewed by some accident. And it is clearer than the day that, if these bodies are not renewed, they will not last. The way to renew them is, as has been said, to bring them back to their beginnings, because all the beginnings of republics and kingdoms must contain in themselves some excellence, by means of which they obtain their first reputation and make their first growth. And as in the progress of time this excellence becomes corrupted, unless something intervenes which restores it to its primary condition, these bodies are necessarily destroyed."

Such is the general rule for the guidance of a reformer. As isolation would involve failure, he must, in order to realise his object, make it his first business to secure the favour of the people. However difficult this might be, without some measure of popularity success would be an impossibility. "I reckon unhappy those princes who, to secure their State, are obliged to employ extraordinary methods, having the many for their enemies; for he who has the few for his enemies, readily and without serious difficulties secures himself; but he who has for enemy the whole people never secures himself, and, the more cruel he is, the weaker his rule becomes. So the best remedy within his reach is to try to make friends with the people." To win popularity and yet to conduct a thorough reform might seem hopeless; but Machiavelli found a solution of the difficulty in the blind ignorance of the people, who may easily be deluded by the appearances of liberty. "He who desires or intends to reform the government of a city must, if this reform is to be accepted and carried on with general approval, retain at least the semblance of the ancient methods, lest it should appear to the people that their constitution has changed, although in reality the new institutions are entirely different from the old; for the mass of mankind is fed with appearances as much as with realities; indeed, men are frequently more stirred by what seems than by what is." *Populus vult decipi et decipiatur.* There will, of course, be some few men who cannot be cheated; the new prince must not hesitate to kill them. "When men individually, or a whole city together offend against the State, a prince for a warning to others and for his own safety has no other remedy than to exterminate them; for the prince, who fails to chastise an offender so that he cannot offend any more, is reckoned an ignoramus or a coward." Elsewhere the language is even more explicit: "he who is dead cannot think about revenging himself." But such violence would only be necessary in the early stages of a reformer's career, and a wise prince will so manage that the odium shall fall on his subordinates; he may thus secure a reputation for clemency, and in any case all cruelty must be finished at one stroke, and not subsequently repeated at intervals. Such a course would be less obnoxious than to confiscate property, for men would sooner lose their relatives than forfeit their money. Dead friends may sometimes be forgotten; the memory of lost possessions always survives.

It is clear that the task of a reformer, as Machiavelli understood it, would require a very unusual combination of gifts and qualities. It appeared unlikely that any one could be found with the ability and the will to act without reference to traditional standards, and without concession to the ordinary feelings of humanity. Machiavelli was not blind to the difficulties of the case. It had, first, a moral and an emotional side. Whoever was to accomplish the salvation of Italy must be ready to sacrifice his private convictions and to ignore the rights of conscience. The methods which Machiavelli advocated were, he readily admitted, opposed to the life of a Christian, perhaps even to the life of a human being. Were the morally good to be set side by side with the morally evil, no one would ever be so mad or so wicked, that if asked to choose between the two, he would not praise that which deserved praise and blame that which deserved blame. Machiavelli recognised with regret that " it very seldom happens that a good man is willing to become prince by bad means, though his object be good." The desire for posthumous fame and the knowledge that a retrospective judgment would approve were powerful inducements, but, after all, something weightier was required. Machiavelli was prepared to be logical. An extraordinary problem cannot be solved by a tender conscience; " honest slaves are always slaves, and good men are always paupers." Deceit and cruelty and any other instrument of empire, if they led to success, would be understood and forgiven; " those who conquer, in whatever way they conquer, never reap disgrace." Success became the solvent of moral distinctions, and judgment must follow results. And in the particular case of Italy, a further sanction for the reformer's acts might perhaps be found in the desperate condition of the country, and in the high end in view: " where the bare salvation of the motherland is at stake, there no consideration of justice or injustice can find a place, nor any of mercy and cruelty, or of honour and disgrace; every scruple must be set aside, and that plan followed which saves her life and maintains her liberty."

Supposing any one prepared to accept this solution of the intellectual difficulties, it remained doubtful whether a man could be found with the practical ability and steadiness of nerve necessary to accomplish Machiavelli's design. He was sometimes sanguine, but at other times ready to despair. The condition of success would be thoroughness, and in the history of Rome he found evidences that men may, though rarely, avoid half-measures, and " have recourse to extremities." He knew that to halt between two opinions was always fatal, and that it was moreover not only undesirable, but impossible, to follow a middle course continuously. Unfortunately, human nature is apt to recoil from the extreme of evil and to fall short of the ideal of good; " men know not how to be gloriously wicked or perfectly good; and, when a crime has somewhat of grandeur and nobility in it, they flinch." Yet a great crisis often brings to the front a great man, and in 1513 Machiavelli believed the moment had come: " this opportunity must not be allowed to slip by, in order that Italy may at last see her redeemer appear." The right man was, he believed, a Medici, who, with far greater resources, might succeed where a Borgia had failed. His example was Cesare Borgia, who at the time had alone in any sort attempted the work of consolidation, and while shrinking from no convenient crime had damned himself intelligently.

*The Prince* was not published in Machiavelli's lifetime, was almost certainly never presented either to Giuliano or to Lorenzo de' Medici, and as a practical manifesto with a special purpose in view had no influence whatever. But the book summed up and interpreted the converging temper of political thought, and found an echo in the minds of many generations. When *The Discourses* were known only to political theorists, when *The Florentine Histories* were read only by students, and *The Art of War* had become extinct, *The Prince* still continued to find a ready welcome from men immersed in the practical business of government. Later thinkers carried on the lines of reasoning suggested by Machiavelli, and reached conclusions from which he refrained. At last it became clear, that the problems associated with Machiavelli's name were in fact primitive problems, arising inexorably from the conditions of all human societies. They form part of larger questions, in which they become insensibly merged. When the exact place of Machiavelli in history has been defined, the issues which he raised will still subsist. The difficulties can only ultimately disappear, when the progress of thought has determined in some final and conclusive form the necessary relations of all men to one another and to God.

# CHAPTER VII.

## ROME AND THE TEMPORAL POWER.

WE are to describe the consolidation, at the end of the fifteenth and beginning of the sixteenth century, of the Temporal Power of the Popes which had existed amid the greatest vicissitudes since the alliance of the Papacy with the Frankish Kings in the eighth, but had hitherto been rather a source of humiliation than of strength to the Holy See. It must be shown how this transformation of a feeble and distracted State into one firmly organised and fairly tranquil arose from the general tendency to union and coalescence under a single ruler which prevailed among most European nations at this period, but to which, except in this instance, Italy, unfortunately for herself, remained a stranger: how, in the second place, it was forced upon the Popes by the weakness and insecurity of their temporal position: but how, in the third, it was fostered in an unprecedented degree by the inordinate nepotism of one Pope, and the martial ambition of another. Were the story prolonged, it would appear how these impure agencies were overruled for good, and how, when everything else in Italy lay prostrate before the foreign conqueror, the Temporal Power preserved at least a *simulacrum* of independence until the revival of the aspiration for national unity not only superseded the symbol by the reality, but swept it away as an obstacle in its own path.

Much of the history of Europe in the fifteenth century may be expressed in a single word,—coalescence. A movement, as spontaneous and irresistible as those which had in former times lined the Mediterranean coasts of Asia Minor with Greek colonies, and impelled the Northern nations against the decaying Roman Empire, was now agglomerating petty States and feudal lordships into nations; a process involving vast social as well as political changes. Ancient liberties too often disappeared, but ancient lawlessness also; the tall poppies fell before the sword of the Tarquins of the age; and the mercantile class, which had hitherto only asserted itself under the aegis of the free institutions of independent urban communities, became a powerful element in every land. Everywhere the tendency was towards centralisation, clans and districts massing into nations, semi-independent jurisdictions merging themselves into a single dominant Power. The necessity and the salutary effect of this evolution are proved by the happier fortune of the nations which conformed to it. England, France, Spain, the Scandinavian North, and after a while Russia, became great Powers. Where the movement towards coherence was but partial, as in Germany, the nation remained feeble and distracted; where it proved mainly abortive, as in Italy, the country fell under the sway of the foreigner.

In one important portion of Italy, the impulse towards unity was practically effective, and produced results extending far beyond the narrow stage to which it was in appearance confined. The growth of the Temporal Power of the Papacy is as much a phase of the general tendency towards coalescence which we have described as is the beating down of the feudal aristocracy in England, or the consolidation of France under Louis XI. The conduct of the Popes in incorporating petty independent or semi-independent principalities with the patrimony of St Peter did not materially differ from the line of action adopted by Louis or Henry towards their overpowerful vassals. In all these cases the sovereign was urged on by the spirit and necessities of his age, and contended with the influences that made for disintegration, as in former times he might have contended with the Saracens. There was indeed nothing of the spirit of the crusader in him; and yet, unconsciously, he was leading a crusade against a state of things salutary in its day, but which, at the stage to which the world had progressed, would have fettered the development of Europe. In the case of the Popes, however, one obvious consideration compels us to consider their policy and its consequences from a point of view elsewhere inapplicable. They were spiritual as well as secular sovereigns. Their actions were never confined to a merely political sphere, and could not fail to produce the most important effects upon the greatest spiritual institution the world has ever seen,—an institution which at one time had seemed to pervade the entire social as well as religious fabric of the Middle Ages, and to concentrate every civilising influence within itself.

One distinction between the consolidating activity of a merely temporal sovereign and that of a Pope, though obvious, must not be left without notice, since it accounts in a measure for the special obloquy which the Popes have incurred for obeying the general instinct of their time. The monarch was exempt from all suspicion of nepotism, the interests of his heir were inseparable from the interests of the State. Granted that the former were in fact the more influential with him, the circumstance was really immaterial: he could neither work for himself without working for his successor, nor work for his successor without working for himself. The Pope, on the other hand, as an elected monarch, could not have a legitimate heir, while he was by no means precluded from having nephews or still nearer relatives whose interests might come into collision with the interests of the Church. After his death these relatives would no longer be anything, except in so far as he had been able to create a permanent position for them, and this, rather than the public good, was too likely to be the goal of his exertions. Hence the papal aggrandisement has brought an odium upon the Popes of this age unshared by the contemporary secular sovereigns, and which, in so far as they were actuated by private motives, cannot be said to be undeserved. Sixtus IV, though the era of papal conquests dates from him, and though no Pope wrought more persistently or unscrupulously to secure for the Papacy a commanding position in Italy, must rank rather as an accidental promoter than as a deliberate creator of the Temporal Power, since the mainspring of his policy was manifestly the advantage of his nephews. This cannot be said of one of the two great architects of the Temporal Power—Julius II; whether it applies to his precursor is one of the problems of history. Before, however, the question could arise concerning Alexander VI, there was to be an interval of quiet under a feeble Pope who did little for his family and nothing for the Church, but who admirably suited the circumstances of his time.

Sixtus IV had succeeded well in promoting the interests of his house. Imola and Forlì made an excellent establishment for one nephew, Girolamo Riario; another, Giuliano della Rovere, was one of the most commanding figures in the College of Cardinals. In every other point of view the policy of Sixtus had been a failure; he had lowered the moral authority of the Papacy without any compensating gain in the secular sphere, and had only bequeathed an example destined to remain for a while inoperative. The election of his successor Innocent VIII (August, 1484) was blamed by contemporaries, and pronounced by the Notary Infessura worse even than that of Sixtus, in which bribery had a notorious share. The Notary's charges, notwithstanding, are wanting in definiteness; and it seems needless to look beyond the natural inclination of powerful competitors, neither of whom could achieve the Papacy for himself, to agree upon some generally acceptable person. It is also generally observed that, as the human frailties which in some shape must beset every Pope are especially manifest at the time of his decease, the choice naturally tends towards someone apparently exempt from these particular failings, and hence towards a person different in some sort from his predecessor. As Calixtus had been unlike Nicholas, and Pius unlike Calixtus, and Paul unlike Pius, and Sixtus unlike Paul, it was but in accordance with precedent that the passionate imperious unscrupulous Franciscan should give place to a successor who might have sat for the portrait of an *abbé* in *Gil Blas*. On August 29, 1484, Cardinal Giovanni Battista Cibò became Pope under the name of Innocent VIII. There was probably no more colourless figure in the Sacred College. He had owed the Cardinalate, which he had enjoyed for eleven years, to his Genoese origin and his episcopate over the city of Savona, Sixtus's birthplace. The same circumstances recommended him to the nephew of Sixtus, the able and powerful Cardinal della Rovere, who naturally wished to see one of his uncle's creatures seated on the papal throne; and when two such potent Cardinals as he and the Vice-Chancellor Borgia had agreed, there was but little need for illegitimate modes of action beyond the bestowal of legations and palaces,—almost indispensable concomitants of a papal election in that age. The arrangements thus made, which are enumerated in the despatches of the Florentine envoy Vespucci, were mostly regulated directly or indirectly by Cardinal della Rovere, who found his account in becoming *Papa et plusquam Papa.* The new Pope, indeed, as described by Vespucci, hardly appeared the man to stand by himself. "He has little experience in affairs of State, and little learning, but is not wholly ignorant." As Cardinal he had been distinguished by his affability, and was thought to have let down the dignity of the office. His morals had not been irreproachable, but the attacks of the epigrammatists are gross exaggerations, and, save for a too public manifestation of his affection for his daughter, more criticised by posterity than by contemporaries, his conduct as Pope appears to have been perfectly decorous.

Innocent's part in the evolution which made the Bishop of Rome a powerful temporal sovereign was not conspicuous or glorious, but it was important. It consisted in the demonstration of the absolute necessity of a great extension and fortification of the papal authority, if the Pope was to enjoy the respect of Christendom, or was even to continue at Rome. Never was anarchy more prevalent, or contempt for justice more universal; and the cause was the number of independent jurisdictions, from principalities like Forlì or Faenza down to petty barons established at the gates of Rome,—none of them too petty not to be able to set the Pope at defiance. The general confusion reacted upon the finances, and chronic insolvency accredited the accusations, in all probability calumnious, brought against the Pope "of conniving at the flight of malefactors who paid him money, and granting licenses for sins before their commission." The Pope himself was conscious of his discreditable position, and in a remarkable speech to the Florentine ambassador pronounced by anticipation the apology of his vigorous and unscrupulous successors. "If," he said, "none would aid him against the violence of the King of Naples, he would betake himself abroad, where he would be received with open arms, and where he would be assisted to recover his own, to the shame and scathe of the disloyal princes and peoples of Italy. He could not remain in Italy, if deprived of the dignity befitting a Pope; but neither was he able, if abandoned by the other Italian States, to resist the King, by reason both of the slender military resources of the Church and on account of the unruly Roman barons, who would rejoice to see him in distress. He should therefore deem himself entirely justified in seeking refuge abroad, should nothing less avail to preserve the dignity of the Holy See. Other Popes had done the like, and had returned with fame and honour."

If such was the situation,—and Innocent certainly did not exaggerate it,—the Popes of his day are clearly not to be censured for endeavouring to put it upon a different footing. It might indeed be said that they ought to have renounced the Temporal Power altogether, and gone forth scripless into the world in the fashion of the Apostles; but in their age such a proceeding would have been impracticable, nor could the thought of it have hardly so much as entered their minds. The incurable vice of their position was, that the mutation in things temporal absolutely necessary for the safety and well-being of the Church could not be brought about by means befitting a Christian pastor. The best of men could, upon the papal throne, have effected nothing without violence and treachery. Innocent's successors were not good men, and recourse to means which would have shocked a good man cost them nothing. But they were indisputably the men for the time.

The mission which we have attributed to Innocent of practically demonstrating the need for a strong man in the chair of St Peter, was worked out through a troubled and inglorious pontificate, whose incidents are too remotely connected with the history of the Temporal Power to justify any fulness of treatment in this place. They turn principally upon his relations with Naples and Florence. Having in 1485 entered upon an unnecessary war with Naples, Innocent soon became intimidated, and made peace in 1486. This led to the temporary disgrace of Cardinal della Rovere; and the marriage of the Pope's illegitimate son to the daughter of Lorenzo de' Medici brought him under the influence of the Florentine ruler. It was the best thing that could have happened for the tranquillity of Italy. Lorenzo was a miniature Augustus, intent, indeed, on personal ends in the first instance, but with a genuine fibre of patriotism, and not insatiable or even rapacious. Alone among the rulers of Italy he had the wisdom to discern when acquisition had reached its safe limits, and thenceforth to dedicate his energies to preservation. Hence he was the friend of peace, and the influence he had obtained with the Pope and the King of Naples was devoted to keeping them on amicable terms. In pursuance of this policy he prevented the Pope from allying himself with Venice, and successfully laboured to induce the King to pay to Rome the tribute which he had endeavoured to withhold. No wonder that a course so conducive to the material prosperity of Italy earned Lorenzo her thanks and blessings: yet the unity of Italy, in the last resort her only safety, could only have sprung from national strife. During the generally uneventful decade of 1480–90 the power of France and Spain was growing fast, and a land partitioned between petty principalities and petty republics was lost so soon as two great ambitious Powers agreed to make her their battlefield.

For a time, however, the alliance of Lorenzo and Innocent seemed to have brought about a period of halcyon repose. The Pope's financial straits frequently rendered his position embarrassing and undignified, and his attempts to mitigate these by the multiplication of venal offices aggravated the corruption of his Court. Important events, nevertheless, were as a rule favourable to him. Chance gave the Papacy a certain prestige from its relations with the chief ruler of the Mohammadan world. Upon the death of the conqueror of Constantinople, the incurable vice of all Oriental monarchies revealed itself in a fratricidal contest for the succession between his sons. Bayazid, the elder, gained the throne ; his defeated competitor Jem sought refuge with the Knights of St John of Jerusalem at Rhodes, who naturally detained him as a hostage. The value of the acquisition was proved by the apprehensions of Bayazid, who offered to pay an annual pension so long as his brother should be detained in safe custody. The envy of other Christian States was excited, and every ruler found some reason why the guardianship of Jem should be committed to himself. At length the prize was by common consent entrusted to the Pope, whose claim was really the best, and who actually rendered a service to Christendom by keeping Bayazid in restraint, at least so far as regarded the Mediterranean countries ; nor does he appear to have been wanting in any duty towards his captive. So long as Jem remained in the Pope's keeping, Bayazid observed peace at sea, and paid a pension hardly distinguishable from a tribute ; and it is hard to understand why Innocent's action in the matter should have been condemned by historians. It was further justified in the eyes of his contemporaries by what was then considered a great religious victory, comparable to Augustus's recovery of the standards of Crassus,—the cession by the Sultan of the lance said to have pierced the Saviour's side as He hung upon the cross. Some Cardinals betrayed a sceptical spirit, remarking that this was not the only relic of the kind ; and though received with jubilation at the time, it does not seem to have afterwards figured very conspicuously among the treasures of the Roman See.

A more important success which reflected lustre upon Innocent's pontificate, although he had in no way promoted it, was the fall of Granada on January 2, 1492. The news reached Rome on February 1, and was welcomed with festivals and rejoicings which would have been moderated, if the influence of the event on European politics could then have been comprehended, and the transactions of the next half century foreseen.

When the tidings of the victory arrived, Innocent was already beginning to suffer from the progress of a mortal disease. During the early summer his health grew desperate ; he with difficulty repressed the unseemly contests of Cardinals Borgia and della Rovere, quarrelling in his presence over the steps to be taken after his decease. Strange stories, probably groundless, were told of boys perishing under the surgeon's hands in the endeavour to save the dying Pope's life by transfusion of blood, while he lay in a lethargy. The scene closed on July 25, and on the following day the Pope was interred, in the sarcastic words of a contemporary diarist, *lasso singultu, modicis lacrimis et ejulatu nullo.* Little, indeed, had his life left posterity to applaud or to condemn. His pontificate is only redeemed from absolute insignificance by his docility to the wise counsels of Lorenzo de' Medici,—almost the last occasion in history when it has been possible for a Pope to lean upon a native Italian prince. Lorenzo had preceded him to the tomb by a month; and from Milan to Naples no ruler remained in Italy who was capable of following any other policy than one of selfish aggrandisement.

The election of a Pope (as was remarked above) has frequently resulted in the choice of a successor strongly contrasted in every respect with the previous occupant of the chair of St Peter. It might have been expected that the vacant seat of Innocent would not be filled by another feeble Pope: yet little attention seems to have been paid at first to the prospects of the two ablest and strongest men in the College of Cardinals. Cardinal della Rovere, indeed, might seem excluded by the unwritten law which almost forbade a Cardinal intimately connected with the late Pope to aspire to the Papacy on the first vacancy. The Cardinal was not indeed a relative of Innocent's, but he had been his minister, and was his countryman. Had he been chosen, three Genoese Popes would have worn the tiara in succession,—a scandal to the rest of the peninsula. Moreover, Innocent's promotions of Cardinals had been few and unimportant; he had left no posthumous party in the College. Rodrigo Borgia, Vice-Chancellor and Senior Cardinal, seemed, on the other hand, the man especially pointed out for the emergency. His long occupation of the lucrative Vice-Chancellorship had given him enormous wealth; great capacity for affairs was associated in his person with long and intimate experience; the scandals of his private life counted for little in that age; and, although a Spaniard by birth, he might almost be regarded as a naturalised Italian. If, however, a foreign ambassador may be believed, haughtiness and the imputation of bad faith had ruined his chances at the last election; and it may have been thought that these causes would continue to operate. At all events, his name finds no place in the first speculations of the observers of the conclave. Two of its most respectable members, the Cardinals of Naples and of Lisbon, are apparently the favourites,—when, all on a sudden, on August 11 Rodrigo Borgia is elected by the nearly unanimous vote of the Sacred College, and takes the name of Alexander VI.

Contemporary diarists and letter-writers leave us in no doubt as to the cause of this event. Cardinal Borgia had simply bought up the Sacred College. The principal agent in his elevation was Ascanio Sforza, a Cardinal of the greatest weight for his personal qualities and because of his connexion with the reigning house of Milan, but too young both as a man and a Cardinal to aspire as yet to the Papacy. Borgia's election would vacate the lucrative Vice-Chancellorship, and Sforza was tempted with the reversion. Other Cardinals divided among themselves the archbishoprics, abbacies, and other preferments demitted by the new Pope ; but Sforza's influence was the determining force. His motives were unquestionably rather ambitious than sordid ; he looked to the Vice-Chancellorship to pave his path to the Papacy ; and the tale deserves little credence, that a man who in every subsequent passage of his life evinced magnanimity and high spirit was further tempted by mule-loads of silver. There is, in truth, absolutely no trustworthy evidence as to any money having passed in the shape of coin or bullion, and, although Alexander's election was without question the most notorious of any for the unscrupulous employment of illegitimate influences, it is difficult to affirm that it was in principle more simoniacal than most of those which had lately preceded it or were soon to follow. If the bias of personal interest suffices to invalidate elections decided by it, the age of Alexander cannot be thought to have often seen a lawful Pope. If a less austere view is to be taken, no broad line of demarcation can well be drawn between the election of Alexander and that of Julius.

Whatever the flaw in Alexander's title, he seemed in many respects eminently fit for the office. At the mature age of sixty-two, dignified in personal appearance and in manner, vigorous in constitution, competently learned, a lawyer and a financier who had filled the office of Vice-Chancellor for thirty-six years, versed in diplomacy and well qualified to deal vigorously with turbulent nobles and ferocious bandits, he appeared the aptest possible representative of the Temporal Power while his shortcomings on the spiritual side passed almost unnoticed in an age of lax morality, when religion had with most men become a mere form. Some of the far-seeing, indeed, shook their heads over the Pope's illegitimate offspring, and predicted that the strength of his parental affection, and the imperious vehemence of his character, would lead him further and more disastrously than any predecessor on the paths of nepotism. To most, however, the experienced statesman and diligent man of business, genial and easy-tempered when not crossed, who knew how to combine magnificence with frugality, and whose deep dissimulation was the more dangerous from the perfect genuineness of the sanguine, jovial temperament beneath which it lay concealed, seemed precisely the Pope needed for restoring the Church's tarnished dignity. Nor was it long before Alexander justified a portion of the hope reposed in him by his energy in reestablishing public order and in reinvigorating the administration of justice.

It must always be a question how far Alexander can be said to have ascended the papal throne with a definite intention, either of aggrandising his children or of consolidating his authority as a temporal ruler by the subjugation of his petty vassals. That he meant to promote his children's interests in every practicable manner may well be believed; but that he did not contemplate their elevation to sovereign rank seems manifest from his making the most able and promising of them, his second son Cesare, a Prince of the Church, by exalting him to the cardinalate at the age of eighteen. The Pope's views for his family, however, had necessarily to be expanded in proportion as his secular policy became one of conquest; and, supposing him to have succeeded to the papal throne without any definite intention of subduing his turbulent barons, the need for such a course was soon impressed upon him. A seemingly quite harmless provision made by Innocent VIII for his natural son Franceschetto Cibò gave the first occasion for disturbance. Cibò, a peaceable and insignificant person, recognising his inability to defend the lands with which he had been invested, prudently sold them, and escaped into private life. But the purchaser was Virginio Orsini, a member of a great baronial house already far too powerful for the Pope's security, and whose alternate quarrels and reconciliations with the rival family of the Colonna had for centuries been a chief source of disturbance in the patrimony of St Peter. What was still more serious, the purchase-money was believed to be supplied by Ferdinand King of Naples, whom Orsini had aided in his war with Innocent VIII, and who thus obtained a footing in the Papal States; and the Cardinal della Rovere espoused the cause of Orsini so warmly as to find it prudent to retire (January, 1493) to his bishopric of Ostia at the mouth of the Tiber, where he threatened to intercept the food supplies of Rome. Alexander naturally allied himself with Milan, Venice, and other States inimical to the King of Naples, and a general war seemed about to break out, when it was composed (July) by the intervention of Spain, which had penetrated the designs of the young French King, new to the throne and athirst for glory, for the conquest of Naples, and dreaded the opportunity and advantage that would be afforded him if Naples became embroiled with the Pope. A singular change of relations followed. The King of Naples became to all appearance the Pope's most intimate ally. Alexander's third son married a Neapolitan princess. He became estranged from his recent allies in Venice and Milan, and the Milanese Cardinal Sforza, till now apparently omnipotent at the papal court, lost all credit, notwithstanding the marriage of the Pope's daughter Lucrezia to the despot of Pesaro, a prince of Sforza's house. Yet within two months things took another aspect, when Alexander ignored Ferdinand's wishes in a nomination of Cardinals which gratified the Sforza and drove the freshly reconciled Cardinal della Rovere into new enmity. The entire series of transactions reveals the levity and faithlessness of the rulers of Italy. Alexander had more excuse than any other potentate, for he alone was menaced with serious danger; and he might have learned, had he needed the lesson, the absolute necessity of fortifying the Pope's temporal authority, if even his spiritual authority was to be respected.

The signal for the woes of Italy was given by an event which at another time might not have displeased an Italian patriot,—the death of Ferdinand (or Ferrante), King of Naples, in January, 1494. Ferrante was a monarch after the approved pattern of his age, crafty, cruel, perfidious, but intelligent and well understanding how to make the most of himself and his kingdom. While he lived, the prestige of his authority and experience, combined with the youth of the King of France, may have assisted to delay the execution of French designs upon Naples. Upon his death they were carried forward with such warmth that, as early as February 3, Alexander, whose alliance with Naples remained unimpaired, thought it necessary to censure them in a letter to the French King. A bull assigned by most historians to this date, encouraging Charles to come to Naples in the capacity of a crusader, really belongs to the following year. Whether in obedience to the interests of the hour, or from enlightened policy, Alexander's conduct at this time contrasted favourably with that of other leading men of Italy. Ludovico Sforza, playing with the fire that was to consume him, invited the French King to pass the Alps. The Florentine people favoured Charles VIII, although their unpopular ruler Piero de' Medici seemed on the side of Naples. Venice pretended to espouse Sforza's cause, but could in no way be relied upon. Cardinal della Rovere, whose old feud with the Pope had broken out anew, fled to France where, striving to incense Charles against the Pope, he unchained the tempest against which he was afterwards to contend when too late. Alexander alone, from whatever motive, acted for a time as became a patriotic Italian sovereign. Had he possessed any moral authority, he might have played a greater part. But papal dignity had been decaying since the days of Dante, and Alexander himself had impaired it still further. When his tone seemed the most confident he secretly trembled at the weapons which he had himself put into his enemies' hands by the scandals of his life, and the simony of his election.

Nothing in Charles VIII, either in the outer or in the inner man appeared to betoken the Providential instrument as which he stand forth in history. His ugly and diminutive person bore so little resemblance to his parents that many deemed him a supposititious child; his mind was narrow and uninformed; he was equally destitute of political and of military capacity. He knew, however, how to make himself beloved, *si bon*, deposes the shrewd and observant Commines, *qu'il n'est point possible de voir meilleure créature*. His intentions were good; while unconsciously misled by the noble if perilous passion for glory, he was yet fully convinced that Naples was his of right, for he had inherited the ancient pretensions of the House of Anjou.  He went to war rather in the spirit of a knight-errant than in that of a conqueror, much less of a statesman.  Neither he nor his counsellors dreamed that he was about to bring the political organisation of Italy down like a house of cards, and to launch France on the false path in which she was to persist for centuries without earning in the end anything but humiliation and defeat.  He had already yielded Artois and Franche Comté to Maximilian of Austria for his son, under the terms of the treaty of Arras, and ceded Roussillon and Cerdagne to Ferdinand of Aragon, in order to remove every obstacle to his expedition, which he designed to be the first stage of a Crusade, headed by himself, against the Turks. He had bought the imperial rights of the Paleologi, and aimed at reviving the Byzantine Empire in his own person.  With this anticipation he was determined to demand from Alexander VI the custody of the Sultan's brother Jem ; whether he distinctly contemplated the deposition of the Pope is very doubtful.

Alexander VI might have secured himself by siding with France ; it is to his credit that he remained faithful to his Neapolitan alliance and to the interests of Italy.  A joint plan of operations was agreed upon among the Italian States ; but the French, though so ill provided with money that Charles was obliged to pawn his jewels, carried everything before them by land and sea.  Their land expedition was memorable as the first in which an army bound on a long march had taken with it a train of artillery.  Their maritime superiority gave into their hands Ostia, so lately recovered from Cardinal della Rovere ; the Colonna revolted at the gates of Rome ; and Neapolitan troops, which ought to have moved northward, had to remain in order to protect the Pope.  The terrified Head of Christendom sought the aid of the Turk, and employed Charles's design of setting up the captive Jem against Bayazid as an instrument for recovering the arrears of the pension paid by the Sultan in consideration of his brother's safe custody.  The discovery of the negotiation involved him in obloquy ; yet other Popes have preferred heretical allies to orthodox adversaries.  The genuineness of his instructions to his envoy seems certain ; that of Bayazid's letters urging Jem's removal by poison is very questionable : at all events the proposal, if ever made, was not entertained by Alexander.

The French meanwhile advanced rapidly.  They had entered Turin on September 5 ; by November 8 they had reached Lucca almost without fighting.  Italy was supposed to possess the most scientific generals of the age, but her soldiers were mercenaries who fought for booty as well as pay, and who thought it folly to slay an enemy who might be good for a rich ransom.  An Italian battle had consequently become almost as bloodless as a review.  The barbarity of the French, who actually strove to smite their antagonists hip and thigh, inspired the Italian warriors with nearly as much disgust as dismay : for the first time, perhaps, in history, armies fled although and because they despised the enemy. "The French," said Alexander, "have conquered Italy *con gesso*,"—in allusion to the proceedings of the quartermaster, who simply chalks off the chambers and stables he thinks fit to appropriate. The political disorganisation was worse than the military, and evinced even more clearly the condition to which centuries of selfish intrigue had reduced Italy. Except the King of Naples, who could not abandon Alexander's cause without deserting his own, no Italian prince gave any material aid to the Pope. Piero de' Medici, the feeble and unpopular successor of the great Lorenzo, professed to be the ally of Rome and Naples. But ere the French had appeared before Florence, he made his submission in the hope of preserving his rule, which was nevertheless overthrown by a popular movement a fortnight afterwards (November 9). The Florentines acted partly under the inspiration of the Dominican Savonarola, who could hardly but perceive the fulfilment of his own prophecies in Charles's expedition, and might plead the precedent of Dante for the ruinous error of inviting a deliverer from beyond the Alps.

Alexander showed as much resolution as could be expected, mustering troops, fortifying Rome, arresting Cardinals of doubtful fidelity, and appealing to the rest to accompany him in case of his being compelled to withdraw. But here lay the essential weakness of his position : he could not withdraw. Some authority must exist at Rome to negotiate with Charles VIII upon his entry, now plainly inevitable. If the King did not find the lawful Pope in possession, he might set up another. The need of a reformation of the Church *in capite et membris* had never appeared more urgent, and although the irregularities of Alexander's life might be exaggerated by his enemies, they still afforded ground for doubting whether the *caput* at least was not beyond cure; while his election might be plausibly represented as invalid. If, on the other hand, Charles found Alexander in Rome, he might not only depose him but seize his person. The more violent the alarm into which Alexander was thrown—and so intense it was that a convention with the King of Naples providing for his removal to Gaeta was drawn up and approved, though never signed—the more credit he deserves for his perception that to await Charles would be the lesser peril of the two, and for his resolution in acting upon it. The lesson, that for his own security the Pope must be a powerful temporal sovereign, was no doubt fully impressed upon him : the still more important lesson, that spiritual authority cannot exist without allegiance to the moral code, was less easy of inculcation.

It soon appeared that the Pope's policy was the right one for his present emergency. Charles VIII entered Rome on December 31, and Alexander shut himself up in the Castle of St Angelo. He seemed at the King's mercy, but Charles preferred an accommodation. Men said that Alexander had bribed the French ministers; probably he had, but, corrupt or incorrupt, they could scarcely have advised Charles otherwise. The Pope could not be formally deposed except through the instrumentality of a General Council, which could not easily be convoked, and which, if convoked, would in all probability refuse to take action. Spain might be expected to take the side of the Spanish Pope, and there seemed no good reason for anticipating that other nations would take part with France. The imputations on Alexander's morality were not regarded very seriously in so lax an age: and if, as a matter of fact, he had bought the papacy, the transaction could only be proved by the evidence of the sellers. If, on the other hand, Charles simply imprisoned the Pope without displacing him, he threw Christendom into anarchy, and incurred universal reprobation. To attempt the regeneration of the Church would imperil other projects nearer to Charles's heart, and would be as wide a departure from the original purposes of his expedition as in the thirteenth century the capture of Constantinople had been from the aim of the Fourth Crusade. These considerations might well weigh with Charles's counsellors in advising an agreement with the Pope, although they must have known that conditions extorted by compulsion would bind no longer than compulsion endured. They might indeed have obtained substantial security from the Pope, if they could have constrained him to yield the Castle of St Angelo; but this he steadfastly refused. Cannons were twice pointed at the ramparts; but history cannot say whether they were loaded, and only knows that they were never fired. It was at length agreed that the Pope should yield Cività Vecchia, make his Turkish captive over to the King, and give up his son Cesare as a hostage. Nothing was said of the investiture of Naples, and although Charles afterwards urged this personally upon the Pope at an interview, Alexander, with surprising constancy, continued to refuse, expressing however a willingness to arbitrate upon the claims of the competitors. On January 28, 1495, Charles left Rome to march upon Naples, and two days afterwards was taught the value of diplomatic pledges by the escape of Cesare Borgia, and by Alexander's refusal to surrender Cività Vecchia. A month afterwards the much-coveted Jem died,—of poison, it was said, administered before his departure from Rome; but this is to attribute to poison more than it is capable of performing. Others professed to know that the Prince had been shaved with a poisoned razor; but his death seems sufficiently accounted for by bronchitis and irregularity of living. Jem's death took place at Naples, which Charles had already entered as a conqueror. King Ferdinand's successor, Alfonso, timorous as cruel, and oppressed by a consciousness of the popular hatred, had abdicated and fled to Sicily, leaving his innocent son Ferrante (or Ferrantino) to bear the brunt of invasion. The fickle people of Naples, who had had ample reason to detest the severity of the late King

Ferrante's government, and were without sufficient intelligence to appreciate the wisdom and care for the public welfare which largely compensated it, hastened to acclaim Charles, and Ferrantino retired with touching dignity. Within two months the Neapolitans became as weary of Charles as they had ever been of Ferrante, and a dangerous League was formed in Italy behind his back. Ludovico Sforza had come to perceive how great a fault he had committed in inviting the French King; for the claims of the Duke of Orleans to Milan were at least as substantial as Charles's pretensions to Naples. Maximilian and Ferdinand were no less perturbed at the rapidity of the French conquests; the Pope's sentiments were no secret; and even the cautious Venetians saw the necessity of interference. Between these five Powers a League was concluded (March 31, 1495), whose object was veiled in generalities, but which clearly contemplated the expulsion of the French from Naples. The menace sufficed; on May 20, eight days after his solemn coronation as King of Naples, Charles quitted it, never to return. He did indeed leave a garrison, which was soon dislodged by Spanish troops sent from Sicily, aided by a popular rising, and the young King, so lately deserted by all, was welcomed back with delight. Charles, meanwhile, had proceeded towards Rome, professing an unreciprocated desire to confer with the Pope. Alexander withdrew first to Orvieto, then to Perugia. Charles, after a short stay in Rome, renewed his march northwards. On July 5 an indecisive engagement with the forces of the League at Fornovo, near Parma, insured him a safe retreat, and he was glad to obtain even so much. Notwithstanding the inglorious termination of an expedition which had begun so brilliantly, it forms an epoch in the history of Italy and Europe. In revealing the weakness of Italy, the decay of her military spirit, the faithlessness and disunion of her princes and republics, it not only invited invasion, but provided Europe with a new battlefield. It set up an antagonism between France and Spain, and, while alluring both Powers with visions of easy conquest, ruined the latter State by imposing sacrifices upon her to which she would in any case have been unequal, just at the time when her new acquisitions in America taxed her to the uttermost. It preserved Europe from France by diverting the energies which, wisely exerted, would easily have subdued the Low Countries and the Rhine provinces. Most important of all, the condition of general unsettlement which it ushered in greatly promoted all movements tending to the emancipation of the human intellect. Great was the gain to the world in general, but it was bought by the devastation and enslavement of the most beautiful region of Europe.

The close of Charles's expedition is also an eventful date in the history of Alexander VI. Up to this date he appears the sport of circumstances, which he was henceforth in some manner to shape and control. It was to his credit not to have been seduced into conduct incompatible with his character of a good Italian. Some passages in his conduct might appear ambiguous; in the main, however, whether impelled by honourable or by selfish motives, he had acted as became a patriotic Italian prince, and he was the only Italian prince who had done so. He had been tortuous, perfidious, temporising under stress of circumstances : yet in the main he had obeyed the first and great commandment, to keep the foreigner out of Italy. Had he not afterwards, with what extenuations it will remain to enquire, adopted a different course, the judgment of history upon him as Italian statesman and sovereign must have been highly favourable. A new chapter of his reign was now about to open, pregnant with larger issues of good and ill. He meanwhile manifested his content with the past by causing the most striking episodes of the French invasion of Rome to be depicted in the Castle of St Angelo by the pencil of Pinturicchio. Full of authentic portraits, and costumes and lively representations of actual incidents, these pictures would have been one of the most interesting relics of the age. Their subjects have been preserved by the Pope's German interpreter, who saw them ere they were destroyed by the vandalism of a successor.

Alexander's first step after his return to Rome was the obvious one of strengthening the Castle of St Angelo, which even before the French invasion he had connected with the Vatican by a covered way. His general policy presented no mark for censure. He appeared to aim sincerely at union among the Italian States, and not to be as yet estranged from the public interest by the passion for aggrandising his family. His efforts to bring Florence into the national alliance were laudable; and, if Savonarola obstructed them, it must be owned that in him the preacher predominated over the patriot, and that his tragic fate was in some measure a retribution. This painful history, the right and wrong of which will be perpetually debated, does not however concern the history of the Temporal Power. Alexander's first important step towards the confirmation of the papal authority was the legitimate one of endeavouring to reduce the Orsini, who, though bound to himself by vassalage and to the King of Naples by relationship, had abandoned both during the French invasion. It was nevertheless of evil omen that the papal forces should be commanded by the eldest of Alexander's illegitimate children, the Duke of Gandia, dignified by the title of *Gonfaloniere* of the Church. The war began in October, 1496; and notwithstanding a severe defeat in January, 1497, Alexander was able to conclude a peace in February, by which he recovered Cervetri and Anguillara, the fiefs whose alienation to the Orsini by Franceschetto Cibò had four years before been the beginning of trouble. He was now at liberty to attack Ostia, still in the occupation of the French, who menaced the food-supplies of Rome. The fortress was reduced by Spanish troops, brought from Sicily by Gonzalo de Cordova. Their presence in Rome excited tumults, almost a solitary instance of any open expression of public discontent with Alexander's policy. Personally, indeed, he was never popular ; but his efficiency as an administrator formed the brightest side of his character, and his care for the material interests of his subjects was exemplary. Years afterwards those who had most detested the man wished back the ruler " for his good government, and the plenty of all things in his time."

Unhappily for Alexander's repute, the glory which he might acquire as a just and able ruler was nothing in his eyes compared with the opportunities which his station afforded him for aggrandising his family. Up to this time he had been content with the comparatively inoffensive measures of dignified matrimonial alliances and promotions in Church and State, and had not sought to make his children territorial princes; but, profiting by the death of King Ferrante of Naples, who was succeeded by his uncle Federigo, he now revived papal claims on the territory of Benevento, and erected it into a duchy for the Duke of Gandia. This was to despoil the Church, supposing her claims to have been well founded ; so complete, however, was Alexander's ascendancy over the Sacred College that only one Cardinal dared to object. Simultaneously, Alexander pushed forward his schemes for the advancement of his daughter Lucrezia by divorcing her from her husband Giovanni Sforza, Lord of Pesaro, whose dignity now seemed unequal to the growing grandeur of the Borgia, and who moreover belonged to a family politically estranged from the Pope. A colour of right was not wanting, the divorce, which was decreed by the College of Cardinals after a professedly searching investigation, being grounded upon the alleged impotence of the husband. It is indeed noticeable that Lucrezia, who bore children to both her subsequent husbands, bore none to Giovanni Sforza. The transaction also serves to discredit in some measure the charges brought against the Borgia of secret poisoning, which would have been more easily and conveniently employed than the disagreeable and scandalous method of a legal process.

While Alexander seemed at the summit of success, the wrath or warning of Heaven descended upon him. On the morning of June 15, 1497, the Duke of Gandia was missed from his palace ; soon afterwards his body, gashed with frightful wounds, was taken from the Tiber. Returning the night before from a banquet at the house of his mother, Vanozza, in the company of his brother the Cardinal and other guests, he had separated himself from the party to ride with a masked person who had several times been observed in his company ; and he was never again seen alive. After many had been named as the probable assassins, the popular voice at length proclaimed Cesare Borgia, who certainly profited by the deed ; and most people thought this enough. History cannot convict on such a ground alone, and must rank this picturesque crime among her unsolved problems. After the first paroxysms of grief had subsided, Alexander made a public confession of penitence, which was

probably at the time quite sincere.   With all his dissimulation, he was
a man of vehement emotions.   A commission of Cardinals was appointed
to deliberate upon ecclesiastical reforms ; but by the time when they
reported, Alexander's contrition had vanished.   Their proposals, indeed,
admirable in the abstract, were such as the Church was with difficulty
induced to adopt at the Council of Trent, after having been scourged by
the Reformation for half a century.   Nothing could be more commendable than the prohibition of the sale of spiritual offices ; but it urgently
raised the question how, in that case, was the Pope's government to be
carried on ?

The Duke of Gandia's death is chiefly important on account
of the character of his successor.   There is nothing to prove the
murdered prince anything but an ordinary patrician of his age ; Cesare
Borgia, however, was the complement of his father.   Alexander, an
indefatigable man of business, could never have wasted his time in
inactivity : yet it is conceivable that, had he been without near relations,
he might have applied himself to developing the papal estate as he found
it, and attempted no ambitious conquests, beyond what was necessary
for his own security.   But Cesare seemed driven on by an indwelling
demon,—insatiable, implacable, uncontrollable.   Experience itself could
never have given him his father's wisdom and prudence, but his devouring
energy was even more intense.   From the time of his assumption of a
leading part in affairs the papal policy becomes distinctly one of
conquest.   The profession of care for the general weal of Italy which
had marked the first years of Alexander's pontificate disappeared, and
any foreign alliance was welcome which seemed to insure another principality for Cesare Borgia.   How far this implied a permanent modification in the Pope's views, and how far it was a temporary plan to be
discarded in its turn, is an interesting and a difficult question.   But
certain it is that from this time dates that deliberate creation of a
strong Temporal Power as an auxiliary of the Spiritual which the
present chapter has to record.   Alexander and Cesare might, or might
not, intend that the petty principalities of the Romagna successively
subverted by Cesare should eventually become an independent kingdom
under his government : the only right he could claim to them was by
assignment from the Pope ; and the only condition on which the Pope
could grant this was Cesare's obligation to continue his vassal, and act
as his lieutenant.   It was a great gain to the Holy See to replace a
number of unruly liegemen by a single capable deputy ; but even this
was but a transition stage in the process which must eventually bring
these dependencies under the direct sway of Rome, and constitute by
their aggregation the considerable political entity which has until
recently existed as the Temporal Power.

Thirst for family aggrandisement was not the sole motive which
impelled Alexander to ally himself with the foreigner.   The task of

maintaining order at his own doors had been too hard for him. During the earlier half of 1498 the Roman territory was distracted by the feuds of the Colonna and Orsini, who pursued their strife in total disregard of the authority of the Pope. It was necessary to enlist support from some quarter; nor did Alexander turn to France until he had tried an Italian sovereign. Lucrezia Borgia, emancipated from her real or nominal husband, espoused Alfonso di Biseglia, an illegitimate scion of the House of Naples: but Alexander's ambition went much further, and he demanded the hand of the King's daughter for Cesare, then a Cardinal, but soon to be released from his Orders, which were, in fact, only sub-diaconal. This would have placed him in the direct line of the Neapolitan succession, and have effectually estranged the Pope from France and Spain. Every consideration of sentiment disinclined the King from a step recommended by every consideration of policy; sentiment triumphed, and Naples was lost. Determined to secure an illustrious alliance for his son, Alexander now turned to France, where an event had occurred fraught with mischief to Italy. In April, 1498, Charles VIII died suddenly from the effects of an accident. His only son had died before him, and he was succeeded by Louis XII, Duke of Orleans, a distant cousin, who thought more of his own family claims on Milan than of the title which he had inherited to Naples. It happened also that he was in particular need of the good offices of the Pope, who alone could free him from a marriage forced upon him in his youth, which as he declared had never been consummated by him. This assertion was probably true, and Alexander could afford to act with fairness by referring the question to a commission, which decided in Louis XII's favour. Cesare Borgia, released from his Orders, travelled to France at the head of a brilliant retinue, bringing with him to the King a decree of divorce from his former marriage and a dispensation to contract a new one with his predecessor's widow. He received in return the duchy of Valentinois in Dauphiny. Alexander, who still clung to the Naples marriage-project, expected the French King to use his influence to promote it, and the disappointment of his hopes seemed at one time likely to carry him back to the side of Spain. At last, however (May, 1499), tidings came that Louis had found Cesare another royal bride in the person of Charlotte d'Albret, a princess of the House of Navarre, and Alexander was now fully committed to the French policy, which aimed at nothing less than the subjugation of the duchy of Milan. Venice was to be bribed by a share of the spoil, and Alexander was to be aided in subduing the petty despots who, nominally his vassals, tyrannised over the Romagna and all but besieged the Pope himself in Rome. The undertaking would have been laudable, had not its chief motive been the exaltation of Cesare Borgia.

The fate of Ludovico Sforza was soon decided. Unable to resist the combination of France and Venice, he fled into the Tyrol. Personally he could inspire little sympathy; he had gained his sovereignty by usurpation, coupled, as was very widely believed on evidence which has however failed to convince history, with secret murder; and he had been the first to invite the French into Italy. It was nevertheless shocking and of most inauspicious augury to see an Italian prince dispossessed by the foreigner, with the active aid of one of his own allies and the connivance of another, and deserted by all the rest, who had not like Alexander the excuse of deriving substantial advantage from their perfidy. The French occupied Milan in October, 1499; in December Cesare Borgia, at the head of troops raised by his father and Gascon soldiers and Swiss mercenaries lent by France, commenced the operations which were to result in the constitution of the States of the Church as a European Power.

Theoretically, the Pope was already supreme over the territories of which, three centuries later, the French Revolution was to find him in possession: practically, his authority was a mere shadow. With law and reason on their side, the Popes had rarely been able to reduce their rebellious vassals. Thrice had this apparently been accomplished,—by Cardinal Albornoz as the legate of Innocent VI in the middle of the fourteenth century; by Boniface IX in the very midst of the Great Schism; and by Martin V after its termination. All Martin's gains had been lost under Eugenius IV; and Sixtus IV, with all his unscrupulous energy, had achieved nothing beyond carving out a principality for his own family. Alexander's projects went much further; he wished to crush all the vassal States, and build out of them a kingdom for his son,—with what ulterior aim is one of the problems of history. He must have known that no alienation of the papal title in Cesare's favour could be valid, or would be respected by his successors. He may—so rapidly was he filling the Sacred College with Spanish Cardinals—have looked forward to a successor who would consent to a partnership with Cesare, receiving military support on the one hand, and according spiritual countenance on the other. He may have looked still higher, and regarded the conquest of the Romagna as but a stepping-stone to the acquisition of the Kingdom of Naples for his son; perhaps even to the expulsion of the foreigner, and the sway of the House of Borgia over a grateful and united Italy. Machiavelli evidently thought that Cesare Borgia was the one man from whom the deliverance of Italy might conceivably have come; and the bare possibility that his dark soul may have harboured so generous a project has always in a measure pleaded with Italians for the memory of the most ruthless and treacherous personality of his age.

There was little generosity in Cesare's first movements, which were directed against a woman. Every petty sovereign in the Romagna had given the Pope ample pretext for intervention by withholding tribute, or oppressing his subjects. It was natural, however, to begin with the princes of the House of Sforza, now brought low by the ruin of the chief among them.  Cesare attacked Imola and Forlì, which Sixtus had made the appanage of his nephew Girolamo Riario, and which since the assassination of that detestable tyrant had been governed by his widow, Caterina Sforza.  The courageous spirit of this princess has gained her the good word of history, which she is far from deserving on any other ground.  She was a feudal ruler of the worst type, and in her dominions and elsewhere in the Romagna Cesare was regarded as an avenger commissioned by Heaven to redress ages of oppression and wrong.  The citadel of Forlì surrendered on January 12, 1500.  Caterina was sent to Rome, where she was honourably treated; and though suspected of complicity in an attempt to poison the Pope, was eventually allowed to retire to Florence.  Cesare made a triumphal entry into Rome, but his projects received a temporary check from a revolution in Milan, where Ludovico Sforza recovered his dominions in February, only to lose them again with his liberty in April.  The captive Duke and his brother the Cardinal were sent into France, and Cesare could resume his expedition against the other Romagnol vassals placed upon the Pope's black list as " vicars" in default, the Lords of Pesaro, Rimini, Faenza, and Camerino.

The summer of 1500, nevertheless, passed without further prosecution of Cesare's enterprise, partly because of the difficulty of obtaining the consent of the Venetians to an attack upon Faenza and Rimini; partly, perhaps, from the necessity of replenishing the treasury.  It fitted well with the projects of the Borgia that 1500 was the Year of Jubilee.  Rome was full of pilgrims, every one of whom made an offering, and the sale of indulgences was stimulated to double briskness.  Money poured into the papal coffers, and thence into Cesare's; religion got nothing except a gilded ceiling.  Twelve new Cardinals were created, who paid on the average ten thousand ducats each for their promotion, and the traffic in benefices attained heights of scandal previously unknown.  On the other hand Alexander is not, like most of his immediate predecessors and successors, reproached with any excessive taxation of his people.  The progress which the Turks were then making in the Morea favoured his projects; he exerted himself to give the Venetians both naval and financial aid, and they in return not only withdrew their opposition to his undertakings, but enrolled him among their patricians.  In October, 1500, Cesare marched into the Romagna at the head of ten thousand men.  The tyrants of Rimini and Pesaro fled before him.  Faenza resisted for some time, but ultimately surrendered; and after a while its Lord, the young Astorre Manfredi, was found in the Tiber with a stone about his neck.  Florence and Bologna trembled and sought to buy Cesare off with concessions; the sagacious Venetians, says a contemporary, "looked on unmoved, for they knew that the Duke's conquests were a fire of straw which would go out of itself."  Cesare returned in triumph to Rome (January 17, 1501), and was received "as though he had conquered the lands of the infidels."

He arrived on the eve of one of the most important transactions in Italian history. The refusal of the King of Naples to give his daughter to Cesare had alienated the Pope, and the murder of Lucrezia Borgia's Neapolitan husband in August, 1500, undoubtedly effected through Cesare's agency, has been looked upon as a deliberate prologue to a rupture with Naples. It was more probably the result of a private quarrel; the Pope seems to have honestly tried to protect his son-in-law, and the secret treaty between France and Spain for the partition of Naples was not signed until November, or published until June, 1501. An idle pretext was found in King Federigo's friendly relations with the Sultan; but the archives of European diplomacy register nothing more shameful than this compact, and of all the public acts of Alexander's pontificate his sanction of it is the most disgraceful and indefensible. This sanction was probably reluctant; for he cannot have wished to see two formidable Powers like France and Spain established upon his frontier, and he may have excused himself by the reflexion that there was no help for it, and that he was securing all the compensation he could. Nothing could really compensate for the degradation of the Spiritual Power by its complicity in so infamous a transaction; but this was a consideration which did not strongly appeal to Alexander. It is only just to observe, however, that at bottom this humiliating action sprang from the great cause of humiliation which he was endeavouring to abolish,—the Pope's weakness as a temporal sovereign. This could not be remedied without foreign alliances, and they could not be had unless he was prepared to meet his allies half-way.

The conquest and partition of Naples were effected in a month, Spain taking Apulia and Calabria. The consideration for Alexander's support had been French countenance in the suppression of the turbulent Colonna and Savelli barons who had disquieted the Popes for centuries, but who were now compelled to yield their castles, a welcome token of the disappearance of the feudal age. The Pope's good humour was augmented by the success of his negotiations for the disposal of his daughter Lucrezia, who was betrothed to Alfonso, son of the Duke of Ferrara, in September, and married with great pomp in the following January. The Ferrarese princes only consented through fear; they probably knew that Alexander had only been prevented from attacking them by the veto of Venice. They now obtained a receipt in full and something more, for the Ferrarese tribute was remitted for three generations. The marriage proved happy. Lucrezia, a kindly, accomplished and somewhat apathetic woman, took no more notice of her husband's gallantries than he took of the homage she received from Bembo and other men of letters. Nothing could be less like the real Lucrezia than the Lucrezia of the dramatists and romancers.

The year 1502 beheld a further extension of Cesare's conquests. He

appeared now at the head of a large army, divisions of which were
commanded by the most celebrated Italian mercenary captains.  In June
he conducted an expedition against Camerino, but turned aside to make
a sudden and successful attack on Urbino—a mistake as well as a piece
of perfidy ; for the people of Urbino loved their Duke, and Cesare's sway
was not heartily accepted there as in the Romagna.  It was otherwise
with Camerino, which was acquired with little difficulty.  Negotiations
followed with Florence and the French King, who was then in Italy ;
but while Cesare was scheming to extend his influence over Florence,
and to persuade France to help him to new conquests, he was placed in
the most imminent danger by a conspiracy of his *condottieri*, who had
entered into relations with the Orsini family at Rome.  The plot was
detected, and the incident seemed to have been closed by a reconciliation,
which may have been sincere on the part of the mutinous *condottieri* ;
but Cesare's mind was manifested when on December 31, immediately
after the capture of Sinigaglia, he seized the ringleaders and put them all
to death.  Embalmed in the prose of Machiavelli, who was present in
Cesare's camp as an envoy from Florence, this exploit has gone down to
posterity as Cesare Borgia's masterpiece, matchless in craft and perfidy ;
but it also had more justification than the perpetrators of such actions
can often urge.  In Rome Cardinal Orsini was arrested, and sent to
St Angelo, where he soon expired.  A vigorous campaign against the
castles of the Orsini was set on foot, and they were almost as completely
reduced as those of the Colonna had been.  Alexander might, as he did,
felicitate himself that he had succeeded where all his predecessors had
failed.  The Temporal Power had made prodigious strides in the last
three years, but it was still a question whether its head was to be a Pope
or a secular prince.

With all his triumphs, Alexander was ill at ease.  The robber Kings
who had partitioned Naples had gone to war over their booty.  The
Spaniards were prevailing in the kingdom; but the French threatened to
come to the rescue with an army marching through Italy from north to
south, and Alexander trembled lest they should interfere with his son's
possessions, or with his own.  He began to see what a mistake had been
committed in allowing powerful monarchs to establish themselves on his
borders.  " If the Lord," he said to the Venetian ambassador, " had not
put discord between France and Spain, where should we be ? "  This
utterance escaped him in one of a series of interviews with Giustinian
reported in the latter's despatches, which, if Alexander's sincerity could
be trusted, would do him honour as a patriotic Italian prince.  He
appears or affects to have entirely returned to the ideas of the early
years of his pontificate, when he formed leagues to keep the foreigner
out of Italy.  He paints the wretched condition of Italy in eloquent
language, declares that her last hope consists in an alliance between
himself and Venice, and calls upon the Republic to cooperate with him

ere too late. It was too late already; had it been otherwise, the cautious, selfish Venetians would have been the last to have risked anything for the general good. Alexander must have allied himself either with Spain or with France; he might have decided the contest, but would himself have run great risk of being subjugated by the victor. A quite unforeseen stroke delivered the Papacy from this peril, and, annihilating all Alexander's projects for the grandeur of his house, placed the great work of consolidating the Temporal Power in more disinterested though hardly more scrupulous hands. On August 5 he caught a chill while supping with Cardinal Corneto; on the 12th he felt ill; and on the 18th a fever carried him off. The suddenness of the event, the rapid decomposition of the corpse, and the circumstance that Cesare Borgia was simultaneously taken ill, accredited the inevitable rumours of poison, and his decease became the nucleus of a labyrinthine growth of legend and romance. Modern investigation has dispelled it all, and has left no reasonable doubt that the death was entirely natural.

Alexander's character has undoubtedly gained by the scrutiny of modern historians. It was but natural that one accused of so many crimes, and unquestionably the cause of many scandals, should alternately appear as a tyrant and as a voluptuary. Neither description suits him. The groundwork of his character was extreme exuberance of nature. The Venetian ambassador calls him a carnal man, not implying anything morally derogatory, but meaning a man of sanguine temperament, unable to control his passions and emotions. This perplexed the cool unimpassioned Italians of the diplomatic type then prevalent among rulers and statesmen, and their misapprehensions have unduly prejudiced Alexander, who in truth was not less but more human than most princes of his time. This excessive "carnality" wrought in him for good and ill. Unrestrained by moral scruples, or by any spiritual conception of religion, he was betrayed by it into gross sensuality of one kind, though in other respects he was temperate and abstemious. In the more respectable guise of family affection it led him to outrage every principle of justice; though even here he only performed a necessary work which could not, as one of his agents said, have been accomplished "by holy water." On the other hand, his geniality and joyousness preserved him from tyranny in the ordinary sense of the term; considering the absolute character of his authority, and the standard of his times, it is surprising how little, outside the regions of *la haute politique*, is charged against him. His sanguine constitution also gave him tremendous driving power. "Pope Alexander," says a later writer, censuring the dilatoriness of Leo X, "did but will a thing, and it was done." As a ruler, careful of the material weal of his people, he ranks among the best of his age; as a practical statesman he was the equal of any contemporary. But his insight was impaired by his lack of political morality; he had nothing of the higher wisdom which comprehends the characteristics and foresees the drift of an epoch, and he did not know what a principle was. The general tendency of investigation, while utterly shattering all idle attempts to represent him as a model Pope, has been to relieve him of the most odious imputations against his character. There remains the charge of secret poisoning from motives of cupidity, which indeed appears established, or nearly so, only in a single instance; but this may imply others.

Cesare Borgia afterwards told Machiavelli that he deemed himself to have provided against everything that could possibly happen at the death of his father, but had never thought that he himself might at the same time be disabled by sickness. He succeeded in seizing the Pope's treasure in the Vatican, but failed in securing the Castle of St Angelo, and was obliged to adopt a deferential tone towards the Cardinals. Alexander had gone far towards filling the Sacred College with his own countrymen, and although the Conclave is said by a contemporary to have been more decried for venal practices than any before it, the influence of Ferdinand of Aragon, conjoined with that of Cardinal della Rovere, who found the pear not yet ripe for himself, decided the election in favour of one who assuredly had no share in these practices, the upright Cardinal of Siena. Something may be ascribed to the law already noticed, which frequently fills the place of a deceased Pope with his entire opposite. This may be deemed to have been exemplified anew when, after a sickly pontificate of twenty-seven days, the mild Pius III was replaced (November 1) by the most pugnacious and imperious personality in the Sacred College, Cardinal della Rovere, who evinced his ambition of rivalling if not excelling Alexander by assuming the name of Julius II. His election had not been untainted by simoniacal practices, but cannot like Alexander's be said to have been mainly procured by them. It was rather due to an arrangement with Cesare Borgia, who had the simplicity to expect others to keep faith with him who had kept faith with none, and permitted the Cardinals of his party to vote for della Rovere, on condition that he should be confirmed as *Gonfaloniere* of the Church. History has never made it a reproach to Julius that he soon incarcerated Borgia in St Angelo, and applied himself to stripping him of his possessions in the Romagna. In some cases the exiled lords had reinstated themselves; in others difficulties arose from the fidelity of Cesare's castellans, who refused to obey even the orders extorted from him to surrender their castles. When at last everything had been got from him that could be got, Julius, instead of secretly putting him to death as Alexander would have done, permitted him to depart to Naples, where he was arrested and sent prisoner into Spain. His career was yet to be illustrated by a romantic escape and a soldier's death in an obscure skirmish in Navarre. The Romagna could not forget that he had been to her one just ruler in the place of many tyrants, and he retained partisans there to the last. Had he survived until the new Pope's war with his brother-in-law the Duke of Ferrara, he would probably have commanded the latter's troops, and a new page of conquest might have opened for him.

Julius had hated Alexander above all men; but it was now incumbent upon him to resume Alexander's work, repair the damage it had sustained, and prosecute it to a successful conclusion. His record as Cardinal had not been a bright one. When in favour with Pope Innocent, he had failed to inspire him with energy except for an unjust war, or to reform any abuse in the papal administration. As the enemy of Alexander, he had put himself in the wrong by turbulence and unpatriotic intrigue. If he had not done Italy infinite harm by his invitations to France to invade her, the reason was merely that the French would have come without him. When ostensibly reconciled to Alexander, he had shown much servility. His private life had been licentious; though not illiterate, he was no proficient in literature; and one looks in vain for any service rendered by him as Cardinal to religion, letters, or art. Yet there was always something in him which conveyed the impression of a superior character; he overawed others, and was never treated with disrespect. There was indeed a natural magnanimity in him which adverse circumstances had checked, but which came out so soon as he obtained liberty of action. Unlike his predecessor, he had an deal of what a Pope should be,—defective indeed, but embodying all he qualities particularly demanded by the age. He thought far more of the Church in her temporal than in her spiritual aspect; but Luther was not yet, and for the moment the temporal need seemed the more pressing. He possessed a great advantage over his predecessor in his freedom from nepotism: he had no son, and was content with a modest provision for his daughter, and not only seemed but was personally disinterested in the wars which he undertook for the aggrandisement of the Church. The vehemence which engaged him in such undertakings made him terrible and indefatigable in the prosecution of them; but, as he was deficient in the prudence and discernment of his predecessor, it frequently hurried him into inconsiderate actions and speeches, detrimental to his interests and dignity. Transplanted, however, to another sphere, it secured him a purer and more desirable glory than any that he could obtain by conquest. Having once determined it to be a Pope's duty to encourage the arts, he entered upon the task as he would have entered upon a campaign, and achieved results far beyond the ambition of his most refined and accomplished predecessors. His treatment of individual artists was often harsh and niggardly, but of his dealings with art as a whole Bishop Creighton rightly declares: "he did not merely employ great artists, he impressed them with a sense of his own greatness, and called out all that was strongest and noblest in their own nature. They knew that they served a master who was in sympathy with themselves."

While Julius was ridding himself of Cesare Borgia, a new enemy appeared, too formidable for him to contend with at the time. In the autumn of 1503 the Venetians suddenly seized upon Rimini and Faenza. The aggression was most audacious, and Venice was to find that it was also most unwise. It was no less disastrous to Italy, giving the policy of Julius an unhappy bent from which it could never afterwards free itself. Notwithstanding the errors of his younger days, there is no reason to doubt that he was really a sound patriot, to whom the expulsion of the foreigner always appeared a desirable if remote ideal, and who had no wish to ally himself more closely than he could help with Spain or France. He now had before him only the alternatives of calling in the foreigner or of submitting to an outrageous aggression, and it is not surprising that he preferred the former. He was aware of the mischief that he and Venice were perpetrating between them. " Venice," he said, " makes both herself and me the slaves of everyone— herself that she may keep, me that I may win back. But for this we might have been united to find some way to free Italy from foreigners." It would have been wiser and more patriotic to have waited until some conjunction of circumstances should arise to compel Venice to seek his alliance; but when the fire of his temper and the magnitude of the injury are considered, it can but appear natural that he should have striven to create such a conjuncture himself. This was no difficult matter: every European State envied Venice's wealth and prosperity and her uniformly selfish policy had left her without a friend. By September, 1504, Julius had succeeded in bringing about an anti Venetian League between Maximilian and Louis XII of France, which indeed came to nothing, but sufficiently alarmed the Venetians to induce them to restore Ravenna and Cervia, which had long been in their possession, retaining their recent acquisitions, Faenza and Rimini The Duke of Urbino, the Pope's kinsman, undertook that he would not reclaim these places: Julius dexterously evaded making any such pledge and the seed of war went on slowly ripening.

During this period Julius performed two other actions of im portance. He restored their castles to the Colonna and the Orsini a retrograde step whose ill consequences he was himself to experience and he promulgated a bull against simony in papal elections. His own had not been pure, and the measure may have been intended to silence rumours, but it is quite as likely to have been the fruit of genuine compunction. In any case it distinguishes him favourably from his predecessor, who regarded such iniquities as matter of course, while Julius signalised them as abuses to be rooted out Nor were his efforts vain; though bribery in the coarse form of actual money payment is known to have been attempted at more recent papal elections, it does not appear to have actually determined any.

While nursing his wrath against Venice, Julius sought to compensate the losses of the Church by acquisitions in other quarters. Upon the fall of Cesare Borgia, Urbino and Perugia had reverted to their former lords. Ferrara had now lost the protection insured to it by the Borgia marriage, and the tyranny of the Bentivogli in Bologna incited attack. The Duke of Urbino was Julius's kinsman, and Ferrara was too strong; but the Pope thought he might well assert the claims of the Church to Perugia and Bologna, especially as their conquest could be represented as a crusade for the deliverance of the oppressed, and no imputation of nepotism could be made against him as against his predecessors. Yet he could not avoid exposing himself to the reproach incurred by an alliance with foreigners against Italians. Bologna was under the protectorate of the French King, and Julius could do nothing until he had dissolved this alliance and received a promise of French cooperation. This having been obtained through the influence of King Louis's prime minister, Cardinal d'Amboise, procured by the promise of three cardinalships for his nephews, Julius quitted Rome in August, 1506, at the head of his own army, a sight which Christendom had not seen for ages. Perugia was yielded without a contest, on the stipulation that the Baglioni should not be entirely expelled from the city. Julius continued his march across the Apennines, and on October 7 issued a bull deposing Giovanni Bentivoglio and excommunicating him and his adherents as rebels. Eight thousand French troops simultaneously advanced against Bologna from Milan. Bentivoglio, unable to resist the double attack, took refuge in the French camp, and the city opened its gates to Julius, who might boast of having vindicated his rights and enlarged the papal dominions without spilling a drop of blood. His triumph was commemorated by Michael Angelo's colossal statue, destined to a brief existence, but famous in the history of art. But Julius was a better judge of artists than of ministers, and the misconduct of the legates successively appointed by him to govern Bologna alienated the citizens, and prepared the way for fresh revolutions.

The easy conquest of Bologna could not but whet the Pope's appetite for revenge upon Venice, and ought to have shown the Venetians how formidable an enemy he could be. They continued, nevertheless, to cling with tenacity to their ill-gotten acquisitions in the Romagna, unaware of or indifferent to their peril from the jealousy of the chief states of Europe. No other Power, it was true, had any just cause of quarrel with them. Their most recent acquisitions in Lombardy had indeed been basely obtained as the price of cooperation in the overthrow of Ludovico Sforza: the Neapolitan cities, though acquired by the grant of Ferrantino, had been retained by connivance at the destruction of Federigo; they were, notwithstanding, the stipulated price of these iniquities, which the conquerors of Milan and Naples had no right to reclaim. Their late gains from Maximilian had been made in open war, and confirmed by solemn treaty. These considerations weighed nothing with him or with France; and at Julius's instigation these Powers concluded on December 10, 1508, the famous treaty known as the League of Cambray, by which the continental dominions of Venice were to be divided between them, reservation being made of the claims of the Pope, Mantua, and Ferrara. Spain, if she acceded, was to have the Neapolitan cities occupied by Venice; Dalmatia was to go to Hungary; even the Duke of Savoy was tempted by the bait of Cyprus. It seemed to occur to none that they were destroying "Europe's bulwark 'gainst the Ottomite."

Julius, though the mainspring of the League, avoided joining it openly until he saw that the allies were committed to the war. His assent was given on March 25, 1509; on April 7 the Venetians offered to restore Faenza and Rimini. But the Pope was too deeply engaged, and probably thought that the offer was only made to divide the allies, and would be withdrawn when it had served its purpose. On April 27 he published a violent bull of excommunication. His troops entered the Romagna; but the Emperor and Spain held back, and left the conquest of Lombardy to France. It proved unexpectedly easy. The Venetians were completely defeated at Agnadello on May 14, and the French immediately possessed themselves of Lombardy as far as the Mincio. They halted there, having obtained all they wanted. Maximilian had not yet appeared on the scene, and the extraordinary panic into which the Venetians seemed to fall is to be accounted for not so much by the severity of their defeat as by the mutiny or dispersion of the Venetian militia. They hastened to restore the disputed towns in the Romagna to the Pope,—an act right and wise in itself, but carried out with unthinking precipitation. If the towns had been bravely defended, Julius would probably have met the Venetians half way; as they had no longer any hold upon him, he remained inexorable, and vented his wrath with every token of contumely and harshness. They were equally submissive to Maximilian, who was by this time in partial occupation of the country to the east of the Mincio; nor was it until July 17, that, encouraged by the scantness of his troops and the slenderness of his pecuniary resources, they plucked up courage to recover Padua. Stung by this mortification, Maximilian succeeded in assembling a formidable army; but Venice had in the meantime reorganised her scattered forces, and obtained fresh recruits from Dalmatia and Albania. Padua was besieged during the latter half of September; but the siege was raised early in October. Most of Maximilian's conquests were recovered by the Venetians, and their spirit rose fast, until it was again humbled by the destruction of their fleet on the Po by the artillery of the Duke of Ferrara.

All this time Julius had been browbeating the Venetians. No

content with the recovery of his territory, he demanded submission on all ecclesiastical questions. Venice was to surrender its claims to nominate to bishoprics and benefices, to entertain appeals in ecclesiastical cases, and to tax or try the clergy. Freedom of trade was also demanded, with other minor concessions. It seems almost surprising that the Venetians, who had no great cause to fear the Pope's military or naval strength, and knew that he was beginning to quarrel with the King of France, should have yielded. In fact this resolution was only adopted by a bare majority in the Council, and they guarded themselves by a secret protest as respected their ecclesiastical concessions. The Pope's successors soon found that *non ligant foedera facta metu.* Venice never permanently recovered her possessions in the Romagna; but most of her territorial losses in other quarters were regained by the Treaty of Noyon in 1516. A blow unconnected with Italian politics, and against which war and diplomacy were powerless, had nevertheless been struck by the diversion to Lisbon of her gainful Oriental traffic, consequent upon the doubling of the Cape of Good Hope. A brilliant period in letters and the arts lay yet before her; she was still to war with the Turk in Cyprus and the Morea; but she soon ceased to rank as a first-class Power.

Absolution was formally granted to Venice on February 24, 1510, and Julius thus became openly detached from the League of Cambray. The incident marks the definitive consolidation of the Papal States; for although districts were occasionally lost and others occasionally added during the agitations of the following confused years, such variations were but temporary, and it was long ere the papal territory was finally rounded off by the acquisition of Ferrara and Urbino. From his own point of view Julius had done great things. By dexterous diplomacy and martial daring he had preserved or recovered or augmented Alexander's conquests, and given no suspicion of any intention of alienating them for the benefit of his own family. He was now, what so many Popes had vainly sighed to be, master in his own house, and a considerable temporal sovereign. Yet, if he was at all accessible to the feelings with which he has been usually credited, he must have reflected with remorse that this end had only been accomplished by allying himself with foreigners for the humiliation, almost the ruin, of the only considerable Italian State. He might naturally wish to repair the mischief he had done by humbling the foreigners in their turn. Other causes concurred,—his dread of the preponderance of the French in Northern Italy, his grief at the subjugation of his own city of Genoa by them; above all, it must be feared, his desire to aggrandise the Church by annexing the dominions of the Duke of Ferrara, who was protected by France. Alfonso of Ferrara had been a useful ally in the Pope's attack upon Venice, but he had declined to follow his example in making peace with her; he was personally obnoxious as Alexander VI's son-in-law; and his salt-works at Comacchio competed with the Pope's own. It is remarkable that Julius should be indebted to the least justifiable of his actions for much of his reputation with posterity. It would be difficult to conceive anything more scandalous than his sudden turning round upon his allies so soon as they had helped him to gain his ends. But he proclaimed, and no doubt with a certain measure of sincerity, that his ultimate aim was the deliverance of Italy from the foreigner; and Italian patriots have been so rejoiced to find an Italian prince actually taking up arms against the foreigner instead of merely talking about it, that they have canonised him,—and canonised he will remain. It is also to be remarked that the transactions of the remaining years of his pontificate were on a grander scale than heretofore, and better adapted to exhibit the picturesque aspects of his fiery and indomitable nature.

The War was precipitated by an incident which seemed to give the Pope an opportunity of beginning it with advantage. Louis XII had refused to grant the Swiss the terms which they demanded for the renewal of their alliance with him, which insured him the services, on occasion, of a large number of mercenaries. Julius stepped into his place, and the Swiss agreed to aid him with fifteen thousand men (May, 1510). Elated at this, he resolved to begin the War without delay, though his overtures to other allies had been coldly received, and even the grant of the investiture of Naples, a studied affront to the French King, had failed to bring Ferdinand of Aragon to his side. The Venetians, however, still unreconciled to France, and thirsting for revenge on the Duke of Ferrara, espoused the Pope's cause. The first act of hostility was a bull excommunicating the Duke of Ferrara which, Peter Martyr says, made his hair stand on end, and in which the salt-trade was not forgotten. The Popes failed to perceive how by reckless misuse they were blunting the weapon which they would soon need for more spiritual ends. Louis paid Julius back in his own coin, convoking the French clergy to protest, and threatening a General Council. Modena was reduced by the papal troops; but when, in October, Julius reached Bologna, he received the mortifying intelligence that the Swiss had deserted him, pretending that they had not understood that they were to fight against France. This left the country open to the French commander Chaumont, who, profiting by the division of the Pope's forces between Modena and Bologna, advanced so near the latter city that with a little more energy he could have captured Julius, who was confined to his bed by a fever. While the French general negotiated, Venetian reinforcements appeared and rescued the Pope, wellnigh delirious between fever and fright. When he recovered, he undertook the reduction of the castles of Concordia and Mirandola, commanding the road to Ferrara. Mirandola held out until the winter, and the Pope, enraged at the slowness of his generals, proceeded thither in person and busied himself with military operations, tramping in the deep snow, lodging in a kitchen, swearing at his officers, joking with the soldiers, and endearing himself to the camp by his fund of anecdote and his rough wit.  Mirandola fell at last; but the Pope could make no further progress.  Negotiations were set on foot, but came to nothing.  In May, 1511 the new French general Trivulzio made a descent on Bologna, which was greatly exasperated by the misgovernment of the Legate Alidosi, expelled the Pope's troops, and reinstated the Bentivogli.  Michael Angelo's statue of Julius was hurled from its pedestal, and the Duke of Ferrara, though a reputed lover of art, could not refrain from the practical sarcasm of melting it into a cannon.  Alidosi, gravely suspected of treachery, was cut down by the Duke of Urbino's own hand.  Mirandola was retaken, and Julius returned to Rome apparently beaten at every point, but as resolute as ever.  All Europe was being drawn into his broils.  He looked to Spain, Venice, and England to aid him, and this actually came to pass.

Before, however, the "Holy League" could take effect, Julius fell alarmingly ill.  On August 21 his life was despaired of, and the Orsini and Colonna, whom he had inconsiderately reinstated, prepared to renew their ancient conflicts.  One of the Colonna, Pompeio Bishop of Rieti, a soldier made into a priest against his will, exhorted the Roman people to take the government of the city upon themselves, and was ready to play the part of Rienzi, when Julius suddenly recovered in spite of, or because of, the wine which he insisted on drinking.  His death would have altered the politics of Europe; so important a factor had the Temporal Power now become.  It would also have saved the Church from a small abortive schism.  On September 1, 1511 a handful of dissentient cardinals, reinforced by some French bishops and abbots, met at Pisa in the guise of a General Council.  They soon found it advisable to gather more closely under the wing of the French King by retiring to Milan, whose contemporary chronicler says that he does not think their proceedings worth the ink it would take to record them.  The principal result was the convocation by Julius of a genuine Council at the Lateran, which was actually opened on May 10, 1512.  A step deserving to be called bold, since there was in general nothing that Popes abhorred so much as a General Council; significant, as an admission that the Church needed to be rehabilitated; politic, because Julius's breach of his election promise to summon a Council was the ostensible ground of the convocation of the Pisan.

Julius would have commenced the campaign of 1512 with the greatest chances of success, if his operations had been more skilfully combined; but the Swiss invasion of Lombardy on which he had relied was over, before his own movements had begun.  Scarcely had the Swiss, discouraged by want of support, withdrawn across the Alps, when Julius's army, consisting chiefly of Spaniards under Ramon de Cardona, but with a papal contingent under a papal legate, Cardinal de' Medici,

afterwards Leo X, presented itself before Bologna. In the ordinary
course of things Bologna would have fallen; but the French were
commanded by a great military genius, the youthful Gaston de Foix,
whose life and death alike demonstrated that human personality
counts for much, and that history is not a matter of mere abstract
law.   By skilful manœuvres Gaston compelled the allies to withdraw
into the Romagna, and then (April 11) entirely overthrew them in
the great fight of Ravenna,—most picturesque of battles, pictorial in
every detail, from the stalwart figure of the revolted Cardinal Sanseverino
turning out in complete armour to smite the Pope, to the capture of
Cardinal de' Medici by Greeks in French service, and the death of the young
hero himself, as he strove to crown his victory by the annihilation of the
solid Spanish infantry.   Had he lived, he would soon have been in Rome,
and the Pope, unless he submitted, must have become a captive in France
or a refugee in Spain.   Julius resisted the Cardinals who beset him with
clamours for peace, but his galleys were being equipped for flight when
Giulio de' Medici, afterwards Clement VII, arrived as a messenger from
his cousin the captive legate, with such a picture of the discord among
the victors after Gaston's death that Pope and Cardinals breathed again.
Within a few weeks the French were recalled to Lombardy by another
Swiss invasion.   The German mercenaries, of whom their forces largely
consisted, deserted them at the command of the Emperor, and the army
that might have stood at the gates of Rome actually abandoned Milan,
and with it all the conquests of recent years.   The anti-papal Council
fled into France, and Cardinal Medici was rescued by the Lombard
peasantry.   The Duke of Urbino, who, estranged from the Pope by the
summary justice he had exercised upon Cardinal Alidosi, had for a time
kept aloof and afterwards been on the point of joining the French,
now came forward to provide Julius with another army.   The Bentivogli
fled from Bologna, and the papal troops further occupied Parma and
Piacenza.   But Julius thought nothing done so long as the Duke of
Ferrara retained his dominions.   The Duke came in person to Rome
to deprecate his wrath, protected by a safe conduct, and accompanied by
his own liberated captive, Fabrizio Colonna.   Julius received him kindly,
freed him from all spiritual censures, but was inflexible in temporal
matters;   the surrender of the duchy he must and would have.
Alfonso proving equally firm, the Pope so far forgot himself as to
threaten him with imprisonment; but Fabrizio Colonna, declaring his
own reputation at stake, procured his escape, and escorted him safely
back.   Such instances of a nice sense of personal honour are not infrequent in the annals of the age, and afford a refreshing contrast to the
general political immorality.

An event was now about to happen which, although he was not the
chief agent in it, contributed most of all to confer on Julius the proud
title of Deliverer of Italy.   It was necessary to decide the fate of the

Duchy of Milan, which Ferdinand and Maximilian wished to give to their grandson the Archduke Charles, afterwards the Emperor Charles V. Julius had not driven the French out in order to put the Spaniards and Austrians in. He demanded the restoration of the expelled Italian dynasty in the person of Massimiliano Sforza. Fortunately the decision of the question lay with the Swiss, who from motives of money and policy took the side of Sforza; and he was installed accordingly. All must have seen that this arrangement was a mere makeshift; but the restoration, however precarious, of an Italian dynasty to an Italian State so long usurped by the foreigner was enough to cover Julius with glory. He had unquestionably in this instance done his duty as an Italian sovereign, and men did not over-nicely consider how impotent he would have been without foreign aid, and how substantial an advantage he was obtaining for himself by the annexation of Parma and Piacenza, long held by the ruler of Milan, but now discovered to have been bequeathed to the Church by the Countess Matilda four hundred years before.

A deplorable contemporary event, meanwhile, passed almost unnoticed in the general joy at the expulsion of the French, and the unprecedented development of the Pope's temporal power. This was the subversion of the Florentine republic and the restoration of the Medici, discreditable to the Spaniards who achieved it and to the Pope who permitted it, but chiefly to the Florentines themselves. Their weakness and levity, the memory of the early Medicean rulers, the feeling that since their expulsion Florence had been no strong defence or worthy example to Italy, and the fact that no foreigner was placed in possession, mitigated the indignation and alarm naturally aroused by such a catastrophe. It was not foreseen that in after years a Medicean Pope would accept the maintenance of his family in Florence by way of consideration for the entire sacrifice of the independence of Italy.

The time of Julius's removal from the scenes of earth was approaching, and it was well for him. The continuance of his life and of his reputation would hardly have been compatible. He was about to show, as he had shown before, that, however attached in the abstract to the liberty of Italy, he was always willing to postpone this to his own projects. He had two especially at heart, the subjugation of Ferrara and the success of the Lateran Council, which he had convoked to eclipse the schismatical Council of Pisa. For this the support of the Emperor Maximilian was necessary; for the Council, which had already begun to deliberate, might appear hardly more respectable than its rival, if it was ignored by both France and Germany. As a condition, Maximilian insisted on concessions from the Venetians, whom the Pope ordered to surrender Verona and Vicenza, and to hold Padua and Treviso as fiefs of the Empire. The Venetians refused, and Julius threatened them with excommunication. Fortunately for his fame, the stroke was delayed until it was too late. He had long been suffering from a complication of infirmities. At the end of January, 1513, he took to his bed; on February 4 he professed himself without hope of recovery; on February 20 he received the last sacraments, and he died on the following day. Goethe says that every man abides in our memory in the character under which he has last been prominently displayed; the last days of Julius II exhibited him to the most advantage. He addressed the cardinals with dignity and tenderness; he deplored his faults and errors without descending to particulars; he spoke of the schismatics with forbearance, yet with unbending resolution; he ordered the reissue of his regulations against simony in pontifical elections; and gave many wholesome admonitions respecting the future conclave. On foreign affairs he seems not to have touched. His death evoked the most vehement demonstrations of popular sorrow. Never, says Paris de Grassis, who as papal master of the ceremonies was certain to be well-informed, had there been at the funeral of any Pope anything like the concourse of persons of every age, sex and rank thronging to kiss his feet, and imploring with cries and tears the salvation of him who had been a true Pope of Rome and Vicar of Christ, maintaining justice, augmenting the Church, and warring upon and putting down tyrants and enemies. " Many to whom his death might have been deemed welcome lamented him with abundant tears as they said, 'This Pope has delivered us all, all Italy and all Christendom from the hands of the Gauls and Barbarians.'"

This enthusiastic panegyric would have been moderated if the secret springs of Julius's policy had been better known; if it had been understood how Fortune, rather than Wisdom, had stood his friend through life; and if the inevitably transitory character of his best work had been perceived. A national dynasty might be restored to Milan, but it could not be kept there, nor could it prove aught but the puppet of the foreigner while it remained. The fate of Italy had been sealed long ago, when she refused to participate in the movement of coalescence which was consolidating disjointed communities into great nations. These nations had now become great military monarchies, for which a loose bundle of petty States was no match. A Cesare Borgia might possibly have saved her, if he had wrought at the beginning of the fifteenth century instead of the end. Venice did something; but she was essentially a maritime Power, and her possessions on the mainland were in many respects a source of weakness. The only considerable approach to consolidation was the establishment of the Papal Temporal Power, of which Alexander and Julius were the chief architects. While the means employed in its creation were often most condemnable, the creation itself was justified by the helpless condition of the Papacy without it, and by the useful end it was to serve when it became the only vestige of dignity and independence left to Italy.

# CHAPTER VIII.

## VENICE.

THE beginning of the fifteenth century offers a convenient point whence to survey the growth of the Venetian Republic. Venice had by that time become the Venice of modern European history; a great trading city; a mart for the exchange of goods between East and West; committed to a policy destined to make her one of the five Italian Powers and eventually to raise up against her a coalition of all Italy and Europe. Her constitution was fixed; her colonial system developed; her position towards the Church defined; her aggrandisement on the Italian mainland initiated; her wealth, her splendour, her art were beginning to attract the attention of the civilised world. The various threads of Venetian history are drawn together at this epoch. The Republic was about to move forward upon a larger, more ambitious career than it had hitherto followed; a career for which its various lines of development,—the creation of a maritime empire, expansion on the mainland, efforts for ecclesiastical independence, growth and solidification of the constitution, —had been slowly preparing it. An examination of each of these lines in turn will enable us to understand the nature of the Venetian Republic as it emerged from the Middle Ages and became, for a time, one of the greatest factors in European history.

The growth of Venetian maritime empire in the Levant and supremacy in the Mediterranean falls into four well-defined periods. The Venetians began by moving slowly down the Dalmatian coast and establishing their power in the Adriatic; they then pushed out eastward and acquired rights in Syrian seaports, such as Sidon, Tyre, Acre; they seized many of the islands in the archipelago as their share of the plunder after the Fourth Crusade; finally they met, fought, and defeated their only serious maritime rivals the Genoese.

The Adriatic is the natural water avenue to Venice. If her commerce was to flourish, it was essential that she should be mistress in this sea. But the eastern coast of the Adriatic, with its deep gulfs and numerous islands, had for long sheltered a race of pirates who never ceased to molest Venetian traffic. It was necessary to destroy this corsairs' nest, and Venice embarked on the first great war she undertook as an independent State in her own individual interests. This war was entirely successful. The Dalmatian coast towns recognised the Doge as "Duke of Dalmatia" and submitted to a nominal tribute in recognition of the supremacy of the Republic. Venice, it is true, did not remain in undisturbed and continuous possession of Dalmatia, but she acquired a title which she subsequently rendered effective. She thus took the first step towards that indispensable condition of her commercial existence, supremacy in the Adriatic. The Dalmatian cities were now open to her merchants. The Dalmatian sea-board furnished a food supply which the Lagoons could not; Dalmatian forests yielded timber for building ships and houses.

With the period of the Crusades Venice achieved a still wider expansion in the Levant. The eyes of Europe had been attracted to the little city in the Lagoons which had attacked and subdued the Narentine pirates, challenged and fought the Normans, and rendered striking services to the Eastern Emperor himself. When the Crusaders began to look about for a port of embarcation and for transport-service to the Holy Land, the three cities of Genoa, Pisa, and Venice offered themselves. Venice was not only the most powerful; she was also the most easterly of the three. Her geographical position naturally led to the choice of Venice as the port of departure. The issue of the Crusades proved that the Republic entered upon those enterprises in a purely commercial spirit. When Sidon fell, the Venetians received from Baldwin, King of Jerusalem, in return for their assistance, a market-place, a district, a church, and the right to use their own weights and measures in that city. This was in fact the nucleus of a colony of merchants living under special treaty capitulations; and the privileges of the Sidon treaty we find repeated and extended when Acre, Tyre, and Ascalon were successively occupied.

The siege and capture of Tyre mark the close of the second period in the history of Venetian maritime expansion. With the erection of factories in Constantinople and in the chief cities of the Syrian sea-board the Republic may be said to have embarked upon the construction of that greater Venice, which was to be completed after the Fourth Crusade.

But the course of Venetian expansion was not uninterruptedly smooth. The rapid growth of her power in the Levant procured for the Republic an enemy in the person of the Eastern Emperor. The Emperors had always viewed with suspicion the whole movement of the Crusades and more especially the professedly commercial attitude assumed by Venice, who was obviously bent upon acquiring territory and rights inside the Empire. They were aware that they could chastise her by favouring her rivals Pisa and Genoa. The growing wealth and importance of Venetian colonists in Constantinople, where they are said to have numbered two hundred thousand, increased the imperial jealousy. The Venetians were accused of being troublesome, brawling neighbours, who kept the town in an uproar. In March, 1171, all Venetians in the Empire were placed under arrest and their property confiscated. Popular indignation at Venice swept the Republic into war with the Emperor. One hundred galleys and twenty ships were manned in the course of a hundred days. The issue of the campaign was disastrous for the Venetians. The Emperor's Ambassadors induced the Doge to temporise. The plague decimated and nearly annihilated the fleet. The shattered remnants returned to Venice where the Doge was slain by the mob.

With the reign of Enrico Dandolo and the Fourth Crusade we approach a memorable period in the history of Venetian maritime empire. When Dandolo came to the throne the affairs of the Republic as regards their maritime power stood thus. In the imperial city their position was precarious, liable to violent changes, exposed to the machinations of their commercial and naval rivals, Pisa and Genoa. Their communications with their Syrian factories were not secure. Zara and the Dalmatian coast were still in revolt. In the year 1201 the Republic discovered that the usurping Emperor, Alexius III, was in treaty with the Genoese and meditated conferring on them ampler trading rights. The immediate objects of the Republic were the recovery of Zara and the suppression of their commercial rivals in Constantinople. The story of the Fourth Crusade is the story of the way in which the Republic accomplished its aims.

Zara was recovered and on the fall of Constantinople, in 1204, the Republic reaped material advantages of a preponderating kind. Her portion of the booty gave her solid riches, with which she bought the rights of Boniface over Crete and Salonika, and obtained leave for Venetian citizens to occupy as fiefs of the Empire any Aegean islands not already owned by the Republic. In this way she became possessed of the Cyclades and Sporades, and held the seaports of Thessaly and the island of Crete. Zara and other Dalmatian towns now became hers both by conquest and by title; and thus the Republic acquired an unbroken line of communication from Venice down the Adriatic to Constantinople and round to the seaports of the Syrian coast.

But the possession of this large maritime empire had to be made good. Venice was unable to undertake at one and the same time the actual conquest and settlement of so many scattered territories. She adopted a method borrowed from the feudal system of her Frankish allies, and granted investiture of the various islands, as fiefs, to those of her richer families who would undertake to render effective the Venetian title and to hold the territories for the Republic at a nominal tribute.

We have no evidence as to how these feudatories established their title and governed their fiefs; but when we come to deal with the growth of the Venetian constitution we shall find that a great increase in private wealth resulted from this partition of the Levant islands. We do know, however, the system adopted for the colonisation of the large island of Crete, which the Republic kept directly in its own hands. Venetian citizens were tempted to settle in the island by the gift of certain villages with their districts. These they were expected to hold for the Republic in the case of a revolution. The Governor of the island, who bore the title of Duke of Candia, was a Venetian noble elected in the Great Council at Venice; he was assisted by two Councillors. Matters of importance were decided by the Great Council of Crete, which was composed of all noble Venetians resident in the island and all noble Cretans. The remaining magistracies were formed upon the Venetian model; and the higher posts, such as those of Captain-General, Commander of the Cavalry, Governors, and military commanders in the larger towns, were filled by Venetians. The minor offices were open to Cretans. Absolute equality was granted to both Roman and Orthodox rites. In fact the Republic displayed at once the governing ideas of her colonial policy, namely to interfere as little as possible with local institutions; to develop the resources of the country; to encourage trade with the metropolis; to retain only the very highest military and civil appointments in her own hands as a symbol and guarantee of her supremacy.

For the defence of these widely scattered possessions and for the preservation of communications between Venice and her dependencies the Republic was obliged to organise a service of patrol squadrons. The Captain of "the Gulf," that is the Adriatic, had his head-quarters at the Ionian islands, and was responsible for the safety of merchantmen from Venice to those islands and in the waters of the Morea as far as Modon and Coron. From the Morea to the Dardanelles the safety of the sea route was entrusted to the Venetian feudatories in the Greek islands; while the Dardanelles, the Sea of Marmora, the Bosphorus, and the Black Sea were patrolled by the Black Sea squadron.

It is obvious that the outcome of the Fourth Crusade was of vast importance for the expansion of Venetian maritime empire; and we are now in the presence of a Venice quite different from anything we have encountered hitherto. The Republic assumed the aspect of a naval Power with a large mercantile marine and organised squadrons of warships for her protection. The crews of Venetian warships were at this period free citizens, serving under the command of a Venetian noble. Condemned prisoners or galley-slaves were not employed till much later, —first because the State was hardly large enough to furnish sufficient criminals to serve the oar, and secondly because, as long as boarding formed an important operation in naval tactics, condemned criminals could not be employed with safety as it was dangerous to entrust them with arms. When ramming took the place of boarding, the galley-slave, chained to his bench, could be used precisely as we use machinery.

The expansion of Venetian maritime empire as the outcome of the Fourth Crusade roused the jealousy of her great rival Genoa. It was inevitable that the Genoese and the Venetians, both occupying neighbouring quarters in the Levantine cities, each competing for a monopoly of Eastern commerce, should come to blows. The Republic was now committed to a struggle with her western rival for supremacy in the Levant—a deplorable conflict fraught with disaster for both parties.

A long period of naval campaigning ensued, the fortune of war leaning now to one side, now to the other. The breathing-space between each campaign and the next was devoted by the Republic to the development of her commerce. Treaties were stipulated with Milan, Bologna, Brescia, Como. Trade with England and Flanders by means of the Flanders galleys was developed. Venetian merchants brought sugar from the Levant, and exchanged it for wool in London. The wool was sold in Flanders and cloth bought, which was placed on the markets of Italy and Dalmatia, as the ships sailed east again to procure fresh cargoes for the London market. Industries also began to take root in the city. Refugees from Lucca introduced the silk trade, and established themselves in a quarter near the Rialto. The glass manufacture of Murano received an impetus. The population of the city numbered 200,000; the males fit for arms, that is between the ages of twenty and sixty, were reckoned at 40,000.

There is proof that, in spite of defeats by Genoa at Ayas and at Curzola, Venice had achieved a high position in the eyes of European Princes. Edward III asked for Venetian aid in his wars with Philip of France; he offered extensive privileges, and invited the Doge to send his sons to the English court. Alfonso of Sicily apologised for insults offered to Venetian merchants. The Pope proposed that Venice should undertake the protection of Christians against the Ottoman Turks, who were now beginning to threaten Europe, in return for which the Republic was to enjoy the ecclesiastical tithes for three years.

But Genoa was not yet driven from the field. It was impossible that commercial rivalries should not lead to fresh explosions. The fur trade in the Crimea gave rise to differences. The Venetians sent an embassy to Genoa to protest against alleged violations of a compact by which both Republics had pledged themselves to abstain from trading with the Tartars. The Genoese gave Venice to understand that her presence in the Black Sea was only permitted on sufferance. War broke out. The Republics were now embarked upon a struggle to the death, from which one or other of the combatants must emerge finally victorious.

In the course of that struggle the recuperative power of Venice was amply demonstrated. She lost Negroponte; she was defeated in the Bosphorus; her whole fleet was annihilated at Sapienza. But the result of her one great victory at Cagliari was sufficient to counterbalance her losses, for by it she forced Genoa to surrender her liberties to Visconti. And so, while Venice after each disaster, after Curzola and Sapienza, was able to devote her whole energies to replacing her fleet and reestablishing her commerce, the case was very different with her rival. The Genoese Republic had accepted the lordship of Visconti at a moment of great peril, and was compelled to devote any interval of peace with Venice, not to the increase of her wealth and the augmentation of her fleet, but to efforts for the recovery of that freedom she had surrendered. Genoa could only stand by and watch with jealous eyes the reconstitution of her antagonist.

The steady advance of Venice brought about the final rupture. On the threat that they would join the Sultan Murad I and expel the Emperor John Paleologus from his throne, the Venetians wrung from the Emperor the concession of the island of Tenedos. The position of that island, commanding the mouth of the Dardanelles, made it intolerable to the Genoese that it should pass into the hands of their enemies. War was declared again in 1378. In the following year Vettor Pisani, the Venetian commander, was utterly defeated at Pola, though the Genoese lost their admiral in the battle. This delayed their attack on the Lagoons; and while they awaited the arrival of a new commander, the panic in Venice subsided and the Republic set to work to protect the home waters from an assault which seemed imminent day by day. In July Pietro Doria, the Genoese admiral, reconnoitred Chioggia, and it was clear that he intended to make that Lagoon city his head-quarters and thence to blockade and starve Venice to surrender. Chioggia lay close to the mainland, and Doria counted on abundant supplies from Francesco Carrara, Lord of Padua, who was at that time at open war with the Republic and blockading her on the land side. But Chioggia had yet to be captured. On August 11, 1379, the assault began and was renewed till the 18th, when the town fell into the hands of the Genoese. Carrara urged Doria to push on at once to Venice, only about twenty miles away; and had he done so there can be little doubt but that the flag of St George of Genoa would have floated in the Piazza, and Carrara would have carried out his threat of bitting and bridling the horses on St Mark's. But the Genoese admiral decided to abide by his plan of a blockade and his decision proved the salvation of Venice. At Venice, in the face of this imminent peril, the whole population displayed coolness, courage and tenacity. The magistrates forewent their pay; new imposts were borne without complaint; the people, invited to express their wishes on the question of continuing the war, replied: "Let us man every vessel in Venice and go to fight the foe." The public voice designated Vettor Pisani as leader, in spite of the disastrous defeat he had suffered at Pola, and the government withdrew their own candidate, Taddeo Giustinian. Thirty-four galleys were put together, and Pisani took the command. Meanwhile Doria had resolved to withdraw his whole fleet into Chioggia for winter quarters. Pisani grasped the situation and seized the opportunity. He resolved to blockade the blockaders. All the channels which gave egress from Chioggia to the sea were rendered useless by sinking across them galleys filled with stones. Pisani then drew up his fleet in the open sea opposite the Chioggian entrance to the Lagoons, in order to intercept any reinforcements which might be sent from Genoa. The Genoese in Chioggia were all the while straining every nerve to break through Pisani's lines; his crews were kept on guard by turns day and night; it was winter time, and a storm from the east or south-east might easily spring up such as would probably drive Pisani on to the lee shore. The strain on the Venetians was very great. But just when they were on the point of abandoning the blockade, Carlo Zeno's fleet, which had been cruising down the Adriatic, hove in sight. The reinforcements enabled Pisani to land troops and to occupy the point of Brondolo, whence his two great guns, the "Trevisana" and the "Vittoria," opened on the town. A shot from one of them brought down the Campanile and killed the Genoese admiral Doria. His successor, Napoleone Grimaldi, withdrew all his troops into Chioggia, and abandoned the design of cutting a new canal from the Lagoons to the sea. Carlo Zeno with a company of mercenaries disembarked on the mainland and eventually succeeded in cutting off the supplies which Carrara was sending into Chioggia. The Genoese began building light boats in which they hoped to be able to sail over the obstacles in the channels that led to the Adriatic. Twice they attempted a sortie and failed. Famine came to close the long list of their disasters, and on June 24, 1380, the Genoese fleet surrendered to Venice.

The successful issue of the war of Chioggia left the Republic of Venice the supreme naval Power in the Mediterranean. Genoa never recovered from the blow. She fell a prey to internal feuds, and in 1396 she renounced her independence, receiving from Charles VI of France a governor who ruled the State in French interests. Venetian predominance in the Mediterranean was confirmed by the recovery of Corfu in 1386, and by the purchase of Argos and Nauplia in the Peloponnese. But at the very moment when her power seemed indisputably established a new and formidable rival began to loom on the horizon. Sultan Bayazid's victory at Nikopolis in 1392 planted a Muslim mosque and a Cadi in Constantinople and presaged for Venice that long series of wars, which were destined eventually to drain her resources and to rob her of her maritime supremacy.

The expansion of Venice on the mainland of Italy began somewhat later than the creation of her maritime dominion, and was in a certain way the result of that dominion. The Republic was originally a sea-Power whose merchants brought to her port the various products of Eastern countries, all *de transmarinis partibus orientalium divitias.* The geographical position of Venice as the seaport nearest to the centre of Europe indicated her as a great emporium and mart for the distribution and exchange of goods; and, further, her situation in the shallow waters of the Lagoons gave her a monopoly of salt. Cassiodorus, Theodoric's secretary, when describing the growing State, points to salt as the real riches of the young Republic; "for men may live without gold," he says, "but no one ever heard of their being able to do without salt." Venice however required an outlet for her commodities; and this led at first to the establishment of factories in the districts of Belluno and Treviso, along the banks of the Piave and on one of the high-roads into the heart of Europe (991), and subsequently at Ferrara (1100), and again at Fano (1130).

But these factories did not, strictly speaking, constitute territorial possessions. They were merely colonies of Venetian merchants living in foreign cities under special treaty rights which conferred extra-territoriality on the Venetian quarter. Indeed, the early policy of the Republic was to keep as far aloof as possible from all the complications of the Italian mainland. Her real interests lay in the East,—in the Levant, in Constantinople, in Syria. Her character was oriental rather than Latin. When Pippin, the son of Charles the Great, attempted to compel the Republic to recognise the Frankish suzerainty he received for answer: "$\dot{\eta}\mu\epsilon\hat{\iota}\varsigma$ $\delta o\hat{\upsilon}\lambda o\iota$ $\theta\acute{\epsilon}\lambda o\mu\epsilon\nu$ $\epsilon\hat{\iota}\nu\alpha\iota$ $\tau o\hat{\upsilon}$ $\beta\alpha\sigma\iota\lambda\acute{\epsilon}\omega\varsigma$ $\tau\hat{\omega}\nu$ $^{\prime}P\omega\mu\alpha\acute{\iota}\omega\nu$ $\kappa\alpha\grave{\iota}$ $o\dot{\upsilon}\chi\grave{\iota}$ $\sigma o\hat{\upsilon}$"; and to the spirit of that answer the Venetians remained faithful throughout their early career.

It is not till the year 1300 that the Republic took a decisive and acquisitive step on the Italian mainland. In Ferrara, as we have seen, Venice had established a commercial colony protected by treaty rights. These were swept away when Salinguerra held the city for the Emperor Frederick II, who was hostile to Venice on account of the part she was playing in the Lombard League, for which she acted as banker. Pope Gregory IX, while endeavouring to recover the city, which he claimed as part of Countess Matilda's legacy to the Church, applied to Venice for help. The Republic was largely instrumental in expelling the Imperial troops and recovered all her privileges and interests in the mainland city. These privileges and interests were destined to entangle her in the complications of mainland politics.

The d'Este family was established at Ferrara and held it as a fief of the Holy See. But the Republic had been growing steadily in wealth, and strength, thanks to her expansion in the Levant and to the consolidation of her constitution as an oligarchy by the closing of the Great Council in 1297. She had before her the example of other lordships rising to power on the mainland,—Scala, Visconti, Carrara, all in her neighbourhood. It seems certain from the attitude of the Doge, Pietro Gradenigo, that the government entertained the idea of taking the place of the d'Este should a fitting occasion present itself. That moment appeared to have arrived when Azzo d'Este lay on his death-bed. The Republic sent three nobles to Ferrara with instructions to see that the succession was directed in a way consonant with its aims. Azzo had no legitimate offspring; the d'Este succession seemed likely to pass through his brothers Francesco and Aldobrandino. But Azzo had a bastard named Fresco who had a son Folco; and Azzo named Folco his heir. On his death the uncles of Folco tried to unseat him and his father Fresco, who in his straits applied for help to Venice which was given. But now the Pope, as overlord, claimed the right to direct the succession and sent his troops into Ferrara to support Francesco and to take over the city in the name of the Church. Thereupon Fresco in the name of his son Folco ceded to Venice Folco's claims in Ferrara. The papal troops entered the city; but the Venetians held the fortress and commanded the town. The Pope ordered the Venetians to evacuate the castle. The Doge's speech on this occasion clearly indicates the political conceptions of the party in power and points most emphatically to an expansion of Venice on the mainland of Italy. Gradenigo urged that it was the duty of a loyal citizen to lose no opportunity for the aggrandisement of his native State. In spite of opposition the Doge's policy carried the day, and it was resolved to retain Ferrara. On March 27, 1309, the Pope launched the excommunication and interdict. The clergy were ordered to leave Venetian territory. But, more than this, the jealousy of Venice which had been roused by her expansion and preponderance in the Levant broke loose now; under the papal sanction, in England, in Asia Minor, in Italy, Venetian merchants were threatened in their lives and despoiled of their goods. The government held firm and ordered its officers in Ferrara to withdraw into the castle, promising relief from Venice. But plague broke out in the city. The papal arms pressed the castle closer and closer, till it fell and all the Venetians were put to the sword. These disasters precipitated the great conspiracy of Bajamonte Tiepolo—with which we shall deal when discussing the Venetian constitution—and in 1311 the Republic made its peace with the Pope, paid an indemnity, and received permission to resume its trading rights in Ferrara.

This first attempt of Venice to establish herself in possession of mainland territory proved a failure. But the rise of the great Lords of Verona, Padua, Milan, the Scala, Carraresi, and Visconti, and the struggles which took place between them, could not fail to disturb the quiet of the Lagoons and to draw Venice once more into the mesh of Italian politics. It was impossible for Venice to be indifferent to events which were affecting cities so close to herself and so necessary for her commerce as Padua and Treviso.

Padua, thanks chiefly to the ability of Jacopo da Carrara, had made herself mistress of Vicenza, and had thus been brought into close proximity with the possessions of the powerful family of della Scala, Lords of Verona. The Paduans in return for Jacopo's services elected him as her Lord. When Jacopo da Carrara died, Can Grande della Scala attacked Marsilio da Carrara, who had succeeded his uncle, and wrung from him Padua and the Padovano; thence the Scala spread to Feltre, Belluno, and the territory at the foot of the Alps, and finally Treviso came to their possession in 1329. The Republic of Venice could not be indifferent to the growth of a Power which threatened to enclose the Lagoons and to block all exits for Venetian merchandise. Moreover her natural position rendered her incapable of supporting herself if food supplies from the mainland were cut off. A contingency of this kind, if it should happen to coincide with such a defeat at sea as Venice had sustained at Curzola or Sapienza, would, in a very short time, have placed the Republic at the discretion of her enemies. It was obvious therefore that Venice was face to face with a rival whom she must either crush or be ruined. War was inevitable.

The crisis was of vital importance to the Republic. It is true that in the War of Ferrara she had made an attempt to establish herself on the mainland; but in attacking the Lord of Verona, Vicenza, Brescia, Treviso, Feltre, Belluno, and Padua she was embarking on a far more serious enterprise. Failure meant peril to her very existence; success would compel her to occupy the nearer mainland and therefore to sacrifice one of her great advantages, the absence of a mainland frontier to protect. The party of the Doge, the party opposed to the War, was met and overcome by the argument that war was the only alternative to starvation; the want of corn for feeding the city could not be supplied in any other way. Moreover it was urged that if Venice once attacked the Scala she would be joined by all who were jealous of the growing power of Verona and its Lords. Such proved to be the case. The declaration of war by Venice at once created so strong a combination—Florence, Parma, and Venice—that Mastino della Scala was forced to negotiate for peace. With singular want of judgment he chose as his ambassador to Venice Marsilio da Carrara, the very man whom the Scala had already deprived of the lordship of Padua. That lordship the Doge promised to restore to the Carraresi, if Marsilio would admit the troops of the league into Padua, which he held in the name of Mastino della Scala. Marsilio kept his word, and in August, 1337, Pietro de' Rossi, general of the confederate forces, entered the city.

For her own part, the Republic by the peace of 1338, thus gained possession of the marches of Treviso, with the districts of Bassano,

Castelfranco, Conegliano and Oderzo,—her first mainland possession; and the family of Carrara held Padua—which had been captured in the name of the Republic—as a quasi-fief of Venice. She was now in command of a corn-growing district and was sure of an abundant meat supply. But on the other hand the mainland frontier which she now acquired exposed her to attack from the Patriarch of Aquileia or the Counts of Görz; while she was bound to protect her dependent Carrara beyond whom lay the growing power and ambition of the Visconti of Milan. An attack on Carrara was necessarily a threat to Venice, and in fact if not in appearance the Republic had by the fall of the Scala become conterminous with Visconti.

We have seen how the Republic dealt with her maritime colonies, especially in the instance of Crete; we may now observe her method towards her newly acquired mainland possessions. Her mild and provident sway was fruitful of many results favourable to the Republic, and it brought her dependencies back to her of their own accord after the disastrous wars of the League of Cambray. To use the words of the Senate, the Republic of Venice in her relations towards her dependencies set herself to provide *taliter quod habeamus cor et amorem civium et subditorum nostrorum*, and she succeeded. Her rule was just, lenient and wise. Alike in her maritime and in her mainland acquisitions her object was to interfere as little as might be with local institutions, provided her own tenure and the supremacy of the capital were maintained. In each of the more important dependent cities she placed a civil governor, called the Podestà, and a military commandant, called the Captain, whose duty it was to raise levies and look after the defence of the city; these two when acting together were called the Rectors. The local municipal councils, varying in numbers, were left undisturbed and retained the control of such matters as lighting, roads, local taxation. The police and imperial taxation were in the hands of the Rectors, and they were in constant communication either with the Senate, or, in very grave emergencies, with the Council of Ten. The smaller towns were governed by a *Podestà*, a *Capitano*, or a *Provveditore*. Each town possessed its own special code, called the *Statuto*, which the Rectors swore to observe. The *Statuto* dealt with octroi dues, roads and bridges, wells, lighting, doctors, nurses, fires, guilds, sanitary matters,—in short with all the multifarious details of municipal and even of private life. Peace, encouragement of trade, and comfort of living were the chief objects aimed at. In the Courts of Justice the Podestà or one of his three assessors merely presided; he did not constitute the Court, which was composed of citizens. Provision was made for public instruction in the humanities, in canon and civil law, and in medicine; primary education was supplied by what were called schools of arithmetic. The cost of education was charged on the revenues of the province.

The expansion of Venice on the mainland, while it increased the prestige of the Republic, likewise augmented her dangers. Hitherto she had been engaged in a duel with Genoa for supremacy at sea. No other Italian Power had any motive for interfering in the combat. But now that Venice had acquired a mainland territory she became possessed of something that her mainland neighbours coveted, and of which they were ready to despoil her if occasion offered. Thus during the final phases of her war with Genoa we find the Republic called upon to face Carrara and Hungary, banded together with Genoa to destroy the mighty city of the Lagoons (1369). Louis I, King of Hungary, was ready to attack Venetian mainland territory with a view to wringing from the Republic a renunciation of Dalmatia. The Counts of Görz viewed with alarm Venetian expansion eastward and were ready to join the Hungarians. The Carraresi, though restored to the lordship of Padua by the Republic, were impatient under the suzerainty which Venice imposed, and were aspiring to an absolute independence; they too joined the Hungarians. From their conduct at this moment Venice learned that she would not be safe until Padua was in her possession; and thus she found that having once touched the mainland she could not stop, but was, by the very nature of the situation, forced further and further into the Italian *terra ferma*, and along a line of action which was destined to land her in the disasters of Cambray.

It was obvious that Carrara would not remain quiet if he found an opportunity of attacking Venice with any prospect of success. Such an occasion presented itself in the War of Chioggia (1379). Carrara assisted the Genoese by all the means in his power; he bombarded Mestre and maintained the land blockade of Venice; he sent twenty-four thousand troops to the neighbourhood of Chioggia, and supplied the Genoese forces when they took up their quarters in that town. But the surrender of the Genoese left Carrara single-handed against Venice. He was still in possession of the Trevisan marches and was pressing Treviso so closely that its fall was momently expected. Rather than allow it to pass into the hands of Carrara, Venice made a formal surrender of the city to Duke Leopold of Austria, who immediately occupied it. All parties, however, were weary of the war. Venice was exhausted by her continual struggles against Hungary, Carrara, Genoa; Carrara disgusted at being baulked of Treviso; Genoa crushed by the loss of her fleet. Amadeo of Savoy found little difficulty in negotiating the Peace of Turin (1381).

That Peace left Venice little cause for self-congratulation. She resigned Tenedos, the occupation of which had been the immediate cause of the War of Chioggia; she lost Dalmatia; Treviso she had surrendered to Duke Leopold of Austria; on the mainland all that she now possessed was a narrow strip of territory round the edge of the Lagoon. But the respite granted by the peace was devoted to the reestablishment of commerce and trade. Petrarch, from his windows on the Riva degli

Schiavoni, noted the extraordinary movement of the port: the huge
vessels "as large as my house, and with masts taller than its towers."
They lay like mountains floating on the waters; and their cargoes were
wine for England; honey for Scythia; saffron, oil, linen for Assyria,
Armenia, Persia, and Arabia; wood went to Egypt and Greece. They
brought home again various merchandise to be distributed over all
Europe. "Where the sea stops the sailors quit their ships and travel
on to trade with India and China. They cross the Caucasus and the
Ganges and reach the Eastern Ocean."

And in the history of Venetian mainland extension there was one
task to which all this accumulation of wealth and resources was to be
dedicated; the destruction of the Carraresi and the acquisition of Padua.
Venice knew that the Lords of Padua were permanently hostile. The
action of Francesco Carrara soon proved that the Republic could not,
even if it would, leave him alone. In 1384 Carrara bought from the
Duke of Austria, Treviso, Ceneda, and Feltre, commanding the great
northern road into the Pusterthal by Cortina d'Ampezzo; he was now
master of all the mainland between the Alps and the Lagoons; nothing
remained for him to seize in that direction. But westward, between him
and the Visconti of Milan, lay the territories of Vicenza and Verona,
feebly held by Antonio, the last of the Scala family. Visconti and
Carrara entered into a league to despoil Antonio. Verona was to be
added to Milan, Vicenza to Padua. The attack was delivered simultaneously and Visconti's general entered Verona, but instead of halting there
he pushed on to Vicenza, and captured that city in his master's name.
When too late Carrara saw what his alliance with Visconti implied. He
appealed to Venice for help. But although the Republic had no desire
to see the powerful Lord of Milan so near the Lagoons, she had still less
intention of supporting Carrara whom she knew to be treacherous.
Visconti's emissaries were already in Venice offering to restore Treviso,
Ceneda, and Feltre if the Republic would assist him to crush Carrara.
The terms were accepted and Padua fell to Visconti.

Such a powerful prince as Gian Galeazzo was not likely to prove a
less dangerous neighbour to Venice than Carrara had been. But his
rapid advance in power, and his obvious intention to create a North-
Italian kingdom, immediately produced a coalition against him of all
the threatened Princes. Venice joined the league but she had no
intention of challenging Visconti on the mainland herself; she adopted a
less costly plan and invited the Carraresi to return to Padua promising
to support their enterprise; Sir John Hawkwood, the Florentine General,
was pressing Visconti on the Adda; Visconti's forces were scattered; the
Paduans weary of his rule rose in revolt and the Carraresi recovered
possession of their city (1390).

The Peace of Genoa which ensued (1392) was highly satisfactory to
Venice. Without any cost to herself she had recovered Treviso, Ceneda,

Feltre, and consequently the passes; she had removed Visconti from the immediate neighbourhood of the Lagoons; and replaced him by a Carrara whom dread of Visconti would certainly keep submissive to his protector. But in 1402 Gian Galeazzo died suddenly, and the whole aspect of the situation underwent a change. The reason for Carrara's loyalty to Venice, his dread of Visconti, disappeared. The value of Carrara to Venice, as a buffer between herself and Visconti, no longer existed. The moment had arrived for Venice to consolidate her landed possessions by the absorption of Padua. The pretext was soon found. The Visconti possessions were now held by his Duchess as regent for Gian Galeazzo's infant children. The Duchess was weak. Gian Galeazzo's generals began to divide their late master's dominions. This dissolution of the Visconti duchy roused the cupidity of Carrara. He claimed Vicenza and had an eye on Verona. He sat down before Vicenza; but the people, weary of the uneasy, shifting rule of these personal Lords, Scala, Visconti, Carrara, declared that if they must yield to some one, they would hand their city over to Venice. Moreover the Duchess had already invited Venice to hold Carrara in check and the Republic had demanded as the price of her interference Bassano, Vicenza, Verona. The Duchess consented. Armed with this double title, Venice requested Carrara to raise the siege of Vicenza. He refused, and mutilated the Venetian herald by cropping his ears and slitting his nose. War was declared. Carrara was gradually beaten back into Padua. A long siege followed. Carrara held out with great courage, hoping that aid might come from Florence, and that his partizans in Venice might succeed in carrying into effect a plot which they had concerted in that city. But the plague and the fury of the populace broke down his pertinacity. The Venetians delivered an assault and with the help of the people they entered the town (November 17, 1404). Francesco and his son were taken to Venice, where they were tried and condemned to be strangled.

As the defeat of Genoa secured Venetian maritime supremacy, so the fall of the Carraresi consolidated her mainland possessions. She now held Treviso, Padua, Vicenza, Verona, and their districts. The boundaries of the Republic were, roughly speaking, the sea from the mouth of the Tagliamento to the mouth of the Adige, the river Tagliamento to the east, the Alps to the north, the Adige to the west and south. This territory she retained with brief exceptions, down to the League of Cambray. She now entered the community of Italian States and enjoyed all the prestige, but also confronted all the dangers, of an Italian principality.

On the sea the Turk was already in sight; on the mainland the Visconti of Milan, with their claim to Verona and Vicenza, had to be faced. But before proceeding to narrate the history of the full-grown Republic during the period of her greatest brilliancy, we must consider for a moment two important points, her relations to the Church, and the nature of the Venetian constitution which played so striking a part in the creation and preservation of her glory.

The political independence of the early Venetian State is reflected in her relations towards the Roman Church. The fact that, through the first centuries of her career, she was in closer touch with the Eastern Empire than with the Italian mainland, conduced to that independent attitude towards the Curia which characterises the whole of Venetian history.

Some flavour of an ecclesiastical quality seems to have attached to the office of Doge; we find that on certain great occasions he bestowed his benediction, and the earlier Doges claimed the right to nominate and to invest Bishops. This right was, however, challenged at Rome.

The head of the Church in Venice was the Patriarch of Grado. That See had been called into existence by the same causes which created the city of Venice itself. When Aquileia was destroyed by Attila, the Patriarch of that city and his flock found an asylum in the Lagoons of Grado. After the return to Aquileia a Bishop was left behind in the Lagoon City, and his flock was continually increased—partly by the schism of the Three Chapters which divided the mainland Church, partly by refugees from the repeated barbarian incursions. The Bishop of Grado obtained from Pope Pelagius II a decree which erected his See into the Metropolitan Church of the Lagoons and of Istria, though Aquileia disputed the validity of the act. During the Lombard invasion and under the Lombard protection the mainland Bishoprics became Arian, the Lagoon See remained orthodox. The Metropolitan of Grado then claimed that his See was the real Patriarchal See of the Lagoons in opposition to Arian and heretical Aquileia. A long series of struggles between the two Patriarchates ensued. The Republic of Venice supported the Lagoon Bishopric. Finally the Lateran Council in 732 decreed the separation of the two jurisdictions, assigning to Aquileia all the mainland and to Grado the Lagoons and Istria, and recognised the Patriarchal quality of that See. In 1445 the seat of the Patriarch as well as his title was changed from Grado to Venice and the Beato Lorenzo Giustinian was the first Patriarch of Venice, an office henceforth always filled by a Venetian noble.

The Cathedral Church of Venice was San Pietro di Castello, not St Mark's. That magnificent basilica was technically the Doge's private chapel, and was served by the Doge's chaplain, called the Primiciero, and a chapter of canons; an arrangement not without significance, for the shrine of the patron Saint of Venice, the most splendid monument in the city, the home of its religion, was thereby declared to belong to the State, not to the Curia Romana, whose outward and visible abode was that comparatively insignificant building San Pietro di Castello, at the extreme north-eastern corner of the City.

The anti-Curial attitude of the Republic is obvious all down her history. In 1309, during the War of Ferrara, when Venice was lying under an interdict, the Doge Gradenigo enunciated the principle that the Papacy had no concern in temporal affairs, and that a misinformed Pope could not claim obedience.

She again asserted her adherence to the Conciliar principle when in 1409 she recognised Alexander V, the Pope elected by the Council of Pisa, against her own citizen Gregory XII (Angelo Correr), who was deposed by that Council; and yet again when she sent three ambassadors to the Council of Constance, who solemnly pledged the Republic to accept its decrees. By these acts she accepted the principle that Councils are superior to Popes, from whom an appeal may lie to a future Council; as well as the doctrine that an appeal may lie from a Pope ill-informed to a Pope better informed. In spite of "Execrabilis" the Republic more than once availed herself of these rights. When Sixtus IV placed the Republic under an interdict during the Ferrarese war in 1483, Diedo, the Venetian Ambassador in Rome, refused to send the bull to Venice. The Patriarch was instructed to present it to the government; he feigned to be ill, and secretly informed the Doge and the Ten that the bull was in Venice. The Ten ordered all clerics to continue their functions, and announced their intention to appeal to a future Council. Five experts in Canon Law were appointed to advise the government, and the formula of appeal was actually fixed on the doors of San Celso in Rome.

Again, in 1509, Julius II, preparing for the combined attack of all Europe upon Venice, placed the Republic under an interdict by the bull of April 27. The College and the Council of Ten which undertook to deal with the situation, forbade the publication of the bull, the guards were ordered to tear it down if it were affixed to the walls; doctors in Canon Law were again appointed to advise, and once again an appeal to a future Council was affixed, this time to the doors of St Peter's in Rome.

The position of the Church in Venice as defined by the close of the fourteenth century was as follows. The parish clergy were elected by the clergy and the people, and inducted by the Ordinary. Bishops were elected in the Senate. Candidates were balloted for until one obtained a majority. He was then presented at Rome for confirmation. But in 1484 the Senate decreed that the temporal fruits should not fall to any one who was not approved of by the government. This really made the State master of the situation; and its position was further strengthened by a law of 1488 rendering all foreigners ineligible for the episcopate. Venetian nobles who were beneficed were excluded from the Maggior

Consiglio ; and when ecclesiastical matters were under discussion in the Maggior Consiglio or the Senate all members who were related to any one holding an appointment from the Curia were obliged to retire. The minutes were marked *expulsis papalistis.*

The excessive accumulation of Church property had been regulated by a law passed as early as 1286, which provided that all legacies to monastic establishments must be registered, and the property taxed like any other.

The question of the jurisdiction of the secular Courts over ecclesiastics was a fruitful source of differences with the Curia. Originally it would seem that clerics were subject to the secular Courts in civil as well as in criminal cases. Jacopo Tiepolo granted jurisdiction to the Bishops but reserved punishment to the secular Courts. This arrangement gave rise to constant disputes, and in 1324 a commission was appointed to draw up regulations on the question. Finally a convention was reached between the Patriarch of Grado and the secular authorities, whereby it was agreed that in the case of injury done by a cleric to a laic the secular Courts should denounce the offender to the ecclesiastical Courts, which should try and sentence him in accordance with existing laws ; and *vice versa* in the case of injury inflicted by a laic on a cleric. By the bull of Paul II in 1468 those clerics who had been tonsured after the committal of a crime with a view to securing benefit of clergy were handed over by the Church to the secular Courts ; so too were the clerics caught *in flagrante* and unfrocked. Sixtus IV, in view of the growing frequency of crime—especially of counterfeit coining and of conspiracy—on the part of clerics, instructed the Patriarch to hand over all such offenders to the secular Courts, but to assist at the trial in the person of his Vicar.

The independent attitude of the Republic in matters ecclesiastical is illustrated once again in the position occupied by the Inquisition at Venice. When the Pope, with a view to crushing the Albigensian and Patarinian heresies, endeavoured to establish everywhere in Italy the Dominican Inquisition, the Republic resisted its introduction into Venice. But in 1249, in the reign of the Doge Morosini, the Holy Office was admitted, though only in a modified form. The State charged itself to discover heretics, who when caught were examined by the Patriarch, the Bishop of Castello, or any other Venetian Ordinary. The examining Court was confined to a return of fact. It was called on to state whether the examinee was or was not guilty of heresy. Punishment was reserved to the secular authority. This arrangement did not satisfy the Court of Rome, and in 1289 a modification took place. An Inquisitor was appointed by the Pope, but he required the Doge's *exequatur* before he could act, and a board was created of three Venetian nobles, to sit as assessors to the Holy Office. Their duty was to guard the rights of Venetian citizens against ecclesiastical encroachment ; without their presence and their sanction no act of the Holy Office was valid in Venice. The archive of the Sant' Uffizio is now open to inspection. Heresy was not the sole crime submitted to the jurisdiction of this Court; witchcraft and scandalous living furnished a large number of cases; but among all the trials for heresy pure and simple only six cases of capital punishment can be found, which were in each instance to be carried out by drowning or strangulation, and in none by fire. The Inquisition in Venice was certainly no sanguinary Office, thanks no doubt in a large degree to the independent attitude of the State, which insisted upon the presence of lay assessors at every trial.

But a large part of this independence in matters ecclesiastical, along with much else, was sacrificed at the disastrous epoch of Cambray. In order to detach Julius from the League, the Venetians agreed to the following conditions. The Republic renounced its appeal to a future Council, acknowledged the justice of the excommunication; abolished the taxes on ecclesiastical property; surrendered its right to nominate Bishops; consigned criminous clerics to ecclesiastical Courts; granted free passage in the Adriatic to papal subjects. But in secret the Council of Ten entered a protest against all these concessions and declared that their assent was invalid, as it had been extorted by violence;—a reservation of which Venice availed herself in her subsequent struggle with Pope Paul V, when, championed and directed by Fra Paolo Sarpi, the Republic undertook to defend the rights of secular princes against the claims of the Curia Romana.

The Venetian constitution, which, on account of its stability and efficiency, compelled the envy and admiration of all Italian and numerous foreign statesmen, was a product of the growth of Venice, slowly evolved to meet the growing needs of the growing State.

Democratic in its origin, the constitution of the Lagoon islands was at first a loose confederation of the twelve principal townships each governed by its Tribune; all the Tribunes meeting together for the discussion and discharge of business which affected the whole Lagoon commonwealth. The jealousies and quarrels of the townships and their Tribunes led to the creation of a single supreme magistrate, the Doge. The Doge was elected in the *Concione*, or assembly of the entire Venetian people; his was a democratic magistracy in its first intention; but it soon became apparent that there was considerable danger lest the Doge should attempt to establish an hereditary tyranny. Any such effort was resented by the people and resulted in the murder, blinding, or expulsion of several of the earlier Doges. On the other hand, as the State developed and pushed out beyond the Lagoon boundaries, across to the Dalmatian coast, down the Adriatic, and away eastward, the more able and enterprising citizens began to accumulate wealth, and a division of classes made itself apparent, more especially after such periods of expansion as the reign of Pietro II, Orseolo, the capture of Tyre, and the Fourth Crusade. This wealthier class gradually drew together and formed the nucleus of a plutocracy. The policy of this powerful class, embracing as it did all the leading citizens, naturally pursued the lines along which Venetian constitutional development consistently moved. This policy had a twofold object: first, to curtail the ducal authority; secondly, to exclude the people, and to concentrate all power in the hands of the commercial aristocracy. The history of the Venetian constitution is the history of the way in which the dominant party attained its ends.

The primitive machinery of the Venetian Republic consisted, as we have seen, of the General Assembly and the Doge. Very soon, however, under the pressure of business, two ducal Councillors were added to aid the Doge in the discharge of his ever-growing obligations. Further, it became customary though not necessary, that he should invite (*pregare*) some of the more prominent citizens to assist him with their advice upon grave occasions, and hence the name of what was eventually known as the *Consiglio dei Pregadi*, the Venetian Senate.

But constitutional machinery of so simple a nature could not prove adequate to the requirements of a State whose growth was as rapid as that of Venice. In 1172 the disastrous conclusion of the campaign against the Emperor Manuel, into which the Republic had rushed at the bidding of the *Concione* or General Assembly, called the attention of Venetians to their constitution and its defects. It seemed to them that reforms were required on two grounds: first, because the position of the Doge was too independent, considering his discretionary powers as to whether and as to whom he would ask for advice; secondly, because the people in their General Assembly had become too numerous, unruly and rash to allow of their being safely entrusted with the fortunes of their country. A deliberative assembly of manageable size was required; and its establishment implied a definition of the Doge's authority on the one hand and of the popular rights on the other. The evolution of these two ideas forms the problem of Venetian constitutional history down to the year 1297, when that constitution became stereotyped as a close oligarchy after the famous " Closing of the Great Council."

The reforms of the year 1172 were threefold:

(1) In order to create a manageable deliberative assembly each *sestiere* of the city was required to elect two representatives; and each couple in their turn nominated forty of the more prominent members of their district. Thus a body of four hundred and eighty members was created. They held office for one year and at the end of the first year the General Assembly itself named the two nominating representatives of each *sestiere*.

The functions of this new Assembly were to appoint all officers of

State and to prepare business to be submitted to the General Assembly. This is virtually the germ of the *Maggior Consiglio* (the Great Council), the basis of the Venetian oligarchical constitution. It had its origin in a double necessity :—that of limiting the electorate, and that of securing adequate deliberation and debate in a rapidly growing State. Its prime function of appointing to office belonged to it from the first. Its origin was democratic, for it sprang from election by the whole people ; but an element of a close oligarchy was contained in the provision whereby the Assembly itself at the end of the first and of all subsequent years elected the twelve representatives of the six quarters of the city.

(2) The Doge continued to summon the *Pregadi* to assist him ; but seeing that the newly created Council undertook election to office and many matters of internal policy, foreign affairs were chiefly reserved for the Senate; though that body did not become organised and permanent till the Tiepoline reforms of 1229-44.

(3) With a view to restricting the Doge's authority, four Councillors were added to the two already existing. Their duty was to check any attempt at personal aggrandisement on the part of the Doge ; and gradually the ducal authority was withdrawn from the chief of the State and placed as it were, in commission in his Council. The coronation oath or *promissione* of the Doge was subjected to constant modification in the direction of restricting his authority, till at last the Doge himself lost much of his original weight. As his supreme power was withdrawn from him, bit by bit, the pomp and ceremony surrounding him were steadily increased.

These reforms of 1172 display the inherent nature of the Venetian constitution. The ducal authority is gradually curtailed ; the Council shows a tendency to become a close oligarchy ; the people are removed from the centre of government, although the complete disfranchisement of the mass of the population was not effected at once. The newly appointed Council did indeed endeavour to elect a chief magistrate without any appeal to the people, and a riot ensued which was only quieted by the electors presenting the new Doge to the General Assembly with the words "This is your Doge, an it please you,"—a formula which deluded the people into a belief that they still retained some voice in the election of the Doge.

The tendency displayed in the reforms of 1172 continued to make itself felt during the next hundred years, until we come to the epoch of the Closing of the Great Council, whereby Venice established her constitution as a close oligarchy.

The growing wealth of the State, especially after the Fourth Crusade, served to increase the influence of those families into whose hands the larger share of Venetian commerce had already fallen. We find certain family names such as Contarini, Morosini, Foscari, recurring more and more frequently and preponderating in the Council which the law of

1172 had established.   But the oligarchy was not closed yet; the yearly election of forty members from each quarter might always bring some new men to the front.   The Closing of the Great Council, however, which actually took place in 1297, is not to be regarded as a *coup d'état*; it was rather the last step in a long process.   In 1286 a motion had been made that only those whose paternal ancestors had sat in the Great Council should be eligible to that Council.   The measure was rejected; but was brought up again ten years later by the Doge Pietro Gradenigo, a strong partisan of the growing oligarchy.   The measure was again rejected; but early in the next year the Doge succeeded in carrying the following resolutions:

(1)   The Council of Forty, that is the Judges of the Supreme Court, are to put up to ballot the names of all who have, at any time during the last four years, had a seat in the Great Council.   Those who receive twelve votes and upwards are to be included in the Great Council.

(2)   On return from absence abroad a fresh ballot is requisite.

(3)   Three members shall be appointed to submit names of new candidates for election.   These electors are to hold office for one year.

(4)   The present law may not be revoked, except with the consent of five out of six ducal Councillors, twenty-five members of the Council of Forty, and two-thirds of the Great Council.

The result of these resolutions was to create a specially favoured class, those who had during the last four years sat in the Great Council.   By the third resolution admission to that caste was still left open; but the action of the Committee of three soon completed the *Serrata del Maggior Consiglio*, and rendered the oligarchy virtually a close caste; for they laid down for themselves the rule that no one was eligible to the Great Council unless he could prove that a paternal ancestor had sat in the Council subsequent to its creation in 1172.   By this regulation all those—and they were the vast majority—who had neither sat themselves nor could prove that a paternal ancestor had sat in the Great Council, were virtually disfranchised, for that Council was the root of political life in the State, and exclusion from it meant political annihilation.   In 1315 a list of all those who were eligible for election was compiled, and only legitimate children of parents belonging to the favoured class were allowed to appear in this register, known as the Golden Book.   Thus the Venetian aristocracy was created, and was established as the sole power in the State.

The exclusion of so many Venetians from all share in the government of their State led to the only revolution which ever seriously endangered the Republic,—the Conspiracy of Bajamonte Tiepolo (1310). Thanks, however, to the decisive step then taken, this conspiracy was crushed and the constitution of Venice was never again in any grave peril. For it was at this moment of danger to the State that the constitution received its final touches by the creation of the Council of Ten.

The accumulated difficulties and dangers brought about by the War of Ferrara, the Interdict, and the Tiepoline Conspiracy taught the Republic that the existing machinery of the State was too cumbersome, too slow, too public, to meet and deal successfully with extraordinary crises. A special committee to direct the affairs of Ferrara had been appointed early during that War. When the movements of Tiepolo and his fellow-conspirators, after their defeat, caused grave anxiety to the government, it seemed that some more rapid, secret, and efficient body than the Senate was required to track the operations of the traitors and to watch over the safety of the State. It was accordingly proposed that the Committee on Ferrarese affairs should be entrusted with the task (1310). The proposal was rejected on the ground that the committee was fully occupied. It was then suggested that the Great Council should elect ten of its members, and the Doge, his Council, and the Supreme Court, should elect another ten, and that from this body of twenty the Great Council should afterwards elect ten; not more than one member of the same family might sit on the board, which was at once entrusted with the protection of the public safety and the duty of vigilance against the Tiepoline conspirators. The committee acted so admirably and its services proved so valuable that its term of office, originally only for a few months, was extended and it finally became permanent in 1335.

As eventually modified the Council took the following shape and was governed by its own code of procedure. The members were elected in the Great Council for one year only, and were not re-eligible till a year had elapsed. Every month the Ten elected three of its members as "Chiefs" (*Capi*). The "Chiefs" opened all communications, prepared all business to be submitted to the Council, and acted as its executive arm; they were obliged during their month of office to stay at home, so as to avoid exposure to bribery or other illegitimate influences.

Besides the ten actual members the Council included *ex officio* the Doge and his six Councillors, to whom were added on very grave occasions a certain number of prominent citizens, called the Zonta. Of the normal seventeen Councillors twelve made up a quorum. One at least of the Law-officers of the State—the *Avogadori di comun*—was always present, though without a vote, to prevent the Council from taking any illegal step.

The sittings opened with the reading of letters addressed to the Ten. Then followed the list of denunciations which were either public, that is signed, or secret, that is anonymous. If public, the Council voted whether they should take the accusation into consideration; if four-fifths voted "Aye" the case was entered on the *agenda*. If the denunciation was secret the Doge and his Council and the "Chiefs" were bound, before the question of taking it up came forward, to declare unanimously that the matter of the accusation was of public concern; and such a declaration required confirmation by a vote of five-sixths of the whole Council. This being obtained, the question of taking the matter into consideration next arose, and was decided as in the case of public denunciations. The denunciation list having been discharged, the first case on the trial list then came on for hearing. The Law-officers of the State (*Avogadori*) read a report on the case and submitted the form of warrant for arrest. The Council voted "to proceed" or not. If the vote was affirmative the warrant was issued and the "Chiefs" gave it execution. When the accused was in the hands of the Ten, a sub-committee or *Collegio*, as it was called, was appointed to draw up the case; they were empowered to use torture only by a special vote. The presumption was against the prisoner; he was called on to disprove the charge—*intimare le difese*. He was confronted neither with his accuser nor with witnesses. If he pleaded incapacity he was allowed to consult one of the official advocates established in 1443. The report of the sub-committee was read to the Council, and a vote was taken as to whether sentence should be pronounced. If the vote was affirmative sentence was proposed, any member being free to move a sentence or an amendment to one. On the result of the voting the fate of the prisoner depended. In cases of crime committed outside Venice but within the competence of the Ten, that Council could delegate its powers and procedure (its *rito*) to the local magistrates who sent in the minutes of the trial to the "Chiefs."

With the Closing of the Great Council and the establishment of the Council of Ten, the Venetian constitution reached its maturity. Some slight developments, such as the evolution of the Three *Inquisitori di Stato*, of the *Esecutori contro alla Bestemmia*, and the *Camerlenghi*, took place it is true; but on the whole the form was fixed, and it stood thus:

(1) The Great Council contained the whole body politic. Out of it were elected almost all the chief officers of State. At first it possessed legislative and even some judicial powers, but these were gradually delegated to the Senate, or the Ten, as the Council became unmanageable in size, until at last it was left with hardly any attributes save its original chief function, that of the electorate of the State.

(2) Above the Great Council came the Senate, consisting nominally of one hundred and twenty members, not including the Doge, his Council, the Judges of the Supreme Court, and many other officials, who sat *ex officio* and raised its numbers higher. The Senate was the great legislative body in the State; it also had the chief direction of ordinary foreign affairs and of finance; it declared war, made peace, received despatches from ambassadors, and sent instructions. It possessed a certain judicial authority which, however, was seldom exercised.

(3) Parallel with the Senate, but outside the main lines of the constitution, came the Council of Ten. It had been established as a committee of public safety to meet a crisis, and to supply a defect in the constitution, the want of a rapid, secret, executive arm. Its

efficiency and rapidity led to a gradual substitution of the Ten for the Senate upon many important occasions. An order of the Ten was as binding as a law of the Senate. Ambassadors reported secretly to the Ten; and the instructions of the Ten would carry more weight than those of the Senate. The judicial functions of the Ten were far higher than those of the Senate; and indeed in its capacity as a permanent committee of public safety and guardian of public morals there were few departments of government or of private life where its authority would have been disallowed.

(4) Above both Senate and Ten came the cabinet or *Collegio*. It was composed of the *Savii* or Ministers. The six *Savii grandi*, the three *Savii di terra ferma*, the three *Savii agli ordini*, the Secretaries, of finance, of war, and of marine. The *Savii grandi* took their functions in turn week and week about. All business of State passed through the hands of the *Collegio* and was prepared by them to be submitted to the Great Council, the Senate or the Ten according to the nature and importance of the matter. The *Collegio* was the initiatory body in the State and also the executive arm of the Maggior Consiglio and the Senate. The Ten, as we have stated, possessed an executive of its own in its three "Chiefs."

(5) Above the Collegio came the lesser Council composed of the six ducal Councillors; immediately connected with the Doge; both supervising him and representing him in all his attributes. The Doge could do nothing without his Council; a majority of the Council could perform all the ducal functions, without the presence of the Doge.

(6) At the head of all came the Doge himself; the point of greatest splendour though not of greatest weight, the apex of the constitutional pyramid. He embodied and represented the majesty of the State; his presence was necessary everywhere, in the Great Council, in the Senate, in the Ten, in the College. He was the voice of Venice and in her name he replied to all ambassadors. As a statesman long practised in affairs and intimately acquainted with the political machinery of the Republic he could not fail to carry weight by his personality; and at a crisis the election of a Doge, as in the case of Francesco Foscari or, later still, as in the case of Leonardo Donato, might determine the course of events. But theoretically he was a symbol, not a factor in the constitution; the outward and visible sign of all that the oligarchy meant.

Such was the Venetian constitution, which, thanks to its efficiency and strength, commanded the admiration and the envy of Europe and enabled Venice to assume that high place among the nations which was hers during the fifteenth century.

The fifteenth century is the period of greatest splendour in the history of the Republic. Mature in her constitution, and with a dominion firmly established by sea and land, Venice presented a brilliant spectacle to the eyes of Europe. Yet this period contains the germs of her decadence. Supreme in the Mediterranean by the defeat of Genoa, Venice was almost immediately called upon to face the Turks and to wear herself out in a long and single-handed contest with their growing power; firmly planted on the mainland, the Republic discovered that, with jealous neighbours around her and frontiers to be attacked, she could not stand still; she was compelled to advance, and found herself exposed to all the dangers implied in the use of mercenary arms, and committed to that policy of aggression which summoned up against her the League of Cambray.

Her mainland territory was probably a drain on the financial resources of the Republic, not a fountain of wealth. That territory was only acquired and held by paying for costly troops and more costly captains of adventure. It is doubtful whether the revenue derived from the provinces covered the cost of possession and administration. True, on occasion, the Republic applied to her land territories for a loan, as in 1474, when 516,000 ducats were advanced to the government; but the fact remains that the contentment of her mainland possessions was essential to Venetian supremacy, and that this contentment could not be secured if they were heavily taxed.

The real wealth of Venice, the wealth which enabled her to adorn the Capital and retain her provinces, depended upon the sea. It was derived from her traffic as a great emporium and mart of exchange fed by a large mercantile marine. The State built the ships and let them out to the highest bidder at auction. Every year six fleets were organised and despatched: (1) to the Black Sea, (2) to Greece and Constantinople, (3) to the Syrian ports, (4) to Egypt, (5) to Barbary and the north coast of Africa, (6) to England and Flanders. The route and general instructions for each fleet (*muda*) were carefully discussed in the Senate. Every officer was bound by oath to observe these instructions and to maintain on all occasions the honour of the Republic. The government prescribed the number of the crew for each ship, the size of the anchors, quality of rope, etc. A compulsory load-line was established. New vessels were allowed to load above the line for the first three years, but to a diminishing extent each year. The ships were all built upon government measurements for two reasons; first, because ships of identical build would behave in the same way under stress of weather and could more easily be kept together; secondly, because the consuls in distant ports could be sure of keeping a refit of masts, rudders, sails, etc., when they knew the exact build of all Venetian ships which would touch their ports. The ships were convertible from merchantmen to men-of-war; and this explains to a certain extent how Venice was able to replace her fleets so rapidly after such losses as those of Curzola or Sapienza. The six State fleets are estimated to have numbered 330 ships with crews to the amount of 36,000 men.

Venetian commerce covered the whole civilised world. The city was
a great reservoir of merchandise, constantly filled and constantly emptied
again, with eastern luxuries flowing westward and western commodities
flowing east. Upon export and import alike the government levied taxes
(*tavola dell' entrada e tavola dell' insida*); these, with the salt
monopoly and the taxation of the guilds (*tansa della milizia, tansa
insensibile,* etc.), furnished the main source of her ordinary revenue, which
in the year 1500 was estimated at 1,145,580 ducats. The importance of
the sea in the economy of Venice is obvious; but during the fifteenth
century her naval and commercial sea-power both received a fatal blow.
Wars with the Turks exhausted her fighting capacity and the discovery
of the Cape route to the Indies tended to divert the whole line of the
world's traffic from the Mediterranean into the Atlantic, out of the hands
of the Venetians into the hands of the Portuguese.

The century opened, however, with a series of triumphs for the
Republic. The development and extension of her land empire continued; her prestige at sea increased. Dalmatia, which the Republic
had surrendered by the treaty of Turin, was recovered after a struggle;
and by 1420 Venice was in possession of the whole of Friuli. Thanks
to the mountainous frontier of the province this acquisition gave the
Republic a defensible position towards the east, where she had hitherto
been very weak; it largely increased her land empire and whetted her
appetite for more.

Nor was her achievement by sea less brilliant. The quarrels among
the sons of Sultan Bayazid I ended in the concentration of the Ottoman
power in the hands of Mohammad (1413). Venice had no desire to embark
on a campaign against the victorious Turk. She hoped to trade with
them, not to fight them, and, through her ambassador Francesco Foscari,
a treaty was signed whereby she believed herself to have secured her
colonies from molestation. But Mohammad was not able, even if he
desired, to prevent his followers from regarding all Christians as dogs.
Treaty or no treaty, they chased some Venetian merchantmen into
Negroponte and menaced the island. The Venetian admiral Loredan came
to a parley with the Turkish commander, at Gallipoli (1416). But while
the leaders were in consultation, the crews fell to, and a battle became
inevitable. The Venetians were brilliantly victorious; and the Republic
secured an advantageous peace, as well as the applause of Europe, only
too ready to believe that it need not mind about the Turk as long as
Venice was there to fight him.

But contemporaneously with this fresh expansion of Venice, by the
conquest of Friuli and the heightening of her prestige after the victory
of Gallipoli, events fraught with grave consequences for the Republic
were maturing to the west. On the sudden death of Gian Galeazzo
Visconti (1402), his dominions had been seized and partitioned by his
generals. Gian Galeazzo's son, Filippo Maria, patiently, slowly, but surely,

recovered the Visconti territories. In this task he was greatly assisted by the military skill of Francesco Bussone, called Carmagnola from his birthplace near Turin. By 1420 the task was accomplished, and a Visconti was once more Lord of Milan, Cremona, Crema, Bergamo, Brescia, and Genoa, as powerful as ever Gian Galeazzo had been and not one whit less ambitious. Florence took alarm at Visconti's attitude and asked Venice to join her in a league against Milan. The position was a difficult one for the Republic; Filippo Maria was undeniably menacing and he had a claim in virtue of his father's conquest to both Verona and Vicenza, now Venetian territory; on the other hand Venice was extremely unwilling to embark upon the troubled waters of Italian mainland politics, and to find herself, in all probability, committed to costly mainland campaigns which would consume the wealth she was sweeping in from the sea.

The Florentine proposals revealed two parties in the State. The Doge Mocenigo and his friends held that it was still possible to avoid a rupture with Visconti, that Venice might remain on good terms with her powerful neighbour and trade with Milan instead of fighting it. Opposed to the Doge was Francesco Foscari, head of the party of young Venice, in favour of expansion, elated by the recent acquisition of Friuli. But Mocenigo was dying, and on his death-bed he called the principal statesmen of the Republic about him and reminded them of the position of the community, which had never been more flourishing. He pointed to the merchant marine, the finest in the world, to the rapid reduction of the national debt, from ten millions to six; to the vast commerce with the territories of the Duke of Milan which represented ten million ducats capital with a net profit of two millions; he insisted that at this rate Venice would soon be mistress of the world, but that all might be lost by a rash war. Everything would depend, he said, upon the character of the man who succeeded him. He uttered a solemn warning against Francesco Foscari as a braggart, vainglorious, without solidity, grasping at much, securing little; certain to involve the State in war, to waste its wealth and leave it at the mercy of its mercenary captains. Prophetic words, but powerless to avert the doom they foretold. Foscari was elected (1423); and instantly set himself to support the Florentine request for an alliance. He did not carry his point at once, for the Mocenigo party could always urge that an alliance with Florence against Milan would draw Visconti and Sigismund together against the Republic. But Filippo Maria's successes were continuous; his troops were in the Romagna, and he had defeated Florence in battle after battle, Zagonara, Val di Lamone, Rapallo, Anghiari. In desperation the Florentines declared that if the Venetians would not help them to retain their liberties, they would pull the house about their ears. "When we refused," they said, "to help Genoa, she made Visconti her Lord; if you refuse to help us we will make him King." This threat coupled with the desertion of

Visconti's great general, Carmagnola, turned the scale. The Florentine League was concluded and Carmagnola received the command of the Venetian forces.

Thus the Republic embarked upon a struggle for supremacy as a land-Power in northern Italy. But she was soon to prove the truth of Mocenigo's dying words. The first campaign ended in the acquisition of Brescia and the Bresciano by Venetian troops, but not by Carmagnola. He had no sooner brought his forces under Brescia than he asked leave to retire for his health to the Baths of Abano ; and his conduct from the very first roused those suspicions which eventually led to his doom. The second campaign gave Bergamo to the victorious Republic. But the suspicions of Venice were increased by finding that the Duke of Milan was in communication with Carmagnola and was prepared to conclude a peace through him as intermediary, suspicions confirmed by the dilatory conduct of their general after the victory at Maclodio, when nothing lay between him and Milan. At the opening of the third campaign against Visconti, the Republic endeavoured to rouse their general to vigorous action by making him large promises if he would only crush the Duke and take his capital. But nothing would stir Carmagnola from his culpable inactivity. The truth was that he cared not a jot for Venetian interests ; like all mercenaries he was playing his own game, and that did not counsel him to press Visconti too hard, for it was always possible that he might one day find himself again in the Duke's service.

The patience of the Republic was exhausted at last. Carmagnola was summoned to Venice on the plea that the government wished to consult him. He was received with marked honour. His suite was told that the general stayed to dine with the Doge and that they might go home. The Doge sent to excuse himself from receiving the Count on the score of indisposition. Carmagnola turned to go down to his gondola. In the lower arcade of the palace he was arrested and hurried to prison. He was tried by the Council of Ten on the charge of treason and executed in the Piazzetta of St Mark (1432).

Notwithstanding their difficulties with their mercenary commander, the Venetians had made very solid acquisitions during these wars with Visconti. Brescia and Bergamo were now permanently added to the land empire of the Republic, and the title was confirmed by an imperial investiture at Prague in 1437, in which Venetian dominions are defined as all the land *di quà*, that is east of the Adda,—very nearly the extreme limit of mainland possession ever touched by the Republic.

But the possession of Brescia and Bergamo was not likely to be left undisputed by Filippo Maria Visconti ; and a long series of campaigns, conducted by such generals as Gonzaga and Gattamelata, exhausting to the treasury and unprofitable to the State, was only brought to an end by the death of the Duke of Milan in 1447. During this period, however,

Venice had converted her guardianship of Ravenna into actual possession as remainder-heir to the Polentani, Lords of that city; a step which brought into the field against her the Roman Curia, and was not without important bearings on the final combination of the Papacy with her other enemies at the League of Cambray.

The death of Filippo Maria Visconti left Milan and the Visconti possessions without a Lord. Visconti's only child Bianca was married to Sforza, and in right of her he claimed succession; but the city of Milan declared itself a republic. Venice seized Lodi and Piacenza and offered to support the Milanese Republic if it would recognise the capture. Milan declined. But that city was soon forced to open its gates to Sforza; and shortly afterwards Venice and Sforza came to terms in the Peace of Lodi (1454), by which the Republic was confirmed in possession of Bergamo and Brescia and acquired Crema and Treviglio as well, thereby affording her enemies fresh proofs for that charge of insatiable greed which they were already beginning to move against her.

But Visconti's death produced another result still more momentous not only for Venice but for all Italy as well. Filippo Maria had left no heirs male; and the French claim,—that of the house of Orleans based upon the marriage of Valentina Visconti with the father of Charles of Orleans,—was immediately advanced. It opened a new epoch in Italian history, preparing the way for the complications inseparable from the advent of foreign princes in Italian politics.

There were two reasons which induced Venice to accept gladly the Treaty of Lodi. The long War with Visconti, though it had brought her a large accession of territory, had also cost her very dear; but it was of even greater significance that all Europe and Venice especially, as the power most nearly concerned, had been startled by the news that the Turks had captured Constantinople and that the Eastern Empire was at an end for ever. This event took place in 1453, the year before the Peace of Lodi.

We have seen already that the real desire of the Republic was to trade with the Turks, and not to fight them; from the very outset when she made a treaty with Sultan Mohammad in 1410 and again after the victory of Gallipoli, her whole energies had been directed to securing her colonies and insuring freedom of traffic. But now, with the Mussulmans established in Constantinople and spreading down the Levant, it was inevitable that Venice should be brought into hostile relations with their growing power.

The fall of Constantinople was the last external event of moment in the brilliant reign of Francesco Foscari. Internal events also contributed to render his Dogeship remarkable. He seems to have come to the throne as the embodiment of the new oligarchy which had taken final shape at the closing of the Great Council, and which had consolidated its authority by the creation of the Ten. He was the first Doge in whose election the people had no part. In presenting him to his subjects the old formula

"This is your Doge, an it please you," was changed to "This is your Doge." But, furthermore, Foscari's election is the first in which we find any suggestion of bribery. He was accused of having applied, while holding the office of Procurator, a sum of money, which he found in the coffers of that magistracy, to securing support among the poorer nobility, a class destined to become both famous and dangerous under the name of the Barnabotti, but of whom we hear now for the first time. Political corruption showed itself again in 1433, when a wide-spread conspiracy to arrange election to offices was discovered among the nobles of the Great Council. The obscure case of Jacopo Foscari, the Doge's son, showed to what lengths intrigue might be carried; and the dramatic end of the Doge's reign, his deposition after so long and so brilliant an occupation of the throne, demonstrated the absolute authority of the Council of Ten as sovereign in Venice.

The epoch was one of great outward splendour. Commines, who came to Venice some years later, describes it as "the most triumphant city I have ever seen; the city that bestows the greatest honour on ambassadors and on strangers; the city that is most carefully governed; the city wherein the worship of God is most solemnly conducted."

It was thus that Venice struck a competent observer towards the close of the fifteenth century, and Commines is only one of the earliest in a long list of testimonies to the vivid impression created by the Capital of the Lagoons. Venice was at the zenith of her splendour; a city of pleasure, sumptuous in her reception of "ambassadors and strangers"; a commonwealth of surprising solidity and power, "most carefully governed"; a palace of pomp where the arts flourished and where the "worship of God," in churches, processions, pageants "was most solemnly conducted." Everything connected with the city, external as well as internal, contributed to the indelible impression she produced. Her singular site; her water streets; the beauty of her public and private buildings; the Doge's palace so audaciously designed, glowing with the rose and cream coloured marbles; St Mark's, a precious casket of porphyry, mosaic and oriental cupolas; the Hall of the Great Council adorned with records of Venetian prowess; the rich Gothic of the Porta della Carta; the Piazza with its noble bell-tower; the opening of the Piazzetta, the vista of San Giorgio Maggiore, the sweep of the Riva degli Schiavoni leading away to San Nicolo and the great sea avenue of Venice; the domestic architecture of the private palaces, that lined the Grand and the smaller canals; the slender columns, the ogee windows, the balconies with their sea lions for brackets, the perforated stone tracery above the windows, the glowing colour of the plaster on the walls—all combined to arrest attention. But more than this; behind the external splendour and deep down as the cause of it, Venice had something further to offer for the study and the contemplation of the stranger. Her constitution was almost an ideal for European statesmen. Her declared object was "to win the heart and the affection of her people," and this could only be brought about by attention to their interests; in the interests of commerce consuls had been established as early as 1117; in those of finance public funds and government stock had been created in 1171; in those of order the census was introduced about the year 1300; in those of property each holding was numbered and registered; in those of justice the law was codified in 1229. A factory act forbade the employment of children in dangerous trades where mercury was used. The nautical code provided for a load-line on all shipping and insisted on the proper treatment of crews. In most departments of practical government the Republic of Venice preceded all other States of Europe, and offered material for reflexion to their politicians, to whom was presented the phenomenon of a fully-matured and stable constitution, and of a people fused together in one homogeneous whole.

For though the Closing of the Great Council had rendered the governing class a close oligarchy, it had not produced class hatred; Venice showed no trace of the feudal system with its violent divisions of the State into hostile camps; every Venetian was still a Venetian first and foremost, and though excluded from the functions of government was still in all likelihood closely connected with those who exercised them. The palace of the patrician was surrounded by a network of small alleys filled with his people, his clients. The merchant prince in his office was served by a staff of clerks who had their share in the success of his ventures. The arrival of any merchant's galleys was a matter for rejoicing to the whole community and was announced by the great bell of St Mark's. Venice, in short, from the commercial point of view was a great joint-stock company for the exploitation of the East, and the patricians were its directors.

The life of a Venetian noble could be filled to the full if he so desired. Politics, diplomacy, trade, arms were all open to him; and he frequently combined two or more of these professions. At the age of twenty-five he took his seat in the Great Council and became eligible for any of the numerous offices to which that Council elected. He might serve his apprenticeship in the department of trade, of finance, of health; passing thence to the Senate, he might represent his country in Constantinople, Rome, Prague, Paris, Madrid, London. On his return he would be made a *Savio* and member of the cabinet, or serve his turn of a year on the Council of Ten, ending his days perhaps as a Doge, at least as Procurator of St Mark. And throughout the whole of this official career he was probably directing with the help of his brothers and sons the movement of his private family business, trade, or banking. Nothing is commoner than to find an ambassador petitioning to be recalled, because his family business is suffering through his absence from Venice. There was, of course, another aspect of the patrician class. The vicious nobles became poor, the poor corrupt, and political and social life both suffered in consequence. The Council of Ten was frequently called upon to punish the betrayal of State secrets and the unbridled license of the nobility.

On the other hand, if the people were excluded from the direction of State affairs they found abundant scope for their energies in trade and industries and the guild-life which these created and fostered. Every art and craft and trade in Venice, down to the very sausage-makers, was erected into a guild. They were self-supporting, self-governing bodies, supervised, it is true, by a government office whose approval was necessary for the validity of the bye-laws. They were carefully fostered by the State, which saw in them an outlet for the political activities of the people. At his coronation each new Doge was expected to entertain the guilds, who displayed specimens of their handiwork in the ducal palace; on great State occasions, when Venice entertained distinguished guests, the guilds were called upon to furnish part of the pageant; but they never acquired, as in Florence, or other Italian cities, a voice in the government of the State. The guilds of most Italian towns represented and protected the people against a nobility of arms and of territory. In Venice such a nobility never existed; the patrician was himself a merchant and very probably a member of a trade guild.

And the decorative and cultured side of all this teeming life found expression in the arts. Murano produced the earliest masters of that school of painting which was to adorn the world by the hands of the Vivarini, Carpaccio, the Bellinis, Mantegna, Giorgione, Veronese, Titian, Palma, Cima da Conegliano, Tintoretto, Tiepolo. Dramatic in conception, gorgeous in colour, untrammelled by the effort to express philosophic ideas or religious emotion, the art of Venice was essentially decorative, and was dedicated to the adornment of public and private life in the city. The great colonnade at the Rialto, the very heart of Venetian traffic, was already covered with frescoes and possessed that famous planisphere, or Mapamondo, showing the routes followed by Venetian commerce throughout the world. The study of letters received a vital stimulus, thanks to the asylum which Venice offered to refugees from Constantinople. Cardinal Bessarion made St Mark's Library the legatee of his inestimable treasures. The brilliant history of the Venetian printing press was inaugurated by John of Speyer and Windelin his brother (1469), by Nicolas Jenson, by Waldorfer and Erhardt Radolt, and carried on by Andrea Torresano to the glories of the Aldine Press. Coming third in chronological order, preceded by Subiaco and Rome, the press of Venice surpassed all its Italian contemporaries in splendour and abundance, in range of subjects, in service to scholarship.

Of literature in the sense of belles-lettres there was but little; but the *Annali* of Malipiero, the *Diarii* of Sanudo and the Diaries of Priuli afford us a full, vivid, and veracious narrative of Venetian history, of life in the city, of the wars and intrigues of the Republic during her splendour and the beginning of her decline (1457–1535). No other Italian State can show such a monumental record of its doings as this. Written by capable men of affairs, the first a soldier, the second an official, the third a great merchant-banker, all of whom took a large part in the deeds and events they recount; written, not for publication, but to the honour and glory of that beloved San Marco "whom" to use the phrase of a later Venetian ambassador "each of us has engraved upon his heart"; written in dialect racy of the soil and of the people,—we have here a story, vigorous, vivacious, humorous; direct and simple as a ballad; a monument to the city-State that produced it; an illustration of the central principle of Venetian life that the Republic was everything, while her individual sons were of no account.

But this appearance of prosperity, of splendour, of pomp, during the latter half of the fifteenth century, masked the germs of incipient decline: the corruption of the nobles, the suspicious tyranny of the Ten, the first signs of bank failures, the drop in the value of funds, the rise of the national debt from six to thirteen millions. Land wars continued to drain the treasury; the Turkish wars, conducted by Venice single-handed, curtailed her Levant trade and entailed a continual outlay; worst of all, in 1486 came the news that Diaz had discovered the Cape of Good Hope, and in 1497 that Vasco da Gama had rounded it, thereby cutting the tap-root of Venetian wealth, its Mediterranean carrying-trade, and drawing the great trade-lines of the world out of the Mediterranean into the Atlantic. Venice could alter neither her geographical position nor her policy. She endeavoured to come to terms with the Turk, and she continued to expand on the mainland. This course of action brought down upon her the charge of infidelity on the one hand and of insatiable greed on the other, and ended in the disastrous combination of Cambray.

After the fall of Constantinople the Turkish advance was steadily continued both south and east. Athens surrendered to the Turks in 1457; so did Sinope and Trebizond; and the loss of the Morea in 1462 brought them into immediate collision with the Republic. Venice perfectly understood that a struggle for her possessions in the Levant was inevitable sooner or later; she therefore gladly embraced Pope Pius II's proposals for a crusade. But the lamentable failure of the undertaking, and the Pope's death at Ancona, left the Republic to carry on, single-handed, a war she had undertaken on the promise and in the expectation of European support. Antonio Michiel, a Venetian merchant resident in Constantinople, had warned his government, in 1466, that the Sultan was mustering large forces. "I take it the fleet will number two hundred sail," he says, "and every one here thinks Negroponte its object." He continues in a note of serious warning that matters must not be treated lightly to the deceiving of themselves. The Turk has a way of exaggerating the enemy's strength and arming regardless of expense. Venice had better do the same. This was in 1466; three years later the blow was ready to fall, and again Venice received warning through another merchant, Piero Dolfin, resident in Chios. Let the government, he wrote, fortify its places in the Levant and lose no time about it; "on this depends the safety of the State, for Negroponte once lost the rest of the Levant is in peril."

But Venice, exhausted by the drain of the land wars against Visconti, was unwilling to face another and more terrible campaign by sea unless she were forced to do so. She endeavoured to open negotiations at Constantinople on the pretext that she was acting in the name of Hungary. But in 1470 Negroponte fell. The War had already cost considerably over a million ducats, and the government was reduced to suspending either two-thirds or a half of all official salaries which were over twenty-five ducats per annum. In spite of this she rejected, as extravagant, terms of peace offered her in 1476; and faced the struggle once more. Scutari was attacked by the Sultan in person, who, in his determination to enter the town, blew besieged and besiegers alike to atoms before his siege guns. But the Republic could not hold out for ever unaided; Scutari was at the last extremity; a large army was rumoured to be on its way to attack Friuli. Venice was forced to recognise the facts, and in 1479 she proposed terms of peace. Scutari, and all Venetian possessions in the Morea were ceded to the Turk. Venice agreed to pay ten thousand ducats a year for the privileges of trading, and one hundred thousand in two years, as a war indemnity; and received permission to keep an Agent (*Bailo*) in Constantinople.

The Peace of 1479 marks an epoch in the history of Venetian relations with the East, and indicates a return to her original policy of peaceable dealings, whenever possible, with the Turk.

In truth, the Republic had every reason to complain of the conduct of Europe. After sixteen years of continuous warfare, which she had undertaken on the strength of European promises, Venice concluded a ruinous peace, by which she lost a part of her Levantine possessions and was reduced to the position of a tributary. Yet instantly all Europe attacked her for her perfidy to the Christian faith, and the princes of Italy professed to believe that Venice had abandoned the Turkish War, merely in order to devote herself to the extension of her power on the mainland. Had she received any support from Europe or Italy, she would never have closed the War with such a balance against herself. In truth the Republic was too exhausted to continue the struggle. It was not her fault that, the year after the conclusion of the Peace, Italy and all Europe were alarmed by the news that the Turks had seized Otranto. This was the inevitable result of the withdrawal of Venice from the struggle,—a withdrawal in its turn due to lack of any support from Italy or Europe. When invited by the Pope to join an Italian league against the Turk, Venice, mindful of the results which had followed on her acceptance of the last papal invitation, replied that she had made peace with the Sultan, and confirmed the suspicion that she was in secret understanding with the Turk. Her next step emphasised the further suspicion that her object in coming to terms with the Turk had been to allow herself a free hand to extend in Italy.

We have seen that in 1441 Venice had occupied Ravenna—under protest from Rome—as heir of the Polentani, Lords of Ravenna. She now (1481) attacked the Marquis of Ferrara on the ground that he was infringing a Venetian monopoly by the erection of salt-pans at the mouth of the Po. As the territory of Ferrara lay between the Venetian frontier and Ravenna it looked as if Venice desired to unite her possessions in that direction by the acquisition of Ferrara. This policy induced the Duke of Milan, the Pope, and the King of Naples to combine in support of Ferrara against Venice. The War was popular with the Venetians at first, but the strain on both treasury and private purses soon became insupportable, and no success crowned the Venetian arms. The distressed condition of the Republic is described by Malipiero. Payment of the interest on the funds was partially suspended; the shops on the Rialto were mortgaged; private plate and jewellery compulsorily called in; salaries cut down. The revenue from the mainland was falling off. The arsenal was nearly empty. Famine and plague were at the door. "We shall be forced to sue for peace and restore all we have gained."

Malipiero was partially right. Venice was forced to sue for peace, but not till she had taken the ruinous step (which other Italian princes took before and after her) of suggesting to the French that they should make good their claims on certain Italian provinces,—Charles VIII his claim on Naples, the Duke of Orleans his claims on Milan. Two members of the hostile League, Milan and Naples, were thus threatened in their own possessions, with the result that peace was concluded at Bagnolo in 1484. Venice retained Rovigo and the Polesine, but was forced to surrender the towns she had taken in Apulia during the course of the War.

This invitation to foreigners was fatal to all Italian princes, as events were soon to demonstrate. The five Great Powers of Italy, Venice, Milan, Florence, the Pope and Naples, were able to hold their own against each other, but the moment the more potent ultramontane sovereigns appeared upon the scene, nominally in support of one or other of the Italian States, really in pursuit of their own aggrandisement, the balance was irretrievably upset. The sequence of these events, culminating in the Wars of the League of Cambray, after which Venice never again recovered her commanding place among the political communities of Europe, has been narrated in a previous Chapter.

# CHAPTER IX.

## GERMANY AND THE EMPIRE.

It is a commonplace to contrast the political condition of Germany on the eve of the Reformation with that of the great national States of Western Europe. In Germany the dangerous confusion of the national monarchy with the tradition of the Roman Empire had continued fatal to the German Kingdom, even after the imperial idea had ceased to exert any commanding influence over men's minds. The royal power in consequence became the merest shadow of its former self. Central organisation ceased to exist. Private war and general anarchy were chronic. The national life waxed cold, when uncherished by a strong national monarchy; and in the end salvation was to come from the development of the rude feudal nobility of the Middle Ages into an order of small independent rulers, so extraordinarily tenacious of their sovereign rank that more than a score of them have preserved it even amidst the changed conditions of the nineteenth century. While in France, Spain, and England national monarchies, both autocratic and popular, were establishing national unity, ordered progress, and strong administration, Germany was forced to content herself with the loosest and most impotent of federal governments.

Looking at the course of German history in the fifteenth century with knowledge of what happened later, it would be hard to deny the strength of this contrast. Yet there was no very great or essential dissimilarity between the condition of Germany under Frederick III and that of the France of the Armagnac and Burgundian feuds. The elements of political life were in each case the same. There was a monarchy whose great history was still remembered even in the days of its impotence and ruin. There was a real sense of national life, a consciousness so strong that it could bend even the selfish instincts of feudal nobles into cherishing an ambition wider and more patriotic than that of making themselves little kings over their own patrimony. The strongest of the German feudal houses was less well organised on a separatist basis than the Duchy of Britanny or the Duchy of Burgundy. And few indeed of them could base their power on any keenly felt local or national tradition, or upon anything more solid than the habit of respect for an ancient house. Moreover, the ecclesiastical States might have been, and both the small nobility and the wealthy numerous and active free towns actually were, permanent counterpoises to the absolute supremacy of the greater feudatories in a way to which French history supplies no parallel. All medieval history shows how the possibilities of despotism lurked even in the most decrepit of feudal monarchies, and how the most disorderly of feudal barons could be constrained to use their swords to further national ends.

Even in its worst decay the German kingship still counted for something. "The King of the Romans," as the German King was styled before the papal coronation gave him the right to call himself "Roman Emperor," was still the first of earthly potentates in dignity and rank. The effective intervention in European affairs of a German King so powerless as Sigismund of Luxemburg would have been impossible but for the authority still associated with the imperial name. The German Kings had indeed no longer a direct royal domain such as gave wealth and dignity to the Kings of France or England. They were equally destitute of the regular and ample revenue which ancient custom or the direct grant of the Estates allowed the Kings of France and England to levy in every part of their dominions. But the habit was now established of electing on each occasion a powerful reigning prince as Emperor, and a virtually hereditary empire was secured for the House of Luxemburg and afterwards for its heir and sometime rival, the House of Habsburg. The Emperors thus possessed in their personal territories some compensation for their lack of imperial domain proper. And feudalism was still sufficiently alive in Germany to make the traditional feudal sources of income a real if insufficient substitute for grants and taxes of the more modern type. The imperial Chancery issued no writ or charter without exacting heavy fees. No family compact between members of a reigning house, no agreement of eventual succession between neighbouring princes, was regarded as legitimate without such dearly purchased royal sanction. Even where the Emperor's direct power was slight his influence was very considerable. He no longer controlled ecclesiastical elections with a high hand; but there were few bishoprics or abbeys in which he had not as good a chance of directing the course of events as the strongest of the local lords, and his influence was spread over all Germany, while the prince was powerless outside his own neighbourhood. All over Germany numerous knights, nobles, ecclesiastics, and lawyers looked forward to the Emperor's service as a career, and hope of future imperial favour often induced them to do their best to further the imperial policy. If indirect pressure of this sort did not prevail, the Roman Court more often than not lent its powerful aid towards enforcing imperial wishes. There was no great danger that the feeble monarchs of this period would excite general opposition by flagrant attacks on the traditional authority of their vassals; and in smaller matters it was more to the interest even of the greater princes to keep on good terms with Caesar, than to provoke his hostility by wanton and arbitrary opposition to his wishes.

Another weighty advantage accrued to the German monarch from the circumstance that his chief rivals were every whit as badly off in dealing with their vassals as he was with his. The well-ordered territorial sovereignties of a later generation had not yet come into existence. The strongest of the imperial vassals were still feudal lords and not sovereign princes. The resources at their disposal were those of a great feudal proprietor rather than those of an independent ruler. Outside their own domains they had few means of exercising any real power. Their vassals were as hard to keep in hand as they were themselves impatient of control by their sovereign. When even the imperial Court was destitute of the appliances of a modern State, the smaller princes could only govern in a still ruder and more primitive fashion. Their revenue was uncertain; their means of raising money were utterly inadequate; their army consisted of rude feudal levies; and they had no police, no civil or diplomatic service. Although they could be trusted to struggle stoutly and unscrupulously for their immediate interests, they were the last body of men to frame a general policy or depart from their traditional principles in order to suit the temper of the coming age. The very numerous small princes were infinitely worse off than their greater brethren. The free towns, though much better able to protect themselves than the weaker princes, were powerless for aggression.

The Diet of the Empire (*Reichstag*) was the ancient and traditional council of the Emperor. It remained a purely feudal body in which none save tenants-in-chief (*Reichsunmittelbare*) had any right to appear. Its powers were sufficiently extensive, but its constitution was only very gradually settled, and there was no real means of carrying out its resolutions. The method of its convocation was extraordinarily cumbrous. Besides sending out regular writs, it was the custom for the Emperor to despatch various officials throughout the Empire to request the magnates' personal appearance at the Diet. In the case of the more important princes, this process was often several times repeated. Yet it was seldom, save perhaps at the first Diet of a new King or when business of extraordinary importance was to be discussed, that many princes condescended to appear in person. In their absence they were represented by commissioners, who often delayed proceedings by referring to their principals all questions on which they had not been sufficiently instructed. This habit was so strong with the delegates of the towns that it seriously delayed their recognition as an Estate of the realm, which they had claimed as a right more than fifty years before it was formally conceded. When the preliminaries were over, there was always, in consequence of the lateness of the appearance of some of the representatives, a considerable delay before proceedings could be opened. Very often the early comers went home before the last arrivals appeared at all. Proceedings began when the Emperor or his commissioners laid the royal proposition before the Estates. For ordinary debates the Diet was divided into three *curiae*, colleges, or Estates. But it was not until 1489 that the Estate of the free and imperial towns definitely secured its right to appear in all Diets beside the higher Estates of Electors and princes. Procedure was extraordinarily complicated and cumbrous. It was not until the end of the fifteenth century that such elementary principles as the right of the majority to bind a minority, or the obligation of absent members to abide by the proceedings of those that were present, were definitely established. It was often after many months' discussion that the imperial recess (*Abschied*) was issued, which concluded the proceedings; and the great expense involved in prolonged residence at the seat of the Diet was a real burden even on the richest princes. In all the colleges voting was by individuals; but so personal was the right of representation, that the splitting up of a principality among the sons of a prince gave each ruler of a part a voice equal to that of the ruler of the whole. The smaller tenants-in-chief, the imperial knights, were not regarded as an Estate of the Empire and were excluded from all part in the Diet. Neither the custom which secured that the voting power of a much divided house should be no greater than that of a family whose power was vested in a single hand, nor that which gave only collective votes to the counts, prelates and towns, had as yet sprung into existence.

The incompetence and costliness of the Diet made it very ineffective in practice. The Emperors hesitated to convoke an assembly which, by its theoretical powers, might effectually tie their hands, while the Estates were averse to wasting time and money in fruitless and unending deliberations. Side by side with the constitutional representation of the Empire, divers local and private organisations had gradually come into being to discharge efficiently some at least of the duties that the Estates were incompetent to perform. The oldest among these was the meeting of the six Electors (*Kurfürstentag*). Of these high dignitaries the three Archbishops of Mainz, Cologne and Trier and the Count Palatine of the Rhine commonly acted together, while the two eastern Electors, the Duke of Saxony and the Margrave of Brandenburg, had more discordant interests. The seventh Elector, the King of Bohemia, was excluded as a foreigner from all electoral functions save the actual choice of the King. The *Golden Bull* of 1356 had given privileges which raised the Electors above their brother princes into the first Estate of the Empire. They had such full jurisdiction over their territories that it became the ideal of all other princes to obtain the electoral privileges. Succession to their lands was to go by primogeniture, and every Easter they were to hold an electoral Diet. Regular yearly meetings of the

Electors as prescribed by the *Golden Bull* did not become the fashion ; but the habit of common deliberation became firmly established, and the carelessness of the Luxemburg Emperors, as to all matters not affecting their hereditary dominions, gave the Electoral College an opportunity of playing a foremost part in national history.  The Electors claimed to be the successors of the Roman Senate, if not the representatives of the Roman people as well.  The attitude of a Wenceslas, a Sigismund, or a Frederick made possible a real sharing of the functions of government between Emperor and Senate, such as is imagined to have existed in the primitive division of power between Augustus and the Senate of his day. The six Electors deposed the incompetent King Wenceslas in 1399, and formed in 1424 the Electoral Union (*Kurfürstenverein*) of Bingen in which they pledged themselves and their successors to speak with one voice in all imperial affairs.  Fourteen years later the same Electoral Union was strong enough to adopt for imperial elections the precedent, already commonly set in ecclesiastical elections, of prescribing the direction of the policy of their nominee.  The conditions imposed on Albert II before his election prepared the way for the formal *Wahlkapitulation* which assumes so great an importance in imperial history with the election of Charles V in 1519.  In the same way it was the close understanding between the Electors that made possible the programme of imperial reformation championed by Berthold of Mainz.  It was only after grave differences of policy had permanently divided the Electors that Berthold's dream of a united Germany became impossible.

Less constitutional were the extra-legal combinations of those minor Estates whose members found that without corporate union they were powerless to resist their stronger neighbours.  Before the end of the fourteenth century the Imperial Knights had formed a number of clubs or unions, each with its captain, and regular assemblies, to which King Sigismund had given a formal legitimation.  Of these the most important were the Knights of St George, an organisation of the chivalry of Swabia which took conspicuous part in creating the Swabian League. Even earlier were the associations of the towns.  Of the unions of the thirteenth century, the Hanse League alone remained, and this was now steadily on the decline.  But the southern and western cities formed local leagues with periodical deliberative assemblies.  In course of time other general Diets of town representatives were established Even after the cities had definitively won their right to a limited representation in the Diets these meetings continued, being held often, fo the saving of expense and trouble, side by side with the imperia assemblies.  It was well for the princes that the antagonism of knight and cities was as a rule too strong to enable them to work togethe The strength of the Swabian League was in no small measure due t the fact that towns and knights had both cooperated with the princes i its formation.

Neither Emperors, nor Diets, nor the voluntary associations of classes and districts sufficed to give peace and prosperity to the Empire. The unwieldy fabric had outgrown its ancient organisation and no new system had arisen capable of supplying its needs. Every aspect of fifteenth century history shows how overwhelming and immediate a need existed for thoroughgoing and organic reform. The area of imperial influence was steadily diminishing. Italy no longer saw in the Emperor any one but a foreigner, who could sometimes serve the turn of an ambitious upstart by selling him a lawful title of honour that raised him in the social scale of European rulers. Even the Hundred Years' War did not prevent the spread of French influence over the Middle Kingdom, and the Arelate was now no more an integral part of the Empire than was Italy. But parts of the old German kingdom were falling away. The outposts of Teutonic civilisation in the east were losing all connexion with the Power which had established them. Imperfect as the union established between the Scandinavian kingdoms at Calmar proved to be, it had dealt a mighty blow to the power of the Hansa, while the choice of the Danish king as Duke of Schleswig and Count of Holstein had practically extended the Scandinavian Power to the banks of the Elbe. In the north-east the Teutonic Knights had been forced by the Treaty of Thorn to surrender West Prussia to the Polish kings outright, and to hold as a fief of the Slavonic kingdom such part of Prussia as the Poles still allowed them to rule. Bohemia under George Podiebrad had become an almost purely Slavonic State, whose unfriendliness to German nationality and orthodox Catholicism might well threaten the renewal of those devastating Hussite invasions from which Germany had been saved by the Council of Basel. In Hungary German influence had disappeared with the extinction of the House of Luxemburg; the Magyar King Matthias Corvinus conquered the Duchy of Austria from the Habsburg Emperor, and died master of Vienna. The Swiss Confederacy was gradually drifting into hostility to the Empire; and the House of Burgundy was building up a great separatist State in the Low Dutch and Walloon provinces of the Netherlands. The utter defencelessness of Germany was seen by the devastations of the Armagnacs in Elsass. No prince of the Empire arrested their progress. The stubborn heroism of the Swiss League alone stayed the plague. And beyond all these dangers loomed the terrible spectre of Ottoman aggression.

Matters were equally unsatisfactory in the heart of Germany. Private war raged unchecked, and the feeble efforts made from time to time to secure the Public Peace (*Landfriede*) were made fruitless by the absence of any real executive authority. The robber knights waylaid traders, and great princes did not scruple to abet such lawlessness. The very preservation of the Public Peace had long ceased to be the concern of the Emperor and Empire as a whole, and local and voluntary unions (*Landfriedensvereine*) had sought with but scant result to uphold it within the limits of local and precarious conditions. The lack of imperial justice brought about such grave evils that the Estates sought to provide some sort of substitute for it by private agreements (*Austräge*) referring disputed matters to arbitration, and by that quaint etiquette which made it a breach of propriety for a prince to prefer the solemn judgment of his suzerain to such arbitration of his neighbours. The beginnings of an economic revolution threatened the ancient rude prosperity of the peasant, and embittered the relations of class and class within the towns.

The need for reform was patent. From what source however was the improvement to come? Little was to be expected from the Emperors. Yet even the careless Wenceslas of Bohemia had prepared the way for better things when he not only renewed once more the publication of a universal *Landfriede*, but also invested with imperial authority the local assemblies representative of the various Estates that were entrusted with its execution. Things were worse under Sigismund (1410–37), who could find no middle course between fantastic schemes for the regeneration of the universe and selfish plans for the aggrandisement of his own house. When his inheritance passed to his son-in-law Albert II of Austria (1438–9), the union of the rival houses of Habsburg and Luxemburg at least secured for the ruler a strong family position such as was the essential preliminary for the revival of the imperial power. Albert II's device for securing the general Public Peace of Germany rested upon an extension and development of the local executive authorities, and thus contained the germ of the future system of dividing the Empire into great territorial circumscriptions known as Circles (*Kreise*), destined ultimately to become one of the most lasting of imperial institutions. But Albert passed away before he was so much as able to visit the Empire, and in the long reign of his kinsman and successor Frederick III (1440–93) the imperial authority sunk down to its lowest point. A cold, phlegmatic, slow and unenterprising prince, Frederick of Austria busied himself with no great plans of reform or aggression, but seemed absorbed in gardening, in alchemy, and in astrology rather than in affairs of State. Under his nerveless rule the Luxemburg claims over Bohemia and Hungary passed utterly away. A large proportion of the Habsburg hereditary lands, including Tyrol and the scattered Swabian estates, were ruled by a rival branch of the ruling house represented by the Archduke Sigismund, while Austria itself fell into the hands of Matthias Corvinus. Yet in his cautious and slow-minded fashion Frederick was by no means lacking in ability and foresight. If he were indifferent to the Empire, he looked beyond the present distress of his house to a time when politic marriages and cunningly devised treaties of eventual succession would make Austria a real ruler of the world. Even for the Empire he did a little by his proclamations of a general *Landfriede*, while his settlement of the ecclesiastical relations of Germany after the failure of the Conciliar movement at Basel implied, with all its renunciation of high ideals, the establishment of a workable system that kept the peace until the outbreak of the Reformation. The *Vienna Concordat* of 1448 put an end to that tendency towards the nationalisation of the German Church which had been promoted so powerfully by the attitude of the prelates of the German nation at the Council of Constance, and which had been maintained so long when, under the guidance of Emperor and Electors, the Germans had upheld their neutrality between both the disorderly fathers at Basel and the grasping papal Curia at Rome. In the long run this nationalising tendency must have extended itself from ecclesiastical to political matters. Even in the decline of the Middle Ages the union within the Church might well have prepared the way to the union of the State. In accepting a *modus vivendi* which gave the Pope greater opportunities than now remained to the Emperor of exercising jurisdiction and levying taxation in Germany, Frederick proved himself a better friend to immediate peace than to the development of a national German State.

Three signal successes gilded the end of Frederick's long reign. The power of the House of Burgundy threatened to withdraw the richest and most industrial parts of the Empire from the central authority. But the sluggish Emperor and the inert Empire were at last roused to alarm, when Charles the Bold made the attack on their territory that began with the siege of Neuss. It was an omen of real possibilities for the future when a great imperial army gathered together to relieve the burghers of the Rhenish town. The "New League" of the Alsatian cities which was formed to ward off Charles' southern aggressions was a step in the same direction. And even the "Old League" of the Swiss Highlanders, which finally destroyed the Burgundian power, was not as yet avowedly anti-German in its policy. But, as in Church affairs, Frederick stepped in between the nation and its goal. At the moment of the threatened ruin of his ancient enemy's plans, he cleverly negotiated the marriage of his son Maximilian with Mary, the heiress of Charles the Bold. Soon after the last Duke of Burgundy had fallen at Nancy, Maximilian obtained with the hand of his daughter the many rich provinces of the Netherlands and the Free County of Burgundy (1477). It was not however for the sake of Germany or the Empire that Frederick sought a new sphere of influence for his son. The Burgundian inheritance remained as particularistic and as anti-German under the Habsburgs as it had ever been under Valois rule. But the future fortunes of Austria were established by an acquisition which more than compensated the dynasty for the loss of Hungary and Bohemia.

The other late successes of Frederick were likewise triumphs of Austria rather than victories of the Empire. The Duke of Bavaria-Munich had profited by the internal dissensions of the House of Habsburg and won the goodwill of the aged Archduke Sigismund of Tyrol. It was arranged that, on Sigismund's death without legitimate issue, Tyrol and the Swabian and Rhenish Habsburg lands should pass to the lord of Munich. Frederick bitterly resented this treason, but alone he could hardly have prevented its accomplishment. Yet the prospect of such an extraordinary extension of the Wittelsbach power frightened every petty potentate of Bavaria and Swabia. In 1487 the princes and bishops, abbots and counts, knights and cities of Upper Germany united to form the Swabian League, to maintain the authority of the Emperor and to prevent the union of Bavaria and Tyrol. Its action was irresistible. Tyrol passed quietly under Frederick's direct rule, and an armed Power was set up in the south which enormously strengthened the effective authority of the Emperor. The subsequent expulsion of the Hungarians from Vienna after the death of Matthias (1490), followed as it was by a renewal of the ancient contracts of eventual succession with Wladislav of Bohemia, who now succeeded Matthias in Hungary, restored the might of Habsburg in the east as effectively as the Burgundian marriage had extended it in the west. It was characteristic of the old Emperor that he grudged his son any real share in his newly won power. The third Habsburg triumph, the election of Maximilian as King of the Romans, was carried through the Diet of 1486 in despite of the opposition of the Emperor. In consequence Maximilian entered upon his public career, as the leader of the opposition, and as favouring the plans of imperial reform to which Frederick had long turned a deaf ear.

The purely dynastic ambitions of Frederick were reflected in the policy of the strongest princes of the Empire. We have seen how anti-German were the ideals of such great imperial vassals as Charles the Bold of Burgundy, and the Dukes of Bavaria. Equally anti-national was the policy of the elder or Palatine branch of the Wittelsbach House, then represented by the Elector Frederick the Victorious (1449–76). A magnificent and ambitious ruler, who gathered round his Court doctors of Roman law and early exponents of German humanism, Frederick pursued his selfish aims with something of the strength and ability as well as with something of the recklessness and unscrupulousness of the Italian despot. He made friends with the Cech Podiebrad and with the Frenchman Charles of Burgundy. He was not ashamed to lure on the Bohemian with the prospects of the Imperial Crown, and anticipated the Emperor Frederick's boldest stroke in his scheme to marry his nephew Philip to Mary of Burgundy. Not even Albert IV of Munich was more clearly the enemy of the Empire than his kinsman the "Wicked Fritz." The dominions of the Elector Palatine were indeed scattered and limited. Yet he was not only the strongest but the most successful of the imperial vassals of his time. The failure of his dearest projects showed that the day of princely autocracy had not yet come.

Two great families had won a prominent position in northern

Germany in the early years of the fifteenth century, and had somewhat pushed aside more ancient houses, such as the Guelfs of Brunswick, whose habit of subdividing their territories for a long time grievously weakened their influence. The financial distress of the Emperor Sigismund had forced him to pledge his early acquisition, Brandenburg, to the wealthy and practical Frederick of Hohenzollern, who as Burgrave of Nürnberg was already lord of Kulmbach and of a considerable territory in Upper Franconia. Despairing of redeeming his debt, Sigismund was in 1417 compelled to acquiesce in the permanent establishment of that house in the electorate of Brandenburg. Albert Achilles, Frederick's younger son, had shown in his long strife against Nürnberg and the Wittelsbachs rare skill as a warrior and shrewd ability as a statesman, even when his material resources were limited to his ancestral Kulmbach possessions. Called to the electoral dignity in Brandenburg after his brother Frederick II's death in 1471, Albert held a position among the northern princes only paralleled by that of Frederick of the Palatinate among the lords of the Rhine. As long as he lived he made his influence felt through his rare personal gifts, his courage, and his craft, and his fantastic combination of the ideals of the knight-errant with those of the statesman of the Renaissance. The welfare of Germany as a whole appealed to him almost as little as to Frederick the Victorious. All his pride was in the extension of the power of his house, and his most famous act was perhaps that *Dispositio Achillea* of 1473 which secured the future indivisibility of the whole Mark of Brandenburg and its transmission to the eldest male heir by right of primogeniture. Yet Albert died half conscious that his ambition had been ill-directed. All projects and all warlike preparations, declared the dying hero, were of no effect so long as Germany as a whole had no sound peace, no good law or law-courts, and no general currency. But with Albert's death in 1486 the power of Brandenburg, based purely on his individuality, ceased to excite any alarm among the princes of the north.

The House of Wettin, which had long held the margravate of Meissen, acquired with the district of Wittenberg and some other fragments of the ancient Saxon duchy, the electorate and duchy of Saxony (1423). The dignity and territories of the House now made it prominent among the princes of Germany, but the division of its lands, finally consummated in 1485, between Ernest and Albert, the grandsons of the first Wettin Elector, Frederick the Valiant, limited its power. The singular moderation and the conservative instincts of the Saxon line saved it from aspiring to rival Albert Achilles or Frederick the Victorious. The most illustrious representative of the Ernestine House, Frederick the Wise, who became Elector in 1486, was perhaps the only prince of the first rank who, while giving general support to the Emperor, ultimately identified himself with the plans of imperial reform which were now finding spokesmen among the princes of the second class. As a rule, however, the princes of strongest resources and most individual character were precisely those who were most quickly realising the ideals of localised and dynastic sovereignty, which, in the next century, became the common ambition of German rulers of every rank.

Though the power of the strongest of the German princes was thus limited, yet it was in regions under the influence of such great feudatories that the nearest approach to order prevailed. Habsburg rule in the south-east, Burgundian rule in the north-west, were establishing settled States, though rather at the expense of Germany as a whole than by way of contributing to its general peace. In a similar fashion Bavaria and the north-eastern Marchland between Elbe and Oder attained comparative prosperity under Wittelsbachs, Wettins, and Hohenzollerns. But in the other parts of Germany affairs were far worse. Even in the ancient duchy of Saxony the dissipation of the princely power had become extreme: but the Rhineland, Franconia, and Swabia were in an even more unhappy condition. The scattered Estates of the four Rhenish Electors, and powers such as Cleves and Hesse, were in no case strong enough to preserve general order in the Rhineland. The Elector of Mainz, the bishops of Würzburg and Bamberg, and the abbot of Fulda were, save the Kulmbach Hohenzollerns, the only rulers over even relatively considerable territories in Franconia. Würtemberg and Baden alone broke the monotony of infinite subdivision in Swabia. The characteristic powers in all these regions were rather the counts and the knights, mere local lords or squires with full or partial princely authority over their petty Estates. In such regions as these economic prosperity and ordered civil existence depended almost entirely on the number and importance of the free imperial cities.

Neither from the lesser immediate nobility nor from the city communities was any real contribution to be expected towards imperial reform. The counts and knights were too poor, too numerous, and too helpless, to be able to safeguard even their own interests. Their absurd jealousies of each other, their feuds with the princes and the towns, their chronic policy of highway robbery, made them the chief difficulty in the way of that general *Landfriede* which had been proclaimed so often but never realised. The towns were almost equally incompetent to take up a general national policy. They were indeed wealthy, numerous, and important: but despite their unions with each other they never advanced towards a really national line of action. Their intense local patriotism narrowed their interest to the region immediately around their walls, and their parochial separatism was almost as intense as that of their natural enemies the lesser nobles. While they had thus scanty will to act, their power to do so was perhaps much less than is often imagined. Machiavelli's glowing eulogies of their liberty and capacity of resistance has misled most moderns as to the true position of the German cities. In no way is their position comparable to that of the towns of Italy.

The great Italian cities largely owed their political influence to the fact that they ruled without a rival over districts as large as most German principalities. But in Germany the territory of many of the strongest among the free cities, such as Augsburg, was almost confined to the limits of their city walls. There were very few towns which dominated so wide a stretch of the countryside as Nürnberg, but how insignificant was the Nürnberg territory as compared with that of Florence! Even the population and wealth of the German towns have probably been exaggerated. Careful statistical investigation suggests that none of the cities of upper Germany had more than 20,000 inhabitants, and those which may have been of larger size, such as Cologne or Bremen or Lübeck, are of more importance in the commercial than in the political history of Germany. Though the financiers of Augsburg and Frankfort, and the merchants of Nürnberg or Basel or Cologne, were acquiring vast wealth, building palaces for their residence and through their luxurious ways raising the standard of civilisation and comfort for all ranks of Germans, they were not yet in a position so much as to aspire to political direction. Yet it was in the towns only that there could be found any non-noble class with even the faintest interest in politics. The condition of the country population was steadily declining. Feudalism still kept the peasant in its iron grip, and the rise in prices which opened the economic revolution that ushered in modern times was now beginning to destroy his material prosperity. In the upper Rhineland the condition of the agricultural population seems to have been very similar to that of the French peasantry before the outbreak of the Revolution. While their Swiss neighbours were free and prosperous, the peasant of Elsass or of the Black Forest was hardly able to make a living through the over-great subdivision of the little holdings. It was in this region that the repeated troubles of the *Bundschuh* and the revolts of "Poor Conrad" showed that deep-seated distress had led to the propagation of socialistic and revolutionary schemes among men desperate enough and bold enough to seek by armed force a remedy for their wrongs. Outside this region there was very little active revolutionary propaganda, or actual peasant revolt. However, in 1515, formidable disturbances broke out in Styria and the neighbouring districts.

The beginnings of a more national policy at last came from some of the princes of the second rank. Counts, knights, towns, and peasants were too poor, divided, and limited in their views, to aim at common action. But among the princes of secondary importance were men too far-seeing and politic to adopt a merely isolated attitude, while their consciousness of the limitation of their resources left them without so much as the wish of aspiring to follow from afar the example of Charles the Bold or Albert IV of Munich. To the abler German lords of this type the feudal ideal of absolute domination over their own fiefs was less satisfying in itself and moreover less probable of realisation. Their

territories were so small, and so scattered, their resources were so meagre
and so precarious, that feudal independence meant to them but a limited,
localised, and stunted career, and afforded them few guarantees of protection against the aggressions of their stronger neighbours.　In such
men there was no strong bias of self-interest to prevent their giving
rein to the wholesome sentiment of love of fatherland which still
survived in German breasts.　But personal pride, traditional feuds with
neighbouring houses, the habit of suspicion, and a general low level
of political sagacity and individual capacity made it difficult for this
class as a whole to initiate any comprehensive movement.　All through
the weary years of Frederick's reign projects of reform had been constantly shattered by the violence and jealousy of the greater princes
and by the indifference and want of unanimity of the petty ones.　A
leader of ability and insight had long been wanted to dominate their
sluggish natures and quicken their slow minds with worthier ideals.
Such a leader was at last found in Count Berthold of Henneberg, who
in 1484 became Elector of Mainz at the age of 42.　He soon made
himself famous for the vigour, justice, and sternness, with which he
ruled his dominions, for his eloquence in council, and for the large and
patriotic views which he held on all broad questions of national policy.
With him the movement for effective imperial reform really begins.

Berthold of Mainz had little of the churchman about him, and
his life was in nowise that of the saint; but he stands out among all
the princes of his time as the one statesman who strove with great
ability and consummate pertinacity to realise the ideal of a free, national
and united German State.　His courage, his resourcefulness, his pertinacity, and his enthusiasm carried for a time everything before them.
But soon grave practical difficulties wrecked his schemes and blasted
his hopes.　It is even possible to imagine that his policy was vicious in
principle.　It was a visionary and an impossible task to make petty
feudalists champions of order, law, and progress.　It involved moreover
an antagonism to the monarchy, which after all was the only possible
centre of any effective national sentiment in that age.　But whatever
may be thought of Berthold's practical insight, the whole history of
Frederick III and of his successors shows clearly that the German
monarchy, far from being as in England or France the true mainspring
of a united national life, persistently and by deliberate policy operated as
the strongest particularistic influence.　After all, Germany was a nation,
and Berthold strove by the only way open to him to make Germany
what England and France were already becoming.　It was not his fault
that the method forced upon him was from the beginning an almost
hopeless one.

To students of English medieval history Berthold's position seems
perfectly clear.　His ambition was to provide Germany with an efficient
central government; but also to secure that the exercise of this authority

should be in the hands of a committee of magnates, and not under the control of the German monarch. This design has been described as an attempt at federalism; but the word suggests a more conscious partition of power between central and local authority, and a more organised and representative control of the supreme power than ever Berthold or his associates dreamed to be necessary. A more complete analogy with Berthold's ideals is to be found in the policy of the great prelates and earls of England against the more neglectful or self-seeking kings of the thirteenth and fourteenth centuries. The Clares and the Montforts, the Bohuns, Bigods, and Lancasters, the Cantilupes, the Winchelseas, and the Arundels of medieval England had no trace of properly feudal ambition. They accepted the centralised institutions of the monarchy as ultimate facts, and aspired only to keep the centralised power under their own control. The heroes of the Provisions of Oxford, the Lords Ordainers, and the Lords Appellant, while upholding the representative legislative and taxative body by frequent sessions of Parliament, sought to put the executive power which properly belonged to the Crown into the hands of a commission roughly representative of the great houses. It was a nobler ambition and a finer career for a Clare or a Bohun or a Fitzalan to take his share in controlling the central power than to strive to put a ring fence round his estates and govern them as he had long administered his Welsh Marcher lordships. Even the lord of a great Palatinate might prefer to have his share in ruling England as a whole, rather than limit his ambition to playing the part of a petty king on his own estates. An Anthony Bek was a greater man as minister of Edward I than as the mere sovereign of the lands of St Cuthbert.

Berthold and his associates were in the same position as the English baronial leaders. As Archbishop of Mainz Berthold might either be a petty prince holding sway over scattered regions of the Rhineland and of Franconia, or a great political ecclesiastic like Arundel or Wykeham or George of Amboise. The wider career appealed alike to his patriotism, his interests, and his ambition. As feudal sovereigns the Rhenish Electors stood but in the second rank of German rulers. As prelates, as councillors of their peers, as directors of the Diets, and as effective and not merely nominal Chancellors of their suzerain's domains, they might well emulate the exploits of a Hanno or a Rainald of Dassel. Under the guidance of an aristocracy that was neither feudal nor particularist, and in which the ecclesiastical element was so strong that the dangers of hereditary influence were reduced to a minimum, a German State might have arisen as united and strong as the France of Louis XI or Francis I, while as free as Lancastrian England. Rude facts proved this ambition unworkable. Monarchy, and monarchy only, could be practically efficient as the formative element in national life. Since German monarchy refused to do its duty, German unity was destined not to be achieved. Nevertheless the attempt of Berthold is among the most interesting experiments in history, and the spectacle of the feudal potentates of Germany reversing the rôle of their French or Spanish compeers and striving to build up a united German nation, despite the separatist opposition of the German monarch, shows how strong were the forces that made for nationality during the transition from medieval to modern times. And it was no small indication of the practical wisdom of Berthold that he won over the whole Electoral College to his views. Less dignified princes were as a rule content to follow their lead. Only the Dukes of Bavaria held aloof, obstinately bent upon securing Bavarian interests alone. But perhaps the greatest triumph of the reformers was to be found in the temporary adhesion of the young King of the Romans to their plans.

Berthold of Mainz laid his first plan of reform before the Diet of Frankfort of 1485. He proposed a single national system of currency, a universal *Landfriede*, and a Supreme Court of Justice specially charged with the carrying out of the Public Peace. After the election of Maximilian in 1486, the demand of a special grant to carry on war against the Turks gave a new opportunity for insisting on the policy which the cold and unsympathetic Emperor had done his best to shelve. But the princes now rejected the proposed tax, on the ground that the cooperation of the cities was necessary towards granting an aid, whereas no cities had been summoned to this Diet. The result was before long the final establishment of the right of the cities to form an integral part of every assembly of the German national council. The Diet of 1489 saw every imperial town summoned to its deliberations. Within a generation the city representatives had become the Third Estate of the Empire side by side with Electors and princes.

Frederick gave way both on the question of the rights of the cities and on the programme of reform. He procured his Turkish grant in return for the promise to establish the *Landfriede* and an imperial court of justice. But he did nothing to give effect to his general assurances; and the Estates, closely brought together by their common aim, continued to press for the carrying out of Frederick's concessions. Their first real victory was at the Diet of Frankfort in 1489, when Maximilian, intent on getting help to make himself master of the Netherlands, and now also involved in his fantastic quest of the hand of Anne of Britanny, promised the Diet to do his best to aid it in obtaining an effective constitution of the imperial court of justice. A further step in advance was made at the important Diet of Nürnberg of 1491, where Maximilian declared that the *Landfriede*, already proclaimed for ten years, should be proclaimed for ever, and that for its execution a competent tribunal should be set up at his father's Court.

Even Maximilian's adhesion failed to secure the lasting triumph of the Estates. So long as the old Emperor lived, nothing practical was done; but on Frederick's death in 1493 the open-minded heir became the actual ruler of the Empire. Maximilian was young, restless, ambitious, and able. He had already embarked in those grandiose schemes of international intervention which remained the most serious political interest of the rest of his life. To these he now added his father's care for the development and consolidation of a great Austrian State. Having however nothing of Frederick's self-restraint, he ever gave free rein to the impulse of the moment, and was willing not only to sacrifice the Empire, to whose interests he was indifferent, but even his own Austrian lands to obtain some immediate military or diplomatic advantage in the prosecution of his more visionary ideals. Since he had become King of the Romans he had won his share of successes; but his incurable habit of keeping too many irons in the fire made it impossible for him to prevail in the long run. It was something that, despite the recent ignominy of his Bruges captivity, he was steadily increasing the influence which he wielded in the Netherlands on behalf of his young son, Philip. But he was still involved in great difficulties in that quarter, and the hostility of France, which had robbed him of his Breton wife, still excited powerful Netherlandish factions against him. A new trouble arose with Charles VIII's expedition to Italy in 1494. The triumphant progress of the French King gave the last blow to the imagined interests of the Empire in the Peninsula. Maximilian who had at first hoped to fish on his own account in the troubled waters, became intensely eager to afford all the help he could to the Italian League which was soon formed against the French. In 1495 he formally adhered to the confederacy. But effective assistance to the Italians could only be given by Maximilian as the price of real concessions to the party of imperial reform. Though the promises made by him in his father's lifetime sat but lightly on the reigning monarch, impulse, ambition, and immediate policy all combined to keep him in this case true to his word.

On March 26, 1495, Maximilian laid his first proposition before a Diet at Worms, to which despite the urgency of the crisis the princes came slowly and negligently. He appealed strongly to the Estates to check the progress of the French in Italy. An immediate grant for the relief of Milan, a more continued subsidy that would enable him to set up a standing army for ten or twelve years, could alone save the Empire from dishonour.

It was the opportunity of the reformers, and on April 29 Elector Berthold formulated the conditions upon which the Diet would give the King efficient financial and military support. The old ideas—Public Peace, imperial Court of Justice and the rest—were once more elaborated. But Berthold's chief anxiety was now for the appointment of a permanent imperial Council, representative directly of the Electors and the other Estates of the Empire, without whose approval no act of the King was to be regarded as valid. The only solid power Berthold wished to reserve to the King was that of supreme command in war; but no war was to be declared without the sanction of the Council. Matters of too great difficulty for the Council to determine were to be referred not to the King alone, but to the King and Electors in conjunction; and both here and on the projected Council the King counted but as a single vote. If Maximilian accepted this scheme, a Common Penny was to be levied throughout the Empire and an army established under the control of the Council.

To Maximilian Berthold's proposals must have seemed but a demand for his abdication. But he cleverly negotiated instead of openly refusing, and finally made a counter-proposal, which practically reduced the suggested Council to a mere royal Council, whose independent action was limited to the periods of the King's absence, and which otherwise sat at the King's Court and depended upon the King's pleasure. Long and wearisome negotiations followed, but a final agreement issued on August 7 showed that Berthold's plan had essentially been abandoned in favour of Maximilian's alternative propositions. The reformers preferred to give up their Executive Council altogether rather than allow it to be twisted into a shape which would have subordinated it to the royal prerogative. They went back on the old line of suggestions,—Public Peace, Common Penny, imperial Court of Justice, and the rest. Maximilian had already professed his acceptance of these schemes, so that on such lines agreement was not difficult. Even this mutilated plan of reform was sufficiently thorough and drastic. It makes the Diet of 1495 one of the turning-points in the constitutional history of the Empire.

The *Landfriede* was proclaimed without any limitation of time, and private war was forbidden to all Estates of the Empire under pain of the imperial ban. A special obligation to carry out this Public Peace was enjoined on those dwelling within twenty miles of the place of any breach of it. Were this not enough, the vindication of the peace rested with the Diet. Law was now to supersede violence, and an adequate Supreme Court was at last to be established. Frederick III had converted his traditional feudal Court (*Hofgericht*) into an institution styled the Cameral Tribunal (*Kammergericht*), without in any very material way modifying its constitution. A very different Imperial Cameral Tribunal (*Reichskammergericht*) was now set up. Its head, the *Kammerrichter*, was indeed the King's nominee, but the sixteen assessors, half doctors of law, half of knightly rank, who virtually overshadowed his authority, were to be directly nominated by the Estates. The law which the new Court was to administer was the Roman Law, whose doctrines soon began to filter downwards into the lower Courts, with the result that its principles and procedure speedily exercised a profound influence on every branch of German jurisprudence. The new Court was not to follow the King, but to sit at some fixed place (at first Frankfort), which could only be changed by vote of the Estates. Its officers were to be paid not by the Emperor but by the Empire. Thus independent of the monarch and responsible to the Estates alone, they were to exercise supreme jurisdiction over all persons and in all causes, and immediate jurisdiction over all tenants-in-chief. The Diet was henceforth to meet annually, and no weighty matters were to be decided, even by the King, without the counsel and consent of the Estates. This was practically the compensation which Maximilian offered to the reformers for rejecting their plan of a permanent executive Council. Frequent parliaments might be endured ; but a cabinet council, dependent upon the Estates, was, as Max saw, fatal to the continuance of his authority. A general tax called the Common Penny (*Gemeine Pfennig*) was to be levied throughout the Empire. This was a roughly assessed and rudely graduated property-tax, which had also some elements of an income-tax and a poll-tax. It was now established for four years, and was to be collected by the local princely or municipal authorities, but to be handed over to officials of the Empire and ultimately entrusted to seven imperial Treasurers, appointed by King and Estates and established at Frankfort. Max was authorised to take 150,000 florins from the Common Penny to defray the expenses of his Italian expedition.

In September the Estates separated. Both King and Diet were mutually satisfied, and it seemed as if brighter days were to dawn for the Empire. But dark clouds soon began to gather on every side. Maximilian was bitterly disappointed with his unfortunate Italian campaign of 1496. The German reformers soon found that it was easier to draw up schemes of reform than to carry out even the slightest improvement.

It was not that the Edict of Worms was wholly inoperative. The proclamation of the *Landfriede* was a real boon, though of course it did not change by magic a lawless into a law-abiding society. The *Kammergericht* provided justice in many cases where justice would have been impossible before. But the collection of the Common Penny proved the real difficulty. Even princes who were well disposed towards Berthold's policy showed no eagerness to levy a tax which other men were to spend. In many districts nothing whatever was done to collect the money. The knights as a body refused all taxation, inasmuch as their service was military and not fiscal. The abbots declined to recognise the jurisdiction of a court so exclusively secular as the *Kammergericht*. The princes not represented at Worms repudiated altogether laws passed by an assembly in which they had taken no part.

The weak point of the new constitution was its lack of any administrative authority. Maximilian was in Italy, and his representatives ostentatiously stood aloof from any effort to enforce the new laws. Events soon showed that Berthold was right in demanding the establishment of an executive Council. The yearly Diets were too cumbrous, expensive, and disorganised, to be of any value in discharging administrative functions. The first Diet under the new system, which was to meet in February, 1496, and complete the new constitution, never came into being, neither Max nor the princes thinking it worth their while to attend. Before long want of money and want of coercive power vitiated the whole scheme of reform. The imperial Chamber ceased to be efficient when its decisions could not be enforced, and when its members, seeing no prospect of their promised salaries from an empty treasury, compensated themselves by taking bribes from suitors or transferred themselves to more profitable employments.

The next few years were marked by a series of strenuous efforts on the part of Berthold to carry through in practice what had already been accepted in name. Max's need for money soon gave him his chance. The Diet was summoned to meet the Emperor at Chiavenna; and, when the princes refused to cross the Alps, its meeting-place was fixed for Lindau on the Lake of Constance. The remote and inconvenient little island city was, to the great disgust of the Estates, selected because of its nearness to Italy. The princes were ordered to bring with them their share of the Common Penny and their quota of troops to support the Emperor in Italy. But the Diet, which was opened in September, 1496, was very scantily attended. The princes who appeared came to Lindau without either money or men. In Maximilian's absence Berthold of Mainz stood forth more conspicuously than ever as the leader of the Estates. He passionately exhorted the Germans to follow the example of the Swiss, who through union and trust in one another had made themselves respected and feared by all the world. His special object was to insist upon the execution of the Edict of Worms in the Austrian hereditary dominions, where but slight regard had hitherto been paid to it. He also secured the passing of a resolution that the Common Penny should be paid to the imperial Treasurers by March, 1497, and that its disposition should be determined by a new Diet to be summoned for the spring. By promptly providing for the salaries of its members, Berthold also prevented the dissolution of the *Kammergericht*, which the Diet now transferred to Worms, because that city was regarded as a more accessible place than Frankfort for the doctors of the Rhenish Universities.

The Diet reassembled in the spring of 1497 at Worms; but again the Emperor did not appear. Despite the *Landfriede* the Elector of Trier waged a fierce war against Boppard, and with the help of his neighbour reduced the town to his obedience. The Swiss refused to recognise a decision of the *Kammergericht*. The Common Penny came in but slowly. But external political complications once more helped forward the schemes of the German reformers. Louis XII succeeded Charles VII as King of France. Before long he had occupied the Milanese and forced Maximilian's own son Philip, as ruler of the Netherlands, to make separate peace with him by which the young Archduke formally left Burgundy in French hands for Louis's life. Reduced to desperation by these troubles, Max was again forced to have recourse to the Estates. The Diet, which had been dragging on its lengthy and unimportant sittings at Worms, was transferred at the Emperor's request to his own city of Freiburg in the Breisgau. Max complained bitterly that the Estates were indifferent to his foreign policy and careless of the glories of the Empire. "I have been betrayed by the Lombards," he declared, "I have been abandoned by the Germans. But I will not again suffer myself to be bound hand and foot as at Worms. I will carry on the war myself, and you can say to me what you will. I would sooner dispense myself from my oath at Frankfort; for I am bound to the House of Austria as well as to the Empire." With King and Estates thus utterly at variance, no great results were to be expected. Maximilian desired to carry out his spirited foreign policy: the Estates wished to secure the peace and prosperity of Germany. It was to little purpose that Berthold and many of the cities brought in their contributions towards the Common Penny. Max betook himself to the Netherlands to wage war against Charles, Count of Egmont, the self-styled Duke of Gelderland, who upheld the French cause on the Lower Rhine. With war everywhere it was useless to go on with the farce of assembling the Estates. In 1499 an attempt to hold a Diet at Worms broke down, and, though Max went back from Gelderland to Cologne to meet the Estates, the rump of a Diet assembled at Worms refused to transfer its sittings to Cologne. Berthold lay dangerously sick. The helplessness and disorder of the Empire were as great as ever.

A trouble that had long been imminent now came to a head. The Swiss Confederacy, though still nominally a part of the Empire, had long been drifting into independence. It now refused to be bound by the new policy of strengthening the links that connected the various parts of the Empire with each other. The Swiss who had recently given great offence by declining to join the Swabian League, now forbade the collection of the Common Penny and rejected the jurisdiction of the *Kammergericht.* They renewed their connexion with France at the very moment when France went to war with the Empire, and threatened to absorb the confederated towns of Elsass, as in 1481 they had absorbed Freiburg and Solothurn. The eagerness of Max's Tyrolese government now forced him into open war with the Swiss. But the princely champions of reform would not lift a hand against the daring mountaineers who defied the authority of the Empire. Only the Swabian League gave Max any real help. Before long his armies were beaten and there was no money to raise fresh ones. In despair Max concluded the Peace of Basel (1499) in which he gave the Swiss their own terms. They were declared freed from the Common Penny and from the imperial Chamber and all other specific imperial jurisdiction. A vague and undefined relationship between the Swiss and the Empire was still allowed to remain until the Peace of 1648. And in the following years

matters were made worse by the constant tendency of the south German
States to fall away from the Empire and attach themselves to the
Confederacy, of which in 1501 Basel and Schaffhausen, and Appenzell
in 1513, were formally admitted as full members. It was the mere
accident of some unsettled local disputes as to criminal jurisdiction over
the Thurgau that prevented Constance from following in their steps.
Such of the Estates of Upper Swabia as had hitherto preserved their
freedom now hastened to become "confederate" or "protected" or
"allied" to the strenuous Confederacy, which now dominated the whole
region between the Upper Rhine and the Alps, and had also established
friendly relations with the Rhaetian Leagues that were now taking shape.

It cost Maximilian little to renounce the rights of the Empire over the
Swiss. He looked upon the Confederates as most useful to him in helping his designs on Italy, and now trusted with their assistance to restore
his father-in-law to Milan. But in 1500 came the second conquest of
Milan by the French, and Ludovico's lifelong captivity in a French
dungeon. In the same year the agreement between Louis and Ferdinand
of Spain for the partition of Naples still further isolated Maximilian.
He was as unsuccessful in his schemes of foreign conquest as was Berthold
in his plans of internal reformation. Within a few years he had fought
against Florentines and French, against Gelderland and Switzerland, and
on each occasion had lost the day. And each failure of Maximilian threw
him more and more completely on the mercy of the German reformers.

In April, 1500, the Diet assembled at Augsburg. Maximilian himself
now offered important concessions. Everybody hated the Common Penny,
and neither the princes nor the cities were so rich or public-spirited as to
submit permanently to the waste of money and time, and to the withdrawal
from their own proper local work, involved in the assembling of annual
Diets. As an alternative to the first of these hitherto necessary evils
the King revived a proposal made at Frankfort in 1486, by which the
Estates were to set on foot a permanent army of 34,000 men, and to
provide means for its maintenance. In place of the annual Diets a
permanent committee might be established. On this basis the Estates
began to negotiate with the King, and by July 2 an agreement was
arrived at. In this, instead of the standing army suggested by Maximilian,
an elaborate scheme was devised for setting on foot an army for six
years. Every four hundred property-holders or householders were to
combine to equip and pay a foot-soldier to fight the King's battles.
For the assessment of this burden the parochial organisation was to be
employed, and the sums levied were to be roughly proportionate to the
means of the contributor. The clergy, the religious Orders, and the citizens of imperial towns were to pay one florin for every 40 florins of income.
The Jews were taxed at a florin a head. Counts and barons of the
Empire were to equip a horseman for each 4000 florins of income, while
knights were to do what they could. The princes of the Empire were

to provide at least 500 cavalry from their private resources. It was hoped that these arrangements would give the King an army of 30,000 men; and the leaders of the Diet probably thought it a clever stroke of policy that, while they were themselves let off very lightly, the greater part of the burden fell upon the smaller property-owners.

The obligation to summon a yearly Diet was not formally repealed, but, while legislation and supreme control of finance still remained the special functions of the assembled Estates, the executive business with which they were so incompetent to deal devolved upon a Council of Regency (*Reichsregiment*). This was to consist of twenty-one members. At its head was the King or a deputy appointed by the King. The further representation of the King's interests was provided through an Austrian and a Netherlandish member of the Council. But the other eighteen Councillors were entirely outside the King's control. Each of the six Electors had an individual voice in the Council. One of them was always to be present in person, being replaced by a colleague after three months. Each of the five absent Electors personally nominated a member of the Regency. The representation of the other Estates was divided into two categories. Certain eminent imperial vassals were singled out and granted a personal right of occasional appearance. Thus twelve princes, six spiritual and six lay, were specified as having the privilege of sitting in the Council, by two at a time. Similarly there were one representative of the prelates (abbots and other lesser dignitaries), one of the Counts and two of the Free and Imperial Towns, arranged in groups for the purpose. Besides the six Councillors chosen from this first category, there were six others representing the Estates of six great circumscriptions or Circles into which Germany, excluding the electoral lands, was now for this purpose divided. No names were given to these districts, but roughly they corresponded to the later Circles of Franconia, Bavaria, Swabia, the Upper Rhine, Lower Saxony and Westphalia. The whole constitution was so arranged that the preponderance of power was altogether with the princes, and especially with the Electors. The inferior Estates were as scantily represented as was the King himself.

The establishment of the Council of Regency marks the highest moment of Berthold's triumph. Germany had obtained her centralised institutions, her *Kammergericht*, her annual Diets, her national army, and her imperial taxation. She now also had an executive government as directly dependent upon the Estates as a modern English Cabinet or as the royal Councils, nominated in the English Parliament, in the days before the Wars of the Roses had destroyed Lancastrian constitutionalism. The events of the last five years had demonstrated that, without such executive authority, the reforms were unworkable. But did the circumstances and temper of the times allow such a system as this any reasonable prospects of success? Lancastrian constitutionalism had failed miserably and had but paved the way to Tudor monarchy. What chance was there of Berthold's system prevailing under far worse conditions in Germany?

Maximilian was not likely to acquiesce in being deprived of all that made monarchy a reality. The knights with their passion for lawless freedom, the cities with their narrow outlook and strong local prejudices, might be likewise expected to have no good will towards a system in which the former had no part and the latter but a very small one. But a still greater difficulty lay in the princes, whose sectional ambitions and want of settled national policy wholly unfitted them for carrying out so delicate and difficult a task. Could a group of turbulent nobles, trained in long traditions of private warfare and personal self-seeking, provide Germany with that sound government which lands with better political prospects could only obtain from the strong hand of an individual monarch? The answer to these questions was not long in coming. In a few years the Council of Regency broke down utterly, bearing with it in its fall the strongest pillars of the new German constitution.

A final struggle between Maximilian and the Estates arose as to the meeting-place of the Council of Regency. But Max had gone too far on the way of concession to be able to succeed in enforcing his wish that the Council should follow the Court. The Estates resolved that it should meet in the first instance at Nürnberg. Full of anger and scorn the King left Augsburg, seeking the consolations of the chase in Tyrol. Berthold betook himself to Nürnberg, in order to take his turn as resident Elector on the Council of Regency. The choice of Frederick, Elector of Saxony, as the imperial deputy, made Berthold's task as easy as was possible. But Frederick was very commonly absent from the Council. He was too great a prince to be able to devote his whole time to the reform of the Empire. Upon Berthold alone fell the burden of the new system. Yet he was broken in health and spirits, and even at best only one prince among many. It was due to him that the Council had so much as a start. No political genius could have given it a long life.

Difficulties arose almost from the beginning. Maximilian grew indignant when he discovered that there was no probability of an army being levied to fight the French, and still more wrathful when the Council entered into negotiations on its own account with Louis XII, with whom it concluded a truce without any reference whatever to Italy. This seemed, and perhaps was, treason. But Maximilian was at the same time treating with Louis, and, though for a long time he refused to ratify the compact between the French King and the Estates, he made a truce on his own behalf and finally accepted also that arranged by the Council. But a new difference of opinion at once arose as to the proclamation of the papal Jubilee of 1500 in Germany. King and Council opened separate negotiations with Cardinal Perraudi the papal Legate, and Max much resented the agreement made between Legate and Council, that the profits derived from the Jubilee in Germany should be devoted exclusively to the Turkish War.  He avenged himself by allowing the Pope to proclaim the Jubilee without reservation and by quarrelling with the Legate.  Meanwhile the Council was failing in the impossible task of governing Germany.  The crisis came to a head in 1501 at the Diet of Nürnberg, from which Maximilian was absent.  The King now broke openly with the Council, and did his best to make its position impossible.  Not only did he refuse to attend its sittings, but he neglected to appoint a deputy to preside in his absence.  He would not even nominate the Austrian representative.  He denounced Berthold as a traitor and schemer, and strove to raise an army, after the ancient fashion, by calling upon the individual princes to supply their contingents.

In the struggle that ensued both King and reformers gave up any attempt to observe the new system.  Berthold fell back upon the venerable expedient of a Union of Electors (*Kurfürstenverein*).  He has been reproached with lack of policy in thus abandoning the infant constitution, but his action was probably the result of inevitable necessity.  As he had to fight the King, he naturally chose the most practical weapon that lay to hand.

After the fashion of the Luxemburg period, an Electoral Diet was now held at Frankfort.  The Elector Palatine Philip (1476–1508), nephew and successor of Frederick the Victorious, who had hitherto been at feud with the Elector of Mainz, now made terms with him and attended the meeting.  Alarmed at the unity of the Electors, Maximilian ordered them to adjourn to Speyer, where he would meet them in person.  But the Electors quitted Frankfort before the King's messenger could arrive.  Before separating, however, they renewed the ancient Union of the Electors, and pledged each other to act as one man in upholding the reforms of 1495 and 1500.  It was afterwards believed that the Electors talked of deposing Maximilian, or at least of obtaining still more drastic reforms.  This however does not seem to have been the case.  It was futile to seek further changes, when the innovations already approved of could not be carried out in practice.

The Electors resolved that, if the King did not summon a Diet, they would themselves meet in November at Gelnhausen, and invite the other Estates to join them.  Before this parliamentary convention of the German Estates, they resolved to lay a programme of policy that far surpassed in comprehensiveness any previous plan of reformation.  This scheme provided not merely for the maintenance of the *Landfriede*, the restoration of the *Kammergericht*, and the strengthening of the *Reichsregiment*.  It distinguished itself from its predecessors by going beyond the interests of the princes and taking some thought of the welfare of the ordinary poor man, whom it sought to protect from the personal services, taxes, ecclesiastical Courts and other grievances weighing heavily upon him. But a body which could not carry through a simple political programme showed temerity in dealing with schemes of social reformation. Meanwhile the relations between King and princes became more and more embittered. "The King," said a Venetian ambassador, "speaks ill of the princes, and the princes speak ill of the King."

Maximilian had grown wiser with experience. He at last saw that to maintain a stiff attitude of resistance and to dwell upon his prerogative only served to unite his vassals against him. About this time he gradually drifted into a more temporising, but also a more dangerous, attitude. He was now content to bide his time and wait on events. In the long run the single will of the King was more likely to prevail than the divided wills of a host of magnates. Maximilian now endeavoured to break up the Electoral Union, and to make a party for himself among the younger princes. He employed all his rare personal talents, all the charm and fascination which belonged to him, in order to attract to himself on personal grounds the devotion of the rising generation. He cleverly sowed dissension between the mass of the immediate nobility and the little knot of reformers, who practically controlled the whole of the opposition. Why should a small ring of elderly princes of the second rank deprive the younger generation of all power at home or prospect of distinction abroad? He appealed to the particularistic interests, which were endangered, like his own, by the unionist policy of the Electors. He invoked the chivalrous and adventurous spirit which might well find a more glorious career in fighting Turks and French under the brilliant ruler than in wrangling about constitutional reform at home. He exerted all his interest at episcopal and abbatial elections, and not seldom succeeded in carrying his candidate. He sought to win over Alexander VI to his side, and with that object did not hesitate to negotiate directly with the papal Curia over the head of the Legate. A few years of hard work in these directions wrought a surprising difference in Maximilian's position. With increasing prosperity he grew more cheerful and good-tempered. Only against Berthold of Mainz did he show any great bitterness, and he now sought to obtain the Archbishop's resignation on the ground of ill-health in favour of one of his young followers, the Margrave Casimir of Brandenburg-Kulmbach. The very Electors began to despair of their policy of opposition. They resolved that it was but a waste of time and money to hold Diets in the absence of the King. Two years before it had been the highest goal of their ambition to summon the Estates without waiting for the formality of the royal writ.

Concurrently with these new developments, Maximilian forged other weapons against the reforming oligarchy. So long as he possessed but a purely personal authority, he was powerless against the new system. He therefore resolved to start counter-organisations, emanating from the royal prerogative, which might be taken into account against those established by the Estates at the expense of his supreme authority. Besides this general motive, he found a particular object for such action in the condition of his Austrian territories, which were as disunited and disorderly as feudal States were ever wont to be. He had already begun to combine the ordered administration of his hereditary lands with a rival imperial system that sprang from the royal initiative. The first great step was Maximilian's *Hofrathsordnung* of 1497. Since the ancient *Hofrath* of the Middle Ages had been merged in the *Kammergericht* of Frederick III, which had in its turn been superseded by the *Reichskammergericht* of the reformers, there was no royal Court adequate to support and represent the Crown either in the Empire or the hereditary lands of the House of Austria. Maximilian now set up a permanent Aulic Council (*Hofrath*), competent to deal with "all and every business that can flow in from the Empire, Christendom at large, or the King's hereditary principalities." This body was to follow the royal Court, was to be appointed by the King, and was to decide on all matters by a majority. It was not only a High Court of Justice, exercising concurrent jurisdiction with the *Reichskammergericht*. It was also a supreme administrative body. It was to stand to the Empire and the Estates as the *Concilium Ordinarium* of the late medieval English Kings stood to England and the English Parliament. Next year, Maximilian further improved his executive government. The *Hofkammerordnung* of 1498 set up a separate financial administration, dependent on the Emperor, and subordinated also to the Aulic Council, which heard appeals from its decisions. This body, which was to sit at Innsbruck, was to centralise the financial machinery of Empire and hereditary dominions alike under four Treasurers, one for the Empire, one for Burgundy, and two for Austria. About the same date the *Hofkanzleiordnung* completed these monarchical reforms by setting up a Chancery or Office of State on modern lines and with powers such as could never be given to hereditary Chancellors like the Rhenish Archbishops. In these measures the King offered to his subjects rival guarantees for order, peace, and prosperity to those procured for them by the Diet. After the Gelnhausen meeting he proceeded still further on the same course. He set up a new *Kammergericht*, consisting of judges appointed by himself, and this body actually had a short and troubled life at Ratisbon. He also talked of a new *Reichsregiment*, which was to be a Privy Council dependent on King alone; but this scheme never came into being.

Had Max been a great statesman, aiming at one thing at a time, this system might have been the beginning of a centralised bureaucracy that would have soon pervaded the whole Empire with monarchical ideas of administration. But he was neither persevering, nor whole-hearted, nor far-seeing enough to pursue deliberately the policy of making himself a despot; and his reforms soon showed themselves to be but the

temporary expedients of an ingenious but superficial and temporising
waiter on events.  In a few years fresh royal ordinances upset the system
as easily as it had been called into being; and in practice Maximilian's
reforms were not much better carried out than those of the Diet.
The Aulic Council ceased to exist, and its revival was only forced upon
Maximilian by the Estates of his own dominions, which saw in a standing
council of this sort a means of checking arbitrary prerogative.  Max
died before the renewed Aulic Council came into working order.  Later,
its permanent establishment was secured, and as time went on it proved
a rather formidable rival to the imperial Chamber.  In after ages it
was found more advantageous to take suits before the Emperor's Court
than before the Court of the Empire, because justice was cheaper,
quicker, and more certain in the Aulic Council than in the imperial
Chamber.

Maximilian soon ceased to take much interest in reforming the Empire
by royal prerogative.  But he continued to busy himself with schemes
for strengthening and unifying the administration of his hereditary
dominions.  He had long ago chased away the Hungarian conquerors of
Vienna, and put an end to the division of the Austrian lands between
two rival branches of the Habsburg House.  The Aulic Council and the
Innsbruck Chamber had a less direct bearing on the Empire than on the
hereditary dominions, for the whole of which the Chamber might well have
been the source of a single financial system.  But Maximilian soon set
up, in place of the single *Hofkammer*, two Chambers sitting at Vienna
for Lower Austria (*i.e.* Austria, Carinthia, Carniola, Styria and Istria),
and at Innsbruck for Upper Austria (Tyrol, Vorarlberg and East
Swabia), with perhaps a third organisation for the scattered *Vorlande*
in the Black Forest and Elsass.  In 1501 followed an elaborate plan of
administrative reform for Lower Austria, which established six executive,
judicial, and financial bodies at Linz, Vienna, and Wiener Neustadt.
These are the first signs of a reaction from Maximilian's centralising
policy which became stronger towards the end of his reign.  It is hard
to determine how far this proceeded from his instability, and how far
from the pressure of the local Estates of the Austrian dominions to
which his financial embarrassments ever made him peculiarly liable.  In
the end, however, it was the Estates that took the lead, in Austria as in
the Empire.  The meeting at Innsbruck in 1518, famous in Austrian history, of deputations from the various *Landtage* of the hereditary lands,
is justly regarded as the first establishment of any organic unity within
the Austrian dominions.  Maximilian shared with the Estates the merit
of convoking the meeting; and it was this body that sanctioned the
scheme for the erection of a *Reichshofrath*, to which reference has
already been made.  Of the eighteen members of this Aulic Council of
the Empire, five were to be presented by the Empire, nine by the
various Austrian lands, and the remainder were to consist of great

officials. Side by side with it a Chancery for the Empire and hereditary lands was erected, whose Chancellor was to act with the help of three secretaries, one for the Empire, one for Lower, and one for Upper Austria. Finance was once more to be reorganised, and the Innsbruck Chamber restored to something of its old position. Tribunals were instituted to hear complaints against officials; the prince's domain was not to be alienated, and three local administrations were set up, at Bruck on the Mur for Lower Austria, at Innsbruck for Upper Austria, and at Ensisheim for the *Vorlande*. Maximilian's death within a few months prevented these schemes from being carried out, and the history of the Emperor's Austrian, as of his German policy, ends with the characteristic note of failure. Nevertheless he had truly won for himself the position of founder of the unity of the Austrian dominions. If he accomplished little for Germany, he had done much for Austria.

The soundness of the newer imperial policy of Maximilian was soon to be tested. On the death of George the Rich, Duke of Bavaria-Landshut (1504), a contest arose as to the succession. By family settlements and by the law of the Empire, the next heirs to the deceased Duke were his kinsmen, Albert and Wolfgang, Dukes of Bavaria-Munich. But differences had arisen between the Munich and Landshut branches of the ducal House of Wittelsbach, and George, in the declining years of his life, had formed a scheme for the succession of his nephew and son-in-law, the Count Palatine Rupert, second son of the Elector Palatine Philip, by his wife, George's sister, and the husband of Elizabeth, the Duke of Landshut's only child. On his death he left his wealth and dominions to Rupert and Elizabeth, who at once entered into possession of their inheritance.

The Dukes of Munich immediately appealed to Max, and the newly-constituted royal *Kammergericht* speedily issued a decision in their favour. All the dominions of Duke George were to go to the Dukes of Munich, except those in which the King had an interest. Maximilian at once put Rupert and his wife under the ban of the Empire, and prepared to vindicate by arms the decision of his lawyers. For the first time since his accession the young princes of Germany flocked to his standard. It was in vain that the Elector Palatine appealed to his French and Swiss allies to help his son. A few French nobles fought on his side; but Louis XII preferred to profit by Maximilian's need to obtain recognition as Duke of Milan. The struggle was too one-sided to be of long duration, and the death of Rupert and his wife made its termination the more easy. The mass of the Landshut dominions was now secured to the Dukes of Munich, henceforth the sole lords of the Bavarian duchy. But Maximilian himself appropriated considerable districts for himself, while he compensated the Elector Palatine by the region of Sulzbach and Neuburg—the so-called *Junge Pfalz*. With Maximilian's triumph in the Landshut Succession War died the last hopes of the constitutional reformers of the Empire. Their best chance had ever been the necessities of their King's enterprising foreign policy; but these years also saw the realisation of the brightest dreams of the House of Austria. The Archduke Philip was wedded to Joanna, the heiress of Ferdinand and Isabella of Spain. On Isabella's death in 1504 Philip became King of Castile. To this great dignity was added the prospect of the inheritance of the aged Ferdinand in Aragon and in Naples. With such an extension of his European influence it seemed unlikely that Maximilian would again come before his Estates the helpless suitor that he had been of old.

The history of the Diet of Cologne of 1505 brings out clearly the different position now attained by King and Estates respectively. To this Diet Maximilian came triumphant from his hard-earned victory in Gelderland, attended by a great crowd of enthusiastic nobles and soldiers. He had no longer to face his ancient enemies. Berthold of Mainz had died in the midst of the Landshut troubles, worn out with disease and anxiety, and already conscious of the complete failure of his plans. His former ally, John of Baden, Elector of Trier, had died before him in 1503. Their successors, Jacob of Liebenstein at Mainz and Jacob of Baden, at Trier, were mere creatures of the King, and the latter Maximilian's near kinsman. Hermann of Hesse, the Elector of Cologne, had never been of much personal importance, and was now quite content to float in the royalist tide. The Count Palatine Philip, the chief of the secular opposition since his reconciliation with Berthold, had suffered so severely during the Landshut Succession War that he dared no longer raise his voice against the King. The young Elector Joachim of Brandenburg, who had succeeded to his dignity in 1499, was eager to put his sword at the service of Maximilian. Of the old heroes of the constitutional struggle only Frederick the Wise of Saxony remained, and without Berthold's stimulus Frederick was too passive, too discreet, and too wanting in strenuousness to take the lead. Yet his pleading for the disgraced Elector Palatine, unsuccessful as it was, was the only sign of opposition raised from among the Electors in this Diet. Even more devoted to the Crown were the princes who had won their spurs in the Bavarian War, and the prelates who owed their election to Court influence. Well might the Venetian ambassador report to his Republic, that his imperial Majesty had become a true Emperor over his Empire.

Encouraged by the prospect of the unwonted support of his Estates, Maximilian took a real initiative in the question of imperial reform. In a speech in which he could not conceal his bitter hatred of the dead Elector of Mainz, he urged the establishment of a new Council of Regency, dependent upon the Crown, resident at the imperial Court, and limited to giving the King advice and acting under his direction. But the Diet had had enough of new-fangled reforms. "Let his Majesty," said the Estates, "rule in the future as he has ruled in the past." They also rejected the scheme when Maximilian put it before them in a modified form, which allowed the Electors and princes a large voice in the appointment of the Council. Equally averse was the Diet to the novel method of taxation. Maximilian soon withdrew a proposal for a new Common Penny, and cheerfully contented himself with the proffer of an army of 4000 men, which he proposed to employ to protect his ally Ladislas of Hungary from the revolted Hungarian nobles under John Zapolya. For the expenses of this and for other supplies, money was to be raised by the *matricula*, that is by calling upon the various Estates of the Empire to pay lump sums according to their ability. The *matricula* ignored the union of the Empire and the obligation of the individual subject, which had been emphasised by the Common Penny. But King and subjects had alike ceased to look upon the Empire as anything but a congeries of separate States.

Save in the matters of the Council of Regency and the Common Penny, the Augsburg reforms were once more confirmed by King and Estates. The *Landfriede* of 1495 was solemnly renewed, and orders were given to revive the *Kammergericht*, which had ceased to meet during the recent troubles. For two years, however, the restoration remained on paper, until at last the Diet of Constance of 1507, which in more than one way completed the work of the Diet of Cologne, approved of an elaborate scheme for its reconstitution. By this ordinance the imperial Chamber took its permanent shape. At its head was still to be a *Kammerrichter* chosen by the King, and sixteen assessors representative of the Estates. But while at Worms in 1495 the assessors had been appointed by the King with the counsel and consent of the Estates, the method by which their election was now arrived at was particularist rather than national. The assessors were henceforth to be nominated by the chief territorial powers. Two were named by Maximilian as Duke of Austria and Lord of the Netherlands. The six Electors similarly had each a nomination to a seat, and the remaining eight assessors were to be appointed by the rest of the Estates, grouped for the purpose into six large Circles. The place for the session of the Court was still to be fixed by the Estates. After a year at Regensburg it was to be established at Worms. To please Maximilian, who preferred an ecclesiastic, the Bishop of Passau was the first *Kammerrichter*. His successor, however, was to be a count or a secular prince. The judge was to be paid by the King, and the assessors by the authorities that presented them to their offices. Thus the *Kammergericht* became a permanent institution, which, after various wanderings and a long stay at Speyer, finally settled down at Wetzlar, where it remained until the final dissolution of the Empire. But no care was taken to secure that the Court should administer a reasonable law or adopt a rapid or an economical procedure. The delays of the *Kammergericht* soon became a bye-word, and the ineffectiveness of its methods very materially attenuated the permanent gain accruing from the establishment of an imperial High Court. Nor were any efficient means taken at Cologne or Constance to secure the execution of the sentences of the imperial Chamber. Max himself was not chiefly to blame for this. He renewed at Constance a wise proposal that had fallen flat at Cologne. This was a plan for the nomination by the King of four marshals to carry out the law in the four districts of the Upper Rhine, Lower Rhine, Elbe and Danube respectively. Each marshal was to be assisted by twenty-five knightly subordinates and two councillors. An under-marshal, directly dependent on the Chamber, was to execute criminal sentences. But the princes feared lest this strong executive should intrench upon their territorial rights. Now that the Emperor and not the Estates controlled the Empire, a prince had every inducement to give full scope to his particularistic sympathies. Very weak, however, was the system of execution that found favour at Constance. It was thought enough that the *Kammerrichter* should be authorised to pronounce the ban of the Empire against all who withstood his authority. If the culprit did not yield within six months, the Church was to put him under excommunication. If this did not suffice, then Diet or Emperor was to act. In other words, there was no practical way of carrying out the sentence of the Chamber against over-powerful offenders.

The Diet of Constance placed on a permanent basis the closely allied questions of imperial taxation and imperial levies of troops. Brilliant though the prospects of the House of Austria now seemed, Maximilian's personal necessities only increased with the widening of his hopes. It cost him much trouble to maintain Wladislav of Hungary on his throne, though in the end he succeeded ; and the betrothal of Anne, Wladislav's daughter and heiress, to one of Maximilian's grandsons, an infant like herself, further guaranteed the eventual succession of the Habsburgs in Hungary and Bohemia (March, 1506). The death in the same year (September) of his son Philip of Castile, had involved him in fresh responsibilities. Philip's successor, the future Charles V, was only six years old, and it taxed all Maximilian's skill to guard the interests of his grandson. He now felt it urgently necessary that he should cross the Alps to Italy, and should receive the imperial Crown from the Pope. With this object he besought the Estates at Constance for liberal help. He gave his word that, if an army of thirty thousand men were voted to him, all conquests he might make in Italy should remain for ever with the Empire ; that they should not be granted out as fiefs without the permission of the Electors ; and that an imperial Chamber should be established in Italy to secure the payment by the Italians of their due share in the burdens of the Empire. But these glowing promises only induced the Diet to make a grudging grant of twelve thousand men with provision for their equipment. The matricular system, already adopted at Cologne, was again employed to raise the men and the money. Henceforward, so long as imperial grants continued, this method alone was employed. But grave difficulties arose as to the quotas to be contributed by the various States. One of the chief among these related to princes, who were tenants-in-chief for some part of their territories, while they held the rest mediately of some other vassal of the Empire. None of these problems was settled during Maximilian's life.

The chief interest of German history shifts for the next few years more and more to questions of foreign policy. Maximilian's War with Venice, his share in the League of Cambray and the renewal of hostilities with France, which followed the dissolution of that combination and the establishment of the Holy League, absorbed his energies and exhausted his resources. Very little success attended his restless and shifting policy. He did not even obtain the imperial Crown for which he sought. Unable to wait patiently until the road to Rome was open to him, Max took on February 4, 1508, a step of some constitutional importance. He issued a proclamation from Trent, where he then was, declaring that henceforward he would use the title of Roman Emperor Elect, until such time as he received the Crown in Rome. Julius II, anxious to win his support, formally authorised the adoption of this designation. For the next few years the Venetian War blocked his access to Rome, and later he made no effort to go there. He was now universally addressed as Emperor; and the time had passed when the form of papal coronation could be expected to work miracles. Maximilian's assumption of the imperial title without coronation served as a precedent to all his successors. Henceforward the Elect of the seven Electors was at once styled Roman Emperor in common phrase, Roman Emperor Elect in formal documents. During the three centuries through which the Empire was still to endure, Maximilian's grandson and successor was the only Emperor who took the trouble to receive his Crown from the Pope. As time went on, the very meaning of the phrase "Emperor Elect" became obscure, and was occasionally thought to point to the elective nature of the dignity rather than to the incomplete status of its uncrowned holder.

During these years of trouble in Italy, Maximilian was constantly demanding men and money from the German Estates and was involved in perpetual bickering with the numerous Diets which received his propositions coldly. The royal influence, which had become so great after 1504, broke down as hopelessly as had the authority of the Estates. The conditions of the earlier part of the reign were renewed when the Emperor's financial necessities once more led him to make serious proposals of constitutional reform. The most important of them was the scheme which in March, 1510, Maximilian laid before a well-attended Diet at Augsburg. As usual the Emperor wished for a permanent imperial army, and long experience had convinced him that this could only be obtained by great concessions on his part. He now suggested that a force of 40,000 foot and 10,000 horse should be raised by the Estates of the Empire, including in them the Austrian hereditary dominions. In return for this he promised once more to establish an efficient imperial executive. The Empire was to be divided into four Quarters, over each of which a Captain (*Hauptmann*) was to be appointed as responsible chief of the administration. From these Quarters eight princes, four spiritual and four temporal, were to be chosen, who, under the presidency of an imperial Lieutenant, were to act as a central authority. This body was to sit during the Emperor's absence in the same place as the imperial Chamber. While the Emperor was in the Empire, he had the right to summon it to take up its residence at his Court.

This proposal, although it has been described as the most enlightened plan of fundamental imperial reform that the age produced, nevertheless found little favour with the Diet of Augsburg, which shelved it after the traditional fashion by referring its further consideration to another Diet. Fears for their territorial sovereignty may have partly induced the princes to bring about this result. But it seems probable that distrust of Maximilian was the real motive which led to the rejection of the scheme. Bitter experience had taught the Estates that the Emperor could be tied down to no promises, and could be entrusted with the execution of no settled policy. The best proof of this is that, as soon as Maximilian died, the Diet went back to the ideas of Berthold of Mainz and restored the *Reichsregiment*.

The obligations involved by Maximilian's participation in the Holy League speedily forced upon him once more the necessity of consulting his Estates. In April, 1512, the Emperor travelled to Trier to meet the Diet. Much time was now wasted and finally Max, in despair as to any transaction of business, went to the Netherlands, taking with him many of the assembled princes. A remnant of the Diet lingered on at Trier until Maximilian, returning from the Netherlands, prorogued it to Cologne. Here the Emperor once more brought forward the plan of 1510. As it met with little approval, he proposed as an alternative that a Common Penny should once more be levied after the fashion adopted at Augsburg in 1500, and that, by way of improvement on the Augsburg precedent, a levy of one man in a hundred should provide him with an adequate army. It was ridiculous to expect that the Estates would grant an army four times as large as the levy of 1500, when no great concession like that of the *Reichsregiment* was offered in return. The Emperor gradually reduced his terms, but after much haggling obtained no permanent assistance and only inadequate temporary help.

One result of future importance came from the Diet of Cologne. This was a scheme for the extension of the system of Circles into which portions of the Empire had been divided since 1500. Maximilian now proposed to add to the existing six further new Circles, formed from the electoral and Habsburg territories which had been excluded from the earlier arrangement. A seventh Circle, that of the Lower Rhine, was to comprise the dominions of the four Rhenish Electors. An eighth Circle of Upper Saxony took in the lands of the Electors of Saxony and Brandenburg, together with those of the Dukes of Pomerania and some other minor Powers transferred from the original Saxon Circle. Archbishop Berthold's greatest wish was realised in the proposal to include Max's hereditary dominions in the ninth and tenth Circles of Austria and Burgundy. Thus every large tract of imperial territory became part of a Circle, save only the foreign kingdom of the Cechs. Definite names were given to the older Circles, and in each Circle a Captain appointed by it was empowered to carry out with the help of a force of cavalry the decisions of the imperial Chamber. The Estates however took alarm at the proposal to put the Captains of the Circles at the head of an armed force; and the result was that the division of the Empire into ten Circles never came into working order until after Maximilian's death, and even then certain small districts were left outside the system.

The Diet of 1512 was practically the last of the reforming Diets. The chief interest in the immediately succeeding period centred round the renewal of the Swabian League. This confederacy had for a generation powerfully contributed towards the peace and welfare of South Germany. It had extended its limits, until it included not only the Estates of Swabia, but Rhenish and Franconian magnates such as the Elector Palatine, the Elector of Mainz, and the Bishop of Würzburg. But it comprehended within it very diversified elements, and the lesser Estates looked with jealousy upon the increasing influence of the greater princes upon its policy. Conspicuous among these magnates was Ulrich, the turbulent and unruly young Duke of Würtemberg. The split declared itself when the princes refused to take a share even in paying the cost of the destruction of the robber-nest of Hohenkrähen in the Hegau, which the League, inspired by the Emperor, now captured after a short siege. Accordingly when the League was renewed for ten years in October, 1512, the Duke of Würtemberg with his allies, the Elector Palatine, the Bishop of Würzburg, and the Margrave of Baden, were excluded from it. The excluded princes promptly set up a counter-league, which in 1515 received the adhesion of Frederick the Wise of Saxony. Thus the element of disunion, which had prevented any organised combination of the Empire as a whole, now also threatened to destroy the most successful of the local unions of parts of the Empire. In the midst of this confusion, the last Diets of Maximilian's reign were even more incompetent than their predecessors. The characteristic features of these years were the war of Franz von Sickingen against Worms and the feud between Ulrich of Würtemberg and the Swabian League. The Emperor was now conscious of his impending end. In the hope of furthering his grandson's election as his successor, he relieved Sickingen from the ban which had been pronounced against him. The aggrieved Estates refused in their turn their help against the disobedient Ulrich. New troubles now arose to complicate the situation. The early triumphs of Francis I deprived Maximilian of his last hopes of acquiring influence or territory in Italy. After Marignano his military impotence was clearly demonstrated to all the world, while his shifty and tortuous diplomacy became a bye-word for incompetence. Since 1517 ecclesiastical troubles had assumed an acute shape by the crusade of Martin Luther against papal Indulgences. But the old Emperor still calmly pursued his way, finding amusement with his literary and artistic schemes, and occupying himself more solidly in preparing the way for the world-Empire of his grandson Charles, and in setting the administration of the Austrian hereditary lands on a more satisfactory basis. He was still as full of dreams as ever and talked so late as 1518 of leading a crusade against the Infidel. But the contrast between his projects and achievements was never more strikingly brought out than in the last months of his life. The great schemes of the Diet of Innsbruck were in no wise carried out. The imperial coffers were so empty that Maximilian could not pay the tavern bills of his courtiers. Bitterly vexed at the indignities to which his poverty exposed him, he left Tyrol and travelled down the Inn and Danube to Wels. There, prostrated by a long-threatened illness, he breathed his last on January 19, 1519.

A review of the political history of Germany brings out Maximilian's character almost at its weakest. Yet the impression derived from his calamitous European wars, his ineffective negotiations, and his pitiable shifts for raising money is even more unfavourable. Nevertheless the unsuccessful ruler was a man of rare gifts and many accomplishments. " He was," says a Venetian, " not very fair of face, but well proportioned, exceedingly robust, of sanguine and choleric complexion, and very healthy for his age." His clear-cut features, his penetrating glance, his dignified yet affable manner, marked him as a man of no ordinary stamp. He lived simply and elegantly, loving good cheer and delicate meats, but always showing the utmost moderation, and being entirely free from the hard drinking habits of most of the German rulers of his time. He was the bravest and most adventurous of men, risking his life as freely in the rough chase of the chamois among the mountains of Tyrol as in the tiltyard or on the field of battle. He was an admirable huntsman, and a consummate master of all knightly exercises. Good-humoured, easy-going, and tolerant, he possessed in full measure the hereditary gift of his house for combining kingly dignity with a genial kindliness that took all hearts by storm. He was equally at home with prince, citizen, and peasant. He had so little gall in his composition that, save Berthold of Mainz, he had hardly ever made a personal enemy. Frederick of Saxony eulogised him as the politest of men, and the

Countess Palatine found him the most charming of guests. The personal devotion of the younger generation of princes to the Emperor did more than anything else to break up the party of constitutional reform. The rough *Landsknechte* called him their father; the artists and scholars looked to him for liberal support and discriminating sympathy; the Tyrolese peasantry adored him, and he was ever the favourite of women, whether of high-born princesses, or of the patrician ladies of Augsburg or Nürnberg. He relieved the tedium of his attendance at long Diets by sharing fully in the life of the citizens of the town at which the assembly was held. He attended their dances, their mummings, their archery-meetings, himself often winning the prize through his skill with the cross-bow and arquebus. Yet he was as readily interested in serious subjects as in his pleasures. His quickness was extraordinary, and the range of his interests extremely wide. He could discuss theology with Geiler and Trithemius, art with Dürer or Burgkmaier, letters with Celtes or Peutinger. On all matters of horsemanship, hunting, falconry, fortification, and artillery, he was himself an authority. Yet all these gifts were rendered ineffective by his want of tenacity and perseverance, by his superficiality, and by his strange inability to act with and through other men.

Maximilian was ever restless, a hard and quick, though by no means a thorough, worker, with real insight into many knotty problems and no small power of judging and knowing men. Keenly conscious of his own ability, and morbidly jealous of his own authority, he strove to keep the threads of affairs in his own hands, and seldom or never gave implicit confidence even to his most trusted ministers. He was a good-humoured and indulgent master, blind to the vices of his servants so long as they pleased him or were found useful to him. But the same habit of mind that impelled him to act on his own initiative led him to prefer ministers of lowly origin who owed everything to his favour. These he treated indulgently and well, but regarded as mere secretaries, or agents for carrying out the policy which his master mind had conceived. Few princes of the Empire enjoyed his confidence, and among these none of the first rank. Yet among his better known servants were two Counts of the Empire, Henry of Fürstenberg, and Eitelfritz of Hohenzollern, Swabians both, as were so many of Maximilian's favourites. As diplomatists he preferred Burgundians to Germans. The smaller posts he commonly filled up with his favourite Tyrolese. But the most famous of his ministers was Matthaeus Lang, an Augsburg burgher's son, by profession a churchman and a lawyer, who early became his secretary, and served him with great fidelity for the rest of his life. Maximilian rewarded him nobly, forced the well-born Canons of Augsburg to accept their social inferior as Provost, and soon procured for him the bishopric of Gurk, the archbishopric of Salzburg, and a Cardinal's hat. Leo X compared Lang to Wolsey, and wrongly supposed that both ruled their masters. Like Wolsey, Lang was accused of arrogance and venality, and became exceedingly unpopular. A like fate befel Maximilian's minor ministers, the Tyrolese Serntein and Lichtenstein, and the Augsburger Gossembrot, head of the Tyrolese financial administration. Public opinion regarded them as corrupt and greedy and as ill-advisers of the popular Emperor. "His counsellors were rich," said a contemporary, "and he was poor. He who desired anything of the Emperor took a present to his Council and got what he wanted. And when the other party came, the Council still took his money and gave him letters contrary to those issued previously. All these things the Emperor allowed." The removal of Maximilian's counsellors was one of the conditions imposed on Charles V before his election. Nor was their lot an easy one during the life of their lord. They often had a very hard task in finding out what the wishes of their fickle and inconstant master really were, and they were sometimes quite at a loss as to the direction of the policy which they were expected to carry out. Yet the Emperor was ever ready to trim the sails of his statecraft to suit any passing wind of casual counsel. As Machiavelli said of him, he took advice of nobody and yet believed everybody, and was in consequence badly served. His mind was always running over with fresh ideas and impulses, which, when half carried out, were displaced by other whims of the moment. What he said at night he repudiated in the morning. No promises could bind him; not even self-interest could keep him straight in a single course for any length of time. True child of the Renaissance as he was, his emotional, sensitive, superficial, susceptible, and capricious nature stood in the strongest contrast to the pursuit of statecraft for its own sake by the politic and self-seeking princes of Italy, who used the giddy and volatile Caesar as an easy tool of their purposes. Yet few of the most ruthless of Italians had occasion to stoop to greater meanness, more wanton lying, and more barefaced deceit, than this model of honour and chivalry. And Maximilian's wiles were easily seen through and seldom effected their object. Too open-minded to hold strongly to his opinions, too versatile and universal in his tastes to deal with any subject thoroughly, he remained to the end of his life a gifted amateur in politics. He was at his best when strong personal interest gave free scope to his individuality.

As a general Maximilian was scarcely more successful than he was as a statesman. But as a military organiser he did much to further the revolution in the art of war that attended the growth of the modern system of States. He improved the weapons and equipment of his cavalry, though the lightly armoured horsemen of the Empire never seem in his days to have been able to hold their own against the heavier cavalry of France and Italy. More famous by far was the rehabilitation of German infantry, which owed so much to his personal impulse. In his early Burgundian Wars, he began the reorganisation of the German foot-soldier, which soon made the German *Landsknecht* a terror to all Europe. Turbulent, undisciplined, and greedy, Maximilian's infantry proved admirable fighting material, brave in battle, patient of hardship, and passionately devoted to the King, whom they regarded as their father. For their equipment he discarded the useless and cumbersome shield, and gave them as their chief weapon an ashen lance, some eighteen feet long, though a certain proportion were armed with halberds, and others with firearms that were portable and efficient, at least as compared with earlier weapons of the same sort. The rejection of the heavy armour that still survived from former days made Maximilian's infantry much more mobile than most of the cumbrous armies of the time, while, when they stood in close array, their forest of long spears easily resisted the attacks of cavalry. However disorderly after victory, the *Landsknecht* preserved admirable discipline in the field. Maximilian's inventive genius was at its best in improving the artillery of his time. However poor he was, he always found the means for casting cannon of every calibre. He invented ingenious ways of making cannon portable, and it was largely through his talents as a practical artillerist that light field-pieces were made as serviceable in pitched battles in the open as heavy pieces of ordnance had long been in the siege of fortified places.

Maximilian played no small part in the intellectual and artistic life of his time. The religious movement which burst out at Wittenberg and Zürich in the last years of his life lay outside his sphere. Though he was wont to discuss theological problems with interest and freedom, he was in his personal life, as in his ecclesiastical policy, orthodox and conservative. Yet this orthodox Emperor discussed the temporal dominion of the Popes as an open question, and argued that the Lenten fast should be divided or mitigated, since the rude German climate made the rigid observance of the laws of the Church dangerous to health. He urged on the Papacy the reformation of the Calendar very much on the lines afterwards adopted by Gregory XIII. He was pious and devout after his fashion, and was specially devoted to the Saints whom he claimed as members of the House of Habsburg. He had also inherited some of his father's love for astrology. More important, however, than these things is the large share taken by him in the spread of the New Learning of the humanists in Germany. He reorganised the University of Vienna, and established there chairs of Roman law, mathematics, poetry, and rhetoric. He fostered the younger Habsburg university at Freiburg in the Breisgau. Under the direction of Conrad Celtes, he set up a college of poets and mathematicians as a centre for liberal studies in Vienna. He called Italian humanists over the Alps to his service. He was the friend of Pirkheimer, Peutinger and Trithemius. He was devoted to music, and his Court-chapel was famous for its singing. In art he was a most magnificent patron of the wood engraver. He had friendly relations with Dürer, while Burgkmaier did some of his best work for him.  He loved history, and was a great reader of romances.  He regretted that the Germans were not in the habit of writing chronicles, and interested himself in the printing and composition of works illustrating the history of Germany and especially that of his own House.  His vanity, perhaps the most constant feature in his character, led him to project a long series of literary and artistic undertakings; but, as was usual with him, his designs were far too comprehensive to be ever carried out.  One only of his literary enterprises saw the light during his lifetime.  This was *The Dangers and Adventures of the famous Hero and Knight, Sir Teuerdank,* which Melchior Pfintzing published in 1517 at Nürnberg, and which sets forth in dull and halting German verse, illustrated by Schäufelein's spirited woodcuts, an allegorical account of Maximilian's own exploits during the wooing of Mary of Burgundy.  What part of the composition belongs to Maximilian himself and what the final redaction owed to the earlier designs of his secretary, Max Treitzsaurwein, and of his faithful counsellor Sigismund von Dietrichstein, is not clear, but at least the general scheme and many of the incidents are due to the Emperor.  At his death, he left behind him masses of manuscripts, fragments of proofs, and great collections of drawings and wood-blocks to represent the other compositions which he had contemplated.  In comparatively recent times the piety of his descendants has given these works to the world in sumptuous form.  *Weisskunig,* drawn up by Treitzsaurwein and illustrated by Burgkmaier, describes in German prose the education and the chief exploits of Maximilian.  In the *Triumph of Maximilian* the vast resources of Albert Dürer's art nobly commemorate the Emperor in one of the most grandiose compositions that the wood-engraver has ever produced. In *Freydal* Maximilian's joustings and mummeries are depicted with the help of Burgkmaier's pencil.  Other literary projects, such as the lives of the so-called "Saints of the House of Habsburg," were only very partially carried out.  In the last years of his life Maximilian planned the erection of a splendid tomb for himself at Wiener Neustadt, and called upon the best craftsmen of Tyrol to adorn it with a series of bronze statues.  The Austrian lands were not able to supply his wants, and before long he was ransacking Germany for artists capable of carrying out his ideas.  To this extension of his plan we owe the magnificent statues of Theodoric and Arthur, which Peter Vischer of Nürnberg cast by his orders.  But this scheme too remained incomplete at his death. His last wishes were carried out as imperfectly as he had himself carried out his designs during his life.  His request to be buried at Wiener Neustadt, the town of his birth, was forgotten.  But, among the ornaments of the sumptuous tomb erected over his remains by his grandsons in the palace chapel at Innsbruck, room was found for the works of art which he himself had collected to adorn his last resting-place.  In the heart of his favourite Tyrol, under the shadow of the mountains that he loved, the most glorious monument of the German Renaissance worthily enshrines the prince, who, with all his faults and failures, had no small share in bringing his country into the full blaze of modern light.

Was any real progress achieved by Germany during the reign of Maximilian? The failure both of the Emperor and of the Estates is painfully obvious; yet so much strenuous activity, so much preaching of new political doctrine could not pass away without leaving its mark in history. Very few actual results were at the moment obtained; but the ideal was at least set up, which later generations were able in some slight measure to realise. The policy of imperial reform seemed to have hopelessly broken down; but it was something gained that the *Landfriede* had been proclaimed, the constitution and powers of the Diet settled, and the *Kammergericht* established. The next generation took up and made permanent some of the measures which during Maximilian's lifetime had been utterly abandoned. The division of the Empire into ten Circles was actually carried out. The Aulic Council became the rival of the imperial Chamber. Even the Council of Regency was for a short time revived. In the worst days of disunion these institutions remained, the decrepit survivals of the age of abortive reformation, which with all their feebleness at least faintly embodied the great idea of national union that had originally inspired them. And if all these institutions—such as they were—made for order and progress, the peace and well-being of Germany were much more powerfully secured by the strengthening of the territorial sovereignties which accompanied the reaction from the reformers' policy. The example set by Maximilian in unifying and ordering the government of the Austrian dominions was faithfully followed by his vassals, both great and small. The stronger princes become civilised rulers of modern States. The lesser princes at least abandon their ancient policy of warfare and robbery. The improved condition of Germany displays itself most clearly in the extraordinary development of the towns, which Maximilian had himself helped to foster. Thus the population of Nürnberg seems to have doubled during the sixteenth century; while the growth of material comfort, and of a high standard of living, were as marked as was the undoubted advance in spiritual and intellectual interests, in art and in letters. But most important of all was the great fact that the national idea had survived all the many failures of the attempts made to realise it. Nowhere was its force felt more strongly than in Elsass and along the Rhine, where a genuine though mainly literary enthusiasm responded to Maximilian's efforts at keeping a watch over the national borderlands. And if the age of the collapse of the German State was simultaneously the period of the revival of national scholarship, historical learning, literature, art, and language, it was the national idea that gave unity of direction and aim to the German Renaissance, and inspired all that was best in German Protestantism. To this national idea the Reformation, while completing the political break-up of the

German national State, gave new life, endowing Germany with a common language and inspiring her with fresh motives for independence. It was in no small measure due to these influences—the influences of Maximilian's time and in a measure of Maximilian himself—that in the long and dreary centuries when there was no German State there remained a German nation, able to hand on the great traditions of the past to a happier age which could realise, though in a fresh shape, the ancient ideal of Berthold of Mainz, that side by side with the German nation there should also be a German National State.

# CHAPTER X.

## HUNGARY AND THE SLAVONIC KINGDOMS.

IN the generation preceding the rise of the Reformation, the Magyar and Bohemian kingdoms underwent an internal decay that finally, in 1526, led to their incorporation with the empire of the Habsburgs, while Poland, although far from being sound or strongly organised, continued to maintain her imposing position against Turks and Tartars on the one hand, and Muscovites and Germans on the other. The decay of Hungary and Bohemia was unexpected and has always offered one of the most perplexing problems of modern history. About the middle, and still more during the sixth and seventh decades of the fifteenth century, both kingdoms seemed firmly established, the one (Hungary) in the immense basin of the middle Danube; the other (Bohemia, together with Moravia and Silesia) on the vast plateau of the great watershed of central Europe. Their rulers had real international importance; their armies were numerous and well disciplined; and their administration and revenues furnished them with ample means for making war or securing peace. Yet within a comparatively short period the prospects of the two kingdoms were blighted, their independence as national States was lost, and both were made to swell the rising imperial power of a dynasty that, a few years previously, had seemed to have lost the last vestige of its pretensions to greatness, and that had moreover repeatedly been worsted in the field and in diplomacy by both Bohemia and Hungary.

The power of the Habsburgs during the sixteenth and seventeenth centuries is intimately connected with, and conditioned by, their acquisition of the Crowns of Bohemia and Hungary in 1526; and, since that central fact of Austrian history has at the same time also told on most of the international currents of European history, its cause, that is to say the decay of Hungary and Bohemia during the last years of the fifteenth and the first twenty-six years of the sixteenth century, must necessarily be viewed as possessing a more than local or temporary importance. A glance at the map of Europe in the period just indicated will suffice to show that there were, in central and east-central

Europe, no less than four serious aspirants for a comprehensive monarchy, which should comprise all the fertile countries of the middle Danube, the upper Elbe, and the upper Oder. The Dukes of Bavaria, the Archdukes of Austria, the Kings of Bohemia, and the Kings of Hungary, had long been bidding, intriguing, and warring for the great prize. The spoils went to the House of Habsburg. The burden of the narrative to be attempted in this chapter is implied in this one historic result; and only by a comprehension of its gradual accomplishment can the more or less incoherent events which passed over the scene of south-eastern Europe before the advent of Luther, Charles V, and the great Popes of the Counter-Reformation, be made really intelligible.

Thus a clear solution, one might almost say a technical answer, may be found for the problem, why Austria, and not Bavaria, Bohemia, or Hungary, was to become, in 1526, the political centre of gravity of a part of Europe, where for geographical and historical reasons small independent States could not well hope for enduring existence, and out of which Poland was to retreat behind the Oder, leaving central Europe unaffected by her influence. All personal or accidental events and causes were overruled by one potent general cause, working on behalf of the Habsburgs. However bad the tactics of the Austrian rulers, however insufficient or dishonourable their means, they surpassed their rivals in respect of political strategy, more particularly in the strategy of foreign or international policy, and thus carried the day in a period when, all over Europe, international forces had a decided ascendancy over local or national influences. To this remarkable result the shortcomings of their rivals contributed perhaps more than their own superiority in political insight. The glaring and fatal mismanagement, or rather neglect, of foreign policy by Austria's three rivals rendered fruitless all their efforts for the consolidation of their States.

In approaching the melancholy history of Hungary and Bohemia from 1490 to 1526, one cannot but be struck with the analogies, amounting to complete resemblance, both in the circumstances and in the institutions of the Cech and Magyar kingdoms in the fifteenth century. In natural conditions, in number and quality of population, and in the conjuncture of circumstances historical and historico-geographical, there is indeed a great difference between the two countries. The Magyars are a Turanian, the Cechs an Aryan people. In their languages, their customs, their music, they have little in common. The Cechs have always been, and were especially in the earlier half of the fifteenth century, profoundly troubled by religious movements of their own; while we can detect no parallel in Hungary to the rise and progress of the Bohemian Hussites. The international position of Bohemia was centred in a close, if latently hostile relation to the Holy Roman Empire, the King of Bohemia being one of the seven Electors. The claims to overlordship over Hungary put forward by earlier Emperors were mere pretences. Bohemia, after the fashion of small States hard pressed on all sides by an overpowering empire, was naturally led to intensify her powers of resistance by fanatic nonconformity, and her religious warriors (Ziska, the two Procops) held large parts of central Germany in terror for several years (1419–34). In Hungary there were no such motives for religious isolation and fanaticism, and the relations of the Kings of Hungary to the German Emperors were purely international or political.

Yet notwithstanding all these differences there is, in historical antecedents and in institutions, an unmistakable similarity between Bohemia and Hungary. Until the beginning of the fourteenth century both these countries were under native Kings, Hungary till 1301, Bohemia till 1306. Then followed in both of them foreign dynasties,— in Hungary the Angevins, in Bohemia the Luxemburgs; and so it came about that in both the Crown was made elective. In both countries, during the latter half of the fourteenth and the former half of the fifteenth century, the Estates won political ascendancy, and in both the protectorate of successful leaders in war or politics led to the throne,—in Hungary in the person of Matthias Corvinus, in Bohemia in that of George Podiebrad. Neither of these very able princes was, however, fortunate enough to found a new dynasty ; and both were succeeded by two princes of the Polish House of the Jagellos, Wladislav and his son Louis, each of whom, though incapable and unworthy of his position, became King of Bohemia and of Hungary at the same time.

This profound parallelism, indicated by the mere external sequence and form of rule, becomes still more striking and symptomatic of deeper analogies when we turn to the social and political structure of the two kingdoms.

In the last quarter of the fifteenth century Bohemia consisted legally of Bohemia proper, together with the margravate of Moravia, the duchy of Silesia, and Lower Lusatia. Since the Peace of Olmütz in 1477, most of Moravia, Silesia, and Lusatia were under Hungarian sovereignty, Matthias Corvinus having forced Wladislav of Bohemia to cede these territories. The population of Bohemia was not over 400,000; and then, as now, it was made up of German and of Slav-speaking inhabitants. The Bohemians were settled in the centre, and the "Germans" around them.

Hungary was in 1490 a very large kingdom, stretching from the eastern portion of the modern kingdom of Saxony through Silesia and Moravia, to Hungary proper, occupying wide tracts of fortified lands on the Drave, Save, Una, Bosna and Drina, as far as the Aluta or Olt river, thus comprising large portions of modern Bosnia, Servia and of western Rumania. The population of Hungary amounted towards the end of the sixteenth century to about 1,100,000; we may therefore assume that at the end of the fifteenth it had reached about 800,000. Venetian diplomatic agents were, it is true, repeatedly assured by the Magyars of the time of Wladislav (1490–1516) that Hungary could muster an army of no less than 200,000 men. This assurance, however, cannot be taken as a basis for serious computations of the population, and undoubtedly possesses patriotic and political interest rather than any statistical value. Hungary was then, as it is now, the meeting-ground of a very large number of nationalities. The towns were mostly inhabited by Germans who, as a rule, could not even speak the language of their masters. The mountainous regions in the north were thinly inhabited by Slav peoples, those in the south-east by Romance-speaking Rumanians, by Dalmatians, Servians, Armenians, Cumanians, etc. All social and political prestige and power was with the Magyars—or, to speak more correctly, with the Magyar noblemen.

The political structure of either country was likewise analogous to that of the other. In both, the aristocracy was the paramount element, endowed with chartered or traditional *privileges*, to the practical exclusion from political power of certain classes of citizens endowed with *rights* in the modern sense of the term. In Hungary the ruling Order was, in general terms, the nobility. It consisted of the great prelates of the Church (*Domini Praelati, főpapok*), the magnates (*Barones et Magnates, zászlósurak és országnagyok*) and the common gentry (*nobiles, nemesek*). To these three classes of personal nobles were, since 1405, added the corporate nobles of the free royal towns (*szabad királyi városok*), which as corporations enjoyed some of the rights of Hungarian nobility. Of the prelates, the first in dignity and power was the Archbishop of Esztergom (in German, Gran) who was the Primate of Hungary, the *legatus natus* of the Pope, and the Chancellor of the King; next to him ranked the Bishops of Eger, of Veszprém, of Agram, of Transylvania, and the Abbot of Pannonhalma, in the county of Győr (*Germanicè:* Raab). The magnates were not, with just two exceptions (the Eszterházys and the Erdődys), distinguished from the common gentry in the way of title;—for such titles as "Baron," "Count" or "Prince" were first introduced into Hungary by the Habsburgs, after 1526. They consisted of noblemen who were either very wealthy, or incumbents of one of the great national offices of the country. In perfect keeping with the medieval character of the entire social and political structure of Hungary, these great offices implied immense personal privileges rather than constituting their bearers definite organs of an impersonal State. The highest office was that of the Count Palatine (*Regni Palatinus, nádor*), the King's legal representative, and when he was a minor his legal guardian; judge and umpire on differences between King and nation; Captain-general of the country, and Keeper of the King's records. After the Count Palatine followed the *Judex Curiae regiae;* the *Banus,* or Seneschal, of Croatia; the *Tavernicorum regalium magister* (*főtárnokmester*) or Chancellor of the Exchequer; the *vajdák* or Seneschals of Transylvania and the minor border-provinces on the Danube; and the Lord-lieutenants of the counties (*főispánok*).

The common gentry, about 15,000 families, consisted of persons forming the *populus* as distinguished from the *plebs.* They alone possessed real political rights; they alone enjoyed the active and passive franchise; their estates could not be taken away from them (a right called *ősiség*); they were exempt from taxation; they alone were the leading officials of the county-government, and their chief duty lay in their obligation to defend the country against any enemy attacking it. Even in point of common law they were, unlike Roman *patricii* or English gentry, in a position very much more advantageous than that allowed either to the urban population, called *hospites,* or to the rest of the unfree peasantry (*jobbágyok*).

On this stock of privileged nobility was grafted a system of local and national self-government closely resembling that of England, although the similarity holds good far more with regard to the Hungarian county-system than in respect of the Diet. In the former the local nobility managed all the public affairs with complete autonomy, and there was, especially in the fifteenth century, a strong tendency to differentiate each county as a province, unconcerned in the interests of the neighbouring counties, if not positively hostile to them. Inter-municipal objects, such as the common regulation of the unbridled Tisza river, proved as impossible of achievement as was the uniform assertion in all counties of recent legislative acts. Yet it was the county organisation, itself the outcome of the rapid conquest of all Hungary by one victorious people in the last decade of the ninth century, which preserved the unity of the Magyar kingdom.

The Diet (*országgyűlés*) on the other hand differed from the English Parliament in two essential points. It consisted, not of delegates or deputies, but of the mass of the nobles assembled in full arms on the field of Rákos, near Budapest, or elsewhere. Examples of delegates at Diets are, it is true, not entirely unknown in the period preceding the disaster of Mohács (1526); yet as late as 1495, and repeatedly in 1498, 1500, 1518, special acts were passed enjoining every individual noble to attend the Diet in person. It may readily be seen that such an assembly possessed the elements neither of statesmanlike prudence nor of sustained debate. The poorer members, always the great majority, soon tired of the costly sojourn far away from their homes, and hastened back to their counties. The other essential difference from the English Parliament lay in the fact that down to the end of the period under review (1526) the Hungarian Diet consisted of a single Chamber only. Thus both in structure and in function, the

Diets, although very frequent, very busy and very noisy, remained in a rudimentary state.

This short sketch of the political constitution of pre-Reformation Hungary would, however, be incomplete without laying special stress on the fact that there was no trace of Western feudalism either in the social or the political institutions of the country. Medieval no doubt the structure of Hungary was, even in the opening period of modern history; it was, however, a type of early, almost pre-feudal times, tempered by strong and wholesome elements of the modern national State. The adherence of Hungary to this medieval type rendered her less capable of progressing by the side of the far advanced and modernised States of the West with anything like equal rapidity; the factors of national life, on the other hand, afforded her the possibilities of a greater, if belated, future. Thus the Magyar kingdom stood in point of time between the Middle Ages and modern times; just as in point of space it lay between the Orient and the Occident.

In Bohemia, again, only noblemen enjoyed the actual rights of full citizenship. However, owing to the constant intercourse between Bohemia and Germany, German feudal ideas penetrated into the Cech kingdom; and in the fifteenth century Cech noblemen were divided, not merely *de facto*, as in Hungary, but *de lege*, as in Germany, into two classes—the *Vladyks* or magnates (in Cech also: *páni, šlechtíci*), and the knights (in Cech, *rytierstvo*, meaning the Estate or Order of the knights). The most important *gentes* of the Bohemian magnates were the Vitkovici, Hronovici, Busici, Markwartici (to whom belonged in the seventeenth century the famous Wallenstein), Kounici, each branching off into a number of noble families, frequently with German names (Riesenburg, Schellenberg, etc.). The tendency to make of the *Vladyks* or magnates a real caste, differing in rights, power, and prestige not only from the burgesses and unfree classes, but also from the knights, was so strong, and was so much aided by the terrible Hussite movement, from which the magnates contrived to derive more benefit than any other section of the population, that by the end of the fifteenth century they had in Bohemia proper monopolised the whole government of the country, and were possessed of most valuable and almost regal rights as lords on their estates. The Moravian high gentry, by a convention of 1480, entered on the statute-book, actually went so far as to restrict the number of *Vladyks* to fifteen, and thus practically established themselves as a closed caste. In Hungary, as we have seen, the magnates were never able to assert similar privileges at the expense of the ordinary gentry.

The Bohemian peasantry (in Cech: *sedlák, rolník*) were, previous to the Hussite Wars, in a tolerable position, although there always was among them a very large number of villains and half-serfs (in Cech: *chlap, sluh*). The introduction of German law into Bohemia undoubtedly helped to mitigate the condition of the rural population. The burgesses of the towns, mostly Germans, played,—as in Hungary and Poland,—a very subordinate part, and were admitted to the Diet only after the great Hussite upheaval, in the middle of the fifteenth century. The Diet of Bohemia (*sném*), and that of Moravia, were considerably better organised for efficient work than was the case with the Diet in Hungary. In Moravia there were four Estates (magnates, prelates, knights, and towns), in Bohemia only three, the clergy having here, as in England about the same time, disappeared as a separate Estate from the Diet. The assemblies were not frequented by unmanageable numbers, and were accordingly less tumultuous and more efficient than the national assemblies in Hungary. Yet the proper sphere of the influence wielded by the gentry was the Privy Council (*rada zemská*), where the *Kmets*, or *Seniores*, advised and controlled the King. When we reach the period specially treated here, we find Bohemia practically governed by a caste-like oligarchy, and uncontrolled either, as in Hungary, by a numerous and strong minor gentry, or, as in England, by a strong King.

From 1458 to 1490 Hungary had been ruled by King Matthias Corvinus, son of John Hunyadi, the great warrior and crusader. Matthias was in many ways the counterpart of his contemporary Louis XI of France, except that he surpassed the French ruler in military gifts. Both of them were, like so many of their fellow-monarchs of that time, historical illustrations of Machiavelli's Prince:—unscrupulous, cold, untiringly at work, filled with great ambitions, orderly, systematic, and patrons of learning. Matthias, whom the popular legend in Hungary has raised to the heights of an ideally just ruler ("King Matthias is dead, justice has disappeared" said the common people) had, as a matter of fact, made short work of many of the liberties and rights of his subjects. He controlled and checked the turbulent oligarchs with an iron hand; and his "black legion" of Hussite and other mercenaries,—his standing army, in a word, and as such an illegal institution in Hungary,—was employed by him with the same relentless vigour against refractory Magyars as against Turks or Austrians. In his wars he was particularly fortunate. On the Turks he inflicted severe punishment, and his Herculean general Paul Kinizsi, aided by Stephen Bátori, completely routed them at Kenyérmező near Szászváros (Broos) on the Maros river in Transylvania, October 13, 1479.

It has already been seen how in 1477, Matthias, after a successful war against Wladislav of Bohemia, obtained by the Treaty of Olmütz the larger portion of the territory of the Bohemian Crown. In 1485 the great Corvinus was still more successful. On May 23 of that year, Vienna capitulated to him as victor over the Emperor Frederick III; and thus he added Lower Austria to his vast domain. Nor were his successes gained only by laborious fighting. His diplomatic activity was hardly less comprehensive and elaborate than were his numerous campaigns. Yet, with all his successes and triumphs, Matthias, like the Emperor Charles V at a later date, belongs to a class of rulers more interesting by their personality than important by reason of their work. Like Charles, Matthias triumphed over persons rather than over causes. He humbled nearly all his opponents, and his statue or image was set up at Bautzen as well as at Breslau, in Vienna, and in the border-fortress of Jajcza, far down in Bosnia. When on April 6, 1490, Matthias breathed his last, he left the interests of his only, but il-legitimate son, John Corvinus, and those of his realm, in so insecure a condition that no less than four or five rival candidates were striving for the Crown which he had fondly hoped to secure for his amiable but weakly son.

The oligarchs decided to confer the Crown upon Wladislav of Bohemia, a prince of the Polish House of the Jagellos, whose indolent character promised well for their ardent desire of retrieving the ascendancy which they had long since lost under Matthias' stern rule. The campaign of his competitor Maximilian, the Emperor's son, broke down, while Wladislav's other competitor, his brother Albert, since 1592 King of Poland, was persuaded by him to withdraw. Thus began the period of Wladislav II's reign over Hungary (1490–1516) during which the country, both at home and abroad, was rapidly falling into ruin. The King, commonly called "*Dobzse László*" from his habit of saying "*dobzse*" ("all right") to everything, was a mere plaything in the hands of Thomas Bakócz, the all-powerful Primate, of George Szakmáry, the Bishop of Pécs, and of Emericus Perényi, the Palatine. This Primate is the Hungarian Cardinal Wolsey. Like the great English prelate he commanded all the resources of clerical subtlety, and knew how to humiliate himself for a season. Like Wolsey, he aimed at the highest object of ecclesiastic ambition, the Papacy, and because of the same fatal conflict within him of two contradictory ambitions failed alike to render good service to his country, and to fulfil his hierarchical aspirations.

The Court-party centring in Bakócz was opposed by the adherents of the powerful House of the Zápolyai, who after Stephen Zápolyai's death in 1499, put up his son John as the national candidate for the Crown. John's friends, chiefly the childless and wealthy Lawrence Ujlaky, counted on the King's imbecility in council and war; and finally John proposed to Wladislav repeatedly, and even in threatening fashion, a marriage between him and the King's first child Anne. Wladislav, however, with the cunning which often accompanies dulness, contrived to obtain delay after delay, together with new treaty-assurances from the Emperor Maximilian, until his French wife, Anne de Candale, a kinswoman of Louis XII, King of France, bore him in 1506, a son, Louis, whose birth put an end to the intrigues of John Zápolyai.

All through these years the achievements in arms of the kingdom, if
not of the King, were by no means altogether unsatisfactory.  In the early
years of Wladislav's reign, the old hero Paul Kinizsi still continued to
inflict heavy losses on the ever aggressive Turk; and John Zápolyai, too,
earned some military glory.  Ujlaky's rebellion was put down by the
King's general Drágfy in 1495.  The internal dissensions, however, were
sapping the very foundation of the kingdom; and in 1514 Hungary was
afflicted with one of the terrible peasant revolts then not infrequent
in Austria and Germany, which invariably led to the most inhuman as
well as illegal treatment of the defeated peasants.  A crusade against
the infidel Turk, announced by Bakócz as legate of the Pope, gave rise
to vast gatherings of peasants and other poor people who, on finding
that the nobles refrained from joining them, took umbrage at this refusal, and speedily turned their pikes on the nobility as their oppressors.
A large number of noble families were cruelly and infamously murdered
by the Hungarian Jacquerie led by George Dózsa.  The untrained
masses of the insurgents, however, fell an easy prey to John Zápolyai's
soldiers.  Dózsa was roasted alive, and the peasants were by a special
statute degraded to everlasting serfdom.

After the death of Wladislav II (March, 1516) his son, a boy of ten
years, became King, under the name of Louis II.  He had been brought
up under the baneful influence of his cousin Margrave George of
Brandenburg (Prince of Jägerndorf), and knew only of untrammelled
indulgence in pleasures and pastimes.  Under such conditions there
was no vigorous reform to be expected, and the new Sultan, Sulayman
the Magnificent, occupied in 1521 the important border-fortresses of
Szabács and Nándorfehérvár (Belgrade), after their Hungarian garrisons
had exhausted every effort of the most exalted heroism.  However,
even the loss of these places, the two keys to Hungary, failed to produce a sensible change in the indolence and factiousness of the people.
In vain was Verbőczy,—an able and truly patriotic statesman,—made
Palatine in 1525; in vain good laws were passed to meet the imminent
danger at the hands of the victorious Sultan.  The disaster of Mohács,
August 29, 1526, described in an earlier chapter of this volume, showed
but too clearly that the Sultan's destructive plans were prompted
and aided rather by the fatal disorganisation of Hungary than by the
number and valour of his troops.  The Jagellos ceased to exist, and at
the same time an integral portion of Hungary, soon to be increased to
one-third of the whole country, fell into the hands of the Turk.  Other
nations before this had suffered their Cannae, Hastings, or Agnadello;
but either the victor was equal if not superior in degree of civilisation
to the vanquished, or the latter afterwards found means at home or
abroad to shake off the torpor of defeat.  Hungary, with the exception
of Transylvania, was after Mohács not only defeated but paralysed;
and for three centuries she could not resume her historical mission,

inasmuch as she was able to repel her foreign enemy only by the aid of her domestic oppressor, Austria, and of Austria's allies. Cannae steeled Rome, and Hastings made England an organic part of Europe; Mohács buried the greater part of Hungary for more than nine generations.

Passing now to events in Bohemia, we find them full of similar perturbations. Here, since 1476, the *Vladyks* were involved in interminable struggles with the towns. The common people, especially the German settlers, had suffered exceedingly at the hands of the Hussites who, by impoverishing or massacring the industrial population of their own country, paved the way for an uncontrolled oligarchy. Of these class-wars, the cruel, not to say inhuman, campaign waged by the Vladyk Kopidlansky of Kopidlno against the city of Prague, from 1507 onwards, is perhaps the most remarkable. It was not until October 24, 1517, that the higher gentry and the towns arrived at an arrangement in the so-called Treaty of St Venceslas. The leading politicians and generals of those internecine troubles were John Pashek of Wrat, William of Pernstein, Zdenko Lew of Rozmital, and Peter of Rosenberg. After 1520 the old religious dissensions, now intensified by the introduction of Luther's ideas, were resuscitated. The Kings, Wladislav and Louis, were quite unable, and it is doubtful whether they were willing, to stem the tide of internal strife. At any rate, they appear to have counted for nothing, and Bohemia as well as Moravia was practically handed over to a very limited number of aristocrats, uncontrolled either by the small gentry, as was the case in contemporary Hungary, or by the towns or peasants. Even without a battle of Mohács Bohemia had reached the stage when any bold and able foreign prince might very well hope to possess himself of a country important alike by its situation and its resources. The Habsburgs were not slow to see and appreciate their opportunity.

The political and moral gloom weighing upon Hungary and Bohemia during the reign of the Jagello Kings is undeniable. At the same time it is easy to exaggerate its consequences. The historians of both countries, and more especially the Magyar authors writing on the reigns of Wladislav II and Louis II, seem at a loss for sufficient terms of reproach and recrimination with which to assail the Hungarians of this period ; and they agree in tracing its catastrophe entirely to the moral and unpatriotic shortcomings of the Zápolyais and their contemporaries. Yet these authorities abound in statements implying high-spirited actions of good and great men, and serious and well-meant efforts for the preservation of the country. It is precisely in dark periods such as this that an advance in statesmanship and earnest patriotism is apt to make itself manifest. Any age of Hungarian history might have been proud of a patriot, jurist and statesman such as Stephen Verbőczy, the author of the first authoritative if not strictly official codification of Magyar law, written and unwritten, the *Decretum Tripartitum juris consuetudinarii inclyti regni Hungariae:* (*Hármaskönyv*). Utterances nobler and truer than the speeches delivered by him at the Diets never fell from the lips of a sincere and wise patriot. Nor was Bornemisza a commonplace or mediocre politician: while Paul Tomory, Archbishop of Kalocsa, both as an ecclesiastic and as a commander, to whom the defence of the south of the country was entrusted, deserved highly of his country.

The existence of an ample stock of public and private virtues even in those dark times becomes, however, more evident still when we study the collective actions of the Diets. After making all due allowance for their ultimate barrenness, one cannot but acknowledge that the public of that time, that is to say, the bulk of the magnates and common gentry, were at least very anxious to bring about in the government of the country a tolerable equilibrium between the powers possessed by the legislative, executive and judiciary authorities respectively. As to the legislative, they carried two great principles which in any other age would have been considered a distinct gain for any liberal constitution. One was the law that taxes can be levied by decree of the Diet alone; the other was the equally important law contained in the decrees of 1495, 1498, and especially 1507, by virtue of which the common gentry (not knights, there being no such Order in Hungary) were always to have an equal share with the magnates in the government of the nation, particularly in the Privy Council. Other important laws, salutary in themselves though still-born, were passed in great number; and immediately before the disastrous campaign of Mohács the gentry of their own accord temporarily abandoned their exemption from taxation. Highly commendable from the same point of view are the motives discoverable in numerous measures of the time, endeavouring to regulate the working of the county organisation; and the very high reputation of Verbőczy, who was rewarded by a national gift for his codification, tends to show the genuine interest taken by the commonalty in the important work of legal reform.

The Renaissance, it must be admitted, left but a faint impression on Hungary. The magnificence with which Matthias had patronised Italian scholars and artists, and established his famous collection of books, the Corvina, was only feebly imitated by a few noblemen and churchmen. As late as 1491 we find that the *Judex Curiae* (Lord Chief Justice) of Hungary, Stephen Bátori, was so illiterate as to be unable to sign his name at the treaty negotiations between Maximilian and Wladislav II at Pozsony (Pressburg). In the field of architecture there was some progress. Thus the largest and most beautiful cathedral in the Gothic style in Hungary, that of Kassa, was finished under the Jagello

22—2

Kings; and Bakócz embellished the great cathedral of Esztergom with much exquisite work. Nor were the seats of the nobles neglected, and the pleasant manor-style of fifteenth century Italy may still be admired in the northern counties of Zemplén and Abauj, whither the Turk seldom extended his ravaging expeditions.

But if, as will be noted below in connexion with other equally deplorable facts, the Renaissance proper can scarcely be regarded as having attained to any national importance in Hungary, the Reformation soon penetrated into the various regions and social strata of the country. Already in 1518 traces appear of the influence of the teachings of Luther and Melanchthon in Bártfa, Eperjes, Lőcse, and other towns of northern Hungary. Even among the magnates we find several adherents or patrons of the new creed, such as Peter Perényi, Th. Nádasdi, Valentine Török. The bulk of the population, however, remained faithful to the old religion, and in 1523, 1524, and 1525 very stringent laws were passed against the " *Lutherani.*"

In Bohemia the Hussite movement and the aspirations of the Utraquists, which were not appeased before the Diet of Kuttenberg in 1485, paved the way for the Reformation. Gallus Cahera, a butcher's son, who became vicar of the great Teyn-church at Prague, and John Hlawsa of Libočan were the chief leaders of a religious revival in the sense of Lutheranism.

There can thus be little doubt that, with all the undeniable drawbacks of oligarchic or aristocratic misgovernment, both Hungary and Bohemia still possessed numerous elements of prosperity, and that the relatively sudden downfall of both kingdoms, while certainly connected with some moral failing in rulers and ruled alike, cannot be attributed to ethical deficiencies. These were certainly not so exceptional as to account for the disappearance of national independence after a single great defeat on the battlefield. As was remarked at the outset of this chapter, the unexpected dissolution of the two kingdoms and their absorption by a Power not very much better organised than themselves and suffering from many similar evils, remains one of the great difficulties besetting this earliest period of modern history. To seek to remove such difficulties by moralising on the selfishness or greed of this Palatine or that magnate, supplies no historic synthesis of the true relation of facts. Whenever a disaster like that of Mohács stands at the end of a long series of events, it is only fair to assume that the country in question must have been terribly misgoverned. The neglect, not so much of one or the other of the ordinary virtues indispensable under all circumstances, but rather of one of the directive forces of national life and progress, will—except when a nation is specially protected by nature, as for instance by the geographical configuration of the country—invariably land it in serious predicaments, and eventually in political ruin. One of those directive forces is what is commonly called foreign policy. In Europe at any rate, and most certainly since the downfall of the Byzantine Empire in 1453, the action and reaction of its several countries on one another have been so powerful, that Giuseppe Ferrari's suggestion of writing history in a binary form ought to have been carried out long since for every one of them, as fortunately it actually has been for some.

In the latter half of the fifteenth century the whole tenor and nature of state-craft and policy changed from what it had been in the preceding centuries. The Middle Ages knew only of two "universals" in politics, the Empire proper, that is, the Holy Roman Empire, and the Catholic Church; the Byzantine Empire having little if anything to say in questions of Western policy since the days of Charlemagne. Of those two empires that of the Church alone possessed adequate organisation and means for the purpose of efficient government. The Holy Roman Empire was a fiction, or at best an ideal, lacking all the realities of power. In the face of that vague "Empire," the less ambitious but more practical smaller sovereigns and lords in Germany, France, Spain, and Italy, and likewise those of Bohemia, Hungary, and Poland, endeavoured during the twelfth, thirteenth, and fourteenth centuries, to build up well-knit and well-organised smaller realms. In this some of them succeeded but too well; and by about 1475 Europe was again divided into two groups,—but groups of a character totally different from the medieval classification.

Instead of a loose fiction, such as the Holy Roman Empire, and the Church, Europe then displayed a series of relatively large and fairly centralised monarchies, such as England, France, Aragon, Bohemia, Poland, and Hungary on the one hand; and small semi-monarchies or still smaller but highly organised city-States, such as the duchy of Bavaria, the electorate of Saxony, the free imperial towns and the Italian city-States on the other. The old political "universals" however, the Empire and the Church, were not yet extinct. The Church, although undermined by deleterious influences, internal as well as external, could still draw on vast resources of policy, treasure, and men; the Empire, although antiquated as an institution, still possessed stores of vitality as a diplomatic contrivance and a political allurement. Owing to the "universal" character of both Emperor and Pope, nothing but an international policy could be expected from either; but all the minor sovereigns who were constantly striving to enlarge their domain were likewise inevitably driven into the maze of this species of policy. However, there was a great difference (though hitherto this has remained almost unnoticed) between the realms east and west of the Oder and the March. All the States west of these rivers, especially Austria, Saxony, Bavaria, Burgundy and France—to mention only the most important ones—consisted not of continuous territory, but of larger or smaller *enclaves*, broken territory straggling irregularly over several latitudes, and sometimes severed by hundreds of miles. Austria since the acquisitions of Archduke Leopold III in the fourteenth century had *enclaves* on the Rhine, in Swabia, in Würtemberg, not to mention those in Switzerland, Tyrol, and Friuli. Bavaria's map in the fourteenth century is as bewildering as Italy's in the thirteenth, or that of the Thuringian Princes in our days. The same remark holds good as to Burgundy, France, and even England, with her *enclaves* in France, Ireland, and Scotland.

To this singularly disjoined state of the territory in all the sovereignties west of the Oder and March rivers (with the solitary exception of Bohemia), the realms east of that boundary, such as Poland and Hungary, offer a remarkable and suggestive contrast. Whether Hungary extended, as it did under Louis the Great in the fourteenth century, from Pomerania to Bulgaria, or as under Matthias, from Saxony to Servia, the Magyar kingdom always had an unbroken continuity of territory such as is in our own times possessed only by the several great States of Europe. The same remark applies to Poland, with a few insignificant allowances, and also to the kingdom of Bohemia.

This then is the chief difference between the States of Bohemia, Poland and Hungary as they are found at the end of the fifteenth century, and the rest of the western States of Europe. The unbroken continuity of those eastern States might have seemed to imply a greater unity, and thus greater strength. In reality, however, the effect was entirely different. The western sovereigns, from a natural desire to round off their far outlying possessions, and the western peoples from an equally natural desire to render their nationality coextensive with their land, were constantly anxious to improve and strengthen their organisation at home, while at the same time taking a deep, practical, and incessant interest in the affairs of their neighbours and rivals. The very fact of the situation of their States, and of the fundamental desires and needs to which it gave rise, thus made the western monarchs of the fifteenth century at the same time better or at any rate more efficient rulers at home, and trained diplomatists abroad. They soon learned the lesson, so indispensable in all foreign policy, that no dependence can be placed on any alliance unless it is based on substantial and mutual " consideration,"—to use a lawyer's term. To render themselves valuable, that is, eventually dangerous, was their first and most pressing object, and their subjects could not but feel that at a time when a consistent treatment of foreign policy was the supreme need of their country, the monarch and his counsellors justly claimed absolute power.

The intimate connexion, then, which existed in the case of the western monarchies between the discontinuity of their territories, and absolutism on the one hand, and their spirited foreign policy on the other, goes far to explain the political failure of Hungary and

Bohemia at the end of the fifteenth century, in spite of their brilliant beginnings fifty years before. Precisely at the times when the western States, even England, practically abandoned their faith in parliamentary institutions, and fell into more and more complete subjection to an efficient absolutism, the eastern countries were intent upon weakening the central power and drifted into a quite modern system of Diets and Parliaments. Their territory being continuous and large, neither their Kings nor the peoples underwent any pressure from the outside urging them to undertake the consolidation of their political fabric at home with any degree of superior efficiency, or to devote careful study and effort to the cultivation of foreign policy. Without such pressure from the outside no nation has ever persisted in the arduous work of reform for any lengthy period. In the times of Matthias, it is true, we notice that foreign policy was made a subject of constant and rigorous attention on the part of the King, who even tried to bring up a trained body of diplomatists, such as Balthasar Batthyányi, Peter Dóczi, Gregory Lábatlan, Benedictus Túroczi, and others. These were, however, mere beginnings, and very inferior indeed to the systematic work of the foreign representatives of Burgundy, or Austria, not to speak of Venice and the Pope. Under the Jagellos even these feeble attempts were abandoned, and Hungary and Bohemia were from 1490 to 1526 quite outside the main current of the international policy of Europe; alien to all the great interests then at issue; neither valued as allies, nor dangerous to any one except to minor countries in their immediate neighbourhood. When therefore the Turk in 1526 invaded Hungary with overwhelming forces, no serious attempt whatever was made to save Hungary on the part of any of the Powers, and the Turk, instead of meeting a European coalition, like that which he was to encounter at Lepanto in 1571, when he planned the ruin of Venice, was only confronted by a tiny Magyar army which he easily destroyed.

One has only to compare the incessant activity in foreign policy of Maximilian, or Ferdinand I of Austria, with that of Wladislav II and Louis II of Hungary and Bohemia, in order to see how utterly inferior Magyar political strategy was to that of the House of Habsburg. Maximilian's great wars with Venice, France, and Switzerland, his incessant diplomatic campaigns with the Curia of Rome, with the princes of Germany, with Venice, are all discussed in other parts of this work. It will be sufficient here to limit our attention to Maximilian's eastern policy. In addition to his repeated action in favour of the Teutonic Knights in what was afterwards known as East Prussia, he made several treaties with the "White Czar," such as those of 1490, 1491, and especially that of August 9, 1514, concluded at Gmunden with Czar Wasiliei Ivanovič, through an embassy previously sent to Russia and intended to bring pressure upon Sigismund, King of Poland, who tried to thwart Maximilian's plans in Hungary. With the Jagellos of Hungary he carried on several wars, all of them being in point of fact designed on one pretext or another to renew and improve upon the original treaty, dated July 19, 1463, between the Emperor Frederick III and King Matthias, in virtue of which the Habsburgs were eventually entitled to claim the crown of St Stephen. The Treaty of Pozsony (Nov. 7, 1491) as well as the negotiations of March, 1506, leading to the Treaty of July 19, 1506, and the "Congress" of Vienna (July, 1515), all terminated at the last-named date in an arrangement according to which Wladislav's daughter Anne was to marry Ferdinand, Maximilian's grandson, and Wladislav's son Louis was to become the husband of Maximilian's grand-daughter Mary. By these double marriages the Habsburg claim to the kingdom of Hungary was brought within measurable distance of consummation. It is impossible here to do more than indicate the immense diplomatic activity of Maximilian in this the most lasting of his achievements. All the levers of the international policy then in operation were put in motion by him. His policy towards Louis XII of France, and that towards the Dukes of Milan ; his European league against Venice (the so-called League of Cambray), all and everything was utilised by him to flatter, threaten, bribe or cajole Hungary into accepting his House as the eventual heir of the Jagellos. In July, 1510, his ambassadors, together with those of France and Venice, pleaded before the Hungarian Diet at Tata, pretending to be very anxious for the participation of Hungary in the league against Venice.

As against this business-like and powerful policy of the ingenious Habsburg, what do we find in Hungary? Nothing. Hungary had neither standing ambassadors at the various Courts, nor any class of trained diplomatists. At Tata the assembled gentry listened with self-complacency to the eloquent foreign orators, but as usual the noblemen soon lost patience and dispersed. Venice rightly judged the nullity of Hungary's international position, when even in the midst of her danger she refused to make any concessions whatever to the "Venetian" party amongst the Magyar nobles. The Popes, whose still very valuable countenance Hungary might have secured by a more aggressive policy against Venice in Dalmatia, or in Friuli, likewise dropped Hungary. Ignorant of what passed beyond the Carpathian Mountains ; unable to avail themselves of the currents and counter-currents of the international policy ; rendering no service to the chief Powers of the day,—the Hungarians were left in the hour of their greatest danger to their own slender resources as against the most formidable military Power of the time. The Habsburgs, both from having worn the imperial dignity for ages, and because their countless *enclaves* brought them into incessant conflicts with nearly all the Powers of Europe, had by long and patient study learned the priceless value of a sound and sustained foreign policy. In that vital point neither the Bavarian Dukes, from the exiguity of their domain, nor the Bohemian or Hungarian Kings, from their totally different habits of political thought, could vie with them. Even Matthias could not, in the end, have prevailed against Maximilian, inasmuch as the Hungarians from the very nature of their unbroken, self-sustaining territory would neither have understood, nor have readily followed a Habsburg policy carried out by a Magyar King. Mohács, then, was the necessary outcome of the neglect of foreign policy at a time when it was most needed; and this neglect again cannot but be ascribed chiefly to habits of political thought inevitable in a nation which lacked all those geographical and economic incentives to the maturing of a foreign policy that raised the nations ruled by the Valois and Habsburgs above all other nations of the continent. It is infinitely more becoming to lament Mohács as an unavoidable calamity, than to use it as a text on which to lecture an unfortunate nation.

The fatal failings of Hungarian policy may be traced in Poland also. In the first quarter of the fifteenth century the great Prince of Lithuania, Vitovt, had had indeed far-reaching ideas about the foundation of a vast Cech-Polish empire, which was to dominate the whole east of Europe. However he failed, chiefly because he was antagonistic to the Catholic or national Church of Poland. Kasimir IV (1445–92), father of Wladislav II of Hungary and Bohemia, successfully combated the Teutonic Order and other neighbouring Powers. Doubtless, like his contemporary Matthias Corvinus, he had clear views about the necessity of reorganising his country on the basis adopted by the monarchs of the West. However, both he and his sons and successors after him, John Albert (1492–1501) and Alexander I (1501–6), tried in vain to break the power of the magnates by countenancing the minor gentry (*szlachta*). In 1496 the peasants were completely disfranchised; against the urban population, mostly Germans, and termed *hospites*, several very damaging laws were passed; and the royal power was seriously reduced by the magnates. After suffering more particularly from the Statute of Nieszava, 1454,—the *Golden Bull* rather than the *Magna Charta* of the Polish oligarchs,—and from the Constitution "*Nihil novi*" of 1505, the monarchy became practically helpless in the hands of Sigismund I (1506–48), brother to his predecessors. It was during this period that both the General Diet (*izba poselska*, Chamber of Deputies) of all the various absolutely autonomous provinces of Poland, and the several Provincial Diets, acquired the fulness of actual authority in the legislative and administrative branches of government. The King might appoint, but might not remove officials. The *nuntii terrae* or representatives at the national Diets were inviolable and omnipotent. Thus in Poland too, Parliamentarism in a rather extreme form arose at the very conjuncture when it had proved inefficient in all the occidental countries. As in Hungary and Bohemia, so in Poland, its undue development crippled any consistent and sound foreign policy; and we accordingly find that although during the whole of the sixteenth century Poland still appears imposing and still achieves many a remarkable success, yet she can neither stop the growth of hostile Russia in the east, nor the insidious rise of Prussia in the west; she can neither amalgamate her population into one nation, nor endow it with a less anarchical constitution.

With a country three times as large as modern France, and territorially unbroken, besides possessing a fair outlet to the sea, the Poles were in possession of many of the factors that contribute to establish a State, and to give an assured balance to its position. That pressure from the outside, however, which has probably done more for the good of nations than most of their virtuous and patriotic qualities, was wanting. In proverbial prodigality and pleasure-seeking, the nobility of Poland spent the intervals of war on their neglected estates, leaving the great sea commerce to the German patricians of Danzig, the internal trade to the Jews, what little industry there was to the German burgesses, and the schools to the priests. Although most Polish noblemen of the wealthier classes had received a careful education at the universities of Italy, and many of them were imbued with the spirit of the classics, and fired by the ideals of true patriotism, yet all these and many other fine qualities of this most distinguished of Slavonic nations, were rendered useless and barren by the apathy and indolence of the great body of the nobles. Surely in a nation which could produce a Copernicus and so many great poets, there must have been much natural endowment even for the highest spheres of thought. In the midst of general indifference, however, the richest soil must lie fallow. The Poles, like the Hungarians, were utterly without any power of self-orientation in matters to the west of their vast country; they neglected European interests—both the Renaissance, the new international movement in the realm of intellect, and the new international policy of contemporary monarchs. In return, Europe, indifferent to Poland, as she was to the Magyars, suffered her to sink slowly but surely into inevitable dissolution.

# CHAPTER XI.

## THE CATHOLIC KINGS.

CUT off from the world by the Pyrenees and the still unnavigated ocean, broken up into small kingdoms, largely absorbed in their quarrels and in the reconquest of the land from the Saracens, Spain for many centuries played a comparatively small part in the affairs of Europe. Down to 1479 the peninsula contained five independent kingdoms: Castile, with Leon, occupying 62 per cent. of the entire surface; Aragon, with the kingdom of Valencia and the principality of Catalonia, occupying 15 per cent.; Portugal 20; Navarre 1; and Granada, the last stronghold of the Saracens, occupying 2. The marriage (1469) of Isabel, daughter of John II of Castile, with Ferdinand, son of John II of Aragon, united the two branches of the House of Trastamara, and merged the claims of husband and wife to the Crown of Castile. Isabel succeeded her brother, Henry IV, in 1474. Ferdinand, who had already received from his father the Crowns of Sicily and Sardinia, inherited in 1479 the remaining dominions of Aragon. Aragon and Castile remained distinct, each keeping its separate laws, parliaments, and fiscal frontier. Isabel, as queen in her own right, retained the Crown patronage and revenues within Castile, but general affairs were transacted under a common seal. In Aragon Ferdinand's authority was not shared by his queen. The Spanish possessions in Italy belonged to Aragon exclusively, as America afterwards belonged to Castile. A common policy, and the vastly increased resources of a kingdom uniting under its sway 77 per cent. of the peninsula, at once gave preponderating weight at home. During the greater part of the sixteenth century Spain was the chief Power in the world. The half century from 1474 to 1530, which witnessed the rise of this Power, may be subdivided into periods distinguishable as that of organisation and reconstruction, 1474–1504; that of lawlessness and revolution, 1504–23; that of absolute monarchy, 1523–30.

The reforms of Ferdinand and Isabel, "the Catholic Kings," put an end to anarchy, and formed the bridge between the division of power of the Middle Ages and the absolute monarchy of the sixteenth century.

To understand them, we must briefly recall some peculiarities of the institutions of the larger States of the united kingdom. The organisation of the kingdom of Castile was the direct result of its gradual reconquest from the Saracens. Including in its population Asturians, Galicians, and Basques, as well as Castilians and the mixed peoples of Andalucía, the land is divided ethnologically and geographically into well-marked districts, never thoroughly welded together. Castile was governed by traditional municipal usages and local charters, rather than by national laws. Conquered lands were retained by the Crown, or granted to lords temporal or spiritual, or to corporations. The Crown in some cases retained feudal rights, but in others alienated the whole authority. The owners in the latter case became almost independent princes. Lands conquered without his help owed nothing to the King. Their conquerors divided them, and elected a chief to rule and defend them. Thus were formed *behetrías* (*benefactoria*), independent communities boasting that they could change their lord seven times a day, and distinguished according as the lord might be chosen among all subjects of the Crown or only among certain families. At the end of the fifteenth century the *behetrías* were disappearing. Their factions made them an easy prey to their neighbours, the great nobles or the Crown. Unclaimed lands became the property of those who settled on them. The great estates of the Crown and titled nobles were subdivided among the free men (*hidalgos*) of their following. Those who settled on owned lands became the vassals of the owner. The power of a lord over his vassal was unlimited, unless defined by charter: down to the thirteenth century the law ran " he may kill him by hunger, thirst, or cold." Under these conditions it was impossible to attract settlers to newly conquered and dangerous lands near the frontier. King and noble vied with one another in the attempt to attract population by grant of charter (*fuero*). To grant a *fuero* is to define the obligation of vassals to their lord. Under the local *fueros* sprung up the municipalities, electing their magistrate to administer public lands and to carry out the laws of the *fuero*. As the power of the municipalities increased, that of the nobles or the Crown shrank within the district. The municipalities were the basis of political organisation of the commons. By siding with the Kings in their long struggle with the nobles they increased their liberties as against the nobles, but fell more under the authority of the Crown. The royal judge and tax-gatherer replaced the officers of the overlord or municipality. The King interfered in local matters, nominating the magistrates and appointing a president over them, the *corregidor*, whose vast and undefined powers gradually superseded municipal authority.

The legal and political classification of persons corresponded to the division of the land. The three Estates were formed by ecclesiastics; nobles, including the titular nobility, and the minor free or feudal holders (*hidalgos*); and commons, in many cases the descendants of the serfs of the soil.

The privileges of the first two Orders were enormous. They were exempt from direct taxation: their lands were inalienable: they were liable neither to arrest for debt nor to torture. The nobles were bound to the King only by the lands they held from him. The law recognised their right of formally renouncing their allegiance and making war upon the King. Their rights, like those of the municipalities, had been granted to settlers on the frontier. When the frontier moved forward, the right remained undiminished; and the result was anarchy. Under weak Kings the nobles extended their authority over the municipalities, and extorted large grants of lands and incomes guaranteed on the royal patrimony. Strong Kings exacted restitution.

The commons, while still paying as vassals certain dues to the Crown or to nobles, had, by the middle of the fifteenth century, won the right of changing lords, and the ownership of the land on which they lived, with right of transferring it by sale or bequest. Their condition was notably better under the Crown than under the nobles. In order to check desertion, the nobles were forced to follow the more liberal policy of the Kings. Slaves were rare, consisting in the main of foreigners, captives in the Saracen Wars, or negroes imported through Portugal. Jews and Moslems enjoyed the special protection of the Crown.

The Castilian Cortes originated in a Council of prelates and nobles advising the King on all matters civil and religious. In the thirteenth century the commons of the municipalities won the right of assisting, by deputies, at the Council. At first, neither the number of municipalities represented, nor the number of their deputies was limited; for they had no vote. They assembled merely to receive communication of royal decrees, to swear allegiance to the successor to the throne, and to receive confirmation of their charters at the beginning of a new reign. Later, the representatives of the municipalities won the control of direct taxation, to which their Order alone was subject. But by this time many of them, by delegating their powers to their neighbours, or through neglecting the royal summons, had lost the right of representation. Thus by the middle of the fifteenth century the right of sending two deputies to parliament belonged only to the cities of Burgos, Toledo, Leon, Seville, Córdova, Murcia, Jaen, Segovia, Zamora, Ávila, Salamanca and Cuenca, and the towns of Toro, Valladolid, Soria, Madrid and Guadalajara. Granada was added after the Conquest. The privileged municipalities successfully resisted any addition to their numbers. Large districts remained practically unrepresented; the little town of Zamora spoke in the name of the whole of Galicia. The Proctors were chosen among the municipal magistrates, by vote or lot according to local custom. In some towns the choice was restricted to certain families. At first the Proctors were merely mandataries commissioned to give certain answers to questions set forth in the royal summons. If further matters were proposed, they were obliged to refer to their electors. No law prescribed the interval at which Cortes should be called; but extraordinary supply was generally voted for three years, and at the end of that time parliament was summoned to vote a fresh supply. When the King was in no need of money and the succession was secured, the intervals were longer; no parliament met between 1482 and 1498. The time, place, number of sessions, and subjects for discussion were fixed by the King.

Cortes were general or particular, according as the three Estates, or the commons alone, were summoned. The three Orders deliberated separately. General Cortes met to take the oath of allegiance, and to receive confirmation of privileges. When supply was the only business, the commons alone attended. As exempt from taxation, the nobles and clergy finally ceased to attend after 1538. The King swore to maintain the liberties of his subjects only after receiving their oath of allegiance; nor was it till after voting supply that the commons presented their petition demanding redress of grievances, extension of privileges, and fulfilment of promises. The articles of these petitions ranged from the widest reforms to trivial local matters; they were severally granted, refused, or evaded by the King according to his own judgment or the advice of his Council. The only remedy of the Cortes was to refuse or reduce supply on the next occasion. In order to secure their subservience, the Kings sought to usurp the right of nominating Proctors; to dictate an unlimited commission in a prescribed form; to win over the Proctors themselves by bribes; and to impose an oath of secrecy with regard to their deliberations.

The Cortes had no legislative power. Their suggestions, if accepted by the King, at once became law. But the King was the sole lawgiver, and consent of parliament was not necessary to the validity of his decrees.

Besides being lawgiver, the King was the sole fountain of civil and criminal justice. His powers were delegated (1) to his Council, as supreme Court of Appeal; (2) to the *alcaldes de corte*, a judicial body, part of which held irregular assizes, while part accompanied the royal Court, superseding local tribunals; (3) to the Chancery, or Court of Appeal, of Valladolid (a second for Spain south of the Tagus was founded in 1494 and established at Granada, 1505; in the sixteenth century these *audiencias* or High Courts superseded the *adelantados* and *merinos*); (4) to the *corregidores*; (5) to municipal judges locally elected under the *fuero*. Besides these there existed ecclesiastical Courts partially independent of the Crown.

Since its feudal oligarchy had been broken down (1348) Aragon had enjoyed a constitution capable, under an energetic King, of securing

good government. It differed from that of Castile in its more aristocratic theory and more democratic, or rather oligarchic, practice. The
free population was divided into four Estates,—the clergy, the greater
nobility, the petty nobility, and the citizens or commons. Each of these
Orders was represented in parliament. The numbers of their deputies
varied; in 1518 we find the clergy with fifteen; the greater nobles (*ricos
homes*) with twenty-seven; the petty nobility (*infanzones*) with thirty-six;
and the commons with thirty-six. The parliament thus formed had far
greater power than that of Castile. Custom demanded that it should
meet every two years, and that the King should attend all its sessions.
Absolute unanimity was required to give validity to its decisions. It
exacted confirmation of liberties before swearing allegiance, and redress
of grievances before voting supply. So exorbitant did its claim seem
to the Castilian Isabel, as to cause her to declare that she would rather
conquer the country than suffer the affronts of its parliament. When
parliament was not sitting, its place was taken by a permanent
commission of two members of each Estate, which jealously watched
over the public liberties and the administration of the public moneys.
Below the four Estates stood the serfs of the Crown and of the nobles,
who formed the majority of the population. They were little more
than chattels, without legal or political privileges.

The *Justicia* was originally an arbiter between King and the nobles.
He afterwards came to be regarded as the personification and guardian
of the liberties of the Aragonese. He was appointed by the Crown, but
after the middle of the fifteenth century held office for life. His powers
consisted of the right of *manifestación*, or removal of an accused person
to his own custody until the decision of his case by the proper Court;
and of that of granting *firmas*, or protection of the property of litigants
until sentence was given. The office of *justicia*, the importance of which
has been greatly exaggerated, was similar to that of "inspector of
wrongs" among the Arabs. The municipal liberties were of high
significance. Some communities had the right of owning vassals and
administering public revenues, as well as that of jurisdiction. The
municipalities elected their magistrates, generally by lot; but privileges
differed locally, and in some districts the powers of the nobles were
almost unlimited.

The constitution of Catalonia bore traces of the ancient and close
connexion of this principality with France, and formed the most complete type of feudalism south of the Pyrenees. As such it resembled that
of Aragon more closely than that of Castile. The preponderance of the
nobles was very great, though the three Estates were represented in
parliament. The vassals remained in a condition of the harshest
serfdom, until it was ameliorated by John II in his struggle with the
nobles (1460–72). The "evil customs" under which they groaned were
finally swept away by King Ferdinand (1481).

Valencia at the time of its conquest in the thirteenth century received a constitution modelled on that of Catalonia. The land was shared among the great nobles : its Saracen cultivators became their vassals, and the main source of their wealth and power. In the towns a mixed and busy Christian population sprang up, drawn from Italy and France as well as from Catalonia and other provinces of Spain.

Of the three Basque provinces Biscay was a semi-independent principality until the end of the fourteenth century, when marriage made the King of Castile its *Señor*. Álava and Guipuzcoa were originally *behetrías*; the Kings of Castile became their overlords after the beginning of the thirteenth century. The former was incorporated as a province of Castile in 1332. While the local liberties of other provinces were sacrificed to the centralising policy of Ferdinand and Isabel, the Basques of Biscay and Guipuzcoa, owing partly to respect for tradition, and partly to the necessity of securing the loyalty of a frontier people, obtained the confirmation of their privileges and the right of self-government. Their contribution to the revenue was a " free gift " granted only after redress of grievances. In royal decrees they are called " a separate nation "; as such they upheld their freedom from direct taxation and their right of bearing arms,—the special marks of nobility. It is to be noted that certain Castilian towns enjoyed a similar privilege.

The first two years of Ferdinand and Isabel's reign were occupied by a war of succession. Many of the Castilian grandees, supported by the Kings of Portugal and France, maintained the claim of Juana, called *la Beltraneja*, whom Henry IV had acknowledged as his daughter and successor, but whose legitimacy was doubtful. Aragon took no share in the war; for in this kingdom Ferdinand had not yet succeeded his father. The Portuguese and the Castilian malcontents overran the western frontier, and seized Burgos and strong positions in the Douro valley. The battle of Toro (1476) put an end to the danger, and left leisure for reforms. During the two preceding reigns Castile had been given up to anarchy ; the municipalities had become almost independent; the nobles had usurped the privileges of royalty and devastated the country by their private wars. Centralisation, repression, and assertion of the supremacy of the Crown, were the remedies applied. The primary need was personal security. Outside the walls of the towns all men were at the mercy of the lawless nobility, or of robber bands. As far back as the thirteenth century the municipalities of Castile had formed leagues or " brotherhoods " for defence in time of war, or to resist encroachments by Kings or nobles. Isabel's first parliament (Madrigal, 1476) revived and generalised this practice by founding the Holy Brotherhood. Throughout Castile each group of a hundred houses furnished a horseman for the repression of crimes of violence in the open country and for the arrest of criminals who fled from the towns. Judges of the Brotherhood resided in all important towns and summarily tried offenders. Their sentences, of mutilation or death, were carried out by the troopers on the scene of the crime. The whole organisation was placed under a central assembly appointed by the municipalities, whose president was a bastard brother of King Ferdinand. The nobles at first objected to this curtailment of their right of exercising justice; but their opposition was overcome. A few years later the *Hermandad* was extended to Aragon. Lawlessness disappeared, and the 2,000 trained troops of the Brotherhood, together with its treasury, were made use of in the Conquest of Granada. So well had the Holy Brotherhood fulfilled its purpose, that within twenty years of its foundation it had become unnecessary. In 1492 the Cortes of Castile complained of its cost. The Crown hereupon took over its troops, and in 1495 it was reduced to the standing of a country constabulary; in Aragon it was abolished in 1510.

The resources of the Crown were outweighed by the enormous wealth and power of the nobility. The danger of a combination between the grandees had been proved by the War of Succession, when a mere section of them came near to imposing its will on the country. The reduction and humiliation of the whole Order was undertaken and made easy by its continual feuds. The grandees had wrested from Henry IV almost the whole of the royal patrimony, adding Crown lands to their own, trespassing upon common lands, and extorting huge pensions guaranteed upon the revenue. It was urgently necessary to set free the royal revenues; and in accomplishing this the Crown was sure of the support of the people, which groaned under the burden of taxation made necessary by the loss of these resources. As soon as Ferdinand and Isabel felt their position assured, they revoked the whole of the grants made by their predecessor (Cortes of Toledo, 1480). All titles were subjected to review, and only property held on ancient tenure, or as a reward for public service, was left to the nobles.

The power of the grandees was still excessive. One of its chief sources was the wealth of the Crusading Orders, at once military and religious, which had long neglected the vows of poverty and obedience, imposed at the time of their foundation in the latter half of the twelfth century. The purpose of that foundation itself, the work of reconquest, was wellnigh forgotten. The Grand Masterships conferred on their holders the independent command of an army, and the disposal of many rich commanderies; nor had they been wrongly called the chains and fetters of the Kings of Spain. Instead of crushing them, as the Templars had been crushed, Isabel took over their power. In 1476 she brought forward her husband for the Grand Mastership of Santiago. On this occasion she allowed the election to go against him; but afterwards, as vacancies occurred, he became successively Grand Master of Santiago, Alcántara and Calatrava. The Pope granted investiture on each occasion, with reversion to Isabel. Adrian VI (1523), and Clement VII (1530), attached the Grand Masterships perpetually to the Crown. The King gained the respect due to their semi-religious character, as well as their riches and authority.

Many of the great offices of State, such as those of Constable, Admiral and *Adelantado*, were hereditary. Shorn of their powers, these titles now became merely honorary in families of proved loyalty. The grandees were compelled to lay aside the insignia of royalty which they had usurped, and their mutinous spirit was checked by a few startling examples of royal justice. Their children were educated under the eye of the Queen, and learnt to respect the Crown. Careers were found for them in the Moorish and Italian wars or as officers of a stately Court. The class which had broken the power of Álvaro de Luna, deposed Henry IV, and disputed Isabel's succession, ceased in a few years to be formidable. Isabel revived the custom of administering justice in person. During a progress through Andalucia (1477) she stamped out the great factions whose wars had devastated the land. A royal commissioner, accompanied by an army, suppressed the lawlessness of Galicia, and razed the castles of its robber barons.

At the time of the War of Succession the only regular force at the disposal of the Crown was a bodyguard of 500 men-at-arms and 500 light horse. During the war against Granada this was increased, and received the addition of the trained troops of the Holy Brotherhood. The rest of the army was made up of feudal contingents and local militias, arrayed each under its own banner and commanded by district governors, Grand Masters, grandees, or captains chosen by the municipalities. The period for which these militias could be kept in the field was limited by law and by the scanty royal revenues. Accordingly, they could not be moved far from home, and wars were local in character. The burden as well as the reward of the Conquest of Granada fell chiefly to the Andalucians. At its close, a guard of 2500 horse was retained in the royal service, and the powerful force of artillery that had been brought together was carefully kept up. When the troops of the Holy Brotherhood were disbanded, this force was found insufficient, and the local militias were revived upon a better plan. The old law binding all citizens to provide themselves with arms according to their condition having fallen into disuse, a decree was promulgated (at Valladolid in 1496) declaring one-twelfth of the males between the ages of twenty and forty-eight liable to military service at home or abroad. Captains were appointed, and the militias were mustered and drilled on holidays. But victories abroad made soldiering popular, and volunteers in abundance were found to submit to the discipline and learn the new tactics of the Great Captain. The militia was neglected; taxation had taken the place of personal service, and the municipalities refused to bear a double burden.

The Castilian navy dates its origin from the Moorish Wars, when the Cantabrian sailors sailed round the coast and cooperated with the land forces. Together with the Catalans they were afterwards employed in stopping communications between the Moriscos and their African brethren. The connexion with Italy, Flanders and Africa, increased the importance of the service, and the convoys required by the trade of the Indies rapidly developed a formidable fleet.

The vast powers centred in the Crown were exercised through the royal Council. Originally a deliberative assembly of members of the royal family, prelates, and nobles, it was entirely reformed by Ferdinand and Isabel (1480). Its former members were not excluded, but their votes were taken from them, and their places supplied by lawyers nominated by the Crown. The president, generally a bishop, was the second person in the kingdom. The new Council was organised into departments, the chief of which were the Council of State, controlling the public forces and foreign affairs, and the Council of Castile, the supreme Court of justice, and the centre of the executive. The royal authority was no longer shared by grandees and prelates of noble rank; a professional class, midway between nobles and people, and entirely dependent on the Crown, had sprung up. The lawyers of the Council formed the real legislature; their education had steeped them in Roman law, and their efforts were directed to the unification and centralisation of authority. As the powers of the Council rose, those of the Cortes dwindled.

Over the clergy too the royal authority was extended, and the civil and the ecclesiastical power were united to such a degree, that the separation of Church and State even now remains inconceivable to Spaniards. The morals and discipline of the clergy had become much relaxed. Preferment in Spain was obtained by intrigues at Rome; and those who obtained it often neglected to visit their sees or benefices. Public opinion supported the Crown in its desire for reform. In 1476 the Cortes protested against the abuses of the ecclesiastical Courts, which usurped jurisdiction in civil matters and enforced their sentences by religious penalties. The enormous and ever-increasing estates held by the Church in mortmain had now come to be looked upon with jealousy and anxiety. The revenues of the great sees were immense; the Archbishops of Toledo and Santiago nominated the governors of their provinces. Little by little they were shorn of part of their wealth, and of the whole of their civil jurisdiction and military power. The annexation of the Grand Masterships of the Military Orders by the Crown weakened the Church as well as the nobles. At the same time the sees were filled by men of learning and piety, and ceased to be an appanage of the nobility. At Toledo the turbulent Archbishop Carillo was succeeded by the soldier and statesman Mendoza, known from his influence as "the Third King" (1483). The next Archbishop, the Franciscan Ximenes de Cisneros, though still a statesman and a warrior, was a crusader instead of a leader of faction, a prelate of saintly life, and a lover of learning, as is proved by his foundation (in 1508) of the University of Alcalá

23—2

(Complutum). By a diligent reform of the mendicant orders, he purified and strengthened the Church. In 1482 Ferdinand and Isabel wrested from the Pope the right of supplication in favour of their nominees to bishoprics. This right at a later date, Adrian VI, urged by Charles V, converted into one of presentation. In the kingdom of Granada and in the Indies, ecclesiastical patronage, together with part of the tithes, was reserved by the Crown. In 1493 a decree forbade the publication of bulls without the royal *exequatur*. In general, it may be noted that after the death of Isabel, the attitude of the Spanish Kings towards the papacy became more and more independent. Ferdinand and Charles, when opposed, openly threatened to break with Rome; and the latter obtained large assignments of ecclesiastical revenues. The Inquisition was an ecclesiastical instrument in the hands of the civil power; and when, in 1497, the Pope abandoned the right of hearing appeals, this power became supreme. Thus religious was added to civil despotism; indeed, the majority of Spanish clergy were always found to side with the King against the Pope.

The natural products of Spain are as varied as her climates, but her chief riches have always been cattle, corn, wine, and minerals. Cattle breeding was specially favoured by legislators, because of the ease with which its stock could be put beyond reach of invaders. Climate made a change of pasturage necessary in spring and autumn. So long as the land was thinly populated this was an easy matter. When agriculture became general, the rich owners of the migratory flocks formed a guild for the protection of their traditional rights, and obtained many privileges injurious to cultivators. The enclosure of waste lands was forbidden, and broad tracks were reserved, even through the richest valleys, to provide pasturage for the travelling flocks. In spring and after harvest they ranged at will through corn-lands and vineyards. Nevertheless, at the end of the fifteenth century Castile still exported corn, while Aragon, and even Valencia, in spite of the fabulous richness of its irrigated fields, were forced to import from the Balearic Islands and Sicily. In 1480 the export duty on food passing from Castile to Aragon was abolished. The result was a revival of agriculture, particularly in Murcia; but the flocks diminished, and the policy of protecting them was resumed. For many years the Spaniards in America, intent upon nothing but the finding of gold, imported the necessaries of life from the mother-country. Until 1529 the trade with the Indies was reserved exclusively to Seville, and the result was a great development of corn and wine growing in parts of Andalucia. But agriculture was ruined by the *alcabala*, a tax of one-tenth on all sales. Bread paid three times over, as corn, as meal, and as manufactured. To remedy this the *alcabala* was assessed at a fixed sum levied by districts (1494); but now a larger horizon was beginning to dawn, brilliant actions took place in the New World and in Italy, and agriculture still remained neglected. Gold began to b imported in large quantities, and prices trebled. The evil was further increased by disturbances among the industrious Moriscos, by bad seasons, and by the ruinous policy of fixing a maximum price, which still further depressed the greatest national industry and drove the country population to the towns, which overflowed with beggars.

Spain's position made her a natural half-way-house for sea-borne trade between the Mediterranean and Atlantic. Her exports were chiefly raw products—silk, fruit, and oil from the south; iron, wool, wine, and leather from the north. By prohibiting the export of gold and silver, and by the imposition of heavy export and import dues, it was sought to encourage manufactures and to prevent the necessity of buying back home products manufactured abroad. In spite of repeated protests of the Cortes, the settlement of foreign artisans was encouraged by the Kings. Manufactures, chiefly wool and silk, increased tenfold in the course of a century; the great fairs drew buyers from foreign lands; it seemed as though the inborn Spanish dislike of commerce and industry had been overcome. But the progress which thus manifested itself was not destined to endure. The Revolt of the *Comuneros*, to be noticed below, ultimately resulted in the partial ruin of a rising middle class; the most enterprising of the population emigrated as soldiers or settlers; and the great discoveries of precious metals in America raised prices to such a pitch that Spanish goods could no longer compete in foreign markets. A mistaken economic policy led to a neglect of the objects in favour of the means of exchange, and encouraged the accumulation of unproductive wealth. Nevertheless, a fictitious prosperity was for a time maintained. The period of Spain's greatest commercial energy falls within the reign of Charles I.

It has been supposed that Spanish population sank rapidly during the first half of the sixteenth century. The data on which this calculation was made have, however, been proved to be misleading. It is probable that population remained nearly stationary at about eight millions, or somewhat less than half its present amount.

Trade was hampered by a coinage made up of foreign pieces of various values, and of debased money issued from local and private mints. Ferdinand and Isabel asserted their exclusive right of minting, and established a high standard in their ducats (1476). These ducats were coined at the rate of $65\frac{1}{3}$ from a mark of gold of the standard of $23\frac{3}{4}$ carats. The silver coin of these sovereigns was the *real* (67 to the mark of silver, the standard being 67 parts out of 72). The *maravedi* ($\frac{1}{375}$ of the ducat) was the basis of calculation; there was, however, no actual coin of this value or name, but the *real* was worth 34 *maravedis*. In 1518 the money of Aragon was made uniform with that of Castile.

The chief sources of revenue were the dues and rents of the Crown lands, and the *alcabala*. The last-named, a tax of a tithe on all sales, was in 1494 commuted for a fixed sum assessed on districts. Isabel's will forbade alteration of its amount, but a new assessment was made in 1512. To these sources of revenue has to be added extraordinary supply,—the one direct impost. In Castile this amounted to 50 millions of *maravedis* yearly. Under Charles, an additional supply was demanded. The total supply received by the Crown of Aragon amounted to less than one-fifth of that received by the Crown of Castile, and the whole sum was less than a quarter of that produced by the *alcabala*. Customs-dues, the sale of indulgences under a constantly renewed Bull of Crusade, the revenues of the Grand Masterships, the tax of two-ninths on ecclesiastical tithes, and the King's fifth of the gold of the Indies, brought up the revenue at the beginning of Charles' reign to about 600 millions *maravedis*. Almost the whole of this was farmed by Jews and Genoese, and above all by the Fuggers. When it proved insufficient, fines were levied for a renewal of the assessment of the *alcabala*, and loans were raised at high rates of interest. The law forbidding alienation of the royal patrimony was constantly infringed. Charles sold royal and municipal offices, letters of naturalisation and legitimacy, and patents of nobility. Though the sum produced by the taxes increased thirtyfold within sixty years, the burdens on the people were not augmented in like proportion. Much alienated revenue was recovered; the value of gold sank to less than a third; industry and commerce had vastly increased. The exemption of the nobles and of certain districts and towns from direct taxation was, financially, not very important.

A source of much injustice was the lack of a recognised code of laws. Since the promulgation (1348) of the *Partidas* and *Ordenamiento de Alcalá* as supplementary to municipal law, a great number of statutes had been enacted, while others had fallen into disuse without being repealed. Isabel sought to remedy the confusion by ordering the scattered decrees to be collected and printed in the *Ordenamiento de Montalvo* (1485). But neither this nor a further collection (1503) proved satisfactory. Montalvo's book left many important matters doubtful, and the laws it contained were not faithfully transcribed. Isabel's will (1504) provided for the continuation of the work of unification. The result was the Laws of Toro (1505), a further attempt to reconcile conflicting legislation. The Cortes of 1523 still complained of the evil; nor was it remedied until the publication of the *Nueva Recopilación* (1567).

Under firm government the country recovered rapidly from its exhaustion, and reconquest was again taken in hand. For ten years (1481–91) it was carried on untiringly by the heroic resolution of Isabel and the stubborn valour of Ferdinand. In spite of disasters, like that of the Axarquía (1483), and obstinate resistance, like that of Baza (1489), and notwithstanding the enormous difficulties of transport, the slender resources of the Crown and the unserviceable nature of their feudal army, the kingdom of Granada fell piecemeal into the hands of the Catholic Kings. Owing to internal feuds and the treachery of the last of its Naserite dynasty, not more than half of its natural defenders were ranged at one time against the Christians. Some cities, like Malaga, were treated with great harshness, while others capitulated on favourable terms; for the victor was eager to press forward and it lay with him to decide whether or not he would be bound by his word. At last the city of Granada, isolated and helpless, submitted almost without a struggle (1492). The terms of capitulation included a guarantee of the lives and property of the citizens, with full enjoyment of civil and religious liberty, the right to elect magistrates to administer the existing laws, and exemption from increase of the customary taxation. Ferdinand thus sought to gain time to establish his authority over the excitable and still formidable population.

Even before the fall of Granada the problem of the alien races had presented itself. Living under the special protection of the Crown, the Jews in Spain, in spite of occasional massacres and repressive edicts, enjoyed great prosperity and were very numerous. They controlled finance, and had made their way even into the royal Council. The noblest families were not free from the taint of Jewish blood, and it was known that many professing Christians shared their beliefs. In 1478 a bull granted at the request of Ferdinand and Isabel established in Castile the Inquisition—a tribunal founded in the thirteenth century for the repression of heresy. Its object was now to detect and punish Jews who had adopted Christianity, but had afterwards relapsed. Two years of grace were allowed for recantation. In 1481 the Inquisition began its work at Seville; in 1483, in spite of protests on the ground of illegality, it was extended to Aragon, where the first Inquisitor, St Peter Arbues, was murdered in the cathedral of Saragossa (1485). Under the presidency of Torquemada (1482–94) the Inquisition distinguished itself by the startling severity of its cruel and humiliating *autos* and reconciliations.

Sixtus IV made several attempts (1482–3) to check the deadly work, but was obliged by pressure from Spain to deny the right of appeal to himself. The Inquisitors were appointed by the Crown, which profited by their ruthless confiscations. Their proceedings checked instead of promoting conversion, and a large body of professing Jews remained isolated and stubborn among the Christian population. Against these was turned the religious and national enthusiasm that greeted the fall of the last stronghold of the Infidel. The achievement of political unity made the lack of religious unity more apparent. It was rumoured that the Jews were carrying on an active propaganda; old calumnies were revived; they were accused of plotting against the State, of sacrificing Christian children, and of torturing and insulting the Host. In 1478 an edict expelled them from Seville and Córdova; the severest repressive measures were renewed in 1480; and in March, 1492, in spite of

Ferdinand's protest, the Jews of Castile were bidden to choose within four months between baptism and exile. On the strength of an existing law prohibiting the export of precious metals, they were stripped of a great part of their wealth, and many hundred thousands quitted Spain. The treasury seized their abandoned property; but Spain was the poorer for the loss of a thrifty and industrious population. The work of the Inquisition now increased. Many of the exiles returned as professing Christians, while many suspected families of converts had been left behind. Pedigrees were subjected to the closest scrutiny; not even the highest position in the Church, or the most saintly life, secured those whose blood was tainted from cruel persecution. Even if their faith was beyond suspicion, they were made social outcasts. Statutes as to purity of blood excluded them, in spite of the protests of the Church, at first from universities, Chapters, and public offices, and later even from religious Congregations and trade guilds. Torquemada died in 1498; but the persecution went on until Córdova rose against the fierce and fanatical Lucero (1506–7). Ximenes became Grand Inquisitor (1507), and the tribunal became less savage, while its sphere of activity widened. At the beginning of the century the baptised Saracens had been placed under its authority. When Islam was proscribed throughout Castile (1502), the Inquisition stamped out its last embers, by methods hardly less rigorous than those directed against the Jews; afterwards, it was employed to further absolutism in Church and State. Such are the passions roused by the very name of the Inquisition, that it is difficult to judge its work. The Jesuit Mariana, a bold and impartial critic, calls it " a present remedy given by Heaven against threatened ills." He admits, however, that the cure was a costly one; that the good name, life, and fortune of all lay in the hands of the Inquisitors; that its visitation of the sins of fathers upon children, its cruel punishments, its secret proceedings, and prying methods caused universal alarm; and that its tyranny was regarded by many as " worse than death."

For nearly eight years after its conquest the kingdom of Granada was ruled with firmness and moderation by its Captain-general, the Count of Tendilla, and by Talavera, Archbishop of the newly-created see. The capitulation had been respected; men's minds were reassured; and many, who had at first preferred exile to submission, had returned. Talavera, a man of earnest but mild temper, devoted all his energies to the conversion of the Muslims; he secured their confidence and respect, and, by encouraging the study of Arabic, partly broke down the barrier of language. Already the results of his good work were apparent, when his persuasive and forbearing policy was abandoned.

To the religious advisers of the Queen the results attained seemed paltry: shocked at what they considered a stubborn rejection of evident truths, they regarded the respect shown to the religious and social peculiarities of the Muslims as impious trafficking with evil, while the salvation of thousands was at stake. Ximenes shared the fanaticism of his age and country. Having obtained a commission to aid the Archbishop in his work, he assembled the Muslim doctors, harangued, flattered, and bribed them till many received baptism (1499). Still unsatisfied, he adopted more violent measures. He began to ill-treat the descendants of renegades and to tear their children from them; he imprisoned the more obstinate of his opponents, and confiscated and publicly burned all books treating of their religion. A savage revolt within the city was quelled only by the influence of the Captain-general and the Archbishop. Ximenes, when recalled to Court to be reprimanded for his high-handed action, succeeded in winning over the Queen to his views. A commission was sent to punish a revolt provoked by the infraction of guaranteed rights. It was evident that the capitulation was no longer to be respected, and while thousands, cowed but unconvinced, received baptism, others quitted Spain for Africa. The districts round Granada showed none of the submissive spirit of the city. On hearing of the injustice done to their fellow-countrymen the mountaineers of the Alpujarras revolted, and the Count of Tendilla, with Gonzalo de Córdova, then a young soldier, undertook a difficult and dangerous campaign in an almost inaccessible region. In the spring of 1500 Ferdinand himself assumed the command, and the rebellion was crushed out by irresistibly superior forces. Each little town perched upon its crag had to be stormed. Men taken with arms in their hands were butchered as rebels; the survivors were punished by enormous fines, and cajoled or forced to receive baptism.

No sooner was this rising repressed, than a still more formidable one broke out in the Sierra Bermeja on the western side of the kingdom. Christians were tortured and murdered, and the alarm was increased by the belief that the rebels were in communication with Africa. A splendid force, hastily raised in Andalucia, marched into the fastnesses of the mountains; but, becoming entangled among passes where the heavy-armed horsemen were helpless, it was nearly exterminated at Rio Verde (March, 1501). The rebels, however, were terrified by their success; the revolt spread no further; and when Ferdinand hurried to Ronda, prepared for a campaign, they sued for peace. Again the choice between baptism and exile was offered, and thousands quitted the country.

In July, 1501, the whole kingdom of Granada was declared to be Christian; and the only Muslim element left within the realms of Castile consisted of small groups settled in cities even as far north as Burgos and Zamora, under the protection of the Crown. These Mudéjares were now forbidden to communicate with their newly converted brethren of the south. Six months later, all who refused to become Christians were banished. In Aragon and Valencia the Mudéjares were allowed, for a time, the private exercise of their religion.  The harsh treatment of the Saracens seemed justified by fear of their numbers and of their intrigues with the African corsairs.  They sank into a state of serfdom, being left dependent for protection upon the landowners who throve on their industry.  Even so they clung to their faith, and the Inquisition found a hundred years insufficient for rooting it out.  The results of intolerance are still to be traced in the wide wastes, once rich in corn, vine, and olive, of central and southern Spain.  While the rest of the land had been won back in a half-ruined and desolate state, Granada was seized in full prosperity, but even she was not spared.

Profiting by the eagerness of the King of France to settle outstanding differences before invading Italy, Ferdinand in 1493 recovered by negotiation the counties of Roussillon and Cerdagne, which had been pledged by his father to Louis XI.

In 1494, following the traditions of the Crown of Aragon, he began actively to interfere in European politics by forming the League of Venice for the purpose of driving the French out of Italy.  A period of peace followed the death of Charles VIII (1498).  When the War was resumed the Crown of Naples was added by the Great Captain, Gonzalo de Córdova, to those of Castile, Aragon and Sicily (1503).  The New World had been discovered, but its supreme importance was misunderstood; Spain was embarked upon the current of European politics, which was to drag her to her ruin.  Defeated in Italy and baffled in negotiation, the French King decided to carry the war into the enemy's country.  In the autumn of 1503 two armies set out to invade Spain, one through the western passes of the Pyrenees, and the other, supported by a fleet, through the eastern.  The former never reached its destination.  The latter entered Roussillon unopposed; but wasted time in besieging the castle of Salsas near Perpignan, until Ferdinand marched to its relief.  The French retreated to Narbonne without fighting.  The loss of the fleet in a storm completed the disaster of the French, and a humiliating peace ended the War.

In 1496 were negotiated the marriages which eventually gave the Crown of Spain to the House of Austria.  Juan, only son of Ferdinand and Isabel, married Margaret, daughter of Maximilian, Archduke of Austria and King of the Romans.  His sister, Juana, married Maximilian's son Philip the Fair, who had inherited (1493) from his mother, the Netherlands, Flanders, Artois, and Franche-Comté.  The death of the Infante Juan left his sister, Isabel, Queen of Portugal, heiress apparent to the throne of Castile (1497).  By her death (1498) and that of her infant son (1500) the hope of the union of the whole Peninsula under one Crown was defeated.  The succession fell to Juana and her husband Philip.  From the first their marriage had been an unhappy one.  Philip gave his wife abundant cause for jealousy, and repressed her violent outbreaks by making her a prisoner within her palace.  Her mind became disordered, and she soon showed signs of the intermittent insanity which later overtook her.  It became necessary for Juana and Philip to visit Spain to receive the oath of allegiance as heirs to the Crown.  But Philip delayed till the end of the year 1501, and caused additional displeasure by seeking the friendship of Louis XII and doing formal homage to him as he passed through France.  The Cortes of Castile swore allegiance to Juana and her husband at Toledo (1502).  The Cortes of Aragon, which had previously refused to acknowledge her sister Isabel, alleging that females were excluded from the succession, now took the usual oath.  At the beginning of 1503 Philip quitted Spain, leaving his wife with her parents.  He again passed through France, and concluded a peace with King Louis.  But this peace Ferdinand, on hearing news of the victories of the Great Captain, repudiated, alleging that Philip had exceeded his instructions.  The War in Italy went on as before.

After the birth of Ferdinand, her second son, Juana's insanity increased.  In March, 1504, she quitted Spain against her mother's will, leaving her in feeble health.  Isabel was broken by long years of toil, and by family sorrows.  She died of dropsy at the end of the year.  The character of the great Queen is well described in the simple words of Guicciardini : "a great lover of justice, most modest in her person, she made herself much loved and feared by her subjects.  She was greedy of glory, generous, and by nature very frank."  Her will named Juana as her successor; but a codicil directed "that Don Fernando should govern the realm during the absence of Queen Juana, and that if, on her arrival, she should be unwilling or unable to govern, Don Fernando should govern."  Ferdinand proclaimed Juana and Philip, and undertook the regency; but Isabel's death marks the beginning of a period of anarchy which lasted until Charles established his rule (1523).

The year 1505 was spent in plots and counter-plots.  Philip, supported by a strong party in Spain, attempted to drive out Ferdinand.  Instigated by Don Juan Manuel, he intrigued with Gonzalo de Córdova, and with the King of France.  Ferdinand, on his side, was ready to sacrifice the union of Spain to private ambition : his first plan was to marry and revive the claims of Princess Juana, *la Beltraneja.*  When this failed, he married Germaine de Foix, niece to the King of France (October, 1505).  King Louis made over to her as dowry his claims on the disputed portions of the kingdom of Naples, with reversion to the French Crown should the union prove childless.  In this way Ferdinand broke up the dangerous alliance between Louis, Philip, and Maximilian; but he also alienated from his cause a large portion of the Castilians, who regarded his hasty marriage as an insult to the memory of their Queen.  At the same time Philip's agents in Spain were undermining Ferdinand's authority, and had won over many of the nobles of Andalucia; for he was still regarded as a foreigner in the land which he had so long ruled, and his harsh, suspicious and niggardly nature increased his unpopularity.

By the Treaty of Salamanca (November, 1505) it was agreed that Ferdinand, Juana, and Philip should rule jointly, and divide the revenues and patronage. In the following spring Philip was obliged by stress of weather to land at Corunna. It had been his intention to sail round to Seville and collect his partisans, since neither party meant to abide by the agreement. Ferdinand hastened to meet his son-in-law; but Philip evaded an interview, for every day more grandees joined him, and he would soon be able to dictate his own terms. When the meeting actually took place (June), Ferdinand's following was reduced to three or four old friends, and he was compelled to declare that, owing to Juana's infirmity, her interference would be disastrous to the kingdom. In consideration of a pension he gave up the regency, and sulkily withdrew into Aragon with his young wife, and otherwise unaccompanied, "holding it unworthy to exercise delegated powers in realms over which he had been absolute King." He was welcomed by the Aragonese, who rejoiced to have shaken off the union with the preponderating power of Castile. Shortly afterwards he sailed for Naples, where the conduct of Gonzalo de Córdova had excited his suspicions.

In July Philip met the Castilian Cortes at Valladolid. Aided by Ximenes, he attempted to have his wife declared incapable of governing; but he was successfully opposed by a party led by the Admiral of Castile. Juana was acknowledged as Queen in her own right, Philip as King by right of marriage, and their infant son Charles as heir to the throne. Acting in his wife's name, Philip hereupon conferred the offices of State and wardenships of the royal castles on members of his own party. The malcontents began to draw together to liberate the Queen, whom they believed to be sane and a prisoner in the hands of her husband. The threatened rebellion was, however, for the moment arrested, and Philip was called away northward to watch the frontier. He evaded the danger of invasion by means of a treaty with the French King, from which Ferdinand was excluded. In September, 1506, Philip died suddenly at Burgos leaving Spain in a ferment of rival factions. Within Castile no authority existed; for Juana refused to act. The grandees nominated Ximenes with six members of the Council to carry on the regency until the guardianship of the infant heir to the throne should be decided. They summoned the Cortes; but their summons was disregarded as unconstitutional. Ferdinand had already reached Italy, when the news overtook him. He sent a commission to Ximenes to carry on the government during his absence. On his return to Spain (July, 1507) he crushed the party, headed by Juan Manuel, which supported the claim of Maximilian to act as regent for his daughter-in-law and grandson. Ferdinand's position was a strong one, for the event foreseen in Isabel's will had come to pass: Juana, wandering from village to village with the weird procession that bore her husband's corpse, stubbornly refused to sign papers of State. Most of the Flemish party fled; then Burgos and Jaen, held for a time in Maximilian's interest, submitted, and "calm fell upon Castile"; for the majority welcomed the prospect of speedy repression of the disorder which had broken out during Ferdinand's absence. After a meeting with Juana, who refused to lend herself to his schemes by marrying Henry of England, he gave out that she had resigned the government to him, and thus remained undisputed master of the kingdom. Ferdinand showed no wish to avenge himself upon those who had driven him with ignominy from the kingdom, but bore himself ruthlessly towards those who now questioned his authority. Don Juan Manuel had fled. The Duke of Nágera refused to deliver up his fortresses; but, when an army was sent against him, he submitted, and his lands and titles were given to his eldest son. At Córdova the Marquis of Priego revolted. Ferdinand called out all Andalucia to crush him. He threw himself on the King's mercy, but was condemned to death. The interest of the Great Captain, his kinsman, availed only to obtain a commutation of his sentence to confiscation, fine and banishment.

Although the suspicions against him were probably groundless, the Great Captain felt the weight of Ferdinand's jealousy. They had returned from Italy together, and Ferdinand had shown him all deference and had promised him the Grand Mastership of Santiago. But the promise was never fulfilled; he was treated with marked coolness, and withdrew to his estates near Loja, where he ended his days in haughty and magnificent retirement. Once only—after the battle of Ravenna (1512), when it was believed that he alone could save Spain's possessions in Italy, he received a commission to enlist troops. Thousands had already joined his banner, when the danger passed away, and Ferdinand, alarmed and jealous, withdrew his commission.

The Barbary pirates not only rendered the sea unsafe, but acting in concert with the Moriscos, made frequent descents upon the Spanish coast, spreading terror and devastation far inland. In 1505, at the instigation of Ximenes, Mers-el-Kebir, one of their strongholds, had been captured. The disturbed condition of Spain made it impossible immediately to follow up this success, but Ximenes had not lost sight of his policy of African conquest. A war against the Infidel always stirred the crusading spirit of the Spaniards, and Ferdinand saw in it a way of turning public attention from late events. In 1508 a small expedition under Pedro Navarro captured Peñon de la Gomera. In the following year a larger one was prepared. Ximenes lent money out of the vast revenues of his see, and himself accompanied the army of 14,000 men to Oran (May, 1509). The city was captured, and many Christian captives were set free; but the glory of the victory was stained by a brutal massacre of unarmed inhabitants. Within a month Ximenes was back in

Spain.  He had quarrelled with Pedro Navarro, the general in command of
the expedition, and was moreover alarmed by reports that Ferdinand was
plotting to deprive him of his archbishopric in favour of his illegitimate
son, the Archbishop of Saragossa.  Pedro Navarro remained behind, and
in a few months effected a series of brilliant conquests.  Bugia fell after
a siege; Algiers and Tlemcen surrendered; Tripolis was stormed.  Grown
overbold, Navarro fell into an ambuscade among the sandhills of the
waterless island of Gelves; the greater part of his army perished;
and the tide of Spanish conquest in Africa was stayed for a time
(August, 1510).

The recovery of Roussillon and Cerdagne gave Ferdinand command of
the eastern passes of the Pyrenees; but Spanish unity was still incomplete, while the kingdom of Navarre lying astride of the western end
of the range held the keys of Spain.  Torn by the continual wars of
her two great factions, the Beaumonts and Grammonts, and crushed by
the neighbourhood of more powerful States, Navarre could not hope to
preserve her independence.  She was, moreover, ruled by a feeble
dynasty that had not taken root in the soil.  Navarre had belonged to
Ferdinand's father in right of his first wife, but had passed by right
of marriage to her great-grandson François Phébus Count of Foix, and,
later, to his sister Catherine.  Ferdinand sought to secure the prize
by marrying his son to Catherine.  The scheme was frustrated by
her mother Madeleine, sister of Louis XII; and Catherine married
Jean d'Albret, a Gascon nobleman whose large estates lay on the border
of Lower Navarre.  Nevertheless Ferdinand found means of frequently
interfering in the affairs of his neighbours.  He protected the Beaumont
faction and the dynasty against King Louis, who supported the claims
of a younger branch of the House of Foix, represented first by the
Viscount of Narbonne, and later by Gaston Phébus, brother of Ferdinand's second wife.

In 1511 Pope Julius II, the Emperor, the Venetians, Ferdinand, and
Henry VIII of England formed the Holy League for the purpose of
crushing France.  Bent on his scheme of recovering Guyenne Henry sent
an army to Guipuzcoa to cooperate with the Spaniards (1512).  Ferdinand's opportunity had now come.  He demanded a free passage for his
troops through Navarre, and the surrender of fortresses as a guarantee of
neutrality.  Jean d'Albret tried to evade compliance by allying himself
with the French.  Ferdinand retaliated by a manifesto declaiming
against his faithlessness and ingratitude, and by ordering the Duke
of Alva to invade Navarre (July, 1512).  Five days later the Spaniards,
aided by the Beaumontais, encamped before Pamplona, and Jean d'Albret
fled to seek help from the French army encamped near Bayonne.
Pamplona surrendered on receiving guarantees of its liberties, which it
held dearer than its foreign dynasty.

Failing to get help from the French, Jean d'Albret, though his capital was already in the enemy's hands, attempted negotiation, professing his readiness to accept any terms that might be dictated. Ferdinand, however, insisted on his claim to hold Navarre until he should complete his holy enterprise against France. Most of the Navarrese towns and fortresses now surrendered; Tudela was besieged by the Aragonese under the Archbishop of Saragossa. Early in August Ferdinand renewed his promise to give up the kingdom at the end of the war. His messenger was seized and imprisoned, and on the 21st of the month he published at Burgos the bull *Pater ille coelestis*, excommunicating all who resisted the Holy League, and declaring their lands and honours forfeited to those who should seize them. Although Jean d'Albret and Catherine were not named, the bull specially mentioned the Basques and Cantabrians, and dread of its threats brought about the surrender of the few places that still held out in Upper Navarre. Ferdinand now threw off the mask and took the title of King of Navarre. Meanwhile Alva had crossed the mountains, and summoned the Marquis of Dorset from his camp near San Sebastian to aid in the conquest of Lower Navarre. The English, however, declared that they had come to conquer not Navarre but Guyenne; and since it was now too late in the year for that purpose they sailed home after plundering a small part of the frontier. A French army advanced against Alva, who recrossed the mountains without fighting and shut himself up in Pamplona. But, after two fierce assaults, the French in turn withdrew on the approach of Spanish reinforcements. The whole of Upper Navarre and the district of Ultrapuertos north of the mountains remained in Ferdinand's hands. In 1513 the Navarrese Cortes swore allegiance to him, and the French King abandoned his allies by concluding a truce. Navarre was incorporated with Castile (1515); Ultrapuertos was however afterwards abandoned on account of the expense of keeping up an outpost beyond the mountains (1530).

The last three years of Ferdinand's life were uneventful, so far as Spain is concerned. Although he was involved in the tangled skein of alliances and plots by which the fate of Italy was decided, his interest in politics was no longer active. His chief anxiety was to leave a son to succeed to his patrimony. One had been born of his second marriage, but had died shortly after birth. Although he was eager to become a father once more, he was not destined to undo his life's work,—Spanish unity. He fell ill (1513), and with the restlessness of a dying man, wandered through the mountain villages of Castile pursuing his favourite occupation of hunting. A strong Spanish party, led by Don Juan Manuel and supported by France, still opposed him, scheming in favour of Maximilian's claim to govern Spain as regent for his grandson. King Ferdinand held them in check, and set up against Charles his younger brother Ferdinand, who had been brought up in Spain and was now regarded as the probable successor to the united Crowns, or, at least, to that of Aragon.  In 1515 King Ferdinand visited Aragon for the last time, and held Cortes at Calatayud.  His arbitrary temper had grown upon him, and, when supply was refused, he struck a last fierce blow at his country's liberties by angrily dismissing the deputies and imprisoning their president.  When his end was known to be near (September, 1515) the Flemish party sent to Adrian of Utrecht to act in the name of his former pupil, the Infante Charles.

King Ferdinand died in the village of Madrigalejo (January, 1516) leaving behind him a reputation for political wisdom, astonishing when it is remembered that he was an unlettered man.  But it was his unscrupulousness that left the deepest mark upon the age.  During Isabel's lifetime he had screened his grasping policy behind her religious enthusiasm, and had used her haughty and upright spirit as an instrument for attaining his selfish ends.  He had never sought to be loved, and after her death his character stood revealed in its native harshness.  "No reproach attaches to him," says Guicciardini, "save his lack of generosity and his faithlessness to his word."  Shortly before his death he revoked a will which favoured his younger grandson and namesake, and now bequeathed to him only a pension so modest as to preclude all chance of rivalry with his brother.  He left the Crowns of Aragon and the two Sicilies to his daughter Juana, Queen of Castile, appointing her son Charles regent in her name.  To Ximenes he entrusted the government of Castile, and to his bastard son, the Archbishop of Saragossa, that of Aragon.

Ximenes, although more than eighty years old, undertook the charge with his wonted energy.  Acting under instructions from Flanders, and disregarding the protests of the Castilians, he proclaimed Charles as King conjointly with his mother (May, 1516).  He reformed the household of Queen Juana, who had been ill-treated by a brutal governor. He fixed the seat of government at Madrid, on account of its central position.  He secured the person of the Infante Ferdinand, whose discontent was being fomented by interested advisers.  By sheer force of character he set aside Adrian of Utrecht, who had been sent to share the regency. He revoked all grants of lands and pensions made since Isabel's death; when a commission of grandees waited upon him to enquire by virtue of what power he had taken this step, he pointed to the artillery massed below his palace.

Not content with the regular forces of the Crown, he attempted to revive in more efficient form the old militia, and sent commissioners to enrol a force of 31,000 men.  Exemption from taxation was promised to all who gave in their names.  A certain number in each district were to be armed and drilled, and to receive pay when called out.  The nobles took alarm, and stirred up the municipalities to resist what was represented as a new burden and an encroachment on their liberties. Valladolid and other cities rose in revolt, and forwarded a protest to

Charles in Flanders. The matter was ordered to stand over until his arrival. Four years later, the municipalities had reason to regret their lack of military organisation.

Thinking to profit by the unsettled state of Spain Jean d'Albret invaded Navarre and laid siege to St Jean Pied-de-Port. He was supported by native exiles, who broke in through the pass of Roncal, hoping for a rising within the country. They were met before effecting a junction with the King, and were utterly defeated (March, 1516). Jean d'Albret gave up the enterprise; he died three months later, leaving his claims to his son Henri. Ximenes began to fortify Pamplona as a stronghold for the Castilian garrison, while he dismantled a number of outlying castles which might give protection to invaders.

In pursuit of his policy of African conquest Ximenes sent an expedition against Algiers, which had been seized by Barbarossa, the famous renegade corsair (September, 1516). In consequence of the incapacity of its leader, the expedition met with a crushing defeat, and was almost annihilated.

Ximenes' schemes were everywhere thwarted by Charles' Flemish councillors. With their chief, William de Croy, Seigneur de Chièvres, he had tried unsuccessfully to establish a good understanding. Flemish interests required alliance with France, and in pursuit of this object they were ready to sacrifice Spanish interests in Italy and Navarre. For a time they were successful. By the Treaty of Noyon (October, 1516) Charles became betrothed to Francis' infant daughter, promising to satisfy the claims of the Albrets in Navarre and to give up Queen Germaine's dowry. Moreover, a growing feeling of discontent was provoked in Spain by the shameless traffic in Spanish offices of dignity and profit carried on by Flemish courtiers. The grandees, who writhed under Ximenes' strong hand, flocked with their complaints to Flanders and obtained a ready hearing. The people were persuaded that Juana was sane and shut out from her rights by a cruel plot. Ximenes, surrounded by difficulties, wrote repeatedly urging Charles to come to Spain, and warning him of the rising discontent of the municipalities. At last, in September, 1517, Charles landed on the Asturian coast. He was only seventeen years old; his health was delicate; and his diffidence had been increased by his being brought up under such masterful spirits as Chièvres and his aunt Margaret. He found himself in a strange country seething with half-repressed rebellion; he could not speak a word of Spanish. The grandees hastened to welcome the King; but access to his presence was barred by the Flemings. Ximenes too journeyed northward to meet the prince whom he had so manfully served. He wished before his death to explain the policy by which the mutinous spirit of Castile might be appeased and the anarchy of Aragon quelled. The Flemings, foreseeing that their influence would be at an end, if Charles fell under the influence of the Cardinal's powerful will, did their utmost to prevent a meeting. Ximenes was accordingly checked by a letter in which Charles thanked him for his services and invited him to an interview, after which he was ordered to retire to his diocese and take such rest as his health demanded. Ximenes did not survive his political downfall. His death (November 8) left Spain entirely in the hands of the foreigners, among whom his honours were speedily divided. Adrian was made Cardinal, Chièvres became chief minister of the Crown; his youthful nephew, William de Croy, Archbishop of Toledo; and Jean le Sauvage, Chancellor. Ximenes' policy had been directed to assure the supremacy of the Crown while giving to the people such rights and cohesion as should balance the power of the nobles. He had also attempted to found a Spanish empire in Africa. The latter scheme was intermittently prosecuted after his death; but its special importance was lost sight of amid dreams of universal empire. The natural development of the political rights of the people was checked, and their hardly-won municipal liberties were crushed, in the struggles that followed. Charles aimed from the first at the absolute power which in the end swallowed up the liberties of nobles and commons alike.

After a brief visit to his mad mother at Tordesillas, where she passed fifty years of her life, Charles made a triumphal entry into Valladolid (November, 1517). Here, in the following spring, the Castilian Cortes assembled. The grandees were disgusted to find that all favours fell to foreigners. The sessions opened stormily; for Spanish jealousy had been aroused by the appointment of a Fleming to preside in conjunction with the Bishop of Badajoz, a known ally of the foreign party. Two legal assessors watched the proceedings on behalf of the Crown. The commons had hoped to profit by the inexperience of the prince in order to extend their rights. Led by Dr Zumel, proctor of Burgos, they adopted a haughty tone, reminded Charles of his duties as King and actually addressed him as "our hireling." They claimed, contrary to custom, that he should swear to observe their liberties before receiving the oath of allegiance, and should hear petitions before they granted supply. Charles submitted to the former demand, and was acknowledged as sovereign in conjunction with his mother. This was a disappointment; for he had hoped to rule alone. The Cortes voted a supply of somewhat more than the usual amount, spread over three years. In answer to a long list of petitions, the King promised to learn to speak Spanish; to forbid illegal exportation of gold and silver; to grant no further offices or letters of naturalisation to foreigners; to keep his brother in Spain till the succession should be assured; not to alienate Crown property; and not to give up Navarre.

Charles then hurried on to hold Cortes at Saragossa. The Aragonese proved more stubborn. Freed from Ferdinand's strong hand, the nobles had shaken off all respect for the Crown, and moreover, Charles was thoroughly distrusted. Regardless of his late promises, he had sent his brother Ferdinand to Flanders, and, on the death of Jean le Sauvage, had appointed another foreign Chancellor (Arborio de Gattinara). The Aragonese first disputed Charles' right to call Cortes; they next demanded proof of Juana's incapacity; and when, finally, they consented to acknowledge him as King in conjunction with her, they insisted on declaring that, if she should recover, she alone would be Queen in Aragon. Charles was forced to adopt a submissive attitude; he sought to win over the people by breaking down the usurped privileges of the nobles; but it cost him eight months, and he had to undergo many affronts, before he could obtain a grant of money so small that it was insufficient for paying his expenses. In order to replenish the treasury, the supply voted by the Castilians was farmed; offices were sold; and the Inquisition was urged to ruthless confiscation. The tide of discontent rose higher than ever.

At Barcelona objection was again taken to swearing the oath of allegiance to Charles during his mother's lifetime. Only after ten months were bribery and flattery able to break down opposition and elicit a moderate grant. Charles was preparing to meet the Parliament of Valencia (January, 1520), when news was brought of his election as King of the Romans in succession to his grandfather Maximilian. The report that the King was about to quit Spain roused the indignation against him to the highest pitch. The Castilian cities were jealous of the time he had spent in Aragon and Catalonia, haggling to obtain small supplies, while loyal Castile, which had voted an extra sum, was neglected. There was now reason to fear that Spain would sink to the level of a mere province of the Empire. Already in November, Toledo had sent a circular letter to the cities possessing votes in the Cortes, urging them to combine in order to prevent the departure of the King, the export of gold, and government by foreigners. Some made no reply; others, like Salamanca, joined eagerly in the protest. A commission was appointed to lay before Charles the demands of the kingdom, whereupon he sent to Toledo a new and more energetic *corregidor* to check the spirit of mutiny. Wishing to obtain money and at the same time to tranquillise the public mind by explanations and promises, he summoned Parliament to meet him at Santiago de Compostela (February, 1520). As he hurried northward, he was overtaken at Valladolid by the commissioners from Toledo and Salamanca, who insisted, in spite of his orders, on fulfilling their charge. He bade them follow the Court until he could find time to attend to them. A report that Queen Juana was to be carried out of the country provoked a riot and a rash attempt to check the King's departure from Valladolid. The cruelty with which these excesses were avenged still further irritated the people. At Villalpando the promised audience was granted to the commissioners of the cities; but Charles was in no mood for yielding. He harshly bade them await the meeting of Parliament to lay their wishes before him. Meanwhile the

24—2

Court party was doing its utmost to secure submissive deputies. A royal decree directed that an unlimited commission should be given to the proctors according to a prescribed form. Toledo refused to comply; her proctors were instructed merely to hear and report on the proposals of the King. Other cities, while granting a commission in the prescribed form, limited it by secret instructions to resist all demands for money.

It was amid the gloomiest forebodings that the Cortes met at Santiago (March, 1520). The selection of a place so far removed from the centre of Spain was suspicious; even if promises were wrung from the departing King, their fulfilment was unlikely: at such a distance from their electors deputies might easily be bribed or intimidated. The chief cause of complaint, however, was the demand for further supply, while the grant of 1518 had still a year to run. An attempt was made to soothe irritation by the appointment of a Spanish president; and a conciliatory speech from the throne was read by the Bishop of Badajoz in the presence of Charles himself. Toledo was unrepresented, having refused to grant the prescribed commission; the deputies of Salamanca were excluded for refusing to take the oath before petitions had been heard. The nobles, disgusted at their exclusion from the royal favour, had quitted the Court. Charles hurried on to Corunna, in order to be able to embark at a moment's notice and reach England (April). The remaining deputies followed, and were cajoled and threatened until, by a narrow majority, they voted a supply of 300 millions of *maravedis*. They petitioned for a Spanish regent; for the speedy return of the King; for the better administration of justice; against the nomination of deputies by the Crown, and the exaction of unlimited commissions; that the Cortes should meet every three years; that the summons should contain a list of the matters to be discussed; and that deputies should be compelled to render an account to their electors within a stated time. Most of these petitions were refused, or left unanswered; the Cortes were dismissed; and in May Charles set sail, leaving nobles and people equally discontented. Adrian of Utrecht was appointed by him regent in his absence.

The return of the deputies from Corunna was the signal for rioting in many cities. Some who had voted supply contrary to instructions were murdered by the mob. Led by Toledo, the cities, from Leon to Murcia and from Burgos to Jaen, formed a league under the name of the Santa Comunidad, and expelled their *corregidores* to the cry of "Long live the King; down with the bad ministers!" Ávila was chosen on account of its central position as the meeting-place of their Junta (July, 1520), which included nobles and ecclesiastics as well as commons. It began by declaring itself independent of the Regent and Council, and organising the levies of the cities under the command of Juan de Padilla, a nobleman of Toledo. Adrian's attempts to check the revolt were feeble and unsuccessful. A small body of troops, sent with Ronquillo, a judge of notorious severity, to punish Segovia, where the outbreak had been specially violent, was easily beaten off. An attempt made by Fonseca, one of the royal captains, to seize the artillery which Ximenes had kept in readiness at Medina del Campo, not only failed, but resulted in the destruction by fire of the town, one of the richest in Spain. Adrian was obliged to disband Fonseca's army and disavow his action. A more serious blow to the royal cause followed. Padilla seized Tordesillas, and with it the person of Queen Juana (August 29). The Santa Junta now removed to Tordesillas, and proclaimed that the Queen was sane and approved its actions. Valladolid, the seat of the regency, was captured; some members of the royal Council were imprisoned; others, among them Adrian himself, fled (October 18). The Great Seal of the kingdom and the State papers fell into the hands of the rebels. Led by Adrian, who despaired from the first, the friends of Charles in Spain wrote to him that all was lost, unless he returned at once and came to terms with the *Comuneros.* But Charles never yielded. His cause was aided more by the incapacity of its opponents than by the energy of the royalists. Instead of setting up a government in the place of that which it had overthrown, the Junta continued to declare its loyalty; unable to conceive any authority other than that of the monarchy, it wasted its time in trying to persuade the imbecile Queen to confirm its acts. Juana had received its members, when they broke into Tordesillas, with some show of favour; but her steady refusal to sign documents was not to be shaken. The main theory of the revolution—that the Queen was sane, and that her faithful commons were to deliver her and shake off the hated yoke of the foreigner—had broken down. Juana's obstinacy acted as a physical obstacle. Disheartened and irresolute, the Junta betook itself to the only other source of legitimate authority, and sent a deputation to Flanders to assure the King of its loyalty and beg confirmation of its acts. At the same time it forwarded a long list of petitions. These included Charles' return to Spain and marriage; the reform of the Court on the model of Ferdinand and Isabel's; the reduction of taxes to the standard of 1494; the better administration of justice; together with demands that *corregidores* should not be appointed without a request on the part of the municipality concerned, and then only for two years; that municipalities should elect their proctors without interference; that the commission of the proctors should not be prescribed, and that death should be the penalty for accepting bribes; that the Cortes should meet every three years, and that the three Orders should be represented; that nobles should be excluded from municipal and financial offices, and from the exclusive use of waste and common lands; that such lands as they had seized should be restored within six months; that Isabel's will and Charles' own oath forbidding the alienation of any part of the royal patrimony should be observed, so as to obviate the necessity for extraordinary taxation. These petitions never reached Charles, for the messengers' hearts failed them, and they turned back; but they show that the Junta utterly misunderstood its position and the character of the King. The last two clauses mark a change of spirit; they are directed against the nobles, some of whom had acquiesced in or favoured the insurrection. So soon as their usurped privileges were threatened, they began to rally round the throne. This tendency was furthered by a masterly stroke of policy. Urged by Adrian's despairing appeals for help, Charles nominated two Spanish grandees, the Constable and the Admiral of Castile, to share the regency: he bade them temporise and dissimulate, call Cortes in his name if advisable, but sanction no curtailment of the royal authority. The Constable raised an army in the north under the command of his son, the Count of Haro; and, aided by Zumel, who a year before had figured as a champion of popular rights, but had been brought over by a bribe, he recovered the city of Burgos, where jealousy of Toledo's leadership was strong. The Admiral joined Adrian at Rioseco, which forthwith became the rallying-place of the royalists, and began to treat with the *Comuneros*. These appointments silenced the complaints of the grandees as to the neglect of their order; nor could the popular party any longer complain that the land was left to the government of strangers.

Internal quarrels still further weakened the *Comuneros*. Flattered by the adhesion of Pedro Giron, a nobleman with a private grievance, they made him captain in place of Padilla (November). This was considered as a slight by the Toledans, and their contingent marched home. The loss of Padilla and his men was compensated by the arrival of Alonso de Acuña, Bishop of Zamora, one of the boldest and most skilful captains of the time. Giron marched against Rioseco; but, either betraying the cause he served or fooled by sham negotiations, he let his opportunity slip. His army melted away; the Count of Haro relieved Rioseco and recaptured Tordesillas together with the Queen and some members of the Junta (December 5). The cry of treachery was raised, and Giron became a fugitive.

An amnesty and a few conciliatory measures would now have put an end to the movement; but the Regents were hindered by Charles' obstinacy. He not only sternly forbade further concession, but disavowed the moderate conditions under which Burgos had returned to its loyalty. He seemed utterly reckless, leaving his agents to fight alone, and even allowing their letters to remain unanswered. But the Regents had now the nobility on their side, for the *Comuneros* became daily more democratic and radical.

When the Junta reassembled at Valladolid, its disorganisation was more than ever apparent; its authority was lost; it had not even a definite rallying-cry. Now that his rival was gone, Padilla returned with his troops from Toledo. Though his unfitness for command was

known, he was elected captain by popular acclaim.   A French army was
on the point of invading Navarre, and a powerful noble, the Count of
Salvatierra, had revolted in the north.   But again the forces of the
*Comuneros* were divided ;  for Bishop Acuña, hearing that the see of
Toledo was vacant, marched southward, hoping for the second time in
his life to win a mitre by force of arms.   The royalist party was not
more united ;  Adrian wrote " that any one of the grandees would gladly
lose an eye, in order that his fellow might suffer the same."   The
Constable and the Admiral had fallen out as to the proper course of
action ;  the former advocated force, the latter the continuation of
negotiations.

In the spring of 1521 Padilla led out his ill-equipped forces and,
by a stroke of fortune, captured the strong castle of Torrelobaton.
Instead, however, of following up his success, he lingered while the
Constable, after defeating the Count of Salvatierra in the north, marched
with a fresh army to join his son at Tordesillas.   Fear, and a suspicion
that their leaders were busy making terms, spread confusion in the
*Comuneros*' ranks.   Many of the soldiers deserted, others betook
themselves to indiscriminate plunder.   Convinced that to risk a battle
with the remainder of his disheartened force would be madness, Padilla
retired as the Count of Haro advanced.   While making his way down
the valley of the Douro to the protection of the castle of Toro, he was
overtaken at Villalar (April 23, 1521); his troops were easily dispersed,
and, though he sought death, he was himself captured alive.   On the
following day he was put to death, together with his second in command.
An enthusiastic but not unselfish supporter of the popular cause, he had
devoted his valour to its service ;  but his jealousy and incompetence
unfitted him alike for command and for the rank of hero to which
latter-day liberals have raised him.   Bishop Acuña, after one or two
skirmishes in the neighbourhood of Ocaña, wasted his time and popularity in an attempt to compel the Chapter of Toledo to accept him
as Archbishop.   On receipt of the news of the disaster of Villalar he
fled.   Padilla's widow, whose family connexions and high spirit gave
her great authority, held out at Toledo for a few months.   After a
useless struggle she escaped to Portugal, and the War of the *Comuneros*
was at an end.

When Charles returned to Spain (July, 1522) he was received, as he
states, "with much humility and reverence."   But he came accompanied
by a foreign guard, and determined to punish ruthlessly.   At Palencia
the Regents laid before him their proposals for amnesty.   Not only were
these rejected, but pardons granted in his name were withdrawn.   On
All Saints' Day at Valladolid he mounted a dais and declared that he
would be justified in punishing all who had shared in the late rebellion,
—the municipalities by deprivation of their liberties, and individuals
by confiscation and death ;  nevertheless, he promised to pardon all save

three hundred. This proscription in the form of an amnesty was mercilessly carried out. The list contained the names of many members of noble families. The supplications of relatives who had fought on the royalist side availed nothing; and the sum brought into the treasury by confiscation amounted to two million ducats. Many executions followed, and even as late as 1528 the Cortes still prayed for mercy on fugitives.

The revolt of the *Comuneros* originated in indignation against particular acts of misgovernment, and hatred of foreigners, rather than in any meditated scheme for winning popular liberties. It has been represented as an attempt to resist the encroachments of the Crown, but was really an attempt to limit its traditional privileges. Under the weak Kings of the fifteenth century, the Castilian Cortes had neglected to secure the abolition of the antiquated forms which represented the King as everywhere paramount. Under strong Kings the strict letter of the law was enforced. Ferdinand and Isabel were despots with the consent of their subjects; Charles was strong enough to disregard the popular will. The movement never spread beyond Castile. The Andalucians offered to suppress it, but their aid was not required; it was crushed by Castilian troops. So soon as its democratic character became pronounced, it was opposed by the nobles, whose aid, or acquiescence, was essential to its success. It failed through local jealousy, respect for tradition, and lack of a leader, and of a plan. It was not openly directed against the Crown. The Junta denied the accusation of disloyalty, asserting that "never did Spain breed disobedience save in her nobles, nor loyalty save in her commons" (January, 1521). The failure of the movement so depressed the popular cause, that until the beginning of the nineteenth century the Spanish commons but rarely again raised up their heads beneath the sceptre of their absolute Kings.

While the rising of the *Comuneros* stirred Castile into a ferment, a distinct and much more violent rebellion was in progress in Valencia. This was entirely social in character. The city population was composed of restless and turbulent artisans, descendants of the adventurers who had settled here, when the land was won back from the Saracens. The country population was chiefly made up of Saracen peasants, vassals of the nobles. Between nobles and people stood the rich burgesses, despised by the former and envied by the latter. The industry of the Saracens, stimulated by a heavy burden of taxation, pressed hard on the Christians. In the autumn of 1519, while most of the magistrates were absent on account of the plague, the forty-eight trade-guilds of the city took up arms to resist an expected attack of the Barbary pirates. The contemplation of their own strength gave rise to a feeling of independence among the commons; they began to claim a larger share in the government, and appointed a Junta of thirteen members to rule over them. The nobles sought to interfere, but the guilds formed a brotherhood (*Germanía*) to resist them, and petitioned Charles to prevent the dispersion of their forces. On receipt of a favourable reply the movement spread to such an alarming degree, that the nobles called upon the King to come in person and check the disorder. A commission was sent to examine the situation, and, in accordance with its report, the *Germanía* was ordered to lay down its arms. By this concession Charles thought to persuade the Valencian nobles to take the oath of allegiance, and to vote supply without insisting on his presence at their Cortes. On their refusal he again changed his policy, favouring the *Germanía* and sending Adrian of Utrecht to enquire into its grievances (February, 1520). In view of their danger the nobles, when Charles was on the point of quitting Spain, consented to receive his oath by deputy; and, in answer to their appeal, he sent Diego de Mendoza, a nobleman of haughty temper, to restore order (April, 1520). After an interval of quiet riots broke out again. In June the city was left in the hands of the *Germanía* by the flight of the governor. Shortly afterwards he was driven from Játiva to Denia, while all the cities of the kingdom of Valencia, with the exception of Morella, rose against their magistrates and appointed Juntas like that of the mother city. The movement spread as far as the Balearic Islands, and now began to show itself in its true light. The grievances originally put forward were, that the people were deprived of their rightful share in the government, that taxes were excesssive, and that justice was badly administered. But when the rabble gained the upper hand, instead of attempting political reforms, they plundered the houses of the nobles, and called upon them to produce the titles by which they held their estates. This attack on property alienated the burgesses, who henceforth sided with the nobles; and the action of the *Germanía* became more violent and fanatical than before. Despairing of help from the regency, the nobles armed their vassals. The army of the *Germanía* marched out against them, but was crushingly defeated at Oropesa and Almenara (June and July, 1521). The governor, however, was again routed at Gandía and driven to seek refuge at Peñíscola. Meanwhile, owing to the frantic excesses of the populace, which now openly avowed its intention of exterminating nobles and infidels, the moderate party was increasing. At its head was the Marquis of Zenete, a nobleman of well-known benevolence and impartiality. Negotiating between the opposing factions he succeeded in obtaining the submission of the city and bringing back the governor. But the more violent members of the *Germanía* were still encamped at Játiva. Having imprudently put himself into their power he was treacherously imprisoned, but escaped to Valencia, rallied all the moderate citizens, seized and executed the ringleaders of the mob, and after a fierce fight remained master of the city. Játiva and a few outlying towns were not subdued until after Charles' return. In March, 1523, the Queen Dowager, Germaine, was sent as regent to punish the guilty. The pardons granted in return for submission were revoked; a ruthless proscription and many executions followed; thousands fled; and the guilds were ruined by heavy fines. Like the *Comuneros* the *Agermanados* never ceased to proclaim their loyalty. The two revolts were simultaneous, and were at all events directed against the same enemy; but cooperation was never attempted. Local jealousy and traditional hatred were still strong; the Castilian in the eyes of a Valencian was, nay, is to this day, a foreigner.

The rebellion of the *Comuneros* had hardly been suppressed, when Navarre was invaded by Henri d'Albret with the connivance of Francis I. Charles had engaged to restore Navarre to the House of Albret; but negotiations had failed to bring about fulfilment, or confirmation of the promise. Henri d'Albret entered into communication with the *Comuneros*, with a view to combined action; but his army came too late. It was commanded with more courage than discretion by a scion of the exiled family, André de Foix d'Asparros, or Lesparre. The garrison of Navarre had been greatly weakened by the withdrawal of troops to crush the revolt in Castile. St Jean Pied-de-Port was easily captured, the fortifications of Pamplona were not yet sufficiently strong to offer more than a feeble resistance. Henri d'Albret was welcomed by his partisans within the kingdom, and the whole of Navarre was overrun. Elated by his easy conquest, Asparros crossed the frontier of Castile and laid siege to Logroño. The Duke of Nágera, viceroy of Navarre, had hurried south to obtain assistance from the Regents. Logroño made a heroic defence, while he marched to its relief with the troops lately victorious at Villalar. Meanwhile Sangüesa had been recaptured in the rear of the French, who now retired towards Pamplona fearing to have their retreat cut off. They were overtaken by the Spanish army, two leagues from the city; the garrison which they had left for its defence was unable to join them. Driven to bay, Asparros ordered an immediate attack while the Spaniards were resting after their long march. He was utterly defeated and taken prisoner at Noain (June, 1521). The Albrets never again attempted to win back their kingdom by force of arms.

Charles returned to Spain (1522), no longer a diffident and delicate young man, passive in the hands of his advisers. His views had broadened, and his temper was haughty and autocratic. Spain was now part of a larger whole. The accident of the possessions of the Aragonese Crown in Italy, the election to the Empire, and the inheritance of the House of Burgundy checked and warped her development as an African and Atlantic Power; but foreign courtiers were no longer allowed to treat her as a conquered country. The Emperor learnt to know and respect the Spaniards; Spanish statesmen sat in his Council; Spanish soldiers formed the mainstay of his power abroad. The overthrow of the *Comuneros* had compelled their fear and respect; association in world-wide schemes of universal monarchy and championship of the Church endeared him to them, and roused them from their natural lethargy and absorption in provincial and class differences. Military glory turned away attention from the burden and sufferings of the land and increased the national contempt for all professions save that of arms. The middle class which under the Catholic Kings was struggling into existence almost disappeared. But Charles attempted to found his world-wide power on submission, and not on political, social, and economic well-being. Spain was indeed formally united, and political unity was based on religious unity as Isabel had intended; but the vigorous provincial and municipal life, checked by harsh centralisation, became a source of weakness instead of a reserve of strength.

A memorable intellectual, literary, and artistic development accompanied the political expansion and the growth of military glory. The striking originality of the new generation contrasts with the effete imitation that sufficed for its predecessor. The predominance of the Castilian dialect was already secured; but even in the fifteenth century poets sought models in Provençal, Gallegan, and Italian. Ausias March (who died in 1466), the most notable among them, wrote in his native Lemosin. Literature was an exotic cultivated at Court; hardly a poem of the hundreds collected into the *Cancioneros* of Baena, Stuñiga, and Hernando del Castillo (published in 1511) possesses more than historical interest. The frivolity, artificiality, and disorder of the reigns of John II and Henry IV were reflected by their poets, and their tragedy by the chronicles,—probably, too, by ballads now modernised beyond recognition.

The introduction of printing coincides with the accession of the Catholic Kings, and the next half century produced translations of the Latin and Italian classics in abundance. Though the Revival of Learning influenced Spain, it bore no fruit there till later. The scholars who brought the new learning to the Peninsula were mostly foreigners, or Spaniards trained abroad. Peter Martyr of Anghera, the two brothers Geraldino and Marineus Siculus, were Italians; Arias Barbosa, a Portuguese, taught Greek by the side of Fernan Nuñez de Guzman, a Spanish nobleman; but Spain produced no Hellenists of note. Luis Vives, the humanist, tutor to William de Croy, the boy Archbishop of Toledo, and to Mary of England, was Spanish only by the accident of his birth. Antonio de Nebrija, or Lebrija, the most distinguished native scholar of his age, was educated at Bologna, though his teaching was, like his Latin Dictionary (1492) and Spanish and Latin Grammars, addressed to his fellow-countrymen. His daughter Francisca was one of a company of learned women who carried their teaching even to the universities and the Court. Ferdinand himself was all but illiterate, but Isabel had a taste for learning. After her accession she acquired some knowledge of Latin; so carefully were her children educated, that Queen Juana could make impromptu speeches in the learned tongue. Isabel's schemes of reform included the education of the nobility; by her command Peter Martyr opened a school at Court. His success exceeded his hopes, and learning became so fashionable that the sons of grandees lectured at the universities. The Church, though impoverished, aided the cause with splendid benefactions. Schools were founded at Toledo (1490); the decayed *studium generale* of Valencia was revived (1500); Barcelona followed suit (1507). The noble college of Santa Cruz at Valladolid was finished in 1492; that of Santiago at Salamanca some thirty years later. Both were founded by Archbishops of Toledo. As a patron of learning no less than as a statesman Ximenes de Cisneros led the way. In 1508 he founded the University of Alcalá (Complutum), *alma mater* of so many famous Spaniards, with professorial chairs of grammar, philosophy, and medicine. Its chief purpose, however, was the study of the Holy Scriptures, and its first-fruits were the earliest Polyglot Bible (of which the First Part was published in 1514). The Semitic text is the work of converted Jews; a Greek cooperated with Spanish scholars on the Latin and Greek texts. The level of education was raised, and foundations were laid from which the Golden Age of Spanish Literature could take its rise.

But the notable books of the period owe little or nothing to classical or foreign influence. Play-acting did not become popular till the time of Lope de Rueda (about 1550) and even then its methods were rude and simple; but the secular drama emerged from the religious early in the century. In the *annus mirabilis* 1492 the first drama was publicly acted by a regular company. The "representations" of Juan del Encina (1468–1534), the "comedies" of Torres de Naharro (published in 1517), and those of Gil Vicente (1470–1534), are much more than mere dialogues without action, like the one in which Princess Isabel had taken the part of a muse on a birthday of her brother Alfonso (who died in 1468). Gil Vicente was a Portuguese, and the other two lived long in Italy; but, although there the drama was already established, the Spaniards took their own line. Encina calls his simple plays "eclogues"; Torres de Naharro cites Horace for method, and awkwardly divides drama into fact (*noticia*) and fiction (*fantasía*); but these classical reminiscences are merely superficial. Figures of everyday life were put upon the stage, and dialogue was cast in Castilian octosyllabic verse instead of in foreign hendecasyllables.

A book that may be read for its own sake as well as for its historical importance is the *Tragicomedy of Calixto and Melibea* (published in 1499), generally known as *La Celestina*. The authorship of the first part is disputed; but probably the whole is the work of Fernando de Rojas. *La Celestina* is a story told throughout in dialogue, and divided into twenty-two acts. Its length is only one of the circumstances that unfit it for acting; but its vivacious and natural dialogue furnished a model for the drama. Its hero and heroine are the typical lady and gallant, the stock romantic characters of the comedy " of cloak and sword," the primitive Romeo and Juliet. Celestina, witch and go-between, with her train of thieving lackeys, low women and bullies, more than foreshadows the realistic and comic characters of the drama and novel, the rogues (*pícaros*) and buffoons (*graciosos*) who in later days were to play so prominent a part. The book was translated into many tongues; its influence at home and abroad is incalculable.

Another masterpiece solitary in its kind, and contrasted in its noble earnestness with the artificiality of the other poems of its author and his generation, is the *Coplas de Manrique*,—verses by Jorge de Manrique on the death of his father (which occurred in 1476, two years before his own). Longfellow has done all that a translator can do for this unsurpassed elegy; but half its beauty is lost with the language in which it is written. Its stately pageant of mourning and final resignation realise Christian chivalry as poets have dreamed of it, and the solemn knell of the majestic verse is worthy of " the noblest daughter of Latin." At the beginning of the sixteenth century the knightly chronicle degenerated into the romance of chivalry. *Amadis of Gaul*, the first and best of the kind, perhaps originated in a French *fabliau*. More than one allusion to it is found in Spanish writers, before it was published (1508) by García Ordoñez de Montalvo as a translation from the Portuguese. The success produced many imitations and " continuations " dealing with exploits of " the innumerable lineage of Amadis." These heroes of the romances of chivalry are impossible beings, living in a shadowy and impossible world. The first of them exhausted the capability of the species; the others surpass it only in absurdity, while the abuse of the supernatural makes their stories tame and uninteresting. A Cervantes was hardly needed to dispel this fantastic dream of a debased chivalry.

The advance from chronicle to history due to the Revival of Learning was not made in Spain till the middle of the sixteenth century. The story of the reign of the Catholic Kings down to 1492 was written by their official chronicler Hernando del Pulgar in the form of annals. Despite some graphic descriptions and florid speeches, it is in general heavy and arid, lacking in the simple dignity of its kind, and inferior to the *Claros Varones de Castilla*, a gallery of contemporary portraits drawn with skill and energy by the same pen. Andres Bernaldez, curate of Los Palacios, expanded his memoirs into a history of his time. He is at his best, when he forgets the gravity of his subject and is content to gossip about the events of which he was an eyewitness. Nebrija condensed Pulgar's Chronicle; Peter Martyr left a collection of letters on contemporary events, a rich but untrustworthy and puzzling mine of information. These books, like the *De Rebus Hispaniae* of Marineus Siculus, are Latin exercises upon historical subjects.

Spain has never lacked learned men; but, except perhaps in theology, the Spaniards have never been a learned nation. The foreigners who came with Charles V were struck by the ignorance and contempt of letters prevalent in Spain, as well as by the semi-savagery of the bulk of its people. The Revival of Learning could not at once produce fruit on soil so scorched and seamed by centuries of war. Moreover the richest fruits of Spanish genius are indigenous. Inspiration for the noblest poetry of Spain was found in the Bible and in her own history rather than in Latin and Italian writers; her novel and drama sprang from her own rough but teeming soil.

With the exception of painting, which was still in its infancy, the arts had already reached the fullest expression to which they have at any time attained in this country. In architecture, in sculpture, in pottery, in gold, silver and iron work, and in embroidery Spain never improved upon the skill of the Saracens and the masterpieces of the fourteenth and fifteenth centuries. The influences which moulded her art are to be found partly in race, partly in climate, and partly in history. Possessing great power of adaptation, she set her mark upon all that she produced. In the northern and central regions design and initiative in architecture are mostly French; but the influence of the Saracens leavens this northern style and informs it with richer beauty, "the songs and shrines being equally tinged with the colouring of northern piety and oriental fancy." Introduced at first as a mere accessory in vestments and jewelry, and in Moorish caskets which guarded the relics of saints, little by little this more gorgeous ornamentation permeated the whole building. It was still a Christian cathedral; yet the lavishness with which the minor arts were used in decoration produced a result that is not to be found elsewhere, and is known as the *plateresque* or silver-smith's style. Typical examples are the Puerta del Perdón of Seville Cathedral, the horseshoe arch of a mosque overlaid with Christian emblem and decoration (1519), and, in less mixed form, San Marcos of Leon (1514). To this period belong some of the choicest works of expiring Gothic and dawning renaissance building. The Church of San Juan de los Reyes at Toledo perpetuates the memory of the battle of Toro. Cathedrals were planned for Salamanca, Segovia, Plasencia, and Granada; but the most valuable work of the age was the completion and decoration of the splendid designs of an earlier time at Burgos, at Toledo, and at Seville. To it belong also the church set down in the midst of the great mosque of Córdova, and the splendid but incongruous palace of Charles V on the Alhambra Hill.

Sculpture in Spain is usually associated with religious architecture. It is often in bolder relief and of more intense expression than elsewhere, and attains its greatest perfection in altar-pieces and sepulchral monuments. Such are the marvels of marble and wood created by Philip de Vigarny or de Boloña (about 1500–43), Alonso de Berruguete, a Spanish pupil of Michael Angelo (about 1520), and Damien Forment of Valencia (about 1511–32), the tombs of King Juan II in the Cartuja de Miraflores, that of the Infante Don Juan at Ávila, those of Iñigo de Mendoza and his wife at Burgos, and the kneeling statue of Padilla. They are, it must be confessed, delicate and gorgeous rather than grand. Marble and alabaster are treated like metal and lace; beauty is sought in details and no longer in grand and simple lines. To the Spanish Saracens belongs the invention of a dwelling combining with convenience and suitability to their climate a high degree of beauty. Nowhere else has a fortress been made a home of strength and beauty like the Alhambra (mainly fourteenth century) and the other *alcazars* of Spain. The semi-oriental domestic architecture adopted by the Christians of Andalusia is seen at its best in the so-called *Casa de Pilatos* at Seville (1521). Here there is no need to guard against the weight of snow, no cold to be kept out, no smoke to blacken; so the roof becomes a terrace, the arch is reared in fairy lightness, the glaze and colour of brilliant tiles replace the heavy wainscot and arras; stucco moulded into geometrical designs and harmoniously coloured makes up for the lack of pictures and for the scantiness of the furniture. The *Lonja* or Silk-Exchange at Valencia (1482) is an example, not without parallel, of the successful wedding of late Gothic design to Saracen detail of window (*ajimez*) and decoration. As a subject race the Saracens continued almost to monopolise the more delicate industrial arts. Theirs are the pottery of metallic sheen, and the exquisite designs of lace and filigree, damascening and inlaying—which with the rich silks and velvets testify to their skill as handicraftsmen and to their exquisite taste in form and colour.

# CHAPTER XII.

## FRANCE.

FOUR reigns almost fill up the space of time from Agincourt to Marignano. In that century the slow consistent policy of four Kings and their agents raises France from her nadir almost to her zenith. The institutions and the prosperity built up by Louis the Fat, Philip Augustus, Louis IX, and Philip the Fair had been shattered under the first two Valois; the prosperity had been in part restored, the institutions further developed under Charles V. In the long anarchy which we call the reign of Charles VI, all bonds had been loosened, all well-being blighted, all order overwhelmed. Slowly the old traditions reassert themselves, the old principles resume their domination, and from chaos emerges the new monarchy, with all and more than all the powers of the old.

Communal, feudal, representative institutions have proved too weak to withstand the stress of foreign and civil war. The monarchy and the monarchical system alone retain their vitality unimpaired, and seem to acquire new vigour from misfortune. Under Charles VII the new *régime* was begun; under Louis XI and his daughter the ground was ruthlessly cleared of all that could impede regal action at home, while the wars of Charles VIII and Louis XII, purposeless and exhausting as they were, without seriously diminishing domestic prosperity, satisfactorily tested the strength and solidity of the new structure.

Thus equipped and prepared, France enters on the race of modern times as the most compact, harmonious, united nation of the European continent. All that she has suffered is forgotten. The sacrifice of individual and local liberty is hardly felt. In the splendour and power of the monarchy the nation sees its aspirations realised. Nobility, clergy, commons, abandon their old ideals, and are content that their will should be expressed, their being absorbed, their energy manifested in the will and being and operations of the King.

Institutions of independent origin give up their strength to feed his power, and exist if at all only by his sufferance. Time had been when clergy, nobility, even towns, had been powers in the State with which the King needed to reckon, not as a sovereign, hardly as a superior. Before the Reformation two of these powers had been yoked in complete submission, and the third was far on the way to final subjugation.

Critical in all respects, the period of Charles VII and his three successors was not least so in respect of the King's relations with the Church and the Papacy. The Conciliar movement, fruitless on the whole, had an important effect in France. It initiated a fresh stage in the struggle between Church and State in France; and for a time Gallican liberties were conceived as something different from the authority of the French King over the French Church, and especially over her patronage.

From the beginning the King played a conspicuous part, and in the end he succeeded in seizing the chief share of all that was won from the Pope. But at first he assumed the air of an impartial and sovereign arbiter between Council and Pope. In 1438 the majority of the Council of Basel were in open rupture with the Pope, Eugenius IV. Charles VII, while negotiating on the one hand with the Fathers of the Council, and on the other with the Pope, and outwardly maintaining his obedience to Eugenius, was careful to preserve his liberty of action. In the same year a deputation of the Council waited upon Charles and communicated to him the text of the decrees of reform adopted up to that time by the Fathers. The King called an assembly of the clergy of his kingdom to meet at Bourges, where, together with himself and a considerable number of his chief councillors, ambassadors of Pope and Council were present. The result was the royal ordinance issued on July 7, 1438, and known as the Pragmatic Sanction of Bourges.

In this solemn edict, issued by the sovereign authority of the prince, but supported by the consent and advice of the august assembly which he had summoned, more of conciliar spirit is observable than of royal ambition. The superiority of the Council to the Pope was acknowledged in matters touching the faith, the extirpation of schism, and the reform of the Church in Head and members. Decennial Councils were demanded. Election by the Chapter or the Convent was to be the rule for the higher ecclesiastical dignities; but the King and the magnates were not debarred from recommending candidates for election. The general right of papal reservation was abolished, and a strict limit placed on the cases in which it was permissible. No benefice was to be conferred by the Pope before vacancy under the form known as an expectative grace.

Provisions were made in favour of University graduates. In every cathedral church one prebend was to be given on the earliest opportunity to a graduate in theology, who was bound to lecture at least once a week. Furthermore, in every cathedral or collegiate church one-third of the prebends were to be reserved for suitable graduates, and the same principle was to obtain in the collation of other ecclesiastical benefices. Graduates were also to be entitled to a special preference in urban parish churches.

No appeals or evocation of causes to Rome were to be allowed until the other grades of jurisdiction had been exhausted. Moreover, where the parties should be distant more than four days' journey from the Curia, all ordinary cases were to be judged by those judges *in partibus* to whom they belonged by custom and right. The decree of the Council limiting the number of Cardinals to twenty-four was approved. Annates were abolished with a small reservation in favour of the existing Pope. A number of edicts of the Council, relating to the order of divine service and the discipline of the clergy, were confirmed. The decrees of the Council accepted without modification were to be put in force immediately within the kingdom, and the assent of the Council was to be solicited where modifications had been introduced. These purport to have been the decisions of the Council of Bourges, and the King at its request ordered that they should be obeyed throughout the kingdom and in Dauphiné, and enforced by the royal Courts.

Yet republican as is the constitution of the Church as sanctioned at Basel and Bourges, it must be noticed that the sovereign authority of the King is expressly invoked by the Council of Bourges as necessary to secure execution of the reforms proposed; and in so far the Church of France is subordinated to the State, and the ultimate issue of these developments foreshadowed. The usurpation of authority is patent; and forgery was needed to support it. Few now believe in the Pragmatic Sanction of St Louis, which seems first to have seen the light after 1438. On the other hand the freedom of election conferred meant little more than the freedom to entertain recommendations from the King and other great personages. For the conflict of intrigue at the Court of Rome was substituted a conflict of influence within the kingdom, and the share of patronage obtained in this by the King was not destined long to satisfy him.

The position of the clergy and people was so far improved that the drain of treasure from France to Rome caused not only by the annates, but also in great measure by the receipts of non-resident beneficiaries, by the fees incident to litigation at Rome, and by the presents required from suitors and petitioners for favour, was under the Pragmatic greatly diminished. But the abuses in the Church, due to the holding of benefices in plurality, were not directly touched by the decree. The holding of abbeys and priories *in commendam*, so detrimental to the discipline of the religious orders, remained unaffected. The University received considerable privileges, and the power of the *Parlement* over the Church was greatly increased.

Charles VII, though consistent in supporting Eugenius against the Council's Anti-Pope, as steadily maintained the Pragmatic against the repeated protests of successive Popes, and a very liberal Concordat offered by Eugenius for some reason never came into effect. The King did not however always respect the liberty of election which he had restored to the Church, and we even find him approaching the Pope to solicit his nomination for certain benefices. Louis on his accession went further. It was said that during his exile at Genappe he had promised to abolish the Pragmatic Sanction. No doubt he hoped in cooperation with a friendly Pope to secure more complete control over the appointment to prelacies than was possible under the system of elections established by the Sanction. He hoped at the same time, by making a favour of the repeal, to secure the Pope's support for the Angevin claims on Naples against Ferrante. Accordingly, towards the end of 1461 the Pope was in possession of his formal promise to abolish the obnoxious edict; and the *Parlement* was forced to register the letter of abolition as a royal ordinance. But the Pope was too deeply pledged to Ferrante, and saw too clearly the danger of French intervention in Naples. John of Calabria, the representative of the Angevin claims, met an open enemy in Pius II. Neither did Louis find that promotion in France proceeded entirely according to his wishes. Thus from 1463 an anomalous situation prevailed.

The Pragmatic was not formally restored, but a series of edicts were passed against the oppression and exactions of papal agents, against those who applied at Rome for expectative graces or the gift of prelacies, against papal jurisdiction in questions relating to the possession of benefices, and against the export of treasure. In 1472 a Concordat was arranged between Louis and Sixtus IV for the division of patronage between the Ordinary and the Pope, and to regulate other matters of dispute; but hardly any attempt seems to have been made to carry this agreement into effect. On the whole, the policy of Louis seems to have been to keep the whole question open; to resist as far as possible the export of treasure; to discourage the independent exercise by the Pope of his power to provide for prelacies; to oppose reservations and expectative graces; to keep the jurisdiction in question of prelacies and benefices in the hands of the royal judges; and thus, sometimes by suggestion at the Court of Rome, sometimes by election under pressure, sometimes by means of the King's influence on the *Parlement* and other Courts, and not infrequently by the blunt use of force, to retain all important ecclesiastical patronage at his own disposal;—and this without any acute breach with Rome or with the Gallican clergy. His means were various and even inconsistent, but his general policy is clear.

The great Estates of Tours in 1484 showed the trend of feeling, both lay and ecclesiastical. The Estate of the Church demanded the restitution of the Pragmatic Sanction. And the third Estate speaks feelingly of the " *évacuation de pécune* " resulting from the papal exactions, and prays for reform. The Bishops indeed protested in defence of the authority of the Holy See. But the King's Council took no decisive step. The old confusion continued; it was impossible to say whether the Pragmatic was or was not in force.

Louis XII on his accession confirmed the Pragmatic, and the *Parlement* as before seized every opportunity to enforce it by its decisions. But so long as the King and the Pope were on good terms no serious question arose; for Amboise held continuously the office of legate for France and was in effect a provincial Pope. Julius promised to nominate to prelacies in France only titularies approved by the King. After the breach between Louis and Julius the kingdom was in open disobedience, and the law was silent. It was left for Francis I and Leo X to put aside the principle of free election so long defended by *Parlement* and clergy, and to agree upon a division of the spoils, which ignored the liberties of the Gallican Church, while conferring exceptional privileges on the King of France.

The result was the Concordat of 1516. Elections were abolished. The King was to nominate to metropolitan and cathedral churches, to abbeys and conventual priories, and if certain rules were observed the papal confirmation would not be refused. Reservations and expectative graces were abolished. The third of benefices was still reserved to University graduates. The regular degrees of jurisdiction were to be respected, unless in cases of exceptional importance. By implication though not by open stipulation annates were retained. The Lateran Council accepted this agreement. The Pragmatic was finally condemned. Although the *Parlement* and the University of Paris protested energetically, resistance was in vain. No power in France could withstand this alliance of King and Pope, by which the material ends of each were secured, without any conspicuous tenderness being shown for the spiritual interests of the Church.

During the same period the proud independence of the University of Paris was successfully attacked. In 1437 the exemption from taxation claimed for its numerous dependents was abolished. In 1446 it was first made subject to the jurisdiction of the *Parlement*. In 1452 the Cardinal d'Estouteville, acting in concert with the King and the King's *Parlement*, imposed upon it a scheme of reformation, and its independence of secular jurisdiction was at an end. Under Louis XII the old threat of a cessation of public exercises was used in resistance to royal proposals of reform. The scholars soon found that the King was master, and were like the rest of the kingdom obliged to submit. The condemnation of the Nominalists by Louis XI is a grotesque but striking proof that even the republic of letters was no longer exempt from the interference of an alien authority.

The Church, whose independence was thus impaired by progressive encroachments, could not claim that its privileges were deserved by virtues, efficiency, or discipline. Plurality, non-residence, immorality, neglect of duty, worldliness, disobedience to rule, were common in France as elsewhere. Amboise did something for reform in the Franciscan, Dominican, and Benedictine Orders; but far more was needed to effect a cure. Unfortunately the Concordat of Francis I tended rather to stimulate the worldly ambitions and interests of the higher clergy, than to aid or encourage any royal attempts in the direction of reform.

Passing to those secular authorities that were in a position to refuse obedience to the King, we have first to notice the appanaged and other nobility of princely rank. The successful Wars of 1449–53 drove the English from the limits of France, extinguished the duchy of Aquitaine, and left only Calais and Guines to the foreigner. The English claims were still kept alive, but the only serious invasion, that of 1475, broke down owing to the failure of cooperation on the part of Burgundy. The duchy of Aquitaine was revived by Louis XI as a temporary expedient (1469–72) to satisfy the petulant ambition of his brother, while separating him by the widest possible interval from his ally of Burgundy. On the death of Charles of Aquitaine the duchy was reoccupied. But during the English Wars a Power had arisen in the East which menaced the very existence of the monarchy. In pursuance of that policy of granting escheated or conquered provinces as appanages to the younger members of the royal house, which facilitated the transition from earlier feudal independence to direct royal government, John had in 1363 granted the duchy of Burgundy to his son, Philip, and the gift had been confirmed by Charles V. By marriage this enterprising family added to their dominions Flanders, Artois, the county of Burgundy, Nevers and Rethel, Brabant and Limburg; by purchase Namur and Luxemburg, and, mainly by conquest, Hainault, Holland, and Zeeland. Enriched by the wealth of the Low Countries, fortified by the military resources of so many provinces, animated against the house of France by the murder of his father (1419), released from his oath of allegiance and further fortified by the cession of the frontier fortresses along the Somme by the Treaty of Arras in 1435, during thirty years after the conclusion of that treaty Philip the Good (1419–67) had been content to maintain a perfect independence, and to gather his strength in peace. Then, as the old man's strength failed, his son's opportunity came. Enraged that Louis had been allowed in 1463 to repurchase the towns on the Somme under the terms of their original cession, Charles the Bold contracted a League with the discontented princes and nobles of France, and in 1465 invaded the kingdom, and with his allies invested Paris.

The Treaties of St Maur des Fossés and of Conflans dissolved the League of the Public Weal, but restored to Burgundy the Somme towns, and established Charles of France in the rich appanage of Normandy. Then in four campaigns Liége and the other cities of her principality, which in reliance on French support had braved the power of Burgundy, were brought low, and in 1468 the episcopal city was destroyed in the forced presence of the King of France. Meanwhile, in 1467 Charles the Bold succeeded to the duchy whose policy he had controlled for two years, and in 1468 he married the sister of Edward IV, the hereditary enemy of France.

The fortunes of Charles of Burgundy perhaps never stood higher than at the fall of Liége. Louis XI, his prisoner at Peronne, had been forced to promise Champagne to Charles of France, the ally of Burgundy, which would have made a convenient link between the northern and the southern dominions of Charles the Bold. But in the war of intrigue and arms that filled the next four years Louis on the whole gained the advantage. Charles of France was persuaded to give up Champagne. The old League was almost, but never quite, revived. The death of Charles of France in 1472 came opportunely, some said too opportunely, for his brother the King. Charles the Bold, who had recently established a standing army of horse and foot, determined to force the game and invaded France. But Louis avoided any engagement, and Charles consumed his forces in a vain attack on Beauvais. He retreated without any advantage gained. Meanwhile Britanny had been reduced to submission.

From that time Charles' ambition seems to look rather eastwards. In 1469 he had received from Sigismund of Austria, as security for a loan, the southern part of Elsass with the Breisgau. In 1473, after the conquest of Gelders and Zutphen, he entered on fruitless negotiations with the Emperor Frederick III with a view to being crowned as King, and recognised as imperial Vicar in the West. He even hoped to be accepted as King of the Romans. In 1474 he interfered in a quarrel between the Archbishop of Cologne and his Chapter, and laid siege to the little town of Neuss. Eleven months his army lay before this poor place. Imperial hosts gathered to its relief, and Charles was baffled. Meanwhile his chance of chances went by. When, as the result of long-continued pressure, Edward IV at length invaded France, Charles, who had just raised the siege of Neuss, was exhausted and unable to take his part in the proposed operations. Edward made terms with Louis and retired. In the autumn (1475) Charles scored his last success by overrunning Lorraine. At length his northern and his southern dominions were united.

But meanwhile his acquisitions in Elsass and the Breisgau had involved him in quarrels with the Swiss. Swiss merchants had been ill-treated. The mortgaged provinces were outraged by the harsh rule of Peter von Hagenbach, the Duke's governor. The Swiss took up their quarrel, instigated by French gold. A revolt ensued, and the Swiss assisted the inhabitants to seize, try, and execute Hagenbach (May, 1474). In his camp before Neuss Charles received the Swiss defiance. Soon afterwards, the Swiss invaded Franche Comté and defeated the Duke's forces near Héricourt. In March, 1475, Pontarlier was sacked, and later in the same year the Swiss attacked the Duchess of Savoy and the Count de Romont, the Duke's allies, and were everywhere victorious.

These were insults not to be borne. Charles marshalled all his strength, crossed the Jura in February, 1476, and advancing to the shore of Neuchatel, assaulted and captured the castle of Granson. Moving along the north-western verge of the lake, a few miles further he was attacked by the Swiss. An unaccountable panic seized his army; it broke and fled. All the rich equipment of Charles, even his seal and his jewels, fell into the hands of the Swiss; and the Duke himself fled. At Lausanne, under the protection of the Duchess of Savoy, he reorganised his army. In May he was ready to set forth once more against the Swiss and especially against Bern. His route this time led him to the little town of Morat, S.E. of the lake of Neuchatel. Here he lingered for ten days in hopes to overpower the garrison and secure his communications for a further advance. But the little place, whose walls still stand, held out. Time was thus given for the enemy to collect. On June 21 their last contingent arrived. The next day they moved forward in pouring rain to attack. The Burgundians awaited their arrival in the neighbourhood of their camp to the south of Morat. The battle was fierce, but the shock of the Swiss phalanx proved irresistible. This time the Duke's army was not only scattered, but destroyed, after being driven back upon the lake. But few escaped, and no prisoners were made.

Once more the Duke threw himself on the mercy of the Duchess of Savoy, whose kindness he soon afterwards ill repaid by making her his prisoner. After a period of deep depression, bordering on insanity, Charles was roused once more to action by the news that René of Lorraine was reconquering his duchy. Nancy and other places had already fallen, when Charles appeared at the head of an army. René, leaving orders to hold Nancy, retired from the province to seek aid abroad. The Swiss gave leave to raise volunteers; the King of France supplied him with money; and, while Nancy still held out, René at length, in bitter weather, set out from Basel. As he approached Nancy, Charles met him with his beleaguering army to the south of the town (January 5, 1477); but the Swiss were not to be denied. Once more Charles was defeated; this time he met with his death. His vast plans, which had even included the acquisition of Provence by bequest from the Duke of Anjou, so as, with the control or possession of Savoy, to complete the establishment of his rule from the Mediterranean to the mouth of the Rhine, were extinguished with him.

The King of France, who hitherto had left his allies to fight alone, now took up arms, and occupied both the duchy and the county of Burgundy, the remaining Somme towns, and Artois with Arras. But Mary, Charles' heiress, gave her hand to Maximilian of Austria, who succeeded in stemming the tide of Louis' conquests, and even inflicted a defeat on him at Guinegaste (1479). Louis lost and recovered the county of Burgundy. At length a treaty was concluded at Arras

(1482). Early in the same year Mary had died, leaving two children. The duchy of Burgundy was lost for ever to her heirs and incorporated with the royal domain. Artois, the county of Burgundy, and some minor lands were retained by Louis as the dowry of Margaret of Burgundy, who was betrothed to the infant Dauphin. After this marriage had been finally broken off in 1491, Charles VIII restored Artois and Franche Comté to the house of Burgundy by the Treaty of Senlis (1493).

Thus ended the great duel of war and intrigue between Louis XI and Charles the Bold. The struggle had taxed the strength of France, which had hardly yet recovered from the Hundred Years' War. But the result was all or nearly all that could be wished. The old feud reappears in a new form in the rivalry of Charles V and Francis I. The danger was however then distinctly foreign; Charles the Bold, on the other hand, was still a French prince and relied on French territory and French support.

Second, but far inferior in power, to the Duke of Burgundy came the Duke of Britanny,—Duke by the grace of God. His duchy was indeed more sharply severed from the rest of France by conscious difference of blood; his subjects were not less warlike and of equal loyalty. But his province stood alone, and was not, like that of Charles the Bold, supported by other even more rich and populous territories forming part of France or of the Empire. The undesirable aid of England could be had for a price, and was occasionally invoked, but could never be a real source of strength. On the other hand, like Burgundy, Britanny was exempt from royal *taille* and *aides*, and was not even bound to support the King in his wars. The Duke of Britanny did only simple homage to the King for his duchy. The homage of his subjects to their Duke was without reserve. He had his own Court of appeal, his "great days," for his subjects. Only after this Court had pronounced, was resort allowed to the *Parlement*, on ground of *déni de justice*, or *faux jugement*.

Britanny sent no representatives to the French States-General. She had her own law, her own coinage, of both gold and silver. In 1438 she refused to recognise the Pragmatic. Yet French had here since the eleventh century been the language of administration. The Breton youth were educated at Paris or Angers. Breton nobles rose to fame and fortune in the King's service. In 1378 Jean IV was driven out for supporting too warmly the English cause. French tastes and sympathies were thus consistent with obstinate attachment to Breton independence.

To preserve this cherished independence, the Dukes maintained a long and unequal struggle. Charles V had attempted to annex the duchy by way of forfeiture, but soon found the task beyond his powers. In all the intrigues of the reign of Louis XI, the Duke of Britanny was either an open or a covert foe. His isolated position exposed him to the King's attacks, and although at one time, when allied with Charles, then Duke of Normandy, his armies occupied the western half of that province, the close of Louis' reign showed him distinctly weaker. The character of the last Duke, Francis II, was not such as to qualify him for making the best of a bad position. Weak, unwarlike, and easily influenced, he provoked a hostility which he was not man enough to meet.

In the intrigues against the government of Anne of Beaujeu during the minority of Charles VIII, Francis of Britanny was leagued with the Duke of Orleans, the Count of Angoulême, René of Lorraine and other discontented princes. Unfortunately the Duke's confidential minister, Landois, by his corrupt and oppressive rule, alienated a large part of his subjects, and provoked a revolt, which was supported by the Court of France. The Duke of Britanny was helpless. Louis of Orleans, who was already scheming for a divorce and an aspirant for the hand of Anne of Britanny, could render little assistance, and his undeveloped character was unequally matched with the political wisdom of Madame de Beaujeu. English aid was hoped for; but Richard III was fully occupied at home. Bourbon and d'Albret, who supported the coalition, were too distant to render effective aid. Thus the only result of the "Guerre Folle" was that Landois fell into the hands of the rebels, and was hanged. The hollow Peace of Beaugency and Bourges (1485) decided nothing, but gave the government time to strengthen its position. Henry Tudor, who had in the interval established himself in England, was indebted to France for opportune support and protection, and remembered his obligation for a time.

Landois removed, the Bretons remained disunited. French influence was disliked by all, and annexation to France abhorred. The Estates of Britanny (February, 1486) declared that the succession to the duchy belonged to the Duke's two daughters in order of birth, thus barring the rights of the House of Penthièvre\*, which Louis XI had purchased in 1480. But the Duke's attachment to his French advisers kept in vigour the Breton opposition, which was forced to lean upon the Court of France, and hoped nevertheless (by the Treaty of Châteaubriant, 1487) to secure the liberties of Britanny. For his part the Duke allied himself with Maximilian, recently elected King of the Romans, who began hostilities on the northern frontier of France in the summer of 1486, and, later in the same year, with Orleans, Lorraine, Angoulême, Orange, and Albret. Dunois, Lescun (now Comte de Comminges and Governor of Guyenne), Commines, and others, lent the weight of their experience and personal qualities. Bourbon this time stood aloof, and the French government promptly threw its whole force on the south-western Powers, who were forced to submit. Lescun was replaced in the government of

---

\* Under the Treaty of Guérande (1365) the House of Blois, now represented by Penthièvre, was to succeed, in default of male heirs of the House of Montfort, of whom Duke Francis II was the last.

Guyenne by the Sire de Beaujeu (March, 1487). The French army was then directed against Britanny, remaining in concert with the opposition within the duchy. A desultory campaign ensued, while des Querdes acted boldly and brilliantly against Maximilian in the north of France. The Sire de Candale, Beaujeu's lieutenant in Guyenne, prevented Albret from bringing aid to Francis, and forced him to give hostages for good behaviour. The Breton opposition under the Sire de Rohan held the north-west of the country and captured Ploermel. The French army met with little serious resistance except at Nantes, where they were forced to raise their siege; Norman corsairs blocked the coast, and the land was ravaged by friend and foe.

Early in 1488 the Duke of Orleans recovered for Francis Vannes, Auray, and Ploermel. Rohan was forced to capitulate. D'Albret obtained assistance from the Court of Spain, and joined the Duke's army with 5000 men; Maximilian had previously sent 1500 men. The young French general, La Trémouille, delayed on the borders of the duchy until his forces were complete. An English force landed under Lord Scales. On the other hand the Roman King was busy with rebellious Flanders, supported by des Querdes, and d'Albret was pushing his claims to the hand of the heiress of Britanny, which conflicted with the hopes of Maximilian, and of Louis of Orleans. At length La Trémouille was satisfied with his army of 15,000 men, including 7000 Swiss, and equipped with an admirable artillery. He gave battle (July, 1488) at St Aubin du Cormier, defeated the Breton host, and captured the Duke of Orleans. By the Peace of Le Verger (August) the Breton government pledged itself to dismiss its foreign allies, and to marry the Duke's daughters only with the King's consent. Four strong places and a substantial sum were to be given as guarantee. A few days after Francis II died. An amnesty was granted to d'Albret, Dunois, Lescun, and others; but the Duke of Orleans was kept a prisoner till 1491, as a penalty for his share in the rebellion.

Francis had left the guardianship of his daughters to the Marshal de Rieux, but this was promptly claimed by the royal Council. The French armies advanced to take possession of the duchy. Foreign powers intervened. Alliances were concluded in February, 1489, between Henry VII, Maximilian, and the Duchess Anne. Ferdinand and Isabel demanded the restitution of Roussillon, and on its refusal joined the league. Hereupon 2000 Spaniards and 6000 English landed in Britanny. But the Breton leaders were themselves divided. Rieux favoured the marriage proposals of d'Albret, who was with him at Nantes. The English, after first upholding d'Albret, advanced a candidate of their own. Dunois and others, with whom were the young princesses, opposed d'Albret, to whose unattractive person Anne took a strong dislike. Rohan had hopes for one of his sons.

The Peace of Frankfort (July, 1489) proved abortive so far as regards the affairs of Britanny, though it gave Maximilian a breathing space for making favourable terms with the cities of the Netherlands. Meanwhile the state of war in Britanny continued. Like Mary of Burgundy before her, Anne sought a deliverer from unwelcome suitors and the stress of war in the Austrian Archduke. Covetous as usual of a profitable marriage, Maximilian snatched a moment from the claims of other business, and caused full powers to be made out for the conclusion by proxy of a marriage-contract on his behalf. Ten days afterwards the King of Hungary and conqueror of Austria, Matthias Corvinus, died (April 6, 1490). The prospect of recovering Vienna and acquiring Hungary opened before the eyes of Maximilian. He was at once immersed in correspondence and preparations, then in war. Successes were followed by difficulties, difficulties by reverses. The War in Hungary was closed in November, 1491, by the Peace of Pressburg. Meanwhile his emissaries had not found their course quite clear in Britanny. A Spanish suitor was in the field, and a series of delays followed. At length (December, 1490) the wedding of Maximilian to the Breton heiress was solemnly concluded by his proxy. But while to protect his bride, even to make the bond secure, his personal presence was needed, the bridegroom lingered in Eastern lands, and the French pressed on. Albret, disgusted at his own rebuff, surrendered the castle of Nantes to the suzerain, and the town was shortly occupied. Henry VII and Ferdinand sent no aid. The Duke of Orleans was liberated and reconciled to the King, who was beginning to act on his own behalf. The Duchess was besieged at Rennes and was forced to accept the French terms, consisting of the rupture of her marriage with the Roman King, and her union with the King of France. Without waiting for the needful dispensations the contract was concluded, and the marriage followed (December, 1491).

The marriage with Anne involved a breach of the Treaty of Arras (1482), which stipulated that Charles should marry Margaret of Austria (indeed, the marriage had been solemnised, though not consummated), and led to the retrocession in 1493 to Maximilian of Franche Comté, Artois and minor places. Yet the gain was adequate. Britanny was not as yet united to the French Crown, but preserved its liberties and separate government. It was, however, agreed that Anne, if she survived her husband, should be bound to marry the successor, or presumptive successor, to the Crown. Louis XII, on his accession, realised his early wish, obtained a divorce from his saintly, unhappy wife, and became Anne's third royal consort. Dangerous plans were at one time pushed by Anne for the marriage of her daughter to the heir of Burgundy, Spain, and Austria, but these plans fortunately broke down, and the marriage of her elder daughter and heiress Claude to Francis of Angoulême prevented the separation of Britanny from France. In 1532 the Estates of Britanny under pressure agreed to the union of the province to the Crown; and its formal independence actually came to an end on the accession of King Henry II in 1547.

The Duke of Anjou, as holding in addition Lorraine, Provence, the titular crown of Naples, and the family appanage of Maine, was another powerful rival to the King. But Charles VII had married an Angevin wife, and was in intimate alliance with the House of Anjou. Throughout his long reign the Duke René (1431–81), more interested in literature and art and other peaceful pastimes than in political intrigue, gave little trouble to France. His son, John of Calabria, joined in the League of the Public Weal, but was afterwards reconciled to Louis XI. He lost his life in an adventurous attempt to win a crown in Catalonia (1470). The grandson, Nicolas of Calabria, was one of the aspirants to the hand of Mary of Burgundy, but died in 1472. The independence of Anjou, like that of most of the later appanages, was strictly limited. The Duke received neither *taille* nor *aides*, but generally drew a fixed pension. Strictly he had not the right to maintain or levy troops, though this rule inevitably failed to act in time of revolution. But the domain profits were considerable, and the lack of direct royal government was a considerable diminution of the King's authority, and might at any time become a serious danger. In 1474 Louis XI took over the administration of Anjou, and in 1476, as it was reported that René had been meditating the bequest of Provence to Charles of Burgundy, the King forced on the old Duke a treaty whereby he engaged never to cede any part of that province to the enemies of France. On the Duke's death in 1480, his nephew Charles succeeded, but only survived him for a year, when by his will all the possessions of Anjou except Lorraine reverted to the Crown. The process of consolidation was proceeding apace. Provence had never hitherto been reckoned as part of France.

The tradition of feudal independence was nowhere stronger than in Guyenne. The revolt of the South against the Black Prince was occasioned by the levy of a *fouage* at a time when France was accepting a far more burdensome system of arbitrary taxation almost without a murmur. The great principalities of the South were Armagnac, Albret, and Foix. The Counts of Armagnac had been associated with the worst traditions of the anarchical period. Jean V carried into private life the lawless instincts of the family. Imprisoned by Charles VII for correspondence with the English government, he was liberated and treated with favour by Louis XI. He requited his benefactor by revolt and treachery in the War of the Public Weal. Pardoned, he continued his game of disobedience and intrigue. The King's writ could hardly be said to run in Armagnac and its appendant provinces; the King's taxes were collected with difficulty, if at all; the Count's men-at-arms owned no restraint. Driven out in 1470, Jean returned under the protection of the King's brother, the Duke of Guyenne.

In 1473 a fresh expedition was sent against him; Lectoure was surrendered; and the Count killed, perhaps murdered. His fate deserves less sympathy than it has found. The independence of Armagnac, Rouergue and La Marche was at an end.

His brother, Jacques, had a similar history. Raised to the duchy of Nemours and the *pairie* by Louis XI, he became a traitor in 1465, and was implicated in all the treacherous machinations of his brother. His fate was delayed till 1476, when he was arrested. His trial left something to be desired in point of fairness, but there can be little doubt that substantial justice was done, when he was executed in 1477. Charles VIII restored the duchy to his sons, one of whom died in the King's service at the battle of Cerignola. With him the male line of Armagnac became extinct.

The House of Albret was more fortunate. Though implicated in the League of the Public Weal, and in the Breton rebellion, this House incurred no forfeiture. But the long rule of Alain le Grand (1471–1522) illustrates pathetically the humiliations, vexations, and losses that so great a prince had constantly to endure through the steady pressure of the King's agents, lawyers, and financiers, and, in some cases, through the ill-will of his own subjects. In spite of his vast domains, his appeal Courts, his more than princely revenue, he was unable to meet his still greater expenses, swelled by the new luxury and by legal costs, without a heavy pension from the King. A man, reckoned to have received from the Crown in his fifty years no less than six millions *l.t.*, cannot, however powerful he was, be regarded as independent. By marriage his House in the next generation acquired Navarre with Foix, and was ultimately merged in Bourbon, and in the Crown.

Other appanages call for little remark. Bourbon, with its appendants, Auvergne, Beaujolais, Forez, and (1477) La Marche, was the most important. It was preserved from reunion to the Crown by the influence of Anne of Beaujeu, who secured it for her daughter and her husband, the Count of Montpensier. The duchy of Orleans with the county of Blois was united to the Crown at the accession of Louis XII. None of these important fiefs were free from the royal taxes or authority, though they enjoyed some administrative independence.

Princes and minor nobles alike were gradually brought into the King's obedience by the King's pay. While the poor gentlemen entered the King's service as guards, as men-at-arms, or even as archers, the great princes drew the King's pensions, or aspired to the lucrative captainship of a body of *ordonnances*. If of sufficient dignity and influence they might hope for the still more valuable post of governor in some province. When they had once learnt to rely on the mercenary's stipend, they could not easily bring themselves to exchange it for the old honourable, though lawless, independence. Gradually the provincial nobility became dependent on the Court, and in large measure resident there. This process begins in early times, but advances more rapidly under Charles VII and his successors, and is nearly completed under Francis I.

The third Order, that of the *bourgeois* of the *bonnes villes*, has lost all the political independence that it had ever possessed. The free communes of the North and North-east had succumbed as much by their own financial mismanagement as from any other cause. Throughout the fourteenth century the intervention of the King in the internal affairs of the towns became a normal experience, and Charles V actually suppressed a number of communes. A considerable degree of municipal liberty is left, but the power of political action is gone. The government is as a rule in the hands of a comparatively small number of well-to-do *bourgeois*, who support the King's authority, and from whom is drawn the most efficient class of financiers and administrators. In time of need they help the King with loans and exceptional gifts. Many of the towns are exempt from *taille*, but the *aides* fall heavily upon them. Louis XI continued on the same lines. He granted abundant privileges to towns—fairs, markets, nobility to their officers, and the right of purchasing noble fiefs. But their intervention in politics was not encouraged. On a slight provocation the King took the town government into his hands, and heavy was the punishment of a town like Reims or Bourges, that ventured to rebel.

The position of the peasants can only be faintly indicated here. Personal servitude still exists, though probably a majority of the serfs have been enfranchised. In either case the rights of the lord have as a rule become fixed. The peasants are for the most part holders at a quit rent or in *métayage*, though bound to the *corvée*, and to the use of the lord's mill and of his bakehouse. If serfs, they are *mainmortables*, that is, their personal property belongs to their lords on their decease. Such a right obviously cannot be strictly exercised. Necessary agricultural stock must at least be spared. The lord can no longer tallage his peasants at will. His Courts are rather a symbol of his dignity and a source of petty profit, than a real instrument of arbitrary authority. Everywhere the King's power makes itself felt.

Thus the peasant was beginning to be more concerned in the character and policy of the King than in those of his lord, though, if the latter was imprudent, his peasants' crops might be ravaged. The rate of the King's *taille* made the difference between plenty and want. The *taille* cut the sources of wealth at their fountain-head, while the *seigneur* only diverted a portion of their flow. The *taille* was liable to more momentous variation than seigniorial dues; as imposed by Louis XI, it was almost, though not quite, as ruinous as the English War. Under Charles VIII and still more under Louis XII, the cessation of internal war, and the remission of *taille*, made these reigns a golden

memory to the French peasant. Seyssel says that one-third of the
land of France was restored to cultivation within these thirty years.
Moreover, it was not until the reign of Louis XII that the peasant felt
the full benefit that he should have received from the establishment of
a paid army. Under Louis XI the discipline of the regulars was still
imperfect; and the *arrière-ban* was even worse. For good government
and for bad government alike the peasant had to pay; to pay less for
better government was a double boon.

But what of that institution, the Estates General, that attempted to
bring the three Orders (in which the peasants were not included) into
touch with the central government? The representative institutions of
France had always been the humble servants of the monarchy. At the
utmost for a moment in the time of Etienne Marcel they had ventured to
take advantage of the King's weakness, and to interfere in the work of
government. The interesting ordinance of 1413, known as the *Cabochienne*, is not the work of the Estates, but of an alliance between the
University, the people of Paris, and the Duke of Burgundy. As a rule,
the Estates approach the King upon their knees. They supplicate, they
cannot command. Legislation is not their concern; even if a great
ordinance, as that of 1439, is associated with a meeting of Estates, it
cannot be regarded as their work. Their single important function, that
of assenting to the *taille*, is taken from them almost unobserved in
1439. The provincial Estates of central France continue to grant the
*taille* till 1451, when their cooperation also ceases. Normandy, and
more definitely Languedoc and the later acquisitions, retain a shadow of
this liberty. But with the power of the purse the power of the people
passes slowly and surely to the King.

Parliamentarism was doomed. Louis XI only summoned the Estates
once, in 1468, to confirm the revocation of the grant of Normandy which
he had made to Charles. The Treaty of 1482, which required the consent of the Estates, was sanctioned by not less than 47 separate local
assemblies of Estates. On his death an assembly was summoned to
Tours (1484), which was perhaps the most important meeting of Estates
General previous to 1789. Each Estate was here represented by elected
members. Thus the freedom of the assembly was not swamped by the
preponderance of princes and prelates. The persons who took the lead
were distinctly of the middle class, gentlemen, *bourgeois*, clerks. Three
deputies were as a rule sent from each *bailliage* or *sénéchaussée*; but to
this there were many exceptions. The assembly was divided into six
sections, more or less corresponding to the *généralités*,—Paris with the
North-east, Burgundy, Normandy, Guyenne, Languedoc with Provence
and Dauphiné, and Languedoil, which comprised the whole of the centre
of France together with Poitou and Saintonge. Each section deliberated
separately. Then the whole met to prepare their bills of recommendations (*cahiers*), which were presented separately by the three Estates.

The recommendations are business-like and strike at the root of many abuses. They suggested or foreshadowed many reforms actually carried out in the next thirty years. But they had no binding force. Their execution depended on the goodwill of the King's government. With such high matters as the constitution of the Council of Regency and the settlement of the rivalry between Beaujeu and Orleans the Estates ventured at most timidly to coquette. Finally they decided to take no part in the controversy and to leave all questions of government to be determined by the princes of the blood, who alone were competent to deal with them. They ventured however humbly to recommend that some of the wisest of the delegates should be called in to share the counsels of the government. In the matter of the *taille* they showed more earnestness, begging, indeed almost insisting, that a return should be made to the lower scale of Charles VII. Large concession was made to them in this respect; but the government neither resigned, nor had ever intended to resign, the absolute control over finance which it had acquired. Parliamentarism had perhaps a chance in 1484; but the tradition of humility and obedience, the sense of ignorance and diffidence in things political, were too strong, and the opportunity slipped away.

The assembly of Estates in 1506 was summoned to confirm the government in abandoning the marriage agreement already concluded between the eldest daughter of Louis XII, and the infant Duke of Luxemburg. Louis knew that his change of policy was popular, and was glad to strengthen his feeble knees with popularity against opposition in exalted quarters. But the royal will was decisive with or without the sanction of popular support.

After the battle of Nancy the King had no longer any single formidable rival within the limits of France. After the Wars of Britanny he needed no longer fear any coalition. His direct authority was enormously extended. Burgundy, Provence, Anjou, Maine, Guyenne with the dominions of Armagnac, had been annexed by the Crown, and Britanny was in process of absorption. Orleans and Blois were soon added. His power was at the same time gaining, and not only in extension, as the organs of his will became more fitted for its execution. Legislation was in his hands; the *ordonnances* were his permanent commands. In the business of making laws he was assisted by his Council, a body of sworn advisers, to which it was usual to admit the Princes of the Blood, though the King could summon or exclude whom he pleased at his discretion.

The amount of authority entrusted to the Council varied. It was said of Louis XI that the King's mule carried not only the King but his Council. It is certain that the Council never dominated him, and that he kept all high matters of State to himself and a few confidential advisers, though he made extensive use of the Council's assistance for less important things. Under a powerful minister like Georges d'Amboise the Council's advice might be useful, even necessary, but its wishes might be neglected. On the other hand, during the youth of Charles VIII the support of the Council was a valuable prop to Anne, who skilfully introduced into it men of her own confidence. The Princes of the Blood, with few exceptions, were irregular and fitful in their attendance. The professional men of affairs, legists and financiers, by their knowledge, industry, and regular presence, must have effectively controlled the business. And this was of the most varied and important character. Not only legislation, but all manner of executive matters came under its notice; police, foreign policy, ecclesiastical matters, finance, justice,—nothing was excluded from its purview. The members of the Council were numerous, their total amounting to fifty, sixty or more. After the death of Louis XI some attempt was made to limit the numbers to twelve or fifteen, and the name *Conseil étroit* was applied to this smaller body; but the endeavour, if serious, was unsuccessful; the numbers soon rose again, and were further swelled by the great men's habit of bringing with them their own private advisers.

The exercise of jurisdiction by this body often brought it into collision with the *Parlement* of Paris, whose decisions it sometimes quashed, and whose cases it evoked while still *sub judice*. Apparently under Louis XI first, and afterwards under his successors, a judicial committee of the King's Council was created to deal with contentious litigation. The specific name of *Grand Conseil* seems to attach to this tribunal, which was especially occupied with questions relating to the possession of benefices, and to the right of holding offices under the Crown. It is probable that the *Parlement*, always favourable to the Pragmatic, could not after its revocation be trusted in beneficiary actions to give judgments satisfactory to the Crown. Hence this extension and regularisation of the exceptional jurisdiction of the Council. The Estates of 1484 complained of the frequency of evocations, and interference with the ordinary course of justice, but in 1497 the *Grand Conseil* was consecrated by a new ordinance, making it in the main a Court of administrative justice. It then had in its turn to suffer the encroachments of the King's ordinary Council.

The *Parlement* of Paris was the supreme constitutional tribunal of law for the chief part of the kingdom. The jurisdiction of the King's Council sprang out of the plenitude of the royal power, and was hardly, except so far as the ordinance of 1497 extended, constitutional. For Languedoc the *Parlement* of Toulouse was created in 1443, for Dauphiné that of Grenoble in 1453, that of Bordeaux for Guyenne in 1462, and that of Dijon for conquered Burgundy in 1477. Aix was the seat of a similar tribunal for Provence after 1501, and in 1515 the Exchequer of Normandy took the style of *Parlement*. Outside the limits of these jurisdictions the *Parlement* of Paris was the sovereign Court of appeal, and a Court of first instance for those persons and corporations which

26

enjoyed the privilege (*committimus*) of resorting to it direct. *Ordonnances* required to be registered and promulgated by the Court of the *Parlement* before they received the force of law. The Court assumed the right to delay the registration of objectionable laws; and its protest was in some cases effectual even under Louis XI; but as a rule, in response to its protests, peremptory *lettres de jussion* proceeded from the King, to which they yielded. The Court had succeeded to the rights of the *Cour des pairs*, to whom belonged the exclusive power of judging those few members of the highest nobility, who were recognised as *pairs de France*. When such a peer came before the Court, a few peers took their seat with the other Counsellors, and the Court was said to be *garnie de pairs*.

Besides the peers, there were in the *Parlement* eight *maîtres des requêtes*, and 80 counsellors, equally divided since the time of Louis XI between clerical and lay. The counsellors were appointed by the King on the nomination of the members of the Court. It was usual at this time for the *Parlement* to present three selected candidates, the King to name one. But it is difficult to say how far this really held good under Louis XI. Authors of the time speak as if the King had it in his hands to nominate counsellors at his will. But a counsellor would not infrequently resign in favour of some relative, who was allowed to continue his tenure as if no vacancy had taken place. The magistracy was thus in some measure heritable. Louis XI promised (in 1467) not to remove any counsellor except for misconduct, and instructed his son to respect this decision. It is doubtful whether the venality of offices in *Parlement*, whether by counsellors selling their seats to successors, or by the King, had begun to establish itself before the reign of Francis I.

The *Parlement* was an august and powerful body. It could on occasion show a high degree of independence and even of obstinacy. But it was accessible to influence. To push a case, to avoid delay, to secure delay, even to obtain a favourable decision, the letter or the personal intervention of a great man was powerful, the half-expressed desire of the King almost irresistible. In the highest criminal cases the jurisdiction of the *Parlement* was often, especially under Louis XI, superseded by the establishment of a special commission appointed for the case. Such commissions could hardly deliver an independent judgment, especially when, as sometimes happened, the prospective confiscation of the prisoner's property had been distributed beforehand among the members of the Court.

Subordinate jurisdiction was exercised in the first instance on the royal domain by *prévôts*, *vicomtes*, or *viguiers*. Above them stood the *baillis* or *sénéchaux**, who acted as judges of appeal for their districts,

---

* The whole of France was divided into some twenty-four *bailliages* and *sénéchaussées*, varying greatly in size. Roughly speaking, the former term is used in the North, the latter in the South.

which were considerable in size, not only from the royal judges, but also from the seigniorial courts within the limits of their authority. They held periodical assizes, and were bound to appoint lieutenants under them. The *baillis* and *sénéchaux* had by this time lost their financial attributes, but they still duplicated military and judicial functions. When the *ban et arrière-ban* was called out, these officers assumed the command, and it was not till a later time that the office was divided so as to suit the two somewhat incompatible duties. Frequent edicts were passed to secure the residence of these important functionaries, but we not infrequently find the office held by a courtier, or by a soldier on campaign.

Among the great legislative acts of Charles VII the ordinance of Montils-lèz-Tours ranks high, and settles the general rules of judicial procedure for the kingdom. The reign of Louis XII saw considerable reforms in the detail of judicial machinery (1499 and 1510), but the outline of the judicial constitution was not seriously changed. The codification of local customs projected by Louis XI was begun under Charles VIII, and carried on vigorously under Louis XII, but not completed at his death. More than a century elapsed before this great task was finally achieved. This reform affected the northern part of France which was governed by *droit coutumier*, as opposed to those provinces (Dauphiné, Provence, Languedoc, Guyenne and Lyonnais), which were dominated by *droit écrit*, a modified form of Roman law.

There were many officers of more dignity than real authority, whose posts were a heritage from the more primitive organisation of feudal times. The foremost of these was the Constable of France, whose sword of office was coveted by the greatest nobles of the realm. Great nobles were also given the rank and style of governors of provinces with vice-regal powers; but the functions of such governors were not an essential part of the scheme of rule. More humble, but perhaps not less important, were the secretaries and notaries of *bourgeois* rank attached to the King's chancellery. Many of these, Bourré, for instance, and Balue, rose to great authority, wealth, and influence. The tendency to give real power and confidence rather to *bourgeois*, clerks, and poor gentlemen than to the highest nobility is marked both in Charles VII and Louis XI. Of poor gentlemen so elevated Commines and Ymbert de Batarnay are conspicuous examples.

The multiplication of offices, especially of financial offices, is a cause of complaint at least from the time of Louis XI onwards. That King, regarding himself, in virtue of his consciousness of supreme political wisdom, as emancipated from all rules that experience teaches to small men, would, when anxious to reward a useful servant, create without scruple an office for his sake, as readily as he would alienate for him a portion of domain, or fix a charge upon a *grenier* of salt. The complaints of the Estates of 1484 suggest that the venality of offices, even judicial, had already begun. Certainly it was an evil day for France, when the sale of offices was first adopted as a financial expedient, whether by Louis XII in 1512, or by another sovereign.

The efficiency of the King's officers throughout the land is chiefly shown by their zeal for his interests and their own. Under Louis XII a considerable improvement is evident in the matters of public order and police, but on this side very much still remains to be desired. The police is in the hands of the *prévôts* and *baillis* assisted by their *sergens*. The *prévôt* of Paris also exercised a singular police jurisdiction throughout the land; and Louis XI made extensive use of the summary jurisdiction of the *prévôt des maréchaux*, whose powers properly extended only over the military.

Complicated as is the financial system of France at the end of the Middle Ages, an effort to understand it is not wasted. The life of the Middle Ages for the most part escapes all quantitative analysis; and even the detail of anatomy and function must in great measure remain unknown. It is much then that we are permitted to know the main outlines of the scheme which supplied the means for the expulsion of the English, for the long struggle with Charles the Bold and Maximilian, and for the Italian campaigns, as well as for the not inconsiderable luxury and display of the French Court in this period. It is much that we are able to give approximate figures for the revenue, and to guess what was the weight of the public burdens, and how and on whom they pressed. Moreover, the financial institutions are themselves of rare historical interest; for each anomaly of the system is a mark left on the structure of the government by the history of the nation.

The history of French finance in the fourteenth and fifteenth centuries can be summed up with relative accuracy in a few words. When Philip the Fair first felt the need of extraordinary revenue, he endeavoured to secure the consent of the *seigneurs* individually for the taxation of their subjects. Afterwards the Estates made grants of imposts, direct and indirect, to meet exceptional emergencies. As the result of masked or open usurpation, the Kings succeeded in making good their claim to levy those taxes by royal *fiat* over the greater part of the kingdom.

In the earlier half of the fifteenth century it was still usual to secure the consent of the provincial Estates of at least the centre of France for the *taille*. Under Charles VII this impost, the last and the most important, became, definitely and finally, an annual tax, and the fiction of a vote by the Estates, whether general or provincial, was almost entirely given up in Languedoil. From that time till the reforms of Francis I no important change in method was introduced. The screw was frequently tightened, and occasionally relaxed. New provinces were added to the kingdom, and received exceptional and indulgent treatment. But the main scheme of finance was fixed. Many of its features, indeed, were to remain unaltered till the Revolution.

The revenue, as collected in the latter half of the fifteenth and the beginning of the sixteenth century, is classed as ordinary and extra-ordinary. The ordinary revenue is the ancient heritage of the Kings of France, and comes from the domain lands and rights, being increased on the one hand by the acquisitions of the sovereigns, and diminished on the other by war and waste, extravagant donations, and from time to time by grants of appanages to the members of the royal house. A variety of profits accrue to the King from his position as direct proprietor of land, or as suzerain. Rents and fines, reliefs and escheats, sale of wood, and pay-ments made in kind form one class of domain receipts; while the official seal required to authenticate so many transactions brings a substantial income, and the King still makes a profit by the fines and forfeitures decreed by his *prévôts* and *baillis* in his local courts. The inheritance of foreigners (*aubaine*), and of bastards, is yet another valuable right. *Régales, francs-fiefs, droits d'amortissements*, are further items in a long list bristling with the technicalities of feudal law, as developed by the Kings with a single-minded attention to their own interest. Language, if not public feeling, still insists that this revenue is to be regarded as ordinary, while other revenue is in some sort extraordinary, if not ille-gitimate; but a King who should attempt to live upon his ordinary receipts would be poor indeed. The expenses of collecting the *domaine* are heavy, the waste and destruction of the Hundred Years' War and the extravagant administration of successive Kings have reduced the gross returns, until under Charles VII the *domaine* is estimated at no more than 50,000 clear annual *livres tournois**; and although under Louis XI it may have risen to 100,000, under Louis XII to 200,000 or more, the total is insignificant compared with the needs even of a pacific and economical King.

To his assistance come the *aides, gabelle*, and *taille*. The *aides* are indirect taxes, formerly imposed by the Estates General, but levied since Charles V by royal authority. There is a twentieth levied on the sale of goods, and an eighth, sometimes a fourth, on liquors sold retail. There are many kinds of duties and tolls levied on goods in transit, not only on the frontiers of the kingdom, but at the limits of the several provinces and elsewhere. These imports, multiplex as they are, and oppressive as they seem, bring in, from the farmers who compound for them, no more than 535,000 *livres tournois* in 1461; and in 1514 their return has not risen above 654,000 *l.t.* Languedoc has its separate excise duty on meat and fish, known as the *équivalent*, and collected by the authority of the Estates.

The *gabelle du sel*, once a local and seigniorial tax, has, since the time of Philippe de Valois, become a perpetual and almost universal

* An exact equation is impossible; but the purchasing power of the *livre tournois* in the later fifteenth century was probably not much greater or less than that of the pound sterling to-day.

royal impost. As a rule the salt of the kingdom is brought into the royal warehouses, *greniers*, and left there by the merchants for sale, this taking place in regular turn. A fixed addition for the royal profit is made to the price of the salt as it is sold; and heads of houses are required to purchase a fixed annual minimum of salt. In Languedoc the tax is levied on its passage from the salt works on the sea coast, and the black salt of Poitou and Saintonge gets off with a tax of 25 per cent.; but the general principle is the same. From a quarter upwards is added to the price of a necessary of life, and the product is in 1461 about 160,000 *l.t.*, rising in the more prosperous times and with the more accurate finance of Louis XII to some 280,000 *l.t.*

Finally there is the *taille, fouage*, hearth or land-tax. The gradual process by which the right of the *seigneurs* to levy *taille* on their subjects had passed into the exclusive possession of the King is too long to admit of being followed here. Here as in other cases the Estates at first permitted what the King afterwards carried on without their leave. Under the agonising pressure of foreign and civil war Charles VII was allowed,—we can hardly say that he was authorised,—to transform the *taille* into an annual tax levied at the King's discretion. The normal total was fixed at 1,200,000 *l.t.*; but Charles VII established a precedent by imposing *crues*, or arbitrary additions to the tax, levied for some special emergency. The intervention of the Estates in Languedoil and Outreseine ceased; in Normandy it became a mere form; in Languedoc it was reduced to a one-sided negotiation between the province and the King, in which he might show indulgence, but the deputies could hardly show fight. Yet resistance was not infrequently tried, and was sometimes successful even with the inexorable Louis XI. On the other hand even in Languedoc a *crue* is sometimes ordered and paid without a vote, though never without protest. The *taille* fell only on the *roturiers*, and spared the privileged orders of clergy and *noblesse*. In Languedoc the exemption followed the traditional distinction of tenements into noble and non-noble; in Languedoil the peasant paid if occupying a noble fief, the noble was exempt, although in actual possession of a villain holding.

Thus the clergy and the nobility escaped, except in a few cases, the direct burden of the principal tax. Speaking generally, they did not escape the burden of the *aides* and *gabelle*, though they had certain privileges. Royal officers for the most part escaped not only *taille* but *gabelle*. Many of the principal towns also escaped the former. Such were Paris, Rouen, Laon, Reims, Tours, and many others. There were other inequalities and injustices. Normandy paid one-fourth of the whole *taille*,—a monstrous burden upon a province which had suffered not less than any other from the War. The proportion of one-tenth fixed on Languedoc was probably also excessive. In the *recherche* of 1491 it was calculated that Languedoil paid 19 *l.t.* per head, Outreseine 27, Normandy 60, and Languedoc 67,—an estimate which may be very far from the facts, but gives the result of contemporary impression. Guyenne, when added to the direct dominion of the Crown, escaped in large measure the *aides*, and was allowed to vote a small contribution by way of *taille*. Burgundy compounded for her share of *taille* by an annual vote of about 50,000 *l.t.*, contributing also to *aides* and *gabelle*. Provence was allowed to keep her own Estates and to vote a moderate subsidy. The independent and privileged position of Britanny was not altered until after the death of Louis XII. Dauphiné was treated with a consideration even greater than was warranted by its poverty. Thus the main tax, unevenly distributed as it was, pressed the more heavily on the cultivators of the less fortunate regions. It is not uncommon to hear of the inhabitants of some district under Charles VII or Louis XI preferring to leave home and property rather than bear the enormous weight of the public burdens. The taxable capacity of the people was constantly increasing in the latter half of the fifteenth century; but under Louis XI the burdens increased with more than equal rapidity. The *taille* increased from 1,035,000 *l.t.* in 1461 to some 3,900,000 in 1483. From the pressing remonstrances of the Estates in 1484 a great alleviation resulted. The *taille* was reduced to 1,500,000 *l.t.* and although the expedition of Naples, the War of Britanny, and other causes, necessitated a subsequent rise, the figures remained far below the level of Louis XI's reign. Louis XII was enabled, in spite of his ambitious schemes, to effect further reductions; but the War of Cambray and its sequel swept away nearly all the advantage that had been gained. The revenue raised in 1514 was as high as the highest raised under Louis XI. But the *aides* and *domaine* were more productive; the *taille* was less, and weighed less heavily on a more prosperous nation.

Under Philip the Fair and his successors down to Charles VII a considerable though precarious revenue had often been realised by the disastrous method of tampering with the standard of value. In the latter years of Charles VII and under his three successors this device was rarely employed. A considerable depreciation may be indeed observed between the standard of Louis XII and that of Charles VII; but the changes were far less important and frequent than those of the earlier period. A certain revenue was obtained by legitimate seigniorage, and the illegitimate profits of debasement and the like may be almost neglected.

The system of collection was still only partially centralised, and marked the imperfect union of the successive acquisitions of the monarchy. For the collection and administration both of *domaine* and extraordinary revenue the older provinces were distributed into four divisions. Western Languedoil was administered with Guyenne; but the parts of Languedoil beyond Seine and Yonne, when reunited to the

Crown, about 1436, were organised as a separate financial group (Outreseine). Normandy formed a third and separate administrative area. Administrative Languedoc, that is to say the three *sénéchaussées* of Carcassonne, Beaucaire, and Toulouse, forms the fourth. Picardy, Burgundy, Dauphiné, Provence, Roussillon and of course Britanny, were not included in the general scheme. Milan had its separate financial establishment, and maintained 600 lances.

In these last-mentioned provinces the ordinary and extraordinary revenue were administered together; elsewhere *domaine* and extraordinary revenue were separated. For the administration of the *domaine* each of the four main divisions had a separate treasurer, who was practically supreme in his own district. Under them were as administrators on the first line the *baillis* or *sénéchaux*, on the second, the *prévôts, vicomtes,* or *viguiers.* The separation of the receipt from the administration of funds is a principle that runs through the whole system of finance both ordinary and extraordinary. Accordingly, there is a *receveur* for each *prévôté* or other subdivision, and a general receiver for the whole domain, known as the *changeur du Trésor.* But the actual collection of cash at the central office was in large measure avoided, partly by charging the local officer of receipt with all local expenses, and partly by a system of drafts on local offices adopted for the payment of obligations incurred by the central government. The beneficiary presented his draft to the local *receveur* or *grenetier,* or discounted it with a broker, who forwarded it to his agent for collection. The same plan was adopted in the extraordinary finance, and made an accurate knowledge of the financial position, and correct supervision of the accounts, a matter of extreme difficulty. Contentious business was either settled by the *baillis* or *prévôts,* or by a central tribunal of *domaine* finance, the *Chambre du Trésor,* or in some cases by the *Chambre des Comptes* or the *Parlement.*

The same regions of France were similarly divided for extraordinary finance into four *généralités.* At the head of each were two *généraux,* one *pour le fait des finances,* the other *pour le fait de la justice.* The four *généraux de la justice* met together to form the *Cour des Aides,* an appeal Court for contentious questions arising out of the collection of the extraordinary revenue. There are other *Cours des Aides,* at Montpellier for Languedoc, and at Rouen for Normandy. Each *général des finances* was supreme in the administration of his own *généralité.* Associated with each *général* there was a *receveur général,* who guarded the cash and was accountable for it. In Languedoc the partition and collection of *taille* and the collection of *aides* was managed by the Estates of the province. The other three *généralités* (except Guyenne, which was administered by commissioners) were divided into *élections,* a term reminiscent of the earlier system when the Estates collected the sums they had voted and elected the supervising officers. The *élus,* who stood at the head of each *élection*, and whose duty it was to apportion the *taille* over the several parishes, to let out the *aides*, and to act as judges of first instance in any litigation that might arise, were now, as they had long since been, the nominees of the King. Beside them stood the *receveurs*, who as a rule handled the product both of *taille* and *aides*. As a general rule each *receveur*, whether of ordinary or extraordinary finance, was doubled with a comptroller, whose business it was to check his accounts, and fortify his honesty. The *aides* were let out at farm. The actual collection of the *taille* was carried out by locally appointed collectors, who received five per cent. for their trouble. The assessment on individuals was the work of locally elected *asséeurs*. The collection of the *gabelle* was in the hands of special officers. Each *grenier* had a receiver called *grenetier* and the inevitable *contrerôleur*.

All accounts of the area so circumscribed were inspected and passed by a superior body, the *Chambre des Comptes*. Separate Courts were also set up at Nantes, Dijon, Aix, and Grenoble for their respective provinces. The *Chambre des Comptes* of Paris was differently composed at different times but consisted in 1511 of two presidents and ten *maîtres des Comptes*. It had power to impose disciplinary penalties on financial officers, and claimed to be a sovereign Court, exempt from the controlling jurisdiction of the *Parlement*, but this claim was not always successfully maintained. All alienations of domain, and pensions for more than a brief period of years, had to be registered in the *Chambre des Comptes*,— a form which gave this Court the opportunity to protest against, and at any rate to delay, injudicious grants.

As will be seen, this financial system by no means lacked checks and safeguards; rather perhaps it erred on the side of over-elaboration. Although an immense improvement is perceptible since the time of Charles VI, there can be little doubt that the system suffered from considerable leakage. The men employed in the King's finance were mostly of *bourgeois* rank; Jacques Cœur, Guillaume and Pierre Briçonnet, Jacques de Beaune, Étienne Chevalier, Jean Bourré, are among the most famous names; in many cases they were related to each other by blood or marriage, and they all, almost without exception, became very rich. In some cases this need be thought no shame; thus Jacques Cœur no doubt owed his wealth to the inexhaustible riches of oriental trade. But as a rule servants only grow rich at the expense of their master; and it is a sign of evil augury when the servant lends his master money, as for instance Jacques de Beaune did on a large scale. This great financier was in the ambiguous position of a banker who himself discounted the bills just signed by him for his King. The business was legitimate, and lucrative because of its very hazardousness; but it comported ill with a position of supreme financial trust and responsibility.

Not only was the system of control imperfect, and the tradition of honesty unsatisfactory, but the scheme lacked unity of direction. There was no single responsible financial officer. Jacques de Beaune (sieur de Semblençay, 1510-23) enjoyed a certain priority of dignity, but exercised no unifying authority. Once a year the treasurers and *généraux*, "*Messieurs des finances*," met in committee and drew up in concert the budget for the year. So much being expected as receipt from *domaine, aides,* and *gabelle,* and so much anticipated as expenditure,—then the *taille* must be so much to meet the balance. And to a certain extent the Council of State kept its hand on finance, assisted at need by the financial officers specially convened. But unity of management and administration was conspicuously wanting.

The expenditure of the four Kings cannot, on the whole, if tried by a royal standard, be called extravagant. The most questionable item is that of pensions. Pensions were not only used to reward services, and gratify courtiers, but were also given on a large scale to Princes of the Blood and considerable nobles. Historically such pensions may be regarded as some compensation for the loss of the right of raising *aides* and *taille* in their own domain, which had once belonged to personages holding such positions, but which since 1439 had remained categorically abolished. With the fall of Charles the Bold and the absorption of Britanny the last examples of princes enjoying such rights unquestioned disappeared. Politically such pensions were intended to conciliate possible opponents and enemies, for the great princes, though stripped by law of their chief powers, still possessed in spite of the law sufficient influence and authority to raise a war. How strong such influence might be we see in 1465, when not only Britanny and Burgundy, but Bourbon, Armagnac, and d'Albret, found their subjects ready to follow them against the King.

Such pensions were an old abuse. Louis XI found in them one of his most powerful political engines, and distributed them with a lavish hand. The pensions bill rose under him from about 300,000 *l.t.* to 500,000. In addition there were the great English pensions, and the pensions to the Swiss. The totals were probably not much less under Charles VIII; but Louis XII reduced them at one time so low as 105,000 and seems to have effected a substantial average diminution. However, the practice of charging pensions on local sources of revenue, especially the *greniers* of salt, prevents the whole magnitude of this waste from coming into view.

The expenses of the Court, largely military, rose under Louis XI from about 300,000 to 400,000 *l.t.*; and seem to have been reduced by half or more by Louis XII. Military expenses are of course the chief item of the budget. The constantly increasing expenditure of Louis XI is chiefly due to the cost of the army. The establishment rose from 2000 lances to 3,884 in 1483, when there was also a standing army of 16,000 foot at Pont de l'Arche in Normandy, including 6,000 Swiss. The cost of the army on a peace footing is not less in this year than 2,700,000 *l.t.*

The difficulties of Louis XI were very great, and the results of his military expenditure on the whole commensurate with the sacrifices, but he seems in his later years to have been driven by nervous fear to excessive precaution.

The military budget of the succeeding Kings was conspicuously less. The War of Naples was chiefly waged on credit, and at the death of Charles VIII a deficit of 1,400,000 remained unliquidated, but in no year can the totals of Louis XI have been passed; perhaps in 1496 they may have been reached. Louis XII carried on his wars very economically until the deserved disasters of the War of Cambray. The *taille* of these years speaks for itself. It rises steadily from 2,000,000 *l.t.* in 1510 to 3,700,000 in 1514, and the father of his people left an additional deficit of a million and a half.

The new conditions, political and social, of the fourteenth and fifteenth centuries in France had long demanded a reorganisation of the army. Service by tenure had lost its meaning since, in the time of Philip the Fair, the practice of paying the contingents had been adopted. There is little that is feudal in the organisation of the French army during the Hundred Years' War, much more that is anarchical, and a little that is royal. At most the feudal aristocracy supplies some of the *cadres* in which the troops are embodied. But the aristocracy is not a necessary but an accidental feature of the scheme. The organisation of the host and of its units does not follow the lines of the feudal hierarchy. The King is a rallying-point, giving rise to a delusive sense of unity of direction; chance and the love of fighting accomplish the rest. For a few years the centralising purpose of Charles V warranted better hopes, which perished with his death.

As the War continues, the professional soldier, the professional captain, becomes all in all. This soldier or captain may be a noble, born to the art of arms, but side by side with him are many adventurers sprung from the lower orders. They are glad to receive pay if pay is forthcoming; if not, they will be content with loot; in any case they are lawless, landless, homeless mercenaries, who live upon the people, and are the terror rather of friend than of foe. This lack of even feudal discipline in France is the cause of the success of the better-organised armies of England. It is also the principal cause of the horrors of the endless War. When a respite intervenes, the country knows no peace till the mercenaries are sent to die abroad,—in Castile, in Lorraine, or against the Swiss.

To have put an end to this misrule is the conspicuous service of Charles VII and his successors. In 1439, on the occasion of a great meeting of the Estates at Orleans, the King and his Council promulgated a notable edict. The number of captains was henceforth to be fixed, and no person was under the gravest penalties to entertain soldiers without the King's permission. A pathetic list follows of customary outrages, which are now forbidden; and the captains are made responsible for the good conduct of their men. The seneschals and bailiffs are given authority, if authority suffices, to punish any military crimes whatsoever, and wheresoever committed. The financial side of the measure is indicated by a clause prohibiting all lords from levying *tailles* in their lands without the King's leave, impeding the collectors of the King's *taille*, or collecting any increment on their own account. The King intends to have an army, to have the only army, to have it disciplined and obedient, and to have the money for its pay.

Unfortunately the revolt known as the *Praguerie*, which broke out soon after, impeded the development of this plan. The *Armagnacs* were then sent to be let blood in Lorraine and Switzerland. The warlike operations of 1444 having been carried out, the scheme took effect in the following year. Fifteen companies of one hundred "lances" were instituted, each under a captain appointed by the King. It would seem that five more were to be supported by Languedoc. Each "lance" was to consist of one man-at-arms, two archers, a swordsman, a valet, and a page, all mounted and armed according to their quality. The page and the valet were the servants of the man-at-arms, but the valet at least was a fighting man. The method of organisation is strange, but has an historical explanation. It had long been customary for the man-at-arms to take the field accompanied by several armed followers; the ordinance adopted the existing practice. Its effect was to establish several different sorts of cavalry, light and heavy, capable of manœuvring separately, and useful for different purposes; but tradition required that they should be grouped in "lances," and it was long before the advantage of separating them was understood. For a time the superstitious imitation of English tactics made the men-at-arms dismount for the shock of battle; but they learned their own lesson from experience, and found that few could resist the weight of armoured men and heavy horses charging in line.

At first the new companies were quartered on the several provinces, and the task of providing for them was left to the local Estates. But before long the advantage of regular money payment was perceived, and a *taille* was levied to provide monthly pay, at the rate of thirty-one *livres* per lance.

The force of standing cavalry so formed became the admiration of Europe. Their ranks were mainly filled with noblemen, whose magnificent tradition of personal courage and devotion to the practice of arms made them the best possible material. In four campaigns they mastered and expelled the English. In Britanny, in Italy, on a score of fields they proved their bravery, their discipline, their skill. They had undoubtedly the faults of professional soldiers, but their virtues no body of men ever had in a higher degree. Even the moral tone of an army that trained and honoured Bayard could not be altogether bad.

Fortunately perhaps for Europe, the King's efforts to form an adequate force of infantry were not equally successful. In 1448 each parish was ordered to supply an archer fully armed for fighting on foot. The individual chosen was to practise the bow on feast-days and holidays, and to serve the King for pay when called upon. In return he was freed from the payment of *taille*, whence the name *francs archers*. Later the contingent was one archer to every fifty *feux*, and under Louis XI it was reckoned that there were some 16,000 men in this militia. Four classes were then differentiated; pikemen, halberdiers, archers, cross-bowmen. They were organised in brigades of 4,000 under a captain-general, and bands of 500 under a captain. They did not however prove efficient, and in 1479 disgraced themselves at Guinegaste. Louis XI then dismissed them and established a standing army of 16,000 foot at Pont de l'Arche in Normandy, of whom 6,000 were Swiss. To meet the expense and provide regular pay, an extra *taille* was imposed.

The cost of this army led to its disbandment in the next reign, and Charles VIII tried to revive the institution of free archers. Free archers fought on both sides in the Wars of Britanny. But they were not taken to Naples, and although they are still mentioned occasionally, they saw no further service in the period now under review.

Louis XII relied largely on Swiss, and afterwards on Germans. But he also organised bands of French *aventuriers* under the command of gentlemen. Those who guarded the frontier of Picardy were known as the *bandes de Picardie*. Levies were also made in Gascony, Britanny, Dauphiné, and Piedmont. But they were usually disbanded on the conclusion of a war. For garrison duty a force of veterans was kept on foot known as *morte-paies*. But the infantry arm of the service continued to be unsatisfactory. The general levy of all those bound to bear arms, known as *ban et arrière-ban*, was not infrequently called out by Louis XI, but proved disorderly and unserviceable.

The artillery was first organised under Charles VII by the brothers Bureau. The French artillery was distinguished by its comparative mobility, and discharged iron shot. It was under the command of the *grand maître de l'artillerie*, and served as a model to the rest of Europe. We find under Louis XI, and afterwards, an organised force of sappers.

The navy depended still in large measure on the impressment of merchant vessels and seamen. Normandy, Provence, and afterwards Britanny, were the chief recruiting grounds. In the Italian Wars we find the French Kings chiefly dependent on Genoa for galleys. But under Louis XII a few war vessels were built and owned by the King. The French mounted heavy guns on large ships with excellent results.

Everywhere we find invention at work, directed for the most part to practical construction and consolidation. Commerce was stirring. The

French were directing their attention to the oriental trade, in which Jacques Cœur and the Beaune family founded their fortunes. Breton sailors went far afield, traded with the Canaries and Madeira, and were fishing cod off Iceland, perhaps on the Banks of Newfoundland, long before the recognised discovery of the New World. But internal trade was more prosperous than foreign. In spite of paralysing tariffs on the frontiers of provinces and the myriad *péages* which the Kings in vain attempted to keep down, steady progress was made. The misfortunes of Bruges and Ghent, Liége and Dinant, left a gap in home markets which French traders partly succeeded in filling. The silk trade took root at Tours and Lyons, and was encouraged by Louis XI. Reviving agriculture stimulated commercial and industrial life in many a country town, and small fortunes were frequently made. The marvellous recuperative power of France was never more clearly seen than in the half century after the English wars.

The middle of the fifteenth century saw a national revival of art in France. French miniaturists had long explored the resources and perhaps reached the limits of their charming art. The *Hours* of the Duke of Berry, dating from the early fifteenth century, are hardly to be surpassed. But Jean Foucquet (1415–80) was not only a master among masters of miniature, but a painter prized even in Italy. His work is interesting as showing the taste for classical architecture in works of fancy long before it had begun to influence the constructions of French builders. It is probable that the competition of Italian painters for the patronage of the great, which begins immediately after the Italian wars, checked the growth of an indigenous French school of painting, which might have fulfilled the promise of French miniaturists. In sculpture a school arose at Dijon under Charles VI, which is original and fruitful. In this school was trained Michel Colombe (who died in 1512); his masterpiece is perhaps the tomb of Francis II at Nantes.

Gothic ecclesiastical architecture had lost itself in the meaningless elaborations of the decadent "*Flamboyant*." But in domestic architecture the *corps de métier* were still capable of producing such masterly work as the house of Jacques Cœur at Bourges, and, in the reign of Louis XI, the castles of Langeais and Le Plessis Bourré, still standing solid and reminiscent of the necessities of defence. Amboise, of a still later date, shows the same characteristics. Gradually classical influence begins to modify, first detail, then construction. The results may be seen in Louis XII's part of the castle of Blois. But the golden age of French Renaissance architecture is the reign of Francis I, when first the castle put off its heavy armour, and assumed the lightness, grace, and gaiety, so well known to travellers on the Loire.

In literature, the excellence of the best is so great that it makes us the less willing to remain content with the dull mediocrity of the mass.

Charles of Orleans' melancholy, musical verse fixes in perpetuity the fragrance of the passing ideals of chivalry. Villon, closely conversant with the pathos and humours of the real, veils it gracefully and slightly in transparent artificialities. Commines, naïf, for all his dignified reserve, cold wisdom, and experienced cynicism, ranks alike with those who have rediscovered the art of history, and with those who have assisted to perfect French prose. Chastelain, burdened with cumbrous rhetoric and prone to useless sermonising, can on occasion tell a stirring tale, and proves his faults to be not of himself, but of his school. For the rest, in poetry and prose, whether the tedious allegories learnt from the *Roman de la Rose* prevail, or the not less tedious affectations of classical imitation, or the laboured tricks of a most unhappy school of verse, there are few names that deserve to be remembered.

In the world of thought the French clung longer than other nations to the traditions of Scholasticism. But the school of Nicolas of Cusa, which represents a transitional movement from medieval to Renaissance philosophy, had its followers in France, of whom the first was Jacques le Fèvre d'Étaples, and the most distinguished Carolus Bovillus.

To deal adequately with the men whose accumulated endeavours restored order, unity, and prosperity to France after the English wars would need a volume, not a chapter. Many of them, humble, obscure, energetic, faithful, escape the notice of the historian. Valuable monographs have been written upon some, but no adequate memorial exists of the most powerful French minister of the time, Georges d'Amboise, without whom nothing of moment whether good or bad was done during the best years of Louis XII. One figure stands out above all others,— Louis XI, of the four Kings the only one who both reigned and governed. Whether we condemn or whether we condone the remorseless rigour with which that King pursued his public ends, whether we regret the absolute monarchy which he established, or accept it as having been the only possible salvation of France, we cannot deny to him the name of great. Great he was in intellect and in tenacity of purpose, great in prosperity and even greater in misfortune. Whatsoever he did had its determined end, and that end was the greatness of France,—or, if the expression be preferred, of the French monarchy. The universal condemnation which he has incurred may be ascribed chiefly to two causes: the unrelenting sternness with which he visited treachery in the great, and the severity of the taxation which he found it necessary to impose. The world was shocked by the fate of Jean d'Armagnac, Jacques de Nemours, Louis de St Pol, Cardinal Balue, and by the cynical methods which achieved their ruin. Looking back without passion, we pronounce their sentence just. The burden of taxes was cruel, and the stories we read in Brantôme and elsewhere of lawless and inhuman executions are probably not without foundation. These methods may be supposed to have been required to bring the enormous taxes in. The

Estates of 1484 speak of five hundred executions for offences against the *gabelle*. We need not accept the number; the Estates believed many strange tales; but the suggestion is instructive, and helps to explain the legends of apparently meaningless slaughter wrought upon the humble. In the struggle for life and death in which France was engaged those taxes and perhaps those executions saved her; the King's crimes were national crimes, and national crimes are not to be judged by the standards of domestic morality. The France of Louis XII is the justification of Louis XI.

# CHAPTER XIII.

## THE NETHERLANDS.

WHEN after the catastrophe of Nancy the cautious doubts of Louis XI as to the personal fate of his adversary had at last been set at rest, many of Charles the Bold's former subjects refused to believe him dead; and from Burgundy to the Flemish communes the rumour ran that he but lay concealed in some sure retreat whence sooner or later he would issue forth in the full blaze of his accustomed grandeur. Some had seen him in Lorraine, others in Germany; others in Portugal, to whose nationality he had laid claim as descending to him from his mother, and in England, of whose throne he had loved to describe himself as the next heir; yet others in Jerusalem, which he and his father had vainly hoped to reach as crusaders, and in Rome. Men of business lent out large sums of money to one another to be repaid on the day of his return, on which strange to say even those fixed their hopes who had previously testified to having seen him dead in the snow and ice of his last battlefield. A delusion was upon them all, says the chronicler Molinet in his bombastic way, like that possessing the Jews who await the coming of the Messiah in Judæa, or the English who expect King Arthur back in their island; but what wonder, he asks, since there never was in the Burgundian dominions a duke more magnificent, more warlike, more terrible than he, the scourge of the rebels, the alarum of Germany, the exterminator of the folk of Liége, and the terror of France? Of so strong and splendid a prince it might indeed seem hard to understand so great a fall. Yet even more difficult to grasp than the fact of his personal overthrow was this other fact, that with him had been pulled down suddenly, and to all seeming irrecoverably, the mightiest and wealthiest monarchy known to the West in the fifteenth century. This vast inheritance, welded together by the policy of his ancestors and above all of his father, and augmented by his own ambition, to which Charles had allowed so many princes to aspire as suitors for his daughter's hand, he had left to her precarious tenure as a mutilated, dislocated, and disorganised heap of territories. Furthermore, in those centres of civic life, whose mercantile and industrial prosperity had in the Europe of the later Middle Ages been the real source of the importance of the Netherlands and of the Burgundian monarchy, that prosperity was except in certain specially favoured seaports helplessly and hopelessly on the wane; and the great communes which had of old been its most favoured seats, were, in the truthful words of a modern historian, smitten to the heart.

### I.

The territories under the dominion of the House of Burgundy, which had formed part of the northern division of ancient Lotharingia, and were known to later political geography as the provinces of the Netherlands, were for the most part acquired by the fortune of marriage and inheritance; but a settled plan of policy had from an early date continuously directed and developed the process of annexation. The inheritance brought by Margaret of Maele to the French prince, who was the founder of the ducal dynasty, included the county of Artois, with its capital of Arras, a city of great mercantile prosperity as early as the thirteenth century, and the whole of Flanders. To the latter on the eastern side Malines (Mechlin) and Antwerp had been yielded by Brabant, and on the south certain Walloon districts, long united with France and including Lille and Douay, had been restored so as likewise to be left to his daughter by the last Count of Flanders of the native line. Without the support of the good towns of Flanders—Bruges, Ghent, and Ypres—Philip the Bold could not have secured the hand of the richest heiress in Europe; and of the political greatness achieved by his dynasty the true foundations are to be sought in the resources of the great communes themselves, with whom it was engaged in perennial conflict, and, in a less degree, of the other towns around them. There is no indication, on the other hand, that even during the Burgundian period agriculture, except perhaps pasture, reached a high level in Flanders; in a considerable proportion of its villages, the inhabitants gained their livelihood by manufacturing industry, the villages aiming at becoming small towns, and the small towns at becoming large in their turn.

Artois and Flanders remained fiefs of the French Crown, although by the Peace of Arras (1435) Philip the Good was relieved for his own person of all obligations of homage to his French overlord. The great acquisitions, which ensued in the course of his long reign, were not altogether due to his own resolution and statecraft. He shared the credit of them with his grandfather and namesake who had induced Joan, heiress of Brabant and aunt to his wife Margaret of Flanders, to designate his second son Anthony as her heir; and who married his daughter, another Margaret, to the future Count William VI of Hainault, Holland, Zeeland, and Friesland. But they could not have been actually accomplished except by the extraordinary strength of will and perseverance displayed by Philip the Good in the course of the long and momentous struggle carried on by Jacqueline of Bavaria for the maintenance of her rights as William VI's heiress.

Philip began the systematic extension of his dominions by the business-like purchase of the county of Namur (Namen) (1422), of which he came into actual possession eight years later by the death of the last female representative of the House of Dampierre. This district was of some consequence by reason of its mining industry, whose products the Meuse carried north, after uniting the waters of the Sambre to its own at the capital. Brabant fell into his hands in 1430 on the death of the young Duke Philip, the brother of Jacqueline's unhappy husband. To the duchy of Brabant that of Limburg had been annexed (1288), with its chief town of Maestricht, the "higher ford" of the Romans and the residence of many Caroling Kings, over which the Bishop of Liége claimed joint rights of sovereignty with the Dukes of Brabant. Unlike the Flemish Counts these Dukes had consistently remained on friendly terms with their towns, where the patriciate (*geslachten*) vigorously maintained itself throughout the fourteenth century. Ample and solid liberties were conceded to his towns and nobility by Duke John II in the compact known as the Letter of Cortenberg (1312), enlarged by later charters, and above all, when the accession of Wenceslas of Luxemburg offered an irresistible opportunity by the famous *Joyeuse Entrée* (*blyde inkomste*) (1356), which remained the chief pillar of the liberties of the two united duchies down to the tempestuous times of Philip II of Spain. At the beginning of this century Louvain (Leuven) had still regarded herself as the foremost city of Brabant, mindful of the day when she had numbered a hundred thousand inhabitants, and the cloth-industry and the linen-trade had alike flourished within her walls. Soon, however, though she became the seat of the first Netherlands University (1426), a large emigration set in to Brussels, whither the Court likewise transferred its seat. Here the active lower town, and the residences of the nobility lining the descent from the Castle to St Gudule, together contained all the chief elements in the Brabançon population, while the French tastes and manners introduced together with the use of the French tongue by the new dynasty familiarised its favourite residence with an exotic license of life. But, owing to the decay of the cloth industry early in the century, the democratic ascendency of the trades was short-lived in the capital of Brabant; and, like the great Flemish cities themselves, Brussels, though other industries flourished here, was commercially distanced by Antwerp.

Over Hainault, Holland, Zeeland, and (more or less nominally) Friesland, Philip's sovereignty was definitively established in 1433, five years after the resistance of Jacqueline had finally collapsed, at the very time when the fury of the *Kabeljaauws* had risen to fever-pitch

27—2

against her supporters, the *Hoeks*; their last fleet had been annihilated, and he was preparing for a decisive campaign against his seemingly indomitable adversary. At that time the recognition of Philip as next heir had been voted even in chivalrous Hainault, where Jacqueline had always been able to count on ardent loyalty, and where, amidst feudal conditions of life, only one or two towns—Valenciennes, and more recently Mons,—had developed their communal institutions. In Holland and Zeeland the towns attained to an advanced condition of prosperity and importance later than in Brabant, just as the latter had lagged behind Flanders. Yet, though the growth of the towns in the Northern Netherlands was relatively slow, neither was their commercial and industrial progress hampered, as was the case in Germany, by too close a control on the part of transmitted interests, nor was their political life, like that of the Flemish communes, handed over to the gusts of the market-place. As a rule, practical considerations led them from more to less broadly popular methods of government.

In matters of trade, on the other hand, the towns of Holland generally favoured freedom as against privilege and protection, and towards the close of the Middle Ages the single port in the Northern Netherlands which retained any staple-rights of consequence was Dort, whose ancient monopoly of all goods carried on the main rivers of Holland nominally outlasted the Burgundian period. But long before this Amsterdam, converted into a seaport by the formation of the Zuiderzee in the thirteenth century, had risen into prominence, and by the middle of the fifteenth she had left behind all the older towns of importance—Dort, Delft, Haarlem, Alkmaar, Middelburg, and Zierikzee—while among the younger Gouda, Leiden, Schiedam, and Rotterdam were likewise active centres of industrial and mercantile life. Few great noble families remained either in Holland or in Zeeland; but in the latter the small nobility was still numerous in the days of Jacqueline, and it was from them that the main strength of the *Hoeks* had been recruited in her wars, while that of the *Kabeljaauws* lay with the ruling classes in the towns. The vanquished cause, however, was consecrated in the memory of the people as having been that of resistance against the dominion of the stranger.

In no instance had his hand been heavier than in his treatment of the peninsula now known as North Holland, stretching out between the North Sea and the Zuiderzee, where dwelt the Kennemer, a primitive race of great and tried vigour, who clung to their liberties as they held fast to the fragments of land left to them by the waters. In Kennemerland proper Alkmaar was the only town; with thriving Haarlem on their borders these peasants were constantly engaged in petty warfare, and it was from here that Philip proceeded on his expedition of vengeance which reduced them to the condition of overtaxed dependents. A few of the mercantile settlements along the western coast of the

Zuiderzee came in the Burgundian period to rank among the busiest towns of Holland—Hoorn as the chief market in the Netherlands for dairy produce and cattle, Enkhuizen as a centre of the herring-fishery. Friesland proper, on the north-eastern shore, over which Philip asserted his claims as Count of Holland and Zeeland, was not actually absorbed by him. Here the party-name of the *Schieringers* mainly applied to the lower population settled round the waters of the ancient Westergao, and that of the *Vetkoopers* to the men of substance in and around Groningen, which town held a position so distinctive that it afterwards became eponymous of a whole province (officially called *stadt en landen*). Philip the Good might possibly have been acknow-ledged as Lord of Friesland, like John of Bavaria before him, had he been prepared to bind himself to respect the liberties of the population. But this he consistently refused, and the remote region was once more left to itself. Even the subsequent recognition by Groningen of the overlordship of the Bishop of Utrecht was purely nominal; as was the episcopal protection claimed by her against the attempt of Charles the Bold to assert the ducal authority over all West-Friesland (1469.) From the renewed internal party-conflicts in Friesland Groningen dis-creetly held aloof, intent upon the advancement of her commercial prosperity, by whose side that of ancient "golden" Stavoren was passing away, while that of Leeuwarden had hardly yet begun.

Philip's last important territorial acquisition was that of the duchy of Luxemburg, a sparsely peopled land of mountains and forests whose capital derived importance from the incomparable natural strength of its position. It had been twice temporarily united with Brabant—first under Wenceslas, upon whom it had been bestowed by his brother, the great Emperor Charles IV, and who was married to the heiress Joan; and then under Elizabeth, niece of the second Wenceslas, King of the Romans, who had left it very much to itself and the protection of its natural outworks, the wild Ardennes. To her (commonly called Elizabeth of Görlitz) he had, after her marriage to Duke Anthony of Brabant, Philip's younger brother, made over his rights in Luxemburg; and since both Anthony and her second husband, John of Bavaria, formerly Bishop-elect of Liége, left her a childless widow, her duchy was plainly marked out for incorporation in the Burgundian dominions. In 1445 Philip purchased it from Elizabeth, who, after he had averted an extraneous attack and established his authority in every part of the duchy, made a formal donation to him of the whole.

Of the four great dioceses into which the Netherlands were up to the time of Charles V divided, Liége and Utrecht retained the character of self-governed ecclesiastical principalities beyond the dura-tion of Philip's reign. Liége (Luik) was one of the most important sees in the Empire, and the spiritual authority of its Bishop extended over parts of Brabant and Hainault, as well as over Namur, Limburg, and Upper Gelderland. In the principality the Diets were composed of representatives of clergy, nobility, and towns, but these last were in enjoyment of liberties resembling those possessed by the Flemish communes. In the city of Liége itself the struggle which had long been carried on between the old patrician families, relatively few in number but favoured by the Bishops, and the mass of the Walloon population, had been decided in favour of the latter, even before "a city of priests had been changed into one of colliers and armourers." The faction feuds between the *Awans* and the *Waroux* had ended with the utter extrusion of the patrician element from the city; and Liége became a democracy of the most advanced type, with a governing body based directly upon the suffrage of all the thirty-two trades. It was as a community swayed by leaders who gloried in their rupture with the past (*haydroits*), that Liége, with the support of the other "good towns" of the principality revolted against the Bishop-elect, John of Bavaria. The terrible chastisement inflicted by this "pitiless" prince, in which his kinsman the "fearless" John of Burgundy had hastened to have his share (1408), was followed by a reconstitution of the government, from which the trades were absolutely excluded (1414); but some concessions were made to them a few years later.

Half a century later the Liégeois, instigated by Louis XI of France, waged another struggle against another bishop, Louis of Bourbon, a nephew of Duke Philip of Burgundy. His son, the future Duke Charles, forced the principality to acknowledge the Burgundian Dukes as its hereditary protectors (*mambourgs*) (1465); but another insurrection speedily broke out, nor was the defiant spirit of the artisans who were masters of the city broken even by the bloody sack of Dinant, hitherto the seat of a flourishing industry in the working of copper and brass. In 1467, after defeating the Liégeois in the field, Charles, now Duke in his father's place, annihilated their privileges and re-established the Bishop, but at the same time reduced the principality to the condition of a Burgundian fief. In the following year, when Louis XI had placed himself in the power of Charles at Péronne, and a fresh rising had taken place at Liége, the recalcitrant city was overtaken by a fearful doom, at the wreaking of which the French King assisted perforce. *Leodensium clades et excidium* became the most flagrant of Charles the Bold's titles to fame; and the pillaged churches, in which, formerly, according to Commines, as many masses had been daily said as at Rome, were virtually all that, after a seven weeks' sack, was left standing of Liége. But the principality, which had never been formally annexed by Charles, after his death recovered its political independence; and, with characteristic vitality, the great Walloon city rose rapidly from its ruins.

At Péronne Charles also made use of his strange opportunity to strengthen his hold over the series of towns along the line of the Somme, extending from St Quentin to St Valéry at the mouth of the river. These Picard towns, "the key of France," had been left in pledge by France to Burgundy already in the Treaty of Arras (1435), which first impressed upon western Europe a sense of the magnitude of the Burgundian power; redeemed by Louis, in 1463, at a time when Philip and his heir were on ill terms with one another, they had been recovered in 1465 for the Netherlands and the protection of their southern frontier.

The temporal power of the Bishops of Utrecht covered, at least in name, the later provinces of Overyssel and Drenthe (called the Upper See), Groningen, and Utrecht (called the Lower). Although much restricted by the "five Chapters," whose deputies took the first place in the Diets, the episcopal system of government, as well as the institutions of the city of Utrecht, showed considerable lasting power; largely because, while the representatives of the trades controlled the civic Council, members of the noble families residing at Utrecht had been frequently placed on the roll of the trades themselves. Conflicts, however, repeatedly broke out on the occasion of the filling up of the see, and in Jacqueline's times the factions of the *Lichtenbergers* and the *Lockhorsts* respectively supported the *Hoeks* and the *Kabeljaauws*. In 1425 the question of the episcopal succession gave rise to a protracted contest, in which Philip took part; and when, after this had come to an end on the expulsion of one of the claimants and the death of the other, the succession was again disputed, he menaced Utrecht with a large armada, and thus managed to secure the see for his illegitimate son David, who kept possession of it till the death of Charles the Bold. From 1456 onwards to that date Utrecht was entirely under Burgundian influence; but though, as will be seen, Maximilian in 1483 assumed the administration of the principality, and though from 1517–24 another of Philip the Good's bastards was put in possession of the bishopric, it was not till 1529 that the temporal government of the Upper and Lower See was definitively assumed by Charles V as the sovereign of Brabant and Holland.

It was still later that Gelderland in its turn acknowledged the authority now established over all the rest of the Netherlands. The dynastic broils of the House of Gelders had been tragic enough while they merely affected its own dominions and the neighbouring duchy of Juliers—brother supplanting brother, and sister striving against sister. The contending factions in the duchy of Gelders, whose fury survived the occasion of their origin, went by the names of the *Heckerens* and the *Bronkhorsts*. The spheres of English and Burgundian influence in the Netherlands were respectively enlarged, when Duke William IX of Juliers and Gelders, himself the grandson of an English princess, opposed the efforts of Joan of Brabant, the friend of Burgundy, and defied the power of France. His reign, which lasted till 1402, marked an important advance in the prosperity of the chief Geldrian towns, Nymwegen, Roermonde, Zutphen, and Arnhem, where the rise of a considerable cloth industry connects itself with his firm attachment to the English alliance. Under his brother and successor, who remained childless like himself, the diet of the duchy resolved that no Duke should henceforth be acknowledged in Gelderland unless approved by the majority of the knightly Order (many of whose members down to the close of the fifteenth century were virtually independent), and by the smaller towns, with the unanimous assent of the above-mentioned chief towns of the "four quarters"; while any partition of the duchy, or alienation of any section of it, was made conditional on the sanction of the diet. Thus in 1423, on the death of Duke Rainald IV, the towns raised to the ducal dignity his sister's grandson Arnold of Egmond, who was still a boy in years. Although the Emperor Sigismund had invested the Duke of Berg with the duchy of Gelders, Arnold retained the confidence of the Estates by enlarging their privileges, and enjoyed the support of Duke Philip of Burgundy, to whose niece, the daughter of Duke Adolf of Cleves, he was betrothed, and afterwards united in marriage. Subsequently, however, Duke Arnold fell out with his ally as to the succession to the see of Utrecht; whereupon Philip joined with the four chief towns of Gelderland in the successful attempt of Arnold's son Adolf to substitute his own for his father's authority. But when in 1467 Charles the Bold became Duke of Burgundy, who could not bring himself to befriend a friend of the towns, Adolf after rejecting a compromise was thrown into prison, and his incapable father, against the will of the towns and the law of the land, pledged his duchy to Charles for 300,000 Rhenish florins (1471). On Arnold's death two years later, Charles took possession of the duchy. Nymwegen, whose stout resistance he had overcome by force, was subjected to a heavy fine; and only such of the towns as had voluntarily submitted to the Burgundian *régime* were confirmed in certain of their privileges. During the rest of the reign of Charles the Bold Arnold's son Charles and his sister were kept at the Burgundian Court, and Gelderland was ruled with an iron hand; but the Burgundian system of administration was probably to the advantage of the Geldrian population at large, though it had to furnish troops for his wars. As will be seen, a long and troublous interval of rebellion and war was to ensue, before in 1543, William of Juliers, whom Charles of Egmond had named his successor, resigned his claims to Gelders and Zutphen, and the entire Netherlands were united in the hands of the Emperor Charles V.

The extension by the Dukes of Burgundy of their territorial dominion over the Netherlands necessitated the establishment by them of a strong monarchical authority. A number of States, of which each had a history and institutions of its own, while the most important of them abounded in large and populous towns, were brought under the control of one and the same dynasty. The physical and economic conditions of these several provinces varied greatly; while in the country at large two very dissimilar races continued to dwell side by side, and to employ two forms of speech differing from one another as well as from the language spoken at the ducal Court. But the Dukes of Burgundy from the first were intent upon something more than securing to themselves a strong control over all their Netherlands dominions. They had come into the Low Countries as strangers; they had no traditional sympathy with the memories, no inborn respect for the rights and liberties, of any section or class of their subjects; and the last two of these Dukes in particular were deliberately resolved on setting up a centralised system of rule in the face of all claims, legal, historical, or other. Herein they followed both the traditions of the royal line from which they sprang, and the political instinct which apprised them, that, unless their strength was at least equal to that of their overlords, the struggle against these could only end in the absorption of their own dominions in a united France.

While, for reasons to be given below, the endeavour of the Dukes of Burgundy to advance and consolidate their princely power in the Netherlands met with goodwill and cooperation on the part of the nobility and clergy, its chief adversaries were the great communes of Flanders, and in a less degree those of Brabant. This conflict was in itself inevitable; for the political and social development of the chief Flemish towns only typified on a large scale what had taken or was taking place in other Provinces. The terrible blow inflicted at Roosebeke with the aid of France upon the communes, and upon Ghent in particular, was not absolutely mortal; and although their prosperity in the fifteenth century never again reached the height to which it had previously attained, yet their importance in the whole body politic was still paramount. As early as the thirteenth century Bruges, practically a port by means of its control of Sluys, had become a world's fair, and Ghent in Eastern and Ypres in Western Flanders had grown with amazing rapidity into great industrial centres of population surrounded by many other flourishing towns of which the names are now in part forgotten. With their activity and wealth had grown a sense of power and an impatience of external control for which in the Middle Ages no complete parallel could have been found on the hither side of the Alps. The civic governments which in this earlier period asserted their authority against that of the Counts were purely oligarchic; and it was only gradually that the artisans, since the organisation of the trades as guilds had been elaborated and was for a long time controlled by the patriciates, came to essay a trial of strength with them. The determining factor is to be sought in the irresistible ascendency of the trade of the weavers and of the minor trades connected with it, when the cloth industry of Flanders was at its height. When the patricians in their turn had thrown themselves upon the support of the French Crown (*leliaerts*), the massacres known as the *mette* (*matines*) of Bruges began the great democratic revolution which triumphed in the utter overthrow of the chivalry of France on the field of Courtray (1302). The honours of that day belonged to the trades of Bruges, assisted by those of Ypres and Ghent in defiance of the prohibitions issued by their patrician authorities. And during the entire epoch of the political ascendency of the communes, their self-government was striving to establish itself on broad popular foundations. The elder Artevelde was the Pericles of Ghent, whose extraordinary self-confidence was mainly due to the hope of an effective political alliance with England, based on free commercial intercourse with her, as the chief provider of the raw material of Flemish industry. After his death evil times began for Ghent, which had become the chief of " the three members of Flanders " (*de dry leden*), and had charged itself with the executive on behalf of the towns and other districts of the country at large. The visitations of Heaven seemed to descend upon the land in the form of tempests and inundations and the Black Death. The Anglo-Flemish alliance was a thing of the past. Bruges, whose jealousy of Ghent was ineradicable, was inclined to support the manœuvres of the territorial prince; and in many of the communes a reaction set in towards oligarchical government. But Ghent stood firm, and when the banners of her crafts had been unfurled for the critical struggle, and the Whitehoods once more streamed forth from her gates, Bruges, Ypres, Courtray, and all the other Flemish towns once more fell into line for the final struggle. With their overthrow at Roosebeke (1382) the political greatness of the communes came to an end; but the resistance of Ghent was only slowly extinguished.

Yet to Philip the Good, as to his father (notwithstanding the part which he played at Paris) and to his grandfather before him, and his son after him, the Flemish communes were, as Commines says of Ghent in especial, a thorn in the flesh. Not that he was unaware of the fact that his European position depended upon the prosperity of the Flemish towns even more than upon that of the Dutch, who always regarded the ally of the *Kabeljaauws* as their friend, or upon that of Brussels, his favourite place of residence. He sought to arrest the decay of Ypres, and his commercial policy towards England was dictated by the interests of Flanders. But he was resolute in asserting his political supremacy at any cost; and the first occasion, on which he showed himself conscious of the fact that the destruction of his subjects was his own loss, was when he had crushed the last resistance of the Ghenters at Gavre (1453). Until the Peace of Arras he mainly (though not entirely, as Ypres learnt to its cost) confined himself to sowing discord between the towns; but afterwards, when the communal militia had deserted him at the siege of Calais, the conflict first broke out between him and

Bruges (1436). Patched up by the grant of two new charters, it burst forth again in the insurrection known as the Terrible Whit-Wednesday (1438); and after meeting the Duke's forces in the open field, the city, which was suffering from the devastations of a pestilence, was in the end forced to give way. Bruges was only saved from destruction by the intervention of the foreign merchants; but, while the new charters were revoked or modified, the trades were deprived of their cherished right of unfurling their banners without waiting for the display of the Duke's—in other words of the right of taking up arms without his summons—and the sinews of future resistance were cut by the abolition of the communal contribution to the trades (*mœndtgelt*).

The turn of Ghent came a little later. On her refusal to pay a salt-tax to which Bruges and Ypres had submitted, a conflict began which lasted for four years (1449). After the Duke had twice stopped the ordinary administration of justice, the whole body of the people took the power into its hands, appointed three captains (*hooftmannen*), and at the sound of the bell assembled under arms on the *Vrydags-markt*. The Duke retorted by a decree of blockade and outlawry against Ghent. Bruges and the other towns jealously held aloof; and, though the Ghenters appealed both to the French suzerain and to the government of Henry VI of England, they had to fight out the contest virtually alone. In the city a ruthless terrorism maintained an unreasoning enthusiasm, till a long and sanguinary campaign ended, within sight of her towers, by the carnage of Gavre (1453). The settlement which ensued established the ducal authority as paramount in every important function of the administration of the city, abolished the most cherished guarantees of its previous independence, and among other humiliations inflicted on its representatives that of confessing the guilt of the suppressed rebellion in the French tongue. Some of the privileges of the prostrate city were indeed renewed in a new charter, the powers of the royal bailiff were restricted, and no mention was made of the obnoxious salt-tax. But the victory was not the less complete, and was followed by the revocation of the charters of other towns, although they had abstained from supporting Ghent.

The overthrow of the greatness of the Flemish communes was due in part to the anarchical spirit which more and more took possession of them as their public life passed into the ochlocratic stage, and which could not but impair their military discipline and defensive strength. What had here—and the state of things was not very different in Brabant—remained of the authority of the territorial prince was con-fined to the influence exercised by his *bailli* upon the administration of justice, and when possible upon the choice of magistrates and upon legislation. The patriciate—the *poorters* at Bruges and Ghent, to which the *lignages* corresponded in Brabant—still ordinarily deter-mined the choice of the magistrates or aldermen; but in any season of agitation this power was sure to be swept out of their hands with all the judicial, financial, and other functions of government. Not unfrequently such outbursts of popular fury were provoked by the venality of the ruling classes, and the fear of their recurrence naturally inclined the patricians towards the ducal authority, unless when their advances were blindly repelled by the harshness of the sovereign, as in the later days of Charles the Bold. The real holders of power in the Flemish communes were now the working population at large, divided on a system varying in the several towns into trades or handicrafts (*ambachten*); in Brabant these trades had before the accession of Philip effected a compromise with the *lignages*; in Holland and Utrecht their authority was great but not overwhelming; in Liége, as has been seen, it was paramount. In the three great Flemish towns, the great mass of the trades ordinarily asserted their power by the votes of their representatives, and on critical occasions by the organised resort to arms under their banners in the market-place (*wapeninghe*). By itself each trade formed not only a military, but also a social and religious unit, with its common purse for purposes of business, pleasure and charity, and often with a chapel and a hospital of its own. In the course of the fourteenth century the great craft of the Weavers had effected its predominance in each of the three cities, and became omnipotent at Ghent. Next to them came the Fullers, with whom they had many a sanguinary conflict. At Ghent there were besides these two great crafts 52 smaller crafts; and in one of them even the *poorters*, who constituted a guild without political power, had to inscribe themselves if desirous of becoming eligible for a magisterial office. At Bruges there were four great crafts—Weavers, Fullers, Shearers and Dyers—and the famous muster of October 10, 1436, included 48 smaller, from the butchers and bakers to the paternoster-makers; all these were combined into eight "members," with a ninth consisting of the four "free trades" of merchants, while the Ghent trades made up three "members" only. Each "member" (elsewhere called "nation") was presided over by a Grand Dean; and these officers were always, however its composition might from time to time vary, included in the representative committee (called *collatie* at Ghent) of the entire commune. The approval of this committee was doubtless asked by the commune, when in moments of supreme excitement *hooftmannen* or captains were chosen by or for it—a term which seems in the first instance to have meant merely the heads of a *poorters'* guild.

The absence of any durable league or alliance between the several communes was due to the narrow jealousy which they cherished towards one another and which has already been illustrated in the case of the relations between Bruges and Ghent. In 1423 Ghent successfully thwarted the attempt of Ypres to divert to herself the water-transport of wine and cereals; half a century later the Yprois joined the Ghenters in ignoring the apprehensions of Bruges as to the sanding-up of the Zwyn. To this pernicious jealousy was added the ill-will of the large against the *smalle steden*, and the tyrannous arrogance of the towns towards the rural districts; nor was it till 1438 that Duke Philip restored the rights of the *Vrije* (*le Franc*) of Bruges as a "fourth member" of Flanders.

The economic decline of Flanders in the fifteenth century has been obscured by the glowing descriptions of luxurious life in which the Court chroniclers of Philip and Charles abound. The great industry which had filled the famous Cloth-hall of Ypres steadily declined; till about the time of the death of Mary a city population which had formerly amounted to something like 100,000 had fallen to about one-twentieth of that total. Ypres, like some other of the Flemish towns, had suffered from special causes, but there was one which fundamentally affected them all. The fabrication of cloth in England had endangered the chief industry of Flanders already at the close of the fourteenth century; and, profiting alike by the instruction derived from the Flemish immigration which the troubles of the fifteenth century had superadded to earlier immigrations in the twelfth and fourteenth, and by the facilities of export offered by the Hanseatic merchants, she gradually drove Flemish cloth from the staple at Calais. The crucial question whether it were better to attract to the Flemish market the sale of this exported English cloth, or to exclude it altogether from competition with the native industry, was settled by a sort of compromise in favour of protection. But the repeated prohibitions of the importation of English cloth (1436–64) remained ineffectual, and the cloth industry was paralysed in the Flemish cities; though it maintained itself for a considerable time in the open country. Ghent was able to some extent to fall back upon its resources as a staple of corn; and at Bruges, where the banking business of Europe was in the hands of foreign merchants, a busy traffic continued to be carried on. In the struggle pertinaciously maintained by the latter city, from the close of the thirteenth century onwards, against the transference of her foreign trade to Antwerp, interest in the end prevailed over habit. The English Merchant Adventurers, who had set up a house at Antwerp early in the fifteenth century, by the middle of it had transferred themselves thither in a body. While the great transmarine trade was thus drawn away from Flanders proper to Brabant, and the depopulation of the former, which assumed alarming proportions under Charles the Bold, had begun already in the last years of his predecessor, the prosperity of the Northern Netherlands continued to increase. Navigation, with the great fishing and other industries, flourished; and little troubled by the remote wars of Charles the Bold, the Hollanders and their neighbours took consolation for his exactions in the cheapness of comforts which they came to reckon among the necessaries of life.

In the struggles of the Dukes with the communes the nobles ranged
themselves readily on the side of the former down to the close of
Philip's reign—notably in Flanders, where Courtray had never been
forgotten.  Only very gradually under him, though more abruptly under
his successor, the modern notion of the sovereign throned in majestic
isolation superseded the feudal conception of the prince among his
peers.  To a large extent the change was doubtless due to the influence
of the most splendid of contemporary Western courts.  The pictures
of its magnificence and luxury drawn by Jacques du Clercq and the
elaborate episodes of feast and tournament, with which Olivier de la
Marche loves to intersperse his narrative, bear out the assertion of
Commines, that in the prodigality of enticements it surpassed any other
Court known to his experience.  In the Court guide composed by
Olivier during the siege of Neuss where Charles displayed in the midst
of war the stately ceremonial in which his pride delighted, he details
the official system, and the elaborate etiquette which became the model
of many generations.  But the completeness of the external machinery
furnished no safeguard against the venality and corruption inseparable
from despotic rule, or against a dissoluteness of manners usually fostered
by formal restraint.  The lasciviousness, that pervaded the Court of
Charles VII of France and made that of Edward IV a seminary of
pleasant vice, readily found its way into the surroundings of Philip the
Good, who had a large family of bastards, and mistresses by the score.
The extravagant delights in which the nobles might share when not
engaged in warlike service impoverished many and ruined some; and
Charles the Bold's relations with his nobility were strained to the utmost
by the military burdens which he imposed on them.  Numerous de-
fections followed, and suspicions of treason on the unfortunate field of
Morat; only a handful of his nobles fought by his side at Nancy, and
hardly any held out by his daughter in her hour of distress.

Of the relations between the Dukes and the clergy it must suffice
to say that they were largely determined by considerations of interest,
and drawn closer by the unpopularity of both prince and priesthood
in the towns.  Duke Philip contrived to place his illegitimate brother
John in the see of Cambray, while two of his own bastards held the
great ecclesiastical principality of Liége.  Notwithstanding the Church's
acquisitions of landed property, which here as elsewhere legislation
sought to stay, the secular arm occasionally appealed to the spiritual
for its aid against civic recalcitrance, and now and then supported the
clergy when at issue with the towns.  Yet such was the perversity of
Charles the Bold, which left no section of his subjects to lament his
downfall, that he, who at the beginning of his reign had protected the
churches of Liége from sharing in the general doom of the city, was at
its close generally hated by the Netherlands clergy, for having overtaxed them as he had their flocks.

The principles and policy of the Burgundian dynasty found their most skilful agents in the highly-trained lawyers who, after studying in France, at Louvain, or in the University founded by Philip in Franche Comté, held high judicial office in the Netherlands. The ground had been in some measure prepared for them, at all events in Flanders, though it was precisely here that the judicial innovations of this period met with the most stubborn resistance. The so-called *Audiences of the Count,* based to some extent on the ancient usage of conveying "quiet truths" to him, led the way to the establishment of the Count's Council, which in 1385 Philip the Bold transformed into the Chamber of the Duke's Council in Flanders, subdividing it into a judicial and a financial Chamber. The latter remained at Lille, whence Philip the Good extended its operations to Namur, Hainault, and the towns on the Somme, while the two financial chambers of Holland and Zeeland, and of Brabant, were united by him at Brussels in 1463. The judicial Chamber on the other hand, which came to be generally known as the Council of Flanders, was, after many shiftings of place, finally brought back to Ghent in 1452; the Council of the Counts of Holland, and that of the Dukes of Brabant, having been alike reformed on the acknowledgment of Philip's sovereignty. In each case the substance of the reform lay in the introduction, by the side of the great lords and officials previously composing the Council, of trained lawyers, devoted to the maintenance of the ducal authority, and inclined to stimulate its self-consciousness. In order, however, to make this authority really supreme, and to avoid the possibility of any appeal to the Parliament of Paris, Philip in 1446, without putting an end to the Privy Council which ordinarily attended him, established a Grand Council, attached to his own person and entrusted with supreme judicial as well as political and financial functions. The centralising process was carried to its final stage by Charles the Bold's settlement of 1473, which maintained the Grand Council as a Council of State for the whole of his dominions, but transferred its financial functions to a Chamber finally fixed at Malines, absorbing into this the Brussels Chamber of Accounts. Charles also established a central judicial Court at Malines, which he sought to surround with all possible external dignity, frequently presiding in person at his sittings. But it remained unpopular, by reason of its slow Roman procedure, and the use of the French language to which it adhered; nor did it survive his fall.

As a matter of course, both Philip and Charles had from time to time to summon the "States" of the several lands; for there was no other way of obtaining the extraordinary aids (*beden*) required more especially for their wars. In the meetings of these "States" the attendance of the nobles gradually slackened, and (notably in Holland) only the larger towns were regularly represented. For the rest, no town or "State" was bound except by its own vote. It was again no innovation when, in 1428, Philip caused his settlement with Jacqueline to be confirmed by a meeting of representatives of all the lands whose allegiance she had formerly claimed. And it was only a step further when, after two previous meetings in 1463–4 he in 1465 formally called upon all the States of the Low Countries assembled at Brussels to recognise his son as his successor and *Lieutenant général,* and at the same time obtained from them a supply enabling him to carry on effective war against Louis XI. Charles the Bold thrice assembled these States-General; but they do not appear to have regularly comprised representatives of the whole of his Netherlands dominions. Thus this all-important institution never passed beyond an initial stage under either of the last two Burgundian Dukes; though Philip had faithful servants who advised him to trust those trusted by his subjects. Indeed, an outline of the constitutional system to which the occasional convocation of the States-General pointed has actually been preserved, dating from an early period of his reign.

After Philip had, like his father before him, found the communal militia of the Flemish towns untrustworthy in foreign war, he had for his military needs fallen back on the feudal services upon which the first two Burgundian Dukes had placed a precarious dependence; but the forces which he employed for the overthrow of the liberties of Ghent, and which his heir led forth against Louis XI on behalf of the League of the Common Good, already comprised a considerable element of mercenary soldiers—Picards and English in particular. The *bandes d'ordonnance* of Charles the Bold, a modified imitation of the new French model, were partly recruited among the nobility, partly made up of Italian heavy infantry and the indispensable English archers; and a select body-guard was formed on a similar basis. In 1471 he raised a permanent force of 10,000 men. The towns had to equip contingents at their own expense, but under officers named by the Duke. He improved his artillery, and paid attention to the fighting qualities of his navy. Though Charles was both an unskilful and an unfortunate commander, he was the creator of the standing army which proved so formidable under the rule of his descendants; much of his military expenditure was unavoidable, since the superiority of regular troops over feudal levies was already proved; and he deserves credit for his consistent maintenance of discipline, more especially as it only increased his unpopularity.

It has frequently been assumed that the progress of art and literature in the Netherlands must have benefited by the patronage of an open-handed dynasty and a sumptuous Court. But, although the Renaissance owed not a little to the goodwill of Philip the Good and his family, they either used its culture as a political expedient or (in Voltaire's phrase) treated it as a *passe-temps.* The triumphs of a late and rich variety of the Gothic style attested by so many municipal and ecclesiastical edifices of the fifteenth century are due to the towns, although in so many instances their decadence had already set in. The case was different with the sister-art, which in Flanders was emancipated from Byzantine models (introduced by the Crusades) by the great painters to whom the miniaturists had formed a characteristic transition. When Hubert van Eyck died in 1420, he bequeathed the completion of the masterpiece of the school of Bruges to his younger brother John. Within fourteen further years the latter, who was soon made a member of Duke Philip's household, perfected a form of art that clothed its simple ideals of faith and devotion in the golden splendour of the age of its origin. Its latest great master, Memling, carried far beyond the borders of his native land the purest and profoundest pictorial expression of the mystic depth of religious sentiment.

Leaving aside other forms of art—among which something might be said of the attention paid by both Flemings and Walloons to that of music—we find that already under the House of Dampierre, the French literature patronised by the Counts, and the Flemish that was dear to the people, had gone far asunder. In the latter part of the fourteenth century, French historic prose as it were annexed the Netherlands as part of its proper domain. Froissart, the chief prophet of the last phase of chivalry radiating from the Court of the Burgundian Dukes and the exemplar of a whole line of chroniclers devoted to their dynasty, was himself a native of Hainault and spent the last quarter of a century of his life in retirement in Flanders. After him it became indispensable that every important Court or great noble household should possess its *indiciaire* or historiographer, and the House of Burgundy fostered a series of such literary officials, who placed on record every step in its advance, inflated its pride, and enhanced its fame. The list includes, besides Enguerrand de Monstrelet, on the whole a fairly candid writer, Jacques Lefèvre de Saint-Remy, who in the main borrowed or abridged from him, the graphic Jacques du Clercq, Georges Chastellain, by his literary gifts as well as by his masculine outspokenness the most notable of Froissart's successors, and Jean Molinet, whose turgid artificiality and Euphuistic affectations render him a fit narrator of the decay and downfall of Burgundian greatness. All these (except Monstrelet) were officials of the ducal House, which was abandoned by Commines, the one narrator of the great struggle who writes in the spirit of practical statesmanship. Edmond of Dynter, who came into the service of Philip the Good from that of the Dukes of Brabant, furnished a long pragmatic history of the Jacqueline troubles and the complicated course of events in Gelderland.

Against the influences of a French-speaking Court and its literary mouthpieces, the native language and literature had to rely upon a power of resistance strengthened by movements springing from the heart of the people. Thus, though the so-called Chambers of Rhetoric, whose members went by the name of *Rederijkers,* derived their title from France, the institution itself was clearly a continuation or renewal of the old confraternities or guilds devoted to the performance of religious plays which flourished in various parts of the Netherlands in the fourteenth and fifteenth centuries. The *Rederijkers,* whose activity cannot safely be asserted to have begun much before the fifteenth century, abandoned the domain of ecclesiastical tradition, thereby rendering collision with the Church inevitable sooner or later, and, as at the same time the critical spirit asserted itself and the influence of the Renaissance enlarged the choice of materials, in their dramatic allegories or moralities (*spelen van zinne*) paid increasing attention to the treatment of their subjects and the form of their plays. Connecting their performances with the festivals that formed so material a part of the popular life of the Netherlands, they at the same time more and more acquired the character of literary associations whose activity extended to a wide variety of forms of composition. The most ancient of the Belgian Chambers, the *Alpha et Omega* of Ypres, seems to date from a time rather before the beginning of the fifteenth century; the famous *In liefde bloeyende* of Amsterdam was not instituted till 1517. Their number ultimately grew to an extraordinary extent, more especially in the Southern Netherlands; and the elaborate arrangements for establishing an organic union among them culminated in the meeting of deputies of all the Chambers at Malines in 1493 on the summons of Philip the Fair, and the setting-up in 1503 of a supreme Chamber at Ghent. But this late effort of a centralising policy was vehemently opposed, and its practical result was small. The Reformation found the Chambers instinctively sensitive to impulses moving the heart of the people—with what consequences is well known.

The popular religious movements noticeable in the Netherlands up to the close of the fourteenth century had on the whole remained ominously out of touch with the organisation of the Church. On the other hand, the Béguines and Beghards and Lollards had little or nothing to say against the doctrines of the Church of Rome; and neither the Wicliffites nor afterwards the followers of Hus seem to have attempted any propaganda in the Low Countries. The beginnings there of mystical speculation, of which the revered Johannes Rusbroek, born near Brussels in 1283, can in his age hardly have been a solitary representative, may possibly be traceable to the teachings of the "Master" Eckhart at Cologne. To Rusbroek's teachings both Tauler and Gerard Groote were listeners; they became a profound source of personal inspiration to many generations; nor has their echo died out to this day. To Geert (Gerard) Groote and his friend Florentius Radevynszoon, unlike him an ecclesiastic by profession, was due the establishment of the *frater-huis* at his native town of Deventer, which became the model of a series of similar foundations, intended as the homes of pious followers of God resolved to lead a common life of prayer and labour, unencumbered by any hierarchical organisation and free from any system of irrevocable vows. A happy accident suggested that some of the young members of the Deventer settlement should contribute towards its support by clubbing together their earnings as copyists of manuscripts of the Scriptures and the Church Fathers, to which work they had as pupils of the Latin school in the town been encouraged by Groote. Hereby he had from the very outset of his endeavours blended the pursuit of learning and the furtherance of education with a life of piety and devotion. While extending and consolidating the system of the *fraterhuizen*, Florentius also carried out a cherished earlier design of his friend by the foundation, at Windesem near Zwolle, of a convent of canons regular. The half-century of the reigns of Philip and Charles witnessed a continuous extension in almost every part of the Netherlands, as well as in many districts of Northern Germany, both of the Houses of the Brethren of the Common Life and of the convents called the Windesem Congregations. The Church had come to recognise the agency of the Brethren as useful and praiseworthy; among those who extolled their labours was the Minorite Johannes Brugmann, the greatest popular preacher of his age in the Netherlands, and they were favoured by Duke Philip's brother, Bishop David of Utrecht.

The value of the Brethren's labours in the transcription of manuscripts has not been overestimated; but these labours belonged to a period that was passing away, and were only slightly supplemented by use of the new invention of the printing-press. On the other hand the work of education had always formed a chief purpose and essential part of the existence of the fraternity. The very large numbers of scholars attending its schools signally contributed throughout the Netherlands to lay the foundations of an enduring literary culture, and the fact that the teaching and training of these scholars was everywhere impregnated with the spirit of religious devotion determined the significance, to the most illustrious as well as to the humblest of them, of the advance of the New Learning. They met it less in the spirit of an enthusiastic humanism than in that of a steady demand for serviceable lore, such as already gives so much substance to the writings of Cardinal Cusanus, a pupil of Deventer in its earlier days.

But a new educational epoch began with Alexander Hegius, who in 1474 was appointed head of the school at Deventer, and died near the close of the century, leaving behind him nothing but his clothes and his books, and a name which may fairly be called that of one of the great schoolmasters of the world. The list of the scholars trained at Deventer by him, or in his time, and that of his Paris fellow-student Badius Ascensius (Bade of Asche), includes, besides its chief and incomparable glory, the name of Erasmus, those of Conrad Mutianus, the pride of Erfurt in her brightest days, and Hermann von dem Busche, whom

Strauss calls "the missionary of humanism." Johannes Sintius (Sintheim), who taught with Hegius at Deventer and was himself a member of the Brotherhood, rendered a signal service to education in the Netherlands and in Germany by the successful revision of the Latin grammar which had held its own for centuries. But the schools of the Brethren were not seminaries of that narrower humanism which made the study of the classical tongues the sole method and all but the supreme object of education. They encouraged the reading of the Bible and the use of the service-books in the vulgar tongue, cherished the careful use and even the study of the vernacular, and thus brought about the beginning of a new educational movement which on the Upper Rhine was to lead to results such as it could hardly expect to command on the Lower. Many links connect the labours of the Brethren and the great movement which in the fifteenth century strove to quicken the religious life of the German people by bringing learning and education, and literature and art, into living harmony with it. Such a link may be found in the life of Rudolf Agricola, who died in 1485, and, although apparently not a pupil of the Brethren, was a native of the neighbourhood of Groningen, where one of their seminaries was placed. The last years of his life were spent at Heidelberg and Worms. He was a man of three tongues; but it was in theological rather than in philological study that he found the crown of his labours.

Of a very different character were the relations, in the Netherlands, between the Renaissance and University studies. The complete separation of academical from municipal government at Louvain, and the special attention devoted there to legal studies intended to prepare for the service of the central government, went some way towards estranging that University from popular and provincial interests; but the part which she was long to play in the history of the intellectual culture of the country was determined by the identification of her interests with those of Church and Clergy. The most illustrious of the earlier students and teachers of Louvain, Pope Adrian VI, in a sense typifies both her influence and that of the Brethren's school in which he had been previously trained. In matters concerning the Church he thought with vigour and honesty; but for "poetry" he had scant sympathy to spare. Especially in consequence of the influence exercised by the monastic orders, Louvain's academical character was even more conservative than that of Cologne. For the rest, the relations between Church and people in the fifteenth century were in the Netherlands affected by the general causes in operation throughout western Europe. The deep religious feeling of the people remained proof against the excesses alike and the shortcomings of the clergy; against a corruption which led even Philip the Good to approve of the attempt to divert the administration of charity into lay hands, and a license of life on the part of both seculars and regulars which defied repeated attempts at reform. Few protests against the doctrines and usages of the Church are noticeable in the course of the fifteenth century.

A more lasting influence was however being quietly exercised by a school of religious thinkers, to which in the latter half of the century two notable Netherlanders belonged. The theology of John (Pupper) of Goch in the duchy of Cleves, who is believed to have been educated in one of the Brethren's schools, and who for nearly a quarter of a century presided over a priory of Austin canonesses founded by him at Malines in 1451, rejected the pretensions of mere outward piety and dead formalism. There is no proof that his writings which were read by few were known to Luther; but they must have come under the notice of Erasmus. The step to the assertion of the universal priesthood of Christian believers was taken by a bolder thinker, John Wessel (Goesevort), who, born at Groningen about the year 1420, was educated in the school of the Brotherhood at Zwolle, but afterwards studied in most of the chief universities of Europe. He was honoured by both Luther and Melanchthon, but he never took Orders, and his academic distinction is his chief title to fame (*magister contradictionum*). He enjoyed the patronage of Bishop David of Utrecht; but his favourite residence seems to have been the Frisian convent of Adwert, to which a species of high school was attached. Lover of truth as he was, and in one respect at least (viz. as to the doctrine of the Eucharist) even further advanced than Luther, he disliked any appeal to the passions of the people, and had as little thought as Bishop David himself of an open rupture with the Church.

## II.

When the death of Charles the Bold at Nancy was ascertained, Louis prepared to seize those parts of the ducal dominions which were nearest to his hand and indispensable for the future of the French monarchy, while keeping in view the ultimate acquisition of them all. He proclaimed his anxiety for the interest of Charles' daughter and heiress whom he had held at the font; but the project of a marriage between Mary, now close upon her twenty-first year, and the Dauphin, a boy of eight, was full of difficulty, more especially as the suit of Maximilian had already reached an advanced point. This prince's father was naturally not less anxious to preserve the cohesion of the Burgundian inheritance than Louis XI had been prompt to impair it; and from him no revival was to be apprehended of those questions as to male or female fiefs which had of old divided the Netherlands. All the more important was the attitude of the country itself towards the French intervention.

Almost simultaneously with the prompt mission of the Count of Craon into Burgundy, Louis had despatched to Picardy and Artois the

High Admiral of France (the Bastard of Bourbon), accompanied by Commines, to demand the surrender of all fiefs of the French Crown, and in the first instance of the towns on the Somme. His plans were vast, but according to Commines the reverse of vague. Namur, Hainault, and other parts near his borders were to be made over to some of his French vassals, and Brabant and Holland to German princes whom he would thus bind to his alliance. The French fief of Flanders he must have intended to secure for his Crown, of which it would still have been one of the brightest jewels. The towns on the Somme were one after the other—some by golden keys—opened to him ; and the defection of Philip de Crèvecœur placed him in possession of the Boulonnais. Mary's letter of January 23 to the ducal council at Dijon, protesting against French encroachments in the duchy of Burgundy and the Franche Comté, held out no prospect of armed resistance on her own part ; and indeed any attempt of the kind was out of the question. At Ghent, where she was detained whether she would or not, and in the other towns of Flanders and Brabant, the confirmation of the tidings of her father's death had been received with general feelings of relief and joy, and throughout the Netherlands it was resolved to make the most of the opportunity.

By the beginning of February, the Four Members of Flanders, the three Estates of Brabant and Hainault, and the deputies of the States of Holland were assembled at Ghent. In the hands of these representatives of the *vier landen*, who explicitly took it upon themselves to act on behalf of the country at large, the executive remained till the Austrian marriage, and their united action imposed upon the lady of Burgundy the grant of the great charter of Netherlands liberties, and of the special charters which supplemented it. The importance of the promises comprised in the *Groote Privilegie* of February 10, 1477, lies not so much in its sweeping invalidation of all previous ducal ordinances antagonistic to communal privileges, or even in the assertion of principles more or less indigenous to all the Low Countries under Burgundian rule, as in the announcement of a definite machinery for their future government. It was, no doubt, of moment to provide that no war could be declared and no marriage concluded by the ducal sovereign without the consent of the States; to establish the necessity of their approval for fresh taxes, to confine the tenure of office to natives, to insist on the use of the national tongue in all public documents, to secure to the several provinces the control of the government's commercial policy and a check upon the use of its military force. But the chief political significance of the new constitution was directly constructive. While abolishing the central judicial Court or Parliament of Malines, it reorganised the Grand Council, attached to the person of the sovereign, on a broad representative basis. It was to consist, in addition to the princes of the dynasty,

of the Chancellor and twenty-three other members named for life
by the sovereign, nobles and trained lawyers in equal proportions,
and assigned on a fixed scale to each of the provinces of the land.
Every precaution was used for ensuring a paramount regard on the
part of the Council for the privileges and usages of provinces and
towns, and every facility provided for the assembling on their own
motion of the States of the whole of the ducal dominions—the States-
General.

The Great Privilege was supplemented by several special applications of its principles to the needs of particular provinces. These
were the Flemish Privilege, obtained on the same day by the Four
Members of Flanders, upon whose unanimous consent it made any future
constitutional change depend, while no Flemish business was to be
transacted except on Flemish soil and in the Flemish tongue; the Great
Privilege of Holland and Zeeland (February 17), which contained
similar provisions and granted full liberty to the towns to hold "Parliaments" of their own, in conjunction with the other States of the
Netherlands or not; the Great Privilege of Namur (May), and the
*Joyeuse Entrée* granted to Mary on the occasion of her being acknowledged at Leuven as Duchess of Brabant (May 29), which, while
returning to the usages confirmed at the accession of Philip the Good,
added new liberties and doubled the measure of restrictions upon the
ducal power.

That fear of France rather than any affection for the Burgundian
dynasty, or even any warmth of feeling towards Mary herself, had
induced the representatives of the *vier landen* to come to terms with
her, was shown by the military preparations upon which they simultaneously agreed. In place of the ducal army which had ceased to
exist, 100,000 men were to be levied, of whom Flanders contributed
more than one-third, and the rest in proportion. Raised by means of
half-obsolete feudal obligations, or as communal or rural militia, this
army, though its numbers were helped out by a system of substitutes,
proved inadequate to its purpose; but the fact of its levy not the
less shows that the mind of the Netherlands had been made up to
resist the French advance.

Meanwhile Mary, still uncertain in which direction to turn for
preservation, had sent an embassy to Louis XI, apparently just before
her relations with the Flemish towns had been settled. She had
little personal advice to depend upon. Her step-mother, the high-
spirited Duchess Dowager Margaret, still relied on delusive hopes of
English support. Mary's kinsman, Adolf, Lord zum Ravenstein and
brother of the Duke of Cleves, was both loyal to her and popular
with her subjects, but as yet chiefly intent upon securing her hand
for his own son. The time for taking the matronly advice of her
former governess, Jeanne de Commines, Dame de Hallewin, had not yet

come. Very naturally, therefore, she fell back upon the counsel of the men who had been faithful to his father's interests in his last and worst days, and who still sat in her Privy Council, though differing in their policy from the majority of its members. The Chancellor Hugonet (to leave out his other titles) and the Sire d'Himbercourt, Count of Meghem—the former a Burgundian, the latter a Picard by birth—persuaded the youthful Duchess to allow them to negotiate with France. They were animated by the spirit common to lawyers and nobles in the heyday of the Burgundian rule, and shared by the Church (William de Clugny, protonotary of the Holy See, was afterwards arraigned for complicity with them). Towards France they were attracted by a sympathy which needed no stimulus of sordid interests, whether or not they had from the first resolved that the end must be the acceptance of Louis XI's marriage-scheme and the reabsorption of the Burgundian in the French dynasty; while they detested a policy of concessions to the several portions of the crumbling monarchy of Charles the Bold.

Louis, on his side, was resolved to secure a party in Flanders. The agent whom he had first, in spite of Commines' warning, sent to Ghent for the purpose—no other than the notorious Olivier le Dain—had indeed been obliged to depart discomfited, and had only partially redeemed his credit by cleverly bringing into his master's power the city of Tournay, always well disposed towards France. Louis, however, when Mary's embassy reached him at Péronne, was at particular pains to show courtesy towards the Flemish towns in the person of the distinguished *hooftman* of Bruges, a member of the great patrician family of Gruuthuse. Little importance attached to the ambassadors' offers of the cession of all the possessions given up by Louis in the Treaty of Péronne, and the recognition of his suzerainty in Artois and Flanders; and as to the real *nodus* of the transaction, the question of a marriage engagement between Mary and the Dauphin, they declared themselves to be without instructions. While, therefore, the embassy returned to Flanders to report, Louis seems to have, by private communications with Hugonet and d'Himbercourt, secured their adherence to the marriage-scheme. At Arras, of which he took possession in March, 1477, he received a deputation from Ghent, and—playing the kind of double game which his soul loved—revealed to them the confidence reposed by Mary in the privy councillors detested by the city.

Thus, on the return of the civic deputies to Ghent, the storm broke out. The city was already in a condition of ferment; some of the partisans of the old *régime* had been put to death; and the agitation, which had spread to Ypres and as far as Mons, was increased by the claims put forward at Ghent on behalf of the restoration of Liégeois independence by the Bishop of Liége, urged on by William of Aremberg, Sire de la Marck, the "Boar of the Ardennes," and the terror of all who respected the ordinances of either God or man. Distracted by her fears, Mary seems actually to have countenanced Hugonet's final proposal that she should quit Flanders and place herself under the protection of the French King, when at the last moment Ravenstein induced her to reveal the design. He immediately informed the representatives of the *vier landen*, and the deans of the trades of Ghent, and on the same night (March 4) Hugonet, d'Himbercourt and de Clugny were placed under arrest. A rumour having been spread that their liberation was to be attempted, and news having arrived of the resolute advance of the French forces, new disturbances followed; and Mary issued an ordinance naming a mixed commission of nobles and civic officials to try the accused with all due expedition (March 28). She afterwards interceded in favour of one or both of the lay prisoners (for de Clugny was saved by his benefit of clergy), and at a later date expressed her sympathy with the widow and orphans of d'Himbercourt, the extent of whose share in the Chancellor's schemes remains unknown. After being subjected to torture, both were executed on April 3. They met with short shrift at the hands of their judges; but they cannot be said to have been sacrificed to a mere gust of democratic passion; and Mary and her Council, and the other Estates of the Netherlands assembled at Ghent, were with the city itself and the sister Flemish towns one and all involved in the responsibility of the deed.

There was now no solution left but war, and at Eastertide Louis XI advanced from Artois into Hainault. At the same time no doubt could remain as to the way in which the question of Mary's marriage must be settled. An English engagement such as the Duchess Dowager desired was hopelessly impeded by the disagreement between the factions at Edward's Court, one of which favoured the claims of the Duke of Clarence, while the other supported Earl Rivers, the brother of Queen Elizabeth. At Ghent there was for a time a strong wish that Mary would bestow her hand upon Adolf of Gelders, the friend of the towns, who had been liberated from prison on Charles' death, and proclaimed Duke notwithstanding Mary's protest. He had entered himself as a member of one of the trades of Ghent, and had been named commander of the Flemish levies against France. But, instead of gaining Mary's hand, he was destined to fall fighting in her service before Tournay (June), leaving his children Charles and Philippa as hostages in her hands, though the former had been proclaimed Duke in Gelderland. Of Mary's kinsmen of the Cleves family two were still talked of for her hand—the Duke's son and subsequent successor, John, and Philip, the son of his brother Adolf zum Ravenstein. Philip had been brought up with Mary, whose father was said to have at one time favoured the idea of their future union, agreeably it was rumoured to Mary's own wishes. But after the English project had come to naught the Duchess Dowager transferred all her influence to the only remaining suitor, the selection of whom promised high political advantage; and the choice actually fell upon Archduke Maximilian of Austria.

The vigilance of the Emperor Frederick III had long prepared this match, and even the catastrophe of Nancy had been unable to baulk his purpose. Now, while at Bruges Mary was seeking to satisfy a clamorous demand for a suppression of the pretensions of *le Franc*, the imperial envoys arrived to urge upon her the acceptance of the Austrian suit (April 18); and Mary formally accorded it. On May 21 Maximilian, who had been delayed by the slackness of the response made by the Estates to the imperial appeal for support of his enterprise (the Wittelsbachs were jealous about Hainault and Holland, while the King of Bohemia remembered the Luxemburg connexion), at last started on his expedition; and after passing through Louvain and Brussels, where he was well received, at the head of a body of near 8000 horsemen, arrived at Ghent. At six o'clock on the following morning his marriage with Mary was solemnised by the Bishop of Tournay, in the presence of the Count of Chimay and the *hooftman* of Bruges, "min jonker" of Gelders and his sister bearing the tapers before the bride. He had not come a day too soon. Part of Hainault was already in Louis' hands, and Brabant and Flanders were alike threatened; but, now that the political situation had so decisively altered to his disadvantage, he paused. Mary, in securing the protection of which she stood in need against the contending influences around, and the popular bodies confronting her, had at the same time gained for the Netherlands the alliance of a House not less resolved upon withstanding the encroachments of France in the West of the Empire, than it was upon resisting Hungarian ambition and the Turkish danger in the East. On no other conditions could the House of Austria command support from the princes of the Empire, or continue to hold authority there. With England also the Austrian marriage at once placed the Netherlands government on close terms of friendship.

At first things went smoothly with Archduke Maximilian in the Netherlands. Born in 1459, he was but a boy in years and little else than a boy in mind, notwithstanding the completeness of the education which he afterwards professed to have received through the care of the old *Weisskunig*, and the solemn purposes which he ascribed to himself as the "dear hero" *Tewrdanck*. But at no time of his life was he wanting either in courage or in elasticity of disposition. On September 18 Louis was found ready to conclude a favourable truce at Lens, having enough on his hands in consequence of the reconciliation of the Swiss to the House of Austria, and the menace of an English as well as an Aragonese invasion. And though in 1478 the campaign recommenced with much show of ardour, it only ended in another truce (July). The Flemish army under Maximilian's command, reinforced by Swiss mercenaries and English archers, had driven the French back upon Arras; Tournay had been retaken; and Louis promised to restore all towns taken by him in Hainault.

But already there were signs of impatience in Flanders. Maximilian had immediately on his marriage sworn to respect the privileges of Ghent and Bruges; and loud complaints were now heard of the misconduct of the German and other foreign soldiery, while Ghent was wroth at the imposition of a war-duty on small-beer. This led to an outbreak, in which three of the trades were involved and which, if Molinet is to be believed, had some curiously Catilinarian characteristics. It was quenched, chiefly through the exertions of Jan van Dadizeele, a loyal Flemish noble who now or afterwards was named *Bailli* of Ghent, and who in the following year (1479) so effectively reorganised the Flemish forces, of which he was named captain-general, that Olivier de la Marche describes these well-disciplined levies as the largest army he ever saw put into the field by Flanders. Town and country had combined to furnish it forth; and not less than five hundred nobles served with it on foot. With this truly national force the young Archduke gained his first victory at Guinegaste near Térouanne (August, 1479); but it could not be followed up, and the capture of the Holland herring-fleet caused renewed discouragement. Though in 1480 Maximilian gained possession of Luxemburg and in 1481, mainly through his general Count Adolf of Nassau, reduced Gelderland, where the insurgents had actually entered into alliance with France, the principal struggle made no progress, and the Archduke refused to be led away by the daring schemes of the Duchess Dowager for an Anglo-Burgundian invasion and partition of France.

His position was already growing difficult, and though the popularity of Mary, who in June, 1478, after the death of their first infant, had borne him a son, seems to have been on the increase, ill-will accumulated against her German consort. Maximilian's, doubtless reluctant, consent to place himself up to a certain point under the guidance of the Members of Flanders, and to allow the communal authorities of Ghent to interfere as to appointments in his household, had no conciliatory effect. In October, 1481, a grievous catastrophe occurred in the murder of Jan van Dadizeele, whose services to the House of Burgundy had not ended at Guinegaste. The arrest by Maximilian's orders of persons unsuspected of complicity with this dark crime, while others actually suspected of it were left untouched, led to an open quarrel between the ducal government and the Ghent magistrature. Such had been the jealousy of the Archduke excited in the Ghenters that after the birth of his third child Margaret (February, 1480) they had attempted to secure the control of both her and her brother Philip; and though it had finally been arranged that the children were to reside in the several chief provinces in succession, the Ghenters refused to give them up to Brabant when the first term of four months was at an end. In

September, 1481, a third son was born; but he survived for a few months only.  His mother's death soon followed.  On March 27, 1482, the results of a neglected fall from her horse proved fatal to the Duchess Mary.  Pitiable as was the decease of one so young, and so full of life and happiness, from a political point of view it threatened to prove disastrous to those whom she left behind her.

In accordance with the declaration put forth immediately before their marriage, Maximilian's authority in the Netherlands had come to an end with the life of his consort; and his claims to its continuance must be based on his parentage of their two surviving children, and Philip the young heir in particular.  But these children were in the power of Ghent, where, as throughout Flanders, Maximilian was profoundly unpopular.  Moreover, the feeling was widespread that apart from his personal prowess the advantages looked for from his union with the Duchess Mary had proved illusory.  Neither the Emperor nor England had come forward as allies against the French invasion; and at home all was disturbance and disorder.  Holland and Zeeland were once more torn by the old faction-feuds; in Gelderland Arnhem was ready to give the signal for renewed revolt; Utrecht had driven out its Burgundian Bishop.  Meanwhile Flanders was exposed to the full force of the French advance; her trade and industry were at a standstill.  Ghent and her sister-towns had no desire for annexation to France; but neither did they wish to bear the burden of a war which must end either thus or by covering the hated German prince with glory.  They therefore resolved to force him into a peace with France which would leave them free, under the nominal rule of his youthful son.  In the three years' struggle which ensued before Ghent lay at Maximilian's mercy, he was obliged to all intents and purposes to rely upon himself.  Lower Austria, with parts of Styria and the adjoining duchies, were in the grasp of King Matthias Corvinus, and the Emperor had to depend upon the scant sympathy and goodwill which he could find among the electors at Frankfort.  A loud cry arose in the Austrian dominions for the presence of the valiant and vigorous Archduke; but instead of giving way, as so often afterwards, to his natural impetuosity, he resolved so far as his hereditary interests were concerned to bide his time.

While in Holland and Zeeland as well as in Hainault Maximilian was at once acknowledged as guardian of his son and regent on his behalf (*mambourg*), Flanders and Brabant refused to concede this position to him, except under the control in each case of a Council named by the province.  Yet on every side faction was raging.  At Liége William de la Marck savagely murdered the Bishop and thrust his own son into his place, defying Maximilian and the nobles of Brabant and Namur so long as he knew himself supported by France; nor was it till 1485 that after new outrages he fell into the Archduke's hands and was righteously put to death at Maestricht.  New troubles had begun at

Utrecht; in Holland the leaders of the government set up at Hoorn by the *Hoeks* were put to death by the *Kabeljaauws* and the town pillaged; and Haarlem only escaped similar treatment by payment of an onerous fine. In the midst of this confusion, Maximilian had to allow the States of the Netherlands, assembled at Alost with the exception of Luxemburg and Gelders, to open a formal negotiation with Louis XI (November), with whom they had been for some time in secret communication. Nor was he able to refuse his assent to the basis on which, in December, 1482, the Peace of Arras was actually concluded, viz. the marriage of his daughter Margaret to the Dauphin, with Artois and Burgundy for her dowry. It was further settled by this peace that Philip should do homage to Louis for Flanders, so that the old relation of vassalage against which Charles the Bold and his father had so long struggled was restored, and a pretext for fresh intervention established. But the Flemish communes, satisfied with the restoration of free commercial intercourse with France, would probably have been prepared to sacrifice Namur and Hainault into the bargain, and Louis, now near his end, seemed to have lived long enough to master the House of Burgundy. Maximilian, who had been left out of the Council of four, appointed, with Ravenstein at its head, to carry on the government of Flanders with the Estates on behalf of Philip, was powerless, and unable to obtain the annual pension granted to him about this time except by compliance. In March, 1483, he finally accepted the Peace of Arras, and without any interposition on his part, his daughter was transferred into the guardianship of the French King, and on June 23 solemnly betrothed to the Dauphin.

Soon after this Maximilian was able to strengthen his personal position by a successful intervention against the *Hoek* revolt at Utrecht. On returning to his capital Bishop David had been brutally insulted and imprisoned at Amersfoort, and Engelbert of Cleves had been set up in his place. At the head of a force of 12000 men, commanded by a staff of celebrated captains, the Archduke laid siege to Utrecht, which capitulated in September and was condemned to pay a heavy fine. Bishop David once more held his entry into the prostrate city as the spiritual ruler of his see (he died peacefully as such at Wyk in 1496); but Maximilian was acknowledged as the administrator of its temporalities. It was in the course of this successful campaign that he received the news of the death of Louis XI. Though this event could hardly lead to the undoing of the Peace of Arras, it could not but reassure him as to the future relations between France and the Flemings, for he was not aware how much of her father's spirit survived in Anne de Beaujeu, under whose control the government of Charles VIII was carried on during the first eight years of his reign. He now declared the powers of the Council of Flanders to have determined, and a storm of protests and charges ensued, in the course of which the Flemings invoked the authority of Charles VIII, which Maximilian refused to acknowledge. Towards the end of 1483, after the French government had ingratiated itself with the great Flemish towns by renouncing for ten years the appellate jurisdiction claimed by the Parliament of Paris, negotiations for an alliance ensued between the States of Flanders and Brabant and the assembly which, under the name of States-General, met at Tours in 1484. But the popular *entente* of earlier days was not to be renewed between the decaying communes and a people over which the power of the monarchy was already paramount.

Meanwhile the quarrel between Maximilian and the Flemings became more acute. The Knights of the Golden Fleece at Termonde declared his headship of their Order at an end, though he might still preside over its meetings during his son's minority. Bruges refused him admission if attended by more than a dozen companions, and sent to the block several persons who had laid a plot on his behalf. Rumours of a similar plot were rife at Ghent; and Maximilian had clearly accepted the challenge of a people resolved upon completely throwing off his authority. He began by sending the faithful Olivier de la Marche to lodge complaints with the French government against the communes, and succeeded in provoking so much distrust in Flanders that, though a French as well as a Flemish army took the field in 1484, no decisive blow was struck. The Flemings however flooded Brabant, where the Archduke's appeal for support of the dynasty was very coolly received, and Count de Romont, the commander of the Flemish levies, proclaimed himself lieutenant-general of Duke Philip against his father. In January, 1485, Maximilian by taking Oudenarde showed his determination to make himself master of Ghent. But after defeating the Ghenters under their own walls, and capturing their great banner, he was obliged by a mutiny for pay among his troops to retreat, while the French under Crèvecœur (des Querdes) entered the city. Soon nothing remained to the Archduke but Brabant and Hainault. Fortunately, however, for him with the Ghenters the powers that were could never be in the right; and such a storm of popular indignation was raised by the misconduct of the French soldiery, that Crèvecœur in his turn retired upon Tournay.

The French faction were now at the mercy of their adversaries. On June 21 Maximilian held his entry into Bruges, which had set the example of recognising him as *mambourg*. At Ghent, William Rin and another leader of the French faction were decapitated, while Coppenole (said to be in actual enjoyment of a pension as a member of the royal household) and the rest only saved themselves by flight. On June 28 Maximilian, while confirming the privileges of Ghent and Bruges, was by the former also recognised as *mambourg*, and declared a general amnesty, with however some important exceptions. On July 6 Duke Philip was delivered into his father's hands at a

village near Ghent, which they hereupon entered at the head of 5000
men, instead of the stipulated 500. Before night the trades were under
arms on the *Vrydagsmarkt*, and in the morning a terrible conflict must
have ensued, had not Maximilian listened to counsels of moderation and
delay. Sending his son out of Ghent, he returned for a final settlement; and the end was the complete submission of the city, which
was carried out on July 22. Thirty-three ringleaders were executed,
many more sent into banishment, and a heavy fine was inflicted. Many
of the old charters were destroyed, and the entire constitution of the
city was subjected to revision by a commission. After taking Philip to
Malines, there to be educated under the superintendence of the Duchess
Dowager, and judiciously declining an offer of the Liégeois to put him in
possession of their city, Maximilian at last departed to Germany. He
left the Netherlands under the military guardianship of Philip of Cleves
and his other captains.

When, in the summer of 1486, Maximilian returned to the Netherlands as Roman King, the glamour of this new dignity ensured him a
good reception in Brabant and the other provinces through which, as
*mambourg*, he accompanied Duke Philip on a sort of progress; and he
was more than ever intent upon taking vengeance on France. But,
though he openly broke the Peace of Arras by occupying Omer, which
was again taken by Crèvecœur with Térouanne in the following year,
these campaigns were of no real importance; his chief designs were
concerned with the future of Britanny—a vital question for France. It
was the fear of a war no longer defensive and of measurable proportions which, together with the slow rate of his military progress
in the Low Countries, notwithstanding the oppressive presence of his
large bodies of alien troops—German and Swiss mercenaries in particular
—led to the renewal of agitation in Flanders against the Austrian
*régime*. Of what advantage had it proved to the economic interests
of the good towns? In 1478 the *intercursus* had indeed been concluded
which placed commerce and navigation between England and the Netherlands on a new footing of security, and King Richard III had granted
to the Netherlands merchants in England the lower tariff of duties
enjoyed by their German competitors (a privilege taken away again
by his successor). But, for reasons already stated, the English trade
had more and more passed to Brabant and Holland, and Flanders found
her industry and commerce increasingly dependent upon her relations
with France.

Stirred up by the return of Adrian Vilain, Lord of Rasenghien, who
had fled from the city at the time of the execution of William
Rin, the *mordans laingages* at Ghent, as Molinet calls them, com-
plained more loudly than ever of imposts and military oppression, and
Maximilian was fain to summon the States of the chief provinces to
Ypres, while at the same time he met the deans of the trades in

person at Bruges and promised—sincerely or not—to enter into peace negotiations with France. But the Ghent democracy, brooking no delay, sent forth a force which seized Courtray, obliging it to take the oath to Duke Philip and Ghent, and holding it against Philip of Cleves. On February 1, 1488, the trades of Bruges in their turn took up arms, and the Carpenters occupied the gate towards Ghent. Then ensued the strangest and most humiliating episode in the whole history of Maximilian's experiences in the Netherlands. The market-place was turned into a fortified camp, and for the better part of four months the Roman King was detained, first in his own lodging; then, as an actual prisoner in the Cranenburg, a house by the market; afterwards, when his soldiery had been driven out of the city, in the fortified mansion of Ravenstein. Bruges itself, afraid of Antwerp and plied with advice by Ghent (whence at one time several thousands arrived before the gates, and later Coppenole appeared to proclaim the Peace of Arras), passed gradually into a state of terrorism, during which a series of executions of the King's followers took place under his very eyes. In the midst of these proceedings the Brughelins sent forth their levies against Maximilian's garrisons in other towns, seizing Middelburg and putting several nobles of his party to death; while the Ghenters on their own account committed similar excesses. Maximilian, although he at first gave fair words to the trades and afterwards made a pathetic appeal for consideration, bore himself throughout with courage and dignity.

At last, after Pope Innocent VIII had issued his censures at Bruges, it became known there that the Emperor in person was marching upon Flanders for the delivery of his son. Hitherto the States assembled round Duke Philip at Malines had transacted in a very business-like way with the other States at Ghent; but by the middle of May it was understood that now or never an arrangement must be made with the captive King. He was liberated on condition that he would withdraw from Flanders within four days of his deliverance, and that he approved, as did his son-in-law the King of France, the solemn League and Union entered into on May 1 by the States of several of the provinces for the sake of peace and good government, and for the maintenance of the Treaty of Arras.

He had thus yielded everything. But, though he had sworn a solemn oath and accepted a heavy pecuniary payment, it was felt that the *nodus materiae* lay in the question of hostages; nor was it till Philip of Cleves had arrived at Bruges in this capacity that the King was at last allowed to depart. On May 24 the Emperor arrived at Louvain at the head of a well-appointed army, and Maximilian, as a prince of the Empire (not "for his own quarrel"), felt himself compelled to take part in the punitive campaign against Flanders. On both sides the necessity was put forward of protecting the rights of Duke Philip; and, after the Germans and Walloons had seized Deinze,

Ravenstein protested that he must take up arms in defence of his liege lord even against the Emperor. Henceforth the hostage became the guiding spirit of Flemish resistance to Maximilian. In September, 1488, he was received with acclamation at Brussels; soon Louvain and the smaller towns of Brabant fell into his hands. Flanders had likewise remained unreduced, while Maximilian was operating on the Lys and in Zeeland; Ypres was occupied by French troops, and the siege of Ghent, begun by the Emperor in person, had been abandoned. By October Frederick III had returned to Germany, and in the last days of the year Maximilian followed. In vain he had assembled the loyal States at Malines; for the time his field of action lay elsewhere. The Duke of Britanny had died in September, and the struggle with France would have to be resumed on a perhaps more favourable field. But his present task was to reconquer Austria.

Maximilian left behind him as governor-general, with full powers, Duke Albert of Saxony (*Albertus Animosus*, founder of the Albertine line), who in the organisation and conduct of armies was unsurpassed by any German commander of his age. With resources inferior to those which had been at Maximilian's disposal, Albert had in the first instance to suppress a fresh outbreak of the *Hoeks* in Holland, who, under the leadership of young Francis van Brederode, after surprising Rotterdam, organised a petty warfare in the style of the *gueux* of later days. But the States of Holland resolved on putting an end to this *Jonker-Franzen* war, and the rebel fleet was finally all but annihilated at Brouwershaven (July, 1490), Brederode himself dying soon afterwards of his wounds. Several of the other *Hoek* leaders died a violent death at Delft; but one of them threw himself into Sluys, which was in the hands of Philip of Cleves. In 1489 Albert restored the authority of Maximilian in Brabant, where the Peace of Frankfort, concluded for temporary purposes with France by the Roman King, was eagerly welcomed, for Bruges and Louvain had suffered unspeakably from war and pestilence. But it was some time before, at Montils-les-Tours, Maximilian's *mambournie* over Flanders was likewise acknowledged, and Ghent, Bruges, and Ypres undertook to sue to him for pardon, a commission being appointed to ascertain and restore the privileges enjoyed by them under Philip the Good and his successor.

The ink, however, was hardly dry upon the so-called Treaty of Flanders when, during Albert's temporary absence in Germany, the communal insurrection broke out afresh. At Bruges George Picquanet, elected *hooftman*, held out for a time against famine and Engelbert of Nassau, by whose soldiery he was ultimately killed. At Ghent, in May, 1491, a cordwainer named Remieulx, after admitting some of Philip of Cleves' adherents, slew the Grand Dean, and Coppenole was put in his place. A strange conflict ensued between this demagogue and one Arnoul Leclercq, a labourer who had been named *hooftman* by a body of 5000 peasants previously organised under arms by Coppenole and his brother, both of whom were in the end put to death. Then a deputation of notables waited upon Duke Philip at Malines; the usual penalties were once more inflicted, the wearing of white hoods was prohibited for ever, and a Peace of Ghent was once more proclaimed (June, 1492). Meanwhile, Albert had on his return been occupied with a rising in Kennemerland, Friesland, and the Texel, stirred up by emissaries from Alkmaar, where followers of Brederode had seized the power. The insurgent peasants bore banners of our Lady and certain saints of local repute, together with a strange ensign consisting of a loaf of rye-bread and a large lump of green cheese. (Arnoul Leclercq at Ghent had borne a plough in his banner, and we remember the *Bundschuh*.) After much debate they were admitted into Haarlem, which had itself been disaffected; but on the approach of Albert the peasant host, left to itself, was massacred at Hemskerke. Haarlem, Alkmaar, and the smaller towns all humbled themselves before him; and the *Landsknechte*, with the art-treasures of Haarlem stuck in their hats, prefigured their comrades of the *sacco di Roma* (May). It remained for Albert to finish his task by the reduction of Sluys, where Philip of Cleves, whom the death of his father during the siege made Lord zum Ravenstein, still held out. The slow progress of the siege, even after in July English vessels, sent by Henry VII, had arrived to take part in it, finds its explanation in the tenderness invariably shown by the House of Burgundy, and by Maximilian, to his wife's kinsman. In October Ravenstein very leisurely surrendered Sluys, and three years later he was formally acquitted of any imputation against his honour.

Meanwhile, Maximilian had (towards the end of 1490) made the great cast, and married by proxy Anne, the heiress of Britanny. Shortly before this he had concluded a close alliance with Henry VII, mediated by Ferdinand of Aragon. (For Flanders this was all the more important, since in 1486 Bruges had sought to gain English support by granting free importation of English cloths and in 1488 had entreated the new King to aid her against the Emperor and concluded a new commercial treaty with this object.) Although this had been a fortunate year for Maximilian, he could not expect that his successes would be crowned by the tame submission of France to such a provocation. In November, 1491, Anne of Britanny surrendered Rennes, and in the following month she gave her hand to Charles VIII. But Margaret of Burgundy was still detained in France, and nothing had been said as to the restitution of her dowry. Yet in the Netherlands there was little sympathy with the insulted Regent; and early in 1492 the French Court provided him with a new difficulty in the shape of a pretender in Gelderland. Charles of Egmond had in 1487 been taken prisoner at Bethune and carried off to France. The Geldrian towns eagerly came forward to pay the ransom demanded by the French government; but without its support they had not sufficient resources to place Charles in the seat of his ancestors. His struggle against the Burgundian authority accordingly proved long and arduous. At first Maximilian showed himself willing to take the unusual course of referring the question of the government of Gelderland to the arbitration of the Empire; then a truce was concluded in 1497, with a view to a partition of the duchy; but soon afterwards war broke out again, Maximilian taking the field in person. In 1505 Philip, now King of Castile, consented to a compromise at Rosendal, which left Charles in possession of the Nymwegen and Roermonde districts. But he played fast and loose with the treaty, and as the ally of France by 1514 at last succeeded in possessing himself of the entire duchy. His later struggles which only terminated with his death in 1538, and in the course of which he actually sought to make over his duchy to France, must be left unnoticed here.

The recovery of Artois, whose capital Arras was surprised by the *Landsknechte* after the fall of Sluys, would, together with his reconquest of Franche Comté, have encouraged Maximilian to attempt to secure the whole of his daughter's dowry, notwithstanding the pacifications concluded by Charles VIII's government with the Kings of England and Aragon (November, 1492—January, 1493). But the unwillingness of the Netherlands to continue the War, added to his other cares, induced him to accept Swiss mediation for the conclusion of a truce with France, followed in May, 1493, by the Peace of Senlis. The territorial question was settled as nearly as possible on the *uti possidetis* basis; so that Artois (and the Franche Comté) remained with the House of Burgundy, though Arras was ultimately to revert to France in exchange for certain towns now occupied by her. Margaret, all obligations between her and King Charles having been cancelled by the treaty, returned home joyously, calling out *Vive Bourgogne* to the people who flocked round her at St Quentin, and receiving at Valenciennes a popular welcome. After narrowly escaping a design of the *Landsknechte* to seize her in pledge for outstanding pay, she took up her residence at Namur.

In 1494, the year after that of his father's death, Maximilian returned to the Netherlands. His immediate purpose was to superintend the transfer of their government to Philip, now fifteen years of age, and also to settle affairs in Gelderland; but the Eastern Question was now uppermost in his mind, as was shown by his solemn assumption at Antwerp of the insignia of the crusading Order of St George, and by his appeal to all Christian potentates to follow his example (October—November). Flanders was tranquil; Crèvecœur lay dead; Ravenstein was among those who paid their respects to the young Duke on his solemn entry into the great mercantile city. The presence there of another visitor—the pretended Richard Duke of York—which gave rise to an unseemly *fracas*, reflected little credit on the discretion of the House of Burgundy. He was the *protégé* of the Duchess Dowager, and Maximilian was quite ready to risk a quarrel with England on the chance of the dethronement of the faithless Tudor. Henry VII replied by removing the staple for English wool, tin, and other products to Calais, stopping all intercourse between his subjects and the Netherlands, and expelling all Flemings from England. The Burgundian government retorted (April, 1494, and January, 1495) by prohibiting the importation of English cloth; and for two years there was a complete cessation of commercial dealings between the two countries. Finally, Duke Philip was prevailed upon to promise not to admit any enemy of England into his dominions; and in February, 1496, the *Magnus Intercursus* proclaimed on both sides freedom of trade, *i.e.* the right of trading without special license or pass, and that of fishery. Though there was nothing novel in this famous treaty, it offered a solid foundation for the establishment of satisfactory mercantile relations; but time could hardly fail to be on the side of the English, to the sale of whose cloth the Netherlands were now open—with the important exception however of Flanders, where restrictions were still maintained. Even here it soon became difficult to confine this sale to the staples of Antwerp and Bruges—or from 1501 to Bruges alone—to limit it to large pieces, and to prevent the wearing of it by natives. And Philip's well-meant endeavours to revive the sunken prosperity of Bruges were seen to be hopelessly out of date. After in 1502 the *Magnus Intercursus* had been solemnly renewed, Henry VII, angered by the refusal of the Netherlands government to assist him in laying hands on the fugitive Earl of Suffolk (Edmund de la Pole), brought about a fresh stoppage of trade between the two countries, which lasted till 1506.

It was not only in commercial matters that Duke Philip and his advisers showed a disposition to emancipate themselves from his father's control. Maximilian had placed at the head of the Privy Council, composed of fourteen members, Count Engelbert of Nassau, the faithful servant of three generations of the House of Burgundy, but the leading voice in it was that of William de Croy, Seigneur de Chièvres. He and those who thought with him resented as strongly as the Flemish and Brabançon towns the continuance in the land of the German soldiery, to whose chief commander Albert of Saxony the ducal treasury had pledged Haarlem and several other important places pending the payment of a heavy debt. The influence of de Chièvres and the great nobles in general was accordingly in favour of maintaining peace with France, although in the Gelders difficulty above all she showed so little regard for Netherlands interests; and Philip on the whole inclined to follow these pacific counsels.

In May, 1494, Maximilian had at Kempten intervened in a dispute between Groningen and the rural districts of West-Friesland encroached upon by the city. His decision had been in favour of Groningen; and though he was anxious to keep the peace, further encroachments on her part induced the *Schieringers* of the Westergao in their straits to invite the redoubtable Albert of Saxony to assume authority as governor. The end came three years later when Albert was once more offered the governorship by the terrified towns of Sneek and Franeker, and his lieutenants subjugated the land by a series of manœuvres, crafty and cruel like those of a campaign against savages, and ending with a battle of artillery against pikes, and the capture of Leeuwarden (June—July, 1498). Maximilian now bestowed the whole of Friesland, including Groningen, upon Albert with the title of hereditary governor (*potestat*), reserving to himself the right of redeeming West-Friesland on the payment of 100,000 florins. The greater part of his own debt to Albert, which amounted to more than treble this sum, had been taken over by Philip; but an ugly suspicion remains as to Maximilian's motives in the transaction. After Albert, who had been detained by the Gelders War, had himself arrived in Friesland, the rough insolence of one of his sons drove the country into rising once more against his yoke; and he was laying siege to Groningen, which this time had joined hands with its former adversaries, when death overtook him at Emden (September, 1500). Edzard of East-Friesland, to whom Groningen and the *Ommelande* now did homage, summoned Charles of Egmond to his aid and was supported by a native rising under a peasant known as the Great Pier, who afterwards rejoiced in the title of " Admiral of the Zuiderzee." At last, in 1515, Duke George of Saxony agreed to dismiss the " Black Band " of soldiery, formerly in Egmond's service, which had carried fire and sword through the land, and to accept the redemption of the country on payment of the sum agreed upon between his father and the Roman King. Charles, who in this very year assumed the government of the Netherlands, at last solved the Frisian problem by the reduction of the country, followed by the submission of Groningen to the imperial authority.

Slight indeed had been the importance of that problem on the horizon of Maximilian's speculations. The great matrimonial plan, which he seems to have devised in part as early as 1491, was fully carried out within six years. In August, 1496, the infanta Juana was wedded at Antwerp to Duke Philip, and on Palm Sunday of the following year his sister Margaret, after intrepidly encountering many dangers on the way, gave her hand at Burgos to the infante Don John. Soon however a tragic succession of deaths—those of Don John, his posthumous child, Juana's elder sister Queen Isabel of Portugal, and her son Don Miguel, left Juana heiress-apparent of the united kingdoms of Castile and Aragon (1500). In the same year her eldest son Charles was born at Ghent; and the city, with no foreknowledge of what she was afterwards to suffer at his hands, was loud in her rejoicings. But vast as was the prospect now opened before Philip, he was, so far as the conduct of Netherlands affairs was concerned, brought little nearer to the schemes of Maximilian's foreign policy. An interview between father and son arranged by Ravenstein and others in May, 1496, seems indeed for a time to have made Philip swerve from his policy of friendliness towards France, and soon afterwards he dismissed from his council Francis van Busleyden, Provost of Liége, supposed to be an active adversary of the Austrian influence. But already in 1497 he helped to thwart the exertions of Maximilian in Gelderland, and, on the accession of Louis XII in 1498, crossed the endeavours of his father, who had actually invaded Burgundy, by opening negotiations with the new French King. In the Treaty of Brussels Philip promised homage for Artois and Flanders (performed in 1499), and personally renounced all claims on the duchy of Burgundy, in return for the restoration of the Picard towns reserved at Senlis; while Maximilian, after taking Franche Comté, gradually became inclined to treat in his turn for peace with France.

Thus it was that during the first years of the new century father and son came to cooperate in the scheme for a marriage between Philip's son Charles (Duke of Luxemburg) and Claude, the elder daughter of Louis XII, which was to transfer both Britanny and Burgundy to Philip as the dowry of his future daughter-in-law. The purposes of this extraordinary design being purely dynastic, except that Maximilian seems honestly to have counted on its success for French aid against the Turks, it could not find much favour in the Netherlands, where in February, 1505, the States-General at Malines showed little willingness to grant a large *bede* demanded for the Turkish War by the Roman King in the absence of his son. Involved in a network of manœuvres, besides being obliged to nurse his Spanish expectations, Philip was in these years constantly away from the Low Countries—in 1501 with his consort in Spain, where their succession was assured in Castile and, should King Ferdinand die without a male heir, in Aragon, and negotiating on his way out and home with King Louis in France; in 1503 in the Empire. It was on their second voyage to Spain that King Philip and his Queen —once more on kindly terms with one another—were obliged by a fearful storm (January, 1506) to land at Southampton, and placed for a time in the power of Henry VII. The goodwill of that prince—highly important to Philip by reason of his desire to arrive at a permanent understanding with Ferdinand of Aragon—had, together with his personal liberty, to be purchased by a commercial treaty. Philip had a heart for the Flemings, and for Bruges in particular; and in the negotiations which followed her interests were eagerly pressed; but so also were the divergent interests of Antwerp. The so-called *Malus Intercursus* was inevitably to the advantage of English trade, which it freed from oppressive tolls on the way to Antwerp or Bruges, Middelburg or Mons, while it left the sale and use of English cloth absolutely free except to a certain extent in Flanders. The unpopularity of the compact there was no secret to Philip, and notwithstanding the representations of de Chièvres he had not yet ratified it, when the news arrived of his

death at Burgos (September 25, 1506).　Evil rumours accompanied the
tidings; for the young King's light and profuse ways were odious to the
Castilians, agreeing better with the preferences of the Low Countries,
and the traditional habits of the Burgundian House.　Philip the Fair
had something of his mother's docility in council and of his father's
high spirit in the field, and was not wholly without the popular fibre
which commended each of them to the respective lands of their birth;
but, so far as can be judged from his short career, he gave no proof
of the profound conscientiousness and high aspirings that make it
difficult to deny the epithet of great to his eldest son, notwithstanding
all his failures.

Five months after Philip's death the unhappy Juana gave birth to a
third daughter, and then sank into hopeless insanity.　Maximilian
showed himself from the first perfectly prepared to enter on a second
course of regency, this time on behalf of his elder grandson, now a boy of
six years of age.　Personally he was as unpopular as ever in the Netherlands, where it was perceived that neither his authority in the Empire
nor his influence in European affairs corresponded to his still expanding
ambition; and where a strong feeling survived in favour of maintaining
friendly relations with France.　It was therefore a judicious as well as
a necessary step on his part, when, after accepting the offer made to him
by the States-General on the motion of the States of Holland and
Brabant (October, 1506), he empowered his daughter Margaret to receive
in his stead the oaths due to him as Guardian of his grandchildren and
Regent; and on her being proclaimed as such by the States-General at
Leuven (April, 1507), he appointed her his sole governor-general in the
Netherlands.

The office which Margaret had originally been intended by her
father to hold only temporarily she filled with honour and credit during
eight eventful years (1507–15).　After her troubled experiences in
France she had in 1501 bravely gone forth to serve the imperial interest
by becoming the bride of Duke Philibert (called the Fair) of Savoy, and,
once more a widow, had escaped the doom of being united to Henry VII
of England.　She was now, though saddened by her sufferings, prepared
to devote her remarkable talents and even higher gifts of character
to the service of her House.　Her correspondence with her father,
occasionally grotesque in form, since neither had really mastered the
language of the other, proves her candour and courage, her moderation
more especially in the earlier years of her government, and her spirit of
self-sacrifice throughout its course.　She began by promptly declaring
the so-called *Malus Intercursus* invalid, thus putting pressure on Henry
VII, who had no mind for the stoppage of commercial relations, besides
being desirous of influencing the political action of Margaret's government and at this moment himself posing as a candidate for her hand.　A
commercial treaty, drafted on the lines of the *Intercursus* of 1496, but

with the English cloth-trade clauses left out, was at once returned
with her signature; and on these terms trade was carried on between
the two countries during the remainder of Henry VII's reign.

Maximilian might therefore look forward hopefully to the explanation of his relations with England which he invited Margaret to lay
before the States-General early in 1508, when notifying to them the
proposed marriage between Charles and Mary Tudor. Not long before
this he had enquired of her whether the Netherlands were to be regarded
as included in his present war with France. Margaret knew how even
the Gelderland trouble was insufficient to counteract the desire of the
States for peace with France, and therefore persuaded her father by
concluding a truce with Charles of Egmond, which left Gelderland provisionally in his hands, to conciliate his French ally, whose cooperation
he needed for his project of vengeance upon Venice. The ill-omened
League of Cambray, concluded in December, 1508, was as a matter
of fact in a large measure Margaret's work. Soon Maximilian was
wrapped up in its progress; but in the ensuing four years he by no means
left his daughter to carry on her government without his supervision.
Not only was he extremely sensitive of any supposed want of deference
by her to his supreme authority, but he was constantly intervening in
the matter of appointments in Church and State—from the bishopric of
Cambray to the aldermanship of *le Franc*. And through all goes the
call for money, culminating in July, 1510, with a demand for an annual
pension of 50,000 crowns for which Margaret was obliged to tell him
the time had not yet come. Her task of mediating between the States
and the requirements of Maximilian's complicated Italian policy was
a very arduous one.

With the advent on the scene of Henry VIII a new chapter may
be said to begin in the political activity of Margaret, to whom the
alliance between him and her father was mainly due. The variations
of Maximilian's European policy in these years of surprises were little
to the taste of the Netherlanders, and occasionally ran a risk of conflicting with their interests. Thus when he had been tardily induced
to take the side of the Head of the Hansa in her quarrel with John,
King of Denmark, the latter (in 1507 or rather later) sought to strike
a blow at Lübeck's commercial supremacy in the Baltic by inviting
the Holland merchants to make the Sound one of their trade-routes.
The Lübeckers insisted on the Holland and Friesland vessels confining
themselves to the passage of the Great Belt, as leading more directly to
their own city. Hence the outbreak of hostilities between the Hansa
and the Netherlands, many of whose ships were taken up the Trave as
prizes, and in 1511 the capture of the entire Dutch Baltic fleet by the
Lübeckers and Wismarers. Strong pressure was put by the States upon
Margaret to induce the Emperor to equip a fleet for the protection
of the interests of Holland in the Baltic; in the end, though the Peace of

Malmoe (1512) maintained Lübeck's ascendency there, it secured free navigation for Netherlands vessels, except when carrying contraband of war.  But to the schemes of the Emperor-Elect (as he now called himself) against France, with which was curiously mixed up a project for a marriage between Charles and Louis XII's second daughter Renée, the provinces turned a deaf ear.  Not even against Charles of Egmond, though Holland and Brabant were dreading his approach, would they grant aids, unless assured of a general peace.  With the exception of Antwerp, Malines, and Hertogenbosch, Margaret wrote, the States were *d'une si maulvaise nature* that nothing short of the Emperor's own presence could manage the business.  But even this expedient seems to have failed; and when in April, 1513, he concluded an offensive alliance with Henry VIII against France, the Netherlands were declared neutral. They took advantage of their neutrality to supply the French with arms and ammunition, but at the same time allowed Henry after he had commenced the siege of Térouanne (June, 1513) to levy both foot and horse in the country.  Maximilian approved, but he held no independent command, and the capture of Tournay following on the brilliant victory of Guinegaste was treated by Henry as an English acquisition. But though for a time it seemed as if Margaret's programme of a close alliance against France of England, Spain, and the Austro-Burgundian interest would carry everything before it, Henry was at last estranged by the delay of the marriage between his sister and Prince Charles, due in part at least to the de Chièvres influence, and finally entered into an alliance with Louis XII, to whom the English Princess was now wedded. As the project of marriage between the French King and Charles' sister Eleanor was now likewise abandoned, Charles was in his turn left in a humiliating position, and, though the Netherlands were *ex post facto* admitted to the new French alliance, all cordiality between the English and Burgundian Courts was at an end.  The commercial relations between the two countries had meanwhile made but little advance; the duties levied upon English trade, especially in Zeeland, had again been raised; and a commission summoned to Bruges in 1512 had effected nothing.

Thus Margaret's foreign policy had proved unsuccessful before (January, 1515) Charles assumed the government of the Netherlands; and in the course of the year she found herself virtually excluded from the more intimate counsels of the nephew over whose interests she had so tenderly watched in his younger days, and for whom to the last she was ready to make any personal sacrifice.  Charles, who in 1520 fitly recognised her services by assigning to her as her own domain the loyal city of Malines and the adjoining territory, was during the first years of his government still entirely under the influence of de Chièvres, who, in the course of this very year, contrived to send away Adrian of Utrecht to Spain in the interests of the Prince's succession.  The death of Louis XII on January 1, 1515, and the accession of Francis I had offered an opening for the advancement of those friendly relations with France which de Chièvres and the Netherlands statesmen were so anxious to cultivate; and even after the death of Ferdinand of Aragon a year later had left to Charles the inheritance of the Spanish monarchy and its Italian dependencies, he continued in spite of Margaret's action to follow the same policy. Nor was it till the imperial succession loomed largely on the horizon that the three generations, Maximilian, Margaret and Charles were reunited in their efforts for a common end.

A heavy price was paid by the Netherlands for the preservation of the greater part of the monarchy of Charles the Bold. Like the House of Burgundy into which he had married, Maximilian (so popular at Nürnberg and Augsburg) showed scant regard for the rights and usages of provinces or towns in its dominions, though it was only exceptionally that he ventured on such an act as the decapitation of the burgomaster of Dort, who had upheld a meeting of the States on their own motion, as allowed by the *Groote Privilegie*. Philip the Fair went the logical length of limiting his renewal of this famous Charter by a reservation which rendered his acceptance nugatory. That these sentiments had descended to Charles V was shown by the chastisement inflicted by him in 1540 upon his native city of Ghent—the most far-reaching, though not the most sanguinary of any to which in the course of her history she was subjected. In the face of these experiences the gradual growth of the practice of summoning the States-General, long resisted by Charles, but resumed during the governor-generalship (from 1531) of his sister Maria, Queen Dowager of Hungary, seemed of little account. The sufferings of the country—of Holland in particular—in the period preceding that of the rule of Philip the Fair were unforgotten by the next generation. In 1494 a new valuation of income (*verponding*) was made throughout the Netherlands, in order to rectify the *modus* under which the contributions to the *bedes* had hitherto been assessed on the several towns and villages; and this had to be again revised in 1514. A most distressful state of things was hereby revealed in many parts of the country—more especially south of Utrecht and Gelderland, where there had hardly been a break in the presence of the German soldiery. The number of the homesteads here had dwindled, the cattle had on many pastures diminished by half; along the coasts navigation and fisheries had declined. In some of the Zuiderzee ports the stillness was beginning to set in from which, owing to natural causes, there was to be no later awakening. What wonder that under Philip and afterwards during Margaret's governorship all classes in the Netherlands should have been practically unanimous in their desire for peace, and that even the Gelders War, upon a successful termination of which the achievement of political unity depended, was held a burden? And what favour could the endeavours expect to find which, set on foot by

Maximilian, were carried out by Charles V for establishing in a new form an organic connexion between the whole of the provinces and the Empire at large? The States took very coolly the inclusion in 1512 of the so-called Burgundian Circle (Gelderland and Utrecht were afterwards added to the Westphalian) in the system of Circles established as it were incidentally twelve years earlier, and persistently declined to acknowledge the right claimed by the Emperor of taxing the provinces for imperial purposes. On the other hand the imperial Diet held fast to the pretension, as was shown at Nürnberg in 1543; and in 1548—just a century before the political bond between the United Provinces and the Empire was finally severed—the entire group of the "Burgundian hereditary lands" was included as the Burgundian Circle in the *nexus* of the Empire. It was in this shape that, with the proper safeguard of a reservation of the privileges and liberties of the several provinces, the undivided Netherlands were by the Pragmatic Sanction of 1549 settled upon Philip, then intended by Charles to succeed him on the Imperial as well as on the Spanish throne.

Although, notwithstanding the Gelders War, the Netherlands recovered something of their prosperity during the governorship of Margaret, the downfall of the trade and industry of Flanders was irremediable. Public feeling in England continued to favour the Netherlands, just as of old the Flemish towns had upheld the English alliance; but no substantial change took place for many a long year in the mercantile relations between the two peoples. In consequence of the decline of the Venetian and Genoese trade after the discovery of the Cape route to India, Antwerp, where the Portuguese and Spaniards found the facilities and the security they required, and whither they were followed by the other foreign "nations" from Bruges, gradually became the chief commercial port of Europe; while not a rivulet from the current of trade could be turned back into the sands of the Zwyn. Before the middle of the century the proportion of the total exports of the Netherlands, estimated at between six and six and a half million of pounds Flemish, assignable to Antwerp was reckoned at eighty per cent.—that to Bruges at one-half per cent. While Antwerp had supplanted Bruges, the advance of Amsterdam was beginning to emulate that of the great Belgian city, and the mariners of Holland and Zeeland were in the North Sea and the Baltic learning to play their destined part of carriers on the ocean.

The great religious movement the eve of which this summary has reached, found the intellectual life of the Netherlands in a condition of stillness sufficiently accounted for by its political experiences. But the stillness was not stagnation. University studies were in fetters; but in the schools education was largely in the hands of men anxious to prevent any divorce between theological and grammatical teaching. Among the people at large publications against the sale of indulgences

—an abuse with which the Netherlands had been familiarised during the previous half century—circulated before the date of Luther's *theses*; and the book of appeal, the Bible, had spread very notably in its Latin form, even before (some time after a version of the body of the Old Testament) the first Dutch New Testament appeared in 1523. The activity of the Windeshem convents continued till the advent of the Reformation, when the *Fraterhuizen* themselves, many of whose members adopted the doctrines of the reformers, fell into disuse. For the rest, although Erasmus had reason enough for remembering the monks of his native land, the monasticism denounced by him is not so much of a local as of a general type; so too was the disregard by the secular priesthood of one at least of the laws most conspicuously imposed upon their lives by the Church. Yet in the Netherlands, formerly a seedplot of attempts to purify life and morals which too often took a fanatical form and thus came to be branded as heresies, the Reformation had few immediate precursors. John Wessel, as has been seen, died in a convent. The Austin friars at Dort had been influenced by Hendrik of Zutphen, appointed their prior in 1515 after being a pupil of Staupitz and a fellow-student of Luther. Nor do we meet with many enquirers upon whom the Free Spirit, which had formerly likewise had its Brotherhood and Sisterhood, might be thought to have descended. The only heretic of this sort whom Jacob van Hoogstraten, himself of Brabançon origin, tracked to his death in the Netherlands before the Reformation was Hermann of Ryswyk, burnt in 1512.

The share of the Netherlands in the history of the Renaissance, on the other hand, is, insofar as it has not already come under notice here, comprehended in a single name—Erasmus. The ducal Court, as has been seen, was not indifferent to intellectual abilities of many sorts and kinds; the examples of his father and half-brother were in a sense bettered by Bishop David of Utrecht, and a fresh impulse was given to the patronage of learning and its appliances by the English consort of Charles the Bold. The relations between Maximilian and the Renaissance were neither perfunctory nor casual, and justify the warmth of feeling towards him on the part of scholars, poets, and artists which was one of the truest foundations of his popularity; but no traces remain of his having found leisure to encourage a similar devotion in the Burgundian lands, except that among the statues for his own mausoleum (originally meant to be erected at Vienna) he gave orders for two—one of them very likely his own—to be cast in the Netherlands. What he left undone was not supplied either by his son Philip, careless of most of the graver interests of life, or by his daughter Margaret who, poetess as she was, needed all her strength for the business of her life. Thus amidst depressing influences the care of learning and letters, arts and science, was in the main left to the population itself, and chiefly of course to the towns; and from the midst of one of these, trained under influences which more than any other strengthened popular and civic life, came forth Erasmus, a born citizen of the world of letters of which he became the glory.

His early education, as has been seen, he received at Deventer under Alexander Hegius; but after this he had to learn by bitter experience how evil is the corruption of that which is good. For it may be taken as proved that the Collationary Brethren, in whose House he and his brother were placed to be prepared for the assumption of monastic vows, and whom in his celebrated letter he describes as so many decoys for the monastic orders proper, were Brethren of the Common Life under another name. A few years after he had been liberated from the cloister, he began his cosmopolitan career, and the Netherlands could no longer more than transitorily claim him as their own; and when at the height of his fame, he had by the Emperor's desire fixed his residence at Louvain, there was probably no place in the world which swarmed so thickly with his enemies, who hated him at least as bitterly for his actual learning as for his supposed heresy. But cosmopolite as he was, more especially in the years preceding this date, he was such rather in the sense that all countries were after a fashion alike to him, than that, notwithstanding occasional rhetorical flights, he identified himself with any. His position towards peoples as well as princes was a European one, and has not inaptly been compared to that of Voltaire in the eighteenth century; and though the Renaissance was not *his* movement, nor that of any one other man, yet his influence over its course was incomparable—even in Germany by the side of Reuchlin, and in England as developing the work of Colet. His earlier publications were mainly linguistic and literary; but it would not be difficult to show that in all, or nearly all of them, the educational purpose proper to the Renaissance movement in his native land maintained itself. In his *Education of a Christian Prince*, designed primarily for the use of the future Emperor Charles V, he advances political doctrines in harmony with the progress of the constitutional life of his own native land, and effaces the futile distinction between political and Christian morality. Thus, too, there is a real continuity between the whole of these writings and his great biblical and patristic labours—from which of course his one late excursion into the field of dogmatic controversy stands apart. It was not by chance that he was led to theological enquiry, as he had of his own choice addressed himself to ethical problems. He believed that a new era was dawning for the Church and the Christian religion, and that to hasten its advent was eminently a concern of his. But he had made up his mind that a calm and reasonable progress, in which scholar and statesman should go hand in hand, was the only way by which victory could be secured and a real and enduring reformation accomplished. Had he thought differently of his task, he would probably in many ways have proved ill-suited for the leadership of a great popular movement. But in truth, he had no desire in his heart to be reckoned on either side. He was content to stand by himself—herein a true representative of the Renaissance, whose supreme purpose it was after all to vindicate to every man the right of remaining true to his individuality by means of self-education and self-development. Whether or not, from this point of view also, he was in some respects a typical product of his native land, the Reformation as it presented itself to the Netherlands, and as they gave admittance to it with consequences so vital for their future history, was not the Reformation of Erasmus.

# CHAPTER XIV.

## THE EARLY TUDORS.

THAT which gave the death-blow to feudalism in England was undoubtedly the Battle of Bosworth. The Normans, after their invasion and conquest, had drilled and disciplined the English people with so thorough a comprehension of the capabilities of the Saxon population, and so full an appreciation of their solid merits, that the sense of subjugation was soon effaced and a harmonious system established which time could not entirely destroy. The courtesy of the upper classes and the respectful subordination of the lower alike contributed to the strength of an English nationality, which, as it became more and more entirely insular, became more and more unique; so that even the decay and demoralisation which followed the loss of continental possessions in the fifteenth century, were accompanied by a compensation which was very real though but little appreciated at the time. With the loss of France, England was released from a burden which she was quite unable to bear; and when, a century later, she lost Calais also, she was all the more able to negotiate effectually with Scotland, and lay firm the foundations of a United Kingdom which a future age was to build up.

The expulsion of the English from both Normandy and Gascony in the days of Henry VI had led naturally to mutual recriminations among the nobility and gentry, who looked upon France as a playground to which they had an obvious right. These feelings mixed themselves with the great dynastic struggle of the Wars of the Roses; and the House of York owed not a little of its popularity to the fact that their party was not responsible for disaster abroad. But when Edward IV taxed his subjects severely for a new invasion of France, which was to revive the glories of the Black Prince and of Henry V, and when, instead of prosecuting his claims in the field, he listened to a seductive offer of an annual tribute from Louis XI and returned home from a bloodless campaign, it was already clear to discerning minds that the reconquest of France was a dream and an impossibility. Edward, indeed, though an excellent soldier when events compelled him to act, was constitutionally indolent; nor did he win the hearts of his people by pocketing what seemed very like a bribe from an enemy, after impoverishing his own subjects for the purpose of making war. But he was anxious to bequeath to his children a quiet succession, untroubled by serious difficulties either abroad or at home. Unhappily, he was no politician, and failed to foresee the clouds which darkened the horizon in both quarters just before his death.

England might have done very well without France, and even the quarrels of the nobility might have been left to settle themselves, had they not shaken the throne itself. But the security of the throne depended on the support of great families with large landed possessions, who could put large forces of their retainers into the field at need. Warwick the King-maker had been the great ally of Edward IV and of his father, and it was to him more than any other man in England that Edward owed his kingdom. It was by Warwick also that he was afterwards driven out of it, and that Henry VI was reinstated there for a time. Edward's own brother Clarence was won over by Warwick to assist in driving him out; and, though afterwards he changed sides again and helped in his brother's restoration, mutual distrust still remained, and Clarence was ultimately put to death as a traitor. Strange to say, Edward seems to have retained his confidence in his younger brother Richard, who after his death proved a worse traitor still; for he supplanted Edward's two sons, and then murdered them after getting himself proclaimed King as Richard III. But a conspiracy was formed between confederates both in England and in Britanny, where Henry, Earl of Richmond, lived in exile, by which it was arranged that he should invade the kingdom, and after winning the Crown by the defeat of Richard in battle, should marry Elizabeth, eldest daughter of Edward IV, thereby uniting the claims of the House of York to those of the House of Lancaster.

## I.

## HENRY VII.

## (1485-1509.)

It was thus that the Earl of Richmond after the victory of Bosworth became King Henry the Seventh. He indeed claimed the throne in his own right by a Lancastrian title; but, as that title seemed open to some objections, he could not have hoped to win it apart from the pledge he had given to marry the heiress of York; still less could he have retained it without actually marrying her. During nearly the whole of his reign he was troubled with Yorkist conspiracies; and it was with great wisdom that, in his second Parliament, he procured the institution of the Court of the Star Chamber—a Court of evil repute in later times, but of great value in that day for the correction of irregularities in the administration of justice, caused by the excessive power of local magnates, partial sheriffs, and corrupt juries. The name of this Court was derived from the chamber in which the Privy Council had been accustomed to sit at Westminster, and the Act only delegated to a Committee of that Council powers which had been always exercised, when thought fit, by the Council as a whole. An Act was also passed to make murderers always amenable to prosecution by the Crown, without waiting, as had been usual, a year and a day during which the next of kin might prosecute. The responsibility of coroners and townships was also increased in all cases of slaughter. The King, moreover, with the Pope's assent, imposed some restrictions on the privileges of sanctuaries, especially in cases of treason, and on those of the clergy when convicted of crime.

But faction at home was unhappily reinforced by movements outside the country; for foreign princes joined continually in the game, and Ireland afforded, especially at the commencement of Henry's reign, a basis of operations against England of which these princes were not slow to take advantage. For Ireland had been a stronghold of the Yorkist party, where in past days Richard, Duke of York, proscribed in England, had ruled as the King's lieutenant in defiance of the very authority he professed to represent. It was not a country which a Lancastrian King could hope to reduce very speedily to obedience; and yet we shall see that, notwithstanding the most unpromising commencement, Henry's success in this matter was far beyond expectation.

The first rumour of disturbances after his accession arose out of the escape of Viscount Lovel and the two brothers Stafford from sanctuary at Colchester in the spring of 1486. The leaders, however, still lay hid, and it was not till the beginning of 1487 that some far-reaching plots developed themselves. Lovel fled to Flanders—a hotbed of conspiracy against Henry—and a boy named Lambert Simnel was set up in Ireland, first as a son of Edward IV (the murder of the two young princes in the Tower being held doubtful by some), afterwards as the Earl of Warwick, son of the ill-fated Duke of Clarence, whom Henry, just after his accession, had lodged in the Tower to prevent any rising in his favour. Then John de la Pole, Earl of Lincoln, who had attended a meeting of the Privy Council at Sheen on February 2, escaped to Flanders also. He was probably the originator of the whole conspiracy; for he was the eldest son of the Duke of Suffolk by Elizabeth, sister of Edward IV, and had been nominated by Richard III as his successor on the throne. His hopes had thus been blighted by Henry's accession; and, having prepared a fleet, he now took counsel in Flanders with his aunt, Margaret, Duchess Dowager of Burgundy (another sister of Edward IV), how to dispossess Henry of the kingdom. He then went to Simnel in Ireland, whose pretensions he recognised, though he had the best reason to know their falsehood, as a means of clearing the ground for himself. Simnel was crowned in Christchurch Cathedral, Dublin, in the presence of the Earl of Kildare, then Deputy of Ireland, and of his brother the Lord Chancellor, and of nearly all the judges, nobility, and bishops of the land. Supported by Lincoln, Kildare, and a body of German mercenaries under one Martin Swart, the pretender invaded England. But he was defeated at Stoke-upon-Trent (June 16, 1487); his leaders, including Lincoln and Lord Thomas Fitzgerald, were slain, and he was himself taken prisoner.

So ended the first great crisis in Henry's reign. And he was stronger now than he had been, not only by the death of Lincoln and the overthrow of the conspiracy, but because his Queen Elizabeth in the year preceding had borne him a son, to whom, in respect of his old British descent, he gave the name of the fabled King Arthur. As a further counterpoise to faction he now caused the Queen to be crowned (November 25). But at this very time he had also to appeal urgently to Parliament (it was his second Parliament) for aid in the shape of taxation for the defence of the realm. The continual danger of invasion made it an object of supreme importance to him to study carefully the aims and policy of foreign princes; for his own security upon the throne depended quite as much on what was done abroad as on anything that he could do at home. The Spanish sovereigns, Ferdinand and Isabel, were anxious to draw him into a war with France; and the marriage of Prince Arthur to their daughter, Katharine of Aragon, was already arranged in 1488. Henry was unwilling to make war upon a country whose government had really assisted him to obtain the Crown; but he had been scarcely less indebted, as an exile, to the Duke of Britanny, and France was menacing the independence of that duchy. Henry endeavoured to mediate, while a band of volunteers under Lord Woodville crossed the Channel unauthorised, and shared the disastrous defeat of the Bretons in the battle of St Aubin (July 28, 1488). Henry strongly disowned responsibility for this expedition; but ill-feeling had been already aroused both in France and England, and on April 1, 1489, he fully committed himself to the defence of the duchy by a treaty with the Duchess Anne. Moreover, a state of war between England and France had existed when he came to the throne, and he had only suspended it by a truce, which he from time to time renewed, till circumstances were at last too strong for him. The treaty for the marriage between Arthur and Katharine was fettered with conditions which really obliged England to make actual war upon France for the benefit of Spain. This was the understanding from the first, and it was distinctly expressed in the treaty which

Henry's ambassadors negotiated at Medina del Campo in March, 1489. Henry was making preparations, though he was anxious to put off the event to the last. In February Parliament granted him a very special subsidy of one-tenth of the annual value of lands and one-eightieth part of the whole value of men's goods. The levying of this impost created disturbances in Yorkshire, in attempting to suppress which the Earl of Northumberland was slain ; but resistance was at length put down. Henry did his best for some time to assist Britanny without engaging otherwise in hostility with France ; but his efforts were all thrown away. In December, 1491, the Duchess Anne married Charles VIII and the first step was taken towards a union of Britanny with France. Next year, in fulfilment of obligations, alike to Spain and to Maximilian, King of the Romans, Henry crossed the Channel and besieged Boulogne (October). The season was late, and he was quite unsupported by his allies ; but he fulfilled his treaty obligations to them ; and, moreover, finding Charles VIII quite willing to pay him an annual tribute of 50,000 francs, he followed the example of Edward IV and made a peace very profitable to himself (the Treaty of Étaples, November 3, 1492), after having taxed his subjects highly and drawn "benevolences" from them for an energetic war.

However unpopular this result might be in England, it certainly strengthened Henry's hands in dealing with foreign Powers. He was no longer under special obligations to Spain, and France had consented to buy his friendship. The prince who was most dissatisfied with the result was Maximilian, King of the Romans, to whom Henry had already rendered very important aid, and who seemed to consider him bound to fight his battles in France, though he had himself been by no means a steady and faithful ally. Maximilian's animosity from this time was persistent ; yet it was perhaps not more injurious to Henry in particular than it was inconvenient to other Powers, when, in 1495, Spain, Venice and the Pope would have been glad to draw England into a league with Maximilian against France.

Maximilian's infant son Philip, called Archduke of Austria, was to govern the Netherlands when he came of age. But the Council which meanwhile governed in his name had very little respect for his father, who in fact was at one time not allowed the guardianship of his own son. Much more influential was Margaret Duchess of Burgundy, widow of the young Prince's grandfather, Charles the Bold ; who, being a sister of Edward IV, and having sustained considerable loss of revenue by the accession of Henry VII, laboured assiduously for his overthrow. She harboured at her Court disaffected Yorkists who fled from England, and assisted their conspiracies against the new King. Her nephew, John de la Pole, Earl of Lincoln, who supported Simnel and was killed at the battle of Stoke (1487), had first escaped over sea and held conference with her. And, notwithstanding the disastrous failure of that rebellion, the refugees at her Court had ample facilities for the formation of fresh conspiracies.

It is questionable, however, whether the new impostor who now appeared on the scene received his original stimulus from her. Perkin Warbeck, a native of Tournay, was a young man who had been much in the Low Countries and in Portugal, and having finally taken service with a Breton named Prégent Meno, landed in Cork in 1491, arrayed in fine clothing belonging to his master. The Irish took him for a prince of royal birth; if not Warwick, the son of Clarence, he must be a bastard son of Richard III. But after he had denied both characters, they persuaded him to personate Richard Duke of York, the younger of the two princes murdered in the Tower, telling him he would be supported by the Earls of Kildare and Desmond, who were both, in spite of recent professions of loyalty, wholly bent on the King's destruction. He remained some little time in Ireland, learning to speak English fluently and to play the part assigned to him, when Charles VIII, knowing that Henry was preparing to make war on France, invited him to his Court. There for a brief time he was honoured as a prince; but on the conclusion of the Peace of Étaples (1492) he was dismissed and went to Flanders, where Margaret received him with open arms, acknowledging him as her nephew. Next year, when Maximilian visited the Low Countries, Henry sent an embassy to him and to the Archduke Philip to remonstrate against the countenance given to the Pretender; but it produced no result, the Council of the young Archduke replying that Margaret was free to do as she pleased within the lands of her jointure.

Thus it was clear that the government of the Low Countries intended to allow conspiracies to be matured in those parts against Henry VII. He met this by forbidding commerce with Flanders and removing the mart of the Merchant Adventurers from Antwerp to Calais (September 18, 1493). This was a step quite against his ordinary policy, for no King was ever more studious of the interests of commerce, and though aimed at the Flemings it produced inconvenience on both sides, thus leading to a riot in London, as the German merchants of the Hansa had certain privileges by charter, which enabled them to carry on the traffic forbidden to Englishmen. Perkin, however, soon afterwards repaired to Maximilian at Vienna, where at the funeral of the Emperor Frederick III a place was assigned to him corresponding to his pretensions. Next year he returned with Maximilian to Flanders, where he was recognised as King of England. But Henry had intelligence of those implicated in the conspiracy at home, and a number of arrests were made, the most startling of which was that of Sir William Stanley. To him King Henry had owed not only his crown but his life, when it was in serious danger at Bosworth; in reward for which, among other things, Stanley had been appointed the King's Chamberlain. Yet he had sent over to Flanders to encourage Perkin one Sir Robert Clifford, who, turning informer, revealed his intrigues to the King. Stanley was beheaded on Tower Hill (February 16, 1495). This disconcerted for a time a plan for the invasion of England which had been formed in the Low Countries and was nearly ripe for execution. On July 3, however, Warbeck appeared with a little fleet off Deal, and some of his followers landed, but were presently taken, sent up to London and hanged. Perkin himself had wisely refrained from landing, and sailed to Ireland, where he attacked by sea the loyal town of Waterford, which Desmond's followers at the same time besieged by land. After eleven days, however, he was compelled to withdraw with loss, and later in the year he found a better asylum in Scotland, which had long been prepared to receive him.

Influenced, no doubt, by Maximilian and by Margaret of Burgundy, James IV of Scotland had committed himself to Perkin's cause before he came, and now not only acknowledged him as Duke of York, but gave him in marriage his cousin, Katharine Gordon, daughter of the Earl of Huntly. In September, 1496, when the young man had been nearly a year his guest in Scotland, James invaded England with Perkin in his company. But it was a mere brief border raid, from which the Scots returned in three days on hearing of a force sent from Newcastle to oppose them; and all that came of it was that a truce was broken, and that Henry now made preparations to punish a neighbour whom he had been anxious to conciliate. He assembled a great council which, anticipating the action of Parliament, promised him £120,000 for the War, and authorised the raising of £40,000 in loans. Parliament met in January, 1497. Two fifteenths and tenths were imposed, to be levied in May and November following. But the first attempt to collect the money in Cornwall met with serious opposition. A lawyer named Thomas Flammock told the people that they were not bound to pay, as the King had a right to the services of his feudal tenants for military purposes, without burdening his subjects generally. Flammock and a blacksmith named Michael Joseph became the leaders of an army of malcontents, which marched on towards London. They were joined at Wells by Lord Audeley, but were refused admittance into Bristol. At last they encamped upon Blackheath, and actually overlooked London. But here at length they were defeated with great slaughter (June 17), and the survivors delivered themselves up as prisoners.

This result was not obtained without the aid of a force under Lord Daubeney, which had been raised to proceed against Scotland, but was hastily recalled to meet the Cornishmen. Henry's troubles made him the more anxious to come to terms with James, if he could only be got to deliver up Perkin, or even to cease to countenance him. But just at the time when he despatched Bishop Fox to Scotland to make these demands (July, 1497), James was sending off Warbeck by sea from Ayr with a view to his landing among the disaffected population in Cornwall and getting them to aid his pretensions. Before sailing, however, Warbeck had received a message from a turbulent Irish chieftain named Sir James Ormond, which induced him to take Ireland on his way. This was a mistake; for both Kildare and Desmond were now reconciled to the King. But he landed at Cork and was received warmly by an old friend, John Walter, or John à Water as he is called by the chroniclers, who had lately been mayor. Sir James Ormond had by this time been killed in a private encounter; and Perkin wasted precious time while the loyal citizens of Waterford not only despatched across the Channel news of his arrival and design of invading Cornwall, but did their best, first to seize him, and, afterwards, when he sailed in September, to intercept him on his passage.

He not only escaped capture, however, but landed at Whitesand Bay near the Land's End on September 7, and speedily drew after him a very considerable following. On September 17 he appeared before Exeter and for two days attempted to storm the town. Failing here, he went on towards Taunton, where, hearing that an army under Daubeney was advancing to meet him, he stole away in the night and, riding hard across country with one or two companions, took refuge at Beaulieu Sanctuary in Hampshire. The Sanctuary being soon afterwards surrounded, he surrendered on promise of the King's pardon and was brought back to Taunton where the King had now arrived. He was compelled to confess his imposture before his wife, who had accompanied him to Cornwall, and who was sent for from St Michael's Mount, where he had left her. The King, pitying her misfortunes, sent her with an escort to the Queen; while he himself followed slowly to Westminster, where he arrived in the latter part of November.

With him came Perkin, whose career was now virtually finished, and the King seems at this time to have had no other thought than to expose him to public derision as a rebuke to factiousness. Misled by the Duchess Margaret, it is quite possible that Maximilian and some other foreign princes had believed in Perkin; but it is clear that most of them valued him merely as a pawn by which to gain their own ends with Henry VII. And this was really his whole significance. In England he had never the courage to play his part effectively. At Deal he refused to land; in Northumberland he only pitied the ravages committed by his Scotch allies; in Devonshire he stole away from his own followers in search of an asylum. And now the Londoners flocked to see him "as he were a monster," while he was made to repeat his confession in public and conveyed on horseback through the streets, one day to the Tower and another day to Westminster. His life was spared for two years longer.

His dismissal from Scotland, though certainly not a concession to English demands, is commonly considered to have cleared the way for a peace between the kingdoms. And no doubt it did so, but not at once.

Owing to the Cornish rebellion James had for a time escaped retribution for his infraction of the truce in the preceding year; and, just after sending Warbeck away, he proceeded to besiege Norham Castle on the Tweed. The Earl of Surrey, however, whom Henry had some years before appointed lieutenant of the North, hastened to its relief, and James was obliged to retire. Surrey then advanced into the Borders, destroyed some fortresses and took the castle of Ayton, where (September 30, 1497) by the mediation of the Spanish Ambassador, Pedro de Ayala, another seven years' truce was arranged between the two countries, with a stipulation, to which both kings afterwards agreed, that matters in dispute between them should be referred to Spanish arbitration. Spain had a very deep interest in promoting friendly relations between England and Scotland, in order that the former country might still be a check upon France; and Ayala was a most efficient instrument in the reconciliation. Next year, an unfortunate incident on the Borders threatened for a moment to disturb the new settlement. Some Scotch-men visiting Norham Castle in armour created suspicion. Haughty words led to blows, and the Scots fled. The English, too, killed a number of Scots, apparently in some raid which followed. But both sovereigns were so anxious to preserve the peace that the matter was satisfactorily arranged by Bishop Fox, who was sent to James at Melrose, and who there apparently concluded with him a long-talked-of project for his marriage with Henry's daughter Margaret.

Henry had now seemingly surmounted his most serious difficulties; but there were still troubles in store for him. Before relating these, however, something must be said of his remarkable success in the pacification of Ireland. How, it will be asked, had that country, after supporting Lambert Simnel with such strange enthusiasm and unanimity in 1487, become so loyal ten years later that hardly the slightest Irish encouragement was then afforded to Perkin Warbeck? This result was certainly due to a patience and sagacity on the King's part, characteristic of that "politic governance" for which he bore so high a name among princes. Even after the victory of Stoke he could not afford to punish Simnel's adherents in Ireland, who were virtually the whole Irish people. In 1488, the year after Simnel's coronation, he sent Sir Richard Edgecombe to Ireland, to receive the submissions of Kildare and the other Irish lords, and administer oaths of allegiance; and it required great adroitness in the envoy to succeed in such a mission. They took the oath, however, and Kildare was continued as Lord Deputy. But new Yorkist plots were brewing in England, and, in order to be safe as regards Ireland, Henry desired to win Kildare over to a personal interview with him. He sent him a private message promising great favours if he would come, with a renewal of the dignity of Lord Deputy for ten years; and he also wrote to him on July 28, 1490, expressly desiring his presence within ten months. But all this was nothing to Kildare. He allowed the time granted him to expire, and then not only wrote himself, but induced a number of the Irish lords to write in his excuse to the King, that his continued presence in Ireland at that time was absolutely indispensable. The King, however, they declared, might rest assured of the Earl's complete loyalty.

Henry could not well have remained satisfied with this assurance. Next year Kildare and his cousin Desmond encouraged Perkin Warbeck; and in 1492 the King made a complete change in the government of Ireland, appointing Walter Fitzsimmons, Archbishop of Dublin, as Lord Deputy in Kildare's place. Some Irish feuds broke out, and there was fighting in the streets of Dublin; but at last in 1493 Kildare was induced by a promise of pardon to go over and seek the King's presence. He and some Irish lords who went with him were invited by the King to a feast, at which Simnel served them with wine; and witnessing the shame on each of their faces when they saw their cupbearer, Henry remarked sarcastically "My masters, you will crown apes some day!" Kildare received his pardon on June 22, but was not restored to his old office. After some other changes the King (September 11, 1494) appointed his second son Henry as Lord Lieutenant (a mere honorary title), with Sir Edward Poynings as his Deputy. Poynings was a good soldier but found desultory warfare with Irish chieftains unsatisfactory, and tried to secure their loyalty by money payments. He then opened at Drogheda, on December 1, 1494, the Parliament which passed the celebrated Acts called by his name, whereby for the next three centuries all legislation submitted to the Irish Parliament required first to be approved by the English Council. Other enactments in this Parliament were conceived in the same spirit as laws passed in England, to put down armed retinues and the war-cries of hostile factions. But having established a new system of government, Poynings was recalled in January, 1496; and on August 6 following Kildare, who had curiously regained the King's confidence by his frankness, was reinstated as Deputy. From that day he held the office till his death and was faithful both to Henry and to his son. The King seems to have believed from the first that nothing but a little personal intercourse with him was required to make him a loyal subject; and he was right in the belief.

Warbeck's imposture being now at an end, the King did not at first care to keep him in very close confinement. But on June 9, 1498 (the year after his capture), he created some alarm by escaping at night from the King's Court, where he had been only watched by keepers. He got no further, however, than Sheen, where he again took sanctuary and prevailed upon the prior to intercede for him. He was placed in the stocks for several hours, one day at Westminster and another day in Cheapside; after which he was shut up in the Tower, where he remained the greater part of next year. But meanwhile the King had been disquieted by a new impostor, a young man named Ralph Wilford, who suddenly appeared in Kent, first telling people privately that he was the Earl of Warwick just escaped from the Tower; while one Friar Patrick, by whom he was accompanied, confirmed the story and at last declared it from the pulpit. Both the young man and the friar were soon apprehended, and the former was hanged on Shrove Tuesday (February 12, 1499). A few weeks later it was observed, that Henry seemed to have grown twenty years older, and was spending much time in religious observances, while also accumulating money, of which he had an unequalled store. That he was brooding over danger to himself is hardly doubtful.

Later in the year Warbeck managed to corrupt some of his keepers, with whom he formed a conspiracy to kill Sir John Digby, the Lieutenant of the Tower, and liberate himself and the Earl of Warwick, who, having been a prisoner from boyhood and knowing nothing of the world, gave too easy an assent to the project. Warbeck was tried and hanged at Tyburn in November with his old associate, John à Water, Mayor of Cork. The Earl of Warwick was arraigned at Westminster before the Earl of Oxford as Constable of England, confessed the indictment in his simplicity, and was beheaded on Tower Hill.

Warwick's confinement had been all along justified only by the danger of leaving him at liberty; but his execution was felt to be nothing less than a judicial murder. One thing, however, was made clear to Yorkist intriguers; neither counterfeit Warwicks nor any other counterfeits would avail them now. If they took further action, it must be in their own names.

The year 1500 was a year of Jubilee at Rome, and in England a period of domestic peace seemed to have begun. Henry was much stronger now in his relations with foreign princes. The stoppage of trade with the Netherlands, owing to the support given to Warbeck there in 1493, had been long since ended. From the first it had been found intolerable, especially on the other side of the Channel, and on February 24, 1496, a commercial treaty was concluded in London between the two countries. This did not, indeed, prove a complete settlement, and was followed by further treaties in July 1497 and May 1499; but a better understanding was growing up, and in 1498 the English merchants returned to Antwerp, where they were received with a general procession. On May 8, 1500, Henry VII with his Queen crossed to Calais, where they remained till June 16. On June 9 they had a meeting with Archduke Philip, in which most cordial relations were established and marriages proposed between the two families, which, however, did not take effect.

This meeting seems to have quickened the anxiety of Ferdinand and Isabel of Spain at length to give effect to the long-talked-of match of their daughter Katharine, which they had repeatedly delayed till they should be convinced of the stability of Henry's throne. She was sent to

England in 1501, landed at Plymouth on October 2, and after travelling slowly up to London entered the city on November 12. She was received with a vast amount of pageantry and scenic displays, and the marriage took place at St Paul's on Sunday the 14th. Amid the rejoicings which followed, came ambassadors from Scotland to negotiate another marriage, that, namely, of James IV with Margaret, the treaty for which was concluded on January 24, 1502. Next day the marriage was celebrated by proxy at Richmond. But on April 2 following, to the inexpressible grief of Henry and his Queen, Prince Arthur died at Ludlow; and next year (1503) on February 11, died his mother the Queen, leaving Henry a widower. In the following summer he conducted his daughter as far as Northamptonshire on her way to Scotland, and she was married to James at Edinburgh on August 8.

Meanwhile a new danger for Henry had sprung up. Edmund de la Pole, the brother of the Earl of Lincoln who had supported Simnel, had succeeded on his father's death to the dukedom of Suffolk; but, as the family estate had suffered seriously from his brother's attainder, he arranged with the King, on the restoration of a part of the property, to bear the title of "Earl of Suffolk" only. In 1498 he killed a man in a passion, but after being indicted received the King's pardon. In the summer of 1499 he escaped over sea to Calais, and was going on to the Court of Margaret of Burgundy in Flanders, when ambassadors on their way from Henry VII to the Archduke Philip persuaded him to return. He was with the King at his meeting with Philip in 1500. But in August, 1501, he escaped abroad again, together with his younger brother Richard, relying on a promise which Maximilian, King of the Romans, had made to Sir Robert Curzon, that he would help him to obtain the Crown of England. Sir Robert had been captain of Hammes Castle, but had a desire to go and fight for Maximilian against the Turks; and he obtained leave of the King to give up his post for that purpose on August 29, 1499. This date must have been just after Suffolk's first flight, and there is reason to suspect that leave to give up his post was granted to him on an understanding that he would act as a spy on Suffolk for the King, and ascertain whether the factious Duchess Margaret was disposed to encourage him as she had encouraged Simnel and Warbeck in Flanders. In fact, he simulated flight like one out of favour with his King. But the Duchess Margaret had already been obliged to apologise for the countenance she had given to Warbeck, and it does not appear that she was prepared to encourage Suffolk. At all events, it was by convincing the Earl that he would receive no support from foreign princes, either from France, Spain, Portugal, Scotland, or even from Philip (who was no less an ally of Henry than were the others), that the King's ambassadors persuaded him to return. This, however, was just before the judicial murder of Warwick,—an act which aroused a good deal of resentment in England; and Curzon, when he reached the Court of Maximilian, gave expression to the general feeling about the "murders and tyrannies" of the King of England. And it was then that Maximilian declared himself willing to help Suffolk to obtain the Crown.

The Earl reached Maximilian in the Tyrol, and was most kindly received; but he was put off with repeated excuses on account of the amity between England and Maximilian's son, Philip. He was sent to Aachen for aid, and various schemes fell through. Maximilian, in truth, since the day he promised to help him, had been drawn by overtures from Henry, and, though he still had the will to some extent, his means were not equal to his will. Meanwhile several friends of Suffolk in England were imprisoned, and the Earl himself along with Curzon and other fugitives abroad were denounced as traitors at Paul's Cross (November 7, 1501) and excommunicated on the strength of a papal bull. Suffolk ran into debt at Aachen even for the necessaries of life, while of course all his property in England was confiscated. But on June 20, 1502, a treaty was made at Antwerp between Henry and Maximilian, in which the latter was promised £10,000 for his war against the Turks, on condition that he would not harbour any English rebels, even of ducal dignity (to which Suffolk still laid claim); and the money was paid to him at Augsburg on July 28, the day on which he confirmed the treaty. Aachen, however, was a free city of the Empire and Maximilian was slow to fulfil his pledges and procure Suffolk's banishment.

And now, notwithstanding Henry's treaties with foreign princes, some would have been glad to get Suffolk into their hands, in order to use him like Warbeck as a check upon England. Spain demanded his surrender from the city of Aachen under the specious guise of friendship to Henry, but was refused. In the spring of 1504, however, the Earl had hopes of assistance from Duke George of Saxony, hereditary governor of Friesland, who apparently desired to get him into his hands only as a means of bargaining for Henry's assistance against the town of Groningen, which still withstood his authority. The Earl obtained a passport from the Duke of Gelders to enable him to pass through his country to Friesland, and was permitted to depart from Aachen, leaving his brother Richard as a hostage to his creditors for payment of his debts. But notwithstanding his safe-conduct the Duke of Gelders caused him to be taken and confined at Hattem. So the Duke of Saxony was foiled of his prize, and it was feared that the Duke of Gelders would make use of him in the same way, to bid for Henry's assistance in his quarrels with his neighbour the Archduke Philip, who since the death of Queen Isabel in November, 1504, was called King of Castile in right of his wife Juana. Gelders, however, appears to have got nothing out of Henry, when in July, 1505, King Philip's forces captured Zutphen and Hattem. Suffolk thus had a new custodian; but, peace being immediately made between Philip and Gelders, the former did not like to retain the fugitive in the teeth of his treaties with Henry, who was at that very time advancing money to him for his prospective voyage to Spain. He accordingly sent Suffolk back to Wageningen, where he was again in the Duke of Gelders' hands. Suffolk tried to escape, and then implored Philip to reclaim him; which apparently Philip did indirectly after receiving the last instalment of Henry's loan; whereupon Suffolk, coming into his hands again, was shut up in the castle of Namur.

But early in 1506, Philip and his Queen Juana, having set sail for Spain, were driven by tempest on the coast of England. Henry at once saw his advantage, hospitably received them at his Court, and wrung from Philip not only the surrender of the unhappy Suffolk (whose life he promised to spare) but a very important commercial treaty with Flanders, which settled some long-standing tariff disputes in a way that the Flemings continually resented afterwards as unjust and onesided.

Meanwhile the deaths of Prince Arthur and the Queen had given rise to new marriage projects. As soon as the former event was known to Ferdinand and Isabel they sent a special ambassador to England empowered to demand repayment of the first instalment (all that was yet paid) of Katharine's dower, and that Katharine herself should be sent back to Spain, or, if Henry preferred it, to conclude a new marriage for her with his second son Henry, soon afterwards created Prince of Wales. This last was clearly their aim, and as early as September 24, 1502, a draft treaty for the new marriage was drawn up in England; but it was not concluded till June 23, 1503. Application was made to Rome for a dispensation, both by Spain and by England; but its issue was delayed first by the deaths of two Popes within one year, and then by the necessity of special enquiry into the case. A brief, ante-dated December 26, 1503, was at length sent to Spain for the satisfaction of Queen Isabel on her death-bed; and a bull, almost verbally the same, was afterwards issued with the same date. But, owing to continual disputes between Henry VII and Ferdinand, the marriage did not take place during the life of the former King.

The fact that Katharine remained in England gave Henry a great advantage over Ferdinand in these diplomatic squabbles. When Henry found himself a widower in 1503, a shameful suggestion was brought forward that he might himself marry her instead of his son. It was probably meant only to alarm the Spanish Court, and Isabel tried to meet it by offering him as a bride her niece, Juana Queen of Naples, the younger of two dowager princesses who bore the same title and lived together at Valencia. After some time Henry asked for this lady's portrait, and when, on Isabel's death, he sent three gentlemen to Spain to ascertain what hold Ferdinand still had upon Castile, he commissioned them also to visit the princess and to report, rather too minutely, on her personal qualities. Offers were further held out to him of a French match, either for his son or for himself; and Maximilian and Philip encouraged him to look for the hand of Maximilian's daughter, Margaret of Savoy. When Philip went to Spain, Margaret was left as Regent of the Netherlands, and since his marriage with her would have given Henry the government of that country, this scheme was more than once the subject of negotiations; but she could not herself be induced to agree to it. A more repulsive match was for some time talked about, owing to Philip's early death (September 25, 1506), namely with his widow, the mad Queen Juana of Castile; which Henry could only have contemplated as a means of obtaining the control of her kingdom. But another project was afterwards set on foot, which tended the same way, and excited the most serious jealousy in Ferdinand. As Philip's son Charles, heir alike to the lands of the House of Austria, the dukedom of Burgundy and the throne of Castile, was but a child under tutelage of his grandfather Maximilian, Henry won the Emperor over to an alliance; and a treaty was concluded at Calais, December 21, 1507, for the marriage of Prince Charles to the King's second daughter, Mary. Bonds were taken from various princes and towns in the Netherlands for the fulfilment of this treaty when the prince should come of age; and, on December 17, 1508, the Sieur de Bergues, who came over at the head of a distinguished embassy, married the Princess by proxy. On the 21st a rich jewel of the Emperor, called the *fleur-de-lis*, was given in pawn to Henry for 50,000 crowns of gold.

King Henry, who had been subject for some time to attacks of gout, died on April 21, 1509. He had made his will on March 30, leaving large bequests for masses and charitable objects, with strict injunctions to his executors to make restitution for wrongs done in answer to all complaints. He was buried, according to his direction, in the gorgeous chapel he had himself built in Westminster Abbey. During his life he had amassed, it was said, as much gold as all other Kings in Christendom put together. A more distinct and apparently well-founded statement is that at his death he left in bullion four and a half millions, besides abundance of plate and jewels. Doubtless he had studied to keep a large reserve for his own security, and he made rebellions pay their own expenses in fines. But he had permitted agents, of whom the most notorious were Sir Richard Empson and Edmund Dudley, further to fill his exchequer by extortions, founded generally on antiquated processes of law, for which at the last he expressed remorse. The two great ministers, Cardinal Morton and Sir Reginald Bray, who had paved his way to the throne, had died long before him. They had no doubt given much judicious counsel during the anxieties of the first part of his reign. But in his latter years he was strong both at home and abroad, his friendship being sought after by all European princes.

## II.

### HENRY VIII.

#### (1509–19.)

It was a new world altogether when Henry VIII, in his eighteenth year, succeeded his father upon the throne. With a full exchequer and an undisputed title, the young King was at the commencement of his reign liberal and generous; and being handsome in person, highly accomplished and fond of manly exercises, he was abundantly popular. The old King just before his death had desired to atone for past severities, and had issued a general pardon, which his successor at once renewed, excepting from it, however, among others, those instruments of extortion, Empson and Dudley, who were arrested the very day after his accession. By his father's dying advice, moreover, the unfriendly policy towards Ferdinand of Aragon was dropped at once, and the King married Katharine on June 11. He was crowned with her on the 28th at Westminster.

Dudley was found guilty of constructive treason at the Guildhall of London on July 18, 1509, and Empson at Northampton on August 8. The treason in both cases consisted in their having written to friends to come up to London armed, in anticipation of the old King's death, to help them to maintain their influence. Both Empson and Dudley were attainted in the Parliament which met in January, 1510, and both were beheaded on Tower Hill on August 17 following. The bonds which they had wrung from many on various legal pretexts were one by one brought into Chancery, and cancelled. It is noteworthy that Dudley during his imprisonment composed a treatise called *The Tree of Common Wealth*, in which he pointed out the chief dangers of the time, including that of the cruel administration of penal laws, in which he himself had taken so much part.

The first two years of the King's reign were peaceful and happy. There were no events to chronicle but Court pageants and tournaments, Christmas revels and May games; and when, on January 1, 1511, Katharine bore to the King a son named Henry, a new stimulus was given to these displays. But, though a household was appointed for the royal infant, he died on February 22. That same month the King received a request from his father-in-law, Ferdinand of Aragon, for the aid of fifteen hundred archers to make war on the Moors of Barbary. The men were easily found, and were placed under the command of Lord Darcy. But the expedition was unfortunate; for they had scarcely landed at Cadiz when they found that Ferdinand, pressed by France, had been obliged to make a truce with the Moors, and their services were not required.   The men, too, were ill-disciplined, became intoxicated with Spanish wines, had frays with the natives, and returned home in ill-humour.   Another expedition of fifteen hundred archers sent under the command of Sir Edward Poynings to the assistance of Margaret of Savoy and the Burgundians against Gelders was at first more satisfactory; for with their aid some places were captured and destroyed (August).   But when, after these successes, siege was laid to Venloo and had continued twenty-nine days, Poynings began to feel that their allies were making undue use of the detachment, and it obtained leave to return home. Hereupon, the river being swollen by heavy rains, the Burgundians raised the siege and retired for the winter, wasting the country round about.

Shortly before this began a misunderstanding with James IV of Scotland, on account of acts of piracy stated to have been committed by his sea captain, Andrew Barton.   The King sent out against him Lord Thomas Howard, eldest son of the Earl of Surrey, with his younger brother Edward, soon afterwards knighted and created Lord Admiral.   In the Downs, Lord Thomas overtook Andrew Barton, who after a fierce fight fell into his hands, mortally wounded, his ship the *Lion* being captured with her crew by the Englishmen, who after a further chase also took the bark *Jenny Pirwyn*, the *Lion's* consort, and brought them both to Blackwall on August 2.   The Scotch prisoners appealed to the King for mercy, confessing their offence to be piracy, and were sent out of the country; but James was exceedingly angry, and demanded redress for Barton's death and the capture of his two ships.

In this year (1511) King Henry VIII was also first drawn into continental politics.   In 1508 the leading Powers on the Continent had combined against Venice in the League of Cambray; but France, the prime mover in the game, very soon alarmed her confederates, and especially Pope Julius II, by her successes in Northern Italy.   Pope Julius thereupon made friends with the Seigniory, and in April, 1510, sent a golden rose to Henry VIII.   The surrender of Bologna to the French in May, 1511, and the attempt, in which Louis XII secured the concurrence of the Emperor Maximilian, to set up a Council at Pisa enraged the Pope still more, and drew other princes to his aid. The Holy League was proclaimed at Rome on October 4 between the Pope and Ferdinand of Aragon; and Henry joined it on November 13, promising to make active war against France in the following spring. The recovery of Guyenne, which had now been lost to England for sixty years, was the reward held out to him by the treaty.   Accordingly in May, 1512, while the French seemed still to be making head in Italy, having on Easter Sunday cut to pieces the papal and Spanish forces at Ravenna, an expedition was despatched to Spain under the

Marquis of Dorset for the invasion of Guyenne, in the hope of its being supported by Spanish troops. It landed in Biscay on June 7; but it was even more unfortunate than Lord Darcy's expedition. No preparation had been made in Spain for its reception, not even by way of supplying the soldiers with victuals, or with carriage for their ordnance. They were exposed to the weather, and the diet and wines of Spain disagreed with their English habits of body. Moreover, while hundreds died of diarrhœa, the force was kept idle for months, expecting the Duke of Alva to join it. But Alva was engaged on Ferdinand's work in the conquest of Navarre, in which he succeeded perfectly; and the only effect of the English expedition was to hamper the French in Italy, where they soon completely lost their footing. Dorset's troops at last mutinied, and at a council of war on August 28 resolved to return home without leave,—in fact, against orders. The King was very indignant, but was unable to punish where so many were in fault.

It had been arranged that, while Dorset sought to recover Guyenne, English ships were to keep the Channel as far as Brest, and the Spaniards the sea thence to the Bay of Biscay. Sir Edward Howard was appointed Admiral of the English fleet on April 7, and after cruising about the Channel and chasing French fishing-boats he accompanied Dorset's fleet as far as Brest. He then landed on the Breton coast, burning towns and villages ruthlessly over a circuit of thirty miles, and returned home. But the Spanish fleet did not come to join the English till September, when it was really useless; and French ships were meanwhile got ready both in Normandy and Britanny, and placed under the command of the redoubted Prégent de Bidoux, summoned hastily from the Mediterranean. Thus by August, when another expedition sailed from England for Brest harbour, the French had a pretty fair squadron there, and on the 10th a fierce action took place between the two fleets. The *Regent*, the largest vessel on the English side, grappled with her chief opponent the *Cordelière* (called by the English the Great Carrack of Brest), till by some means both vessels took fire, and were totally consumed with the loss of nearly all their crews. Sir Thomas Knyvet, commander of the *Regent*, was among the victims. The King at once determined to repair the loss of the *Regent* by building a still larger ship called the *Henry Grace de Dieu*, or "The Great Harry," which was launched two years later.

In April, 1513, Sir Edward Howard again sailed to the entrance of Brest harbour, intent on avenging Knyvet's fate. He found drawn up in shallow water a line of French galleys, which rained shot and square bolts upon him from guns and crossbows. Putting himself in a row-barge he faced this tremendous fire and boarded Prégent's galley, while his men cast the anchor on to the galley's deck. But the cable was either let slip or cut by the French; and Sir Edward, left in the hands of the enemy, was thrust overboard and perished. The attack was foolhardy; but Howard's gallantry retrieved the honour of the English nation.

For several months preparations had been in progress for an invasion of France by the King in person. It may have been in order to prevent any possible conspiracy at home that the unhappy Earl of Suffolk, whose brother Richard de la Pole was now in the French King's service, was beheaded on April 30, notwithstanding the promise given by Henry VII that his life should be spared. The first portion of the invading army went over to Calais in the latter part of May, and the King himself landed there on June 30, having left the Queen behind him as Regent in his absence. Siege was laid to the fortified city of Térouanne on June 22; but it still held out on August 4, when the King joined the besiegers. On the 11th he left the camp and had a meeting with the Emperor Maximilian, between Térouanne and Aire, in very foul weather; of which, indeed, there had been much already. Next day the Emperor visited the trenches and returned for a time to Aire. He was afterwards content, instead of joining the King under his own banner, to serve with his company at the King's wages under the banner of St George; for he was always glad of money, while his great military experience was unquestionably of service to the King. On the night of the 11th Lyon King of Arms arrived with a message from James IV, setting forth various complaints against England and requiring Henry to desist from the invasion of a country which was James' ally. To this an appropriate answer was next day returned by Henry.

On the 16th the King removed his camp to Guinegaste in order to defeat any attempt on the part of the French, who were mustering south of Térouanne, at victualling the place. They were presently descried and, after a brief encounter, took to flight, leaving in the hands of the English some most illustrious prisoners, among whom were the Duke of Longueville and the renowned Chevalier Bayard. The engagement received the name of "the Battle of the Spurs" from the speedy flight of the French. A week later, on the 23rd, Térouanne surrendered. The fortifications which had made it so formidable were then blown up, and the invading army passed on to Tournay, which likewise surrendered a month later, on September 23. These conquests were not valuable to England unless she had an interest in Belgium; but Henry looked forward to the marriage of his sister Mary to young Charles of Castile, which, as we have seen, had been arranged in Henry VII's time. The city of Térouanne, as belonging to the House of Burgundy, was made over to the Emperor, whose soldiers ruthlessly destroyed it by fire. On the way to Tournay Henry paid a visit to Margaret of Savoy at Lille, which was within the territory of Flanders; and after the capture of the city she returned the visit, bringing with her the young Prince, then in his fourteenth year. Yet another meeting was held at Lille, where on October 17 it was arranged that the marriage should take place at Calais in the following year in presence of the Emperor, Margaret of Savoy, Henry VIII, and Queen Katharine. Provisions were also made for the defence of Artois and Hainault in the winter, and for the further prosecution of the War next year.

The ungracious declaration of war by the Scotch King had not been unexpected. Notwithstanding his treaties with England James had formed a new league with France in 1512, and had given most unsatisfactory answers as to his evident preparations for war to the English ambassador, West, Bishop of Ely. Before embarking at Dover, Henry had accordingly conferred the command of the North upon Thomas, Earl of Surrey, who conducted the Queen back to London, and thence in the end of July proceeded to his charge. Even in August the Scots made a raid into Northumberland under Hume, the Lord Chamberlain of Scotland, in which they came off so badly that they themselves called it "the Ill Raid"; for they were met by Sir William Bulmer and driven home with great slaughter and the loss of all their booty. But on the 22nd James himself entered Northumberland with as large an army as he could collect, won Norham Castle after a six days' siege, and razed it to the ground; after which he took some other fortresses. Hearing of this at Durham, Surrey advanced with the banner of St Cuthbert to Newcastle, where he had ordered musters from all the Northern counties to be held on September 1. On the 4th he despatched a herald to the King of Scots, reproaching him with his bad faith and offering to give him battle on the Friday following (September 9). James awaited his attack on ground very well chosen. The deep river Till lay between the armies. But Surrey bade his vanguard with the ordnance cross it at Twizel bridge near its junction with the Tweed, while the rear crossed at another point, threatening to cut off the retreat of the Scotch army. Hereupon the Scots made an onslaught which for a time was successful; but the fortune of the day changed, and the invaders were disastrously defeated. The King and the flower of the Scottish nobility were left dead upon the field of Flodden. In reward for this victory Surrey was some months later created Duke of Norfolk, and his son was made Earl of Surrey in his own right.

The success of the English arms in France and in Scotland produced important results both abroad and at home. The disgrace which had attended Dorset's expedition to Spain was now more than wiped out and it was clear that, even as a military Power, England had to be reckoned with. But the belief still generally prevailed that she was an easy dupe. She had been doing the work of Ferdinand in Spain; in France she had been winning conquests for Maximilian; and by more than one treaty she had been subsidising that needy Emperor, really to keep him true to his engagements as to his grandson's marriage with Mary. Henry's military successes compelled scheming politicians to change their tactics.   His father-in-law, Ferdinand, did not relish them at all; for he had already made secret overtures for peace to France. Nor had he ever loved the project of an English princess marrying Charles of Castile, which would have afforded Henry opportunities for interference in Spain.   And although in October, 1513, his ambassador at Lille made a treaty with the Emperor and Henry for continuing the War against France, the year could scarcely have run out before he had persuaded Maximilian to join him in coming to terms with the enemy, and leaving England in the lurch.   Thus in the spring of the following year the War was really between England and France only ; and Admiral Prégent burned the small fishing village of Brighthelmstone (Brighton), while Wallop committed similar havock on the coast of Normandy.

Early in 1513 Louis XII and his Queen, Anne of Britanny, had in vain attempted to break up the confederacy against France by offering their second daughter Renée to the Prince of Castile, with the duchy of Britanny as her dowry.   Anne of Britanny died in January, 1514; but Louis renewed the offer, and appeared to meet with less resistance. There was, indeed, always a French party in Flanders; and though Margaret of Savoy was strongly opposed to a breach of faith with England in this matter, she was overborne by her father Maximilian, who, under the influence of Ferdinand, invented excuses for putting off the match with Mary, which plainly proved that there was no intention of concluding it.

But Henry was less of a dupe than men supposed.   He had one counsellor, especially, not so famous yet as he was soon to become, whose eye was keen to detect false dealing and treachery abroad, and who well knew in what direction to look for a remedy.   The abilities of Thomas Wolsey as a diplomatist had already been discovered by Henry VII, who made him his Chaplain and also Dean of Lincoln; and though the new King, at the commencement of his reign, was more largely under the influence of others, it was Wolsey whose energies had planned and organised the naval and military expeditions of the last three years.   In fact he was rapidly becoming in most matters the King's sole counsellor. He accompanied Henry in the French campaign; and after the capture of Tournay the King obtained for him by papal bull the bishopric of that city, the see being newly vacant, though another bishop had been nominated by France.   In February, 1514, the more substantial bishopric of Lincoln was also bestowed upon him; and, before many months were over, the death of Cardinal Bainbridge at Rome enabled the King to advance him from Lincoln to the archbishopric of York.

Under Wolsey's direction it was not difficult for Henry to chastise the perfidy of Ferdinand and the instability of Maximilian.   While King Henry, deserted by his allies, seemed resolute to carry on the War alone, secret negotiations were opened with France through the prisoners taken in English hands by the battle of the Spurs; and there was no enemy whom France was so anxious to conciliate as England. The death of Anne of Britanny cleared the way for Louis to enter the state of matrimony again at the age of fifty-two, and Henry had no scruple about giving him the hand of his own sister Mary, a beautiful girl of eighteen. On August 7 there were concluded in London a treaty of peace with France and another for the marriage, a pledge being given by French commissioners for the payment of 1,000,000 gold crowns by half-yearly instalments of 50,000 francs. The marriage was actually celebrated at Abbeville on October 9.

This new alliance with France astonished the world, and spread serious alarm in many places. Henry certainly harboured deep designs in connexion with it, especially against his father-in-law; while Louis considered that he should now be able most effectually to prosecute his claim to the duchy of Milan. But Europe had scarcely had time to consider what might come of these arrangements, when they were virtually at an end. Louis XII died on January 1, 1515; and, as he left no sons, the Count of Angoulême succeeded him as Francis I. There was, indeed, no disposition, at all events on the part of Francis, to break off the amity with England; but it was clear from the first that that young and chivalrous King would be a rival, and not a help, to Henry in his European schemes. The embassy sent to him from England on his accession was headed by Charles Brandon, Duke of Suffolk, in whom the hope had been raised of marrying the widowed French Queen. Unfortunately for the other purposes of the Duke's mission, Francis found out his secret, and, after putting him to the blush, promised every possible assistance in the matter he had most at heart. The King was as good as his word; but the impatience of the young couple, who feared strong opposition in England, induced them to be married in France before they left. On their return Suffolk was in serious danger from the indignation of King Henry and his nobles; but by Wolsey's intercession he procured his pardon.

Suffolk's indiscretion had, in fact, entailed the failure of some secret diplomacy with which he had been charged; and succeeding ambassadors could not remedy the result of his mismanagement. Francis renewed the treaty made with Suffolk's predecessor, and took his departure for Italy in order to assert his claim to Milan, evading an inconvenient demand that he should prevent the Duke of Albany from proceeding to Scotland.

John Duke of Albany was the son of Duke Alexander, who had tried to supplant his brother James III in Scotland, and had been driven into exile in France. There his son had been brought up and was now living,—a Frenchman in birth and feeling, but next heir to the Crown of Scotland after the two children of James IV. For this reason the Scottish people desired his coming. Immediately after the battle of Flodden, it is true, the widowed Queen Margaret was recognised, under her late husband's will, as Regent for her infant son James V. But in this she was evidently intended to be controlled by a Council, and even then Albany's presence was desired; but Louis XII would not allow him to leave France. It was only natural, however, that Francis I should refuse to give any pledge to detain him; and events in Scotland meanwhile had certainly made his going thither more desirable. For Margaret, after giving birth to a posthumous child— Alexander, Duke of Ross—very speedily married young Archibald Douglas, Earl of Angus, and thereby made herself a partisan among the opposing factions of the Scotch nobility. She was considered to have by this act forfeited both the regency and the control of her children; and the Council (August 26, 1514) were unanimous that Albany should be called in to assume the government. Margaret's position became intolerable, and in November she wrote to Henry from Stirling, where she had shut herself up with Angus, to send forces by sea and land for her deliverance. The country was indeed full of feuds and conspiracies; but Henry's treaties with France forbade open interference with Scotland, and he advised his sister to escape to England instead, and bring her husband and her children with her. This however was not to be easily effected, even had it been desired by Margaret herself, which at first was very likely not the case. Albany arrived in Scotland in May, 1515, and, being afterwards confirmed as governor by the Scottish Parliament, was quite resolved on obtaining possession of the children. To this end a deputation of Scotch lords approached the Queen at Stirling; but they were compelled to deliver their message outside the gates, the portcullis being dropped. The castle was besieged, and Albany himself appeared before it on August 4 with formidable artillery. Margaret, deserted by her friends, put the keys of the castle into the young King's hands and delivered both him and his brother to the Duke. Next month, by means of skilful arrangements made for her by Lord Dacre, she contrived to escape to Harbottle in Northumberland, where, on October 7, she was delivered of a daughter, Margaret Douglas, afterwards the mother of Lord Darnley. Here the Queen was obliged to remain for the winter, removing no further than Morpeth in November, as her confinement had been followed by a long illness, during which the news of her second son's death at Stirling was for a time concealed from her; and she only visited her brother's Court in the following spring.

Meanwhile the influence of Henry VIII at Rome had procured for Wolsey the title of Cardinal, which was bestowed upon him by Leo X on September 10. On December 24 following the King appointed him Lord Chancellor, and ambassadors noted that the whole power of the State appeared to be lodged in him. The King, indeed, reposed very complete confidence in him, but always required frequent conferences with him as to the aims and methods of policy, and the Cardinal always found it necessary to carry out the objects of a very intelligent master, whether he quite approved of them himself or not. Henry VIII might hunt and take his pleasure; but there was no department of the State's business which he failed to look into or which he did not fully command.

In September, 1515, Francis I won the battle of Marignano, to the confusion of the Pope, and the Spaniards, and the Swiss. Nor was the news more acceptable to Henry, who read the letters presented to him by the French ambassador with ill-concealed mortification. He had no reasonable cause, however, for a rupture with France, and Wolsey and Suffolk were eager to assure the ambassador that nothing of the kind was in contemplation. But not only had he just (October 19) made a new treaty (though a defensive one only) with Ferdinand of Aragon, but he had also been listening with interest to a secretary of Maximilian Sforza, Duke of Milan, who urged him to league with the Swiss for the expulsion of the French from Italy. And Wolsey had already despatched his very able secretary, Richard Pace, on a secret mission to hire Swiss mercenaries for this purpose, throwing out a hint that their efforts were likely to be seconded by another English invasion of France. Unluckily, even before Pace had set out, not only had the Swiss been decisively defeated at Marignano, but Milan had opened its gates to the victors, and the Duke, taken prisoner, had resigned his duchy for a French pension. But the plan was not dropped. The Emperor conferred the title of Duke of Milan on Francis Sforza, brother of Maximilian, and it was arranged that the Swiss were to serve the Emperor and to be paid by England.

But a further change very soon took place in the situation. In January, 1516, Ferdinand of Aragon died, and the young Prince Charles was in Flanders proclaimed King of Castile. It was desirable —and became more and more so as time went on—that he should leave the Netherlands for his new dominions, but there were many difficulties to compose. His Council leaned to France, and the Holy League had not much prospect of survival without Spain. England, however, clung to her former policy, and, as it seemed at first, with every prospect of success. The French were driven into Milan, and it was thought that they could not keep the city against the Emperor, who had come down from Trent and joined the Swiss with a view to attacking them. But, when almost at the gates of the city on Easter Monday, March 24, he suddenly changed his mind, refused to advance further, and presently withdrew once more across the Adda towards Germany, alleging the most frivolous excuses to Pace and the English ambassador, Wingfield. Whether he was discontented at not having received English money, or had actually received French money, is uncertain. The Swiss would have gone on without him; but their leaders fell out among themselves, and the whole enterprise was ruined. Still, by Wolsey's policy, the Swiss were kept in pay, and the Emperor was prevented for a time from coming to an understanding with France.

Conscious of his debts to England, Maximilian gravely offered to invest King Henry with the dukedom of Milan, and even to resign the Empire itself in his favour. Henry was not much taken with these offers, but thought it more important that the Emperor should come down to Flanders and correct the French leanings of his grandson's counsellors; or he might come on to Calais, where, in that case, Henry would meet him. The suggestion was agreeable to Maximilian, as it offered a pretext for new demands on Henry's purse for travelling expenses. He delayed the journey, however, for some time, while Charles and his counsellors concluded a treaty with France at Noyon, on August 13, with the object of settling questions about Navarre and Naples, so as to let the young Prince go to Spain with comfort. This was quite disastrous to the policy of England and to the manifest interests of Maximilian, and had a bad effect upon the Swiss. But Maximilian required further aid from England to prevent Verona falling into the hands of the Venetians, and it was apparently with this object mainly that he despatched Matthias Schinner, Cardinal of Sion, into England in October, though there were no doubt more specious pretexts. For, notwithstanding the Treaty of Noyon, even Charles' counsellors admitted the danger of Francis becoming supreme in Italy and putting pressure on the Pope. The Cardinal of Sion conferred with them on the way to England, and a league for the defence of the Church was concluded in London on October 29 between England, the Emperor, and Spain. But the Emperor was still called on to perform his promise; and, being yet far from the Low Countries, he continually required golden arguments to make him advance further. He reached Hagenau in Elsass in the beginning of December; and the Cardinal of Sion, who joined him there on his return from England, continued the begging on his behalf, writing to Wolsey that Charles' counsellors were seriously alarmed at his approach. This was a gross falsehood; for, shameful to say, at that very time the Emperor, by his commissioners at Brussels, had accepted the Treaty of Noyon and given his oath to observe it. Moreover, he had put Verona into the hands of the King of Castile, who, he pretended, could keep it better than himself; but Charles merely handed it over by compact to the French, to be restored by them to the Venetians.

So, in fact, all the King's money bestowed on Maximilian was lost. But under Wolsey's guidance large compensation was obtained ere long. No change was made in external policy. The Emperor was treated still as a friend, till he fell into suspicion with other allies, and lost all influence in Europe: while, on the other hand, England was sought by all parties for the sake of her full coffers. Charles of Castile felt the need of her to advance money to him for his voyage to Spain; and, while Henry was supposed to be still bent on doing France all the mischief in his power, very secret negotiations began between France and England, first for the restoration of Tournay, and ultimately, before the world knew, for a cordial alliance, of which more will be said presently.

Meanwhile the Queen had given birth in February to a daughter named Mary, who was afterwards Queen of England; and in May Margaret, Queen of Scotland, came to her brother's Court at Greenwich. Her stay in England gave Henry very great power in dealing with the Northern kingdom. Even at Harbottle and Morpeth she had fallen under the power of Lord Dacre, a great master of intrigue, who understood the King's general objects and first induced her to prefer demands which were refused by the Scotch lords; then, later, to sign a bill of complaints against Albany, in which it was even insinuated that the King was not safe in his hands, and that the death of the King's younger brother was probably due to the Duke. This, however, was only a State-paper to be used when convenient; for she was at that very time corresponding with Albany, who at her request liberated her friends from prison, agreed to give up her dowry, and showed every desire to satisfy her. Yet, on June 1, 1516, Henry wrote to the Scotch lords a formal demand for Albany's removal; but he was met by an absolute refusal on July 4. Albany, however, was really desirous to revisit France, and to this end he made a treaty with Wolsey on July 24, arranged for a prolongation of the truce and a settlement of Margaret's demands, and proposed to pass through England on his way, and there conclude a perpetual peace. At a later date, he obtained an unwilling permission from the Scotch Parliament to return to France for a time; but the visit to England had to be abandoned.

He returned to France in June, 1517, and in the course of the same month Margaret re-entered Scotland, having left London on May 16. Little more than a fortnight before her departure occurred the formidable riot of the London apprentices called Evil Mayday. It arose out of a conspiracy against foreigners, on whose houses a general attack was made during the night of April 30. This outbreak was not unexpected; but the civic authorities, in spite of a serious warning from Wolsey, who had to protect his own house at Westminster with a guard and artillery, failed to take adequate steps to prevent it. Troops were despatched into the City by various routes, and cannon were used to quell the disturbance. Two hundred and seventy-eight citizens were taken prisoners, of whom sixty were hanged in different parts of the City, and some beheaded and quartered, the offence being counted treason on account of the King's amity with foreign princes. The rest were pardoned at the intercession of the Queen and Wolsey.

Another public calamity which speedily followed was a severe outbreak of the Sweating Sickness—an epidemic which first made notable ravages in England immediately after the accession of Henry VII (1485). Wolsey was dangerously ill of it, and the Court was obliged, both this year and, in the year following (1518), to withdraw from the neighbourhood of London for fear of the infection.

Early in 1517 a conspiracy to poison Pope Leo X was discovered at Rome, in which some Cardinals were implicated—among others, Cardinal Adrian de Corneto, the papal Collector in England, who held the bishopric of Bath and Wells, originally bestowed upon him by King Henry VII. He exercised his office of collector by deputy, and his sub-collector, the celebrated Polydore Vergil, had already been imprisoned by Wolsey for an intrigue, and had only been released at the Pope's urgent intercession. Leo seems to have been equally anxious to spare Adrian himself the full penalty of his guilt; but Henry insisted that he should be deprived alike of his cardinalate and of his English bishopric, intending that the latter should be bestowed on Wolsey *in commendam*, to be held along with the archbishopric of York. The Pope put off the deprivation as long as possible. But both this and another concession he ultimately consented to make, in order to advance a project of his own. For in March, 1517, the Lateran Council, taking advantage of the general peace in Europe, had proposed a Crusade against the Turk, and Leo had before the year was out already sent Legates to some countries to promote it. Henry VIII, however, objected that it was unusual to admit a foreign Legate in England, but said that he would waive the objection if Wolsey also were made Legate *de latere* at the same time. A joint legatine commission was accordingly issued by Leo in May, 1518, to Cardinal Campeggio and to Wolsey; whereupon the former proceeded as far as Calais. But Cardinal Adrian was not yet deprived of his bishopric, and powerful intercession was used in his behalf. At Calais, therefore, Campeggio had to remain some weeks, until certain intelligence was received of Adrian's deprivation, when he was conducted across the Channel in July, and received with great magnificence in London.

Nothing came, indeed, of the expedition against the Turk. The selfishness of princes and the double views of the Popes themselves always interfered with such projects. But the proposal for a general peace had for some time formed an admirable blind for negotiations, which had been secretly in progress for a special alliance between England and France. These arose out of private communications concerning Tournay —first, seemingly about ecclesiastical jurisdiction, for the French Bishop always maintained his claim against Wolsey,—afterwards about the town itself, which the French were anxious to recover. No one yet knew what was going on, when in July, 1518, a protocol was signed by Wolsey and the French ambassador, Villeroy, for the surrender of the city and for the future marriage of the Princess Mary to the Dauphin, born in February of that same year. A magnificent embassy then came over in September, and was received by the King in the presence of Cardinal Campeggio. A treaty of universal peace, as it was called, was signed in London by the French ambassadors and the English Privy Council on October 2, and on the next day the King and the ambassadors swore to it at St Paul's. It was professedly a treaty between Leo X, Maximilian, Francis I, Charles of Spain, and Henry VIII, for mutual defence against invasion; but it was only signed at present by representatives of England and France, time being given to the Pope and the others to confirm it. This in itself, however, made it first of all a closer alliance with France; and two days later further treaties were signed for the marriage, for the surrender of Tournay, and for the settlement of questions about depredations. Bonnivet, the head of the French embassy, then, as proxy for the Dauphin, formally married Mary at Greenwich on October 5, and finally on the 8th another treaty was signed for an interview between the French and English Kings, to take place at Sandingfield near Calais before April 1 of the following year.

Charles of Castile did not like this treaty, but it was for his own interest to confirm it, and he did so in Spain. Thus it formed a fair beginning for a European settlement, and virtually took Campeggio's mission out of his hands, making England the negotiator of the general peace, and consequently the arbiter of continental differences. To England, however, the great immediate advantage was, in the first place, that France was willing to buy her friendship, by means of an understanding that Albany must be kept from returning to Scotland, and of the payment of 600,000 crowns for the surrender of Tournay—a city which had been very expensive to keep, and to secure which the King had, in 1515, begun to build a citadel. Wolsey, too, surrendered his ineffectual claims on the bishopric (whose revenues he had never been able to draw) for a pension of 12,000 *livres*.

Early in the next year (1519) the Emperor Maximilian died (January 12). Charles of Spain and Francis I of France immediately became candidates for the succession; and perhaps these events had their share in putting off the interview between the Kings of France and England. But in May Henry himself became a third competitor, sending Pace (now his own Secretary instead of Wolsey's) to Germany, to suggest in secret objections to both the other candidates and thus win the Electors in his favour. It was a hopeless project, which Wolsey certainly promoted against his own better judgment, because he saw his master set upon it. Moreover, it was a piece of double dealing towards Francis whose candidature Henry had promised to support; and Francis found it out, but did not let the fact disturb the new amity. Charles was elected Emperor (June 28).

This brings us to the threshold of a new epoch, to be treated of in a later volume. During the latter part of the fifteenth and the beginning of the sixteenth century, the constant tendency had been for every kingdom of Europe to consolidate itself and bring feudal lordships into full subjection to the supreme ruler. France felt this necessity most in order to repel the English invader. England herself was made to feel it by the Wars of the Roses. Spain came together under

Ferdinand and Isabel, and drove out the Moors. The House of Burgundy, with its rich inheritance in the Netherlands, was a dangerous neighbour to France and a natural ally of England; but, ending in a female, it became joined with the House of Austria which had already attained to the Empire, and was striving to secure it as a dynastic inheritance. The spirit of the times moved even the Papacy, whose territorial claims in Italy Julius II advanced by a warfare much more earthly than spiritual.

The spirit of the times in political matters had been appreciated by Sir Thomas More whose *Utopia* is described elsewhere in this volume as a classic product of an age of discovery. Such it was in its most striking aspect; but none the less was it in some parts a most faithful transcript of the Machiavellian politics pursued by the princes of Europe, and not least by the King of England. In More's ideal island inhabited by intelligent pagans we find precisely those arts practised which were practised in the Courts of Christian Europe. While kingdoms were advancing, and domestic peace and security should have found a firmer basis, the rulers of Christendom were cheating each other, engaging in unjust wars, or, like England, paying Swiss mercenaries to fight without declaring themselves belligerents. Henry VII had watched continental politics without allowing himself to be drawn into continental wars. It was otherwise with Henry VIII. Young and popular, and seated on a throne as secure as his father's was unstable, to him the glories of war had their attractions, and the practices of the Utopians in the conduct of it were not abhorrent. Such things were merely in the way of statesmanship, and when the King was satisfied there was no one to call him to account.

Yet it was a highly polished age. Many ideas of former days, no doubt, had lost their hold. Chivalry had decayed; the talk of crusades against the Turk had become a mockery; the Eastern Empire had passed away, and the pretensions of the Western Empire had become more unreal than ever. But civilisation had recovered from the disorders of papal schisms, internecine wars, and socialistic insurrections. There was marked progress in art and letters, first in Italy, then over the continent of Europe; and if in England there was little art and the young vernacular literature seemed to have languished since Chaucer's day, yet this country was scarcely behind other nations in cherishing the revived study of the classics. Long before the close of the fifteenth century English monks, like Prior Sellyng of Canterbury, had brought Greek scholarship home from Italian universities; and Erasmus himself, who first came to England in 1497 or 1498, and was set to teach Greek at Cambridge in 1510, found the country a special abode of scholarship. More, Colet, Grocyn and Linacre were the men in whom this culture was most conspicuous; and Archbishop Warham and Bishop Fisher were the leading patrons of learning.

The people, too, were polished in their manners. English urbanity struck even a Venetian who visited the country about the year 1500. But Erasmus found in English social intercourse something more than mere urbanity. "Did you but know the endowments of Britain," he writes to his poetical friend Andrelinus, "you would run hither with winged feet, and if the gout stopped you, you would wish yourself a Daedalus. To mention one thing out of many. There are here nymphs of divine beauty, gentle and kind, whom you may well prefer to your Camoenae. Moreover there is a fashion never sufficiently commended. Wherever you go you are received by every one with kisses; when you take leave you are dismissed with kisses. You return, kisses again are renewed. People come to you and kisses are offered; they take their leave and kisses are again distributed. Wherever you meet there are kisses in abundance; in short wherever you move all things are charged with kisses. And, Faustus, if you once tasted how sweet and fragrant they are, you would be glad to sojourn in England, not for ten years only like Solon, but to your dying day."

Such was English social life before the days of Puritanism; but it must be said, this pleasant freedom of manners was accompanied by much laxity with regard to social ties. Our Venetian visitor found, side by side with English courtesy, an absence of domestic affection which seemed to him altogether amazing: of licentiousness he saw instances in this country, but none of a man in love; and though Englishmen kept jealous guard over their wives, offences against married life could always among them in the end be condoned for money. For their children they seemed to have no affection, sending them out to service in other homes as soon as they reached the age of seven, or nine at the utmost, in order that they might learn manners. These observations are fully confirmed by the evidence of the *Paston Letters*, where, among other things, we read of a young lady of twenty in a respectable family being repeatedly beaten and having her head broken in two or three places at a time, so that she was inclined to marry an elderly and ill-favoured suitor to escape from her mother's tyranny.

This painful absence of natural feeling was largely owing to the feudal system of wardships, by which heirs under age were disposed of in marriage without their own consent, and that union which lays the foundation of all social life was commonly made a matter of bargain and sale. It was anything but an ideal condition of society; yet the nation was polite, well ordered, and, on the whole, very submissive to authority. The people loved their King, and even when their affection came to be sorely tried, honoured him with a respectful obedience which later generations found it impossible to pay to his successors.

# CHAPTER XV.

## ECONOMIC CHANGE.

WE are accustomed to remark on the extraordinary economic changes which have taken place during the last three hundred years. Commercial intercourse has increased enormously; the age of invention has brought about a veritable revolution in the processes of manufacture; and agriculture has been indirectly, but deeply, affected by these influences. Despite the growth, however, in the volume of trade, in the mass of wealth, and in the numbers of the population, similar principles of economic policy and commercial enterprise have been in vogue all this time. The seventeenth, eighteenth, and nineteenth centuries belong to the same period in the world's history. The turning-point was passed when the age of geographical discovery opened up the possibility of communication between all parts of the globe; and when the seventeenth century began, there had been time for the readjustment of the more limited ambitions of the Middle Ages to the new conditions. Rival nationalities were trying then, as they are to-day, to strengthen their naval and military forces with the aid of resources drawn from distant lands; and a close analogy is observable between the practices which were then pursued by the most progressive countries and some of the expedients which are being proposed at the present time. The commercial struggles and the economic controversies of the seventeenth century may seem petty and trivial; but the atmosphere is perfectly familiar, since they are thoroughly modern in character.

The preceding period of three hundred years with which we are concerned at present—the fourteenth, fifteenth and sixteenth centuries —was also a time of rapid movement in the economic sphere; but the changes which occurred in that era contrast forcibly with those of the modern world. There are few indications of steady growth in those troubled times; they were marked, instead, by the break up of medieval society and the reconstruction of economic organisation on entirely different lines. It is probable that according to modern standards no startling change in the total volume of trade occurred between the reign of Philip the Fair and the accession of Henry of Navarre; but during that time the methods of commercial practice had been fundamentally altered, and the institutions which controlled industrial activity had been remodelled. Although the processes of manufacture and agriculture remained almost the same, there was a veritable revolution in commerce at the close of the Middle Ages; and as its result, every aspect of economic life and every member of the body economic was transformed. The drastic character of these changes will be more easily understood, if we try to compare economic life in the earlier part of the fourteenth century, when medieval institutions were at their best, with the state of affairs at the opening of the seventeenth, when the modern period was already beginning.

The area traversed by fourteenth century merchants was very restricted, when compared with the voyages of Dutch or English traders in the seventeenth century. Medieval Christendom was hemmed in on the east and south by Mohammadan lands; and though Europeans ventured to the borders of these territories and founded factories at many points in them, they could not penetrate into the interior or establish direct commercial connexions with the distant regions which supplied spices and silk. Maritime intercourse was confined to the Mediterranean and the Black Sea, the Baltic and the North Sea, and the eastern border of the Atlantic. Within these narrow geographical limits, each commercial community aimed at obtaining a profitable monopoly in some line of trade, and at ousting competitors; this policy gave rise to arbitrary restrictions on trading voyages. The Genoese and the Venetians contended for the possession of the commerce of the Black Sea; Venice succeeded in controlling the trade on the Adriatic and in the valley of the Po; the merchants of the Hanse towns would not admit any rivals in the Baltic. The command of particular harbours carried with it a supremacy in neighbouring waters, and secured the exclusive possession of particular routes so long as coasting voyages were in vogue. The geographical discoveries of the fifteenth century not only opened new regions to maritime intercourse, but they also gave a new form to commercial rivalry. The maintenance of privileged rights at particular ports was less important in the new era when the compass had come into common use; with the wide field for their activities presented by the New World and the now accessible East, merchants no longer confined themselves to struggling for a share of the limited trade which had grown up at special points; statesmen learned to vie with each other in trying to extend the market for goods by establishing factories in remote lands and planting colonies, for this seemed to be the secret of commercial success. Political and commercial considerations were so closely mingled at the opening of the seventeenth century that it is difficult to distinguish the trading enterprise from the military ambition of this period; but at least it may be said that the merchants who were content to abide by the old routes and methods of business were being rapidly deposed from their former supremacy.

As compared with the conditions which prevail in modern days, society in the fourteenth century was very definitely organised in recognised groups. Personal relations were not easily alterable at will; there were few opportunities for change of employment or even for change of residence from one place to another. In rural districts the peasantry were everywhere practically attached to particular estates as serfs; and the artisan classes had but little encouragement to migrate from place to place, though in some callings, such as that of masons, special provision was made for undertaking work in any locality where building was required; while in other instances there seems to have been a recognised period of *Wanderjahre.* Even the merchants engaged in active trade were forced, as we have seen, to keep to certain routes of commercial connexion, and at other times their operations were confined to transactions in some one class of goods and no other; there was comparatively little freedom for change in any department of trading activity. In the most advanced communities such restrictions had not been swept away entirely even at the beginning of the seventeenth century; but they were much criticised, and the difficulty of enforcing them was increasing.

The deeply-marked social distinctions and strong local attachments of the Middle Ages were closely connected with another economic feature, the importance of which is sometimes overlooked. The use of money was not nearly so general in the ordinary affairs of life, as it has come to be in modern times. In many rural districts the peasant's payment for the use of his holding was rendered in service or in kind; labourers were often remunerated, in part at least, by being provided with rations of food, shelter, and necessary wearing apparel. Even when these vestiges of natural economy had passed away and payment in money had been introduced, the terms of exchange were frequently the subject of regulation. There was often a recognised rate at which dues in service, or in kind, could be commuted for money; or attempts were made to determine the prices of goods and the rates of wages by authority, either in the interest of the consumer or, at other times and places, in that of the producer. All sorts of rates, which are now reached by bargaining and by the higgling of the market, were then regarded as the proper subject of official regulation. The circumstances of the day and the limited character of the markets rendered this system convenient; but it had also very strong support in the current morality of the time. So long as theorists maintained that every article had an intrinsic just price which was ordinarily ascertained by "common estimation," and which was, as a matter of fact, closely related to the expenses of production, the strongest prejudice was excited against those who made a living by taking advantage of variations of price in different places or at different seasons of the year. However imperfectly they may have been carried out, these efforts to enforce reasonable prices probably put considerable restraint on certain forms of extortion, while they tended to check the violence of the fluctuations which must occasionally occur in every kind of trade.

In the fourteenth century this elaborate system of economic regulation was organised by civic authorities; it was to a very small extent a matter for royal or national interference. Each town formed a separate economic centre, which not only regulated its own internal affairs, but pursued its own policy in its trading relations with other places. Some cities were banded together for the sake of maintaining common interests and formed confederations like that of the Hanse League; but on the whole they cherished economic independence. Each city had to deal with the problem of its own food supply; some towns, such as Nîmes, could rely on the produce of their own lands, though others, like Bordeaux, were dependent on commerce for the sustenance of the inhabitants; while many erected large granaries, to enable them to tide over occasional periods of scarcity, which might arise from the failure of crops or the interruption of trade. The diverse circumstances in which they were placed rendered it inevitable that each should, more or less consciously, devise its own economic policy, and control the machinery which regulated industrial life; some towns had special advantages for one branch of manufacture and some for others. Florence owed her prosperity to skill in the working and dressing of cloth, Genoa excelled in the production of arms, and Venice was successful in bringing the manufacture of glass and silk to a high state of perfection. The precise *status* of the companies and gilds and lodges of the Middle Ages varied from place to place, and the organisation of one craft might differ considerably from that of another. But this one characteristic held good generally, that all these bodies were municipal institutions which had regard to the welfare of the public, or of the trade, in each particular town.

Civic patriotism not only affected the character of the internal regulation of industry, but it also determined the policy of each town towards outsiders. The jealousy of "foreign" artisans, *i.e.* of those who were not burgesses, gave rise to bitter disputes in the neighbourhood of Bruges and other Flemish towns; and "foreign" merchants were seriously hampered in attempts to trade, unless they could secure special privileges, and particular establishments of their own, with accommodation for residence and for the warehousing of their goods. The cities of Aragon, Provence, and Italy had such factories in the Mohammadan towns of Morocco, Tunis, Egypt, and Syria; the members of the Hanse League had a similar establishment in London, and their settlement at Bergen became so powerful as to dominate over the native portion of the place. In the fourteenth century commerce was intermunicipal rather than international in character: though similar usages prevailed very widely and disputes could be settled according to Law Merchant, which was recognised as generally binding. Trade was carried on to the greatest advantage at the fairs, where the merchants of many cities could meet on equal terms. In the present day free-traders take account of the economic advantage of the world as a whole, and discuss industrial and commercial affairs from a cosmopolitan standpoint, while protectionists are inclined to limit their consideration to the interests of some one particular country. In the Middle Ages, very few merchants or politicians were in a position to take account of national prosperity; they limited their views to a narrower sphere, and were content to concentrate their attention on the welfare of a particular town. With regard both to the administration of industry and to the regulation of commerce, the city was the principal economic unit, in the medieval as it had been in the ancient world.

Such were the chief contrasts between the economic life of medieval and of modern times; were we to seek a phrase which should indicate the general character of the transition from one to the other, we might say that this revolution consisted in the rise of nationalities as the bases of industrial organisation and commercial policy. Economically considered, medieval Christendom consisted of a system of city States, while modern history describes the commercial and colonial rivalries of great nations. During the fourteenth, fifteenth, and sixteenth centuries we can trace the gradual subversion of the older institutions, and we can also see the rise of the newer forms of organisation. The corresponding changes were not of course exactly synchronous in every land; indeed, those places where the older and stereotyped system had the greatest vitality were at a positive disadvantage in accepting modifications and adopting new methods. To follow the course of so widespread and complicated a revolution would be wellnigh impossible, without a clue; but fortunately we can have little doubt as to the factor primarily concerned in producing these momentous changes. Even the fourteenth and fifteenth centuries were marked by the formation of capital, and the process went on with great rapidity in the sixteenth; the whole period furnishes abundant illustrations of the power of moneyed men; and by fixing attention on them and their action, we can most easily trace the influences which were at work in building up the economic system of modern Europe.

Modern economists maintain that there are three requisites of production,—labour, capital, and land; but in the early Middle Ages agricultural and industrial work were both carried on without the intervention of capital, as we now understand the term. A capitalist may be regarded as the owner of a mass of wealth which is constantly altering its form by means of exchange. He tries to get gain by turning over his stock, and is on the look-out for opportunities of applying and replacing it frequently. This is equally true of the capital of the financier and the merchant; and till recently it held good of capital engaged in the processes of manufacture and of tillage. The age of invention has rendered it necessary to lock up large amounts of capital in expensive machinery, or to sink it in permanent improvements of the soil; but, at the beginning of the modern era, capital might be described as a mass of wealth that was constantly being put into circulation and replaced. The financier exchanged his ready money for securities, which he held till the sum was repaid; the merchant bought and exported a cargo of goods which he hoped to sell for money; manufacturers obtained the services of labour by paying wages, and bought materials which were converted into commodities for sale. Facilities for exchange were necessary at every step, before the capitalist administration of industry and agriculture could be introduced; there had been no opportunity for such an introduction, so long as society was organised on a basis of natural economy. In any department of life where payments are made in kind or in service rather than in money, no room remains for the operation of the capitalist. So long as the cultivator continues to live on the produce of his fields and his stock, and only occasionally offers some of his surplus for sale, he is conducting his business in a fashion quite incompatible with the aims of the enterprising capitalist, who desires to dispose of his whole crop at a profit. During the long ages when society had been organised in self-sufficing estates, the *familia* in each being engaged in catering for household needs and not in working for a market, there was no true exchange, and therefore no occasion for a measure of value, or for the use of money, among those engaged in different avocations.

The transition from natural to money economy was a gradual process, and afforded great opportunities of gain to the men whose wealth consisted of coins and bullion. In the twelfth and thirteenth centuries many private persons had large hoards, and received a handsome income by making advances to such wealthy people as were in temporary straits for want of ready money. Much of this business arose in connexion with the revenue system; kings were glad to borrow on the security of the royal jewels, thus making it possible to anticipate the slow collection of taxes and fit out an armed expedition. The financiers also lent money to landed proprietors, to enable them to meet some sudden demand for an aid, and took as security the title-deeds of an estate so as to enjoy the certainty of being reimbursed when rents were due. The lending of the thirteenth and fourteenth centuries was almost entirely for military and other unproductive purposes; it enriched the moneyed men who obtained high interest on their loans, but it did not provide capital or invigorate the industry of the country. Even in those cases where debts were contracted in order to erect magnificent buildings, these costly edifices were not available for promoting the further increase of wealth. Medieval capital was lent for purposes of unproductive consumption. Thus applied, the money failed to bring about an increase of wealth, but remained, as Aristotle would have said, "barren." This fact goes far to account for the long-continued prejudice against Jews and Lombards. Since no addition to the wealth of the community arose through their intervention, it seemed that any gain accruing to them in their operations must have been made at the expense of the borrowers and ought to be condemned as extortionate. Under these circumstances the traditional objection to interest of every kind was strongly maintained, and found expression in the writings of casuists and in the decisions of ecclesiastical Courts against usury.

The unsatisfactory character of the transactions of medieval bankers reacted on the prosperity of their business, and eventually brought about their ruin. It was a constant difficulty for their debtors to scrape together money which would reimburse the Jew or the Lombard for wealth that had been unremuneratively expended; and it was natural enough that the capitalists should suffer in turn from defaulting creditors. The Jews were under such serious disabilities that it was only by special favour that they could recover their debts, and several of the Florentine and other Italian bankers were ruined by breaches of royal faith, about the middle of the fourteenth century; but the failure of the Templars, who had also organised an immense banking business, was due to political rather than economic causes. At that time very few opportunities existed of so using capital that it should not only bring in a return to the owner, but also increase the wealth of the community.

There was, however, all through the Middle Ages one such opening for the profitable employment of capital; and of this the great Italian houses took full advantage. The merchant who engaged in active trade and visited distant markets with a cargo of goods, was rendering a real service to the community. He was enabling the inhabitants of certain districts to enjoy the benefit of products which did not grow on their own soil, or of wares which they had not the skill to manufacture. So long as the merchant confined himself to such operations, no question was raised by the strictest moralist as to the legitimacy of his transactions or as to the lawfulness of gains thus derived; and capitalists, who joined together in taking the risks of useful business of this kind, were held to be perfectly justified in sharing the profits which accrued to them from their enterprise. While nearly all moneyed men were under suspicion of occasional unfairness, the medieval conscience clearly recognised that the capitalist was fully entitled to some gain, so long as he transported commodities without trying to bargain himself out of risks. Capital engaged in active commerce was employed in producing goods at the places where they were most wanted; and it was being applied to facilitate the production of wealth. The importing merchant neither increased the material objects nor altered their intrinsic qualities; but he gave them greater utility, by conveying them to places where they were largely required.

The economic revolution at the close of the Middle Ages was largely due to the discovery of new methods for the productive employment of capital. New lines of commerce were opened; and it was also found that various branches of industry could be prosecuted to greater advantage, when taken up and organised by capitalists. Success in these ventures enabled enterprising men to amass more wealth and to form additional capital, while it tempted those who had hoards lying idle to find means of employing them as capital; by so doing they brought large sums of money into circulation and moreover secured an income for themselves. The formation of new capital and the employment of hoards as capital for facilitating production went on apace in the fifteenth and sixteenth centuries; the lending of capital for purposes of unproductive consumption did not cease, but came to be an entirely subordinate, because it proved to be a less secure and less remunerative, method of employing wealth.

There was no apparent reason, so far as we can see in looking back to the beginning of the fourteenth century, why the material progress which had been steadily maintained for some generations should not have been continued. Medieval society, stereotyped as it was, had been capable of considerable readjustment, as circumstances had changed. It seems as if capital might have gradually found openings in new directions, so that the medieval system would have been slowly transformed without any serious rupture with the past. At Florence, in particular, capitalist organisation existed side by side with the older forms of industrial life at the beginning of the fourteenth century; and as money economy became increasingly prevalent, capitalistic enterprise might have taken advantage of the new fields which were ready for its operation. But circumstances combined to render this impossible; medieval society and its institutions suffered an especially severe blow from the terrible pestilence known as the Black Death, which ravaged Europe in the middle of the fourteenth century. From this shock the various countries of Europe only recovered slowly; and when material prosperity began to be restored, the old institutions were no longer suitable to the changed requirements of the times. The old industrial life had been so far disintegrated by the disturbed conditions of the fourteenth and fifteenth centuries that the change from the medieval to the modern was accomplished, not as a gradual transition but as a violent revolution.

Three principal causes combined to subject the social and economic system of medieval Europe to an overwhelming strain.

Some uncertainty must necessarily attach to conclusions based on the statistics drawn from medieval sources; and there can be little doubt that the estimates of the mortality due to the Black Death, made by contemporary writers, were grossly exaggerated. Many records, however, exist of the deaths in particular places, or among a special class such as the parochial clergy; and these statements appear to be well worthy of credit. It seems to be generally agreed that at least half of the population was swept away by the successive visitations of this pestilence. While we cannot easily conceive what must have been the full effects of such wholesale destruction, we may at least conclude that considerable tracts of country were depopulated, so that the area devoted to tillage was necessarily reduced; we have also abundant evidence of labour agitation in many branches of industry. The whole system of regulated rates and prices was seriously undermined; under the new conditions the old payments had become unsatisfactory; changes of some kind, both as to the terms on which land was rented and as to those on which labour was employed, were inevitable.

The constant wars of the latter half of the fourteenth and the fifteenth centuries were another disruptive force and proved fatal to the maintenance of the highly organised system of medieval times. In the countries which were the scene of frequent warlike operations, immense mischief was done to agriculture; it is difficult to understand how a rural population should have survived in France at all, when we read of the ravages of the English armies, and the devastations caused by the factions. The chronic disorder not only affected tillage and the food-supply, but rendered internal trade so insecure that it was practically suspended altogether. What had been a prosperous kingdom, with many well-organised cities, and with fairs that were frequented by merchants from all parts of Europe, was reduced to utter desolation and ruin. Similar results attended the Hussite Wars in Bohemia, and, to a lesser degree, the Wars of the Roses in England; the Italian cities must also have found their intercivic hostilities a serious drain on their resources. Venice and Genoa had carried on a long-protracted struggle about Chioggia; Pisa was at length forced to succumb to Florence, and Milan gradually established her superiority over her neighbours. Doubtless, to many districts the wars brought profit as well as loss; Swiss and Italian mercenaries often engaged in fighting as a regular trade, in which much booty was to be obtained; and successful cities might recoup themselves for their outlay by securing new avenues of commerce at the expense of their rivals. Still the fact remains that war was a disturbing element; the instability introduced by it into all the relations of life was irreconcilable with the maintenance of the old industrial system or old trading connexions. The countries which for any considerable period enjoyed a relative immunity from external war, such as Flanders, the duchy of Burgundy, the Rhineland, and Bavaria, made rapid progress, while others failed to regain the prosperity they had enjoyed before the Black Death, or sank into deeper and deeper decay. The most obvious and important commercial result of the Wars in France was seen in the diversion of the traffic between Italy and Flanders from the Rhone valley, so as to increase the intercourse over the Alps and by the valley of the Inn. Augsburg, Nürnberg, and the cities of the Rhineland came to be for a time on the great highway of Europe; while there was also increased maritime communication between the Mediterranean and the Low Countries by the Straits of Gibraltar and the English Channel.

Other political causes affected the more distant trading connexions of European cities. The union of the northern kingdoms of Denmark, Norway, and Sweden under Queen Margaret consolidated the opposition to the monopoly asserted by the Hanse League over the commerce of the North; while the rise of the power of Poland, and her successful contests with the Teutonic Order, interrupted the lines of its Eastern communications. When in 1477 Ivan, Czar of Russia, brought Novgorod into complete subjection and it ceased to be an independent city, the merchants of the Hanse League lost their footing at the point where they had established connexions with traders who were engaged in traffic with the East.

There were other movements in eastern Europe which seriously affected the course of merchandise. The advancing power of the Turks destroyed the commercial colonies on the Black Sea, and interrupted the trading intercourse in the Danube valley; in the latter half of the fifteenth century the commerce between East and West was almost entirely confined to the Egyptian and Syrian routes; Venice was the chief *dépôt* on the northern side of the Mediterranean for Eastern spices, and the centre from which these highly-valued commodities were distributed to Germany, Flanders, and the North.

The Turkish conquests had forced the principal trade of the East into restricted channels, and Christian successes were responsible for the increasing difficulties under which the commerce of the western Mediterranean was carried on. The expulsion of the Moors from Spain, which was completed by the conquest of Granada, was followed by an extraordinary development of national vigour and material prosperity in many parts of the peninsula; but the exiled population aroused the sympathy of their co-religionists in Africa; an increase of marauding expeditions by sea ensued, and the difficulties of merchants who trafficked with Morocco were seriously aggravated.

On every side, the old lines of distant trade were greatly modified by political changes; and the prosperity of the towns, which had risen into greatness as centres of commerce, was shaken at its very foundations, while rural and urban districts alike long continued to show the desolation caused directly and indirectly by the Black Death.

From this brief survey of the nature of the revolution and the causes which occasioned the decay of the old order, we may now turn to look for the first signs of reconstruction. No part of Europe had been more ruthlessly devastated than France, during the fourteenth century and the earlier part of the fifteenth; but a turning-point was reached at last, and the reviving prosperity of the country shaped itself upon new lines. Control of industry and commerce was now exercised by national rather than civic authority, while the financial and commercial business of the realm was no longer left to Italians and other strangers, but was organised by native merchants of enterprise and resource. In this new class one figure is preeminent; no other French merchant attained to wealth at all comparable to that of Jacques Cœur of Montpellier; and few experienced such a sudden reverse of fortune as he suffered when the royal master whom he had served so faithfully imprisoned him and allowed him to die in exile. Apart from these elements of romance, the story of Jacques Cœur's rise is interesting because of the important part which he took in the political life of France. By helping to reorganise the finances of the realm he brought the Crown and the *bourgeoisie* in all parts of the country into much closer relations, and contributed to the remodelling of economic life and to the rise of one great nationality. His extraordinary commercial prosperity, though transitory, helps us to understand the circumstances under which a merchant class came into prominence in lands where the active trade had hitherto been prosecuted by aliens; the rapid rise of one man to a pinnacle of greatness as a merchant prince throws considerable light on the opportunities for forming capital and investing it available in his day.

Jacques Cœur's work as a statesman had a permanent value for his country; he was for a time the most influential of the royal advisers; he did much to improve the financial administration, and instituted a reform of the coinage. There can be little doubt, when we regard his position, his preponderating influence, and his financial ability, that the creation of the permanent *taille* was due to his initiative. During the Hundred Years' War France had been subjected not only to the ravages of her enemies, but to pillage by her undisciplined soldiery, who were unpaid and had no other means of obtaining supplies. With the view of removing the excuse for these outrages, the Crown, at the meeting of the Estates in 1439, announced its intention of maintaining a standing army; and the *taille* became a permanent source of income which was practically levied at the royal pleasure. The project answered the immediate expectations of those who devised it; the regular troops, well-disciplined and restrained from the habitual pillage which had proved the ruin of France, expelled the English, and helped to bring large districts of the old Burgundian kingdom within the boundaries of France. But the ulterior effects of the measure were far more important; the basis on which French finance rested was altered so as to place it on a firmer footing. The main resources of the feudal monarchs had been drawn from the royal estates and supplemented by occasional aids; but the institution of a permanent *taille* now furnished to the Crown a regular income from taxation, which was defrayed by the trading and industrial as well as the agricultural classes. The French Crown had been mainly dependent for its revenue on the landed classes; but it henceforth became the direct interest of the King to watch and promote the welfare of industry and commerce. As a result of this financial policy extraordinary pains were taken in regard to the supervision and direction of industrial life. The *corps-de-métier* were revived in one town after another, but they were not permitted to retain the old *status* of mere municipal institutions; they were brought into direct relations with the Crown, so that they became part of a centralised system for the administrative control of the whole of French manufactures. This centralisation and over-regulation came in time to be baneful to industrial interests; but at the outset it was a natural result of the efforts of the royal authority to foster material prosperity. Under Charles VII the foundations were laid of that *bourgeois* policy which was pursued more thoroughly, and in defiance of the expressed disapprobation of the nobility, by Louis XI. We shall be better able to gauge the importance of this change when we come to examine the special character of the subsequent revival of French prosperity in the time of Henry of Navarre.

The far-reaching influence exercised by this fiscal change contrasts curiously with the instability of the great commercial connexion established by Jacques Cœur. He desired to open up a direct trade with the East, and succeeded in obtaining numerous concessions not only from the French Crown, but also from the Pope, and from Muslim Powers in Egypt and Syria. These privileges secured to him the monopoly of many lines of profitable trade; he is said to have had no fewer than three hundred factors at various points on the eastern Mediterranean. This great commercial fabric, however, rested on concessions personal to Jacques Cœur and his representatives; and, on his fall from favour, the whole structure collapsed. Montpellier was the principal seat of his business, and the town enjoyed a period of extraordinary prosperity through the trade which he brought to it; but this brief efflorescence seems to have had little abiding influence on the future of French commerce. The main interest attaching to the career of Jacques Cœur as a merchant lies in the illustration which it furnishes of the possibilities open in the early fifteenth century to men who had the capacity to use them.

At first sight, the conditions of life in that age appear to have been such as to make it impossible to understand how great fortunes could have been amassed. If the career of Jacques Cœur had been absolutely unique, it might be sufficient to say that he was able to take advantage of a great monopoly and to trade at an enormous rate of profit; but he did not stand entirely alone. His case was not altogether solitary; though, like William de la Pole and William Canynges, he was pre-eminent among a considerable number of wealthy men.   It is not easy to see how this class could have come into being in so many places during this particular period; but this difficulty must be faced.   An increasing scarcity of the precious metals would seem to have involved a steady fall in prices; so that, apart altogether from the effects of war and pestilence, the monetary conditions were singularly unfavourable to successful trade.   Commerce between Europe and Asia was carried on by means of a constant drain of silver from the West; there was no other suitable commodity for export in return for silks and spices, nor was the stock of bullion being adequately replenished from European mines.   The trade with Morocco did not result in an importation of African gold, but involved an additional demand on the European supply of silver.   It appears that the value of silver was steadily rising from the middle of the fourteenth century onwards, though the fall of prices was not so great as might have been expected; a counteracting influence was at work which affected the currency and prices in much the same way as an additional supply of silver bullion; there seems to have been a greatly increased rapidity of circulation. Money was not laid by in hoards to the same extent as formerly; and masses of bullion, which had been stored for public or private purposes, were being regularly utilised.   The treasure of the feudal monarchs had been withdrawn from circulation for years; Charles V of France had accumulated a reserve of not less than 17,000,000 *livres*.   But the Kings who borrowed from Jacques Cœur and his contemporaries were less thrifty; they only obtained money when they had need to spend it, and there was no reason that it should ever lie idle.   In the same way it would appear that, as the monopoly of the aliens was broken down, the hoards of humbler citizens were drawn upon and employed in active commerce.

By increased rapidity of circulation the diminishing stock of silver seems to have been rendered available to meet commercial demands, and Europe was saved from the embarrassment of severe financial depression. It is certainly remarkable that, during the century which immediately preceded the discovery of America and the importation of bullion from the New World, there should have been so many instances of men who rose to considerable wealth, and who in some cases amassed very large fortunes.   This phenomenon should be borne in mind, even if we are dissatisfied with attempts to account for it; but it seems to be at least partially accounted for by the shifting of trade into new channels and into the hands of native merchants, and partly by the practical increase of the available currency which resulted from the manner in which hoards of bullion were being brought into circulation.

Success in commerce had apparently been the chief avenue to wealth in the earlier part of the fifteenth century; when we pass to the latter half, there is less difficulty in tracing the means by which fortunes could be amassed. The matter is particularly clear in the case of the group of Augsburg capitalists, who were destined to exercise such a potent influence on the political and economic condition of Europe. They could draw from three sources of wealth; for they had access to many frequented trading centres, they were connected with an important textile industry, and they had the opportunity of engaging in profitable mining speculation. The fresh supplies of silver which they obtained from the mines enabled them to accumulate and store wealth for profitable investment as opportunities arose. The man of frugal habits, with a prosperous self-sufficing household, can lay up supplies against a bad season; but his wealth is not in a form which enables him to avail himself of chances for turning over his capital. Only those who are in the habit of using money or of handling the precious metals are likely to make rapid gains and so to amass a great fortune.

The Fugger family of Augsburg eventually became pre-eminent among European financiers; they were originally interested in the weaving of cloth; but, early in the fifteenth century, they began to take part in the spice and silk trades, and established connexions with Venice; Jacob Fugger, who settled the style and constitution of the firm, received his business training at the German factory in that city. Even before his time, the family had made some profitable speculations in mining; they were engaged in working for silver in Tyrol in 1487, and ten years later they took up copper mining in Hungary; they contrived to combine with other Augsburg merchants and form a ring which controlled the copper market at Venice. The career of the Fuggers was not exceptional; the Welsers attained to great financial eminence by similar methods; they too had laid the foundations of their fortune by trading with Venice, and subsequently engaged in silver mining in Tyrol and in Saxony.

Altogether, there was about this time in different parts of Germany a great development of mining, both for the precious and the useful metals. The working of silver at Schwatz dates from 1448, at Salzburg from 1460, and in Saxony from 1471; while the Bohemian mines, which had been practically closed for eighty years in consequence of the Hussite Wars, were reopened in 1492. Early in the sixteenth century some Nürnberg capitalists established iron forges in Thuringia and they were also actively engaged in copper mining. Apparently, in all these cases, commerce gave these enterprising undertakers their first start; the mineral resources of Germany, though not unknown, had been neglected; but money made in commerce was available in the fifteenth century to work the mines, and large fortunes were gained in connexion with these operations. Even before the discovery of

America, with her extraordinary treasure, there had been considerable additions to the supply of silver in Europe; it is easy to see that the Augsburg merchants were able to secure the means of hoarding, and of thus amassing wealth which they were eager to use as capital in any direction offering a profit.

Though Augsburg and its neighbourhood had afforded excellent facilities for the formation of capital, it gradually ceased to be the best centre for making profitable investments. The changed political conditions of Europe and the new discoveries had to some extent interfered with the traffic on the great route from the Adriatic by the Brenner and the Inn; the commerce of Venice was declining, relatively even to that of some other Italian cities. The Genoese secured a practical monopoly in the wool trade between the North and Italy by the valley of the Rhone; and after the fall of the Greek Empire at Constantinople they had been permitted by the Turks to establish a factory there. Florence, by her victory over Pisa, and her agreement with Genoa as to Leghorn, was becoming a considerable naval Power; and the trade with Morocco offered the opportunity for the rise of a new Florentine commercial aristocracy. Venice had lost much of her old importance as a trading centre; and a large proportion of the traffic which was maintained between the Adriatic and the Low Countries was now conducted by sea. Augsburg, formerly situate on one of the great routes of the world's trade, found that the stream of commerce had been diverted; its merchants recognised the trend of affairs, and began to establish themselves in the Low Countries. They could gather the threads of old connexions there; the Genoese were in the habit of frequenting Bruges; but the Venetians despatched some of their galleys to its rising competitor Antwerp, and in this city an Augsburg capitalist, Ludwig Menting, established a business in 1474. The other leading houses subsequently followed this example, and Antwerp came to be the chief centre for the financial operations of the great German capitalists. Their fortunes were not inseparably linked with the prosperity of the town of their origin; capital is fluid, and can be easily transferred from one city or one employment to another. The Fuggers and Welsers and other Augsburg capitalists were ready to adapt themselves to the changed conditions of business; the centre of the world's commerce was shifting, but they would not submit to be kept back from having a share in the new developments of trade and finance.

At the beginning of the sixteenth century Antwerp afforded unexampled opportunities to enterprising men of any nationality who had wealth at their command and were anxious to engage in commerce. The Portuguese had opened direct trading intercourse with the East; but they were too busily engaged in securing their footing in the Indies, and in prosecuting the distant trades, to have energy to spare for increasing their shipping in northern waters. They left to other merchants the business of distributing to European consumers the spices and other valuable products which were imported to Lisbon; and Antwerp, from her position and still more from her policy, became the chief centre of the capitalists who were ready to take a part in this profitable commerce.

The organisations for intermunicipal commerce in the Middle Ages hampered the enterprising capitalist, as they tended to confine him to dealings in one particular class of goods and to limit the amount of his transactions. The modern capitalist desires to be free to engage in any promising venture, and to push his business as fast as he can; but to this the medieval merchants hardly aspired. To secure a footing at some particular port was a difficult and costly business; and when they succeeded in this they organised the trade with care, so as to avoid flooding the market with their imports, and to ensure that all who joined in maintaining the factory and in contributing to the expenses of the establishment should have a share of the available trade. The old merchant organisations, with their particular privileges, their private factories, and "well-ordered trade," were a mere encumbrance at a time when the main routes of the world's commerce were being shifted; the real chance of rising to fortune lay with the men who were free to adapt themselves to these changing conditions; and Antwerp was a town which imposed little restriction on the employment of capital in any direction. The Merchant Adventurers had transferred their factory from Bruges to Antwerp in 1446; but they were almost the only traders who enjoyed special privileges in the city on the Scheldt. English commerce had given a great impetus to the growth of the town, which also became a staple for the products of Holland, and eventually secured much of the trade in fish, barley, and salt that had been previously carried on at Malines. The men of Antwerp were thus brought into direct antagonism with other Flemish cities, and were forced, almost unconsciously perhaps, to adopt an economic policy in consonance with the requirements of the coming age. The towns which followed the traditional scheme tried to make outside commerce directly subservient to their particular interests as producers or consumers; the men of Antwerp were merely concerned to increase the volume of trade and to take advantage of any benefit that happened to accrue; they bought out the rights of the landowners who took tolls on the Scheldt and made their city a centre of free intercourse, where men of all nations were welcome to engage in trade on equal terms. During the Middle Ages the only opportunities for such unrestricted intercourse had occurred at fairs; Antwerp owed its first importance to one of these gatherings, and so far as its economic institutions were concerned it was not so much a city as a permanent fair. Hence it was most natural that the German capitalists, who saw that traffic was being diverted to new centres, should emigrate to a town which offered the fewest restrictions to their operations as merchants or financiers. Bruges was completely distanced at the close of the fifteenth century; it continued for a time to be the privileged resort of Spanish merchants; but it lay off the line of Portuguese trading connexions. The German merchants, who had been the distributors of the spices imported by the Venetians, now became the principal intermediaries in connexion with the cargoes brought from the East to Lisbon, which was frequented by the factors of the principal German houses, though Antwerp was the chief centre of their commercial operations.

It followed, almost as a necessary consequence of the commercial activity of Antwerp, that this city soon became a great monetary centre; in this respect again it had the character of a permanent fair. The fairs of the Middle Ages had been the great occasions for financial transactions of every kind; rates for making remittances could be easily quoted, and loans could be negotiated to run to the date of the next fair; there was a sort of clearing-house at each fair for settling the transactions that took place during its continuance. One district after another had been the principal scene of these operations; the fairs of Champagne had given place to those of Geneva; Geneva had been superseded by Lyons, which Charles VIII found a convenient place for making payments to his Swiss mercenaries. In the sixteenth century Antwerp took the lead; it was a money-market where there was less organisation and more freedom for negotiating loans than at Lyons; business was carried on with little variation all the year round and was not restricted by the definite dates fixed by the occurrence of the fair; nor was there any attempt to fix a normal rate of exchange, as had been the practice at Lyons. The merchant had far better opportunities here than elsewhere of borrowing capital at the moment when he required it, and for the precise term desired by him; so that mercantile life at Antwerp had many features in common with the commercial centres of the modern era. The discovery of the New World, with its enormous treasure of precious metals, introduced an extraordinary confusion into economic relations in Europe. There are many unsolved problems as to the course of the distribution of the American silver and the effects produced by it in different countries; but at all events we can see that the money-market at Antwerp was so arranged as to be capable of taking a very effective part in the transference of the precious metals from country to country, and in facilitating the application of capital to new enterprises.

These monetary and commercial conditions were favourable to rapid growth; and Antwerp rose quickly from comparative unimportance to be the leading city of Europe. She was enriched by her connexions with Lisbon and the spice-trade of the Portuguese; she did not, however, remain a mere trading city but became a manufacturing town as well.

There was a considerable migration of German industry in the wake of German capital: both the linen and the fustian manufacture were attracted to a region from which there was such easy access to distant markets. The prosperity of the town increased by leaps and bounds, until in 1576 the Spanish Fury dealt it a blow from which it never recovered.

Though her greatness was short-lived, Antwerp occupies a very important place in the transition from medieval to modern commerce; for her merchants are said to have developed the modern system of commission-business. In the Middle Ages every possible obstacle had been put in the way of such transactions. Each merchant travelled personally with his own goods, or consigned them to a factor who acted exclusively as the representative of a single employer. Each city was cautious about admitting outsiders to any trading privileges within its walls; and no merchant, who was free to carry on business himself, was allowed to "colour" the goods of an unfree trader, or to act as his broker. At Antwerp no such jealousy of outsiders existed: any one might settle and commence trade, and there was no objection to his doing business for the men of any city, or on any terms that suited him. This implied an immense reduction in the cost of maintaining agencies and in the incidental expenses of trade; and when once the new system got a fair trial, there could be no doubt that it had come to stay.

The rise of Antwerp is also significant of the change in the centre of gravity of the world's commerce which has occurred, since ocean voyages have become the chief means of mercantile intercourse. The Mediterranean ports were left stranded, and Lisbon failed to take their place. The trade which had been opened up by Portuguese enterprise did not react on home industries, or give increased and profitable employment to productive labourers. The carrying trade between Lisbon and Antwerp was largely taken up by the merchants of Holland, who had ships and sailors engaged in fishing, and these could be easily and remuneratively employed in other waters. The Iberian peninsula offered an immense market for the salt-fish, the cloth, and linen of the Low Countries; Antwerp merchants had the means of purchasing the products brought from the East. While the energies of the Spaniards and Portuguese were thrown into the task of establishing their power in the Indies, and prosecuting distant trade, the Netherlanders reaped much of the profit of carrying goods in European waters, and their industrial and maritime activity was greatly stimulated. Antwerp obtained for a time that supremacy in the world's commerce, which has never since been wrested from northern ports.

The discussion of the application of capital to commerce, and of the changes in business practice which it introduced, have led us far away from the rise of the Augsburg merchants in the fifteenth century. We should have to turn back to a very early time in order to trace the first beginnings of the influence which capital exercised on manufactures; indications of it can be found in the thirteenth century, but it was at that date quite exceptional. Medieval industrial organisation usually consisted of a number of separate gilds, each composed of independent craftsmen; these associations had the power of regulating the trades with which they were respectively connected, subject to the approval by municipal or royal authority of the manner in which they exercised their rights, and of the particular rules which they framed. If we are careful to remember that, while this was the ordinary state of affairs, it was not universal in all cities, that its origin was not the same in all places and that it did not hold good equally in all trades, we may look a little more closely at the economic features and conditions of this type of organisation.

The craft-gild was formed with reference to the requirements of a particular city, and looked to a very limited circle of the public for the demand for goods. Part of its function was to see that the quality of the goods was maintained; but its policy was chiefly determined by a desire to give each member his fair share of the available employment. Each master was to have his chance, and none was allowed, by unduly multiplying the number of apprentices or journeymen, to supplant other workmen. These restrictions told in favour of the good training of apprentices, and improved their chance of employment as journeymen after they had served their time, but the rules hampered any man who was trying to push his business and manufacture on a large scale.

The master workman would be in the habit of buying on his own account the material which he required, or he might have the advantage of purchasing wholesale in association with other members of the craft; he would also sell the finished article to the man who wished to use it—the consumer; in some crafts, such as the tailors', an even more primitive practice was long maintained, and the craftsman worked on materials furnished to him by the consumers. Hence we can see that there were two points at which the intervention of the capitalist would easily occur. In the case of goods exported to a distant market, when an exporting merchant was the customer, he might find it convenient to have them manufactured under his direction and at his time instead of procuring them from an independent craftsman; the transition was easy from the position of a constant purchaser to that of an employer. On the other hand, when goods were made from imported materials, it was convenient for the merchant to retain his ownership in the materials and employ craftsmen to work them up. The effect of drawing any industry into the circle of distant trade with reference either to the materials or to the vent for the product, was to render capitalist intervention almost inevitable; when the capitalist system is thoroughly adopted, the employer owns the materials and also undertakes to act as an intermediary in the disposal of finished goods. It is needless to observe that, when this transition is complete, it becomes the interest of the employer to push his trade and to turn over his capital as rapidly as may be; he has to cater for a varying market, and the restrictions devised for those who have been sharing the employment afforded by a known market would not suit him at all.

There were some industries, however, in great commercial centres, which from their first planting were dependent, either for materials or for the vent of their products, on distant trade. Organisation, in such callings, was almost certain to proceed on capitalist lines; the rules laid down by the leading men were devised by great employers, and not, as in the craft-gilds, by small masters who personally worked at the trade. The working and dressing of cloth at Florence was dependent on the importation of undressed cloths, which were converted into excellently finished fabrics and exported on profitable terms. This *Arte di Calimala* appears to have been organised and regulated as a capitalist industry from the earliest times; and the *Arte di Lana*, which was dependent on the importation of raw wool from the North, was also an association of wealthy employers. The *Arte di Seta* was another long-established industry; it had been improved by immigrants from Lucca in the early part of the fourteenth century, and was conducted on similar lines. Capitalist organisation was not universal in industries of this commercial type; for we find that the silk-trade of Venice in the thirteenth century was regulated by small masters, who were however dependent on the services of merchants for securing a stock of materials to be used in regular work and for selling the fabrics of the looms; it need be no matter of surprise, that a change had occurred before the most flourishing period of the Venetian silk-trade in the fifteenth century, and that merchants were engaged in it as capitalist employers.

The capitalist organisation of industry was not confined to the more advanced communities, but might be found in the most backward countries, when the commercial conditions were favourable. In the twelfth and thirteenth centuries, when there was little export of cloth, weavers' gilds existed in London, Winchester, Beverley, and other centres, and the trade was probably conducted by independent workmen. But the clothing-trade of England was developed with increasing success, so that in the fifteenth century large quantities of woollen cloths were exported; it was evidently assuming the conditions of a capitalist trade, and was being organised by large employers. In England the transition to the new condition of affairs took place with little friction; weaving began to be practised in villages where civic gilds had no jurisdiction, and the quality of the product was inspected by a royal officer, so that the capitalist system of giving out materials to the weavers and buying their cloth was able to make its way imperceptibly.

In continental towns, where there was a large number of independent masters strongly organised in craft-gilds, a very decided antagonism prevailed between the old order and the new that was being gradually introduced. In France the *corps-de-métier* assumed a more and more oligarchical character, as increasing obstacles were being put in the way of journeymen who aimed at attaining the *status* of independent masters. A further indication of the same tendency, and of the differentiation of the journeymen as a permanent class within the trade, is found in the existence of journeyman gilds at Strassburg and elsewhere. The rise of a wealthy capitalist class within a craft-gild tended on the one hand to change the character of the old association and to make it a company of capitalists and traders, each of whom employed a large number of paid workmen; and, on the other hand, to call forth associations among the journeymen who had little hope of attaining to a higher *status* as independent masters, and who were therefore interested in maintaining favourable conditions for a wage-earning class. In other cases the pressure of the changed conditions was most severely felt by the small masters, since the men with large capital and a growing trade were able to pay better wages; the capitalists and journeymen were then united in opposition to the small masters, who desired to retain the restrictions imposed by the old craft-gilds.

Where the conservative policy was successful and the small independent masters held their own, the results were not satisfactory; the craft-gilds could maintain the old rules, but they could not control the course of trade; business migrated to the centres where it could be conducted on capitalistic lines. In Flanders and in England we hear much of the conflict between urban and suburban workmen; this antagonism was partly due to the fact that the journeymen were inclined to migrate to districts where the rules which prevented them from setting up in business or working for capitalist employers could not be enforced. The trend of affairs was going against the old type of craft-gild; and these institutions, in so far as they were incompatible with the investment of capital in industrial occupations, were bound to pass away.

To some extent, however, they proved to be compatible with the new order; the craft-gilds played an important part by exercising a right of search, and by insisting that the wares exposed for sale should be good in quality. Both in France and in England they were retained to some extent as convenient instruments for the royal or parliamentary control of the conditions of work and the quality of the output; occasionally, too, they retained their name and tradition, though they had changed their character and become associations of employers. At the close of the sixteenth century the organisation of industry by capitalists, which had been exceptional in the fourteenth century, had come to be an ordinary arrangement in the principal manufacturing centres.

The freedom thus obtained for capitalist administration proved of immense importance in facilitating the planting of industries at new centres and in undeveloped lands. Under no circumstances is this a simple task; but in the Middle Ages and in the earlier part of modern times it could only be accomplished by transferring skilled labour from one place to another. It was through the migration of great employers, with the labour which followed in their wake, that the silk-trade was developed in Venice, Bologna, Genoa, Florence, and France; that an improved manufacture of woollen cloth was introduced into England under Edward III; that the Spanish cities responded in some degree to the call made upon them by colonial demand, and that the manufactures of linen, glass, and pottery were introduced into France. A most remarkable development of industry in the fifteenth century seems to have been carried through by the Florentine capitalists, who were interested in the dressing and dyeing of cloth. They devoted themselves to encouraging the weaving of cloth in the wool-growing lands of the North, in order to command a supply of the half-manufactured goods which could be so finished at Florence as to be a most valuable article of commerce. In medieval times the industrial system had been intensely local in character; but as capital and capitalist organisation were introduced, the local attachments were severed one by one; in the new era the great employer is prepared to carry on business in any place and under any government where there is good prospect of working at a profit.

In the preceding sections an attempt has been made to show how the rising power of capitalism broke down the medieval forms of commercial and industrial regulation; the capitalists, who could not dominate them, migrated to places where they were free from old-fashioned restrictions. Capital offered facilities for the planting of new industries, the development of trade, and the opening up of mines and other natural advantages; so that the means lay at hand for promoting material progress of every kind. Hence new questions of economic policy came to the front. The efforts of traders were no longer confined to retaining exclusive commercial rights; but they began to consider how the various resources within a given area might be developed, so that by the interaction of different interests the greatest material prosperity might be attained in the community as a whole. We have already seen that in the fifteenth century the French monarchs had come to be directly interested in the welfare of the trading as well as in that of the landed classes; and at this period some of the German princes were becoming alive to the necessity of paying attention to all the different elements in the community. Other influences were at work elsewhere which tended to the growth of a new economic system; many of the cities of Italy and of Germany had become great territorial Powers, and, with a keen eye to business, they were endeavouring to devise schemes of policy which should enable them to reap the greatest advantage from their acquisitions.

It is of course true that many European cities had from the earliest period of their development had landed possessions and agricultural interests, and that the burgesses had enjoyed rights in respect of tillage and pasturage. But the questions which arose under these old circumstances were very different from those which presented themselves to citizens ruling over a large province and controlling the development of a considerable territory. Several of the cities of Italy and of the Rhineland had attained to great political importance in the early part of the fourteenth century; in some cases they were successful in military operations and extended their domain by conquest; in others the power of some city promised protection and attracted neighbours to commend themselves to a civic superior; in other instances land temporarily assigned to some town as a pledge for money borrowed was permanently transferred, when the borrower proved quite unable to repay his debt. In these various ways civic control came to be exercised over considerable areas, and civic authorities were concerned in regulating a large territory, with its distinct and conflicting interests, in such a way as to produce the best results for the commonwealth as a whole.

The great Italian towns, which were the seats of manufactures, had considerable difficulty in obtaining a sufficient food-supply for the very large population which had been attracted to them, or had grown up within their walls. Venice was forced to control the agricultural produce of her own district, and to prevent all other towns, such as Ancona, Ferrara and Bologna, from competing with her in Lower Italy, the district from which she obtained corn, eggs, and other produce; to purchase these commodities, the neighbouring towns were compelled to frequent the Venetian market. Florence and Milan, Bern and Basel, Ulm and Strassburg had alike to give close attention to the question of food-supply, and pursued a similar object, though with such modifications as the special circumstances of each town might suggest.

There was a marked contrast between the expedients adopted by the Venetians and those which commended themselves to the Florentines. The merchant princes of Florence bought large estates in Tuscany, and devoted themselves to agriculture. The conditions of the rural population were such that capitalist farming could be easily introduced; serfdom had entirely disappeared in this neighbourhood, and money dealings permeated the whole fabric of rural society; but agriculture cannot have been a very profitable investment. The policy of the city was that of providing cheap food for the consumer; export was forbidden, and the price at which corn might be sold was fixed by a tariff.

Free access was given to food-stuffs imported from abroad, so that the farmer was not only restricted in his operations, but was obliged to contend with foreign competitors in the home markets. There is reason to believe that this policy must have pressed with great severity on the rural population; a *maximum* was fixed for the wages of labour; and the terms of their contracts were such that the loss from bad seasons fell on the cultivating tenants rather than the proprietor. The depression of the rural inhabitants in the interest of the consumers was disastrous; but many communities besides Florence were tempted to pursue this policy. It seemed as if the peasant could be forced to carry on the work of tillage, whatever pressure was put upon him; there was little danger of his giving up rural occupations altogether, while the advantage of cheap food to an industrial and trading community was obvious.

The cities were also concerned in the wise management of such parts of their territory as were suitable for pasturage, partly for the sake of a supply of meat, but also with the view of procuring wool; the Florentines had large flocks upon the Maremma, for the obtaining of raw material was of primary importance to the *Arte di Lana*. We also find evidences of the introduction of sericulture in the neighbourhood of the towns where the weaving of silk had been introduced. The provision of raw material and of a proper food-supply were the two main points in the economic policy which the towns pursued in the large territories under their control.

This practice of treating town and country avocations as parts of one economic whole was commonly adopted, though it had hardly been definitely formulated in the fifteenth century; but the general principles which it involved had at least been so far thought out that they could be habitually assumed in the political writings of Machiavelli. He is quite clear as to the necessity of subordinating the interest of the citizen to that of the State; the civic policy of the Middle Ages had been that of severing different trading bodies and keeping them from encroaching on one another, rather than of subordinating all to an ulterior object. With Machiavelli the ulterior object towards which all commercial activities should be directed is the power of the prince. He points out that measures which tend to increase the wealth of the prince, without enriching the people, provide the firmest basis for absolute power.

Such ideas were widely current at the beginning of the sixteenth century, and they may easily have affected the statesmen who were guiding the destinies of the rising nationalities of Europe. In many countries all the elements that combine to form true national life were present; for there was a common stock, a common language, and a common law. But the fusion was incomplete and local divisions were deep and real. The ambitions which were opened up by the age of discovery strengthened national sentiment by affording an unlimited field for national rivalries; and the religious differences, which accentuated the divisions of Christendom, rendered the sense of national religion a convenient badge in warfare. These positive elements in the growth of national life were strengthened in any country where a territorial economic policy was adopted, so as to bring out a community of interest among the citizens, and to give solidarity to the whole social system. Definite schemes for the development of material resources, with a view to one supreme object, involved the suppression of local privileges and the increase of commercial intercourse; and this tended in its turn to give the opportunity for the healthy interaction of rural, urban, and commercial life upon each other. As the economic life of a country adapted itself to these new conditions, and as appropriate institutions were organised, the body economic came to be reconstituted on a national, not as of old, on a civic basis. The recognition of ties of common interest throughout a large territory gave definite shape to the groups which were pervaded by similar sentiments of race and religion. The sense of economic welfare as something common to the whole of a country strengthened the bonds which united each rising nationality in a common economic life, that was of importance to all citizens alike.

In the earlier sections of this chapter it has seemed convenient to deal chiefly with the rise of capital and the influence of its growing power over the economic institutions of medieval cities. The city was the type of economic organisation which had flourished in the ancient and in the medieval world; but it was not adequate to the requirements of modern life, and the old associations were disintegrated and destroyed. In the sixteenth century we see the signs of real reconstruction, and the growth of economic institutions and regulations which were compatible with capitalistic enterprise both in industry and commerce; even though this was still restricted within limits that we regard as narrow. One nation after another adopted a territorial economic policy, which implied the conscious subordination of certain private interests to the welfare of the realm, the conscious development of the resources of the country, and the conscious building up of the sinews of national power. The main feature of this territorial economic policy was similar in the case of all nations; all the rivals desired to accumulate treasure, as the means of equipping or of hiring armies; but there were different methods by which this aim could be attained, and different subordinate objects to be pursued, according to the circumstances of each particular country. To these we must now turn; for by briefly tracing the special schemes of territorial development which were adopted in Spain, England, and France respectively, we shall see most clearly the nature of the enlarged body economic which has come into prominence in modern times.

The discovery of America by Colombo gave the Spaniards access to an enormous territory of which they were complete masters, and which they were free to develop on any lines that seemed good to them. It is no part of our present purpose to discuss by itself the colonial policy which the monarchs followed; we have rather to consider the aims pursued by them for their empire as a whole. The large mass of bullion that was imported, together with the great commercial opportunities that were opened up, exercised a remarkable influence upon economic conditions in the peninsula. The amount of gold and silver which the Spaniards acquired was quite unprecedented, and might have been used to form a very large capital indeed. The West India islands supplied increasing quantities of gold from the time of their discovery until 1516. In 1522 the exploitation of Mexico began; silver was acquired in greater and greater masses, and the introduction, in 1557, of a simpler process of reduction of the ore by means of quicksilver diminished the cost of production and still farther augmented the yield of bullion. In 1533 the Spaniards also obtained access to Peru, from which additional supplies of silver were procured. Altogether, an enormous stream of bullion poured into Spain during the whole of the sixteenth century.

The Spaniards were able to rely on the best possible advice as to the organisation of business of every kind. Genoese financiers were ready to give every assistance, and the South-German capitalists, who had so much experience of mining and enterprise of every sort, were closely attached to the interests of Charles V; after his accession to the throne of Spain they were attracted to that country in large numbers, as great privileges were conferred upon them. They were able to take part in colonisation, and to engage directly in mining. The Fuggers undertook to develop the quicksilver deposits of Almaden; they formed business connexions in the New World, and founded settlements in Peru. The Welsers established a colony in Venezuela, and undertook copper-mining in San Domingo. There was at the same time an incursion, chiefly to Seville, of other German capitalists, who were prepared to devote their energies to developing the industrial arts of Spain. With all these material and technical advantages it seems extraordinary that the dreams of Charles V and Philip II were not realised, and that they failed to build up such a military power as would have enabled them to establish a complete supremacy in Europe.

It would be exceedingly interesting if we were able to examine in detail the extent to which the precious metals came into circulation in Spain, and the precise course of economic affairs in different parts of the country; but the material for such an enquiry does not appear to be forthcoming. Yet one thing is obvious; the Spanish colonists devoted themselves almost entirely to mining for the precious metals, and they were largely dependent for their supply of food of all kinds on the mother country. This caused an increased demand for corn in Spain and a rapid rise of prices there, as the colonists were able to pay large sums for the necessaries of life. Charles V, indeed, endeavoured to carry out works of irrigation, and to increase the food-supply by bringing a larger area under cultivation. But tillage could not be developed so as to meet the new demands. The methods of cultivation already in vogue were as high as was generally practicable in the existing state of society; the vine- and olive-growers on the one hand, and the pasture-farmers on the other, resented any encroachments on the land at their disposal, so that it was impossible to bring a larger area under crop. So powerful were the *Mesta*, a great corporation of sheep-farmers, that they were actually able in 1552 to insist that Crown- and Church-land which had been brought under tillage should revert to pasture. The result was inevitable; food became dearer, and the government was forced to recognise the fact by raising the *maximum* limit of price; as a consequence, the necessary outlay of all classes increased, while a large part of the population were not compensated by the profit obtained through the new facilities for trade.

Under ordinary circumstances the increase in the price of food would have been merely injurious to industry; it would necessitate a larger outlay in the expenses of production, and would leave less margin for profit, and no opportunity for the formation of capital. Ultimately, this seems to have been the effect on Spanish manufactures, and the high cost of production in the peninsula rendered it possible for other European countries, where the range of prices was lower, to undersell the Spanish producer in the home market. No serious attempt was made by the government to check this tendency, as the policy pursued was in the main that of favouring the consumer, and protective tariffs were not introduced.

The circumstances which prevailed in Spain at the opening of the sixteenth century were, however, quite exceptional, and as a matter of fact there seems to have been a considerable, though short-lived, development of industry. The colonists not only imported their food, but manufactures as well; there was a sudden increase in the demand both for textile goods and for hardware, to meet the American requirements, and of course there was a great rise of prices. The small independent masters, working on the old industrial system, were unable to cope with this new state of affairs; but the foreign capitalists saw their opportunity. Manufacturing of every kind was organised on a large scale at Toledo and other centres; wages rose enormously, and a great influx of population was attracted into the city. This was doubtless drawn to some extent from the rural districts; but the stream must have been considerably augmented by the immigration of French and Italians. Hence it appears that this rapid industrial development was merely an excrescence, which had no very deep attachment to the country; the

Spaniards themselves appear to have regarded it as an intrusion, and to have resented it accordingly. The Spanish gentry had no means of paying the increased prices which the colonial demand had occasioned, for natural economy was still in vogue in many rural districts. Indeed, this revolution in industry must have given rise to many social grievances; the craftsman of the old school would suffer from the competition of the capitalist in his own trade, while the great rise of prices to consumers was attributed to the greed of the foreigner. The government was persuaded to pass measures which imposed disabilities on foreign capitalists; it succeeded in forcing the withdrawal of the French and Italian workmen, as well as in expelling the *Moriscos*. As these changes ensued, the foreign capitalists were doubtless successful in transferring large portions of their capital to other lands; but the decline of alien competition on Spanish soil did not enable native manufacturers to take their place or to recover the lost ground. With the new scale of outlay they had little opportunity for forming capital, and the *bourgeois* class may not have had the skill for organising business on the new lines. On the whole it appears that the large colonial demands for food on the one hand, and the large supplies of foreign manufactures on the other, prevented a healthy reaction of commercial on agricultural and industrial development; Spain was left exhausted by the feverish activity which had been temporarily induced, and which passed away.

The Spanish government was firmly convinced that the best means of promoting the power of the country was by hoarding the large share of the produce of the mines which came into their possession, and they made frequent efforts to prevent the export of any bullion into other parts of Europe, though the Genoese and German capitalists had special licenses which allowed them to transmit it. It is obviously impossible that the government could have succeeded in enforcing this prohibition, under the existing conditions of trade; most of the bullion which arrived at Seville belonged to the merchants and manufacturers who were concerned in supplying the colonial demand for goods. The ingots which were not taken to the mint may have been hoarded for a time; but the foreign capitalists would not allow their money to lie idle, and much of it must have been exported, in spite of all laws to the contrary, to pay for the cheaper manufactures which were coming in from abroad. Comparatively little coin could have passed into general circulation in Spain itself; payments from the towns for agricultural produce would scarcely overbalance the payments due from the country for the dearer manufactured goods.

The Spanish rulers had ignorantly and unintentionally pursued the precise course of policy recommended by Machiavelli. They had sought to accumulate treasure in the coffers of the State, and they had by their mistaken measures allowed the subjects to continue poor.

The wealth which passed into the country had no steady and persistent reaction on industrial and agricultural life; and when the military exigencies of Philip's policy reduced him to bankruptcy, it became obvious to the world that the Spaniards had completely misused the unique opportunities which lay within their grasp. They had sacrificed everything else to the accumulation of treasure by the Crown, and they had completely failed to attain the one object on which they had concentrated all their efforts.

The permanent gain from the treasure imported into Europe went to those countries which were able to employ it as capital for industrial or agricultural improvement, and Spain could do neither. There was every prospect, at one time, that the greatest advantage would be reaped by Spanish subjects in the Netherlands. The policy of the government, however, and the failure of the Duke of Alva to recognise the importance of trading interests, rendered this impossible. The War in the Low Countries not only caused the migration of industry from that part of Spanish territory, but tended to bring about the collapse of the great capitalists who had allied themselves to the Spanish interest. The foreigners were being gradually excluded from taking any direct part in the new industrial developments in Spain; they confined themselves more and more to banking business, and to financial operations in the government service. But the persistent failure of the Spanish and imperial policy in one country after another had the effect of crippling several of the great Genoese and German houses, and at length drained the resources even of such millionaires as the Fuggers. The decline of these bankers proved that the control of the treasure of the New World was passing into other hands; as a matter of fact it was shifting more and more into the possession of the Dutch, who were making their country a harbour of refuge for persons expelled from the Spanish Netherlands, and who were building up a great centre of commercial and industrial life at Amsterdam. At the beginning of the seventeenth century the people of Holland had succeeded in winning the greater part of the gains which accrued from the Portuguese discoveries, while they had also succeeded in drawing to themselves a large share of the treasure of Spanish America, and in using it as capital in commerce, in shipping, and in industrial pursuits. It was the nemesis of the policy of his Catholic Majesty that his subjects failed to derive real advantage from the much vaunted American possessions, and that the gains which might have enriched the peninsula went to his bitterest enemies.

In the middle of the sixteenth century, England was not a competitor with Spain and France for the sovereignty of the world; her political ambition was far humbler; the dangers that threatened her were so imminent, and her means of defence so insufficient, that it was only by devoting great care to the development of her resources that she could hope to retain political independence. William Cecil found himself called upon to guide the destinies of the realm, at a time when the country was destitute of munitions of war. Elizabeth's Protestantism seriously interfered with the opportunities of procuring military stores; the chief supply of saltpetre and sulphur, which were required for gunpowder, as well as of the metals which were necessary for the making of ordnance, came from ports controlled by the great Roman Catholic Powers. The native mining industries were quite undeveloped, and England could easily have been prevented from purchasing copper and iron from abroad. Woollen cloth was the chief export from the country; but alum, which was used in the processes of dyeing and finishing, was obtained from Ischia, an island which belonged to the Pope. A hoard of bullion, laid up against possible emergencies, was a political luxury which Cecil could not afford; all the resources that the Crown could dispose of, either as personal possessions, or by influence exercised on loyal subjects, were devoted to the planting of industries which directly subserved the strength of the realm and rendered it less hopelessly unprepared for the struggle that could not be indefinitely postponed. When the storm burst at last, and England had to get ready for meeting the Spanish Armada, it was found that the leeway had been entirely made up, and that English guns and gunners were as good as those of Spain, and better too.

It would in any case have been useless for Cecil to imitate the Spanish policy and amass bullion to serve for the payment of mercenaries. England had no access to silver mines, and she was forced to rely on her own sons to man her fleets and to serve in her armies. It was essential to adhere to the policy which was even then traditional in England, and to take pains that there should be a well-diffused and healthy population. With this end in view, the government was specially anxious to maintain tillage, as an avocation which gave employment to vigorous labourers; and agriculture came to be encouraged, not merely on economic but on military grounds. In a similar way, much attention was paid to securing favourable conditions for the maintenance of a large sea-faring population. The fishing trades were important as a source of wealth, but even more so as a school of seamanship and a ready way of training men who should be capable of serving in naval warfare; this employment was artificially stimulated, and people were compelled by law to eat fish on three days in the week. The special exigencies of the situation forced Cecil to devote the greatest possible care to developing native resources of every kind in such a fashion that they should, as much as possible, contribute directly to the national strength. The government was of course aware that the general increase of industrial skill and of commercial activity was likewise of importance; in the actual circumstances of England these were the only means of procuring treasure at all; but, since the supply could only be secured indirectly, it was not treated as an immediate, far less as an exclusive object, as it had been with the Spaniards.

The method which Cecil adopted for carrying out these aims presents another interesting contrast with the course of affairs in Spain. He had, indeed, to obtain assistance from the group of Augsburg capitalists who had taken such a leading part in European finance; but he relied on them rather for their technical skill and enterprise in organising undertakings, than for the capital with which new schemes were carried out. The usual plan was to grant a concession to a company, the capital being subscribed in England, though the management was controlled by the Hochstetters and other German adventurers. By these means, the arts of brass-founding and wire-drawing were planted, and mining for the useful metals was largely carried on. Most important of all was the skill of German engineers; their methods of pumping water were introduced, and rendered mining possible where it had never been practised before. Not only the hardware trades, but whatever other industry was subsidiary to any of the forms of national strength, came under Cecil's special care; among these may be instanced the manufacture of sailcloth, which he was at personal pains to promote.

The government looked with a favourable eye on the introduction of useful industries of any kind; but especially welcomed those which consisted in the working up of native products, and which would save the necessity of importing finished goods from abroad. The favourite mode of encouragement was one which cost the Crown nothing, while yet it encouraged alien adventurers to do their best. Exclusive privileges for the exercise of the trade were granted, and in this way the manufacture of glass, paper, starch, soap, and other commodities of common consumption were successfully established. Circumstances were specially favourable to such attempts at this particular time. England served as a haven of refuge for many of the artisans who were dispersed by the wars in the Netherlands, and skilled workmen emigrated hither even from such distant countries as Greece, Italy, and Spain. Some of them appear to have possessed capital, and many of them were highly skilled in departments of industry which had been practically unrepresented in England.

The dislike felt by Englishmen for foreigners was almost as strong as that of the Spaniards, and there was some little difficulty in disarming the local hostility to these settlers. The new industries were on the whole developed on capitalist lines; the old craft-gilds had ceased to be effective forces, and there was little serious opposition from them. In so far as native industrial organisation was reinvigorated in England towards the close of this reign, it took the form of capitalist associations, and these appear to have been for a time the strongholds of opposition to the alien invasion. The central government, however, was firm in its attitude of encouraging the immigrants, while it also desired so far as possible to merge them with the existing population, and to use them as means for the technical education of Englishmen. In this Cecil, who personally revised the regulations for settling the aliens, was singularly successful; though the Dutch and Walloon colonies were separately organised for social and religious purposes, they soon came to be highly appreciated by their neighbours as an important factor in the economic welfare of the country. Spain had suffered seriously by imposing disabilities on aliens, and England gained immensely by encouraging their immigration and absorbing them as an integral part of the nation.

The improvement of industry had a very favourable reaction on the progress of agriculture. At the beginning of Elizabeth's reign the condition of rural life was eminently unsatisfactory; an increasing area was being diverted from tillage to pasture-farming; the wool which was produced in such large quantities, and the cloth into which it was manufactured, fetched very high prices; this export-trade was un-doubtedly the channel through which a portion of the treasure from the New World began to flow into England. Beneficial as this de-velopment was in many ways, it yet entailed serious grievances in rural districts. The price of corn was relatively low, and there seemed to be a danger that the food-supply would fall short. Measures were devised for giving the farmer the best opportunity for selling his corn in any part of the country, and not unfrequently for exporting it on easy terms. Great pains were also taken to ensure that he should have an adequate supply of labour, and to encourage those particular forms of industry which were subsidiary to agricultural operations. In no other country of Europe were the interests of agriculture put so prominently forward. English statesmen realised that it was necessary to render tillage profitable if it was to be properly maintained, and progress in the industrial arts was treated as a subordinate consideration. As the demands of the industrial population for food increased, and as the improving marine of England gave access to markets abroad, those who were pursuing agriculture as a trade found that they could work at a profit. The revival of agriculture, moreover, was possible without a serious diminution of the area which was devoted to sheep. The conflict between the two rural interests in England was not so keen as in Spain. By the introduction of convertible husbandry, a better return could be obtained from the same acreage. The old common fields were broken up; land was occupied in severalty; and each farmer was free to pursue his avocation to the best of his ability and means. By this new method the land enjoyed long periods of rest, and the soil recovered from the exhausting effects of the persistent, though slovenly, tillage to which it had long been subjected. Enclosure and readjustment afforded the opportunity of greatly increasing the production from the land, without additional expenditure of capital.

The improvement of industry and tillage had very favourable effects on the commerce of the country. There was each year a larger and larger available surplus which could be exported. The export of English cloth came to be entirely in the hands of English shippers; and, when the opportunity at length occurred for England to plant colonies beyond the seas, she was able to meet their immediate necessities without any strain upon her internal condition. Partly through the force of circumstances, but partly also through the wisdom of the government, there was a development of the manufacture of native products, which reacted in a healthy and natural manner on the improvement of agriculture and the increase of trade. The admirable picture given in Hales' *Discourse of the Common Weal*, of the condition of affairs under Edward VI shows us the evils of the transition at a time when both the Crown and the people felt the pressure of poverty. This was in some ways more apparent than real, and was partly due to the debased condition of the coinage. When with the restoration of the currency England began to receive her share of the treasure of the New World, improvement proceeded rapidly. At the close of Elizabeth's reign the people were wonderfully prosperous, and the pauperism of earlier years had ceased to be a serious problem. The political future of England was largely affected by the fact that the industrial population was becoming wealthy while the Crown was relatively poor.

The rapidity with which countries may recover from the ravages of war has been often remarked upon; in no case was it more strikingly exemplified than by the marvellous growth of material prosperity in France, so soon as Henry IV was complete master of the realm. This can hardly be ascribed, however, to a natural recuperation after the removal of the disturbing causes; it was really due to the view which Henry and his advisers took of the duty of government, and the excellent manner in which they discharged their task. It was to the interest of the French monarchy, with its large income drawn from taxation, that measures should be taken to advance internal trade, to plant industries, and to improve agriculture, so that the people might be prosperous and able to contribute their quota to the revenue. Henry IV set himself consciously and deliberately to develop the material resources of France, and his schemes were so well devised that the foundations of the magnificent and powerful monarchy of Louis XIV were successfully laid. The King was admirably assisted by Sully, and profited from the suggestions of Laffemas and Olivier de Serres, who were respectively experts in the organisation of industry and in promoting agriculture; and he possessed, moreover, the means for carrying out the schemes that met his approval. The revival of France was brought about on royal initiative, by royal administrators, and to a large extent by drawing on royal wealth for the necessary capital.

A comparison with the position of the Crown in England, when Cecil was working for the development of the realm, may serve to point the contrast. Elizabeth was very poor, and she was particularly averse to summoning Parliament and levying taxation; she had little money to spare for encouraging improvements in rural and industrial pursuits that would only bring indirect gains to the government. The King of France had a large permanent income from taxation, and it was worth his while to invest a part of it in undertakings that were not directly remunerative; the increase of the wealth of its subjects was the surest method of increasing the prospective income of the Crown.

At the time when Sully became superintendent of finances in 1598, he had to face an enormous burden of debt, entailed by the expenses of the Wars in which Henry had rendered his possession of the throne secure. The debt amounted to no less than 348 million *livres*; loans had been obtained by pledging the personal estates of the King, as well as a large part of the receipts from taxation. Only a comparatively small portion of the *taille* was available for current expenditure. Sully's first care was to reform the abuses in the collection of the revenue; he completely overhauled the fiscal administration and rendered the incidence of taxation more equable; while, by cancelling heavy arrears of *taille*, he relieved the tax-payers from an intolerable burden, and placed them in a position of solvency which rendered it possible for them to meet the current demands of the government. By these means he was able to steadily diminish the burden of indebtedness, while there was money at command, not only for the expenses of the Court, but also for much-needed public works.

The most important undertaking was that of facilitating internal trade by improving the water-communication through different parts of France. Humphry Bradley, who had had much experience in Holland, was the principal engineer employed; in some cases rivers were opened to the passage of barges, while canals were also laid out to connect the river-basins, and thus to provide great channels of through communication; a canal was planned between the Garonne and the Aude to complete a water-way from the Bay of Biscay to the Mediterranean; and another to connect the Loire with the Seine was begun. Great engineering works were also undertaken in the way of banking and draining, so as to recover considerable stretches of land that were lying waste; and attempts were made to improve the facilities for travel by land, especially in the reconstruction of bridges. In many instances the town chiefly concerned defrayed part of this last expense; but the main burden generally lay with the government which had been responsible for initiating these improvements, and no less a sum than a million *livres* a year was devoted to the construction of main roads.

The policy pursued by the French Crown in the planting of industry is open to criticism; but it must at least be allowed to have attained success. France was already richly supplied with the necessaries of life, and considerable progress had been made in the useful arts; but large sums were expended yearly in the purchase of luxuries, and it seemed possible to introduce the manufacture of silk and artistic goods, so that there should be less reason for the drain of treasure, and that the country might be entirely self-sufficing, not only for necessaries, but also for luxuries. Sully was doubtful as to this policy; he would have preferred to check the use of luxuries by sumptuary laws, and to develop those industries in which French products were the materials employed. This objection was partly met by extensive efforts to introduce sericulture on French soil; and, on the whole, experience seems to have proved that the King was well-advised in following the example of Venice and Florence and trying to plant this new industry, even though it required large subventions at first. In the latter part of the seventeenth century it flourished to such an extent as to provide an important and valuable article of export trade, so that foreign customers had to pay a considerable balance in bullion. The manufacture of glass and that of fine pottery were introduced during this reign into various districts of France by persons who had special privileges conferred upon them; the tapestry-manufacture needed still further encouragement, and obtained a royal subvention of 100,000 *livres*, and a sum of 150,000 *livres* was lent to two merchants of Rouen who proposed to undertake the making of fine cloth. While such pains were taken to stimulate exotic and plant new industries, a very careful scheme was devised for the reorganisation of the *corps-de-métier*, so as to provide more effective supervision for the existing trades; attempts were made to check the preposterous claims of the " Kings of the Mercers," and to break down the arbitrary restrictions by which the *status* of master in any trade had been guarded. A Council of Commerce was established, which carried out some useful changes in particular trades, though it did not reconstitute the *corps-de-métier* as completely as might have been desirable. Their powers were, however, limited, and they were not allowed to obstruct enterprising individuals who were trying to introduce improved processes of manufacture; many abuses were checked, and these institutions as modified continued to be a convenient piece of administrative machinery.

The efforts that were made to improve agriculture also resulted in the stereotyping of the old social organisation. The King could not interfere to force on progress in the arts of tillage; all that could be done was to set an example of enterprise on the royal estates, and to bring pressure upon the magnates to follow it. The cultivators could only be effectively reached through the landed aristocracy, and there was a tendency to coerce them for their good by the exercise of seigniorial powers. The preservation of the relics of natural economy was also unfortunate, inasmuch as the *métayers* were thus cut off from the stimulating influence of the independent pursuit of their calling as a trade.

The French government was extraordinarily successful in consolidating the nation by these means. Separate and local interests were cared for; but they were always kept in conscious subordination to the prosperity of the entire realm. The views of Henry were on the whole most judicious, and the suddenness of the revival of French prosperity is a testimony to the effectiveness of the administration. But a heavy price was being paid for these advantages; the national economic life was rendered dependent on royal initiative and royal supervision; in subsequent times French industry suffered from the over-elaboration of administrative machinery, while the commercial and colonial development of the country was destitute of the healthy vigour called out where private enterprise was allowed free play.

The success of the royal policy in England and France presents a marked contrast to the failure of the Spanish monarch, whose ultimate aim was nevertheless the same; each prince desired to raise the whole land over which he ruled into the highest pitch of prosperity. It was impossible for Charles V or Philip II to accumulate the treasure which was so necessary for the country, and with the aid of which each hoped in his turn to become the most powerful ruler in the world. The American silver could not be kept in Spain, and there was so little native capital for use in that widely extended empire, that it declined. England, on the other hand, was consciously developed by the great middle class, who were ready to invest comparatively small sums in promising undertakings, while the government gave active support to the foreign capitalists and workers whose experience was so valuable. The English minister, Cecil, nursed the realm as carefully as if he were the steward of a private estate, but he was hampered by the poverty of the Crown, and his great work lay in stimulating other people to take the initiative and trust to themselves for their own remuneration.

As we have just seen the revival of France was due to the capital in the hands of the King, whose measures were largely innovations and experiments carried out in spite of opposition. In England the development of the country was carried on by the people, in France for the people; but both countries attained a high degree of national prosperity. Huge empires, like those of Macedonia and Rome, had already been familiar in the ancient world, but nations constituted like France and England were something quite new. The intimate union of all parts of such large areas and the interdependence of each part on the other, as well as the conscious subordination of local interests to the larger idea of "the realm,"—these were conceptions not merely distinct from the civic policy of the Middle Ages but equally foreign to the idea of the great polities of ancient days.

The nation is not only a new phenomenon, but it is the characteristic feature of what we are wont to call modern times; and hence the rise of Holland, as the heir of Portugal and a victor over Spain, the increased importance of England and the revival of France, mark an era in economic history. The transition from the medieval to the modern age has been accomplished; we are no longer concerned with the struggle of town with town, but of nation with nation, each trying to secure the greatest material advantages for its own land and its own people. The chief economic interest of the subsequent century lies in the study of the means taken by these three rivals to build up their own strength and to weaken their adversaries. Each had entered on a career of material prosperity, and each had adapted its system with more or less success to modern industrial and commercial conditions. It is worth while, however, to cast a retrospecting glance at some of the places which had been distanced in the race for wealth, and to enquire why so many of the cities which had attained to great prosperity in the fourteenth and fifteenth centuries failed to share in the extraordinary impulse which was given to progress by the discovery of the New World and its treasures. Some of them did not advance, and others distinctly declined.

The change of commercial routes was the most obvious reason for the decadence of some of the magnificent cities of the Middle Ages. Commerce takes the path of the least resistance, and none of the overland routes to the East or passes across the Alps could compare with the convenience of an unbroken voyage from the Moluccas to Amsterdam. The Italian and South-German towns which had been occupied with the Eastern trade, and the Baltic and Lithuanian cities which had been the great *dépôts* of the Hanse League, ceased to be the chief centres of commerce, and from the mere fact of their geographical position were left on a siding. In the case of Stettin and other towns which had been merely mercantile, and where there had been no success in developing industry as subsidiary to commerce, the decline of trade was a desperate blow. The towns which had developed an industrial life, Cologne and Strassburg, Augsburg and Nürnberg, Venice, Genoa, and Florence, did indeed suffer severely. They lost their facilities for access to the best markets or for the most convenient purchase of food and materials; but they were able to re-adapt themselves to their diminished opportunities, and to utilise their resources for the maintenance of a prosperous though less notable economic life.

Certain social conditions prevented some communities from adopting innovations which were necessary for maintaining the continuance of their prosperity. Where society had been very definitely organised and a social system was stereotyped, many insensible hindrances opposed themselves to modification of any kind. Success in the new order of things depended on adaptability. Capitalists were organising industry on other lines, and opening up wider commercial connexions. Those who were unable to adopt the modern methods of business were necessarily distanced in the race. The industrial centres where the craft-gilds had been most vigorous and had retained their power most successfully, were at a positive disadvantage in entering on competition with neighbours who had imposed no such restrictions. Modern nations have incorporated the towns which were formerly so powerful and which failed to maintain the leading position they once held; this has been in part at all events because their very success under the old system rendered them incapable of giving a cordial welcome to the new.

In conjunction with this social obstacle to progress may be specially noticed the antagonism which was felt in many quarters to the introduction or the retention of alien and seemingly incongruous elements of population. The strength of the capitalist system consists in its ability to utilise the most varied elements. Both Holland, and to a less extent England, in receiving immigrants from other countries, increased their industrial resources by that most precious of all national possessions,—great skill in industrial employments of every kind. Varieties of type and of intelligence have been of the greatest importance in introducing new methods of business and improved processes of production; France and Spain, on the contrary, suffered severely from the policy which insisted on assimilating the whole population to conformity in religious and political thought.

Such were the trading and social conditions which placed capital at a disadvantage, and which determined those who controlled it to seek opportunities for investment in other lands. But there was one occupation throughout Europe which offered little attraction to the enterprising capitalist, and which therefore continued to lie almost outside the sphere of his operations. The agricultural system on the Continent in general was highly stereotyped. In Germany and Hungary serfdom remained; in Spain, France, and Italy vestiges of natural economy survived. Such a reorganisation of the population as would have produced better results presented great difficulties; while the introduction of improved methods often involved an outlay of capital and a diminished rate of return. The small proprietary and cultivating peasantry were destitute of the means of introducing improvements, even if the value of the change had been apparent. Some public works for the benefit of agriculture were undertaken by the Crown both in France and Spain; but it was only in Holland where there was a plethora of capital, and in England where the trade of the farmer was encouraged, that private capitalists became interested in the improvement of the soil. There was, as a consequence, little alteration in the condition of the rural population, and the first changes which occurred with the gradual introduction of capitalism were often for the worse. It was left for the social and political revolutions of the last hundred years to sweep away the system which had been previously left untouched by economic progress.

These were the general conditions that determined the ultimate distribution of the treasure which was brought from the New World. Transferred in the sixteenth century, partly in response to military requirements, partly by successful depredation, and partly by mere smuggling, this treasure sooner or later found its way into the hands of agents of commerce, who desired to use it as capital and who employed it in the places and avocations where they had most reason to expect a large profit. The actual return depended partly on social, partly on physical conditions; but the results that followed were curious and unequal, for while some of the more backward countries moved rapidly forward, making huge strides in wealth and material prosperity, whole classes in every community and large districts of continental Europe remained almost stationary, untouched and unaffected by the march of progress.

Nevertheless, though these great economic movements were retarded, they could not be wholly arrested. Capitalism has gradually overcome the medieval obstacles; it has swept away local exclusiveness, and has been the means of developing large economic areas. A revolution has taken place in business practice, and the breaking down of commercial restrictions is a change which has affected the traders in all lands. Industry has become capitalistic, and the whole foundation of trading relations and commercial morality has been altered so as to open indefinite possibilities to every merchant. Civic has given place to national economic life. At the commencement of the seventeenth century neither Germany nor Italy had become true nations, but in the course of time the European peoples have come to conform more and more to the larger type of organisation that had already arisen in England and in France.

# CHAPTER XVI.

## THE CLASSICAL RENAISSANCE.

THE Renaissance, in the largest sense of the term, is the whole process of transition in Europe from the medieval to the modern order. The Revival of Learning, by which is meant more especially the resuscitated knowledge of classical antiquity, is the most potent and characteristic of the forces which operated in the Renaissance. That revival has two aspects. In one, it is the recovery of a lost culture; in another, of even higher and wider significance, it is the renewed diffusion of a liberal spirit which for centuries had been dead or sleeping. The conception which dominated the Middle Ages was that of the Universal Empire and the Universal Church. A gradual decadence of that idea, from the second half of the thirteenth century to the end of the fifteenth, was the clearest outward sign that a great change was beginning to pass over the world. From the twelfth century onwards there was a new stirring of minds, a growing desire of light; and the first large result was the Scholastic Philosophy. That was an attempt to codify all existing knowledge under certain laws and formulas, and so to reconcile it logically with the one Truth; just as all rights are referable to the one Right, that is, to certain general principles of justice. No revolt was implied there, no break with the reigning tendencies of thought. The direct aim of the Schoolmen was not, indeed, to bind all knowledge to the rock of St Peter; but the truth which they took as their standard was that to which the Church had given her sanction. In the middle of the fourteenth century, when Scholasticism was already waning, another intellectual movement set in. This was Humanism, born in Italy of a new feeling for the past greatness of Rome. And now the barriers so long imposed on the exercise of the reason were broken down; not all at once, but by degrees. It was recognised that there had been a time when men had used all their faculties of mind and imagination without fear or reproof; not restricted to certain paths or bound by formulas, but freely seeking for knowledge in every field of speculation, and for beauty in all the realms of fancy. Those men had bequeathed to posterity a literature different in quality and range from anything that had been written for a thousand years. They had left, too, works of architecture such that even the mutilated remains had been regarded by legend as the work of supernatural beings whom heathen poets had constrained by spells. The pagan view was now once more proclaimed, that man was made, not only to toil and suffer, but to enjoy. And naturally enough, in the first reaction from a more ascetic ideal, the lower side of ancient life obscured, with many men, its better aspects. It was thus that Humanism first appeared, bringing a claim for the mental freedom of man, and for the full development of his being. But, in order to see the point of departure, it is necessary to trace in outline the general course of literary tradition in Europe from the fifth century to the fourteenth.

The fall of the Western Empire in the fifth century was followed by a rapid decline of education and of general culture. The later ages of classical antiquity, if comparatively poor in the higher kind of literary genius, were still familiar with the best writers of Greece and Rome, and continued to be prolific in work inspired by good models. They also retained the traditions of that civilisation and social life out of which the classical literature had arisen. But the barbarian invaders of Italy and Gaul were strangers to that civilisation; they brought with them a life in which the ancient culture found no place. The schools of the Roman Empire were swept away, or died out. Such education as survived was preserved by the Church, and was almost wholly confined to ecclesiastics. Monasteries had begun to multiply in the West from the close of the fourth century. Their schools, and those attached to cathedrals, alone tempered the reign of ignorance. The level of the monastic schools was the higher. In the cathedral schools the training was usually restricted to such rudiments of knowledge as were indispensable for the secular clergy, viz., reading, writing, arithmetic, and elementary music. But even in the monastic schools the course was usually meagre and narrow. The superior education of the age was chiefly based on a few jejune text-books, compilations and abridgments from older sources. One of these was the treatise of the African rhetorician, Martianus Capella (flor. c. 420), on the *Septem Artes Liberales*,—grammar, logic, rhetoric, music, arithmetic, geometry, and astronomy. The form is allegorical; Mercury weds Philology, and at their nuptials assigns the Arts to her as handmaids. Capella was, however, regarded with disfavour by those Christian teachers who rigorously proscribed pagan literature; and his book, though it remained an authority down to the Renaissance, was not everywhere admitted. Thus it is absent from Alcuin's catalogue (made c. 770) of the library at York, a fairly representative collection of the books which then were most read. The Seven Arts had been distributed, so early as the fifth century, into the *trivium*, consisting of grammar, logic, and rhetoric, and the *quadrivium*, comprising the other four. Grammar was taught by excerpts from Donatus or Priscian; rhetoric, often with the aid of extracts from Cicero's *De Inventione* and *Topica*, or the treatise *Ad Herennium*. For the *trivium* generally a favourite text-book was Cassiodorus (d. 568), *De Artibus et Disciplinis Liberalium Artium*. For the *quadrivium*, and for the more advanced logic, the standard manuals were the treatises of Boetius (d. 524), which included some Latin transcripts from parts of Aristotle's *Organon*. Boetius, "the last of the Romans," was, indeed, an author of cardinal importance in the higher education of the earlier Middle Ages. Another standard work was an encyclopaedia of arts and sciences by Isidore, Bishop of Seville (d. 636), containing a mass of information in every recognised branch of knowledge (*Originum s. Etymologiarum libri XX*). It is characteristic of education in the Middle Ages that compendia of this poor kind had largely superseded their own classical sources in the ordinary use of the schools. Note should be taken also of the persistent tendency to look for allegorical and mystic senses beneath the literal meaning of a passage. This tendency dates at least from the teaching of Cassian (flor. c. 400), one of the chief founders of Western monachism. It was applied first to the Scriptures, and thence transferred to other books, with an influence which did much to vitiate the medieval study of literature.

The period from c. 500 to the latter part of the eighth century was that during which the general level of knowledge in Europe was probably lowest. Gregory of Tours (d. 595) could declare that "the study of letters" had "perished." Nearly two hundred years later Charles the Great re-echoed the complaint, and sought a remedy. Yet, even in those centuries, there were places of comparative light. Chief among these, on the Continent, were the Benedictine houses. It was in 528 that the Abbey of Monte Cassino was founded by St Benedict. His rule, formulated in 529, provided for regular study. Thenceforth his Order, wherever established, was a powerful agency in the maintenance of knowledge. To the Benedictines is largely due the survival of the Latin classics; indeed, it would be difficult to overrate their services as guardians of books in the darkest age of Europe. In Germany the Benedictine Abbey of Fulda, founded by St Boniface (d. 755), was pre-eminent during the ninth century as a home of literary studies. Meanwhile the condition of letters in the British Islands was somewhat better than that which prevailed on the Continent. This was conspicuously the case in Ireland, the stronghold of Celtic monachism, which was independent of Benedictine influences. The Irish monasteries, many of which arose before 500, were prosperous. They were devoted to learning, derived partly from a monastic community, the once-famous Insulani, planted (c. 400) by St Honoratus in the isle near Cannes which bears his name; and they had the unique distinction of witnessing to an affinity between the Celtic and the Hellenic spirit. Alone among the religious houses of the West in that age, they fostered the study of the Greek Fathers. Ireland sent forth not a few of the scholars and missionaries whose names shine most clearly through the gloom of those centuries; St Columba (d. 597), who made Iona a centre of light for northern Britain; St Columbanus (d. 615), a founder and reformer of monastic houses in Europe; Clement, who succeeded Alcuin (c. 798) as head of the school at Aachen; and John Scotus Erigena (d. c. 875), whose acquirements included some knowledge of Greek, and whose independence as a philosophical thinker renders him the most interesting intellectual figure of the ninth century. England also, from 600 to 800, was probably less dark than the Continent. Augustine, a Benedictine, and his Roman fellow-missionaries, came in 597, bringing with them the Latin language and Latin books. In 668 the Greek Theodore became seventh Archbishop of Canterbury. He was zealous for the promotion of learning, and certainly introduced some knowledge of Greek among his clergy, though the measure and duration of that knowledge are uncertain. Baeda (d. 735), the ascetic monk of Jarrow, was the comprehensive interpreter of all the literature, theological, historical, and educational, which had come into England with Christianity. Alcuin (d. 804), trained in the famous monastery of York, where he afterwards presided over the school, won repute as a theologian, and more especially as a grammarian. He does not seem to have been a man of originality or force, and he inherited the narrow view which was adverse to pagan lore; but, under the auspices of Charles the Great, he did a large work for education.

The reign of that monarch (768–814) saw the first large and systematic effort towards a restoration of letters. The motives which actuated the new Emperor of the West were primarily political and social. He felt that it was of vital moment for his realm to mitigate the mischief and reproach of illiteracy. In 782 he induced Alcuin to leave York and take up his abode at Aachen, as the head of a school in connexion with the Court. With Alcuin's advice and aid, he did his best to stimulate and improve the only educational agencies which existed,—those of the episcopal and monastic schools. Bishops were encouraged to provide elementary instruction for the children of the laity. The Capitulary of 789 directs the more important monasteries to establish higher schools in addition to the ordinary schools provided by religious houses. Not a few of these higher schools became distinguished. Foremost among them was that of the Abbey of Fulda. Others belonged to the Abbeys of Tours, Reims, St Gall, and Corvey. Throughout the ninth century such schools rendered good service to learning. Rabanus Maurus, Abbot of Fulda (d. 856), who was free from any blind prejudice against the classics, did much to liberalise monastic studies. His pupil, Lupus Servatus, had a wide range of reading in good Latin authors, and studied them with a zeal not unworthy of the Renaissance. Many of these monastic schools perished in the tenth century. In the second half of that century, however, the Emperor Otto the Great (936–73) enlarged the horizon and stimulated the culture of the German people. His reign brought security to such seats of study as existed; and their welfare was promoted by his brother, the learned Bruno, Archbishop of Cologne.

Gerbert, afterwards Pope Sylvester II, who died in 1003, shows how much was possible for a gifted scholar in the tenth century. He had not merely read a great deal of the best Latin literature, but had appreciated it on the literary side, had imbibed something of its spirit, and had found in it an instrument of self-culture. His case is, indeed, a very exceptional one. But some knowledge, at least, of the Latin classics was not even then a rare accomplishment. A tradition of learning, derived especially from Fulda, had been created, which descended without a break to the time when the University of Paris arose. Nowhere on the Continent was there such a violent interruption, or such a general blight upon culture, as was caused in England and Ireland by the raids of the destroying Northmen. From about the end of the tenth century onwards culture began to be somewhat more widely diffused. There are indications that the course of Latin reading in the better schools was now no longer confined to meagre text-books, but had become fairly liberal. Thus at the school of Paderborn in Westphalia, early in the eleventh century, the plan of study included Virgil, Horace, Statius, and Sallust. Towards the close of that century, Bernard of Chartres, after teaching his pupils the rules of grammar from Donatus and Priscian, led them on to the Latin poets, orators, and historians, dwelling especially on the rhetorical precepts of Cicero and Quintilian. His method is praised by John of Salisbury, writing in the middle of the twelfth century, who was himself strongly imbued with a love of classical studies, being especially familiar with Horace, and with much of Cicero. Among other classics who found medieval readers may be named Terence (a favourite), Ovid, Lucan, Martial, Caesar, Livy, and Suetonius. The incipient revival of a better literary taste was checked in the thirteenth century by the influence of the Scholastic Philosophy. That discipline, intent on subtleties of logic and metaphysic, was indifferent to literary form, and soon became encumbered with the technical jargon which Erasmus ridicules. Such doctors as Albertus Magnus and Duns Scotus lent the prestige of their authority to barbarous Latin. In the Universities dialectic now shared the foremost place with theology, and their professors were generally adverse to the literary subjects represented by the *trivium*. In England, France, and Germany, during the thirteenth century, the study of ancient literature gained no ground, but rather receded; and the fourteenth century showed no improvement. Italy, meanwhile, where the Scholastic Philosophy had taken less hold, had been showing some signs of a growing interest in the Latin classics for more than a century before Petrarch.

With him the Italian revival of learning began in earnest, and at a time when, owing to the causes above noticed, there were as yet few symptoms of such a movement in the other countries of Europe. The medieval fortunes of the Latin classics differed widely from those of the Greek. The classical Latin language and literature were never wholly lost. But, after the fifth century, a knowledge of classical Greek rapidly faded out of the West, until it became practically extinct. Between the fall of the Western Empire and the Renaissance, no general provision for teaching Greek existed in the West, similar to that which was made in regard to Latin. Charles the Great wished, indeed, to restore Greek, mainly for the practical purpose of intercourse with the East. One of the Capitularies attests his design (" *Graecas et Latinas scholas in perpetuum manere ordinavimus* "); but it is doubtful whether his purpose was anywhere fulfilled. Some study of Greek was fostered, as we have seen, in the Irish monasteries; and a few instances of it occur in other places. Thus in the tenth century Greek was studied by some brethren of the Abbey of St Gall. The Council of Vienne (1311) had proposed to establish chairs of Greek in several cities of Europe; but nothing was done. Several eminent men of western Europe, in the course of those centuries, certainly possessed some knowledge of Greek, though it is often difficult to say how much. After the schism between the Eastern and Western Churches, sporadic settlements of Greeks occurred in the West, especially in France; and Latin controversialists had a new motive for acquiring the language of their opponents. Grosseteste, according to Matthew Paris, was aided by a Greek priest of St Albans in translating the *Testament of the Twelve Patriarchs* into Latin. The Benedictine historians give lists of the persons in each century who were reputed to know Greek; but it may well be that these lists, short though they are, include men who had merely gained some slight knowledge of the language from intercourse with Greeks. In Italy, doubtless, the number of those who knew some Greek was larger than elsewhere, owing to the greater closeness of Italy's relations with the East. But even at Constantinople itself, in the fourteenth century, a sound knowledge of ancient Greek was confined to a narrow circle; and an intelligent appreciation of the ancient Hellenic literature was probably rarer still.

Enough has been said to guard against the notion that the Italian revival of learning was something more sudden and abrupt than it actually was. The movement in the second half of the fourteenth century would appear almost miraculous, if the new light were supposed to have flashed upon Italy, at Petrarch's word, from a background of utter darkness. The fact is rather that the dawn had long been growing in the sky. On the other hand, the revival which dates from Petrarch was, in a very definite sense, the beginning of a new era. The appreciation of classical antiquity which came with it differed in two respects from any which the earlier Middle Ages could show.  In the first place, the excellence of literary form exhibited by the ancient masters of Latin style now became a direct object of study and of imitation.  Such portions of these authors as had been read in the period preceding the Renaissance had been valued chiefly for the facts, or sentiments, or supposed allegorical meanings, which could be drawn from them ; they were, as a rule, but dimly apprehended as literature, and had very little influence on the medieval writing of Latin.  The second difference was still more important.  Ancient literature was now welcomed, not only as supplying standards of form, but as disclosing a new conception of life ; a conception freer, larger, more rational, and more joyous, than the medieval ; one which gave unfettered scope to the play of the human feelings, to the sense of beauty, and to all the activities of the intellect.  Ancient Latin writers used the word *humanitas* to denote the civilising and refining influence of polite letters and of the liberal arts; as they also applied the epithet *humanus* to a character which had received that influence.  The Italian scholars of the Renaissance, to whom the classical literature of antiquity was not merely a model, but a culture, and, indeed, a life, found it natural to employ a phrase not used by the ancients, and to speak of *litterae humanae* or *litterae humaniores*;  meaning by the comparative, not "secular rather than theological," but "distinctively humane";  more so, that is, than other literature.  The "humanist," a term already known to Ariosto, is the student of humane letters.  A man like John of Salisbury, imbued with the loving study of good Latin classics, or even a man like Gerbert, whose genius gave almost a foretaste of the revival, was still divided by a broad and deep gulf from the Italian humanist of the age opened by Petrarch.  Medieval orthodoxy would have recoiled from that view of human life, and especially from that claim of absolute liberty for the reason, which formed part of the humanist's ideal.  Indeed we are continually reminded, throughout the course of the Italian Renaissance, that the new movement has medieval forces to combat or to reconcile.  It is only some of the clearer and stronger spirits, in that time of transition, that thoroughly succeed in harmonising Christian teaching with a full acceptance of the New Learning.

Francesco Petrarca (1304–74),—who thus modified, for euphony's sake, his surname Petracco,—was born at Arezzo.  He was nine years old when his father settled at Avignon, the seat, since 1309, of the Papacy.  At Avignon Petrarch passed his boyhood,—already charmed, at school, by Cicero's periods ; and there, when he was twenty-three, he saw in a church the Laura of his sonnets.  The central interest of his life, from an early age, was in the classical past of Italy.  He longed to see the ancient glories of Rome revived.  Twice, in poetical epistles, he adjured Benedict XII to quit the "Babylon" on the Rhone for the city on the Tiber. In 1336, when he saw Rome for the first time, he was impressed by the contrast between the grandeur of the decaying monuments and the squalor of their medieval surroundings. Then he spent some years in his beautiful retreat at Vaucluse, near Avignon, brooding on Roman history. There he began a Latin epic, *Africa,* with Scipio Africanus for its hero, a poem which slowly grew under his hands, but was never completed; tame in parts, and lacking Virgilian finish, yet full of powerful and musical lines. But it was chiefly, if not wholly, his *Canzoniere,*—where he had reached absolute perfection within a limited sphere,—that won him the honour of being crowned with the laurel on the Capitol at Rome (1341, *aet.* 37). Thenceforth he was recognised as the foremost man of letters in Europe. When, in May, 1347, Rienzi was proclaimed head of "the Holy Roman Republic," Petrarch hailed the "tribune" as a heaven-sent deliverer, who was to rid Italy of the "foreign tyrants," as humanism loved to style the feudal nobles. With many of these "tyrants," such as the Colonnesi and the Visconti, Petrarch lived, then and afterwards, on terms of much cordiality and reciprocal advantage. Patriotic archaeology had inspired that crazy scheme of restoring the Roman Commonwealth. But the same enthusiasm for classical antiquity made Petrarch the leader in a solid and permanent restoration of literature.

He was steeped in the life, the thoughts, and the emotions of the Latin classics. His way of using them might be contrasted with Dante's in the *De Monarchia.* To Petrarch they were real men, his Italian ancestors. He was the first who zealously collected Latin manuscripts, inscriptions, and coins. He was the first typical humanist in his cultivation of Latin style. And with him the *imitatio veterum* was never slavish. In a letter to Boccaccio he remarks that the resemblance of a modern's work to his ancient model should not be that of a portrait to the original, but rather the family likeness of child to parent. He deprecated even the smallest debts of phrase to the ancients, and was annoyed when it was pointed out to him that in one of his *Eclogues* he had unconsciously borrowed from Virgil the words *atque intonat ore.* The Latin letters which he poured out so abundantly were in large part finished essays, in a style founded mainly on Seneca and St Augustine, but tinged (especially in his later period) by Cicero. In them he was ever pleading, directly or indirectly, the cause of humanism. An orthodox Churchman, a student of the Vulgate and of the Fathers, he had nothing in common with the neopaganism of some later men. He advocated the study of the classics as the key to a larger mental life, not contrary to the Christian, but ancillary to it; one which should educate and exercise men's highest faculties. In all subjects he was adverse to pedantic and narrowing methods. If his egotism was absorbing, it was the reflex of a passion for self-culture; here he had a kinship with Goethe. The desire of fame was a ruling motive with him, as with so many Italians of the maturer Renaissance; but in him it was inseparable from the desire to have a new pattern of self-culture recognised.

Nor did he plead in vain. The age was ready for some new kind of intellectual activity; the subtleties of the Schoolmen's dialectic were beginning to pall, and the professional studies of the Universities were unsatisfying. Petrarch, by his great gifts and unique position, succeeded in making countless friends and patrons for humanism among those persons whose favour was indispensable to its earlier progress. For it should be remembered that humanism was not cradled in the bosom of Universities,—which, indeed, for a long while, were mostly hostile to it; nor, again, was it brought in by a sweeping movement of the popular mind. Humanism depended, in its infancy and youth, on encouragement by powerful and wealthy individuals, through whom the humanist gained a footing and an audience in this or that Italian city. Petrarch won the ear of men who became patrons of humanism. But he did more than that. He stimulated an inner circle of disciples, foremost among whom was his devoted friend and admirer, Boccaccio. When, therefore, Petrarch is designated as the "father" or "founder" of humanism, the description is correct, if rightly understood. He was, in his own person, the first brilliant humanist; he was also the first effective propagator of humanism in the world at large; and he inspired chosen pupils who continued the tradition.

In his letter *To Homer*, Petrarch says, "I have not been so fortunate as to learn Greek." But he had at least made some attempt to do so. Barlaam, a Calabrian by birth, who had long resided at Constantinople, came to Italy in 1339 on a mission from the Emperor Cantacuzenus. It was probably in 1342 that Petrarch began to study Greek with him. "I had thrown myself into the work," he says, "with eager hope and keen desire. But the strangeness of the foreign tongue, and the early departure of my teacher, baffled my purpose." The failure, thus shortly told, throws an instructive light on the difficulties which beset a revival of Greek. No aids to the acquisition of Greek then existed in the Latin or the Italian language. The rudiments of grammar and vocabulary could be acquired only from a Greek-speaking teacher. If the learner's aim had been merely to gain some knowledge of the Romaic spoken and written in the daily life of the Levant, tutors in plenty could have been found at Venice, or at any Italian centre of commerce. But a scholarly knowledge of ancient Greek was a rare attainment; rarer still was a scholarly acquaintance with the Greek classics. Even at Constantinople such knowledge was then possessed only by a few persons of superior education, including those who were professional students or men of letters. A Greek teacher of this class could be drawn to Italy, as a rule, only by some definite prospect of honour and emolument. The Italian revival of Greek in the fourteenth and fifteenth centuries was effected mainly by a small number of highly-accomplished Greeks, who were induced to settle as professors at Florence or other centres. The revival was also furthered by the visits which several Italian scholars made to Constantinople for the purpose of studying the language there. In viewing the Italian revival of Greek as a whole, we must remember its essential dependence on these sources. The higher Byzantine level of Greek scholarship in that age was the highest to which Italy could then aspire. Italian students of Greek in the earlier and middle periods of the Renaissance learned the classical language from men to whom its modern form was a vernacular. This was, in one way, a distinct advantage, since there is a large continuity both of idiom and of vocabulary between classical Greek and the more polished modern Greek. On the other hand, the Byzantine feeling for the genius and style of the classical literature had become grievously defective.

Boccaccio is the first Italian of the Renaissance who is known to have made any progress in the study of Greek. He was impelled to it by the advice of Petrarch, a friend to whom his modest and affectionate nature gave an ungrudging and unbounded worship. His teacher was Leontius Pilatus, a pupil of the Barlaam who had been Petrarch's instructor, and, like him, a Calabrian who had migrated to Byzantium. The notion of Leontius to be gathered from Petrarch (who had read with him at Venice), and from Boccaccio, again illustrates the difficulty of finding tolerable Greek teaching in Italy. Leontius evidently knew little or nothing beyond the Byzantine Greek of the day; he was stupid and pretentious; his temper appears to have been morose, and his personal habits were repulsive. Nevertheless Boccaccio received him into his house at Florence, and caused him to be appointed professor of Greek in the Studio there. He made for Boccaccio a bald and faulty translation of Homer into bad Latin prose, which was sent to Petrarch, and received by him as an inestimable boon.

But the first real teacher of Greek in Italy, the man with whom the revival of Greek learning in the West began, was Manuel Chrysoloras, who lectured on Greek at Florence from 1397 to 1400. He was a Byzantine of good family, who had previously visited Italy on a mission from the Emperor Paleologus, for the purpose of seeking aid against the Turks. Some cultivated Florentines, who had then met him, afterwards prevailed on the *Signoria* of Florence to offer him the chair of Greek, which he accepted. His coming made an epoch in the history of European letters. He was a scholar, able to interpret the classical Greek poets and prose-writers; and he was eloquent. The enthusiasm created at Florence must have been remarkable. For the first time, Italians were placed in sympathy with the ancient Greek mind at its best. Ardent students, young and old, including several who afterwards became eminent, crowded the lecture-room. One of these was Lionardo Bruni, well-known in later life for his Latin *History of Florence*, as also for translations from Plato, Aristotle, Demosthenes, and Plutarch. He has described the powerful spell by which the new teacher drew him away from the study of Civil Law. It is especially noteworthy that he speaks of Chrysoloras, without hesitation, as opening a new era. "The knowledge of Greek," he says, "was revived, after an interval of seven centuries." (He might have said, eight or nine.) "Chrysoloras of Byzantium...brought us Greek learning...I gave myself to his teaching with such ardour, that my dreams at night were filled with what I had learned from him by day." Another scholar, who met Chrysoloras at Pavia, Pier Candido Decembrio, speaks of him with a similar enthusiasm. The Greek Grammar of Chrysoloras, in the form of questions and answers (*Erotemata*), was the earliest modern book of the kind. Florence was then the intellectual centre of Italy; and throughout the fifteenth century it continued to be pre-eminently the home of Greek studies, while at the same time taking its full share in the advancement of Latin scholarship. But Chrysoloras did not confine his activities to Florence. He taught Greek at Pavia (for some time between 1400 and 1403); as well as at Milan, at Venice, and perhaps at Rome. He visited Padua also, but did not teach there.

The movement so powerfully and widely initiated by Chrysoloras was continued by several of his compatriots, most of whom came to Italy between 1400 and the capture of Constantinople in 1453. The restoration of Greek letters in Italy preceded the fall of the Eastern Empire, and was not, as has sometimes been supposed, a result of emigrations caused by that event. The Greeks who chiefly effected the revival were drawn westward by the demand for teachers which offered them distinguished and lucrative careers. The subsequent break-up of Byzantine society sent over, no doubt, a fresh stream of exiles, and reinforced the ranks of Hellenism in the West; but by that time Greek studies in Italy were already vigorous.

A few names stand pre-eminent in the series of Greeks who furthered the Hellenic Renaissance. Georgius Trapezuntius (George of Trebizond), who came to Italy about 1420, taught at Venice, Florence, Rome, and elsewhere. His work is more especially associated with Rome, where his criticisms on Plato brought him into controversy with his compatriot, Cardinal Bessarion. While primarily busied with his native language, George of Trebizond also gained the highest repute as a master of Latin style. Theodorus Gaza, arriving in Italy about 1430, taught Greek for some nine years (1441–50) at Ferrara, and afterwards settled at Rome. His best-known works were translations from Aristotle, and a Greek grammar, which was already a classic when printed by Aldus in 1495. The study of Plato and the Neoplatonists at Florence received a marked impetus from the visit in 1438 of Gemistos Plethon, whose mysticism, if eccentric and sometimes extravagant, was allied with power and sincerity. It was his influence which led Cosmo de' Medici to found the Platonic Academy of Florence. Another fruit of his visit was the Latin translation of Plato by Marsilio Ficino (printed in 1482). Among the Greek teachers specially associated with Florence none, perhaps, is more worthy of a place next to Chrysoloras than John Argyropoulos, who held the Greek chair for fifteen years (1456–71), afterwards going to Rome, where one of his best pupils was Reuchlin. Somewhat later the Florentine professorship was held by Andronicus Callistus, who had Politian among his hearers. It was about 1447 that Demetrius Chalcondylas came from Constantinople to Rome. He obtained the chair of Greek at Perugia, where he taught with great success. Other names of high merit might be cited, but perhaps only one remains which is of quite the same rank as those above mentioned. John Lascaris, much of whose work as a teacher was done in Paris, was invited by Leo X to Rome, where he helped to promote Greek studies. After another visit to France, he died at Rome in 1535. These Greek restorers of Greek letters in the West were happy in the season of their labours. The temper of the age is reflected in Bruni's enthusiasm for Chrysoloras, and in the words which a young student at Perugia wrote concerning the lectures of Chalcondylas:—"A Greek has just come, and has begun to teach me with great diligence, while I listen to him with indescribable pleasure, because he is a Greek...It seems to me as if in him were mirrored the wisdom, the refined intelligence, and the elegance of those famous men of old."

Meanwhile the revival of Latin scholarship was following the course on which it had been started by Petrarch. Giovanni di Conversino da Ravenna, who had lived as a pupil in Petrarch's house, became the most eminent Latinist of his time. He was the earliest example of a teacher who went from city to city, communicating his own ardour to successive groups of students; but the chief scene of his labours was Padua, where he was professor of rhetoric from 1392 to about 1405. Among his pupils were two who were destined to become famous as humanist educators, Vittorino da Feltre and Guarino da Verona. Conversino's favourite author was Cicero, but he lectured also on the Roman poets. Though not distinguished as a writer, he contributed by his teaching to that zealous study of Latin style which was a characteristic feature of the Italian Renaissance.

The "imitation of the ancients" was more than a literary fashion or a pedantic exercise. It sprang from the desire of Italians, for whom Latin literature was being opened anew, to recover the tongue of their Roman ancestors,—that language, barbarised in the course of centuries, which bore witness to the ancient glories of the land in which they lived, and to the civilisation whose monuments were around them. Italy had many dialects, and Tuscan, even in the fifteenth century, had only a limited currency, while Latin was an universal language. Practical

utility thus conspired with patriotic sentiment and with the zeal of
scholarship. But it was not easy to lift Latin to a higher level, while
the medieval form of it was still current in the learned professions, in
the offices of the Church, and in ordinary correspondence. Letter-
writing was the department of Latin composition to which the humanists
naturally and properly gave their first attention. It was in this that
Petrarch had especially shown his power. His younger contemporary,
Coluccio de' Salutati, who became Chancellor of Florence in 1375, set
the example of writing classical and elegant Latin in public documents.
The higher standard of official and diplomatic Latinity which he
introduced had the effect of opening employment to professional scholars
in many chanceries and Courts of Italy. A close study of Cicero's
Letters, with a view to correctness and fluency in Latin correspondence,
won a reputation for Gasparino da Barzizza, who, on the invitation of
Filippo Maria Visconti, opened a school at Milan in 1418.

Latin epistolography was now cultivated as a special branch of
literature. The letters exchanged between eminent scholars were, as a
rule, private only in form, being vehicles for the display of style, wit,
and learning. They were usually intended, if not for publication in the
modern sense, at least for a large circulation. The range of topics
was conventionally restricted by a pervading desire to write somewhat
as Cicero might have written to Atticus. Notices of books and manuscripts, literary criticism, introductions or recommendations of friends,
requests and commissions, thanks, compliments, occasional glimpses into
the writer's daily occupations, form the staple of such epistles. There is
seldom any reference to contemporary politics, to questions of theology,
or to any modern subjects which could not be handled without breaking
the classical illusion. Sometimes, indeed, eminent scholars addressed
theological or political pamphlets, in choice Latin, to princes or prelates;
but such efforts lay outside the ordinary province of humanistic letter-
writing. Nor were really private matters often confided to these Latin
letters. "I always write in the vulgar tongue (*alla grossolana*)," says
Filelfo, "those things which I do not wish to be copied." Nevertheless,
the Latin letter-writing of the Renaissance has the interest of exhibiting
with great distinctness the characters of the writers and their friends.
It has also a larger claim on our gratitude. It was an exercise, sufficiently pleasurable to be widely used, by which successive generations
of lettered men gradually rose to the conception of a style which should
be correct, fluent, and easy. In the darker ages the model of a good
prose had been lost. The Italian letter-writers of the Renaissance, the
imitators of Cicero, were labouring to restore it. They achieved their
object; and the achievement bore fruit, not merely in Latin, but
afterwards in the modern languages of Europe.

It was to be expected that, as the cultivation of Latin style
progressed, the imitation of the ancient models should become more

critical. Lorenzo Valla, who died in 1457, was the author of a work *De Elegantiis Latinae Linguae*, which marked the highest level that had yet been reached in the critical study of Latin. He dealt with various points of grammar, with niceties of phrase and idiom, and with the discrimination of synonyms. His book appears to have been reprinted nearly sixty times between 1471 and 1536. After Valla, the next Italian Latinist who became an authority on the more minute refinements of style was Bembo, whose reputation was at its zenith in the pontificate of Leo X (1513–21). But Bembo's scope was much more limited than Valla's. Cicero's usage was a law from which Bembo never consciously swerved. In strong contrast with his timid and even morbid Ciceronianism,—a symptom that the Italian revival had passed its prime,—stands a quality which we recognise in the Latin writing of the more powerful and genial humanists. This is, briefly, the gift of writing Latin almost as if it were a living language. Politian had this gift in an eminent degree, and exhibits it in verse no less than in prose. Poggio, before him, had it too, though his Latin was much rougher and less classical. The same quality may be ascribed to Paulus Jovius (1483–1552), whose vivid and picturesque style in narrative was compared by Leo X,—with some exaggeration, but not without some justice,— to that of Livy. To write Latin as such men wrote it, demanded the union of general correctness with ease and spontaneity. The fact that several Italian humanists attained to this merit is a proof that the *imitatio veterum* was not necessarily lifeless or mechanical, but could serve a truly educative purpose, by helping men to regain a flexible organ of literary expression. Erasmus, though in touch with the Italian Renaissance, belongs to a stage beyond it. His ridicule of pseudo-Ciceronianism falls on the sect of Bembo. But his own Latin style, so admirable in its elasticity, edge, and force, is a result which only the Italian Renaissance had made possible.

Yet the cultivation of Latin style, while it was so salient a trait of the Italian revival, was only one of its manifold energies. The same study of the classical writers which incited men to imitate their form inspired also the wish to comprehend their subject-matter. There was a widespread desire to enter into the ideas and the meaning of the ancient Greek and Roman civilisations. Italians were especially eager to reconstruct an image, as distinct as possible, of the manner in which their ancestors had lived. But the aids to such study, now so abundant, did not yet exist. There were no dictionaries of mythology, of biography, of antiquities, no treatises on classical archaeology, no collections of inscriptions. A teacher in the earlier time of the Renaissance, when he dictated an all-embracing commentary to his pupils, had to rely mostly on the stores gathered by his own reading. The erudite labour done by the Italian humanists was of great variety and volume. Many of the more eminent scholars published notes, critical or exegetical, on the Greek or Latin authors whom they expounded in their lectures; but such work has left comparatively few distinctive traces, having been either absorbed into later books, or superseded. Latin translations from the Greek classics formed an important department of humanistic work, and were of the greatest service, not only at the Renaissance but long afterwards, in diffusing the study of Greek literature. The learned humanist Tommaso Parentucelli, who became Pope Nicholas V in 1447, was especially zealous in promoting such translations, many of which were made at Rome during his pontificate. Greek residents in Italy contributed to the work. But Italians were not less active; indeed there were few distinguished humanists who did not give this proof of their Greek scholarship. In the field of textual criticism mention is due to Politian's edition of the *Pandects* of Justinian, perhaps the earliest work based on a careful collation of manuscripts and on a critical estimate of their relative authority. The manuals of grammar produced at the Renaissance were inevitably of a crude kind; but some of them, at least, had merits which made them standard works for several generations. Thus the earliest of the Renaissance Greek grammars, that of Manuel Chrysoloras (afterwards translated from Greek into Latin by Guarino), held its ground well into the sixteenth century. It was the first text-book used by Erasmus when teaching Greek at Cambridge: the next to which he introduced his pupils was the more advanced Greek grammar of Theodorus Gaza, dating perhaps from about 1445, though first printed in 1495. The Greek grammar of Constantine Lascaris (composed perhaps about 1460, and printed in 1476) also had a high reputation. The Latin grammar of Nicholas Perotti, printed at Rome in 1473, treats grammar in connexion with rhetoric, and is commended by Erasmus as the most complete manual on the subject then extant.

The higher historical criticism is represented by Lorenzo Valla, already mentioned as a fine Latinist. In 1440, when Naples was at feud with the papal See, he published a tract on the Donation of Constantine, proving that the chief document of the temporal power was spurious. Eugenius IV was then Pope. His successor, Nicholas V, a scholar and a statesman, read in Valla's tract a sign of the times. The Council of Florence (1438), where Greeks and Latins met in conference, had lately shown that the history of the early Church could not be fully understood without a knowledge of Greek writings. And now it was plain that the long impunity of ecclesiastical forgery was drawing to an end. Nicholas saw that humanism would be less disastrous to the Vatican as an uncongenial inmate than as an irrepressible critic. He made Valla an official of the Curia. It was a turning-point. The new papal policy was continued, with few breaks, down to the Reformation.

Beyond the limits of strictly literary studies, there was a wide and varied field of interests which the classical revival opened to Italians.

The superstitious awe with which the Middle Ages had viewed the ruins of ancient Rome was not accompanied by any feeling for their artistic worth, or by the slightest desire to preserve them. A Latin epigram by Pius II (1458-64)—the first Pope who endeavoured to arrest their decay—attests the fact, to which there are other witnesses, that even then the citizens of Rome used to strip marbles from the ancient monuments, in order to burn them as lime. Where the Roman remains were capable of conversion into dwellings or strongholds, as was the case especially with some of the baths and tombs, they had often been occupied by medieval nobles, and had thus been exposed to further damage. Many such monuments had been destroyed, and the ruins had then been used as quarries. But a change of feeling came with the spirit of the incipient Renaissance. The first phase of this new feeling was a sense of pathetic contrast between the majesty of the ancient remains and the squalor of the modern city. Petrarch compares Rome to a stately woman, of venerable aspect, but clad in mean and tattered garments. Poggio is reminded of a queen in slavery. He was the first man of the Renaissance who had studied the monuments of Rome with the method of a scholar and an archaeologist, comparing them with the testimony of the Latin classics. His *Urbis Romae Descriptio*—the title commonly given to the first section of his essay *De Varietate Fortunae*—is the clearest general survey now extant of the Roman monuments as they existed in the first half of the fifteenth century. Poggio gives us some idea of the rate at which destructive agencies had been working even in his own lifetime. But a better day was at hand. The interest in Italian archaeology had already become active. Flavio Biondo (Blondus), who died in 1463, compiled an encyclopaedic work in three parts, *Roma Instaurata*, *Roma Triumphans*, and *Italia Illustrata*, on the history, institutions, manners, topography, and monuments of ancient Italy. He lived to complete also more than thirty books of a great work on the period commencing with the decline of the Roman Empire, *Historiarum ab inclinatione Romanorum*. In an age so largely occupied with style, which was not among his gifts, Biondo is a signal example of laborious and comprehensive erudition. He holds indeed an honourable place among the founders of Roman archaeology.

It was just at the close of Biondo's life that Pius II, in 1462, issued his bull designed to protect the remains of ancient Rome from further depredations. The solicitude of which this was the first official expression was not always imitated by his successors. But the period from about 1470 to 1525 was one which saw a notable advance in the care and study bestowed on works of ancient art and architecture. Within that period the Museum of the Capitol and the Museum of the Vatican were founded. The appreciation of classical sculpture was quickened by the recovery of many ancient works. Near the entrance to the garden of the Belvedere, the newly-found Apollo was erected by Julius II (1503–13),—the Pope who perceived how renascent art could add splendour to the See of St Peter, and at whose bidding Bramante replaced the ancient basilica of Constantine by the greatest church of Christendom. Michelangelo saw the Laocoon disinterred from the ruined Baths of Titus. Leo X acquired the reclining statues of the Nile and the Tiber, and the so-called Antinous. These and other specimens of classical art, though not representative of that art at its best, helped to educate Italian taste, already well-disposed towards every form of classical culture. The Latin verse-writers of Leo's age show the impression made by the newly-found works of sculpture. It is more interesting to note the remark of an expert, the Florentine sculptor Ghiberti, who, in speaking of an ancient statue which he had seen at Rome, observes that its subtle perfection eludes the eye, and can be fully appreciated only by passing the hand over the surface of the marble.

The most memorable record of the new zeal for ancient Rome is the letter addressed to Leo X, in 1518, by Raffaelle. He writes as Master of the Works at St Peter's, and Inspector-General of Antiquities, having been appointed to these posts in 1515. For a long time he had been engaged in a comprehensive study of the ancient monuments. In them, he says, he had recognised " the divinity of those minds of the old world." A pitiful sight it is to him, " the mangled corpse of this noble mother, once the queen of the world." " Temples, arches, statues, and other buildings, the glory of their founders," had been allowed to suffer defacement or destruction. " I would not hesitate to say," he continues, " that all this new Rome which our eyes behold, grand and beautiful as it is, adorned with palaces, churches, and other structures, has been built with lime made from ancient marbles." He next recalls, with details, the progress of the havoc during the twelve years which he has passed in Rome. And then he unfolds his project. Mapping out Rome into fourteen regions, he urges that systematic works should be undertaken for the purpose of clearing, or excavating, all existing remains of the ancient city, and then safeguarding them against further injury. His premature death in 1520 prevented the execution of the design. The greatness of that design is well expressed in one of the Latin elegies which mourned his loss: *Nunc Romam in Roma quaerit reperitque Raphaël.* It shows the grasp of his genius, and is also an impressive witness to the new spirit of the Renaissance.

This was a period at which Vitruvius (edited not long before by Fra Giocondo) and Frontinus found many readers. The classical influence was indeed already the dominant one in Italian sculpture and architecture. It was a power which might tend to cold formalism, as in Palladio, or happily ally itself with the native bent of the modern artist, as in Giulio Romano; but, for good or evil, it was everywhere. Meanwhile scholars were producing learned work in various branches of Roman archaeology. A permanently valuable service to Latin epigraphy was rendered by Jacopo Mazochi and his collaborator Francesco Albertini in *Epigrammata Antiquae Urbis Romae* (1521), where some use was made of earlier collections by Ciriaco of Ancona and Fra Giocondo. Andrea Fulvio published in 1527 his *Antiquitates Urbis Romae*. The *Urbis Romae Topographia* of Bartolommeo Marliano appeared in 1537. Such books, though their contents have been mostly absorbed or transmuted in later works, claim the gratitude which is due to indefatigable pioneers.

The buoyancy and animation of the Renaissance in Italy were sustained throughout by the joys of discovery, and of these none was keener than the delight of acquiring manuscripts. Petrarch was the leader in this as in other ways. He was prepared to undertake any trouble, in his own person or through emissaries, for the sake of finding a new classical book, or a better copy of one which was already known. The first of his epistles *To Marcus Tullius Cicero* expresses the feelings stirred in him by reading the orator's Letters to Atticus, Brutus, and Quintus, which he had just been fortunate enough to unearth at Verona: he was not destined to know the *Epistolae ad Familiares*, which were found about 1389 at Vercelli. Petrarch had a quaint and lively way, which was copied by his immediate successors, of personifying the hidden and neglected manuscripts of the classics as gentle prisoners held in captivity by barbarous gaolers. The monastic or cathedral libraries of Italy were the places which first attracted research. Boccaccio's account of his visit to the Abbey of Monte Cassino in Apulia, recorded by a pupil, vividly pictures the scandalous treatment of the books there, which the monks ruthlessly mutilated for the purpose of making cheap psalters, amulets, or anything by which they could earn a few pence. But the quest was not confined to Italy. Italian or foreign agents of the Roman Curia had frequent opportunities of prosecuting research in the libraries of northern Europe. Thus Poggio's journey to the Council of Constance in 1414, in the capacity of Apostolic Secretary, enabled him to visit several religious houses in Switzerland and Swabia. At the Abbey of St Gall he discovered, to his intense pleasure, the *Institutions* of Quintilian, previously known only through a defective copy found by Petrarch at Florence. The place in which the books were kept is described by Poggio as a sort of dungeon, foul and dark, at the bottom of a tower. Quintilian, he says, " seemed to be stretching out his hands, calling upon the Romans," and praying to be saved from the doom to which barbarians had consigned him. Some other classical authors, including Valerius Flaccus, were found by Poggio on the same occasion. He was, indeed, one of the most fortunate of the searchers. Among his rewards were Cicero's speech for Caecina, Lucretius, Silius Italicus, Manilius, Columella, Vitruvius, and Ammianus Marcellinus. Centuries were to elapse before the process of exploration begun by these early humanists was to be finished. Only in our own day has the actual wealth of Europe in classical manuscripts been ascertained with any approach to completeness. But in the period of the Italian Renaissance discoveries more or less important were of frequent occurrence, and no one could tell from what quarter the next treasure-trove might come. Thus in 1425 Cicero's rhetorical treatises were found by Gherardo Landriani in the Duomo at Lodi; and four years later Nicholas of Treves, a fiscal agent of the Vatican in Germany, sent thence to Rome the most complete codex of Plautus. One of the greatest acquisitions was among the latest. Not till 1508 did the modern world recover the first six books of the *Annals* of Tacitus. The manuscript, said to have been found in the monastery of Corvey, was sent from Westphalia to Rome, and was acquired by Giovanni de' Medici, afterwards Leo X.

But it was more especially the quest for Greek classics that engaged the ardent zeal of the earlier humanists. The comparative novelty of Greek literature stimulated curiosity; Greek codices were sought, not only by students eager for knowledge, but also by a much larger world. Commercial houses at Florence, such as that of the Medici, with agencies throughout Europe and the Levant, spared no expense in procuring Greek books. Princes, and sometimes Popes, joined in the competition. A new Greek classic gave not only the kind of pleasure which an expert finds in a rare book, but also the pride of possession, not necessarily allied with knowledge, which a wealthy collector feels in a good picture. In short, classical antiquity, Greek especially, was vehemently the fashion in Italy, if that phrase be not less than just to the earnestness of the movement. A letter-writer of the time has related that, just after the publication of Politian's *Miscellanea* at Florence in 1489, he happened to go into a public office, and found the clerks neglecting their business while they devoured the new book, divided in sheets among them. In an age when the demand for manuscripts had all these forces behind it, the search could not fail to be well-organised, if only as a branch of commerce. For Greek books, Constantinople was the chief hunting-ground. Thither, for at least half a century before the fatal year 1453, many Italian humanists repaired; enjoying, we may suppose, every facility for research. Three such men are foremost among those who brought copies of the Greek classics to Italy. Giovanni Aurispa (1369–1459) went to Constantinople in youth, to study Greek; and, returning to Italy in 1423, carried with him no less than 238 manuscripts. A quiet teacher and student, as he is described by Filelfo, —"*placidis Aurispa Camoenis deditus*,"—he closed his long life at Ferrara. Guarino da Verona (1370–1460), who also acquired Greek at Constantinople, brought back with him a large number of Greek books. But neither he nor Aurispa can have had better opportunities than

Francesco Filelfo (1398–1481), afterwards so conspicuous as a humanist. He studied Greek at Constantinople with John (brother of Manuel) Chrysoloras, whose daughter he married. In selecting the books which he brought home with him, he doubtless had access to the best stores of the Eastern metropolis. Considerable interest therefore attaches to the list of his Greek books which Filelfo gives in a letter to Ambrogio Traversari, written shortly after his return to Venice in 1427. The manuscripts which he enumerates are those which he had carried with him to Italy. He says that he is expecting a few more ("*alios...nonnullos*") by the next Venetian ships from the Bosporus; but we may assume that the catalogue in this letter includes the great bulk of his Greek library. It comprises the principal Greek poets (including the Alexandrian), with the notable exception of the Attic dramatists, who are represented only by "seven plays of Euripides." In prose he has the historians, from Herodotus to Polybius; of the orators, Demosthenes, Aeschines, and "one oration of Lysias"; no dialogue of Plato, but nearly all the more important writings of Aristotle: also much prose literature, good and bad, of the Alexandrian and Roman ages. The list contains no book which is not now extant.

Not all men, however, were in a position to seek manuscripts for themselves at Constantinople or elsewhere. The majority of collectors perforce relied on agents. A typical figure in the manuscript-trade of the Renaissance was Vespasiano da Bisticci of Florence (1421–98), to whose pen we owe vivid portraits of several among his more distinguished clients. He acted as an agent in procuring and purchasing manuscripts. He also employed a staff of copyists which was probably the largest in Europe. But he was not merely a man of business. He was scholar enough to see that his men made correct transcripts. In his later years the printer was beginning to supersede the scribe. Vespasiano regarded this new mechanical contrivance with all the scorn of a connoisseur in penmanship, and of one who grieved that those treasures which he procured for the select few should be placed within the reach of the multitude. Among the eminent men of whom Vespasiano became the biographer was Niccolo de' Niccoli, of Florence, one of the most notable collectors in the earlier Renaissance. Niccoli was an elegant Latin scholar, and held a prominent place in the literary circle of Cosmo de' Medici. His house was filled with choice relics of antiquity, marbles, coins, and gems; in the refined luxury of his private life he seemed to Vespasiano "a perfect model of the men of old"; but the object to which he devoted most of his wealth and thought was the acquisition of Greek and Latin manuscripts. It was to him that Aurispa brought the famous eleventh-century codex now known as the Laurentian, containing Aeschylus, Sophocles, and Apollonius Rhodius. Bred in the days when good copyists were scarce, Niccoli had become inured, like Petrarch, Boccaccio, and Poggio, to the labour of transcribing manuscripts, and a large proportion of those in his library were the work of his own hand. At his death in 1437 he bequeathed 800 manuscripts to Cosmo de' Medici and fifteen other trustees, among whom were Ambrogio Traversari and Poggio.

This noble bequest was worthily used by Cosmo de' Medici, who stands out as the first great founder of libraries at the Renaissance. Already, in his exile from Florence, he had founded at Venice, in 1433, the Library of San Giorgio Maggiore. In 1441, when the new hall of the Convent of San Marco at Florence was ready to receive books, he placed there 400 of Niccoli's volumes. Of the other 400 the greater part passed into his own large collection, which became the nucleus of the Medicean Library. For the new Abbey which he had built at Fiesole he also provided a library, giving a commission to Vespasiano, who set forty-five copyists to work, and produced 200 manuscripts in twenty-two months. The Medicean collection, joined to those of San Marco and of the Abbey at Fiesole, form the oldest part of the books now in the Biblioteca Mediceo-Laurenziana.

Another great library which first took shape in the fifteenth century is that of the Vatican. A papal library of some sort had existed from very early times, and had received from Pope Zacharias (741–52) a large addition to its stock of Greek manuscripts. This old collection had been deposited in the Lateran. When the papal Court was removed to Avignon in 1309, the books were taken thither. The Great Schism, which began in 1378, was closed by the election of Martin V in 1417. The books were subsequently brought back from Avignon to Rome, and placed in the Vatican. Eugenius IV (1431–47), who came next after Martin V, interested himself in this matter. But his successor, Nicholas V (1447–55), has the best claim to be called the founder of the Vatican Library. As Tommaso Parentucelli, he had catalogued the Library of San Marco at Florence for Cosmo de' Medici. He was thus well qualified to build up a great collection for the Vatican. During the eight years of his pontificate, he enlarged that collection with energy and judgment, adding to it several thousands of manuscripts. The number of Latin manuscripts alone was, at his death, 824, as is shown by a catalogue dated April 16, 1455. He had intended also to erect a spacious library, which should be thrown open to the public; but he did not live to execute that design. His successor, Calixtus III (1455–8), added many volumes brought from Constantinople after its capture by the Turks. Sixtus IV (1471–84),—Francesco della Rovere, a Franciscan monk of learning and eloquence,—became the second founder of the library. In 1475 he appointed as librarian the erudite Bartolommeo Sacchi, known as Platina from the Latinised name of his birthplace Piadena. Under the supervision of Platina, to whom Sixtus IV gave a free hand, the collection was lodged in its present abode, a suite of rooms on the ground-floor of a building in the Vatican which had been erected by Nicholas V, but had hitherto been used for other purposes. Before his death in 1481, Platina enjoyed the satisfaction of seeing these rooms suitably furnished and decorated. A catalogue had also been made, and the Vatican Library had been completely established in its new home.

Among private founders of libraries in the fifteenth century mention is due to Federigo da Montefeltro, Duke of Urbino, who created there a great collection of classics, of theology, and of medieval and humanistic literature. Vespasiano states that during fourteen years a large staff of scribes was constantly occupied in adding to this collection, and records with marked satisfaction that no printed book was suffered to profane it. Few private libraries then in existence can have rivalled that of Urbino; but many others must have been very considerable. Such, for instance, was the library of Cardinal Bessarion at Rome, said by Vespasiano to have contained 600 Greek and Latin manuscripts. The owner presented it, in 1468, to St Mark's at Venice; but, with that apathy towards the Classical Renaissance which characterised the Venetian Republic down to the close of the fifteenth century, a generation went by before the munificent gift was worthily housed.

The incessant quest for manuscripts, and the gradual formation of large libraries, slowly improved the external facilities for humanistic study. Much progress was made in this respect during the interval between the death of Petrarch in 1374 and that of Politian in 1494. Yet, even in the latter part of the fifteenth century, good classical texts were far from abundant. It was only by the printing press that such books were made easily accessible to the majority of students. This fact must be remembered if we would understand the part played in Italy by the humanist professors. In the Italian Revival, viewed as a whole, two principal agencies may be distinguished, corresponding with two successive stages of the movement. The first agency is that of oral teaching by a scholar of eminence, who addresses large audiences, including persons of various ages and attainments. Such a lecturer did not, as a rule, confine his labours to any one place, but accepted invitations from several cities in succession. This method of teaching began immediately after Petrarch. In the earlier days of humanism it was a necessity; there was no other way in which the first elements of the new learning could be diffused. Such a lecturer as Manuel Chrysoloras or Giovanni di Conversino appealed to an enthusiasm which was still in its youth. By such men the seeds of humanism were sown far and wide. But meanwhile another agency was coming into existence, better fitted, in some respects, to promote the higher humanism. It was that of private groups or coteries, formed by patrons and students of letters, who held meetings for the purpose of learned converse and discussion. In contrast with the influence of the humanist professor, who often changed his abode, such an Academy was a permanent centre of study in the place where it was formed. In contrast with the professor's large and miscellaneous audience, the members of an Academy were limited in number, and carefully selected; and, while the lecturer was usually constrained to adopt a more or less popular mode of treatment, the work of an Academy was more esoteric.

Among the humanist professors, none were more eminent or successful in their day than Filelfo and Politian. Each is a representative man. Filelfo is a type of the wandering humanist who played so conspicuous a part in the first half of the fifteenth century. Politian, in the latter part of that century, represents the public teaching of the classics in a riper phase: with him, indeed, it reached the highest level to which Italy ever saw it lifted by the union of learning with genius. The zenith of Filelfo's reputation may be placed at the time, in 1429, when, after teaching at Venice and Bologna, he came as professor to Florence. We have already seen that, after studying Greek at Constantinople, he had brought home with him a considerable store of classical manuscripts. He especially prided himself on a comprehensive knowledge of the Greek and Latin literatures, and on his facility in using both languages, alike in prose and in verse. At Florence, for a time at least, he often gave four lectures a day, taking (for instance) Cicero and Homer in the morning, followed by Terence and Thucydides in the afternoon. "My audience," he says, "numbers every day four hundred persons,—perhaps more"; or perhaps less; for his own later recollections reduced the estimate by one half. At any rate the attendance was very large. There were youths (some from France, Germany, Spain, Cyprus), but also middle-aged or elderly men, including the foremost in Florence. This state of things did not, indeed, last long; for Filelfo had a fatal knack of rousing enmities. But it is a good illustration of what was possible for a very eminent humanist at that period. The method of teaching was determined by the peculiar conditions. Among Filelfo's large audience there would be many, possibly a majority, who would regard the lecture mainly as a display of Latin eloquence, and who would not attempt to take notes. But there would also be many serious students, intent on recording what the lecturer said; and of these only a few would possess manuscripts of the author,—Cicero, for example,—whom he was expounding. After an introduction, Filelfo would therefore dictate a portion of Cicero's text, which the students would transcribe. To this he would add a commentary, dealing with grammar, with the usage of words, and with everything in the subject-matter which needed to be explained or illustrated. Thus, at the end of such a course, the lecturer would have dictated a fully annotated edition of the classical book, or portion of a book, which he was treating; and the diligent student would have transcribed it. The migratory habits of the earlier humanists are partly to be explained by the fact that, when a lecturer had exhausted his existing stock of annotated texts, a change of scene and of audience would enable him to use them over again. A lecture by such a man as Filelfo had, in fact, a twofold quality. On the one hand, it was an exposition,—not of an advanced character, judged by modern standards, yet not too elementary for the conditions of the time. On the other, it was a recognised opportunity for the display of oratorical and dialectical skill. The audience were prepared for flashes of lively eloquence, quotations, epigrams, strokes of satire, panegyric, or invective. As scholarship advanced in Italy, the humanistic lecture became more sparing of irrelevant ornament; but it always preserved something of its old rhetorical character.

Angelo Ambrogini, called Poliziano (Politianus) from his birthplace, Montepulciano, was born in 1454. His precocious abilities were shown in boyhood. In 1470 he earned the designation of " Homericus iuvenis" by translating four books of the *Iliad* (ii–v) into Latin. At eighteen he published an edition of Catullus. He attracted the notice of Lorenzo de' Medici, who made him tutor to his children. Before he was thirty he became professor of Greek and Latin at Florence. He held that chair till his death, in 1494, at the age of forty. Like Filelfo, Politian covered in his lectures a wide field of literature in both the classical languages. But his standard of scholarship, best exemplified in his edition of the *Pandects*, was higher and more critical than that of any predecessor. A quality which distinguished him not less than his comprehensive scholarship was his rhetorical genius. Its characteristics were spontaneity, swiftness, fire, with a certain copiousness of matter, poured forth from a rich and prompt memory. This, indeed, even more than his learning, was the gift to which he owed his unique fame with his contemporaries. A vivid idea of his power as a rhetorician, which also helps us to imagine him as a lecturer, is given by four Latin poems comprised in his *Sylvae*. Each of these poems was written in order that he might recite it in his lecture-room as a prelude to a course of lectures. The first piece, entitled *Nutricia,* is an outline of the history of poetry from Homer to Boccaccio, with a peroration in praise of Lorenzo de' Medici. It may justly be called one of the most noteworthy products of the Italian Renaissance. The facility and rapidity of the sonorous hexameters are extraordinary. Politian is said to have been, in all styles, a swift composer; and these verses convince the reader that they flowed forth. The matter is scarcely less remarkable. We observe that this great humanist is far more at home with the Latin poets than with the Greek. Thus, though no less than twenty-seven verses are given to Pindar, these turn wholly on the ancient traditions about his life; there is not a word that proves knowledge of his work or insight into his genius. The three masters of Greek tragedy are dismissed with one verse apiece, purporting to tell how each was killed;—Aeschylus, by a tortoise falling on his head,—Sophocles, by a shock of joy at the success of a play,—and Euripides, by wild dogs in Macedon. This brief passage is quaintly significant of the scant attention given to the Attic drama in the fifteenth century. But nothing in the poem is truer to the feeling of Italian humanism, or better indicates one of its limitations on the critical side, than the estimate of Homer and Virgil. Virgil, says Politian, ranks next to Homer; or, were not Homer the elder, might even rank above him (*vel, ni veneranda senectus Obstiterit, fortasse prior*). The second poem of the *Sylvae*, called *Rusticus*, was an introduction to the author's lectures on Hesiod's *Works and Days*, Virgil's *Eclogues* and *Georgics*, and other bucolic poetry. The third, *Manto*, was a brilliant eulogy on Virgil. The fourth, *Ambra*, was prefatory to lectures on Homer. Politian's Italian lyrics have been deemed by competent critics to possess high poetical merit, entitling him to a place between Petrarch and Ariosto. His Latin verse, brilliant as it is in rhetorical quality, wants the tact in selection of topics, and the artistic finish, which belong to poetry. But it is easy to conceive how powerful must have been the effect of those impetuous hexameters, when Politian, who was skilled in elocution and gifted with a voice of much charm, declaimed them in his crowded lecture-room at Florence, as a proem to discourses full of eloquence and learning. His audience was cosmopolitan, and the fame of his teaching was borne to every country in Europe. Politian's work was cut short by death at an age when most men of comparable eminence in the annals of scholarship have been only at the outset of their career. But his function was to inspire; and his gifts were such that his brief span of life sufficed to render him one of the most influential personalities in the history of Italian humanism.

The teaching by public lecture, of which Filelfo and Politian were such distinguished exponents, gave occupation, throughout the fifteenth century, to a long series of able men. It flourished at almost every considerable centre of Italian life. And, from the second quarter of the century onwards, the humanist professor had found an efficient ally in the schoolmaster, who prepared the ground for him. The Italian Renaissance brought forth no fairer fruit, and none fraught with more important consequences for the liberal culture of the world, than the school-training, based on the ideas of humanism, which took shape at that period. A place of special honour in the history of education is due to the founder of that system, Vittorino da Feltre. Born in 1378 at Feltre, a small town of Venetia, he went at eighteen to the University of Padua, then second in Italy only to the University of Bologna, and sharing with Pavia the distinction, still rare at that time in Universities, of being comparatively favourable to the New Learning. At Padua, Vittorino was the pupil of Giovanni di Conversino and afterwards of Gasparino da Barzizza, scholars whose important services to the study of Latin have already been noticed. Another Paduan teacher of that day whose influence Vittorino doubtless felt was Vergerius, the author of an essay on the formation of character (*De Ingenuis Moribus*) which remained a classic for two centuries, passing through some forty editions before the year 1600. The Renaissance was fertile in educational treatises; but this tractate was the clearest, as it was the earliest, statement of the principles on which humanistic training rested. Vittorino, after holding a chair of rhetoric at Padua, and then teaching privately at Venice, was invited by Gian Francesco Gonzaga, Marquis of Mantua, to undertake the tuition of his children. In 1425 he took up his residence in a villa assigned to him for that purpose at Mantua, where he remained till his death in 1446. Here he created a school of a type previously unknown.

His aim was to develop the whole nature of his pupils, intellectual, moral, and physical; not with a view to any special calling, but so as to form good citizens and useful members of society, capable of bearing their part with credit in public and private life. For intellectual training he took the Latin classics as a basis; teaching them, however, not in the dry and meagre fashion generally prevalent in the medieval schools, where their meaning as literature was too often obscured by artificial and pedantic methods, but in the large and generous spirit of Renaissance humanism. Poetry, oratory, Roman history, and the ethics of Roman Stoicism, were studied in the best Latin writers, and in a way fitted to interest and stimulate boys. By degrees Vittorino introduced some Greek classics also. The scholars were practised in Latin composition, and to some extent in Greek; also in recitation, and in reading aloud. He further provided for some teaching of mathematics, including geometry (a subject which the humanists preferred to the schoolmen's logic), arithmetic, and the elements of astronomy. Nor did he neglect the rudiments of such knowledge as then passed for natural philosophy and natural history. Music and singing also found a place. Unlike some of the contemporary humanists, Vittorino was an orthodox, even a devout churchman, and one whose precepts were enforced by his practice. He was a layman, and the type of education which he was creating might even be contrasted, in some respects, with the ecclesiastical type which had preceded it. But he was entirely exempt from any tendency to neopaganism in religion or ethics; and his ethical influence as a teacher seems to have been thoroughly sound.

With great insight and tact, Vittorino saw how far social education could be given in a school with advantage to morals and without loss to manliness; he inculcated a good tone of manners, and encouraged the acquirement of such social accomplishments as the age demanded in well-educated men. As to physical training, he provided instructors in riding, swimming, and military exercises. He also promoted every kind of healthy outdoor activity. This was a new thing in schools. The ecclesiastical schoolmaster of the Middle Ages had not usually concerned himself with it. The medieval provision for physical training had been chiefly in the households of princes or nobles, where horsemanship, hunting, and martial sports were in vogue. Vittorino was in some sort continuing this old training; many of his pupils were young nobles destined to the life of courts and camps. But his point of view was a novel one. The idea which dominated his whole system was the classical, primarily Greek, idea of an education in which mind and body should be harmoniously developed. The force with which this idea appealed to the humanists was partly due to its contrast with medieval theory and practice. The new type of school-education developed by Vittorino is rightly called humanistic; but the reason for so calling it is not solely or chiefly that the intellectual part of it was based on the Greek and Latin classics. It was humanistic, in a deeper sense, because it was at once intellectual, moral, and physical. Vittorino was resolved that the advantages of his school should be open to all boys who were fitted to profit by them. Pupils were sent to him from several of the Italian Courts to be educated with the young Mantuan princes. But he also maintained at his own cost a large number of poorer scholars, for whom lodgings were found near the villa. The rules of life and study were the same for all. Many of the most distinguished scholars of the century had enjoyed his teaching. Among these were George of Trebizond, Valla, Nicholas Perotti and John, Bishop of Aleria, who prepared for the Roman press (in 1469–71) the *editiones principes* of many Latin classics.

Next to Vittorino must be named the other great schoolmaster of the time, his contemporary and friend Guarino da Verona. Guarino, after studying Latin under Giovanni di Conversino, had learned Greek at Constantinople, where for five years he lived in the house of Manuel Chrysoloras (1403–8). No other Italian of that day was probably Guarino's equal as a Greek scholar. Filelfo and Aurispa were indeed the only contemporary Italians who shared his facility in speaking and writing Greek. It was in 1414 that Guarino opened at Venice the first humanistic school which had been established in that city. Vittorino studied Greek with him there for a year and a half. In 1418 Guarino finally left Venice. He was subsequently invited by Niccolo d' Este, Marquis of Ferrara, to undertake the education of his son and heir, Lionello. After the early death of Lionello, a youth of great promise, Guarino remained at Ferrara, where he enjoyed the highest repute as a teacher, drawing pupils from all parts of Italy. He died there in 1460, aged ninety.

Thus, before the middle of the fifteenth century, school and lecture-room had diffused the influences of humanism throughout Italy. The spirit of humanistic study had given a new bent to the intellectual interests of cultivated society, and had become a potent factor in the education of youth. In all the principal cities there were men who found themselves drawn together by a common taste for ancient literature and art. The time was ripe for raising the new studies to a somewhat higher level by the exercise of a keener criticism, such as is generated by the play of mind upon mind within a limited social circle, to which the only passport is a recognised standard of attainment or genius. The age of Academies was at hand. Florence, the metropolis of humanism, was the place where the earliest of such societies arose. We have seen that the visit of Gemistos Plethon in 1438 had stimulated the Florentine study of Plato, and had impelled Cosmo de' Medici to found his Platonic Academy. But the palmy days of that institution were rather in the time of his grandson, Lorenzo de' Medici, who became head of the State in 1469, and died in 1492.

Lorenzo was remarkable for versatility even among the men of the Renaissance. Few can ever have been more brilliantly qualified, by natural abilities and by varied accomplishments, to adorn the part of a Maecenas. The Platonic Academy usually met in his palace at Florence, or in his villa on the heights of Fiesole. Only a few members of the society can be named here. Platonic studies were more especially represented by Marsilio Ficino, who had given a great impulse to them, though he had no critical comprehension of Plato. Giovanni Pico della Mirandola brought to Lorenzo's circle those varied gifts of mind and character which so strongly impressed his contemporaries. A keen interest in ancient philosophy, and a desire to harmonise it with Christian doctrine, were distinctive of him. He was destined to die, at the age of thirty-one, in 1494. Leo Battista Alberti, architect, musician, painter, an excellent writer in both Latin and Italian, contributed an example of versatile power almost comparable to that of Lionardo da Vinci. There, too, was Michelangelo, already a poet, but with his greatest artistic achievements still before him. Scholarship had several representatives. Foremost among them was Politian, who has commemorated in Latin verse the gatherings at his patron's villa. Another was Cristoforo Landino, an able Latinist, the author of some dialogues, on the model of Cicero's *Tusculans*, which aid us in imagining the kind of discourse to which the meetings of the Academy gave rise. These are the well-known *Disputationes Camaldunenses*, so called because the conversations are supposed to take place at a house of the Camaldulite Order in the Apennines. Landino introduces us to Lorenzo de' Medici and a party of his friends, who have sought refuge there from the summer heat of Florence. The conversation turns on the merits of that active life which they have left behind them in the fair city on the Arno, as compared with the contemplative life of the philosopher or the monk. Alberti argues in favour of the contemplative existence; Lorenzo, of the active: and their hearers pronounce the opinion that both must contribute to form the complete man. So passes their first evening among the hills. On three following days the friends discourse of Virgil. Humanists though they are, they cling (as Petrarch did) to the faith that his poetry is allegorical; and in the veiled meanings which underlie it they discover links with Platonic doctrine. Landino's work in these imaginary conversations must be accepted as true to the general tendency and tone of the circle which he knew so well. It should be added that the cult of Plato by the Florentine Academy included certain ceremonial observances. They kept his birthday with a banquet, after which some portion of his works was read and discussed. The anniversary of his death had also its fitting commemoration. His bust was crowned with flowers, and a lamp was burned before it. Such things, which may seem childish now, were outward signs of the strong and fresh reality which the memory of the illustrious ancients had for the men of the Renaissance, the heirs of the Middle Age, who had not wholly broken, even yet, with its feelings and impulses.

Rome, too, had its Academy. This was founded, about 1460, by Julius Pomponius Laetus, an enthusiast for Latin scholarship, in which Valla had been his master. It was the peculiar ambition of Laetus to imitate as closely as possible the manners, occupations, and even amusements, of the ancients. The Academy founded by him devoted itself especially to the study of Latin antiquities. Its members also followed his bent by celebrating the Palilia on the legendary birthday of Rome,—by acting comedies of Plautus,—and generally by raising, among themselves, such a phantom as they could of ancient life. It is not altogether surprising that a Pope devoid of humanistic sympathies should have regarded such a society with disapproval. The Roman Academy was temporarily suppressed by Paul II. But it was revived under Sixtus IV, and lived on into the age of Leo X, when it greatly flourished. Among its members at that later period were three of the eminent Latin scholars who became Cardinals,—Bembo, Sadoleto, and Egidio Canisio; also the sparkling historian and biographer Paulus Jovius. It could claim also that brilliant ornament of Leo's Court, Baldassare Castiglione, the author of the *Cortegiano*, and himself a mirror of the accomplishments which he describes.

The Academy of Naples differed in stamp both from the Florentine and from the Roman. Alfonso V of Aragon, who made himself master of Naples in 1442, had drawn a number of distinguished scholars to his Court in that city. After his death in 1458 there was no longer a centre at Naples round which such men could gather. Then it was that Jovianus Pontanus, an excellent writer of Latin, and especially of Latin verse, developed an Academy out of what had previously been an informal society of scholarly friends. The distinctive note of the Neapolitan Academy continued to be that which it derived from its origin. It was occupied more especially with the cultivation of style. The activity distinctive of it is represented by a series of Latin versifiers, remarkable for scholarship, for vigour, and also for a neopagan tendency. The Florentine Academy was predominantly philosophic; the Roman was antiquarian; the

Neapolitan was literary. Many similar societies, of more or less note, arose in other Italian cities. At the close of the fifteenth century almost every considerable centre of culture possessed its Academy. The manner in which these institutions contributed to the advancement of scholarship and learning was somewhat different from that associated with more modern bodies of a similar nature. The Italian Academies of the Renaissance had little to show in the way of "transactions" or memoirs which could be regarded as permanently valuable contributions to special branches of knowledge. But the variety and brilliancy of the men whom these societies are known to have brought into sympathetic converse would suffice to establish the importance of the movement. Such Academies raised the classical Renaissance to a higher level.

Cooperation of the academic kind bore a necessary part in that great work which crowned the labours of the Italian revival by securing the Greek and Latin classics against the accidents of time. Aldo Manuzio was aided in the affairs of his press by the "New Academy" (*Neacademia*) which he founded at Venice. In order justly to estimate his achievement, we must recall what had been done in the same field before him. Italy was the country where the recently invented art of printing first became largely fruitful in the service of letters. In the Benedictine House of Santa Scolastica at Subiaco the German printers Schweinheim and Pannartz printed in 1465 the first edition of Lactantius. Removing to Rome in 1467, they began to issue the Latin classics. In 1469 their press produced Caesar, Livy, Aulus Gellius, Virgil, and Lucan; which were shortly followed by Cicero's Letters, with a volume of his Orations, and by Ovid. Some twenty-three Latin authors were published by them in little more than two years. At about the same time printing was begun at Venice by John of Speyer, and by a Frenchman, Nicolas Jenson. They, too, sent forth many Latin authors. Milan seems to have had a press as early as 1469. At Florence, in 1471, Bernardo Cennini printed the commentary of Servius on Virgil's Eclogues. Another Florentine printing-house was that of Giunta, afterwards famed for the *editiones Iuntinae.* The printing of Greek began not long after the first entrance of the art into Italy. In 1476 the Greek Grammar of Constantine Lascaris was printed at Milan by Zarot. At Milan, Theocritus (*Idylls* i—xviii), and Hesiod (*Works and Days*) came from the press in or about 1481; and Isocrates (edited by Demetrius Chalcondylas) in 1493. Venice contributed, in 1484, the Greek Grammar (*Erotemata*) of Manuel Chrysoloras. At Florence, in 1488, Lorenzo Alopa, a Venetian, published a Homer, edited by Chalcondylas. Such was the general situation when Aldo commenced his labours. Most of the greater Latin classics had been printed; but of the Greek, only Homer, Hesiod's *Works and Days*, eighteen Idylls of Theocritus, and Isocrates.

Teobaldo Manucci, who Latinised his name into Aldus Manutius, and is now more usually called Aldo Manuzio, was born in 1450. His aim in youth was to qualify himself for the profession of a humanist. He studied Greek at Ferrara under Guarino da Verona, to whom he afterwards inscribed his Theocritus. At Rome Gasparino da Verona was his master in Latin. Aldo became tutor to the young princes of Carpi, Alberto and Lionello Pio, nephews of his old fellow-student, the brilliant Pico della Mirandola. But he had now formed the great design of printing all the masterpieces of Greek literature, and on that project all his thoughts were intent. He was supplied with the means of executing it by his pupil Alberto Pio, to whom, as τῷ τῶν ὄντων ἐραστῇ, he dedicated the *editio princeps* of Aristotle. In 1490 he settled at Venice, in a house near the church of San Agostino, and entered upon preparations for his task. A Cretan, Marcus Musurus, was the most important of his assistants. The handwriting of Musurus was the pattern from which Aldo's Greek type was cast,—as, in a later day, Porson's hand supplied a model to the Cambridge press. It is noteworthy that another Cretan, Demetrius, had designed the types used by Alopa in the Florentine Homer of 1488. Many of Aldo's compositors were likewise Cretans. His printing establishment at Venice was a Greek-speaking household. There was a separate department for binding books. The printing-ink was made in the house; the excellent paper came from the mills of Fabriano.

In 1493 Aldo began his series of Greek editions with the *Hero and Leander* of Musaeus; whom, as appears from the preface, he identified with the pre-Homeric bard of legend. Thenceforward Aldo's work was prosecuted with steady vigour, though not without some enforced interruptions. The whole of Hesiod, with Theocritus (thirty Idylls), Theognis, and some other gnomic poetry, came out in 1495. Aristotle, in five volumes, appeared in the years 1495–8. Nine plays of Aristophanes were issued in 1498. The year 1502 produced Thucydides, Sophocles, and Herodotus. In 1503 came Xenophon's *Hellenica*, and Euripides; in 1504, Demosthenes; in 1508, Lysias and other orators; in 1509, parts of Plutarch. The year 1513 was signalised by the *editio princeps* of Plato, dedicated to Leo X. In 1514 Pindar was sent forth; also Hesychius and Athenaeus. When Aldo died in 1515, he had produced twenty-eight *editiones principes* of Greek and Latin classics within the space of some twenty-two years. And these editions were of a merit hitherto unequalled. Pains had been taken with the collation of manuscripts and with criticism of the text; and in this respect many of the books, though they may fail to satisfy the modern standard, were superior to any that had preceded them. The printing was of much beauty; and the small form of the volumes was a welcome boon in an age accustomed to folios or quartos. But the most important benefit was the extraordinary cheapness of these editions. The price of an Aldine volume ranged from about a shilling to half-a-crown of our money. It was not without many difficulties and discouragements that such a result had been attained. Aldo suffered from the jealousy of rival printers and the frauds of piratical booksellers. On four occasions (he writes in 1501) the persons in his employment had caballed against him, with the aim of making larger gains at his expense. Then the work of his press was twice stopped by war; first in 1506, and again in 1510–15. But Aldo was sustained by a sober enthusiasm.

He must also have been cheered by the sympathy of the Hellenists whom he had drawn around him. His "Neacademia" was formed at Venice at 1500. Its rules were drawn up in Greek, and that language was spoken at its meetings. The secretary of the society was Scipione Fortiguerra, the author of a once famous essay *In praise of Greek Letters*, who grecised his name as Carteromachus; an example which the other members of the body followed. The eminent scholar John Lascaris was one of several distinguished Greeks resident in Italy who joined Aldo's Academy. Among the subjects with which the Neacademia occupied itself was the choice of books to be printed, the collation of manuscripts, and the discussion of various readings. Some of the members assisted Aldo as editors of particular classics. It was in order to see a new edition of his own *Adagia* through the press that Erasmus became a guest under Aldo's roof in 1508. He has described how he sat in the same room with his host, revising the book, while Aldo and his proof-reader Seraphinus pushed forward the printing. Erasmus became, as was natural, an honorary member of the Neacademia. That distinction was enjoyed also by an Englishman who had studied humane letters under Politian, Thomas Linacre. Aldo's Academy thus stands out among kindred institutions of the Italian Renaissance as a body actively associated with a definite work on a grand scale, the printing of the classics. After Aldo's death in 1515, the business of the press was carried on by his brothers-in-law and partners, the Asolani; and then by his son, Paolo Manuzio, and his grandson, Aldo the younger. The series of Greek classics was continued with Pausanias, Strabo, Aeschylus, Galen, Hippocrates, and Longinus. When Aeschylus had appeared, in 1518, no extant Greek classic of the first rank remained unprinted. Aldo was not only one of the greatest of all benefactors to literature, but also a man whose disinterested ardour and generous character compel admiration. Alluding to the device on his title-pages, the dolphin and the anchor,—symbols of speed and tenacity, with the motto *Festina lente*,—he said (in 1499), "I have achieved much by patience (*cunctando*), and I work without pause." The energy, knowing neither haste nor rest, which carried him to his goal was inspired by the same feeling which, in the dawn of the Renaissance, had animated Petrarch and Boccaccio. Those pioneers, when they ransacked libraries for manuscripts, felt as if they were liberating the master-spirits of old from captivity. So does Aldo exult, in one of his prefaces, at the thought that he has delivered the classics from bondage to "the buriers of books," the misers of bibliography who hid their treasures from the light. And no one was more liberal than Aldo to all who worked with him, or who sought his aid.

At the time when his task was advancing towards completion, Greek learning had already begun to decline in Italy, and the last period of the Italian Renaissance had set in. That period may be roughly dated from the year 1494; and the end, or beginning of the end, is marked by the sack of Rome in 1527. It was in 1494 that Charles VIII of France marched on Naples. He conquered it easily, but lost it again after his withdrawal. A time of turmoil ensued in Italy, which became the battle-ground where foreign princes fought out their feuds. The Medici were driven from Florence, which thereupon was rent by the struggle between the Piagnoni and the Ottimati. Naples was acquired in 1504 by Ferdinand of Aragon. Milan was harassed by the passage of French, Swiss, and German armies. Almost everywhere Italy lay down-trodden under the contending invaders. Only a few of the smaller principalities, such as Ferrara and Mantua, retained any vigorous or independent life. Rome, meanwhile, was wealthy, and still untroubled by war. The papacy was now the chief Italian Power in the peninsula. It was at Rome, therefore, that humanistic culture held its central seat in this closing period of the Italian Renaissance. Erasmus was there in 1509, when Cardinal Grimani pressed him to make Rome his permanent abode; and he has recorded his impressions. He saw a bright and glorious city, an opulent treasure-house of literature and art, the metropolis of polite society, refined luxury, and learned intercourse. Nor was this merely the estimate of a northern visitor. A similar view of Rome brought consolation to contemporary Italians. The *Poetica* of Marco Vida (1489–1566) ends with a panegyric on Leo X, in which he laments, indeed, that Italy has become a prey to "foreign tyrants." The "fortune of arms" has forsaken her. "But may she still excel," he cries, "in the studies of Minerva; and may Rome, peerless in beauty, still teach the nations!" The claim which Virgil made immortal is reversed by Vida. Let others wield the sword, and bear rule; but let Rome be supreme in letters and in arts.

The prevalent tendency of humanism at this period was towards accuracy and elegance of Latin style. That wide range of study which had been characteristic of Politian, and of the greatest humanists before him, was no longer in vogue. Attention was now concentrated on a few models of composition, especially on Cicero and Virgil. Bembo, strictest of Ciceronians, a literary dictator in the age of Leo X, warned the learned Sadoleto against allowing his style to be depraved by the diction of St Paul's Epistles ("*Omitte has nugas*"); advice which did not, however, ultimately deter Sadoleto from publishing a commentary on the *Epistle to the Romans*. Another trait of the time, justly ridiculed by Erasmus, was the fashion of using pagan paraphrases for Christian ideas, or for things wholly modern. Thus the saints are *divi*; the papal tiara is *infula Romulea*. Not merely good taste, but reverence, was often sacrificed to this affectation. With regard to pagan themes, Bembo is a proof that they could now be treated in Latin verse, and by an ecclesiastic, with a frank paganism which no ancient could have outdone.

The central figure in this period is Pope Leo X (1513-21). He had an inborn zeal for the Classical Renaissance. At Rome, under his reign, the cult of the antique engaged a circle much larger, though far less rich in genius, than the group which had surrounded his father Lorenzo de' Medici at Florence. The position of humanism at the Vatican was now very different from what it had been in the preceding century. So far as the earlier humanists came into relations with the papal Curia, it was chiefly because they were required as writers of Latin. Poggio, Lionardo Bruni, and Lorenzo Valla, were employed as Apostolic secretaries; Valla's appointment marked, indeed, as we have seen, a new policy of the Vatican towards humanism: but all three remained laymen; and that was the general rule. In those days, humanists seldom rose to high ecclesiastical office. It was otherwise now. Distinction in scholarship had become one of the surest avenues to preferment in the Church. A youth gained some literary distinction, was brought to Rome by his patron, and attracted the notice of the Pope. Thus Bembo, Sadoleto, and Aleander attained to the sacred purple; Paulus Jovius, Vida, and Marcus Musurus became bishops. Such cases were frequent. Scholars were now in the high places of the Vatican. They gave the tone to the Court and to Roman society. It was a world pervaded by a sense of beauty in literature, in plastic art, in architecture, in painting; a world in which graceful accomplishments and courtly manners lent a charm to daily life. A scholar or artist, coming to Rome in Leo's reign, would have found there all, or more than all, that had fascinated Erasmus a few years before. To Leo and his contemporaries it might well have seemed that their age was the very flower and crown of the Renaissance. The aesthetic pleasures of their existence had been prepared by the labours of predecessors who had brought back the ancient culture. But the humanism of Leo's age had no longer within it the seeds of further growth. The classical revival in Italy had now wellnigh run its course. Its best and freshest forces were spent. It was rather in the literature of the Italian language that the original power of the Italian genius was now seeking expression.

Leo X should not, however, be identified merely with that phase of humanism, brilliant, indeed, yet already decadent, which was mirrored in his Court. He was also, beyond doubt, a man animated by a strong and genuine desire to promote intellectual culture, not only in the form of elegant accomplishment, but also in that of solid learning. Of this he gave several proofs. The Roman University (the "Sapienza") had hitherto been inferior, as a school of humanism, to some others in Italy. It had never rivalled Florence, and it could not now compete with Ferrara. Leo, in the first year of his pontificate (1513), made a serious effort to improve it; and it was not his fault if that effort had little permanent success. He remodelled the statutes of the University; created some new chairs; enlarged the emoluments of those which existed; and induced some scholars of eminence to join the staff. Another way in which he showed his earnest sympathy with learning was by his encouragement of Greek studies. More than forty years before this, editions of Latin classics had begun to issue from the Roman press. But Rome had hitherto lagged behind in the printing of Greek. The first Greek book printed at Rome was a Pindar, published in 1515 by Zacharias Calliergi, a Cretan, who had helped to bring out the *Etymologicum Magnum* at Venice in 1499. A Greek printing press was now established in Rome by Leo. He also instituted the "Gymnasium Caballini Montis," where lectures were given by Aldo's former assistant, the eminent Cretan scholar Marcus Musurus, and also by the veteran John Lascaris. This was perhaps the last considerable effort made in Italy to arrest the incipient decline of Greek studies.

A permanent interest attaches to the profession of faith in humanism left on record by Leo X. When, in 1515, the first six books of the *Annals* of Tacitus appeared in the *editio princeps* of Filippo Beroaldo the younger, the Pope conferred upon the editor a privilege for the sale and reprinting of the book. In the brief which granted this privilege, and which was prefixed to the edition, Leo expressed his estimate of the New Learning. "We have been accustomed," he says, "even from our early years, to think that nothing more excellent or more useful has been given by the Creator to mankind, if we except only the knowledge and true worship of Himself, than these studies, which not only lead to the ornament and guidance of human life, but are applicable and useful to every particular situation; in adversity consolatory, in prosperity pleasing and honourable; insomuch that without them we should be deprived of all the grace of life and all the polish of social intercourse." He then observes that "the security and extension of these studies" seem to depend chiefly on two things,—"the number of men of learning, and the ample supply of excellent authors." As to the first, it has always been his earnest desire to encourage men of letters; and as to the acquisition of books, he rejoices when an opportunity is thus afforded him of thus "promoting the advantage of mankind." The best spirit of Italian humanism finds a noble expression in these words, written by one who, both as Giovanni de' Medici and as Leo X, had proved the sincerity of his devotion to the interests of letters. That sympathy was interwoven with his personal character and temperament; it scarcely needed to be strengthened by the great traditions of his house. We may doubt whether he was conscious that the Classical Renaissance had so decidedly passed its zenith : certainly he can have had no presage of what was to happen a few years after his death.

The capture of Rome by the imperialist troops in 1527 broke up that Roman world of literature and art which, as viewed by the men who were under its spell, had rivalled the age of Pericles or of Augustus. Valeriano, who knew the city both before and after that fatal year, has described, in his dialogue *De Literatorum Infelicitate,* the horror and completeness of the catastrophe. When he asked for the men of letters whom he remembered at Rome, he learned that many of them had perished by the sword, by torture, or by disease. Others had escaped only to end their days in penury and suffering. But some fine scholars were still left in Italy. Petrus Victorius (1499–1584), who taught at his native Florence from 1538 onwards, showed much acuteness in his *Variae Lectiones.* His labours included some good work for the Attic tragedians, Aristotle, and Cicero. Lombardy was now the part of Italy in which classical culture found its chief refuge. At Ferrara humanism was represented especially by Lilius Gyraldus (1479–1552), whose *Historia Poetarum* (1545) was one of the earliest books on the history of classical literature. Robortellus (1516–67), a sound Hellenist, who taught at Pavia and elsewhere, edited Aeschylus and Callimachus ; while by his treatise *De Arte sive Ratione Corrigendi Antiquos Libros* he ranks among the founders of textual criticism. Ever since the days of Politian, the cultivation of Latin verse writing had been popular. Along with much that was mediocre or bad, some admirable work in this kind was produced. Andrea Navagero, of Venice, who died in 1529, might be instanced as a Latin scholar who wrote verse in a really classical taste, untainted by the coarseness which was then too common. A few years after the sack of Rome, Marcantonio Flaminio, of Imola, dedicated to his patron, Alessandro Farnese, a collection of verses by scholars belonging to Venice, Modena, Verona, Mantua, and other North-Italian towns. The condition of Italy at this time was utterly miserable. But Flaminio's elegant verse breathes only a scholar's exultation. " Happy, too happy, are our days, which have given birth to a Catullus, a Tibullus, a Horace, and a Virgil of their own ! Who would have thought that, after the darkness of so many centuries, and the dire disasters of Italy, so many lights could have arisen within the narrow region beyond the Po ? " Such words, written in such days, have an unconscious pathos. They are significant of Italy's patient fidelity to the ideals of the Renaissance, as well as of the price which she paid for it. And now at last the tide was about to turn. The power of the Roman Church, strenuously engaged in combating the Reformation, became adverse also to the aims and the spirit of the New Learning. In 1530 Clement VII and Charles V made their compact at Bologna. Spain, supported by the papacy, effected the pacification of Italy. So far as Italy was concerned, the humanistic movement was now arrested, and a reaction had begun. Writing about 1540, Paulus Jovius lamented that scholarship had migrated from Italy to Germany. His complaint was somewhat premature; but such a process had indeed set in. The most learned Italian of the next generation, Cardinal Baronius (1538–1607), the author of *Annales Ecclesiastici*, was unacquainted with Greek.

The work accomplished by the Italian Renaissance claims the lasting gratitude of mankind. In the interval between the time of Petrarch and that of Leo X, a space of about a hundred and seventy years, ardent and unceasing labours bridged the gulf between the medieval and the modern world. Latin, the universal language, was purged from barbarism. Latin literature was brought back into the full light of intelligent study. Greek was restored to the West. After centuries of intellectual poverty, men entered once more into possession of the poetry and the eloquence, the wisdom and the wit, bequeathed by ancient Greece and Rome. The period of this revival was one in which the general tone of morality was low; and cynicism, bred partly of abuses in the Church, had wellnigh paralysed the restraining power of religion. Some of the humanists were pagans, not as Seneca was, but as Petronius Arbiter; and, far from suffering in public esteem, enjoyed the applause of princes and prelates. Not a little that was odious or shameful occasionally marked their conduct and disfigured their writings. But it is hardly needful to observe that such exponents of humanism were in no way representative of its essence, or even of its inevitable conditions in a corrupt age. Among the foremost Italian scholars were many exemplars of worthy life and noble character, men whose enthusiasm for letters was joined to moral qualities which compel respect and admiration. And no transient phase of fashionable paganism could mar the distinctive merits of the Italian Renaissance, or affect its permanent results. Italian humanism restored good standards of style in prose and verse, thereby benefiting not classical studies alone, but modern literature as well; it did much for erudition, and prepared the ground for more; it founded literary education of a liberal type; it had a wide outlook, and taught men to regard classical antiquity as a whole, a fruitful stage in the history of human development. Lastly, it achieved a result even larger than its work for scholarship, by diffusing a new spirit, the foe of obscurantism, the ally of all forces that make for light, for the advancement of knowledge, and for reasonable freedom.

Long before the Renaissance had run its course in Italy, its influences had begun to pass the Alps. But there is one man who, above all others, must be regarded as the herald of humanism in the North. It is the distinction of Erasmus that by the peculiar qualities of his genius, and by the unique popularity of his writings, he prepared the advent of the New Learning, not in his native Holland alone, but throughout Europe. Before indicating the special directions which the

Renaissance took in particular countries, it is fitting to speak of him whose work affected them all.

Born at Rotterdam in 1467, Erasmus was approaching manhood when Italian humanism, having culminated in the days of Politian, was about to decline. His own training was not directly due to Italy. When he was a schoolboy at Deventer, his precocious ability was recognised by Rudolf Agricola, whom he has designated as " the first who brought from Italy some breath of a better culture." Erasmus avers that, in his boyhood, northern Europe was barbarously ignorant of humane literature. A knowledge of Greek was " the next thing to heresy." " I did my best," he says, " to deliver the rising generation from this slough of ignorance, and to inspire them with a taste for better studies." He made himself a good scholar by dint of hard private work, suffering privations which left him a chronic invalid. In 1498 he visited Oxford, meeting there some of the earliest English humanists. From 1500 to 1505 he was in Paris, working hard at Greek. He spent the years 1506–9 in Italy. From the close of 1510 to that of 1513 he was at Cambridge, where he lectured on Greek, and also held the Lady Margaret Professorship of Divinity. There, in 1512, he completed his collation of the Greek text of the New Testament. In 1516, his edition of it, the first ever published, was brought out by Froben at Basel. He left England in 1514, to return only for a few months somewhat later. His life, after 1514, was passed chiefly at Basel, where he died in 1536. Those twenty-two years were full of marvellous literary activity.

The attitude of Erasmus towards humanism had a general affinity with that of Petrarch and the other leaders of the Italian revival. Like them, he hailed a new conception of knowledge, an enlargement of the boundaries within which the intellect and imagination could move. Like them, he welcomed the recovered literatures of Greece and Rome as inestimable organs of that mental and spiritual enfranchisement. But there was also a difference. To Petrarch, as to the typical Italian humanist generally, the New Learning was above all things an instrument for the self-culture of the individual. To Erasmus, on the other hand, self-culture was, in itself,—greatly though he valued it,—a secondary object, subservient to a greater end. He regarded humanism as the most effectual weapon for combating that widespread ignorance which he considered to be the root of many evils that were around him. He saw the abuses in the Church, the scandals among the clergy, the illiteracy prevalent in some of the monastic Orders. Kings wrought untold misery for selfish aims: " when princes purpose to exhaust a commonwealth," he said, " they speak of a just war; when they unite for that object, they call it peace." The pedantries of the Schoolmen, though decaying, were still obstacles to intellectual progress. The moral standards in public and private life were deplorably low. Erasmus held that the first step towards mitigating such evils was to disseminate as widely as possible the civilising influence of knowledge; and in humanism he found the knowledge best suited for the purpose. He overrated the rapidity with which such an influence could permeate the world. But he was constant to his object, and did much towards attaining it.

Thus, in all his work, his aim was essentially educational. He was an ardent and indefatigable student. But through all his labours there ran the purpose of a practical moralist, who hoped to leave human society better than he had found it. No aspect of the Renaissance interested him which he did not think conducive to that end. He cared nothing for its metaphysics, archaeology, or art. All his own writings illustrate his ruling motive. The *Adagia* are maxims or proverbial sayings, culled from the classics, which he often applies to the affairs of his own day. The *Colloquia* are lively dialogues, partly meant to serve as models of Latin writing, which convey, in a dramatic guise, his views on contemporary questions. The *Apophthegms* are pointed sayings from various authors, largely from Plutarch. An educational and ethical aim also guided his choice of books to be edited. His best edition of a classic was that of his favourite poet Terence. Next in merit, perhaps, stood his edition of Seneca. An equal importance can scarcely be claimed for his editions of Greek classics, belonging chiefly to the last five years of his life; though they did the service of making the authors more accessible, and of supplying improved texts. He also promoted a wider knowledge of Greek poetry and prose by several Latin translations. But that purpose which gave unity to his life-work received its highest embodiment in his contributions to Biblical criticism and exegesis. The Scholastic Theology had been wont to use isolated texts, detached from their context, and artificially interpreted. The object of Erasmus was to let all men know what the Bible really said and meant. We have seen that his edition of the Greek Testament was the earliest. He also made a Latin version of the New Testament, aiming at an accuracy greater than that of the Vulgate. He wrote Latin paraphrases of the books of the New Testament (except *Revelation*), with the object of exhibiting the thought in a more modern form. Lastly, he recalled attention from the medieval expositors of Christian doctrine to the Fathers of the early Church. He edited Jerome, and some other Latin Fathers; he also made Latin translations from some of the Greek Fathers, especially from Chrysostom and Athanasius, and so helped to make their writings better known in the West. He wished to see the Scriptures translated into every language, and given to all. "I long," he said, "that the husbandman should sing them to himself as he follows the plough, that the weaver should hum them to the tune of his shuttle, that the traveller should beguile with them the weariness of his journey."

The more popular writings of Erasmus had a circulation throughout Europe which even now would be considered enormous. When it was rumoured that the Sorbonne intended to brand his *Colloquia* as heretical, a Paris bookseller deemed it well to hurry through the press an edition of 24,000 copies. We hear that in 1527 a Spanish version of his *Encheiridion* (a manual of Christian ethics) could be found in many country-inns throughout Spain. It would probably be difficult to name an author whose writings were so often reprinted in his lifetime as were those of Erasmus. He was not, indeed, a Scaliger, a Casaubon, or a Bentley. He did not contribute, in the same sense or in a similar degree, to the progress of scientific scholarship. But no one else so effectively propagated the influence of humanism. Of all scholars who have popularised scholarly literature Erasmus was the most brilliant, the man whose aims were loftiest, and who produced lasting effects over the widest area. His work was done, too, at the right moment for the North. A genial power was needed to thaw the frost-bound soil, and to prepare those fruits which each land was to bring forth in its own way.

The energies of the Italian Renaissance had been concentrated on the literature and art of ancient Greece and Rome. The Italian mind had a native and intimate sympathy with classical antiquity. For Italy, the whole movement of the Renaissance is virtually identical with the restoration of classical learning. It is otherwise when we follow that movement into northern Europe. Humanism is still, indeed, the principal organ through which the new spirit works; but the operations of the spirit itself become larger and more varied. The history of the Classical Revival passes, on one side, into that of the Reformation; on another, into provinces which belong to modern literature. It might be said that the close of the Italian Renaissance is also, in strictness, the close of the process by which a knowledge of classical antiquity was restored: what remained, was to diffuse the results throughout Europe, and to give them a riper development. But it is desirable to indicate, at least in outline, the general conditions under which humanism first entered the countries of the North. We may begin with Germany.

In the course of the fifteenth century, some German students had resorted to teachers of the New Learning at various Italian centres. Among the earliest of these was Johann Müller (1436-76), born at Königsberg near Coburg, and hence known as Regiomontanus. He was the first who made humanism the handmaid of science. After working at Vienna under the astronomer Purbach, he went with Cardinal Bessarion to Italy, where he spent several years in studying Greek (1462-70). He translated into Latin the works of Ptolemy, the *Conics* of Apollonius of Perga, and other scientific treatises. Settling at Nürnberg in 1471, he founded an observatory, and made several improvements in practical astronomy. His *Ephemerides*, the precursors of nautical almanacs, helped the Spanish and Portuguese explorers to navigate untravelled seas. Another of the German pioneers was Roelof Huysmann, known in literary history as Rudolf Agricola (1443–85). Going to Ferrara in 1476, he attended the Greek lectures of Theodorus Gaza. Through the good offices of Johann von Dalberg, the scholarly Bishop of Worms, he was appointed to a professorship at Heidelberg. There, as also at Worms, he lectured on the Greek and Roman literature. He was an opponent of the scholastic philosophy as it existed in his day, and his best-known work, *De Inventione Dialectica*, was a plea for its reform. But his special claim to remembrance is that he was the first who systematically sought to make classical study an effective force in German education. He, and such as he, when they returned to Germany from their studies in Italy, found themselves in an atmosphere wholly different from that which surrounded the early Italian humanists. Erasmus has described the intellectual torpor which prevailed in Germany during his own boyhood and youth. The teaching of Latin was dull and meagre; Greek was scarcely taught at all. The masters were content with a few old hand-books, and wedded to outworn methods. Scholastic theologians and illiterate monks were equally hostile to the new humanism. It had, however, some powerful protectors, including the Roman King Maximilian; Joachim, the Elector of Brandenburg; Albert, Archbishop of Mainz; and, not least, Frederick, Elector of Saxony. Of the seventeen Universities, some, such as Vienna, Heidelberg, and Erfurt, admitted the New Learning, though in some others, such as Cologne, it was opposed. There were also groups of learned students at several centres, such as Basel, Strassburg, Augsburg, and Nürnberg; and there were some rising societies or academies, devoted to humane letters. But there was, as yet, no general or widely-diffused interest in the New Learning; while, on the other hand, there were powerful influences directly and strongly opposed to it. The first event which roused the public mind to a more active sympathy is connected with an illustrious name.

Johann Reuchlin (1455–1522) studied Greek at Paris, and also at Basel. He afterwards went to Italy. At Rome, in 1482, he heard Argyropoulos lecture on Thucydides, and was noticed by him as a student of great promise. He published some Latin versions from Greek authors, and some elementary Greek manuals which were used in German schools. But after 1492 his chief interest was in Hebrew,—mainly as the key of the Old Testament, but also on account of the *Cabbala*, that medieval system of Jewish theosophy which he regarded as helpful towards reconciling ancient philosophy with Christian doctrine. The same notion had been cherished by Pico della Mirandola (1463–94), who, like Reuchlin, had approached the Cabbala through Neoplatonism. Reuchlin's views on the subject were set forth in his treatises *De Verbo Mirifico* (1494) and *De Arte Cabalistica* (1517). Thus alike on theological and on philosophical grounds Reuchlin was an enthusiast for Hebrew scholarship.  He furnished it with several aids, including the grammar and lexicon (*Rudimenta Hebraica*) which he brought out in 1506.  And it was as a defender of Hebrew letters that he became engaged in a struggle which went far to decide the immediate future of the New Learning in Germany.

In 1509 Johann Pfefferkorn, a converted Jew, sought from the Emperor Maximilian a mandate for the suppression of all Hebrew books except copies of the Bible.  Reuchlin was consulted, and opposed the measure. He was then attacked by Pfefferkorn as a traitor to the Church.  In 1514 he was accused by the Dominicans of Cologne, whose dean was the Inquisitor Hochstraten, in the ecclesiastical Court at Mainz.  The Bishop of Speyer, acting for the Pope, acquitted him, and the decision was confirmed at Rome in 1516.  This was an impressive victory for Reuchlin.  Afterwards, on an appeal of the Dominicans, Rome reversed the previous judgment, and condemned him (1520); but that sentence passed unnoticed, and has come to light only in our own time.

Meanwhile the German humanists had taken up Reuchlin's cause, which, as they saw, was their own.  If Jews should be forbidden to read such an author as Maimonides, who was useful to St Thomas Aquinas, how could Christians be allowed to read Homer, who depicts the immoralities of Olympus?  Never was intolerance a fairer mark for the shafts of ridicule.  The first volume of the *Epistolae Obscurorum Virorum*, written chiefly by Crotus Rubeanus, appeared in 1514; the second, chiefly by Ulrich von Hutten, in 1517.  The writers wield, with trenchant if somewhat brutal force, a weapon which had been used with greater subtlety by Plato, and to which a keener edge was afterwards given by Pascal.  They put the satire into the mouths of the satirised. Bigots and obscurantists bear witness in dog-Latin to their own ineptitude.  Reuchlin's triumph in 1516 had an immediate and momentous effect on German opinion.  A decided impetus was given to Hebrew and to Greek studies, especially in their bearing on Biblical criticism and on theology.  This was the direction characteristic of the earlier humanism in Germany.  Almost all the more eminent scholars were occupied, at least occasionally, with theological discussions.  In 1525, three years after Reuchlin's death, Erasmus wrote a letter to Alberto Pio, prince of Carpi (the pupil and benefactor of Aldo), in which he observes that the adversaries of the New Learning had been anxious to identify it with the Lutheran cause.  They hoped, he says, thus to damage two enemies at once.  In Germany, during the earlier half of the sixteenth century, the alliance between humanism and the Reformation was real and intimate.  The paramount task which the New Learning found in Germany was the elucidation of the Bible.  But the study of the classical literatures also made steady progress, and was soon firmly established in German education.

Foremost among those who contributed to that result was Melanchthon

(1497–1560), though his services to humanism in earlier life are now less prominently associated with his memory than the part which he afterwards bore in the theological controversies of his age. It was from Reuchlin that the precocious boy, Philip Schwartzerd, received the Greek name, a version of his patronymic, under which he was to become famous. After taking his doctor's degree at Tübingen in 1514, Melanchthon won notice by expositions of Virgil and Terence, which led Erasmus to hail him as a rising star of learning. He was only twenty-one when, in 1518, the Elector of Saxony, moved by Reuchlin, appointed him to the chair of Greek in the University of Wittenberg. It was characteristic of the man and of the period that he began with two concurrent sets of lectures, one upon the *Epistle to Titus*, and the other upon Homer; observing, in reference to the latter, that, like Solomon, he sought "Tyrian brass and gems" for the adornment of God's temple. Luther, his senior by fourteen years, derived from him a new impulse to the study of Greek. Melanchthon did very important work towards establishing or improving humanistic education in the schools of Germany. In his *Discourse on Reforming the Studies of Youth*, a work imbued with the genuine spirit of the Renaissance, he advocated a liberal discipline of classical literature as the soundest basis of school-training, in opposition to the methods of instruction favoured by the older scholastic system. Many of the aids to classical study which Melanchthon produced (chiefly at Wittenberg) were popular school-books in their day. Among these were his *Institutiones Linguae Graecae* (1518); his *Grammatica Latina* (1525); Latin versions from Greek classics; and comments on various Greek and Latin authors. After Melanchthon may justly be named his friend and biographer Camerarius (Joachim Kammermeister, 1500–74), a prolific contributor to scholarly literature, whose edition of Plautus (1552) was the first that placed the text on a sound basis.

Thus, in the course of the sixteenth century, the new studies gradually conquered a secure position in Germany. Broad and solid foundations were laid for the classical learning which Germans of a later age were to build up. But, while there was this progress in humane letters, the Teutonic movement showed nothing analogous to the Italian feeling for the aesthetic charm of ancient culture and existence. The German mind, earnest, and intellectually practical, had not the Italian's delight in beauty of literary style and form, still less his instinctive sympathy with the pagan spirit. Germany drew fresh mental vigour and freedom from the Classical Revival, without adopting the Italian ideal of self-culture, or admitting a refined paganism into social life. The Teutonic genius, which had moulded so much of all that was distinctively medieval, remained sturdily itself. A like contrast is seen in the province of art. Michelangelo and Raffaelle are intimately affected by classical influences; Dürer and Holbein, men of the same period, also show a new mastery, but remain Gothic. Thus the first period of Humanism in Germany presents a strongly-marked character of its own, wholly different from the Italian. So far as concerns the main current of intellectual and literary interests, the German Renaissance is the Reformation.

France had received the influences of Italian Humanism with the facility of a country to which they were historically congenial, and had been penetrated by them before the conflict opened by Luther had become a disturbing force in Europe. In France the basis of the national character was Latin, and no admixture of other elements could overpower the innate capacity of a Latin race to assimilate the spirit of classical antiquity. The University of Paris was one of the greatest intellectual centres in Europe, drawing to itself, in some measure, every new form of knowledge, while it promoted communication between Paris and all foreign seats of literary activity. It was in 1494, when the Italian Renaissance was at its height, that Charles VIII made his expedition to Naples. For nearly a century afterwards, until the line of the Valois Kings ended with the death of Henry III in 1589, the intercourse between France and Italy was close and continuous. A tincture of Italian manners pervaded the French Court. Italian studies of antiquity reacted upon French literature and art. Thus, from the beginning of the sixteenth century, France offered a smooth course to the Classical Revival. Greek studies had, however, been planted in France at a somewhat earlier time. In 1458 Gregory Tifernas, an Italian of Greek origin, had petitioned the University of Paris to appoint him teacher of Greek. He received that post, with a salary, on condition that he should take no fees, and should give two lectures daily, one on Greek and the other on rhetoric. The scholastic theology and logic were then still dominant at Paris, while the humanities seem to have occupied an inferior place. But, at any rate, the University had now given official sanction to the teaching of Greek. The eminent Byzantine, John Lascaris, lectured on that language at Paris in the reign of Charles VIII. His teaching was continued at intervals under Louis XII, who once sent him as ambassador to Venice; and also under Francis I, for whom he supervised the formation of a library at Fontainebleau. A still more eminent name in the early history of French humanism is that of the Italian Jerome Aleander, afterwards so strenuous an antagonist of the Reformation. Coming to Paris in 1508, at the age of twenty-eight, he gave lectures in Greek, Latin, and Hebrew, winning a reputation which caused him to be appointed Rector of the University. On his return to Rome in 1516 he became librarian of the Vatican, and in 1538 was made a Cardinal. Aleander, who was fortunate in the time of his work at Paris, has been regarded, probably with justice, as the first scholar who gave a decisive stimulus to philological studies in France.

Just before the arrival of Aleander, Paris had begun to take part in the work of publishing Greek books, a field of labour in which its scholarly printers were afterwards to win so much distinction. The first Greek press at Paris was that of Gourmont, who in 1507 issued the Grammar of Chrysoloras, Hesiod's *Works and Days*, the pseudo-Homeric *Frogs and Mice*, Theocritus, and Musaeus. Portions of Plutarch's *Moralia* followed in 1509, under the editorship of Aleander. After an interval, the length of which perhaps indicates that the demand for Greek classics was still very limited, a text of Aristophanes came from Gourmont's press in 1528. A Sophocles was published by Simon Colinaeus in 1529. Robert Estienne (1503–59), scholar and printer, brought out in 1532 his *Thesaurus Linguae Latinae*, which was much enlarged in the succeeding editions (1536 and 1543). Among his Greek *editiones principes* were those of Eusebius (1544–6), Dionysius of Halicarnassus (1547), Dio Cassius (1548), and Appian (1551). His son, Henri Estienne (1528–98), who had the distinction of first printing the *Agamemnon* in its entirety, is especially remembered by his great work, the *Thesaurus Linguae Graecae* (1572). Before the middle of the century the stream of classical publications had fairly set in at Paris, and thenceforth continued to be abundant. Meanwhile a French scholar had arisen who reflected lustre on his country throughout Europe. Budaeus (Guillaume Budé, 1467–1540), after producing in 1514 an able treatise on Roman money (*De Asse*), gained a commanding reputation by his *Commentarii Linguae Graecae*, published at Paris in 1529. That work proved a mine to lexicographers, and was more particularly useful to students of the Greek orators, owing to the care which the author had bestowed on explaining the technical terms of Greek law. Budaeus was, beyond question, the best Greek scholar of his day in Europe, being superior in that respect to Erasmus, though no rival to him in literary genius. But special knowledge is superseded, while the salt of style lasts for ever; and Erasmus lives, while Budaeus is wellnigh forgotten. The relations between these two distinguished men became somewhat strained, through the fault, as it would seem, of Erasmus, whose sly strictures on the Frenchman are certainly suggestive of a covert jealousy; and French scholars made the quarrel a national one. Another French Hellenist of great eminence at this period is Turnebus (Adrien Turnèbe, 1512–65), who belonged to the generation following that of Budaeus. The Royal College had been founded at Paris by Francis I, in 1531, with the special object of encouraging Greek, Latin, and Hebrew learning. Turnebus was appointed, in 1547, to the chair of Greek at that College. He also held the office of King's printer. One of his chief works was an edition of Sophocles, published at Paris in 1553, which did much to determine the text followed by later editors of that poet before Brunck. Henri Estienne, who had been a pupil of Turnebus, has recorded his veneration for him. A better-known tribute is that paid by Montaigne, his junior by twenty-one years, who declares that "Adrianus Turnebus knew more, and knew it better, than any man of his century, or for ages past." He was entirely free, as Montaigne testifies, from pedantry: "his quick understanding and sound judgment" were equally remarkable, whether the subject of conversation was literary or political. Lambinus (Denys Lambin, 1520–72), who in 1561 became a professor at the Royal College, published editions of Horace and Cicero which made a new epoch in the study of those authors. Auratus (Jean Dorat, 1507–88), poet and scholar, who taught Greek at the College, shone especially in the criticism of Aeschylus. Mention is due also to the ill-fated Estienne Dolet (1509–46), who took up the cause of the Ciceronians against Erasmus, and in 1536, at the age of twenty-seven, published his two folio volumes *Commentariorum Linguae Latinae.* Ten years later, he was unjustly condemned by the Sorbonne on a charge of atheism, and put to a cruel death. It should be noted that French scholars won special distinction in the study of Roman Law. Instead of relying on commentators who had merely repeated the older *glossatores*, they turned to the original Roman texts. Cujacius (Jacques Cujas, 1522–90), the greatest interpreter of the sources of law, struck out a new path of critical and historical exposition. Donellus (Hugues Doneau, 1527–91) introduced systematic arrangement by his *Commentarii Iuris Civilis.* Brissonius (Barnabé Brisson, 1531–91) was pre-eminently the lexicographer of the civil law. Gothofredus (Denys Godefroy, 1549–1621) produced an edition of the *Corpus Iuris Civilis* which is still valued. His son Jacques (1587–1652) edited the Theodosian Code.

During the century which followed the death of Turnebus, the history of French humanism is illustrated by names of the first magnitude. Such are those of Joseph Scaliger, Salmasius, and Casaubon; but these great scholars stand beyond the borders of the Renaissance, and belong, like Bentley, to a maturer stage in the erudite development of classical philology. In them, however, the national characteristics of humanism were essentially the same that had appeared in French scholars of the preceding period. These characteristics are alert intelligence, fine perception, boldness in criticism, and lucid exposition. There is a notable difference between the Italian and the French mind of the Renaissance in relation to the antique. The Italian mind surrendered itself, without reserve, to classical antiquity: the Italian desire was to absorb the classical spirit, and to reproduce it with artistic fidelity. The French mind, on the other hand, when brought into contact with the antique, always preserved its originality and independence. It contemplated the work of the ancients with intelligent sympathy, yet with self-possessed detachment, adopting the classical qualities which it admired, but blending them with qualities of its own; so that the outcome is not a reproduction, but a new result. This may be traced in the French architecture and sculpture of the Renaissance no less than in the criticism and the literature.

The seeds of humanism were brought to the Iberian peninsula by a few students who had visited Italy in the fifteenth century. The Spaniard Arias Barbosa, who had studied under Politian, was regarded by his countrymen as their first effective Hellenist. He lectured on Greek for about twenty years at the University of Salamanca, attracting his hearers not only by " a large and rich vein of learning," but also by his poetical taste. A higher fame, however, was gained by his contemporary, Antonio Lebrixa (" Nebrissensis "). After a sojourn of ten years in Italy, Lebrixa returned to Spain in 1473, and taught successively at the Universities of Seville, Salamanca, and Alcalà. He is described as inferior to Barbosa in Greek scholarship, but wider in his range of knowledge, which included Hebrew. Lebrixa's reputation among his Spanish contemporaries, though not in Europe at large, was comparable to that which Budaeus enjoyed in France. He had some distinguished pupils. One of them was Fernando de Guzman Nunez, better known as " Pintianus " (from Pintia, the ancient name of Valladolid), whose fame even eclipsed his master's. Nunez taught Greek at Alcalà, and subsequently at Salamanca, but in literature was best known by an edition of Seneca which appeared in 1536. Another pupil of Lebrixa, the Portuguese historian and poet Resende, did much to promote classical education at Lisbon.

Thus the early part of the sixteenth century afforded grounds for the hope that in the Peninsula, as in other countries of Europe, humanism was destined to flourish. Cardinal Ximenes, the founder of the College at Alcalà, caused the Greek text of the New Testament to be printed there; a task which was completed in 1514. It formed the fifth volume of the Complutensian Polyglott, published at Alcalà in 1522. That work reflected honour on the country, and might well be deemed a good omen for the future of Spanish learning. But after the compact of Charles V with Clement VII, concluded at Bologna in 1530, Spain was definitely ranged on the side of those forces which were reacting against the liberal studies of the Renaissance. The Spanish humanists had never been anything more than centres of cultivated groups, enabled by powerful patronage to defy the general hostility of priests and monks. Humanism had gained no hold on Spanish society at large; and its foes were now more influential than ever. The Jesuits, who afterwards did so much for classical education elsewhere, were then no friends to it in Spain. The Spanish Inquisition was a terror to every suspected pursuit. It is not strange that, under such conditions, Greek learning did not prosper in the Peninsula; though it still produced good Latinists, such as Francisco Sanchez, of Brozas (1523–1601), who wrote on grammar, and the Portuguese Achille Estaço (Achilles Statius, 1524–81) whose criticism of Suetonius was highly praised by Casaubon. The vigorous

Iberian mind, with its strongly-marked individuality, showed the impetus given by the Renaissance in other forms than those of classical scholarship. It found expression in the romance of Cervantes, in the epic of Camoens, and in the dramas of Lope de Vega; or, not less characteristically, in the wistful ardour of exploration which animated Vasco da Gama and Colombo.

Reactionary Spain, a stepmother to classical studies on her own soil, also delayed their progress in the Netherlands. Little time could be spared to them by men who were struggling against Philip II for political independence and for the reformed religion. But when humanism had once been planted in the Low Countries, its growth was remarkably vigorous and rapid. The University of Leyden became the principal centre of the New Learning. Among scholars of Dutch birth at the period of the Renaissance, Erasmus is the first in time as in rank; but neither his higher training nor his life-work was specially connected with his native land. He was, as we have seen, cosmopolitan. The first great name, after his, in the earlier annals of Dutch scholarship is that of Justus Lipsius (Joest Lips, 1547–1606), who was especially strong in knowledge of the Latin historians and of Roman antiquities. His chief work was his celebrated edition of Tacitus (1575). William Canter (1542–75), of Utrecht, who did good work for Greek tragedy, laid down sound principles of textual criticism in his *Syntagma de ratione emendandi Graecos auctores* (1566). In the next generation, Vossius (Gerard John Vos, 1577–1649) rendered solid services to the historical study of antiquity, more especially by setting the example of treating ancient religions from the historical point of view. In Daniel Heinsius (1580–1655) Holland produced a scholar who had more affinity with the Italian humanists. He excelled in the composition of Latin verse and prose; and, as an editor, in his treatment of the Greek poets. Hugo Grotius (Huig van Groot, 1583–1645) owes his fame to the *De Iure Belli et Pacis* (1625), a work fundamental to the modern science of the law of nature and nations. He wrote *Christus Patiens*, and two other plays, in Latin verse. With regard to the earlier Dutch humanism as a whole, it may be said that its characteristic aim was to arrange, classify, and criticise the materials which earlier labours had amassed, while at the same time it was distinguished by an original subtlety and elegance.

England felt the movement of the Renaissance somewhat later than France, and with less instinctive sympathy, but also without such active repugnance as had to be overcome in Germany. A few Englishmen had been pupils of the Italian masters. One of the earliest was William Selling, an Oxonian, who died in 1495. Erasmus, when he came to Oxford in 1498, found there a congenial group of Hellenists, chief among whom were William Grocyn and Thomas Linacre. Both had heard Politian at Florence: Linacre had also been a member of Aldo's Neacademia at Venice. Another Oxonian who did much for

37—2

the New Learning in England was William Lilly, who had studied Greek in Rhodes, and afterwards at Rome. There were others then at Oxford who had some knowledge of Greek, though the whole number cannot have been large. Few books which could help a beginner with the first rudiments of Greek had as yet found their way to England. An English student desirous of acquiring that language was, as a rule, obliged to go abroad. Erasmus mentions that John Fisher, the Bishop of Rochester, who began Greek late in life, had been dissuaded by Latimer from attempting it unless he could procure a teacher from Italy. John Colet, a scholar of most active mind and of great industry, lamented in 1516 that he had not been able to learn Greek—a deficiency which he afterwards made strenuous efforts to repair. But the Oxford Hellenists, though not numerous, represented a new ideal of humane learning, and had a fruitful influence on its progress in England. At Cambridge the study of Greek received its first impulse from the teaching of Erasmus between 1510 and 1513. He began with the rudiments, using first the *Erotemata* of Chrysoloras, and then the larger manual of Theodorus Gaza. His class was a small one, but included some ardent students, such as his friend Henry Bullock; who, writing to him in 1516, reported that the Greek studies which he had initiated were being vigorously prosecuted. Richard Croke, of King's College, Cambridge, who took his degree in the year 1509–10, studied Greek at Oxford with William Grocyn; went thence to Paris; and subsequently taught Greek at Cologne, Louvain, Leipzig, and Dresden. Returning to Cambridge in 1518 he began a course of lectures there on the Greek language, though without official sanction. In 1519 he was formally appointed University reader of Greek, and delivered a remarkable inaugural address in praise of Greek studies, which is still extant. His successor in the readership was a man of rare ability, Sir Thomas Smith (1512–77), of Queens' College, who afterwards rose to eminence in the public service. Smith lectured on Greek, with great success, from about 1535 to 1540. In the latter year Henry VIII founded the five Regius Professorships of Divinity, Civil Law, Physic, Hebrew, and Greek. Smith received the chair of Civil Law; that of Greek was given to his close friend, John Cheke (1514–57), of St John's College, whose repute already stood very high.

Roger Ascham was Cheke's contemporary, and a member of the same College. Scarcely two years after Cheke's appointment, Ascham wrote an interesting letter from Cambridge to a Fellow of St John's, in which he describes the state of classical studies in the University. Aristotle and Plato, he mentions, are read by the undergraduates; as had, indeed, been the case, at least in his own College, for some five years. "Sophocles and Euripides," he then says, "are more familiar authors than Plautus was in your time" [*i.e.* about 1525–35]. "Herodotus, Thucydides, and Xenophon are more conned and discussed than Livy was then. Demosthenes is as familiar an author as Cicero used to be; and there are more copies of Isocrates in use than there formerly were of Terence. Nor do we disregard the Latin authors, but study with the greatest zeal the choicest writers of the best period. It is Cheke's labour and example that have lighted up and continue to sustain this learned ardour." This was written in 1542. It is perhaps the most precise testimony that exists as to the state of Greek studies at any important English seat of learning at any moment in the sixteenth century. Great progress had evidently been made in the preceding ten or twenty years. Sir John Cheke's services to Greek learning in his day were certainly unequalled in England; but Sir Thomas Smith deserves to be remembered along with him as a man who had also given a new and great impetus to those studies.

Mention is due here to the important part which both these eminent men bore in a controversy which excited and divided the humanists of that age. The teachers from whom the scholars of the Renaissance learned Greek pronounced that language as Greeks do at the present day. In 1528 Erasmus published at Basel his dialogue *De recta Latini Graecique sermonis Pronuntiatione.* His protest was chiefly directed against the modern Greek "iotacism"; *i.e.* the pronunciation of several different vowels and diphthongs with the same sound, that of the Italian *i.* He rightly maintained that the ancients must have given to each of these vowels and diphthongs a distinctive sound; and he urged that it was both irrational and inconvenient not to do so. He also objected to the modern Greek mode of pronouncing certain consonants. His reformed pronunciation came to be known as the "Erasmian"; while that used by modern Greeks was called the "Reuchlinian," because Reuchlin (whom Melanchthon followed) had upheld it. About 1535, Thomas Smith and John Cheke—then young men of about twenty— examined the question for themselves, and came to the conclusion that Erasmus was right. Thereupon Smith began to use the "Erasmian" pronunciation in his Greek lectures—though cautiously at first; Cheke and others supported him; and the reform was soon generally accepted. But in 1542 Bishop Gardiner, the Chancellor of the University, issued a decree, enjoining a return to the Reuchlinian mode. Ascham has described, not without humour, the discontent which this edict evoked. After Elizabeth's accession, the "Erasmian" method was restored.

Meanwhile, in the first half of the sixteenth century, a classical training had been introduced into English schools. In developing this type of education Italy had preceded England by about eighty years. Vittorino's school at Mantua, already described, was the earliest model. Winchester College had been founded when Vittorino was a boy; Eton College arose at a time when his school was in its zenith; but these great English foundations, since so distinguished as seats of classical teaching, came into being long before the humanistic influences of the

Renaissance had begun to be felt in England. The oldest English school which has been humanistic from its origin is St Paul's, founded by Dean Colet, who, in 1512, appointed William Lilly to be the first High Master. Lilly was, as we have seen, among the pioneers of Greek study in England, though he is now best remembered by his Latin Grammar. The statutes of St Paul's (1518) enjoin that the Master shall be "learned in good and clean Latin, and also in Greek, if such may be gotten." The proviso implies some scarcity; and in fact it was not, probably, till about 1560 that Greek was thoroughly established among the regular studies of English schools. The statutes of Harrow School (1590) prescribe the teaching of some Greek orators and historians, and of Hesiod's poems. This seems to be one of the earliest instances in our school-statutes where the directions for Greek teaching are precise, and not merely general. Many large public schools, such as Christ's Hospital, Westminster, Merchant Taylors', and Charterhouse, were established in or near London within a century after the foundation of St Paul's School. In all these the basis of study was humanistic; as it was also in many other grammar schools founded, during the same period, in various parts of the country.

A general survey of English humanism in the sixteenth century supplies abundant evidence of zealous work, and of a progress which, before the year 1600, had secured the future of classical studies in England. There were many able teachers, and a few who were really eminent in their day. Yet, in two respects, a comparison with the leading countries of the Continent is disadvantageous for our country at that period. Britain produced in the sixteenth century no scholar of the first rank; though in George Buchanan (1506–82) Scotland could show a consummate writer of the Latin language. And our press sent forth few books which advanced Greek or Latin learning. Linacre's treatise on certain points of Latin usage (*De emendata structura Latini sermonis*, 1514), a work of the same class as Valla's *Elegantiae*, is one of the very few English books in that department of knowledge which attained to the distinction of being reprinted abroad, having been recommended to German students by Melanchthon and Camerarius. It was in the seventeenth century that English learning first became an important contributor to the European literature of humanism; and the earliest English name of the first magnitude is that of Richard Bentley. It should be recollected, however, that in the sixteenth century the Greek and Latin languages were not the only channels through which England received the humanism of the Renaissance. English versions of the classics, such as Chapman's Homer, Phaer's Virgil, and North's Plutarch, circulated in a world larger than that of scholars. Italian authors who were themselves representative of the Renaissance also became known in English translations. Thus the rendering of Tasso by Fairfax, and of Ariosto by Harrington, enabled

English readers to appreciate the influence of the Renaissance on Italian poetry. Hoby's version of Castiglione's *Cortegiano* brought before them the new Italian ideal of intellectual and social accomplishment. Milton, the greatest humanist among poets of the first rank, best illustrates the various sources of culture, ancient and modern, but more especially Greek and Italian, which had become available for Englishmen not long before his own time. The modern sources had been opened to almost all who cared for literature ; the ancient, as yet, less widely. It is the prerogative of Milton to fuse in a splendid unity both the ancient and the modern elements that have contributed to enrich his genius ; he can be genuinely classical without loss of spontaneity or freshness. His poetry is not, however, the most characteristic expression of the English Renaissance in its larger aspects. That is to be found rather in the Elizabethan drama ; and its supreme exponent is Shakespeare.

While the Revival of Learning thus presents varying aspects in the several countries to which it passed from Italy, the essential gift which it brought was the same for all. That gift was the recovery of an inheritance which men had temporarily lost ; one so valuable in itself that human life would be definitely poorer without it, and also fraught with such power to educate and to stimulate, that the permanent loss of it would have been the annulment of an inestimable agency in the development of human faculty. The creative mind of ancient Greece was the greatest originating force which the world has seen. It left typical standards of form in poetry and prose, as of plastic beauty in art. Ideas which sprang from it have been fruitful in every province of knowledge. The ancient Latin mind also, which received the lessons of Greece without losing its own individuality, was the parent of master-works which bear its character, and of thoughts which are altogether its own ; while both the classical literatures contain a varied wealth of observation and experience. There was a time when men had allowed the best part of these treasures to be buried out of sight, and had almost forgotten their existence. The Italians found them again, and gave them back to those races of Europe on which the future of civilisation chiefly depended.

It may be questioned whether any other people than the Italian would have been equal to achieving this great task. When Greek and Latin studies had once been resuscitated into a vigorous life, it was easy for nations outside of Italy to carry the work further. But wonderful qualities were demanded in the men who initiated and accomplished the revival in the fourteenth and fifteenth centuries. There are cases in which it is easier to apprehend the temper and tone of a past age than to picture the chief actors. Thucydides conveys a more vivid idea of Periclean Athens than of the statesman by whose genius it had been moulded. It is not so with the Italian Renaissance. From letters and other sources, one can form tolerably clear images of many among the foremost personalities, such as Petrarch, Boccaccio, Politian, and Aldo ; even though it may be difficult to conceive such prodigies of versatility as a Battista Alberti or a Lionardo da Vinci. But it is a much harder thing to imagine the general atmosphere of the revival, the pervading enthusiasm, sustained through several generations, which was so prolific in many-sided work, so far-reaching in its influence on other lands. This atmosphere was created, this enthusiasm kindled, by the labours and examples of men extraordinary both in their powers and in their ardour. Yet it may be doubted whether even they could have wrought so effectually, had they not felt the motive which at the Renaissance was peculiar to Italians,—that patriotism which, failing of political expression, was concentrated on restoring the ancestral language and literature. No other country could show a parallel to the zeal with which Latin was cultivated in Italy, as the chief organ of literary expression, from the days of Petrarch to those of Politian. The ancient tongue, not the modern, was that in which the ablest men of letters chiefly aspired to shine. Few masters of Italian prose emerge in the interval of about a century and a half which separates the age of Villani and Boccaccio from that of Machiavelli and Guicciardini. Such men as Petrarch, Aeneas Sylvius, Jovianus Pontanus, and Paulus Jovius, who might have enriched the prose of their vernacular, preferred to write in Latin. The Platonic Academy of Florence was the first influential coterie which gave its sanction to the view that literary taste and skill, disciplined by the ancient models, could be worthily exercised in Italian. Lorenzo de' Medici set an example in his lyrics ; a more authoritative one was given by Politian, especially in his *Orfeo*, the first Italian drama of true literary merit. This larger virtue of the Classical Renaissance, as educating a new capacity for culture in general, which came out in Italy only towards the close of the movement, was manifested in other countries almost as soon as they had been fully brought under the influences of the New Learning. It was conspicuously seen in France, not merely in the work which classicists such as Ronsard and his group did for the French language, but also, for example, in the Aristophanic genius of Rabelais, —the greatest literary representative of the Renaissance for France, in the same large sense that Cervantes was such for Spain, and Shakespeare for England. The historical importance of the Classical Revival in Italy depends ultimately on the fact that it broadened out into this diffusion of a general capacity for liberal culture, taking various forms under different local and national conditions. That capacity, once restored to the civilised world, became a part of the higher life of the race, an energy which, though it might be temporarily retarded here and there by reactionary forces, could not again be lost. Not in literature or in art alone, but in every form of intellectual activity, the Renaissance opened a new era for mankind.

# CHAPTER XVII.

## THE CHRISTIAN RENAISSANCE.

"NUMBERLESS portions of the wisdom of God are wanting to us. Many books of the Sacred Text remain untranslated, as two books of the Maccabees which I know to exist in Greek; and many other books of divers Prophets, whereto reference is made in the books of Kings and Chronicles. Josephus, too, in the books of his *Antiquities,* is altogether falsely rendered as far as concerns the chronological side: and without him nothing can be known of the history of the Sacred Text. Unless he be corrected, in a new translation, he is of no avail, and the Biblical history is lost. Numberless books, again, of Hebrew and Greek expositors are wanting to the Latins: as those of Origen, Basil, Gregory Nazianzen, Damascene, Dionysius, Chrysostom, and other most noble Doctors, alike in Hebrew and in Greek. The Church, therefore, is slumbering. She does nothing in this matter, nor hath done these seventy years; save that my Lord Robert, Bishop of Lincoln, of holy memory, did give to the Latins some part of the writings of St Dionysius and of Damascene, and some other holy Doctors. It is an amazing thing, this negligence of the Church: for, from the time of Pope Damasus there hath not been any Pope, nor any of less rank, who hath busied himself for the advantaging of the Church by translations, except the aforesaid glorious Bishop."

It would be difficult to find a better statement, in the same compass, of those gaps in the knowledge of Western Christendom which the Christian Renaissance was to fill. Roger Bacon, the author of the passage, and Robert Grosseteste, who is in part the subject of it, were the two men who, to all appearance, first realised the scientific needs of the Church. If they did not actually initiate the Christian Renaissance they at least stood very close to its beginnings,—as close, one may say, as Petrarch to the beginnings of the Classical Renaissance.

We shall see reason to believe that their influence upon their contemporaries and successors was very great in this respect: and it must also be said that their actual achievements in the way of preparing materials, and in work done, were far from inconsiderable. They merit a more detailed notice than has commonly been accorded to them.

It is a matter of common knowledge that Grosseteste brought Greek books to England (probably most of them came from Sicily and South Italy), and that in conjunction with at least two other men whose names are known—Nicholas the Greek, and John of Basingstoke—he gave to the world Latin versions of certain Greek documents. Foremost among these were the *Testaments of the Twelve Patriarchs*, a famous and early apocryphal book. The manuscript from which the Latin version was made is now in the University Library at Cambridge. Of the same character was a book whose existence in a Latin dress is almost certainly due to Grosseteste—though his name has not until recently been mentioned in connexion with it. This is the pretty Greek romance which treats of the life of Asenath, the patriarch Joseph's Egyptian wife. Though now forgotten, it was widely known to medieval men, owing to its inclusion in the great *Speculum Historiale* of Vincent commonly called " of Beauvais." The claim is sometimes set up in Grosseteste's behalf that he translated the *Lexicon* of Suidas into Latin ; but when this very curious assertion is examined, we find that all he did was to render into Latin a few of the more important biographical articles in it. The principal one which has survived in his version is the article on Jesus Christ. This is in reality another *apocryphon*, containing the story of an enquiry into the priestly descent of our Lord. However, the undoubted fact that he possessed a manuscript of the *Lexicon* is a sufficiently interesting one.

Far more important in its bearings on Christian literature was the Latin version of that text of the *Epistles of St Ignatius* which is now accepted as presenting them in their most genuine form. This version, too, is reckoned as due to Grosseteste : but it seems to have been the one which attracted least attention of any. Not more than one ancient copy of it is known to exist, and the only medieval writers who show any knowledge of it are Oxford Franciscans, members of the House to which the Bishop bequeathed his library. Not until the seventeenth century were its merits and importance suspected, by Archbishop Ussher.

Of Dionysius the Areopagite, Latin versions were known and widely disseminated long before Grosseteste's day. It was presumably the unsatisfactory character of these that led him to undertake a new one ; and it is improbable that he ever brought it to a conclusion. Versions of the treatise *On the Divine Names*, and of the *Letters*, are very definitely ascribed to him ; and it is also likely that the detached *Letter to Timothy on the Martyrdoms of St Peter and Paul* was rendered into Latin by him or by his assistants. Yet, however much of the work he may have succeeded in finishing, it is certain that in the fifteenth century the need for a fresh translation of the whole was felt in Italy, and that the need was supplied by the indefatigable Camaldulite, Ambrogio Traversari.

The versions of works by John Damascene, of which Bacon speaks, seem upon examination to resolve themselves into a commentary upon the defective Latin version of the treatise *De Fide orthodoxa*, made a century before by Burgundio of Pisa.

Such is the list of Grosseteste's gifts to the Latin Church. If not very large in extent, it is assuredly very remarkable in quality. With the exception of the work of John Damascene, it consists entirely of writings for which a pre-Christian or an apostolic date was claimed. In other words, we see in Grosseteste the beginnings of that interest in the origins of Christianity which is usually regarded as characteristic of a later age. He is a collector of what claims to be ancient and primitive. Others will follow to whom Chrysostom and Basil will seem better worth translating : and their day will be a long one.

We have ample evidence of Grosseteste's knowledge of Greek. Less is known of his attainments in Hebrew : and yet evidence can be produced to show that they were not contemptible. A Franciscan writer of the next century—Henry of Costessey (circa 1336), to whom reference will be made hereafter—had before him, when writing an exposition of the Psalter, a copy of the text of that book in Hebrew with an interlinear translation into Latin. This had been the property, if not the work, of Grosseteste. Little positive proof beyond the common rumour of his contemporaries can be added to this fact ; but even if it stands by itself, it is well worthy of note. It is clear that the Bishop's chief interest centred in his Greek studies : more than a respectable working knowledge of the other sacred tongue is not claimed for him here.

Thus much it has seemed right to say of the work of the earlier of the two men who have been commemorated at the outset of this chapter. Of the other, Roger Bacon to wit, we may speak in shorter compass.

Page after page in his works attests his clear perception of the needs of scientific theology, of the crucial importance of a knowledge of the " original tongues "—Greek, Hebrew, and " Chaldean,"—of the need for a revision of the Latin Bible by the help of the oldest manuscripts, and, as we have seen, of the necessity of re-introducing to the West the works of the great Greek Fathers. And perhaps his greatest service to the Church of his age may have lain in the statement of these needs. Something, it is true, he himself achieved towards supplying them. He wrote grammars of the Greek, Hebrew, and Arabic languages. The first two of these it appears that we possess, and a single copy of a Greek dictionary also survives, which there seems good reason to attribute to him. The third is not known to exist. We have, moreover, part of a series of letters which may with some confidence be regarded as Bacon's. In these he deals at length with points of Hebrew grammar for the benefit of a friend, himself evidently an accomplished Hebraist, who had sought his advice. It must be confessed that the fruit of these labours was not great : yet we shall see that it continued to be produced, if in scanty measure, up to the day of the fuller harvest.

That Grosseteste and Bacon had their precursors we must expect to find. Indeed, it is pretty certain that there was never a time when the knowledge of either Hebrew or Greek was altogether dead in the Latin Church. In almost every generation we can point to some document which bears witness to the possession of such knowledge by scholars scattered here and there. In the middle of the twelfth century, for example, Johannes Burgundio of Pisa executed—badly enough it seems —a whole series of versions from the Greek. Among these were the *Homilies* of Chrysostom *on Matthew,* the tract of Nemesius—then believed to be by Gregory of Nyssa—*On the Nature of Man,* and, above all, the treatise of John of Damascus *On the Orthodox Faith,* of which mention has been made already. Again, in the second half of the same century, an English Odo—his personality remains obscure—dedicates to Gilbert Foliot, Bishop of London, an *Introduction to Theology* in which long passages from the Old Testament are quoted in the original Hebrew. There were also in the latter half of this same century the makings of a Greek school at the Abbey of St Denis. The reason of this is not far to seek. The patron saint of that great House was a Greek, and, as all men believed, the author of a famous group of writings. As early as the eleventh century (in 1022) a copy of the Gospels in Greek had been written for the Abbey. In the twelfth century Odo de Deuil, who succeeded Suger as Abbot, sent one of his monks, William of Gap, to the East on a literary mission, as it seems. William brought Greek books back with him from Constantinople; and made a Latin version of a life of the philosopher Secundus, which was extensively copied. To him also we may assign a Latin version of a set of Greek *Arguments to the Pauline Epistles.* This last piece of work he did when Abbot of St Denis, between 1172 and 1186, at the request of Herbert de Bosham, the friend and biographer of St Thomas of Canterbury. A fellow-monk of William's, Johannes Saracenus, a correspondent of John of Salisbury's, and in after years Abbot at Vercelli, translated into Latin the greater part of the Pseudo-Dionysian writings. A second William, monk of St Denis, did the same for a Greek panegyric on their reputed author. Down to a late date part of the office on St Denis' Day was said in Greek at the Abbey; and the Bibliothèque Nationale possesses a couple of twelfth century Greek manuscripts which belonged to the same House, and may well have been among the spoils brought back by William of Gap.

Yet after all these were isolated phenomena. Bacon's estimate of the needs of his time remains the true one. It is amply confirmed by contemporary literature, and perhaps the readiest and most convincing demonstration of it is furnished by the catalogues of the great libraries which come from this period. The value of these documents for purposes of literary history is self-evident. They provide us in the directest way imaginable with a view of the resources of the learned communities of the time. It will be worth while, therefore, to discuss, in a summary fashion, one typical example.

The passage of Bacon which stands at the head of this chapter was written in or about the year 1271. The author survived the year 1292; and we possess a detailed catalogue of one of the largest libraries in England, which was drawn up within a very few years after the latter date. We may, then, fairly use it as illustrative of the condition of theological learning and of the range of theological literature at the close of Bacon's life. The library in question is that of Christ Church Priory at Canterbury. In extent it rivalled any of its time for it contained close upon two thousand volumes; and, without entering into details as to the method of its formation, we may assert generally that it is possible to a large extent to discriminate the earlier from the later acquisitions, and to arrange these latter in chronological order.

In that portion of the library which dates back to the days of Lanfranc and Anselm fragmentary survivals are traceable of a learning which had no attraction for the mass of clerics in Bacon's day. The best example of these is a copy of the treatise of Irenaeus *Against Heresies*—in all likelihood the only copy then in England. There are indications also of the influence of John of Salisbury in the list of the books bequeathed by St Thomas to his Cathedral; but, as we should expect, this influence is more clearly seen in the presence of certain classical Latin authors than in the province of sacred literature. Coming nearer to the period with which we are chiefly concerned, we notice that Grosseteste has left his mark on the Canterbury Library: copies of most of the texts which he restored to the Latins are to be found in the catalogue. Of Roger Bacon, however, and of his work there is no sign. Not a single Greek or Hebrew book is discoverable. All trace of the learning of Theodore has disappeared. The theologian *par excellence* is, as always, Augustine: and the other three Latin Doctors are present in great force. For the rest, the Divinity library is made up chiefly of glossed books of the Bible, of "*Distinctions*," sermons, the books of Anselm, Alexander Neckam, Peter Lombard, Richard of Préaux, Robert Cursun, Peter Comestor, and the like; while, among the latest accretions, are numbered the works of the great Schoolmen. Thus almost the only aid to the literal interpretation of the Biblical text which the monks of this great House possessed was what they could gather from the works of Jerome. Peter Comestor and Josephus were their teachers in Biblical history; and for the history of the Church they had to turn to Rufinus' version of the *History* of Eusebius, to the *Tripartite History*, and to the numerous lives of Saints.

The state of this one great library must be taken as typical of that of others throughout Europe. Yet, if the darkness was thick, it was already beginning to lift. By means of a recent discovery the present writer has ascertained that in this very library a copy of the books of the Old Testament from Genesis to Ruth in Greek existed early in the fifteenth century. The manuscript, now at Oxford, is of Grosseteste's date, and was very probably brought by him to England.

There were younger contemporaries of Grosseteste and of Bacon, who carried on the work of the great teachers, and that in no unworthy fashion. At Ramsey Abbey (where the influence of the former may fairly be suspected, for it lay in his diocese) a small band of scholars were in possession of the whole of the Old Testament in Hebrew. They had bought up the libraries of the suppressed synagogues at Huntingdon and Stamford. One among them, Prior Gregory, had furthermore studied Greek: a bilingual Psalter remains to attest the fact. At a somewhat later date the stores of Hebrew manuscripts accumulated by his predecessors enabled Laurence Holbeach, a monk of the same House, to compile a Hebrew Lexicon.

Another great work was set on foot in the second half of the thirteenth century,—a work whose existence is hardly suspected now-a-days. This was nothing less than a literal translation from Hebrew into Latin of the greater part of the Old Testament—clearly a work of English scholars, for all the known manuscripts which contain any part of it are of English origin, and are preserved in English libraries. Of the originators of this enterprise, and of the character of their work, we may look to learn more; but even in our present state of knowledge we can very confidently predicate of them that they owed their inspiration to the influence of one or other of the two great champions of the " original tongues."

It must not be supposed that for England alone is claimed the honour of having attempted a scientific treatment of the Sacred Text at this time. The principal impulse to study seems to have been given by Englishmen, it is true; but work was also being done *outre mer*. Before the middle of the thirteenth century the Dominicans of Paris had attempted the task of systematically correcting the text of the Latin Bible. The results, however, were not happy, in the opinion of the man best qualified to judge of them. Bacon is, indeed, unsparing in his strictures. The work had been undertaken without adequate knowledge of the original tongues, and carried on without reference being made to the oldest and best manuscripts of the Vulgate. The consequence is that the Paris "correction," of which there were two editions, is " the worst possible corruption and destruction of the text of God." But Bacon was not merely a destructive critic. It was seemingly a friend and correspondent of his own, William de Mara, who eventually compiled a *Correctorium* based on a sound knowledge of Hebrew. On its composition he spent not less than forty years; and it is believed that he derived material assistance from Bacon himself in the course of his work.

The critical labours of which we have been speaking were chiefly concerned with the text of the Old Testament; and it is a noteworthy circumstance that in the fourteenth century the knowledge of Hebrew, and the application of that knowledge to Biblical studies, was far commoner than the knowledge of Greek. It is not difficult to account for this, so far as Western Europe is concerned. Teachers of Hebrew were, as Bacon tells us, very easily procurable. It is true that he adds that it was equally easy to acquire Greek; but it must be remembered that in the case of Hebrew, books in which the language could be studied, and on which critical and exegetical work could be done, were plentiful. Wherever a community of Jews existed, the Scriptures in Hebrew could be readily obtained. Not so with Greek. The few Greek manuscripts imported into England by Grosseteste, the Greek Gospels which the Byzantine Emperor had sent to St Louis, the two or three volumes at St Denis, were rarities of the first water. The stores of Greek literature in the Basilian monasteries of Southern Italy and Sicily, to say nothing of Greece and of Byzantium, were not yet unlocked. That ancient scholarship to which we owe the Graeco-Latin manuscripts of Southern France, the Laudian manuscript of the *Acts* that Baeda used, and the famous codices of St Gall, had altogether died. The eyes of a few far-sighted scholars were turned towards the Grecian lands; but as yet they could do no more than look and long.

Still, the truths to which Roger Bacon had given expression were not forgotten. Especially in the ranks of his own—the Franciscan— Order, men were found who realised and acted upon them. Scraps of Hebrew and Greek learning—alphabets, transcripts of the Lord's Prayer, and the like—are of not infrequent occurrence in manuscripts of Franciscan origin. These may be only straws showing which way the wind sets. More significant is the appearance among the Franciscans of the greatest exponent of the literal sense of Scripture whom the medieval world can show. This was Nicholas de Lyra, who died in 1340. It is not so much because of his learning that he is important, though his knowledge of Hebrew was highly notable; it is rather his attitude, his desire to ascertain what the words of the Sacred Text actually mean, which differentiates him from the ancient allegorists. The same tendency is seen in the work of a far less famous Franciscan of the same generation. Henry of Costessey is the author of a *Commentary upon the Psalms* which appears to exist in but one manuscript. In this the insistence upon the literal sense, the constant reference to the original Hebrew, and the independence of the writer's judgment, who is for ever canvassing and contradicting the opinions of Lyra, are such as would have rejoiced Bacon's heart. For a considerable time the Franciscan Houses at both Oxford and Cambridge must have kept alive the interest in this "New Learning." We are fairly well informed about the establishment at Oxford; and concerning the Cambridge House we can at least tell who were its teachers of divinity: Henry of Costessey was among them. The Oxford Friars did not, it is true, preserve the traditions of Grosseteste and of Bacon into the Reformation period, for Leland has a sorry tale to tell of the neglected condition of their once noble library. Yet the tradition of learning lingered in the Order; at the beginning of the sixteenth century Richard Brinkley, Provincial of the Grey Friars in England, was a student of Hebrew—he borrowed a Hebrew Psalter from the monks of Bury St Edmunds; and he was moreover the owner of more than one Greek Biblical manuscript: among them, of the Leicester Codex of the New Testament, well known to textual critics.

More is yet to be said of the Franciscans in England, and of their services to sacred literature. They did not confine their attention to the Bible. There is another great literary enterprise, the credit of whose initiation belongs to them, though its subsequent development must be assigned to a Benedictine. Described shortly, it was an attempt to discover and locate all the works of the principal known authors, both sacred and secular, which existed in England. At some time in the fourteenth century circulars were issued, or visits paid, to about one hundred and sixty monasteries. A list of some ninety authors was drawn up, and the writings of each enumerated. The list of libraries and that of books were then fused together in such a way that from the completed work it is possible to ascertain what books by each writer were to be found in England, and in what libraries each book existed. The name given to this compilation is the *Catalogus* or *Registrum Librorum Angliae,* and the indications that in this first form it is the work of a member or members of the Franciscan Order are hardly to be mistaken. Early in the fifteenth century, the work received a most important expansion at the hands of a monk of Bury, John Boston by name. He added a score of names to the list of libraries, and raised to nearly seven hundred the number of authors whose works were enumerated. He gave, moreover, a short biographical sketch of each writer drawn from the best sources at his disposal: so that the book in its completed form might claim to be called a Dictionary of Literature. If this *Catalogue* of Boston's did not serve as a model to Trithemius and his successors (and there is no reason to suppose that it did), it was at least the legitimate ancestor of the later *Bibliothecae*. What is more to the point at present, it furnishes a key to the literary possessions and perhaps still more to the literary needs of England about the year 1400, the importance of which it would be difficult to exaggerate.

It may be necessary to return to the consideration of England's share in the movement; but we must now proceed to extend the range of our outlook. We have to ask whether, in the home of the Classical Revival, any consciousness existed of the needs of the Church corresponding to the feeling that we have seen stirring in the minds of Grosseteste and of Bacon. As far as we can judge, this question must be answered in the negative. Exceptional opportunities for the furthering of Christian scholarship lay ready to the hands of the Italians in the fourteenth century; yet there is strikingly little to show that advantage was taken of them. It has already been hinted that in Italy the knowledge of Greek as a spoken language was far from uncommon. Large portions of the South were, as Bacon says, "purely Greek"; on the Adriatic coast Greek was widely known. The Court of Rome had its relations with the Eastern patriarchates. The points at issue between the Greek and Latin Churches were productive of a long series of controversial writings on both sides. There was, in fact, no good reason why the knowledge of the Greek Bible and of the great Greek Fathers should not have continued to exist at the papal Court, and have been diffused from thence over the West. Yet we do not find that such knowledge existed in any appreciable degree. The thought of applying the knowledge of Greek to the study of the Bible seems hardly to have occurred to the Italian scholars of the fourteenth century. There are, it is true, examples dating from this period of Gospel-books and other parts of the Bible written in Greek and Latin, and emanating from Venice and Florence. It is commonly said, too, that an English Bishop —Adam Easton, Bishop of Norwich and Cardinal of St Cecilia—made a fresh version of the whole Bible from the original while in Italy. But this last assertion stands in need of corroboration; and at best it would indicate, not an activity of Italians in sacred studies, but the existence in Italy of materials by the aid of which such studies could be prosecuted. The difficulty of discovering any symptom of consciousness that the field of theological study needed widening is of more weight than are the isolated examples of a wider learning which have been cited.

Before the fifteenth century has fairly opened we find nothing that can be called a decided current setting in the direction of wider learning or true sacred scholarship. It was not immediately that the rush of new discoveries involved those whose prime interest lay in things sacred. But when we hear of a Queen of Cyprus presenting a copy of the Gospels in Greek to a Pope, of a Greek prelate on his way to the Council of Florence giving another copy to a church at Verona, of a Cardinal (Cusanus) in the same year buying a third at Constantinople, and, within four years more, of copies being written in Italy itself, we feel sure that the movement is well in train.

Once begun, its development can be followed up along many lines. Three in particular suggest themselves as fruitful in indications not likely to be fallacious. First, we may take stock of what was done in the way of collecting ancient texts and forming libraries in which to preserve them. Secondly, we may review the work of the translators and copyists who made the new material accessible to their public; and, in the third place, we may trace the beginnings of criticism as applied to the documents which were already known, and to those which began now to be known for the first time.

Much has been written upon the first of these topics, but chiefly from the point of view of men interested in the Classical Revival. There is not a great deal that can suitably be added in this place to the story of the rediscovery of ancient literature. The work done by the collectors of Greek books was a wholly new work; we shall see the results of it most clearly in the course of our examination of the libraries. With the early literature of the Latin Church the case was different. There were but few Christian writers among those whom Poggio and his fellows rescued from an age-long obscurity; and the welcome accorded to these by the humanists was theirs as Latinists rather than as theologians. Tertullian and Lactantius are the leading names of this class. The first copy of the works of the former was found at Basel by Tommaso Parentucelli (afterwards Nicholas V). Lactantius, never a frequent author in medieval libraries, had hardly found a single copyist between the eleventh and the fourteenth century. A library at Bologna had preserved the earliest and best manuscript of his *Institutions*, and other tracts were yielded up by St Gall and the German abbeys. The most important Latin books apart from these were some of the early versions of Greek patristic works, such as that of Origen's *Homilies on Luke*, the finding of which, at St Cecilia's in Rome, gladdened the heart of Ambrogio Traversari. However, it must be allowed that, upon the whole, the Latin finds of the earlier period were inconsiderable. The work of Irenaeus, though known to exist, attracted very little attention—chiefly, we may conjecture, because of its barbarous style; the Latin version of Hermas was hardly read; and the writings of Arnobius and Minucius Felix, which are of the kind that would have proved most pleasing to the humanists, were reserved for the explorers of the next century.

The libraries which received and preserved the stock of new material claim to be discussed at greater length. The natural centre for the formation of a great Christian library was the papal Court. Private amateurs like Niccolo Niccoli might, and actually did, accomplish much in the way of rescuing and bringing together books of all kinds; but it is a clear and familiar fact that what they prized most were the masterpieces of the pagan literature. It is the clergy, and above all the Pope, whom we expect to find caring for the archives of Christian antiquity. Fortunately, we are in a position to estimate very accurately, by the help of library catalogues, the measure of what was done in this line. The greatest of the early papal bibliophiles was Nicholas V (1447–55). It is not necessary to spend words here upon describing his activity as a collector or his munificence as a patron of letters. We shall run less risk of exaggeration if we draw from so unemotional a document as the inventory of his books, made at his decease. A short survey of the collection, if dry, will at least afford some basis of solid fact.

In 1455, then, the library of Nicholas V consisted of 824 Latin and 352 Greek manuscripts. We must not expect to find in the Latin library any sign that the learning of the schools is losing its interest. The theology and the Canon Law of the later centuries are as fully represented here as in any Abbey library of them all. What we have to note as significant is the presence—partly in old copies newly brought to light, partly in new versions or in manuscripts written to order—of a number of writings whose existence or whose importance was but just beginning to be realised. Of these the most striking may be instanced here. The new version of Chrysostom's *Homilies on Matthew*, by Ambrogio Traversari, side by side with the old and faulty one of Burgundio of Pisa: Cyril of Alexandria upon John, translated by George of Trebizond: several copies of Origen upon Luke, to which allusion has already been made; then—a noteworthy item—a Latin version of Maimonides on the sense of the Scriptures. Later, and after masses of volumes of Augustine, Jerome, and Thomas Aquinas, appear, first, a translation of the *Acts of the Ephesine Council*, and then, disguised as "Nicenus Episcopus Lugdunensis," the work of Irenaeus *Against Heresies*. Worthy of mention also are the following: the *Acts of the Five Great Councils*; the *Praeparatio Evangelica* of Eusebius in George of Trebizond's version; Tertullian, Victor Vitensis, the *Chronicon* of Eusebius, Josephus *Against Apion*, and a version of Philo Judaeus by Lilio of Città di Castello.

Cyprian and Lactantius, and versions, either old or new, of works of Ephrem the Syrian, Athanasius, and Basil, are the remaining indications of the new movement which occur in the catalogue of Nicholas V's Latin library.

The inventory of his Greek books is, of course, in one sense, from end to end a list of novelties; and yet it is rather disappointing. The volumes are shortly and meagrely described. Their contents, if new to the scholars of that day, are just those which are most familiar to us. It is in part consoling to find that Nicholas possessed no great treasure that has since perished; but still the absence of any such entry robs the catalogue of an element of excitement. It is, in truth, some-what commonplace. Chrysostom heads the list with forty volumes, and Gregory Nazianzen, Basil, Athanasius, and Simeon the Metaphrast, are largely represented. There is but one volume of Origen: there are two of Philo, and two copies of what may be the Clementine Homilies. The Bible is represented by some scattered portions of the Old Testament, a fair number of Gospel-books (*Evangelistaria*) and a few copies of the Acts and Epistles. No such thing as a complete Greek Bible occurs, though we know that at this date the famous Vatican Codex (B) was already in the Pope's possession.

The character of the collection did not alter materially during the remainder of the fifteenth century. At the death of Sixtus IV in 1484 it had grown considerably in bulk. Instead of 350 Greek manuscripts there were now about a thousand. Still, we note no specially striking additions to the list of early Church writers. Origen, for example, is just as poorly represented as he was under Nicholas V. One important section, however, shows a marked growth. The Bibles, or parts of Bibles, have swelled to the goodly number of fifty-eight.

The examination of this, the most important library of the West in the fifteenth century, teaches us that the main interest of Christian scholars was centred not on the literature of the first ages, but upon the works of the great doctors of the fourth and fifth centuries,—upon the definers and expositors of developed dogma. This was the natural outcome, perhaps, of the long period spent under the influence of Scholastic Theology. But it was also the inevitable result of the condition of things in the headquarters of Greek learning. The Eastern Church had herself forgotten Justin, Clement of Alexandria, and Irenaeus, and regarded Origen with suspicion. We know now that as late as the sixteenth century a Greek Irenaeus, and a copy of the *Ecclesiastical Memoirs* of Hegesippus were lurking in a Greek island. There they were destined to remain and to perish. Yet, had their existence been known in the time of Nicholas V, it is doubtful whether he and his contemporaries would have been much excited by the announcement. A couple of generations later the case would have been widely different.

The literary treasures of Italy were by no means confined to the Vatican; and, though it would be dreary work to investigate in detail the inventories of all the great collectors, a word must still be said about those of Venice and Florence. At the first-named place Bessarion's great library was deposited, among whose treasures was at least one volume of extraordinary value for the history of Christian beliefs,—our best copy of the treatise of Epiphanius *Against Heresies*. Florence was enriched, not only with the beginnings of the Medicean collection, but with the earlier and hardly less precious library of Niccolo Niccoli (d. 1437), which passed to the Convent of San Marco. In the list of the one hundred and eighty Greek manuscripts which that community owned in the last years of the century we note a few names, and only a few, that we did not meet at Rome, particularly that of Justin Martyr. From this Florence copy Pico della Mirandola must in all probability have made his translation of the *Cohortatio ad Gentes*.

In the Latin collection we find such items as three volumes of Tertullian, all of them copies on paper made from the ancient manuscript which had come into the hands of Cardinal Orsini. Cyprian, Lactantius, and Ignatius too, are there, with of course many of the freshly made versions of Greek books. That of the *Letter of Aristeas*, so-called, from the pen of Matteo Palmieri, is a welcome variation from the everlasting Chrysostoms and Basils. Literature owes much, indeed, to Niccoli; but Christian literature has specially to thank another of its friends, Lorenzo de' Medici, for the preservation of that inestimable monument, the unique manuscript of the *Miscellanies* (*Stromateis*) of Clement of Alexandria.

We turn now from Italy, the centre of light, to ask what was the condition of affairs in the outer darkness beyond the Alps. In France the work of collecting Greek books had hardly begun in the first half of the fifteenth century. There were, as we have seen, what may be called accidental deposits in two or three places, as at St Denis, and the Abbey of Corbie in Picardy. The papal library at Avignon, which owned more than a hundred and twenty Hebrew manuscripts in 1369, could muster only some half-dozen in Greek—another striking testimony to the statement made above that the former language was far more commonly known in that age than the latter. In 1416 one Greek book had found its way into the possession of the Duke of Berri; but his cataloguers cannot give us any notion of the character of its contents. The famous decree of the Council of Venice in 1311 that the Hebrew, Arabic, and Chaldean tongues should be taught at all the greater Universities of Europe had remained absolutely ineffective.

With the arrival of George Hermonymus at Paris in 1476 the work of collection and diffusion of Greek literature really began. Hermonymus himself worked as a copyist alike of the Sacred Text and of secular authors. Still it was nothing more than a beginning that the fifteenth century witnessed. The enormous accumulations, which have ended in making the Bibliothèque Nationale of Paris the depository of more Greek manuscripts than any other library outside Greece can show, were the work of the two centuries that followed.

Of England not much more remains to be said in the present connexion; and yet, as the history of our progress in this field has been but sparsely investigated, more may be said in this place than a consideration of proportion would perhaps seem to justify. We have rather frequent accounts of the importations of valuable collections of books from Italy. Adam Easton, Bishop of Norwich (who has already engaged our attention), was among the earliest of those who collected in this way. He died in the last quarter of the fourteenth century. Thomas Walden gave many foreign manuscripts, notable for age and rarity, to the Carmelites of London. John Gunthorpe, Dean of Wells, deposited a precious collection formed in Italy at Jesus College in Cambridge. It is still possible to trace the greater part of the gifts made by William Gray, Bishop of Ely, to Balliol College. Another Oxford College—Lincoln—possesses a manuscript of the Acts and Catholic Epistles in Greek which was given to it in 1483 by Robert Flemmyng, Dean of Lincoln. Flemmyng was another of those who had travelled in Italy: and he is credited with having compiled a Greek dictionary. At Lincoln College is also a copy of the Gospels in Greek which was the gift of Edmund Audley, Bishop of Salisbury, in 1502.

Gone, alas! are the collections, amounting in all to nearly six hundred volumes, which Duke Humphrey of Gloucester gave at different times to the University of Oxford. Gone, too, for the most part is that imported by William Tilley of Selling, Prior of Christ Church, Canterbury, the friend of Politian and the patron of Linacre. During the two long visits that he paid to Italy, Selling had brought together a number of books. We have no list of them; but his contemporaries evidently accounted them very choice and precious. The tradition was even current (though we must gravely question its correctness) that among them was a copy of the *De Republica* of Cicero. They were deposited in the Prior's lodging on his return and, unfortunately, were never transferred to the main library of the monastery. On the eve of the Dissolution, a royal commissioner—Leighton—and his train were lodged in the building which contained the books: an accidental fire, the responsibility for which is laid by the monks upon Leighton's drunken servants, burst out, and the treasured library of Selling was consumed. A few survivors are enumerated by Leland—notably a copy of Basil's *Commentary on Isaiah* in Greek: a few which he does not name can be traced in our libraries now. Among them must in all probability be reckoned the first copy of Homer whose presence can be definitely traced in England since the days of Theodore of Tarsus.

That copies of the newly-recovered writings of the Latin Fathers and of the new translations from the Greek made their way to England among these various collections is not surprising. Both among Selling's books, and among those which Bishop Gray gave to Balliol College, we find translations by Aretinus and by Traversari. In Gray's list Lactantius and Tertullian are also represented. His copy of the *Apology* of the latter suggests a curious question. It is enriched with marginal notes, which in the opinion of the antiquaries of an older day were due to the pen of a twelfth century critic,—no less a person indeed than William of Malmesbury. But the manuscript which contains them is of the fifteenth century and is the work of a foreign scribe; and the notes themselves afford no clue to their author.

The library of St Augustine's Abbey at Canterbury, again, possessed the *Apology* of Tertullian; but we can only guess at the date of the manuscript; and a wide range is open to us, since the catalogue in which it is entered was drawn up in the last years of the fifteenth century. It is to be feared that this country did not contribute in any important degree to the stock of new material which was being made available for the world's use. Poggio's visit to England was a failure in this as in other respects. Had he been able to explore the libraries of the great monasteries of the West or of the North—Glastonbury, Worcester, and the scenes of Baeda's activity—he would not have returned empty-handed. Many books lay in hiding there which he would have been glad to secure. In after years we find the English scholars actively playing their part in the matter of accumulating books. At present we must leave them, in order to enquire, rather more briefly, into the records of the movement in Germany and Switzerland.

The Council of Basel (1431) had in one respect a remarkable and far-reaching influence on literature. A Dominican, John of Ragusa, afterwards Cardinal, who figured there, left in the Dominican convent of the city a collection of books which in later years acquired a peculiar importance. They included three manuscripts of parts of the New Testament in Greek: and others were subsequently added to their number by purchase by the brethren of the House. These manuscripts were not only the first Greek books to which Johann Reuchlin had access, but were in after years wellnigh the sole authorities used by Erasmus for the constitution of the first published text of the Greek Testament. Few cities outside Italy could at that time have supplied even such facilities as this to an intending editor of the Sacred Text; and we may be grateful for the accident on which their presence at Basel depended. Another of this Cardinal's books, which since his day has found a home at Eton College, is still the only known source of a tract of some celebrity, current under the name of Athanasius.

It seems not unfair to say that Germany—the country which in the middle of the fifteenth century gave to the cause of enlightenment its mightiest weapon, in the shape of the printing press—did little more for that cause, at least of her own initiative, in the course of that century. To the learning of the next her contributions were enormous; but for the moment she is conspicuous not by bringing to light her own hidden treasures but by parting with them to strangers. The number of ancient texts, both classical and patristic, which were exported from German Abbeys to Italy was very large: and scarcely less remarkable was the number and quality of those which remained undiscovered, until native scholars of a later generation scented them out. Yet there were German book-collectors before 1450: and to one of them it may be well to devote a few words. In the letters of Poggio and his contemporaries there is not unfrequent mention of one Nicholas of Trier as a successful collector and discoverer. It is a probability, and indeed it has been accounted nearer a certainty, that he is identical with Nicholas of Cusa, afterwards Cardinal, who became famous as a politician, as a mathematician and reformer of the Calendar, and as a writer against Islam. Cusanus died in 1464, and bequeathed to a hospital he had founded at Cues on the Mosel, his native town, the books brought together by him during his residence in Italy and his journeys to the Greek lands. At Cues a good many of them still remain. The collection has, to some extent, suffered from an exchange of old lamps for new, which was effected in the last century to the advantage of the Harleian Library: but the books which are now at the Hospital of St Nicholas at Cues are both individually and collectively worthy of notice.

Two Graeco-Latin Psalters, of the eighth and ninth centuries, three other Greek manuscripts (one being an early and famous *Catena* on St John's Gospel), and two copies of most of the Old Testament in Hebrew are the striking features among the Biblical books. In the patristic section is a volume transcribed for the Cardinal which contains certain works then of very rare occurrence: Optatus of Milevis *Against the Donatists*, Origen *De Principiis*, Tertullian's *Apology*, and *The Shepherd* of Hermas. There are moreover two early Cyprians, and copies of the Latin versions, old or recent, of works of Athanasius, of Eusebius' *Praeparatio Evangelica*, of Cyril, of Philo, of Aristeas, and of Dionysius. In addition to these, the presence of the earlier polemics against the Mohammadans, of works of Raymond Lull in great profusion, and of the new versions of Plato and Aristotle, gives a special character to this forgotten storehouse. In spite of the losses it has suffered, the library of Cues is to be reckoned among the most perfect and unadulterated examples that have survived of the collection of a single scholar of the middle of the fifteenth century.

So much as to the formation of libraries in various parts of Europe, and of its relation to the Christian Renaissance. We have designedly devoted a considerable space to this side of our subject, inasmuch as it has not as yet been adequately appreciated by the generality. To most men the study of inventories and catalogues seems dry work; but the evidence derivable from it is of a kind not easily to be upset. It must be remembered, besides, that the existence of these libraries did not affect their possessors only. Most of them were thrown open to students of all classes; so that they were centres not only for the preservation of literature, but for a wide and rapid diffusion of knowledge. We may have occasion to recur shortly to the topic of book-preservation. At present two other subjects intimately connected with the development of learning in the fifteenth century appear to require comment.

The first is the work of those who made translations of the newly imported Greek literature. The fact that very many of those who welcomed the fresh materials for study were unable to use them in their original forms needs little explanation. Petrarch himself never mastered Greek. But, whichever of several readily intelligible causes it was that gave rise to the demand for translations, it is certain that they were actually made in great numbers. There was, as we have noted, a considerable stock of them, of older date, already in circulation. Works of Origen, Athanasius, Basil, Gregory Nazianzen, and Chrysostom were all available. Many of these, and particularly those by Burgundio of Pisa, were, or were accounted, obscure and barbarous: many other works of the same authors had never been current in Latin at all. There was thus room for a fresh translation of a whole literature. We have already encountered by the way the names of some of those who put their hands to the work. Probably the most important labourer in this field was Ambrogio Traversari, General of the Camal-dulite Order who died in 1438. To him the Church owed an improved version of the *Homilies* of Chrysostom *on the Pauline Epistles*, of other tracts by the same Father, of the Greek *Vitae Patrum*, of Dionysius the Areopagite, of Aeneas of Gaza, and not a few other books. His joy in his labour of translating, which was the great object of his life, appears over and over again in the hundreds of letters we possess from his pen. The interruptions in his work, which his appointment to the Generalship of his Order occasioned, were a constant grievance. Bitter were his regrets when he had yielded to the persuasions of Cosmo de' Medici, and undertaken to make a Latin version of Diogenes Laertius : not solely because the task distracted his attention from the holy Doctors, but because the lives of the pagan philosophers were not a subject upon which a Christian monk should spend his time. Of all the prominent translators, Traversari is perhaps the one who has most clearly before him the thought that it is a worthy task to reopen to the Latins the mines of Greek theology. We see of course in him the same rather disappointing want of interest in the writers of the very earliest Christian period that we have noticed in studying the library catalogues—disappointing, because the conviction can hardly be resisted that, had the scholars of the fifteenth century made special and definite enquiries, they would have been in time to recover writings which have since perished.

It is impracticable to discuss at any length the productions of the multitude of translators contemporary with or subsequent to Traversari. We may mention but one of the most notable among them. Next to the *Stromateis* of Clement of Alexandria, no patristic treatise is more remarkable for the number and value of the ancient authorities whom it quotes than the *Praeparatio Evangelica* of Eusebius. It therefore naturally attracted the attention of the lover of pagan antiquity as well as of the smaller band who desired to learn more of the origins of Christianity ; and to the men of the Middle Ages it had been absolutely unknown. The Latin version of it, by George of Trebizond, was one of the most important additions to learning which that age could have seen. It opened up a whole realm of forgotten history. From it men first learned the names of such writers as Sanchoniathon, Manetho, and Berosus ; indeed, the publication of the book may very probably have paved the way for the once famous forgeries of Annius of Viterbo. Translations of some part of Philo's works, and of the venerable Hellenistic forgery known as the *Letter of Aristeas,* were also produced before the middle of the fifteenth century.

Much, then, had been done towards reopening the ancient store-houses before the date at which it was long fashionable to say that the revival of Greek learning began—the taking of Constantinople in 1453 ; much, too, before the printing press had been set up. Great libraries had been formed, and translators had been at work, and to such good purpose that a very representative collection of Greek theology was readily accessible to any studious Western.

The next development that we look for is the rise of the critical instinct. The fifteenth century produced one critic who died before its close, Lorenzo Valla. He, though uninspired by any interest in the Christian religion, did a considerable service to the cause of truth by pointing out the falsity of certain documents which had long taken high rank among the archives of the Church.

One of these was the "Donation of Constantine," a forgery easy to detect when attention was once drawn to it, but yet a monument whose apparent importance was so great that the fate of Uzzah might have seemed likely to await the man who first laid hands upon it. The other was the group of works which passed under the name of Dionysius the Areopagite. We have seen something of the popularity of these books, as attested by the multiplicity of versions in which they were current; and indeed so important are they in themselves as a meeting-ground of Christian theology and Greek philosophy that they may be considered not unworthy of the pains lavished upon them by Erigena, Saracenus, Grosseteste, and Traversari. The last word has not yet been said as to their origin and history; but it is clear enough that the first word was spoken by Lorenzo Valla. No one before him had questioned the claim of these writings to be regarded as works of the Apostolic age. Hardly any one since his time has had a word to say in defence of that claim. The story of Grocyn's relation to them, of the high value he set upon them at first, and of his later conviction that Valla's estimate of them was the true one,—a conviction which, with characteristic honesty, he hastened to make public,—forms as good an illustration as any that could be found of the spirit that was abroad. New estimates of the old documents were being formed, as a direct result of the accession of new materials for study.

One question of the highest importance to our subject has been left out of consideration in the preceding remarks. What was the condition of things as regards the text of the Scriptures, the fountain-head of Christian science? Since 1455 the Church had had in its hands a printed Bible in Latin; and more than one vernacular version had seen the light. The Old Testament also had been printed in Hebrew by Italian Jews. But what was the quality of these texts? Had Roger Bacon's aspirations for a Latin Bible corrected according to the oldest copies, and for the multiplication and distribution among the clergy of the Scriptures in the original tongues, been satisfied? The question must be answered in the negative. Of the many printed Vulgates none offered a text constructed on critical principles; and it is probable that of the earliest Hebrew Bibles, such as that of Soncino, few copies made their way into Christian hands. The first important attempt to present the world with a complete Bible in the original was made in Spain:—a country which in after years contributed less than most to the cause of Christian science. The Complutensian Polyglot gave us the first printed Septuagint, and the first printed, though not the first published, New Testament in Greek. For the formation of the text of the Septuagint and of the Latin Vulgate, great pains were taken to collect early manuscript authorities. Two Septuagint manuscripts were borrowed from Rome. The Vatican Bible of the fourth century was not among them, probably because its age and importance were not known to Ximenes and his colleagues. For the Latin text Spain itself possessed authorities as early as could readily be found elsewhere. The Greek text of the New Testament was formed from less good sources: and not one of the manuscripts used can now be identified with certainty. No praise is too high for the design of Ximenes; and, as regards the execution, it is doubtful whether the best scholarship of all Europe, had it been mustered at Alcalà for the work, could have produced a much better result. The science of textual criticism was scarcely born. At this time, and for years afterwards, scholars such as Erasmus had no hesitation as to printing a text from a single manuscript, and from sending that manuscript as "copy" to the press.

Though printed in 1514, the Complutensian New Testament was not published for some years. It seems indeed that copies of the whole work were not procurable earlier than 1522. The story of the preparation of the Greek New Testament which was actually the first in circulation is well known. Neither in its object, the anticipation of the Complutensian text, nor in the manner of its preparation, does it seem to us deserving of praise. Hurried through the press of Froben between September and March, it was formed on the authority of six manuscripts at most, the best of which Erasmus neglected almost entirely to consult. We have already traced the history of some of these manuscripts and have seen them in the hands of Johann Reuchlin. Four of them are still at Basel; a fifth, now in the Oettingen-Wallerstein Library at Mayhingen, was the one authority available for the *Apocalypse.* The last six verses of the last chapter are missing; and Erasmus was reduced to translating them into rather surprising Greek from the Latin Vulgate. The sixth authority was not a copy of the New Testament, but of Theophylact's commentary on the Gospels, apparently still at Basel. It is this Theophylact, Archbishop of Bulgaria, who is designated in Erasmus' preface by the mysterious name Vulgarius.

Faulty as was the Erasmian edition, it was a truly epoch-making book. It was the ancestor of the *textus receptus*, and the channel by which the Greek text of the New Testament was most widely diffused. This was natural not only because Erasmus was first in the field, but because his text, in its many editions, was far cheaper and more convenient than the huge Polyglot, of which but six hundred copies in all were printed.

To trace the history of the printed Greek Testament through the various editions of Erasmus, of Aldus, of Simon de Colines, and of the Estiennes is beyond the scope of this chapter. We must be content with noticing that in Robert Estienne's third edition, that of 1550, known as *Editio Regia*, a considerable advance in textual criticism is perceptible. Estienne employed not less than fifteen manuscripts for the correction of his text. Most of these have been identified : eleven are at Paris, and two at Cambridge.

Since the original text of the New Testament had been allowed to remain so long unprinted, it was hardly to be expected that the older oriental versions should be very quick in making their appearance. Indeed it was not until just after the middle of the century that one of the most important—the Syriac—first saw the light. In 1555 the Austrian Chancellor of Ferdinand I, Johann Albrecht Widmanstetter, enabled a native Syrian priest, Moses of Mardin, to publish an edition of the Peshitta Version of the New Testament at Vienna. Widmanstetter had himself been interested in Syriac before this : a rather famous Syrian monk, Theseus Ambrosius, had been his teacher. It is commonly said that the eccentric and possibly insane Guillaume Postel had a hand in the production of this first Syriac New Testament, of which three hundred copies were sent to the Maronite patriarch and him of Antioch.

It is our task to deal chiefly with beginnings : but it is impossible to pass entirely unnoticed the Roman edition of the Septuagint Version which appeared in 1587. Its text was based mainly on the great Vatican manuscript, and the committee of scholars who superintended its production included the Cardinals Sirleto and Caraffa, as well as Latino Latini, and Pierre Morin. This was not an *editio princeps*, but to Biblical scholars it was of enormous importance. The version had been already twice printed, first in the Complutensian Polyglot, and next by Aldus in 1518; but in the Roman edition a manuscript of first class value was for the first time utilised. Until the nineteenth century, indeed, the text of the Vatican manuscript was only known by means of this book. The attempts of Sixtus V and Clement VIII to supply the Church with an authoritative text of the Latin Vulgate, were, as we know, not brought to a satisfactory issue; but the fact that the attempt was made deserves at least a passing notice.

With the translators and expounders of the Bible it is simply impossible to deal. With regard to the first, it can only be said broadly that the sixteenth century saw innumerable new versions of the Scriptures; many were in Latin (*e.g.* that of Sanctius Pagninus) and attempted either fidelity or elegance of style, or both. Others were in the vernacular of this or that country, and these were naturally in most cases the off-spring of the reforming movement. The high standard of knowledge which was attainable can be most readily indicated to Englishmen by reference to the "Authorised Version" of 1611. The scholars whose work we see in this were essentially men of the sixteenth century.

As to the commentators, it is even more hopeless to attempt to enter into detail. Lefèvre d'Étaples, Colet, Sadoleto, Erasmus, were all of them men who advanced the cause of sacred learning by trying to ascertain the actual meaning of the words of Scripture, instead of presenting their readers with a *réchauffé* of the *Glossa Ordinaria* or fashioning every sentence into a weapon of controversy. But besides these there were innumerable writers who contributed to the elucidation of both Testaments. They were confined to no one sect or country; but their names must not be sought here.

Something must now be said of the growth of Hebrew studies among Christian scholars. The thirteenth, fourteenth, and fifteenth centuries had produced a number of men who for the purpose either of Biblical study or of controversy had acquired a knowledge of Hebrew; and from time to time the Church had attempted to encourage and foster such students. The close of the fifteenth century saw a new development in this as in other branches of sacred learning. The brilliant young noble and scholar, Pico della Mirandola, may not unfairly be singled out as the beginner of the movement. His training in classical philosophy, coupled with his deep interest in theological study, made him eagerly seek and warmly welcome a system of learning which professed to be the fountain-head of both subjects. This system was the Jewish Cabbala. Ostensibly as old as the patriarch Abraham, its principal documents are now known to be productions of the thirteenth century; and intrinsically they are wholly unworthy of the reverence which has been paid to them by many great minds. The influence they exercised may be compared with that of the pseudo-Dionysian writings, though it was less widely felt, and less enduring. Pico saw no reason to doubt the claim of the Cabbalistic books to a reverend antiquity; and he did his best to impart to the world the treasure he thought he had found. His work is mainly important because of the effect it had upon Johann Reuchlin.

We have had occasion already to mention Reuchlin as a student of Greek; but in popularising the study of that language and literature he did little as compared with Erasmus and many others. In Hebrew, however, he was the teacher of the modern world. By personal instruction and by the compiling of grammars, reading-books, and a rudimentary lexicon, he became unconsciously the first who carried into effect the aspirations of Roger Bacon. And it is unquestionable that he owed the interest he felt in the sacred tongue in a large measure to the work of Pico della Mirandola. By this he was attracted to the study of the Cabbala; and in praise of the Cabbala his most voluminous works were written. Nor can his famous defence of the Rabbinic books be wholly dissociated from the consequences of Pico's influence, though in this respect the debt he owed to his Jewish instructors must evidently be taken into account.

Reuchlin, it should be further noted, was wellnigh the first German

Hebraist. Though in England, France, and Italy it has been easy to name scholars throughout the medieval period who had more or less knowledge of the language, such has not been the case as regards Germany. Yet this slowness to receive the New Learning was more than compensated by the ardour and thoroughness with which it was utilised when once its value had been recognised.

If the beginnings of a revival in Christian learning can be traced to Bacon and Grosseteste in the thirteenth century, there can be little doubt that the central figure of the whole movement is Erasmus. This is a commonplace : and when it has been set down, the difficulty of deciding how much detail should be added to the bare statement is very great. His personality cannot be adequately set forth within the limits of a single chapter. His career has been shortly traced elsewhere in this volume. The most that can be done here is to summarise the work done by him in reopening the long-closed pages of the Church's early literature.

We have spoken already of what is usually accounted his greatest service in that department, the publication of the Greek text of the New Testament. But we have seen that his best work was not put into this. It was a hurried production ; and the task of forming a really good Greek text of a set of documents, with so long and complex a history as the books which compose the New Testament, was a task beyond the powers of any individual. Many generations of textual critics were destined to collect materials and to elaborate theories before the principles on which the work must be done were formulated ; and even in our own day perfection has not been attained.

Erasmus was far more at home, and far more successful, in dealing with patristic texts. His hero among Christian scholars was St Jerome. Before the close of the fifteenth century we find him giving expression to his desire that he might be enabled to improve the text of this Father's works, and, in particular, that of his *Epistles.* In these, as is well known, there is a multitude of Greek and Hebrew quotations. Any one who has looked at, say, a twelfth century manuscript of the Letters will remember what a scene of confusion is certain to take place when the scribe is confronted with one of these passages. The best that one can hope for is an unintelligent imitation of the Greek uncial characters, upon which conjecture more or less scientific may be founded. Too often the copyist's courage deserts him, and a blank is left. The earlier editions of Jerome were no better than the manuscripts. Erasmus is never tired of saying that before his time Jerome could not be read. Johann Amerbach the printer had set on foot the enterprise of a new issue of Jerome's writings, and had engaged the services of Reuchlin and others to emend the text. Reuchlin's work— which had to do more especially with the Greek and Hebrew quotations just mentioned—was, it seems, done more by conjecture than upon the authority of manuscripts. More successful was Johann Cono, a Dominican, of Nürnberg, who made use of such ancient copies as he could find. At Amerbach's death the edition was incomplete. It was continued by his two sons in conjunction with Johann Froben; and at this point Erasmus' services were called in. In 1516 the work was published, and dedicated by Erasmus to Warham, Archbishop of Canterbury. The prefaces to this and to the other editions of patristic texts which Erasmus superintended contain perhaps the most instructive expressions of his attitude as a Christian scholar which can readily be found. Irenaeus, Origen, Athanasius, Basil, Chrysostom among the Greeks, Cyprian, Hilary, Augustine, and Arnobius *On the Psalms*, among the Latins, all benefited by his critical care. He is the first, perhaps, who had a glimpse of the true greatness of Origen. One page of Origen, he says, is preferable to ten of Augustine: and yet such all-important books as the *Commentary upon John* and the tract *On Prayer* were unknown to him. Nothing is more conspicuous in him than the acuteness of his critical sense. In his preface to Hilary he dwells at some length upon the corruptions and interpolations of his manuscript authorities. His conjectural emendations are most noteworthy: one, the substitution of *auxesin faciens* for *aures infaciens* in the pseudo-Arnobius, is worthy of a Bentley. His sense of style is wonderfully keen: over and over again he detects and rejects tracts wrongly fathered on one or other of his authors. Not that he is free from error in these matters. He is not sure whether Irenaeus wrote in Greek or Latin: he identifies Arnobius, the author of a *Commentary on the Psalms*, with Arnobius the Apologist; and he is inclined to repudiate Chrysostom's *Homilies on the Acts*, a genuine, though poor work of that Father's. *En revanche*, he rightly pronounces the *Opus imperfectum in Matthaeum* to be the production of an Arian; yet this work, by the irony of fate, had during the Middle Ages been far more widely disseminated under Chrysostom's name among the Latins than anything that Chrysostom really wrote.

In the preface to Hilary is a passage which sums up the position of Erasmus towards the ancient and the scholastic learning far better than we could do it for ourselves. "We have no right to despise the discoveries or improvements which have originated in the minds of our contemporaries; yet it is an unscrupulous intellect that does not pay to antiquity its due reverence, and an ungrateful one that rejects those to whose industry the Christian world owes so much. What would sacred learning be without the labours of Origen, Tertullian, Chrysostom, Jerome, Hilary, and Augustine? I do not hold that even the works of Thomas (Aquinas) or Scotus should be entirely set aside. They wrote for their age, and delivered to us much that they drew from the writings of the ancients and expounded most acutely. On the other hand, I cannot approve the churlishness of those who set so much store by authors of this class, that they think it necessary to protest against the providential revival of good literature all over the world. There are many kinds of genius: each age has its different gifts. Let every man contribute what he can, and let none envy another who does his best to make some useful addition to the common stock of knowledge."

"To the ancients reverence is due, and in particular to those who are commended by holiness of life as well as by learning and eloquence; yet they are to be read with discretion. The moderns have a right to fair play. Read them without prejudice, but not without discrimination. In any case let us avoid heated contention, the bane of peace and concord."

Such was the spirit in which Erasmus strove to work: and some words of his good friend and fellow-worker, Beatus Rhenanus, tell us something of the effect of his work on his own age. "He was sufficiently outspoken on the subject of sacred learning: for, to use his own words in a letter to a friend, he saw that more than enough was made of scholastic theology, and that the ancient learning was quite set at nought. Theologians were so much occupied with the subtleties of Scotus that the fountain-head of Divine wisdom was never reached by them....We begin, God be thanked, to see the fruit of these warnings. Instead of Hales and Holcot, the pages of Cyprian, Augustine, Ambrose, and Jerome are studied by our divines in their due season."

Only the briefest allusion has so far been made to the development of one great department of Christian learning—ecclesiastical history. The men of the thirteenth and fourteenth centuries had in their hands not a few of the authorities which we account as of capital importance. They had the *History* of Eusebius in a Latin version: they had the *Tripartite History*, embodying Socrates, Sozomen, and Evagrius: they had Baeda, Gregory of Tours, and the *Speculum Historiale* of Vincent; and they had innumerable biographies of Saints. In spite of this, it will not be contended that a true and discriminating view of Church history, based on the best sources, was a possession of the Middle Ages. It is clear that highly incorrect views were current as to the development of doctrine, ecclesiastical jurisdiction, and liturgical usage. This could not fail to be the case when such documents as the False Decretals and the Donation of Constantine passed as genuine. And, on the other hand, when their spuriousness became an accepted fact, a reaction was inevitable. We have seen that the first attacks on them did not come from men who had broken with the Roman Church. It was Lorenzo Valla who exposed the Donation of Constantine; and Roman Catholics did not scruple to impugn the Decretals. Cusanus rejects the *Epistles* of Clement and Anacletus:

Erasmus points out (in a Preface to Athanasius) the way in which a letter of Anteros was made up. Naturally, however, the attitude of the "Evangelical" critics towards the credentials of the Latin Church was a far more radical one. Everything, in their eyes, was corrupt. A return to primitive simplicity was essential: and the width of the chasm which separated the Roman usages of their day from those of the Apostolic age could easily be demonstrated by a categorical setting forth of the history and development of those usages from the beginning. With such an object the great compilation of the "Magdeburg Centuriators" was begun; and it has some claim to be looked upon as the first Church History compiled on critical principles. It was of course a *Tendenzschrift*; nothing else was possible; nevertheless, it brought together and laid before the world for the first time an enormous amount of information either dispersed or unknown before. A committee, whose composition varied from time to time, was responsible for the work. The period dealt with was divided into centuries, and the events, literature, doctrine, and other characteristics of each century were separately treated according to a regular plan. The twelfth century was the last that was reached. The moving spirit of the committee was Matthias Flacius Illyricus, who had already made himself a name as a controversialist on the Protestant side. His *Clavis Sacrae Scripturae* sums up the exegetical knowledge of his day. His book on the testimony of earlier ages against the papacy (*Catalogus Testium Veritatis*) gives proof of an enormous range of reading; and among our smaller debts to him may be reckoned the fact that he collected and printed as a supplement to that work a large mass of medieval Latin poetry, largely from a manuscript of English origin.

Whatever the merits or demerits of the *Magdeburg History* may have been, it speedily became a famous and influential book: so famous and so influential, indeed, that those whose position it attacked were compelled to issue a counterblast. A worthy champion was found in Cesare Baronio, Cardinal of the title of SS. Nereus and Achilleus. The twelve volumes of his *Annales Ecclesiastici*, published between 1588 and 1607, cover the same period as the work of the Centuriators. The stores of the Vatican, of which after 1596 he was librarian, furnished an unrivalled stock of material, and his own previous studies, of which some fruit had already been seen in his edition of the Roman Martyrology, enabled him to use this material to advantage. That Baronius, like the Centuriators, was a partisan needs hardly to be said; his accuracy and critical instinct, moreover, leave much to be desired. Still, his erudition was enormous, his services to learning great, and his love of antiquity genuine and fervent. An eloquent witness of this love is the appeal to posterity inscribed in the Cardinal's own titular church, whose ancient arrangements he had himself restored, preserving with a reverence uncommon in his day all that he could find of its original furniture.

A brief parenthesis may be allowed at this point on the application of the science of archaeology to things Christian. For more than a century had the remains of classical art and architecture been studied and treasured before it occurred to scholars that the Church possessed antiquities which merited consideration. Probably the first book entirely devoted to the consideration of Christian monuments was that of Onofrio Panvinio on the older Roman basilicas, published in 1554. Rome was thus the parent of Christian as of classical archaeology. In 1578 the reopening of the Catacombs began, and the discoveries of ancient paintings and inscriptions excited a keen interest, though it was not until 1632 that the first great work on " *Roma sotterranea* "—that of Bosio—saw the light. The study was carried on and developed during the seventeenth century chiefly by Italians : it is probably fair to say that no work of real importance in this department was done outside Italy before 1700.

To return to the wider field of Church history. In this, the Centuriators and Baronius may be regarded as pioneers. Theirs were, of course, not the only works of the kind that appeared, but they deserve special prominence in view of their large design and the extent of the new ground they broke.

We ought to glance briefly at the progress made in two subdivisions of this great subject. One is the study of the lives of the Saints. Most people have some idea of the character of the popular medieval collections of such Lives. The *Legenda Aurea* of Jacobus de Voragine was, of all, the most widely diffused both in manuscript and print, and it was one which made no pretensions either to completeness or critical selection. The later collections, that of Mombritius, for example, or the *Catalogus Sanctorum*, were of the same character, though of larger compass. Criticism of these ancient documents other than stricture could not well be expected from the Protestant side ; save perhaps in the case of the Acts of some of the earliest martyrs. The first man who attempted seriously the task of collecting the best accessible texts of the Lives of the Saints was probably Aloysius Lippomannus, who was assisted by such scholars as Gentianus Hervetus, and Cardinal Sirleto. His copious employment of Greek authorities is a principal mark of his superiority to his predecessors. His collection filled eight volumes, and was a worthy beginning of the work which in later centuries was continued by Bolland, Papebroch, Surius, Ruinart, and a host of others.

The other department of Church history of which it was our intention to speak was the bibliography of Christian literature. Jerome had set the fashion of compiling notices of Christian writers and their works. Gennadius had supplemented his book, and the tracts of both had been widely read. The Middle Ages had, as we have seen, done something towards continuing the tradition in such works as the *Catalogus Scriptorum* of John Boston. It was natural that it should occur to the men of the Renaissance period to take stock of the mass of writings newly brought to light; and very useful work was done by several in classifying and cataloguing the writers of all ages up to their own. Johann Trithemius (Trittenheim), Abbot of Sponheim, wrote a catalogue of Church writers about 1492. In 1545 Conrad Gesner printed his *Bibliotheca*, a far larger book, not confined to ecclesiastical authors. The *Bibliotheca Sancta* of Sixtus of Siena (1586) is rather an encyclopaedia of literature connected with the Bible. All three books are interesting and remarkable achievements. That of Trithemius is a guide—not always a safe one—to the literary possessions of dying medievalism. He knows less accurately than Gesner what books actually exist and are accessible; but he is invaluable as marking a stage in the period of rediscovery and revival. It is most interesting to compare his list of authors with that derivable from the more scientific Gesner. Sixtus of Siena's book, lastly, is still valuable, not only because it presents us with a comprehensive view of the standard of Biblical and patristic knowledge at a certain period, but because the author apparently had access to documents of early date which have since disappeared.

The greatest man who continued the work of Trithemius during the sixteenth century was no doubt Cardinal Bellarmin. His book on ecclesiastical writers, produced during his early years, gives evidence of his great power, and in particular of his critical ability; but though it may be intrinsically better than the works of Trithemius or Gesner, it does not occupy so important a place in the history of this special form of literature. Of more enduring value were the bibliographies devoted to particular countries, notably that of Bale, in which are embodied his own collections and those of Leland. It gives a really amazing *conspectus* of the literary history of medieval England.

The progress of the formation of libraries, which we traced roughly during the period preceding the invention of printing, demands our attention again in the earlier part of the sixteenth century. There is no need to dwell at length upon the obvious fact, that the possession of a library of reasonable extent was now within the power of nearly all students. In the fourteenth century a man might be proud of owning thirty manuscripts; he could now for the same money purchase one or two hundred printed books.

Most prominent scholars possessed in addition a certain number of manuscripts; but these were in most cases late in date, and, in proportion as the critical sense was developed, the productions of the fifteenth century scribes lost their value as compared with the correct and beautiful texts issued by Aldo or Froben, and supervised by

Erasmus or Beatus Rhenanus. Still, a long time must needs elapse before complete editions of the greater Greek Fathers—Chrysostom say, or Basil—could be produced; and for the purposes of studying these unprinted texts, manuscripts were still indispensable: nay, they continued to be multiplied. This was especially the case with Greek texts. Numberless are the sixteenth century manuscripts of Greek authors, pagan and Christian alike. The relics of Grocyn's library at Corpus Christi College, Oxford, afford a ready instance, or the books given by Cardinal Pole to New College. A glance at the Catalogue of the Greek manuscripts at Paris is yet more instructive in this respect. Vergecius, Darmarius, Valeriano of Forlì, and a score of others were gaining great names as copyists in the service of princes, secular and ecclesiastical. Every noble and every prelate was in honour bound to be the owner of as brilliant a collection as he could. In these libraries the Greek classics were doubtless more prominent and more valued than the Greek Fathers; yet these latter held their place also, especially on the shelves of the princes of the Church. In England, for example, Warham, Pole, and Cranmer had no inconsiderable stores of such books; and there is no lack of similar instances on the Continent. Representative examples of the libraries of individual scholars of humbler position can also be cited. We have the catalogue of the books possessed by Grocyn at his death; and the library of Beatus Rhenanus forms the nucleus of the town library of Schlettstadt.

We have spoken incidentally of the work done by such men as Erasmus in the publication of patristic texts. Before we close this imperfect survey of the movement which we have called the Christian Renaissance, it will be right to ask what progress was made during the sixteenth century in the task of bringing together the literature of the early Christian centuries and making it accessible in print. It appears to us that the most effective way of answering this question will be to review the actual work done in certain selected instances, and we shall not shrink from entering upon bibliographical detail to a somewhat larger extent than we have hitherto done. Our survey will naturally not be complete; its aim will be to give an idea of the activity of those engaged, and to show in what quarters this activity was specially noticeable. It will be convenient to adopt an order mainly depending on the dates, supposed or real, of the writings concerned. A place apart may be assigned to the two great Jewish writers of the first century whose works have had so potent an influence on Christian learning, to wit, Philo and Josephus.

A tract by Philo in a Latin version was first printed at Paris in 1520 by Agostino Giustiniani. A further instalment, likewise in Latin, appeared at Basel in 1527. One of the Philonian writings in this volume—a fabulous chronicle of Biblical events from Adam to Saul—is a spurious book. In spite of its remarkably sensational conents, and of the fact that it was reprinted at least thrice during the century, this early *apocryphon* suffered the singular fate of being absolutely forgotten until a year or two ago, when attention was called to it once more.

Not until 1552 did any of Philo's works appear in Greek. It was Adrien Turnèbe who produced the first collection. John Christopherson, afterwards Bishop of Chichester, Sigismund Gelenius, Frederic Morel, and David Hoeschel were the scholars who contributed most to the publication and elucidation of this author during the second half of the century; but no great collective edition of his works was brought out before the seventeenth century.

Josephus, as we have seen, was known during the medieval period through the medium of ancient Latin versions. As late as the year 1524, indeed, doubts were expressed by scholars as to whether the Greek originals of his writings were still in existence. Many editions in Latin were produced from about 1470 until 1544. One of these (that of Basel, 1537) had been superintended by Erasmus. In 1544 the first Greek Josephus appeared—also at Basel, and from Froben's press. The text was supplied mainly by a manuscript, then the property of Diego Hurtado Mendoza, which, with other of his books, found a home in the Escurial. An Orleans edition, printed in 1591 by de la Rovière, also gave the Greek text. Exactly a century later Thomas Ittig superintended a Leipzig edition, and Edward Bernard issued a portion of one at Oxford.

We may next say something of the apocryphal literature; and in so doing we will confine ourselves to that connected with the New Testament. The Old Testament *pseudepigrapha*, other than those which were circulated with the Vulgate or the Septuagint—the Fourth Book of Esdras, for example, or the Prayer of Manasses—were almost wholly unknown during our period; of the one really important exception, the *Testaments of the Twelve Patriarchs*, we have already spoken. On the other hand there were spurious Gospels, Epistles, and Acts of Apostles which continued to influence popular imagination and sacred art both in East and West. The *Gospel of Nicodemus*, so-called, the letters of Paul and Seneca, the correspondence of our Lord with Abgarus of Edessa, had never been forgotten. Narratives of the Infancy of the Virgin and of Christ enjoyed a certain repute; and the fabulous Passions of the Apostles were taken seriously by the mass of readers.

The first document of this class which had been previously unknown to the West was the important so-called *Protevangelium*. This had been brought from the East by Guillaume Postel, who insisted that it was a genuine work of James, the brother of the Lord, and contained authentic history; for these assertions he was soundly castigated by Henri Estienne, who seems to have suspected, wrongly, that Postel himself was the author. The book was printed in Latin in 1552, and in Greek in 1563 by Michael Neander in the first collection ever made of Christian *Apocrypha.* Grynaeus' *Orthodoxographa* of 1569, and Glaser's *Apocrypha* of 1614 are the only subsequent collections of texts which deserve mention before 1703. In that year appeared the *Codex Apocryphus* of John Albert Fabricius, eclipsing all previous attempts, and still an indispensable authority on the subject of the spurious Christian literature.

The next group of writings to be considered are those conventionally classed as the Apostolic Fathers; that is, the Epistles of Barnabas, Clement, Ignatius, and Polycarp, and *The Shepherd* of Hermas. Occupying a place midway between them and the Apocryphal literature are the pseudo-Clementine Recognitions and Homilies, the Apostolic Constitutions, and the Liturgies current under the names of various Apostles. We will notice them in order.

It was long before the two first-named authors made their appearance at all: Barnabas, at Paris in 1645, in a posthumous publication of Hugues Menard superintended by Dachery; Clement, in 1633 at Oxford, edited by Patrick Young.

The letters of Ignatius—extant, as is well known, in two recensions, one copiously interpolated—were known in Latin versions in medieval times: and the Letter of Polycarp was preserved with them. The longer Latin version was first printed at Paris in 1498 along with the pseudo-Dionysian works. The editor was Jacques Lefèvre d'Étaples. They did not appear in Greek until 1557, when Valentine Frid (Paceus) edited them at Dillingen. About a century later (in 1644) the first great critical exposition of the vexed Ignatian question was made by Archbishop Ussher.

The bulky allegory called the *Shepherd* of Hermas was current, like the last-named documents, in Latin versions. The Greek original, indeed, was only discovered in the middle of the nineteenth century. The Latin appeared first in 1513 at Paris. Lefèvre d'Étaples was in this instance again the editor. He rather obscured the true character of his text by discarding its old name of *Pastor,* and substituting one apparently of his own devising: *Liber trium virorum et trium spiritualium virginum.*

Last come the important pseudonymous works associated with the name of Clement of Rome: the two romances, called the *Recognitions,* and the *Homilies* of Clement: and the manual of ecclesiastical usages known as the *Apostolic Constitutions.* The first of these had been early popularised in the Latin version of Rufinus, in which form alone it has survived complete. Lefèvre d'Étaples printed it first at Paris in 1504: the *Homilies,* which we only have in Greek, were not given to the world until 1672. Bovius and Turrianus in 1563 produced editions of the *Constitutions,* the former in Latin, the latter in the original Greek.

The whole series of documents which we have been describing was brought together and edited in a masterly manner by J. B. Cotelier of Paris in 1672.

The Greek Apologists form a convenient class, and we may survey their destinies next. The only one who was introduced to the West in the fifteenth century was one of the obscurest, Athenagoras. Large portions of his book *On the Resurrection* were rendered into Latin by Ficino and also by G. Valla, and printed in 1488. The Greek appeared in 1541. The *Apology* was edited by Gesner at Zurich and by Robert Estienne at Paris in 1557.

The first portion of Justin Martyr's works that saw the light was the *Address to the Greeks*, printed in the Latin version of Pico della Mirandola in 1507. In 1551 Robert Estienne brought out a *corpus* of this writer's works, genuine and spurious, which for most of them— notably the two *Apologies* and the *Dialogue with Trypho*—was the *editio princeps*.

Tatian and Theophilus first appeared at Zurich in 1546: the unimportant tract of Hermias in 1553 at Basel. The editor of the first two was Gesner, of the third Raphael Seiler.

All the extant works of Clement of Alexandria, with a few unimportant exceptions, were placed in the hands of scholars together, in the Florentine edition of 1550, superintended by Pietro Victorio. But the best work done on the text of this Father was that of Friedrich Sylburg, who brought out his writings at Heidelberg in 1592. The printer was Commelin.

The first nine editions of Irenaeus, ranging in date from 1526 to 1567, all give a text constructed by Erasmus, and improved to a certain extent by him in those which were published during his lifetime. The Erasmian text, however, never attained a very high pitch of excellence. A step forward was taken by Gallasius, who brought out an Irenaeus at Geneva in 1570, and more decided progress by Feuardent of Paris, whose best edition was printed at Cologne in 1596. Nothing of any great importance was done for the elucidation of this writer before the publication of Grabe's great work at Oxford in 1702.

The works of Origen, largely preserved in old Latin versions, were never wholly unrepresented in Western libraries. It is a curious fact that, in spite of the deep interest which this great thinker excited in the minds of men like Erasmus, no portion of his writings appeared in the original Greek during the sixteenth century. As early as 1475 some Homilies were printed in Latin, and the books *Against Celsus*, also in Latin, in 1481. A collective edition in the same language was brought out by Merlin at Paris in 1512. Erasmus was engaged on another when he died in 1536, and Beatus Rhenanus completed it in that year. Genebrard, Archbishop of Aix, produced a third in 1574. The first attempt at a complete edition in Greek and Latin was that of Peter Daniel Huet (afterwards Bishop of Avranches), which appeared at Rouen in 1668. It included only the exegetical works, and was never completed. Herbert Thorndike, of Trinity College, Cambridge, had made large preparations about the same period as Huet for a collective edition, no part of which was printed. His manuscripts, among which is the unique copy of the important treatise *On Prayer*, are preserved in the Library of his College. The first editor of one of the longer treatises in Greek was David Hoeschel, who published the books *Against Celsus* in 1605.

We have no right to inflict a complete patristic bibliography on our readers. One more Greek father only shall be mentioned, namely, Eusebius of Caesarea. His *Praeparatio Evangelica* has been mentioned more than once in the body of this chapter. George of Trebizond's Latin version of it—faulty as it was—was printed again and again before 1500. The Greek text appeared at Paris in 1544 from the press of Robert Estienne. The same indefatigable worker brought out in the same year the *History* of Eusebius in Greek for the first time, along with the later Greek ecclesiastical historians. In Latin the history had long been current, and the sixteenth century had seen at least two fresh Latin versions, made by Wolfgang Musculus and by Christopherson. It was reserved for Valesius (Valois), in 1659, to produce the first really great illustrative edition of this priceless record of Christian origins.

The Latin Fathers demand a briefer treatment than those of the Greek Church. A good deal has been said already as to the reappearance of those authors who had been forgotten, and as to the labours of scholars upon the text of some who had always been studied. We may, therefore, in this place confine ourselves to a select few of the earlier Latin writers. The *Apology* of Tertullian was printed in 1483 ; but the first edition of any considerable part of his works was supervised by Beatus Rhenanus in 1521. Gagnaeus of Paris added some eleven tracts to those previously known, in 1545; and Sigismund Gelenius improved the text. By 1625 the whole of the writings we possess had appeared in print, and the editions were numerous. Those of Rigault, of which the first appeared in 1633, did most for the text of this earliest of the great Christian Latinists. Rigault had access to all the principal manuscripts, whether preserved in France, as those of Pithou and Dupuy, with the famous "Agobardian" Codex, in Germany, as that of Fulda, or in Italy, as that of Fulvio Orsini.

Cyprian, in a gravely interpolated text, was read throughout the medieval period, and five editions of his works appeared between 1471 and 1500. He was one of the host of writers who profited by the scholarship of Erasmus; the first Basel edition came out in 1520, and was often reprinted. Latino Latini undertook to edit the works, but was prevented from completing them ; the results of his labours, taken up by others, saw the light in 1563 at Rome. The same decade witnessed the appearance of Morel's Paris edition (1564), and of that of J. de Pamèle (Antwerp, 1568); the former is said to have improved the text, the latter to have corrupted it by the use of interpolated manuscripts. An "epoch-making" edition was that of Nicholas Rigault in 1648.

The Latin Apologists alone remain to be discussed. Lactantius, first printed in 1465, was one of those writers who appealed most strongly to the humanists; and the number of reprints of his works, belonging to the fifteenth and sixteenth centuries, is correspondingly great. The first critical edition worth mentioning is probably that of Basel (1563) with the commentary of Xystus Betuleius.

Arnobius and Minucius Felix go together. The only two manuscripts of their writings which we possess have handed down the *Octavius* of the latter as if it were part of the *Disputationes* of the former; and two editions appeared before the mistake was detected. The first was that of Faustus Sabaeus of Brescia (Rome, 1543), librarian of the Vatican, to whom our oldest manuscript (now at Paris) belonged. The second was by Sigismund Gelenius, three years later, at Basel.

Of the great post-Nicene Fathers, Eastern or Western, we have decided not to speak in this place. It has already been said that they had attracted attention from the first moment of revival; and, though much notable work was done in collecting and publishing their writings during the sixteenth century, a review of that work would swell the present chapter to an undue size.

We prefer to notice the rise of those great collections of the minor Christian writings which are generically known as the *Bibliothecae Patrum*. It was the chief merit of these that they brought together, and put into the hands of a large circle, a number of brief tracts of the most diverse ages, which ran the risk either of passing unnoticed or dropping out of existence altogether. That the texts of the works thus published were uniformly good we neither expect nor find; but of their extreme value to the men of their time there can be no doubt. Even now they are the best available authorities for a good many writings.

The series is headed by a publication of Sichard of Basel (1528), called *Antidotum contra diversas...haereses*. It contains treatises by twenty authors, the earliest of whom is Justin Martyr.

The *Micropresbyticon* of 1550, also a Basel book, numbers thirty-two writers. Aristeas, the fabulous Chronicle of "Philo," and the Letters of Ignatius and Polycarp, are among its contents. Five years later appeared the *Orthodoxographa*, edited by Herold, with seventy-six headings. The collection of Grynaeus, issued with the same title in 1569, includes eighty-five. The printer of these four was Henricus Petri.

Basel, then, began the work with credit. Zurich produced somewhat similar publications, between 1546 and 1572, under the auspices of Conrad Gesner and Simler. But the productions of the two Swiss cities were surpassed, if not superseded, by the issue in 1575 of the first edition of the Paris *Bibliotheca Veterum Patrum.* Its editor was Marguerin de la Bigne, and the collection appeared in eight sections or classes arranged according to the character of the writings in each. In the first, for example, were Epistles, in the sixth Commentaries, and so forth. A supplementary volume was issued in 1579. Something over 220 writers of all ages, from the first to the sixteenth century, are represented altogether; and the whole work is in Latin. It was dedicated to Gregory XIII. In 1589 came a second edition, in nine volumes, increased by the addition of a good many treatises, but marked also by the omission of several which had called forth the censure of the authorities. Among these were the works of Nicholas de Clemanges, whose animadversions on ecclesiastical matters had seemed to surpass the bounds of fair criticism. So dangerous, indeed, did the collection appear to some minds that the Jesuit Possevin declares that it is impossible, *salva conscientia*, to keep either of the first two editions of the *Bibliotheca* on one's shelves, and more than one detailed censure of the book was issued. In the editions of 1610 and later, efforts were made to remedy the faults that had been noted; and in 1624 appeared the first of a series of publications in which the Greek texts of some of the authors hitherto only published in Latin were given. This first *auctarium* was edited by the Jesuit Fronton le Duc (Ducaeus). The final and largest form of de la Bigne's *Bibliotheca* was issued in 1644, in seventeen volumes. It contained writings of about two hundred additional authors.

A rival to the Paris *Bibliotheca* soon appeared, in the shape of the *Magna Bibliotheca* of Cologne. The first fourteen tomes, with preface by Alard Wyel, were published in 1618: a fifteenth by Andreas Schott in 1622. Their appearance provoked the publication of an *auctarium* to the Paris collection by Gilles Morel at Paris in 1639. A noticeable point about the Cologne *Bibliotheca* is that its contents are digested in chronological order, each volume comprising the writers of a century. Similar arrangements were adopted in most of the subsequent *Bibliothecae*. Cologne did not continue the rivalry; and the last great work of the seventeenth century in this department was again the product of a French press. It was the *Maxima Bibliotheca*, issued at Lyons in 1677, in twenty-seven parts. The next century witnessed the appearance of a still more comprehensive *corpus* of patristic literature in the shape of Gallandi's *Bibliotheca* (Venice, 1766); but the publication of Migne's enormous *Patrology*—never likely to be surpassed in extent—in the middle of the nineteenth century has largely superseded the earlier collections which we have been reviewing.

Let us attempt, in a few closing paragraphs, to sum up the results of an investigation which has covered, however incompletely, a wide range both in space and in time. We have seen reason to place the first symptoms of a revival of Christian learning as far back as the thirteenth century, and to connect the beginnings of the movement with England. In the fourteenth century the scene of activity is shifted to Italy, where the impulse given to classical studies reacts upon theology. Not until late in the fifteenth century are the effects of this awakening visible to much purpose in France or in Germany, in the Low Countries or in Switzerland; but throughout the succeeding centuries these countries continue to produce indefatigable workers and noble monuments of learning, while Italy, and more evidently Spain, gradually lose the predominance they had once held. The rapidity with which the light spread in Germany has been the subject of comment already: France's achievements are not less noteworthy. Lefèvre d'Étaples, Michel Vatable the Hebraist, Gentien Hervet the translator, the Estiennes, who cover the whole field of Greek and Latin literature, de la Bigne, Rigault, Dachery, Fronton le Duc, Combefis—all strenuous workers in the patristic and medieval departments—these form an imposing list, and one that might be largely increased without difficulty. Nor does the succession of scholars cease with them: it continues throughout the seventeenth century, and culminates in the noble erudition of the Congregation of St Maur.

It is dangerous to attempt to characterise the work of whole centuries in single phrases; but there are cases, and this seems to be one of them, where the progress of a movement can be marked out with approximate accuracy, and its stages defined, in such a way. The three centuries, from the fifteenth to the seventeenth, with which we have been principally occupied, had each its special form of contribution to the movement which we have called the Christian Renaissance. The fifteenth century was the age of collection: the documents were brought together, and the great libraries formed. The sixteenth century was the age of publication. What had been recovered was given to the world by the great scholar-printers. And the seventeenth century was the age of criticism: with the documents now before them, men settled themselves down to the improvement of texts and the elucidation of subject-matter, to an extent which had been impossible for their predecessors.

The names of Niccoli and Poggio, of Erasmus and de la Bigne, of Ussher and Valois, give a fair indication of the several activities which seem to us to have characterised the periods we have passed under review.

# CHAPTER XVIII.

## CATHOLIC EUROPE.

So far back as the Council of Vienne in 1311, William Durandus, nephew of the "Resolute Doctor," when commissioned by Clement V to advise him on the method of holding that assembly, had answered in a volume which we may still consult that "the Church ought to be reformed in head and members." The phrase was caught up, was echoed during the Great Schism at Pisa (1409), in the stormy sessions of Constance (1414–18), at Basel (1431–49), and to the very end of the fifteenth century. It became a watchword, not only in the manifestos of French or German princes at issue with the Apostolic See, but on the lips of Popes themselves and in official documents. But though searching and sweeping, the formula had its limits. Reformation was conceivable of persons, institutions and laws; it could not, on Catholic principles, be admitted within the sphere of dogma, or identified with Revelation; it must leave untouched the root-idea of medieval Christendom that the priesthood possessed a divine power in the Mass and in the Sacraments, conferred by the episcopal laying-on of hands. It affected nothing beyond discipline or practice; and only that portion of the Canon Law might be revised which was not implicitly contained in the Bible or in the unanimous teaching of the Fathers as expounded by the Church. Foxe of Winchester, writing to Wolsey in 1520, well defined the scope of amendment; he had found, he says, that everything belonging to the primitive integrity of the clergy, and especially to the monastic state, was perverted either by dispensations or corruptions, or else had become obsolete from age or depraved by the iniquity of the times. Thus even Alexander VI, startled into momentary penitence by the murder of his son, the Duke of Gandia, appointed a committee of Cardinals in 1497, to draw up a scheme for the reformation of morals which, he declared, must begin with the Roman Curia. The mere summary of abuses to be corrected, or of better dispositions to be taken, in the government of the Church, extends to one hundred and twenty-eight heads, as set forth in the papal Letters beginning, "*In apostolicae sedis specula.*" Julius II, addressing the Fifth Lateran Council (1512) reckons among its chief objects ecclesiastical reform; before its opening he had named a commission which was to set in order the officials of his Court. Leo X, in 1513, accepted the rules which had been laid down by these Cardinals with a view to redressing the grievances of which complaint was made, and published them during the eighth session of Lateran as his own. Nevertheless, not until the Fathers at Trent had brought their labours (1545-64) to an end did the new discipline, promulgated by them in twenty-five sessions and explicitly termed a reformation, take effect in the Roman Church. By that time the Northern peoples had fallen away; Christendom was rent into many pieces, and the hierarchy, the religious Orders, and the Mass, had been abolished wherever Lutherans or Calvinists prevailed.

It does not enter into the scope of the present chapter to enlarge upon a subject treated elsewhere in this volume,—the causes which led up to the Protestant Reformation. But, as was made clear by the rise of the Jesuits, the decrees of Trent, the acts and virtues of a multitude of Saints, the renewed austerity of the papal Court, and the successful resistance to a further advance on the part of Lutheranism in Germany, and of Calvinism in France and the Belgic Provinces, there also existed a Catholic Reformation, within the Church, not tinged with heresy, but founded on a deeper apprehension of the dogmas in dispute, and on a passionate desire for their triumph. In one sense, this great movement might be described as a reaction, since it aimed at bringing back the past. In another, it was merely a development of principles or a more effectual realisation of them, whose beginnings are discernible long before Trent. Thus we may regard the fifteenth century as above all an era of transition. It exhibits violent contrasts, especially among the high clergy and in religious associations, between a piety which was fruitful in good works and a worldliness which has never been surpassed. Corruption on a scale so wide as, in the opinion of many, to justify revolt from Pope and bishops, was matched by remarkable earnestness in preaching necessary reforms, by devotion to learning in the service of religion, by an extraordinary flow of beneficence, attested by the establishment of schools, hospitals, brotherhoods, gilds, and asylums for the destitute, no less than by the magnificent churches, unrivalled paintings, and multiplied festivals, and by the new shrines, pilgrimages, miracle-plays, and popular gatherings for the celebration of such events as the Jubilees of 1475 and 1500, which fling over the whole period an air of gaiety and suggest that life in the days of the Renaissance was often a public masquerade.

Catholic tradition, in the shape of an all-pervading and long-established Church, towered high above the nations. It was embodied in a vast edifice of laws. It kept its jurisdiction intact, its clergy exempt, and held its own Courts all over Christendom. It owned from a fifth to a third of the soil in mortmain. It had revenues far exceeding the resources of kings, to which it was continually adding by fresh taxation. It offered enormous prizes to the well-born in its bishoprics, abbacies, and cathedral Chapters, which carried with them feudal dominion over lands, serfs, and tribute-yielding cities. It opened a career to clever ambitious lads of the middle and lower class. Within its cloisters women might study as well as pray, and rule their own estates, wielding the crozier and equalling prelates in dignity and power. The Church, too, maintained her pre-eminence, though shaken once and again, in the old Universities, at Paris, Oxford, and Bologna, while founding new seats of learning at Louvain (1426) or along the Rhine; as far east as Ingolstadt (1472) or even Frankfort-on-the-Oder (1506), and as far south as Alcalà (1499). Her authority was still strong enough to put down the Hussites for a time, though not without conceding to them points of discipline. It showed no dismay at the light which was dawning in humanism. And it gave back to ruined and desolate Rome the Augustan glory of a capital in which letters, arts, manners, attained to a fulness of life and splendour of expression, such as had not been witnessed in Europe since the fall of the Empire.

From the days of Nicholas V down to those of Leo X, Rome was the world's centre. The Popes held in their hands the key of religion; they aspired to possess the key of knowledge. Along every line of enterprise and from every point of the compass, except one, they were visible. They would not dedicate themselves to the long-sought reformation in head and members, although they allowed its necessity again and again in the most emphatic terms. The plans which were laid before them by ardent churchmen like Cesarini we shall consider as we proceed. But they declined to take those measures without which no lasting improvement of the Curia was to be anticipated. They were loth to summon a representative Council; they refused to cross the Alps and meet the German people, or to listen when it drew up its grievances in formal array. Had the Fifth of Lateran fulfilled its task, instead of leaving it to the Council of Trent half a century later, the Diet of Worms might have never met, and Luther would perhaps have lingered out his years in a cell at Wittenberg.

Two series of considerations may explain why the papacy shrank from calling a fresh parliament of Western prelates and sovereigns, and why it relegated these questions of discipline to a secondary place. One was that the Holy See felt itself engaged in the necessary and therefore just enterprise of recovering its temporal independence, shattered since the migration to Avignon. That plea has been urged on behalf of Sixtus IV, and still more of Julius II. The other was that it had not long emerged from a period of revolution. In Rome the Church had been constantly regarded as a monarchy with the Pope at its head; he was the supreme judge of spiritual causes, from whom there could be no appeal. But in the fourth and fifth sessions of Constance (1415) another view had prevailed,—a view unknown to earlier ages and impossible to carry out in practice,—that of the superiority to the Pope of the Church in Council assembled. This doctrine, put forward by Cardinal d'Ailly, by Gerson, and by the followers of William Occam, might be welcome to lawyers ; but it had no roots among the people ; it had never flourished in the schools deemed orthodox ; and it irritated as much as it alarmed the Pontiff. At Basel it led to repeated and flagrant violations of the ancient canons. During the eighteen years of its existence (1431–49) this convention had deposed one Pope, Eugenius IV, elected by lawful scrutiny; it had chosen another, Felix V, Duke of Savoy, who was hardly recognised beyond the valley of the Rhone. It had compelled bishops to sit and vote, not only with simple priests but with laymen, on questions which concerned the Catholic faith. It had submitted to the feeble Emperor Sigismund ; its president was D'Allemand, the Cardinal of Avignon—an ominous title ; and for ten years it sat in permanent schism. Professing to do away with abuses, it enacted them once more in the shape of commendam, annates, and pluralities. When the large-minded reformers, Cardinal Julian Cesarini and Nicholas of Cusa, forsook its tumultuous sittings ; when Aeneas Sylvius, that politic man of letters, looked round for a wealthier patron and joined himself to Eugenius; and when the German prelates could no longer hold it up as a shield against the strokes of the Curia, the Council came to an end, and with it all hopes of reform on the parliamentary system. Felix V, last of the anti-Popes, laid down the keys and the tiara (April, 1449) in the house called La Grotte at Lausanne, under the roof of which Gibbon was afterwards to complete his History of *The Decline and Fall.* Henceforth it was evident that the spiritual restoration of Christendom would come, if ever it came, from the zeal of individuals. For the Council had failed ; no Pope would risk his supreme authority by a repetition of Basel ; and the rules of the Roman Chancery which Martin V had confirmed were, as a matter of course, approved by his successors.

Private effort could do much, so long as it refrained from calling dogma in question or resisting the legal claims of Pope and bishops. But the creed was not in danger. So far as we can judge from the local Councils and the literature of the years before us, in no part of Europe did men at this time cast away their inherited beliefs, with the exception of a humanist here and there, like Pomponazzo at Rome—and even these kept their denials to themselves or acquiesced in the common practices of religion. In 1466 groups of the Fraticelli were discovered and put down by Pius II at Poli near Palestrina. In the same year a German sect, of which the chiefs were Brothers Janko and Livin von Wirsberg, was denounced to Henry, Bishop of Ratisbon, by the papal Legate. The Fraticelli appeared again in 1471 on the coast of Tuscany; and notices are extant of heretics in the diocese of Reims and at Bologna.

The Maraños, or crypto-Jews, in Spain deserve separate consideration. Nor did the Waldensians ever cease to exist in Italy. But obstinate unbelief was rare: even a reprobate like Sigismondo Malatesta, the monstrous tyrant of Rimini, would not die without the last Sacraments. Machiavelli, who writes as if the Christian faith were an exploded superstition, had a priest with him when he expired. Of Caterina Sforza, whose crimes and profligacies were notorious, it is on record that, while she sinned, she endowed convents and built churches. Other examples of repentant humanists are Giovanni Pontano and Antonio Galatea. Among Germans who, after quarrelling with the papal authorities or questioning articles of the creed, came back to offer their submission, may be remarked Gregor Heimburg and in the next generation Conrad Mutianus of Erfurt. It has been stated elsewhere that the famous Wessel spent his last days in the cloister of the Agnetenberg. Revolt, followed by repentance, was a common feature in the Italian genius. But indeed the rules of the Inquisition, which allowed of easy retractation, imply that few heretics would persist in their opinion after once being called to account. During the ninety years with which we are concerned no popular uprising against the authorities of the Church on purely dogmatic grounds is recorded to have taken place anywhere outside Bohemia.

Intolerance was not a characteristic feature of an age abounding in hope, dazzled with discoveries and inventions, and far from ascetic in its habits of life, its outdoor spectacles, its architecture, painting, music, and popular diversions. The later fifteenth century was eclectic rather than critical. At Rome itself, an "incredible liberty" of discussion was allowed under all the Popes of the Renaissance. And though Paul II dealt severely with Platina and the Roman Academicians, whom he accused of unbelief, his motives seem to have been personal or political rather than religious. Philosophy, too, was undergoing a serious change. Plato had supplanted Aristotle in his influence over men's minds; and the high Doctors of the School—Aquinas, Bonaventura, and Scotus—had lost no little of their power since Occam brought into repute his logic of scepticism, which fixed between religion and metaphysics an impassable gulf where every human system disappeared in the void.

It is not, therefore, without significance that the chief reformer of the age, Cardinal Nicholas of Cusa, exhibits in his action and writings not only the pious enthusiasm which he learned from the Brethren of the Common Life, but a passion for every kind of knowledge; or that his method of apologetics sought in every form of religion its affinities with the Christian, as we learn from his *Dialogue of Peace, or The Concord of Faith.* His speculations, afterwards used or abused by Giordano Bruno in building up a system of pantheism, cannot be drawn out here. Nicholas Krebs was the son of a fisherman, born, probably in 1401, at Cues on the Mosel. He belonged to that Low-Dutch race, first cousins, so to speak, of the English, which has done such notable things for science, religion, and government, by its tenacious grasp of realities, its silent thought and moderation of speech, its energetic action that scorns the trammels of paper logic. Dwelling along the rivers of Germany and on the edge of the North Sea, this trading people had amassed riches, cultivated a Fine Art of its own which vies with the Italian, created a network of municipal liberties, and lived a deep religious life, sometimes haunted by visions, which might be open to the suspicion of unsoundness when the formal Inquisitor from Cologne looked into it with his spying-glass.

Yet no one has ventured to brand with that suspicion Thomas à Kempis. From this Low-Dutch people we have received the *Imitation of Christ*; when a Catholic Reformation is spoken of, that little volume, all gold and light, will furnish its leaders with a standard not only of spiritual illumination but of piety towards the Sacrament of the Altar which took for granted the whole Catholic system. Since it was finally given to the world in 1441 it has been the recognised guide of every generation in the Western Church. But with its author we must associate Cusanus and Erasmus, both of the same stock; these three fill the spaces of transition between the decadent luxury of Avignon and the stern reaction which followed hard upon Trent. By their side appears Cardinal Ximenes, who attempted among Spaniards the same work of renovation that Cusanus set on foot among Germans and Netherlanders. To the *Imitation* corresponds, almost as an art to its theory, the *Spiritual Exercises* of St Ignatius Loyola. And if Erasmus left no successor equal to himself, he trained a host of disciples or plagiarists in the Company of Jesus, where his memory has always evoked a fierce antagonism, and his writings have been put to the ban.

Spain and the Netherlands thus became rival centres in a movement which was profoundly Catholic. It sprang up in Northern Europe under the influence of the Dominican Friars; south of the Pyrenees it was due to the Benedictines and Franciscans. A third element, derived from the writings of St Augustine and the Rule called after his name, is more difficult to estimate. St Augustine had ever been the chief Western authority in the Schools as in the Councils. He, though no infallible teacher, formed the intellect of medieval Europe. But the Cathari or Waldensians were fond of quoting him as the patron of their anti-sacerdotal principles, and in the vehement polemics of Luther he is set up against Aquinas. From Deventer, then, we may trace the origin of a reforming tendency which, passing by Alcalà and Toledo, takes us on to the Council of Trent. In that assembly Spanish divines, Laynez or Salmeron, vindicated the scholastic tradition, while Popes under Spanish protection tightened discipline and recovered, though late, their lost moral dignity. But from Deventer likewise another movement issued forth, in which John of Goch, Wesel, and Gansfort led up to Erfurt and Wittenberg—to the new doctrine of justification by faith alone, and to an independent type of religion.

In these two Reformations, Catholic and Protestant, it will be observed that England, France and Italy play secondary parts. To the ideas which inspired Thomas à Kempis, Luther, or Loyola—creative or revolutionary as they might be—no English thinker except Occam contributed. Nor did a single French writer anticipate Calvin. And the Italians, almost wholly given up to art or letters, and at no time much troubled with the problems which divided the Schools in Paris, might seem to have been incapable of grasping a spiritual principle in its pure form, until they were subjugated by the Jesuit masters who came in with the Spanish dominion.

Yet, as in England religion had no quarrel with learning but was revived in its train, so among Italians the impressive figure of Savonarola warns us that prophets after the manner of the Old Testament were not wanting, even to the heyday of a Classical Renaissance. True, the English humanism did but serve to usher in a period, Elizabethan or Jacobean, which was not Catholic according to the Roman style; and Savonarola was burnt. Yet on the eve of the Reformation these more spiritual influences were not extinct in the Church; they might have been turned to a saving use; and for a while the orthodox hoped it would be so. Frà Girolamo, Bishop Fisher, Sir Thomas More, have always been regarded by those who shared their faith as martyrs in the cause of a true Christian morality and as harbingers of a reform which they did not live to see.

In the Low Countries, therefore, from the appearance of Tanchelin, about 1100, and after the growth of Waldensian opinions, though these were by no means peculiar to the Netherlands, much had been done by authority to suppress or convert dissidents. The Black Friars of St Dominic were called to Antwerp as early as 1247. They acquired almost at once a power which was chiefly exercised in spiritual direction; their many disciples followed a way of life pure, detached, and simple—the way of the heart rather than the intellect. Another sign which accompanied them was the multiplying of Third Orders, in which men and women, not bound by vow or shut up within a cloister, strove to lead the higher life. These sodalities must not be confounded with the Turlupins, Beghards, or Brethren of the Free Spirit—ecstatic, perhaps antinomian fraternities—condemned by Pope John XXII and abhorred of all good Catholics. If we would understand what precisely was the Dominican training, a delightful instance has been left us in the correspondence of Christine de Stommelin (1306). But the finest example as the most celebrated of Flemish masters in the fourteenth century is the "admirable" Ruysbroek, an earlier Thomas à Kempis, who adorns the period which lies between 1283 and 1381, and whose son in the spirit, Gerard Groot, gave a new and lasting significance to the school of Deventer.

That "flight of the alone to the Alone," which we call Christian mysticism, had found no unworthy expression in St Thomas Aquinas, the Angel of the Schools, who reasons by set syllogism on all things in heaven and earth. He had sealed with his authority the books, translated by Scotus Erigena, which were long attributed to Dionysius the Areopagite, but which are now known to be a production of the fifth century and of the Alexandrian, or even Monophysite, metaphysics. With severe negations, not wholly foreign to Plotinus, they limit, by exceeding them, the affirmations of the School theology; in the paradoxical phrase of Cusanus, their teaching is a "learned ignorance"; but they exalt the earthly as a shadow of the heavenly hierarchy; and they leave to our adoring worship the man Christ Jesus. From the defilements of sense, the scandals of history, the misuse of holy things, they turn to an inward, upward vision and celebrate the hidden life. It is well known that Eastern hermits joined the work of their hands to prayer; that cenobites under the Rule of St Basil copied manuscripts, studied the Scriptures, and taught in schools, especially the children of the poor. Brought from the plains of the Euphrates to the wild heaths or grassy meadows of Rhine and Yssel, this secret doctrine found in Ruysbroek an Areopagite, in Gerard Groot and Florentius Radevynzon the masters of its practice, who combined meditation with handicraft, and both with sacred and secular studies.

Of these men mention has already been made in another chapter of the present volume, which deals with the Netherlands. Groot's institution, closely resembling in idea the first thought of St Francis, was at Constance opposed by the Dominican Grabo, but defended by Gerson. It may be remarked in passing, that Gerson—unfairly according to the best judges—criticised the language of Ruysbroek's *Ornament of the Spiritual Marriage* as tainted with pantheism. In 1431 Eugenius IV approved the Brethren of the Common Life. Pius II and Sixtus IV showed them much kindness. Florentius, after establishing his Austin Canons at Windeshem, died in 1400; but his scheme of education prospered. Gerard Zerbold of Zutphen governed and taught in a similar spirit. The communities of Sisters fell off in some measure. On the other hand, Groot's foundation at Zwolle developed into a house of studies under John Cele, and drew scholars from every side—from Brabant, Westphalia, and even Saxony. In 1402 seven monasteries looked up to Windeshem as their mother-house. The congregation spread into Germany. In 1409 tumults at Prague, with which University Groot's leading disciples had been associated, drove out thence a multitude of students who had embraced the system of Nominalism. They flocked to Deventer, Zwolle, and the other Flemish towns where that system was upheld against the extravagances of an overbearing Realism. The convent and library of le Rouge Cloître, in the Forest of Soignies, became very celebrated. In these retreats of contemplatives, kept wholesome by hard manual labour, the Scriptures were copied and read; the text of the Vulgate was corrected; a treasure of devout wisdom was silently gathered up, whose most precious jewel is the book written by Thomas à Kempis, though it did not bear his name. Within thirty years Windeshem had given rise to thirty-eight convents, of which eight were sisterhoods and the rest communities for men of a strict yet not unreasonable observance. To the Austin Canons established by Florentius we may trace a main current in the Catholic Reformation; the Austin Hermits ended in Staupitz and Luther.

Education was the daily work of many among the Brethren. Their school at Hertogenbosch is said to have numbered twelve hundred pupils. In Deventer they taught in the grammar-school, and "here in the mother-house I learned to write," says Thomas Hemerken, who came thither from Kempen as a lad of twelve. Florentius gave him books, paid his school fees, was a father to him. Unlike Groot, who had taken his degree at Paris, Thomas attended no University. He was taught singing; he practised the beautiful hand in which he copied out the whole Bible; he travelled on business for the monastery, but was away only three years altogether; at Mount St Agnes he spent just upon seventy years. The key-note of his life was tranquillity; he perhaps called his book not, as we do, the *Imitation of Christ*, but the *Ecclesiastical Music*. A reformer in the deepest sense, he accepted Church and hierarchy as they existed, and never dreamed of resisting them. Everything that the sixteenth century called into question is to be found in his writings. He availed himself of an indulgence granted by Boniface IX; he held the Lateran teaching on the Eucharist; he speaks without a shadow of misgiving of the veneration of Saints, of masses for the dead, lay Communion in one kind, auricular confession and penance. To him the system under which he lived was divine, though men were frail and the world had fallen upon evil days. Those, therefore, who seek in *The Imitation* vestiges of Eckhart's pantheism, or prophesyings of Luther's justification by faith alone, fail to apprehend its spirit, nor have they mounted to its origin. For Ruysbroek is emphatic in asserting free-will, the necessity of works as fruits of virtue, the Grace which makes its recipient holy. Such is the very kernel of Thomas à Kempis, in whom no enthusiast for antinomian freedom would find an argument. And in a temper as active, though retiring, as dutiful though creative, the movement went on which had begun at Deventer. Thomas records in a series of biographical sketches how his companions lived and wrought. When we arrive at Cusanus, we feel that there could have been no worthier preparation for measures of amendment in the Church at large than this quiet process of self-discipline.

As a pupil of Deventer, Nicholas Krebs had been brought up in a devout atmosphere. The times drove reformers to take sides with a Council which was certain, against a Pope who was doubtful; and while Archdeacon of Lüttich, Cusanus at Basel in 1433 repeated and enforced the deposing maxims which he had learnt from Pierre d'Ailly. His pamphlet *On Catholic Concord* gave the Fathers in that assembly a text for their high-handed proceedings. But events opened his eyes. Though he had contributed not a little to the "Compact" by which peace was made with the Bohemians, yet, like Cesarini, this learned and moderate man felt that he could no longer hold with a democratic party pledged to everlasting dissensions. He submitted to Eugenius IV. At Mainz and Vienna in 1439 he appeared as an advocate of the papal claims. Two years later Eugenius associated him with Carvajal, of whom more will be said below, on the like errand. Nicholas V in 1451 gave him a legatine commission to Bohemia; and again he was united with a vehement Church reformer, the Neapolitan Capistrano, who was preaching to great multitudes in Vienna and Prague.

This renowned progress of Cusanus which, beginning in Austria, was extended to Utrecht, certainly sheds lustre on the lowly-born Pope, who had invested him with the Roman purple, appointed him Bishop of Brixen, and bestowed on him the amplest powers to visit, reform, and correct abuses. Yet the Council of Basel, so anarchical when it attempted to govern the Church, must share in whatever credit attaches to the work of the Legate. For the Conciliar decree which ordered Diocesan Synods to be held every year and Provincial every three years, set on foot a custom fraught in the sequel with large and admirable consequences. We possess information with regard to some two hundred and twenty Synods which were held in various parts of Europe between 1431 and 1520. Of these Germany claims the larger number; France follows no long way behind; but Italy reckons few in comparison, nor are these so important as the Councils which were celebrated beyond the Alps. At Florence, indeed, East and West for a moment joined hands. But the union of the Churches was one of name rather than of fact; it melted away before popular hatred in the Greek provinces; and its gain to Latins may be summed up in the personality, the scholarship, and the library of Bessarion, who spent his days on the futile embassies by which he hoped to bring about a new crusade. The reform of discipline, which in almost every diocesan or provincial Synod became the chief subject of argument and legislation, was not undertaken at Florence.

Not doctrine but canon law occupied the six local assemblies at Terguier between 1431 and 1440; the two held at Beziers in 1437 and 1442; and that which met at Nantes in 1445 and 1446. Italy had its Council of Ferrara in 1436; Portugal in the same year met in Council at Braga under Archbishop Fernando Guerra. German Synods were held frequently about this period, at Bamberg, Strassburg, Ratisbon, and Constance. At Salzburg in 1437 a code of reform was drawn up which other Councils repeated and enforced. It dealt with Reservations,—that deadly plague of papal and episcopal finance; with the moral disorders of the clergy; and with many abuses the effects of which have been strongly depicted in Protestant satires. The Synod of Freising in 1440 condemned usury and was loud in its denunciation of Jew money-lenders. There was a Synod of London in 1438; Edinburgh held another in 1445. The numerous and well-considered statutes of Söderköping, over which the Archbishop of Upsala presided in 1441, and of other assemblies in Scandinavia between 1443 and 1448, reveal the widespread evils from which religion was suffering; they insist on prayers in the vernacular, on frequent preaching, on a stricter discipline among the clergy. A French Synod at Rouen in 1445, which enacted forty-one canons, condemned in emphatic terms witchcraft and magic and many other popular superstitions, together with the non-residence of beneficiaries and the tax which prelates were not ashamed to gather in from priests who kept concubines. At Angers in 1448 a severe attack was made upon the traffic in spurious relics and false indulgences. Many strokes might be added to this picture; but there is an inevitable monotony, as in the abuses painted, so in the remedies proposed for them, none of which laid the axe to the root. Unless princes and nobles could be hindered from masquerading as bishops, though destitute of piety, learning, and vocation, the ancient evils must continue to flourish. The odious charges laid on a poverty-stricken clergy, at once too numerous and too heavily burdened, which took from them their first-fruits, their tenths, their fifteenths, were not abolished in a single one of these Councils. Nor was the abominable practice of charging money-dues on every office of religion abandoned, until the floods came and the great rains fell which threatened the house with destruction. The master-idol which it was impossible to pull down was Mammon. Culture was ruined by immorality, and religion itself by simony; while for the sake of a living crowds professed rules of perfection which they made little or no attempt to observe.

Yet Cusanus showed them a more excellent way. In February, 1451, he began to execute his legatine commission at Salzburg, where he presided over a local Synod. He travelled in unpretending guise, preached wherever he came, and displayed zeal and even tact, which was not his special quality, in reconciling the parish clergy with the Mendicants, and in bringing back monastic discipline to its former purity. At Vienna, in March, he appointed three visitors to the Austrian houses of St Benedict, then by no means attached to Rome. Fifty convents, in due time, accepted the reform. Cusanus took in hand the Augustinian Canons, held a Synod at Bamberg, and endeavoured to regulate the troublesome question of Easter Confession to the parish priest, on which strife was constantly arising with the friars. At Würzburg he received the homage of seventy Benedictine Abbots, who promised obedience to his decrees; though all did not keep their engagement. The Bursfelde Congregation, which brought under strict observance as many as eighty-eight abbeys and several nunneries, was already flourishing. It had been set up by John Dederoth of Minden, who became Abbot of Bursfelde in 1433, and was closely allied with another zealous reformer, John Rode of St Matthias at Trier. But the original impulse appears to have been derived from the Augustinian houses which had adopted the rule of Windeshem, and the famous John Busch may be named in the present connexion. This indefatigable preacher visited and succeeded in reforming a large number of convents in Thuringia and the adjacent parts. Cusanus examined and approved the statutes of Bursfelde in May, 1451. He appointed visitors to the convents of Thuringia, and in June opened the Synod of Magdeburg, which passed the usual decrees touching reform of the monasteries, concubinary priests, and economic oppression as practised by Hebrew money-lenders. But his next proceeding, an attempt to put down the pilgrimage to the "Miraculous Host" of Wilsnack, was the beginning of great troubles and met with no success.

Archbishop Frederick of Magdeburg, who had supported the Cardinal in this attempt, was however an opponent of John Busch, and in 1454 the latter returned to Windeshem, so that the decrees of Cusanus were not in the end carried out. He, meanwhile, continued his visitation at Hildesheim and Minden. In August he was at Deventer, whither much business followed him. The Holy See extended his legatine powers to Burgundy and England; but in what manner this part of his mission was fulfilled does not seem clear. That he fell into a serious illness, from which he did not recover until February, 1452, may be ascribed to his apostolic labours and journeyings. It had been his intention to preside at the Synod of Mainz, which was opened in his absence by Archbishop Dietrich, in March, 1452, and which repeated the enactments of Magdeburg against usury, clerical concubines, vagrant collectors of alms, and the holding of markets on feast-days. Other decrees imply that superstition was rife, and that crime was not unknown in holy places. The Cardinal confirmed these statutes, which were published in many diocesan Synods. In March, 1452, he presided over a gathering at Cologne in which twenty-one decrees were published, all indicating how deep and wide were the wounds of religion in the German Church, the wealthiest and the most feudalised in Christendom, and how little prospect there was of healing them. It is not the way of religious Councils to legislate for evils which do not exist or have attained only slender proportions; and we must conclude from the reiterated acts of authority that all over the West the bonds of discipline were loosened; that clerics in various places broke their vows with the connivance of bishops; that into some convents vice had found an entrance; and that many more had lapsed into ease and sloth. Yet in the largest houses immorality was rare; nor did Lutheranism receive its first impulse from the relaxation of conventual rule. That the clergy as a body were throughout this period corrupt or immoral, is an assumption unsupported by definite evidence.

When the century was ending, Trithemius, Abbot of Sponheim, celebrated Cusanus as an angel of light appearing to the fatherland. He restored, said Trithemius, the unity of the Church and the dignity of her Head; his mind embraced the whole circle of knowledge. The Cardinal, while not disdaining the tradition of the Schools, had busied himself in Italy with Plato and Aristotle; he encouraged the study of the classics, during his embassy to Constantinople collected Greek manuscripts, and won a reputation in astronomy and physics which entitles him to be named as a forerunner of Copernicus. With George Peurbach and John Müller of Königsberg, who died Bishop of Ratisbon, he kept up a correspondence on scientific and literary topics. His designs for the exaltation of the imperial power, though somewhat chimerical, stamp him as a patriot who would have prevented by timely changes the disorders which Charles V, a Fleming or a Spaniard rather than a true German Emperor, could not overcome. But he failed in politics, and his other reforms bore little fruit. Of the hundred and twenty-seven abbeys which accepted his statutes, not more than seventy observed them in 1493.

Cusanus had been appointed Bishop of Brixen directly by the Pope, without the local Chapter being consulted. This was a violation of the Concordat, and the Chapter appealed to Archduke Sigismund, Count of Tyrol. But the Cardinal was peacefully installed; and when he came back from his legatine mission in 1452, he set about reforming his diocese, which stood greatly in need of it. He began with a visitation of the convents. At Brixen he turned the unruly Sisters out of their house. The Benedictine nuns of Sonnenburg pleaded exemption and, like the Chapter, called upon Sigismund who, though notorious for his profligacies, took up their defence. Very unwisely, Cusanus, by way of answering the Duke, laid claim to a temporal jurisdiction and enforced it by anathema and interdict, which were little heeded. The Tyrolese detested strangers and wanted no reform. In 1457 the Cardinal fled from Wilten, declaring that his life was in danger: Calixtus III interdicted Sigismund; and the Duke, prompted by Heimburg, a lifelong enemy of the Holy See, appealed to the Pope better informed. This did not avail with Cusanus. He proceeded with his censures, hired troops out of Venetia, and cut to pieces a band of forty men who were in the pay of the Sonnenburg Sisters. In 1459, Pius II undertook to mediate. He was not successful. On the contrary, Sigismund, who had pleaded his own cause in Mantua, went away dissatisfied and was preparing an appeal to a future Council, when Pius launched the bull *Execrabilis* (January, 1460), by which all such appeals were condemned and forbidden.

Here, we may remark, is evidence of the motives on which the Popes distrusted Conciliar action, because, if it could be invoked at any time and for any reason against them, their jurisdiction was paralysed.

A year later the Duke made the Cardinal his prisoner at Bruneck, and demanded a surrender of the points in dispute. Cusanus yielded, escaped, fled to Pius at Siena, and cried aloud for satisfaction. The Pope, after fruitless negotiations, excommunicated Sigismund, laid his dominions under interdict, and brought Gregor Heimburg once more into the field, who drew up a formal appeal to the Council. A war of pamphlets followed, bitter in its personalities on all sides, but especially damaging to Pius II, whose earlier years were little fitted to endure the fierce light of criticism now turned upon them. Heimburg's language, though moderate, was unsound from the papal point of view; it was coloured also by his personal dislike of Aeneas Sylvius Piccolomini, with whom he had a long-standing quarrel. "Prelates of Germany," he exclaimed, "insist on the Council as the stronghold of your freedom. If the Pope carries it, he will tax you at his good pleasure, take your money for a Crusade, and send it to Ferrante of Naples." The Bishop of Feltre replied on behalf of Pius, while the German princes took part with Sigismund. No one regarded the interdict. Diether of Mainz, after being excommunicated and deposed, took up arms against the Curia, and a miserable war laid waste Germany. The Cardinal's death brought his troubles to an end in 1464. Heimburg passed over to George Podiebrad and the Bohemians, only at last to seek reconciliation with Rome. Sigismund received absolution. The Curia triumphed in the conflict at Mainz. An interval of quiet followed, during which the movement of learning went its way prosperously and religion kept the peace with humanism.

This humanism or, as it may be termed, the earlier Renaissance, flourished at many centres. Realist and Nominalist were of one mind in promoting classical studies, although Ulrich von Hutten has persuaded the world that Cologne, the head-quarters of monasticism and the Inquisition, loved to dwell in Egyptian darkness. The inveterate quarrel, which is as old as Plato, between poets, or men of letters, and philosophers who seek wisdom by process of dialectic, must not be overlooked, when we read the judgments of the later humanists on a scholasticism that they despised without always understanding it. To them technical terms were a jargon, and the subtle but exquisite distinctions of Aquinas spelt barbarism. But now printing with moveable types had been invented. From Mainz it was with incredible rapidity carried over Europe to Rome, London, Lisbon, and even Constantinople. The clergy—to quote the words of Archbishop Berthold of Mainz (Henneberg)—hailed it as a divine art. They endowed printing-presses, crowded the book-markets, almost impoverished themselves by the purchase of their productions—if we may believe Coberger's unwilling testimony; they composed as well as distributed innumerable volumes of which the purport was to teach, to explain, and to enforce the duties of religion. The first book printed by Gutenberg was the Latin Bible. We will pursue the story of its editions and translations in due course. Here it is seasonable to record that many prelates, like Dalberg at Worms and Heidelberg, were munificent patrons of the new art; that others, like Scherenberg and Bibra, published indulgences for the benefit of those who bought and sold printed books ; but that if we would measure the depth and extent of civilisation as due to the diffusion of literature through the press, we must look to the wealthy middle class and the Free Cities of Germany, to Augsburg, Nürnberg, Ratisbon, and the Rhine bishoprics.

Once more Deventer solicits our attention. Its occupation with the copying of manuscripts was to be ruined by Gutenberg's types; but so long as the Brethren lasted they did no small service to education, whether we regard its matter or its methods. To their school has been referred the illustrious Rudolf Agricola. Alexander Hegius presided over it ; and among its disciples were Rudolf von Langen and Desiderius Erasmus of Rotterdam. Agricola is often called the German Petrarch on the ground that he laboured incessantly during a short life (1443–85) to spread classical learning north of the Alps. With a passionate love of the ancients he combined deep devotion to the Sacred Scriptures ; his last years were spent in religious meditation. Hegius, though an older man, looked up to him as a guide in all learning. And while it must be admitted that Hegius did not understand Greek, and was not an accomplished Latin scholar, yet, in the thirty-three years (1465–98) during which he ruled as headmaster at Deventer, he led the way to better things by his improvement of the German manuals. As is elsewhere told, he died poor, leaving only his books and his clothes. Rudolf von Langen, provost of the cathedral in Deventer, new-modelled the schools of Westphalia, drew crowds of students to Münster, and sent out teachers as far as Copenhagen, in which capital a University had been founded in 1479. He was sent on a mission to Rome in 1486, where his amazing knowledge of Latin excited the admiration of Sixtus IV. Not only the ancient classics, but their native antiquities, poetry and topography, engaged the attention of these Teutonic masters; but they were zealous above all to diffuse the knowledge of the Bible in the vernacular as in the Latin Vulgate, and are aptly termed the Christian Humanists.

None among them was more celebrated than Wimpheling. Born at Schlettstadt in 1450, living down to the tumultuous period of the Reformation, he is a fine example of the priest, scholar, teacher, journalist, and patriot, as Germans then conceived of such a figure. Strassburg was proud to own him; Reuchlin became his pupil; with equal heat and eloquence he denounced unworthy friars, the greedy

Curia, Jewish financiers, and the "poets" or literary pagans, as he deemed them, who were leading the Renaissance astray from orthodox paths. But education in theory and practice was his proper mission. Of his writings on the subject forty thousand copies, it is estimated, had been thrown into circulation by the year 1500. His *Isidoneus Germanicus* (Guide of the German Youth), dated 1497, is accounted the first methodical treatise on teaching by a German hand. It was followed three years later by a second work entitled *Adolescentia,* which marks an era in the science of pedagogics. His pamphlet *On the Art of Printing* (1507), offers a lively sketch of German culture; warns his countrymen against perils which were then rapidly approaching; and contains a hearty expostulation with princes, nobles, and lawyers, who were unprincipled enough to sacrifice the old freedom of their people to the Roman Law, and the national prosperity to their own covetousness.

Wimpheling offended many interests. As an Alsatian, he sounded the alarm against French ideas and French invasions. It was not to be expected that he would find favour in the eyes of Hebrews whom he charged with usury, of Roman courtiers, Lutheran controversialists, or self-indulgent men of letters, all of whom he assailed. Somewhat narrow in his views, and pedantic or harsh in expressing them, this vigorous partisan has suffered in the esteem of posterity. He may, nevertheless, be classed with Reuchlin as an enthusiastic student whose researches left his religion intact. He desired to see Germany free and independent, neither enslaved to the King of France nor burdened with the hundred *gravamina,* due to a bad ecclesiastical system of taxation, to papal nepotism, and other enormities, against which he reiterated the strong national protest of 1457. Had such men as Wimpheling been admitted to the confidence of the Roman Court; had their knowledge of German law and custom been turned to good account by Julius II or Leo X, a peaceful reformation might still have been effected. They resisted the encroachments of the new imperial legislation which was destroying the liberties of their towns, and the comfort of their yeomanry; they desired to protect the farmer from the money-lender; they abhorred paganism, even when it brought the gift of culture; and they taught every rank to read, to pray, to make fuller acquaintance with the open Bible. When the Church parted asunder and the War of the Peasants broke out, many must have looked up to Wimpheling as a true prophet. But his day was gone by.

Meanwhile, the clergy had education in their hands. Scholars flocked wherever Churchmen ruled, along the Rhine as in Rome itself; freedom to learn, to teach, to print, was unbounded. The greatest of medieval Universities had been Paris. Not to pursue its earlier and informal beginnings, it had grown up on the Isle de la Cité since 1155, when the Abbot of Ste Geneviève appointed a Chancellor whose duty it was to license teachers of schools in that district. Its statutes were compiled about 1208 ; its first appearance as a corporation is traced to Innocent III and the year 1211. In perpetual conflict with Chancellor, Bishop, and Cathedral-chapter, the University owed its triumph to the Popes, one of whom, Gregory IX, in his bull *Parens Scientiarum* of 1231, established the right of the several Faculties to regulate their own constitution. Down to the Great Schism in 1378, the Pontiffs were on amicable terms with Paris and did not encourage the erection of chairs of theology elsewhere, except in Italy, where they were introduced at Pisa, Florence, Bologna, and Padua. But they encouraged the Faculties of Roman or Canon Law on the pattern of Bologna, as extending their own jurisdiction. With a divided papacy came the rise of Gallicanism, already foreshadowed by the writings of Occam and Marsilius of Padua, the *Defensor Pacis*. It was Paris that directed the antipapal measures of Constance and Basel. The Holy See replied by showing favour to other academies such as Cologne, which from its foundation in 1388 had always been ultramontane. Some four-and-twenty Universities were established during the period under review, of which those of Wittenberg and Frankfort-on-the-Oder were the last. That their organisation was not independent of the Church, or opposed to its authority, is clear on the evidence of the diplomas and papal bulls to which they owe their origin. Even Wittenberg, though set up by an imperial decree, received an endowment from Alexander VI ; and the Curia showed everywhere remarkable zeal in helping forward the new centres of learning.

In France, Poitiers was founded by Charles VII in 1431, by way of retort on Paris which had declared for the English King. Caen, Bordeaux, Nantes disputed the monopoly of the French capital, which was further lessened by long and venomous wranglings between the Realist divines who were conservative in temper as they were Roman in doctrine, and the Nominalists, or King-and-Council men, determined at all costs to support the Crown. Prague, also, which had become the *Studium Generale* of Slavonia, drew to itself students from Paris ; and Louvain exercised no small influence even on the banks of the Seine. A striking episode is the journey of Wessel to Paris (1452) in the hope of converting from their Nominalist errors his fellow-countrymen, Henry van Zomeren and Nicholas of Utrecht. But they converted him from Realism ; Wessel adopted the philosophy of Plato and plunged into the quarrels of the day as to the extent of the Pope's jurisdiction and the abuses of the Curia. He lived in his new home sixteen years. Among his associates were Guillaume de Phalis, John of Brussels, and Jean Haveron the Picard, who in 1450 became Rector of the University. In 1473 Wessel after a tour in Italy returned to Paris. That was the year in which Louis XI proscribed the doctrines of Nominalism as unedifying to the Church, dangerous to faith, and unfitted for the training of youth. That Occam's principles ended in a system sensuous at once and sceptical, it would not be easy to deny ; and this consideration furnished a sufficient motive, though by no means the only one on which its adversaries went. All professors were now bound by oath to teach the old scholastic tradition. Jean Bochard, Bishop of Avranches, who had been the adviser of Louis in this proceeding, still however sought the aid of Wessel; it is said that the Flemish divine was appointed Rector and by judicious measures restored the credit of the great School, endangered during a long intellectual anarchy. Peace was secured; the edict which forbade the teaching of Nominalist views was repealed in 1481. Reuchlin studied Greek in Paris, where the first professor of that language had been nominated in 1458; and in the Collège Montaigu Erasmus underwent those experiences of which he has left us so amusing an account. But the Renaissance can scarcely be described as having made a commencement in France until Charles VIII came back from his Italian expedition; its foremost leader and representative, the mighty-mouthed Rabelais, belongs to a period many years beyond the limits of this chapter. Neither saints nor scholars adorned an age which wasted itself in political strife, in contentions between the Crown-lawyers and the champions of Church-privileges, in the abortive Council of Pisa, in the enforcement or the revocation of the Pragmatic Sanction. No serious thought of reform occupied the public mind in France. Local synods denounced abuses which they were powerless to remedy. But though Erasmus did not conceive a high opinion of German culture in his youth, the new era had dawned with Agricola and his contemporaries across the Rhine.

An immense number of schools, elementary or advanced, are known to us from these years as existing in German regions. Nine Universities were opened. Brandenburg alone lagged behind; Berlin had no printing-press until 1539. Cologne, which was Realist and Dominican, the first among older foundations, still deserved its fame; Ortuin Gratius, despite the *Letters of Obscure Men*, was not only a good scholar but in his own way liberal-minded. John von Dalberg, appointed in 1482 Curator of Heidelberg and Bishop of Worms, divided his time between the University and the bishopric; he helped to establish the first chair of Greek, and he began the famous Palatine library. Reuchlin came to Heidelberg in 1496; he was made librarian and in 1498 professor of Hebrew. The Palatinate was likewise the head-quarters of the Rhenish Literary Sodality, set on foot in 1491 by Conrad Celtes. At Freiburg in the Breisgau, Zasius, an exceedingly zealous Catholic, taught jurisprudence. Gabriel Biel, last of the medieval Schoolmen (though by no means of the scholastic philosophers), an admirable preacher, occupied for many years the pulpit at Tübingen (1495). At Basel resided John Heynlin, who persuaded Gering, Cranz, and Freiburger to set up a printing-press within the walls of the Sorbonne in 1470, while he was Rector of Paris University. Sebastian Brant, author of *The Ship of Fools*, an ardent defender of papal claims, dwelt at Basel until he settled in his native city of Strassburg. John Müller, otherwise Regiomontanus (from his birthplace Königsberg, in Thuringia), lectured on physical science in Vienna and Nürnberg, prepared the maps and calendars of which Colombo made use in crossing the Atlantic, and died Bishop of Ratisbon. He met at Rome in 1500 Copernicus, already a member of the Chapter of Frauenburg, and at the time engaged in mathematical teaching. These names, to which many might be added, will serve to indicate the union of orthodoxy with erudition, and of a devotion to science with the spirit of Christian reform. In none of these men do we perceive either dislike or opposition to the sacerdotal system, to sacraments, or to the papacy. Sebastian Brant, in particular, published his widely-read and popular poem with intent to counteract the party of rebellion which was then rising. He defended the doctrine of the Immaculate Conception ; and in the height of his satire he is careful to spare the priesthood. On the whole, it appears that the German Universities flourished rather in the years which immediately preceded the Reformation than in those which followed it ; and if we except Wittenberg and Erfurt, they almost all took sides with the ancient religion and the Holy See. The spirit of literature, as of science, is however, in its nature, obviously distinct from the dogmatic method cultivated by all theologians in the sixteenth century.

"In papal times," said Luther towards the close of his life, "men gave with both hands, joyfully and with great devotion. It snowed of alms, foundations, and testaments. Our forefathers, lords and kings, princes and other folk, gave richly and compassionately, yea, to over-flowing,—to churches, parishes, schools, burses, hospitals." Examination in detail proves that this witness of Luther is true. There never had been in Germany, since the days of St Boniface, such a season of beneficence directed to the fostering of scholarship and piety. Churches, of which a long list remains, were built in towns and villages, often on a splendid scale. German architects, like German printers, invaded all countries ; they were found in Spain at Barcelona and Burgos ; they were called in to complete the Duomo at Milan. The Gothic style in Italy was recognised to be of German origin. But it was especially on works of benevolence or education that gifts were lavished. Endowments, no small portion of which came from the clergy, provided for universities and almshouses, for poor scholars and public preachers, for the printing of works by well-known authors, such as Wimpheling and Brant. Cloisters became the home of the press ; friars themselves turned printers. Among other instances may be cited Marienthal (1468), St Ulrich in Augsburg (1472), the Benedictines in Bamberg (1474), the Austin Hermits in Nürnberg (1479), and the Minorites and Carthusians who assisted Amerbach in Basel. Typography was introduced in 1476 at Brussels by the Brethren of the Common Life and also at Rostock. They were energetic in spreading the new art ; they called themselves preachers not in word but in type, *non verbo sed scripto predicantes.* Their activity extended through the dioceses of Lübeck, Schleswig, and Denmark; they gave out books to be printed, which betokens a demand that they could scarcely satisfy; and in Windesheim and other houses lending-libraries were opened. In the district of Utrecht alone, wrote John Busch the reformer, more than a hundred free congregations of Sisters or Beguines had a multitude of German books for their daily reading. This was earlier than 1479.

The demand fell into five or six large categories. The public wanted grammars and aids to learning. They were eager to be told about their own history and antiquities. They welcomed every edition of a Latin classic. But above all they cried out for books of devotion and the Bible in their mother-tongue. To sum up with one of the biographers of Erasmus, the early printed books of Germany were in the main of a popular educational or a religious character.

All that is left from the immense shipwreck of libraries and literature which happened during the sixteenth and seventeenth centuries bears out this statement. It may be convenient to introduce at this point a brief general survey of the first Bibles printed, whether in Latin or the vernacular, down to the eve of the Reformation. As the educated classes read and corresponded on learned topics in the language of Rome, and monasteries were great consumers of religious works in Latin, we should expect frequent publication and large editions of the Vulgate which had been from before St Jerome's day the authorised Western version. Accordingly, Gutenberg set it up in type as his first production. It was finished by 1456; under the name of the Mazarin Bible, it still survives in several copies. The Mainz Psalter is the first printed volume with a date, 1457. The first dated Bible (fourth Latin) came out at Mainz from the office of "Fust and Schoeffer" in 1462. No book was more frequently republished than the Latin Vulgate, of which ninety-eight distinct and full editions appeared prior to 1500, besides twelve others which contained the *Glossa Ordinaria* or the Postils of Lyranus. From 1475, when the first Venetian issue is dated, twenty-two complete impressions have been found in the city of St Mark alone. Half a dozen folio editions came forth before a single Latin classic had been printed. This Latin text, constantly produced or translated, was accessible to all scholars; it did not undergo a critical recension; but it might be compared with the Hebrew Psalms printed in 1477; the Pentateuch printed in 1482; the Prophets in 1485; the Old Testament in 1488, by Abraham ben Chayim at Soncino in the duchy of Milan. The Hebrew Hagiographa had come out at Naples in 1486. The Rabbinic Bible, from the Bomberg press at Venice, was edited in four parts by Felix Pratensis and dedicated to Leo X in 1517. The firm of Aldus in 1518 published the Septuagint; Erasmus had brought out the Greek New Testament in 1516. But it was first printed in 1514 in the

Polyglot of Cardinal Ximenes at Alcalà (Complutum) which, however, did not appear until 1520.

The earliest Bibles printed in any modern language were in German, issued by Mentelin and Eggesteyn of Strassburg not later than 1466. In 1471 appeared at Venice two Italian translations, the first by Malermi, a Camaldulese monk who died as far back as 1421, the second by Nicholas Jenson. Buyer at Lyons is responsible for the first French New Testament in 1477; the Old Testament in Dutch came out at Delft the same year. In 1480 the Low German Bible appeared at Cologne. The entire Bible, done into French paraphrase by Guiars de Moulin in the thirteenth century, was committed to type in 1487, and went through sixteen editions. The Bohemian version belongs to 1488. The Spanish had been made about 1405 by Boniface, brother of St Vincent Ferrer; it was printed at Valencia in 1478, and republished in 1515, of course with the imprimatur of the Inquisition. The standard French version of Jacques Lefèvre (1512 to 1523–7) was revised by Louvain theologians and passed through forty editions down to the year 1700. Fourteen translations of the Vulgate into German, and five into Low Dutch, are known to have existed before Luther undertook the task; from a collation of these with his Bible, it is evident that the reformer consulted previous recensions, and that his work was not entirely original. Prior to his first complete edition in 1534 no fewer than thirty Catholic impressions of the entire Scriptures or portions of them had appeared in the German vernacular. Eleven full Italian editions, with permission of the Holy Office, are counted before 1567. The Polish Bible was printed at Cracow in 1556 and many times afterwards with approbation of the reigning Popes.

Translations of the Psalms and Sunday Gospels had long been in use. From the Council of Constance, or even earlier, provincial synods laid the duty on priests of explaining these portions during Mass; and Postils or Plenaria which comment upon them in the vernacular meet us everywhere. Metrical versions, such as that of de Moulins in France, or of Maerlant in the Netherlands (1225–1300), were well-known among all classes. But to what an enormous extent the Bible was now read the above dates and figures may indicate, not to mention the forms in which it was speedily issued, pocket or miniature editions for daily use. It is not until we come within sight of the Lutheran troubles, that preachers like Geiler of Kaisersberg hint their doubts on the expediency of unrestrained Bible-reading in the vernacular. One remarkable fact would seem to tell the other way. In this extensive catalogue we have not been able to discover a solitary English Bible. How did it happen, we must ask, that before Tyndale's New Testament of 1526 none was printed in our native tongue?

A dense darkness hangs over the origin and authorship of the translation ascribed to Wyclif. It is certain that Archbishop Arundel, at the Council of Oxford in 1408, prohibited the making or keeping of unauthorised English versions, and that he condemned "any book, booklet, or tract of this kind made in the time of the said John Wyclif or since." It is equally certain that manuscript copies of an English Bible were in possession of such orthodox Catholics as Thomas of Woodstock, Henry VI, Humphrey Duke of Gloucester, and the Brigittine nuns of Syon. English Bibles were bequeathed by will, and given to churches or religious houses. From all this it has been argued, on the one hand, that authority tolerated the use of a version which was due to Wycliffite sources; on the other, that a Catholic version must have existed, and that the copies mentioned above contain it. Sir Thomas More, disputing against Tyndale, affirms that no translations executed prior to the Lollards were forbidden. "I myself have seen and can show you," he says in his *Dyalogue*, "Bibles fair and old, written in English, which have been known and seen by the bishop of the diocese, and left in the hands of lay men and women whom he knew to be good and Catholic people." More himself was decidedly in favour of vernacular versions; but "the New Testament newly-forged by Tyndale, altered and changed in matters of great weight," he judged worthy of the fire. The extant copies of an earlier Bible, to whomsoever due, exhibit no traces of heretical doctrine. Cranmer and Foxe the martyrologist both allude to translations of the whole body of Scripture, "as well before John Wyclif was born as since," says the latter. In the destruction of libraries these have perished and nothing of them is now known.

To Latin readers the Bible would be familiar. Coberger of Nürnberg had set up in London a warehouse for the sale of the Vulgate as early as 1480. To English readers Caxton offered the *Golden Legend* in 1483; it contained nearly the whole of the Pentateuch and a large portion of the Gospels. The *Liber Festivalis* included Scripture paraphrases. But it was in Germany that the printer had become the evangelist. No censorship interfered with the ordinary course of instruction; and this contemplated the whole duty of a Christian man; it was a comment on Holy Writ which all were at liberty to keep in their hands. Fifty-nine editions of the *Imitation of Christ* were brought out in less than fifty years. Prayer-books in heartfelt and instructive speech, the *Gate of Heaven*, the *Path to Paradise*, and a hundred more, were sold in all book-markets. Numerous as are the specimens that survive, those who have examined them agree that on points afterwards violently disputed,— as the doctrine of indulgences and prayers to the Saints,—they lend no countenance to superstition or excess. Were we to form our view of German religion from these prayers, hymns, and popular manuals, it would be eminently favourable. In language as in sentiment they have never been surpassed. The *Deutsche Theologie*, named and published in part by Luther (1516–18) is an admirable instance, perfectly orthodox and profoundly spiritual, by an unknown author, perhaps of the fourteenth century. We must look to other sources of information—among them Innocent VIII's bull *Summis desiderantes affectibus* against witchcraft (1484) and the *Malleus Maleficarum* of Jacob Sprenger and Heinrich Krämer (Institoris) (before 1487) hold a conspicuous place—if we would understand that with much outward ceremony and not a little genuine devotion, the phenomena of diseased fancies, ancient heathenism and growing luxury, were mingled in unequal proportions. But there is no reason for alleging that the Hierarchy or the religious Orders in general directly opposed themselves to the progress of learning. They considered that the Christian faith had much to gain and nothing to lose by the arts, inventions, and discoveries which the new inspiration called the Renaissance had carried to so marvellous a height. The enemy was not erudition but unbelief.

It would be as unreasonable to suppose that the rank and file of the monks were classical scholars, as that the personal influence of the prelates was for the most part edifying. But bishops who lived in open defiance of decency enacted excellent laws in synod; and there were few monasteries in which a serious effort to attain learning would be absolutely in vain. The scholastic philosophy was now overladen with futile expositions and had sunk to unprofitable wrangling. But Erasmus, the glory of Deventer, is a witness beyond exception to the spirit which prevailed among churchmen of high degree, from Oxford to Basel, and from Cambray to Rome. In his *Colloquies*, his *Encomium Moriae*, and throughout his correspondence, he mocks or argues against many superstitions, irregularities, and fantastic opinions, which he had observed in the course of his travels. But nowhere does he hint, under no provocation is he tempted to imagine, that authority frowns upon "good letters," while he addresses the Archbishop of Mainz and the Pope himself in favour of reform. On these subjects the evidence of his residence in England is particularly instructive.

Erasmus (1466–1536) owed a little to Hegius; he had been re-marked by Rudolf Agricola; his patron was the Bishop of Cambray. After making trial in Paris of the student's joys and sufferings, since he despaired of reaching Italy, he came in 1499 to Oxford, and tarried there two or three months. He won the friendship of Colet and More; he became acquainted with Grocyn and Linacre. These were the lights of English learning, the chief guides in English religion, before the King's "great matter" brought in a new world. "Colet's erudition, More's sweetness," to which an Erasmian letter alludes, have become proverbial. But the movement had not begun with them. Out of the new impulse, during or after the mid-course of the century, colleges at Oxford had sprung into existence or received a fresh life. They were rivalling or surpassing the monastic *hospitia*. In the classic revival Oxford rather than Paris took the lead. Grocyn, More's teacher, was not the first Englishman who studied Greek. He received lessons, indeed, from the exile Chalcondylas in 1491; but twenty-five years earlier two monks of Canterbury, Hadley and Selling, were students at Padua, Bologna, and Rome (1464–7). According to Leland, Selling attended the lectures of Politian; at Bologna the Greek masters appear to have been Lionorus and Andronicus. To Canterbury the Benedictine monk brought Greek manuscripts and converted his monastery into a house of studies, from which the knowledge of Hellenic literature was carried in more than one direction.

His most celebrated pupil was Linacre. Sent to Oxford about 1480, Linacre studied in Canterbury College, became Fellow of All Souls', and went with Selling in 1486 on an embassy from Henry VII to Pope Innocent. At Florence he shared in the lessons given by Politian to the children of Lorenzo de Medici. From Chalcondylas he learned more Greek than Selling had taught him. It was when Linacre had passed a year in Italy that he persuaded William Grocyn, whom he had known in Oxford, to come out and share his studies. Such was the origin of those famous lectures attended by Sir Thomas More. Of the names we have mentioned two, therefore, represent the Benedictine cloister at Canterbury; Grocyn was a doctor in theology, "almost superstitiously observant," says Erasmus, "of ecclesiastical custom"; Linacre, after graduating in the medical schools at Padua, became physician to Henry VIII, and in the decline of life took priest's orders. Selling translated a sermon of Chrysostom's from Greek into Latin as early as 1488. And the complete Homer as well as the plays of Euripides, once associated with the memory of Archbishop Theodore, which are still preserved in the library of Corpus Christi, Cambridge, may have been among the manuscripts which Selling brought from Italy. In like manner the Livy, the Greek Psalter of the fifteenth century, and the Hebrew and Latin Psalms, in Trinity College Library, were Benedictine treasures.

With this learned Prior we may reckon his friend Langton, in 1483 Bishop of Winchester, from whose "domestic school" came the still more learned Robert Pace, well known as a diplomatist and man of letters. Langton sent Pace to study at Padua and Rome; he was assisted by Cuthbert Tunstal and William Latimer, and was taught by Leonicus. Few among Englishmen, except the clergy, were, as a Venetian traveller observed in 1500, at this time addicted to literature. In religious houses, as at Reading, Ramsey, and Glastonbury, distinct evidence is forthcoming of zeal in scholarship. To these examples may be added Richard Charnock, Prior of St Mary's, Oxford, with whom Erasmus stayed. The registers of the University from 1506 to 1535, the era of Dissolution, prove that the Benedictines kept up a high average of graduates. To the same effect are details gleaned elsewhere, as at Gonville Hall, Cambridge, between 1500 and 1523. Help was constantly given to poor students by monastic houses; hence, when these were swept away, not only did the secular clergy lack recruits, but the

Universities showed a falling off in their scholars. It is remarked that in 1547 and 1550 not a single degree was taken at Oxford. In 1545 Cambridge petitioned the Crown for fresh privileges in apprehension of the total decay of learning. Latimer in Edward VI's time, and Edgeworth under Mary, contrast this lamentable change with former flourishing years. Under Henry VIII the numbers fell off; the spirit of independence was broken; the Universities lay at the King's mercy. True, the Reformation had allied itself with Humanism; but these two great movements were not destined to follow the same path. Erasmus had complained of the harm which Luther was inflicting on letters; Bembo was all astonishment at the piety of Melanchthon. Neither the literary nor the scientific spirit was in its essence Protestant.

Colet (1466–1519), who strikes us as entirely English, downright, straightforward, and impatient of scholastic subtleties and pagan license, had come home from Italy in 1498 with a contempt for its ungodly refinements. He lectured without stipend in Oxford on the Epistles of St Paul, after a new method which attracted many, but was a stone of offence to some of the elders. Colet preached a return to primitive discipline; he preferred the Fathers before their commentators; and he despised much of the current usage as tending to overlay the Gospel with human inventions. In 1504 Henry VII named him Dean of St Paul's. Here he endowed the public school of which he made William Lilly headmaster; its governors were to be married citizens, not monks or clerics. It furnished a pattern to other foundations, including the grammar-schools of Edward VI and Elizabeth, but was much decried by teachers of the ancient stamp. In Archbishop Warham Colet, as afterwards Erasmus, found an unfailing friend and benefactor. By him the Dean was enabled to address the Convocation of Canterbury, in 1512. Colet inveighed against the worldliness of bishops, the accumulation of benefices, the evils of non-residence. He attacked no dogma. But he was at once accused before the Primate as disparaging celibacy and as being himself a heretic. Warham dismissed the charges. If we consider who Colet's friends were the accusations against him seem scarcely probable. He had been for a number of years More's spiritual director. He strongly approved of Erasmus when he brought out his Greek New Testament. But he praised quite as strongly Melton's *Exhortation to Young Men entering on Orders,* printed by Wynkin de Worde, in which it is laid down that a priest should say his Hours and his Mass every day, as well as meditate on the writings of the Fathers and read the Scriptures. It was not dogma, but the superfluous contendings of "neoteric divines" which provoked the indignation of those moderate reformers with whom Colet thought and acted. As a patristic student he is termed by Erasmus "the assertor and champion of the old theology,"—a phrase which defines his position, but which does not exhibit him as favouring the Reformation.

Foxe, Bishop of Winchester, founded Corpus Christi, Oxford, in 1516, with special reference to the study of Greek. Three years later, sermons and speeches were made against this innovation, but More and Pace engaged the King easily on their own side, and the "Trojans" were laughed out of court. At Cambridge, Fisher, the Chancellor, recalled his *protégé* Richard Croke from Leipzig in 1519 to carry on the work of Erasmus, who had taught Greek in the University between 1511 and 1513. In the great humanist's flattering judgment, Cambridge had become equal to the best academy abroad since it had discarded the old exercises in Aristotle and put away Scotus. On the appearance of his New Testament, Warham assured Erasmus in an all but official letter that it had been gladly received by all the bishops to whom he had shown it. Fisher and More in 1519 helped in the correction of the second edition. Leo X accepted its dedication. The alarm which was raised in some parts, as if Greek studies were a prelude to Lutheranism, found no echo in England. Few signs of an approaching catastrophe in Church and State can be noted until the fall of Wolsey. The Lollards were extinct. Benevolence still continued to flow in ecclesiastical channels. As in Germany, schools, colleges, and gilds were multiplied. The people, who had during the last fifty or sixty years rebuilt so many parish churches, now adorned, endowed, and managed them. Printing-presses were set up under clerical patronage. Religious literature was in constant demand. Missals, manuals, breviaries, for the use of the clergy ; special treatises like *Pars Oculi*, dealing with their duties ; and primers, prayer-books, *Dives et Pauper*, for the laity, were printed in great abundance. Sermons were much in request. Paul's Cross attracted famous preachers and vast audiences. But there was another side to the picture.

That religious men in England had somewhat degenerated from their ancient strictness and fervour of spirit, is one reason alleged by Cresacre More why Sir Thomas did not join the Carthusians or Franciscans. Unlike Erasmus, who suffered from the intemperate zeal which thrust vows upon him in his youth, More was a devoted adherent of monasticism. His biographer's judgment, however, is far too mild ; on the other hand, the sweeping inferences which have been drawn from the indictment laid before Cardinal Morton in 1489 against the Abbot of St Albans, cannot be accepted without proof.

Disorder and dilapidation enough were shown to justify Wolsey in taking out the Legatine commission in 1518, which later on was turned against the clergy, whom it did not amend, as bringing them into a praemunire. Wolsey could have reformed others, himself not at all,— or not until his dignities were stripped off and death stared him in the face. A magnificent pluralist ill-famed for his unclerical living, and a Cardinal who did not shrink from proposing to buy the papal tiara, he had always been the friend of learning since he completed Magdalen

Tower at Oxford in his bursar's days. With a revival of monastic discipline he intended to combine large schemes of study founded on the classics. Bishops as severe as Foxe of Winchester welcomed his clerical reform, which could not imply designs on the Catholic Faith. The nation did not repulse an English Legate. Various Benedictine houses put into Wolsey's hands the election of their superiors. The Dominicans would not resist. But with the Observantines there was great difficulty. For his own Province of York Wolsey drew up a Constitution (1515 or 1518) which has been termed a model of ecclesiastical government; how far it was carried out we have scanty means of determining. His measures with regard to education are better known. In 1515 the University of Oxford surrendered to him all its powers. He proceeded to found seven lectureships, one of which was held by Ludovico Vives. He planned the "College of Secular Priests" for five hundred students, which was then styled Cardinal College and is now Christ Church. It was to be fed from a richly-endowed school at Ipswich, where only a gateway remains to tell of that splendid undertaking. Twenty-two small convents, with less than six inmates apiece, were suppressed and their revenues applied to defray these enterprises. It was remarked afterwards that Wolsey's Legatine autocracy had paved the way for Henry's assumption of the Supreme Headship; and that a precedent had been given in dissolving the small monasteries for the pillage and spoliation that speedily followed by Act of Parliament. On the other side, if reformation was necessary, Wolsey's dealing can scarcely be judged inhumane; his hand would have been lighter than Thomas Cromwell's; and while he protected the ancient creed he was lenient with such dissenters as fell under his jurisdiction.

In truth, it was not the Revival of Learning that shook Europe to its base, but the assault on a complicated and decaying system in which politics, finance and privileges, were blended with religion. Of the twelve Popes who sat in St Peter's Chair between 1420 and 1520 not one was a man of transcendent faculty or deep insight. Martin V broke his solemn engagement to reform the Curia. Eugenius IV trifled with the Council of Basel and squandered a great opportunity. Cesarini warned him in vain that the German clergy were dissolute, the lay people scandalised; that the Holy See had fallen from its high estate. He pleaded for a serious amendment, if, "the entire shame were not to be cast on the Roman Curia, as the cause and author of all these evils." When the anarchy of Basel drove him from it he did what in him lay at Florence (1439) to promote the short-lived union with the Greeks. And he perished in Hungary at the battle of Varna, still fighting on behalf of a united and reformed Christendom. Nicholas V, though intent chiefly on restoring literature, sent Cusanus with ample powers, as we have seen, into the North. But his own desire was that Rome should be a missionary of culture, when what the world needed was an economic and moral restoration. Pius II, whose character stands forth so individually in the long succession, had been a dissolute young man, but as a Pontiff he was grave and enthusiastic; his zeal for the Crusade denoted some far-off touch of greatness. He, too, spoke of reform. The learned Venetian, Domenichi, drew up a project which was to cure the ills of simony, to correct the vices of churchmen, and "other uncleanness and indecency." Cusanus, on being consulted, took a wider range in his fourteen Articles; primitive discipline should be restored, and three visitors, clothed in dictatorial power, were to deal with the whole Church, beginning from the Pope and Curia. At least, he observed significantly, their state need not be worse than in the time of Martin V. Of all this nothing whatever came.

Pius II began once more the bad old custom of nepotism. He advanced his kinsfolk to high positions in the Church, regardless of their age or attainments. But he distinguished some good men, as Calandrini, the Grand Penitentiary; the two Capranicas; Oliva, General of the Augustinians, known as the Angel of Peace; and the stern Carvajal, who survived as an example of austere virtue into the shameful years which tolerated Cardinals like Borgia and della Rovere. Judged by ethical standards, Italy exhibited during the whole of the fifteenth century a deeper decline than any other country in Europe. Private depravity and political debasement followed the most brilliant culture like a shadow; violence, craft, cruelty, were mingled with the administration of holy things. Yet the descent was broken, though not arrested, by religious revivals, especially in the north and centre, of which the credit is due to the Observantine Friars, the Austin Hermits, and the Benedictines. A catalogue of eighty Saints, men and women, chiefly in these communities, has been made out; it covers the period from 1400 to 1520. None are of the first rank; but Bernardino of Siena (1444) and Giovanni Capistrano (1456), Observantines, preached repentance with great if not lasting effect, to multitudes. Antoninus, Archbishop of Florence (1459), taught Christian doctrine successfully; denounced usury; and was a welcome peacemaker. Lorenzo Giustiniani, Patriarch of Venice (1456), abounded in good works. Frà Angelico da Fiesole, the Dominican (1455), perhaps the most purely religious painter that ever lived, was himself a vision of innocence and joy. Bernardino da Feltre (1494), by way of rescuing the poor from usurers, against whom he waged an incessant warfare, established in Rome the first Monte di Pietà, with the concurrence of Innocent VIII. The whole story of his benevolent campaigns is replete with interest. A series of preachers— the most famous were Franciscans—from Roberto da Lecce to Gabriele da Barletta, thundered against the vices of the age and its growing paganism. The Third Order of St Francis counted thousands of members, especially in the middle class, not so tainted as nobles or clergy. For, whatever may be said in defence of the priesthood elsewhere, in the Italian Peninsula it had lost its savour. Documentary evidence from almost every district and city leaves no doubt on this melancholy subject. The clergy were despised; so patent was their misconduct that proposals to abrogate the law of celibacy began to be put forward. Pius II may have entertained such a thought. But he contented himself with an endeavour to correct the religious Orders. The Observantines, who were strict, deserved and obtained his favour. But continual strife for precedence, which meant disciples and influence, raged between these and the Conventuals, nor could any Pope reconcile them. Santa Giustina, the Benedictine house at Padua (1412), became an Italian Bursfelde ; its reform was accepted in Verona, Pavia, Milan ; Pius II brought under it many monasteries which required better discipline. He deposed Auribelle, the unworthy General of the Dominicans. He took severe measures with the convents of Vallombrosa, the Humiliati in Venice, the Carmelites in Brescia, the Religious in Siena and Florence. Other Popes, Paul II, Sixtus IV, even Alexander VI did in like manner. Such efforts had been stimulated by earnest and cultivated men, of whom the most capable were Traversari, General of the Camaldulese (1386–1439), Baptista Mantuanus (1448–1516), and Aegidius of Viterbo, Augustinian and Cardinal, whose decrees in the synod of Santa Sabina afforded a scheme of reformation to the Fifth Lateran.

The correspondence of Alessandra degli Strozzi (1406–71), the biographies of Bisticci, the note-books of Rucellai, Landucci's *Diary*, Domenichi's work on the government of the household, reveal a sincere spirit of piety in many families, and correct the hard impression we should otherwise receive, especially of life at Florence under the Medici. Vittorino da Feltre's school at Mantua is estimated in another chapter. With him as a Christian teacher may be named Agostini Dati of Siena (1479), and Maffeo Vigeo, the latter of whom wrote six books on education and was a friend of Pius II, devout, cultivated, and practical. St Antoninus published a manual of confession, which is but a specimen of a very large class, and which instructs all professions, from magistrates to weavers and day-labourers, in their several duties. Gilds and brotherhoods were a feature of the time. Their objects were mainly secular, but religious and charitable foundations were almost invariably associated with them. Strict rules, enjoining daily prayer, the use of the Sacraments, the observance of Sundays and holidays, are incorporated in their statutes. Care of the poor and sick members was obligatory ; every gild had its physician ; pensions were often provided for widows and children, and dowries for maidens. The wealthier brotherhoods built each their *Scuola*, and embellished or erected churches. In Italy, even more than among Germans, church-building was a passion and an art, lending itself sometimes to strange ends,—witness the Isotta Chapel at Rimini,—but serving religion on a grand scale, according as it was then interpreted. Plague and sickness called forth many confraternities, such as the great Misericordia dating from 1244, revived at Florence in 1475 ; San Rocco at Venice (1415); the Good Men of St Martin (1441) due to Archbishop Antoninus ; and the Sodality of the Dolorosa yet existing in Rome (1448). Torquemada in 1460 established in the Minerva dowries for girls,—the Annunziata. Florence towards 1500 had seventy-three municipal associations, and at Rome there were many more, dedicated to religious observances, but likewise to charity. Such was the Brotherhood in the Ripetta established in 1499 by Alexander VI, which had its own hospital and took charge of sailors. Again, trade-gilds of every description flourished, native and even foreign ; and these were accustomed to act the miracle-plays called *divozioni*, which had sprung up in Umbria. The great hospitals, of which there were thirty-five in Florence alone, are the special honour of the fifteenth century. In Rome, the Popes Martin, Eugenius, and Sixtus, the latter of whom rebuilt Santo Spirito, showed them constant favour. Most of the old foundations were kept up, many new ones added. Over the whole of Italy, in the period between 1400 and 1524, fresh hospitals, alms-houses, orphanages, schools, and other institutions of a charitable nature, have been reckoned up to the number of three hundred and twenty-four ; but this calculation does not exhaust the list.

From these things it is clear that Savonarola (1452–98), as happens to great men, did no more than sum up in his preaching a world of ideas and aspirations with which his audience,—the early contemporaries of Michelangelo,—were already familiar. Converted to the Order of St Dominic by a sermon which he heard from the lips of an Austin hermit at Faenza (1474); filled with a lofty Platonism learned from Aquinas ; sickened by the public depravity, and prescient as his poem *De Ruina Mundi* shows of coming disasters, he nourished himself on the Bible and the Apocalypse ; fasted, prayed, wept, and became a visionary. At Florence, to which he was transferred in 1484, he saw the Brethren of San Marco losing themselves in the pedantries of the old school, and the upper classes of society in the frivolities of the new. His rudeness of speech and violence of gesture told against him in the pulpit at first. He was always sighing for " that peace which reigned in the Church when she was poor." Then at San Gemignano there came to the Friar his large prophetic vision, " the Church will be scourged and renewed, and that in our day." He made no allowance for perspective. He came back, took Florence by storm, and ruled it like a king. His mind grew to be a place of dreams. This was not astonishing in the countryman of Dante and Buonarotti. Italians saw their religion painted and sculptured ; for them it lay outside books and filled their eyes. But Florence was before all things a city of political scheming. The papacy aimed at temporal dominion; it was capable, so Machiavelli judged, of becoming the first power in the land. The pulpit was at once platform and newspaper. Spiritual censures were employed as weapons of war; Sixtus IV laid an interdict on Florence for the conspiracy of the Pazzi, with which his remembrance is indelibly bound up. How should a prophet not be a politician? Savonarola could not see his way to an answer in the negative. He foretold the coming of the French under Charles VIII. He did his utmost to keep Florence in a line of policy which Alexander VI rejected with disdain, although he accepted it two years after Savonarola's death. In this confusion of ideas and interests the preacher of righteousness fell under excommunication; he was tortured, degraded, hanged, and burnt, by a *coup d'état*.

Savonarola had invoked a General Council to depose Alexander VI. He fell back upon Pierre d'Ailly and the decrees of Constance. For his prophesyings he never claimed infallible authority. His moral teaching was taken from Aquinas; in expounding the Scriptures he followed the allegorical method; on points of dogma he was at one with his Dominican masters. Like the Brethren of Deventer he was friendly to learning, art, and science. Among his disciples were Pico della Mirandola, Frà Bartolommeo, Michelangelo. It would not be impossible to demonstrate that the sublime and simple grandeur with which the mightiest of Florentines has painted his Prophets and Sibyls on the vault of the Sistine chapel is in perfect accord with the melancholy and majesty of Savonarola's teaching. Nor in the "Burning of the Vanities" are we to imagine a spirit resembling that of John Knox. It was an *auto de fe* of vicious or unseemly objects, not a judgment on Christian art. Frà Girolamo was, in a word, the last of the great medieval Friars.

But the restoration which he longed for began in Spain. Flushed with her victory over Jews and Muslims; baptised a nation by her unity in the faith; exalted in a moment to the foremost place among European Powers, Spain was destined to rule, and sometimes to tyrannise over, Catholicism. The telling names here are Ferdinand and Isabel, Ximenes and Loyola. Feudal rights went down before the monarchy in Castile; the Estates of Aragon were no match for Ferdinand. The great Military Knighthoods were absorbed by the Sovereign. From Barcelona the Inquisition was carried to Seville and Toledo. By papal bull, yet in despite of papal protests, it became the Supreme Court before which nobles and prelates lost countenance. Spiritual, orthodox, independent, politic, and cruel, it played with lives and properties, but created one Spain as it upheld one Church. Thus it exercised an authority from which there was no escape. Even Sixtus IV lodged his appellate jurisdiction in the hands of the Archbishop of Seville (1488). No Church could be more arrogantly national than the Spanish, fenced round as it was with exemptions, royal, episcopal, monastic. But none was more Catholic. It bred neither heresy nor schism. The reform which it needed came by the hands of a saintly Queen, and of her ascetic director—Cisneros or Ximenes (1436–1517).

Other names deserve honourable mention. Cardinal Mendoza, Primate of Spain, had lived up to his high duties. Corillo, his predecessor, at the Synod of Aranda in 1473, had laid down twenty-nine chapters of reformation. Talavera, who held the see of Granada, would have converted the Moors by kindness and put into their hands a vernacular Bible, for which he fell under grave suspicion and was censured by Ximenes. Yet this ascetic Franciscan, who had been a secular priest, was himself a lover of learning, not cruel by temperament, though severe with the ungodly as in his own person. He lived like a hermit on the throne of Toledo, which he had accepted only out of obedience to the Pope. In 1494, with the aid of Isabel, against Alexander VI's terrified protestations, he corrected the Observantines with such rigour that thousands fled to Morocco sooner than obey. Of Arabic manuscripts deemed antichristian he made a famous holocaust. He risked his life at Granada in 1499; offered the Moors baptism or death; and brought over many thousands. His services to sacred and secular erudition were perpetuated in the restored University of Alcalà and the Polyglot Bible, first of its kind since Origen's *Hexapla*. Like Wolsey, the Spanish Cardinal obtained unlimited legatine faculties; he would hear of no exemptions and, being Primate, Grand Inquisitor, and chief of the government, he became irresistible. In two synods, of Alcalà in 1497 and Talavera in 1498, he published his regulations. Spain had been suffering from ruffianly nobles, undisciplined monks, immoral and insolent clerics. Bishops attempted to withstand Queen and Cardinal; they were compelled to give way. The result may be briefly stated. The worst abuses were purged out of the Iberian Church; and while other European clergy were accused of gross licentiousness, the Spanish priests became for the most part virtuous and devout.

As early as 1493 the Benedictine Abbey of Monserrat accepted under compulsion the stricter rule of Valladolid. Its new Abbot, Garcias Cisneros, nephew of the Cardinal, composed a *Book of Spiritual Exercises*, from which Ignatius of Loyola may have borrowed the title for his very different and much more scientific treatise, when he retired to this convent and was guided by the Benedictine Chanones. As is well known, he received his celebrated wound in fighting the French, who were then at war with the Pope, at the siege of Pampeluna in 1512. The pseudo-Council of Pisa was shortly to be answered by the Fifth of Lateran. In 1511 King and Bishops at Burgos uttered a series of demands which came to this;—that reformation must begin at Rome, the reign of simony end, dispensations no longer make void the law of God; that learning must be encouraged, Councils held at fixed times, residence enforced, pluralities abolished. An unsigned Spanish memorial of the same date is bolder still. It paints in darkest hues the evils tolerated by successive Pontiffs; it proposes sweeping measures which were at last carried into execution by the Council of Trent, aided by the course of events. For the Fifth of Lateran came to naught. Though admonished by Cajetan and Aegidius of Viterbo, dissolute prelates could not reform disorderly monks; Leo X cared only to rid himself of the Pragmatic Sanction. Popes, Cardinals, Curia went forward headlong to the double catastrophe of the Diet of Worms and the sack of Rome.

That which revolutionaries aimed at,—John of Goch, John Rucherath of Oberwesel, Gansfort of Groningen, and finally, Luther, was the pulling down of the sacerdotal, Sacramental system;—hence the abolition of the Mass and the Hierarchy. That which Catholic reformers spent their lives in attempting, was to make the practice of clergy and faithful harmonise with the ideals inherited from their past. Shrines, festivals, pilgrimages, devotions, brotherhoods, new religious Orders like the Minims of St Francis of Paola, and the Third Orders of Regulars, had no other design except to carry on a tradition which came down from St Benedict, St Augustine, St Jerome, the Fathers of the Desert, the ancient Churches. Justification by faith alone, the unprofitableness of Christian works and virtues, the right of free enquiry, with no appeal to a supreme visible tribunal, were all ideas unknown to the Catholic populations, abhorrent and anarchic in their eyes. From the general view which has been taken we may conclude that no demand for revolution in dogma was advanced save by individuals; that the daily offices and parochial ministrations were fulfilled with increasing attention; that abuses, though rife, were not endured without protest; that the source of mischief was especially in the Roman Court, which encouraged learning but made no strenuous effort to restore discipline; that the true occasions, whether of rebellion or reform, were not the discoveries and inventions of a progressive age, but deep-seated moral evils, and above all the avarice and ambition of worldly-minded prelates, thrust upon the sees of Christendom against the express injunctions of Canon Law; that the Bible was open, antiquity coming to be understood, an immense provision of charity laid up for the sick, the indigent, the industrial classes, for education and old age; that decrees of many Synods in every country of the West pointed out the prevailing diseases and their various remedies; and that if in course of time the Council of Trent yielded the essence and the sum of all these efforts, it is entitled to the glory of the Catholic Reformation.

# CHAPTER XIX.

## THE EVE OF THE REFORMATION.

As the sixteenth century opened, Europe was standing unconscious on the brink of a crater destined to change profoundly by its eruption the course of modern civilisation. The Church had acquired so complete a control over the souls of men, its venerable antiquity and its majestic organisation so filled the imagination, the services it had rendered seemed to call for such reverential gratitude, and its acknowledged claim to interpret the will of God to man rendered obedience so plain a duty, that the continuance of its power appeared to be an unchanging law of the universe, destined to operate throughout the limitless future. To understand the combination of forces which rent the domination of the Church into fragments, we must investigate in detail its relations with society on the eve of the disruption, and consider how it was regarded by the men of that day, with their diverse grievances, more or less justifying revolt. We must here omit from consideration the benefits which the Church had conferred, and confine our attention to the antagonisms which it provoked and to the evils for which it was held responsible. The interests and the motives at work were numerous and complex, some of them dating back for centuries, others comparatively recent, but all of them growing in intensity with the development of political institutions and popular intelligence. There has been a natural tendency to regard the Reformation as solely a religious movement; but this is an error. In the curious theocracy which dominated the Middle Ages, secular and spiritual interests became so inextricably intermingled that it is impossible wholly to disentangle them; but the motives, both remote and proximate, which led to the Lutheran revolt were largely secular rather than spiritual. So far, indeed, as concerns our present purpose we may dismiss the religious changes incident to the Reformation with the remark that they were not the object sought but the means for attaining that object. The existing ecclesiastical system was the practical evolution of dogma, and the overthrow of dogma was the only way to obtain permanent relief from the intolerable abuses of that system.

In primitive society the kingly and the priestly functions are commonly united; the Church and the State are one. Development leads to specialisation; the functions are divided; and the struggle for supremacy, like that between the Brahman and Kshatriya castes, becomes inevitable. In medieval Europe this struggle was peculiarly intricate, for, in the conversion of the Barbarians, a strange religion was imposed by the conquered on the conquerors; and the history of the relations between Church and State thenceforth becomes a record of the efforts of the priestly class to acquire domination and of the military class to maintain its independence. The former gradually won. It had two enormous advantages, for it virtually monopolised education and culture, and, through its democratic organisation, absorbed an undue share of the vigour and energy of successive generations by means of the career which it alone offered to those of lowly birth but lofty ambition. When Charles the Great fostered the Church as a civilising agency he was careful to preserve his mastership; but the anarchy attending the dissolution of his empire enabled the Church to assert its pretensions, as formulated in the False Decretals, and, when the slow process of enlightenment again began in the eleventh century, it had a most advantageous base of operations. With the development of scholastic theology in the twelfth century, its claims on the obedience of the faithful were reduced to a system under which the priest became the arbiter of the eternal destiny of man, a power readily transmuted into control of his worldly fortunes by the use of excommunication and interdict. During this period, moreover, the hierarchical organisation was strengthened and the claims of the Pope as the Vicar of Christ and as the supreme and irresponsible head of the Church became more firmly established through the extension of its jurisdiction, original and appellate. The first half of the thirteenth century saw the power of these agencies fully developed, when Raymond of Toulouse was humbled with fleshly arms, and John of England with spiritual weapons, and when the long rivalry of the papacy and Empire was virtually ended with the extinction of the House of Hohenstaufen. The expression of the supremacy thus won is to be found in the Gloss of Innocent IV on the Decretals and was proclaimed to the world by Boniface VIII in the bull *Unam Sanctam.*

This sovereignty was temporal as well as spiritual. The power of the Pope, as the earthly representative of God, was illimitable. The official theory, as expressed in the *De Principum Regimine,* which passes under the name of St Thomas Aquinas, declared the temporal jurisdiction of kings to be simply derived from the authority intrusted by Christ to St Peter and his successors; whence it followed that the exercise of the royal authority was subject to papal control. As Matthew of Vendôme had already sung—

Papa regit reges, dominos dominatur, acerbis
Principibus stabili jure jubere jubet.

The arguments of Marsiglio of Padua, intended to restore the imperial system of a Church subordinate to the State, were of some assistance to Louis of Bavaria in his long struggle with the papacy; but at his death they virtually disappeared from view. The Councils of Constance and Basel were an effort on the part of the prelates and princes to limit the papal authority, and if they had succeeded they would have rendered the Church a constitutional monarchy in place of a despotism; but the disastrous failure at Basel greatly strengthened papal absolutism. The superiority of Councils over Popes, though it continued to be asserted by France in the Pragmatic Sanction of 1438, and from time to time by Germany, gradually sank into an academic question, and the Popes were finally able to treat it with contempt. In 1459, at the Congress of Mantua, Pius II, in his speech to the French envoys, took occasion to assert his irresponsible supremacy, which could not be limited by general councils and to which all princes were subject. In his extraordinary letter to Mohammad II, then in the full flush of his conquests, Pius tempted the Turk to embrace Christianity with the promise to appoint him Emperor of Greece and of the East, so that what he had won by force he might enjoy with justice. If the Pope could thus grant kingdoms, he could also take them away. George Podiebrad, King of Bohemia, committed the offence of insisting on the terms under which the Hussites had been reconciled to the Church by the Fathers of Basel; whereupon Pius II in 1464, and Paul II in 1465, summoned him to Rome to stand his trial for heresy; and the latter, without awaiting the expiration of the term assigned, declared him deprived of the royal power, released his subjects from their allegiance and made over his kingdom to Matthias Corvinus of Hungary, with the result of a long and devastating war. Julius II, in his strife with France, gave the finishing blow to the little kingdom of Navarre by excommunicating in 1511 those children of perdition Jean d'Albret and his wife Catherine, and empowering the first comer to seize their dominions—an act of piety for which the rapacious Ferdinand of Aragon had made all necessary preparations. In the bull of excommunication Julius formally asserted his plenary power, granted by God, over all nations and kingdoms; and this claim, amounting to a quasi-divinity, was sententiously expressed in one of the inscriptions at the consecration of Alexander VI in 1492—

> Caesare magna fuit, nunc Roma est maxima. Sextus
> Regnat Alexander: ille vir, iste Deus.

While it is true that the extreme exercise of papal authority in making and unmaking Kings was exceptional, still the unlimited jurisdiction claimed by the Holy See was irksome in many ways to the sovereigns of Europe and, as time wore on and the secular authority became consolidated, it was endured with more and more impatience. There could be no hard and fast line of delimitation between the spiritual and the temporal, for the two were mutually interdependent, and the convenient phrase, *temporalia ad spiritualia ordinata*, was devised to define those temporal matters, over which, as requisite to the due enjoyment of the spiritual, the Church claimed exclusive control. Moreover it assumed the right to determine in doubtful matters the definition of this elastic term and the secular ruler constantly found himself inconveniently limited in the exercise of his authority. The tension thence arising was increased by the happy device of legates and nuncios, by which the Holy See established in every country a representative whose business it was to exercise supreme spiritual jurisdiction and to maintain the claims of the Church, resulting in a divided sovereignty, at times exceedingly galling and even incompatible with a well-ordered State. Rulers so orthodox as Ferdinand and Isabel asked the great national council of Seville, in 1478, how they could best prevent the residence of legates and nuncios who not only carried much gold out of the kingdom but interfered seriously with the royal pre-eminence. In this they only expressed the desires of the people; for the Estates of Castile, in 1480, asked the sovereigns to make some provision with respect to the nuncios who were of no benefit and only a source of evil.

Another fruitful source of complaint, on the part not only of the rulers but of the national Churches, was the gradual extension of the claim of the Holy See to control all patronage. Innocent III has the credit of first systematically asserting this claim and exploiting it for the benefit of his cardinals and other officials. The practice increased and, in 1319, Villani tells us that John XXII assumed to himself the control of all prebends in every collegiate church, from the sale of which he gathered immense sums. Finally the assertion was made that the Holy See owned all benefices and in the rules of the papal Chanceries appear the prices to be charged for them, whether with or without cure of souls, showing that the traffic had become an established source of revenue. Even the rights of lay patrons and founders were disregarded and in the provisions granted by the popes there was a special clause derogating their claims. Partly this patronage was used for direct profit, partly it was employed for the benefit of the cardinals and their retainers, on whom pluralities were heaped with unstinted hand, and the further refinement was introduced of granting to them pensions imposed on benefices and monastic foundations. Abbeys, also, were bestowed *in commendam* on titular abbots who collected the revenues through stewards, with little heed to the maintenance of the inmates or the performance of the offices. In the eager desire to anticipate these profits of simony, vacancies were not awaited, and rights of succession, under the name of expectatives, were given or sold in advance. The deplorable results of this spiritual commerce were early apparent and formed the subject of bitter lamentation and complaint, but to no purpose. In the thirteenth century Bishop Grosseteste and St Louis assailed it in vigorous terms; in the fourteenth, Bishop Alvar Pelayo, a penitentiary of John XXII, was equally fearless and unsparing in his denunciation. In 1385 Charles V of France asserted in an *ordonnance* that the Cardinals had absorbed all the preferment in the kingdom—benefices, abbeys, orphanages, hospitals etc.—exacting revenue to the utmost and leaving the institutions disabled and the fabric to fall into ruin. At the Council of Siena, in 1423, the French prelates declared that all the benefices in France were sold by the Curia, so that the churches were reduced to desolation. In 1475 the Abbot of Abbots of the great Cistercian Order complained that all the abbeys in France were held *in commendam*, and consequently were laid waste. England in self-defence had enacted, in the fourteenth century, the Statutes of Provisors and Praemunire; while in 1438 France protected herself with the Pragmatic Sanction, but other nations lacked the strength or the resolution to do likewise and the resultant irritation continued to grow ominously. In Spain, which refused to throw off the yoke as late as 1547, the Primate Siliceo of Toledo asserted, in a memorial to Charles V, that there were then in Rome five or six thousand Spaniards engaged in bargaining for benefices, "such being, for our sins, the present custom"; and he added that in every cathedral chapter in the land the majority of canons had been either hostlers in Rome or traders in benefices who scarce knew grammar enough to read their hours.

In this absorption of patronage the feature most provocative of friction with the sovereigns was the claim gradually advanced to nominate bishops; for these prelates were mostly temporal lords of no little influence, and in the political schemes of the papacy the character of its nominees might well create uneasiness in the State. Quarrels over the exercise of this power were of frequent occurrence. Venice, for instance, which was chronically in open or concealed hostility to Rome, was very sensitive as to the fidelity of its acquisitions on the mainland, where a bishop who was the agent of an enemy might be the source of infinite mischief. Thus, in 1485, there was a struggle over the vacant see of Padua, in which Venice triumphed by sequestrating other revenues of Cardinal Michiel, appointed by Innocent VIII. Again, in 1491, a contest arose over the patriarchate of Aquileia, the primatial see of Venetia, resulting in the exile of the celebrated humanist Ermolao Barbaro, on whom Innocent had bestowed it, and the see remained vacant until Alexander VI accepted Niccolò Donato, the Venetian nominee. In 1505 Julius II refused to confirm a bishop appointed by the *Signoria* to the see of Cremona, as he designed the place for his favourite nephew Galeotto della Rovere; he held out for two years and finally compromised for a money payment to the Cardinal. So, when the latter died in 1508, Venice filled his see of Vicenza with Jacopo Dandolo, while Julius gave it to another nephew, Sisto Gara della Rovere, and the unseemly contest over the bishopric lasted for years. Matters were scarce better between the Holy See and its crusader Matthias Corvinus. A serious breach was occasioned, in 1465, by the effort of Paul II to enforce his claims; but Matthias took a position so aggressive that finally Sixtus IV conceded the point and confirmed his appointments. The quarrel was renewed in 1480, over the see of Modrus, which Sixtus wanted for a retainer of his nephew, Cardinal Giuliano della Rovere. The King told Sixtus that Hungary, in her customary spirit, would rather, for a third time, cut herself loose from the Catholic Church and go over to the infidel than permit the benefices of the land to be appropriated in violation of the royal right of presentation ; but, after holding out for three years, he submitted. He was more successful, in 1485, when he gave the archbishopric of Gran to Ippolito d'Este, who was a youth under age, and when Innocent VIII remonstrated he retorted that the Pope had granted such favours to many less worthy persons; any person appointed by the Pope might bear the title, but Ippolito should enjoy the revenues. He carried his point and, in 1487, Ippolito took possession.

Spain was still less patient. Even under so weak a monarch as Henry IV Sixtus failed to secure for his worthless nephew, Cardinal Piero Riario, the archbishopric of Seville, which fell vacant in 1473 through the death of Alfonso de Fonseca. Although he had been regularly appointed the Spaniards refused to receive Riario, and the see was administered by Pero Gonzalez Mendoza, Bishop of Sigüenza, until 1482, when it was filled by Iñigo Manrique. The stronger and abler Ferdinand of Aragon was even more recalcitrant. He adopted the most arbitrary measures to secure the archbishopric of Saragossa for his natural son Alfonso against Ausias Dezpuch, the nominee of Sixtus IV. Still more decisive was the struggle in Castile over the see of Cuenca, in 1482, to which Sixtus appointed a Genoese cousin. Ferdinand and Isabel demanded that Spanish bishoprics should be filled only with Spaniards of their selection, to which Sixtus replied that all benefices were in the gift of the Pope and that his power, derived from Christ, was unlimited. The sovereigns answered by calling home all their subjects resident at the papal Court and threatening to take steps for the convocation of a General Council. This brought Sixtus to terms; he sent a special nuncio to Spain, but they refused to receive him and stood on their dignity until Cardinal Mendoza, then Archbishop of Toledo, intervened, when, on Sixtus withdrawing his pretensions, they allowed themselves to be reconciled. Ferdinand and his successor Charles V displayed the same vigour in resisting the encroachments of the cardinals when they seized upon vacant abbacies which happened to belong to the patronage of the Crown. It marks the abasement to which the Holy Roman Empire had fallen when we hear that Sixtus confirmed to Frederick III and his son Maximilian a privilege granted by Eugenius IV to nominate to the sees of Brixen, Trent, Gurk, Triest, Coire, Vienna, and Wienerisch-Neustadt, adding thereto the presentation to three hundred benefices.

These cases have a double interest as illustrating the growing tension between the Holy See and secular potentates and the increasing disposition to meet its claims with scant measure of respect. It was constantly arrogating to itself enlarged prerogatives and the sovereigns were less and less inclined to submission. But, whether exercised by King or Pope, the distribution of ecclesiastical patronage had become simple jobbery, to reward dependents or to gain pecuniary or political advantage, without regard to the character of the incumbent or the sacred duties of the office. These evils were aggravated by habitual and extravagant pluralism, of which the Holy See set an example eagerly imitated by the sovereigns. Bishoprics and benefices were showered upon the Cardinals and their retainers, and upon the favourites of the Popes in all parts of Europe, whose revenues were drawn to Rome, to the impoverishment of each locality; while the functions for which the revenues had been granted remained for the most part unperformed, to the irritation of the populations. Rodrigo Borgia (subsequently Alexander VI), created Cardinal in his youth by his uncle Calixtus III, accumulated benefices to the aggregate of 70,000 ducats a year. Giuliano della Rovere (Julius II) likewise owed his cardinalate to his uncle Sixtus IV, who bestowed on him also the archbishopric of Avignon and the bishoprics of Bologna, Lausanne, Coutances, Viviers, Mende, Ostia, and Velletri, with the abbeys of Nonantola and Grottaferrata. Another Cardinal nephew of Sixtus was Piero Riario, who held a crowd of bishoprics yielding him 60,000 ducats a year, which he lavished in shameless excesses, dying deeply in debt. But this abuse was not confined to Rome. A notable example is that of Jean, son of René II, Duke of Lorraine. Born in 1498, he was in 1501 appointed coadjutor to his uncle Henri, Bishop of Metz, after whose death in 1505 Jean took possession in 1508, and held the see until 1529. He then resigned it in favour of his nephew Nicholas, aged four, but reserved the revenues and right of resumption in case of death or resignation. In 1517 he became also Bishop of Toul and in 1518 of Térouanne, besides obtaining the cardinalate. In 1521 he added the sees of Valence and Die, in 1523 that of Verdun. Then followed the three archbishoprics of Narbonne, Reims, and Lyons in 1524, 1533 and 1537. In 1536 he obtained the see of Alby, soon afterwards that of Macon, in 1541 that of Agen, and in 1542 that of Nantes. In addition he held the abbeys of Gorze, Fécamp, Cluny, Marmoutiers, St Ouen, St Jean de Laon, St Germer, St Médard of Soissons, and St Mansuy of Toul. The see of Verdun he resigned to his nephew Nicholas on the same terms as that of Metz and when the latter, in 1548, abdicated in order to marry

Marguerite d'Egmont, he resumed them both. The archbishopric of Reims he resigned in 1538 in favour of his nephew Charles, and Lyons he abandoned in 1539. In spite of the enormous revenues derived from these scandalous pluralities his extravagance kept him always poor and we can imagine the condition, spiritual and temporal, of the churches and abbeys thus consigned to the negligence of a worldly prelate whose life was spent in Courts. It was bad enough when these pluralists employed coadjutors to look after their numerous prelacies, but worse when they farmed them out to the highest bidder.

Another ecclesiastical abuse severely felt by all sovereigns who were jealous of their jurisdiction and earnest in enforcing justice was the exemption enjoyed by all ranks of the clergy from the authority of the secular tribunals. They were justiciable only by the spiritual Courts, which could pronounce no judgments of blood, and whose leniency towards clerical offenders virtually assured to them immunity from punishment—an immunity long maintained in English jurisprudence under the well-known name of Benefit of Clergy. So complete was the freedom of the priesthood from all responsibility to secular authority that the ingenuity of the doctors was taxed to find excuses for the banishment of Abiathar by Solomon. The evil of this consisted not only in the temptation to crime which it offered to those regularly bred to the Church and performing its functions, but it attracted to the lower orders of the clergy, which were not bound to celibacy or debarred from worldly pursuits, numberless criminals and vagabonds, who were thus enabled to set the officers of justice at defiance. The first defence of a thief or assassin when arrested was to claim that he belonged to the Church and to display his tonsure, and the episcopal officials were vigilant in the defence of these wretches, thus stimulating crime and grievously impeding the administration of justice. Frequent efforts were made by the secular authorities to remedy these evils; but the Church resolutely maintained its prerogatives, provoking quarrels which led to increased antagonism between the laity and the clergy. The *Gravamina* of the German Nation, adopted by the Diet of Nürnberg, in 1522, stated no more than the truth in asserting that this clerical immunity was responsible for countless cases of adultery, robbery, coining, arson, homicide, and false-witness committed by ecclesiastics; and there was peculiar significance in the declaration that, unless the clergy were subjected to the secular Courts, there was reason to fear an uprising of the people, for no justice was to be had against a clerical offender in the spiritual tribunals.

Venice was peculiarly sensitive as to this interference with social order, and it is well known how her insistence on her right to enforce the laws on all offenders led to the prolonged rupture between the Republic and Paul V in the early years of the seventeenth century. It was a special concession to her when, in 1474, Sixtus IV admitted that, in view of the numerous clerical counterfeiters and State criminals, such offenders might be tried by secular process, with the assistance, however, of the vicar of the Patriarch of Aquileia. The extent of the abuse is indicated by an order of Leo X, in 1514, to the governor of Ascoli, authorising him, for the sake of the peace of the community, to hand over to the secular courts all criminal married clerks who did not wear vestment and tonsure. What exasperating use could be made of this clerical privilege was shown, in 1478, in the Florentine conspiracy of the Pazzi, which was engineered, with the privity of Sixtus IV, by his nephew Girolamo Riario. The assassins were two clerics, Stefano da Bagnoni and Antonio Maffei; they succeeded in killing Giuliano de' Medici and wounding Lorenzo, during the mass, thus adding sacrilege to murder, while Salviati, Archbishop of Pisa, was endeavouring to seize the palace of the *Signoria*. The enraged populace promptly hanged Salviati, the two assassins were put to death, and Cardinal Raffaelle Sansoni Riario, another papal nephew, who was suspiciously in Florence as the guest of the Pazzi, was imprisoned. Sixtus had the effrontery to complain loudly of the violation of the liberties of the Church and to demand of Florence satisfaction, including the banishment of Lorenzo. The Cardinal was liberated after a few weeks, during which he was detained as a hostage for the Florentines who were in Rome, but this did not appease Sixtus. He laid Florence under an interdict, which was not observed, and a local Council was assembled which issued a manifesto denouncing the Pope as a servant of adulterers and a vicar of Satan and praying God to liberate His Church from a pastor who was a ravening wolf in sheep's clothing. The pretensions of the Church were evidently becoming unendurable to the advancing intelligence of the age; it was forfeiting human respect and there was a dangerous tendency abroad to treat it as a secular institution devoid of all special claim to reverence.

This was not the only manner in which the papacy interfered with secular justice, for, towards the end of the fifteenth century, the papal jurisdiction spread its aegis over the crimes of the laity as well as of the clergy. Since the early thirteenth century the papal Penitentiary had been accustomed to administer absolution, in the forum of conscience, to all applicants. In the fourteenth this came to be a source of profit to the Curia by reason of the graduated scale of fees demanded and the imposition of so-called pecuniary penance by which the sinner purchased pardon of his sins. When the Castilian Inquisition began its operation in 1481, the New Christians, as the Jewish converts were called, hurried in crowds to Rome where they had no difficulty in obtaining from the Penitentiary absolution for whatever heretical crimes they might have committed; and they then claimed that this exempted them from subsequent inquisitorial prosecution. Even those who had been condemned were able to procure for a consideration letters setting aside the sentence and rehabilitating them. It was no part of the policy of Ferdinand and

Isabel to allow impunity to be thus easily gained by the apostates or
to forego the abundant confiscations flowing into the royal treasury,
and therefore they refused to admit that such papal briefs were valid
without the royal approval.   Sixtus, on his part, was not content to lose
the lucrative business arising from Spanish intolerance, and, in 1484, by
the constitution *Quoniam nonnulli* he refuted the assertion that his briefs
were valid only in the *forum conscientiae* and not in the *forum conten-
tiosum* and ordered them to be received as absolute authority in all
Courts, secular as well as ecclesiastical.   This was asserting an appellate
jurisdiction over all the criminal tribunals of Christendom, and, through
the notorious venality of the Curia, where these letters of absolution
could always be had for a price, it was a serious blow to the administration of justice everywhere.   Not content with this, the power was
delegated to the peripatetic vendors of indulgences, who thus carried
impunity for crime to every man's door.   The St Peter's indulgences,
sold by Tetzel and his colleagues, were of this character and not only
released the purchasers from all spiritual penalties but forbade all
secular or criminal prosecution.   These monstrous pretensions were
reiterated by Paul III in 1549 and by Julius III in 1550.   It was
impossible for secular rulers tamely to submit to this sale of impunity
for crime.   In Spain the struggle against it continued with equal
obstinacy on each side, and it was fortunate that the Reformation came
to prevent the Holy See from rendering all justice, human and divine, a
commodity to be sold in open market.

There was another of the so-called liberties of the Church which
brought it into collision with temporal princes—the exemption from
taxation of all ecclesiastical property, so vigorously proclaimed by
Boniface VIII in the bull *Clericis laicos*.   Although, under pressure
from Philip the Fair, this declaration was annulled by the Council of
Vienne, the principle remained unaffected.   The piety of successive
generations had brought so large a portion of the wealth of Europe—
estimated at fully one-third—into the hands of the Church, that the
secular power was becoming more and more disinclined to exempt
it from the burdens of the State.   Under Paul II (1464–71) the
endeavours of Venice and of Florence to subject such property to taxation were the cause of serious and prolonged difficulties with Rome.
In fact, the relations between the papacy and the sovereigns of Europe
were becoming more and more strained in every way, as the transformation took place from the feudal institutions of the Middle Ages to the
monarchical absolutism of the modern era.   The nationalities were
becoming organised, save in Germany, with a consciousness of unity
that they had never before possessed and with new aims and aspirations
necessitating settled lines of policy.   Less and less they felt themselves
mere portions of the great Christian commonwealth under the supreme
guidance of the Vicar of Christ, and less and less were they inclined to

submit to his commands or to permit his interference with their affairs. In 1464 Louis XI forbade the publication of papal bulls until they should be submitted to him and receive the royal *exequatur*. Spain followed his example and this became the settled policy of all sovereigns able to assert their independence.

The incompatibility between the papal pretensions and the royal prerogative was intensified not only by the development of the monarchies but by the increasing secularisation of the Holy See. It had long been weighted down by its territorial possessions which led it to subordinate its spiritual duties to its acquisitive ambition. When, about 1280, Nicholas III offered the cardinalate to the Blessed John of Parma, he refused it, saying that he could give good counsel if there was any one to listen to him; but that in Rome salvation of souls was of small account in comparison with wars and intrigues. So it had been and so it continued to be. The fatal necessity of defending the Patrimony of St Peter against the assaults of unscrupulous neighbours and the even more fatal eagerness to extend its boundaries governed the papal policy to the virtual exclusion of loftier aims. Even the transfer to Avignon did not serve to release the Holy See from these chains which bound it to the earth, as was seen in the atrocious war waged by Clement V to gain Ferrara, in the long contest of John XXII with the Visconti, and in the bloody subjugation of revolted communities by Cardinal Albornoz as legate of Urban V. The earlier half of the fifteenth century was occupied with the Great Schism and the struggle between the papacy and the General Councils; but, on the final and triumphant assertion of papal absolutism, the Popes became to all intents and purposes mere secular princes, to whom religion was purely an instrument for supplementing territorial weakness in the attainment of worldly ends. Religion was, in fact, a source of no little strength, increasing the value of the papacy as an ally and its power as an enemy. Among the transalpine nations, at least, there was still enough reverence felt for the Vicar of Christ to render open rupture undesirable. Then there remained the sentence of excommunication and interdict, a force in reserve always to be borne in mind by hostile States. There was also the supreme authority to bind and to loose, whereby a Pope could always release himself from inconvenient agreements and was absolved from observing any compacts, while, if the conscience of an ally chanced to be tender, it could be relieved in the same manner. Still more important was the inexhaustible source of revenue derived from the headship of the Church and the power of the keys—the levying of annates and tithes and the sale of dispensations, absolutions and indulgences. These were exploited in every way that ingenuity could suggest, draining Europe of its substance for the maintenance of papal armies and fleets and of a Court unrivalled in its sumptuous magnificence, until the

Holy See was everywhere regarded with detestation. It was this temporal sovereignty which rendered possible the existence of such a succession of pontiffs as disgraced the end of the fifteenth and commencement of the sixteenth century—such careers as those of Alexander VI and Cesare Borgia, such a catastrophe as the sack of Rome in 1527. Even before these evils had grown to such appalling magnitude, Dante had expressed the opinion of all thoughtful men in deploring the results which had followed the so-called Donation of Constantine. By the middle of the fifteenth century Lorenzo Valla, in his demonstration of the fraud, assumed that the corruption of the Church and the wars which desolated Italy were its direct consequence, and few more eloquent and powerful indictments of the papacy are to be found than the bold utterances in which he warned the Holy See that princes and peoples could not much longer endure its tyranny and wickedness. Remonstrances and warnings were in vain; the papacy became more and more secularised, and, as the pressure grew more inexorable, men asked themselves why, if the headship of St Peter were founded on Christ's injunction to feed His sheep, St Peter's successor employed that headship rather to shear and slaughter.

Papal history, in fact, as soon as the Holy See had vindicated its supremacy over general councils, becomes purely a political history of diplomatic intrigues, of alliances made and broken, of military enterprises. In following it no one would conclude, from internal evidence, that the papacy represented interests higher than those of any other petty Italian prince, or that it claimed to be the incarnation of a faith divinely revealed to ensure peace on earth and goodwill to man—save when, occasionally in a papal letter, an unctuous expression is employed to shroud some peculiarly objectionable design. The result of this, even in the hands of a man like Pius II, not wholly without loftier impulses, is seen in his complaint, March 12, 1462, to the Milanese envoy. All the States of Italy, he said, were hostile, save Naples and Milan, in both of which the existing governments were precarious; his own subjects were always on the brink of revolt, and many of his Cardinals were on the side of France, which was threatening him with a Council and was ready to provoke a schism unless he would abandon Ferdinand of Naples for René of Anjou. France, moreover, dragged Spain and Burgundy with her, while Germany was equally unfriendly. The powerful Archbishop of Mainz was hostile and was supported by most of the princes, who were offended at the papal relations with the powerless Frederick III, and he, again, was at war with the King of Hungary, while the King of Bohemia was half a heretic. The position was no better under his successor, Paul II, who, at his death in 1471, left the Holy See without a friend in Italy; everywhere it was regarded with hatred and distrust. Under Sixtus IV there was no improvement; and, in 1490, Innocent VIII threatened to leave Italy and find a refuge elsewhere. He had not a friend or an ally; the treasury was exhausted; the barons of the Patrimony were rebellious; and Ferdinand of Naples openly talked of entering Rome, lance in rest, to teach the Pope to do justice. The Church had conquered heresy, it had overcome schism, there was no question of faith to distract men's minds, yet this was the antagonistic position which the Head of Christendom had forced upon the nations whose allegiance it claimed.

During the half-century preceding the Reformation there was constant shifting of scene; enemies were converted into allies and allies into enemies, but the spirit of the papacy remained the same, and, whatever might be the political combination of the moment, the Christian nations at large regarded it as a possible enemy, whose friendship was not to be trusted, for it was always fighting for its own hand—or rather, as the increasing nepotism of successive pontiffs ruled its policy, for the aggrandisement of worthless scions of the papal stock, such as Girolamo Riario or Franceschetto Cibò or Cesare Borgia. Julius II, it is true, was less addicted to nepotism, and made and broke treaties and waged war for the enlargement of the papal territories, producing on the awakening intelligence of Europe the impression which Erasmus condenses in such a way as to show how threatening was the spirit evoked by the secularisation of the Holy See. In the *Encomium Moriae*, written in 1510, he describes the spiritual and material weapons employed by the Popes, against those who, at the instigation of the devil, seek to nibble at the Patrimony of St Peter, fighting not only with bulls of excommunication but with fire and sword, to the shedding of much Christian blood, and believing themselves to be defending the Church against her enemies,—as if she could have any worse enemies than impious pontiffs. Leo X followed with a pale imitation of the policy of Alexander VI, his object being the advancement of the Medici family and the preservation of the papal dominions in the fierce strife between France and Spain. To him the papacy was a personal possession out of which the possessor was expected to make the most, religion being an entirely subordinate affair. His conception of his duties is condensed in the burst of exultation attributed to him on his election,—Let us enjoy the papacy since God has given it to us!

Under the circumstances the Holy See could inspire neither respect nor confidence. Universal distrust was the rule between the States, and the papacy was merely a State whose pretensions to care for the general welfare of Christendom were recognised as diplomatic hypocrisy. When, in 1462, Pius II took the desperate step of resolving to lead in person the proposed Crusade, he explained that this was the only way to convince Europe of his sincerity. When he levied a tithe, he said, for the war with the infidel, appeal was made to a future Council; when he issued indulgences he was accused of greed; whatever was done was attributed to the desire to raise money, and no one trusted the papal word; like a bankrupt trader, he was without credit. This distrust of the papacy with regard to its financial devices for the prosecution of the war with the Turk was universally entertained, and it lent a sharper edge to the dissatisfaction of those called upon to contribute. At the Diet of Frankfort in 1454 and at the Congress of Mantua in 1459, the overwhelming danger to Europe from the Turkish advance failed to stimulate the princes to action; for they asserted that the papal purpose was to get their money, and not to fight the infidel. In this some injustice was done to Calixtus III and Pius II who at heart were earnest in the crusading spirit, but it was justified in the case of their successors. Men saw large sums raised ostensibly for that object by tithes on ecclesiastical revenues, and by the innumerable crusading indulgences which were preached wherever the secular authorities would permit, while no effective measures were adopted to oppose the Turk. It is true that in 1480 the capture of Otranto caused a panic throughout Italy which forced the Italian States to unite for its recovery; but scarce was this accomplished, in 1481, when Sixtus IV, in alliance with Venice, plunged into a war with Naples, and, after he had been forced to make peace, turned his arms against his ally and gave 50,000 ducats to equip a fleet against the Republic—ducats probably supplied by the crusading indulgence which he had just published.

Such had in fact been the papal practice, since in the thirteenth century Gregory IX had proclaimed that the home interests of the Holy See were more important than the defence of the Holy Land and that crusading money could be more advantageously expended in Italy than in Palestine. There was no scruple about applying to the needs of the moment money derived from any source whatever and, in spite of the large amounts raised under the pretext of crusades which never started, the extravagance of the papal Court and its military enterprises left it almost always poor. Popes and Cardinals rivalled each other in the sumptuousness of their buildings. Never were religious solemnities and public functions performed with such profuse magnificence, nor was greater liberality exercised in the encouragement of art and literature. Paul II had a *sedia gestatoria* built for the Christmas ceremonies of 1466 which was an artistic wonder, costing, according to popular report, more than a palace. Yet this Pope so managed his finances that on his death, in 1471, he left behind him an enormous treasure in money and jewels and costly works of antique art; we hear of pearls inventoried at 300,000 ducats, the gold and jewels of two tiaras appraised at 300,000 more, and other precious stones and ornaments at 1,000,000. All this was wasted by Sixtus IV on his worthless kindred and on the wars in which he was involved for their benefit; and he left the treasury deeply in debt. His successor, Innocent VIII, was equally reckless and was always in straits for money, though his son, Franceschetto Cibò, could coolly lose in a single night 14,000 ducats to Cardinal Riario, and in another 8000 to

Cardinal Balue. The pontificate of Alexander VI was notorious for the splendour of its banquets and public solemnities, as well as for the enormous sums consumed in the ambitious enterprises of Cesare Borgia. Julius II lavished money without stint on his wars as well as on architecture and art; yet he left 200,000 ducats in the treasury besides jewels and regalia to a large amount. The careless magnificence of Leo X, his schemes for the aggrandisement of his family, and his patronage of art and letters, soon exhausted this reserve as well as all available sources of revenue; he was always in need of money and employed ruinous expedients to raise it; when he died he left nothing but debts, through which his nearest friends were ruined, and a treasury so empty that at his funeral the candles used were those which had already seen service at the obsequies of Cardinal Riario. When we consider that this lavish and unceasing expenditure, incurred to gratify the ambition and vanity of successive Vicars of Christ, was ultimately drawn from the toil of the peasantry of Europe, and that probably the larger part of the sums thus exacted disappeared in the handling before the residue reached Rome, we can understand the incessant complaints of the oppressed populations, and the hatred which was silently stored up to await the time of explosion. Thus, we may reasonably conclude that in its essence the Reformation was due more largely to financial than to religious considerations. The terrible indictment of the papacy which Ulrich von Hutten addressed to Leo X, December 1, 1517, contains not a word about faith or doctrine; the whole *gravamen* consists in the abuse of power—the spoliations, the exactions, the oppression, the sale of dispensations and pardons, the fraudulent devices whereby the wealth of Germany was cunningly transferred to Rome, and the stirring up of strife among Christians in order to defend or to extend the Patrimony of St Peter.

In every way the revenues thus enjoyed and squandered by the Curia were scandalous and oppressive. To begin with, the cost of their collection was enormous. The accounts of the papal agent for first-fruits in Hungary, for the year 1320, show that of 1913 florins collected only 732 reached the papal treasury. With a more thorough organisation in later periods the returns were better; but when the device was adopted of employing bankers to collect the proceeds of annates and indulgences, the share allotted to those who conducted the business and made advances, was ruinously large. In the contract for the fateful St Peter's indulgence with the Fuggers of Augsburg, their portion of the receipts was to be fifty *per cent*. Even worse was it when these revenues were farmed out, for the banker who depended for his profits on the extent of his sales or collections was not likely to be overnice in his methods, nor to exercise much restraint over his agents. Europe was overrun with pardon-sellers who had purchased letters empowering them to sell indulgences, whether of a general character or for some church or hospital; and for centuries their lies, their frauds, their exactions, and their filthy living were the cause of the bitterest and most indignant complaints.

Even more demoralising were the revenues derived from the sale of countless dispensations for marriage within the prohibited degrees, for the holding of pluralities, for the numerous kinds of "irregularities" and other breaches of the canon law; so that its prescriptions might almost seem to have been framed for the purpose of enabling the Holy See to profit by their violation. Not less destructive to morals were the absolutions, which amounted to a sale of pardons for sin of every description, as though the Decalogue had been enacted for this very purpose. There was also a thriving business done in the composition for unjust gains, whereby fraudulent traders, usurers, robbers, and other malefactors, on paying to the Church a portion of their illegal acquisitions, were released from the obligation of making restitution. In every way the power of the keys and the treasure of the merits of Christ were exploited, without any regard for moral consequences.

Deplorable as was this effacement of the standards of right and wrong, all these were at least voluntary payments which perhaps rather predisposed the thoughtless in favour of the Church who so benignantly exercised her powers to relieve the weakness of human nature. It was otherwise however with the traffic in benefices and expectatives which filled the parishes and chapters with unworthy incumbents, not only neglectful of their sacred duties but seeking to recoup themselves for their expenditure by exactions from their subjects. A standing grievance was the exaction of the annates, which, since their regulation by Boniface IX and the fruitless effort of the Council of Basel to abolish them, continued to be the source of bitter complaint. They consisted of a portion, usually computed at one-half, of the estimated revenue of a benefice, worth twenty-five florins or more, collected on every change of incumbents. Thus the archbishopric of Rouen was taxed at 12,000 florins and the little see of Grenoble at 300; the great abbacy of Saint Denis at 6000 and the little Saint Ciprian of Poitiers at 33, while all parish cures in France were rated uniformly at 24 ducats, equivalent to about 30 florins. As though these burdens were not enough, pensions on benefices and religious houses were lavishly granted to the favourites of Popes and Cardinals; for the Pope was master of all Church property and was limited in its distribution by nothing but his own discretion. Thus the people on whom these burdens ultimately fell were taught to hate the clergy as the clergy hated the Holy See. Of all its oppressions, however, that which excited the fiercest clerical antagonism was the power which it exercised of demanding a tithe of all ecclesiastical revenues whenever money was needed, under the pretext, generally, of carrying on the war with the infidel. As early as 1240, Gregory IX called for a twentieth to aid him in his struggle with Frederick II, and his Legate at the Council of Senlis forced the French Bishops to give their assent; but St Louis interposed and forbade it.  Nevertheless, Franciscan emissaries were sent to collect it under threats of excommunication, causing, as St Louis declared, so great a hatred of the Holy See that only the strenuous exercise of the royal power kept the Gallican Church in the Roman obedience.  He subsequently took measures to protect it from these exactions without the royal assent, but Germany was defenceless and the papal demands were here the source of bitter exasperation and resistance.  When in 1354 his Italian wars caused Innocent VI to impose a tithe on the German clergy, the whole Church of the Empire rose in indignation, and was ready to resort to any extremity of opposition.  Frederick, Bishop of Ratisbon, seized the papal collector, and confined him in a castle, while the papal Nuncio, the Bishop of Cavaillon, with his assistant, narrowly escaped an ambush set for his life.  A similar storm was aroused when, in 1372, Gregory XI repeated the levy; the clergy of Mainz bound themselves by a solemn mutual agreement not to pay it, while Frederick, Archbishop of Cologne, pledged his assistance to his clergy in their refusal to submit.  Despite this resistance, the papacy prevailed, but, with the decline of respect for the Holy See in the second half of the fifteenth century, it was not always able to enforce its demands.  When at the Congress of Mantua, in 1459, Pius II levied a tithe for his crusade, the German princes refused to allow it to be collected and he prudently shrank from the issue.  In 1487, Innocent VIII repeated the attempt, but the German clergy protested so energetically that he was forced to abandon his intention.  When, in 1500, Alexander VI adopted the same expedient, Henry VII permitted the collection in England; but the French clergy refused to pay.  They were consequently excommunicated; whereupon they asked the University of Paris whether the excommunication was valid and, on receiving a negative answer, quietly continued to perform their sacred functions. The University, in fact, had long paid little respect to papal utterances.  When Eugenius IV and Nicholas V ordered the prosecution as heretics of those who taught the doctrines of John of Poilly respecting the validity of confessions to Mendicant Friars, the University denounced the bulls as surreptitious and not to be obeyed; and this position it held persistently until the Holy See was obliged to give way.  There evidently were ample causes of dissension in the Church between its head and its members and the tension continued to increase.

An even more potent, because more constant, source of antagonism was the venality of the Curia and its pitiless exactions from the multitudes who were obliged to have recourse to it.  This had always been the case since the Holy See had succeeded in concentrating in itself the supreme jurisdiction, original and appellate, so that all questions concerning the spirituality could be brought before it.  At the Council of St Baseul, in 992, Arnoul of Orleans unhesitatingly denounced Rome as a place where justice was put up to auction for the highest bidder; and similar complaints continue through the Middle Ages with ever-increasing vehemence, as its sphere of operations widened and its system became more intricate and more perfect. As Dietrich of Nieheim says, it was a gulf which swallowed everything, a sea into which all rivers poured without its overflowing, and happy was he who could escape its clutches without being stripped. Even Aeneas Sylvius, before he attained the papacy, had no scruple in asserting that everything was for sale in Rome and that nothing was to be had there without money. The enormous business concentrated in the holy city from every corner of Christendom required a vast army of officials who were supported by fees and whose numbers were multiplied oppressively, especially after Boniface IX had introduced the sale of offices as a financial expedient. Thus, in 1487, when Sixtus IV desired to redeem his tiara and jewels, pledged for a loan of 100,000 ducats, he increased his secretaries from six to twenty-four and required each to pay 2600 florins for the office. In 1503, to raise funds for Cesare Borgia, Alexander VI created eighty new offices and sold them for 760 ducats apiece. Julius II formed a "college" of a hundred and one scriveners of papal briefs, in return for which they paid him 74,000 ducats. Leo X appointed sixty chamberlains and a hundred and forty squires, with certain perquisites for which the former paid him 90,000 ducats and the latter 112,000. Places thus paid for were personal property, transferable by sale; and Leo X levied a commission of five *per cent.* on such transactions, and then made over the proceeds to Cardinal Tarlato, a retainer of the Medici family. Burchard tells us that in 1483 he bought the mastership of ceremonies from his predecessor Patrizzi for 450 ducats, which covered all expenses, and that in 1505 he vainly offered Julius II 2000 for a vacant scrivenership; but soon afterwards he bought the succession to an abbreviatorship for 2040. As Burchard was still master of ceremonies and Bishop of Orta it is evident that this was simply an investment for the fees of an office which carried with it no duties.

The whole machinery was thus manifestly devised for the purpose of levying as large a tax as possible on the multitudes whose necessities brought them to the Curia, and its rapacity was proverbial. The hands through which every document passed were multiplied to an incredible degree and each one levied his share upon it. Besides, there were heavy charges which do not appear in the rules of the Chancery and which doubtless enured to the benefit of the papal Camera, so that the official tax-tables bear but a slender proportion to the actual cost of briefs to suitors. Thus certain briefs obtained for the city of Cologne, in 1393, of which the charge, according to the tables, was eleven and a half florins, cost when delivered 266, and, in 1423, some similar privileges for the abbey of St Albans were paid for at forty times the amount provided in the tables. Thus the army of officials constituting the Curia not only cost nothing to the Holy See, but brought in revenue; and its exactions rendered it an object of execration throughout Christendom.

The administration of justice was provocative of even greater detestation. The business flowing in from every part of Europe was necessarily enormous, and the effort seems to have been not to expedite, but to prolong it, and to render it as costly as possible to the pleader. We hear incidentally of a suit between the Teutonic Order and the clergy of Riga, concerning the somewhat trivial question whether the latter were privileged to wear the vestments of the Order, in the course of which, in 1430, the agent of the Order writes from Rome that he had already expended on it 14,000 ducats, and that 6000 more would be required to bring it to a conclusion. The sale of benefices and expectatives was in itself a most lucrative source of profit to the Roman Courts; for, in the magnitude and complexity of the business, mistakes, accidental or otherwise, were frequent, leading to conflicting claims which could be adjudicated only in Rome. The Gallican Church, assembled at the Council of Bourges, in 1438, declared that this was the cause of innumerable suits and contentions between the servants of God; that quarrels and hatreds were excited, the greed of pluralities was stimulated, the money of the kingdom was exhausted; pleaders, forced to have recourse to the Roman Courts, were reduced to poverty, and rightful claims were set aside in favour of those whose greater cunning or larger means enabled them to profit through the frauds rendered possible by the complexities of the papal graces. France protected herself by the Pragmatic Sanction, until its final abrogation, in 1516, by the Concordat between Francis I and Leo X excited intense dissatisfaction and was one of the causes which favoured the rapid spread of the Lutheran heresy there. Germany had not been so fortunate, and among the grievances presented, in 1510, to the Emperor Maximilian was enumerated the granting of expectatives without number, and often the same to several persons, as giving rise to daily law-suits; so that the money laid out in the purchase and that expended in the suit were alike lost, and it became a proverb that whoever obtained an expectative from Rome ought to lay aside with it one or two hundred gold pieces to be expended in rendering it effective. Another of the grievances was that cases, which ought to have been decided at home where there were good and upright judges, were carried without distinction to Rome. There was, in fact, no confidence felt in the notoriously venal Roman Courts, and their very name was an abomination in Germany.

The pressing necessities of the papacy had found another source of relief which did not bear so directly on the nations but was an expedient fatally degrading to the dignity and character of the Holy See. This was the sale of the highest office in the Church next to the papacy itself —the red hat of the cardinalate. The reputation of the Sacred College was already rapidly deteriorating through the nepotism of the Pontiffs, who thrust their kinsmen into it irrespective of fitness, or yielded to the pressure of monarchs and appointed their unworthy favourites in order to secure some temporary political advantage. Thus its decadence and secularisation were rapid through the second half of the fifteenth century; but a lower depth was reached when, in 1500, Alexander VI created twelve Cardinals from whose appointment Cesare Borgia secured the sum of 120,000 ducats, and whose character may readily be surmised. In 1503, with the same object, nine more were appointed and again Cesare obtained between 120,000 and 130,000 ducats. Even Julius II, in his creation of Cardinals in April, 1511, did not scruple to make some of them pay heavily for the promotion and in this he was imitated by Leo X in 1517, on the notorious occasion of the swamping of the Sacred College. It was only a step from this to the purchase of the papacy itself, and both Alexander VI and Julius II obtained the pontificate by bribery. So commonly known, indeed, was the venality of the Sacred College that, at the death of Innocent VIII, in 1492, Charles VIII was currently reported to have deposited 200,000 ducats and Genoa 100,000 in a Roman bank in order to secure the election of Giuliano della Rovere; but Rodrigo Borgia carried off the prize. Under a similar conviction, when, in 1511, Julius II was thought to be on his death-bed, and the Emperor Maximilian conceived the idea of securing his own election to the expected vacancy, his first step was to try to obtain a loan of 200,000 or 300,000 ducats from the Fuggers' bank on the security of his jewels and insignia. That Maximilian should have entertained such a project is a significant illustration of the complete secularisation of the Holy See.

Under such influences it is no wonder that Rome had become a centre of corruption whence infection was radiated throughout Christendom. In the middle of the fourteenth century Petrarch exhausts his rhetoric in describing the abominations of the papal city of Avignon, where everything was vile; and the return of the Curia to Rome transferred to that city the supremacy in wickedness. In 1499 the Venetian ambassador describes it as the sewer of the world, and Machiavelli asserts that through its example all devotion and all religion had perished in Italy. In 1490 it numbered 6000 public women—an enormous proportion for a population not exceeding 100,000. The story is well known, how Cardinal Borgia who, as Vice-Chancellor, openly sold pardons for crime, when reproved for this, replied, that God desires not the death of sinners but that they should pay and live. If the Diary of Infessura is suspect on account of his partizanship, that of Burchard is unimpeachable, and his placid recital of the events passing under his eyes presents to us a society too depraved to take shame at its own wickedness. The public marriage, he says, of the daughters of Innocent VIII and Alexander VI set the fashion for the clergy to have children, and they diligently followed it; for all, from the highest to the lowest, kept concubines, while the monasteries were brothels. The official conscience was illustrated in the Hospital of San Giovanni in Laterano where the confessor, when he found that a patient had money, would notify the physician, who thereupon would administer a deadly dose and the two would seize and divide the spoils. Had the physician contented himself with this industry, he might have escaped detection; but he varied it by going into the streets every morning and shooting with a cross-bow people whose pockets he then emptied, for which he was duly hanged (May 27, 1500). The foulness of the debaucheries in which Alexander VI emulated the worst excesses of the pagan empire was possible only in a social condition of utter corruption; and, as a knowledge of the facts filtered through the consciousness of Europe, contempt was added to the detestation so generally entertained for the Holy See. This was ominously expressed, in 1501, in a letter to Alexander VI from a knight and two men-at-arms who had despoiled the convent of Weissenburg and had disregarded the consequent excommunication. Under the canon law this rendered them suspect of heresy, for which they were summoned to Rome to answer for their faith. They replied in a tone of unconcealed irony; the journey, they say, is too long, so they send a profession of faith, including a promise of obedience to a Pope honestly elected who has not sullied the Holy See with immoralities and scandals.

In fact, one of the most urgent symptoms of the necessity of a new order of things was the complete divorce between religion and morality. There was abundant zeal in debating minute points of faith, but little in evoking from it an exemplary standard of life—as Pius II said of the Conventual Franciscans: they were generally excellent theologians but gave themselves little trouble about virtue. The sacerdotal system, developed by the dialectics of the Schoolmen, had constructed a routine of external observances through which salvation was to be gained not so much by abstinence from sin as by its pardon through the intervention of the priest, whose supernatural powers were in no way impaired by the scandals of his daily life. Except within the pale of the pagan Renaissance, never was there a livelier dread of future punishment, but this punishment was to be escaped, not by amendment but by confession, absolution, and indulgences. This frame of mind is exemplified by the condottiere Vitelozzo Vitelli who, when after a life steeped in crime, he was suddenly strangled by Cesare Borgia, in 1502, felt no more poignant regret than that he could not obtain absolution from the Pope—and that Pope was Alexander VI. Society was thoroughly corrupt—perhaps less so in the lower than in the higher classes—but no one can read the Lenten sermons of the preachers of the time, even with full allowance for rhetorical exaggeration, without recognising that the world has rarely seen a more debased standard of morality than that which prevailed in Italy in the closing years of the Middle Ages. Yet at the same time never were there greater outward manifestations of devotional zeal. A man like San Giovanni Capistrano could scarce walk the streets of a city without an armed guard to preserve his life from the surging crowds eager to secure a rag of his garments as a relic or to carry away some odour of his holiness by touching him with a stick. Venice, which cared little for an interdict, offered in vain ten thousand ducats, in 1455, for a seamless coat of Christ. Siena and Perugia went to war over the wedding-ring of the Virgin. At no period was there greater faith in the thaumaturgic virtue of images and saintly relics; never were religious solemnities so gorgeously celebrated; never were processions so magnificent or so numerously attended; never were fashionable shrines so largely thronged by pilgrims. In his *Encheiridion Militis Christiani*, written in 1502 and approved by Adrian VI, then head of the University of Louvain, Erasmus had the boldness to protest against this new kind of Judaism which placed its reliance on observances, like magic rites, which drew men away from Christ; and again, in 1519, in a letter to Cardinal Albrecht of Mainz, he declared that religion was degenerating into a more than Judaic formalism of ceremonies, and that there must be a change.

A priesthood trained in this formalism, which had practically replaced the ethical values of Christianity, secure that its supernatural attributes were unaffected by the most flagitious life, and selected by such methods as were practised by the Curia and imitated by the prelates, could not be expected to rise above the standards of the community. Rather, indeed, were the influences, to which the clergy were exposed, adapted to depress them below the average. They were clothed with virtually irresponsible power over their subjects, they were free from the restraints of secular law, and they were condemned to celibacy in times when no man was expected to be continent. For three hundred years it had been the constant complaint that the people were contaminated by their pastors and the complaint continued. After the death of Calixtus III, in 1458, the Cardinals about to enter the Conclave were told in the address made to them by Domenico de' Domenichi, Bishop of Torcello, "The morals of the clergy are corrupt, they have become an offence to the laity, all discipline is lost. From day to day the respect for the Church diminishes; the power of her censures is almost gone." In 1519, Briçonnet, Bishop of Meaux, in his diocesan synod, did not shrink from describing the Church as a stronghold of vice, a city of refuge from transgression, where one could live in safety, free from all fear of punishment. The antagonism towards the priesthood, thus aroused among the people, was indicated in the career of Hans Böheim, a wandering musician, who settled in Niklashausen, where he announced revelations from the Virgin. She instructed him to proclaim to her people that she could no longer endure the pride, the avarice, and the lust of the priesthood and that the world would be destroyed because of their wickedness unless they should speedily amend their ways. Tithes and tribute should be purely voluntary; tolls and customs dues and game-preserving should be abolished; Rome had no claim to the primacy of the Church; purgatory was a figment and he had power to rescue souls from hell. The fame of the inspired preacher spread far and wide between the Rhineland and Meissen; crowds from all quarters flocked to hear him and he frequently addressed assemblages rated at twenty or thirty thousand souls who brought him rich offerings. In 1476 Rudolf Bishop of Würzburg put an end to this dangerous propaganda by seizing and burning the prophet, but belief in him continued until Diether of Mainz placed an interdict on the church of Niklashausen in order to check the concourse of pilgrims who persisted in visiting it.

Perhaps the most complete and instructive presentation which we have of the opinions and aspirations of the medieval populations is embodied in the ample series of the Spanish Cortes published by the *Real Academía de la Historía*. In the petitions or *cahiers* of these representative bodies we find an uninterrupted expression of hostility towards the Church, unrelieved by any recognition of services, whether as the guardian of religious truth or as the mediator between God and man. To the Castilian of the fourteenth and fifteenth centuries it was simply an engine of oppression, an instrument through which rapacious men could satisfy their greed and inflict misery on the people by its exactions and its constantly encroaching jurisdiction, enforced through unrestricted power of excommunication. Bitter were the reiterated complaints of the immunity which it afforded to criminals, and there was constant irritation at clerical exemption from public duties and burdens. In short, it seems to have been regarded as a public enemy, and the slight respect in which it was held is amply evidenced in the repeated complaints of the spoliation of churches which were robbed of their sacred vessels, apparently without compunction.

The popular literature of the period similarly reflects this mingled contempt and hatred for the priesthood. The Franciscan Thomas Murner, who subsequently was one of the most savage opponents of Luther, in the curious rhymed sermons which, in 1512, he preached in Frankfort-on-the-Main, and which, under the names of the *Schelmen-zunft* and the *Narrenbeschweerung*, had a wide popularity, is never tired of dwelling on the scandals of all classes of the clergy, from bishops to monks and nuns. All are worldly, rapacious, and sensual. When the lay lord has shorn the sheep, the priest comes and fairly disembowels it, the begging friar follows and gets what he can and then the pardoner. If a bishop is in want of money he sends around his fiscal among the parish priests to extort payment for the privilege of keeping their concubines. In the nunneries the sister who has the most children is made the abbess. If Christ were on earth to-day He would be betrayed,

43—2

and Judas would be reckoned an honest man. The devil is really the ruler of the Church, whose prelates perform his works; they are too ignorant to discharge their duties and require coadjutors—it would be well for them could they likewise have substitutes in hell. The wolf preached and sang mass so as to gather the geese around him, and then seized and ate them; so it is with prelate and priest who promise all things and pretend to care for souls until they get their benefices, when they devour their flocks. The immense applause with which these attacks on the abuses of the Church were everywhere received, and others of a similar character in Eulenspiegel, Sebastian Brant's *Narrenschiff*, Johann Faber's *Tractatus de Ruine Ecclesie Planctu*, and the *Encomium Moriae* of Erasmus, their translation into many languages and wide circulation throughout Europe, show how thoroughly they responded to the popular feeling, how dangerously the Church had forfeited the respect of the masses, and how deeply rooted was the aversion which it had inspired. The priests hated Rome for her ceaseless exactions and the people hated the priests with perhaps even better reason. So bitter was this dislike that, in 1502, Erasmus tells us that among laymen to call a man a cleric or a priest or a monk was an unpardonable insult.

This antagonism was fostered by the pulpit, which, until the invention of printing and the diffusion of education, was the only channel of access to the masses. Neglected by the bishops, involved in worldly cares and indulgence, and by the parish priests, too ignorant and too indolent to employ it, the duty of preaching fell, for the most part, to volunteers who, like Thomas Murner, were usually Mendicant Friars and consequently hostile to the secular clergy. Their influence on public opinion was great. With coarse and vigorous eloquence they attacked abuses of all kinds, whether in Church or State, and with an almost incredible hardihood they aroused the people to a sense of their wrongs. A favourite topic was the contrast between the misery of the lower classes and the luxury of the prelates—their hawks and hounds, their splendid retinues and the lavish adornment of their female companions. The licentiousness of the clergy was not spared—according to one of them the wealth of the Church only serves as a pair of bellows to kindle the fires of lust. The earliest of these bold demagogues of whom we have authentic details was Foulques de Neuilly, who, in the closing years of the twelfth century, traversed France, calling the people to repentance and listened to by immense crowds. He was especially severe on the vices of the clergy, and it is related of him that at Lisieux, to silence him, they threw him into prison and loaded him with chains; but his saintliness had won for him thaumaturgic power, and he walked forth unharmed. Thomas Connecte, a Carmelite of Britanny, was another wandering preacher who produced an immense impression wherever he went, and we are told that his invectives against the priesthood won him especial applause; but when, in 1432, he went to Rome to lash the vices of the Curia he was speedily found to be a heretic and he perished at the stake. Although St Bonaventura deprecated, on account of the scandals and quarrels which it provoked, the Mendicant preachers' habit of attacking the corruption of the priesthood, it was ever a favourite topic; and the preaching of such men as Olivier Maillard, Geiler von Kaisersberg, Guillaume Pepin, Jean Clérée, Michel Menot, and a host of others, unquestionably contributed largely to stimulate the irresistible impulse which finally insisted on reform. With the invention of printing their eloquence reached larger audiences; for their sermons were collected and printed and received a wide circulation.

That a reform of the Church in its head and its members was necessary had long been generally conceded. For more than a century Europe had been clamouring for it. For this it had gathered its learning and piety at Constance, 1414–18; the Curia had skilfully eluded the demand and the assembly delegated the task to future Councils which, by the decree *Frequens*, it decreed should be convoked at regular intervals of seven years. In obedience to this decree a Council met at Pavia and Siena in 1423–4, where the effort was again made and again frustrated. When the term came around in 1431 and the Church, assembled at Basel, determined not to be balked again, the resolute energy of the reformers speedily caused a rupture with the papacy, and the Basilian canons, aimed at some of the more crying abuses, were stedfastly ignored. The responsibility thus devolved upon the papacy, which had rendered abortive the efforts of the Councils and, after its bitter experience at Basel, had successfully resisted the constantly recurring demands for the enforcement of the decree *Frequens*. To meet this responsibility successive Popes, from Martin V to Leo X, issued reformatory decrees, the promulgation and non-observance of which only served as an acknowledgment of the evil and of the impossibility of its correction.

At length, in 1511, the schismatic Council of Pisa, held by the disaffected Cardinals under the auspices of Louis XII, forced the hand of Julius II, and to checkmate it he issued a summons for a General Council to assemble in Rome, April 19, 1512, to resist the schism, to reform the morals of laity and clergy, to bring about peace between Christian princes and to prosecute the War with the Turk. Not much was to be hoped of a Council held in Rome under papal presidency; but Europe took the project seriously. The instructions of the Spanish delegates ordered them to labour especially for the reformation of the Curia; for the chief objection of the infidels to Christianity arose from the public and execrable wickedness of Rome, for which the Pope was accountable. It was apparently to forestall action that, in March, 1512, Julius appointed a commission of eight Cardinals to reform the Curia and its officials and, on March 30, he issued a bull reducing the heavy burden of fees and other exactions. The Fifth Council of the Lateran assembled a little later than the time appointed, and its earlier sessions were devoted to obliterating the traces of the schism and attacking the Pragmatic Sanction of France. Julius died, February 21, 1513, and to his successor, Leo X, was transferred the management of the Council. To him Gianfrancesco Pico addressed a memorial recapitulating the evils to be redressed. The worship of God, he said, was neglected; the churches were held by pimps and catamites; the nunneries were dens of prostitution; justice was a matter of hatred or favour; piety was lost in superstition; the priesthood was bought and sold; the revenues of the Church ministered only to the vilest excesses, and the people were repelled from religion by the example of their pastors. The Council made at least a show of attacking these evils. On May 3, 1514, it approved a papal decree which, if enforced, would have cured a small portion of the abuses; but all subsequent efforts were blocked by quarrels between the different classes to be reformed. The Council sat until March, 1517, and the disappointment arising from its dissolution, without accomplishing anything of the long-desired reform, may well have contributed to the eagerness with which the Lutheran revolt was soon afterwards hailed; for thoughtful men everywhere must have been convinced that nothing short of revolution could put an end to corruption so inexpugnably established. It was the emphatic testimony of interested observers that the Roman Curia, in its immovable adherence to its evil ways, was the real cause of the uprising. The papal nuncio Aleander, writing from the Diet of Worms in 1521, says that the priests are foremost in the revolt, not for Luther's sake but because through him they can gratify their long-cherished hatred of Rome; nine Germans out of ten are for Luther, and the tenth man longs for the destruction of the Roman Curia. Cardinal Albrecht of Mainz, about the same time, wrote to Pope Leo that it was rare to find a man who favoured the clergy, while a large portion of the priests were for Luther, and the majority were afraid to stand forth in support of the Roman Church,—so deep was the hatred felt for the Curia and the papal decrees. When Dr Eck found that his disputatious zeal was a failure, he told Paul III that the heresy had arisen from the abuses of the Curia, that it had spread in consequence of the immorality of the clergy, and that it could only be checked by reform. Adrian VI, in his instructions to his legate at the Diet of Nürnberg in 1522, admitted the abominations habitual to the Holy See and promised their removal, but added that it would be a work of time; for the evil was too complex and too deeply rooted for a speedy cure. Meanwhile he demanded the execution of the papal sentence against Luther without awaiting the promised reform; but the German princes replied that this would simply cause rebellion, for the people would then despair of amendment.

While thus the primary cause of the Reformation is to be sought in the all-pervading corruption of the Church and its oppressive exercise of its supernatural prerogatives, there were other factors conducing to the explosion. Sufficient provocation had long existed, and since the failure at Basel no reasonable man could continue to anticipate relief from conciliar action. The shackles which for centuries had bound the human intellect had to be loosened, before there could be a popular movement of volume sufficient to break with the traditions of the past and boldly tempt the dangers of a new and untried career for humanity. The old reverence for authority had to be weakened, the sense of intellectual independence had to be awakened and the spirit of enquiry and of more or less scientific investigation had to be created, before pious and devout men could reach the root of the abuses which caused so much indignation, and could deny the authenticity of the apostolical deposit on which had been erected the venerable and imposing structure of Scholastic Theology and papal autocracy.

It was the New Learning and the humanistic movement which supplied the impulse necessary for this, and they found conditions singularly favourable for their work. The Church had triumphed so completely over her enemies that the engines of repression had been neglected and had grown rusty, while the Popes were so engrossed in their secular schemes and ambition that they had little thought to waste on the possible tendencies of the fashionable learning which they patronised. Thus there came an atmosphere of free thought, strangely at variance with the rigid dogmatism of the theologians, and even in theology there was a certain latitude of discussion permissible, for the Tridentine decrees had not yet formulated into articles of faith the results of the debates of the Schoolmen since the twelfth century. It is a remarkable proof of the prevailing laxity that Nicholas V commissioned Gianozzo Manetti to make a new translation of the Bible from the original Hebrew and Greek, thus showing that the Vulgate was regarded as insufficient and that it enjoyed no such authority as that attributed to it at Trent. In view of this laxity it is not surprising that in Italy the New Learning assumed various fantastic shapes of belief— the cult of the Genius of Rome by Pomponio Leto and his Academy, the Platonism of Marsiglio Ficino, the practical denial of immortality by Pomponazzi, and the modified Averrhoism of Agostino Nifo. So long as the profits of the Curia or the authority of the Pope remained undisputed there was little disposition to trouble the dreamers and speculators. Savonarola declares, with some rhetorical exaggeration, that culture had supplanted religion in the minds of those to whom the destinies of Christianity were confided, until they lost belief in God, celebrated feasts of the devil, and made a jest of the sacred mysteries. In the polite Court circles of Leo X, we are told, a man was scarce accounted as cultured and well-bred unless he cherished a certain amount of heretical opinion; and after Luther's doctrines had become rigidly defined Melanchthon is said to have looked back with a sigh to the days before the Reformation as to a time when there was freedom of thought. It is true that there was occasional spasmodic repression. Pico della Mirandola, because of thirteen heretical propositions among the nine hundred which he offered to defend in 1487, was obliged to fly to Spain and to make his peace by submission; but, as a rule, the humanists were allowed to air their fancies in peace. When the disputations of the schools on the question of the future life became overbold and created scandal, the Lateran Council, in 1513, forbade the teaching of Averrhoism and of the mortality of the soul; but it did so in terms which placed little restraint on philosophers who shielded themselves behind a perfunctory declaration of submission to the judgment of the Church.

In the intellectual ferment at work throughout Europe, it was, however, impossible that many devout Christians should not be led to question details in the theology on which the Schoolmen had erected the structure of sacerdotal supremacy. Gregor Heimburg was a layman who devoted his life to asserting the superiority of the secular power to the ecclesiastical, lending the aid of his learning and eloquence to the anti-papal side of all the controversies which raged from the time of the Council of Basel until he died in 1472, absolved at last from the excommunication which he had richly earned. In 1479 the errors of Pedro de Osma, a professor of Salamanca, were condemned by the Council of Alcalà; they consisted in denying the efficacy of indulgences, the divine origin and necessity of confession, and the infallibility and irresponsible autocracy of the papacy. The same year witnessed the trial at Mainz, by the Cologne inquisitor, of Johann Rucherath of Wesel, a professor in the University of Erfurt and one of the most distinguished theologians of Germany. Erfurt was noted for its humanism and for its adherence to the doctrine of the superiority of councils over popes, and Johann Rucherath had been uttering his heretical opinions for many years without opposition. He would probably have been allowed to continue in peace until the end but for the mortal quarrel between the Realists and the Nominalists and the desire of the Dominican Thomists to silence a Nominalist leader. He rejected the authority of tradition and of the Fathers; he carried predestination to a point which stripped the Church of its power over salvation and he even struck the word *Filioque* from the Creed. He was of course condemned and forced to recant; but the contemporary reporter of the trial apparently considers that his only serious error was the one concerning the procession of the Holy Ghost, and he cites various men of learning who held that most of the condemned articles could be maintained. More fortunate was Johann Wessel of Groningen, a prominent theological teacher who entertained heretical notions as to confession, absolution, and purgatory, and denied that the Pope could grant indulgences, for God deals directly with man—doctrines as revolutionary as those of Luther—yet he was allowed to die peacefully in 1489, held in great honour by the community. Still more significant of the spiritual unrest of the period was a *Sorbonnique*, or thesis for the doctorate, presented to the University of Paris, in 1485, by a priest named Jean Laillier, whose audacity reduced the hierarchy, including the pope, to simple priesthood and rejected confession, absolution, indulgences, fasting, the obligation of celibacy, and the authority of tradition. The extreme difficulty encountered in procuring the condemnation of these dangerous heresies, which finally required the intervention of Innocent VIII, is a noteworthy symptom of the time, and equally so is the fact that the Bishop of Meaux, selected by Innocent as one of the judges in the case, was at that moment under censure by the University for reviving the condemned doctrine of the insufficiency of the sacraments in polluted hands. In 1498, an Observantine Friar named Jean Vitrier, in sermons at Tournay, went even further and taught that it was a mortal sin to listen to the mass of a concubinary priest. He also rejected the intercession of saints, and asserted that pardons and indulgences were the offspring of hell and the money paid for them was employed in the maintenance of brothels. The Tournay authorities were apparently powerless, and referred these utterances to the University of Paris, which extracted from them sixteen heretical propositions; but it does not appear that the audacious preacher was punished. It was still more ominous of the future when men were found ready to endure martyrdom in denial of the highest mysteries of the faith, as when, in 1491, Jean Langlois, priest of St Crispin in Paris, while celebrating mass, cast the consecrated elements on the floor and trampled on them, giving as a reason that the body and blood of Christ were not in them and persisting in his error to the stake. Similar was the obstinacy of Aymon Picard in 1503, who at the feast of St Louis in the Sainte Chapelle snatched the host from the celebrant and dashed it on the floor, for he, too, refused to recant and was burnt.

To what extent humanism was responsible for these heresies it would not be easy now to determine, save in so far as it had stimulated the spirit of enquiry and destroyed the reverence for authority. These influences are plainly observable in the career of Jacques Lefèvre d'Étaples, the precursor of the Reformation in France, who commenced as a student of philosophy and, in 1492, visited Italy to sit at the feet of Marsiglio Ficino, Hermolao Barbaro, Pico della Mirandola, and Angelo Poliziano, but who, when he turned to the study of Scripture, expressed the pious wish that the profane classical writings should be burnt rather than be placed in the hands of youth. His *Commentary on the Pauline Epistles*, printed in 1512, was the first example of casting aside the scholastic exegesis for a treatment in which tradition was rejected and the freedom of individual judgment was exercised as a matter of right. This led him to a number of conclusions which Luther only reached gradually in the disputations forced upon him in defence of his first step; but this protest against the established sacerdotalism brought no persecution on Lefèvre until the progress of the Reformation in Germany aroused the authorities to the danger lurking in such utterances, when the Sorbonne, in 1521, had no difficulty in defining twenty-five heretical propositions in the *Commentaries*. Proceedings were commenced against him, but he was saved by the favour of Francis I and Marguerite of Navarre.

There were other humanists, less spiritual than Lefèvre, who exercised enormous influence in breaking down reverence for tradition and authority and asserting the right of private judgment, without giving in their adhesion to the Reformation. They had a narrow and a perilous path to tread. Wilibald Pirckheimer was no Lutheran, but his name stood first on the list of those selected for excommunication by Eck when he returned from Rome as the bearer of the portentous bull *Exsurge Domine*. More fortunate was the foremost humanist, Erasmus, whose unrivalled intellect rendered him a power to be courted by Popes and princes, though he was secretly held responsible as the primary cause of the revolt. In 1522 Adrian VI adjured him to come to the rescue of the bark of the Church, struggling in the tempest sent by God in consequence mainly of the sins of the clergy, and assured him that this was a province reserved to him by God. Yet, in 1527, Edward Lee, then English ambassador to Spain and subsequently Archbishop of York, drew up a list of twenty-one heresies extracted from the writings of Erasmus, ranging from Arianism to the repudiation of indulgences, the veneration of saints, pilgrimages, and relics. At this very moment, however, Erasmus, frightened at the violence of the reformers, was writing to Pirckheimer that he held the authority of the Church so high that at her bidding he would accept Arianism and Pelagianism, for the words of Christ were not of themselves sufficient for him.

Luther himself had in some sort a humanistic pedigree. The Franciscan Paul Scriptoris, professor at Tübingen, learned in Greek and mathematics, used confidentially to predict that a reformation was at hand in which the Church would be forced to reject the scholastic theology and return to the simplicity of primitive belief, but when he permitted these views to find expression in his sermons the chapter of his Order took steps to discipline him, and he fled, in 1502, to Italy where he died. He was the teacher of Johann von Staupitz, Conrad Pellican, and others subsequently prominent in the movement; Staupitz became the Vicar of Luther's Augustinian Order and was warmly esteemed by the Elector Frederick of Saxony; so that he was enabled to afford to Luther efficient protection during the earlier years of the revolt. He was a humanist, strongly imbued with the views of the German mystics of the fourteenth century, and all mysticism is, in its essence, incompatible with sacerdotalism. In his *Nachfolgung des Sterbens Jesu Christi*, printed in 1515, he denied, like Erasmus, the efficacy of external observances, condemning the doctrine as a kind of Judaism. In 1516, at Nürnberg, he preached a series of sermons warning against reliance on confession, for justification comes alone from the grace of God. These were greeted with immense applause; they were printed in both Latin and German and a *Sodalitas Staupitiana* was organised, embracing many of the leading citizens, among whom Albrecht Dürer was numbered. The next year at Munich he inculcated the same doctrines with equal success and he embodied his views in the work *Von der Liebe Gottes*, dedicated to the Duchess Kunigunda of Bavaria, of which four editions were speedily exhausted, showing the receptivity of the popular mind for anti-sacerdotal teachings. It was some time before Luther advanced as far as Staupitz had already done, and then it was largely through the study of the fourteenth century mystics and Staupitz's work *On the love of God*.

There was no product of humanistic literature, however, which so aided in paving the way for the Reformation as the *Narrenschiff*, or *Ship of Fools*, the work of a layman, Sebastian Brant, chancellor (city clerk) of Strassburg. Countless editions and numerous translations of this work, first printed at Basel in 1494, showed how exactly it responded to the popular tendencies, and how wide and lasting was its influence. One of the foremost preachers of the day, Geiler von Kaisersberg, used its several chapters or sections as texts for a series of sermons at Strassburg, in 1498, and the opinions of the poet lost none of their significance in the expositions of the preacher. The work forms a singularly instructive document for the intellectual and moral history of the period. Brant satirises all the follies and weaknesses of man; those of the clergy are of course included and, though no special attention is devoted to them, the manner in which they are handled shows how completely the priesthood had forfeited popular respect. But the important feature of the work is the deep moral earnestness which pervades its jest and satire; man is exhorted never to lose sight of his salvation and the future life is represented as the goal to which his efforts are to be directed. With all this, the Church is never referred to as the means through which the pardon of sin and the grace of God are to be attained; confession is alluded to in passing once or twice, but not the intercession of the Virgin and saints and there is no intimation that the offices of the Church are essential. The lesson is taught that man deals directly with God and is responsible to Him alone. Most significant is the remark that many a mass is celebrated which had better have been left unsung for God does not accept a sacrifice sinfully offered in sin. Wisdom is the one thing for which man should strive,—wisdom being obedience to God and a virtuous life, while the examples cited are almost exclusively drawn from classic paganism—Hercules, Pythagoras, Socrates, Plato,

Penelope, Virgil—though the references to Scripture show adequate acquaintance with Holy Writ. As the embodiment of humanistic teaching through which Germany, unlike Italy, aspired to moral elevation as well as to classical training, the *Narrenschiff* holds the highest place alike for comprehensiveness and effectiveness.

It is not to be supposed that these influences were allowed to develop without protest or opposition. The battle between humanism and obscurantism had been fought out in Italy, in the middle of the fifteenth century, in the strife between Lorenzo Valla and the Mendicant Friars backed by the Inquisition. In Germany the struggle took place, in the second decade of the sixteenth century, over Reuchlin, on the occasion of his protesting against Pfefferkorn's measures for the destruction of objectionable Hebrew books. It arrayed the opposing forces in internecine conflict, and all the culture of Europe was ranged on the side of the scholar who was threatened with prosecution by the Inquisition. The New Learning recognised the danger to which it was exposed and its disciples found themselves unconsciously organising for self-defence and for attack. Religious dogma was not really involved; but the authority of the Schools was at stake, and the power to silence by persecution an adversary who could not be overcome in argument. The bitterness on both sides was intense and victory seemed to perch alternately on the opposing banners; but the quarrel virtually sank out of sight in the larger issues raised by the opening years of the Reformation. Technically the obscurantists triumphed, but it was a Pyrrhic victory; for the discussion had done its work and incidentally it had given occasion for blighting ridicule of the trivialities of the Schools and the stupid ignorance of the Schoolmen in the *Epistolae Obscurorum Virorum*, 1514, a production that largely contributed to the popular contempt in which the ancient system was beginning to be held.

The whole of this movement had been rendered possible by the invention of printing, which facilitated so enormously the diffusion of intelligence, which enabled public opinion to form and express itself and which, by bringing into communication minds of similar ways of thinking, afforded opportunity for combined action. When we are told that bibliographers enumerate thirteen German versions of the Bible anterior to Luther's and that repeated editions of these were called for, we can measure not only the religious earnestness of the people but the degree in which it was stimulated by the process which brought the Scriptures within reach of the multitude. Cochlaeus complains that when Luther's translation of the New Testament appeared, in 1522, every one sought it without distinction of age or station, and they speedily acquired such familiarity with it that they audaciously disputed with doctors of theology and regarded it as the fountain of all truth. Tradition and scholastic dogma had under such circumstances small chance of reverence. When therefore, on October 31, 1517, Luther's fateful theses were hung

on the church-door at Wittenberg, they were, as he tells us, known in
a fortnight throughout Germany; and in a month they had reached
Rome and were being read in every school and convent in Europe—a
result manifestly impossible without the aid of the printing-press. The
reformers took full advantage of the opportunities which it afforded,
and, for the most part, they had the sympathies of the printers themselves. The assertion of the *Epistolae Obscurorum Virorum*

> Sed in domo Frobenii
> Sunt multi pravi haeretici

is doubtless true of all the great printing offices. It was a standing
grievance with the papalists that the printers eagerly printed and
circulated everything on the Lutheran side, while the Catholics had
difficulty in bringing their works before the public, and had to defray
the cost themselves; but this is doubtless rather attributable to the fact
that there was a steady demand for the one and not for the other.

It had not taken the Church long to recognise the potential dangers
of the printing-press. In 1479, Sixtus IV empowered the University of
Cologne to proceed with censures against the printers, purchasers, and
readers of heretical books. In 1486, Berthold, Archbishop of Mainz,
endeavoured to establish a crude censorship over translations into the
vernacular. Alexander VI, in 1501, took a more comprehensive step,
reciting that many books and tracts were printed containing various
errors and perverted doctrines, wherefore in future no book was to be
printed without preliminary examination and license, while all existing
books were to be inspected and those not approved were to be surrendered. The fifth Lateran Council adopted, with but one dissenting
voice, a decree laid before it by Leo X constituting the Bishop and
Inquisitor of each diocese a board of censors of all books: printers
disregarding their commands were visited with excommunication, suspension from business and a fine of a hundred ducats applicable to the
fabric of St Peter's. In obedience to this, Cardinal Albrecht of Mainz, in
1517, appointed his vicar, Paul, Bishop of Ascalon, and Dr Jodocus
Trutvetter as Inquisitors and Censors of the Press. These measures,
which were the precursors of the Index, were in vain. When, in 1521,
Charles V, in the Edict of Worms, ordered all Luther's books to be
surrendered and burnt, Cochlaeus tells us that they were only the more
eagerly sought for and brought better prices.

The dissemination of the Scriptures and the propagation of the
anti-sacerdotal views of the humanists naturally led to questioning the
conclusions of scholastic theology and to increased impatience of the
papal autocracy, these being regarded as the source of the evils so
generally and so grievously felt. The new teachings found a wide and
receptive audience, fully prepared to carry them to their ultimate

conclusions, in the numberless associations, partly literary and artistic, partly religious, which existed throughout the Teutonic lands. In the Netherlands there were everywhere to be found " Chambers of Rhetoric," exercising a powerful influence on public opinion, and these had long been hostile to the clergy whose vices were a favourite subject of their ballads and rondels, their moralities and farces. Less popular, but still dangerously influential, were the so-called Academies which sprang up all over Germany with the Revival of Learning, and which cherished tendencies adverse to the dogmas of the Church and to her practical use of those dogmas. In 1520, Aleander includes among the worst enemies of the papacy the grumbling race of grammarians and poets which swarmed everywhere throughout the land. There were also numerous more or less secret societies and associations, entertaining various opinions, but all heretical to a greater or less degree. These were partly the representatives of mysticism which, since the days of Master Eckart and Tauler, had never ceased to flourish in Germany; partly they were the survivors of Waldensianism, so pitilessly persecuted yet never suppressed. Zwingli, Oecolampadius, Bucer, and other leaders of the reform had received their early impressions in these associations, and the sudden outburst of Anabaptism shows how numerous were the dissidents from Rome who were not prepared to accept the limitations of the Lutheran creed. The Anabaptists, moreover, were but a portion of these Evangelicals, as they styled themselves; for adult baptism was not a feature of their original tenets, and when it was adopted as a doctrine it led to a division in their ranks. The influence of art as well as of literature in stimulating opposition to Rome is seen in the number of artists belonging to the Evangelical bodies. When, in 1524, the Lutherans, under the lead of Osiander, obtained control in Nürnberg, the heretics whom they arrested included Georg Pencz, Barthel and Sebald Behem, Ludwig Krug, and others. By Luther as well as by Rome Albrecht Dürer was accounted a heretic.

The combination of all these factors rendered an explosion inevitable, and Germany was predestined to be its scene. The ground was better prepared for it there than elsewhere, by the deeper moral and religious earnestness of the people and by the tendencies of the academies and associations with which society was honeycombed. In obedience to these influences the humanistic movement had not been pagan and aesthetic as in Italy, but had addressed itself to the higher emotions and had sought to train the conscience of the individual to recognise his direct responsibility to God and to his fellows. But more potent than all this were the forces arising from the political system of Germany and its relations with the Holy See. The Teutonic spirit of independence had early found expression in the *Sachsenspiegel* and *Sächsische Weichbild*—the laws and customs of Northern Germany—

which were resolutely maintained in spite of repeated papal condemnation. Thus not only did the Church inspire there less awe than elsewhere in Europe, but throughout the Middle Ages there had been special causes of antagonism actively at work.

If Italy had suffered bitterly from the *Tedeschi*, Germany had no less reason to hate the papacy. The fatal curse of the so-called Holy Roman Empire hung over both lands. It gave the Emperor a valid right to the suzerainty of the peninsula; it gave the papacy a traditional claim to confirm at its discretion the election of an Emperor. Conflicting and incompatible pretensions rendered impossible a permanent truce between the representatives of Charlemagne and St Peter. Since the age of Gregory VII the consistent policy of Rome had been to cripple the Empire by fomenting internal dissension and rendering impossible the evolution of a strong and centralised government, such as elsewhere in Europe was gradually overcoming the centrifugal forces of feudalism. This policy had been successful and Germany had become a mere geographical expression—a congeries of sovereign princes, petty and great, owning allegiance to an Emperor whose dignity was scarce more than a primacy of honour and whose actual power was to be measured by that of his ancestral territories. The result of this was that Germany lay exposed defenceless to the rapacity and oppression of the Roman Curia. Its multitudinous sovereigns had vindicated their independence at the cost of depriving themselves of the strength to be derived from centralised union. Germany was the ordinary resource of a Pope in financial straits, through the exaction of a tithe, the raising of the annates, or the issue in unstinted volume of the treasure of the merits of Christ in the form of an unremitting stream of indulgences which sucked up as with a sponge the savings of the people. Nor could any steady opposition be offered to the absorption of the ecclesiastical patronage by the Curia, through which benefices were sold or bestowed on the cardinals or their creatures, and no limits could be set on appeals to the Holy See which enlarged its jurisdiction and impoverished pleaders by involving them in interminable and ruinous litigation in the venal Roman Courts.

It was in vain that in 1438 the Roman King Albert II endeavoured to emulate Charles VII of France by proclaiming a Pragmatic Sanction defining the limits of papal authority. He died the next year and was followed by the feeble Frederick III, during whose long reign of fifty-three years the imperial authority was reduced to a shadow. It was probably to procure a promise of papal coronation that, in 1448, he agreed to a Concordat under which the reservation of benefices to the Pope, as made by John XXII and Benedict XII, was assured; the election of bishops was subjected to papal confirmation with the privilege of substituting a better candidate by advice of the Sacred College; canonries and other benefices falling vacant during the six uneven months were conceded to the Pope and a promise was made that the annates should be moderate and be payable in instalments during two years. This was a triumph of Italian diplomacy, for the leaven of Basel was still working in Germany, and the Basilian anti-Pope, Felix V, was endeavouring to secure recognition. But Aeneas Sylvius notified Nicholas V that this was only a truce, not a permanent peace, and that the utmost skill would be required to avert a rupture, for there were dangerous times ahead and currents under the surface that would call for careful piloting.

Advantageous as the Concordat was to Rome, the Curia could not be restrained to its observance and, in 1455, the three Spiritual Electors of Mainz, Trier, and Cologne, united in complaint of its violation. With other bishops and princes of the Empire they bound themselves to resist a tithe demanded by Calixtus III and to send his pardoners back across the Alps with empty purses; they agitated for the enforcement of the canons of Constance and Basel and urged Frederick III to proclaim a Pragmatic Sanction. Various assemblies were held during the next two years to promote these objects and, in 1457, Dr Martin Meyer, Chancellor of the Archbishop of Mainz, in a letter to Aeneas Sylvius, bitterly complained of the papal exactions, whereby Germany was drained of its gold and that nation which, by its valour, had won the Roman Empire and had been the mistress of the world was reduced to want and servitude, to grief and squalor. Calixtus met the German complaints with a serene consciousness of the weakness of his adversaries. To the prelates he wrote threatening them with punishment, spiritual and temporal. To Frederick he admitted that mistakes might have been made in the pressure of business but there had been no intentional violation of the Concordat. It was true that the Holy See was supreme and was not to be fettered by the terms of any agreement; but still, out of liberality and love of peace and affection for the person of the Emperor, the compact should be observed. No one must dare to oppose the Roman Church; if Germany thought it had reason to complain it could appeal to him. The result corresponded to the expectations of Calixtus; the confederates suspected their leader, Archbishop Dietrich of Mainz, of desiring to sell them; and after some further agitation in 1458 the movement fell to pieces.

It was promptly followed by another of even more dangerous aspect. Dietrich of Mainz died, May 6, 1459, and was succeeded by Diether von Isenburg. Pius II, then Aeneas Sylvius, had negotiated the Concordat of 1448 which stipulated that annates should be moderate and be payable by instalments, yet he refused to confirm Diether except on condition that he would satisfy the demands of the Camera for his annates. Diether's envoys agreed, and the cost of the confirmation was fixed at 20,550 *gulden*, to be advanced on the spot by Roman bankers. These accordingly paid the shares of the Pope, the Cardinals, and the lower officials, taking from them receipts which bore that they would refund the money in case Diether failed to meet the obligations given by his agents.  He claimed that the amount was largely in excess of all precedent, repudiated the agreement, and disregarded the consequent excommunication.   The result of this scandalous transaction was a series of disturbances which kept Germany in turmoil for three years.  Leagues were formed to replace Frederick III by George Podiebrad, and to adopt as the laws of the land the Basilian canons, one of which abrogated the annates.  Gregor Heimburg was sent to France to arrange for common action against the Holy See, and there seemed to be a prospect that Germany at last might assert its independence of the Curia.  But the papal agents with profuse promises detached one member of the alliance after another, and finally Diether was left alone.  He offered submission, but Pius secretly sent to Adolf of Nassau, one of the Canons of Mainz, a brief appointing him Archbishop and removing Diether.  This led to a bloody war between the rivals until, in October, 1463, they reached a compromise, Adolf retaining the title and conceding to Diether a portion of the territory.  Thus the papacy triumphed through its habitual policy of dividing and conquering.  There could be no successful resistance to oppression by alliances in which every member felt that he might at any moment be abandoned by his allies.  Yet this fruitless contest has special interest in the fact that Diether issued, May 30, 1462, a manifesto calling upon all German princes to take to heart the example of injustice and oppression of which they might be the next victims, and this manifesto, we are told, was printed by Gutenberg—an omen of the aid which the new art was to render in the struggle with Rome.

Even more bitter was the conflict, lasting from 1457 to 1464, between Sigismund Duke of Tyrol and Cardinal Nicholas of Cusa, as Bishop of Brixen, arising from his praiseworthy attempt to reform his clergy.   In this struggle Sigismund had the support of both clergy and people and was able to disregard the interdicts freely launched upon the land, as well as to resist the Swiss whom Pius II induced to take up arms against him.  He held out bravely, and the matter was finally settled by an agreement in which he asked for pardon and absolution, thus saving the honour of the Holy See.

If this was a drawn battle between the secular power and the Church, it did not lessen the effect of the triumphs which the Curia had won in the contests with the great Archbishops of Mainz.  Unsuccessful resistance leads to fresh aggression and it is not to be supposed that Rome failed to make the most of her victories over the German Church. At the great assembly of the clergy at Coblenz, in 1479, there were countless complaints of the Holy See, chiefly directed against its violations of the Concordat, its unlawful taxation, the privileges granted to the Mendicant Orders, and the numerous exemptions.   It was doubtless this demonstration that led, in 1480, to the negotiation of an agreement between Sixtus IV and the Emperor Frederick, in which the latter was pledged to keep Germany obedient to the Pope, while the Pope was to sustain the Emperor with the free use of censures.  This meant encouragement to fresh aggressions; and the indignation of the clergy found expression in the grievances presented, in 1510, to the Emperor-Elect Maximilian.  They asserted with scant ceremony that the papacy could be restrained by no agreements or conventions, seeing that it granted, for the benefit of the vilest persons, dispensations, suspensions, revocations, and other devices for nullifying its promises and evading its wholesome regulations; the elections of prelates were set aside; the right of choosing provosts, which many Chapters had purchased with heavy payments, was disregarded; the greater benefices and dignities were bestowed on the Cardinals and Prothonotaries of the Curia; expectatives were granted without number, giving rise to ruinous litigation; annates were exacted promptly and mercilessly and sometimes more was extorted than was due; the cure of souls was committed by Rome to those fitted rather to take charge of mules than of men; in order to raise money, new indulgences were issued, with suspension of the old, the laity being thus made to murmur against the clergy; tithes were exacted under the pretext of war against the Turks, yet no expeditions were sent forth; and cases which should be tried at home were carried without distinction to Rome.  Maximilian was seriously considering a plan for releasing Germany from the yoke of the Curia, and for preventing the transfer to Rome of the large sums which Julius II was employing to his special detriment; he thought of the withdrawal of the annates and of the appointment of a permanent legate, who should be a German and exercise a general jurisdiction.  But Jacob Wimpheling, who was consulted by the Emperor-Elect, while expressing himself vigorously as to the suffering of Germany from the Curia, thought it wiser to endure in the hope of amendment than to risk a schism.  Amendment, however, in obedience to any internal impulse, was out of the question.  The Lateran Council met, deliberated, and dissolved without offering to the most sanguine the slightest rational expectation of relief.  The only resource lay in revolution, and Germany was ready for the signal.  In 1521 the Nuncio Aleander writes that, five years before he had mentioned to Pope Leo his dread of a German uprising, he had heard from many Germans that they were only waiting for some fool to open his mouth against Rome.

If Germany was thus the predestined scene of the outbreak, it was also the land in which the chances of success were the greatest.  The very political condition which baffled all attempts at self-protection likewise barred the way to the suppression of the movement.  A single prince, like the Elector Frederick of Saxony, could protect it in its infancy.  As the revolt made progress other princes could join it, whether moved by religious considerations, or by way of maintaining the allegiance of their subjects, or in order to seize the temporalities and pious foundations, or, like Albrecht of Brandenburg, to found a principality and a dynasty. We need not here enquire too closely into the motives of which the League of Schmalkalden was the outcome, and may content ourselves with pointing to the fact that even Charles V was, in spite of the victory of Mühlberg, powerless to restore the imperial supremacy or to impose his will on the Protestant States.

The progress of the Reformation, and still more so that of the Counter-Reformation, lie outside the limits of the present chapter; but it may be concluded by a few words suggesting why the abuses which, in the sixteenth century, could only be cured by rending the Church in twain, have to so large an extent disappeared since the Reformation, leading many enthusiasts to feel regret that the venerable ecclesiastical structure was not purified from within—that reform was not adopted in place of schism.

The abuses under which Christendom groaned were too inveterate, too firmly entrenched, and too profitable to be removed by any but the sternest and sharpest remedies. The task was too great even for papal omnipotence. The attempt of Adrian VI had broken down. In 1555, the future Cardinal Seripando, in announcing to the Bishop of Fiesole the death of Marcellus II, who, in his short pontificate of twenty-two days, had manifested a resolute determination to correct abuses, says that perhaps God, in thus bringing reform so near and then destroying all hope of it, has wished to show that it is not to be the work of human hands and is not to come in the way expected by us, but in some way that we have not been able to conjecture. In truth the slow operation was required of causes for the most part external. So long as the Roman Church held the monopoly of salvation it inevitably followed the practice of all monopolies in exacting all that the market would yield—in obtaining the maximum of power and wealth. When northern Europe had definitely seceded, and a large proportion of the rest of the Continent was trembling in the balance,—when what was lost could not be regained and a strenuous effort was required to save the remainder,—the Church at length recognised that she stood face to face with a permanent competitor, whose rivalry could only be met by her casting off the burdens that impeded her in the struggle. To this the Council of Trent contributed something, and the stern purpose of Pius V, followed at intervals by other pontiffs, still more. The permanent supremacy of Spain in Italy checked the aspirations of the Holy See towards enlarging its temporal dominions. The chief source of cause of advance, however, is the action of the secular princes who sustained the cause of the Church during a century of religious wars. The Reformation had emancipated their power as well as the

44—2

spirit of Protestantism. If the Church required their support she must yield to their exigencies; she could no longer claim to decide peremptorily and without appeal as to the boundary-line between the spiritual and the temporal authority in the dominions of each of them; and she could no longer shield her criminals from their justice. Together with the progress of the Reformation, a phase of absolute monarchy had developed itself through which the European nations passed, and the enforcement of the *regalia* put an end to a large part of the grievances which had caused the Church of the fifteenth century to be so fiercely hated. Whether or not the populations were benefited by the change of masters, the Church was no longer responsible; and for the loss of her temporal authority and the final secularisation of her temporalities she has found recompense tenfold in the renewed vigour of her spiritual vitality.

# BIBLIOGRAPHIES.

## CHAPTERS I AND II.

### THE AGE OF DISCOVERY AND THE NEW WORLD.

#### I. COLLECTIONS OF DOCUMENTS, TEXTS AND PAPERS.

Academia Real das Sciencias (Lisbon).  Collecção de Monumentos Ineditos para la Historia das Conquistas dos Portugueses.  1858, etc.
—— Collecção de Opusculos Reimpresos relativos á Historia das Navegações, Viagens, e Conquistas dos Portugueses.  1844–58.
—— Conferencias acerca dos Descobrimentos dos Portuguezes na Africa.  1877, etc.
—— Torre do Tombo, Alguns Documentos do Archivo National da.  1892.
Academia Real de la Historia (Madrid).  Documentos Ineditos relativos al Descubrimiento, Conquista, y Organizacion de las antiguas Posesiones de Ultramar.  1885, etc.
Aguiar y Acuña, R. de.  Recopilacion de las Leyes de los Reynos de las Indias.  Mexico.  1677.
American Anthropologist.  Washington.  1888–98.
—— New Series.  1899.
American Antiquarian.  Cleveland, etc.  1878, etc.
American Ethnological Society.  Transactions.  New York.  1845, etc.
Américanistes, Congrès International des.  Comptes Rendus.  Europe.  1875, etc.
Angelis, P. de.  Obras y Documentos relativos á la Historia de las Provincias del Rio de la Plata.  Buenos Aires.  1836–7.
Barcia, A. G. de.  Historiadores de las Indias Occidentales.  Madrid.  1749.
Biblioteca de los Americanistas.  Madrid.  1882–5.
Bry, J. T. de.  Collectiones Peregrinantium.  Frankfort.  1590–1634.
Cartas de Indias.  Madrid.  1877.
Coleccion de Libros Raros o Curiosos que tratan de America.  Madrid.  1891–7.
Espada, M. J. de la.  Relaciones Historicas de Indias.  Madrid.  1881.
Fracanzo, M.  Paesi novamente Retrovati.  Vicenza.  1507.
Gama Quatercentenary, Commission for Celebration of.  Various Publications.  Lisbon.  1897, etc.
Hakluyt, R.  Principal Navigations, Voyages, and Discoveries, etc.  London.  1589; 1599–1600.
Hakluyt Society.  Publications.  London.  1848, etc.  Vols. II. VII. XXI. XXX. XXXIII. XXXIV. XL. XLI. XLII. XLV. XLVII. XLVIII. LIII. LV. LX. LXI. LXII. LXVIII. LXIX. LXXXVI. XC. XCV. XCVIII. XCIX. C.

Icazbalceta, J. G. de.  Documentos para la Historia de Mexico.  Mexico.  1852–7.
——— Nueva Coleccion.  Mexico.  1858–70.
Jomard, E. F.  Monuments de la Géographie.  Paris.  1854–6.
Kingsborough, Viscount, and Aglio, A.  Antiquities of Mexico.  London.  1831–48.
Mexico, Anales del Museo Nacional de.  Mexico.  1877–97.
Mexico, Junta Colombina de.  Antiguedades Mexicanas.  Mexico.  Ed. A. Chavero.
    1892.
Navarrete, M. F. de, and others.  Coleccion de Documentos Ineditos para la
    Historia de España.  Madrid.  1842, etc.
——— Coleccion de Viajes y Descubrimientos.  Madrid.  1825–37.
Cardenas, J. F. Pacheco de, Mendoza, Torres de, and others.  Documentos Ineditos
    relativos al Descubrimiento, Conquista y Colonizacion de las Posesiones Espa-
    ñolas.  Madrid.  1864–84.
Peabody Museum (Cambridge, Massachusetts), Reports of.  1868, etc.
Peñafiel, A.  Codice Fernandez-Leal.  Mexico.  1895.
Ramusio, G. B.  Navigationi et Viaggi.  Venice.  1554–65.
Rio de Janeiro, Museo Nacional de.  Archivos.
Smith, B.  Documentos para la Historia de la Florida.  1857.
Smithsonian Institution.  Reports of the Bureau of Ethnology.  Washington,
    Columbia.  1881, etc.
Ternaux-Compans, H.  Voyages, Relations, et Mémoires Originaux pour servir à
    l'Histoire de la Découverte de l'Amérique.  Paris.  1837–41.
Vedia, E. de.  Historiadores de Indias.  In Ariban's Biblioteca.  Madrid.  1852–3.
Vera, F. H.  Coleccion de Documentos Eclesiasticos de Mexico.  Amecameca.  1887.


## II.  EARLIER HISTORIES, MEMOIRS, AND TREATISES.

Acosta, J.  De Procuranda Indorum Salute.  1596.
——— Historia Natural y Moral de las Indias.  Seville.  1590.
Albuquerque, A. de.  Commentarios.  Lisbon.  1557.
Angleria, Peter Martyr de.  De Orbe Novo Decades Octo.  Alcalà.  1530.
——— Opus Epistolarum.  Alcalà.  1530.
Argensola, B. L. de.  Conquista de las Islas Molucas.  Madrid.  1609.
Arriaga, P. J. de.  Extirpacion de la Idolatria del Piru.  Lima.  1621.
Azurara.  See Zurara.
Bandini, A. M.  Vita e Lettere di A. Vespucci.  Florence.  1745.
Barcia, A. G.  (Cardenas y Cano, G. de.)  Ensayo Cronologico para la Historia de
    la Florida.  1723.
Barros, J. de, y Couto, D. de.  Decadas da Asia.  Lisbon.  1552–1636.
Benzoni, G.  La Historia del Mondo Nuevo.  Venice.  1565.
Bernaldez, A.  Historia de los Reyes Catolicos.  Seville.  1870.
Betanzos, J. de.  Suma y Narracion de los Incas.  Madrid.  1880.
Bienewitz, P.  (Apianus.)  Cosmographicus Liber.  Antwerp.  1529.
Bremen, Adam of.  Libellus de Situ Daniae.  Leyden.  1629.
Bustamante, C. M. de.  Cronica Mexicana Tesamoxtli.  Mexico.  1821–2.
Calancha, F. A. de.  Cronica Moralizada del Orden de San Augustin en el Peru.
    Barcelona.  1638.
Casas, B. de Las.  Brevissima Relacion de la Destruccion de las Indias.  Seville.
    1552.  (And other pamphlets.)
——— Historia Apologetica.  In Coleccion de Documentos Ineditos para la Historia
    de España.  Madrid.  1876.

Casas, B. de Las. Historia de las Indias. In Coleccion de Documentos Ineditos para la Historia de España. Madrid. 1875–6.

Castillo, Bernal Diaz del. Conquista de la Nueva España. Madrid. 1632.

Chimalpahin, D. de S. A. Annals. Ed. R. Siméon. Paris. 1889.

Cieza de Leon, P. Cronica del Peru. Parte I. Seville. 1553. Parte II. Madrid. 1880.

Clemente, C. Tablas Cronologicas. Valencia. 1689.

Cobo, B. Historia del Nuevo Mundo. Ed. de la Espada. Seville. 1890–6.

Colden, C. History of the Five Nations. New York. 1727.

Colombo, C. Autografos y Papeles de America. Ed. Duquesa de Berwick y de Alba. Madrid. 1892.

—— Scritti publicati ed illustrati da C. de Lollis. Reale Commissione Colombiana. Rome. 1892–4.

Colombo, F. Historie. Venice. 1571.

Cordeyro, A. Historia Insulana. Lisbon Occidental. 1717.

Cortés, Hernan. Cartas de Relacion. 1522–5.

Duran, D. Historia de las Indias de Nueva España. Ed. Ramirez. Mexico. 1867–80.

Eden, R. Decades of the New World, etc. London. 1555. Reprinted by E. Arber (The First Three English Books on America). Birmingham. 1885.

Edrisi. Geography. Translated by P. A. Jaubert. Paris. 1836.

Esmeraldo. De Situ Orbis. Ed. R. E. de Azevedo Basto. Lisbon. 1892.

Faria-y-Sousa, M. Asia Portuguesa. Lisbon. 1666–75.

Fernandez, D. Historia del Peru. Seville. 1571.

Four Elements, the. In W. C. Hazlitt's edition of Dodsley's Old Plays. Vol. I. London. 1874.

Galvão, A. Descubrimentos Antigos e Modernos. Lisbon. 1563.

Gama, V. da. Roteiro (da Viagem que fez em 1497). Ed. D. Kopke e A. da Costa Paiva. Oporto. 1838.

Goes, Damião de. Chronica del Rei Dom Emanuel. Lisbon. 1566.

—— Chronica del Rei João II. Lisbon. 1567. (And other works.)

Gómara, F. L. de. Conquista de México. Saragossa. 1552.

—— Historia de las Indias. Saragossa. 1552.

Gomez, D. De Prima Inventione Guineae. Ed. Schmeller. 1845.

Guzman, L. de. Historia de las Missiones de la Compania de Jesus en la India Oriental. Alcalà. 1601.

Herrera Tordesillas, A. de. Historia General (1492–1554). Madrid. 1601–15.

Ibn Batuta. Travels. Translated by S. Lee. London. 1829.

Jovius, P. Historiae sui Temporis. Florence. 1550–2.

La Croze, V. Histoire du Christianisme des Indes. The Hague. 1724.

Léry, J. de. Histoire d'un Voyage faict en la Terre du Brésil. La Rochelle. 1578.

Lescarbot, M. Histoire de la Nouvelle France. Paris. 1609.

Lopez de Castanheda, F. Descobrimento e Conquista da India pelos Portugueses. Coimbra. 1552–61.

Mendieta, G. de. Historia Ecclesiastica Indiana (1596). Mexico. 1870.

Morisot, C. B. Orbis Maritimi Historia. Dijon. 1643.

Motolinia, T. de. Historia de los Indios de Nueva España. Mexico. 1858.

Muñoz Camargo, D. Historia de Tlascala. Ed. A. Chavero. Mexico. 1892.

Münster, S. Cosmographia. Basel. 1544.

Munzer, H. De Inventione Africae Maritimae. Ed. F. Kunstmann. 1854.

Oliva, A. Histoire du Pérou. Ed. H. Ternaux-Compans. Paris. 1857.

Osorius, H. De rebus Emmanuelis R. Lusitaniae...gestis. Lisbon. 1571.

Oviedo y Valdes, G. F. de. Historia General de las Indias. Venice. 1534. Also 1851–5.

Pereira, J. de Solorzano.　De Indiarum Jure.　Madrid.　1629.
——　Politica Indiana.　Antwerp.　1703.
Piedrahita, F. de.　Historia de las Conquistas del Nuevo Reyno de Granada.　Antwerp.　1688.　Also Bogota.　1881.
Pigafetta, A.　Primo Viaggio intorno al Globo.　Ed. Amoretti.　Milan.　1800.
Pizarro y Orellana, F.　Varones Illustres del Nuevo Mundo.　Madrid.　1639.
Politianus, A.　Opera.　Basel.　1553.
Polo, Marco.　Liber de Consuetudinibus et Conditionibus Orientalium Regionum.　Antwerp.　1485 (?).　Trans. by H. Yule.　London.　1871.
Rafn, C. C.　Antiguedades Americanas.　Havana.　1845.
Resende, G. de.　Chronica del Rey Dom João II.　Lisbon.　1622.
Sahagun, B. de.　Historia General de Nueva España.　Ed. Bustamante.　Mexico.　1829-30.
Salcamayhua, J. de S. P.　Relacion...del Piru.　1613?.　See Espada, M. J. de la.
Santillan, F. de.　Relacion...de los Incas.　1572.　See Espada, M. J. de la.
Sepulveda, J. G. de.　Opera Omnia.　Cologne.　1602.
Simon, P.　Conquistas de Tierra Firme.　Cuenza.　1627.
Solis, A. de.　Conquista de Mexico.　1684.
Sousa, L. de.　Annaes de el Rei Dom João III.　Ed. A. Herculano.　Lisbon.　1844.
Tevius, J.　Opuscula.　Paris.　1762.
Tezozomoc, H. A.　Cronica Mexicana (1598).　Ed. Orozco y Berra.　Mexico.　1878.
Toledo, F. de.　Relacion Sumaria.　Ed. De la Espada.　Madrid.　1884.
Torfaeus, T.　Historia Vinlandiae Antiquae.　Copenhagen.　1705.
Torquemada, J. de.　Monarchia Indiana.　Madrid.　1723.
Vega, G. de la.　Commentarios Reales.　Lisbon.　1608.
——　Historia General del Peru.　Madrid.　1723.
——　La Florida del Inca.　Madrid.　1723.
Vetancurt, A. de.　Teatro Mexicano.　Mexico.　1697-98.
Walzemüller, M.　(Hylacomylus.)　Cosmographiae Introductio.　Strassburg.　1509.
Wyrcestre, William of.　Itinerarium.　Cambridge.　1778.
Xeres, F. de.　Conquista del Peru.　Salamanca.　1547.
Zarate, A. de.　Descubrimiento y Conquista del Peru.　Seville.　1577.
Zurara, G. E. de.　Chronica do Descobrimento e Conquista de Guiné.　Ed. Santarem.　Paris.　1841.

## III.  MODERN WORKS.

Acosta, Joaquin.　Compendio Historico del Descubrimiento y Colonisacion de la Nueva Granada.　Paris.　1848.
Alcedo, A. de.　Diccionario Geografico-historico de las Indias Occidentales o America.　5 vols.　Madrid.　1786-9.
Alves, A.　Dom Henrique o Infante.　Oporto.　1894.
Anderson, A.　Historical and Chronological Deduction of the Origin of Commerce.　Ed. W. Combe.　4 vols.　London.　1787-9.
Avalos, F. A. de Christophoro d'.　Essai sur le Commerce et les Intérêts de l'Espagne et de ses Colonies.　Paris.　1819.
Avézac-Macaya, M. A. P. d'.　Découvertes dans l'Océan Atlantique.　Paris.　1845.
——　Martin Hylacomylus Waltzemüller.　Paris.　1867.
Bancroft, H. H.　The Native Races of the Pacific States of North America.　New York.　1875.
——　The Pacific States of North America.　San Francisco.　1882.
Bandelier, A. F.　Archaeological Tour in Mexico.　Boston.　1885.
Barradas, M.　O Infante D. Henrique.　Lisbon.　1894.

Bastian, A. Die Culturländer des alten America's. 3 vols. Berlin. 1888.

Beazley, C. R. The Dawn of Modern Geography. 2 vols. London. 1897.

—— John and Sebastian Cabot. In Builders of Greater Britain Series. 1898.

—— Prince Henry the Navigator. In Heroes of the Nations Series. 1890.

Becher, A. B. The Landfall of Columbus. London. 1856.

Biddle, R. Memoir of Sebastian Cabot. London. 1831.

Brehm, R. B. Das Inka-Reich. Jena. 1885.

Brinton, D. G. Ancient Nahuatl Poetry. 1887.

—— The American Race. New York. 1891.

—— Essays of an Americanist. Philadelphia. 1890. (And other publications.)

Brühl, G. Die Culturvölker Alt-Amerikas. St Louis. 1877–87.

Bunbury, E. H. History of Ancient Geography. 2 vols. London. 1879.

(Burke, E.) Essay towards a History of the Commerce of the Several Nations of
Europe to the East-Indies. In Dodsley's History of the East-Indies. Vol. ii.
1757.

—— Account of European Settlements in America. London. 1757.

Canale, M. G. Storia del Commercio, dei Viaggi, etc., degl' Italiani. Genoa.
1866.

—— Nuova Istoria della Rep. di Genova. 4 vols. Florence. 1858–64.

—— Vita e Viaggi di C. Colombo. Florence. 1863.

Charnay, D. Ancient Cities of the New World. London and New York. 1887.

Church, G. E. Costa Rica. Geographical Journal. 1897.

—— Presidential Address, British Association, Geographical Section, 1898.

Clavigero, F. S. Storia Antica del Messico. Cesena. 1780–1.

Cooley, W. D. History of Maritime and Inland Discovery. Lardner's Cabinet
Cyclopaedia. London. 1830.

Cronau, R. Amerika; die Geschichte seiner Entdeckung. 2 vols. Leipzig. 1892.

Danvers, F. C. The Portuguese in India. London. 1894.

Döllinger, J. J. I. von. Fables respecting the Popes of the Middle Ages.
(Transl. by A. Plummer.) London. 1871.

Echevarria y Veytia, F. de. Historia Antigua de Mejico. Mexico. 1836.

Fiske, J. The Discovery of America. 1892.

Forster, J. R. Geschichte der Entdeckungen und Schifffahrten im Norden.
Frankfort a. d. O. 1785.

Gaffarel, P. Histoire de la Découverte de l'Amérique. Paris. 1892.

Grasset, E. Cuarto Centenario del Descubrimiento de America. (Organo oficial
de la Exposicion Internacional de Madrid.) 1893.

Gravier, G. Découverte de l'Amérique par les Normands. Rouen. 1874.

Gravière, J. P. A. J. de la. Les Marins du xv. et du xvi. Siècle. Paris. 1879.

Haebler, C. Amerika. In Weltgeschichte, herausg. von H. F. Helmolt. Eng.
Transl. vol. i. London. 1899.

Harrisse, H. Bibliotheca Americana Vetustissima. New York. 1866. Additions.
Paris. 1872.

—— Christophe Colomb. Paris. 1884.

—— Jean et Sébastien Cabot. Paris. 1882.

—— John Cabot the Discoverer of North America. London. 1896.

—— The Diplomatic History of America. London. 1897.

—— The Discovery of North America. A critical, documentary and historic
investigation. London. 1892.

Hélie, A. Discours sur l'Histoire Moderne des Deux Mondes. 2 vols. Paris.
1854.

Humboldt, A. von. Histoire de la Géographie du Nouveau Continent. Paris.
1836–39.

—— Vues des Cordilleras. 2 vols. Paris. 1816.

Jal, A.   Archéologie Navale.   2 vols.   Paris.   1840.

Jourdain, C. M. G. B.   Influence d'Aristote et de ses Interprètes sur la Découverte du Nouveau-monde.   Paris.   1861.

Kohler, J.   Das Recht der Azteken.   1892.

Kretschmer, K.   Die Entdeckung Amerikas.   Berlin.   1892.

Kunstmann, F.   Die Entdeckung Amerikas.   Munich.   1859.

——— Die Kenntniss Indiens im xv. Jahrhunderte.   Munich.   1863.

Lacroix.   Pérou.   In L'Univers.   Paris.   1843.

Larenaudière, P. F. de.   Mexique et Guatemala.   In L'Univers.   Paris.   1843.

Lelewel, J.   Histoire de la Géographie au Moyen-âge.   Brussels.   1852–7.

Major, R. H.   Life of Prince Henry of Portugal.   London.   1868.

Marin, C. A.   Storia del Commercio de' Veneziani.   8 vols.   Venice.   1798–1808.

Markham, Sir C. R.   Life of Christopher Columbus.   London.   1892.

——— Cuzco and Lima.   London.   1856.

——— History of Peru.   Chicago.   1892.

——— Peru.   In Foreign Countries Series.   London.   1880.   And other publications.

Martins, J. P. O.   Os Filhos de Dom João I.   Lisbon.   1891.

——— Navegaciones y Descubrimientos de los Portugueses anteriores al Viage de Colon.   Madrid.   1892.

Mayer, B.   Mexico, Aztec, Spanish, and Republican.   2 vols.   Hartford.   1853.

Molina, G. I.   Saggio sulla Storia Civile del Chili.   Bologna.   1787.

Monte y Tejada, A. del.   Historia de Santo Domingo.   Havana.   1853.

Morgan, L. H.   League of the Iroquois.   Rochester, N.Y.   1851.

——— Ancient Society.   New York.   1877.

——— Houses and House-life of the American Aborigines.   1881.

Morton, S. G.   Crania Americana.   Philadelphia.   1839.

Müller, J. G.   Geschichte der Amerikanischen Urreligionen.   1855.

Muñoz, J. B.   Historia del Nuevo-Mundo.   Madrid.   1793.

Nadaillac, Marquis de.   Prehistoric America.   Trans. by N. d'Anvers.   London.   1885.

Navarrete, M. F. de.   Opusculos.   Madrid.   1848.

Orbigny, A. D. d'.   L'Homme Américain.   Paris.   1839.

——— Voyage Pittoresque dans les Deux Amériques.   Paris.   1836.

Orozco y Berra, M.   Geografia de las Lenguas de Mexico.   Mexico.   1864.

——— Historia Antigua y de la Conquista de Mexico.   Mexico.   1880.

Payne, E. J.   History of the New World called America.   Oxford.   1892–9.

——— Voyages of the Elizabethan Seamen to America.   Oxford.   1893–1900.

Peet, S. D.   Prehistoric America.   Animal Mounds.   Chicago.   1890.

Peñafiel, A. de.   Nombres Geograficos de Mexico.   Mexico.   1885.

——— Monumentos del Arte Mexicano Antiguo.   3 vols.   Berlin.   1890.

Peragallo, P.   Cristoforo Colombo in Portogallo.   Genoa.   1882.

Peralta, M. M. de.   Costa Rica, Nicaragua y Panama en el Siglo xvi.   Madrid.   1883.

Pertz, G. H.   Der aelteste Versuch zur Entdeckung des Seewegs nach Ostindien.   1859.

Peschel, O. F.   Abhandlungen zur Erd- und Völkerkunde.   Ed. Löwenberg.   Leipzig.   1877.

——— Geschichte des Zeitalters der Entdeckungen.   Stuttgart and Augsburg.   1858.

——— Geschichte der Erdkunde.   Munich.   1878.

——— Völkerkunde.   Leipzig.   1875.

Pimentel, F.   Cuadro de las Lenguas Indigenas de Mexico.   Mexico.   1874–5.

Prescott, W. H.   History of the Conquest of Mexico.   London.   1843.

Prescott, W. H.   History of the Conquest of Peru.   London.   1847.

Quintana, M. J.   Lives of Balboa and Pizarro.   Trans. by Mrs Hodson.   Edinburgh.   1832.

Reynoso, A.   Agricultura de los Indigenas de Cuba y Haiti.   1881.

Rio Branco, Baron de.   Esquisse de l'Histoire du Brésil.   Paris.   1889.

Roa Barcena, J. M.   Historia Anecdotica de Mexico.   Mexico.   1862.

Robertson, W.   Historical Disquisition concerning the Knowledge which the Ancients had of India.   London.   1791.

—— History of America.   London.   1777–96.

Santarem, M. F., Visconde de.   Essai sur l'Histoire de la Cosmographie.   Paris.   1849–52.

—— Recherches sur Vespuce et ses Voyages.   Paris.   1842.

Sapper, C.   Das Nördliche Mittel-Amerika.   Brunswick.   1897.

Scherer, H.   Allgemeine Geschichte des Welthandels.   Leipzig.   1852.

Schoolcraft, H. R.   Archives of Aboriginal Knowledge.   Philadelphia.   1860.

Shaler, N. S.   Nature and Man in America.   Cambridge, Mass.   1892.

Southey, R.   History of Brazil.   London.   1810.

Souza Holstein, Marquez de.   A Escola de Sagres.   Lisbon.   1877.

Squier, E. G.   Peru: Incidents of Travel and Exploration.   London.   1877.

Squier, E. G. and Davis, E. H.   Ancient Monuments of the Mississippi Valley.   New York.   1848.

Steffen, M.   Die Landwirthschaft bei den Altamerikanischen Kulturvölkern.   Leipzig.   1883.

Stephens, H. M.   The Story of Portugal.   Story of the Nations Series.   1891.

St Martin, Vivien de.   Histoire de la Géographie.   Paris.   1873.

Tschudi, J. J. von.   Organismus der Khetschua-Sprache.   Leipzig.   1884.   (And other works.)

Tylor, E. B.   Anahuac.   London.   1861.   (And other works.)

Uzielli, G.   La Vita e i Tempi di P. dal P. Toscanelli.   Rome.   1894.

Varnhagen, F. A. de.   Historia General do Brazil.   Madrid.   1854–7.

—— Amerigo Vespucci.   Lima.   1865.

Winsor, J.   Narrative and Critical History of America.   8 vols.   London and Cambridge, Mass.   1886–9.

# CHAPTER III.

## THE OTTOMAN CONQUEST.

### I. DOCUMENTS.

#### (ORIGINAL AUTHORITIES OF ALL KINDS.)

Alberi, E.   Relazioni degli Stati Ottomani.   Vol. I.   1840.   Vol. III.   Florence. 1855.

Albinus.   De gestis regum Neapolitanorum ab Aragonia (1495).   Naples.   1588.

Angiolello, G. M.   Breve narrationi della Vita et Fatti del Signor Ussuncassano. In Ramusio's Viaggi.   Vol. II.   Venice.   1574.

Annius [Nanni de Viterbo].   De futuris Christianorum triumphis in Turcos et Saracenos.   Nürnberg.   1480.

[Anonymus Albanensis, used by] Biemmi, Istoria di Giorgio Castriota.   Brescia. 1742.

[Aubusson, P. d'.]   Epistola ad Papam de Obsidione insulae Rhodus [sic] a Turcis [1480].   In Ludewig's Reliquiae Manuscriptorum.   v.   Frankfort, etc.   1723.

Behem, M.   Chronik.   In Quellen und Forschungen zur vaterländischen Geschichte, Litteratur und Kunst.   1849.

Bembo, P. (Card.).   Lettere.   4 vols.   Venice.   1552–75.

Bogdan, I.   Cronice inedite atting. de istoria Romînilor.   Bucharest.   1895.

—— Vechile cronice moldovenesci pana la Urechia.   Bucharest.   1891.

Bosio, G.   Istoria della Sacra Religione et Militia di San Giovanni Gierosolimitano. Vol. II.   Rome.   1594.

Breviarium rerum gestarum Turcarum et Sophi Persarum imperatoris de anno 1514. 1514.

Caoursin and Khodgia Afendy.   The History of the Turkish War with the Rhodians, Venetians, Egyptians, Persians and other nations.   1683.

Cepione, C. (Cippicus).   De Petri Mocenici imperatoris gestis.   1544.   (Italian version in Sathas, Documents, vol. VII. pp. 262 sqq.)

Chalcocondylas, L.   Historia de rebus Turcicis.   Ed. I. Bekker.   Bks VIII.—x.   In Byzantin. Hist. Scriptores.   Bonn.   1843.

Charrière, E.   Négotiations de la France dans le Levant.   In Collection des documents inédits.   Ser. I.   Vol. I.   Paris.   1850.

[Costin.]   Une Histoire inédite de la Moldavie (described by Hase).   In Notices et extraits des manuscrits de la Bibliothèque du Roi.   XI.   1827.

[Damaskenos Studites.]   Historia Politica Constantinopoleos.   In M. Crusius, Turco-Graecia, pp. 1 sqq.   Basel.   1584.

[Damaskenos Studites, not Manuel Malaxas.]   Patriarchica Constantinopoleos Historia.   In Crusius, ib. pp. 107 sqq.

Ducas. Historia Byzantina. Chaps. 42—45. In Byzantin. Hist. Script. Vol. xxi. Bonn. 1834.

Ekthesis Chronikê. In Sathas, Bibl. Graeca medii aevi. vii. pp. 557 sqq. Venice. 1894.

Esarcu, C. Stefanu cellu Mare. Bucharest. 1874.

Filelfus, F. Epistolare. s.l. 1495.

Gévay, A. Urkunden und Actenstücke zur Geschichte der Verhältnisse zwischen Österreich-Ungarn und der Pforte. Vol. i. Vienna. 1838.

Gobellinus, J. Pii Secundi Commentarii. 1614.

Hadji-Khalifa. History of the Maritime Wars of the Turks, tr. by J. Mitchell. London. 1831.

Katona, I. Historia critica Regum Hungariae stirpis mixtae. Vols. vii.—xii. Buda-Pest, etc. 1792–3.

—— Historia critica Regum Hungariae stirpis Austriacae. Vol. i. (Vols. xiii.— xx. of the collective work.) Buda-Pest, etc. 1792–3.

Kemal Pasha. History of the Campaign of Mohács; (*a*) Turkish, with French transl. by Pavet de Courteille, Paris, 1859; (*b*) in Thúry's Török történetírók, in Hungarian transl., vol. i. Pest.

Konstantinović. History (ili ljetopisi turski). In Glasnik srp. uč. druzhtva. xviii. (pp. 1—188). 1865.

Koronaios, T. Ἀνδραγαθήματα Μερκουρίου Μπούα. In Sathas, Ἑλληνικὰ ἀνέκδοτα. i. pp. 4 sqq. Venice. 1867.

Kritobulos. History. In Mueller's Fragmenta Historicorum Graecorum. Vol. v., Part 2. Paris. 1870.

Lamansky, V. I. Secrets d'état de Venise. St Petersburg. 1884.

Lanz, K. Correspondenz des Kaisers Karl V. Vol. i. Leipzig. 1844.

Leunclavius [and Spiegel]. Annales Sultanorum Othmanidarum. Frankfort. 1596.

Lonicerus, P. Chronica Turcica. 3 vols. Frankfort a. M. 1578.

Magyar diplomacziai emlékek Mátyás király korából, 1458–90. i.—iv. 1875–8.

Magyar történelmi okmánytár. Vols. i. and v. 1857 and 9.

Makushev, V. Monum. histor. Slavorum meridionalium. i. ii. Warsaw. 1874, 1885.

Malipiero, D. Annali Veneti dell' anno 1457 al 1500. In Archivio storico Italiano. vii. 1843–4.

Manfredo Repeta. Extracts from Chronicle of (1464–89). By D. Bortolani. Vicenza. 1887.

Matthias Corvinus. Letters (ed. Fraknói). In Monumenta Vaticana Hungariae historiam illustrantia. Series i. Vol. vi. Pest. 1891.

Miklosich, F. Monumenta Serbica. Vienna. 1858.

Miklosich, F. and Müller, J. Acta et diplomata Graeca medii aevi. 3 vols. 1860, etc.

Müller. Documenti sulle Relazioni delle città Toscane coll' Oriente Cristiano e coi Turchi. 1879.

Novaković, S. Odlomak Srpskoga Ljetopisa. In Starine of the South Slavonic Academy. vi. pp. 19 sqq. Agram. 1874.

Paoli, S. Codice diplom. del sacro militare ordine Gerosolimitano. Lucca. 1737.

Phrantzes, G. Chronicle. Bk iv. Bonn. 1838.

Piccolomineus, Jacobus (Cardinalis Papiensis). Commentarii et epistolae. Appended to Gobellinus, pp. 348 sqq. 1614.

(Pius II.) Aeneas Sylvius Piccolomini. Epistolae. Opera, pp. 500 sqq. 1571.

—— Opera inedita. Ed. Cugnoni. In Atti della R. Accademia dei Lincei. Series iii. Vol. viii. pp. 319–686. 1883.

Rački, F. Dubrovački Spomenici. In Starine of the South Slavonic Academy. vi. pp. 1 sqq. Agram. 1874.

Raynaldus, O. Annales Ecclesiastici. Vols. xviii. xix. xx. Cologne. 1694, etc.

Relazione della presa di Otranto. In Archivio storico per le provincie Napolitane. VI. fasc. 1, pp. 74—162 and 169—176. Naples. 1880.

Rizzardo, J. La presa di Negroponte. Ed. Cicogna. Venice. 1844.

Sa'd ad-Din:

   (1) Chronica, Ital. transl. by Bratutti. Vol. I. Vienna, 1649. Vol. II. Madrid, 1652;

   (2) Annali Ottomanici, Part I. (to death of Selim), translated by Podestà: (*a*) German, with Turkish text facing. Nürnberg. 1671. (*b*) Italian and Latin. Vienna and Nürnberg. 1672;

   (3) [Parts relating to Hungarian history] in Hungarian transl. by Thúry. *See below.*

Sacy, Baron S. de. Pièces diplomatiques (from Archives of Genoa). In Notices et extraits des manuscrits de la Bibliothèque du Roi. XI. 1827.

Sanuto, Marino (1) I diarii. Vols. I. etc. 1879–80, etc. (2) Parts relating to Hungary, to end of Bk 42 (1526). In the Magyar történelmi Tár. Vols. XIV. XXIV. XXV. Pest. 1869, 1877–8.

Sathas, C. N. Documents inédits. Vols. I. IV. VI. VII. IX. 1880, etc.

Schafárik. Acta Archivi Veneti spectantia ad historiam Serborum et reliquorum Slavorum meridionalium. II. 1862.

Schwandtner, J. G. Scriptores rerum Hungaricarum. 3 vols. Vienna. 1746–8.

Servian Annals. (*a*) Ed. Jagić. In Archiv für slavische Philologie. II. Berlin. 1880. (*b*) Ed. Bogdan. Ib. XIII. 1891.

Șincai, G. Chronica Românilor. Bucharest. 1886.

Spandugino Cantacusino. Della Origine dei principi Turchi. In Sansovino's Historia Universale. 1564. And in Sathas, Documents. Vol. IX.

Sulayman, Sultan. Diary of his Hungarian campaigns; translated in (*a*) Hammer's Histoire de l'empire ottoman, notes to vol. V.; (*b*) Thúry's Török történetírók, vol. I. (as above).

Teleki, Count J. Hunyadiak kora Magyarországon. Vol. X. 1853. Vol. XI. Pest. 1855.

Theiner, A. Vetera monumenta Slavorum meridionalium Historiam illustrantia. I. Rome. 1863. II. Agram. 1875.

Török történetírók. Hungarian translations by J. Thúry. In Török magyarkori történelmi emlékek (of the Magyar Academy). Series II. Vols. I. and II. Pest. 1893, 1896.

Tractatus quidam de Turcis prout ad presens Ecclesia Sancta ab eis affligatur. 1481.

Urechi, G. Chronique de Moldavie (with Fr. tr. by Picot). Paris. 1878.

—— Documente istorice. 1878.

Zinkeisen, J. W. Drei Denkschriften über die orientalische Frage von Pabst Leo X, König Franz I, und Kaiser Maximilian I (1517). Gotha. 1854.

It should be noted that Hammer has used a large number of oriental sources which have never been printed. A French translation of Sa'd ad-Din's history by A. Galland lies in manuscript in the Bibliothèque Nationale, and has been consulted by several French writers. Feridun's collection of Turkish state papers has been printed at Constantinople in two volumes (1848–9), but is not in the British Museum. Angiolello's Historia turchesca (from 1429 to 1513) lies unpublished in the Bibliothèque Nationale (fonds ital. no. 1238). Only extracts have been published from Percichi's Le quattro incursioni dei Turchi nel Friuli, which must be consulted at Padua.

The publication of the rich stores of the archives of Ragusa, well begun by Rački, has been less well continued by Gelcich (Monumenta Ragusina, vols. III. IV. 1895–6); but vol. IV. comes down only to 1396. Thus it will be some time before our period is reached.

## II. GENERAL HISTORIES.

### A. Of the Ottomans.

Cantemir, D.   History of the Growth and Decay of the Ottoman empire [tr. by N. Tindal].   1734.

Esprinchard, J.   Histoire des Ottomans.   Paris.   1609.

Hammer-Purgstall, Baron J. von.   Geschichte des osmanischen Reiches.   I. II. Pest.   1834.

Knolles, R.   The generall Historie of the Turkes.   London.   1603.

La Jonquière, Vicomte A. de.   Histoire de l'Empire ottoman.   1881.

Leunclavius, J.   Historia Musulmana Turcorum.   Frankfort.   1591.

Mignot, V.   Histoire de l'empire Ottoman.   I.   Paris.   1771.

Poole, S. Lane.   Turkey.   London.   1886.

Sagredo, G.   History of the Ottoman Empire [French tr. by M. Laurent].   I. II. Paris.   1732.

Sansovino, F.   Historia Universale dell' Origine et Imperio de' Turchi.   Venice. 1560.

Zinkeisen, J. W.   Geschichte des osmanischen Reiches in Europa.   I. II. III. Gesch. d. europ. Staaten.   Gotha.   1854–5.

### B. Of other Lands.

Andrić, A.   Geschichte des Fürstentums Montenegro.   Vienna.   1853.

Coquelle, P.   Histoire du Monténégro et de la Bosnie.   Paris.   1895.

Engel, J. C. von.   Geschichte von Serwien und Bosnien.   Halle.   1801.

——   Geschichte des Freystaats Ragusa.   Vienna.   1809.

Fallmerayer, J. P.   Geschichte des Kaisertums Trapezunt.   Munich.   1829.

——   Geschichte der Halbinsel Morea.   2 vols.   Stuttgart.   1830–6.

Finlay, G.   History of Greece.   Ed. H. F. Tozer.   v.   Oxford.   1877.

Gopčević, S.   Montenegro und die Montenegriner.   Leipzig.   1877.

Gregorovius, F.   Geschichte der Stadt Athen im Mittelalter.   II.   Stuttgart.   1889.

Hopf, K. H.   Geschichte Griechenlands.   In Ersch und Gruber's Encyklopädie. Vol. LXXXVI.   1868.

Horváth, M.   Geschichte der Ungarn (tr. from Hungarian).   I.   Pest.   1851.

Klaić, V.   Geschichte Bosniens.   Leipzig.   1885.

Lebedev, A. P.   Istoriya greko-vostochnoi tserkvi pod vlastiyu turok ot padeniya Konstantinopolya do nastoyashchago vremeni.   I.   Moscow.   1896.

Malcolm, Sir J.   History of Persia.   II.   London.   1815.

Mendelssohn-Bartholdy, C.   Geschichte Griechenlands.   I.   Leipzig.   1870.

Nakko, A. K.   Histoire de la Bessarabie.   2 vols.   1876.

Romanin, S.   Storia documentata di Venezia.   VI.   Venice.   1858.

Szalay, L.   Geschichte Ungarns (tr. from Hungarian).   I.   Pest and Vienna.   1866.

Vertot, Abbé de.   Histoire des Chevaliers Hospitaliers de St Jean de Jérusalem. II. and III.   Paris.   1726.   [English translation, 1728.]

Xénopol, A. D.   Histoire des Roumains.   Translated.   I.   Paris.   1896.

## III.  AUXILIARY WORKS.

### On Ottoman Institutions, etc.

Baudier, M.　Histoire générale du Serrail et de la Cour de l'Empereur des Turcs. 2 vols.　Paris.　1624.　Eng. tr. by Grimeston.　1735.

Belin, F. A.　Du Régime des Fiefs militaires dans l'Islamisme et particulièrement en Turquie.　Paris.　1870.

—— Histoire de la Latinité de Constantinople.　2nd ed.　Paris.　1894.

Djevad-Bey (Ahmad-Jawad).　État militaire ottoman (Fr. tr. by G. Macrides). Paris.　1882.

Gycaud.　De la généalogie du Grand-Turc et la dignité des officiers et ordre de sa Cour...　1570.

Hammer-Purgstall, Baron J. von.　Staatsverwaltung des osmanischen Reiches. 2 vols.　Vienna.　1815.

Lacroix, de.　État général de l'Empire ottoman, par un solitaire Turc.　(French tr.) 3 vols.　Paris.　1695.

Libellus de moribus conditionibus et nequitia Turcorum [by a Christian captive] (appended to Ricoldus de Monte Crucis, Contra sectam mahumeticam libellus...).　1511.

Marsigli, L. F.　L'état militaire de l'Empire Ottoman (in French and Italian).　The Hague.　1732.

Ohsson, I. de.　Tableau général de l'Empire Ottoman.　3 vols.　Paris.　1787–1820.

Postel, G.　De la république des Turcs et des mœurs et loys de tous Muhademistes. Poitiers.　1560.

Ranke, L. von.　Die Osmanen etc. im 16ten und 17ten Jahrhundert.　4th ed. Vol. xxxv. of Sämmtliche Werke.　Leipzig.　1874, etc.

Rycaut, Sir P.　The present state of the Ottoman Empire, containing the maxims of the Turkish politie...　London.　1668.

Saint-Maurice.　La cour othomane ou l'interprète de la Porte.　1673.

## IV.  MONOGRAPHS, ETC.

Asbóth, J.　Official tour through Bosnia and Herzegovina.　London.　1890.

Bain, R. N.　Siege of Belgrade by Muhammad II.　English Historical Review. vii. pp. 235 sqq.　1892.

Berchet, G.　La republica di Venezia e la Persia.　Turin.　1863.

Biancus.　Vita G. Castrioti.　1636.

Bonhours.　Histoire de Pierre d'Aubusson.　1676.

Cataneo, T.　Vita di S. Giovanni da Capistrano.　Parma.　1691.

Chassin, C. L.　Jean de Hunyad.　In La Hongrie, son génie et sa mission, pp. 223 sqq.　Paris.　1856.

Cornet, E.　Le guerre dei Veneti nell' Asia (1470–4).　Vienna.　1856.

[Ferrari, Antonio de].　Successi dell' Armata Turchesca nella città d' Otranto dall' anno mccclxxx.　1612.

Fincati, L.　La deplorabile Battaglia Navale del Zonchio (1490).　Rivista maritima, fasc. 2, pp. 185 sqq.　1883.　[See also appendix thereto by Cecchetti.　Archivio Veneto.　xxv., fasc. 50, pp. 415 sqq.]

Fraknói, V. (Frankl).　Carvajal bibornok magyarországi követségei.　Pest.　1889.

—— Mathias Corvinus.　(German transl.)　Freiburg i. B.　1891.

Grigorović, V. I.  O Serbii v eya obnosheniyach k sosyednim derzavam v xiv. i xv. stolyetiyach.  1859.

Guérard, P.  S. Jean de Capistran et son temps.  Bourges.  1865.

Guillet de Saint-George, G.  Histoire du Règne de Mahomet II, empereur des Turcs.  2 vols.  Paris.  1681.

Hammer-Purgstall, Baron J. von.  Mémoire sur les premières relations diplomatiques entre la France et la Porte.  In the Journal Asiatique.  Paris.  1825.

—— Wiens erste aufgehobene türkische Belagerung.  Pest.  1829.

Hermann.  Capistrano triumphans.  1700.

Hopf, K. H.  Veneto-byzantinische Analekten.  1860.

Kabdebo, H.  Bibliographie zur Geschichte der beiden Türkenbelagerungen Wien's 1529 und 1683.  Vienna.  1876.

Kiss, K.  Hunyadi János utolsó hadjárata.  Pest.  1857.

Kupelwieser, L.  Die Kämpfe Ungarns mit den Osmanen.  Vienna.  1895.

Levec.  Die Einfälle der Türken in Krain und Istrien.  1891.

Makushev, V.  Istoricheskiya razyskaniya o slavyanach v Albanii.  1871.

Manfroni, C.  Storia della Marina Italiana della caduta di Costantinopoli alla battaglia di Lepanto.  Livorno.  1897.

Marion.  François Ier et Soliman le Grand.  1853.

Meldeman.  Rundansicht der Stadt Wien während der Türkenbelagerung im Jahre 1529.  1863.

Musoni.  Sulle incursioni dei Turchi in Friuli.  (3 pamphlets.)  1890–2.

Paganel, C.  Histoire de Scanderbeg.  Paris.  1855.

Pisko, J.  Skanderbeg.  Vienna.  1894.

Pontanus z Praitenberka, J. B.  Historia G. Castrioti.  Hanover.  1609.

Rački, F.  Bogomili i Patareni.  Rad of the South Slavonic Academy.  vii. pp. 84—179.  viii. pp. 121—87.  x. pp. 160—263.  Agram.  1869–70.

Rosmini, C. de.  Vita di Francesco Filelfo.  Milan.  1808.

Sathas, C. N.  Τουρκοκρατουμένη Ἑλλάς.  Athens.  1869.

Sauli, L.  Della colonia dei Genovesi in Galata.  Turin.  1831.

Tercier, C. A. de.  Mémoire sur la Prise de Rhodes.  In the Mémoires de l'Académie des Inscriptions.  xxvi.  Paris.  1759.

Thuasne, L.  Djem-Sultan.  Paris.  1892.

—— Gentile Bellini et Sultan Mohammed II.  Paris.  1888.

Torr, C.  Rhodes in modern times.  Cambridge.  1887.

Valentinelli, G.  Esposizione di Rapporti fra la republica Veneta e gli Slavi meridionali.  Venice.  1863.

Vast, H.  Le Cardinal Bessarion.  Paris.  1878.

Vlastos, Χιακά.  ii.  1840.

Voigt, G.  Enea Silvio de' Piccolomini als Papst Pius der Zweite und sein Zeitalter.  3 vols.  Berlin.  1856–63.

—— Johannes Capistranus.  Historische Zeitschrift.  x.  1863.

Zeller, Jean.  Quae primae fuerint legationes a Francisco Imo in orientem missae.  Paris.  1881.

# CHAPTER IV.

## ITALY AND HER INVADERS.

*(For a bibliography of the historical literature dealing with this period, very full within its limits, see* Pastor, Geschichte der Päpste, vol. III.)

### I. CONTEMPORARY CHRONICLES, MEMOIRS, AND PRINTED HISTORICAL DOCUMENTS.

*(For further indications on the contemporary authorities for this period, see* Potthast, Bibliotheca Historica Medii Aevi, Berlin, 1895-6.
*See also Bibliographies of Chapters V. VI. VII. VIII. XII. in this Volume.)*

#### A. FLORENCE.

Buonaccorsi, B.   Diario de' successi più importanti seguiti in Italia e…in Fiorenza, 1498-1512.   Florence.   1568.
Guicciardini, F.   Opere inedite.   10 vols.   Florence.   1857-67.
Landucci, L.   Diario Fiorentino, 1450-1516.   Ib.   1883.
Macchiavelli, N.   Arte di guerra.   Vol. IV. of edition "Italia.   1813."
—— Historie Fiorentine (fragments).   Ed. Passerini and Milanesi.   Vol. II.
—— Legazioni e Commisarie.   Ed. Passerini and Milanesi.   In Opere di N. M. III. IV.   Florence and Rome.   1874.
Nardi, J.   Istorie della Città di Firenze.   Ed. Gelli.   2 vols.   Florence.   1858.
Scala, B.   Historia Fiorentina.   In Graevius, Antiq. Ital. VIII. I.
Vettori, F.   Sommario dell' istoria d' Italia, 1511-27.   Arch. Stor. Ital. App. VI. B, pp. 261—387.

#### B. FRANCE.

*See also* G. Monod.   Bibliographie de l'Histoire de France.   Paris.   1888.

Arcuate, J. F. de.   Memorabilia in Adventu Caroli VIII in Ital.   Rome.   1514.
Auton, J. d'.   Chronique de Louis XII.   Ed. R. Maulde la Clavière.   Soc. hist. Fr. Paris.   1890 sqq.
Bayard, Histoire du Chevalier.   Par le loyal serviteur.   Soc. hist. Fr.   Paris.   1878.
Bouchet, J.   Panégyrique du Chevalier sans reproches (Louis de la Trémouille). Coll. Michaud et Poujoulat, vol. IV.
Champier, S.   Les grans Croniques des…ducs et princes de Savoye et Piémont. Paris.   1516.

Champier, S.   Les gestes ensemble la vie du Preulx Chev. Bayard.   In Cimber and Danjou, Archives Curieuses.   Ser. I. vol. II.

Desjardins, A.   Négotiations diplomatiques de la France avec la Toscane.   Documents inédits.   XXXVI.   Vols. I. and II.   Paris.   1859–61.

Ferronus, A.   De rebus gestis Gallorum libri IX.   Paris.   1550.

Fleurange, R. de.   Mémoires (1501–21).   Collection Michaud et Poujoulat.   Vol. V.

Gilles, N.   Les tres élegantes et copieuses Annales des modérateurs des belliqueuses Gaules.   (History of Louis XII.)   Paris.   1534, etc.

La Vigne, A. de.   Extrait de l'histoire du Voyage de Naples du roy Charles VIII, 1494–5.   In D. Godefroy, Hist. de Charles VIII.   No. 3.

——   Vergier d'Honneur de l'entreprise et voyage de Naples.   In Cimber and Danjou, Archives Curieuses.   Ser. I. vol. I.   Paris.   1834.

Le Grand.   Lettres de Charles VIII concernant la Bataille de Rapallo.   Bibl. Ec. des Chartes, LV. p. 143.

Louis XII.   Lettres de Louis XII et du Cardinal d'Amboise.   4 vols.   Brussels. 1712.

Pélissier, L. G.   Documents sur la première année de Louis XII.   Paris.   1890.

——   Un régistre de Lettres missives de Louis XII.   Rome.   1891.

Villeneuve, G. de.   Mémoires (1494–6).   Collection Michaud et Poujoulat.   Vol. IV.

## C.   Milan.

Ambrogio da Paullo, P.   Cronaca Milanese, 1476–1515.   Misc. di Storia Ital. XIII.

Argellati, F.   Bibliotheca scriptorum Mediolanensium.   2 vols.   Milan.   1745.

Burigozzo, G. M.   Cronaca Milanese, 1500–44.   In Arch. Stor. Ital. III.   1842.

Cagnola, G. P.   Cronaca Milanese, 1023–1497.   In Arch. Stor. Ital. III.   1842.

Corio, B.   Storia di Milano—1500.   Ed. E. de Magri.   3 vols.   Milan.   1855–7.

Florus, G. (of Milan).   De bello Italico et rebus Gallorum praeclare gestis.   In Burmanni Thesaurus Antiquit. Italic. IX. and D. Godefroy, Histoire de Charles VIII, p. 216.

Grumello, A.   Cronaca Pavese, 1467–1529.   In Raccolta di cronisti e documenti storici Lombardi inediti.   Ed. Müller.   Milan.   1856.

Muraltus, F. (of Como).   Annalia, 1492–1519.   Ed. Dominius.   Ib.   1861.

Odovici, F.   Il processo dei congiurati Bresciani, 1512.   Published in Raccolta di cronisti etc. Lombardi inediti.   Vol. II.   Ib.   1857.

Osio, L.   Documenti diplomatici tratti dagli archivi Milanesi, e coordinati p. c. L. Osio et C. Cantu.   Ib.   1864.

Pélissier, L. G.   Analyse de 3 régistres de lettres ducales de Louis XII à Milan. Bulletin du Comité des travaux historiques.   Paris.   1892.

——   Inventaire des Régistres Panigarola et du Gridario generale de l' archivio di Stato di Milano, 1499–1513.   Revue bibliograph.   1895–7.

——   Lettres inédites sur la Conquête du Milanais par Louis XII.   Atti della reale Accademia delle Scienze di Torino, XXIX.   1893–4.

——   Trois régistres de lettres ducales de Louis XII aux Archives de Milan. Paris.   1892.

——   Trois relations sur la situation de la France, 1498–9.   (L. Sforza to the Duke of Ferrara.)   Montpellier.   1894.

Prato, G. A.   Cronaca Milanese, 1499–1519.   In Arch. Stor. Ital. III.   1842.

## D. Naples.

Albini, J.  De gestis regum Neapol. ab Aragonia...—1495...sive de Caroli VIII... expeditione in regnum Neapolit.  Naples.  1588.

Caracciolo, T.  Opuscula historica.  Muratori, Script. xxii.

Chronicon anon. Neap. 1434–1506.  In Pratilli, Historia princip. Langobard. iv. p. 132.

Giornali Napoletani.  Muratori, Script. xxi.

Jovius, P.  Vitae illustrium virorum ; Elogia virorum illustrium ; Historiae sui temporis (to the death of Francis I).  Basel.  1577.

Notar, Giacomo.  Cronica di Napoli.  Ed. Garzelli.  Naples.  1845.

Passero, G.  Journal of Naples.  Naples.  1785.

Pelliccia, A. A.  Raccolta di varie Chroniche appartenenti alla storia del Regno di Napoli.  Vol. i.  1780.

Pulgar, H. P. del.  Crónica del Gran Capitan don Gonzalo de Cordoba.  Sevilla. 1527.  Ed. Martinez de la Rosa.  Madrid.  1834.

Pulgar, H. del.  Crónica llamada las dos conquistas dal reyno de Napoles.  Saragossa.  1559.

Trinchera, F.  Codice Aragonese ossia lettere regie, ordinamenti etc. dei sovrani Aragonesi in Napoli.  Naples.  1866.

Volpicella, G. G.  Diurnali.  Ed. Scipione Volpicella.  Ib.  1846.

Volpicella, S.  Regis Ferdinandi I instructionum liber.  Ib.  1861.

—— Collezione di opere inedite o rare di storia Neapolitana.  Ib.  1859.

## E. Rome.

Burcardus, J.  Diarium, sive rerum urbanarum Commentarii, 1483–1506.  Ed. Thuasne.  3 vols.  Paris.  1883–5.

Fabroni, A.  Vita Leonis X.  Pisa.  1797.

Giustiniani, A.  Dispacci (from Rome to Venice), 1502–5.  Ed. Villari.  Florence. 1876.

Gottlob, A.  Aus der Camera apostolica des xvten Jahrhunderts.  Innsbruck.  1889.

Infessura, L.  Diario della Città di Roma.  Ed. O. Tommasini for Istituto Storico Italiano.  1890.

Paris de Grassis.  Diary (during the Papacy of Leo X).  Ed. M. Armellini.  Rome. 1884.

Pélissier, L. G.  Alcuni documenti relativi all' Alleanza d' Alessandro VI e Luigi XII.  Arch. Storico Romano.  Società Romana di stor. patria, xvii. p. 303. 1894–5.

Sigismondo dei Conti da Foligno.  Le Storie dei suoi tempi 1475–1510.  2 vols. Rome.  1883.

Volaterranus, R.  Commentariorum urbanorum libri 38.  Ib.  1506, etc.

—— Historia de vita quattuor pontificum (Sixtus IV, Innocent VIII, Alexander VI, Pius III).  1511.

## F. Venice.

Alberi, E.  Relazioni degli ambasciatori Veneti al Senato.  Series i. 1, 4, 6. Series ii. 3.  Florence.  1846–62.

Arluni, B.  De bello Veneto Libri vi.  In Graevius, Thesaurus Antiquitatum. Tom. v.

Bembus, P. (Card.). Historiae Venetae libri xii. 1486–1513. Venice. 1551. Milan. 1809, etc.

Benedetti, A. Diarium de bello Carolino, 1495. Venice, 1496. In Eccard Corp. hist. medii aevi, ii. pp. 1577–1628.

Cronache Veneziane Antichissime. Ed. G. Monticolo. Fonti per la St. d' Italia, Ser. i. No. 9, etc. Istituto Storico Italiano.

Cordo, B. La obsidione di Padua, 1509. Ed. A. Medin. Bologna. 1892.

Malipiero, P. Annali Veneti. Arch. Stor. Ital., Ser. i. vol. vii.

Mas Latrie, le Comte L. de. Commerce et expéditions militaires de France et de Venise au Moyen Âge. Doc. inéd., 2nd series, Mélanges historiques. 1846.

Mocenigo, A. Bellum Cameracense. In Graevius, Thesaurus Antiquitatum. Vol. v.

Navagero, A. Historia Veneta to 1498. Muratori, Script. xxiii.

Pacantius, A. B. Diaria de bello Carolino. Venice. 1496.

Porto, L. da. Lettere Storiche, 1509–8. Ed. B. Bessan. Florence. 1857.

Sanuto, M. Commentarius de Bello Gallico, 1494–1500. Muratori, Script. xxiv.

Sanuto, M. Diari, 1496–1533. 58 vols. Venice. 1879, etc.

## G. Miscellaneous.

Alfani, T. Memorie Perugine, 1502–27. Arch. Stor. Ital. xvi. 2. 1851.

Allegretto Allegretti. Ephemerides Senenses, 1450–96. In Muratori, vol. xxiii.

Anshelm, V. Berner Chronik. Bern. 1825–33. 6 vols. Also Bern. 1884.

Bernouilli, A. Eine Schweizerische Chronik, 1499–1516. Anzeiger für Schweiz. Gesch. 6.

Bianchi, Jacopino and Tommasino dei. Cronaca Modenese, 1469–1554. In Monumenti di storia patria delle provincie Modenesi. Cronache. Vol. i. Parma. 1861.

Carpesan, F. (Parma). Commentaria sui temporis (1470–1526). Martène, Collectio Amplissima. Vol. v.

Chmel, J. Briefe und Actenstücke der Herzoge von Mailand von 1451–1513. Notizenblatt of the Academy of Vienna. vi. 1856.

——— Urkunden, etc. zur Gesch. Maximilians I. u. seiner Zeit. Bibl. d. lit. Ver. x. Stuttgart. 1845.

Coccinius, M. (Köchlin). De rebus gestis in Italia, 1511 et 1512. In Freher, Germ. rer. script. ii.

Cronaca di Genova, 1507. In Atti della Società Ligure di Storia patria. x. Genoa. 1874.

Cyrnaeus. Historia insulae Corsicae, 1506. In Muratori, Script. xxiv. pp. 413—506.

Diarium Ferrariense, 1409–1502. Muratori, Script. xxiv. pp. 143—408.

Donatus, H. Oratio ad Caesarem pro re Christiana. Venice. 1501.

Du Mont, J. Corps universel diplomatique du Droit des Gens. Amsterdam. 1726.

Foscari, F. Dispacci al senato Veneto presso l' imperatore Massimiliano, 1496. Arch. Stor. Ital. vii. 2, pp. 723—948.

Gaddi, Agnolo and Francesco. In Arch. Stor. Ital. iv. 1844.

Guicciardini, F. Storia d' Italia. 4 vols. Milan. 1884.

Le Glay, R. Correspondance de l'empereur Maximilien et de Marguerite d'Autriche, 1507–19. 2 vols. Paris. 1839.

——— Négotiations diplomatiques entre la France et l'Autriche, 1501—30. Collection des documents inédits. xliv. 2 vols. Ib. 1845.

Lettres de Charles VIII, Louis XII et François I aux communes de Gènes et de Florence. Coll. des doc. inédits. viii. Vol. i.

Matarazzo, F.  Cronaca della Città di Perugia, 1492–1503.  Arch. Stor. Ital.  xvi. 2. 1851.

Molini, G.  Documenti di Storia Italiana.  Vol. i.  Florence.  1836.

Morone, G.  Lettere Miscell. di Storia Ital.  ii.

Oricellarius, B. (Rucellai).  Commentarius de Bello Italico.  London.  1724.

Pélissier, L. G.  Documents pour l'histoire de l'établissement de la Domination Française à Gènes 1498.  Genoa.

—— Le Traité d'Alliance de Louis XII et de Philibert de Savoie, 1499.  Mémoires de la section de lettres, Ac. des Sciences et Lettres de Montpellier, Sér. 2. Montpellier.  1893.

Perizolo da Pisa.  Ricordi 1422–1510, in Arch. Stor. Ital. vi. 2, pp. 387—396. 1845.

Petrus Martyr d'Anghiera.  Opus Epistolarum.  Amsterdam.  1670.

Porto Venere, G.  Memoriale come il Re di Francia passa in Italia per aquistare il reame di Napoli.  1494–1502.  Arch. Stor. Ital. vi. 2.

Ricciardi da Pistoia, F.  Ricordi Storici, 1494–1500.  Ed. P. Vigo.  Bologna. 1882.

Ruscelli, G.  Lettere di Principi.  Venice.  1562.

Sadoletus, J.  Epistolae.  Vol. ii.  Rome.  1760.

Saige, M. J. J. G.  Documents historiques relatifs à la Principauté de Monaco depuis le quinzième Siècle.  Monaco.  1888.

Segesser, A. P. von.  Ämtliche Sammlung der alten eidgenössischen Abschiede. Lucerne.  1863.

Senarega, B.  De rebus Genuensibus Commentaria, 1488–1514.  Muratori, Script. xxiv.

Silvestro, T. di.  Diario.  Ed. L. Fumi.  Orvieto.  1891, etc.

Tubero, L.  Commentarii de rebus...in Pannonia et Turcia et finitimis regionibus gestis, 1490–1522.  In Schwandtner, Script. Rer. Hungaricarum. ii.

Zurita, G.  Los annales de la Corona d'Aragon.  Saragossa, 1610–21, etc.

## II.  LATER HISTORICAL WORKS.

### A.  General.

Balan, P.  Storia d' Italia.  Tom. v.  Modena.  1877.

Baschet, A.  La Diplomatie Vénétienne.  Paris.  1862.

Bréquigny, O. F. de.  Histoire des révolutions de Gènes.  1752.

Burckhardt, J.  Die Cultur der Renaissance in Italien.  Basel.  1860.

Busch, W.  England unter den Tudors.  Stuttgart.  1892.

Buser, B.  Beziehungen der Mediceer zu Frankreich, 1434-94.  Leipzig.  1879.

Canale, M. G.  Nuova storia della Republica di Genova.  Florence.  1886.

Canestrini, G.  Della Milizia Italiana del Secolo xiii. al xvi.  Florence?.  1857.

Capponi, G. A. G. G.  Storia del Reame di Napoli.  1846.

Cherrier, C. de.  Histoire de Charles VIII.  2 vols.  Paris.  1868.

Cipolla, C.  Storia delle Signorie Italiane, 1313–1530.  Milan.  1881.

Costanzo, A. di.  Istoria del Regno di Napoli.  3 vols.  Milan.  1805.

Dändliker, C.  Geschichte der Schweiz.  Zurich.  1884–7.

Dierauer, J.  Geschichte der schweiz. Eidgenossenschaft.  (Gesch. d. europ. Staaten.)  Vol. ii.  Gotha.  1892.

Fuchs, I.  Mailändische Feldzüge der Schweizer.  2 vols.  St Gallen.  1810.

Giustiniani, A.  Annali della Republica di Genova.  Genoa.  1854.

Gothein, E.   Culturentwickelung Süd-Italiens.   Breslau.   1886.

Gregorovius, F.   Geschichte der Stadt Rom im Mittelalter.   Vols. vii. and viii.
Stuttgart.   1872.

Hardy, M. J. F. E.   Les Français en Italie.   Paris.   1880.

Havemann, W.   Geschichte der italienisch-französischen Kriege, 1494–1515.
Hanover.   1833.

Heyd, W.   Geschichte des Levantehandels im Mittelalter.   Stuttgart.   1879.
French edition (amplified).   Paris.   1885–6.

Jähns.   Handbuch einer Geschichte des Kriegswesens von der Urzeit bis zur
Renaissance.   Leipzig.   1880.

Lamansky, V.   Secrets d'État de Venise.   St Petersburg.   1884.

Lichnowski, C. M.   Geschichte des Hauses Hapsburg bis zum Tode Maximilians I.
Vienna.   1844.

Maulde la Clavière, R.   La Diplomatie au temps de Machiavel.   3 vols.   Paris.
1892–3.

Pastor, L.   Geschichte der Päpste.   Vol. iii.   2nd ed.   Freiburg i. B.   1891.

Perrens, F. T.   Histoire de Florence.   Paris.   1890.

Perret, P. M.   Histoire des relations de France avec Venise du xiii^e Siècle à
Charles VIII.   2 vols.   Paris.   1896.

Ranke, L. von.   Die römischen Päpste.   Vols. xxxvii.—ix. of Sämmtliche Werke.
Leipzig.   1874, etc.

—— Geschichte der romanischen und germanischen Völker, 1494–1514, 1824.
Vols. xxxiii.–iv. of Sämmtliche Werke.   Leipzig.   1874, etc.

Raumer, F. L. G. von.   Geschichte Europas seit dem Ende des fünfzehnten
Jahrhunderts.   Ib.   1832–50.

Reumont, A. von.   Beiträge zur italienischen Geschichte.   6 vols.   Berlin.
1853–7.

—— Geschichte der Stadt Rom.   Berlin.   1867–70.

Ricotti.   Storia delle Compagnie di Ventura in Italia.   4 vols.   Turin.   1845.

Romanin, S.   Storia documentata di Venezia.   Vol. v.   Venice.   1856.

Rosmini, C.   Dell' istoria di Milano.   4 vols.   Milan.   1820–1.

Ségur, P. de.   Histoire de Charles VIII.   1855.

Sugenheim, S.   Entstehung u. Ausbildung des Kirchenstaates.   Leipzig.   1854.

Symonds, J. A.   Renaissance in Italy.   7 vols.   London.   1875–86.

Ulmann, H.   Kaiser Maximilian I.   2 vols.   Stuttgart.   1884 and 1891.

Vecchi, A. V.   Storia generale della Marina militare.   3 vols.   Leghorn.   1895.

Verri, P.   Storia di Milano.   Florence.   1851, etc.

## B.   Special.

Alvisi, E.   Cesare Borgia.   Imola.   1878.

Brosch, M.   Julius II und die Gründung des Kirchenstaats.   Gotha.   1878.

Cantu, C.   Milano e il suo Territorio.   Milan.   1844.

—— Gli Sforza e Charles VIII.   Arch. Stor. Lombardo xv.   1888.

Carutti, D.   Diplomazia di Savoia.   Turin.   1875.

Cérésole, V.   La république de Venise et les Suisses.   Venice.   1890.

Baldi, B.   Della vita e fatti di Guidobaldo I da Montefeltro, duca d' Urbino.
Libri xii.   2 vols.   Ib.   1821.

Cambi, G.   Historie.   In Delizie degli eruditi Toscani.   Vol. xxi.   Florence.
1785.

Cian, V.   Catarina Sforza.   Turin.   1893.

Delaborde, H. F.  Expédition de Charles VIII en Italie.  Paris.  F. Didot.  1888.

—— Négotiations entre Charles VIII et Ludovico Moro.  Rapport à l'Académie des Inscr. et Belles-Lettres, 1879.

Elgger, C. von.  Das Kriegswesen der schweiz. Eidgenossenschaft im xiv. xv. und xvi. Jahrhundert.  Lucerne.  1873.

Escher, H.  Der Verrat von Novara.  Jahrbuch für schweiz. Gesch. xxi. pp. 71—194.  Zurich.  1897.

Fabretti, A.  Biographie dei Capitani venturieri dell' Umbria.  5 vols.  Montepulciano.  1842–6.

Filippi, G.  Il Convegno in Savona tra Luigi XII e Ferdinando il Cattolico.  Savona. 1890.

Formentini, M.  Il Ducato di Milano.  Milan.  1877.

Fraknói, W.  Ungarn und die Liga von Cambrai, 1509–1511.  Budapest.  1883.

Gisi, W.  Antheil der Eidgenossen an der europ. Politik, 1512–6.  Schaffhausen. 1866.

Giulini, G.  Memorie spettanti alla Storia, al Governo, ed alla Descrizione della Città e della Campagna di Milano ne' secoli bassi.  Milan.  1760.

Gozzadini, G.  Memorie per la vita di Giulio II.  Bologna.  1839.

Höfler, C. A. C. von.  Rodrigo di Borgia.  Vienna.  1888.

Jarry, E.  Les origines de la Domination Française à Gènes.  Paris.  1896.

Kohler, C.  La conquête du Tessin, 1500–3.  Rev. Hist. March and April, 1891.

—— Les Suisses dans les guerres d'Italie.  Mémoires et documents de la Soc. hist. de Genève.  Ser. ii., Vol. iv.  1896.

La Pilorgerie, J. de.  Campagnes et Bulletins de Charles VIII.  Paris.  1866.

Leonetti, A.  Papa Alessandro VI, secondo documenti e cartezzi del tempo.  3 vols. Bologna.  1880.

Leonii, L.  Vita di B. di Alviano.  Todi.  1858.

Luzio, A. and Renier, R.  Relazioni d' Isabelle d' Este ed Elizabetta Gonzaga con Ludovico e Beatrice Sforza.  Arch. Stor. Lombardo.  1890.

—— Mantova e Urbino.  Isabella d' Este ed Elizabetta Gonzaga nelle relazioni famiglieri e nelle vicende politiche.  Turin.  1893.

—— Fr. Gonzaga alla Battaglia di Fornovo, secondo i documenti Mantovani. Florence.  1890.

Maulde la Clavière, R.  Conquête du Tessin par les Suisses.  Turin.  1890.

—— L'Entrevue de Savone, 1507.  Rev. Hist. dipl.  1890.  Also separate.  Paris. 1890.

Mülinen, N. F.  Gesch. der schweizerischen Söldner bis zur Errichtung der ersten stehenden Garde, 1497.  Bern.  1887.

Pasolini dell' Onda, Count.  Caterina Sforza.  3 vols.  Rome.  1893.

Pélissier, L. G.  La politique du Marquis de Mantoue, 1498–1500.  Annales de la Faculté de Lettres de Bordeaux.  1892.

—— La Politique de Trivulce au début du règne de Louis XII.  Revue des Quest. histor. lvi.  Paris.  1894.

—— Louis XII et Ludovic Sforza, 1498–1500.  2 vols.  Bibl. des Écoles Franç. d'Athène et de Rome, fascc. 75—6.  Paris.  1896.

Piollet, A.  Étude sur Geoffroy Carles, Président de Dauphiné et du Sénat de Milan.  Grenoble, 1882.  Anz. für schweiz. Gesch. 1884, pp. 279—82.

Porzio, C.  Congiura dei Baroni del Regno di Napoli.  Rome.  1565, etc.

Ranke, L. von.  Zur Kritik neuerer Geschichtschreiber.  1824.  Vol. xxxiv. of Sämmtliche Werke.  Leipzig.  1874, etc.

Rosmini, C.  Dell' istoria…di J. J. Trivulzio.  Ib.  1815.

Scardovelli, G.  Battaglia di Taro, 1495.  Mantua.  1888.

Schneider, J.  Die kirchliche und politische Wirksamkeit des Legaten Raimond Péraud, 1496–1505.  Halle.  1882.

Thuasne, L.   Djem-Sultan.   Paris.   1892.

—— Texte du traité entre Charles VIII et la République de Florence, 25 Nov. 1494.   Rev. Hist. diplom.   1887.

Ugolini, F.   Storia dei Conti e Duchi d' Urbino.   Florence.   1859.

Ulmann, H.   Kaiser Maximilians Absichten auf den Papstthron in den Jahren 1507–11.   Stuttgart.   1888.

Valentinelli, G.   Esposizione di rapporti fra la Rep. Veneta e gli Slavi meridionali. Venice, 1863.   Vol. I.   (1496–1515.)

Verga, E.   Concessioni fatti da M. Sforza alla Città di Milano, 1515.   Arch. Storico Lombardo, Ann. XXI. (1894), fasc. 4.

Yriarte, C.   César Borgia; sa vie, sa captivité, sa mort.   2 vols.   Paris.   1889.

# CHAPTER V.

## FLORENCE (I): SAVONAROLA.

### I. CONTEMPORARY WORKS AND DOCUMENTS.

#### A. WORKS OF SAVONAROLA.

It would be impossible here to give a bibliography of the numerous early editions of Savonarola's sermons and tracts. Bibliotheca Savonaroliana, the catalogue recently published by L. S. Olschki, of Florence and Venice, will be found useful. The works of Savonarola mentioned here are those recently published and generally accessible.

Poesie di Girolamo Savonarola: ed. by C. Capponi and C. Guasti. Florence. 1862.
Alcune lettere di Frà G. Savonarola: ed. by C. Capponi. Florence. 1858.
Opere di Frà G. Savonarola. Sermons on the First Epistle of St John and on the Psalm Quam bonus. 1845.
Prediche di Frà G. Savonarola. The Sermons of 1496: ed. by G. Baccini. Florence. 1889.
Scelta di Prediche e Scritti di Frà G. Savonarola con nuovi Documenti intorno alla sua Vita (including the Epistola of Frà Placido Cinozzi and the Cronaca di Simone Filipepi). P. Villari and E. Casanova. Florence. 1898.
Trattato circa il Reggimento e Governo della Città di Firenze. 1847.
Œuvres Spirituelles Choisies de Jérôme Savonarola. 3 vols. E. C. Bayonne. Paris. 1879.
Lettere inedite di Frà G. Savonarola. V. Marchese. Arch. Stor. It. App. VIII. 1850.
Il Trionfo della Croce (the Latin and Italian texts): ed. by L. Ferretti. Siena. 1900.
L' ultimo Scritto di Frà Girolamo Savonarola. Il Salmo Miserere mei Deus, commentato in carcere. (Italian translation with Introduction and Notes.) L. Ferretti. Milan. 1901.

#### B. SOME WORKS OF SAVONAROLA'S DISCIPLES.

Bertuccio (Frà Benedetto), Cedrus Libani. Edited by V. Marchese. Arch. Stor. It. App. VII. 1849.
Molti devotissimi Trattati. (Savonarolist pamphlets.) Venice. 1535-8.
Riforma santa et pretiosa. By Domenico Cecchi. 1496. (Extremely rare, but is in the British Museum.)

Benivieni, D.   Dialogo della Verità della Doctrina, etc.   1495 (?).
—— Epistola responsiva, etc.   1496 (?).
—— Tractato in defensione.   1496.
  (These tracts are in the British Museum.)
Lauda per Frà Girolamo Savonarola scritta da uno dei Piagnoni.   1865.


### C.  Contemporary Writers and Documents.

Acciajoli, V.   Vita di Piero Capponi; with documents, including extracts from the
  Priovista of A. and F. Gaddi.   Arch. Stor. It.   Vol. iv. 2.   1853.
Bacci, P.   Due Documenti pistoiesi sopra Frà G. Savonarola.   1894.
Benivieni, G.   Defence of Savonarola to Clement VII.   At close of G. Milanesi's ed.
  of B. Varchi.   Florence.   1858.
Bonaini, F.   Annali del Convento di Sta Caterina di Pisa.   Arch. Stor. It.   vi. ii.
  1845.
Bongi, S.   A letter to the Government of Lucca on the Jews.   Ibid., iii.
Burcardus, J.   Diarium.   Ed. L. Thuasne.   3 vols.   Paris.   1883–5.
Burlamacchi, P.   Vita del P. F. Girolamo Savonarola (first published by D. M. Mansi
  in Addizioni alla Miscellanea del Baluzio).   Lucca.   1761.
Cambi, G.   Istorie.   In Delizie degli eruditi Toscani.   xxi.—xxiii.   Florence.
  1785 sqq.
Cappelli, A.   Frà G. Savonarola e Notizie intorno il suo tempo.   Reprinted from
  Atti e Memorie della R. Deputazione di Storia Patria per le provincie Modenesi
  e Parmensi.   Vol. iv.   Modena.   1869.
Capponi, C.   L' ufficio proprio per Frà G. Savonarola.   Arch. Stor. It.   New
  Series, xii.   1860.
Commines, P. de.   Mémoires.   Paris.   1843.
Conti, A.   A narrative of the Ordeal.   Arch. Stor. It.   3rd Series, xiii.   1871.
—— The Controversy with the Franciscans.   Ibid.
Conti, Sigismondo de'.   Le Storie de' suoi tempi dal 1475 al 1510.   Rome.   1883.
Desjardins, A.   Négociations diplomatiques de la France avec la Toscane.   Vols. i.
  and ii.   Paris.   1859–61.
Gherardi, A.   Nuovi Documenti e Studi intorno a Girolamo Savonarola.   2nd ed.
  Florence.   1887.   (An invaluable collection of documents critically examined,
  with a bibliography.)
Giustiniani, A.   Dispacci.   Ed. P. Villari.   3 vols.   Florence.   1876.
Guasti, C.   Il Savonarola ed i Lucchesi.   Nuovi documenti.   1862.   (A reprint
  from Giornale Storico degli Archivi Toscani.   vi.)
Guicciardini, F.   Storia Fiorentina.   Opere inedite, iii.
—— Del Reggimento di Firenze.   Opere inedite, ii.
—— Various writings.   Opere inedite, x.
—— Storia d' Italia, i.
Landucci, L.   Diario Fiorentino dal 1450 al 1516.   Florence.   1883.
Lungo, I. del.   Documents on the Excommunication, and the letters of the
  Milanese envoys Somenzi and Tranchedino.   Arch. Stor. It.   New Series,
  xviii. i. and ii.   1863.
—— Canzona d' un Piagnone pel Bruciamento delle Vanità, etc.   Florence.   1864.
Lupi, C.   Pratiche and other documents.   Arch. Stor. It.   3rd Series, iii. i.   1866.
—— Pisan documents.   Arch. Stor. It.   3rd Series, xiii.   1871.
Machiavelli, N.   Il Principe, ed. L. A. Burd.   Oxford.   1891.   (For passages from
  Machiavelli's works relating to Savonarola, see Appendix i.)
Nardi, J.   Istoria della Città di Firenze.   Florence.   1838.

Nerli, F.　Commentari.　Augsburg.　1728.

Passerini, L.　Reports of trials of Frà Domenico and Frà Silvestro and Apologia di Marsilio Ficino.　Giornale Storico degli Archivi Toscani.　Vols. ii. and iii. 1858 and 59.

Pico della Mirandola, G. F.　Vita R. P. Fr. Hieronymi Savonarolae.　Ed. by J. Quétif. 3 vols.　Paris.　1874.　(Vol. iii. contains Savonarola's letters.)

Pitti, J.　Istoria Fiorentina dal 1215 al 1529.　Arch. Stor. It.　Vol. i.　1842.

—— Apologia de' Cappucci.　Arch. Stor. It.　Vol. iv. 2.　1853.

—— Vita di A. Giacomini Tebalducci.　Arch. Stor. It.　Vol. iv. 2.　1853.

Politianus, A.　Epistolae Jacopo Antiquario.　Book iv.　May, 1492.　(As to Savonarola and the death of L. de' Medici.)

Portioli, A.　Nuovi documenti su G. Savonarola.　Arch. Stor. Lomb. i. iii.　1874.

Renier, R.　I Sonetti del Pistoia.　1889.　(A passage representing the "Temperance" influence of Savonarola.)

Rinuccini, A.　Ricordi Storici dal 1460.　Florence.　1840.

Rossi, T.　Ricordanze.　In Delizie degli eruditi Toscani.　xxiii.　1785, etc.

Sanuto, Marino.　I Diarii.　Venice.　1879– .

—— La Spedizione di Carlo VIII in Italia.　Venice.　1883.

Tizio, S.　An extract from the Sienese Chronicler, by G. Rondoni.　Arch. Stor. Ital.　5th Series, ii.　1888.

Vaglienti, P., Fr. G. Savonarola giudicato da.　By L. Randi.　Florence.　1893. (Extracts from the chronicler relating to Savonarola.)

Cerretani, B.　Storia Fiorentina.　MS.　Bibliotheca Nazionale, Florence.

Parenti, P.　Storia Fiorentina.　MS.　Bibliotheca Nazionale, Florence.

> (These two manuscripts have not been printed, but have been much utilised. Parenti is of the highest value.)

> *For Documents see also* Villari; Meier; Ranke; Cittadella; Bayonne; Luotto (*below*).

## II.　LATER WRITINGS.

*(Certain of these are included less for their intrinsic importance than as representing different schools of opinion.)*

Ammirato, S.　Istorie Fiorentine.　Part ii.　Florence.　1641.

Armstrong, E.　English Historical Review.　iv.　1889.

Athenaeum.　Jan. 19, 1889.

"Anon."　The Irish Rosary.　June to October, 1898.

Barry, W.　Saint Peter's.　June, 1898.

Bayonne, E. C.　Étude sur Jérome Savonarole d'après de nouveaux documents. Paris.　1879.

Bollettino Bimensale per le Onoranze Cattoliche del P. G. Savonarola.　Ed. by Magri.　Borgo S. Lorenzo.　1898.

Brosch, M.　Zur Savonarola-Kontroverse.　Deutsche Zeitsch. für Geschichtswissenschaft.　January, 1898.

Burckhardt, J.　Cultur der Renaissance in Italien.　Vol. ii.　Leipzig.　1877–8.

Burr, G. L.　American Historical Review.　1896.

Canestrini, G.　La Scienza e l' Arte di Stato.　Florence.　1862.

Capponi, G.　Storia di Firenze.　Vol. iii.　Florence.　1875.

Cipolla, C.　Frà G. Savonarola e la Costituzione Veneta.　Arch. Ven.　1874.

Cittadella, L. N.   La nobile famiglia Savonarola in Padova ed in Ferrara.   Ferrara. 1867.

Civiltà Cattolica, La.   November, 1897.

Comba, E.   I nostri Protestanti avanti la Riforma.   Florence.   1895.

Cosci, A.   G. Savonarola e i nuovi Documenti.   Arch. Stor. Ital.   Fourth Series. iv.   1879.

Creighton, M. (Bishop).   History of the Papacy.   Vol. iii.   London.   1887.

Danne, E.   Jérome Savonarole prédicateur.   (A thesis for Faculty of Protestant Theology at Paris.)   1894.

Delaborde, H. F.   L'Expédition de Charles VIII en Italie.   Paris.   1888.

Döllinger, J. J. I. von.   Der Weissagungsglaube und das Prophetenthum in der christlichen Zeit.   In Riehl's Hist. Taschenbuch.   1871.   Also in Döllinger's Kleinere Schriften, ed. by F. H. Rensch.   Stuttgart.   1890.

Ferretti, L.   Per la Causa di Frà G. Savonarola Fatti e Testimonianze.   Milan.   1897.

Frantz, E.   Sixtus IV und die Republik Florenz.   Ratisbon.   1880.

—— Fra Bartolomeo della Porta.   Ratisbon.   1879.

Galassi, L. M.   Girolamo Savonarola.   Fu egli vittima del Clericalismo?   1898.

Gaspary, B.   Geschichte der ital. Literatur.   Vol. ii.   Berlin.   1888.

Gebhart, E.   L'Italie mystique.   Paris.   1890.

Giannotti, D.   Della Repubblica Fiorentina libri iv.   1722.

Giorgetti, A. and Baretti, C.   Savonarola e la critica tedesca.   (Italian translation of articles cited by H. Grauert, J. Schnitzer, M. Brosch and "Spectator": with Preface by P. Villari and Introduction by F. Tocco.)   Florence.   1900.

Glossner, M.   Savonarola als Apologet und Philosoph.   Paderborn.   1898.

Goetz, W.   Deutsche Zeitsch. für Geschichtswissenschaft.   April, 1898.

Grauert, H.   Wissenschaftliche Beilage zur Germania.   June 3, 1898.

Gregorovius, F.   Geschichte der Stadt Rom.   Vol. vii.   Stuttgart.   1894.

Grisar, H.   Zeitsch. für kath. Theologie.   iv.   1880.

Gruyer, A.   Les illustrations des écrits de Jérome Savonarole.   Paris.   1879.

Guicciardini, F. de'.   Profezie politiche e religiose di Frà H. Savonarola ricavate dalle sue Prediche.   Florence.   1863.

Hardy, G. Mᶜ.   Girolamo Savonarola.   (The World's Epoch Makers.)   Edinburgh. 1901.

Hartwig, O.   Hist. Zeitschr.   Vol. lxiv.   1890.

Hase, K.   Neue Propheten.   ii.   Leipzig.   1861.

Hergenröther, J. (Card.)   Conciliengeschichte.   Vol. viii.   Freiburg i. B.   1887.

Höfler, C. von.   Die romanische Welt und ihr Verhältniss zu den Reformideen des Mittelalters.   Vienna.   1878.

Horsburgh, E. L. S.   Girolamo Savonarola.   (Little Biographies.)   London.   1901.

Lottini, G.   Fu veramente scommunicato il Savonarola?   Milan.   1898.

Lucas, H.   Fra Girolamo Savonarola.   London.   1899.

Luotto, P.   Il vero Savonarola ed il Savonarola di L. Pastor.   (Includes copious extracts from Savonarola's sermons.)   Florence.   1897.

Manen, G.   Essai sur Jérome Savonarole d'après sa prédication.   1897.   (A thesis for the Faculty of Protestant Theology at Montauban.)

Marchese, V.   Storia del Convento di San Marco in Scritti varii.   3rd edition. Florence.   1892.

Meier, K.   Girolamo Savonarola.   Berlin.   1836.   (Contains numerous documents.)

Michael, E.   Zeitschr. für kath. Theol.   ii.   1898.

Monnet, A.   Jérome Savonarole jugé par sa Réforme.   1880.   (A thesis for Faculty of Protestant Theology at Montauban.)

Müntz, E.   Revue bleue.   December, 1896.

Newman, J. H. (Card.)   On the Mission of S. Philip Neri.   Sermons preached on various occasions.   1870.

Pagnini. Della Decima. Vol. ɪ. Lisbon and Lucca. 1765–6.

Pastor, L. Geschichte der Päpste. Vol. ɪɪɪ. English translation. Vol. v. London. 1898.

—— Zur Beurtheilung Savonarola's. Freiburg i. B. 1898. (An answer to P. Luotto; *see above.*)

Pélissier, L. G. Louis XII et Ludovic Sforza. 1897.

Pellegrini, F. Arch. della R. Soc. Rom. xɪ. 1887.

—— Giorn. Stor. della Letteratura Ital. x. xɪɪ.

Perrens, F. T. Histoire de Florence. Vol. ɪɪ. Paris. 1888.

—— Jérome Savonarole, sa vie, ses prédications, ses écrits. 2 vols. Paris. 1856.

—— Révue Historique. 1888.

Piccolo Messaggiere, il, per il 4° centenario di Frà G. Savonarola. No. 6. May, 1898.

Pometti, F. Nuova Antologia. June, 1898.

Procter, J. The Dominican Savonarola and the Reformation. A reply to Dean Farrar. 1895.

Ranke, L. von. Savonarola und die florentinische Republik. In Historisch-bio-graphische Studien. (Containing extracts from Parenti and Cerretani.) Vols. xʟ. and xʟɪ. of Sämmtliche Werke. Leipzig. 1874, etc.

Reumont, A. von. Lorenzo de' Medici. Eng. transl. Vol. ɪɪ. London. 1876.

Rohr, J. Die Prophetie im letzten Jahrhundert vor der Reformation. Hist. Jahrbuch xɪx. 1, 3. 1898.

Rondoni, G. Arch. Stor. Ital. Ser. v. ɪ. 1888.

Rudelbach, A. G. Hieronymus Savonarola und seine Zeit. Hamburg. 1855.

Saturday Review. Jan. 26, 1889.

Schnitzer, J. Savonarola im Lichte der neuesten Literatur.

—— Historisch-politische Blätter für das katholische Deutschland. Vol. cxxɪ. 1898. Vol. cxxv. 1900.

Sickinger, C. Savonarola, sein Leben und seine Zeit. In Katholische Studien, Jahrg. ɪɪɪ. 1877.

"Spectator." Allgemeine Zeitung, Beilage, November 2, 1898.

Tocco, F. La Vita italiana nel Rinascimento. Vol. ɪɪ. Milan. 1893.

Tommasini, O. La Vita e gli Scritti di Niccolò Machiavelli. Turin. 1883.

Villari, P. Arch. Stor. It. Ser. v. ɪ. 1899.

—— Girolamo Savonarola e l' ora presente: a speech in celebration of the cen-tenary. Rivista d' Italia. No. 7. Also separately printed.

—— La Storia di G. Savonarola. 2 vols. Florence. 1887. (Contains a large number of rare or unpublished documents.) Translation, Linda Villari. (Con-tains some additions, but omits the documents.) London. 1890.

—— On the early Biographies. Rivista Stor. Ital. No. ɪ. 1884.

—— Reply to Pellegrini. Arch. Stor. Ital. Ser. v. ɪ. 1888.

—— Reply to Perrens. Révue Historique. 1888.

Zardo, A. La Tirannide secondo il Savonarola e l' Alfieri. Rassegna Nazionale. ʟxxxɪɪɪ.

Ziegler, H. Savonarola, ein Vorläufer der Reformation. Berlin. 1870.

# CHAPTER VI.

## FLORENCE (II): MACHIAVELLI.

### A. COLLECTIVE EDITIONS OF MACHIAVELLI'S WORKS.

Tutte le opere di Nicolo Machiavelli Cittadino et Secretario Fiorentino, divise in V. parti, et di nuovo con somma accuratezza ristampate. 1550. The first Testina edition: the imprint "In Geneva, Presso Pietro Chouet" was added by hand after the printing of the work. This is the earliest edition of the collected works. It contains neither the Legazioni, nor the Lettere Familiari.

Opere di Niccolò Machiavelli: Italia, 1813. 8 vols. The least incomplete of all the editions; it was issued by Piatti of Florence: the preparation of the text was superintended by Reginaldo Tanzini and Francesco Tassi.

Opere di Niccolò Machiavelli, per cura di L. Passerini e G. Milanesi: Florence. 1873-7. 6 vols. The first volume was prepared for publication by P. Fanfani and L. Passerini; the other five by Passerini and Milanesi. This ed. contains the Istorie Fiorentine, Legazioni, and some of the minor works, but not the Principe, Discorsi, or Arte della Guerra. The publication was discontinued in 1877 on the death of Passerini.

Scritti Inediti di Niccolò Machiavelli risguardanti la Storia e la Milizia (1499–1512), ed illustrati da Giuseppe Canestrini. Florence. 1857.

### B. *EDITIONES PRINCIPES* OF MACHIAVELLI'S CHIEF WORKS.

Il Principe di Niccholo Machiavello al Magnifico Lorenzo di Piero de' Medici. La Vita di Castruccio Castracani da Lucca...Il modo che tenne il Duca Valentino per ammazar Vitellozo, etc....Antonio Blado. Rome. 1532.

Discorsi...sopra la prima deca di Tito Livio: Per A. Blado de Asola. Rome. 1531.

Historie Fiorentine. Florence. 1532.

Libro della Arte della Guerra di Niccolò Machiavegli. Florence. 1521.

### C. MODERN BIOGRAPHIES, CRITICAL ESSAYS AND EDITIONS.

Amico, G.   La Vita di Niccolò Machiavelli; commentari storico-critici.   Florence. 1875–6.

Angelini, A.   Nicolò Machiavelli nel suo Principe.   Milan.   1869.

Anon. Machiavel. Neue Monatsschrift für Deutschland, historisch-politischen Inhalts. Herausg. von Friedrich Buchholz. Vol. xii. pp. 302—40. Berlin. 1823.

Artaud de Montor, A. F. Machiavel, son génie et ses erreurs. 2 vols. Paris. 1833.

Barthélemy-Saint-Hilaire, J. Politique d'Aristote, traduite en français. 2 vols. Paris. 1837. (Preface and notes.)

Baudrillart, H. J. L. J. Bodin et son temps. Paris. 1853. pp. 17—24, 225 sqq.

Bollmann. Vertheidigung des Machiavellismus. Quedlinburg. 1858.

Boullier, A. Études de Politique et d'Histoire étrangères. Paris. 1870. pp. 249 —82.

Buhle, J. G. Geschichte der neuern Philosophie seit der Epoche der Wiederherstellung der Wissenschaften. Göttingen. 1800. Vol. ii. p. 929.

Burd, L. A. Il Principe di N. Machiavelli, edited by L. A. Burd, with an Introduction by Lord Acton. Oxford. 1891.

—— Le Fonti letterarie di Machiavelli nell' "Arte della Guerra." Rome. 1897.

Capponi, Gino. Storia della Repubblica di Firenze. 3 vols. Florence. 1888. Vol. ii. Bk vi. ch. vii.

Castelnau, A. La Faune politique et Machiavel. In La Philosophie Positive. Revue dirigée par É. Littré et G. Wyrouboff. Ser. ii., vol. xix. Paris. 1877. pp. 103—22, and pp. 469—75.

Cattaneo. Niccolò Machiavelli. Trieste. 1877.

Cipolla, C. Storia delle Signorie Italiane dal 1313 al 1530. Milan. 1881. pp. 929 —37.

Deltuf, P. Essai sur les œuvres et la doctrine de Machiavel. Paris. 1867.

Ebeling, F. W. Niccolo d. B. dei Machiavelli's politisches System zum erstenmal dargestellt. Berlin. 1850.

Ellinger. Die antiken Quellen der Staatslehre Machiavelli's. Tübingen. 1888.

Etienne, L. Une autobiographie de Machiavel. Revue des deux Mondes. Vol. cviii. pp. 37—60. Ib. 1873.

Falco, F. Nicolò Machiavelli, suo carattere e suoi principj. Lucca. 1896.

Fehr, J. Ueber die Entwickelung und den Einfluss der politischen Theorien. Innsbruck. 1855. pp. 103—44.

Ferrari, G. Machiavel, juge des Révolutions de notre temps. Paris. 1849.

Ferri, L. Aristote et Machiavel. Revue des Cours Littéraires de la France et de l'Étranger. Paris. July 29, 1865. pp. 572—77.

Feuerlein, E. Zur Machiavellifrage. Historische Zeitschrift. Vol. xix. pp. 1—24. Munich. 1868.

Fichte, J. G. Über Machiavelli als Schriftsteller, und Stellen aus seinen Schriften. Nachgelassene Werke. 3 vols. Bonn. 1834. Vol. iii. p. 403.

Fleury, C. Réflexions sur les œuvres de Machiavel. Droit public de France; Ouvrage posthume de M. l'Abbé Fleury, etc. Paris. 1769. Vol. i. pp. 35—64.

Franck, A. Réformateurs et Publicistes. Vol. i. pp. 287—335. Paris. 1864.

Frapporti, G. Sugli Intendimenti di Nicolò Machiavelli nello scrivere il Principe. Vicenza. 1855.

Galanti, G. M. Elogio di Niccolò Machiavelli...con un discorso intorno alla costituzione della Società ed al governo politico. Milan. 1779. (Part of a projected edition of Machiavelli's works.)

Gamba, B. Serie dei Testi di Lingua, etc. Venice. 1839.

Gaspary, A. Die italienische Literatur der Renaissancezeit. pp. 341 sqq. Berlin. 1888.

Gebhart, E. L'honnêteté diplomatique de Machiavel. Séances et travaux de l'Académie des Sciences morales et politiques. 37e année; Nouv. Sér. vol. vii. Paris. 1877. pp. 290—308.

Gervinus, G. G.   Florentinische Historiographie.   Historische Schriften.   Frankfort.   1833.

Giambelli, C.   Niccolò Machiavelli : saggio critico e filosofico.   Il Gerdil, vol. II.   Turin.   1867.   pp. 294, etc.

Ginguené, P. L.   Histoire littéraire d'Italie.   Paris.   1819.   Vol. VIII. pp. 1—184.

Gioda, C.   Machiavelli e le sue opere.   Florence.   1874.

Hallam, H.   Literature of Europe.   3 vols.   London.   1854.   Vol. I. pp. 264—302.

Heidenheimer, H.   Machiavelli's erste römische Legation.   Ein Beitrag zur Beleuchtung seiner gesandtschaftlichen Thätigkeit.   Darmstadt.   1878.

Helps, Sir A.   Friends in Council: A Series of Readings and Discourses thereon.   New series.   2 vols.   London.   1859.   Vol. II. ch. x. pp. 202—72.

—— Thoughts upon Government.   London.   1872.   pp. 107 sqq.

Hinrichs, H. F. W.   Die Könige.   Entwickelungsgeschichte des Königthums von den ältesten Zeiten bis auf die Gegenwart.   Leipzig.   1853.   pp. 227—39.

Janet, P.   Histoire de la science politique dans ses rapports avec la morale.   3rd ed.   Paris.   1887.   Vol. I.   pp. 491—601.

Kellermann.   Commentatio de Nicolai Machiavelli Principe.   Leipzig.   1831.

Knies, C. G. A.   Niccolò Machiavelli als volkswirthschaftlicher Schriftsteller.   Zeitschrift für die gesammte Staatswissenschaft.   Tübingen.   1852.   Vol. VIII. p. 251.

Lafayette.   Dante, Michel-Ange, Machiavel, par Charles Calemard de Lafayette.   Paris.   1852.

Lavollée, R.   La Morale dans l'Histoire.   Paris.   1892.   pp. 74 sqq.

Leo, H.   Studien und Skizzen zu einer Naturlehre des Staates.   Halle.   1833.   pp. 31—9.

Lerminier, J. L. E.   Philosophie du Droit.   Paris.   1831.   Vol. II. ch. v. pp. 93—111.

Lisio, G.   Il Principe di Niccolò Machiavelli.   Testo critico con introduzione e note, a cura di Giuseppe Lisio.   Florence.   1899.

Lutoslawski, W.   Erhaltung und Untergang der Staatsverfassungen nach Plato, Aristoteles, und Machiavelli.   Breslau.   1888.

Macaulay (Lord).   Essay on Machiavelli.   Edinburgh Review, March, 1827.

Mackintosh, Sir J.   On the writings of Machiavel.   Miscellaneous Works.   3 vols.   London.   1846.   Vol. II. p. 749.

Macun, J.   Niccolò Machiavelli als Dichter, Historiker und Staatsmann.   Grätz.   1875.

Mancini, P. S.   Machiavelli e la sua dottrina politica: pp. 221—318 of vol. XIV. of Biblioteca delle scienze giuridiche e sociali.   Naples.   1873.

Matter, M. J.   Histoire des Doctrines morales et politiques des trois derniers siècles.   3 vols.   Paris.   1836.   Vol. I. pp. 68—88.

Maulde la Clavière, M. A. R. de.   La diplomatie au temps de Machiavel.   3 vols.   Paris.   1892.

Mazères, F.   De Machiavel et de l'influence de sa doctrine...pendant la Révolution.   Paris.   1816.

Meyer, E.   Machiavelli and the Elizabethan Drama.   Literarhistorische Forschungen.   Berlin.   1897.

Meyncke.   Machiavelli's Verhältniss zum griechischen Alterthum.   Beilage zur Allgemeinen Zeitung.   Munich.   No. 188, July 7, 1878, and no. 189, July 8, 1878.

"μικρός."   Di quante spezie sono le repubbliche e di quale fu la repubblica romana.   La Rassegna Settimanale di politica, etc.   Florence.   Vol. IV. no. 103, Dec. 21, 1879, p. 444.

Mohl, R. von.   Die Geschichte und Literatur der Staatswissenschaften.   Erlangen.   1855-8.   Vol. III. pp. 521—91.

Mordenti, F.   Diario di Niccolò Machiavelli.   Florence.   1880.

Morellet, A.   Du Machiavélisme.   In Mélanges de littérature et de philosophie du 18ᵉ siècle.   4 vols.   Paris.   1818.   Vol. iv. pp. 346—56.

Morelli, P.   Sul Principe del Machiavelli.   Cesena.   1879.

Morley, J.   Machiavelli.   Romanes Lecture (June 2, 1897).   London.   1897.

Mundt, T.   Macchiavelli und der Gang der europäischen Politik.   2nd ed.   Leipzig. 1853.

Nitti, F.   Machiavelli nella vita e nelle dottrine studiato.   Vol. i.   Naples.   1876.

Nourrisson, J. F.   Machiavel.   Paris.   1883.

Numan, H.   Diatribe in Nicolai Machiavelli opusculum del Principe inscriptum. Utrecht.   1833.

Owen, J.   The Skeptics of the Italian Renaissance.   London.   1893.   pp. 160—78.

Plato, H.   Machiavelli's religiöse und politische Gesinnung.   Frankfort on the Main and Leipzig.   1855.

Quinet, E.   Les Révolutions d'Italie.   Paris.   1848.   Vol. ii. Part i.   pp. 94—157.

Ranke, L. von.   Zur Kritik neuerer Geschichtschreiber.   Vol. xxxiv. of Sämmtliche Werke.   Leipzig.   1874, etc.   pp. 150 sqq.

Rathery, E. J. B.   Influence de l'Italie sur les lettres françaises, depuis le xiiiᵉ siècle jusqu'au règne de Louis XIV.   Paris.   1853.   pp. 129—50.

Rathmann, H.   Machiavelli und seine Lehre im Verhältniss zum Christenthum und zu den Bestrebungen der Gegenwart.   Nordhausen.   1862.

Reumont, A. von.   Zur Charakteristik Machiavelli's.   Blätter für literarische Unterhaltung.   Vol. i.   (Januar bis Juni.)   Leipzig.   1850.   p. 234.

Ricca-Salerno, G.   Di alcune Opinioni finanziarie del Machiavelli e del Guicciardini. La Rassegna Settimanale etc.   Florence.   Vol. vii. no. 167.   March 13, 1881.

Ricci, G.   Sui Discorsi di Niccolò Machiavelli sopra la prima deca di T. Livio. Civitanove-Marche.   1876.

Ridolfi, A.   Pensieri intorno allo Scopo di Nicolò Machiavelli nel libro Il Principe. Milan.   1810.

Roscoe, W.   The Life and Pontificate of Leo the Tenth.   2 vols.   London.   1846. Vol. ii. p. 291 sqq.

Sanctis, F. de.   Storia della Letteratura Italiana.   2 vols.   Naples.   1879.   Vol. ii. pp. 60—122.

Schirren, C.   Rede über Machiavelli.   Kiel.   1878.

Sclopis, F.   Montesquieu et Machiavel.   Revue historique du Droit français et étranger.   Vol. ii. pp. 15—28.   Paris.   1856.

Settembrini, L.   Lezioni di Letteratura Italiana.   4th ed.   3 vols.   Naples.   1897. Vol. ii. pp. 133—48.

Symonds, J. A.   The Age of the Despots.   London.   1875.   Vol. i. pp. 264—302.

Thudichum, F.   Promachiavell.   Stuttgart.   1897.

Tommasini, O.   La Vita e gli Scritti di Niccolò Machiavelli nella loro relazione col Machiavellismo.   Vol. i.   Turin.   1883.

Tréverret, A. de.   L'Italie au xviᵉ siècle.   1ᵉʳᵉ série.   Paris.   1877.

Triantaphulles, C.   Nicolò Machiavelli e gli scrittori greci.   Venice.   1875.

——— Nuovi Studii su Nicolò Machiavelli: il Principe.   Venice.   1878.

Twesten, C.   Machiavelli.   Berlin.   1868.

Vannucci and Contini.   Quarto Centenario di Niccolò Machiavelli; discorso di Atto Vannucci, e relazione di Efisio Contini.   Florence.   1869.

Venedey, J.   Machiavel, Montesquieu, und Rousseau.   Berlin.   1850.

Villari, P.   Niccolò Machiavelli e i suoi Tempi illustrati con nuovi documenti. 2nd ed.   3 vols.   Milan.   1895-7.   Translated.   2 vols.   London.   1878.

Vorländer.   Geschichte der philosophischen Moral, Rechts- und Staats-Lehre. pp. 88—136.   Marburg.   1855.

Waille, V.   Machiavel en France.   Paris.   1884.

Weizel, J.  Geschichte der Staatswissenschaft.  2 vols.  Stuttgart and Tübingen. 1832.  Vol. i. p. 133.

Windelband, W.  Die Geschichte der neueren Philosophie.  2 vols.  Leipzig. 1878, 1880.  Vol. i. pp. 32 sqq.

Wolff, F.  Betrachtungen über den Fürsten des Machiavelli.  Berlin.  1828.

Zambelli, A.  Considerazioni sul libro del Principe.  Milan.  1840.

Zeller, J.  Italie et Renaissance.  Vol. ii. pp. 127 sqq.  Paris.  1883.

Zimmermann.  Macchiavel in seiner historischen Bedeutung für Italien.  Berlin. 1856.

Zirardini, G.  L' Italia letteraria ed artistica…con cenni storici di Giuseppe Zirardini.  Paris.  1850.  pp. 314—23.

## D.  AUTHORITIES FOR CONTEMPORARY HISTORY.

Buonaccorsi, B.  Diario de' Successi più importanti seguiti in Italia, e particolarmente in Fiorenza dall' anno 1498 in sino all' anno 1512.  Florence.  Appresso i Giunti.  1568.

Cambi, G.  Istorie.  4 vols.  Florence.  1786.  Delizie degli Eruditi Toscani, vols. xx.—xxiii.

Giannotti, D.  Della Repubblica Fiorentina libri quattro.  Opere politiche e letterarie di Donato Giannotti, ed. by Polidori.  2 vols.  Florence.  1850. Vol. i. pp. 59—289.

Guicciardini, F.  Storia d' Italia.  4 vols.  Milan.  1884.

—— Opere Inedite.  10 vols.  Florence.  1857–67.

Nardi, J.  Istorie della Città di Firenze.  2 vols.  Florence.  1888.

Nerli, F. de.  Commentarj de' Fatti civili occorsi dentro la Città di Firenze dall' anno mccxv. al mdxxxvii.  Augsburg (Florence).  1728.

Pitti, J.  Istoria Fiorentina sino al 1529.  Arch. Stor. It. vol. i.  Florence.  1842.

Varchi, B.  Storia Fiorentina.  5 vols.  Milan.  1803.

Vettori, F.  Sommario della Storia d' Italia dal 1511 al 1527.  Archivio Storico Ital.  Appendix 22.  Florence.  1848.

*Modern histories of Florence:*

Capponi, G.  Storia della Repubblica di Firenze.  3 vols.  Florence.  1888.

Napier, H. E.  Florentine History.  6 vols.  London.  1847.

Perrens, F. T.  Histoire de Florence depuis la domination des Médicis jusqu'à la chute de la République (1434–1531).  3 vols.  Paris.  1888-90.

Reumont, A. von.  Tavole cronologiche e sincrone della Storia Fiorentina. Florence.  1841.

*See also*

Burckhardt, J.  Die Cultur der Renaissance in Italien.  2 vols.  Leipzig.  1885.

Canestrini, G.  Documenti per servire alla Storia della Milizia italiana dal xiii. Secolo al xvi.  Arch. St. It. vol. xv.  Florence.  1851.

Ricotti, E.  Storia delle Compagnie di Ventura in Italia.  4 vols.  Turin.  1845.

## E.  EARLY CRITICISM OF MACHIAVELLI, HISTORY OF MACHIAVELLISM, AND GROWTH OF THE COMMON OPINION OF MACHIAVELLI.

### *In chronological order.*

Augustini Niphi medices philosophi Suessani de Regnandi Peritia ad Carolum V imper. Caesarem semper Augustum.  Naples.  1523.

Buonaccorsi, B.  Letter prefixed to a manuscript copy of The Prince in the Laurentian Library at Florence: printed in Introduction to Machiavelli, Opere, Italia 1813.  Vol. i. p. xlii.

Busini, G. B.  Lettere di Gio. Batista Busini a Benedetto Varchi.  Pisa.  1822.
p. 75.  (Letter of Jan. 23, 1549.)

Guicciardini, F.  Considerazioni intorno ai Discorsi del Machiavelli.  Opere inedite.
Vol. i.  Florence.  1857.

Varchi, B.  Storia Fiorentina.  Milan.  1803.  Vol. i. p. 210.

Introductory letter (May 8, 1532) prefixed to the Giunta editions of The Prince.
Florence.  1532, 1540.

Preface to the Giunta edition of The Discourses.  Florence.  1543.

Letter to the Reader, prefixed to the Palermo ed. of The Discourses.  "Palermo,"
1584 (really printed in London).

Pole, R. (Card.)  Epistolarum Reginaldi Poli S. R. E. Cardinalis, et aliorum ad
ipsum Pars i.  Brescia.  1744.  pp. 133 sqq.

Catharinus, A. (Lancelotto Politi).  Enarrationes in quinque priora capita Geneseos,
et alii Tractatus.  Rome.  1552.  (The part concerning Machiavelli occurred
under the heading Quam execrandi sint Machiavelli Discursus et Institutio sui
Principis, beginning in column 340, ending in column 343.  It may be read
*in extenso* in: Lo spirito del Machiavelli, ossia Riflessioni dell' Abate D. Antonio
Eximeno sopra l' elogio di Niccolò Machiavelli detto nell' Accademia Fiorentina
dal Sig. Gio. Battista Baldelli.  Cesena.  1795.  pp. 27 sqq.)

Muzio, G.  Lettere Catholiche del Mutio Iustinopolitano.  Venice.  1571.  p. 99.
(Letter of Nov. 11, 1550.)

Whitehorne, P.  The Arte of Warre, Written first in Italiã by Nicholas Machiauell
and set forthe in Englishe by Peter Whitehorne, etc.  1560.  (Dedication to
Queen Elizabeth.)

Osorius, J.  De Nobilitate Christiana.  Florence.  1552.

Paolo Giovio.  Elogia doctorum virorum.  Antwerp.  1557.

Ascham, Roger.  The Scholemaster.  London.  1570.

Gentillet, I.  Discours sur les moyens de bien gouverner et maintenir en bonne
paix un Royaume ou autre Principauté; Contre Nicolas Machiavel, Florentin.
Lausanne.  1576.  (English translation by Simon Patricke, 1602: in German,
with title "Antimachiavellus," by Nigrinus, 1624: in Latin, De regno adversus
Nic. Machiavellum, 1647.)

Giovanni Matteo Toscano.  Peplus Italiae.  Paris.  1578.  Bk ii. p. 52.

Gentili, S.  De Legationibus libri tres.  London.  1585.  Bk iii. ch. 9.

Possevin, A.  Judicium de Nua, Iohan. Bodino, Ph. Morneo, N. Machiavello.
Rome.  1592.

Bozius, T.  De imperio virtutis.  Cologne.  1594.—De robore bellico.  Ib. 1594.—
De Italiae statu.  Ib.  1595.—De ruinis gentium ac regnorum.  Ib.  1598.

Ribadeneyra, P.  Tratado de la Religion y Virtudes que debe tener el Principe
Christiano, para governar y conservar sus Estados.  Contra lo quo N. Machiavelo y los Politicos deste tiempo enseñan.  Madrid.  1595.

Justus Lipsius.  Politicorum sive Civilis Doctrinae libri sex.  Antwerp.  1605.

Shakespeare, Marlowe, Greene, Ben Jonson, Gabriel Harvey, Richard Harvey, etc.
See Meyer, E. (cited above); Ward, A. W., English Dramatic Literature
(2nd ed.), vol. i. p. 339.

Bedingfield, T.  Epistle Dedicatory to English Translation of Machiavelli's Florentine Histories.  London.  1595.

Hooker, R.  Laws of Ecclesiastical Polity.  1597.  (See vol. iii. p. 435 of Clar.
Press ed., viith ed., 1888.)

Bacon's works: *passim* (cf. E. A. Abbott's ed. of Bacon's Essays, 2 vols., 1876;
T. Fowler, Francis Bacon, 1881, pp. 40 sqq.; Abbott's Appendix to his Francis
Bacon, 1885; Fowler, Preface to his second ed. of the Novum Organum).

Naunton, T.  Fragmenta Regalia.  1641.  (Arber's English Reprints, p. 29.)

Fitzherbert, Sir R.  A Treatise concerning Policy and Religion...  Douay.  1606 and 1615. The ed. of 1696 has the title, A Treatise of Policy and Religion, Part II., containing Instructions to a young Statist... London. 1696. The same in Latin, An sit utilitas in scelere, vel de infelicitate principis Machiavellici contra Machiavellum et politicos ejus sectatores. Rome. 1610.

Donne, J. Conclave Ignatii. London. 1611. (Introduces Machiavelli first as an opponent of Loyola, and then as endeavouring to conciliate him by flattery.)

Hume, David (of Godscroft). Le Contr' Assassin, ov Response a l'apologie des Iesvites, faite par vn pere de la compagnie de Iesus de Loyola: & refutee par vn tres-hvmble servitevr de Iesus Christ, de la compagnie de tous les vrais Chrestiens, D. H.—Imprimé l'an M.DC.XII. (See esp. p. 37.)

—— Apologia Basilica sev Machiavelli Ingenivm, examinatvm in libro, quem inscripsit Principem... Paris. 1626. (There is a perfect copy of this very rare book in the Bodleian library; the British Museum copy is mutilated.)

Boccalini, T. De' Ragguagli di Parnaso. Milan. 1613. p. 418.

Campanella, T. Atheismus Triumphatus, seu Reductio ad religionem per scientiarum veritates. Paris. 1636.

Dacres, E. Introductions and notes to his translations of The Prince and The Discourses. London. 1636 and 1640.

Osborne, Francis. A discourse upon Nicolas Machiavell; or An impartiall examination of the justnesse of the Censure commonly laid upon him. (Forms part of a volume with the title Politicall Reflections upon the Government of the Turks. London. 1656.)

Harrington, J. The Commonwealth of Oceana. London. 1656.

Sancroft, W. (Archbishop of Canterbury). Modern Policies, Taken from Machiavel, Borgia, and other choise Authors, by an Eye-Witness. London. 1652.

Sexby, E. Killing No Murder. London. 1657. (Connects Machiavelli and Oliver Cromwell.)

Machiavelli, N. De' Discorsi Politici, e Militari Libri Tre, Scielti (*sic*) fra gravissimi Scrittori, da Amadio Niecollucci, Toscano...In Venetia MDCXXXXVIII. Presso Marco Ginammi. Con Licenza de' Superiori & Privilegio. 4to. pp. 346. (Expurgated ed. of The Discourses. The order of the chapters is re-arranged, and things offensive to the Church are omitted, and what seemed immoral is softened down.)

Nevile, Henry. The Publisher, or Translator of Nicholas Machiavel's Whole Works out of Italian, faithfully into English; concerning the following letter of Nicholas Machiavelo...Printed in the year 1688. (Also appended to Nevile's anonymous translation, 3rd ed. 1720.)

Clarendon, Earl of. History of the Rebellion, etc. Oxford. 1849. Vol. IV. p. 334 (Bk x. 168).

Scioppius, G. (Caspar Schoppe). Paedia politices, sive Suppetiae logicae scriptoribus politicis latae contra ἀπαιδευσίαν et acerbitatem plebeiorum quorundam judiciorum. Rome. 1623. (The best account of Scioppius' manuscript works on Machiavelli is given in Bandini. See Aug. Mar. Bandini Commentariorum de vita et scriptis Iohannis Bapt. Doni Patricii Florentini olim sacri Cardinal. Collegii a Secretis Libri Quinque Adnotationibus illustrati, etc. Florence. 1755.)

Naudé, G. Science des Princes ou Considérations politiques sur les Coups d'État. Strassburg. 1673. (First edition, 1639.)

Conring, H. Animadversiones politicae in N. M. librum de Principe. Helmstädt. 1661.

Matchiavel Junior, or the Secret Arts of the Jesuits, etc. London. 1683.

Amelot de la Houssaie, A. N. Le Prince de N. M. Traduit et commenté par A. N. Amelot, Sieur de la Houssaie. Amsterdam. 1685.

L'Estrange, Sir R.    Fables of Æsop, and other eminent mythologists: with Morals
    and Reflexions.   London.   1692.   pp. 468, etc.
Lucchesini.    Saggio della Sciocchezza di Nicolo Machiavelli.   Rome.   1697.
    (Reviewed in Acta Eruditorum for 1698.)
Feuerlin, C. F.   Missus Thesium Machiavellisticarum de ipso Nicolao Machiavello
    eiusque scriptis et censuris...   Schwabach.   1714.
Reimmann, J. F.    Historia universalis Atheismi et Atheorum falso & merito
    suspectorum, etc.   Hildesheim.   1725.   pp. 355 sqq.
William Nicholls.   The Religion of a Prince...In opposition to the Irreligious
    Principles of Nicholas Machiavel, Hobbs, etc.   London.   1704.—A Conference
    with a Theist...with the addition of Two Conferences; the One with a Machia-
    velian, the Other with an Atheist.   2 vols.   London.   1723.   Vol. II. pp. 309—
    435.
Frederick II of Prussia.   Réfutation du Prince de Machiavel.   Preuss, Œuvres
    de Frédéric.   Vol. VIII. pp. 61—163.   Cf. Dohm, C. W., Denkwürdigkeiten
    meiner Zeit, Hanover, 1817.   Vol. V. pp. 89—113; and Trendelenburg, A.,
    Machiavell und Antimachiavell, in Monatsberichte der K. Preuss. Akademie
    der Wissenschaften zu Berlin, Jan. 25, 1855.   pp. 47—71.
Brucker, J. J.   Historia critica Philosophiae a tempore resuscitatarum in occidente
    litterarum ad nostra tempora.   Leipzig.   1744.   Vol. IV. Part 2, pp. 784—93.
Robinet, J. B. R.   Dictionnaire Universel des Sciences Morale, Économique,
    Politique, ou Bibliothèque de l'homme-d'état et du citoyen.   London.   1777.—
    Discours préliminaire, pp. xxxiii. sqq.
Hume, D.   Essays.   Essay III: That Politics may be reduced to a Science.   Essay XI:
    Of Civil Liberty.—See also, The Philosophical Works of David Hume, ed. by
    T. H. Green and T. H. Grose.   London.   1875.   Vol. IV. p. 391: Essay on
    the Study of History.
Bolingbroke, Viscount.   The Idea of a Patriot King.   1738.   (The Miscellaneous
    Works of the Right Hon. Henry St. John, Lord Viscount Bolingbroke.
    Edinburgh.   1768.   Vol. IV. p. 207 sqq.   Cf. vol. I. 34 sqq.; vol. II. 18, 38 sqq.;
    vol. III. 278.)
Stewart, Dugald.   Supplement to the 4th, 5th, and 6th editions of the Encyclo-
    paedia Britannica.   Vol. I.   Dissertation I., exhibiting a general view of the
    progress of Metaphysical, Ethical, and Political Philosophy.   Edinburgh.   1824.

(*See also Bibliographies of Chapters IV. V. VII. VIII.*)

# CHAPTER VII.

## ROME AND THE TEMPORAL POWER.

### I. DOCUMENTS AND CONTEMPORARY WORKS.

Anecdota Litteraria ex MSS. codicibus eruta. 4 vols. Rome. 1772–83.

Archivio della Società Romana di Storia Patria. Rome. 1878, etc.

Archivio Storico Italiano. Florence. 1842, etc.

Archivio Storico Lombardo. Milan. 1874, etc.

Archivio Veneto. Venice. 1870, etc.

Bullarium Romanum, cura A. Tomasetti. Vol. v. Turin. 1860.

Burcardus, Joannes. Diarium sive rerum urbanarum Commentarii 1483–1506. Edidit L. Thuasne. 3 vols. Paris. 1883–5.

Commines, Philippe de. Mémoires. Vol. ii. Paris. 1843.

Conti, Sigismondo de'. Le storie de' suoi tempi. Rome. 1883.

Giustinian, A. Dispacci, 1502–5, pubblicati da P. Villari. 3 vols. Florence. 1876.

Grassis, Paris de. Diarium [manuscripts in the British Museum, Bibliothèque Nationale, and elsewhere. Extracts in Döllinger's Beiträge and the Documenti e studii per la provincia di Romagna. Vol. i. Bologna. 1886].

Infessura, S. Diario della Città di Roma. In Tommasini, Fonti per la Storia d' Italia, 1890.

Maffeius, Raphael, Volaterranus. Commentariorum urbanorum libri 38. Paris. 1536.

Muratori, L. A. Rerum Italicarum Scriptores. Vol. xxiii. Milan. 1750.

Rebello da Silva, L. A. Corpo diplomatico Portuguez. Vol. i. Lisbon. 1862.

Römische Quartalschrift für christliche Alterthumskunde und für Kirchengeschichte. Rome. 1887.

Theiner, A. Codex diplomaticus dominii temporalis s. sedis. Vol. iii. Rome. 1862.

### II. LATER HISTORICAL WRITINGS.

#### A. PRINCIPAL HISTORIES.

Alvisi, E. Cesare Borgia Duca di Romagna. Imola. 1878.

Brosch, M. Papst Julius II und die Gründung des Kirchenstaates. Gotha. 1878.

Creighton, M. (Bishop). History of the Papacy during the period of the Reformation. Vols. iii. iv. London. 1887.

Gregorovius, F. Geschichte der Stadt Rom im Mittelalter. Vols. vii. viii. Stuttgart. 1880.

Gregorovius, F. Lucrezia Borgia. 3rd ed. Stuttgart. 1875.

Guicciardini, F. Storia d' Italia. Vol. i. Capolago. 1836.

Hergenröther, J. (Card.). Conciliengeschichte. Vol. viii. Freiburg i. B. 1887.

Pastor, L.   Geschichte der Päpste seit dem Ausgang des Mittelalters.   Vol. III.
   Eds. 3 and 4.   Freiburg i. B.   1899.
Reumont, A. von.   Geschichte der Stadt Rom.   Vols. II. III.   Berlin.   1867–70.
Sanuto, Marino.   Diarii.   Vols. I.–XV.   Venice.   1879, etc.


B.   Auxiliary Information.

Alberi, E.   Le Relazioni degli Ambasciatori Veneti al Senato durante il secolo
   decimosesto.   3rd Series.   Florence.   1839–55.
Balan, P.   Gli Assedii della Mirandola.   Mirandola.   1876.
Bembus, P. (Card.).   Historiae Venetae libri XII.   1486–1513.   Venice 1551, etc.
   Italian tr. : Istoria Vineziana.   2 vols.   Venice.   1790.
Brosch, J.   Alexander VI und Lucrezia Borgia.   Historische Zeitschrift.   Vol.
   XXXIII.   Munich.   1878.
Cardo, G.   La Lega di Cambray.   Venice.   1885.
Delaborde, H. F.   L'expédition de Charles VIII en Italie.   Paris.   1888.
Dennistoun, J.   Memoirs of the Dukes of Urbino.   3 vols.   London.   1851.
Döllinger, J. J. I. von.   Beiträge zur politischen, kirchlichen, und Culturgeschichte
   der letzten sechs Jahrhunderte.   Vols. II. III.   Ratisbon.   1863.
Dumesnil, M. A. J.   Histoire de Jules II.
Fabronius, A.   Laurentii Medices Magnifici vita.   2 vols.   Pisa.   1784.
Gebhardt, B.   Adrian von Corneto.   Breslau.   1886.
Gozzadini, G.   Memorie per la vita di Giovanni II Bentivoglio.   Bologna.   1839.
Höfler, C. von.   Don Rodrigo de Borja (Pabst Alexander VI) und seine Söhne.
   Vienna.   1889.
Lamansky, V.   Secrets de l'État de Venise.   St Petersburg.   1884.
La Pilorgerie, J. de.   Campagnes et bulletins de la grande armée d'Italie commandée
   par Charles VIII, 1494–5.   Nantes.   1866.
Leonetti, A.   Papa Alessandro VI.   3 vols.   Bologna.   1880.
Leopardi, M.   Vita di Niccolò Bonafede, Vescovo di Chiusi.   Pesaro.   1832.
L'Épinois, H. de.   Le Pape Alexandre VI.   Revue des questions historiques.
   Vol. XXIX.   Paris.   1881.
Machiavelli, N.   Opere.   Florence.   1853.
Maulde la Clavière, M. A. R. de.   La Diplomatie au temps de Machiavel.   3 vols.
   Paris.   1892–3.
Pasolini, P. D.   Caterina Sforza.   3 vols.   Rome.   1893.
Perrens, F. F.   Histoire de Florence.   Vols. I. II.   Paris.   1877.
Ranke, Leopold von.   Die römischen Päpste in den letzten vier Jahrhunderten.
   Vols. XXXVII. and XXXIX. of Sämmtliche Werke.   Leipzig.   1874, etc.
Reumont, A. von.   Lorenzo de' Medici il Magnifico.   2nd ed.   2 vols.   Leipzig.
   1883.
Romanin, S.   Storia documentata di Venezia.   Vols. IV. V.   Venice.   1855.
Roscoe, W.   Life and Pontificate of Leo X.   Vol. I.   London.   1878.
Serdonati, F.   Vita d' Innocenzo VIII.   Milan.   1829.
Sismondi, J. S. de.   Histoire des républiques italiennes.   Vols. XII.–XIV.   Paris.
   1826.
Thuasne, L.   Djem-Sultan.   Paris.   1892.
Vialardi, F. M.   Historia delle Vite de' sommi pontefici Innocenzio VIII, Boni-
   fazio IX, etc.   Venice.   1613.
Villari, P.   Girolamo Savonarola.   2nd ed.   2 vols.   Florence.   1887–8.
Villari, P.   Niccolò Machiavelli.   2nd ed.   2 vols.   Milan.   1895–6.
Yriarte, C.   César Borgia, sa vie, sa captivité, sa mort.   Paris.   1889.
Yriarte, C.   Autour des Borgia.   Paris.   1891.

# CHAPTER VIII.

## VENICE.

## BIBLIOGRAPHIES.

Cicogna, E.   Saggio di Bibliografia Veneziana.   Venice.   1847.
Cobham, C. D.   An attempt at a Bibliography of Cyprus.   4th ed.   Nicosia.
    1900.
Sarfatti, A.   I Codici Veneti nelle Biblioteche di Parigi.   Rome.   1888.
Soranzo, G.   Bibliografia Veneziana.   Venice.   1885.

## I. MANUSCRIPTS.

The Reggio Archivio di Stato, ai Frari, Venice, contains a very large quantity of unpublished material relating to all departments of the Venetian Republic.

The Reggia Biblioteca Marciana, San Marco, Venice, contains many unpublished Chronicles.

The Museo Civico, Fondaco dei Turchi, Venice, contains some archives of private families and the documents of several of the Venetian Gilds, as well as a series of manuscripts belonging to E. A. Cicogna.

## II. CONTEMPORARY AUTHORITIES.

### A. CHRONICLES.

Altinate.   Chronicon Venetum quod Altinate nuncupatur.   In Mon. Germ. Hist.
    Script., vol. xiv., also in Archivio Storico Italiano.   Vol. viii.   Florence.   1845.
Canal, Martino da.   La Cronaca dei Veneziani.   In Archivio Storico Italiano.
    Vol. viii., ut sup.
Caresini, Raphayni.   Continuatio Chronicorum Danduli.   In Muratori, Rer. Ital.
    Script.   Vol. xii.
Chinazzi.   Cronaca della Guerra di Chioggia.   Milan.   1865.   Also in Muratori,
    Rer. Ital. Script.   Vol. xv.
Cortusii Historia.   In Muratori, Rer. Ital. Script.   Vol. xvii.
Dandolo, Andrea.   Chronicon Venetum.   In Muratori, Rer. Ital. Script.   Vol. xii.
Da Porto, Luigi.   Lettere Storiche dall' anno 1509 al 1528.   Florence.   1857.
Diario della Guerra di Chioggia.   (Anonymous.)   Pub. per le Nozze Cittadella-
    Papafava.   Padua.   1859.
Gattari.   Istoria Padovana.   In Muratori, Rer. Ital. Script.   Vol. xvii.
Lorenzo de Monacis.   Chronicon.   Venice.   1758.

Malipiero, Domenico. Annali Veneti, 1457–1500. In Archivio Storico Italiano. Vol. vii. Florence. 1843–4.

Priuli, Girolamo. Chronicon Venetum, 1494–1500. In Muratori, Rer. Ital. Script. Vol. xxiv. This is the first volume of Priuli's Diarii. The rest is still inedited.

Sagornino, sive Johannes Diaconus. Chronicon Venetum. Venice. 1765. Also in Mon. Germ. Hist. Vol. vii. Hanover. 1848. Also in Monticolo, Cronache Veneziane Antichissime. Rome. 1890.

Sanuto, Marino. Vitae Ducum Venetorum. In Muratori, Rer. Ital. Script. Vol. xxii. Also in Parts 3, 4 and 5 of the new edition of Muratori by G. Carducci. Sanuto is edited by G. Monticolo. Città di Castello. 1900.

—— Diarii, 1496–1533. Venice. 1879–1902. (In course of publication.)

Villehardouin, G. La Conquête de Constantinople. Paris. 1872.

B. Collections of Documents.

Alberi, E. Relazioni degli Ambasciatori Veneti. 3rd Series. Vol. xv. Florence. Continued by Nicolò Barozzi and Guglielmo Berchet. Vol. vii. Venice. 1864.

Archivio Storico Italiano. In course of publication. Florence. 1842, etc.

Archivio Veneto. Venice. 1871, etc. (In course of publication.)

Baschet, A. Les Archives de Venise. Paris. 1870.

Berchet, G. La Republica di Venezia e la Persia. Turin. 1865.

Calendar of State Papers, Venetian. 1202–1607. Vol. x. London. 1900.

Castellani, C. I privileggi di Stampa. Venice. 1888.

Cicogna, E. Iscrizioni Veneziane. Vol. vi. Venice. 1824.

Constitutiones Patriarchales Patriarchatus Venetiarum. Venice. 1522.

Cornet, E. Le guerre dei Veneti nell' Asia, 1470–74. Vienna. 1856.

—— Barbaro, giornale dell' Assedio di Constantinopoli. Vienna. 1856.

Fulin, R. Documenti per servire alla storia della Tipografia Veneziana. Venice. 1882.

Gallicciolli, G. Memorie Venete. Vol. viii. Venice. 1795.

Hopf, C. Chroniques Gréco-Romanes. Berlin. 1873.

Lamansky, V. Secrets d'État de Venise. Petersburg. 1884.

Ljubič, S. Commissiones et relationes Venetae. Vol. ii. Agram. 1876.

Mas Latrie, le Comte J. de. Histoire de l'Île de Chypre. Vol. iii. Paris. 1855.

Monticolo, G. I Capitolari delle Arti Veneziane. Rome. 1896.

—— Cronache Veneziane Antichissime. Rome. 1890.

Morelli, J. Monumenti Veneziani di varia letteratura. Venice. 1796.

Mutinelli, F. Storia Arcana. Vol. iv. Venice. 1855.

Ongania, F. La Basilica di San Marco. Vol. iii. Venice. 1877.

Orford, Lord. Leggi e Memorie Venete sulla prostituzione. Venice. 1870.

Schels, G. B. Österreichische militärische Zeitschrift. Vienna. (Nos. i. and iii. contain an account of the siege of Padua, 1509; Nos. x. and xii. an account of the war of Chioggia. 1378–81.)

Simonsfeld, H. Der Fondaco dei Tedeschi. Vol. ii. Stuttgart. 1887.

Storia Patria, R. Deputazione per la. Venice. 1876. (The publications of this Venetian Society are of very high importance.)

Tafel, G. and Thomas, G. Urkunden zur älteren Handels- und Staatsgeschichte der Republik Venedigs. In Fontes rer. Aust. Vol. iii. Vienna. 1856–7.

Thomas, G. Capitular des deutschen Hauses in Venedig. Berlin. 1874.

Villari, P. Dispacci di Antonio Giustinian. Vol. iii. Florence. 1876.

## III. SECONDARY WORKS.

### A. General Histories.

Brown, Horatio F.   Venice: A Historical Sketch of the Republic.   London.   1893.

Cappelletti, G.   Storia della Republica di Venezia.   Vol. XIII.   Venice.   1850.

Daru, P.   Histoire de la République de Venise.   2nd edit.   Vol. VIII.   Paris. 1821.   (The only edition containing the historical bibliography of Venetian manuscripts.)   Italian translation by Bianchi-Giovini, Capolago, 1837 (with valuable notes).

Filiasi, G.   Memorie Storiche de' Veneti primi e secondi.   Vol. IX.   Venice.   1796.

Hazlitt, C.   The Venetian Republic.   Vol. II.   London.   1900.

Hodgson, F.   The early history of Venice.   London.   1901.

Laugier, M.   Histoire de la République de Venise.   Vol. XII.   Paris.   1759, etc.

Musatti, E.   Storia di un Lembo di Terra.   Padua.   1886.

Mutinelli, F.   Annali Urbani.   Venice.   1841.

Paoletti, E.   Il Fiore di Venezia.   Vol. IV.   Venice.   1837.

Romanin, S.   Lezioni di Storia Veneta.   Vol. II.   Florence.   1875.

—— Storia documentata di Venezia.   Vol. X.   Venice.   1853.   (By far the most important general history of the Republic.)

Sandi, V.   Principii di Storia civile della Republica di Venezia.   Vol. VI.   Venice. 1755.

Sismondi, S.   Storia delle Republiche italiane.   Vol. XVI.   Capolago.   1846. Translation of Histoire des Républiques Italiennes du moyen âge.   Paris. 1809, etc.

Tentori, C.   Storia Veneta.   Vol. XII.   Venice.   1785.

Venezia e le sue Lagune.   Vol. II.   Venice.   1847.

Verci, G.   Storia della Marca Trevigiana.   Vol. XX.   Venice.   1786.

### B. Official Histories.

Bembo, P. (Card.).   Historiae Venetae Lib. XII.   Venice.   1551.

Paruta, P.   Historia Vinitiana.   Venice.   1605.

Sabellico, M. A.   Rerum Venetarum ab urbe condita ad sua usque tempora Lib. XXXIII.   Venice.   1487.

### C. Special Works.

#### (1) *Political.*

Armignaud, J.   Venise et le Bas-Empire.   Paris.   1886.

Battistella, A.   Il Conte Carmagnola.   Genoa.   1889.

Caro, G.   Genua und die Mächte am Mittelmeer.   Vol. II.   Halle.   1895–9.

Cittadella, G.   Storia della dominazione Carrarese in Padova.   Vol. II.   Padua. 1842.

Gloria, A.   Padova dopo la Lega stretta in Cambrai.   Padua.   1863.

Hopf, C.   Der Rath der Zehn.   Leipzig.   1865.

Lazzarini, V.   La Congiura di Marin Falier.   Venice.   1897.

Lenel, W.   Die Entstehung der Vorherrschaft Venedigs an der Adria.   Strassburg. 1897.

—— Studien zur Geschichte Paduas und Veronas im XIII. Jahrhundert.   Strassburg. 1893.

Macchi, M.   Storia del Consiglio dei Dieci.   Vol. II.   Milan.   1864.

Pears, E.   The fall of Constantinople.   London.   1885.

Pélissier, L.   Sur les dates de trois lettres inédits de Jean Lascaris.   Paris.   1901.

Romanin, S.   Bajamonte Tiepolo e le sue ultime vicende.   Venice.   1851.

Rubieri, E.   Francesco Primo Sforza.   Vol. II.   Florence.   1879.

Santalena, A.   Veneti e Imperiali.   Venice.   1896.

Spangenberg, H.   Can Grande della Scala.   Vol. II.   Berlin.   1892–5.

Tentori, C.   Il vero carattere politico di Bajamonte Tiepolo.   Venice.   1798.

## (2)  *Constitutional.*

Alletz, E.   Discours sur la puissance et la ruine de la République de Venise.   Paris.   1842.

Cecchetti, B.   Il Doge di Venezia.   Venice.   1864.

Contarini, G.   Della Republica et Magistrati di Venezia.   Venice.   1591.

Crasso, N.   De forma Reipublicae Venetae.   In Thes. Ant. Italiae.   Vol. v.   Lyons.   1722.

Giannotti, D.   Libro della Republica de' Viniziani.   Vol. II.   Florence.   1850.

La Houssaye, de, A.   Histoire du Gouvernement de Venise.   Vol. II.   Paris.   1677.

Stella, A.   Il servizio di Cassa dell' antica Republica Veneta.   Venice.   1890.

The financial documents of the Republic are to be published by the Italian Government on the initiative of the minister Luzzatti ; Vol. I. is to appear shortly. Prof. Fabio Besta's report on the plan to be adopted has been lithographed but not published.

## (3)  *Commercial.*

Formaleoni, V.   Saggio sulla Nautica antica de' Veneziani.   Venice.   1785.

—— Storia filosofica e politica della Navigazione, del Commercio e delle Colonie degli Antichi nel Mar Nero.   Venice.   1788.

Heyd, W.   Le Colonie commerciali degli Italiani in Oriente nel Medio Evo. Dissertazioni rifatte dall' autore e recate in italiano dal Prof. G. Müller. Vol. II.   Venice.   1866.

—— Geschichte des Levantehandels im Mittelalter.   Stuttgart.   1879.

Lattes, E.   La Libertà delle Banche a Venezia dal secolo XIII. a XVII.   Milan.   1869.

Marin, C.   Storia civile e politica del Commercio de' Veneziani.   Vol. VIII.   Venice.   1798–1808.

Mutinelli, F.   Del commercio dei Veneziani.   Venice.   1835.

Padovan, V.   Le monete della Repubblica Veneta.   1879.

Papadopoli, N.   Sulle origini della Veneta Zecca.   Venice.

Simonsfeld, H.   Der Fondaco dei Tedeschi.   Vol. II.   Stuttgart.   1887.

Soresina, A.   Il Banco Giro di Venezia.   Venice.   1889.

Tafel, G. and Thomas G.   Vortrag über die Herausgabe urkundlicher Quellen zur venetianischen Handelsgeschichte.   In Transactions of the Kaiserliche Akademie der Wissenschaften in Wien.   Vol. v.   Vienna.   1852.   (This series contains other valuable publications by the same authorities.)

## (4)  *Artistic and Literary.*

Berenson.   Lorenzo Lotto.   London.   1895.

—— Venetian Painters of the Renaissance.   London.   1894.

Bernoni, D.   Dei Torresani, Blado e Ragazzoni.   Milan.   1890.

Brown, H.   The Venetian Printing Press.   London.   1891.

Brown, R.   Ragguaglii intorno alla Vita di Marin Sanudo.   Vol. II.   Venice.   1837–8.

Castellani, C.   La Stampa in Venezia alla Morte di Aldo Manuzio Seniore.   Venice.
    1889.
Cattaneo, G.   L'Architettura in Italia.   Venice.   1889.
Crowe, J. and Cavalcaselle, G.   Tiziano, la sua vita e i suoi tempi.   Vol. ii.
    Florence.   1877.
Didot, F.   Alde Manuce.   Paris.   1875.
Foscarini, M.   Della Letteratura Veneziana.   Padua.   1752.
Ongania, F.   La Basilica di S. Marco.   Vol. iii.   Venice.   1877.
——   L' Arte della Stampa.   Venice.   1895.
Paoletti, P.   L' Architettura e la Scultura del Rinascimento in Venezia.   Vol. ii.
    Venice.   1893.
Renouard, A.   Annales de l'imprimerie des Aldes.   Vol. iii.   Paris.   1803.
Ridolfi, C.   Le Maraveglie dell' Arte overo le Vite degli illustri Pittori Veneti.
    Vol. ii.   Venice.   1648.
Rivoli, duc de.   Bibliographie des Livres à figures Venétiennes.   Paris.   1892.
Ruskin, J.   The Stones of Venice.   Vol. iii.   London.   1873.
Simonsfeld, H.   Andreas Dandolo und seine Geschichtswerke.   Munich.   1876.
——   Venetianische Studien.   Munich.   1878.
Somborn, C.   Das Venezianische Volkslied Die Villotta.   Heidelberg.   1901.
Symonds, J. A.   The Renaissance in Italy.   Vol. iii: The Fine Arts.   London.   1877.
Yriarte, C.   Venise.   Paris.   1878.
Zwiedineck-Südenhorst, H. von.   Venedig als Weltmacht und Weltstadt.   Bielefeld
    und Leipzig.   1899.

### (5) *Social.*

Bernoni, G.   Canti, Fiabe, Leggende, Credenze popolari.   Venice.   1872–4.
Casola, P.   Viaggio a Gerusalemme.   Milan.   1855.
Cecchetti, B.   La Vita dei Veneziani.   Venice.   1886.
Molmenti, P.   I Banditi della Republica Veneta.   Turin.   1898.
——   La Dogaressa.   Turin.   1884.
——   La Storia di Venezia nella vita privata.   Turin.   1880.
——   Vecchie Storie.   Turin.   1882.
——   Studii e Ricerche.   Turin.   1892.
Saint Disdier, de.   La Ville et la République de Venise.   Paris.   1680.
Yriarte, C.   La vie d'un Patricien de Venise.   Paris.   s. d.

### (6) *Ecclesiastical.*

Cappelletti, G.   Storia della Chiesa di Venezia (incomplete).   S. Lazzaro.   1849–55.
Cecchetti, B.   La Republica di Venezia e la Corte di Roma.   Vol. ii.   Venice.   1874.
Cornaro, F.   Ecclesiae Venetae antiquis monumentis nunc etiam primum editis
    illustratae.   Vol. xv.   Venice.   1749.
——   Ecclesiae Torcellanae, etc.   Vol. iii.   Venice.   1749.
Sarpi, Fra Paolo.   Opere.   Vol. viii.   Helmstädt and Verona.   1768.

### (7) *Topographical.*

Barbari, J. de'.   A large wood-cut plan of Venice.   Now in the Museo Civico.   1500.
Coronelli, V.   Isolario.   Venice.   1696.
Molmenti, P. and Mantovani, D.   Calli e Canali in Venezia.   Venice.   1893.
Sansovino, J.   Venezia Città nobilissima e singolare.   Venice.   1663.
Tassini, A.   Curiosità Veneziane.   Venice.   1863.
Temanza, T.   Antica pianta dell' inclita Città di Venezia.   Venice.   1781.

# CHAPTER IX.

## GERMANY AND THE EMPIRE.

The chief Historical Bibliographies on the subject are: Dahlmann-Waitz, Quellenkunde der deutschen Geschichte, 6th ed. 1894; and Lorenz-Goldmann, Deutsche Geschichtsquellen im Mittelalter, 2 vols. 1886–7. More general bibliographical works such as H. Oesterley, Wegweiser durch die Litteratur der Urkundensammlungen, Part I., Berlin, 1885; and A. Potthast, Bibliotheca Historica Medii Aevi, 2 vols., Berlin, 1896, may also be consulted with advantage. Indications of the more recent literature will be found in the following: J. Jastrow, Jahresberichte der Geschichtswissenschaft (since 1895 edited by E. Berner), Berlin, 1878, etc.; Masslow and Sommerfeldt, Bibliographie zur deutschen Geschichte, in Deutsche Zeitschrift für Geschichtswissenschaft, 1889–97, from 1898 by O. Masslow in Historische Vierteljahrsschrift. F. Förster's Kritischer Wegweiser durch die neuere deutsche historische Literatur, Berlin, 1900, puts the recent literature conveniently together.

## I. ORIGINAL AUTHORITIES AND COLLECTIONS.

### A. GENERAL.

Alberi, E. Le Relazione degli ambasciatori Veneti al Senato nel secolo XVI. Florence. 1839–62. 1st Series. Vols. I. II. and VI.

Altmann-Bernheim. Ausgewählte Urkunden zur Erläuterung der Verfassungsgeschichte Deutschlands im Mittelalter. 2nd ed. Berlin. 1895.

Andlau, P. von. De Imperio Romano, cum notis M. Freheri. Strassburg. 1612.

Bergenroth, G. A. Calendar of Spanish State Papers. Vols. I. II. London. 1862–6.

Brant, Sebastian. Das Narrenschiff. Herausg. von F. Zarncke. Leipzig. 1854.

Brewer, J. S. Calendar, Letters, and Papers of the Reign of Henry VIII. Vols. I. II. London. 1862–4.

Brown, R. Calendar of Venetian State Papers. Vols. I. II. London. 1864–7.

Burgermeister, J. S. Codex diplomaticus equestris. Ulm. 1721.

(Cusanus, Card.) Cues, Nicolaus v. De Concordantia Catholica libri tres. Basel. 1566.

Erdmannsdörffer, B. Auszüge der ven. Relationen in Berichte über die Verhandlungen der k. sachs. Gesellsch. der Wiss., Philol.-hist. Classe, vol. IX. Leipzig. 1857.

Faber, A. Europäische Staatskanzlei. Nürnberg. 1697.

Freher, M., and Struve, B. G.   Germanicarum Rerum Scriptores.   Vols. ii. and iii. Strassburg. 1717. (Contain many chronicles, letters, panegyrics, State papers, and other documents of this period.)

Gebwiler, H.   Libertas Germaniae, qua Germanos Gallis...imperasse probatur. Strassburg. 1519.

Grimm, J., and Schröder.   Weistümer.   7 vols.   Göttingen.   1840–78.

Harpprecht, J. N. von.   Staatsarchiv des kays. Kammergerichts.   Frankfort. 1759–69.   Ulm.   1785–9.

Kluckhohn, A.   Deutsche Reichstagsakten.   Jüngere Reihe.   (From 1519.)   Vol. i. pp. 1—140.   Gotha.   1893.

Koch, C. G.   Neue und vollständige Sammlung der Reichsabschiede.   4 Parts. Frankfort. 1747.

Liliencron, R. von.   Die histor. Volkslieder der Deutschen, vom 13. bis 16. Jahrh. 5 vols.   Leipzig.   1865–9.

Lorenzi, de.   Geiler v. Kaisersbergs ausgewählte Schriften.   4 vols.   Trier.   1881.

Lünig, J. C.   Das deutsche Reichsarchiv.   24 vols.   Leipzig.   1713–22.

——   Thesaurus iuris der Grafen und Herren des heil. röm. Reichs.   Leipzig.   1725.

Moser, F. C.   Sammlung sämtlicher Kreisabschiede.   Leipzig.   1747.

Moser, J. J.   Teutsches Staatsrecht.   50 vols.   1737–54.

——   Neues teutsches Staatsrecht.   Frankfort.   1766–75.

——   Vermischte Nachrichten von reichsritterschaftlichen Sachen.   Nürnberg. 1773–4.

——   Beiträge zu reichsritterschaftlichen Sachen.   Ulm.   1775.

Müller, J. J.   Reichstagsstaat, 1500–8.   Jena.   1708.

——   Reichstagstheatrum unter Keyser Friedrich V.   3 Parts.   Jena.   1713.

——   Reichstagstheatrum unter Keyser Maximilian I.   2 Parts.   Jena.   1718–9.

Sanuto, Marino.   Diarii.   Venice.   1879–92.

Schilter, J. S.   Scriptores Rerum Germanicarum.   Vol. i. Aeneas Sylvius, Hist. Frid. Imp.   Vol. ii. Boecleri Specimen Annotationum in Aeneae Sylvii historiam.   Vol. iii. Diplomata res gestas Frid. III illustr.   Vol. xiv.   Index Diplom. Frid. III.   Strassburg.   1702.

Weizsäcker, J., etc.   Deutsche Reichstagsakten, 1376–1435.   11 vols.   Munich and Gotha.   1868–88.

Wimpheling, J.   Works, to a large extent printed in Riegger, Amoenitates Litterariae Friburgenses.   Ulm, 1775 and Freiburg, 1779.

## B. Territorial and local.

Anonymi Carmen de obsidione et expugnatione arcis Hohenkrayen.   1512.

Anshelm.   Berner Chronik, herausg. von E. Stierlin u. J. R. Wyss.   Bern.   1825–33.

Barack, K. A.   Zimmersche Chronik herausg. von.   Freiburg i. B.   1881.

Burkhardt, C. A. H.   Quellen zur Geschichte des Hauses Hohenzollern.   Das funftt merckisch Buech des Churfuersten Albrecht Achilles, 1471–3.   Jena.   1857.

Fontes Rerum Austriacarum.   Part i. Scriptores.   Vol. i.   Kirchmair, Herbersteins Selbstbiographie, Tichtels Tagebuch, 1477–95, and other important chronicles.

——   Part ii. Diplomataria et acta.   Vol. ii.   Diplomatarium Habsburgense seculi xv. 1850.   Vol. xxx.   Relationen venetianischer Botschaften über Deutschland und Österreich im 16. Jahrh.   Vol. xlii.   Urkunden und Actenstücke zur österr. Geschichte, 1440–71.   Vol. xliv.   Briefe und Acten zur österr.-deutschen Gesch. im Zeitalter K. Friedrich III.   Vol. xlvi.   Urkundliche Nachträge zur österr.-deutsch. Gesch. im Zeitalter K. Fried. III.   Vienna.

Fugger, J. J.   Spiegel der Ehren des Ertz-Hauses Österreich, erweitert durch S. von Birken.   Bk vii.   Nürnberg.   1668.

Goerz, A.  Regesten der Erzbischöfe v. Trier, 814–1503.  Trier.  1859, etc.

Gudenus, V. F.  Codex diplomaticus Moguntinus.  Göttingen.  1743–68.

Hanauer.  Les constitutions des Campagnes de l'Alsace.  1864.

Hegel, K. von.  Die Chroniken der deutschen Städte vom 14. bis zum 16. Jahrhund.  Baier. Academie der Wissenschaften, 25 vols.  Leipzig.  1862, etc. Among the most important of these are Nürnberg's Krieg gegen Albrecht Achilles, II. 95–530, H. Deichsler's Nürnberger Kronik and Chr. Scheurl's Epistel über die Verfassung der Reichsstadt Nürnberg, both in XI., J. Koelhoff's Cronica van der heiliger Stat van Coellen, XIII. and XIV., C. Wierstraat, Histori des beleegs van Nuis, XX., H. Mülich's Augsburger Chronik, XXII., Cl. Sender's Augsburger Chronik, XXIII.  The elaborate introductions by Hegel and others, and occasional notes, such as Hegel's note Über Nürnbergs Bevölkerungszahl, II. Beilage IV., are very useful.

Höfler-Minutoli.  Das kaiserliche Buch des Markgr. Albrecht Achilles, 1440–70. Bayreuth, 1850.  1470–86.  Berlin, 1850.

Janssen, J.  Frankfurts Reichscorrespondenz nebst andern verwandten Actenstücken.  Vol. I.: 1376–1439: Freiburg i. B. 1863.  Vol. II. Part I.: 1440–86: Ib. 1866.  Part II.: 1486–1519: Ib. 1872.

Klüpfel, C.  Urkunden zur Gesch. des schwäbischen Bundes, 1488–1533.  2 vols. Bibliothek des lit. Vereins, XIV. XV.  Stuttgart.  1846.

Krenner.  Baierische Landtagshandlungen, 1429–1513.  Munich.  1804.

Lacomblet.  Urkundenbuch für die Gesch. des Niederrheins.  Vols. III., IV.  Düsseldorf.  1853–8.

Lemnius, S.  Raeteis.  Der schweizerisch-deutsche Krieg von 1499.  Epos in IX. Gesängen herausg. v. P. Plattner.  Chur.  1874.

Österreichische Weistümer.  7 vols.  1870–86.

Priebatsch, F.  Politische Korrespondenz des Kurfürsten Albrecht Achilles. Leipzig.  1894, etc.

Quellen und Erörterungen zur bayer. und deutsch. Geschichte.  Vols. II. and III. Quellen zur Geschichte Friedrichs I des Siegreichen.  Regesten zur Gesch. Fried. I des Siegreichen.  Munich.  1857–63.

Regesta Archiepiscoporum Moguntinensium, 742–1514.  Innsbruck.  1877.

Riedel, A. F.  Codex diplomaticus Brandenburgensis.  Berlin.  1838–58.

Schäfer.  Hanserecesse.  1477–1530.

Schönherr, D.  Urkunden u. Regesten aus d. k.-k. Staatsarchive in Innsbruck, 2 vols.  Wien, 1883–4.

Serarius, N.  Rerum Moguntinarum lib. quinque.  Mainz.  1604.

Trithemius, J.  Annales Hirsaugienses.  1690.

——— Historia Belli Bavarici A.D. 1504 in Freher-Struve, III.

Weinrich, C.  Danziger Chronik.  Hirsch's Script. Rerum Prussicarum, IV. 725— 800.  Leipzig.  1870.

Würdinger, J.  Urkundenauszüge zur Gesch. des Landshuter-Erbfolgekriegs.  Verhandlungen des hist. Vereins v. Niederbaiern, VIII.

Zimerman, H.  Urkunden u. Regesten aus d. k.-k. Staatsarchiv.  Vienna.  1885. The last-named three books are in Jahrbücher der kunsthistor. Sammlungen des Kaiserhauses.

Zimerman, H. and Kreyczki, F.  Urkunden u. Regesten aus d. k.-k. Reichsfinanzarchiv.  Vienna.  1885.

## C.  Special works on Maximilian I and his age.

Birk.  Urkunden-Auszüge zur Geschichte K. Fried. III, 1452–67.  Archiv f. österr. Geschichte, X.–XI.

Chmel, J.  Urkundliches zur Gesch. K. Fried. IV.  Archiv f. österr. Geschichte, III.

Chmel, J.   Regesta Friderici III.   Vienna.   1859.

—— Urkunden, Briefe und Actenstücke zur Gesch. Maximilian's I und seiner Zeit. Bibl. des lit. Vereins, vol. x.   Stuttgart.   1845.

Cuspinian, J.   Diarium de congressu Maximiliani et trium regum apud Viennam 1515.   In Freher-Struve, ii.

Dürer, A.   Randzeichnungen aus dem Gebetbuche des Kaisers Maximilian I.   1850.

Gachard, L. P.   Lettres inédites de Maximilien I sur les affaires des Pays-Bas. 2 vols.   Brussels.   1851–52.   Cf. Compte-rendu de la Commission Histor. Ser. ii. p. 263.   1851.

Glay, E. Le.   Correspondance de l'Empereur Maximilien I et de Marguerite d'Autriche sa fille.   Soc. de l'histoire de France.   Vols. i.–ii.   1839.

Grünbeck.   Hist. Frid. et Maximiliani, in Chmel, Östreichischer Geschichtsforscher, i.

Images des Saints et Saintes issus de la famille de l'Empereur Maximilien I, par H. Burgmaier.   Vienna.   1799.

Karajan, T. G. von.   Kaiser Maximilians geheimes Jagdbuch.   Vienna.   1858.

Keller, A. von.   Geschichten und Thaten Wilwolts v. Schaumburg.   Bibl. des lit. Vereins.   Stuttgart.   1859.

Kraus, V. von.   Maximilians vertraulicher Briefwechsel mit Sigmund Prüschenk. Innsbruck.   1875.

Leitner, Q. von Freydal.   Des Kaisers Maximilians I Turniere und Mummereien. Vienna.   1880–2.

Machiavelli, N.   Ritratti delle cose della Magna, etc.   Opere, vi. 119—230.   Milan. 1811.

—— Legazione al imperatore.   Opere, xi., 15—124.

Monumenta Hapsburgica.   Sammlung von Actenstücken und Briefen zur Gesch. des Hauses Hapsburg im Zeitraume 1473–1576.   Vols. i.–iii.   Vienna.   1853–7.

Pfintzing, M.   Die geuerlichkeiten und einsteils der geschichten des loblichen streytparen und hochberümbten Helds und Ritters herr Tewrdanckhs.   Nürnberg.   1517.

Pirkheimer, B.   De bello Helvetico, in Freher-Struve, iii. or separately edited in Rück. W. Pirckheimer's Schweizerkrieg.   Munich.   1895.

(Pius II.) Aeneas Sylvius Piccolomini.   Hist. rer. Friderici III.   Strassburg.   1685.

Proposals of Knights in 1494.   Archiv für öster. Geschichte, xi.

Saint-Génois.   Lettres de Maximilien à l'abbé de Saint-Pierre à Gand.   Messager hist. de la Belgique.   1845.

Scheurl, Chr.   Briefbuch, 1505–40, herausgegeben von Soden und Knaake. Potsdam.   1867–72.

—— Geschichtsbuch der Christenheit 1511–21, herausgegeben von Knaake. Leipzig.   1872.

Teuerdank.   Herausg. von K. Goedeke.   (Goedeke and Tittmann's Deutsche Dichter des 16. Jahrh.)   Leipzig.   1878.

Treitzsaurwein, M.   Weisskunig.   Eine Erzählung von den Thaten Kais. Maximilians I nebst den Holzschnitten von Hans Burgmair.   1775.

Trithemius, J.   Curiositas regia.   Libb. octo quaestionum ad Maximilianum. 1534.

Triumph des K. Maximilians, der.   Vienna.   1796.

Ulmann, H.   Der Traum des Hans v. Hermannsgrün.   Forschungen zur deutsch. Geschichte, xx. 67—92.   1880.

Villari, P.   Dispacci di A. Giustinian.   1876.

Zasius, Faber, and others.   Funeral orations on Maximilian.   In Freher-Struve, ii.

Zeibig.   Der Ausschusslandtag der österr. Erblande im J. 1518.   Archiv für öster. Geschichte, xiii. 203—316, cf. Sitzungsberichte der k. Acad., philos.-histor. Classe, x. 518, xi. 485.   Vienna.   1853.

The original editions of Maximilian's half-autobiographical works have been sumptuously facsimiled and those previously unpublished have been issued in equally magnificent form in the Jahrbücher der kunsthistor. Sammlungen des Kaiserhauses, I. II. III. IV. V. VI. VII. VIII. IX., with Introductions, of which S. Laschitzer's to Teuerdank (VIII.) is particularly important. Compare also the Holbein Society Facsimiles of Teuerdank, ed. 1519 (1884), and the Triumph (1883). Cf. also R. von Liliencron, Der Weisskunig, in Raumer's Histor. Taschenbuch, Ser. v., Jahrg. 3, and Schönherr, Über M. Treitzsaurwein, Archiv f. österr. Geschichte, XLVIII.

## II.  LATER WORKS.

### A.  GENERAL HISTORIES.

Allgemeine deutsche Biographie.    See, among many useful articles, especially Frederick III by G. Voigt, Frederick the Victorious by K. Menzel, Frederick the Wise by Th. Flathe, Dürer by Woltmann, M. Lang by H. Ulmann, Berthold of Mainz by K. Klüpfel, Maximilian I by H. Ulmann.

Altmann, W.  Die Wahl Albrecht's II zum römischen Könige.   Jastrow's Historische Untersuchungen.   Berlin, 1886.

Aschbach, J.  Geschichte Kaiser Sigmunds.  4 vols.  Hamburg.  1838–45.

Bachmann, A.  Deutsche Reichsgeschichte im Zeitalter Friedrichs III und Max. I. 1884.  Fontes Austr., vol. XLIV.  Vienna.  1885.  With Supplement, 1892.

Bezold, F. von.  Geschichte der deutschen Reformation, pp. 1—161.  (Allgemeine Geschichte in Einzeldarstellungen.)  Berlin.  1890.

Jähns, M.  Geschichte der Kriegswissenschaften vornehmlich in Deutschland. First Part.  Munich.  1889.

Janssen, J.  Geschichte des deutschen Volkes seit dem Ausgange des Mittelalters. Vols. I.—IV.  Freiburg i. B. 1878, etc.  English translation by A. M. Christie : History of the German People at the close of the Middle Ages.  (In course of publication.)

Nitzsch, K. W.  Geschichte des deutschen Volkes, vol. III. pp. 312—416.  Leipzig. 2nd ed.  1892.

Ranke, L. von.  Deutsche Geschichte im Zeitalter der Reformation.  Vol. I. of Sämmtliche Werke, pp. 1—147.  1874, etc.

—— Geschichte der romanischen und germanischen Völker, 1494–1514.  Vols. XXXIII. and XXXIV. of Sämmtliche Werke.  Leipzig.  1874, etc.

### B.  TERRITORIAL AND LOCAL HISTORIES.

Berlichingen-Rossach, F. W. G. Graf von.  Geschichte des Ritters Götz von Berlichingen.  Leipzig.  1861.

Bode, W. J. L.  Geschichte des Bundes der Sachsenstädte bis zum Ende des Mittelalters.  Forschungen zur deutsch. Gesch., II. 203—292.  1862.

Boos, H.  Geschichte der Stadt Basel, I.  Basel.  1877.

Burckhardt-Finsler, A.  Basels Eintritt in den Schweizerbund, 1501.  Denkschrift d. hist. Gesell.  Basel.  1890.

Dierauer, J.  Geschichte der schweizerischen Eidgenossenschaft.  Vol. II.  (Gesch. der europäischen Staaten.)  Gotha.  1892.

Droysen, J. G.  Geschichte der preussischen Politik, vol. II.  Berlin.  1868–70.

Eberstein, L. F. Freiherr von.  Fehde Mangolds v. Eberstein gegen Nürnberg. Nordhausen.  1868.

Ehses, S.  Quellen und Literatur zur Geschichte des bairisch-pfälzischen Erbfolgekriegs.  1880.

Häusser, L.  Geschichte der rheinischen Pfalz, vol. i.  Heidelberg.  1845.

Hefner, v.  Geschichte der Regierung Albrechts IV von Baiern.  Oberbair. Archiv, xiii.

Hegel, C.  Köln im letzten Zeit des Mittelalters.  Histor. Zeitschrift, xxiii. 277—88.  1870.

Heyd, L. F.  Ulrich Herzog zu Württemberg.  Tübingen.  1841–4.

Höfler, C. von.  Über die politische Reformbewegung in Deutschland im 15. Jahrhundert und den Antheil Baierns an derselben.  Munich.  1850.

Huber, A.  Geschichte Österreichs, vols. iii. iv.  (Gesch. der europ. Staaten.) Gotha.  1885, etc.

Klüpfel, C.  Der schwäbische Bund.  Raumer's Histor. Taschenbuch, No. 866.

—— Die Lostrennung der Schweiz von Deutschland.  Histor. Zeitschrift, xvi. 1–47, 1866.

Köllner, A.  Der Landshuter Erbfolgekrieg.  Landshut.  1847.

Krones, F. X.  Handbuch der Geschichte Österreichs.  Berlin.  1876–9.

Langenn, F. A. v.  Herzog Albrecht der Beherzte.  Leipzig.  1838.

Lichnowsky, E. Fürst.  Geschichte des Hauses Habsburg, vol. viii.  Vienna. 1836–44.

Menzel, K.  Kurfürst Friedrich der Siegreiche v. d. Pfalz, 1454–64.  Munich. 1861.

Neudecker and Preller.  Friedrichs des Weisen Leben u. Zeitgeschichte nach Spalatin's Handschrift herausg.  1851.

Oechsli.  Die Beziehungen der schweiz. Eidgenossenschaft zum Reiche, in Hilty's Polit. Jahrbuch.  v.

Osann, E.  Zur Geschichte des schwäb. Bundes, 1487–93.  Giessen.  1861.

Probst, T.  Die Beziehungen der schweiz. Eidgenossenschaft zum deutschen Reich. 1486–99.  Archiv f. schweizer. Gesch. xv.

Redlich, O.  Zur Belagerung von Kufstein im Jahre 1504.  Mittheilungen des Inst. f. öster. Geschichtsforschung, ix. 104—113.  Innsbruck.  1888.

Riezler, S.  Geschichte Baierns, vols. ii. iii.  (Gesch. der europäischen Staaten.) Gotha.  1878, etc.

Schröder, R.  Kurmainz unter B. v. Henneberg, etc.  Zeitschrift f. Rechtsgeschichte, xviii.

Schweizer, P.  Vorgeschichte und Gründung des schwäbischen Bundes.  Zürich. 1876.

Stälin, Chr. F. v.  Wirtembergische Geschichte, vol. iv.  Stuttgart.  1841–73.

Stälin, P. F.  Geschichte Württembergs, vol. i.  (Gesch. der europ. Staaten.) Gotha.  1882.

Tutzschmann, M. M.  Friedrich der Weise.  Grimma.  1848.

Ulmann, H.  Fünf Jahre würtembergischer Geschichte unter Herzog Ulrich, 1515–9.  Leipzig.  1867.

—— Der unbekannte Verfasser der Geschichten und Thaten Wilwolts v. Schaumburg.  Histor. Zeitschrift, xxxix. 193—229.  1878.

—— Ueber die Quellen zur Geschichte des Feldzugs des schwäbischen Bundes gegen Ulrich v. Wurtemberg 1519.  Forschungen zur deutsch. Gesch. vii. 281—90.  1867.

Wagner, F.  Der schwäbische Bund und die fränkischen Hohenzollern.  Forschungen zur deutsch. Gesch. xxii. 259—328, 1882, and xxv. 463—510, 1885.

—— Die Aufnahme der fränkischen Hohenzollern in den schwäb. Bund.  1880.

—— Das dritte kaiserliche Buch der Markgr. v. Brandenburg.  Forschungen zur deutsch. Gesch., xxiv. 475—564.  1884.

Würdinger, J.  Kriegsgeschichte von Bayern, etc. v. 1347 bis 1506.  Munich.  1808.

C. Monographs on Maximilian I and his age.

Ammann, H. Versuch einer Charakteristik K. Maximilians I. 1892.

Bachmann, A. Zur deutschen Königswahl Maximilians I. Arch. für öster. Gesch. LXXVI. 1890.

—— Nochmals die Wahl Maximilians I zum deutschen König. Histor. Vierteljahrschrift. IV. Jahrgang 453—480. 1901.

—— Deutsche Reichsgeschichte unter Friedrich III und Max. I.

Boehm, W. Hat Kaiser Maximilian I im Jahre 1511 Papst werden wollen? 1873.

Brunner. Kaiser Max und Augsburg. Prog. der Studienanstalt v. St Stephan. 1877.

Busson, A. Die Sage von Max auf der Martinswand, und ihre Entstehung. Sitzungsberichte der k. Acad., philos.-histor. Classe, CXVI. 455—500. Vienna. 1888.

Calvi, F. Bianca Maria Sforza. Milan. 1888.

Chmel, J. Geschichte Kaisers Friedrichs IV und seines Sohnes Maximilians I. 2 vols. Hamburg. 1840-3.

Fiedler, J. Die Allianz zwischen K. Maximilian I und Russland, 1514. Sitzungsberichte der k. Acad., philos.-histor. Classe, XLIII. 183—289. Vienna.

Gar, T. Lettera dell' Imp. Massimiliano I ai suoi oratori...di Roma 1503. Archivio Veneto, I. 84—95. 1871.

Geiger, L. Maximilian I in seinem Verhältnisse zum Reuchlinschen Streite. Forschungen zur deutsch. Gesch., IX. 203—216. 1869.

Hegewisch, D. H. Geschichte der Regierung Kais. Maximilians I. Hamburg. 1782-3.

Herberger, Th. Konrad Peutinger in seinem Verhältnisse zum K. Maximilian I. Augsburg. 1851.

Höfler, C. von. Das Journal des A. del Burgo, kais. Gesandten zu Blois 1504, und Ph. Haneton's Denkschrift über die Verhandlungen K. Philipp's und K. Ludwigs 1498-1506. Sitzungsberichte der k. Acad., philos.-histor. Classe, CVIII. 411—502. 1885.

Jäger, A. Der Uebergang Tirols vom Erzh. Sigmund an Maximilian. Archiv f. österr. Geschichte, LI.

—— Ueber K. Maximilians I Verhältniss zum Papstthum. Sitzungsberichte der k. Acad., philos.-histor. Classe, XII. 195—236, 409—40. Vienna. 1854.

Karge, P. Friedrichs III und Maximilians I Ungarische Politik und ihre Beziehungen zu Moskau, 1486-1506. Deutsche Zeitschr. f. Geschichtswissenschaft IX. 259-87. 1893.

Klüpfel, K. Kaiser Maximilian I. Deutsche National Bibliothek. Vol. XII.

Kraus, V. von. Maximilian's Beziehungen zu Sigmund von Tirol in den Jahren 1490-96. Vienna. 1879.

Liske, X. Der Congress zu Wien im Jahre 1515. Forschungen zur deutsch. Gesch., VII. 463—558. 1867.

—— Der Wiener Congress und die Politik Maximilians I gegenüber Preussen und Polen. Forschungen zur deutsch. Gesch., XVIII. 445—68. 1878.

—— Zur Geschichte des Augsburger Reichstages, 1518. Forschungen zur deutschen Gesch. XVIII. 638—48. 1878.

Pauli, R. Diplomatie im Jahre 1516. Ein Beitrag zur Charakteristik Maximilians I. Histor. Zeitschrift, XIV. 269—94. 1865.

Rausch, K. Die burgund. Heirath Maximilians I quellenmässig dargestellt. Vienna. 1880.

Schels, J. B.   Die Feldzüge Maximilians I.   Öster. militar. Zeitschr. III. IV. v.
    IX. x.   1839–41.
Schönherr, D.   Der Krieg K. Maximilians mit Venedig, 1509.   Organ der mili-
    tärwissenschaftl. Vereine, vol. XIII.   1876.
Schreiber, H.   Maximilian I auf dem Reichstag zu Freiburg, 1498.
Schweizer, P.   Die Verträge von Blois, von 22 Sept. 1504.   Forschungen zur deut-
    schen Gesch., XIX. 1—32.   1879.
Seemüller, J.   Zur Geschichte Maximilians I.   Mittheilungen d. Instit. f. öster-
    reich. Geschichtsforschung, XVIII.   Innsbruck.   1897.
Spielberg, H. von.   Maximilian I und das deutsche Reich.   Preuss. Jahrbücher,
    March, 1884.
Stälin, Ch. F. von.   Aufenthaltsorte Maximilians I, 1493–1519.   Forschungen zur
    deutsch. Gesch., I. 347—383.   1862.
——   Bericht über die Annahme der Kaiserwürde durch Maximilian I im J. 1508.
    Forschungen zur deutsch. Gesch., I. 67—73.   1862.
Stoewer, R.   Herzog Albrecht der Beherzte als Reichsfeldherr gegen die Ungarn,
    1487.   1882.
Ulmann, H.   Kaiser Maximilian I.   2 vols.   Stuttgart.   1884–91.   (The best general
    authority for the period covered by this chapter.)
——   Die Opposition Groningens gegen die Politik Maximilians I in Westfries-
    land.   Hansische Geschichtsblätter, II.
——   Studie über Maximilians I.   Plan einer deutschen Kirchenreform im Jahre
    1510.   Zeitschrift für Kirchengesch. III. 199—219.   1879.
——   Die Wahl Maximilians I.   Forschungen zur deutschen Gesch., XXII. 131—
    158.   1882.
——   Maximilian I in dem Conflicte zwischen d. deutschen Orden und Polen,
    1513–5.   Forschungen zur deutschen Gesch. XVIII. 89—110.   1878.
——   K. Maximilian's Absichten auf den Papstthron.   Stuttgart.   1888.
Voltelini, Hans von.   Die Bestrebungen Maximilians I um die Kaiserkrone, 1518.
    Mittheilungen des Instit. für österreich. Geschichtsforschung, XI. 41—85,
    574—626.   Innsbruck.   1890.
Watson, R. W. S.   Maximilian I, Holy Roman Emperor.   London.   1902.
Wiedemann, F.   Die Reichspolitik des Grafen Haug von Werdenberg, 1466–86.
    1883.
Wolf, P. P.   Geschichte Maximilians I.   3 vols.   Munich.   1807–11.


D.   CONSTITUTIONAL AND LEGAL.

Adler, S.   Die Organisation der Centralverwaltung unter Maximilian I.   Leipzig.
    1886.
Ægidi, L. K.   Article on Austräge in Ersch and Gruber's Encyklopädie.
Arnoldi, J.   Aufklärungen in der Geschichte des deutschen Reichsgrafenstandes.
    Marburg.   1802.
Bachmann, A.   Die ersten Versuche zu einer röm. Königswahl unter Fried. III.
    Forschungen zur deutschen Gesch., XVII. 275—332.   1877.
Becker, W.   Ueber die Theilnahme der Städte an den Reichsversammlungen unter
    Fried. III.   Bonn.   1891.
Bidermann, H. J.   Geschichte der landesfürstlichen Behörden in und für Tirol.
    Archiv f. Gesch. Tirols, III.   1866.
Boretius, A.   Die Verwandlung des deutschen Rechtslebens durch die Aufnahme
    des römischen Rechts.   Preus. Jahrbücher.   1883.
Brandenburg, E.   Der Binger Kurverein.   Deutsche Zeitschr. f. Geschichtswis-
    senschaft, XI.   1894.

Danke, W.  Die Virilstimmen im Reichs-Fürstenrath 1495–1654.  Gierke's Untersuchungen zur deutschen Staats- und Reichsgeschichte, xi.  Breslau.  1882.

Datt, J. P.  De Pace Imperii Publica.  Ulm.  1698.

Fellner, Th.  Zur Geschichte der österreichischen Centralverwaltung.  Mittheilungen des Instituts für österr. Geschichtsforschung, viii. 258—352.  Innsbruck.
1887.

Fischer.  Die Landfriedensverfassung unter Karl IV.  1883.

Franklin, Otto.  Das Reichshofgericht im Mittelalter.  Weimar.  1869.

—— Das königl. Kammergericht vor 1495.  Berlin.  1871.

—— Beiträge zur Geschichte der Reception des römischen Rechts in Deutschland.
Hanover.  1863.

Gothein, E.  Der gemeine Pfennig auf dem Reichstag zu Worms.

Hürbin.  Peter von Andlau, der Verfasser des ersten deutschen Reichsstaatsrechts.
Strassburg.  1897.

Jäger, A.  Geschichte der landständ. Verfassung Tirols, ii.  Innsbruck.  1885.

Kerner, J. G.  Staatsrecht der unmittelbaren Reichsritterschaft in Schwaben,
Franken, und am Rhein.  1786–9.

Keussen, H.  Die politische Stellung der Reichsstädte, 1440–57.  Bonn.  1885.

Kraus, V. von.  Das Nürnberger Reichsregiment.  Innsbruck.  1883.

Küffner, K.  Der Reichstag von Nürnberg, 1480.  Würzburg.  1892.

Kulpis.  Vorrede zu eines hochlöbl. schwäb. Kreises alten und neuen Kriegs-
ordnungen und Reglementen.  Stuttgart.  1737.

Leitner and Reumann.  Das Kriegswesen des heiligen röm. Reichs deutscher
Nation.  Leipzig.

Lorenz, O.  Reichskanzler und Reichskanzlei.  Preussische Jahrbücher, vol. xxix.
Berlin.  1872.

Philipps, G.  Deutsche Reichs und Rechtsgeschichte.  Munich.  1845.

Pütter, J. S.  Historische Entwickelung der heutigen Staatsverfassung des d.
Reichs.  3rd ed.  3 vols.  1798–9.  English translation by J. Dornford: An
historical development of the present political constitution of the German
Empire.  3 vols.  London, 1790.  Book iv. deals with Max. I's reign.

Schmidt, C. A.  Die Rezeption des römischen Rechts in Deutschland.  Rostock.  1868.

Schreckenstein, K. H. Freiherr Roth von.  Geschichte der ehemaligen freien
Ritterschaft in Schwaben, Franken und am Rheinstrom.

Schröder, R.  Lehrbuch des deutschen Rechtsgeschichte.  (Parts of 3rd and 4th
Periods.)  3rd ed.  Leipzig.  1898.

Seeliger, G.  Erzkanzler und Reichskanzleien.  Innsbruck.  1889.

—— Das deutsche Hofmeisteramt im späteren Mittelalter.  Innsbruck.  1885.

Simmern, E. Langwerth von.  Die Kreisverfassung Maximilians I und der schwäbische Reichskreis bis 1648.  Heidelberg.  1896.

Stintzing, R. v.  Zur Geschichte des römischen Rechts in Deutschland.  Sybel's
hist. Zeit. xxix. 408—38.  1873.

Tomaschek, J. A.  Die höchste Gerichtsbarkeit des deutschen Königs und Reichs
im 15 Jahrh.  Sitzungsberichte der philos.-hist. Classe d. k. Acad. der Wissen.
Vienna.  1865.

Treuer, G. S.  Bericht von der wahren Gelegenheit und dem rechten Ursprung
der Reichskreise.

Weckerle, J. B.  De Bertholdi Hennebergensis archiep. Moguntini studiis politicis.
1868.

Weigel, M.  Die Landfriedensverhandlungen unter König Siegmund.  1884.

Weiss, J.  Berthold v. Henneberg Erzbischof v. Mainz.  Freiburg i. B.  1889.

Weizsäcker, J.  Der Strassburger Fascikel v. 1431.  Ein Beitrag zur Geschichte
der Reichstagsverhandlungen etc.  Forschungen zur deutschen Gesch., xv.
399—456.  1875.

Wolf, G.  Deutsche Geschichte im Zeitalter der Gegenreformation.  Vol. I.
Berlin.  1899.  (See especially pp. 1—113 for account of the constitutional
position of the Empire about the time of the Reformation.)

Wülcker, E.  Reichstag und Reichsregiment zu Anfang der Reformationszeit.
Preuss. Jahrbücher.  April 1884.

## E.  Literary and educational.

Aschbach, J.  Die Wiener Universität und ihre Humanisten im Zeitalter Kais.
Maximilian I.  Vienna.  1877.

Bezold, F. v.  K. Celtis, der deutsche Erzhumanist.  Histor. Zeitschrift, XLIX.
1—45, 193—228.  1883.

——  Die armen Leute und die deutsche Literatur des späteren Mittelalters.
Histor. Zeitschr., XLI. 1—37.  1879.

Böhme, J. G.  Dissertatio de insigni favore Maximiliani I in poesin.  Leipzig.  1756.

Geiger, L.  Renaissance und Humanismus in Deutschland.  (Allgemeine Geschichte
in Einzeldarstellungen.)  Berlin.  1882.

Hartfelder, K.  Der Zustand der deutschen Hochschulen am Ende des Mittelalters.
Histor. Zeitschrift, LXIV. 50—107.  1890.

Knod.  Jakob Spiegel.  (Two programmes of the Schlettstadt gymnasium.)  Strassburg.  1884 and 1886.

Linton, W. J.  The Masters of Wood Engraving.  1889.

Marggraft, R.  K. Maximilian I und Albrecht Dürer in Nürnberg.  1840.

Martin.  Die Germania von Wimpheling, übersetzt und erläutert.  Strassburg.
1885.

Pastor, L.  Erläuterungen und Ergänzungen zu Janssens Geschichte des deutschen
Volkes, herausgegeben von L. Pastor, Freiburg i. B. 1898; among these essays
see especially J. Knepper, Nationaler Gedanke und Kaiseridee bei den elsässi-
schen Humanisten, with a bibliography illustrating the growth of the national idea
under Maximilian, and J. Gény, Die Reichsstadt Schlettstadt etc. 1490–1536.

Schmidt, Charles.  Histoire littéraire de l'Alsace à la fin du xv$^{ième}$ et au commencement du xvi$^{ième}$ siècle.  2 vols.  Paris.  1879.

Schönherr, D.  Zur Geschichte des Grabmals Kaiser Maximilians.  Archiv f. Geschichte und Alterthum Tirols.

Schreiber, H.  Geschichte der Albert-Ludwigsuniversität in Freiburg.  Freiburg i. B.
1857.

Struver.  Die Schule von Schlettstadt.  Leipzig.  1880.

Thausing, M.  Dürer, Geschichte seines Lebens und seiner Kunst.  2nd ed.  1884.

Voigt, G.  Enea Silvio de' Piccolomini und sein Zeitalter.  3 vols.  Berlin.  1856–63.

Ward, A. W.  Tewrdanck und Weisskunig, and their historical interest.  In an
English Miscellany presented to Dr Furnivall.  Oxford.  1901.

Wegele, Fr.  Geschichte der deutschen Historiographie seit dem Auftreten des
Humanismus (ch. I.–IV. as to Maximilian's encouragement of historical
research, etc.).  Munich.  1885.

Wiskowatoff.  Jakob Wimpheling, sein Leben und seine Schriften.  Berlin.  1867.

## F.  Ecclesiastical.

Dacheux, L.  Un réformateur Catholique, Jean Geiler de Kaisersberg, prédicateur
à Strasbourg.  Paris.  1876.

Gebhardt, B.  Die Gravamina der deutschen Nation gegen den römischen Hof.
Breslau.  1884.

Gothein, E.   Politische und religiöse Volksbewegungen vor der Reformation. Breslau.  1878.

Scharpff, F. A.   Der Cardinal und Bischof Nicolaus von Cusa als Reformator in Kirche, Reich und Philosophie.  Tübingen.  1871.

Schneider, J.   Die kirchliche u. politische Wirksamkeit des Cardinals R. Peraudi. Halle.  1882.

Stumpf, Th.   Die politische Ideen des Nicolaus von Cues.  Cologne.  1865.

## G.  Social and economic.

Gothein, E.   Die Lage des Bauernstandes am Ende des Mittelalters in S. W. Deutschland.  Westdeutsche Zeitschrift für Gesch., vol. iv.

Haupt, H.   Ein oberrheinischer Revolutionär aus dem Zeitalter Kais. Maximilians I. Westdeutsche Zeitschr. für Geschichte, Ergänzungsheft viii.

Jastrow, J.   Die Volkszahl deutscher Städte zu Ende des Mittelalters.  Historische Untersuchungen.  Berlin.  1886.

Lamprecht, K.   Deutsche Geschichte, vol. v. pp. 1—217.  Berlin.  1894.  (Especially for the social and economic aspects of history.)

—— Die Entwickelung des rheinischen Bauernstandes.  Westdeutsche Zeitschrift für Geschichte, vol. vi.

Mayer, F. M.   Der innerösterreichische Bauernkrieg im Jahre 1515.   Archiv f. österr. Gesch., Band lxv.

Schultz, A.   Deutsches Leben im xiv. und xv. Jahrhundert.  Vienna.  1892.

Ulmann, H.   Franz von Sickingen.  Leipzig.  1872.

# CHAPTER X.

## HUNGARY AND THE SLAVONIC KINGDOMS.

### BIBLIOGRAPHIES.

Krones, F., Ritter von Marchland. Grundriss der österreichischen Geschichte. Vienna. 1882. Index of subjects and names, pp. 926 sqq.; for the period treated in this Chapter, see pp. 390—440. (Up to the date of its publication the most complete bibliography of Austro-Hungarian history.)

Chevalier, U. Répertoire des sources historiques du Moyen Âge. Part II.: Topo-Bibliographie. Montbéliard, 1894, etc. See s. vv. Bohème, Hongrie, Pologne (published 1901). (Useful lists.)

Potthast, A. Bibliotheca historica medii aevi. Second revised edition. Berlin. 1896. (Contains in Appendix, nos. 17, 18, 19, the chief sources of the history of Bohemia, Hungary and Poland respectively; while the literature on those sources is given in the body of the work.)

Horváth, E. (Jenő) de Róna. Magyar hadi krónika (Hungarian military annals). Published by the Hungarian Akadémia. Budapest. 1895. (Contains full lists of the literature bearing on the military events of the period, pp. 245, 331.)

Havass, R. Bibliotheca Hungariae geographica. (Contains a full bibliography of local historiography.)

Finkel, L. Bibliografia historyi Polskiej, I. (Polish historical bibliography.) Lemberg. 1891.

Zeissberg, H. Die polnische Geschichtsschreibung im Mittelalter. Leipzig. 1873.

As to Bohemia the most complete bibliographical indications will be found in Krones (see above): and in E. Denis, Fin de l'indépendance de la Bohème. 2 vols. Paris. 1890.

Jastrow's Jahresberichte der Geschichtswissenschaft contain ample material to bring up the bibliography within two years of the present date. For current literature, i.e. such as appeared not earlier than three months previously, consult English Historical Review, Deutsche Zeitschrift für Geschichtswissenschaft, Historische Zeitschrift, and the publications of the Academies of Science at Vienna, Budapest, Cracow and Prague.

For the reign of Matthias Corvinus, covering the period of thirty-two years previous to that treated of in this chapter, see the full list of the sources bearing on the reign, in Hadtörténeti Közlemények (Annals of military history), published by the Hungarian Academy, in Part for 1890, pp. 252—264; and in Part for 1894, pp. 695—698.

## I. LAWS, CHARTERS, DOCUMENTS, DESPATCHES OF AMBASSADORS.

### A. Laws.

All the statutes of the period from 1490 to 1526 will be found, together with Verbŏczy's Tripartitum, in the great edition, published in 1896, under the title Corpus Juris Hungarici 1000–1895. The short, but very useful, juristic and historic notes to the statutes of the period 1490–1526 are by Professors C. Óvári and A. Kolosvári.

### B. Charters, Documents.

The Central Archives at Budapest contain over 35,000 documents and charters from the time previous to 1526, and the majority of those documents date from the fifteenth century. There are also numerous and important charters to be found both in the archives of towns like Pécs, Kassa, Arad and the Transylvanian towns, and in the private archives of the great families, such as the Csákys, the Forgáchs, the Eszterházys, the Bornemiszas, etc. For all these documents there are now various periodical publications, including genealogy and heraldry, edited or subsidised by the Hungarian Academy.

For our period nearly all the important charters and documents will be found in:

Acta Tomiciana, temp. Sigismundi regis Poloniae (a vast collection of documents made by Archbishop Peter Tomicki in the sixteenth century). Edited by Gorski, from 1852. (Very important for Poland, Bohemia and Hungary.)

Analecta saeculi XVI. (A manuscript in the library of the Budapest University.)

Engel, J. C. Monumenta Ungrica. Vienna. 1809.

Fejér, G. Codex diplomaticus Hungariae ecclesiasticus et civilis. Buda. 1829–44. Rendered more available by the chronological Tabula of F. Knauz, 1862, and the Index alphabeticus of M. Czinár, 1866. (It does not extend beyond 1440.)

Firnhaber, F. Beiträge z. Gesch. Ungarns unt. d. Regierung König Wladislaw's u. Ludwig's II. In Archiv f. Kunde österr. Geschichtsquellen. Published by the Vienna Academy of Science, 1849. See pp. 375—552, covering period 1490–3, containing 109 charters.

Katona, S. S. J. Historia critica regum Hungariae. Buda. 1778–1817. 8vo. 42 vols. (Contains a very great number of documents printed from the originals.) To our period refer vols. XVII. XVIII. XIX.

Kovachich, M. G. Vestigia comitiorum apud Hungaros, Buda, 1790; and especially the Supplementa, ib., 1798–1801. 3 vols. (Many of the numerous charters and documents collected by Kovachich and his son are printed in the Vestigia and other works by them.)

Pray, G. S. J. Epistolae procerum regni Hungariae (1490–1531). Vol. I. Vienna. 1806. (A valuable compilation.)

Theiner, A. Vetera monumenta historica Hungariam sacram illustrantia......ex tabulariis Vaticanis deprompta. Rome. 1859–60. 2 vols.

Vatikáni Magyarországi Okirattár. (Hungarian archives from the Vatican Library, a periodical publication of the Hungarian Academy.) See especially the part published in 1884.

In addition to the preceding works, there is much material to be found in the Archives of Vienna and Modena, and also in those of Mantua.

In the Monumenta Hungariae historica published by the Hungarian Academy in four divisions (Diplomataria, Scriptores, Monumenta comitialia, Acta externa) are many charters and documents bearing on the reigns of Wladislav II and Louis II.

## C. Ambassadors' Despatches.

Several of these are in Pray's Epistolae (see above); the most abundant collection of such material is however to be found in the Despatches of the Venetian ambassadors, contained chiefly in the Diari of Marino Sanuto the younger. 58 vols. 1496–1533.

A useful extract of the whole has been published for the years 1496–1515, by Valentinelli, 1863, in Esposizione di rapporti fra la Repubblica Veneta e gli Slavi meridionali. Extracts from the Diari bearing on Hungarian history have been printed by G. Wenczel, in the Publications of the Hungarian Academy.

For many important events of the period under question (1490–1526), Sanuto is not only the chief but the sole source of information.

## II. CHRONICLERS AND HISTORIANS.

For Bohemia the most important contemporary history is the work of John Dubravius, Historiae regni Bohemiae......ab initio......libri xxxiii., in Freher, Scriptores rer. Bohem., 1602, more particularly for our period.

With regard chiefly to Hungarian affairs see:

Bonfinius, Antonius (died 1502). Rerum Hungaricarum decades libris xlv. comprehensae, covering the years 364–1495, but important only for the fifteenth century. Best edition, Leipzig, 1771.

Cuspinianus, Joannes. Conventus Maximiliani I Caes. cum Vladislao Hungariae, Sigismundo Poloniae ac Ludovico Bohemiae Regibus (in Freher, Germ. rer. Script. ii. pp. 304–320); and especially his Tagebuch, covering the years 1502–27 (in Fontes rer. Austriac. Script. i. pp. 397–416).

Istvánfi, N. Regni Hungarici historia libris xxxiv......ab anno 1490...... Vienna, 1758. (Istvánfi, who died in 1615, although not strictly contemporary, is still very important for the period 1490–1526.)

Tubero, L., a Dalmatian. Commentariorum de rebus suo tempore in Pannonia et Turcia et finitimis regionibus gestis libri xi., covering the years 1490 to 1522. In Schwandtner, Script. rer. Hung. ii. pp. 107—381.

## III. MODERN WORKS.

### A. General.

The general histories of the Austro-Hungarian empire by Krones, Handb. d. Gesch. Österr. and Huber, Gesch. Österr. vol. iii. (Gesch. d. europ. Staaten), and in the general histories of Hungary by L. Szalay, M. Horváth, Engel, Fessler (ed. E. Klein), and Sayous (in French), contain some useful chapters; while the fifth volume of Palacky's Geschichte von Böhmen (Prague, 1865) is still fairly exhaustive for the period after 1490. The best general history of our period, however, is that written for the "millennial," A Magyar nemzet története (Hist. of the Magyar nation), ed. by Alex. Szilágyi. Vol. iv., by W. Fraknói, who has published a series of authoritative monographs on the chief events of the period, comprises all the aspects of Hungarian history from 1458 to 1526.

### B. Monographs.

Fraknói, W. Mátyás Király élete (1890), (Life of King Matthias); Magyarország a mohácsi vész előtt (Hungary before the disaster of Mohács), 1884; Bakócz Tamás életrajza (Biography of T. B.).

Márki, A.    Dózsa György és forradalma (George Dózsa and his rebellion), 1886.
Neustadt.    Ungarn's Verfall am Beginn des xvi. Jahrhunderts.    Ungarische Revue
    for 1885.
Thury, J.    Török történetirók (Turkish historians).    Budapest.    1890.

Minor monographs can easily be reached by means of the bibliographies under (I).

## IV.  HISTORICAL MAPS;  BATTLE-PLANS.

There are as yet no special Historical Atlases for the history of Hungary, Bohemia, or Poland.  For Hungary a historical gazetteer is supplied in D. Csánki's very elaborate Magyarország Földrajza a Hunyadiak korában (The topography of Hungary in the time of the Hunyadis: fifteenth century).  Consult also the map of Hungary in 1490 in article Magyarország in the Hungarian Encyclopedia Pallas.  Some battle-plans will be found in the Hadi krónika mentioned above.  See also the general Historical Atlases of Spruner-Menke and Droysen, and the Oxford Historical Atlas.

The best general history of Poland in Polish is Bobrzynski's Dzieje Polski n zarysie (Sketch of Polish history), Warsaw, 1879.  There is much historico-geographical material in Lelewels' work Polska dziej (1868); and the great Polish History of Adam Naruszewicz in Polish is always helpful, chiefly in the Lelewel edition with the atlas (1803).  In German the most authoritative History of Poland is the Geschichte Polen's by R. Roepell, continued by J. Caro in vols. i.–v., Hamburg and Gotha, 1840–86 (Gesch. d. europ. Staaten).  All the requisite details for closer research will be found in the bibliographical work of Finkel (see above); and in Pawinski's report in Jastrow for 1891.

On early Russian history consult A. Rambaud, Histoire de la Russie, new ed. Paris.  1893.

# CHAPTER XI.

## THE CATHOLIC KINGS.

### I. MANUSCRIPTS.

Accounts of some of the chief collections of Spanish historical manuscripts are contained in :

Altamira y Crevea, R.  Historia y Arte.  Madrid.  1898.

Beer, R.  Handschriftenschätze v. Spanien.  Vienna.  1894.

Diaz Sanchez, F.  Villa y Archivo de Simancas.  Madrid.  1885.

Gallardo, B. J.  Biblioteca Española.  Madrid.  4 vols.  1863–89.

Gayangos, P. de.  Catalogue of Spanish Manuscripts in the British Museum.  London.  1875.

Morel-Fatio, A.  Catalogue des MSS. Espagnols dans la Bibliothèque Nationale.  Paris.  1881.

Ochoa, E. de.  Manuscritos Españoles en la Biblioteca de Paris.  Paris.  1844.

### II.  PRINTED COLLECTIONS OF DOCUMENTS ; CONTEMPORARY WORKS ; CHRONICLES.

Academia de la Historia.  Memorias de la R. Academia de la Historia.  Vols. iv. vi. viii.  Madrid.  1796–1852.

—— Cortes de Leon y Castilla.  Vol. iv.  Madrid.  1882.

—— Cortes de Aragon, Valencia y Cataluña.  Madrid.  1897.

—— Boletín de la R. Academia de la Historia.  Madrid.  1877–1900.

Alberi, E.  Relazioni degli Ambasciatori Veneti.  Vols. i. ii.  Florence.  1839–40.

Alcocer, P. de.  Relación sobre las Comunidades, ed. Gamero.  Seville.  1872.

Almakkari.  Mohammedan Dynasties in Spain (trans. by P. de Gayangos).  Oriental Translations Fund.  London.  1840.

Argensola, B. L. de.  Anales de Aragón.  Saragossa.  1630.

Bergenroth and Gayangos.  Calendar of Letters, etc. relating to Negociations between England and Spain.  Vols. i.–iv.  London.  1862–82.

Bernaldez, A.  Historia de los Reyes.  In Crónicas de los Reyes de Castilla.

Bleda, J.  Corónica de los Moros de España.  Valencia.  1618.

Bofarull y Mascaro, P. de.  Documentos inéditos de la Corona de Aragón.  Barcelona.  1847–61.

Castillo, D. Enriquez de.  Crónica del Rey Enrique IV.  Ed. J. M. de Flores.  Included in :

Crónicas.  Coleccion de las Crónicas y Memorias de los Reyes de Castilla.  7 vols.  Madrid.  1779–87.

Crónicas de los Reyes de Castilla.   Vol. III.   In Rivadeneyra Biblioteca, vol. LXX. Madrid.  1878.

Dormer, D. J.   Anales de Aragón.   1516–40.   [Saragossa?]  1697.

Eguilaz Yanguas, L. de.   Conquista de Granada.   Granada.   1894.

Epistolario Español.   In Rivadeneyra Biblioteca, vols. XIII. and LII.   Madrid.  1870, 1884.

Gachard, L. P.   Correspondance de Charles-Quint et Adrien VI.   Brussels.   1859.

—— Voyages des Souverains des Pays-Bas.   Comm. Roy. d'Histoire.   Brussels. 1885.

Galindez Carvajal, L.   Anales Breves.   Navarrete, etc., Documentos Inéditos, vol. XVIII.

Gomez de Castro, A.   De Rebus Gestis Francisci Ximenii.   In A. Schott, Hispaniae Illustratae.

Guevara, A. de.   Epístolas Familiares.   Salamanca.   1578.   In Epistolario Español.

Guicciardini, F.   Legazione di Spagna.   Opere Inedite, vol. VI.   Florence.   1864.

Hinojosa, R. de.   Despachos de la Diplomacia Pontífica en España.   Madrid.  1896.

Jovio, P.   Vita Hadriani VI.   Basel.   1578.

Lanz, K.   Correspondenz des Kaisers Karls V.   Vol. I.   Leipzig.   1844.

Le Glay, A. J. G.   Négociations diplomatiques entre la France et l'Autriche. Collection de documents inédits.   Paris.   1845.

Maldonado, J.   El Movimiento de España.   Madrid.   1840.

Marinaeus Siculus, L.   De Rebus Gestis Hispaniae.   Reprinted in A. Schott, Hispaniae Illustratae.

Mejía, P.   Relación de las Comunidades.   In Rivadeneyra Biblioteca, vol. XXI. 1852.

—— Historia Imperial y Cesárea.   Madrid.   1655.

Moret, J. de.   Anales de Navarra.   12 vols.   Tolosa.   1890–2.

Navarrete, Zabálburu and others.   Documentos Inéditos para la Historia de España. Vols. I. II. III. VII. IX. XI. XII. XIV. XVII. XVIII. XXIII. XXIV. XXV. XXXVI. XXXVIII. XXXIX. L. LI. CVI. CXII.   Madrid.   1842–92.   Index.   Madrid.   1891.

Oviedo, G. Fernandez de.   Las Quinquagenas de la Nobleza de España.   Ed. La Fuente.   R. Academia de la Historia.   Madrid.   1880.

Peter Martyr.   (Vermigli, P. M. de.)   Opus Epistolarum.   1670.

Pulgar, H. P. del.   Crónica de los Reyes Católicos.   Rerum Hispanicarum Scriptores.   Frankfort.   3 vols.   1579–81.

—— Claros Varones de España.   In F. Gomez de Cebdareal, Centon Epistolario. Madrid.   1775.

Quintanilla y Mendoza, P.   Fray Francisco Ximenes de Cisneros.   Palermo.  1653.

Rivadeneyra, M.   Biblioteca de Autores Españoles.   71 vols.   Madrid.   1849–80.

Salazar de Mendoza, P.   Crónica del Gran Cardinal.   Toledo.   1625.

Sandoval, P. de.   Historia del Emperador Carlos V.   Pampeluna.   1634.

Sayas, F. D.   Anales de Aragón.   1520–25.   Saragossa.   1666.

Schottus, Andreas.   Hispaniae Illustratae.   4 vols.   Frankfort.   1603–8.

Sepúlveda, J. G. de.   De Rebus Gestis Caroli V.   1780.

Simpson, L. F.   Autobiography of Charles V.   London.   1862.

Ulloa, A.   Vita dell' Imperatore Carlo V.   Venice.   1562.

Valera, D. de.   Crónica de Hyspaña.   Burgos.   1487.

Verardus, C.   Expugnatio Regni Granatae.   In A. Schott, Hispaniae Illustratae.

Weiss, C.   Papiers d'État du Cardinal de Granvelle.   Collection de documents inédits.   Vol. I.   Paris.   1841.

Ximenes de Cisneros, F.   Cartas.   In Epistolario Español.

Zurita, G. de.   Anales de Aragón.   Vol. VI.   Saragossa.   1620.

## III. LATER GENERAL HISTORIES, MONOGRAPHS, AND BIOGRAPHIES.

Álvarez de Araujo, A.   Las Cuatro Órdenes Militares.   Madrid.   1866.

Amador de los Rios, J.   Historia crítica de la Literatura Española.   Vol. VII. Madrid.   1865.

—— Los Judios de España y Portugal.   3 vols.   Madrid.   1875–6.

Balaguer, V.   Reyes Católicos.   In Historia general de España by A. Canovas del Castillo.   Madrid.   1894.

Baumgarten, H.   Geschichte Karls V.   3 vols.   Stuttgart.   1885.

Bofarull, A. de.   Historia de Cataluña.   1876.

Boissonade, P.   Réunion de la Navarre à la Castille.   Paris.   1893.

Carderera y Solano, V.   Iconografía Española.   2 vols.   Madrid.   1855–64.

Cean Bermudez, J. A.   Diccionario Histórico de los más ilustres Profesores de las Bellas Artes en España.   6 vols.   Madrid.   1800.

Clemencín, D.   Elogio de la Reina Isabel.   Real Academia, etc.   Madrid.   1796.

Clonard, de.   Historia de las Armas de Infantería y Caballería.   16 vols.   Madrid. 1851.

Danvila y Collado, M.   La Germanía de Valencia.   Real Academia, etc.   Madrid. 1884.

—— La Expulsión de los Moriscos.   Madrid.   1889.

—— Las Comunidades de Castilla.   Real Academia, etc.   Madrid.   1897.

Davillier, Baron.   Les Arts décoratifs en Espagne au Moyen Âge.   Paris.   1879.

Ebert, A.   Germania der Handwerke Valencias.   Kassel.   1849.

Fernandez y Gonzalez, F.   Los Mudéjares de Castilla.   Madrid.   1866.

Ferrer del Rio, A.   Levantamiento de las Comunidades de Castilla.   Madrid.   1850.

Fitzmaurice-Kelly, J.   History of Spanish Literature.   (Short Histories of the Literature of the World, v.)   London.   1898.

Flores, H.   Reinas Católicas.   2 vols.   Madrid.   1770.

Ford, R.   A Handbook for Travellers in Spain.   London.   1845.

Gachard, L. P.   Jeanne la Folle.   1858.

Graetz, H.   Geschichte der Juden.   Vol. VIII.   Leipzig.   1864.

Haebler, K.   Der Streit Ferdinands u. Philips um die Regierung.   Dresden.   1888.

Havemann, W.   Darstellungen aus der inneren Geschichte Spaniens.   Göttingen. 1850.

Hefele, C. J. von.   Der Cardinal Ximenes.   Tübingen.   1851.

Höfler, K. von.   Depeschen des Botschafters Vicenzo Quirino.   1884.

—— Aufstand der castilianischen Städte.   Prague.   1876.

—— Don Antonio de Acuña.   Vienna.   1882.

—— Donna Juana, Königin v. Leon, etc.   Denkschr. d. k. Akad. d. Wiss., Abth. Phil.-Hist.   Vol. XXXV.   Vienna.   1885.

—— Monumenta Hispanica.   Abhandl. d. k. böhm. Ges. d. Wiss.   Ser. VI. Vol. II. No. 3.   Prague.   1882.

—— Quellenkunde der ersten Regierungsjahre Karls V.   Denksch. d. k. Akad. d. Wiss., Abth. Phil.-Hist.   Vols. XXV. XXVII. XXXIII.   Vienna.   1876–78–83.

Janer, F.   Condición Social de los Moriscos.   R. Academia de la Historia.   Madrid. 1857.

Juste, T.   Charles-Quint et Marguérite d'Autriche.   Brussels.   1858.

Lafuente, M.   Historia General de España.   26 vols.   Madrid.   1850.

Llaguno y Amirola, F.   Arquitectos y Arquitectura de España.   4 vols.   Madrid. 1829.

Mariana, J. de, and Miniana, J. M.   Historia General de España.   10 vols. Madrid.   1794.

Mariéjol, J. H.　Pierre Martyr d'Angleria.　Paris.　1889.

―― L'Espagne sous Ferdinand et Isabelle.　Paris.　1892.

Menendez y Pelayo, M.　Historia de las Ideas estéticas in España.　Madrid.　1883.

Mignet, F. A. M.　Rivalité de François I$^{er}$ et de Charles-Quint.　Madrid.　1875.

Moratín, L. Fernandez de.　Orígenes del Teatro Español.　In Rivadeneyra Biblioteca.　1846.

Müller, M. J.　Die letzten Zeiten von Granada.　Munich.　1863.

Navarro y Rodrigo, C.　El Cardinal Cisneros.　1862.

Orti y Lara, M.　La Inquisición.　1897.

Prescott, W. H.　Ferdinand and Isabella.　London.　Edited by J. F. Kirk.　1887.

La Primaudaie, F. E. de.　Occupation Espagnole en Afrique.　Algiers.　1875.

Ranke, L. von.　Die Osmanen u. die spanische Monarchie.　Vols. xxxv. and xxxvi. of Sämmtliche Werke.　Leipzig.　1874, etc.

Riaño, J. F.　The industrial Arts in Spain.　South Kensington Museum.　London. 1879.

Robertson, W.　Charles the Fifth.　Ed. W. H. Prescott.　London.　1857.

Rodriguez Villa, A.　Doña Juana la Loca.　Madrid.　1892.

―― Don Francisco de Rojas.　Madrid.　1896.

Schack, A. F. von.　Geschichte der dramatischen Literatur u. Kunst in Spanien. Berlin.　1845.

Schirrmacher, F. W.　Geschichte Spaniens.　Vol. vi.　1893.

Stirling-Maxwell, Sir W.　Annals of the Artists of Spain.　Vol. i.　London (reissued).　1891.

Street, G. F.　Gothic Architecture in Spain.　London.　1865.

Ticknor, G.　History of Spanish Literature.　3rd ed.　3 vols.　London.　1863.

## IV.  WORKS ON CONSTITUTIONAL, LEGAL, ECONOMIC AND ECCLESIASTICAL HISTORY.

Antequera, J. M.　Historia de la Legislación Española.　Madrid.　1874.

Arias y Miranda, J.　Influjo que tuvo en España su Dominación en América. R. Academia de la Historia.　Madrid.　1854.

Blancas, G.　Commentarii Rerum Aragonensium.　Translated by M. Hernandez, for the Diputacion Provincial.　Saragossa.　1876.

―― Coronaciones de los Reyes de Aragon.　Saragossa.　1641.

Bonn, M. J.　Spaniens Niedergang während der Preisrevolution des 16. Jahrhunderts. Munich.　1896.

Cárdenas, F. de.　Historia de la Propiedad Territorial en España.　Madrid.　1873.

Castillo de Bovadilla, G.　Política para Corregidores.　Barcelona.　1624.

Colmeiro, M. de.　Cortes de Leon y Castilla.　Madrid.　1885.

―― Historia de la Economía Política en España.　Madrid.　1863.

Coroleu, J., and Pella, J.　Las Cortes Catalanas.　1876.

Danvila y Collado, M.　Las Libertades de Aragón.　Madrid.　1881.

―― El Poder Civil en España.　1896.

Du Hamel, V.　Histoire Constitutionelle de la Monarchie Espagnole.　Paris.　1845.

Escosura y Heira, A. de.　El Feudalismo en España.　Madrid.　1856.

Fuente, V. de la.　Historia eclesiástica de España.　Vols. iv. v.　2nd ed.　Madrid. 1873-4.

Gallardo y Fernandez, F.　Rentas de la Corona de España.　7 vols.　Madrid.　1805.

Gams, P. B.　Kirchengeschichte von Spanien.　Vols. iv. v.　Ratisbon.　1876-9.

Gonzalez, T.　Censo de la Población en el Siglo xvi.　Madrid.　1829.

Gounon-Loubens, J.　Administration intérieure de la Castille au xvi. siècle.　Paris. 1860.

Haebler, K. Die wirtschaftliche Blüte Spaniens im xvi. Jahrhundert. Berlin. 1888.

Llorente, J. A. Historia crítica de la Inquisición. 10 vols. Madrid. 1870.

Mariana, J. de. Del Rey y de la Institución real. In Rivadeneyra, Biblioteca. Barcelona. 1880.

Marichalar, A., and Manrique, C. Historia de la Legislación de España. Madrid. 1868.

Marina, F. M. Ensayo sobre la Legislación de Leon y Castilla. 2 vols. Madrid. 1834.

Martinez Alcubilla, M. Códigos Antiguos de España. 2 vols. Madrid. 1885.

Mendoza, P. Salazar de. Dignidades seglares de Castilla. Toledo. 1618.

Menendez y Pelayo, M. Los Heterodoxos Españoles. 3 vols. Madrid. 1880.

Paramo, L. de. De Origine et Progressu officii Sanctae Inquisitionis. Madrid. 1598.

Ramirez, J. Las Pragmáticas que están fechas para buena Gouernación del Reino. 1503.

Ribera, J. Orígenes del Justicia de Aragon. 1897.

Sempere, J. Histoire des Cortes d'Espagne. 1815.

—— Grandeur et Décadence de la Monarchie Espagnole. 2 vols. Paris. 1826.

(*See also Bibliographies of Chapters I. II. and IV.*)

# CHAPTER XII.

## FRANCE.

### BIBLIOGRAPHIES.

Chevalier, U.   Répertoire des sources historiques du moyen âge.   Bio-bibliographie. Paris.   1877–88.   Topo-bibliographie.   Paris.   1894–5.

Franklin, A.   Les Sources de l'histoire de France.   Paris.   1877.

Langlois, C. V., and Stein, H.   Les Archives de l'histoire de France.   Paris.   Picard. 1893.

Monod, G.   Bibliographie de l'histoire de France.   Paris.   1888.

Potthast, A.   Bibliotheca historica Medii Aevi.   2nd ed.   2 vols.   Berlin.   1895.

Vidier, A.   Répertoire méthodique du moyen âge français.   1894 sqq.   (Annual.) Extr. from the Moyen Âge.

## I.   CONTEMPORARY CHRONICLES, COLLECTIONS OF DOCUMENTS, ETC.

Amboise, Card., Lettres de, à Louis XII.   1504–14.   4 vols.   Brussels.   1712.

Ammanatus, J., called Piccolomini.   Epistolae et Comm. Jacobi Piccolominei, Card. Papiensis (1479).   Milan.   1506.

Arcq, Douet d'.   Comptes de l'Hôtel aux XIVᵉ et XVᵉ siècles.   Soc. Hist. de France.   Paris.   1851.

Auton, J. d'.   Chroniques 1498–1515.   Ed. R. Maulde la Clavière.   Soc. Hist. de France.   Paris.   1889.

Basin, T. (Bishop).   Histoire de Charles VII et de Louis XI.   Ed. J. Quicherat. Soc. Hist. de France.   Paris.   1854–9.

Baude, H.   Éloge de Charles VII.   Ed. Vallet de Viriville.   Paris.   1855.

Belcarius (Beaucaire).   Rerum Gallicarum commentarii 1461–1530.

Berry (Gilles le Bouvier).   Les Croniques du feu roi Charles VII.   Paris.   1528, etc.

Bonnardot, François.   Histoire générale de Paris.   Registre des délibérations du Bureau de Paris, 1499–1526.   Paris.   1866, etc.

Bouchard, A.   Les grandes chroniques de Bretaigne—1488.   Paris.   1514, etc.

Bourgeois de Paris.   Journal d'un, 1404–49.   Ed. Tuetey.   Paris.   1881.   Soc. Hist. de Paris.   Also Michaud et Poujoulat, II.

——   Journal d'un, 1515–36.   Ed. Lalanne.   Soc. Hist. de Fr.   Paris.   1854.

Champier, S.   Trophaeum Gallorum.   Lyons.   1507.

——   Le recueil ou croniques......de Lorraine, de Hierusalem, de Cicile, et de Bar—1510.   Lyons.   s. d.

Charles VIII. Letters. Ed. P. Pélicier. Soc. Hist. de France. Vol. I. Paris. 1898.

Chartier, J. Histoire de Charles VII. Ed. Vallet de Viriville. Paris. 1858–9.

Chastelain, G. Chronique des ducs de Bourgogne. Ed. Kervyn de Lettenhove. Brussels. 1863–5.

Collection des documents inédits. Series 1.
    VIII. 2. Lettres, etc., relatives à la Guerre du bien public. Ed. Quicherat.
    XX. Documents relatifs à l'histoire du tiers état. Ed. Thierry. 4 vols.
    XXVII. 2. Lettres des Rois, Reines, et autres personnages des cours de France et d'Angleterre (1301–1515). Ed. Bréquigny.
    XLII. Journal des États Généraux, 1484, par Masselin. Ed. A. Bernier.
    XLIII. Procès-verbaux des séances du Conseil de Régence de Charles VIII. 1484–5. Ed. A. Bernier.
    XLIV. Négotiations diplomatiques entre la France et l'Autriche, 1500–30. Ed. Le Glay. 2 vols.
    XLVI. 1. Négotiations de France dans le Levant. Ed. E. Charrière. Introduction.

Commines, P. de. Mémoires contenant l'histoire des rois Louis XI et Charles VIII, 1464–98. Ed. Dupont. Soc. Hist. de France. Paris. 1840–7. Also with documents by Godefroy, 1649, and Langlet Dufresnoy, 1747.

—— Lettres et négotiations. Ed. Kervyn de Lettenhove. 3 vols. Brussels. 1867.

Coville, A. L'Ordonnance Cabochienne (May, 1413). Publiée avec une introduction et des notes. Paris. Picard.

Desrey, P. Grandes Chroniques de Charles VIII. Paris. 1517.

Documents sur les règnes de Charles VIII, Louis XII et François I. Michaud et Poujoulat, v.

Du Clercq, J. Mémoires 1448–67. Petitot, XI. Michaud et Poujoulat, New Coll., III.

Escouchy, M. d'. Histoire d'une partie du règne de Charles VII, 1444–61. Ed. de Beaucourt. Soc. Hist. de France. Paris. 1863–4.

Gaguin, R. Epistolae. Paris. 1498.

—— Les Chroniques de France. Paris. 1514.

Gilles, N. Les Annales et Chroniques de France. Charles VIII. Paris. 1492, etc.

Gingins la Sarraz, F. de. Dépêches des ambassadeurs Milanais sur les Campagnes de Charles le Hardi duc de Bourgogne. 2 vols. Paris and Geneva. 1858.

Godefroy, Denis II. Histoire de Charles VIII. Paris. 1684. (Collection of Chronicles, etc.)

Godefroy, T. Histoires de Charles VIII et Louis XII. Paris. 1615, 1620, 1622. (Collection of Chronicles, etc.)

Jacqueton, G. Documents relatifs à l'administration financière en France de Charles VII à François I. Paris. 1891.

Jaligny, G. de. Histoire de plusieurs choses…du règne de Charles VIII, 1486–8 and 1498. In Godefroy, Hist. de Charles VIII. No. 1.

La Marche, O. de. Memoires, 1435–92. Ed. Beaune et d'Arbaumont. Soc. Hist. de France. 1883–.

La Trémouille, L. de. Correspondance. Ed. Duc de la Trémouille. Paris. 1875.

Legrand, J. Vie et histoire de Louis XI. Manuscript of Bibl. Nationale. 2 vols. With 31 vols. of documents.

Le Roux de Lincy. Recueil de chansons du XIVe et XVe siècles. Paris. 1857.

Leseur, G. Histoire de Gaston IV, C. de Foix. Chron. fr. inéd. du XVe s. edit. H. Courteault. Soc. Hist. de Fr. 1893, etc.

Louis XI. Letters. Ed. Charavay and Vaesen. 6 vols. Soc. Hist. de France. 1883–98.

Maupoint, J. Journal. Ed. G. Fagniez. Soc. Hist. de Paris. 1877.

Molinet, J.   Chroniques, 1476–1506.   Ed. J. A. Buchon.   Paris.   1827–9.

Monstrelet, E. de.   Cronicques de France, etc., 1400–44.   Ed. Douet d'Arcq.   Soc. Hist. de France.   Paris.   1857–62.

Morice.   Mémoires pour servir de preuves à l'Histoire de Bretagne.   Paris.   1743–. 3 vols.

Ordonnances des Rois de France de la iiiᵉ race jusqu'en 1514.   Paris.   1723–1849. 22 vols. in fol.

Pontanus, Joannes Jovianus.   De bello Neapolitano (Ferdinand v. John of Anjou) libri sex.   Venice.   1518, etc.

Procédures politiques de Louis XII.   Ed. R. Maulde la Clavière.

Rosier des Guerres, le.   Paris.   1522.

Saint-Gelais, J. de.   Histoire de Louis XII (to 1510).   Ed. Godefroy.   Paris.   1622.

Seyssel, C. de.   La grand monarchie de France.   Paris.   1519.

—— Les louanges de…Louis XII, etc.   Ed. Godefroy.   Paris.   1622.

Troyes, J. de.   Les Chronicques du très chrétien…Loys de Valois, 1460–83 (misnamed Chronique scandaleuse).   Petitot, xiii. xiv.   Michaud et Poujoulat, New Coll., iv.

Vigneulles, P. de, des Metzer Bürgers Gedenkbuch, 1471–1522.   Ed. Michelaut. Bibl. des literar. Vereins.   Stuttgart.   1852.

Wavrin du Forestel, J. de.   Anchiennes Cronicques d'Engleterre.   Ed. Dupont. Soc. Hist. de France.   Paris.   1858, etc.

# II.   LATER WORKS.

## A.   General Histories.

Anselme de Ste Marie, le Père.   Histoire généalogique et chronologique de la Maison Royale de France, des pairs et grands officiers, etc.   9 vols.   Paris. 1726–33.

Cherrier, C. de.   Histoire de Charles VIII.   2 vols.   Paris.   1868.

Du Fresne de Beaucourt, G.   Histoire de Charles VII.   6 vols.   Paris.   1880–.

Kirk, J. Foster.   History of Charles the Bold.   3 vols.   London.   1864–8.

Legeay, U.   Histoire de Louis XI.   2 vols.   Paris.   1874.

Leroux de Lincy.   Histoire d'Anne de Bretagne.   4 vols.   Paris.   1860–1.

Martin, H.   Histoire de France.   17 vols.   Paris.   1833–6.

Maulde la Clavière, R.   Histoire de Louis XII.   Paris.   1890.   3 vols.   (Previous to his accession.)

Pigeonneau, H.   Histoire du Commerce de la France, to the fifteenth century. Paris.   1885.

Rainaldus, O.   Annales Ecclesiastici, 1198–1534.   Cologne.   1694, etc.

Schmidt, E. A.   Geschichte Frankreichs.   4 vols.   (Gesch. d. europ. Staaten.) Gotha.   1840.

Schmidt, C.   Précis de l'histoire de l'Église d'Occident pendant le moyen âge. Paris.   1885.

Tailhé.   Histoire de Louis XII.   Milan and Paris.   1755.

Toutey, E.   Charles le Téméraire et la Ligue de Constance.   Paris.   1902.

Vallet de Viriville.   Histoire de Charles VII.   3 vols.   Paris.   1865.

## B.  INSTITUTIONS.

Aubert, F.   Le Parlement de Paris de Philippe-le-Bel à Charles VII.   Paris.   1878.

Aucoc, L.   Le Conseil d'État avant et depuis 1789.   Paris.   1876.

Beaurepaire, R. de.   Les états de Normandie sous la domination Anglaise.   Evreux. 1859.

Bourel de La Roncière, C.   Histoire de la Marine française.   Vol. I.   Origines. Paris.   1899.

Boutaric, E.   Actes du Parlement de Paris.   2 vols.   Paris.   1863–7.

——   Institutions militaires de la France avant les armées permanentes.   Paris. 1863.

Clamageran.   Histoire de l'Impôt en France.   1867.

Coville, A.   Les États de Normandie.   Paris.   1894.

Daniel, G.   Histoire de la Milice française.   Paris.   1721.

Dansin, H.   Histoire du gouvernement de la France sous le règne de Charles VII. Paris.   1858.

Dareste, C.   Traites et droits de douanes dans l'ancienne France, 1304–1714. Bibl. de l'Éc. des Chartes.   VIII.   1846–7.

Garnier, J.   Recherche des Feux en Bourgogne aux XIVe et XVe siècles.   Dijon.   1876.

Glasson, E. D.   Histoire du Droit et des institutions de France.   Paris.   1887, etc.

Guettée, F. R.   Histoire de l'Église de France.   Vols. VII. VIII.   Paris.   1847–56.

Guidon Général des Finances, avec les annotations de V. Gelée.   Ed. S. Hardy. Paris.   1644.

Jacqueton, G.   Le Trésor de l'épargne sous François I.   Revue Historique.   1894.

La Chauvelays, J. de.   Étude sur les armées des ducs de Bourgogne.   Paris.   1881.

Laferrière, L. F. J.   Histoire du Droit français.   Paris.   1836.

Le Chanteur.   Dissertation historique et critique sur la Chambre des Comptes. 1765.

Le Grand, J.   Instruction sur le fait des Finances et Chambre des Comptes. Paris.   1583.

Luçay, H. de.   Les Secrétaires de l'état depuis leur institution jusqu'à la mort de Louis XV.   Paris.   1881.

Moreau de Beaumont.   Traité des impositions.   4 vols.   Paris.   1768.

Pardessus, J. M.   Essai historique sur l'organisation judiciaire de la France et l'administration de la justice depuis H. Capet jusqu'à Louis XII.   Ordonnances des rois de France.   Vol. XXI.   Paris.   1849.   Also separate : Paris.   1851.

Picot, G. M. R.   Histoire des États Généraux...de 1355–1614.   4 vols.   Paris. 1872.

——   Le Parlement de Paris sous Charles VIII.   Paris.   1877.

——   États généraux sous Charles VII.   Cabinet historique.   1878.

Rapport au grand conseil de Louis XI sur les abuses de la cour des aides.   1468. Bibl. Éc. des Chartes.   X.   1848–9.

Sée, H.   Louis XI et les Villes.   Paris.   1892.

Spont, A.   La taille en Languedoc.   Annales du Midi, 1890–1.

——   La gabelle du sel en Languedoc.   Annales du Midi, 1891, October.

——   Une recherche générale des feux, 1490.   Ann. Bull. Soc. Hist. de Fr. Paris.   1892.

——   La Marine française sous Charles VIII.   Rev. des Quest. Hist.   Vol. XV. 1894.

——   La Milice des francs-archers (1448–1500).   Rev. des Quest. Hist. LXI. 2. April, 1897.

Thomas, A.   Les États provinciaux de la France centrale sous Charles VII.   Paris. 1879.

Valois, N. Étude historique sur le Conseil du Roi. Introduction to the Inventaire des arrêts du conseil d'état (Henri IV). Paris. 1886.

—— Le Conseil du Roi aux xiv^e, xv^e, et xvi^e siècles. Paris. Picard. 1888.

Viollet, P. Election des députés aux états généraux en 1468, et 1484, d'après des documents de Bayonne, Senlis, Lyon, Orléans, Tours. Bibl. de l'Éc. des Chartes. xxvii. 1866.

Vuitry, A. Étude sur le Régime Financier de la France. Nouvelle Série. 2 vols. 1285–1380. Paris. 1883.

## C. Provincial.

Argentré, B. d'. L'histoire de Bretaigne jusques aux temps de Madame Anne, dernière duchesse. Paris. 1588.

Barante, A. de. Histoire des Ducs de Bourgogne. 12 vols., etc. Paris. 1824–6.

Bouchet, J. Annales d'Aquitaine et Poitou. 1524.

Boutaric, E. Organisation judiciaire du Languedoc au moyen âge. Bibl. de l'Éc. des Chartes. xvi. 1854–5. xvii. 1855–6.

Calmet, A. Histoire ecclésiastique et civile de Lorraine. 1728.

Daru, P. A. N. B. Histoire de Bretagne. 3 vols. Paris. 1816.

Dognon, P. Les Institutions politiques et administratives du pays de Languedoc du xiii^e siècle aux guerres de religion. Bibliot. Méridion. Sér. 2. Vol. 4. 1896.

Dom Felibien et Dom Lobineau. Histoire de Paris. 5 vols. Paris. 1725.

Dom Vaissète et Dom Devic. Histoire de Languedoc. 5 vols. Paris. 1733–45. 15 vols. Toulouse. 1872–.

Dupuy, A. Histoire de la réunion de la Bretagne à la France. 2 vols. Paris. 1880.

La Mure, J. M. de. Histoire des ducs de Bourbon et des comtes de Forez. Ed. Chantelauze. 3 vols. Lyons. 1860–8.

Le Moyne de la Borderie. Histoire de Bretagne. Rennes. 1897.

Morice, H., et Taillandier. Histoire ecclésiastique et civile de Bretagne. 2 vols. Paris. 1756.

Plancher, U. Histoire générale et particulière de Bourgogne. 4 vols. 1779, etc.

Ribbe, C. de. La Société provençale à la fin du moyen âge. Paris. 1898.

## D. Biography.

Boislisle, A. de. Notice sur Étienne de Vesc. In Annuaire Bulletin, Soc. Hist. de France. 1883–4.

Bricard, G. Un serviteur et compère de Louis XI : Jean Bourré, Seigneur du Plessis. 1424–1506. Paris. 1893.

Chabannes, H. de. Histoire de la maison de Chabannes. Paris. 1893.

Clément, P. Jacques Cœur et Charles VII. Paris. 1886.

Fierville, Ch. Le Cardinal Jean Jouffroy et son temps. Paris. 1873.

Forgeot, H. J. de la Balue. Bib. de l'Éc. pratique des Hautes Études...Sciences philol. et hist. fasc. 106. Paris. 1895.

La Borderie, A. de. Louis de la Tremoille et la guerre de Bretagne en 1488. Paris. 1877.

Lecoy de la Marche. Le roi René. Paris. 1875.

Luchaire, A. Alain le Grand, sire d'Albret; l'administration royale et la féodalité du Midi. Paris. 1877.

Mandrot, B. de. Jacques d'Armagnac, Duc de Nemours, 1433–77. Revue Historique. xliii. xliv. 1890.

—— Louis XI et Jean V d'Armagnac. Revue Historique. xxxviii. 1888.

Mandrot, B. de. Ymbert de Batarnay, S<sup>r</sup> du Bouchage. 1438–1523. Paris. 1886.

Maulde la Clavière, R. Jeanne de France, Duchesse d'Orléans. Paris. 1883.

Perret, P. M. Malet de Graville, Amiral de France, 1442–1516. Paris. Picard. 1889.

Reilhac, Jean de, Secrétaire des Rois Charles VII, Louis XI et Charles VIII, 1455–99. Paris. 1886–7.

Spont, A. Semblançay, ?–1527. La Bourgeoisie Financière au début du xvi<sup>e</sup> siècle. Paris. 1895.

### E. MISCELLANEOUS.

Beyold. Die Lehre der Volkssouveränität während des Mittelalters. Histor. Zeitschr. xxxvi. Munich. 1876.

Boissonnade, P. Histoire de la réunion de la Navarre à la Castille, 1479–1521. Paris. 1893.

[Brantôme.] Bourdeilles, P. de, S<sup>r</sup> de Brantôme. Œuvres complètes. Ed. M. L. C. Lalanne. Soc. Hist. de France. Paris. 1864–82.

Chérot, H. The social condition of France at the beginning of the xvith century. Revue des Quest. Hist. LVII. 1895.

Delaborde, H. F. La légation du Cardinal Balue en 1485. Bull. de la Soc. Hist. de Paris. Paris. 1884.

Desjardins, A. Louis XI, sa politique extérieure, ses rapports avec l'Italie. Paris. 1874.

Fagniez. Études sur l'histoire de l'Industrie et de la classe industrielle à Paris du xiii<sup>e</sup> au xv<sup>e</sup> siècle. Paris. 1878.

Franck. Réformateurs et publicistes du moyen âge et de la renaissance. Paris. 1863.

Frédéricq, P. Essai sur le rôle politique et social des ducs de Bourgogne dans les Pays-Bas. Ghent. 1875.

Harrisse, H. Jean et Sebastien Cabot. Paris. 1882.

Jacquet, A. Claude de Seyssel. Rev. des Quest. Hist. LVII. 1895.

Jal, A. Archéologie navale. 2 vols. Paris. 1839.

Laborde, L. E. de. Les Ducs de Bourgogne; étude sur les lettres, arts, etc., pendant le xv<sup>e</sup> siècle. Paris. 1849–52.

—— Renaissance des Arts à la cour de France. Vol. I. Peinture. Additions. Paris. 1850–5.

Lacroix, P. Vie militaire et religieuse au moyen âge. Paris. 1873.

—— Le moyen âge et la Renaissance. 5 vols. Paris. 1848–51.

Lecoy de la Marche, A. La Chaire française au moyen âge. 2nd ed. Paris. 1886.

Leroux, A. Nouvelles recherches sur les relations de la France et de l'Allemagne, 1378–1461. Paris. 1892.

Le Roux de Lincy. Paris et ses historiens aux xiv<sup>e</sup> et xv<sup>e</sup> siècles. Paris. 1867.

Lindner, Th. Die Zusammenkunft K. Friedrichs III mit Karl d. Kühnen, 1473, zu Trier. 1876.

Longnon, A. Paris sous la domination anglaise (1420–36). Soc. Hist. de Paris. Paris. 1879.

Mandrot, A. de. Études sur les relations de Charles VII et Louis XI avec les Cantons suisses. Jahrbuch für schweiz. Gesch. 1880–1.

Maulde la Clavière, R. Les origines de la Révolution française au xvi<sup>e</sup> siècle. Paris. 1890.

Moland, L. E. D. Les origines littéraires de la France. Paris. 1862.

Müntz, E. Renaissance à l'époque de Charles VIII. Paris. 1885.

Nerlinger, Ch. P. de Hagenbach et la domination bourguignonne en Alsace. Nancy. 1890.

Palustre, L.   La Renaissance en France.   Paris.   1879.

Pasquier, E.   Les Recherches de la France.   Paris.   1665.

Pélicier, P.   Essai sur le gouvernement de la Dame de Beaujeu.   Chartres.   Garnier.   1882.

Perrens, F. T.   La Démocratie en France au moyen âge.   2 vols.   Paris.   1873.

Petit, E.   Séjours de Charles VIII.   Bulletin hist. et phil. du Comité des Travaux Hist. et Scient.   1897.

Quicherat, J.   Histoire du Costume en France.   Paris.   1875.

Röderer, P. L.   Louis XII et Francis I ou Mémoires pour servir à une nouvelle histoire de leur règne.   Paris.   1825.   2 vols.

Spont, A.   War with France, 1512–3.   Navy Records Society.   1897.   Vol. x.

Thierry, A.   Histoire du Tiers État.   Paris.   1868.

Tuetey, A.   Les Écorcheurs sous Charles VII.   2 vols.   Montpéliard.   1874.

Vallet de Viriville.   Essais critiques sur les historiens originaux du règne de Charles VII.   Bibl. de l'École des Chartes.   1857.

Viollet le Duc, E. E.   Dictionnaire raisonné du Mobilier de l'Époque Carlovingienne à la Renaissance.   Paris.   1865, etc.

Witte, H.   Zur Geschichte der Burgunder Kriege.   Zeitschr. für Gesch. des Oberrheins 47–49.   Also in Jahrbuch der Lothring. Gesch. und Altertums-kunde, 1892–, 116–28, and other papers.

*(See also Bibliography of Chap. IV.)*

# CHAPTER XIII.

## THE NETHERLANDS.

### BIBLIOGRAPHIES.

See, besides the Ghent Bibliotheca Belgica and other collections on the general bibliography of the Netherlands, S. de Wind, Bibliotheek d. Nederlandsche Geschied-schrijvers, vol. I., Middelburg, 1835; L. La Haye, H. Francotte and F. de Potter, Bibliographie de l'histoire de la Belgique, 1830–82, Liége, from 1886; and the invaluable Bibliographie de l'histoire de Belgique by H. Pirenne, 2nd ed., Brussels and Ghent, 1902. Special bibliographies have also been published of the histories of several towns and territories. The short lists in E. Poullet, Les Anciens Pays-Bas, and in Lavisse and Rambaud's Histoire Générale, vol. III. ch. 4 (by L. Pingard) and 8 (by H. Pirenne), will be found useful, together with the names of authorities in P. Fredericq, Les Ducs de Bourgogne. A list of essays and articles in Belgian periodicals, 1830–65, was published by E. van Bruyssel, Brussels, 1869; many Dutch contributions of value are to be found in De Gids, Amsterdam, from 1837.

### I. ORIGINAL DOCUMENTS.

Of the original documents preserved in the national, provincial, municipal, and other archives of Holland and Belgium, numerous inventaires have been published. Those of the Belgian archives, drawn up under the direction of Gachard by himself, C. Piot, A. Pinchart, and L. Galesloot, were begun in 1837 (Gachard's Analectes Belgiques appeared 1830, his Collection de doc. inéd. conc. l'hist. de Belg. in 3 vols., 1833–5); the archives of the Chambres des Comptes, of the Council of Flanders, and of the Feudal Court of Brabant, were successively introduced by Gachard and Pinchart (Brussels, 1837–65), V. Gaillard (Ghent, 1856) and Galesloot (Brussels, 1870); among later inventaires are those of the Bruges archives by E. van den Bussche, 1881, and of the Brussels by A. Wauters, from 1888. Cf. for a general survey La Haye, etc. u. s. The publication of a series of inventaires of the Belgian archives under the direction of the Administr. des Arch. Gén. du Royaume, Part I: Catalogue raisonné, has quite recently (1902) begun. The Nederlandsche Rijksarchiev was inventoried by R. A. Bakhuizen van den Brink, L. Ph. C. van den Bergh, and J. de Jonge, Amsterdam, 1855; other Dutch archives by the above, P. Scheltema (Amsterdam, 1866–74), van den Brandeler (Dort, 1862–4), Rammel-man Elsevier, J. A. Nijhoff, etc.; those of Groningen by H. O. Feith (Groningen, 1853–7). Numerous original documents of Dutch history are to be found in the publications of the Royal Netherlands Inst. and Acad. of Sc. (Class II.), and of Belgian in the mémoires and bulletins of the Acad. Roy., the Comm. Roy. d'Hist. (whose comptes-rendus fill 4 series from 1834), the Comm. Roy. pour la publ. des anc. lois et ordonnances, and the Ghent Acad. Roy. Flamande. The Utrecht Historisch Genootschap, which published the Codex Diplomaticus Neerlandicus in 6 vols. (1853–63), and other historical societies in Leyden and other Dutch as well as in Belgian towns, have likewise been active in printing original documents; cf. also the Annuaire of the Brussels Bibliothèque Royale, edited by Baron de Reiffenberg, 1840–51. Of importance as to ancient statutes and customs are, besides the Liste chronol. des édits et des ordonnances des Pays-Bas (1885), the Recueil des anc. ord. de la Belgique (from 1860) and the Rec. des anc. coutumes de la B. (from 1867), the publications of the Vereeniging t. uitg. der bronnen v. h. oude vaterl. recht, 13 vols., the Hague, from 1880; the Keurboeken of the Dutch towns, and the documents of the Flemish towns ap. Warnkoenig and Ghedolf, A. Wauters, etc.

For documentary illustrations of the relations between the Netherlands and the Empire, France and England respectively, see the ordinary repositories, and especially Janssen, Reichscorrespondenz, vol. ii., Ordonnances des rois de France, vols. xv.–xvi., Lettres de Louis XI, ed. Vaesen et Charavay for Soc. de l'Hist. de France, vols. i.–v., from 1883; Rymer; and State Papers, Henry VIII, calendared by Brewer and Gairdner. The following collections of documents illustrate other special points, and are enumerated in the order in which these are to be found in the text.

Reusens, E. Documents rel. à l'hist. de l'Université de Louvain, 1425–97.

Kervyn de Lettenhove. Progr. d'un gouvernement constit. en Belgique au 15ᵐᵉ siècle. Brussels. s. d.

Limburg-Brouwer, P. A. van. Boergoensche Charters, 1428–82. (Part iii. of Orkoondenboek van Holland en Zeeland; ed. L. Ph. C. van den Bergh.) The Hague. 1869.

Wall, P. H. van der. Handvesten, Vorregten etc. van Dordrecht. 3 vols. Dort. 1790.

Smetius, J. Handvesten en Charters etc. van Nijmegen. 2 vols. Nymegen.

Dodt van Flensborg, J. J. Stukken betr. David van Borgondie en het Sticht, 1456–97; betr. de Geestelijke Broederschappen te U., 1313–1472; tijdp. 1486–1527 d. U. gesch. Utrecht. 1838.

Ram, P. F. X. de. Documents relatifs aux troubles du Pays de Liège, 1455–1505. Brussels. 1844.

Gingins la Sarra, F. de. Dépêches des Ambassadeurs Milanais sur les campagnes de Charles-le-Hardi etc., 1471–7. 2 vols. Paris. 1858.

Kervyn de Lettenhove. Lettres et Négociations de P. de Commines. 3 vols. Brussels. 1867–8.

Chmel, J. Urkunden, Briefe und Actenstücke zur Gesch. Max. I u. s. Zeit. [1493–1508.] Stuttgart. 1845.

Gachard, L. P. Lettres inéd. de Max., duc d'Autr., sur les aff. des Pays-Bas, 1478–1508. Brussels. s. d.

Diegerick, L. A. Corresp. des magistrats d'Ypres, pendant les troubles sous Max. [1483]. Bruges. 1855.

Höfler, C. von. Depeschen d. Venet. Botsch., V. Quirino, bei Erzh. Philipp v. B. 1505–8. Vienna. 1884.

Cartas de Felipe el hermoso. (Coll. des doc. inéd. d'Esp.) Madrid. 1846.

Le Glay, A. Corresp. de l'Emp. Max. I et de Marguérite d'Autr., Gouvernante des Pays-Bas [1507–19]. 2 vols. Paris. 1839.

Bergh, L. Ph. C. van den. Corresp. de Marguérite d'Autr. etc., 1506–28. (Archives de Lille.) 2 vols. Leyden. 1847.

Quinsonas, de. Matériaux p. s. à l'hist. de Marguérite d'Autr. 3 vols. Paris. 1860.

Erasmus, D. Epistolae. (Vol. iii. of Opera, ed. Le Clerc.) Leyden. 1703.

## II. CHRONICLES AND OTHER NARRATIVES WHOLLY OR IN PART CONTEMPORARY.

### A. Collections.

*(Subsequently cited by the abbreviations here appended.)*

Buchon, J. A.   Coll. des Chroniques Nationales Françaises, du 13me au 16me siècle. Paris.   1826–8.   [Buchon.]

Chroniques rel. à l'Hist. de la Belgique sous les ducs de Bourgogne.   Ed. Kervyn de Lettenhove.   3 vols.   1870–3.   [Chron. Belg.]

Coll. de Chroniques Belges inédites, publ. p. o. du Gouvernement.   Brussels. 1836–93.   [Chron. Belg.]

Coll. des Chroniqueurs et Trouvères Belges, publ. p. l'Académie de Bruxelles. Brussels and Louvain.   1863–79.   [Chron. Acad.]

Martène et Durand.   Vet. Script. et Monum. Amplissima Collectio.   9 vols. Paris.   1724–33.   [Ampl. Coll.]

Matthaeus, A.   Vet. Aevi Analecta.   2nd ed.   5 vols.   The Hague.   1738.   [Matth. Anal.]

Petitot, C. B.   Mémoires sur l'Hist. de France.   1e série.   Paris.   1819–26. [Petitot, i.]

### B. Chronicles treating of the general history of the Netherlands.

Basin, T. (Archiep. Caesar.).   De rebus gestis Caroli VII et Ludov. XI ll. xii. Ed. J. Quicherat for Soc. de l'Hist. de France.   4 vols.   1854–9.

Chastellain, G.   Chroniques.   These include: Déclar. des hauts faits du duc de Bourgogne; la Grande Chronique [1420–74]; Chron. de J. de Lalain etc., 8 vols.   Chron. Acad.; Chron. des ducs de B., 3 vols.   Buchon.

Commines, P. de.   Mémoires [1464–98].   3 vols.   Petitot, i.   Ed. Mlle Dupont, for Soc. Hist. de la France.   3 vols.   Paris.   1840–71.   Chantelauze.   Paris.   1881.

Duclercq, J.   Mémoires [1448–67].   Ed. B. de Reiffenberg.   4 vols.   Brussels. 1823.   Buchon; Petitot, i.

Froissart, J.   Chroniques [1326–1400].   Ed. Buchon.   15 vols.   Ed. Kervyn de Lettenhove.   25 vols. in 26.   Chron. Acad.   Ed. S. Luce.   11 vols.   (In course of publication.)   Paris.   1899, etc.

Gachard, L. P. et Piot, C.   Collection des Voyages des Souverains des Pays-Bas. 4 vols.   1877–82.   (Contains int. al.: A. de Lalaing, Le Voyage de Philippe le Beau, 1503.)   Chron. Belg.

Hermannus Goudanus, G.   Hollandiae Geldriaeque Bellum (from 1507).   Matth. Anal. i.

La Marche, O. de.   L'Estat de la Maison du duc Charles de Bourgogne d. le Hardy [1474].   Petitot, i.   A Flemish version of this, *s. t.*: Rationarium Aulae et Imperii Carol. Audac. etc. in Matth. Anal. i.

—— Mémoires [1435–92].   2 vols.   Petitot, i.   Soc. Hist. de la France.   4 vols. Paris.   1883–8.

La Marck, R. de, le s. de Fleuranges.   Mémoires, 1490–1537.   Buchon.

Macquereau, R.   Chronique de la mais. de Bourgogne, 1500–27.   Louvain.   1765.

Magnum Chronicon Belgicum [–1474].   In J. N. Pistorius, Rer. German. Scriptores, vol. iii.   Ratisbon.   1726.

Molinet, J.   Chroniques [–1492] with Supplément [to 1506].   Ed. Buchon.   5 vols. Paris.   1828.

Monstrelet, E. de. Chroniques [1400–44]. Ed. Douët d'Arcq. 7 vols. Paris. 1857–62. With the Suppléments of M. de Coussy, etc. (–1467). 15 vols. Buchon. [From M. are adapted or abridged the chronicles of J. Lefebvre de St Remy and others.]

Pontus Heuterus. Rerum Burgundicarum ll. vi. [the Austrian period from O. de la Marche]. Antwerp, 1584 and later editions.

(Troyes, J. de.) Les Chroniques de Louys XI, autrem. dites La Chronique Scandaleuse [1460–83]. 2 vols. Petitot, i. Paris. 1820.

## C. Provincial and local Chronicles.

*(According to the order of Provinces followed in the text.)*

Histoire et Chronique de Flandre. Ed. Kervyn de Lettenhove. 2 vols. 1879–80. Cont. int. al. : Histoire des Pays-Bas en forme de Journal. Chron. Belg.

Corpus Chronicorum Flandriae. Ed. J. F. de Smet. 4 vols. 1837–65. Chron. Belg.

Kronyk van Vlaenderen (–1467). 2 vols. Ghent. 1840.

Chroniques de Brabant et de Flandre (–1565). Ed. C. Piot. 1846. Chron. Belg.

Dagboek der Gentsche Collatie, 1446–1555. Ed. A. C. Schayer. Ghent. 1842.

Dagboek van Gent, van 1447 tot 1515. Ed. V. Fris. (In course of publication.)

Gedenkschriften van Jan Heere van Dadizeele [1437–80]. Bruges. 1850.

Rombaut de Donpere. Chronique Brugeoise 1491–98. Ed. H. Dussart. Bruges. 1893.

Relations des troubles de Gand sous Charles V. Ed. Gachard. 1846. Chron. Belg.

Dynter, E. van. Chronica duc. Lotharing. et Brabant. et reg. Franc. [–1447]. Ed. P. J. X. de Ram. 3 vols in 4. 1854–60. With the French version by J. Wauquelin. Chron. Belg.

(Heyden, Van der.) P. a Thymo. Hist. Brabantiae diplom. [Continuation of Dynter.] Ed. B. de Reiffenberg. 2 vols. Brussels. 1830.

Barlandus, H. De reb. gest. duc. Brabant. [–1526]. Louvain. 1532.

Monuments p. s. à l'hist. des prov. de Namur, Hainaut et Luxembourg. Edd. de Reiffenberg, Devillers, de Smet et Borgnet. Chron. Belg.

Chronique du Hainaut et de Mons. Ed. A. Lacroix. Mons. 1841.

Cronycke, die, van Hollandt, Zeelandt en Vrieslandt, –1517 ; with continuations to 1530, Antwerp, 1530 ; and to 1555 in vol. i. of Dort edition, 1620. (The so-called Divisie-cronyk.)

Scharlensis, O. Cronycke etc. van Vrieslandt [to 1500]. Leeuwarden. 1597 and 1742.

Stavelot, J. de. Chronique (history of Liége, 1399–1447). Chron. Belg.

(Oudenbosch.) Adrian. de Veteri Busco. Chronicon rer. Leodensium, etc. (1449–83.) Ampl. Coll.

Burlandus, H. Trajectan. Episcop. Catalogus et eorum res gest. Frankfort. 1585.

Erp, H. ab, Abbatiss. v. d. Vrouwen-clooster in suburb. Trajectan. Annales vernaculi, 1421–1549. Matth. Anal. i.

Annales rer. in Holland. et dioeces. Ultrajectan. gest., 1481–3. Ibid.

## III. LATER WORKS.

### A. General history, geography, and institutions.

Bergh, L. Ph. C. van den. Handboek d. Middel-Nederlandsche Geographie. Leyden, 1852 ; the Hague, 1872.

Biographie Nationale, publ. par l'Académie R. de Belgique. Brussels, from 1866.

Blok, P. J. Geschiedenis v. h. Nederlandsche Volk. Vols. i.–iv. (to the Peace of Westphalia). Groningen. 1892–99. Vols. i. and ii., tr. by O. Bierstadt and R. Putnam. New York and London. 1898–1900.

Borchgrave, E. de. Hist. des rapports de droit publ. entre les Provinces Belges et l'Emp. d'Allemagne. Brussels. 1869.

Deventer, J. de. Atlas des Villes de Belgique au xvi^me siècle. Ed. Reutens. (In course of publication.)

Doornik, J. De Magno Mariae Privilegio. Leyden. 1792.

Gachard, L. P. Lettre etc. conc. les anciennes Assemblées Nationales de la Belgique, 1465–1634. In Études et Notices hist. Vol. i. Brussels. 1890.

Guicciardini, L. Descrittione di tutti i Paesi Bassi, altr. della Germania Inferiore. Antwerp. 1588. (Later Dutch and English versions.)

Juste, T. Hist. des États-Généraux des Pays-Bas, 1465–1790. Brussels and Paris. 1864.

Kampen, N. G. van. Geschichte der Niederlande. (Gesch. d. europ. Staaten.) 2 vols. Hamburg. 1831.

Namèche, A. J. Cours d'Hist. nationale. 29 vols. Louvain. 1853–92.

Nijhoff, D. C. Staatkund. Gesch. van Nederland. 2 vols. Zutphen. 1891–3.

Pirenne, H. Geschichte Belgiens. German tr. by F. Arnheim. Vols. i.–ii. (vol. ii., from the beginning of the 14th century to the death of Charles the Bold, tr. from the French manuscript). (Gesch. der europ. Staaten.) Gotha. 1899–1902.

Poullet, E. Origines, développements et transformations des Institutions dans les anciens Pays-Bas. 2me ed. (Vol. ii. compl. by Pr. Poullet.) 2 vols. Louvain. 1882–92.

Pycke, M. Mém. sur les Métiers dans les Pays-Bas. (Mem. Académ.) Brussels. 1827.

Sickesz, C. de. De Schutterijen in Nederland. Utrecht. 1864.

Tarlier, J. et Wauters, A. Géographie et Hist. des communes Belges. 3 vols. Brussels. 1859–74.

Wagenaar, J. Vaderlandsche Historie. 21 vols. Amsterdam, 1749–59; with continuations, and French and German translations.

Wauters, A. Les libertés communales. 2 vols. Brussels. 1878 (vol. of documents, 1869).

Wenzelburger, K. Th. Gesch. der Niederlande. (Gesch. d. europ. Staaten.) 2 vols. Gotha. 1879–86.

Wynne, J. A. Gesch. v. de Nederlanden. Vol. i. (no more publ.). Groningen. 1873.

### B. History of successive periods.

#### (*In chronological order.*)

Mieris, F. van. Hist. d. Nederland. vorsten u. d. h. v. Beijere, Borgonje en Oostenrijk. (With numismatic illustrations.) 2 vols. The Hague. 1732–5.

Deschamps de Pas, L. Essai sur l'Hist. Monétaire des comtes de Flandre de la m. de Bourg. et de la m. d'Autr. 2 vols. Paris. 1863–74.

Barante, A. G. P. B. de. Histoire des Ducs de Bourgogne, 1364–1477. 13 vols. Paris. 1824–6, and later editions.

Praet, J. van. Les Ducs de Bourgogne. In Essais, etc. Brussels. 1867.

Fredericq, P. Essai sur le rôle polit. et soc. des Ducs de Bourgogne dans les Pays-Bas. Ghent. 1875.

Löher, F. von. Jakobaea von Bayern und ihre Zeit. 2nd ed. 2 vols. Nördlingen. 1869.

Löher, F. von. Jak. von B., Phil. von Burgund u. d. Kaiser Sigismund. In Münchner Histor. Jahrb. Munich. 1866.

Vanderkindere, L.　Le Siècle des Artevelde.　Brussels.　1879.

Richter, F.　Der Luxemburger Erbfolgestreit, 1438–43.　Trier.　1889.

Reiffenberg, B. de.　Hist. de l'Ordre du Toison d'Or.　Brussels.　1830.

Kirk, J. F.　Hist. of Charles the Bold, Duke of Burgundy.　3 vols.　London.　1863–8.

Heuvard, P.　Appréciation sur le règne de Charles le Tém. (Mém. cour. par l'Académ. Belg. vol. xxiv.) ; and Les Campagnes de C. le T. contre les Liégeois. · Brussels.　1868.

Freeman, E. A.　Charles the Bold.　In Hist. Essays, 1st ser.　London.　1871.

Petit-Dutaillis, C.　Charles VII, Louis XI et les premières années de Charles VIII. Vol. iv. of E. Lavisse, Histoire de France. (In course of publication.)

Müller, K. E. M.　Die deutschfeindliche Politik Karl's des Kühnen.　Prenzlau.　1872.

Bussierre, J. M. de.　Hist. de la Ligue formée contre Charles le Tém.　Paris.　1845.

Chauvelays, de la.　Étude sur les armées du duc de Bourg.　Paris.　1881.

Guillaume, G.　Hist. de l'Organisation Militaire sous les ducs de Bourg. and Hist. des Bandes d'Ordonnance des Pays-Bas. (Mém. cour. par l'Académ. Belg.) Brussels.　1846 and 1873.

Toutey, E.　Charles le Téméraire et la ligue de Constance.　Paris.　1892.

Nerlinger, Ch.　Pierre de Hagenbach et la domination bourguign. en Alsace. Nancy.　1890.

Daendliker.　Ursachen und Vorspiele der Burgunderkriege.　Zurich.　1876.

Delbrück, H.　Die Perserkriege u. d. Burgunderkriege.　Berlin.　1887.

Paris, A. J.　Louis XI. et la ville d'Arras (1477–83).　Arras.　1868.

Münch, E.　Maria v. Burgund, nebst d. Leben v. Margaretha v. York.　2 vols. Leipzig.　1832.

Paillard, C.　Le procès du chanc. Hugonet et du s. d'Humbercourt. (Mém. de l'Acad. R.)　Brussels.　1880.

Praet, L. van.　Louis de Bruges, s. de la Gruthuuse.　Paris.　1831.

Ulmann, H.　Kaiser Maximilian I, auf urkundl. Grundl. dargest.　2 vols. Stuttgart.　1884.

Huber, A.　Gesch. Österreichs.　Vol. iii. (Gesch. d. europ. Staaten.)　Gotha. 1888.

Smet, J. J. de.　Mém. sur la guerre de Max. roi des Rom. contre les villes de Flandre, 1482–88. (Mém. de l'Académ. Belg.)　Brussels.　1863.

Asch van Wijck, H. M. A. J. van.　Driej. Oorlog t. Max. v. O. en de stad Utrecht, 1481–4.　Vol. i.　Utrecht.　1841. (Papers by the same author on the Boar of the Ardennes, Bishop David of Utrecht, etc.)

Serrure, C. A.　Not. sur Engelbert II, comte de Nassau.　Ghent.　1862.

Le Glay, A.　Maximilien I et Marguérite d'Autriche.　Paris.　1839 (and with Corresp.).

Münch, E.　Margaretha von Österreich.　Leipzig.　1883.

Juste, T.　Charles-Quint et Marguérite d'Autriche.　Brussels.　1858.

Henne, A.　Hist. du règne de Charles V en Belgique.　10 vols.　Brussels. 1858–60.

(*See also Bibliographies of Chapters XII. and XIV.*)

## C.　History of the several Provinces.
(*According to the arrangement adopted in the text.*)

Meyerus, J.　Annales Flandriae (–1471).　Antwerp.　1561.

Oudegherst.　Annales de Flandre.　Antwerp, 1571 and 2 vols. Ghent, 1789.

Kervyn de Lettenhove.　Histoire de Flandre.　6 vols. (Vols. iv. and v.: Les Ducs de Bourgogne.)　Brussels.　1847–50.

Mathieu, A.   Hist. du Conseil de Flandre.   Antwerp.   1879.

Warnkoenig, L. A.   Flandrische Staats- und Rechtsgeschichte, –1305.   3 vols.
    Tübingen.   1835–42.   Tr. and enlarged, so far as it treats Ghent, Bruges
    and Ypres, by A. Ghedolf.   Hist. de la Flandre et de ses institutions civ.
    et polit. 1835–64.

Baecker, L. de.   Chants historiques de Flandre (400–1650).   Lille.   1885.

Custis, C.   Jaerboeken der stad Brugge.   2nd ed.   2 vols.   Bruges.   1765.

Gaillard, J.   Bruges et le Franc.   Bruges.   1864.

Memorieboek der stad Ghendt, 1301–1793.   4 vols.   Ghent.   1852–61.

Vandenpeereboom, A.   Ypriana.   7 vols.   Bruges.   1878–83.

Smet, J. J.   Notice historique et critique sur le pays de Waes.   Brussels.   1878.


Papenbrochius.   Annales Antverpienses.   Ed. F. Mertens and E. Buschmann.
    5 vols.   Antwerp.   1845–8.

Mertens, F. and Torfs.   Gesch. van Antwerpen.   8 vols.   Antwerp.   1845–53.

David, J.   Gesch. v. d. Stad en de Heerl. v. Mechelen.   Louvain.   1854–8.

Cellier, L.   Une commune flamande.   (Val.)   Valenciennes.   1873.

Bouly, H.   Hist. de Cambrai et du Cambrésis.   2 vols.   Cambrai.   1842.

Hennebert.   Hist. générale eccl. et civ. de la ville et du comté de Namur.   6 vols.
    Liége.   1788–91.

Gachard, L. P.   Mém. sur la composition et les attributions des anc. États de
    Brabant.   Brussels.   1843.

Poullet, E.   La Joyeuse Entrée ou Constitution Brabançonne.   Brussels.   1862.

Molanus, J.   Hist. Lovaniensium ll. xiv.   Ed. P. F. X. de Ram.   2 vols.   Brussels.
    1861.

Linden, H. van der.   Hist. de la const. de la ville de Louvain au moyen-âge.
    Ghent.   1892.

Ram, P. F. X. de.   Considérations sur l'hist. de l'Université de Louvain.   In
    Bulletins de l'Académ. R. Belg.

Henne, A. et Wauters, A.   Hist. de la ville de Bruxelles.   3 vols.   Brussels.
    1843–5.


Ernst, S. P.   Histoire de Limbourg.   Vols. i.–v. [to 1427 only].   Annot. E. de
    Laveleye.   Liége.   1837–48.

Vinchaut.   Annales de la prov. et du comté de Hainaut (–1555).   6 vols.   Brussels.
    1848–54.

Delewarde.   Hist. générale de Hainaut.   6 vols.   Mons.   1718–22.

Devillers, L.   Hainaut sous la régence de Maximilien d'Autr., 1483–5.   Brussels.
    1883.


Kluit, A.   Hist. Crit. Comitatus Hollandiae et Zeelandiae.   4 vols.   Middelburg.
    1777–82.

Rammelman Elsevier, W. J. C.   De strijd t. de Hoeckschen en Kabeljaauwschen
    in 1479–83.   Utrecht.   1851.

Floten, J. van.   Nederlandsche Geschiedzangen (–1609).   New ed.   2 vols.
    Amsterdam.   1864.

Wagenaar, J.   Amsterdam in zyne opkomst, aanw. en geschieden.   13 vols.
    Amsterdam.   1760–8.

Gouw, J. ter.   Gesch. van Amsterdam.   Vols. i.–iv. [to abdication of Charles V].
    Amsterdam.   1879–84.

Reyn, G. van.   Geschiedkund. beschrijving d. stad Rotterdam.   2 vols.   Rotterdam.
    1831–74.

Fruin, R.   Een Hollandsche Stad in de middeleeuwen, cont. De midd. Keur-
    boeken d. stad Leiden, ed. H. G. Hamaker.   Amsterdam.   1873.

Blok, P. J.  Eene Hollandsche Stad in de middeleeuwen.  The Hague.  1883.
Eene H. S. onder de Bourgond.-Oostenr. heersch.  The Hague.  1884.  Een
Hollandsch Dorp in de xive eeuw.  Amsterdam.  1856.
Oosten de Bruyn, G. van.  De stad Haarlem en h. geschiedenissen.  Haarlem.  1765.

Woude, C. van der.  Kronyk d. stad Alkmaar.  Amsterdam.  1725.
Hooft.  Friesland en de Friezen in de middeleeuwen.  Leyden.  1883.
Richthofen, K. von.  Untersuchungen über friesische Rechtsgeschichte.  3 vols.
Berlin.  1880–6.
Blok, F. J.  Schieringers en vetkoopers.  n. d.
Diest Lorgion, F. J.  Geschiedkund. beschrijving d. stad Groningen.  2 vols.
Groningen.  1852–7.

Bertholet, J.  Hist. du duché de Luxembourg.  8 vols.  Luxemburg.  1741–3.
Schötter, J.  Gesch. d. luxemb. Landes.  Ed. K. A. Herchem et N. van Werweke.
Luxemburg, from 1882.
Richter, F.  Der Luxemburger Erbfolgestreit in d. J. 1438–43.  Trier.  1889.

Hénaux, F.  Hist. du pays de Liége.  3rd ed.  2 vols.  Liége.  1872–4.
Borman, C. de.  Les Échevins de la souveraine justice de Liége.  Vol. i.  Liége.  1892.
Daris, J.  Hist. du dioc. et de la princ. de Liége pendant le xvme siècle.  Liége.
1887.
Garnier, E.  Louis de Bourbon, évêque-prince de Liége, 1455–82.  Paris.  1860.
Henrard, P.  Les campagnes de Charles le Tém. contre les Liégeois (1463–8).
Annales de l'Acad. d'Archéol.  1867.
Pirenne, H.  Hist. de la const. de la v. de Dinant au moyen-âge.  Ghent.  1889.
Cortgren, J. van.  Stichtsche Cleyne Cronycke, –1578.  Amsterdam.  1745.
Oudegein de Geer, J. J. van.  Bijdr. t. d. gesch. en oudh. d. prov. Utrecht.
2 vols.  Utrecht.  1860.

Pontanus.  Historiae Gelricae ll. xiv.  Harderwyk.  1639.
Nijhoff, J. A.  Gedenkw. uit de Gesch. van Gelderland.  6 vols. (vol. v. : De
Borgondische Heerschappij ; vol. vi. : Karel van Egmond).  The Hague.
1830–75.

## D.  Trade and industry.

Altmeyer, J. J.  Hist. de la Hanse teutonique dans ses relations avec la Belgique.
Brussels.  1835.
Altmeyer, J. J.  Hist. des relations commerciales et dipl. des Pays-Bas avec le
Nord de l'Europe pendant le xvime siècle.  Brussels.  1890.
Ashley, W. J.  An Introduction to English Economic History and Theory.  Vol. ii.
London.  1893.
Bruyssel, E. van.  Histoire du Commerce et de la Marine en Belgique.  3 vols.
Brussels.  1861–5.
Douw van der Krap, K. K.  Gesch. van Nederlands Koophandel.  Zierikzee.  1854.
Ehrenberg, R.  Das Zeitalter d. Fugger: Geldkapital u. Creditverkehr im 16. Jahrh.
2 vols.  Jena.  1896.
Pinchart, A.  E. sur les relations commerciales des Belges avec le Nord d'Italie
et part. a. les Vénitiens (12me–16me siècles).  Ghent.  1851.
Potter, F. de, and Broeckaert, J.  Gesch. v. d. Belgischen Boerenstand t. h. einde
d. xviii. eeuw.  (Mém. Acad.)  Brussels.  1881.
Reiffenberg, B. de.  De l'état de la population, des fabriques et des manuf. des
Pays-Bas pendant le xvme et le xvime siècle.  (Mém. Acad.)  Brussels.  1822.

Rooy, E. W. de.   Geschied. van den Nederlandsche Handel.   Amsterdam.   1854.

Schanz, G.   Englische Handelspolitik gegen Ende d. Mittelalters.   2 vols.   Leipzig.
    1880–1.

Severen, G. van.   Les relations de la Hanse teutonique avec la ville de Bruges au
    commencement du xv^me siècle.   Bull. de la Comm. royale d'hist.   Vol. vii.
    Brussels.   1880.


## E.   Religion.

Acquoy, J. G.   De Kroniek v. h. Fraterhuis te Zwolle.   Amsterdam.   1879.

—— Het Klooster te Windeshem en zyn invloed.   3 vols.   Utrecht.   1875–80.

Altmeyer, J. J.   Les précurseurs de la Réforme aux Pays-Bas.   2 vols.   Brussels.
    1886.

Böhringer, F.   Die Kirche Christi und ihre Zeugen ; vol. ii. part 3 cont. Rus-
    broek, Groote, F. Radevynzoon, T. v. Kempen.   Zurich.   1857.

Delprat, G. H. M.   Verh. o. d. Broederschap van G. Groote, en o. d. invloed d.
    Fraterhuizen.   2nd ed.   Arnhem.   1856.

Friedrich, J.   Johann Wessel.   Ratisbon.   1892.

Moll, W.   Johannes Brugmann, etc.   2 vols.   Amsterdam.   1854.

—— Kerkgeschiedenis van Nederland voor de Hervorming.   5 vols.   Arnhem
    and Utrecht.   1864–71.

Schmidt, G. C.   Étude sur J. Rusbroek.   Strassburg.   1859.

Ullmann, C.   Reformatoren vor der Reformation, vorn. in Deutschland u. d.
    Niederlanden.   2 vols.   Hamburg.   1841.   Vol. ii. contains Brethren of the
    Common Lot and Joh. Wessel.   Eng. tr. by R. Menzies.   2 vols.   Edinburgh.
    1855.


## F.   Manners, letters, and art.

Crowe, J. A., and Cavalcaselle, G. B.   The Early Flemish Painters.   2nd ed.
    London.   1872.

Hellwald, F. von.   Geschichte d. holländ. Theaters.   Rotterdam.   1871.

Hofdijk, W. J.   Ons Voorgeslacht in zijn dagelijksch leven geschildert.   6 vols.
    Haarlem.   1858–62.

Jonckbloet, W. J. A.   Gesch. d. nederlandsche Letterkunde.   4th ed., rev.
    C. Honigh ; vols. i. and ii.   Groningen.   1888–9.

Laborde, L. E. S. J. de.   Les Ducs de Bourgogne.   Essai sur les lettres, les arts
    et l'industrie pendant le 15^me siècle, etc., part ii.   3 vols.   Paris.   1849–51.

Linde, A. van der.   De Costerlegende.   The Hague.   1869 and later editions.

Moke.   Mœurs, usages, fêtes et solennités des Belges.   2 vols.   Brussels.   1847.

Schayes, A.   Histoire de l'architecture en Belgique.   4 vols.   Brussels.   s. d.

Schotel, G.   Gesch. d. Rederijkers in Nederland.   Rotterdam.   1871.

Serrure, C. A.   Gesch. d. Nederlandsche en Fransche Letterkunde in Vlaenderen
    tot het einde d. regeering v. h. Huis v. Burgondie.   Ghent.   1855.

Snellaert, A.   Hist. de la Littérature Flamande.   Brussels.   1847.

Thibaut, F.   Marguérite d'Autriche et Jehan Lemaire de Belges.   Paris.   1888.


*(For the literature of the Renaissance, and of Erasmus in particular, see the
    Bibliographies of Chaps. XVI. XVII. XVIII. and XIX.)*

# CHAPTER XIV.

## THE EARLY TUDORS.

### BIBLIOGRAPHIES.

Gardiner, S. R. and Mullinger, J. B. Introduction to the Study of English History. 3rd ed. London. 1894.

Gross, C. The Sources and Literature of English History from the earliest times to about 1485. London, New York and Bombay. 1900.

### I. DOCUMENTS.

Baga de Secretis in Report III. App. ii. of Deputy Keeper of Public Records. London. 1842.

Calendar of State Papers, Henry VIII. Vols. i.–iv. (Commission for printing and publishing State Papers.) London. 1862–70.

Calendar of Letters and State Papers, Spanish. Vols. i.–iii. 1862–77. With Supplement to vols. i. and ii. London. 1868.

Calendar of State Papers, etc., Venetian. Vols. i.–iii. London. 1864–9.

Campbell, W. Materials for a History of the Reign of Henry VII. Vols. i. and ii. (all published). Rolls Series. London. 1873, 1877.

Collier, J. P. Bull of Innocent VIII for the marriage of Henry VII with Elizabeth of York. Camden Miscellany, vol. i. London. 1847.

Ellis, H. Original Letters. First Series, vol. i. 1824. Second Series, vol. i. 1827. Third Series, vols. i. and ii. London. 1846.

Ellis, Sir H. E. The Pylgrymage of Sir Richard Guylforde to the Holy Land, A.D. 1506. Camden Soc. London. 1851.

English Historical Review. Vol. xiv. 529—34.

Gairdner, J. Memorials of Henry VII. Rolls Series. London. 1858.

—— Letters and Papers illustrative of the Reigns of Richard III. and Henry VII. 2 vols. Rolls Series. London. 1861, 1863.

—— "The Spousells" of the Princess Mary to Charles, Prince of Castile. 1508. (Camden Miscellany, vol. ix.) London. 1893.

Historical MSS. Commission. Report on Duke of Rutland's MSS. at Belvoir Castle. Vol. i. London. 1888.

—— Report on the Marquis of Salisbury's MSS. at Hatfield. Vol. i. London. 1883.

Jerdan, W. Rutland Papers. Camden Soc. London. 1842.

Leland, J. Collectanea. Vol. iv. pp. 179—309. Oxford. 1715, etc.

Nichols, J. G. Chronicle of Calais. Camden Soc. London. 1846.

—— Chronicle of the Grey Friars. Camden Soc. London. 1852.

Paston Letters, the. Ed. J. Gairdner. Vol. III. Westminster. 1895.

Rymer, T. Fœdera. Vols. XII.–XIV. London. 1711–2.

Schanz, G. Englische Handelspolitik gegen Ende des Mittelalters. 2 vols. Leipzig. 1881.

Sheppard, J. B. Christchurch Letters. Camden Soc. London. 1877.

Sneyd, C. A. A relation...of the Isle of England...about the year 1500. Camden Soc. London. 1847.

Stapleton, T. Plumpton Correspondence. Camden Soc. London. 1839.

Will, the, of King Henry VII. Ed. T. Astle. London. 1775.

Wilkins, D. Concilia. Vol. III. London. 1737.


### Relating to Ireland.

Calendar of Carew MSS. (Book of Howth, etc.) London. 1871.

Calendar of Carew MSS., 1515–74. London. 1867.

Calendar of State Papers relating to Ireland. Vol. I. London. 1860.


### Relating to Scotland.

Bain, J. Calendar of Documents relating to Scotland. Vol. IV. Edinburgh. 1888.

Calendar of State Papers relating to Scotland. Vol. I. London. 1858.

Dickson, T. Accounts of the Lord High Treasurer of Scotland, 1473–98. Edinburgh. 1877.

Rotuli Scaccarii Regum Scotorum. The Exchequer Rolls of Scotland. Ed. J. Stuart and G. Burnett. Vols. IX.–XV. Edinburgh. 1886–95.

Ruddiman, T. Epistolae Jacobi Quarti, Jacobi Quinti et Mariae, Regum Scotorum. Vol. I. Edinburgh. 1722.


## II. EARLY HISTORIES AND CHRONICLES.

André, B. Historia Regis Henrici Septimi, in Gairdner's Memorials. Rolls Series. 1858.

Cavendish, G. Life of Wolsey. Hammersmith. 1893.

Cottonian MS. Vitellius A XVI.

Fabyan, R. Chronicle. Ed. H. Ellis. London. 1811.

Hall, E. Chronicle. Ed. H. Ellis. London. 1809.

Holinshed, R. Chronicle. London. 1587.

Polydori Virgilii Historia Anglica. Leyden. 1651. (Book XXVI. treats of the reign of Henry VII; Book XXVII., which is absent in some editions, of the first part of that of Henry VIII.)

Wriothesley, C. Chronicle. Vol. I. Camden Soc. London. 1875.


### Ireland.

Harris, W. Hibernica, pp. 59—77. Dublin. 1770.

Ware, J. Annales. London. 1658.

SCOTLAND.

Buchanan, G. History of Scotland (Translation by Aikman). 4 vols. Glasgow. 1827.
—— Rerum Scoticarum Historia. Edinburgh. 1582.
Pinkerton, J. History of Scotland. 2 vols. 1797.


## III. PRINCIPAL MODERN HISTORIES.

Bacon, F. History of Henry VII (in Spedding and Ellis' edition of Bacon's Works, Vol. VI. 1861, with valuable annotations).
Bagwell, R. Ireland under the Tudors. Vol. I. London. 1885.
Brewer, J. S. The Reign of Henry VIII. Two vols. 1884.
Busch, W. England unter den Tudors, vol. I. (all yet published). Stuttgart. 1892. English translation by A. M. Todd. London. 1895.
Clowes, W. L. History of the Royal Navy. 4 vols. London. 1897–9.
Gairdner, J. Henry the Seventh. (Twelve English Statesmen Series.) London. 1889.
—— The Story of Perkin Warbeck (at end of History of Richard the Third, Cambridge, 1898).
Green, M. A. E. Lives of the Princesses. Vol. IV. London. 1852.
Herbert of Cherbury, Lord. Life and Reign of Henry VIII. In W. Kennett's Complete History of England, vol. II. 1706.
Pauli, R. Geschichte von England. Vol. V. (Gesch. d. europ. Staaten.) Gotha. 1858.
Richey, A. G. A Short History of the Irish People. Dublin. 1887.
Strickland, A. Lives of the Queens of Scotland. Vol. I. Edinburgh and London. 1850.
—— Lives of the Queens of England. Vol. II. London. 1851.
Tytler, P. F. History of Scotland. 9 vols. Edinburgh. 1828–43.


## IV. AUXILIARY INFORMATION.

Busch, W. Drei Jahre englischer Vermittlungspolitik, 1518–21. Bonn. 1884.
—— Cardinal Wolsey und die englisch-kaiserliche Allianz, 1522–5. Bonn. 1886.
Jacqueton, G. La Politique extérieure de Louise de Savoie. Paris. 1892.
Oppenheim, M. Naval Accounts and Inventories, 1485–8, and 1495–7. (Navy Records Soc. vol. VIII.) London. 1896.
Pauli, R. Aufsätze zur englischen Geschichte. Leipzig. 1869. Neue Folge. Leipzig. 1883.
Skelton, J. Poetical Works. Edited by A. Dyce. 2 vols. 1843.
Spont, A. The War with France, 1512–3. (Navy Records Soc. vol. X.) London. 1897.

(*See also Bibliographies of Chapters IX. XI. XII. and XIII.*)

# CHAPTER XV.

## ECONOMIC CHANGE.

The course of economic progress has always been closely linked with that of political change and the sources of information regarding it are not really distinct. An exhaustive list of authorities for this period would necessarily include all collections of Treaties, since they throw much light on commercial relationships, all collections of Statutes and Royal or Civic Ordinances and numberless histories of separate localities. The present list is merely intended to assist the student by calling his attention to some important books and papers, which are primarily of economic interest. Additional bibliographical information will be found in many of these books, and especially in the works distinguished by an obelus (†).

### I. GENERAL.

Beer, A.  Allgemeine Geschichte des Welthandels.  Vienna.  1860–84.

†Cossa, L.  An introduction to the study of political economy, translated from the Italian.  London.  Italian edition, Milan.  1893.

Cunningham, W.  An Essay on Western Civilisation in its economic aspects. Cambridge.  1898–1900.

Delisle, L.  Opérations financières des Templiers.  Mémoires de l'Institut. Académie des Inscriptions et Belles-Lettres.  Vol. xxxiii.  Paris.  1888.

Depping, G. B.  Les Juifs dans le moyen âge.  Paris.  1834.

Ehrenberg, R.  Das Zeitalter der Fugger.  Geldkapital und Creditverkehr im 16. Jahrhundert.  Jena.  1896.

Frignet, E.  Histoire de l'Association Commerciale depuis l'antiquité jusqu'au temps actuel.  Paris.  1868.

Goetz, W.  Die Verkehrswege im Dienste des Welthandels.  Stuttgart.  1888.

Goldschmidt, L.  Handbuch des Handelsrechts.  Vol. i.  (Universalgeschichte des Handelsrechts.)  Stuttgart.  1891.

Heyd, W.  Histoire du commerce du Levant au moyen âge.  Paris.  1885–7. French translation by F. Raynaud from the German, with author's additions. Leipzig.  1885.

Mas Latrie, le Comte J. de.  Relations et commerce de l'Afrique Septentrionale avec les nations chrétiennes au moyen âge.  Paris.  1886.

Miller, K.  Die ältesten Weltkarten.  Stuttgart.  1895.

Naudé, W.  Die Getreidehandelspolitik der europäischen Staaten vom 13. bis zum 18. Jahrhundert.  Acta Borussica.  Berlin.  1896.

Piton, C.  Les Lombards en France.  Paris.  1892.

Ruge, S. Geschichte des Zeitalters der Entdeckungen. (Allgemeine Geschichte in Einzeldarstellungen.) Berlin. 1881.

Schmoller, G. Studien ueber die wirthschaftliche Politik Friedrichs des Grossen. Jahrbuch für Gesetzgebung, Verwaltung und Volkswirthschaft im deutschen Reich. Leipzig. 1884. 1886. 1887. (The chapter on the mercantile system is translated into English and published in Professor Ashley's Series of Economic Classics under the title The Mercantile System and its historical significance. London and New York. 1896.)

Shaw, W. A. The history of Currency 1252–1894, being an account of the gold and silver monies and monetary standards of England and America. London. 1895.

Soetbeer, A. Edelmetallproduktion und Werthverhältniss zwischen Gold und Silber seit der Entdeckung Amerikas bis zur Gegenwart. Mittheilungen aus Justus Perthes geographischer Anstalt. Gotha. 1879.

Wiebe, G. Zur Geschichte der Preisrevolution des XVI. und XVII. Jahrhunderts. 1895. In the Staats- und Socialwissenschaftliche Beiträge, edited by A. von Miaskowski. Leipzig.

## II. MEDIEVAL OPINION AND CONDITIONS.

Ashley, W. J. An introduction to English economic history and theory. London. 1892–3.

†Brants, V. L'Économie politique au moyen âge, esquisse des théories économiques professées par les écrivains des XIIIe et XIVe siècles. Louvain. 1895.

Cibrario, G. A. L. Dell' economia politica nel medio evo. Turin. 1839.

Endemann, W. Studien in der romanisch-kanonistischen Wirthschafts- und Rechtslehre. Berlin. 1874–83.

Kautz, J. Die geschichtliche Entwickelung der Nationalökonomie und ihre Literatur. Vienna. 1860.

Wiskemann, H. Darstellung der in Deutschland zur Zeit der Reformation herrschenden nationalökonomischen Ansichten. In die Preisschriften gekrönt von der Fürstlich Jablonowskischen Gesellschaft zu Leipzig. Leipzig. 1861.

### A. RURAL.

Andrews, C. M. The Old English Manor. Baltimore, Md. 1892.

Bonnemère, E. Histoire des Paysans, depuis la fin du moyen âge. Paris. 1856.

Dareste de la Chavanne, A. E. C. Histoire des Classes Agricoles en France. Paris. 1858.

†Davenport, F. G. A classified list of printed original materials for English manorial and agrarian history during the Middle Ages. In the Radcliffe College Monographs. Cambridge, Mass. 1894.

Delisle, L. Études sur la condition de la Classe Agricole et de l'état de l'Agriculture en Normandie au moyen âge. Évreux. 1851.

Neilson, N. Economic Conditions of the Manors of Ramsay Abbey. Philadelphia. 1898.

Page, T. W. The end of Villainage in England. Publications of the American Economic Association. 3rd Series. Vol. I. Saratoga. 1900.

Walter of Henley. Le dite de Hosebondrie. Edited and translated by E. Lamond. London. 1890.

### B.  Fairs.

Borel, F.   Les Foires de Genève au xv<sup>e</sup> siècle.   Geneva.   1892.

Bourquelot, F.   Étude sur les Foires de Champagne, sur la nature, l'étendue, et les règles du commerce qui s'y faisait aux xii<sup>e</sup>, xiii<sup>e</sup> et xiv<sup>e</sup> siècles.   Mémoires présentés par divers savants à l'Académie des Inscriptions et Belles-Lettres de l'Institut de France.   Series ii.   Vol. v.   Paris.   1865.

†Huvelin, P.   Essai historique sur le droit des Marchés et des Foires.   Paris. 1897.

### C.  Gilds.

Doren, A.   Entwickelung und Organization der Florentiner Zünfte im 13. und 14. Jahrhundert.   In Staats- und Socialwissenschaftliche Forschungen, vol. xv. edited by G. Schmoller.   Leipzig.   1897.

Franklin, A.   Les Corporations Ouvrières de Paris du xii<sup>e</sup> au xviii<sup>e</sup> siècle.   Paris. 1884.

Geering, T.   Handel und Industrie der Stadt Basel.   Zunftwesen und Wirt-schaftsgeschichte bis zum Ende des xvii. Jahrhunderts.   Basel.   1886.

†Gross, C.   Gild Merchant.   Oxford.   1890.

Lespinasse, R. de.   Les Métiers et Corporations de la ville de Paris au xiii.–xviii. siècle.   Paris.   1886–92.

Martin St Léon, E.   Histoire des Corporations de Métiers depuis leurs origines jusqu'à leur suppression en 1791.   Paris.   1897.

Rodocanachi, E.   Les Corporations Ouvrières à Rome depuis la chute de l'Empire romain.   Paris.   1894.

Schanz, G.   Zur Geschichte der deutschen Gesellen-Verbände.   Mit Documenten aus der Zeit des 14<sup>ten</sup>–17<sup>ten</sup> Jahrhunderts.   Leipzig.   1877.

Schmoller, G.   Die Strassburger Tücher- und Weberzunft.   Strassburg.   1879.

Stieda, W.   Zur Entstehung des deutschen Zunftwesens.   In Hildebrands Jahr-bücher für Nationalökonomie und Statistik.   Jena.   1896.

### III.   IN PARTICULAR COUNTRIES.

### A.   France.

Avenel, G. d'.   Histoire économique de la propriété, des salaires, des denrées et de tous les prix en général depuis l'an 1200 jusqu'en l'an 1800.   Paris.   1894–8.

Blancard, L.   Documents inédits sur le commerce de Marseille au moyen âge. Marseilles.   1884.

Clamageran, J. J.   Histoire de l'Impôt en France.   Paris.   1867–76.

Clément, P.   Jacques Cœur et Charles VII, ou la France au xv<sup>e</sup> siècle.   Paris. 1866.

Fagniez, G.   Études sur l'Industrie et la classe industrielle à Paris au xiii<sup>e</sup> et au xiv<sup>e</sup> siècle.   Paris.   1877.

—— L'Économie Sociale de la France sous Henri IV.   Paris.   1897.

—— Documents relatifs à l'histoire de l'Industrie et du Commerce en France. Paris.   1898.

Fréville de Lorme, C. E. de.   Mémoire sur le commerce maritime de Rouen. Paris.   1857.

Hauser, H.   Ouvriers du temps passé.   Paris.   1899.

Levasseur, E.   Histoire des Classes Ouvrières et de l'industrie en France avant 1789.   Paris.   1900.

Malvézin, T.   Histoire du commerce de Bordeaux.   Bordeaux.   1892.

Pigeonneau, H.   Histoire du commerce de la France.   Paris.   1885.

## B. ITALY.

Bini, T.  I Lucchesi a Venezia.  Lucca.  1853.

Broglio d'Ajano, R.  Die venetianische Seidenindustrie.  Münchener Volkswirtschaftliche Studien.  Stuttgart.  1893.

†Dixon, E.  Florentine Wool trade in the Middle Ages.  In the Transactions of the Royal Historical Society, XII.  London.  1898.

Doren, A.  Studien aus der Florentiner Wirtschaftsgeschichte.  Vol. I.  Die Florentiner Wollentuchindustrie vom 14ten bis zum 16ten Jahrhundert.  Stuttgart.  1902.

Knies, K.  Niccolò Machiavelli als volkswirthschaftlicher Schriftsteller.  In the Zeitschrift für die gesammte Staatswissenschaft, p. 251.  Tübingen.  1852.

Lenel, W.  Die Entstehung der Vorherrschaft Venedigs an der Adria.  Strassburg.  1897.

Peruzzi, S. L.  Storia del commercio e dei banchieri di Firenze in tutto il mondo conosciuto dal 1200 al 1345.  Florence.  1868.

Pöhlmann, R.  Die Wirthschaftspolitik der Florentiner Renaissance.  In the Preisschriften d. F. Jablonowskischen Gesellschaft.  Leipzig.  1878.

Sieveking, H.  Genueser Finanzwesen mit besonderer Berücksichtigung der Casa di S. Giorgio.  Freiburg i. B.  1898.

Simonsfeld, H.  Der Fondaco dei Tedeschi in Venedig und die deutschvenetianische Handelsbeziehungen.  Stuttgart.  1887.


## C. GERMANY.

Daenell, E. R.  Geschichte der deutschen Hanse in der zweiten Hälfte des 14. Jahrhunderts.  Leipzig.  1897.

Ehrenberg, R.  Hamburg und England im Zeitalter der Königin Elisabeth.  Jena.  1896.

Hanauer, C. A.  Études économiques sur l'Alsace ancienne et moderne.  Paris.  1876.

Hanserecesse von 1256–1430.  Königliche Baierische Akademie der Wissenschaften.  1870.  Continued by the Verein für Hansische Geschichte, Lübeck.

Hoehlbaum, C.  Hansisches Urkundenbuch.  Lübeck.  1876.

—— Kölner Inventar.  Lübeck.  1896.

Inama Sternegg, C. T. von.  Deutsche Wirthschaftsgeschichte.  Leipzig.  1879–1901.

Lamprecht, K.  Deutsches Wirthschaftsleben im Mittelalter.  Leipzig.  1886.

—— Zum Verständniss der wirthschaftlichen und socialen Wandlungen in Deutschland vom 14. zum 16. Jahrhundert.  In the Zeitschrift für Social- und Wirthschafts-Geschichte.  Freiburg i. B.  1893.

Mayer, M.  Bayern's Handel.  Munich.  1893.

Nuebling, E.  Ulm's Handel im Mittelalter.  Ulm.  1899–1900.

Roth, J. F.  Geschichte des nürnbergischen Handels.  Leipzig.  1800–2.

Schmoller, G.  Die historische Entwickelung des Fleischconsums in Deutschland.  In Zeitschrift für die gesammte Staatswissenschaft, XXVII.  Tübingen.  1871.

Schönberg, G.  Finanzverhältnisse der Stadt Basel im XIV. u. XV. Jahrhundert.  Tübingen.  1879.

Schulte, A.  Geschichte des mittelalterlichen Handels und Verkehrs zwischen Westdeutschland und Italien mit Ausschluss von Venedig.  Leipzig.  1900.

Stieda, W.  Hansisch-Venetianische Handelsbeziehungen im 15. Jahrhundert.  Rostock.  1894.

### D. Netherlands.

Bruyssel, E. van.  Histoire du Commerce et la Marine en Belgique.  Brussels. Leipzig.  Paris.  1861–5.

Finot, J.  Relations commerciales et maritimes entre la Flandre et l'Espagne au moyen âge.  Annales du comité flamand de France, vol. xxiv.  Dunkirk.  1898.

—— Étude historique sur les relations commerciales entre la France et la Flandre au moyen âge.  1894.

Pringsheim, O.  Beiträge zur wirthschaftlichen Entwickelung der vereinigten Niederlande im 17. und 18. Jahrhundert.  1890.  In the Staats- und Social-wissenschaftliche Forschungen, vol. x.  Edited by G. Schmoller.  Leipzig.

Reiffenberg, F. de.  Quel a été l'état de la population, des fabriques et manu-factures et du commerce dans les provinces des Pays Bas pendant les xvᵉ et xviᵉ siècles?  Brussels.  1822.

Witt, Jan de.  The true interest and political maxims of the Republic of Holland and West-Friesland.  Translated from the Dutch.  1702.  London.


### E. Portugal and Spain.

Bernays, J.  Zur inneren Entwickelung Castiliens unter Karl V.  In the Deutsche Zeitschrift für Geschichtswissenschaft.  Freiburg in B.  1889.

Bonn, M. J.  Spaniens Niedergang während der Preisrevolution des 16. Jahr-hunderts.  Stuttgart.  1896.

Capmany de Montpalau, A. de.  Memorias historicas sobre la marina, commercio, y artes de la antigua ciudad de Barcelona.  Madrid.  1779–92.

Cassel, J. P.  Privilegia und Handlungsfreiheiten welche die Könige von Portugal ehedem an deutsche Kaufleute zu Lissabon ertheilt haben.  Bremen.  1771.

Colmeiro, M.  Historia de la economia politica en España.  Madrid.  1863.

†Haebler, K.  Die wirthschaftliche Blüte Spaniens im xvi. Jahrhundert und ihr Verfall.  Berlin.  1888.

—— Die Geschichte der Fuggerschen Handlung in Spanien.  Weimar.  1897.

Saalfeld, J. C. F.  Geschichte des portugiesischen Kolonialwesens in Ost-Indien. Göttingen.  1810.

Veitia Linage, J. de.  The Spanish rule of trade in the West Indies, translated by J. Stevens.  London.  1702.


### F. England.

†Cunningham, W.  The Growth of English Industry and Commerce.  Cambridge. 1893.

—— Alien Immigrants to England.  London.  1898.

†Gross, C.  A bibliography of British Municipal History including Gilds and Parliamentary Representation.  Cambridge, Mass.  1897.

Hulme, E. W.  The history of the Patent System under the Prerogative and at Common Law.  Law Quarterly Review.  London.  1896, and 1900.

Leadam, I. S.  The Domesday of Inclosures.  London.  1897.

Leonard, E. M.  The Early History of English Poor Relief.  Cambridge.  1900.

Marwick, J. D.  Records of the Convention of Royal Burghs of Scotland. Edinburgh.  1870–90.

Ochenkowski, W. von.  Englands wirthschaftliche Entwickelung im Ausgang des Mittelalters.  Jena.  1879.

Rogers, J. E. T.  The History of Agriculture and Prices in England.  Oxford. 1866.

Schanz, G.  Englische Handelspolitik gegen Ende des Mittelalters.  Leipzig. 1881.

## IV. CONTEMPORARY LITERATURE.

*(In chronological order.)*

Crescentiis, Petrus de.  Opus ruralium commodorum.  (–1300.)  [Augsburg.] 1471.

Domenico Lenzi (1320–35).  Narrazioni estratte dal diario de D. Lenzi, ed. P. Fanfani.  Florence.  1864.

Balducci Pegolotti, F.  (Fourteenth century.)  La Pratica della Mercatura published in vol. III. of Della Decima.  Florence.  1766.

Oresme, N.  Tractatus de origine, natura, jure et mutationibus Monetarum. (–1382.)  Edited by L. Wolowski.  Paris.  1864.

Libelle of Englishe Polycye, 1436.  In Political Songs (Rolls Series), London, or ed. with historical introduction by R. Pauli.  Leipzig.  1878.

Débat, le, des héraults d'armes de France et d'Angleterre, edited by L. Pannier and P. Meyer.  (–1456.)  Société des anciens textes français.  Paris.

Sanuto, Marino.  Itinerario per la terra ferma veneziana nell' anno 1483.  Edited by Rawdon Brown.  Padua.  1847.

Ledger of A. Halyburton, Conservator of the privileges of the Scotch nation in the Netherlands.  1492–1503.  Edited by Cosmo Innes.  Edinburgh.  1867.

Dudley, E.  The Tree of the Commonwealth.  1509.  Manchester.  1859.

Tagebuch des Lucas Rem, 1494–1541, edited by B. Greiff in Jahresbericht XXVI d. historischen Kreisvereins im Regierungsbezirke v. Schwaben und Neuberg f. d. J. 1860.  Augsburg.

Armstrong, C.  A Treatise concerning the Staple and the Commodities of this Realme, about 1530.  With two other anonymous memorials dedicated to the Earl of Essex.  Drei volkswirthschaftliche Denkschriften aus der Zeit Heinrichs VIII.  Edited by R. Pauli.  Göttingen.  1878.

Drei Flugschriften über den Münzstreit im 1530.  Brentano und Leser, Sammlung älterer und neuerer staatswissenschaftlicher Schriften.  Leipzig.  1893.

Hales, J.  A discourse of the common weal of this realm of England.  1549. Edited by E. Lamond.  Cambridge.  1893.

Agricola, G.  De re metallica.  Basel.  1556.  Translated into German under the title Vom Bergkwerck XII Bücher darin alle Empter, Instrument, Bezeuge und alles zu diesem Handel gehörig.  Basel.  1557.

Bodin, J.  Discours sur les causes de l'extrème Cherté qui est aujourd'huy en France.  1574.  In the Archives Curieuses de l'histoire de France.  Paris. 1835.

——  Discours sur le rehaussement et diminution des Monnoyes.  [Paris.]  1578.

Olivier de Serres.  Théatre d'agriculture.  Paris.  1600.

# CHAPTER XVI.

## THE CLASSICAL RENAISSANCE.

### I. WORKS ON THE GENERAL HISTORY OF THE CLASSICAL RENAISSANCE.

Burckhardt, J.  Die Cultur der Renaissance in Italien.  Leipzig.  1896.

Bursian, C.  Geschichte der classischen Philologie in Deutschland von den Anfängen bis zur Gegenwart.  Munich and Leipzig.  1883.

Geiger, L.  Humanismus und Renaissance in Italien und Deutschland.  Oncken's Series.  Berlin.  1882.

Hallam, H.  Introduction to the Literature of Europe in the fifteenth, sixteenth and seventeenth centuries.  6th edition.  London.  1860.

Heeren, A. H. L.  Geschichte des Studiums der klassischen Litteratur seit dem Wiederaufleben der Wissenschaften.  In Historische Schriften, vols. IV. V.  Göttingen.  1822.

Michelet, J.  Histoire de France.  Vol. VII.: Renaissance.  Paris.  1855.

Monnier, M.  La Renaissance de Dante à Luther.  Paris.  1884.

Müntz, E.  La Renaissance en Italie et en France à l'époque de Charles VIII.  Paris.  1885.

Symonds, J. A.  The Renaissance in Italy.  London.  1897.

Tiraboschi, J.  Storia della Letteratura Italiana.  11 vols.  Modena.  1772– .

Voigt, G.  Die Wiederbelebung des classischen Alterthums, oder Das erste Jahrhundert des Humanismus.  Berlin.  1859.

### II. OTHER AUTHORITIES.

Antonii Bononiae Beccatelli cognomento Panhormitae Epistolarum Libri v.  Eiusdem Orationes II.  Carmina, etc.  Venice.  1553.

Baldelli, G.  Vita di Giovanni Boccaccio.  Florence.  1806.

Blondus, Flavius.  (Flavio Biondo.)  Opera.  Basel.  1559.

Boccaccio, G.  Opere.  Vols. IV.–VI.  Florence.  1723–4.

—— Lettere edite e inedite, tradotte et commentate con nuovi documenti da Corazzini.  Florence.  1877.

Botfield, B.  Prefaces to the first editions of the Greek and Roman classics.  London.  1861.

Brunus, Leonardus (Arretinus).  Epistolarum libri VIII rec. Mehus.  Florence.  1741.

Bursian, C.  Geschichte der classischen Philologie in Deutschland.  Munich.  1883.

Carmina Illustrium Poetarum Italorum.  Florence.  1719–21.

Carmina quinque Illustrium Poetarum    Bergamo.  1753.

Comparetti, D. Vergilio nel medio evo. 2 vols. Livorno. 1872. Engl. Transl. by E. F. M. Benecke. London. 1895.

Didot, A. Alde Manuce et l'Hellénisme à Venise. Paris. 1875.

Einstein, L. The Italian Renaissance in England. New York. 1902.

Erasmus, D. Opera. Ed. Le Clerc. 10 vols. Leyden. 1703–6.

Geiger, L. Johann Reuchlin. Leipzig. 1871.

Gregorovius, F. Geschichte der Stadt Rom im Mittelalter. 8 vols. Stuttgart. 1859–72. English trans. by Mrs G. W. Hamilton. London. 1900, etc.

Hauréau, J. B. Histoire de la Philosophie scolastique. 2nd edition. Paris. 1872.

Hodius de Graecis illustribus linguae Graecae literarumque humaniorum instauratoribus, eorum vitis, scriptis et elogiis libri duo. Ed. S. Jebb. London. 1742.

Hortis, A. M. T. Cicerone nelle opere del Petrarca e del Boccaccio. Trieste. 1878.

Hutten, Ulrich von. Schriften. Ed. C. Böcking. 5 vols. and 2 supplementary vols. Suppl. vol. I. contains the Epistolae Obscurorum Virorum. Leipzig. 1859–69.

Janitschek, H. Die Gesellschaft der Renaissance in Italien und die Kunst. Vier Vorträge. Stuttgart. 1879.

Jovius, Paulus. Elogia doctorum virorum. Basle. 1556.
—— Elogia virorum bellica virtute illustrium. Basle. 1575.

Kampschulte, F. W. Die Universität Erfurt in ihrem Verhältnisse zu dem Humanismus und der Reformation. 2 vols. Trier. 1858.

Klette, Th. Beiträge zur Geschichte und Litteratur der italienischen Gelehrten-renaissance. I. Johannes Conversanus und Johannes Malpaghini von Ravenna. Nebst Excursus zu Manuel Chrysoloras, etc. Greifswald. 1888. II. Leonardi Aretini ad Petrum Paulum Istrum dialogus. 1889. III. Die griechischen Briefe des Franciscus Philelphus. 1890.

Koerting, G. Petrarca's Leben und Werke. 1878.
—— Boccaccio's Leben und Werke. 1880.

Kyriacus Anconitanus. Itinerarium ed. Mehus. Florence. 1742.

Landau, M. Giovanni Boccaccio, sein Leben und seine Werke. Stuttgart. 1877.

Legrand, É. Bibliographie hellénique, ou description des ouvrages publiés en grec par des Grecs aux xvᵉ et xviᵉ siècles. Vols. I. II. Paris. 1885.

Maehly, J. A. Angelus Politianus. Ein Culturbild aus der Renaissance. Leipzig. 1864.

Maitland, S. R. The Dark Ages. London. 1844.

Maître, L. Écoles épiscopales et monastiques. Paris. 1866.

Mancini, G. Vita di Leon Battista Alberti. Florence. 1882.

Masius, Alfr. Flavio Biondo, sein Leben und seine Werke. Leipzig. 1879.

Meiners, C. Lebensbeschreibungen berühmter Männer aus den Zeiten der Wiederherstellung der Wissenschaften. Vols. I.–III. Zürich. 1795–7.

Memorie e documenti per la storia dell' Università di Pavia. P. II. Pavia. 1878.

Mullinger, J. B. The University of Cambridge from the earliest times to the Royal Injunctions of 1535. 1873. Vol. II. From 1535 to 1625. Cambridge. 1884.
—— The Schools of Charles the Great, and the restoration of education in the ninth century. London. 1877.

Müntz, E. Les arts à la cour des Papes pendant le xvᵉ et le xviᵉ siècle. Ptie I. II. (Bibliothèque des écoles françaises d'Athènes et de Rome, Fasc. IV. IX.) Paris. 1878, 1879.

Müntz, E. et Fabre, P. La Bibliothèque du Vatican au xvᵉ siècle. (Bibliothèque des écoles françaises d'Athènes et de Rome, Fasc. XLVIII.) Paris. 1887.

Nolhac, P. de. Pétrarque et l'Humanisme. Paris. 1892.

Pastor, L. Geschichte der Päpste im Zeitalter der Renaissance bis zur Wahl Pius II. 3 vols. Freiburg in Breisgau. 1886, etc. Translated by F. I. Antrobus. London. 1891, etc.

Philelphus, F. Cent-dix lettres grecques de François Filelfe publ. par Émile Legrand. Paris. 1892. (Publications de l'école des langues orientales vivantes, III. série, vol. XII.)

—— Satyrarum Decades x. Venice. 1502.

—— Convivia Mediolanensia. Speier. 1508.

—— Epistolarum familiarium libri XXXVII. Venice. 1502.

(Pius II.) Aeneas Sylvius Piccolomini. Opera. Basel. 1551.

Platina, B. de (Sacchi). Opus de vitis ac gestis summorum pontificum ad Sixtum IV pont. max. deductum. Venice. 1479, etc.

Poggius, J. F. Historiae de varietate Fortunae libri quattuor ed. a Dominico Georgio. Accedunt eiusdem Poggii Epist. LVII. Paris. 1723.

—— Epistolae. Ed. T. de Tonellis. Vol. I. Florence. 1832. II. 1859. III. 1861.

Politianus, A. Epistolarum lib. XII. Miscellaneorum centuria I. Antwerp. 1567.

Pontanus, J. J. Opera omnia soluta oratione composita. Lib. I.–III. Venice. 1518, 1519.

—— Opera. Tom. I. II. Basel. 1538.

Poole, R. L. Illustrations of the History of Mediaeval Thought. London. 1884.

Rashdall, H. The Universities of Europe in the Middle Ages. 3 vols. Oxford. 1895.

Robinson, J. H. and Rolfe, H. W. Petrarch the first modern scholar and man of letters. Translation of selected letters. New York and London. 1898.

Roscoe, W. Life of Lorenzo de' Medici, called the Magnificent. Liverpool. 1795, etc.

—— Life and Pontificate of Leo the Tenth. Liverpool. 1805, etc.

Rosmini, C. de. Vita di Francesco Filelfo da Tolentino. Milan. 1808.

—— Vita e disciplina di Guarino Veronese e de' suoi discepoli. Brescia. 1805–6.

Salutatus, L. C. P. Epistolae nunc primum in lucem editae a Jos. Rigaccio. P. I. II. Florence. 1741–2.

—— Epistolario di Coluccio Salutati a cura di Francesco Novati. Vol. I. Rome. 1891.

Schaarschmidt, C. Johannes Saresberiensis. Leipzig. 1862.

Shepherd, W. Life of Poggio Bracciolini. Liverpool. 1802.

Strauss, D. F. Ulrich von Hutten. 2 vols. Leipzig. 1857–8. 2nd ed. 1871.

Traversarius, A. Epistolae. Florence. 1759.

Valeriano, J. P. De Litteratorum Infelicitate. Venice. 1620.

Valla, Laurentius. Opera. Basel. 1540.

Vespasiano da Bisticci. Vite di Uomini Illustri del secolo XV. Ed. A. Bartoli. Florence. 1859.

Villani, P. Liber de civitatis Florentiae famosis civibus. Ed. G. C. Galletti. Florence. 1847.

Voigt, G. Enea Silvio de' Piccolomini als Papst Pius II und sein Zeitalter. 1856–63.

Woodward, W. H. Vittorino da Feltre and other Humanist Educators. Cambridge. 1897.

# CHAPTER XVII.

## THE CHRISTIAN RENAISSANCE.

*(The order adopted here is mainly that of the subjects as treated in the text.)*

Bacon, Roger. Opera inedita, ed. J. S. Brewer (Rolls Series). London. 1859. Opus Majus, ed. Bridges. 3 vols. Oxford. 1897–1900. Greek and Hebrew Grammars, ed. E. Nolan. Cambridge. 1902.

Grosseteste's Suidas. See Val. Rose in Hermes, vol. v. p. 155.

Lightfoot, J. B. Ignatius, i. 76. Cambridge. 1885.

Berger, S. Des essais qui ont été faits à Paris au treizième siècle pour corriger le texte de la Vulgate. Paris. 1883.

—— Quam notitiam linguae hebraicae habuerint Christiani medii aevi temporibus in Gallia. Paris. 1893.

Hirsch. Articles on Medieval Hebrew Scholars. In Jewish Quarterly Review, 1899, etc.

Odonis Isagoge. MS. Trinity College, Cambridge, B. 14. 33.

Herbert of Bosham. Willelmus Medicus, etc. Delisle, Journal des Savants, Dec. 1900.

Greek MSS. at S. Denis. Omont, Inventaire Sommaire des MSS. Grecs de la Bibliothèque Nationale, vol. iv. Bibliothèque Nationale. Paris.

Catalogue of Library of Christ Church, Canterbury. Edwards, E. Memoirs of Libraries, i. 122—236. 2 vols. London. 1859.

Greek Octateuch from Canterbury. Bodl. Canon. Gr. 35.

Hebrew and Greek MSS. at Ramsey Abbey. See Chronicon Abbatiae Ramesiensis. Rolls Series, 79. 3 vols. London. 1884–93.

James, M. R. Sources of Archbishop Parker's Collection of MSS. Cambridge Antiq. Soc. 1899.

Vercellone, C. De correctoriis Bibliae.

Martin, J. Roger Bacon et la Vulgate.

Henry of Cosleisey. Expositio super Psalmos. MS. Christ's College, Cambridge, F. 1. 17.

Farrar, F. W. (Dean). History of Interpretation. London. 1886.

Little, A. G. The Grey Friars in Oxford. Oxford Historical Society, 1891.

Monumenta Franciscana. Rolls Series, 4, i. 555. 2 vols. London. 1858–62.

Brinkley, Richard. See J. Rendel Harris, The Leicester Codex. Cambridge. 1887. M. R. James, Two Essays on the Abbey of Bury St Edmunds. Cambridge Ant. Soc. Octavo Series, 28.

Registrum Librorum Angliae. Bodl. MS. Tanner 165.

Borlais, John. Catalogus Scriptorum. See Bibliotheca Britannico-Hibernica, edd. Wilkins and Tanner. London. 1748. Also Univ. Libr. Cambr. MSS. add.

Müntz, E., et Fabre, P.   La Bibliothèque du Vaticane au quinzième siècle (Bibl. des Écoles Françaises d'Athènes et de Rome, 1887).

Catalogue of the Library of St Mark's Convent at Florence: in the State archives at Modena: a transcript made for J. W. Clark, M.A., Registrary.

List of works presented by Duke Humphrey to the University of Oxford: Anstey, Munimenta Academica Oxon., Rolls Series, 50, p. 758.

Selling, William.   See Bibliotheca Britannico-Hibernica, edd. Wilkins and Tanner, s. v. Cellinge.

John of Ragusa's MSS.   See C. R. Gregory, Prolegomena in Nov. Test. Graecum III. 457 etc.   Leipzig.   1869–94.

Cusanus, Nicolas, Card.   Catalogue of the MSS. at Cues.   In Serapeum.   Leipzig. 1864–5.

Metius, L.   Vita et Epistolae Ambrosii Camaldulensis.   Florence.   1759.

Seebohm, F.   The Oxford Reformers.   3rd ed.   London.   1887.

Delitzsch, F.   Handschriftliche Funde [on MSS. used for the Complutensian Polyglot, etc.].   Leipzig.   1861–2.

Scrivener, F. H. A., and Miller, E.   Introduction to the Criticism of the New Testament.   4th ed.   London.   1894.

Swete, H. B.   Introduction to the Old Testament in Greek.   Cambridge.   1900.

Geiger, L.   Johann Reuchlin, sein Leben und seine Werke.   Leipzig.   1871.

Erasmus, D.   Opera.   Ed. Le Clerc.   10 vols.   Leyden.   1703–6.

Bibliotheca Erasmiana (a bibliography of the works of Erasmus, in course of publication by C. Vyt at Ghent).

Grocyn's library: catalogue in Collectanea of Oxford Historical Society, vol. II.

Beatus Rhenanus.   Die Bibliothek zu Schlettstadt.   J. Gèny and G. Knod. Schlettstadt.   1889.

Ittig, T.   De Bibliothecis Patrum.   Leipzig.   1707.

Dowling, T. G.   Notitia scriptorum SS. Patrum.   Oxford.   1839.

*Also:*

Catalogues of MSS. at the British Museum, the Bodleian, the University Library at Cambridge, and in Oxford and Cambridge College Libraries.

Tanner, T.   Bibliotheca Britannico-Hibernica.   Ed. Wilkins.   1748.

Histoire Littéraire de la France.   Paris.   1733, etc.

Tiraboschi, G.   Storia della Letteratura Italiana.   11 vols.   Modena.   1772–95.

*(See Bibliography of Chapter XVI. for other works on the Renaissance period in general.)*

# CHAPTER XVIII.

## CATHOLIC EUROPE.

### I. LITERATURE AND GENERAL HISTORY.

Bessarion, Card. Opera. Migne, Patrologia, Greek Series 161.

Creighton, M. (Bishop). History of the Papacy from the Great Schism to the Sack of Rome. 6 vols. 2nd edition. London. 1897.

Cusanus, N. (Card.). Opera. 3 vols. Basel. 1565.

Döllinger, J. I. von. Die Reformation. 3 vols. Ratisbon. 1846–8.

Hefele, C. J. von, and Hergenröther, I. (Card.). Conciliengeschichte. Vol. VIII. Freiburg i. B. 1887.

Janssen, J. Geschichte des deutschen Volkes seit dem Ausgang des Mittelalters. 14th and 15th editions. Vols. I.–II. Freiburg i. B. 1887.

Mansi, J. D. Sacrorum Conciliorum Collectio. 29–31. Florence.

—— Monumentorum Historicorum Appendix. In Steph. Baluzii Miscellanea. Lucca. 1761.

Muratori, L. Rerum Italicarum Scriptores, XXIII.–XXIV. Milan. 1733–8.

Pastor, L. Gesch. der Päpste im Zeitalter der Renaissance. 6 vols. Freiburg i. B. 1886 seq.

(Pius II.) Aeneas Sylvius Piccolomini. Opera. Basel. 1571.

Platina, B. Vitae Pontificum Romanorum. Venice. 1479.

Raynaldus. Annales Ecclesiastici. VIII.–XII. Lucca. 1752–5.

Reumont, A. von. Lorenzo de' Medici il Magnifico. 2 vols. Leipzig. 1874.

Wessenberg. Die grossen Kirchenversammlungen d. XV.–XVI. Jahrh. Constance. 1840 seq.

### II. BIOGRAPHIES AND SPECIAL TREATISES.

Abert, F. P. P. Eugenius IV. Mainz. 1884.

Altmeyer, J. J. Les Précurseurs de la Réforme aux Pays Bas. 2 vols. Paris and Brussels. 1886.

Altzog, J. Die deutschen Plenarien. Freiburg i. B. 1874.

Ambrosius, F. De Rebus Gestis ac Scriptis Operibus Bapt. Mantuani. Turin. 1784.

Antonius de Vercellis. Quadragesimales. Venice. 1492.

Aschbach, J. Geschichte der Wiener Universität im ersten Jahrhundert ihres Bestehens. 2 vols. Vienna. 1865–77.

—— Die früheren Wanderjahre des Conrad Celtes. Sitzungsberichte der k. k. Academie der Wissenschaften. Vienna. 1868.

Bangen, J. H. Die Römische Curie. Münster. 1854.

Barletta, Gabriele da. Sermones. Lyons. 1511.

Barzelotti, G. Italia mistica e Italia pagana. Rome. 1891.

Bayonne, E. C. Œuvres Spirituelles de J. Savonarola traduites sur le texte original. 3 vols. Paris. 1879–80.

Bernaldez, A. Historia de los Reyes Católicos Don Fernando y Doña Isabel. 2 vols. Seville. 1870–5.

Berger, S. La Bible française au moyen âge. Paris. 1884.

Bianco, J. F. von. Die alte Universität Köln. Cologne. 1855.

Binder, F. Charitas Pirkheimer. Ed. 2. Freiburg im Breisgau, 1878.

Binterim, A. J. Pragmatische Geschichte der Deutschen. National-, Provincial- und Diöcesanconcilien vom 14. Jht. bis auf das Concilium zu Trient. 7 vols. Mainz. 1848.

Bodman, J. F. Rheingauische Alterthümer, oder Landes- und Regimentsverfassung des Nieder-Rheingaues im mittleren Zeitalter. 2 Parts. Mainz. 1819.

Böhringer, F. Die Vorreformatoren des xiv. und xv. Jahrh. Zürich. 1858.

Brentano, L. Die Arbeitergilden der Gegenwart. Leipzig. 1871.

Brewer, J. S. Letters and Papers of the Reign of Henry VIII. Vol. i. London. 1862.

Brosch, M. P. Julius II und die Gründung des Kirchenstaats. Göttingen. 1878.

Brück, H. Die religiöse Unterricht für Jugend u. Volk in Deutschland in der zweiten Hälfte des xv. Jahrh. Mainz. 1876.

Bullen, G. Catalogue of the Loan Collection connected with the Art of Printing (Caxton Celebration). London. 1877.

Burcard, J. Diarium Innoc. VIII et Alex. VI. Florence. 1854.

—— Diarium, sive rerum urbanarum Commentarii, 1483–1506. 3 vols. Paris. 1883–5.

Busch, J. Chronicon Windeshemense. In Scriptores Brunsvic. ed. Leibniz. Vol. ii. Hanover. 1707.

Cantù, C. Gli Eretici d' Italia. I. Turin. 1865.

Cecconi. Studii Storici sul Concilio di Firenze. Florence. 1869.

Cian, V. Caterina Sforza. Turin. 1893.

Cisneros. Tractatus Directorii Horarum Canonicarum et Exercitatorii Vitae Spiritualis. Venice. 1555.

Cornelius, C. A. Die münsterischen Humanisten u. ihr Verhältniss zur Reformation. Münster. 1851.

Cosci, A. Girolamo Savonarola e i nuovi documenti. Archivio storico-italiano. 4ª Serie. Florence. 1879.

Cronaca Sublacense del P. D. Cherubino Mirzio da Treveri. Rome. 1885.

Cruel, R. Geschichte der deutschen Predigt im Mittelalter. Detmold. 1879.

Dacheux, L. Un réformateur catholique à la fin du xv siècle, Geiler de Kaysersberg. Paris and Strassburg. 1876.

Daisenberger, M. Volksschulen der zweiten Hälfte des Mittelalters in der Diöc. Augsburg. 1884–5.

Delprat, G. H. M. Die Brüderschaft des gemeinsamen Lebens. (Translated from the Dutch.) Leipzig. 1840.

Dittrich. Cardinal Gasparo Contarini. Braunsberg. 1885.

Düx. Der deutsche Cardinal Nic. v. Cusa. Ratisbon. 1874.

Empoli, F. L. Bullar. Ord. Eremitar. S. Augustini. Rome. 1628.

Endemann, M. Die Bedeutung der Wucherlehre. Berlin. 1866.

Eubel, K. Geschichte der oberdeutschen Minoriten. Würzburg. 1886.

Evelt, J. Die Anfänge d. Bursfeld Bened.-Congregation. In Zeitschr. für väterl.-Geschichte und Alterthumsk. Vol. iii. Münster. 1865.

Falk, F. Die Druckkunst im Dienste der Kirche in Deutschland bis 1520. Cologne. 1879.

Falk, F.   Dom- und- Hofpredigerstellen in Deutschland im Ausgang des Mittel-
alters.   In Histor.-polit. Blätter.   Munich.   1881.
—— Die Presse zu Marienthal im Rheingau.   Mainz.   1882.
—— Die deutschen Sterbebüchlein.   Cologne.   1890.
Fiorentino.   Pietro Pomponazzi.   Florence.   1869.
Forgeot, H.   Jean Balue, Cardinal d'Angers.   Paris.   1895.
Frantz, E.   Frà Bartolomeo della Porta.   Ratisbon.   1879.
Friedrich, J.   J. Wessel.   Ratisbon.   1862.
Gams, B.   Die Kirchengeschichte von Spanien.   3 vols.   1862-79.
Gasquet, F. A.   The Eve of the Reformation.   London.   1900.
—— The Old English Bible.   London.   1887.
Gebhardt.   Die Gravamina der deutschen Nation gegen den römischen Hof.
Breslau.   1884.
Geffcken, J.   Der Bildercatechismus des xv Jahrh.   Leipzig.   1855.
Geiger, L.   Johann Reuchlin, sein Leben u. seine Werke.   Leipzig.   1871.
Geiler von Kaysersberg.   Opera, Sermones, et varii Tractatus.   Strassburg.   1518-
21.
Gherardi, A.   Nuovi Documenti e Studj intorno a G. Savonarola.   Florence.   1887.
Ginsburg, C. D.   Introduction to the Massoretico-critical Edition of the Hebrew
Bible.   London.   1897.
Goedeke, K.   Das Narrenschiff von Sebastian Brant.   Leipzig.   1872.
Görres, J.   Die deutschen Volksbücher.   Heidelberg.   1807.
—— Altdeutsche Volks- u. Meisterlieder.   Frankfort.   1817.
Gothein, E.   Ignatius v. Loyola u. die Gegenreform.   Halle.   1895.
Grube, K.   Gerhard Groot u. seine Stiftungen.   Cologne.   1883.
Hagen, C.   Deutschlands literarische und religiöse Verhältnisse im Reformation-
Zeitalter.   2nd ed.   3 vols.   Frankfort.   1868.
Hartfelder, K.   Conrad Celtes und der Heidelberger Humanistenkreis.   Histor.
Zeitschr.   Munich.   1882.
Hartzheim, J.   Concilia Germaniae.   Tom. v. vi.   Cologne.   1763-5.
Hase, K.   Savonarola.   Leipzig.   1861.
Hasak, V.   Der christliche Glaube d. deutschen Volkes beim Schluss d. Mittelalters
Ratisbon.   1868.
—— Dr M. Luther und die religiöse Literatur s. Zeit.   Ratisbon.   1881.
Hefele, C. J.   Der Cardinal Ximenes.   Ed. 2.   Tübingen.   1851.
Heidemann, J.   Vorarbeiten zu einer Geschichte des höheren-Schulwesens in Wesel.
Wesel.   1859.
Hettinger, F.   Die Kunst im Christenthum.   Würzburg.   1867.
Höfler, C.   Aegidius von Viterbo.   Die Lebensbeschreibungen der Päpste im
Zeitalter K. Maximilians I.   Archiv für Österr. Geschichtskunde.   Vienna.
1854
—— Kaiserthum u. Papstthum.   Prague.   1862.
Hoffmann v. Fallersleben, A. H. H.   Geschichte des deutschen Kirchenliedes bis
auf Luther.   Hanover.   1854.
Horawitz, A.   Beatus Rhenanus.   Sitzungsber. der k. k. Academie der Wissen-
schaften.   Vols. lxx. lxxi.-iv.   Vienna.   1870-2.
Infessura, Stef.   Diario d. Città di Roma.   Fonti per la Storia d' Italia.   Rome.
1890.
Jacob, G.   Die Kunst im Dienste d. Kirche.   Landshut.   1870.
Janner, F.   Geschichte d. Bischöfe von Regensburg.   Ratisbon.   1886.
Joller.   Cardinal Schinner.   Blätter aus der wallisch. Geschichte.   Sion.   1890.
Jostes, Fr.   J. Veghe, ein deutscher Prediger d. xv. Jahrh.   Halle.   1883.
Kaulen, F.   Geschichte der Vulgata.   Mainz.   1868.
Kehrein, J.   Gesch. der deutschen Bibelübersetzung vor Luther.   Stuttgart.   1851.

Kehrein, J. Katholisch Kirchenlieder, Hymnen, Psalmen. Würzburg. 1859.

Keller, L. J. v. Staupitz u. die Anfänge d. Reform. Hist. Theol. Blätter. Leipzig. 1888.

Kempis, Thos. à. Opera. Antwerp. 1607.

Kerker, M. Geiler v. Kayserberg u. sein Verhältniss zur Kirche. Histor.-Polit. Blätter, 48, 49. Munich. 1861–2.

Kettlewell, S. The Brothers of the Common Life. London. 1882.

Knepper, J. Jakob Wimpfeling. Erläuterungen u. Ergänzungen zu Janssen's Gesch. d. d. V., vol. III. Freiburg i. B. 1902.

Kolde, Th. Die deutsche Augustinercongregation u. J. v. Staupitz. Gotha. 1879.

Krafft, C. Mittheilungen aus der Matrikel d. alten Kölner Universität. In Hassel's Ztschr. für Preussische Gesch. u. Landeskunde. Berlin. 1868.

—— Mittheilungen aus der niederrheinischen Reformationsgesch. Zeitschr. d. Bergischen Gesch. Vereins. Bonn. 1869.

Krafft, C. und W. Hegius u. seine Schüler. In Zeitschr. d. Bergischen Gesch. Vereins. Bonn. 1871.

Kunz, F. X. Jacob Wimpheling. Luzern. 1883.

Landucci. Diario Fiorentino dal 1450 al 1516 da J. della Badia. Florence. 1883.

Lehmann, P. Das pisan. Concil v. 1511. Breslau. 1874.

Lesker, B. Mittelalterliche Volksbildung in Mecklenburg. Der Katholik. Mainz. 1886.

Linsenmann, F. X. Gabriel Biel, u. die Anfänge der Universität zu Tübingen. Tübingen. 1865.

Lucas, H. Frà Girolamo Savonarola. London. 1899.

Luotto, P. Il vero Savonarola. Florence. 1897.

Maeterlinck. L'Ornement des Noces Spirituelles de Ruysbroeck l'admirable. Traduit du Flamand. Brussels. 1893.

Matzke, D. Die Natürliche Theologie des Raymund von Sabunde. Breslau. 1849.

Maurenbrecher, W. Studien u. Skizzen zur Reformationzeit. Leipzig. 1874.

—— Geschichte der katholischen Reform. Leipzig. 1880.

Meuser. Johann Eck. In Diehringer's Kathol. Zeitschr. für Wissenschaft u. Kunst. Cologne. 1846.

Mohnike, G. Ortuinus Gratius. Illgen's Zeitschr. f. d. Histor. Theologie. Leipzig. 1843.

Nettesheim, F. Gesch. der Schulen im alten Herzogthum Geldern. Düsseldorf. 1882.

Nichols, F. M. The Epistles of Erasmus. English Translation. Vol. I. London. 1901.

Panzer, G. W. Nachrichten von den ältesten gedrückten Bibeln. Nürnberg. 1887.

Pasolini, F. O. Caterina Sforza. Rome. 1893.

Paulsen, F. Gesch. des gelehrten Unterrichts auf den deutschen Schulen u. Universitäten vom Ausgang des Mittelalters. Leipzig. 1885.

Pfeiffer, F. Theologia Deutsch. Mit einer neudeutschen Uebersetzung. 4th ed. Gütersloh. 1900.

[Quétif, J.] Vita H. Savonarolae, auctore J. F. Pico Mirandulae principe. 2 vols. Paris. 1674.

Ranke, L. von. Savonarola u. die florentinische Republik. Vol. XL. of Sämmtliche Werke. Leipzig. 1874, etc.

Reichling, D. Johannes Murmellius. Freiburg im Br. 1880.

Riegger, J. A. Udalrici Zasii Epistolae. Ulm. 1774.

Roberto da Lecce. Quadrigesimales de Peccatis. Venice. 1488.

Rodrigo, Fr. J. Historia verdadera de la Inquisicion. 3 vols. Madrid. 1876–7.

Röhrig, T.   Die Schule zu Schlettstadt.   Illgen's Zeitschr. f. d. Hist. Theologie 4, Stück 2.   Leipzig.   1834.

Rösler, A.   Cardinal Johannes Dominici.   Freiburg i. B.   1894.

Ruland, A.   Johannes Trithemius.   Kilianium.   New Series.   I.   Zurich.   1869.

Schmidt, K.   Geiler v. Kaysersberg.   Ersch and Gruber's Realencyc. IV.

Schneegans, W.   Abt J. Trithemius u. Kloster Sponheim.   Kreutznach.   1882.

Schwartz, B.   Jacob Wimpheling.   Gotha.   1875.

Seebohm, F.   The Oxford Reformers, John Colet, Erasmus, and Thomas More.   London.   Ed. 2.   1869.

Silbernagel.   Johann Trithemius.   Landshut.   1868.

Stinzing, R.   Ulrich Zasius.   Basel.   1857.

Tangl, M.   Die päpstlichen Kanzleiordnungen 1200–1500.   Innsbruck.   1894.

Taunton, E. L.   Thomas Wolsey, Legate and Reformer.   London.   1902.

Tocco, F.   Il Savonarola e la Profezia.   Milan.   1893.

Tonini, L.   Rimini nella Signoria dei Malatesta.   Rimini.   1882.

Trithemius, J.   Opera.   Frankfort.   1601.

——   Chronicon Hirsaugiense.   2 vols.   St Gall.   1690.

Ullmann, K.   Die Reformatoren vor die Reformation.   2 vols.   Gotha.   1866.

Villari, P.   Storia di G. Savonarola.   2 vols.   2nd ed.   Florence.   1898.   Eng. trans. by L. Horner.   London.   1863.

Vischer, W.   Gesch. d. Universität Basel, 1460–1529.   Basel.   1860.

Wackernagel, P. H.   Das deutsche Kirchenlied von der ältesten Zeit bis zum Anfang des XVII Jahrh.   2 vols.   Leipzig.   1867.

Wadding, L.   Annales Minorum XIV.–XV.   Rome.   1735.

Walther, W.   Die deutschen Bibelübersetzungen des Mittelalters.   Brunswick.   1889.

Weitbrecht, W.   Das religiöse Leben d. deutschen Volks am Ausgang des M. A.   Heidelberg.   1886.

Wiedemann, Th.   Johann Eck.   Ratisbon.   1865.

Werner, K.   Der Augustinismus des spätern Mittelalters.   Vienna.   1884.

——   Die Scholastik des spätern Mittelalters.   4 vols.   Vienna.   1881–7.

——   Die nachscotistische Scholastik.   Vienna.   1884.

Weiss, J.   Bert v. Henneberg, Erzbischof v. Mainz (1484–1504).   Freiburg i. B.   1889.

Wiskowatoff, P. V.   Jacob Wimpheling.   Berlin.   1867.

Woker, F. W.   Gesch. d. norddeutschen Franciskanermission d. sächsisch. Ordensprovinzen.   Freiburg i. B.   1880.

Zapf, J.   Johannes v. Dalberg, Bischof v. Worms.   Zurich.   1798.

Ziegler, A.   Regiomontanus, ein geistiger Vorläufer des Columbus.   Dresden.   1874.

Zimmermann, K.   Die kirchlichen Verfassungskämpfe des XV. Jahrh.   Breslau.   1882.

(*See also Bibliographies of Chapters XIII. XVI. and XIX.*)

# CHAPTER XIX.

## THE EVE OF THE REFORMATION.

### I.  UNPUBLISHED MATERIAL.

Archivo General de Simancas, Consejo de Inquisicion, Libro iii, fol. 7.
Archivo General de Simancas, Patronato Real, Inquisicion, Legajo único.
Burriel, A. M., S. J.  Vidas de los Arzobispos de Toledo.  Bibliotheca nacional de Madrid, Sección de MSS. Ff. 194.

### II.  CONTEMPORARY AUTHORITIES AND DOCUMENTS.

Acta Concil. Basoliensis.  Arch. Administratives de Reims, vol. i.  Paris.  1839.
Alvarus Pelagius de Planctu Ecclesiae.  Ulm.  1474.
Aquinas, S. Thomas.  De Rebuspublicis et Principum Institutione.  Leyden.  1643.
Arnestus, Archiep. Pragensis.  Statuta.  Höfler, Concilia Pragensia.  Prague.  1862.
Balan, P.  Monumenta Reformationis Lutheranae.  Ratisbon.  1883.
——  Monumenta Saeculi xvi. Historiam illustrantia.  Vol. i.  Innsbruck.  1885.
Baudouin, A.  Lettres inédites de Philippe le Bel.  Paris.  1887.
Bertrandus, Card. Aeduensis.  Liber contra P. de Cugneriis.  Max. Bibl. Patrum. Vol. xiv.  Cologne.  1618.
Boletin de la Real Academia de la Historia.  Vol. xxii.  Madrid.  1893.
Bonaventura, St.  Opuscula theologica.  2 vols.  Venice.  1584.
Bouchel, L.  Decretorum Ecclesiae Gallicanae Libri viii.  Paris.  1649.
Brant, S.  Narrenschiff.  Ed. F. Farnelle.  Leipzig.  1854.
Bullarium Romanum.  Vol. i.  Luxemburg.  1742.
Burcardus, Johannes.  Diarium.  Avec Introduction, Notes, etc. par L. Thuasne. 3 vols.  Paris.  1883–5.
Cherubino, Frà.  Sermones Quadragesimales.  Venice.  1502.
Corio, B.  Historia di Milano.  Venice.  1565.
Epistolae Obscurorum Virorum ad M. Ortuinum Gratium.  London (apud Editorem).  See also Supplementary vol. i. of Ulrich von Hutten's Schriften, ed. E. Böcking.  Leipzig.  1863.
Erasmus, D.  Encomium Moriae.  Leyden.  1641.
——  Epistolarum Libri xxxi.  London.  1642.
——  Instructio Militis Christiani.  Heidelberg.  1662.
——  Lucubrationes.  Strassburg.  1515.
——  The Epistles of, arranged in order of time.  Edited by F. M. Nichols. London.  1901.
Erler, G.  Der Liber Cancellariae Apostolicae vom Jahre 1380.  Leipzig.  1888.
Faber, J.  Tractatus de Ruine Ecclesie Planctu.  Memmingen.  s. a.

Faber, J.   Wie sich Johannis Huszs der Pikarder und Johannis von Wessalia Lehren und Buecher mit Martino Luther vergleichen.   Leipzig.   1528.

Geyler von Kaysersberg.   Navicula Penitentie.   Augsburg.   1511.

—— Navicula siue Speculum Fatuarum.   Strassburg.   1511.

Gravamina Germanicae Nationis.   In vol. ii. of Freher-Struve, Scriptores Germ. Strassburg.   1717.

Grosseteste, R. (Bishop).   Epistolae.   Ed. H. R. Luard.   Rolls Series.   London. 1861.

Gudenus, Val. Ferd. de.   Codex Diplomaticus Anecdotorum.   5 vols.   Göttingen. 1743–68.

Harduinus, J.   Conciliorum Collectio Regia Maxima.   12 vols.   Paris.   1715.

Henricus Archidiaconus.   Historia Calamitatum Ecclesiae Salzburgensis (Migne's Patrol. Latin., vol. 196).

Hergenröther, J. (Card.).   Leonis X. Pontif. Maximi Regesta.   Freiburg i. B. 1884–91.

Hoffmann, Chr. God.   Nova Scriptorum ac Monumentorum Collectio.   2 vols. Leipzig.   1731.

Honorius III.   Epist. ad Archiep. Bituricensem (Martene, Coll. Ampliss. i.).

Hutten, Ulrich von.   Eleutheri Bizerii Joannis Reuchlin Encomion.   c. 1516.

—— Schriften.   Herausgegeben von E. Böcking.   5 vols. and 2 suppl.   Leipzig. 1859–69.

Infessura, S.   Diarium.   Eccardus, Corpus Historicum Medii Aevi.   Vol. ii. Leipzig.   1723.

Innocent IV.   Apparatus super quinque libris Decretalium.   Strassburg.   1488.

Isambert, Recueil général des anciennes Lois Françaises.   30 vols.   Paris.   1822–32.

Jourdain, R.   Contemplationes Idiotae, per Jacobum Fabrum nuper in lucem editae.   Venice.   1538.

Kirsch, J. P.   Die päpstlichen Kollectorien in Deutschland.   Paderborn.   1894.

Le Plat, J.   Monument. ad Hist. Concilii Tridentini.   Vol. ii.   Louvain.   1782.

Ludewig, J. P.   Reliquiae Manuscriptorum.   12 vols.   Frankfort.   1720–41.

Machiavelli, N.   Opere.   6 vols.   Florence.   1782.

Marsilius Patavinus.   Defensor Pacis.   s. l.   1522.

Matthaeus Vindocinensis.   Commendatio Papae.   Migne's Patrol., Latin Series. Vol. 205.

Medina, F. de.   Vida del Cardenal de Mendoza.   Memorial Histórico Español. Vol. vi.

Monstrelet, Enguerrand de.   Chroniques.   Paris.   1842.

Morone, G.   Nunciaturberichte vom deutschen Königshöfe.   1 vol.   Paderborn. 1892.

Murner, T.   Various works.   In Scheible, Das Kloster.   Vols. i. iv. viii. x. Stuttgart.   1845–8.

Ottenthal, E. von.   Regulae Cancellariae Apostolicae.   1 vol.   Innsbruck.   1888.

Petrarca, F.   Liber sine Titulo.   Opera.   Basel.   1554.

Pico della Mirandola (Gianfrancesco).   Opera omnia.   Basel.   1572.

Pietro da Palermo.   Sermones de Poenitentia per Quadragesimam.   Brixen.   1502.

(Pius II.)   Aeneas Sylvius Piccolomini.   Opera quae extant omnia.   Basel.   1571.

—— Opera inedita (Atti della R. Accademia dei Lincei).   Rome.   1883.

Pragmaticae Sanctionis Passio (Baluz. et Mansi Miscell. iv.).

Pulgar, H.   Cronica de los Reyes Don Fernando y Doña Isabel.   Valencia.   1780.

Ragusio, Joh. de.   De Initio et Prosecutione Concil. Basiliensis (Acta et Monumenta Concil. Saec. xv. vol. i.).

Registre Criminel du Châtelet de Paris.   2 vols.   Paris.   1861.

Rigordus.   Gesta Philippi Augusti (Dom Bouquet, xvii.).

Roberto da Lecce.   Sermones Quadragesimales, etc.   Venice.   1479.

Sachsenspiegel, herausgegeben von Jacob Friedrich Ludovici. Halle. 1720.

Sanctio Pragmatica cum Glossis D. Cosmae Guismiev. Paris. 1613.

Theiner, Augustin. Monumenta Slavorum Meridionalium. Vol. I. Rome. 1863.

Theodericus a Niem. Historiarum sui Temporis Libri IV. Strassburg. 1609.

Trithemius, Johannes. Annales Hirsaugienses. 2 vols. St Gall. 1690.

Valla, L. Contra Donationem quae Constantini dicitur cum Ulrici Hutteni Prefatione ad Leonem X. s. l. 1517.

Villani, G. Cronica. 4 vols. Florence. 1823.

Werunsky, E. Excerpta ex Registris Clementis VI. et Innocentii VI. Innsbruck. 1885.

Wimpheling, J. Ad Julianum II. Pont. Max. querulosa Excusatio. Strassburg. 1507 c.

Wimpheling, J. De Vita et Moribus Episcoporum aliorumque Praelatorum. Strassburg. 1512.

## III. LATER WORKS.

Affò, I. Vita del B. Giovanni di Parma. Parma. 1777.

Altmeyer, J. J. Les Précurseurs de la Réforme aux Pays-Bas. 2 vols. Brussels. 1886.

Amabile, L. Il Santo Officio della Inquisizione in Napoli. 2 vols. Città di Castello. 1892.

Argentré, Ch. D. d'. Collectio Judiciorum de novis Erroribus. 3 vols. Paris. 1755.

Benrath, K. Bernardino Ochino von Siena. Leipzig. 1875.

Bisticci, V. da. Vite di Uomini illustri del Secolo XV. Bologna. 1892.

Burmannus, Casparus. Analecta Historica de Hadriano Sexto. Utrecht. 1727.

Ciacconius, Alphonsus. Vitae Pontificum Romanorum. 4 vols. Rome. 1677.

Clemencin, D. Elógio de la Reina Católica Doña Isabel. Madrid. 1821.

Cochlaeus, J. Historiae Hussitarum Libri XII. St Victor, near Mainz. 1549.

—— De Actis et Scriptis Martini Lutheri. Cologne. 1568.

Colmeiro. Cártes de los antiguos Reinos de Leon y de Castilla. Madrid. 1866–82.

Creighton, M. (Bishop). A History of the Papacy during the Period of the Reformation. 5 vols. London. 1882–94.

Denifle, H. Die älteste Taxrolle der apostolischen Pönitentiarie. Archiv für Literatur- u. Kirchengeschichte, vol. IV. 1888.

Döllinger, J. J. von. Beiträge zur politischen, kirchlichen u. Cultur-Geschichte. 3 vols. Ratisbon. 1862–82.

Dorado, Bernardo. Compendio Hist. de la Ciudad de Salamanca. Salamanca. s. d.

Drews, P. Wilibald Pirckheimer's Stellung zur Reformation. Leipzig. 1887.

Emmius. Rerum Frisicarum Historia. Franeker. 1596.

Fisquet, M. H. La France Pontificale, Archevêché de Lyon. Paris. s. d.

Froude, J. A. Life and Letters of Erasmus. London. 1894.

Gebhart, E. Moines et Papes, Essais de Psychologie Historique. Paris. 1897.

Goldast, M. Politica Imperialia. Frankfort. 1614.

Graf, K. H. Jacobus Faber Stapulensis. Strassburg. 1842.

Gratianus, Ortuinus. Fasciculus Rerum expetendarum et fugiendarum. Cum Appendice opera Edwardi Brown. London. 1690.

Gröne, V. Tetzel und Luther. Soest and Olpe. 1864.

Hardt, H. von der. Historia Litteraria Reformationis. Frankfort. 1717.

—— Magnum Oecum. Constantiense Concilium. 4 vols. Frankfort. 1704–42.

Hocsemii Gesta Pontificum Leodiensium (Chapeaville II.). Liége. 1613.

Janssen, J. Geschichte des deutschen Volkes. 13th ed. Vol. I. Freiburg i. B. 1887.

Keller, L. Johann von Staupitz u. die Anfänge der Reformation. Leipzig. 1888.
—— Die Anfänge der Reformation u. die Ketzerschulen. Monatschrifte der Comenius Gesellschaft. Vol. v. 1896.
Lämmer, H. Meletematum Romanorum Mantissa. Ratisbon. 1875.
—— Monumenta Vaticana. Freiburg i. B. 1861.
Lea, H. C. A History of Auricular Confession and Indulgences. 3 vols. Philadelphia. 1896.
—— Studies in Church History. Philadelphia. 1883.
Mariana, Juan. Historia de España. Libros xxiv. xxvi. Valencia. 1783–96.
Menendez y Pelayo. Heterodoxas Españoles. Vol. ii. Madrid. 1880.
Méray, A. La Vie aux temps des Libres Prêcheurs. 2 vols. Paris. 1878.
Mironi, Barbarano dei. Historia di Vicenza. Vol. ii. Vicenza. 1649.
Pastor, L. Geschichte der Päpste im Zeitalter der Renaissance. Vols. i.–iii. Freiburg i. B. 1891–5.
Preger, W. Die Politik des Papstes Johann XXII. Munich. 1885.
Preuves des Libertez de l'Église Gallicane. Paris. 1651.
Raynaldus, O. Continuatio Annalium Caesaris Baronii. 8 vols. Cologne. 1692–4.
Reusch, Fr. Heinr. Der Index der verbotenen Bücher. Vol. i. Bonn. 1883.
Rodriguez, Manuel. Explicacion de la Bula de la Sancta Cruzada. Salamanca. 1597.
Strauss, D. F. Ulrich von Hutten. 2nd ed. Leipzig. 1871.
Tangl, M. Die päpstlichen Kanzleiordnungen von 1200–1500. Innsbruck. 1894.
—— Das Taxwesen der päpstlichen Kanzlei. Mittheilungen des Instituts für österreichische Geschichtsforschung. Vol. xiii. 1892.
Ullmann, C. Reformatoren vor der Reformation. 2nd ed. 2 vols. Gotha. 1866. English translation by Robert Menzies. Edinburgh. 1855.
Villari, P. La Storia di Girolamo Savonarola. 2 vols. Florence. 1887–8.
—— Niccolò Machiavelli e i suoi tempi. 3 vols. Milan. 1895–7.
Voigt, J. Stimmen aus Rom. Raumer's Hist. Taschenbuch. 1833.
Zurita, G. Añales de la Corona de Aragon. Libro xx. Saragossa. 1669.

(*See also Bibliographies of Chapters XVI. XVII. and XVIII.*)

CAMBRIDGE: PRINTED BY J. AND C. F. CLAY, AT THE UNIVERSITY PRESS.